Crime In Society

Crime
In Society

LEONARD D. SAVITZ
Temple University

NORMAN JOHNSTON
Beaver College

JOHN WILEY & SONS
New York
Santa Barbara
Chichester
Brisbane
Toronto

Cover design by Mark E. Safran.
Production was supervised by Joseph P. Cannizzaro.
Copy editing was supervised by Susan Giniger.

Library of Congress Cataloging in Publication Data:

Crime in society.

   1. Crime and criminals—United States—Addresses,
essays, lectures.   2. Criminal behavior, Predic-
tion of—Addresses, essays, lectures.   3. Crim-
inal psychology—Addresses, essays, lectures.
I.   Savitz, Leonard D.   II.   Johnston, Norman
Bruce, 1921-
HV6789.C695   364'.973   78–806
ISBN 0–471–03385–5

Printed in the United States of America

10 9 8 7 6 5 4 3 2 1

Preface

The basic purpose of *Crime in Society* is to provide the student of criminology access to most of the more significant current research and literature in the field. No book of readings can be so broad-based that every teacher and every student finds an abundance of materials fitting his or her own range of interests. On the other hand, a book such as this, attempting to survey the entire field, cannot represent only one point of view or a single version of what is important. In this book and in its companion volume, *Justice and Corrections,* we have attempted to present a range of viewpoints and ideological beliefs that includes both empirical studies and more descriptive selections. The present volume then should be of value to students in a variety of undergraduate or graduate courses in criminology and juvenile delinquency, either as the basic text or as supplemental reading.

We have spent almost two years reviewing an enormous amount of materials, including the usual American and foreign journals as well as governmental and agency reports, books, and relatively inaccessible papers prepared for meetings and private research organizations. In several instances, experts on certain topics have written papers especially for this book, either updating their own earlier work or surveying their fields of expertise anew.

The great majority of items reviewed could not be included due to space limitations. This is particularly true for historical materials. In other instances excellent studies were excluded simply because they were dated, or were too narrow in scope, or were exotically descriptive but not broadly applicable. Some gaps in the areas covered reflect our inability to find appropriate research.

Some criminology readers, including those that we have previously edited, confine the selections to those more or less sociological in orientation. Such an orientation has been consistent with the mainstream of criminological thought in North America. The present volume, however, reflects a broader perspective which presents a more balanced selection for student and teacher and also represents changes in the field of criminology itself. For example, materials in the areas of the biological-genetic bases of crime and special topics such as drug-related offenses, sex crimes, and white-collar crimes exemplify areas of research and description that were largely unavailable before the 1970s. While we have included up-to-the-minute selections, particularly those dealing with such rapidly changing concerns as juvenile gangs, corporate crime, and newer forms of crime such as computer abuse or record piracy, we have rejected no worthy empirical research, theory, or descriptive materials simply because they were not written within the last several years.

The brief section introductions written by the editors of the book are intended to provide a measure of continuity between the subject matter divisions. Individual selections, however, are presented without comment because it is felt that each instructor will make choices and place the selections in context according to course direction and requirements.

Section I, The Field of Criminology, attempts to orient the student to the discipline of criminology, involving both the legal definitions of crime and juvenile delinquency and the speculations by social scientists on the nature of law.

Criminal statistics, Section II, have always had an important place in the speculations of criminologists and are at the very center of controversies concerning proper strategies for the treatment of criminals and the reduction of crime. Although practitioners, researchers, and theorists will continue to rely on police-based statistics, dissatisfaction with such data has led to the development of new forms of data acquisition such as victimization surveys and self-reporting surveys. The frequent use and misuse of crime statistics make it imperative that students of criminology understand how such figures are generated, what they mean, and how they should be used.

Section III, Theory and Criminology, deals with several currently relevant or widely discussed theoretical explanations of crime. Although the period of so-called "grand theories" in criminology seems now past, one cannot ignore the more significant theoretical statements concerning the causes of crime in our society. Within obvious space limitations, we can do little more than include several examples of the more prominent current theoretical perspectives, including opportunity theory, labeling theory, and Marxist economic theories.

The search for the causes of crime has become increasingly complex and sophisticated. The latter sections of the book mirror the range of that complexity. Persons who classify themselves as "criminologists" are most frequently sociologists. Nevertheless, psychologists, biologists, and economists have made very significant contributions to an understanding of crime. Over a period of time the field of criminology follows unpredictable fashions and trends in explanations of crime, with first one discipline and then another in the ascendancy. Given the serious, unresolved issues in the study of crime and delinquency, we feel that a multidisciplinary approach in this book is more than justified.

Practitioners from different disciplines such as biology and economics explain crime from different points of view. Researchers studying newer kinds of crime such as, for example, computer-based offenses or large-scale racketeering enterprises, have found it necessary to develop research techniques quite different from those used in studying more conventional offenses such as burglary or theft. Consequently, after a preliminary section dealing generally with the problems of causation and prediction, we have grouped empirical and descriptive studies from biology, psychology, sociology, and economics. These are followed by sections devoted to special categories of crimes that are sufficiently unlike conventional crimes that we feel they merit separate consideration.

In the past ten years the general public, legislators, the legal profession, and researchers have become increasingly aware of the impact of organized criminal syndicates on communities and the nation. Researchers have begun to study groups rarely portrayed in earlier criminology texts, such as persons who make life careers out of crimes of bank robbery, confidence games, or pickpocketing. Section IX contains selections dealing with some of these skilled and lucrative crimes and pays particular attention to the reality of several of the more spectacular and colorful claims about the existence of a nationwide criminal conspiracy called the "Mafia."

The last four sections of this book emphasize certain types of criminal activities which have either come into existence within the last decade or else have been the object of increased public concern or fear. Thus we have witnessed since 1967 an "epidemic" of drug-related crime which has not disappeared or been seriously reduced even after considerable governmental concern and funding. The section on sex crimes emphasizes newly arising forms of sexual offenses—teenage prostitution, massage parlor prostitutes, and relatively open homosexual prostitution. Crimes of business executives and politicians have recently captured the public's attention due, primarily, to Vice President Agnew's criminal activities, the Watergate scandals, and illegal political contributions by large corporations, all of which have received extensive publicity in the mass media. These "white-collar crimes" are described in Section XII.

The final section contains descriptions of some new forms of crime, including illegal manipulation and use of computers, the piracy of popular music records, and the fraudulant acquisition of welfare payments.

We would like to express our gratitude and respect to the authors and researchers whose work has made this book possible and especially to those who have contributed papers. Finally, we would also like to express our appreciation to our own students who were exposed to many of these and other selections before the book was put together and whose reactions have guided our final selection.

Leonard D. Savitz
Norman Johnston

Philadelphia, 1978

Contents

The Field of Criminology

CRIMINOLOGY AS A FIELD OF INVESTIGATION ENCOMPASSES A NUMBER OF DISCIPLINES and rather distinctive approaches. This introductory section attempts to provide some awareness of its sociological and legal underpinnings. We view criminology as a fundamentally scientific enterprise that aims at determining and perhaps even utilizing patterns of crime and criminal behavior, and that attempts to understand the factors that in some still uncertain manner, seem to be related to the development of criminal behavior.

The first three selections in this section were written by sociologists of quite different philosophic and ideological persuasions. Emile Durkheim, by common consensus, is considered one of the "founding fathers" of sociology and is among the most seminal theorists in the field. It was his belief that crime, in some form, was an inevitable, *normal* phenomenon in all human societies. He argued that even in a society of saints, a minor, venial sin would, in time, be defined as crime and the perpetrator would be "corrected." Beyond this, he contended that crime is necessary and, in fact, useful for human society. A current social theorist, Richard Quinney, who later in this volume will offer his views concerning crime as a product of our capitalist society, details in selection 2 the development of sociological jurisprudence and its historical transition to its present status as the sociology of criminal law. Within his theoretical perspective, society is characterized by diversity, coercion, and change more than by consensus and stability, and social law typically incorporates the interests of specific persons and interest groups. The Canadian sociologist Gwynn Nettler develops a fascinating exposition on the often implicit assumption that "evil [deviance] is illness." From this it follows that bad people perceive the world around them differently than good people do. With selected bodies of data, Nettler finds, surprisingly perhaps, that good people's view of reality is at least as inaccurate as that of "villains."

Criminology essentially examines the creation and violation of legal norms. (Deviance as a field of investigation focuses on the broader area of violation of social norms.) Most data produced in criminological research are based on the violation of misdemeanors and felonies and other legally specified crime categories. From a classic treatise on crime by Clark and Marshall, the next selection depicts the common law requirements for "crime," specifies culpable (blameworthy) parties in a crime (principals and accessories), and illustrates the careful legal description of a specific crime: rape.

The concepts of crime and criminal in our society apply, with rare exception, to adults, persons who are older than the varying age minimums set in different jurisdictions. Juvenile delinquencies, as Levin and Sarri reveal, are events or actions prohibited to all persons *below* specified ages. Some of these prohibitions are delinquent offenses, actions prohibited to both juveniles and adults. Others, however, are status offenses, such as incorrigibility, unruliness, and truancy, forms of behavior that, if performed by an adult, would not be crimes and would not result in intervention by the state.

1. The Normal and the Pathological

EMILE DURKHEIM

CRIME IS PRESENT NOT ONLY IN THE MAJORITY OF societies of one particular species but in all societies of all types. There is no society that is not confronted with the problem of criminality. Its form changes; the acts thus characterized are not the same everywhere; but, everywhere and always, there have been men who have behaved in such a way as to draw upon themselves penal repression. If, in proportion as societies pass from the lower to the higher types, the rate of criminality, i.e., the relation between the yearly number of crimes and the population, tended to decline, it might be believed that crime, while still normal, is tending to lose this character of normality. But we have no reason to believe that such a regression is substantiated. Many facts would seem rather to indicate a movement in the opposite direction. From the beginning of the [nineteenth] century, statistics enable us to follow the course of criminality. It has everywhere increased. In France the increase is nearly 300 percent. There is, then no phenomenon that presents more indisputably all the symptoms of normality, since it appears closely connected with the conditions of all collective life. To make of crime a form of social morbidity would be to admit that morbidity is not something accidental, but, on the contrary, that in certain cases it grows out of the fundamental constitution of the living organism; it

would result in wiping out all distinction between the physiological and the pathological. No doubt it is possible that crime itself will have abnormal forms, as, for example, when its rate is unusually high. This excess is, indeed, undoubtedly morbid in nature. What is normal, simply, is the existence of criminality, provided that it attains and does not exceed, for each social type, a certain level, which it is perhaps not impossible to fix in conformity with the preceding rules.[1]

Here we are, then, in the presence of a conclusion in appearance quite paradoxical. Let us make no mistake. To classify crime among the phenomena of normal sociology is not to say merely that it is an inevitable, although regrettable phenomenon, due to the incorrigible wickedness of men; it is to affirm that it is a factor in public health, an integral part of all healthy societies. This result is, at first glance, surprising enough to have puzzled even ourselves for a long time. Once this first surprise has been overcome, however, it is not difficult to find reasons explaining this normality and at the same time confirming it.

In the first place crime is normal because a society exempt from it is utterly impossible. Crime, we have shown elsewhere,

▶SOURCE: *Rules of Sociological Method (Eighth Edition, translated by Sarah A. Solvay and John H. Mueller and edited by George E. G. Catlin), Glencoe, Ill.: The Free Press, 1950, pp. 65–73. Reprinted by permission.*

[1]From the fact that crime is a phenomenon of normal sociology, it does not follow that the criminal is an individual normally constituted from the biological and psychological points of view. The two questions are independent of each other. This independence will be better understood when we have shown, later on, the difference between psychological and sociological facts.

3

consists of an act that offends certain very strong collective sentiments. In a society in which criminal acts are no longer committed, the sentiments they offend would have to be found without exception in all individual consciousnesses, and they must be found to exist with the same degree as sentiments contrary to them. Assuming that this condition could actually be realized, crime would not thereby disappear; it would only change its form, for the very cause which would thus dry up the sources of criminality would immediately open up new ones.

Indeed, for the collective sentiments which are protected by the penal law of a people at a specified moment of its history to take possession of the public conscience or for them to acquire a stronger hold where they have an insufficient grip, they must acquire an intensity greater than that which they had hitherto had. The community as a whole must experience them more vividly, for it can acquire from no other source the greater force necessary to control these individuals who formerly were the most refractory. For murderers to disappear, the horror of bloodshed must become greater in those social strata from which murderers are recruited; but, first it must become greater throughout the entire society. Moreover, the very absence of crime would directly contribute to produce this horror; because any sentiment seems much more respectable when it is always and uniformly respected.

One easily overlooks the consideration that these strong states of the common consciousness cannot be thus reinforced without reinforcing at the same time the more feeble states, whose violation previously gave birth to mere infraction of convention—since the weaker ones are only the prolongation, the attenuated form, of the stronger. Thus robbery and simple bad taste injure the same single altruistic sentiment, the respect for that which is another's. However, this same sentiment is less grievously offended by bad taste than by robbery; and since, in addition, the average consciousness has not

sufficient intensity to react keenly to the bad taste, it is treated with greater tolerance. That is why the person guilty of bad taste is merely blamed, whereas the thief is punished. But, if this sentiment grows stronger, to the point of silencing in all consciousness the inclination which disposes man to steal, he will become more sensitive to the offenses which, until then, touched him but lightly. He will react against them, then, with more energy; they will be the object of greater opprobrium, which will transform certain of them from the simple moral faults that they were and give them the quality of crimes. For example, improper contracts, or contracts improperly executed, which only incur public blame or civil damages, will become offenses in law.

Imagine a society of saints, a perfect cloister of exemplary individuals. Crimes, properly so called, will there be unknown; but faults which appear venial to the layman will create there the same scandal that the ordinary offense does in ordinary consciousnesses. If, then, this society has the power to judge and punish, it will define these acts as criminal and will treat them as such. For the same reason, the perfect and upright man judges his smallest failings with a severity that the majority reserve for acts more truly in the nature of an offense. Formerly, acts of violence against persons were more frequent than they are today, because respect for individual dignity was less strong. As this has increased, these crimes have become more rare; and also, many acts violating this sentiment have been introduced into the penal law which were not included there in primitive times.[2]

In order to exhaust all the hypotheses logically possible, it will perhaps be asked why this unanimity does not extend to all collective sentiments without exception. Why should not even the most feeble sentiment gather enough energy to prevent all dissent? The moral consciousness of the society would be present in its entirety in all the individuals, with a vitality sufficient to

[2]Calumny, insults, slander, fraud, etc.

prevent all acts offending it—the purely conventional faults as well as the crimes. But a uniformity so universal and absolute is utterly impossible; for the immediate physical milieu in which each one of us is placed, the hereditary antecedents, and the social influences vary from one individual to the next, and consequently diversify consciousness. It is impossible for all to be alike, if only because each one has his own organism and that these organisms occupy different areas in space. That is why, even among the lower peoples, where individual originality is very little developed, it nevertheless does exist.

Thus, since there cannot be a society in which the individuals do not differ more or less from the collective type, it is also inevitable that, among these divergences, there are some with a criminal character. What confers this character upon them is not the intrinsic quality of a given act but that definition which the collective conscience lends them. If the collective conscience is stronger, if it has enough authority practically to suppress these divergencies, it will also be more sensitive, more exacting; and, reacting against the slightest deviations with the energy it otherwise displays only against more considerable infractions, it will attribute to them the same gravity as formerly to crimes. In other words, it will designate them as criminal.

Crime is, then, necessary; it is bound up with the fundamental conditions of all social life, and by that very fact it is useful, because these conditions of which it is a part are themselves indispensable to the normal evolution of morality and law.

Indeed, it is no longer possible today to dispute the fact that law and morality vary from one social type to the next, nor that they change within the same type if the conditions of life are modified. But, in order that these transformations may be possible, the collective sentiments at the basis of morality must not be hostile to change, and consequently must have but moderate energy. If they were too strong, they would no longer be plastic. Every pattern is an obstacle to new patterns, to the extent that the first pattern is inflexible. The better a structure is articulated, the more it offers a healthy resistance to all modification; and this is equally true of functional, as of anatomical, organization. If there were no crimes, this condition could not have been fulfilled; for such a hypothesis presupposes that collective sentiments have arrived at a degree of intensity unexampled in history. Nothing is good indefinitely and to an unlimited extent. The authority which the moral conscience enjoys must not be excessive; otherwise no one would dare criticize it, and it would too easily congeal into an immutable form. To make progress, individual originality must be able to express itself. In order that the originality of the idealist whose dreams transcend his century may find expression, it is necessary that the originality of the criminal, who is below the level of his time, shall also be possible. One does not occur without the other.

Nor is this all. Aside from this indirect utility, it happens that crime itself plays a useful role in this evolution. Crime implies not only that the way remains open to necessary changes but that in certain cases it directly prepares these changes. Where crime exists, collective sentiments are sufficiently flexible to take on a new form, and crime sometimes helps to determine the form they will take. How many times, indeed, it is only an anticipation of future morality—a step toward what will be! According to Athenian law, Socrates was a criminal, and his condemnation was no more than just. However, his crime, namely, the independence of his thought, rendered a service not only to humanity but to his country. It served to prepare a new morality and faith which the Athenians needed, since the traditions by which they had lived until then were no longer in harmony with the current conditions of life. Nor is the case of Socrates unique; it is reproduced periodically in history. It would never have been possible to establish the freedom of thought we now enjoy if the regulations prohibiting it had not been violated before being solemnly abrogated. At that time, however, the violation was a crime, since it was an offense against sentiments still very keen in the average conscience. And yet this crime was useful as a prelude to reforms which daily became more necessary. Liberal philosophy had as its precursors the heretics of all kinds who were justly punished by secular authorities during the entire course of the Middle Ages and until the eve of modern times.

From this point of view the fundamental facts of criminality present themselves to us in an entirely new light. Contrary to current ideas, the criminal no longer seems a totally unsociable being, a sort of parasitic element, a strange and unassimilable body, introduced into the midst of society.[3] On the contrary, he plays a definite role in social life. Crime, for its part, must no longer be conceived as an evil that cannot be too much suppressed. There is no occasion for self-congratulation when the crime rate drops noticeably below the average level, for we may be certain that this apparent progress is as-

sociated with some social disorder. Thus, the number of assault cases never falls so low as in times of want.[4] With the drop in the crime rate, and as a reaction to it, comes a revision, or the need of a revision in the theory of punishment. If, indeed, crime is a disease, its punishment is its remedy and cannot be otherwise conceived; thus, all the discussions it arouses bear on the point of determining what the punishment must be in order to fulfill this role of remedy. If crime is not pathological at all, the object of punishment cannot be to cure it, and its true function must be sought elsewhere.

[3]We have ourselves committed the error of speaking thus of the criminal, because of a failure to apply our rule *(Division du travail social,* pp. 395–96).

[4]Although crime is a fact of normal sociology, it does not follow that we must not abhor it. Pain itself has nothing desirable about it; the individual dislikes it as society does crime, and yet it is a function of normal physiology. Not only is it necessarily derived from the very constitution of every living organism, but it plays a useful role in life, for which reason it cannot be replaced. It would, then, be a singular distortion of our thought to present it as an apology for crime. We would not even think of protesting against such an interpretation, did we not know to what strange accusations and misunderstandings one exposes oneself when one undertakes to study moral facts objectively and to speak of them in a different language from that of the layman.

2. Criminal Law in Politically Organized Society

RICHARD QUINNEY

THE STUDY OF CRIMINAL LAW[1]

PARADOXICALLY, WITH LAW AND SOCIAL SCIENCE gradually converging, we have no greater theoretical understanding of legal matters than we did all of half a century ago. The rapprochement that we are currently witnessing is not novel; a similar trend appeared in the United States shortly after the turn of the century. At that time social scientists, the early American sociologists in particular, were incorporating law into their scheme of things. E. A. Ross referred to law as "the most specialized and highly furnished engine of control employed by society."[2] Lester F. Ward, an advocate of government control and social planning, foresaw a day when legislation would undertake to solve "questions of social improvement, the amelioration of the condition of all the people, the removal of whatever privations may still remain, and the adoption of means to the positive increase of the social welfare, in short the organization of human happiness."[3] The possibility of social reform, through legal means available to the state, was also emphasized by Albion W. Small.[4]

The ideas of the early sociologists directly influenced the school of legal philosophy that became a major force in American legal thought—sociological jurisprudence—in which Roscoe Pound was the principal figure. He drew from the early sociologists in asserting that law should be studied as a social institution.[5] Pound saw law as a specialized form of social control that brings pressure to bear upon each man "in order to constrain him to do his part in upholding civilized society and to deter him from antisocial conduct, that is, conduct at variance with

▶SOURCE: *The Social Reality of Crime*, Boston: Little, Brown, 1970, pp. 29–42. Reprinted by permission.

---

[1]Portions are adapted with the publisher's permission, from the introduction to my *Crime and Justice in Society* (Boston: Little, Brown and Company, 1969), pp. 20–30.

[2]E. A. Ross, *Social Control* (New York: Macmillan, 1922), p. 106 (originally published in 1901).

[3]Lester F. Ward, *Applied Sociology* (Boston: Ginn, 1906), p. 339.

[4]Albion W. Small, *General Sociology* (Chicago: University of Chicago Press, 1925).

[5]The relationship between early American sociologists and the development of Pound's sociological jurisprudence is discussed in Gilbert Geis, "Sociology and Jurisprudence: Admixture of Lore and Law," *Kentucky Law Journal*, 52 (Winter, 1964), pp. 267–293. Also see Edwin M. Schur, *Law and Society* (New York: Random House, 1968), pp. 17–50.

the postulates of social order."[6] Moreover, in his theory of interests, Pound provided one of the few starting points for the study of law as a social phenomenon.

Recent writing and research have documented the role of interest groups in the political process. The techniques and tactics of interest groups, relations between the groups, their internal organization and politics, and overlapping group membership have been examined.[7] In addition, studies have been conducted on how specific groups operate.[8] But almost no research has been directed at finding how much influence the interests have in formulating and administering law.[9] Moreover,

few have attempted to revise Pound's theory of interests to reflect recent sociological developments. As it has been observed, "Sociologists to date have paid virtually no attention to Pound's doctrine, either in terms of rejecting it, refining it for their purposes, or supplementing it with sociological material of more recent vintage."[10]

In the current movement by social scientists toward research into law and the use by lawyers of social science research, in interest approach might well help us to construct a theory of criminal law that would integrate research findings and provide direction for future research. For sociological purposes, however, Pound's approach necessarily requires reformulation and extension into a sociological theory of criminal law.

FROM SOCIOLOGICAL JURISPRUDENCE TO SOCIOLOGY OF CRIMINAL LAW

Law is not merely a complex of rules and procedures; Pound taught us that in calling for the study of "law in action." For some purposes it may be useful to think of law as autonomous within society, developing according to its own logic and proceeding along its own lines. But law also simultaneously reflects society and influences it, so that, in a social sense, it is both social product and social force. In Pound's juristic approach, however, law represents the consciousness of the total society. This *consensus* model of (criminal) law has been described in the following way: "The state of criminal law

[6]Roscoe Pound, *Social Control Through Law* (New Haven: Yale University Press, 1942), p. 18. Earlier statements by Pound are found in Roscoe Pound, *An Introduction to the Philosophy of Law* (New Haven: Yale University Press, 1922); Roscoe Pound, *Outline of Lectures on Jurisprudence* (Cambridge: Harvard University Press, 1928).

[7]Donald C. Blaisdell, *American Democracy Under Pressure* (New York: Ronald Press, 1957); V. O. Key, Jr., *Politics, Parties and Pressure Groups* (New York: Thomas Y. Crowell, 1959); Earl Latham, *Group Basis of Politics* (Ithaca, N.Y.: Cornell University Press, 1952); David B. Truman, *The Governmental Process* (New York: Alfred A. Knopf, 1951); Henry W. Ehrmann (ed.), *Interest Groups on Four Continents* (Pittsburgh: University of Pittsburgh Press, 1958); Henry A. Turner, "How Pressure Groups Operate," *Annals of the American Academy of Political and Social Science,* 319 (September, 1958), pp. 84–93; Murray S. Stedman, "Pressure Groups and the American Tradition," *Annals of the American Academy of Political and Social Science,* 319 (September, 1958), pp. 123–129.

[8]Robert Engler, *The Politics of Oil* (New York: Macmillan, 1961); Oliver Garceau, *The Political Life of the American Medical Association* (Cambridge: Harvard University Press, 1941); Charles M. Hardin, *The Politics of Agriculture: Soil Conservation and the Struggle for Power in Rural America* (New York: The Free Press of Glencoe, 1962); Grant McConnell, *Private Power and American Democracy* (New York: Alfred A. Knopf, 1966); Harry A. Millis and Royal E. Montgomery, *Organized Labor* (New York: McGraw-Hill, 1945); Warner Schilling, Paul Y. Hammond, and Glenn H. Snyder, *Strategy, Politics and Defense* (New York: Columbia University Press, 1962); William R. Willoughby, *The St. Lawrence Waterway: A Study in Politics and Diplomacy* (Madison: University of Wisconsin Press, 1961).

[9]Other social orientations to the law may be found among sociological jurists, among the so-called legal realists, and

among current legal historians. See, in particular, Oliver Wendell Holmes, "The Path of the Law," *Harvard Law Review,* 10 (March, 1897), pp. 457–478; Thurman W. Arnold, *Symbols of Government* (New Haven: Yale University Press, 1935); Jerome Frank, *Courts on Trial* (Princeton: Princeton University Press, 1949); K. N. Llewellyn and E. Adamson Hoebel, *The Cheyenne Way: Conflict and Case Law in Primitive Jurisprudence* (Norman: University of Oklahoma Press, 1941); J. Willard Hurst, *Law and Economic Growth: The Legal History of the Lumber Industry in Wisconsin, 1836–1915* (Cambridge, Mass.: The Belknap Press, 1964).

[10]Geis, "Sociology and Sociological Jurisprudence: Admixture of Lore and Law," p. 292.

continues to be—as it should—a decisive reflection of the social consciousness of a society. What kind of conduct an organized community considers, at a given time, sufficiently condemnable to impose official sanctions, impairing the life, liberty, or property of the offender, is a barometer of the moral and social thinking of the community."[11] Similarly, Pound, formulating his theory of interests, felt that law reflects the needs of the well-ordered society. In fact, the law is a form of "social engineering" in a civilized society:

"For the purpose of understanding the law of today, I am content to think of law as a social institution to satisfy social wants—the claims and demands involved in the existence of civilized society—by giving effect to as much as we may with the least sacrifice, so far as such wants may be satisfied or such claims given effect by an ordering of human conduct through politically organized society. For present purposes I am content to see in legal history the record of a continually wider recognizing and satisfying of human wants or claims or desires through social control; a more embracing and more effective securing of social interests; a continually more complete and effective elimination of waste and precluding of friction in human enjoyment of the goods of existence—in short, a continually more efficacious social engineering."[12]

Thus, the interests Pound had in mind would maintain and, ultimately, improve the social order. His was a *teleological* as well as consensus theory of interests: men must fulfill some interests for the good of the whole society; these interests are to be achieved through law. In Pound's theory, only the right law can emerge in a civilized society.

Jurisprudence has generally utilized a *pluralistic* model with respect to law as a social force in society. Accordingly, law regulates social behavior and establishes social organization; it orders human relationships by restraining individual actions and by settling disputes in social relations. In recent juristic language, law functions "first, to establish the general framework, the rules of the game so to speak, within and by which individual and group life shall be carried on, and secondly, to adjust the conflicting claims which different individuals and groups of individuals seek to satisfy in society."[13] For Pound, the law adjusts and reconciles conflicting interests:

"Looked at functionally, the law is an attempt to satisfy, to reconcile, to harmonize, to adjust these overlapping and often conflicting claims and demands, either through securing them directly and immediately, or through securing certain individual interests, or through delimitations or compromises of individual interests, so as to give effect to the greatest total of interests or to the interests that weigh most in our civilization, with the least sacrifice of the scheme of interests as a whole."[14]

In Pound's theory of interests, law provides the general framework within which individual and group life is carried on, according to the postulates of social order. Moreover, as a legal historian has written, "The law defines the extent to which it will give effect to the interests which it recognizes, in the light of other interests and of the possibilities of effectively securing them through law; it also devises means for securing those that are recognized and prescribes the limits within which those means may be employed."[15] In the interest theory of sociological jurisprudence, then, law is an instrument

[11]Wolfgang Friedmann, *Law in a Changing Society* (Harmondsworth, England: Penguin Books, 1964), p. 143. A similar statement is found in Jerome Michael and Mortimer J. Adler, *Crime, Law and Social Science* (New York: Harcourt, Brace, 1933), pp. 2–3.

[12]Pound, *An Introduction to the Philosophy of Law,* pp. 98–99.

[13]Carl A. Auerbach, "Law and Social Change in the United States," *U.C.L.A. Law Review,* 6 (July, 1959), pp. 516–532. Similarly, see Julius Stone, *The Province and Function of Law* (Cambridge: Harvard University Press, 1950), Part III; Julius Stone, *Social Dimensions of Law and Justice* (Stanford: Stanford University Press, 1966), chaps. 4–8.

[14]Roscoe Pound, "A Survey of Social Interests," *Harvard Law Review,* 57 (October, 1943), p. 39.

[15]George Lee Haskins, *Law and Authority in Early Massachusetts* (New York: Macmillan, 1960), p. 226.

that controls interests according to the requirements of social order.

Pound's theory of interests included a threefold classification of interests, including the individual, the public, and the social:

"Individual interests are claims or demands or desires involved immediately in the individual life and asserted in the title of that life. Public interests are claims or demands or desires involved in life in a politically organized society and asserted in the title of that organization. They are commonly treated as the claims of a politically organized society thought of as a legal entity. Social interests are claims or demands or desires involved in social life in a civilized society and asserted in the title of that life. It is not uncommon to treat them as the claims of the whole social group as such."[16]

Pound warned that the types are overlapping and interdependent and that most can be placed in all the categories, depending upon one's purpose. He argued, however, that it is often expedient to put claims, demands, and desires in their most general form; that is, in the category of social interests.

Surveying the claims, demands, and desires found in legal proceedings and in legislative proposals, Pound suggested that the most important social interest appears to involve security against actions that threaten the social group.[17] Others are interest in the security of domestic, religious, economic, and political institutions; morals; conservation of social resources; general progress, including the development of human powers and control over nature to satisfy human wants; and individual life, especially the freedom of self-assertion. According to Pound, any legal system depends upon the way in which these interests are incorporated into law.

[16]Pound, "A Survey of Social Interests," pp. 1–2.

[17]Pound, "A Survey of Social Interests," pp. 1–39. Other aspects of the theory of interests are discussed by Pound in the following publications: *The Spirit of the Common Law* (Boston: Marshall Jones, 1921), pp. 91–93, 197–203; *An Introduction to the Philosophy of Law*, pp. 90–96; *Interpretations of Legal History* (New York: Macmillan, 1923), pp. 158–164; *Social Control through Law*, pp. 63–80.

My theoretical perspective on criminal law departs from the general tradition of the interest theory of sociological jurisprudence in a number of ways. First, my perspective is based on a special conception of society. Society is characterized by diversity, conflict, coercion, and change, rather than by consensus and stability. Second, law is a *result* of the operation of interests, rather than an instrument that functions outside of particular interests. Though law may control interests, it is in the first place *created* by interests. Third, law incorporates the interests of specific persons and groups; it is seldom the product of the whole society. Law is made by men, representing special interests, who have the power to translate their interests into public policy. Unlike the pluralistic conception of politics, law does not represent a compromise of the diverse interests in society, but supports some interests at the expense of others. Fourth, the theoretical perspective of criminal law is devoid of teleological connotations. The social order may require certain functions for its maintenance and survival, but such functions will not be considered as inherent in the interests involved in formulating substantive laws. Fifth, the perspective proposed here includes a conceptual scheme for analyzing interests in the law. Finally, construction of the perspective is based on findings from current social science research.

LAW IN POLITICALLY ORGANIZED SOCIETY

Authority relations are present in all social collectivities: some persons are always at the command of others. As order is established in a society, several systems of control develop to regulate the conduct of various groups of persons. Human behavior is thus subject to restraint by varied agencies, institutions, and social groupings—families, churches, social clubs, political organizations, labor unions, corporations, educational systems, and so forth.

The control systems vary considerably in the

forms of conduct they regulate, and most provide means for assuring compliance to their rules. Informal means, spontaneously employed by some persons, such as ridicule, gossip, and censure, may ensure conformity to some rules. Control systems may, in addition, rely upon formal and regularized means of sanction.

The *legal system* is the most explicit form of social control. The law consists of (1) specific rules of conduct, (2) planned use of sanctions to support the rules, and (3) designated officials to interpret and enforce the rules.[18] Furthermore, law becomes more important as a system of control as societies increase in complexity. Pound wrote that "in the modern world law has become the paramount agent of social control. Our main reliance is upon force of a politically organized state."[19]

Law is more than a system of formal social control; it is also a body of specialized rules created and interpreted in a *politically organized society,* or the state, which is a territorial organization with the authorized power to govern the lives and activities of all the inhabitants. Though other types of organized bodies may possess formal rules, only the specialized rule systems of politically organized societies are regarded here as systems of law.[20]

[18]F. James Davis, "Law as a Type of Social Control," in F. James Davis, Henry H. Foster, Jr., C. Ray Jeffery, and E. Eugene Davis, *Society and the Law* (New York: The Free Press of Glencoe, 1962), p. 43.

[19]Pound, *Social Control through Law,* p. 20.

[20]The rule systems of societies other than those which are politically organized may be adequately referred to, for comparative purposes, in any number of quasilegal ways, such as nonstate law, primitive law, or "lawways." Perhaps, even better, such systems of rules could be described simply as "tradition," "normative system," or "custom." The concept of law is expanded to include the control systems of other than politically organized society among such writers as Bronislaw Malinowski, *Crime and Custom in Savage Society* (London: Routledge and Kegan Paul, 1926); E. Adamson Hoebel, *The Law of Primitive Man* (Cambridge: Harvard University Press, 1954); William M. Evan, "Public and Private Legal Systems," in William M. Evan (ed.), *Law and Sociology* (New York: The Free Press of Glencoe, 1962), pp. 165–184; Philip Selznick, "Legal Institutions and Social Controls," *Vanderbilt Law Review,* 17 (December, 1963), pp. 79–90.

Law, as a special kind of institution, again is more than an abstract body of rules. Instead of being autonomous within society and developing according to its own logic, law is an integral part of society, operating as a force in society and as a social product. The law is not only that which is written as statutes and recorded as court opinions and administrative rulings, but is also a method or *process* of doing something.[21] As a process, law is a dynamic force that is continually being *created* and *interpreted.* Thus, law in action involves the making of specialized (legal) decisions by various *authorized agents.* In politically organized society, human actions are regulated by those invested with the authority to make specified decisions in the name of the society.

Furthermore, law in operation is an aspect of politics—it is one of the methods by which public policy is formulated and administered for governing the lives and activities of the state's inhabitants. As an act of politics, law and legal decisions do not represent the interests of all persons in the society. Whenever a law is created or interpreted, the values of some are necessarily assured and the values of others are either ignored or negated.

THE INTEREST STRUCTURE

Modern societies are characterized by an organization of differences. The social differentiation of society, in turn, provides the basis for the state's political life. Government in a politically organized society operates according to the interests that characterize the socially differentiated positions. Because varied interests are distributed among the positions, and because the positions are differently equipped with the ability to command, public policy represents specific interests in the society. Politically organized society, therefore, may be viewed as a differentiated *interest structure.*

[21]For this conception of law, as applied to criminal law, see Henry M. Hart, Jr., "The Aims of the Criminal Law," *Law and Contemporary Problems,* 23 (Summer, 1958), pp. 401–441.

Each *segment* of society has its own values, its own norms, and its own ideological orientations. When these are considered to be important for the existence and welfare of the respective segments, they may be defined as *interests*.[22] Further, interests can be categorized according to the ways in which activities are generally pursued in society; that is according to the *institutional orders* of society. The following may then serve as a definition of interests: *the institutional concerns of the segments of society.* Thus, interests are grounded in the segments of society and represent the institutional concerns of the segments.

The institutional orders within which interests operate may be classified into fairly broad categories.[23] For our use, these may be called: (1) *the political,* which regulates the distribution of power and authority in society; (2) *the economic,* which regulates the production and distribution of goods and services; (3) *the religious,* which regulates the relationship of man to a conception of the supernatural; (4) *the kinship,* which regulates sexual relations, family patterns, and the procreation and rearing of children; (5) *the educational,* which regulates the formal training of the society's members; and (6) *the public,* which regulates the protection and maintenance of the community and its citizens. Each segment of society has its own orientation to these orders. Some, because of their authority position in the interest structure, are able to have their interests represented in public policy.

The segments of society differ in the extent to which their interests are organized. The segments themselves are broad statistical aggregates containing persons of similar age, sex, class, status, occupation, race, ethnicity, religion, or the like. All these have *formal interests;* those which are advantageous to the segment but which are not consciously held by the incumbents and are not organized for action. *Active interests,* on the other hand, are manifest to persons in the segments and are sufficiently organized to serve as the basis for representation in policy decisions.[24]

Within the segments, groups of persons may become aware of and organize to promote their common interests; these may be called *interest groups.* Public policy, in turn, is the result of the success gained by these groups.

The interest structure is characterized by the unequal distribution of *power* and *conflict* among the segments of society. It is differentiated by diverse interests and by the ability of the segments to translate their interests into public policy. Furthermore, the segments are in continual conflict over their interests. Interests thus are structured according to differences in power and are in conflict.

Power and conflict are linked in this conception of interest structure. Power, as the ability to shape public policy, produces conflict among the competing segments, and conflict produces differences in the distribution of power. Coherence in the interest structure is thus ensured by the exercise of force and constraint by the conflicting segments. In the conflict-power model, therefore, politically organized society is held together by conflicting elements and functions according to the coercion of some segments by others.

The conflict-power conception of interest structure implies that public policy results from differential distribution of power and conflict among the segments of society. Diverse segments with specialized interests become so

---

[22]The view here that interests are not distributed randomly in society but are related to one's position in society follows Marx's theory of economic production and class conflict. See Ralf Dahrendorf, *Class and Class Conflict in Industrial Society* (Stanford: Stanford University Press, 1959), especially pp. 3–35.

[23]The conception of institutional orders closely follows that of Hans Gerth and C. Wright Mills, *Character and Social Structure* (New York: Harcourt, Brace, 1953), especially pp. 25–26.

[24]The distinction between formal interests and active interests is similar to the distinction Dahrendorf makes between latent and manifest interests. See Dahrendorf, *Class and Class Conflict in Industrial Society,* pp. 173–179.

highly organized that they are able to influence the policies that affect all persons in the state. Groups that have the power to gain access to the decision-making process are able to translate their interests into public policy. Thus, the interests represented in the formulation and administration of public policy are those treasured by the dominant segments of the society. Hence, public policy is created because segments with power differentials are in conflict with one another. Public policy itself is a manifestation of an interest structure in politically organized society.

FORMULATION AND ADMINISTRATION OF CRIMINAL LAW

Law is a form of public policy that regulates the behavior and activities of all members of a society. It is *formulated* and *administered* by those segments of society which are able to incorporate their interests into the creation and interpretation of public policy. Rather than representing the institutional concerns of all segments of society, law secures the interests of particular segments, supporting one point of view at the expense of others.

Thus, the content of the law, including the substantive regulations and the procedural rules, represents the interests of the segments of society that have the power to shape public policy. Formulation of law allows some segments of society to protect and perpetuate their own interests. By formulating law, some segments are able to control others to their own advantage.

The interests that the power segments of society attempt to maintain enter into all stages of legal administration. Since legal formulations do not provide specific instructions for interpreting law, administration of law is largely a matter of discretion on the part of *legal agents* (police, prosecutors, judges, juries, prison authorities, parole officers, and others). Though implementation of law is necessarily influenced by such matters as localized conditions and the occupa-tional organization of legal agents, the interest structure of politically organized society is responsible for the general design of the administration of criminal justice.

Finally, the formulation and administration of law in politically organized society are affected by changing social conditions. Emerging interests and increasing concern with the protection of various aspects of social life require new laws or reinterpretations of old laws. Consequently, legal changes take place within the context of the changing interest structure of society.

INTERESTS IN CONTEMPORARY SOCIETY

Interests not only are the principal forces behind the creation and interpretation of law, but they are changing the very nature of government. For centuries the state was the Leviathan, protector, repository of power, main source of the community's economic and social life. The state unified and controlled most of the activities of the society. In recent times, however, it is apparent that some groups and segments of society have taken over many of the state's functions:

"The question must be raised in all seriousness whether the 'overmighty subjects' of our time—the giant corporations, both of a commercial and noncommercial character, the labor unions, the trade associations, farmers' organizations, veterans' legions, and some other highly organized groups—have taken over the substance of sovereignty. Has the balance of pressures and counter-pressures between these groups left the legal power of the State as a mere shell? If this is a correct interpretation of the social change of our time, we are witnessing another dialectic process in history: the national sovereign State—having taken over effective legal political power from the social groups of the previous age—surrenders its power to the new massive social groups of the industrial age."[25]

[25]Friedmann, *Law in a Changing Society,* pp. 239–240.

Some analysts of the contemporary scene have optimistically forecasted that checks of "countervailing power" will adequately balance the interests of the well organized groups.[26] This pluralistic conception disregards the fact that interest groups are grossly unequal in power. Groups that are similar in power may well check each others' interests, but groups that have little or no power will not have the opportunity to have their interest represented in public policy. The consequence is government by a few powerful private interest groups.

Furthermore, the politics of private interests tends to take place outside of the arena of the public governmental process. In private politics, interest groups receive their individual claims in return for allowing other groups to press for their interests.[27] Behind public politics a private government operates in a way that not only guarantees rewards to well organized groups but affects the lives of us all.

If there be any check in this contemporary condition, it is in the prospect that the "public interest" will take precedence over private interests. Interest groups, if for no other reason than their concern for public relations, may bow to the commonweal. Optimistically, the public interest may become an ideal fulfilled, no matter what the source of private power.

But the fallacy in any expectation of the achievement of the public good through the "public interest" is that the government which could foster such a condition will become again in a new age an oppressive interest in itself. That age, in fact, seems to be upon us. Increasingly, as Reich has argued, "Americans live on government largess—allocated by government on its own terms, and held by recipients subject to conditions which express 'the public interest.'"[28] While the highly organized, scientifically planned society, governed for the social good of its inhabitants, promises the best life that man has ever known, not all of our human values will receive attention, and some may be temporarily or permanently negated.

In raw form we cannot hold optimistically to either government by private interests or public interest by government largess. The future for individual man appears to lie in some form of protection from both forms of government. Decentralized government offers some possibility for the survival of the individual in a collective society. But more immediately, that protection must be sought in procedural law, a law that must necessarily be removed from the control of either the interests of private groups or public government. The challenge for law of the future is that it create an order providing fulfillment for individual values that are now within our reach, values that paradoxically are imminent because of the existence of interests from which we must now seek protection. A new society is indeed coming: Can a law be created apart from private interests which assures individual fulfillment within a good society?

[26]John Kenneth Galbraith, *Modern Capitalism* (Boston: Houghton Mifflin, 1952).

[27]See Theodore Lowi, "The Public Philosophy: Interest-Group Liberalism," *American Political Science Review*, 61 (March, 1967), pp. 5–24.

[28]Charles A. Reich, "The New Property," *Yale Law Journal*, 73 (April, 1964), p. 733.

3. Good Men, Bad Men, and the Perception of Reality

GWYNN NETTLER

WITH THE RISE OF A SCIENTIFIC DETERMINISM AND the associated decline of free will and sin as explanations of deviant behavior, it has become popular to look upon "badness" as sickness. Research designed to increase our knowledge of prostitution, radicalism, homosexuality, dictatorship, race prejudice, crime and delinquency often makes the assumption, implicitly and explicitly, that evil is illness.[1]

▶SOURCE: *"Good Men, Bad Men, and the Perception of Reality," Sociometry (September 1961), 24:3:279–294. Reprinted by permission of the American Sociological Association and the author.*

---

[1]There is a tautological sense in which this is true: if illness is defined as anything bad that is caused.

For present purposes and euphony's sake I should like to use "evil," and "deviant" interchangeably, if it will be recognized that I do not believe that all deviation—even some of which offends society—is evil, and that what is evil according to classical standards includes much that is now acceptable.

This synonymy seems defensible in view of the orientation of Social Problems and Social Disorganization textbooks which, although they do not always say so directly, are "really" concerned with badness. And this remains true even when they are re-titled "Social Deviation," because it is only disapproved difference that one finds in the chapter headings. Thus one doesn't see nor expect discussions in these books of such deviations as being rich, powerful, beautiful, or creative, clear, and intelligent.

Thus saying, this paper will hereafter abandon the defense of placing quotation marks about these useful but fuzzy terms.

These assumptions have not gone unchallenged (10, 18, 35, 56, 65, 66), yet they flourish. Part of their viability flows from the "evil-causes-evil" fallacy (60, page 62), but these assumptions are sustained also in the vogue of psychoanalysis and by the ambiguities that reside in the idea of mental health, ambiguities into which prejudices have stepped. Attempts to define a "healthy personality" carry a load of personal preference and we are prone to call the man "sound" who behaves as we do, or as we like to think we behave (9). These preferences seem not merely idiosyncratic but also class-biased and ethnocentric.[2] They gather ideological support from the Platonic suggestion that goodness, truth, and beauty are the ultimate desirables and that they bear each other an intimate connection. Since this Platonism is part of the academic subculture in which most investigators have been steeped, there have been few dissident voices among sociologists (65) or humanists

---

[2]For example, Witmer and Kotinsky (71) write that ". . . to be happy and responsible is to be healthy in personality." The words "happy" and "responsible" are so glorious that one is loath to question their relevance to mental health, but they *are* suspect simply because we do not expect a man to be happy regardless of circumstance and "responsibility" does not specify for whom nor how nor under what conditions with what limits.

(37), although psychologists seem increasingly reluctant to accept the vaunted relationship of health and goodness (19, 46, 59, 62, 63).

The hope that goodness is friendly to the truth, or, better, that knowing the truth will make us good, has been brewed into our definitions of the healthy man and the concoction then used to justify our values. The California study of the *Authoritarian Personality* is a prime example (1). Maslow makes the logic explicit:

"The neurotic is not only emotionally sick—he is cognitively *wrong!* If health and neurosis are, respectively, correct and incorrect perceptions of reality, propositions of fact and propositions of value merge in this area, and in principle, value propositions should then be empirically demonstrable rather than merely matters of taste or exhortation (36)."

If the scientist can show that bad behavior is a symptom of sickness and if a measure of this sickness is a perverted picture of the world, then the equation of morality (ours) with correctness seems established and certain happy consequences may be inferred, for example:

1. That truth and utility are *not* at war, as Pareto and the inconsistent Plato believed.

2. That science can "prove" values and thus give them the underpinning they lost with the decline of religious authority.

3. That, since evil-is-sickness-is-error, therapy remains what some like to think it is: truth-giving.

4. That we good people are also more factually correct.

But what if these assumptions are questionable? What if evil is a way of responding to an imperfect world by actors with limited resources in a determinate situation? What shall we say to such a sensitive writer as Han Su-yin (Dr. Elizabeth K. Comber) when she tells us, "So I'm not a good woman. If I'd been a good woman, where would I be now? I'll tell you—dead!"? Finally, what will it mean for our notions of psychotherapy and sociotherapy if, in those cases where evil people see a different world from that observed by good men, the evil eye should prove the clearer?

Raising such a possibility is itself an invidious task, but just such a one as the professional student of society must undertake as part of the work of describing how people behave. To the objector who would resist the question and assume its answer in advance of test, the reminder must be given that the conflict between truth and utility is an old one and that, while it remains unresolved, it is of crucial importance for any theory of personal or social improvement. It must also be considered that, while as scientists we protest our preference for truth over error, as culture-bound thinkers we may favor lies when their credentials are of the right sort.

Raising the uncomfortable question of the healthfulness of bad actors may place us, as meliorists, in a "bind" because there are realities which, correctly perceived, are sickening, and we may have to choose between the "health" of the man who behaves badly because he sees accurately and the "health" of the man who behaves nicely because he has learned the popular ways of seeing falsely.

A PARTIAL EXAMINATION OF THE EVIL EYE

There is little doubt that bad people see the world differently from good. Many studies tell us so. Part of this perception involves preferences, tastes, self-conceptions and attitudes, but part of the difference in perception concerns how the world really is, and it is with this that we are concerned.

The differences in what good and bad people see "out there" share a generality because evil has been defined in socio-psychological research as deviation from a humanitarian, "progressive," middle-class, quasi-Christian,[3] Western-

---

[3]The use of the qualifier, "quasi," is not flippant. Western society has moved a long way from the ideals and practices of a Christian community. For a statement of what the Christian mode would mean, see Jones (28) and Russell (54).

urban standard, so that it makes almost no difference which kind of badness one is inspecting—the kinds of belief about the world that allegedly differentiate the good and the bad man are of a persistent piece. In fact, one prominent study consciously explores the possibility that these evils are one morsel, as it attempts to relate political evil ("authoritarianism") to ethnic prejudice, crime, and psychic malfunction (1). What is crucial for present purposes is that these investigators believe the evil eye is astigmatic; they hold political evil (*their* conception) to be an ideology that fails as ". . . an objective appraisal of social reality, (and) tends to resemble a fantasy. . . ." (1, page 845).

The purportedly fantastic world seen by the bad man is a jungle. And a jungle may be defined as a place where strength and cunning decide and win—not "humanness," "justice," "principle," nor any other ethic than force and fraud. It is a place where each against all is truer than all for each or, even, each for himself alone.

Since the perceptions reported as marking off the bad man from the good have this generality, it is not necessary to use the findings of every study, nor to limit our search to one kind of wrong, in order to examine the relative acuity of good and evil perception. A sample of such studies dealing with delinquency (6, 22, 23), juvenile narcotic users (14), fascism (1), and ethnic prejudice (1, 2) has been taken. From the measures which these studies report as differentiating, with some degree of probability, the attitudes of good and bad people, *all* statements relating to "external fact" as opposed to self-evaluation or personal behavior have been listed. The literature has then been scanned for evidence, tentative and partial though it might be, that would permit a grading of these differentiating perceptions, using the bad person's view from his environment as the one to be tested, since it is he who is allegedly unhealthy and who eyes the world through need-distorted lenses.

In fairness to the investigators whose studies have been used, employment of their differentiating items should not be construed as meaning that these authors necessarily subscribe to the notion under question here—that badness is sickness, a symptom of which is a distorted perception of the world. The approach of certain of these investigators has been purely actuarial: what distinctions can be found that allow us to predict? But in other cases, notably those of Allport-Kramer and the Adorno group, the investigators do maintain that "good" perceptions are healthier and more accurate than evil ones.

The reality-perceptions of bad men, and one judge's estimate of their accuracy based on the sources cited, are listed below. To propose one's own estimate of perceptual accuracy is, of course, to run the risk of criticism *ad hominem* and the kind of "tele-psyching" to which even behavioral scientists are not immune. However, this study has been entered with the explicit assumption that socio-psychological observers assessing good and evil conduct and mental health may themselves be wearing class-ethnic blinkers, so that it would hardly be pertinent to put this matter to their vote. Since the present concern lies more heavily with being heuristic than with being right, it would seem sufficient only to make a probable guess as to the state of the "real world" as good and bad people differentially see it, and to cite one's grounds for his estimate.

Some Available Evidence

Ball (6) reports five statements that differentiate between delinquent and non-delinquent perceptions of the prevalence of stealing. The first reads:

"How many people would steal if they had a good chance?"

   a.   *The delinquent believes* "about half, most, or all."

   b.   *Estimate:* Probably accurate; much depends on the meaning of "good chance."

   c.   *Evidence:*
   1. ". . . all employees of a chain-store were run through his (Keeler's) polygraph when the

company complained it was losing more than one million dollars annually through petty thefts. Polygraph records indicated fully three out of four employees were pilfering funds. This and subsequent experiences led Keeler to pronounce a rather cynical dictum generally held by lie-detection experts today: '65 per cent of people who handle money take money. . . .' " (17, pages, 154–155).

2. "Lie detector tests of employees of certain Chicago banks showed that 20 per cent had taken money or property, and in almost all cases the tests were supported by confessions. Similarly, lie detector tests of a cross section sample of the employees of a chain store indicated that about 75 per cent had taken money or merchandise from the store." (40)

3. ". . . the Comptroller of Currency reported that about three-fourths of the national banks examined in one period were violating the national banking laws and that dishonesty was found in 50.5 per cent of the national bank failures in the years 1865–1899, and 61.4 per cent in the years 1900–1919." (16, page 185)

4. "Undersecretary of the Treasury Fred A. Scribner, Jr., reported that a Treasury examination of 1956 income tax returns discovered that taxpayers had failed to report almost $4,500,000,000 of interest and dividends received during that year. . . ." (55)

5. Investigators carefully dropped stamped, addressed postcards, letters, and letters bearing a lead coin simulating a 50-cent piece in various cities of the East and Midwest. Seventy-two per cent of the postcards were returned; 85 per cent of the blank letters; 54 per cent of the "coin-carrying" letters. "We conclude . . . that the public at large is very strikingly altruistic, manifesting obligingness, consideration, and responsibility. A sharp decline in the reliability of the public sets in under the effects of suggestion of financial gain. One-third of the altruistically minded are converted to selfish behavior. It is probable that an even larger proportion of the public at large is unreliable in such a financial matter." (41)

6. "Hume said one could be sufficiently sure about certain aspects of human nature to predict with accuracy what would happen to a quantity of gold left unguarded in a populous place. On the basis of human experience in a free society one can now say the same of anything, of however little value, that is portable. For in all our centers of dense population any possessions left unguarded on the doorstep—roller skates, bicycles, baby carriages, appliances, garbage cans, tools, lawn mowers, trash receptacles and the like—disappear as if by magic." (33)

7. *Reader's Digest* Survey, 1941:
   Of 347 garages visited, 63 per cent were dishonest.
   Of 304 radio shops, 64 per cent were dishonest.
   Of 462 watchmakers, 49 per cent were dishonest (51).

A second of Ball's questions asks, *"Do you think many people have taken things at some time?"*

a. *The delinquent* again believes that "about half, most, or all" have.

b. *Estimate and Evidence:* There is little reliable evidence on this matter. However, one study of a non-criminal population is suggestive. Nettler (48) asked a heterogeneous sample of California residents these questions, among others, concerning their criminal conduct:

—"Since age 16, how many times have you taken hotel towels or blankets as souvenirs?"
—"Since age 16, how many times have you taken a newspaper from a stand without paying for it?"
—"Since age 16, how many times have you taken something from a store without paying for it?"
—"Since age 16, how many times have you kept money for yourself that belonged to someone else?"
—"Since age 16, how many times have you taken another's property such as fruit, tools, library books, or other unsecured objects?"

A majority of the respondents admitted anonymously to one or more of these crimes.

Ball reports three other statements that distinguish good and bad perception: "Do you think many people would steal from their friends?" "Do you think many people would steal from a store if they had a good chance?" ". . . from a school?" Lack of evidence prevents a test of these items.

Chein (14) found that juvenile narcotics users tend to see a different social world than children who are free of this habit:

"Most policemen treat people of all races the same."

a. *Narcotics user* denies.

b. *Estimate:* probably an accurate perception—in the environment in which the question was asked.

c. *Evidence:* (4; 7, pages 158, 164–165; 53; 60, pages 139–140; 64, page 95)

"Most policemen can be paid off."

a. *Narcotics user* agrees.

b. *Estimate and Evidence:* No one knows about "most policemen." But for evidence that this perception is not a fantasy, see (7, pages 245–246; 49, page 73; 60, pages 228–229, 383–389)

"The police often pick on people for no good reason."

a. *Narcotics user* agrees.

b. *Estimate and Evidence:* This must vary with race, class, and the police force. And no one knows, class by class, whether this is "often" true. But for evidence that this perception, again, is not a hallucination, see (7, page 750; 60, pages 331–341).

"I am sure that most of my friends would stand by me no matter what kind of trouble I got into."

a. *Narcotics user* denies.

b. *Estimate and Evidence:* Part of this is tautology; a "friend" is this kind of person.

Again, no one knows how much friendship there is in our society. And such as one finds probably varies socio-economically (13, pages 189–190; 34; 42, *passim*). "When you have no money, nobody takes an interest in you. I never had a friend. For six years it has been like that. We are living in filthy misery on the East Side—nobody can ever help us out of that." (25, page 17)

Jungles, by definition, are not friendly environments and we need to know their protean styles and their prevalence. It is more than one observer's judgment that friendship, as distinct from "clique-ship," is an abnormality on Manhattan's Seventh Avenue or San Francisco's Montgomery Street. And, if one talks as an industrial consultant to the $52-a-week girls straitened desk-after-desk in the offices of Megalopolitan Insurance, he will not be reassured that many abide in the warmth of friendship. Or enter academia and observe the rarity of love and charity. Some participants have described the Academy as a genteel jungle, a microcosm of the competitive, political, envious and even unhappy world we usually associate with the strivers in grey flannel (8, 39, 69)

"Everybody is just out for himself. Nobody really cares about anybody else."

a. *Narcotics user* agrees.

b. *Estimate and Evidence:* As worded, this seems patently false. *Some* people care for others, at least in some milieux.

But this too must be class linked and the delinquent's perception may give an accurate picture of his world.

Such a statement poses, and leaves unanswered, three important questions about people's concern for others:

1. Under what circumstances does altruism develop?

2. How many people do care about how many others? What is the *range* of love by ethnic group and socio-economic status?

3. What is the *quality* of this concern? Love does not often come to us unalloyed. Portions of personal motivation, self-interest, ego are involved in altruism; the question is, "How much?" As Eric Hoffer has put it, "There is no doubt that in exchanging a self-centered for a selfless life we gain enormously in self-esteem."

As "concern for others" becomes a thing one does out of concern for himself—not to uphold self-principle, but to get something or somewhere—the delinquent's perception becomes more accurate. Perhaps he has put the emphasis on *"really* cares." Instance: involvement in a large community's welfare activities will impress one that many (how many?) of the civic-minded altruists do not "really" care for those they are helping. Their concern seems to be a public expression that has status and recreational value, political, and even commercial value. Probably no one who has worked with charities and welfare agencies would dispute the existence (while he may debate the prevalence) of non-loving motives among board members, junior leaguers, service clubs, and other volunteer welfare-dispensers.

In the investigation by Hathaway and Monachesi (23) the following perceptions were found to distinguish predelinquent boys from others:

"My mother was a good woman."

a. *Predelinquent* denies.

b. *No evidence* available. A "good woman" is difficult to define.

"One or more members of my family is very nervous."

a. *Predelinquent* agrees.

b. *No evidence* in either direction.

"The man who had most to do with me when I was a child (such as my father, stepfather, etc.) was very strict with me."

a. *Predelinquent* agrees.

b. *Estimate:* probably true.

c. *Evidence:*
1. Glueck's "Social Factors" Prediction Table (21, p. 260):

	Weighted Failure
#1. Discipline of Boy by Father—	Score:
Overstrict or erratic	71.8
Lax	59.8
Firm but kindly	9.3

2. Anderson (3) reports that parents ranked by psychometrics as high in dominance and low in affection had aggressive and rebellious children.

3. "On every item in the interview in which intensity of punishment was rated, the fathers of the high aggression boys punished more severely than the fathers of the low aggression boys" (67). (This finding is qualified by the possibility that judges may have rated non-verbal punishment as more severe than verbal. Personal communication from the investigator.)

"When a man is with a woman he is usually thinking about things related to her sex."

a. *Predelinquents* affirm.

b. *Estimate and Evidence:* This may be a function of age, but otherwise . . .? It may also vary with status and culture. Much depends on the meaning of "with a woman" and "thinking about things." But, if the delinquent's perception is widely inaccurate, then Hollywood, the ladies' magazines, and American advertisers are also wearing distorting spectacles.

"My parents have often objected to the kind of people I went around with."

a. *Predelinquent* admits.

b. *Estimate:* probably true.

c. *Evidence:* Chwast (15) cites many studies that affirm the relationship between delinquent behavior and parental rejection/disapproval.

Gough and Peterson's items (22) distinguishing those predisposed to crime and those more immune are largely attitudinal and self-descriptive. However, there are two categories of statement that deal with how the world "out there" is perceived; three items are concerned with how "jungley" it is and nine with family life.

The predelinquent is depicted by Gough and Peterson as believing that: *"I would have been more successful if people had given me a fair chance"*; *"Life usually hands me a pretty raw deal"*; and *"A person is better off if he doesn't trust anyone."*

For all of these statements there is thus far no conclusive evidence. These items are, of course, both "objective" and "subjective"—they carry a heavy load of interpretation of what has happened to one—but, for present purposes, it need only be indicated that the predelinquent, particularly if he comes from the lower classes, is probably not distorting his reality greatly. And, in validation of the delinquent perception, one can cite all manner of learned non-delinquents. For example, Charles Stockard, the noted zoologist, believed, erroneously, that ". . . man is the only animal that gives deliberately false signals to his kind," and George Bernard Shaw has been quoted as saying:

Man is the only animal of which I am thoroughly and cravenly afraid. I have never thought much of the courage of the lion-tamer. Inside the cage he is at least safe from other men. There is less harm in a well-fed lion. It has no ideals, no sect, no party, no nation, no class; in short, no reason for destroying anything it does not want to eat. (11)

Myers and Roberts (47) write of their class V (lowest status) patients, "They were reared in an environment where violence, aggression, hostility, and rebellion were accepted. (They) . . . received little warmth or affection."

David Riesman summarizes, ". . . the conditions of lower-class life do not encourage trust" (52)

The pre-criminal, according to Gough and Peterson, sees his family life as unsatisfactory and he is probably right. He believes:

"My family has objected to the kind of work I do, or plan to do."

"My parents were too strict with me when I was a child."

"My parents never really understood me."

"My home life as a child was less peaceful and quiet than those of most other people."

"My parents have often disapproved of my friends."

"I was often punished unfairly as a child."

And he denies that:

"My home life was always very pleasant."

"My parents have generally let me make my own decisions."

"The members of my family were always very close to each other."

The final form of the F (authoritarianism) scale devised by Adorno and associates (1) contains ten statements that describe how the world is or will be and to which the "fascist" subscribes. Of these ten items, one seems false, one true, and four might be correct depending upon the definitions adopted. For the remaining four statements no evidence is available.

Probably false: "Wars and social troubles may someday be ended by an earthquake or flood that will destroy the whole world."

Probably true: "Human nature being what it is, there will always be war and conflict."

See Hanson Baldwin (5) or Freud (20).

Possibly true, depending upon the definitions given:

"People can be divided into two distinct classes, the weak and the strong."

As with all defining statements, the "validity" of this one is a function of someone's purposes in making such a classification. While field theorists warn against such Aristotelian dichotomies, many scientists are convinced of the usefulness of dichotomous assumptions for certain purposes. See, for example, George Kelly (30).

"A person who has bad manners, habits, and breeding can hardly expect to get along with decent people."

As conventionally understood, this is probably a true statement; much depends on who one thinks is "decent."

"Most of our social problems would be solved if we could somehow get rid of the immoral, crooked, and feeble-minded people."

Since there is no agreed-upon roster of social problems, it is impossible to say how many problems would constitute "most." However, see any social problems text.

"The wild sex life of the old Greeks and Romans was tame compared to some of the goings-on in this country, even in places where people might least expect it."

Comparative study of this nature seems insurmountably difficult, although challenging.

See almost any issue of *Playboy, Confidential,* or the daily press. Also, Ben Hecht (24).

No evidence available:

> "*If people would talk less and work more, everybody would be better off.*"

> "*Most people don't realize how much our lives are controlled by plots hatched in secret places.*"

The words "plot" and "secret" make the statement difficult to evaluate; otherwise see Hunter (26) and Mills (42).

> "*The businessman and the manufacturer are much more important to society than the artist and the professor.*"

> "*Familiarity breeds contempt.*"

Most of the items in E (Ethnocentrism) scale devised by the same group of investigators (1, page 142) are too attitudinal and ambiguous to permit test, but one seems quite probably false, and two possibly true:

> *Probably false:* "*The people who raise all the talk about putting Negroes on the same level as whites are mostly radical agitators trying to stir up conflicts.*"

> *Possibly true:* "*The best guarantee of our national security is for America to have the biggest army and navy in the world and the secret of the atom bomb.*"

> This item is dated. If its intent is read as of 1961, our government seems to be acting as if preparedness were "the best guarantee," even though American sociologists may not feel too secure in it.

> Again, see Baldwin: "The right fist of all-out nuclear power must remain ready as a sanction to help ensure limited war" (5, page 43).

> Or, Morgenstern: "The problem, the great problem, of our military planners is to organize and maintain armed forces capable of fighting any kind of war anywhere" (43).

> "*The trouble with letting Jews into a nice neighborhood is that they gradually give it a typical Jewish atmosphere.*"

> This offensive statement is emotionally loaded by the phrase, "The trouble with . . ." and the adjective, "nice." If one discounts these attitudi-

nal indicators and restricts the sentence to its factual representation, to the possibility of ethnic invasion and succession, it seems true in the larger metropolitan areas of the United States (70).

Ambiguous and No Evidence Available:

> "*One trouble with Jewish businessmen is that they stick together and prevent other people from having a fair chance in competition.*"

> "*There may be a few exceptions, but in general Jews are pretty much alike.*"

> "*There is something different and strange about Jews; it's hard to tell what they are thinking and planning, and what makes them tick.*"

> "*Manual labor and unskilled jobs seem to fit the Negro mentality and ability better than more skilled or responsible work.*"

> "*Most Negroes would become overbearing and disagreeable if not kept in their place.*"

> "*The worst danger to real Americanism during the last 50 years has come from foreign ideas and agitators.*"

> "*America may not be perfect, but the American way has brought us about as close as human beings can get to a perfect society.*"

Allport and Kramer (2), testing Ichheiser's psychoanalytic hypothesis about anti-Semitism (27), find that anti-Semites are differentiated from the unprejudiced by their greater fear of swindlers than of gangsters. They say, ". . . those who are more afraid of swindlers also have higher prejudice scores in general. ($\chi^2 = 7.17$, significant at the 1 per cent level). Those who are more afraid of gangsters (may we not say, a more natural and normal fear?) are less prejudiced" (2, pages 33–34).

Allport and Kramer may choose to call the good man's greater fear of gangsters "natural and normal", whatever that means, but such honorific labelling does nothing to root this fear in a clearer perception of reality. Again, the good man, Allport and Kramer included, seems to be looking at the world through distorting spectacles, for the evidence is abundant that good and bad people alike are at least as apt to be defrauded by swindlers as bludgeoned by gangsters. Barnes and Teeters (7, page 69) call it a toss-up, but Nietzsche (32), White (68), and Bernard (12, page 36), among others, see fraud as the more common danger. Sutherland felt it probable that ". . . fraud is the most prevalent crime in America" (60, page 42), Schur calls swindling, ". . . a strongly entrenched national phenomenon. . . ." (57, page 269), and Nettler (48) found "crimes of deceit" to be admitted anonymously by a majority of non-criminal population. Reference to works on white-collar crime (61) and confidence games (38) confirms the suspicion that Allport-Kramer and their un-prejudiced subjects are less able to test the reality about them (in this department at least) than their evil respondents.

A Tally

It appears that good people see the world at least as inaccurately—to put it mildly—as bad ones. Any "score" here is subject to criticism and can only be offered tentatively. For, aside from the quarrels with one investigator's assessment of reality, even where he cites "evidence" for his view, there remains the possibility that good and bad men reside in different "real" worlds and, hence, where they differ they may be equally correct or incorrect. For this reason Table I presents three tallies: one of all 48 items as judged for approximation to actuality in the text above, and two tallies—a "rough" and a "soft" one—of the 37 items that remain after the family history items in the Gough-Peterson and Hathaway-Monachesi studies are discounted.

A reading of these 37 non-personal items shows that the possible residence of good and bad men in different "real" worlds does not explain all the differences in perception; a generalized view of the shared world remains and, from the items and evidence at hand, it cannot be concluded that the evil eye sees it poorly.

DISCUSSION

It has been argued that the conception of evil action as sickness is questionable. Particularly doubtful is the assumption that a prime symptom of the illness that generates badness is a false picture of the world. If this now seems obvious, one wonders how such an idea could have been given professional credence. A few sources of this intellectual infection may be suggested.

It would seem that the notion that bad people must be sick is the spawn of American pragmatic optimism (All problems are soluble if we but think; do something!) bred with the classic values of goodness, truth, and beauty in an atmosphere in which the prestige of religious explanation has been declining while that of popular psychologizing has been rising.

Having "advanced" beyond blaming the bad man for his moral depravity, the middle-class investigator proposes to treat him for his sickness. This proposal is emboldened by the optimistic assumption that goodness and health (which includes telling, seeking, and seeing the truth) are reciprocally related. With faith so set, it follows that evil may be cured, like other infirmities, and that an important part of the cure lies in the bad, sick man's taking psychotherapeutic exercises in correct perception—of what he has done, and why, and of how people "really" are as opposed to what he thought they were.

This tentative study calls into question this popular thoughtway. Bad actors may not be sick—at least no more so than good men—and, particularly, they may not suffer from perverted perception. Rather, if the present tally has validity, it is the good man who sees relatively inaccurately.

Two questions persist:

—How jungle-like is our society?

—To what extent is behavior a function of how one perceives his social world?

Table I. A Tally of the Relative Accuracy of the Perceptions of Good and Bad Men

Tally I: All Items

	Study							
	Ball	*Chein*	*H-M*	*G-P*	*F-Scale*	*E-Scale*	*A-K*	*Total*
Bad man accurate	2	5	3	9	5	2	1	27
Good man accurate	0	0	0	0	1	1	0	2
Evidence lacking or ambiguous	3	0	2	3	4	7	0	19
Total	5	5	5	12	10	10	1	48

Tally II: Family History Items Omitted
"Rough" Version

	Ball	*Chein*	*H-M*	*G-P*	*F-Scale*	*E-Scale*	*A-K*	*Total*
Bad man accurate	2	5	1	0	5	2	1	16
Good man accurate	0	0	0	0	1	1	0	2
Evidence lacking or ambiguous	3	0	2	3	4	7	0	19
Total	5	5	3	3	10	10	1	37

Tally III: Family History Items Omitted
"Soft" Version

	Ball	*Chein*	*H-M*	*G-P*	*F-Scale*	*E-Scale*	*A-K*	*Total*
Bad man accurate	1[a]	1[b]	1	0	1[c]	1[d]	1	6
Good man accurate	0	0	0	0	1	1	0	2
Evidence lacking or ambiguous	4	4	2	3	8	8	0	29
Total	5	5	3	3	10	10	1	37

[a] Calls "many people have taken things" lacking in evidence.

[b] Considers only the delinquent negation of "most policemen treat people of all races the same" as an accurate perception in the environment in which the question was asked.

[c] Calls the four items judged "possible true" lacking in evidence.

[d] Calls the item about "Jews in nice neighborhoods" ambiguous and lacking in evidence.

On the first question our "authorities" give conflicting answers. Freud advises that "Men are not only worse, but also better, than they think they are," but, another time, he writes, *"Homo homini lupus;* who has the courage to dispute it in the face of all the evidence in his own life and history?" (20)

A philosopher reviewing a work on "New Knowledge in Human Values" asks its psychologist-editor, "If Maslow is right in saying that 'our deepest needs are *not* . . . dangerous or evil or bad,' why are our surface appetites often so?" (58)

And Ortega tells us, "The very name, 'society,' as denoting groups of men who live together, is equivocal and utopian." (50)

Relative to the second question, disputes persist concerning the value of accurate perception (44).

—"It is not wholesome to live by illusion," Gordon Allport assures us.

—"Mankind cannot stand too much reality," T. S. Eliot replies.

—The golden virtues are ". . . love, truth, beauty, self-realization . . . (they) conduce to psychological health," Huston Smith retorts.

—But ". . . mental integrity may rest on the capacity for denial, for sustained repression of truth," answers Philip Roche.

If more thorough investigations support present assumptions about the likely answers to our two questions, the result will be unfortunate for those of us who have learned to value truth. With the Existentialists, we may have to agree that some truths are sickening. And with Plato and the many religionists, we may have to agree that men need the control as well as the comfort of myth.

REFERENCES

1.   Adorno, T. W., *et. al.*, *The Authoritarian Personality,* New York: Harper, 1950.

2.   Allport, G., and B. M. Kramer, "Some Roots of Prejudice," *Journal of Psychology,* 1946, 22, 9–39.

3.   Anderson, J. P., "A Study of the Relationships Between Certain Aspects of Parental Behavior and the Attitudes and Behavior of Junior High School Students," *Contributions to Education, #809,* New York: Teachers College, Columbia University, 1940.

4.   Axelrad, Sidney, "Negro and White Institutionalized Delinquents," *American Journal of Sociology,* 1952, 57, 569–574.

5.   Baldwin, H. W., "Limited War," *The Atlantic Monthly,* May, 1959, 203, 35–43.

6.   Ball, J. C., "Delinquent and Non-Delinquent Attitudes Toward the Prevalence of Stealing," *Journal of Criminal Law, Criminology, and Police Science,* 1957, 48, 259–274.

7.   Barnes, H. E., and N. K. Teeters, *New Horizons in Criminology,* New York: Prentice-Hall, 1951.

8.   Barr, Stringfellow, *Purely Academic,* New York: Simon and Schuster, 1958.

9.   Barron, Frank, "Towards a Positive Definition of Psychological Health," paper read to the American Psychological Association, 1955.

10.   Barron, M. L., *The Juvenile in Delinquent Society,* New York: Knopf, 1954.

11.   Basso, H., "Foxy Like a Grandpa," *New Yorker,* 1949, 25, 109.

12.   Bernard, L. L., *Social Control,* New York: Macmillan, 1939.

13.   Broom, L., and P. Selznick, *Sociology,* Evanston: Row-Peterson, 1955.

14.   Chein, I., "Narcotics Use Among Juveniles," *Social Work,* 1956, 1, 50–60.

15.   Chwast, J., "Perceived Parental Attitudes and Pre-Delinquency," *Journal of Criminal Law, Criminology, and Police Science,* 1958, 49, 116–128.

16.   Cressey, D. R., *Other People's Money,* Glencoe: Free Press, 1953.

17.   Deutsch, A., *The Trouble with Cops,* Boston: Little, Brown, 1950.

18.   Frank, L. K., *Society as the Patient,* New Brunswick: Rutgers University Press, 1948.

19.   Freides, D., "Toward the Elimination of the Concept of Normality," *Journal of Consulting Psychology,* 1960, 24, 128–133.

20.   Freud, S., *Civilization and Its Discontents,* New York: Doubleday, 1953, p. 61.

21.   Glueck, S., and E. Glueck, *Unraveling Juvenile Delinquency,* Cambridge: Harvard University Press, 1950, pp. 257–262.

22.   Gough, H., and D. R. Peterson, "The Identification and Measurement of Predispositional Factors in Crime and Delinquency: A First Report," paper read at the 1951 meeting of The Western Psychological Association.

23.   Hathaway, S. R., and E. D. Monachesi, "The Personalities of Predelinquent Boys," *Journal of Criminal Law, Criminology, and Police Science,* 1957, 48, 149–163.

24.   Hecht, B., "Sex in Hollywood," *Esquire,* 1954, 41, 35 and *passim.*

25.   Hellersberg, E. F., *The Individual's Relation to Reality in Our Culture,* Springfield: Thomas, 1950.

26. Hunter, F., *Top Leadership, U.S.A.*, Chapel Hill: University of North Carolina Press, 1959.

27. Ichheiser, G., "Fear of Violence and Fear of Fraud, with Some Remarks on the Social Psychology of Anti-Semitism," *Sociometry*, 1944, 7, 376–383.

28. Jones, W. T., *A History of Western Philosophy*, New York: Harcourt, Brace, 1952, pp. 342–343.

29. Kahn, Jr., E. J., "Annals of Crime," *New Yorker*, 1959, 35, 122–153.

30. Kelly, G. A., *The Psychology of Personal Constructs*, New York: Norton, 1955, vol. I, pp. 109–110.

31. Lambert, W. W., L. M. Triandis, and M. Wolf, "Some Correlates of Belief in the Malevolence and Benevolence of Supernatural Beings: A Cross-Societal Study," *Journal of Abnormal and Social Psychology*, 1959, 58, 162–169.

32. Levy, O. (ed.) *The Complete Works of Friederich Nietzsche, vol. 7, Human, All-too-Human*, London: Fouilis, 1911, pp. 200–201.

33. Lundberg, F., *The Treason of the People*, New York: Harper, 1954, p. 289.

34. Lynd, R. J., and H. Lynd, *Middletown*, New York: Harcourt, Brace, 1929, p. 272.

35. Masling, S. M., "How Neurotic is the Authoritarian?", *Journal of Abnormal and Social Psychology*, 1954, 49, 316–318.

36. Maslow, A. H., *Motivation and Personality*, New York: Harper, 1954, p. 204.

37. Maugham, S., *The Summing Up*, New York: Doubleday, 1938.

38. Maurer, D. W., *The Big Con*, New York: Bobbs-Merrill, 1940.

39. McCarthy, M., *The Groves of Academe*, New York: Harcourt, Brace, 1952.

40. McEvoy, F. P., "The Lie-Detector Goes Into Business," *Reader's Digest*, 1941, 38, 69–72.

41. Merritt, C. B., and E. G. Fowler, "The Pecuniary Honesty of the Public at Large," *Journal of Abnormal and Social Psychology*, 1948, 43, 90–93.

42. Mills, C. W., *The Power Elite*, New York: Oxford University Press, 1956.

43. Morgenstern, O., *The Question of National Defense*, New York: Random House, 1959.

44. Moore, W. E., and M. M. Tumin, "Some Social Functions of Ignorance," *American Sociological Review*, 1949, 14, 787–795.

45. Morris, C. W., *The Variety of Values*, Chicago: University of Chicago Press, 1956.

46. Mowrer, O. H., "Sin, the Lesser of Two Evils," *American Psychologist*, 1960, 15, 301–304.

47. Myers, J. K., and B. H. Roberts, *Family and Class Dynamics in Mental Illness*, New York: Wiley, 1959, page 253.

48. Nettler, G., "Antisocial Sentiment and Criminality," *American Sociological Review*, 1959, 24, 202–218.

49. Nossiter, B. D., "The Teamsters: Corrupt Policemen of an Unruly Industry," *Harper's*, 1959, 218, 70–76.

50. Ortega y Gasset, Jose, *Concord and Liberty*, New York: Norton, 1946, p. 24.

51. Reader's Digest, 1941, 38, July, August, September issues.

52. Riesman, D., "Political Communication and Social Structure in the United States," *Public Opinion Quarterly*, 1956, 20, 60.

53. Robison, S. M., *Juvenile Delinquency: Its Nature and Control*, New York: Holt-Dryden, 1960, p. 211.

54. Russell, B., *Why I Am Not a Christian*, New York: Simon and Schuster, 1957.

55. Sahlman, H., "Taxes: Evasion and Avoidance," *Commentary*, 1959, 28, 447–448.

56. Schuessler, K. F., and D. R. Cressey, "Personality Characteristics of Criminals," *American Journal of Sociology*, 1950, 55, 476–484.

57. Schur, E. M., "Sociological Analysis of Confidence Swindling," *Journal of Criminal Law, Criminology, and Police Science*, 1957, 48, 296–304.

58. Smith, H., review of A. H. Maslow (ed.), "New Knowledge of Human Values," *Saturday Review*, 1959, 42, 25.

59. Smith, M. B., "Research Strategies Toward a Conception of Positive Mental Health," *American Psychologist*, 1959, 14, 673–681.

60. Sutherland, E. H., and D. R. Cressey, *Principles of Criminology*, Philadelphia: Lippincott, 1955.

61. Sutherland, E. H., *White Collar Crime,* New York: Dryden, 1949.

62. Szaz, T. S., "The Myth of Mental Illness," *American Psychologist,* 1960, 15, 113–118.

63. Szaz, T. S., "Naming and the Myth of Mental Illness," *American Psychologist,* 1961, 16, 59–65.

64. Taft, D. R., *Criminology,* New York: Macmillan, 1950.

65. van den Haag, E., "Psychoanalysis and Its Discontents," in S. Hook (ed.), *Psychoanalysis, Scientific Method, and Philosophy,* New York: New York University Press, 1959.

66. Volkman, A. P., "Delinquent and Nondelinquent Personality," *Social Problems,* 1958–59, 6, 238–245.

67. Walder, L. O., "An Attempt at an Empirical Test of a Theory," in *The Application of Role and Learning Theories to the Study of the Development of Aggression in Children,* Washington: American Psychological Association, 1958.

68. White, L. A., *The Evolution of Culture,* New York: McGraw-Hill, 1959, pp. 346–347.

69. Williams, G., *Some of My Best Friends Are Professors,* New York: Abelard-Schuman, 1958.

70. Wirth, L., *The Ghetto,* Chicago: The University of Chicago Press, 1929.

71. Witmer, H. L., and R. Kotinsky, *Personality in the Making,* New York: Harper, 1952, p. xviii.

4. Legal Definitions of Crime, Criminal, and Rape

WILLIAM L. CLARK
WILLIAM L. MARSHALL

DEFINING CRIME

A WIDE VARIETY OF MEANINGS ARE ASSIGNED THE concept labeled "crime." One hears a neighbor say, "The way he treats her is a crime," or "Isn't it a crime the price they charge?" If the speakers were pressed and asked just what they mean by these statements the short retort, no doubt, would be, "You know what I mean." Rarely do either speakers or listeners trouble to identify the terms of reference or context. Such exchanges of verbal utterances having blurred edges are merely shadowy ideas which, on close attention manifest little more than the emotional attitude of the speaker.

A technically accurate, reliable definition of "crime" is unlikely of attainment. Crime is clearly a legal entity, a legalistic classifying device, and not an objective factual entity. Part of the difficulty in framing a sound meaning for that word in the context here arises from a common and persistent failure to keep the functional, separated from the procedural, aspect. Many definitions are pseudo statements reflecting circular reasoning in which, for example, an author without defining "crime" asserts that be-

behavior prosecuted in criminal proceedings is a crime. Of course such an approach contributes nothing in a situation where the central problem requires initial classification of a statutory provision, and behavior described by it, in order to determine whether civil or criminal procedure is appropriate. On the other hand, Callan v. Wilson reflects an early Supreme Court view of the elusive word:

"The third article of the Constitution provides for a jury in the trial of 'all crimes, except in cases of impeachment.' The word 'crime,' in its more extended sense, comprehends every violation of public law; in a limited sense, it embraces offences of a serious or atrocious character. In our opinion, the provision is to be interpreted in the light of the principles which, at common law, determined whether the accused, in a given class of cases, was entitled to be tried by a jury. It is not to be construed as relating only to felonies, or offences punishable by confinement in the penitentiary. It embraces as well some classes of misdemeanors, the punishment of which involves or may involve the deprivation of the liberty of the citizen. It would be a narrow construction of the Constitution to hold that no prosecution for a misdemeanor is a prosecution for a 'crime' within the meaning of the third article, or a 'criminal prosecution' within the meaning of the Sixth Amendment. . . ."

Several modern statutory provisions describe a criminal offense, or a crime, in terms of the requirement of a union, or joint operation, of act and intent.

▶SOURCE: *A Treatise on the Law of Crimes (Seventh Edition, edited by Marian Quinn Barnes), Mundelein, Ill.: Callaghan and Co., 1967, pp. 89–101, 506–516, 752–762. (Editorial adaptations.) Reprinted with permission from Clark and Marshall Crimes (A Treatise on the Law of Crimes) published by Callaghan & Co., 6141 North Cicero Avenue, Chicago, Ill. 60646.*

The word "crime" is also used to describe forbidden behavior and the result of behavior—acts or omissions. A simplified practical working definition of crime, containing the cognitive, volitional and physical elements coupled with the elements of law, but subject to the discussion in the balance of this section:

"A crime is any act or omission prohibited by public law for the protection of the public, and made punishable by the state in a judicial proceeding in its own name. It is a public wrong, as distinguished from a mere private wrong or civil injury to an individual."

The familiar classification of positive and natural law comes into play when Blackstone struggles to explain the differences between offenses "mala prohibita" and "mala in se." Natural law or the so-called "Law Behind the Law" is believed by some to be an assemblage of rules which all laws, ideally speaking, should approach and proximate if the most efficacious regulatory results are to be achieved. He defines "positive offences" as "offences against the municipal law only and not against the law of nature." Blackstone is an excellent example of a source of confusion because he then proceeds to declare that capital punishment as imposed for violating offenses mala in se is, in some instances, inflicted by the command of God. Blackstone's authority for this mandate is the precept delivered to Noah in Genesis 9:6 (A. V.). A bit of analysis discloses some interesting defects in Blackstone's statements. He has used the word "positive" in two different ways. At one time he is speaking about a legislative enactment (municipal law), and the other concerns a code stemming from purely religious sources. In the first instance, human beings frankly admit they are the authors of the municipal law; while on the other hand, the "code" (per Blackstone) has been passed along by tradition from Divine revelation, and reported, and interpreted by human beings. Blackstone obviously failed in fully explaining his meaning of positive law in comparison with natural law when he wrote the following imaginative explanation:

"It is clear, that the right of punishing crimes against the law of nature, as murder and the like, is in a state of mere nature vested in every individual. For it must be vested in somebody; otherwise the laws of nature would be vain and fruitless, if none were empowered to put them in execution: and if that power is vested in any *one*, it must also be vested in *all* mankind; since all are by nature equal. . . .[1]

But all this goes further, for after that statement Blackstone is moved to discuss "offences against the laws of society"—offenses mala prohibita, not mala in se. Clearly the prohibition of murder, which he had so particularly mentioned is as much a law of society as the offenses Blackstone classes as mala prohibita. Driven then to justifying punishment of this latter group of offenses, Blackstone invoked a vague notion about the social contract. Nevertheless, this well-known legal writer epitomizes the difficulties in meanings. Blackstone, like many who follow in his wake, encounters the following situation. Unorganized human organisms pay homage to certain traditional beliefs, obeying particular mandates that have been passed along. Upon disobedience a punishment is inflicted. When communities are formed some of these beliefs persist, accompanied by punishments—and are frequently cast into words forming rules for governing the now organized society. As the community becomes structured, growing in population, communication, and complexity, both internally and externally, more rules for controlling behavior are framed and adopted by the community, and successive human legislators. Both sets of rules merge and are used for regulating conduct. The core of the problem lies in discovering the source of these rules, and the method and reason for promulgating them. Thus, murder was punished before a formal human legislative body enacted what is currently called a statute. But the punishment once varied from death, to fines, depending on the era, geographical location and social values. When certain

[1]Blackstone, Commentaries 7.

homicides are tolerated (e.g., self-defense), it is clear that human legislators are then enacting modifications of an imperative "thou shalt not kill," drawn from reservoirs of religious teachings. At this point, then, it becomes important to notice that statues passed by legislatures are repealed, amended, and extended.

"Immorality" and "crime" are by no means convertible terms. The common law does not undertake to punish a man for his acts *merely* because they are immoral. There must be something more than this. There must be some injury or prejudice to the community at large. A man may be guilty of fornication or adultery in private, or be otherwise guilty of the grossest immorality in his private life, without being amenable to the criminal law, unless his conduct is covered by some penal statute. Public immorality or indecency, however, stands upon a different ground. Because of its manifest tendency to corrupt the morals of the community, or to shock the public sense of morality and decency, public immorality and indecency is a common nuisance and a misdemeanor at common law. It may be laid down as a general rule that any act which has a direct tendency to corrupt the public morals or which tends to shock the public sense of morality and decency, is a misdemeanor, whether covered by any statute or not.

In England, various acts were punished at first in the ecclesiastical courts, and later, by statutes, in the civil courts, as offenses against God, the Christian religion, and the established church, and some acts were punished at common law. Among these were apostasy, or a total renunciation of Christianity by embracing either a false religion, or no religion at all, after having once professed Christianity; heresy, which consists, not in a total denial of Christianity, but in a denial of some of its essential doctrines, publicly and obstinately avowed; offenses against the established church, by reviling its ordinances, or failure to conform to its worship; blasphemy; profane swearing and cursing; witchcraft; religious impostures, such as falsely pretending an extraordinary commission from heaven, and terrifying and abusing the people with false denunciations of judgments; simony, or the corrupt presentation of any one to an ecclesiastical benefice for gift or rewards; Sabbath breaking; drunkenness; and open and notorious lewdness.

In this country, there being no established church as in England, no act is a crime merely because it offends against any church, or against God, or against religious doctrines. Some of the acts mentioned, if committed under such circumstances as to constitute a public nuisance, are indictable in this country as common-law misdemeanors, but this is because they annoy the community or shock its sense of morality and decency, or tend to corrupt the public morals. Blasphemy, profane swearing and cursing, drunkenness, and lewdness are all misdemeanors at common law if committed openly and notoriously, but, as a rule, it is otherwise if they are committed in private. To commit fornication in private, even when accompanied by seduction, or to get drunk in one's own house, was not a common-law offense. There are no such crimes in this country as apostacy, heresy, and nonconformity to the worship of a church.

In a broad sense, all offenses are breaches of the public peace. Unless otherwise provided by statute, every indictment, whether for a common-law or statutory offense, concluded by alleging that the offense was committed "against the peace of the state." Putting to one side the serious crimes, various lesser offenses, for example, forcible entry and detainer, affrays, unlawful assemblies, routs, riots, disturbance of public assemblies, certain kinds of disorderly houses, libel, and malicious mischief, all affect the public peace, and for that reason are punishable at common law. In addition to those specific offenses, it is a general rule that any other act constituting a breach of the public peace, or which has a direct tendency to cause a breach of the public peace, is a misdemeanor at common law. Thus, where a man discharged his gun at wild fowl, with knowledge and after warning that the report would injuriously affect a sick person in the neighborhood, and the report had such effect, it was held that his act was an indictable offense, not only because it was a wanton act of mischief, but also because it was against the public peace and security.

"It is not necessary that there shall be actual force or violence to constitute an indictable offense. Acts injurious to private persons, which tend to excite violent resentment, and thus produce fighting and disturbance of the peace of society, are themselves indictable. To send a challenge to fight a duel is indictable, because it tends directly toward a breach of the peace. . . . A libel even of a deceased person is an offense against the public, because it may stir up the passions of the living, and produce acts of revenge."

Among the various obstacles to a precise definition of crime is the broad meaning commonly assigned to the term "public law." Implicit in the shift from private vengeance to punishment only by the state is the emergence of another attribute of sovereignty—the power to create criminal offenses. Yet in contemporary times conduct of various types is classified as antisocial, consequently prohibited for the protection of the public, and punished on multiple American governmental levels. Which of the regulative measures emanating from Congress, the state legislatures, counties, municipal corporations and administrative agencies, making violators vulnerable to some sort of punishment, creates a crime depends upon several factors. The enumerated bodies also mandate, prohibit, and regulate a wide variety of daily conduct through "public law," which is well outside the ambit of "crimes." Public law, then, without a more explicit statement is an inaccurate benchmark for surveying the area of crime. Blackstone's definition of crime—"an act committed or omitted in violation of a public law, either forbidding or commanding it," although frequently quoted with approval, is inexact. It is not the "act omitted" that constitutes a crime, but the omission to act; and, the term "public law" is too broad, for it includes many other laws besides those which define and punish crimes. An act is not necessarily a crime because it is prohibited by a public law. It is essential to ascertain the ground upon which the act is punished and by whom the punishment is imposed. To constitute a crime, behavior must be punished to protect the public generally, and it must be punished by the state or other sovereign power.

Violations of Ordinances Adopted by Municipal Corporations

Various political subdivisions, such as municipal corporations and counties, are empowered by state legislatures to enact regulatory measures and impose penalties upon violators of such ordinances. The object of these police regulations is to control human behavior within the physical corporate limits and jurisdiction of a county, city, or village. But power to enact such measures only flows from the legislature whose representatives are elected by the people of an entire state of the Union. Under criminal law theory, a crime, viewed in its technical setting, is an offense against the "people," referring to the human population of a state and not merely a transgression against some small segment. Congress and the state legislatures, as representatives of all the people in either the national or state areas, have the power to declare what behavior shall be proscribed and punished. This legislative function cannot be delegated. While municipalities are empowered to enact a variety of police regulations they cannot create criminal offenses in the sense that a sovereign can do so. A violation of a municipal ordinance is not an offense against the state but only runs counter to the local prohibition enacted by the municipality. In a modern complex society the identical course of conduct is frequently prohibited and punished by both a state, in the name of its people, and by a municipality as well. Consequently the problem arises as to whether the violator of such a dualistic prohibition can be subjected to double punishment.

By the weight of judicial decisions, the violation of a municipal ordinance, enacted by a city under legislative authority, as in the case of ordinances prohibiting and punishing gaming, and the keeping of gaming houses or bawdy houses, is not a crime, in the technical sense of the term, for such ordinances are not public laws; punishment for their violation is imposed by the municipality, and not by the state. Since such ordinances are not on the level of public laws, it is usually held, where a state statute prohibits the same act forbidden by a municipal ordinance, that *both* the state and the municipality may punish whoever commits the offense.

FIRST-DEGREE PRINCIPALS AT COMMON LAW

A principal in the first degree is the one who actually commits the crime, either by his own hand, or by an inanimate agency, or by an innocent human agent.

Or, for example, a man may commit a homicide himself (as the principal) through the agency of an innocent third person, as by giving poison to a child, or to an adult who is ignorant of its character, with directions that the latter shall give it to another. The child or other adult are not considered as parties to this principal's crime.

SECOND-DEGREE PRINCIPALS AT COMMON LAW

A principal in the second degree is one who is present when a felony is committed by another, and who aids or abets in its commission. To constitute one a principal in the second degree, (1) there must be a guilty principal in the first degree, (2) the principal in the second degree must be present when the offense is committed, but his presence may be constructive, and (3) he must aid or abet the commission of the offense, for some participation is necessary, though it need not necessarily be active. There cannot be a principal in the second degree unless there is a guilty principal in the first degree. On the trial of a person indicted as a principal in the second

degree, it is necessary to show the guilt of the principal in the first degree.

Presence, actual or constructive, at the time the offense is committed, is necessary to render one a principal in the second degree. If a person procures or counsels the commission of a crime by another, and is absent when it is committed, he is merely an accessory, and at common law he cannot be convicted under an indictment charging him as a principal. Thus, where a servant let a person into his master's house on an afternoon, and concealed him there all night, in order that he might commit a larceny in the house, but left the house early the next morning, and was absent when the larceny was committed, it was held that he was not a principal in the second degree, but an accessory before the fact.

Constructive Presence

It is unnecessary, however, in order to charge one as a principal in the second degree, as distinguished from an accessory before the fact, that there shall be a strict, actual, and immediate presence at the time and place of the commission of the offense. Nor is it necessary that he shall be an eye or ear witness of the criminal act. A person is constructively present, hence guilty as a principal, if he is acting with the person who actually commits the deed in pursuance of a common design, and is aiding his associate, either by keeping watch or otherwise, or is so situated as to be able to aid him, with a view, known to the other, to insure success in the accomplishment of the common enterprise.

A person who watches nearby to prevent surprise or interference while a confederate breaks and enters a house with felonious intent, or robs a man, or sets fire to a building, or commits a larceny, is guilty as a principal in the second degree, though he may not be near enough to see the other commit the offense. And where a servant, whose duty it is to watch over goods, purposely absents himself to facilitate their theft, he is guilty as a principal.

A person may be constructively present, even

though actually at a considerable distance. In an early case, A and B were convicted of an assault with intent to rob a stage, which was alleged to have been committed in a particular county, when the evidence tended to show that A, B and C entered into a conspiracy to commit the robbery, that the attempt to commit the same was actually made by B and C in one county, and that A was at the time in another county, and not within forty miles of the scene of the attempt. It appeared, however, that acting in pursuance of the common plan, he had given the others notice of the departure of the stage from the county where he was, by building a fire on a mountain in that county. Under these circumstances it was held that A was constructively present in the county where the alleged crime was committed, at the time of the attempt, and that he was guilty as a principal in the second degree in that county, and not merely as an accessory before the fact in the county where he actually was.

To be constructively present within this principle, one must at least be in such a situation that he might render assistance in some manner, not necessarily physical, in the commission of the offense.

Participation

To render one guilty as principal in the second degree, he must in some way participate in the commission of the offense, by aiding or abetting the actual perpetrator of the deed. Mere presence at the time the offense is committed, and acquiescence or failure to make any effort to prevent its commission, or to apprehend the offender, is not enough.

"If he be present," said Sir Matthew Hale, "and not aiding or abetting to the felony, he is neither principal nor accessory. If A and B be fighting and C, a man of full age, comes by chance, and is a looker on only, and assists neither, he is not guilty of murder or homicide, as principal in the second degree, but is a misprision, for which he shall be fined, unless he use means to apprehend the felon." Mere mental approval is not enough to render one an aider and abettor.

It is not necessary, however, that actual physical aid shall be given. It is enough to make one a principal in the second degree if he is present in concert with the actual perpetrator of the offense, for the purpose of assisting if necessary, or of watching and preventing interference or detection, or for the purpose of encouragement.

Criminal Intent

To be guilty as a principal in the second degree, a criminal intent is necessary. A person who enters into communication with one who is suspected of criminal acts, and apparently aids or abets him in the commission of an act, is not a principal in the second degree, if he did so, not with a criminal intent, but for the purpose of detecting the other party, and disclosing his guilt for the benefit of the public. And it can make no difference in such a case whether he was a public officer or merely a private person.

When a specific intent is necessary to constitute a particular crime, one cannot be a principal in the second degree to that particular offense unless he entertains such an intent, or knows that the party actually doing the act entertains such intent.

ACCESSORY BEFORE THE FACT

An accessory before the fact is one who procures, commands, or counsels the commission of a felony by another, but who is not present, either actually or constructively, when the felony is committed. To constitute one an accessory before the fact, (1) there must be a guilty principal in the first degree, (2) the accessory must be neither actually nor constructively present when the offense is committed, and (3) there must be some participation by way of procurement, command, or counsel. Mere knowledge that the offense is to be committed, or even mental approval, is not enough.

The person actually committing the deed

must be a guilty party, and not an innocent agent, because one who procures the commission of a felony through the instrumentality of an innocent agent is himself the principal in the first degree. Of course a person who commands or counsels another to commit a felony cannot be an accessory, if the other does not actually commit the felony.

Statutes in some jurisdictions have altered the common-law requirement that the principal be convicted before or simultaneously with the accessory by permitting such convictions prior to the conviction of the principal. Not only must a principal be found guilty but to punish an accessory before the fact by imprisonment it must be shown that the principal is also amenable to such punishment. Therefore it was held that where the principal was a corporation the accessory before the fact could not be sentenced to imprisonment.

Criminal Intent

For one to be guilty of a crime as an accessory he must have a criminal intent. Thus, one who joins a conspiracy to commit a robbery merely for the purpose of exposing it, and honestly carries out the plan, is not an accessory before the fact to the robbery when committed by the others.

"Mere presence, of course, and even mental approbation, if unaccompanied by outward manifestation or expression of such approval, is insufficient." As where defendant is a bystander in a crowd seeking the release of a prisoner, but does not participate in the misconduct of the mob, nor in the shooting that resulted therefrom.

Where defendant assisted another in committing a burglary by boosting the burglar up so that he could enter the burglarized store, and then reported it to the police, and assisted the police in capturing the burglar, the court held that the question of defendant's criminal intent was for the jury, when he explained that he helped the burglar and then reported him to get even with him for stealing his watch.

Procurement, Command, or Counsel

To render one an accessory he must have procured, commanded, or counseled the commission of the act. "And therefore," says Sir Matthew Hale, "words that sound in bare permission make not an accessory; as, if A says he will kill J. S., and B says 'You may do your pleasure for me,' this makes not B accessary." The procurement, however, need not be direct. It is sufficient if it be through the agency of another; and it may be by approbation or consent to an expressed felonious design.

Approbation and consent are something more than "words sounding in bare permission," of which Hale speaks in the above quotation. Bare nondisclosure or concealment of the intention of another to commit a felony is not enough.

*

RAPE

The common-law felony denoted rape is unlawful carnal knowledge of a woman by force and without her consent.

This crime is defined by East as "the unlawful carnal knowledge, by a man, of a woman, forcibly and against her will" and by Hawkins as "unlawful and carnal knowledge of a woman by force and against her will." The usual statutory definition is "the act of sexual intercourse with a female person not the wife of, or judicially separated from bed and board from, the offender, committed without her lawful consent. Emission is not necessary; and any sexual penetration, however slight, is sufficient to complete the crime." The Model Penal Code broadens the definition of rape to cover deviate sexual intercourse enforced upon a woman, recognizing that forcible ravishment of whatever kind or type is a crime of the greatest gravity. The expression "against her will" in the early definitions, meant "without her consent" and the latter expression has been substituted in modern statutes, as has just been seen. Any man who has unlawful carnal knowledge of a woman by force, and without her conscious consent or permission, is guilty of rape, both at common law and under statutes. It is generally agreed that this offense involves want of consent on the part of the woman. If she consciously consents to the act of intercourse, however tardily or reluctantly, and however persistently she may resist for a time, the act is not rape, provided she is of such an age and condition as to be capable of giving a valid consent. In many of the cases it has been said that, to make the act rape, the woman must have resisted "to the uttermost." A court has held that "resistance must be up to the point of being overpowered by actual force, or of inability, from loss of strength, longer to resist, or, from the number of persons attacking, resistance must be dangerous or absolutely useless, or there must be duress or fear of death." Some courts, however, decline to recognize the rule requiring the utmost reluctance and resistance. The important distinction lies in the difference between consent and submission; the latter does not preclude a prosecution for rape.

Obviously rape could be classed, and treated with, offenses against the person, also recall assault with intent to rape and attempts to rape.

The Victim

A requisite of this offense is "unlawful" carnal knowledge of a woman. It follows, therefore, that a man usually cannot be guilty of rape by having carnal knowledge of his wife, and it can make no difference that he does so by force and against her will. Nor can a man be guilty of an attempt to rape his wife, or of an assault with intent to rape her. The same public policy reasons dictating the exclusion of one's wife as a rape victim, namely, the availability of civil remedies for sexual incompatibility, and the legislative and judicial refusal to jeopardize a husband's freedom for an activity occurring within the marital relation, apply, in some degree, to any parties cohabiting as man and wife. Consequently, the Model Penal Code bars prosecution for rape in all cases where the parties have been living together, whether adulterously, bigamously or in any other meretricious manner, for some extended period. He may, however, be guilty as a principal in the second degree, or as an accessory before the fact, in procuring the rape of his wife by another man, or in aiding or abetting another in committing the offense. Subject to the marital status qualification, any female may be the subject of rape. It is not necessary, as has sometimes been contended, that she shall have reached the age of puberty. Nor is it necessary that she shall have been chaste. The fact that she was not chaste may aid, as a matter of evidence, in showing that she consented, but it does not, as a matter of law, prevent the intercourse from being rape, if it was in fact accomplished by force and without her consent.

Problems of Consent

That the female is mentally incapable of consenting or refusing has been held not to be a bar, despite the want of consent requirement, in the case of intercourse with women who are insane, idiotic, insensible, or asleep at the time of the act; but there must be force in accomplishing the act. If a woman is asleep, or is so insane or imbecilic that she does not know the nature of the act, intercourse with her is rape, though she does not resist. For the same reason, unlawful intercourse with a woman who is reduced to a state of insensibility by intoxicating liquors or drugs constitutes rape, if the liquors or drugs were administered by the accused, or by another with his cognizance. If the law were otherwise, any woman in a state of utter stupefaction or unconsciousness, however caused, would be vulnerable to the gravest personal dishonor.

Another apparent exception to the rule requiring force and want of consent in rape is in cases where the woman's consent is induced, or resistance prevented, by fear of personal violence threatened by the man. It is generally agreed that a man is guilty of rape if he so overpowers a woman by threats and an array of force that she does not dare to resist, and has intercourse with her under such circumstances, as the want of consent of the woman is the essence of the offense. The old rule of "resistance to the uttermost" is obsolete and the more modern authorities have repudiated it. The law no longer requires a woman to do more than her age, strength and other circumstances render it reasonable for her to do in order to demonstrate her opposition.

Some of the courts have recognized a further exception to the rule requiring force and want of consent in cases in which the woman's consent is obtained by fraud. On this question there is a conflict in the decisions. It has been held that if a woman is fraudulently induced to submit to sexual intercourse, when she does not understand the nature of the act, as where a physician fraudulently induces a girl to submit to intercourse with him by pretending that it is necessary and proper surgical treatment, the act is rape. But by some authority, if a woman consents to sexual intercourse with a man, understanding the nature of the act, the man is not guilty of rape, though her consent may have been obtained by false and fraudulent pretenses. According to this view, some of the courts in which the question has arisen have held that a man is not guilty of rape in having carnal knowledge of a woman by falsely personating her husband. For the same reasons, if a woman consents to intercourse in the belief that an illegal marriage with the man is legal, upon his fradulent representation to that effect, he is not guilty of rape.

Statutory Rape

Under the old common law it was not regarded as rape to have carnal knowledge of a child, however young, if she consented. By an early English statute, however, it was made a felony to have carnal knowledge of a child under the age of ten years, whether with or without her consent. Similar statutes have been enacted in this country. In some states the statute punishes the carnal knowledge of girls of as much as sixteen years of age, or even more, either with or without their consent. In a few cases it has been held that, independently of any statute, a child under ten years of age is incapable of consenting to sexual intercourse, and that it is rape at common law for a man to have intercourse with her with her consent. The Model Penal Code classifies statutory rape not as rape at all, but as a species of "corruption of minors," and penalizes it by a maximum 5-year prison term. Moreover, the Code requires the male offender to have at least a 4-year age advantage over his female victim and allows him to use the defense of the girl's prior promiscuity with other partners. This recommended law would eliminate the treatment as a statutory rape victim of a consenting, physically mature, perhaps even seducing, teen-aged girl, who is on an age and emotional par with her adolescent attacker.

Intercourse with a girl under 12 constitutes, in some jurisdictions, a crime denominated "aggravated rape." It can be argued that such denomination is a distinct misnomer because the child-victim, although legally incapable of assent, has actually and in fact consented to the intercourse, thereby vitiating the definitional element of force or violence requisite to rape. The wisdom and propriety of straining and stretching the word "rape" to include nonforceful, nonviolent coitus is highly disputable, for such inclusion serves to dilute, diminish and obscure the classic meaning of a universally understood word.

Semantic difficulties in this area do not end here. Some states prohibit intercourse with a willing girl between 12 and 17 years of age by an offense called "statutory rape," likewise a gross misnomer as no violence, force or coercion is involved. In Illinois and in England, still different but perhaps more accurate and distinctive legal phraseology has been adopted to characterize sex relations with a consenting female adolescent. The appellation accorded such offense is "indecent assault." In fact, the Illinois Criminal Code of 1961 eliminates altogether the crime of statutory rape, and substitutes therefor two statutes applicable in such instances, namely, a felony titled "indecent liberty with a child," and a misdemeanor called "contributing to the delinquency of a child."

There is one other grammatical mutation or aberration of note and that is the use of the words "carnal knowledge of a child" or "carnal knowledge of a juvenile" to encompass such nonforceful intercourse with children and adolescents.

Unlawful Carnal Knowledge

To constitute rape, sexual intercourse (carnal knowledge) is essential. It is necessary, therefore, that there shall be some penetration of the female organ by the male. The slightest penetration, however, is sufficient.

In Hill's Case, decided in England in 1781, emission was held to be necessary, as well as penetration, on the theory that there could not be carnal knowledge without it. Prior to this decision, emission was not regarded as necessary, and it has since been declared unnecessary by statute. In this country some of the courts have followed Hill's Case; but others have recognized the earlier rule, and have held penetration, without emission, sufficient; or else statutes have been enacted expressly declaring it unnecessary.

Males Incapable of Committing Rape

In England, at common law, a boy under fourteen years of age was conclusively presumed to be physically incapable of committing rape, and no evidence could be introduced to show capacity in fact. In this country the same rule has been held by some of the courts. Others have repudiated it, however, on the ground that in this country boys do, as a matter of fact, sometimes reach the age of puberty before they are fourteen, and that, as the reason for the rule does not exist, the rule is not applicable. Most of these courts have held that there is a presumption of incapacity, but that the presumption may be rebutted by affirmatively showing capacity in fact. A court went further, and held that there is not even a presumption of incapacity.

An impotent man, if incapable of copulation, cannot commit rape, but if he is capable of penetration, and merely incapable of emission or procreation, he may commit the offense, for, as we have seen, penetration, without emission, is sufficient. He may commit assault with intent to commit rape.

Liability of Nonvictim Females

Accessorial liability has been utilized as the basis for convicting females who have aided and abetted males in raping another woman.

*

5. Delinquent and Status Offenses in American Juvenile Courts

MARK M. LEVIN
ROSEMARY C. SARRI

A COMPARATIVE ANALYSIS OF STATUTES DEALING with the jurisdiction of juvenile courts in the 50 states and District of Columbia reveals great diversity of legislative approaches. After 70 years of experimentation, the states have still not reached consensus on many crucial statutory provisions, such as those governing age and offense definitions.

Federalism has produced dramatic differences, most of which cannot be related to states' sociodemographic conditions. In Connecticut, for example, a 16 year-old is not considered a juvenile. He or she will be tried in an adult criminal court with full constitutional protection. If convicted, however, disposition will probably be handled by a juvenile court, and the youth may be retained in a juvenile institution until age 21. In contrast, the majority of states set 17 years as the maximum for original jurisdiction, and several states provide for transition to adult status under youthful offender statutes.

The statutory differences that result in these startling variations can be sorted into several general areas, each of which will be discussed in some detail: (1) the scope and nature of delinquent and status offense definitions; (2) age; (3) offense limitations on the court's adjudicatory powers; (4) jurisdictional conflicts with the criminal court; and (5) permissible interactions with the adult criminal system, such as waiver, concurrent jurisdiction, and so forth.

DELINQUENT AND STATUS OFFENSES

The juvenile court is vested with the following types of jurisdiction: (1) proceedings involving juveniles who have allegedly committed statutory offenses, where the case has been withdrawn from the ordinary processes of criminal justice because of the offender's age; (2) proceedings involving behavior which if performed by an adult would not be criminal and would not result in state intervention; and (3) proceedings involving the dependent and/or neglected status of juveniles.

In some states, where family and other special courts have been established, the jurisdiction of the court may be extended even further. Our concern in this report is directed toward those behaviors that include statutory violations and status offenses.[1]

The first type of proceedings presents few definitional problems unique to the juvenile justice system. However, states use different labels to denote the same behavior. Thirty-nine

▶SOURCE: *Juvenile Delinquency: A Comparative Analysis of Legal Codes in the U.S. National Assessment of Juvenile Corrections, Ann Arbor, Mich.: The University of Michigan, June 1974, pp. 10–19. (Editorial adaptations.) Reprinted by permission of Mark M. Levin and Rosemary C. Sarri, National Assessment of Juvenile Corrections, University of Michigan, Ann Arbor, Mich.*

[1]Provisions governing the processing of dependent and neglected juveniles are not analyzed in this report unless the statutes did not distinguish between delinquent and dependent youth.

states categorize juvenile lawbreakers as "delin-quent."[2] In the 12 remaining states, the statutes use what are intended to be less stigmatizing names—"offenders," "wards of the courts," or simply "children."[3] Ironically, "delinquent" was originally considered a neutral decriminalized term. Recent statutory provisions have generally retained the use of the "delinquent" category.

The second type of proceedings is currently a source of great controversy. All 51 Juvenile Codes bring within the purview of the juvenile court conduct that is illegal only because of the child's age—"status offenses." Youth so charged have not violated a law applicable to adults. With the exception of truancy and curfew violations, juveniles really come under the court's jurisdic-tion because of their condition, not because of specific conduct. These status offenses are defined in highly subjective terms— "incorrigibility," "immorality," "idling," "beyond reasonable parental control," "unruliness," "waywardness," and "in need of supervision." In many states, status offenses are defined so broadly that any and all children could be brought within the juvenile court's jurisdiction if the judge were so inclined. For example, a re-cently revised statute in Ohio provides that the court may have jurisdiction over a child:

a. "who does not subject himself to the reasonable control of his parents, teachers, guardian, or custo-dian, by reason of being wayward or habitually dis-obedient;

b. who is habitually truant from home or school;

c. who so deports himself as to injure or endanger the health or morals of himself or others;

d. who is found in a disreputable place, visits or patronizes a place prohibited by law or associates with vagrant, vicious, criminal, notorious, or immoral per-sons. . . ."

This provision is representative, rather than unusual, in its scope, vagueness, imprecision, and opportunity for abuse.

In 26 states status violators are not differen-tiated and are classified as delinquents, subject to the same dispositions as juveniles who have committed an adult offense.[4] In 25 states sepa-rate categories have been created for status of-fenders.[5] The labels vary: "children in need of supervision," "unruly children," "incorrigible children," etc.; and unfortunately, the language in these provisions is so ambiguous that depen-dent youth can often be included for processing. Such provisions are likely to produce negative outcomes unless agencies and courts are also en-joined to meet the dependency needs of youth in ways that will enhance their ability to function in normal social roles.

In the 25 states with separate status offense categories, the distinction is generally more than merely semantic. Eighteen of these "separate categorization" states place restrictions on the disposition alternatives available to the juvenile court judge for status offenders;[6] and four states require separate detention housing.[7] Dis-position restrictions are mostly of two types: (1) a flat prohibition on housing status offenders and delinquents together; or (2) a requirement that the judge must first find the child unamen-able to other forms of treatment before commit-ting the child to a training school or other cor-rectional facility.

States where recent Code revisions have been enacted show a definite trend toward adding such separate categories. No special status of-fender provisions can be found in Codes predat-ing 1959.

[2]Ala., Ariz., Ark., Colo., Conn., Del., D. C., Fla., Ga., Ill., Ind., Iowa, Kans., La., Md., Mass., Minn., Miss., Mont., Neb., N. H., N. J., N. Mex., N. Y., N. C., N. Dak., Ohio, Okla., Pa., R. I., S. C., S. Dak., Tenn., Tex., Vt., Wash., W. Va., Wis., Wyo.
[3]Alaska, Calif., Hawaii, Ida., Ky., Me., Mich., Mo., Nev., Ore., Utah, Va.

[4]Ala., Ark., Conn., Del., Ida., Ind., Iowa, Ky., La., Me., Mich., Minn., Miss., Mo., Mont., Nev., N. H., N. J., N. Mex., Ore., Pa., S. C., Tex., Utah, Va., W. Va.
[5]Alaska, Ariz., Calif., Colo., D. C., Fla., Ga., Hawaii, Ill., Kans., Md., Mass., Neb., N. Y., N. C., N. Dak., Ohio, Okla., R. I., S. Dak., Tenn., Vt., Wash., Wis., Wyo.
[6]Alaska, Calif., Colo., D. C., Fla., Ga., Hawaii, Ill., Md., Neb., N. Y., N. C., N. Dak., Ohio, S. Dak., Tenn., Vt., Wis.
[7]Del., Ga., Md., Vt.

AGE LIMITATIONS

Age for Original Jurisdiction

Naturally, one of the most significant limitations on the juvenile court's jurisdiction is the age of the child. The philosophy of the juvenile court movement was premised on the assumption that children, because of their age, are generally incapable of criminal behavior. There is today, however, no agreement on the age at which a child is considered an adult. In fact, many recent statutory changes have occurred in this area—age limits have been both lowered and raised.

Minimum age limitations are infrequently found in juvenile court jurisdictional statutes. However, adult penal codes frequently reflect the common law view, which limits criminal offenses to those who have reached age 7.

As the data in Figure 1 indicate, the *maximum* age for original jurisdiction is 17 years in 33 states.[8] In 12 states the maximum age is 16,[9] and in the remaining states the court can adjudicate only those age 15 and under.[10] There are no longer any states where original jurisdiction extends to age 21, as was true until recently in California. Three states still set a lower maximum age for males than for females, but such a distinction has been held unconstitutional by state tribunals.[11]

Four states set a higher maximum age for those charged with status offenses.[12] In New York, for example, 16 year-old runaways may be found in the juvenile court, but not 16 year-olds charged with adult offenses.

*

MAXIMUM AGE FOR CONTINUING JURISDICTION

Once the juvenile court's jurisdiction has been attached, the maximum age for original jurisdiction is no longer a limitation on the court's authority. Forty-one states grant the juvenile court continuing jurisdiction over offenders until they reach age 21, as Figure 2 indicates.[13] Thus, in California, where the maximum age for original jurisdiction is 17, the court does not lose its authority when an adjudicated delinquent becomes 18 years old. In three states, the court's jurisdiction terminates at age 20.[14] In Michigan, New York, and Vermont, jurisdiction ends at

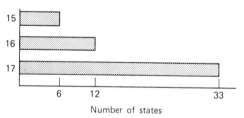

Figure 1.   Maximum age for original jurisdiction.

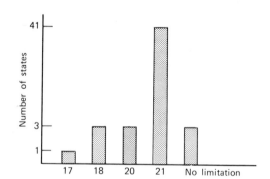

Figure 2.   Maximum age for continuing jurisdiction.

[8]*Alaska, Ariz., Ark., Calif., Colo., Del., D. C., Hawaii, Ida., Ind., Iowa, Kans., Ky., Minn., Miss., Mont., Neb., Nev., N. J., N. Mex., N. Dak., Ohio, Ore., Pa., R. I., S. Dak., Tenn., Utah, Va., Wash., W. Va., Wis., Wyo.*

[9]*Fla., Ga., Ill., La., Me., Md., Mass., Mich., Mo., N. H., S. C., Tex.*

[10]*Ala., Conn., N. Y., N. C., Okla., Vt.* In Vermont and Alabama, the juvenile court can adjudicate children 16 and 17 years old, but only if the prosecutor decides to bring the case into juvenile court.

[11]*Ill., Okla., Tex.*

[12]*Ala., Mich., N. Y., Vt.* All but Michigan set 15 as the maximum age for original jurisdiction.

[13]*Ala., Alaska, Ariz., Ark., Calif., Colo., Del., D. C., Fla., Ga., Hawaii, Ida., Ill., Ind., Iowa, Kans., Ky., La., Md., Mass., Minn., Mo., Nev., N. H., N. Mex., N. C., N. Dak., Ohio, Okla., Ore., Pa., R. I., S. Dak., Tenn., Tex., Utah, Vt., Va., Wash., W. Va., Wis.*

[14]*Me., Miss., Neb.*

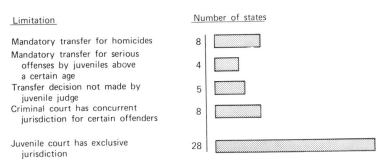

Figure 3. Jurisdictional limitations. Virginia and Pennsylvania are included in two categories because of special code provisions.

age 18. Connecticut, with a maximum original jurisdiction age limitation of 15, allows institutionalization and probation to extend for only two years, which means release is mandatory before the juvenile reaches age 18. Montana, South Carolina, and New Jersey put no maximum age limitations on the continuing jurisdiction for certain serious offenses like homicide and rape.

It is significant that these provisions are phrased in terms of the age of majority.[15] As states move to lower the age of majority, the juvenile court's continuing jurisdiction to supervise delinquent children becomes restricted. Consequently, permissible transfer to the criminal court may become a more attractive alternative to those juvenile judges who do not wish to have serious offenders released shortly after they have committed an offense. More importantly, it may lead legislatures to lower the maximum age for the court's original jurisdiction.

Application of these provisions for continuing jurisdiction is limited. The court has power only to retain a previously adjudicated juvenile offender in an institution or on probation. For example, the court has no jurisdiction over a juvenile probationer who has passed the maximum age limitation on original jurisdiction and commits an additional offense while still on probation.

[15]See Florida Statutes Section 39.02: "The jurisdiction of the court terminates when the offender reaches the age of majority."

In 28 states, as shown in Figure 3, age is the only restriction on the juvenile court's jurisdiction, and the court has exclusive, orginal jurisdiction over all children below a certain age.[16] In the remaining 23 states, however, the juvenile court faces a host of restrictions on whom it can adjudicate.[17] The basis and rationale for mandatory transfer or concurrent jurisdictions are discussed below.

OFFENSE LIMITATIONS

Original jurisdiction of the juvenile court is limited by offense as well as by age in 12 states. The findings in Figure 3 clearly indicate that juveniles must be transferred to adult courts in many states. These provisions proceed from the assumption that, regardless of beliefs about the child's capacity for criminal behavior, the public must be protected from dangerous conduct. In eight states, any juvenile, regardless of age, may be tried in criminal court if he is charged with homicide or other capital or life-term offenses.[18]

[16]*Ala., Alaska, Ariz., Conn., Ga., Hawaii, Kans., Ky., Me., Mass., Mich., Minn., Mo., Mont., N. J., N. Mex., N. Y., N. Dak., Ohio, Okla., Ore., R. I., Tenn., Tex., Utah, Vt., Wash., Wis.*

[17]*Ark., Calif., Colo., Del., D. C., Fla., Ida., Ill., Ind., Iowa, La., Md., Miss., Neb., Nev., N. H., N. C., Pa., S. C., S. Dak., Va., W. Va., Wyo.*

[18]*Colo., Del., Fla., Ind., Miss., N. C., Pa., W. Va.* These statutory provisions are phrased either as an offense limitation on the juvenile court's jurisdiction or as a mandatory waiver of its jurisdiction. This distinction is significant because a mandatory waiver state may require that a probable cause hearing be held first in the juvenile court before trans-

Four states have similar Code provisions affecting a more limited class of juvenile offenders who must be tried in the criminal court.[19] This class is defined jointly in terms of offense and age. For example, in Louisiana, the juvenile court has no jurisdiction over juveniles 15 or older who are alleged to have committed rape or a capital offense. In Maryland, a similar provision sets the age at 14. Under the District of Columbia Code, serious felonies committed by juveniles 16 or over are excluded from the jurisdiction of the juvenile court. Arkansas' juvenile courts cannot hear felony cases if the child has reached age 15. These provisions attempt to strike a legislative balance between the need for protecting the community and the traditional juvenile court philosophy.

JURISDICTIONAL CONFLICT AND OVERLAP

A juvenile may fall within the age and offense limitations of the juvenile court and still be tried in the criminal court. In nearly every state, the juvenile court is empowered to weigh certain competing policy objectives listed in the statute and make a determination that the juvenile would best be tried in the criminal system. In 12 states, however, other procedures allow the criminal court to take jurisdiction over a juvenile: the prosecutor in certain situations is empowered to weigh the competing policies and make the initial decision about which court will try certain juveniles.[20] His decision is often different from that reached by the juvenile court judge, who is powerless to stop the criminal adjudication in these cases. In varying degrees, the scope of the juvenile judge's power is limited by

age and offense characteristics. This type of statutory provision may be phrased either as a grant of authority to the prosecutor or in terms of the concurrent jurisdiction of the criminal court, but they result in identical practices.

In Virginia, for example, the Commonwealth Attorney has discretion to send a case to the grand jury when the juvenile is an "habitual offender," or if "the offense may entail a jail term of over 20 years." The Illinois and South Carolina Codes take a similar approach. In Iowa, a grand jury indictment will automatically deprive the juvenile court of jurisdiction.

In Wyoming, the criminal court has concurrent jurisdiction over juveniles of any age and any offense. Nevada's criminal courts have concurrent jurisdiction over all juveniles who have allegedly committed a capital offense. In Pennsylvania, criminal courts have concurrent jurisdiction over 16 and 17 year-olds charged with capital offenses. In Nebraska, all youths 15 years and older may be subject to the powers of the criminal court.

Curiously, the criminal courts in California, Idaho, and New Hampshire may try juveniles who have fled the state to avoid prosecution, while South Dakota and Virginia have unusual procedures whereby criminal courts have concurrent jurisdiction if it was not know at the beginning of the proceeding that the offender was a juvenile.

Such statutory provisions represent a legislative determination that the juvenile offender must be criminally prosecuted in certain kinds of cases. In this sense, they are identical to the offense limitations on the juvenile courts' jurisdiction discussed above. However, these provisions go further and recognize a need for a degree of discretion not deemed appropriate for the juvenile court judge to exercise. Instead, it is vested in the prosecutor, whose chief concern is presumably the protection of the public rather than the welfare of the individual child and his prospects for rehabilitation.

---

fer, as in North Carolina. In offense limitation states, the juvenile must face a probable cause hearing in the criminal court.

[19]*Ark., D. C., La., Md.*

[20]*Calif., Ida., Ill., Iowa, Neb., Nev., N. H., Pa., S. C., S. Dak., Va., Wyo.*

The Measurement of Crime

THERE ARE SEVERAL METHODOLOGICAL TECHNIQUES CURRENTLY WIDELY USED TO estimate the extent of crime in modern society. Official police statistics involve criminal events that are detected, reported to the police, confirmed by the police, and become part of official tabulations recorded as "Crimes Known to the Police." Second, there are self-report studies in which persons, usually juveniles, admit on a questionnaire to having committed a number of illegal acts, most of which, seemingly, have never become known to public authorities. These may be considered as "Crimes Known to the Criminal or Delinquent." Finally, in recent years we have seen the rise of national victimization surveys, using sample survey techniques that secure information from a large population of households about previous offenses perpetrated against various family members.

The selections in this section represent a range of critical evaluations of these techniques of measuring crime. Black's selection, "The Production of Crime Rates," investigates the situational factors that impact on the police officer and the officer's role in creating official crime records or reports, by reacting to and noting field encounters with complainants. The creation of official crime reports are found to be related to the seriousness of the reported criminal behavior; the complainants's desire for police intervention; the relationship between offender and complainant prior to the crime; deference shown the police officer; and the social status of the complainant. It is important to note that Black finds no evidence of racially discriminatory behavior among the police investigated.

Skogan's selection, "The Dark Figure," deals with the extent and importance of unreported crime; it is a commonplace that of all crimes committed, only a certain percentage become known to the police. Skogan examines data from a national victimization survey that notes all offenses and crimes reported to the police. Discrepancies are found but, generally, unreported crimes contain proportionately fewer serious offenses, involve little financial loss, have comparatively less serious injuries, and are less likely to involve weapons. The final selection, by Savitz, deals with official statistics; it is a broad critique of official law enforcement statistics, primarily of the *Uniform Crime Reports* prepared by the FBI. The seven "major" offenses, which constitute the so-called Index Crimes, are examined, and a detailed statement is made of police statistics generally and to what diachronic changes in rates may be attributable. His conclusion is that with all of its limitations, the *U.C.R.* is still useful and remains perhaps the best and most useful source of regularly produced information on crime in America.

Hardt and Hardt, in the next selection, indicate some professionals' concern with official statistics of juvenile delinquency and their evident inadequacies, which has led to a growing reliance on the use of self-report techniques. They use data from one more self-report study of adolescents and evaluate the quality of this technique, appraising by several procedures. They find some evidence for the high validity of self-reports (for mostly minor delinquencies) and suggest the utility of the technique in some etiological and evaluation studies.

In a careful critique of crime victimization surveys, Levine explicates major sources of error that artificially and incorrectly inflate victimization crime rates. Subject biases (false reporting, memory errors, mistaken interpretation, and erroneous classification of events that might be crimes), interviewer biases, and coding errors are all considered.

The final selection in this section deals with the intriguing case of drug abuse, about which little serious data are available. In recent years figures and numbers regarding drug abuse incidence have been somehow generated and, in time, have become "commonly agreed on." Singer pursues the consequences of accepting these mythical numbers of heroin addicts in New York City and the amount of crime that is, accordingly, attributed to them. He clearly demonstrates the absurdity of these grossly inflated figures whereby, if addicts were assumed to have committed *all* shoplifting, burglaries, and robberies in the city, the total amount of property stolen would still be only a fraction of the property crime that such estimates have assumed they would be required to commit.

6. Production of Crime Rates

DONALD BLACK

SOCIOLOGICAL APPROACHES TO OFFICIAL CRIME rates generally fail to make problematic the production of the rates themselves. Theory has not directed inquiry to the principles and mechanisms by which some technically illegal acts are recorded in the official ledger of crime while others are not. Instead crime rates ordinarily are put to use as data in the service of broader investigations of deviance and control. Yet at the same time it has long been taken for granted that official statistics are not an accurate measure of all legally defined crime in the community (e.g., de Beaumont and de Tocqueville, 1964; Morrison, 1897; Sellin, 1931).

The major uses of official crime statistics have taken two forms (see Biderman and Reiss, 1967); each involves a different social epistemology, a different way of structuring knowledge about crime. One employs official statistics as an index of the "actual" or "real" volume and morphology of criminal deviance in the population. Those who follow this approach typically consider the lack of fit between official and actual rates of crime to be a methodological misfortune. Historically, measurement of crime has been the dominant function of crime rates in social science. A second major use of official statistics abandons the search for "actual" deviance. This is managed either be defining deviance with the official reactions themselves—a labeling approach—or by incorporating the

official rates not as an index of deviant behavior but as an index of control operations (e.g., Kitsuse and Cicourel, 1963; Erikson, 1966; Wilson, 1968). In effect this second range of work investigates "actual" social control rather than "actual" deviance. Hence it encounters methodological problems of its own, since, without question, social control agencies do not record all of their official attempts to counteract or contain what they and others regard as deviant conduct.[1] A striking feature of police work, for instance, is the degree to which officers operate with informal tactics, such as harassment and manipulative human-relations techniques, when they confront law-violative behavior (e.g., Skolnick, 1966; LaFave, 1965; Bittner, 1967; Black, 1968; Black and Reiss, 1970). In sum, when official statistics are used as a *means* of measurement and analysis, they usually function imperfectly. This is not to deny that such methods can be highly rewarding in some contexts.

This selection follows an alternative strategy that arises from an alternative conceptual starting point. It makes official records of crime an end rather than a means of study (see Wheeler,

---

[1] An approach that operationally defines criminal deviance as that which the police record as criminal—and nothing else—is immune to these problems. This would be the most radical "labeling" approach. It would exclude from the category of crime, for example, a murder carried out so skillfully that it goes undetected. It would necessarily exclude most "police brutality," since crimes committed by policemen are seldom detected and officially recorded as such.

▶SOURCE: *"Production of Crime Rates," American Sociological Review* (1970), 35:733–748. Reprinted by permission.

1967; Cicourel, 1968:26–28). It treats the crime rate as itself a social fact, an empirical phenomenon with its own existential integrity. A crime rate is not an epiphenomenon. It is part of the natural world. From this standpoint crime statistics are not evaluated as inaccurate or unreliable. They are an aspect of social organization and cannot, sociologically, be wrong. From the present perspective it nevertheless remains interesting that social control systems process more than they report in official statistics and that there is a good deal more rule-violative behavior than that which is processed. These patterns are themselves analytically relevant aspects of crime rates.

An official crime rate may be understood as a rate of *socially recognized*[2] deviant behavior; deviance rates in this sense are produced by all control systems that respond on a case-by-case basis to sanctionable conduct. This does not say that deviant behavior as a general category is synonymous with socially recognized deviant behavior. As a general category deviance may be defined as any behavior in a *class* for which there is a *probability* of negative sanction subsequent to its detection (Black and Reiss, 1970). Thus, whether or not an agent of control detects or sanctions a particular instance of rule-violative behavior is immaterial to the issue of whether or not it is deviant. Deviance is behavior that is *vulnerable* to social control. This approach generates three empirical types of deviance: (1) undetected deviance, (2) detected, unsanctioned deviance, and (3) sanctioned deviance. It should be apparent that, while every control system may produce a rate of socially recognized deviance, much unrecognized deviance surely resides in every control system.[3] By definition undetected

deviance cannot be recognized by a control system, but, as will become apparent in this presentation, even detected deviance may not be recognized as such. The notion of sanctioned deviance, by contrast, presumes that a social recognition process has taken place. The concept of social recognition of deviance is nothing more than a short-hand, more abstract way of stating what we mean by concrete expressions such as invocation of the law, hue and cry, bringing a suit, blowing the whistle, and so forth.

The concept of deviance should be applied with reference to specific systems of social control. For example, deviance that is undetected from the standpoint of a formal, legal control system, such as the police, may be detected or even sanctioned in an informal control context, such as a business organization, neighborhood or friendship group, or family. Crime rates then are rates of deviance socially recognized by official agencies of criminal-law enforcement. They are official rates of *detection* ("crimes known to the police") and of *sanctioning* (arrest rates and conviction rates).[4] Enforcement agencies handle many technically illegal acts that they omit from their official records. This selection explores some of the conditions under which the police produce official rates of crime detection in field encounters with citizens.

public and private places guarantees contemporary society some volume of secret deviance (Schwartz, 1968; Lofland, 1969:62–68). As far as criminal deviance is concerned, other well-known factors are the failure of citizens to report victimizations to the police and the failure of the police to report what is reported to them.

Evidence from victimization surveys suggests that under-reporting of crime in official statistics is more a consequence of police discretion than of the failure of citizens to notify the police. Citizens claim that they report far more crimes to the police than the police ultimately report; this margin of unreported crime exceeds that which citizens admit they withhold from the police (Biderman, 1967).

[4]The "clearance rate" is a hybrid form of crime rate produced in American police systems. This is the proportion of "crimes known to the police" that have been solved, whether through arrest or some other means (see Skolnick, 1966;164–181).

[2]In his definition of law, Hoebel (1954:28) notes that enforcement of law is a "socially recognized" privilege. In the same vein a crime rate may be understood as a socially recognized product of law enforcement work. Malinowski (1962:79–80) stresses the importance of social recognition of deviant acts for the community as well as for the deviant person.

[3]The moral and physical organization of social life into

SOCIAL ORGANIZATION OF CRIME DETECTION

Detection of deviance involves (1) the discovery of deviant *acts* or behavior and (2) the linking of *persons* or groups to those acts. Types of deviance vary widely according to the extent to which either or both of these aspects of detection are probable. Some deviant acts are unlikely to be discovered, although discovery generally is equivalent to the detection of the deviant person as well. Examples are homosexual conduct and various other forms of consensual sexual deviance. Acts of burglary and auto theft, by contrast, are readily detected, but the offending persons often are not apprehended. These differential detection probabilities stem in part from the empirical patterns by which various forms of violative behavior occur in time and social space. In part they stem as well from the uneven climate of social control.

The organization of police control lodges the primary responsibility for crime detection in the citizenry rather than in the police. The uniformed patrol division, the major line unit of modern police departments, is geared to respond to citizen calls for help via a centralized radio-communications system. Apart from traffic violations, patrol officers detect comparatively little crime through their own initiative. This is all the more true of legally serious crime. Thus crime detection may be understood as a largely *reactive* process from the standpoint of the police as a control system. Far less is it a *proactive* process. Proactive operations aimed at the discovery of criminal behavior predominate in the smaller specialized units of the large police department, particularly in the vice and morals division, including the narcotics squad, and in the traffic division. Most crimes, unlike vice offenses, are not susceptible to detection by means of undercover work or the enlistment of quasi-employed informers (see Skolnick, 1966). Unlike traffic offenses, furthermore, most crimes cannot be discovered through the surveillance of public places. Since the typical crim-inal act occurs at a specifically unpredictable time and place, the police must rely upon citizens to involve them in the average case. The law of privacy is another factor that presses the police toward a reactive detection system (Stinchcombe, 1963). Even without legal limitations on police detective work, however, the unpredictability of crime itself would usually render the police ignorant in the absence of citizens. Most often the citizen who calls the police is a victim of a crime who seeks justice in the role of *complainant*.

Vice control and traffic enforcement generally operate without the assistance of complainants. It appears that most proactive police work arises when there is community pressure for police action but where, routinely, there are no complainants involved as victims in the situations of violative behavior in question. In the average case proactive detection involves a simultaneous detection of the violative act and of the violative person. Proactively produced crime rates, therefore, are nearly always rates of arrest rather than rates of known criminal acts. In effect the proactive clearance rate is 100%. Crime rates that are produced in proactive police operations, such as rates of arrest for prostitution, gambling, homosexual behavior, and narcotics violation, directly correlate with police manpower allocation. Until a point of total detection is reached and holding all else constant, these vice rates increase as the number of policemen assigned to vice control is increased. On the other hand, the more important variable in rates of "crimes known to the police," is the volume of complaints from citizens.

Nevertheless, rates of known crimes do not perfectly reflect the volume of citizen complaints. A complaint must be given official status in a formal written report before it can enter police statistics, and the report by no means automatically follows receipt of the complaint by the police. In the present investigation patrol officers wrote official reports in only 64% of the 554 crime situations where a complainant, but no suspect, was present in the field setting. The decision to give official status to a crime ordinarily is an outcome of face-to-face interaction between the police and the complainant rather than a programmed police response to a bureaucratic or legal formula. The content and contours of this interaction differentially condition the probability that an official report will be written, much as they condition, in situations where a suspect is present, the probability that an arrest will be made (Black, 1968; Black and Reiss, 1970).

Whether or not an official report is written affects not only the profile of official crime rates; it also determines whether subsequent police investigation of the crime will be undertaken at a later date. Subsequent investigation can occur only when an official report is forwarded to the detective division for further processing, which includes the possibility of an arrest of the suspect. Hence the rate of detection and sanctioning of deviant *persons* is in part contingent upon whether the detection of deviant *acts* is made official. In this respect justice demands formality in the processing of crimes. This paper considers the following conditions as they relate to the probability of an official crime report in police-complainant encounters: the legal seriousness of the alleged crime, the preference of the complainant, the relational distance between the complainant and the absentee suspect, the degree of deference the complainant extends to the police, and the race and social-class status of the complainant.

FIELD METHOD

Systematic observation of police-citizen transactions was conducted in Boston, Chicago, and Washington, D.C., during the summer of 1966. Thirty-six observers—persons with law, social science, and police administration backgrounds—recorded observations of routine encounters between uniformed patrolmen and citizens. Observers accompanied patrolmen on all work-shifts on all days of the week for seven weeks in each city. However, the times when police activity is comparatively high (evening shifts, particularly weekend evenings) were given added weight in the sample.

Police precincts were chosen as observation sites in each city. The precincts were selected so as to maximize observation in lower socioeconomic, high crime rate, racially homogeneous residential areas. This was accomplished through the selection of two precincts in Boston and Chicago and four precincts in Washington, D.C.

The data were recorded in "incident booklets," forms structurally similar to interview schedules. One booklet was used for each incident that the police were requested to handle or that they themselves noticed while on patrol. These booklets were not filled out in the presence of policemen. In fact the officers were told that our research was not concerned with police behavior but only with citizen behavior toward the police and the kinds of problems citizens make for the police. Thus the study partially utilized systematic deception.

A total of 5,713 incidents were observed and recorded. In what follows, however, the statistical base is only 554 cases, roughly one-in-ten of the total sample. These cases comprise nearly all of the police encounters with complainants in crime situations where no suspect was present in the field situation. They are drawn from the cases that originated with a citizen telephone call to the police, 76% of the total. Excluded are, first, encounters initiated by policemen on their own initiative (13%). Police-initiated encounters almost always involve a suspect or offender rather than a complainant; complainants usually must take the initiative to make themselves known to the police. Also excluded are encounters initiated by citizens who walk into a police station to ask for help (6%) or who personally flag down the police on the street (5%). Both of these kinds of police work have peculiar situational features and should be treated separately. The great majority of citizen calls by telephone are likewise inappropriate for the present sample. In almost one-third of the cases no citizen is present when the police arrive to handle the complaint. When a citizen is present, furthermore, the incident at issue pertains to a noncriminal matter in well over one half of the cases. Even when there is a criminal matter a suspect not infrequently is present. When a suspect is present the major official outcome possible is arrest rather than a crime report. Finally, the sample excludes cases in which two or more complainants of mixed race or social-class composition participated. It may appear that, in all, much has been eliminated. Still, perhaps surprisingly, what remains is the *majority of crime situations* that the police handle in response to citizen telephone calls for service. There is no suspect available in 77% of the felonies and in 51% of the misdemeanors that the police handle on account of a complaint by telephone. There is only a complainant. These proportions alone justify a study of police encounters with complainants. In routine police work the handling of crime is in large part the handling of complainants. Policemen see more victims than criminals.

LEGAL SERIOUSNESS OF THE CRIME

Police encounters with complainants where no suspect is present involve a disproportionately large number of felonies, the legally serious category of crime. This was true of 53% of the cases in the sample of 554. When a suspect is present, with or without a citizen complainant, the great majority of police encounters pertain only to misdemeanors (Black, 1968). In other words, the police arrive at the scene too late to apprehend a suspect more often in serious crime situations than in those of a relatively minor nature.[5] In police language, felonies

more often are "cold." A moment's reflection upon the empirical patterns by which various crimes are committed reveals why this is so. Some of the more common felonies, such as burglary and auto theft, generally involve stealth and occur when the victim is absent; by the time the crime is discovered, the offender has departed. Other felonies such as robbery and rape have a hit-and-run character, such that the police rarely can be notified in time to make an arrest at the crime setting. Misdemeanors, by contrast, more often involve some form of "disturbance of the peace," such as disorderly conduct and drunkenness, crimes that are readily audible or visible to potential complainants and that proceed in time with comparative continuity. In short, properties of the social organization of crime make detection of felony offenders relatively difficult and detection of misdemeanor offenders relatively simple, given detection of the act.[6]

When the offender has left the scene in either felony or misdemeanor situations, however, detection and sanctioning of the offender is precluded unless an official report is written by the police. Not surprisingly, the police are more likely to write these reports in felony than in misdemeanor situations.[7] Reports were written

[5]It is interesting to note that in ancient Roman law the offender caught in the act of theft was subject to a more serious punishment than the offender apprehended some time after detection of this theft. In the *Laws of the Twelve Tables* these were called "manifest" and "non-manifest" thefts. The same legal principle is found in the early Anglo-Saxon and other Germanic codes (Maine, 1963:366–367). It could well be that a similar pattern is found in present-day

law-in-action. What is formal in one legal system may be informal in another.

[6]The heavier penalties that the law provides for felonies may compensate for a loss in deterrence that could result from the relatively low rate at which felons are apprehended. Likewise, the law of arrest seemingly compensates for the social organization of crime that gives felons a head start on the police. In most jurisdictions the police need less evidence in felony than in misdemeanor situations to make a legal arrest without warrant. By a second technique, then, the legal system increases the jeopardy of felony offenders. The power of substantive law increases as procedural restrictions on legal officials are weakened. By both penalty and procedure, the law pursues the felon with a special vengeance.

[7]Crime situations were classified as felonies or misdemeanors according to legal criteria. These criteria were applied to the version of the crime that prevailed in the police-citizen transaction. The observations reports required the observer to classify the incident in a detailed list of

in 72% of the 312 felonies, but in only 53% of the 242 misdemeanors. It is clear that official recognition of crimes becomes more likely as the legally defined seriousness of the crime increases. Even so, it remains noteworthy that the police officially disregard one-fourth of the felonies they handle in encounters with complainants. These are not referred to the detective division for investigation; offenders in these cases thus unknowingly receive a pardon of sorts.

Now the reader might protest an analysis that treats as crimes some incidents that the police themselves do not handle as crimes. How can we call an event a law violation when a legal official ignores that very event? This is a definitional problem that plagues a sociology of law as well as a sociology of deviance and social control. How is a violation of the "law on the books" properly classified if "in practice" it is not labeled as such? It is easy enough to argue that either of these criteria, the written law or the law-in-action, should alone define the violative behavior in question. No answer to this dilemma

---

categories as well as to write a long-hand description of the incident. The felony-misdemeanor breakdown was made during the coding stage of the investigation.

The major shortcoming of this strategy is that the tabulation allows no gradations of legal seriousness within the felony and misdemeanor categories. This shortcoming was accepted in order to facilitate more elaborate statistical analysis with a minimum of attrition in the number of cases.

It should also be noted that the tabulations do not provide information pertaining to the kind of official report the police wrote for a given kind of crime situation. Occasionally, the police officially characterize the crime with a category that seems incorrect to a legally sophisticated observer. Most commonly this involves reducing the legal seriousness of the crime. However, there are cases where the officer, sometimes through sheer ignorance of the law or inattention, increases the legal seriousness of the crime. In one case, for example, a woman complained about two young men in an automobile who had made obscene remarks to her as she walked along the street near her residence. She claimed she was ready to press charges. After leaving the scene the officer filled out an official report, classifying the incident as an "aggravated assault," the felonious level of assault. Before doing so he asked the observer for his opinion as to the proper category. The observer feigned ignorance.

is true or false. It is of course all a matter of the usefulness of one definition or another. Here a major aim is to learn something about the process by which the police select for official attention certain technically illegal acts while they bypass others. If we classify as crimes only those acts the police officially recognize as crimes, then what shall we call the remainder? Surely the remainder should be conceptually distinguished from acts that are technically legal and which carry no sanctions. For that reason, the present analysis operates with two working categories, crimes and officially recognized crimes, along with an implicit residual category of non-crimes. Crime differs from other behavior by dint of a probability, the probability that it will be sanctioned in a particular administrative system if it is detected. The written law usually—though not always—is a good index of whether that probability exists. "Dead letter" illegal acts, i.e., those virtually never sanctioned, are not classifed as crimes in this analysis. Crime as a *general category* consists in a probability of sanction; official recognition in the form of a crime report is one factor that escalates that probability for a *specific instance* of crime. It is worthwhile to have a vocabulary that distinguishes *between crimes* on the basis of how the police relate to them. Without a vocabulary of this kind police invocation of the law in the face of a law violation cannot be treated as empirically or theoretically problematic. Rather, invocation of the law would *define* a law violation and would thereby deprive sociology of an intriguing problem for analysis. Indeed, if we define a law violation *with* invocation of the law, we are left with the peculiar analytical premise that enforcement of the law is total or universal. We would definitionally destroy the possibility of police leniency or even of police discretion in law enforcement.

THE COMPLAINANT'S PREFERENCE

Upon arriving at a field setting, the police typically have very little information about what they are going to find. At best they have the crude label assigned to the incident by a dispatcher at the communications center. Over the police radio they hear such descriptions as "a B and E" (breaking and/or entering), "family trouble," "somebody screaming," "a theft report," "a man down" (person lying in a public place, cause unknown), "outside ringer" (burglar-alarm ringing), "the boys" (trouble with juveniles), and suchlike. Not infrequently these labels prove to be inaccurate. In any case policemen find themselves highly dependent upon citizens to assist them in structuring situational reality. Complainants, biased though they may be, serve the police as primary agents of situational intelligence.

What is more, complainants not infrequently go beyond the role of providing information by seeking to influence the direction of police action. When a suspect is present the complainant may pressure the police to make an arrest or to be lenient. When there is no available suspect, it becomes a matter of whether the complainant prefers that the crime be handled as an official matter or whether he wants it handled informally. Of course many complainants are quite passive and remain behaviorally neutral. During the observation period the complainant's preference was unclear in 40% of the encounters involving a "cold" felony or misdemeanor. There were 184 felony situations in which the complainant expressed a clear preference; 78% lobbied for official action. Of the 145 misdemeanor situations where the complainant expressed a clear preference, the proportion favoring official action was 75%, roughly the same proportion as that in felony situations. It seems that complainants are, behaviorally, insensitive to the legal seriousness of crimes when they seek to direct police action.

Police action displays a striking pattern of conformity with the preferences of complainants. Indeed, in not one case did the police write an official crime report when the complainant manifested a preference for informal action. This pattern seen in legal perspective is particularly interesting given that felony complainants prefer informal action nearly as frequently as misdemeanor complainants. Police conformity with those complainants who do not prefer official action, however, is not so symmetrical. In felony situations the police comply by writing an official report in 84% of the cases, whereas when the complaint involves a misdemeanor their rate of compliance drops to 64%. Thus the police follow the wishes of officially-oriented complainants in the majority of encounters, but the majority is somewhat heavier when the occasion is a legally more serious matter. In the field setting proper the citizen complainant has much to say about the official recognition of crimes, though the law seemingly screens his influence.[8]

Recall that the raw inputs for the official detection rate are generated by the citizenry who call the police. At two levels, then, the operational influence of citizens gives crime rates a peculiarly democratic character. Here the servant role of the police predominates; the guardian role recedes. Since an official report is a prerequisite for further police investigation of the crime, this pattern also implies that complainants are operationally endowed with an adjudicatory power. Their observable preferences can ultimately affect probabilities of arrest and

[8]Here two general remarks about analytical strategy seem appropriate. One is that the present approach abdicates the problematics of psychological analysis. The observational study does not provide data on the motives or cognitions of the police or the citizens whose behavior is described. Still, findings on patterns of behavior make prediction of police behavior impossible. They also offer opportunities for drawing inferences about the impact or implications of police work for social organization. Much can be learned about man's behavior in a social matrix without knowing how he experiences his behavior. The consequences of behavior, moreover, are indifferent to their mental origins.

Secondly, the strategy pursued in this analysis is not sensitive, except in the broadest terms, to the temporal dimension of police-citizen transactions. Thus, simply because the complainant's preference is treated prior to other variables does not mean that it is temporally prior to other aspects of police-citizen interaction. Like the other variables treated in this investigation, the complainant's preference is prior in time only to the final police response to the encounter.

conviction. While the structure of the process is democratic in this sense, it most certainly is not universalistic. The moral standards of complainants vary to some extent across the citizen population, thereby injecting particularism into the production of outcomes. There appears a trade-off between democratic process and universalistic enforcement in police work. This is an organizational dilemma not only of the police but of the legal system at large. When the citizenry has the power to direct the invocation of law, it has the power to discriminate among law-violators. Moral diversity in the citizen population by itself assures that some discrimination of this kind will occur. This is true regardless of the intentions of individual citizens. When a legal system organizes to follow the demands of the citizenry, it must sacrifice uniformity, since the system responds only to those who call upon it while it ignores illegality that citizens choose to ignore. A legal system that strives for universalistic application of the law, by contrast, must refuse to follow the diverse whims of its atomized citizenry. Only a society of citizens homogeneous in their legal behavior could avoid this dilemma.

RELATIONAL DISTANCE

Like any other kind of behavior, criminal behavior is located within networks of social organization. One aspect of that social organization consists in the relationship existing between the criminal offender and the complainant prior to a criminal event. They may be related by blood, marriage, friendship, neighborhood, membership in the same community, or whatever. In other words, the adversarial relation that is created by a crime may itself be viewed as it is structured within a wider social frame. The findings in this section permit the conclusion that the probability of official recognition of a crime varies with the relational network in which the crime occurs.[9] The greater the rela-

tional distance between citizen adversaries, the greater is the likelihood of official recognition.

Citizen adversaries may be classified according to three levels of relational distance: (1) fellow family members, (2) friends, neighbors, or acquaintances, and (3) strangers. The vast majority of the cases fall into the "stranger" category, though some of these probably would be reclassified into one of the other relational categories if the criminal offender were detected. The complainant's first speculation generally is that a stranger committed the offense in question.

Table I shows that when a complainant expresses a preference for official action the police comply most readily when the adversaries are strangers to one another. They are less likely to comply by writing an official crime report when the adversaries are friends, neighbors, or acquaintances, and they are least likely to give official recognition to the crime when the complainant and suspect are members of the same family. The small number of cases in the "fellow family members" category prohibits comparison between felony and misdemeanor situations. In the other relational categories this comparison reveals that the police follow the same pattern in the handling of both felonies and misdemeanors. With the relational distance between the adversaries held constant, however, the probability of an official report is higher for felony than for misdemeanor situations. The highest probability of an official response occurs when the crime is a felony and the adversaries are strangers to one another (91%); the lowest calculable probability is that for misdemeanors when the adversaries are related by friendship, neighborhood, or acquaintanceship (42%). On the other hand, it appears that relational distance can override the legal seriousness of crimes in conditioning police action, since the

---

[9]Hall (1952:318) suggests that the relational distance between the victim and offender may influence the probability of *prosecution*. The present investigation, following Hall,

seeks to predict social control responses from variations in relational distance. A different strategy is to predict community organization from the relationships between adversaries who enter the legal system, under the assumption that legal disputes bespeak a relative absence of informal control in the relational contexts where they arise (see Nader, 1964).

Table I. Percent of Police Encounters with Complianants According to Type of Crime and Relational Tie between Citizen Adversaries, by Situational Outcome: Complainant Prefers Official Action

	Type of Crime and Relational Tie between Citizen Adversaries								
	Felony			Misdemeanor			All Crimes		
Situational Outcome	Family Members	Friends, Neighbors, Acquaintances	Strangers	Family Members	Friends, Neighbors, Acquaintances	Strangers	Family Members	Friends, Neighbors, Acquaintances	Strangers
Official report	(4)	62	91	(3)	43	74	41	51	84
No official report	(5)	38	9	(5)	57	26	59	49	16
Total percent	...	100	100	...	100	100	100	100	100
Total number	(9)	(16)	(92)	(8)	(23)	(62)	(17)	(39)	(154)

police are more likely to give official recognition to a misdemeanor involving strangers as adversaries (74%) than to a felony involving friends, neighbors, or acquaintances (62%). Here again, therefore, the law screens but does not direct the impact of an extra-legal element in the production of crime rates.

Beyond the importance of relational distance for an understanding of crime rates as such is another implication of these findings. Because a follow-up investigation of the crime report by the detective division may result in apprehension of the criminal offender, it is apparent that the probability of an official sanction for the offender lessens as the degree of social intimacy with his adversary—usually his victim—increases. When an offender victimizes a social intimate the police are most apt to let the event remain a private matter, regardless of the complainant's preference. A more general consequence of this pattern of police behavior is that the criminal law gives priority to the protection of strangers from strangers while it leaves vulnerable intimates to intimates. Indeed, victimizations of strangers by strangers may be comparatively more damaging to social order and hence, from a functional standpoint, require more attention from the forces of control. A victimization between intimates is capsulated by intimacy itself. Furthermore, as social networks are more intimate, it surely is more likely that informal systems of social control operate. Other forms of legal control also may become available in the more intimate social relationships. In contrast there is hardly anyone but the police to oversee relations among strangers. Seemingly the criminal law is most likely to be invoked where it is the only operable control system. The same may be said of legal control in general (see Pound, 1942; Schwartz, 1954; Nader and Metzger, 1963). Legal control melds with other aspects of social organization.

THE COMPLAINANT'S DEFERENCE

Evidence accumulates from studies of police sanctioning that the fate of suspects sometimes hangs upon the degree of deference or respect they extend to policemen in field encounters (Westley, 1953; Piliavin and Briar, 1964; Black, 1968; Black and Reiss, 1970). As a rule, the police are especially likely to sanction suspects who fail to defer to police authority whether legal grounds exist or not. Situational etiquette can weigh heavily on broader processes of social life (see Goffman, 1956 and 1963). This section offers findings showing that the complainant's deference toward the police conditions the official recognition of crime complaints.

The deference of complainants toward the police can be classified into three categories: (1) very deferential or very respectful, (2) civil, and (3) antagonistic or disrespectful. As might be expected, complainants are not often antagonistic toward policemen; it is the suspect who is more likely to be disrespectful (Black and Reiss, 1967:63–65). The number of cases of police encounters with antagonistic complainants is too few for separate analysis of felony and misdemeanor situations. When felonies and misdemeanors are combined into one statistical base, however, it becomes clear that by a large margin the probability of an official crime report is lowest when the complainant is antagonistic in the face-to-face encounter. (See Table II). Less than one-third of the disrespectful complainants who prefer official action see their wishes actualized in a crime report. Because of the small number of cases this finding nevertheless should be taken as tentative. The comparison between the very deferential and the civil complainants, which is more firmly grounded, is equally striking. The police are somewhat more likely to comply with very deferential complainants than with those who are merely civil. In sum, then, the less deferential the complainant, the less likely are the police to comply with his manifest preference for official action in the form of an official crime report.[10]

---

[10]The findings in this section present a problem of interpretation, since no information about the police officer's behavior toward the citizen is provided apart from whether or not he wrote an official report. Therefore, nothing is

Table II also shows that the complainant's degree of deference conditions crime-reporting in both felony and misdemeanor situations. In fact, it seems that the complainant's deference can predict official recognition as well, or even slightly better than the legal seriousness of the crime. The probability of a crime report in misdemeanor situations where the complainant is very deferential (85%) is as high as it is in felony situations where he is only civil toward the police (80%). Still, when we hold constant the complainant's deference, the legal seriousness of the incident looms to importance. In felony situations where the complainant is very respectful, the police satisfy his preference for official action in no less than 100% of the cases.

The findings in this section reveal that the level of citizen respect for the police in field encounters has consequences beyond those known to operate in the sanctioning of suspects. Here we see that the fate of citizens who are nominally

known from the tabulation about whether the officer behaved in such a way as to *provoke* the citizen into one or another degree of deference. Nothing is known about the subtle exchange of cues that takes place in any instance of face-to-face interaction. Other studies of the role of deference in police work are subject to the same criticism. Here, again, no inquiry is made into the motivational dimensions of the pattern. It nevertheless should be emphasized that whatever the motivation of the complainant behavior, the motivation was not the failure of the police to write an official report. In the cities studied the complainant ordinarily did not even know whether or not an official report was written, since the police ordinarily wrote the report in the police car or at the police station after leaving the encounter with the complainant. During the encounter they recorded the relevant facts about the incident in a notebook, whether or not they intended to write an official report. As some officers say, they do this "for show" in order to lead the complainant to believe they are "doing something." Thus, in the average case, it can be assumed that the complainant's deference is not a consequence of the situational outcome. Furthermore, the observers were instructed to record only the level of citizen deference that appeared prior to the situational outcome. A separate item was provided in the observation booklet for recording the citizen's manifest level of satisfaction at the close of the encounter. It therefore remains reasonable to hold that the complainant's deference can aid in calculating the probability of an official crime report.

served, as well as those who are controlled by the police, rides in part upon their etiquette. The official response to an avowed victimization in part depends upon the situational *style* in which the citizen presents his complaint to the control system. Official crime rates and the justice done through police detection of criminal offenders, therefore, reflect the politeness of victims. That sanctions are sometimes more severe for alleged offenders who are disrespectful toward the police can be understood in many ways as a possible contribution to the control function. Perhaps, for example, disrespectful offenders pose a greater threat to society, since they refuse to extend legitimacy to its legal system. Perhaps deterrence is undermined by leniency toward disrespectful suspects. Perhaps not. The point is that rationales are available for understanding this pattern as it relates to the police control function. It should be apparent that such rationales do not apply as readily to the tendency of the police to underreport the victimizations of disrespectful complainants. Surely this pattern could have only the remotest connection to deterrence of illegal behavior. Etiquette, it would seem, can belittle the criminal law.

THE COMPLAINANT'S STATUS

The literature on police work abounds in speculation but provides little observational evidence concerning the relation of social status to police outcomes. The routine policing of Negroes differs somewhat from that of whites, and the policing of blue-collar citizens differs quite massively from that of white-collar citizens. Nevertheless, there is a dearth of evidence that these differences arise from discriminatory behavior by policemen. It appears that more consequential in determining these outcomes are aggregative differences between the races and classes in the kinds of incidents the police handle along with situational factors such as those the present analysis examines (e.g., Skolnick, 1966; Black, 1968; Black and Reiss, 1970). Nevertheless, the research literature remains far

Table II. Percent of Police Encounters with Complainants According to Type of Crime and Complainant's Degree of Deference, by Situational Outcome: Complainant Prefers Official Action

Situational Outcome	Felony Very Deferential	Felony Civil	Felony Antagonistic	Misdemeanor Very Deferential	Misdemeanor Civil	Misdemeanor Antagonistic	All Crimes Very Deferential	All Crimes Civil	All Crimes Antagonistic
Official report	100	80	(2)	85	65	(1)	91	73	30
No official report	...	20	(1)	15	35	(6)	9	26	70
Total percent	100	100	...	100	100	...	100	99	100
Total number	(15)	(127)	(3)	(20)	(79)	(7)	(35)	(206)	(10)

Table III. Percent of Police Encounters with Complainants According to Type of Crime and Complainant's Social-Class Status and Race, by Situational Outcome: Complainant Prefers Official Action and Is Civil Toward Police

Situational Outcome	Felony Blue-Collar Negro	White	Felony White Collar Negro	White	Felony Class Unknown Negro	White	Misdemeanor Blue-Collar Negro	White	Misdemeanor White-Collar Negro	White	Misdemeanor Class Unknown Negro	White	All Crimes and Classes Negro	White
Official report	77	77	(5)	100	(3)	90	69	55	(2)	64	(2)	80	72	76
No official report	23	23	...	...	(5)	10	31	45	...	36	(3)	20	28	24
Total percent	100	100	...	100	...	100	100	100	...	100	...	100	100	100
Total number	(64)	(22)	(5)	(18)	(8)	(10)	(26)	(22)	(2)	(14)	(5)	(10)	(110)	(96)

too scanty to permit confident generalization on these questions.

Studies in the discretionary aspects of police work focus almost solely upon police encounters with suspects. The present sample provides an opportunity to investigate the relation between a complainant's race and social-class status and the probability that the police will give official recognition to his complaint. The tabulation limits the cases to those where the complainant expresses a preference for official action and to those where he is civil toward the police. This section concludes that the race of complainants does not independently relate to the production of official crime rates, but there is some evidence that the police give preferential treatment to white-collar complainants in felony situations.

For all crimes and social-class statuses taken together, the difference between Negroes and whites in the probability of an official crime report is slight and negligible (see Table III); it is a bit higher for whites. Table III also shows that this probability is the same for blue-collar Negroes and blue-collar whites in felony situations, though it is comparatively higher for blue-collar Negroes in misdemeanor situations. Evidence of racial discrimination thus appears weak and inconsistent. It should nonetheless be noted that if there were consistent evidence of a race differential it is not readily clear to whom a disadvantage could be attributed. Considered from the complainant's standpoint, a higher frequency of police failure to comply with complainants of one race could be viewed as discrimination *against* that race. But police failure to write a crime report also lowers the likelihood that the offender will be subjected to the criminal process. Since we may assume that complainants more commonly are victims of offenses committed by members of their own race than by members of another race (Reiss, 1967), then disproportionate police failure to comply with complainants could be viewed as discrimination *in favor* of that race, considered from the offender's standpoint. Race differentials in arrest rates for crimes where there is an identifiable

victim necessarily pose a similar dilemma of interpretation. Definitionally, there always is a conflict of legal interests between offenders and victims. Offender-victim relationships tend to be racially homogeneous. The social organization of crime therefore complicates questions of racial discrimination in law enforcement.[11]

Along social-class lines there is some evidence of discrimination against complainants and offenders. Table III shows that in felony situations the police are somewhat more likely to comply with white-collar complainants than with those of blue-collar status. In fact an official crime report resulted from every encounter between the police and a white-collar felony complainant of either race. The probability of official recognition drops to about three-fourths for blue-collar felony complainants. There does not appear to be a clear social-class differential in misdemeanor situations, however.

Only in felony situations, then, does an inference of discrimination offer itself. In these encounters the police seem to discriminate against blue-collar complainants. Moreover, when both white-collar and blue-collar complainants report felonious offenses, we should be able to assume that the offenders characteristically are of blue-collar status. There is every reason to believe, after all, that white-collar citizens rarely commit the common felonies such as burglary, robbery, and aggravated assault. A possible exception is auto theft, a crime in which youths from white-

[11]It may seem that in criminal matters the costs are slight for the complainant when the police fail to comply with his preference for official action. However, it should be remembered that crimes frequently involve an economic loss for the victim, a loss that can sometimes be recouped if and when the offender is discovered. In other cases, discovery and punishment of the offender may net the victim nothing more than a sense of revenge or security or a sense that justice has been done—concerns that have received little attention in social science. For that matter, social scientists generally examine questions of discriminatory law enforcement *only* from the offender's standpoint. Ordinary citizens in high crime rate areas probably are more interested in questions of discrimination in police allocation of manpower for community protection.

collar families occasionally indulge. Since this study was conducted in predominantly blue-collar residential areas the assumption should be all the more warranted. It would follow that the police discriminate against blue-collar citizens who feloniously offend white-collar citizens by being comparatively lenient in the investigation of felonies committed by one blue-collar citizen against another. In this instance the legal system listens more attentively to the claims of the higher status citizen. The pattern is recorded in the crime rate.

OVERVIEW

The forgoing analysis yields a number of empirical generalizations about the production of crime rates. For the sake of convenience they may be listed as follows:

I.   The police officially recognize proportionately more legally serious crimes than legally minor crimes.

II.   The complainant's manifest preference for police action has a significant effect upon official crime-reporting.

III.   The greater the relational distance between the complainant and the suspect, the greater is the likelihood of official recognition.

IV.   The more deferential the complainant toward the police, the greater is the likelihood of official recognition of the complaint.

V.   There is no evidence of racial discrimination in crime-reporting.

VI.   There is some evidence that the police discriminate in favor of white-collar complainants, but this is true only in the official recognition of legally serious crime situations.

On the surface these findings have direct methodological relevance for those who would put official statistics to use as empirical data, whether to index actual crime in the population or to index actual police practices. Crime rates, as data, systematically underrepresent much crime and much police work. To learn some of the patterns by which this selection process occurs is to acquire a means of improving the utility of crime rates as data.

It should again be emphasized that these patterns of police behavior have consequences not only for official rates of detection as such; they also result in differential investigation of crimes and hence differential probabilities of arrest and conviction of criminal offenders. Thus the life chances of a criminal violator may depend upon who his victim is and how his victim presents his claim to the police. The complainant's role is appreciable in the criminal process. Surely the complainant has a central place in other legal and nonlegal control contexts as well, though there is as yet little research on the topic. Complainants are the consumers of justice. They are the prime movers of every known legal system, the human mechanisms by which legal services are routed into situations where there is a felt need for law. Complainants are the most invisible and they may be the most important social force binding the law to other aspects of social organization.

REFERENCES

Biderman, Albert D.
   1967   "Surveys of population samples for estimating crime incidence." The Annals of the American Academy of Political and Social Science 374 (1967):16–33.

Biderman, Albert D. and Albert J. Reiss, Jr.
   1967   "On exploring the 'dark figure' of crime." The Annals of the American Academy of Political and Social Science 374 (1967):1–15.

Bittner, Egon
   1967   "The police on skid-row: A study of peacekeeping." American Sociological Review 32 (1967):699–715.

Black, Donald J.
  1968   Police Encounters and Social Organization: An Observation Study. Unpublished Ph.D. Dissertation, Department of Sociology, University of Michigan.

Black, Donald J. and Albert J. Reiss, Jr.
  1967   "Patterns of behavior in police and citizen transactions." Pp. 1–139 in President's Commission on Law Enforcement and Administration of Justice, Studies in Crime and Law Enforcement in Major Metropolitan Areas, Field Surveys III, Volume 2. Washington, D. C.: U.S. Government Printing Office.
  1970   "Police control of juveniles." American Sociological Review 35 (February):63–77.

Cicourel, Aaron V.
  1968   The Social Organization of Juvenile Justice. New York: John Wiley and Sons, Inc.

de Beaumont, Gustave and Alexis de Tocqueville
  1964   On the Penitentiary System in the United States and Its Application in France. Carbondale, Ill.: Southern University Press. (orig. pub. 1833).

Erikson, Kai T.
  1966   Wayward Puritans: A Study in the Sociology of Deviance. New York: John Wiley and Sons.

Goffman, Erving
  1956   "The nature of deference and demeanor." American Anthropologist 58 (1956):473–502.
  1963   Behavior in Public Places: Notes on the Social Organization of Gatherings. New York: The Free Press.

Hall, Jerome
  1952   Theft, Law and Society. Indianapolis, Ind.: The Bobbs-Merrill Company (2nd Ed.)

Hoebel, E. Adamson
  1954   The Law of Primitive Man: A Study in Comparative Legal Dynamics. Cambridge: Harvard University Press.

Kitsuse, John I. and Aaron Cicourel
  1963   "A note on the uses of official statistics." Social Problems 11 (1963):131–139.

LaFave, Wayne R.
  1965   Arrest: The Decision to Take a Suspect into Custody. Boston: Little, Brown and Company.

Lofland, John
  1969   Deviance and Identity. Englewood Cliffs, N.J.: Prentice-Hall.

Maine, Henry Sumner
  1963   Ancient Law: Its Connection with the Early History of Society and Its Relation to Modern Ideas. Boston: Beacon Press. (orig. pub. 1861).

Malinowski, Bronislaw
  1962   Crime and Custom in Savage Society. Paterson, N.J.: Littlefield, Adams and Co. (orig. pub. 1926).

Morrison, William Douglas
  1897   "The interpretation of criminal statistics." Journal of the Royal Statistical Society 60 (1897):1–24.

Nader, Laura
  1964   "An analysis of Zapotec Law cases," Ethnology 3 (1964):404–419.

Nader, Laura and Duane Metzger
  1963   "Conflict resolution in two Mexican communities." American Anthropologist 65 (1963):584–592.

Piliavin, Irving and Scott Briar
  1964   "Police encounters with juveniles." American Journal of Sociology 70 (1964):206–214.

Pound, Roscoe
  1942   Social Control Through Law. New Haven: Yale University Press.

Reiss, Albert J., Jr.
  1967   "Measurement of the nature and amount of crime." Pp. 1–183 in President's Commission on Law Enforcement and Administration of Justice, Studies in Crime and Law Enforcement in Major Metropolitan Areas, Field Surveys III, Volume 1. Washington, D.C.: U.S. Government Printing Office.

Schwartz, Barry
  1968   "The social psychology of privacy." American Journal of Sociology 73 (1968):741–752.

Schwartz, Richard D.
1954   "Social factors in the development of legal control: A case study of two Israeli settlements." Yale Law Journal 63 (1954):471–491.

Sellin, Thorsten
1931   "Crime." Pp. 563–569 in Edwin R. A. Seligman (ed.), Encyclopaedia of the Social Sciences, Volume 4. New York: The Macmillan Company.

Skolnick, Jerome H.
1966   Justice Without Trial: Law Enforcement in Democratic Society. New York: John Wiley and Sons.

Stinchcombe, Arthur L.
1963   "Institutions of privacy in the determination of police administrative practice." American Journal of Sociology 69 (1963):150–160.

Westley, William A.
1953   "Violence and the police." American Journal of Sociology 59 (1955):34–41.

Wheeler, Stanton
1967   "Criminal statistics: A reformulation of the problem." Journal of Criminal Law, Criminology and Police Science 58 (1967):317–324.

Wilson, James Q.
1968   Varieties of Police Behavior: The Management of Law and Order in Eight Communities. Cambridge, Mass.: Harvard University Press.

7. The "Dark Figure" of Unreported Crime

WESLEY G. SKOGAN

A GREAT DEAL OF THE CRIMINAL ACTIVITY THAT goes on in the United States evades the attention of monitoring systems devised to measure its volume and distribution and to record the identity of its victims. The existence of this reservoir of unrecorded crime has a number of vexatious consequences. It limits the deterrent capability of the criminal justice system, for it shields offenders from police action. In the increasingly large number of cities which distribute police manpower and equipment in response to demands for service, it contributes to the misallocation of resources and leads to the understatement of protection due certain victims under "equal crime coverage" policies. It may help shape the police role: the selective nonrecognition of certain classes of activity in their own environment may enable the police to avoid the organizational and individual innovations that would be demanded by serious confrontation of these problems. The victims of crimes who do not become "officially known" to the criminal justice system thereby also become ineligible for many of the supportive and ameliorative benefits supplied by public and private agencies. Finally, the pool of unrecorded criminal incidents shapes the "socialized" costs of crime: private insurance premiums and the

public cost of victim compensation programs are affected by the number and character of events that remain hidden from view.

The development of new techniques for measuring crime may shed some additional light on the magnitude of problems associated with the "dark figure" of unrecorded crime. Population surveys can provide new information on one portion of the dark figure, those incidents that were not brought to the attention of the police but are later recalled in an interview. Our knowledge of criminal events is obscured by other sources of error, to be sure, but there is some reason to believe that citizen nonreporting is more important than most police nonrecording practices in determining the magnitude of official crime statistics.[1] This selection explores some of the characteristics of unreported incidents, using data from a national survey of the victims of crime. It examines the social consequences, for victims and for society, of the entry or non-entry of events into the crime recording process. To the extent that the operation of the criminal justice system and related institutions is shaped by demands for service, the volume and character of reported and unreported crime are powerful determinants of the consequences of and responses to criminal victimization.

▶SOURCE: "Dimensions of the Dark Figure of Unreported Crime," Crime and Delinquency (January 1977), 23:41–50. Reprinted with permission of the National Council on Crime and Delinquency.

[1]Wesley G. Skogan, "Measurement Problems in Official and Survey Crime Rates," Journal of Criminal Justice, Spring 1975, pp. 17–31.

KNOWING ABOUT CRIME

The problem is well known: an activity which is by some criterion a crime may occur without being registered in the systems devised to count it, thus reducing the accuracy of inferences from the data. This elusive subtotal was dubbed "the dark figure of crime" by European criminologists.[2] The recognition of the threat to valid inference posed by this pool of unmeasured events has stimulated the development of new procedures for probing its dimensions and greater care by users of official crime data. It is now always necessary to refute systematically all plausible, error-based, rival interpretations of research findings based on reported crime data.

The dark figure of criminality has been examined by the use of techniques that elicit anonymous confessions of delinquency directly from offenders. These self-reporting studies generally suggest that inferences based on arrest data unduly skew the distribution of criminality in the direction of minorities and the poor.[3] While European scholars long insisted that court statistics (which "correct" police errors in construing events and making arrests) were the best measure of the true distribution of crime, observational studies of charging decisions, preliminary hearings, and plea bargaining have laid that argument to rest.[4] Field studies of patrol performance indicate the enormous impact of police organization and tactics upon arrest totals and even on the decision that a crime has occurred.[5] Finally, both proactive and reactive procedures have been developed to provide

ways for the victims or witnesses of crime to register their experiences. "Heroin Hot Lines" and consumer fraud complaint offices are data-collection devices that open channels for citizen-initiated information, while victimization surveys require only the passive participation of those respondents chosen to represent their fellow citizens.

These efforts are important, for errors in the measurement of crime-related phenomena may have serious consequences: they create and conceal major social problems, and they complicate the interpretation of crime statistics and the validity of statistical inferences made from them. Errors in our knowledge of the volume and distribution of criminal incidents may considerably disguise human misery and limit our ability to understand even the most basic facts about society.

The social consequences of the failure of citizens to record their experiences may be considerable. First, failing to register criminal acts with the authorities virtually assures their perpetrators immunity from the attention of the police. While they may be harassed on general grounds or in response to other suspicions, those who prey upon individuals who will not or cannot relate their experiences to the police enjoy considerable advantages. This is well understood by criminals who victimize youths, homosexuals, minorities, or their fellow felons, and it redoubles the burden of the social and economic disadvantages that those victims already bear. While the empirical evidence on deterrence processes is mixed, it is too early to write off the pursuit of a great number (in fact, probably a numerical majority) of offenders.[6]

Those whose victimizations do not enter the

[2] Albert D. Biderman and Albert J. Reiss, Jr., "On Exploring the 'Dark Figure' of Crime," *Annals*, November 1967, pp. 1–15.

[3] Richard Quinney, *The Social Reality of Crime* (Boston: Little Brown, 1970).

[4] F. H. McClintock, "The Dark Figure," in *Collected Studies in Criminological Research*, vol. 4 (Strasbourg, France: Council of Europe, 1970), pp. 7–34.

[5] Donald M. McIntyre, "A Study of Judicial Dominance of the Charging Process," *Journal of Criminal Law, Criminology and Police Science*, December 1968, pp. 463–90; Abraham Blumberg, *Criminal Justice* (Chicago: Quadrangle Books, 1967); Albert J. Reiss, Jr., *The Police and the Public* (New Haven: Yale University Press, 1971); Donald J. Black, "Pro-

duction of Crime Rates," *American Sociological Review*, August 1970, pp. 733–48.

[6] George E. Antunes and A. Lee Hunt, "The Impact of Certainty and Severity on Levels of Crime in American States: An Extended Analysis," *Journal of Criminal Law and Criminology*, December 1973, pp. 486–93; Harold Votey and Llad Phillips, "An Economic Analysis of the Deterrent Effect of Law Enforcement on Criminal Activity," *Journal of Criminal Law, Criminology, and Police Science*, September 1972, pp. 335–42.

system may also receive less routine protection in return. Increasingly, big-city police departments allocate manpower and equipment in response to the distribution of demands for their services. These are measured primarily by crimes known to the police, usually weighted to reflect their "seriousness" or the probability that a swift response will produce an arrest. Victimizations which are not reported to the police can attract neither future deterrent effort in the neighborhood nor event-specific responses from the criminal justice system.

Reporting practices may also shape the police mandate. The self-image of the policeman is that of a "crime fighter"; police officers see themselves as strong, masculine protectors of the weak against criminal predators.[7] In reality, a great deal of their time is spent resolving or suppressing conflicts which have little to do with this role model: assaults in bars, husbands beating their wives (and wives killing their husbands), and disputes between neighbors over land or property. In fact, a large number of behaviorally "illegal" activities take place between persons who know, live with, or are related to each other. There is growing recognition in police circles that traditional forms of police intervention into these relationships may be unproductive and that new styles of police operation may be required.[8] Police officers and police unions, on the other hand, usually resist the grafting of "social work" onto their role and struggle to define their mission in ways more congruent with their preferred self-image.

A problematic aspect of this role conflict is the extent to which differences in reporting rates reinforce one task definition or another. Reporting practices in part set the agenda for police work. If problems brought to the police reflect the universe of problems only selectively, this will have some impact upon police operations. In this case, if the pool of reported crimes is more likely to contain victimizations perpetrated by anonymous assailants, the workload facing the police will favor the perpetuation of the traditional police role; on the other hand, changes in reporting practices might divert from the pool of unreported events those calling for different kinds of skills, making new demands upon police departments.

Nonreporting may also affect the distribution of ameliorative programs designed to confer financial benefits, psychological support, or special protection for the victims of crime. For example, public and private rape crisis intervention units cannot fulfil their intended functions in the absence of information about incidents; special tactical units cannot provide protection for unknown victims or apprehend offenders who prey upon frequently victimized, nonreporting establishments. Funds for the rebuilding of public and private space to render them more "defensive," high-intensity street lighting, and other efforts to physically structure neighborhood safety may be allocated in response to measured need.[9]

Finally, several states are implementing programs for compensation of victims of physical attacks.[10] Like private insurance programs, public victim compensation schemes (which socialize the cost of our inability to protect individuals from violence) depend upon the assertion of claims by those who suffered injury. Variations in victim-reporting practices will affect insurance premium rates and the cost to the taxpayer of public claims, as well as the distribution of individual benefits.

In short, information about the volume and distribution of criminal incidents plays an important role in shaping the response of private agencies and the state to crime. Events which do not register on social indicators—events which are not "officially known"—will evade attempts to redress their dysfunctional consequences.

[7]Arthur Niederhoffer, *Behind the Shield: The Police in Urban Society* (New York: Doubleday, 1967).

[8]Raymond Parnas, "Police Discretion and Diversion of Incidents of Intra-Family Violence," *Law and Contemporary Problems*, Autumn 1971, pp. 539–65.

[9]Oscar Newman, *Defensible Space: Crime Prevention through Urban Design* (New York: Praeger, 1974).

[10]Herbert Edelhertz and Gilbert Geis, *Public Compensation to Victims of Crime* (New York: Praeger, 1974).

THE DATA

The data employed here to probe the dimensions of unreported victimization were gathered through a national sample survey designed to measure the incidence of crimes against households and individuals in the United States. Conducted by the Bureau of the Census, the program involves continuing interviews with all residents twelve years of age and older in a rotating national panel of 60,000 households.[11] The large sample is necessary to uncover a workable number of such events as robbery and rape and to make reasonable inferences from the sample to the population. The interview schedule is designed to elicit self-reports from victims of some of the crimes which the FBI has placed on its Part I list: rape, robbery, assault, larceny, burglary, and auto theft. Homicide, a well-understood and infrequent event (and one which leaves no victim capable of reporting it) was not considered. The survey items have been subjected to an extensive series of methodological tests.[12]

Estimates of the magnitude of unreported crime are based upon respondents' recollections of their actions. After eliciting details of the incidents from their victims, interviewers inquired whether they were brought to the attention of the police. Each incident may thus be treated as "reported" or "unreported," giving us an empirical handle on events that did not become official statistics.

This measure of unreported crime is itself subject to error. In some circles it may be socially desirable to recall that one reported an event to the authorities, and this will inflate survey estimates of "crimes which should be known to the police." More important is the problem of nonrecall. Methodological tests of the victimization survey instrument indicate that certain classes of events, notably rape and assaults between friends or relatives, sometimes are not recalled even in anonymous, face-to-face interviews.[13] This survey's practice of "bounding" the visit of the interviewer with a previous visit to encourage victims to remember their experiences, asking respondents to recall only serious crimes, and requiring brief periods of recall (in the national survey, only six months) alleviates many of the methodological shortcomings of earlier victimization surveys.[14] But the "doubly dark" figure of crime which is reported neither to the police nor to an interviewer remains elusive.

VOLUME AND DISTRIBUTION OF CRIME

According to estimates projected from a national sample of victims of crime in the United States in 1973, there were more than 34-million incidents of auto theft, robbery, burglary, rape, assault, and larceny. (See Table I.) Most of them went unreported, the victims recollecting that less than one-third of these incidents—28 per cent—were reported to the police. Even if the police did not err in classifying and processing incidents which were brought to their attention, it appears that, of every 100 crimes that actually occurred, 72 were not recorded in official statistics.

Table I also indicates that nonreporting varies considerably by offense type, ranging from 32 per cent in incidents of auto theft to 82 per cent for larceny.[15] Robberies and burglaries

[11]Official findings from the National Survey are reported in *Criminal Victimization in the United States: 1973 Advance Report* (Washington, D.C.: National Criminal Justice Information and Statistics Service, Law Enforcement Assistance Administration, May 1975).

[12]U.S. Dept. of Justice, Law Enforcement Assistance Administration, National Institute of Law Enforcement and Criminal Justice, Statistics Division, *San Jose Methods Test of Known Crime Victims,* Statistics Technical Report No. 1., 1971.

[13]*Ibid.*

[14]Philip H. Ennis, *Criminal Victimization in the United States: A Report on a National Survey* (Washington, D.C.: U.S. Govt. Printing Office, 1967); Albert D. Biderman *et al., Report on a Pilot Study in the District of Columbia on Victimization and Attitudes toward Law Enforcement* (Washington, D.C.: U.S. Govt. Printing Office, 1967).

[15]Limited by definition in this survey to thefts from households and individuals.

Table I. Volume and Distribution of Reported and Unreported Crime in the U.S., 1973

Crime	Total No. of Incidents	Reported to the Police		Not Reported to the Police		
		No.	%	No.	%	% of All Nonreported Incidents
Auto theft	1,330,470	904,720	68%	425,750	32%	1.7%
Robbery	950,770	465,877	49%	484,893	51%	2.0%
Burglary	6,433,030	2,959,194	46%	3,473,836	54%	14.0%
Rape	153,050	67,342	44%	85,708	56%	0.4%
Assault	3,517,990	1,407,196	40%	2,110,794	60%	8.5%
Larceny	22,176,370	3,991,747	18%	18,184,623	82%	73.0%
Total	34,561,680	9,796,076	28%	24,765,604	72%	99.6%

Source: Calculated by the author from advance incident tabulations supplied by the Bureau of the Census.

were not reported to the police in a little more than half the instances. Rape was not reported in 56 per cent of the cases; assault, not reported in 60 per cent. Larceny shows the widest gap between actual incidence and official reporting. In 1973, thefts from individuals and households constituted about 64 per cent of all crime, but only about 18 per cent of them found their way into police reports. How significant is this discrepancy?

SOCIAL CONSEQUENCES OF NONREPORTING

Contrary to considerable speculation about the portentous implications of unreported crime, these data indicate that the vast pool of incidents which do not come to the attention of the police does not conceal a large amount of serious crime with immediate social significance and does not further disadvantage groups in the population already burdened with other disabilities.

The first popular hypothesis is that nonreporting works to the disadvantage of racial minorities. It is often argued that the victimization experiences of blacks are less likely to be reported to the police. Traditional police-ghetto

hostility, the unwillingness of many police officers to take complaints by blacks seriously, simple nonresponse by the police to calls for assistance, and outright citizen fear of any encounters with these representatives of the dominant society have all been cited as reasons for the undercounting of the crime experiences of black citizens. While these data cannot speak to the organizational effectiveness of the police once complaints have been entered, they indicate clearly that race is not related in any simple way to patterns of crime reporting.

Table II compares the distribution of reported and unreported household offenses (burglary, larceny, auto theft) across racial categories. For this class of offenses, nonreporting in fact is more commonly found among white victims; unreported crime is fractionally more likely to involve whites than blacks. The extremely low correlation between reporting and race (contingency coefficient = .03) indicates that this cleavage is not substantially related to the burdens and benefits attendant on crime reporting: the effect is similar across many subdivisions of crime (including personal crimes of passion and profit) and across major UCR categories; rarely does nonreporting vary

Table II. The Consequences of Unreported Crime

	U.S. Pop. Est. N^a	All Household Incidents v. Race of Household Head					
		White			Black		
Reported	8,750,960	89.2%			10.8%		
Unreported	20,552,410	91.3%			8.7%		
		C = .03					

	U.S. Pop. Est.	Household Larcenies v. the Value of Stolen Items					
		$1-9	$10-24	$25-49	$50-99	$100-249	$250+
Reported	4,910,530	11.8%	12.1%	17.3%	23.7%	23.6%	11.5%
Unreported	16,695,660	45.4%	24.2%	14.6%	9.0%	5.0%	1.6%
		θ = .62					

	U.S. Pop. Est.	Robbery (without Physical Assault) v. Use of a Weapon		
		Weapon		No Weapon
Reported	243,780	51.8%		48.2%
Unreported	355,480	30.2%		69.8%
		C = .21		

	U.S. Pop. Est.	All Personal Incidents v. Relationship between Victim and Offender		
		Stranger		Not Stranger
Reported	2,080,770	69.3%		30.7%
Unreported	2,972,790	65.8%		34.2%
		C = .04		

[a]The number of incidents for the U.S. as a whole for 1973, as estimated from the survey. Excludes a relatively small number of "don't know" responses.

Source: Advance tabulations supplied by the Bureau of the Census.

by more than 2 per cent across racial lines.

This lack of co-variation suggests that non-reporting does not play a major role in shaping the distribution by race of goods and services made available by governments in response to the crime problem. *Nonreporting* does not deflate the apparent need of blacks for increased police protection, and it does not guarantee greater immunity from apprehension for predators in the black community. Crime remains hidden from the authorities and thus cannot be employed to allocate squad cars or justify foot patrols, but the burden of this misallocation

does not fall along racial lines. Likewise, the data suggest that victim compensation programs are unlikely to reinforce existing disparities between blacks and whites; the "eligibility" of victims from both groups is unaffected by the distribution of officially known events.

Data presented in Table II also indicate that the pool of unreported events does not harbor a great deal of serious crime, incidents which cause substantial social harm but which remain hidden. First, unreported property crime tends to involve relatively small amounts of money. Table II presents the distribution of the value of household goods lost to thieves, divided into reported and unreported categories. The vast majority of unreported larcenies of this type involve small financial loss: in 84 per cent of the incidents the lost merchandise was worth less than $50. Less than 7 per cent of these thefts involved more than $100. It should not be surprising that in this survey, as in other victim surveys, "it wasn't worth the effort," "it was inconvenient," or "it was unimportant" are frequently volunteered excuses for nonreporting. It also should be noted that $50 is usually the lower limit for insurance claims, which may explain why the relative volume of unreported theft drops at that point.

The bulk of unreported personal crime also appears to be less serious than incidents which were brought to the attention of the police. The victims of these events are less likely to be injured, they lose less if there is a robbery or theft (and those incidents are more likely to be unsuccessful attempts), and unreported incidents are less likely than reported ones to breach the security of the victim's home. Table II presents a breakdown of another measure of the seriousness of crime, the use of a weapon. Crimes involving weapons are much more likely to result in injury or death to undermine the morale of the community. These effects are recognized in many states by statutes which impose harsher penalties upon felons who employ guns. Table II indicates that a substantial number of unreported robberies do involve the use of a weapon (about 30 per cent) but that many more (by 22 per cent) reported events can be counted as serious by this measure. While a significant amount of crime involving weapons continues to remain unknown to the police, incidents which come to the attention of the authorities are much more likely to be serious.

To the extent that the police role is shaped by the nature of their task, reporting practices may shape police work by determining the distribution of problems facing officers. If nonreporting reduces the proportion of domestic disturbances or other nonstranger crimes entering the criminal justice system, pressure for the adoption of crisis-intervention or dispute-settlement roles for police officers may be reduced. Table II reports the distribution of unreported and reported crime across the relationship between victims and their assailants. The category "stranger," in this case, includes unknown attackers and those known only "by sight." As Table II illustrates, differences in the distribution of reported and unreported crime were slight: 69 per cent of all personal crimes which were reported to the police involved strangers, while 66 per cent of unreported incidents were of the anonymous variety. Within the personal crime category, only simple rape (not involving theft) differed markedly by offender: unreported rapes were 14 per cent more likely to involve nonstrangers than reported rapes. The comparable difference for personal larceny (picked pockets, purse snatchings) was only 0.8 per cent. It does not appear that general increases in reporting rates would greatly affect the *distribution* of demands for radically different forms of police service, although it certainly would affect their volume.

SUMMARY AND CONCLUSIONS

It has long been argued that official statistics fail to reflect the volume of events which are by some definition a crime. A major source of this error has been attributed to the nonreporting of events to the police. While some types of criminal events are relatively fully reported (homicide, successful auto theft), for others the modal event is not brought to the attention of the authorities. In a 1973 national survey of crime victims, the reporting rate for simple larceny was only 18 per cent.

There has been considerable speculation about nonreporting and its consequences for crime victims and the operation of the criminal justice system. The vast pool of unreported crime (estimated by this survey to approach 24-million incidents in 1973) could conceal a great deal of human misery, isolate deserving victims from the ameliorative activities of the state, shield dangerous criminals from official attention, and shape the operation of the criminal justice system by defining the nature of its day-to-day workload. All the pernicious consequences of nonreporting could overlay existing social cleavages, redoubling the burdens of those who already suffer disproportionately from other social evils.

While it is not possible to speak to all of these issues in detail through the analysis of survey data, figures from the 1973 victimization survey conducted by the Census Bureau suggest that general shifts in reporting rates would not greatly affect the present distribution of known crime across many social and behavioral categories. The pool of unreported crime consists mainly of minor property offenses. Unreported crimes against persons appear to be of less social significance than those which are brought to the attention of the police. The victims of unreported personal crime are much less likely to have been injured, their financial losses are small, and weapons are less likely to have been employed by the offenders. The pool of unreported incidents does not appear to conceal a disproportionate array of intra-acquaintance offenses, and changes in reporting habits may not dramatically affect the relative mix of crime-fighting and social-working demanded of the police. (However, some serious methodological problems cloud the interpretation of this aspect of the data.) Finally, across a number of crime categories, there were virtually no racial differences in the distribution of known and officially unknown incidents. Whatever the burdens of nonreporting, they do not appear to reinforce racial cleavages.

A great deal of research remains to be done on the social and individual *consequences* of nonreporting. Those who report crimes become enmeshed in stressful social and organizational processes. They must confront the police and they may face prosecutors, courts, and the hostile glares of their assailants. Given the debilitating round of appearances and continuances facing victims or witnesses in many criminal courts and the fear that threats of reprisal may generate along the way, it is important to discover whether the ultimate adjustment to their new status arrived at by the victims of crime is any happier than among those whose problems never come to the attention of the state. There is good reason to suspect that it often is not. There also have been no experimental or *post hoc* analyses of the effects of programs aimed at increasing the rate at which citizens report crimes to the police, except for the impact that fluctuation in reporting has on official crime statistics.[16] It is important that we discover the effects of media campaigns, police-community relations programs, and the implementation of victim-compensation schemes upon the rate at which the problems of particular subgroups in the population come to the attention of the police. There simply are no data upon which to estimate the temporal stability of even the simple relationships reported here.

[16]Anne L. Schneider, "The Portland Evaluation Studies: Uses of Victimization Surveys for Evaluation and Planning," paper presented at the National Conference on Patterns of Criminal Victimization, Washington, D.C., June 1975.

8. Official Police Statistics and Their Limitations

LEONARD D. SAVITZ

I. INTRODUCTION

BEFORE UNDERTAKING THE DESCRIPTION AND evaluation of the major sources of criminal statistics in the United States, it is of some importance to conceptualize several basic terms: crime, criminal, and criminal statistics.

Taking the latter first, criminal statistics may be defined as the regular and systematic collection, collation, and publication, with a more-or-less public distribution of a body of data dealing with some specific aspect or phase of the criminal justice or juvenile justice system. Typically this involves a social agency which is directly or indirectly involved in the criminal justice system in some significant capacity beyond the production of statistic reports.

Criminal statistics are produced on a local, state, and federal level; we will concentrate, however, on national criminal statistics, primarily because of enormous variability in the existence, availability and, in all candor, value of many local and state criminal statistic reports. Admittedly some large urban police departments publish annual reports (primarily for public relations purposes), and several judicial and prosecutors' offices also produce relevant annual reports, but they are scattered and very few in number.

Criminal statistics are produced in order to develop reasonably accurate data on the incidence and prevalence of specified types of crime, criminal behavior, and criminals. Such information is useful as an admittedly crude measure of the amount or the "seriousness" of the crime problem within legal jurisdictions or within a cluster of jurisdictions having common geographic or demographic characteristics. Such statistics, of course, can be used for comparison between distinct jurisdictions and for recognition of diachronic changes in official crime rates within a single jurisdiction.

There can be no question that the primary purpose of the gathering and dissemination of statistics, as Wilkins (68) reminds us, is for its *utility*. Statistics are ways of classifying events (crimes) which maximize the power of the information for purposes of social action.

The term "criminal" is often used to embrace four distinct concepts: crime, criminal, delinquency, and delinquent. Yet each of these are quite distinct, as will be made clear in the following discussion.

Crime is legally prohibited and judicially punishable forms of specified behavior. These are defined within a criminal code, and, for a crime to exist, five features theoretically should be present:

1. The act (with very rare exceptions) must consist of a conscious, voluntary, external harm. (Intention is not the deed.)

2. The harm (effect of the act) must be legally prohibited at the time it is undertaken. (There can be, in this country, no ex post facto

69

laws, under Article I, Section 9, paragraph 3, and Section 10, paragraph 1 of the Constitution.)

3. The perpetrator of the act must have had mens rea (criminal intent or guilty mind) at the time of the crime. (If a person commits the act because he is insane, because of a nonculpable accident, because he is below the age of culpability, or because the act was due to an unavoidable coercion, he is deemed to be lacking in mens rea.)

4. The voluntary misconduct must lead to the legally forbidden harm; that is, there must be a causal relationship between the behavior of the actor and the crime for which he is ultimately charged.

5. There must be a legally prescribed punishment.

Criminal is a somewhat more difficult concept to deal with. It is impossible to argue that a criminal is a person who commits a crime whether or not anyone ever becomes aware of the crime. Or a criminal could be thought of as an adult who commits an act which he knows to be a crime. Most usually, criminal is a social label applied to the person who is arrested for a criminal offense. The term here involves an arrestee, a suspect, an accused and, perhaps, in time, a defendant. Much criminological research defines as criminals persons who are thought to be a criminal by some victim/complainant/third party who then solicits police intrusion into the matter (the most usual manner by which police intrude into criminal events); the police respond to the request, agree that a crime has in fact taken place (the crime is "founded"), and sometimes a suspect may be arrested because it appears that a prima facie case can be made against this culpable (blameworthy) individual. The arrest represents, usually, a judgment by some civilian(s) that a crime has occurred and a confirmation of this made by a member of the law enforcement enterprise with the subsequent apprehension of a "likely" perpetrator by official personnel.

But most arrested persons are not subsequently convicted. Evidence is available that about one in five arrests results in conviction in a court of law. Legally, the strongest contention could be made that "criminals" are only culpable adults who are convicted in a court of law. They represent, admittedly, a very small fraction of all perpetrators of crimes and a minority of all arrestees. In an efficiently operating criminal justice system, if a reasonable (prima facia) case can be made against an adult, the arrested suspect would not be legally released until his guilt or innocence is established judicially. There is some force, then, for operationalizing criminal as someone found guilty in criminal court. (But, alas, there are now no national statistics collected on persons convicted in criminal court.)

Delinquency is prohibited behavior encompassing all crimes (with rare exception) which apply to adults, plus a series of "status" delinquencies prohibited to juveniles only so long as they remain below a specified age (e.g., truancy, runaway, incorrigibility).

Delinquent is the most difficult concept of all. A delinquent might represent all juveniles who commit delinquencies (delinquent acts) whether or not detected or the term may represent all children officially entering into the juvenile justice system. But one cannot easily argue that legally a delinquent is simply an underaged adult criminal. Juveniles who are unarguably and proveably perpetrators of delinquent acts which have come to official attention may legally and legitimately exit from the juvenile system at several junctures, if such decisions are made by persons who are *authorized* to eliminate even "guilty" children from the juvenile justice system because further judicial processing is considered unreasonable and without value to the child.

Crimes and criminals (variously defined) become *official* statistics when the event and the perpetrator become known to the police. As indicated above, the most usual sequence involves some citizen who informs the police that a crime has been committed; the police are dispatched to the scene, arrive, confirm the occurrence of a crime, and perhaps apprehend a likely offender. There are offenses which become part of official record because police directly see a crime occurring (an "on-view" offense); but these represent only a minority of all crimes which become official statistics.

II. UNIFORM CRIME REPORTS—CRIME IN THE UNITED STATES

Currently the most important and valuable source of official criminal statistics in the United States is the *Uniform Crime Reports* (U.C.R.). This is, now, an annual publication of the Federal Bureau of Investigation of the reports it receives monthly and annually from the vast majority of, but not all, police departments, in the United States. The Bureau selects a certain body of data submitted to it; it then collates, analyzes, and presents to the public this singularly important body of data.

The primary focus of the *U.C.R.* is on "Crimes Known to the Police" (CKP) which involves crimes which have come to the official attention of the police and which, upon police investigation, are "found" (it is confirmed that a crime had indeed occurred).

For various reasons, the analyses of the *U.C.R.* concentrates, almost to the exclusion of all other offenses, on seven crimes. These are called "Index Crimes" (formerly known as "Part I" crimes) and were chosen because, the FBI argues, they are (among) those crimes most likely to be reported to the police and because they occur with "sufficient frequency" to provide an adequate basis for comparisons. These are, then, defined as serious crimes by virtue of their nature and/or their volume.

The seven offenses as defined by the *Uniform Crime Reporting Handbook* (57) are:

1. *Murder and Nonnegligent Manslaughter:* These are killings of live human beings which are *not* accidental deaths, assaults to murder, attempted murder, nor excusable or justifiable homicide. (Killing persons by gross negligence,

traffic deaths, etc., are subsumed under Manslaughter by Negligence, which is *not* an Index crime.)

2. *Forcible Rape:* This includes rape by force and all attempts to commit forcible rape. The so-called statutory rapes and other sex offenses are excluded. (It may be noted that if several males rape one female, this is counted as a single rape, with several punishable offenders or criminals.)

3. *Robbery:* This is the taking or attempt to take something of value from the care, custody, or control of a person, by use of force, threat of force, or by putting the victim into fear. [Information is secured on the weapon used (firearms/knives/other dangerous weapons/and strong arm), but this is seldom used in *U.C.R.* tabular presentations.]

4. *Aggravated Assault:* This act involves an unlawful attack by a person upon another for the purpose of inflicting severe or aggravated bodily harm. It is usually accompanied by the use of a weapon or by means likely to produce death or great bodily harm. (Once more, the type of weaponry used is secured by the FBI but seldom used.)

5. *Burglary (Breaking or Entering):* This crime is the unlawful entry into a structure to commit or attempt to commit a felony or theft. The types of structure entered could be dwelling houses, garages, churches, schools, trailers, barns, vessels, public buildings, offices, apartments, stables, and ships. (Shoplifting and theft from cars, however, are not burglary in the FBI classification). The types of burglary are: *Forcible Entry* (use of any kind of force to unlawfully enter a structure to commit a felony or theft, including use of tools, breaking of windows, forcing doors, or cutting screens); *Unlawful Entry* (no force used, but the unit is entered through an unlocked door or window). If the area entered is one of "open access," the theft is larceny, not burglary.

6. *Larceny-Theft:* Involved here is the unlawful taking, carrying, leading, or riding away property that is the possession of others. Excluded are car thefts, robbery, burglary, embezzlement, fraud, larceny by check, and check fraud. Whether the amount taken constitutes grand or petty larceny, or if the theft is a felony or misdemeanor is irrelevant; all are larceny-thefts. (The nine types of theft range from pocket-picking through theft of bikes to theft from coin-operated devices.)

7. *Motor Vehicle Theft:* This is the theft or attempted theft of a motor vehicle.

These seven offenses (murder/nonnegligent manslaughter, forcible rape, robbery, aggravated assault, burglary, larceny, and automobile theft) represent the seven Index Crimes, and it is important to recall that for five of these crimes (rape, robbery, forcible entry, theft, and auto theft) *attempts* are included together with *completed* crimes.

In recent years, the *U.C.R.* has presented data on Index Crimes (known to the police) in tabular form with some exposition as regards national totals, both actual reported totals and "estimated" totals. (The *U.C.R.*, curiously, extrapolates or inflates figures reported to them by various police departments to derive an estimate of ALL Index Crimes committed in the United States, even those occurring in areas where the police do not report to the FBI. This "problem" will be dealt with below.)

The *Uniform Crime Reports* typically presents estimated yearly totals, percentage change in rates from previous to current year, percentage change over the last five years, and percentage change from 1960 to current year for each of the seven Index Crimes. Furthermore, for each of the seven crimes, total data are presented by rate per 100,000 persons by degree of urbanization of reporting areas (Standard Metropolitan Statistical Area [S.M.S.A.]-Other Cities-Rural), by region of the country (Northeast-North Central-South-West), by individual states, and

by S.M.S.A.-Other City-and Rural groupings within each state. Information is also presented by several measures of population density. Comparisons are made of cities of over 250,000 with those cities of under 250,000; cities of over 250,000 are subdivided into 250,000-500,000, 500,000-1,000,000, and over 1,000,000 and compared with one another; most analyses, however, are made of areas demographically divided into populations of: over 250,000, 100,000-250,000, 50,000-100,000, 25,000-50,000, 10,000-25,000, under 10,000, "suburban," and "rural."

The FBI also secures annually police information on 22 other non-Index (or Part II) crimes, but these data are not used to construct rates for these offenses but are used primarily as regards arrests and dispositions for these "lesser" crimes. These offenses are: Other Assaults, Arson, Forgery and Counterfeiting, Fraud, Embezzlement, Stolen Property, Vandalism, Weapons, Prostitution and Commercial Vice, Sex Offenses (including adultery, fornication, incest, and intercourse with insane, epileptic, or venereal diseased person), Gambling, Offenses Against Family and Children (desertion, nonsupport, neglect, and abuse), Driving While Intoxicated, Liquor Laws (illegal manufacture and sales), Disorderly Conduct (disturbing peace, disorderly conduct, illegal prize fights), Vagrancy, Miscellaneous (including abduction, abortion, blackmail, bribery, and "suspicion"), Curfew and Loitering Law violations (for juveniles), Runaway (for juveniles), and Narcotic Drug Laws.

*

In the *Uniform Crime Reports* of 1974, non-Index crimes were presented for over-all arrest totals (and occasionally disposition), by various demographic groupings, trends over time, and arrest rates by age, sex, and race. Focusing, as an example, on Narcotic Drug Law violations, the data reveal changes in arrest rates from the previous to the current year, and changes from five years prior to the current year. Tabular data are presented on violation rates by region of the country and type of narcotic involved in the arrest. The *U.C.R.* of 1974 presents the findings of two studies of "Careers in Crime," involving rearrest patterns. The first dealt with persons arrested two or more times between 1970 to 1974, and found that the largest group of recidivists were auto thieves and robbers (79%), while 59% of all persons arrested for narcotic offenses were also repeaters. A follow-up study of persons arrested in 1972 and followed through 1974 determined that 28% of all narcotic offenders were rearrested for their same crime in the two-year period.

Uniform Crime Reports present 30 tables of data involving arrests for all 29 offenses. These tables deal with:

1. Numbers and Rate of Dispositions of Persons Charged by Police (categories being: Guilty of Offense Charged, Guilty of Lesser Offense, Acquitted, and Referred to Juvenile Court).

2. Numbers and Percentages of Persons Charged, by Percentage Arrested and percentaged Summoned, for Current Year.

3. Number of Total *Estimated* Arrests for Current Year.

4. Numbers and Rates of Arrest by Population Groups [Group I (over 250,000), II, III, IV, V, VI (Cities under 10,000), Suburban, and Rural], for Current Year.

5. Total Arrest Trends by Age (Under 18/Over 18), from Previous to Current Year.

6. Total Arrest Trends by Age (Under 18/Over 18), from 5 Years Before to Current Year.

7. Total Arrest Trends by Age (Under 18/Over 18), from 1960 to Current Year.

8. Total Arrest Trends by Age (Under 15/Under 18/Under 21/Under 25), from previous to Current Year.

9. Total Arrests by Age (within 23 separate age categories), for Current Year.

10. Total Arrests by Age (Under 15/Under 18/Under 21/Under 25), for Current Year.

11. Total Arrests by Sex, for Current Year.

12. Total Arrest Trends by Sex and Age (Under 18/Over 18), from Previous to Current Year.

13. Number and Rates of Total Arrest by Race and Age (Under 18/Over 18), for Current Year.

14. City Arrest Trends by Age (Total/Under 18/Over 18), from Previous to Current Year.

15. City Arrests by Age (23 separate age categories), for Current Year.

16. City Arrests by Age (Under 15/Under 18/Under 21/Under 25), for Current Year.

17. City Arrests by Sex, for Current Year.

18. City Arrest Trends by Sex and Age (Under 18/Over 18), from Previous to Current Year.

19. City Arrests by Race and Age (Under 18/Over 18), for Current Year.

20. Suburban Arrests by Age (Under 18/Over 18), for Current Year.

21. Suburban Arrest Trends by Age (23 separate age categories), from Previous to Current Year.

22. Suburban Arrest Rates by Age (Under 15/Under 18/Under 21/Under 25), from Previous to Current Year.

23. Suburban Arrests by Sex, for Current Year.

24. Suburban Arrests by Race and Age (Under 18/Over 18), for Current Year.

25. Rural Arrest Trends, by Age (Under 18/Over 18), from Previous to Current Year.

26. Rural Arrests by Age (23 separate age categories), for Current Year.

27.   Rural Arrests by Age (Under 15/Under 18/Under 21/Under 25), for Current Year.

28.   Rural Arrests by Sex, for Current Year.

29.   Rural Arrests by Race and Age (Under 18/Over 18), for Current Year.

30.   Suburban and Rural Arrest Trends by Sex, from Previous to Current Year.

III. GENERAL LIMITATIONS OF (OFFICIAL) POLICE STATISTICS

There are a number of serious problems associated with any source of official (police-derived) crime statistics. These limitations are described in detail, not because they vitiate the use of official criminal statistics, but because they indicate cautions to their unqualified use.

The relationship between crimes known to the police and the total universe of all crimes committed is unknown. Clearly crimes known to the police represent a percentage of all events which *could* have been classified as crimes. There is an implicit, and probably false, belief that the ratio of crimes known to the police to the universe of all committed crime, while unknown, is probably *stable* and constant, so that changes in the crimes known to the police mirror (through a glass, darkly) similar changes in the totality or universe of crime committed.

From this it would seem to follow that increases in police-determined rates of crime from one time period to another are mirrors of changes in amounts of crime occurring in the universe. In fact, however, there are other factors which could, and likely do, operate to alter official crime rates significantly over time.

A. Demographic Changes

Alterations in the age structure, sex ratio, and degree of urbanization probably significantly influence the amount of crime committed universally, and the amount of crime reported to the police (17).

B. Changes in Police Practices

With an increase in the number of police officers, one would expect greater detection of previously undetected crimes and greater capability of police reaction to previously not-responded-to crimes. Also, enhanced efficiency, professionalism, or sophistication of the police may increase the number of crimes which come to official attention and the accuracy with which these actions are recorded as offenses, (7,18,25). Better record-keeping practices and capabilities are likely to produce more accurate crime statistics. Sagi and Wellford (44) found that the increased percentage of civilian employees within a police department from 1958 to 1964 was associated with increases in reported crime rates; they assume that civilian employees would have considerable impact on crime reported and crime recorded due to their greater talent in report preparation. Also, enormous technological advances and paraphernalia associated with police work would maximize law enforcement efficiency by, for example, improved police response time. Research has shown that quicker police response time is associated with greater chances of police noting, founding, arresting, and clearing the crimes which come to their attention (32).

Administrative changes in police policy focusing police attention and resources on certain crimes rather than on others surely changes the crime rates produced for the newly important and the less important crimes. Similarly, a prosecutor's arbitrary decisions on the types of crimes he will or will not "paper" or prosecute impacts on police practices and the crimes they will note, found, and clear by arrests.

Additionally, Black (9) argues that there are distinctive police "styles," classified as Reactive Police Processing (where much crime is known to the police but police produce low rates of clearances by arrest) and Proactive Police Operations [which would result in higher arrest rates (compared to the Reactive style)].

Pittman and Handy (38) determined that variations in police "founding" practices have considerable impact on crime rates. National statistics reveals that unfounding rates range from 3 to 18% for different types of crimes (the lowest being for larceny and the highest for rape). Not only does founding vary by offense, but there are also enormous jurisdictional variations. The question arises as to how these factors influence the statistics reported by the several police departments.

Furthermore, the accuracy of the original police classification of a crime is said to vary with the officer's legal competence, his desire to get a "good pinch," and his estimates of subsequent plea bargaining practices in his jurisdiction (3).

Some evidence has been adduced showing a large number of errors in police classification of *U.C.R.* offenses (21). Beyond this, police have been accused of bias (13) and dishonesty (38) in their data collection practices. In fact, however, little *evidence* has ever been produced to substantiate these claims. Some commentators believe police themselves are unhappy with police statistics, and it is contended that they are cynical about their validity and use (23). Seidman and Couzens (46) conclude that the police decision to react to the event as a crime is correlated with extralegal factors such as:

1. The desire of the complainant.

2. Relational distance separating parties in the crime.

3. Deference shown toward the police.

4. The status of the complainant.

C. Changes in the Public "Acceptance" of Crime

Alterations in the general public's willingness to intrude hired functionaries (police) into certain types of actions (crimes) which occur against themselves or which they note have taken place against others, will influence official crime rates. Certain events which are legally crimes but are, in some populations considered "private mat-

ters," in time are thought worthy of police intrusion, previous constraints against informing the police are eliminated, and official statistics soar. With rising expectations of the poor and minorities for greater police protection and intervention, what were previously interpersonal concerns become public, official concerns. Also relevant is that increasing American involvement with insurance has led to a greater desire and need to report crimes to the police, in order to collect insurance compensation (18).

Center and Smith (12) speak of the need of developing "tolerance quotients" and "threshold values" of the particular community, which would measure how bad specified crimes must be, before the victim or observer would report it. [Ennis (12) asked a large number of crime victims why they had not reported the crime (and their victimization) to the police; the most usual reasons were that the police were judged to be indifferent or ineffective.]

D. Changes in the Legal Code

When any legislative body criminalizes previously acceptable behavior, decriminalizes current crimes, or alters the classification of a crime (from misdemeanor to felony or the reverse), there should likely be a change in reported crimes in subsequent statistical publications.

E. Changing Criminal Opportunities

Alterations in the physical environment frequently effect temptations and opportunities to commit certain types of crimes (e.g., an increase in the number of parking meters in an area of the city would increase the rate of theft from parking meters in that city sector).

F. Changes in Local Data Needs

When a community decides that there is some peculiar and pressing need for certain forms of criminal information, this is likely to result in the focusing of attention and law enforcement resources on these new priorities and interests (25).

IV. LIMITATIONS OF THE UNIFORM CRIME REPORTS

There are additionally a number of methodological problems peculiar to the *Uniform Crime Reports.*

1.   No federal cases are included, and these involve an appreciable number of crimes.

2.   Police reports are voluntarily submitted by their departments, and the data vary enormously in completeness and accuracy; the FBI states in their *Report* that it does not guarantee accuracy or completeness. They do, however, arithmetically check all reports and examine them for "reasonableness."

3.   Not all police departments submit reports to the FBI and one cannot assume that nonresponding departments have the same crime experiences as reporting departments.

4.   Not satisfied with the data received from responding police departments, the FBI inflates or increases police-reported figures to estimate total crime figures. This arbitrary (and extremely doubtful) practice may be of little consequence when a state has reported police data for 99% of their population (with the FBI adding 1% to this figure). But with lower reporting states, the practice of amplification adds enormously to the reported data. Thus, Mississippi (in 1971) had a total population of 2,342,000. All Standard Metropolitan Statistical Areas police departments in the state reported; 79% of "Other Cities" police departments also reported so their reported figures were increased by 21%. For police departments in rural areas, containing the majority of the state population, only 39.2% reported to the FBI. Thus, in the *U.C.R.* the reported rural Mississippi crime rate was increased by 150%, so that the rural Crime Index rose from 1604 (reported) to 4095 (estimated). (Even more dramatic is the situation in Tennessee, where only 17.2% of the rural areas had their crime experiences reported to the FBI; these figures were increased by over 400%, so

that the rural Tennessee Crime Index rate soared from 1432 (reported) to 8302 (estimated).

5.   The *U.C.R.* openly acknowledges the grave problems of comparability of rates across jurisdictions because of many differences in population, socioeconomic factors, and police characteristics.

6.   The numbers used to construct *U.C.R.* tables vary enormously. Thus one table on "Offense Analysis" in 1974 was based on reports from police who service 165,000,000 persons, while data on "Persons Charged" was based on reports from police servicing only 18,700,000 persons.

7.   Arrest does not equal crime solution. Persons arrested are not guilty by reason of arrest. About 20% of all arrested persons are subsequently found guilty in a court of law.

8.   Much data sent to the FBI by the police are not used in the *U.C.R.,* and much of this is quite important, such as the percentage of arrests that are unfounded. Furthermore, much of the unused data are thought by some to be particularly valuable in ascertaining basic causes of areal crime variations (25, 38).

Problems of Crime Classification

9.   There is only one crime classification given for each criminal event, even if multiple offenses have occurred during the crime. If a crime involves murder, rape, and drug use, it will be classified simply by the most important or serious crime—murder—and there would be no listing of the lesser crimes of rape and Narcotic Drug Law violation (3,17,25).

10.   The number of offenses listed varies by type of crime committed (40); thus for personal crimes the number of listed offenses equals the number of persons injured. If someone enters a bar and assaults six patrons, this could be counted as six assaults. For property crimes, however, each operation is a single offense. The same person who enters a bar and robs six persons would have his criminal action listed for *U.C.R.* purposes as one robbery.

11. The "arbitrary" basis of the seven Index Crimes has been variously attacked (39). Most crimes committed and most crimes brought to the attention of the police do not fall within the Index Crimes. Furthermore, the largest portion of a Total Index Crime Rate is made up of the least serious crimes: larceny and auto theft. It may be recalled that the seven crimes were chosen because they were defined as serious and/or had a high reported volume, but if these were the sole criteria, why, then, are Narcotic Drug Law violations not included (12)?

12. Dissatisfaction has been expressed with the inclusion of auto theft among Index Crimes when 80 to 90% of all stolen cars are recovered and the high reportability of the offense is attributable to insurance requirements and the fact that even without insurance, legal control over the car impels the owner to report any loss.

13. In recent years, larceny of any amount is an Index Crime. The theft of an item worth $.05 is equal in weight to a murder in the Total Crime Index Rate.

14. All Index Crimes are unweighted in the Total Index Crime Rates used in the *U.C.R.* This is apt to produce a false picture of the extent and change in serious crimes. It has been noted that most crimes which produce bodily injury are classified as non-Index Crimes (17).

15. Completed and noncompleted (attempts) acts are lumped equally, for five of the seven Index Crimes.

16. By arbitrarily making these seven offenses major crimes, police have almost of necessity been required to concentrate their attention and effort on these, with comparatively less attention being paid to other non-Index Crimes.

17. Robbery is classified by the *U.C.R.* as a Personal Crime, and is one of four Index Crimes used in the construction of Personal Crime Index Rates. Yet the President's Commission on Violence and the Bureau of Narcotics and Dangerous Drugs seem to agree that robbery could properly be classified both as a personal and a property crime. Indeed, some research sponsored by the B.N.D.D. classified robbery first as a property crime, and then data were remanipulated with robbery reclassified as a personal crime.

18. Relatively few victimless crimes and white-collar crimes are included in the *U.C.R.*

19. Strong disagreements exist between *U.C.R.* and state definitions of specified crimes (12). Under California's Criminal Code, shoplifting constitutes a burglary, whereas the *U.C.R.* requires that burglary must contain the element of unlawful entry. Thus, in California, the reporting officer must first classify shoplifting by state specifications and then someone must later reclassify the same act by *U.C.R. Handbook* requirements.

20. The *U.C.R. Handbook* describes several offenses imprecisely, particularly the narcotic offenses (25,33).

21. There is little if any justification for the inclusion of "suspicion" in *U.C.R.* arrest data as well as very minor juvenile "status" delinquencies such as curfew violations, loitering and runaway.

Problems Relating to the Construction of Crime Rates

22. The *U.C.R.* uses dicennial census information, and populations change often quickly and dramatically within a decade (17).

23. The use of the total adult population in constructing crime rates is absurd in that not all adults are equally open to the risk of certain crimes (11, 17, 40). Thus women should constitute the denominator in any rape rate; women over a certain age for purse-snatching; number of dwelling and commercial units for burglary; and number of cars for auto theft. Boggs (11) has argued that one should use "environmental opportunitites" to determine true risk groups. For aggravated assault and criminal homicide, she suggests the use of *pairs* of person; for auto theft, the amount of space given over to parking (as a measure of untended parked cars); and for highway robbery, the number of square feet of street (as a crude index of the number of people on public streets).

24.   The use of different-size population bases to construct rates of crime causes differential social perceptions of the seriousness of crime (40). Thus a robbery rate of 200 per 100,000 persons is somehow viewed as more serious than an identical rate of 20 per 10,000 persons, while a robbery rate of only 2 per 1000 seems almost no real problem at all in the view of some people.

*

In the face of these problems associated with official police statistics generally and the *Uniform Crime Reports* in particular, one might well ask if these statistics can be used for any serious purpose. The considered answer must be clearly yes. With all of their limitations, the *Uniform Crime Reports* remains among the most valuable sources of criminal statistics currently available. Even serious critics of the *U.C.R.* agree that it is the most adequate general measure available of change in the incidence of criminal behavior (17). Comparing the *U.C.R.* and the National Crime Survey (Law Enforcement Assistance Administration's national panel survey of criminal victimization), Maltz (32) found that the greatest accuracy was achieved by the use of both rather than the use of either. Hindelang (24) compared homicide data from the *U.C.R.* with homicide data developed by the Center for Health Statistics; he also compared a range of *U.C.R.* data with information developed in Ennis' study of *Criminal Victimization in the United*

States in 1967 (20). He determined that the *U.C.R.* and the Center's homicide data both depicted essentially similar patterns over time. He concluded that the *U.C.R.* produced "robust estimates" of relative incidence of police known index offenses; and surprisingly, he found that the unweighted *U.C.R.* statistics produce patterns very similar to those produced when the crimes were weighted.

BIBLIOGRAPHY

1.   Beattie, R. H., "A System of Integrated Criminal Statistics," *Criminologica, 5*(2):12–19 (1967).

2.   Beattie, R. H., "Criminal Statistics in the United States—1960" *Journal of Criminal Law, Criminology, and Police Science, 51*:49–65 (1960).

3.   Beattie, R. H., *Manual of Criminal Statistics.* (New York: American Prison Association, 1950).

4.   Beattie, R. H., "Problems of Criminal Statistics in the United States," *Journal of Criminal Law, Criminology, and Police Science, 46*:178–186 (1955).

5.   Beattie, R. H., "Sources of Statistics on Crime and Correction," *Journal, American Statistical Association, 54*:582–592 (September 1959).

6.   Biderman, A. D., "Surveys of Population Samples for Estimating Crime Incidence," *Annals of the American Society of Political and Social Sciences, 374*:16–25 (1967).

7.   Biderman, A. D., "Social Indicators and Goals," in R. A. Bauer (Ed.), *Social Indicators.* (Cambridge, Mass.: M.I.T. Press, 1966), pp. 111–129.

8.   Biderman, A. D., and A. J. Reiss, "On Exploring the Dark Figure of Crime," *Annals of the American Society of Political and Social Sciences, 374*:1–15 (1967).

9.   Black, D. J., "The Production of Crime Rates," *American Sociological Review, 35*:733–748 (1970).

10.   Bloch, P. B., and C. Ulberg, *Auditing Clearance Rates.* (Washington, D.C.: Police Foundation, December 1974).

11.   Boggs, S. L., "Urban Crime Patterns," *American Sociological Review, 30*:899–908 (1965).

12.   Center, L. J., and T. G. Smith, "Criminal

Statistics—Can They Be Trusted?" *The American Criminal Law Review, 11*:1045–1086 (1973).

13. Chambliss, W., and R. H. Nagasawa, "On the Validity of Official Statistics," *Journal of Research on Crime and Delinquency, 6*:71–77 (1969).

14. Chilton, R. J., "Persistent Problems of Crime Statistics, " in S. Dinitz and W. C. Reckless (Eds.), *Critical Issues in the Study of Crime.* (Boston: Little Brown, 1968), pp. 89–95.

15. Chilton, R. J., and A. Spielberger, "Increases in Crime: The Utility of Alternative Measures," *Journal of Criminal Law, Criminology, and Police Science, 63*:68–74 (1972).

16. Cressey, D., "Criminological Research and the Definition of Crime," *American Journal of Sociology, 56*:546–552 (1951).

17. Cressey, D., "The State of Criminal Statistics," *NPPA Journal 3*:230–241 (July 1957).

18. Doleschal, E., *Criminal Statistics.* Crime and Delinquency Topics. National Institute of Mental Health, Center for Studies of Crime and Delinquency. DHEW Publication No. 72–9094. (n.d.).

19. Engleman, H. O., and K. Throckmorton, "Interaction Frequency and Crime Rates," *Wisconsin Sociologist, 5*:33–36 (1967).

20. Ennis, P. *Criminal Victimization in the United States: A Report of a National Survey.* Field Survey II. President's Commission on Law Enforcement and Administration of Justice. (Washington, D.C.: U.S.G.P.O., 1967).

21. Ferracuti, F., R. Hernandez, and M. E. Wolfgang, "A Study of Police Errors in Crime Classification," *Journal of Criminal Law, Criminology, and Police Science, 53*:113–119 (1962).

22. Frankel, E., "Statistics of Crime," in V. C. Branham, and S. B. Kutash, (Eds.) *Encyclopedia of Criminology.* (New York: Philosophical Library, 1947), pp. 478–489.

23. Griffin, J. L., "New Perspectives in Police Statistics," *Journal of Criminal Law, Criminology, and Police Science, 46*:879–881 (1950).

24. Griffin, J. L., "Current Problems in Police Statistics," *Proceedings of the Social Statistics Section, American Statistics Association, 1960,* pp. 18–20.

25. Hindelang, M., "The Uniform Crime Reports Revisited," *Journal of Criminal Justice, 2*:1–17 (1974).

26. Isaacs, N. E., "The Crime of Present Day Crime Reporting," *Journal of Criminal Law, Criminology, and Police Science, 52*:405–410 (1961).

27. Kitsuse, J., and A. V. Cicourel, "A Note on the Uses of Official Statistics," *Social Problems, 11*:131–139 (Fall 1963).

28. Law Enforcement Assistance Administration, *Crime in the Nation's Five Largest Cities.* (Washington, D.C.: U.S.G.P.O., 1974).

29. Law Enforcement Assistance Administration, National Criminal Justice Information and Statistics Service, *Crime and Victims. A Report on the Dayton-San Jose Pilot Survey of Victimization.* (Washington, D.C.: U.S.G.P.O., 1974).

30. Lejins, P. P., "Measurement of Juvenile Delinquency," *Proceedings of the Social Statistics Section, American Statistics Association, 1960,* pp. 47–49.

31. Lejins, P. P., "Uniform Crime Reports," *Michigan Law Review, 64*:1011–1030 (April 1966).

32. Maltz, M. D., "Crime Statistics: A Mathematical Perspective," *Journal of Criminal Justice, 3*:177–194 (1975).

33. Mandel, J., "Problems of Official Statistics with Official Drug Statistics," *Stanford Law Review, 21*:991–1040 (May 1969).

34. McClintock, F. H., "Criminological and Penological Aspects of the Dark Figure of Crime and Criminality," *Sixth European Conference of Directors of Criminological Research Institutes* (Council of Europe).

35. Morris, A., "What are the Sources of Knowledge About Crime in the United States?" *Correctional Research Bulletin,* No. 15 (November 1965), pp. 6–13.

36. Normandeau, A., and Schwartz, R., "A Crime Classification of American Metropolitan Areas," *Criminology, 9*:228–247 (1971).

37. Park, R. B., "Sources of Limitations of Data in Criminal Justice Research," in J. A. Gardiner and M. A. Mulkey (Eds.), *Crime and Criminal Justice.* (Lexington, Mass.: D.C. Heath and Co., 1975), pp. 31–42.

38. Pittman, D. J., and W. F. Handy, "Uniform Crime Reporting: Suggested Improvements," *Sociology and Social Research, 46*:135–143 (January 1962).

39. Price, J. E., "Testing the Accuracy of Crime Statistics," *Social Problems, 14*:214–221 (Fall 1966).

40. Reiss, A. J., "Measurement of the Nature and Amount of Crime," *Studies in Crime and Law Enforcement in Metropolitan Areas, Volume I.* (Washington, D.C.: U.S.G.P.O., 1967) pp. 1–183.

41. Reiss, A. J., *Methodological Studies in Crime Classification.* Report Prepared for the National Institute of Law Enforcement and Criminal Justice (June 1972).

42. Robison, S., *Can Delinquency Be Measured?* (New York: Columbia University Press, 1936).

43. Robison, S., "A Critical View of the *Uniform Crime Reports,*" *Michigan Law Review, 64*:1031–1054 (April 1966).

44. Sagi, P., and C. F. Wellford, "Age Composition and Patterns of Change in Criminal Statistics," *Journal of Criminal Law, Criminology, and Police Science, 59*:29–35 (1968).

45. Schulman, H. M., "The Measurement of Crime in the United States," *Journal of Criminal Law, Criminology, and Police Science, 57*:483–492 (1966).

46. Seidman, D., and M. Couzens, "Getting the Crime Rate Down. Political Pressure and Crime Reporting," *Law and Society Review, 8*:457–493 (1974).

47. Sellin, T., "Problems of Criminal Statistics," *Correction, 19*:3–9 (1954).

48. Sellin, T., "Problems of National Crime Statistics," *Proceedings, American Prison Association, 62*:300–314 (1932).

49. Sellin, T., "The Significance of Records of Crime," *Law Quarterly Review, 67*:496–504 (1951).

50. Sellin, T., and M. E. Wolfgang, *The Measurement of Delinquency.* (New York: John Wiley and Sons, 1964).

51. Skogan, W. G., "Measurement Problems in Official and Survey Crime Rates," *Journal of Criminal Justice, 3*:17–32 (1975).

52. Sutherland, E. H., and C. C. Van Vechten, "The Reliability of Criminal Statistics," *Journal of Criminal Law, Criminology, and Police Science, 25*:10–20 (1934).

53. Turner, S. H., "Some Methods for Estimating Uncleared Juvenile Offenses," *Journal of Criminal Law, Criminology, and Police Science, 56*:54–58 (1965).

54. United States District Court, Administrative Office, *Federal Offenders in the United States District Courts—1970.* (Washington, D.C.: U.S.G.P.O., 1972).

55. United States Department of Justice, Federal Bureau of Investigation, *Review of the Report of the Consultation Committee on Uniform Crime Reporting. Special Issue of Uniform Crime Reports,* 1958.

56. United States Department of Justice, Federal Bureau of Investigation, *Ten Years of Uniform Crime Reporting, 1930–1939.* (Washington, D.C.: U.S. G.P.O., 1959).

57. United States Department of Justice, Federal Bureau of Investigation, *Uniform Crime Reporting Handbook.* (Washington, D.C.: U.S.G.P.O., 1974).

58. United States Department of Justice, Federal Bureau of Investigation, *Unifrom Crime Reports—1973. Crime in the United States.* (Washington, D.C.: U.S.G.P.O., 1974).

59. United States Department of Justice, Law Enforcement Assistance Administration, National Criminal Justice Information and Statistics Service. *Criminal Victimization Survey in the Nation's Five Largest Cities. National Panel Survey of Chicago, Detroit, Los Angeles, New York and Philadelphia.* (Washington, D.C.: U.S.G.P.O., 1975).

60. United States Department of Justice, Law Enforcement Assistance Administration, National Crime Justice Information and Statistics Service, *Prisoners in State and Federal Institutions on December 31, 1971, 1972, 1973. NPS. National Prisoner Statistics Bulletin.* No. SD-NPS-PSF–1 (May 1975).

61. United States Department of Justice, Law Enforcement Assistance Administration, National Institute of Law Enforcement and Criminal Justice, Statistics Division, *San Jose Methods Test of Known Crime Victims.* Statistics Technical Report No. 1. Washington, D.C. (June 1972).

62. United States, President's Commission on Law Enforcement and the Administration of Justice, "Crime Statistics," in Task Force Report: *Crime and Its*

Impact: An Assessment. (Washington, D.C.: U.S.G.P.O., 1967).

63. Ward, P., "Careers in Crime: The F.B.I. Story," *Journal of Research in Crime and Delinquency,* 7:207–218 (1970).

64. Walker, N., *Crimes, Courts and Figures: An Introduction to Criminal Statistics.* (Baltimore: Penguin Books, 1971).

65. Wellford, C. F., "Age Composition and the Increase in Recorded Crime," *Criminology, 11*:61–70 (1975).

66. Wheeler, S., "Criminal Statistics: A Reformulation of the Problem," *Journal of Criminal Law, Criminology, and Police Science, 58*:317–324 (1967).

67. Wilkins, L. T., "The Measurement of Crime," *Journal of Criminal Law, Criminology, and Police Science, 53*:321–341 (1963).

68. Wilkins, L. T., "New Thinking in Criminal Statistics," *Journal of Criminal Law, Criminology, and Police Science, 56*:227–284 (1965).

69. Wingersky, M. F., "Some Aspects of Criminal Statistics and a Statistical Methodology in Areas of Criminal Law and Procedure," *De Paul Law Review, 3*:199–220 (Spring 1954).

70. Wolfgang, M. E., "Uniform Crime Reports: A Critical Appraisal," *University of Pennsylvania Law Review, 111*:708–738 (1963).

9. Self-Reporting of Delinquency

ROBERT H. HARDT
SANDRA PETERSON-HARDT

THE PHENOMENON OF DELINQUENCY HAS BEEN AS-
sumed to be, for the most part, associated with
the lower class. The strong relationship between
social class and delinquent behavior has been
reported in repeated investigations (Shaw and
McKay, 1942; Kvaraceus, 1944). More recent
research, however, has thrown some suspicion
on the adequacy of the method employed to
measure delinquency in the past, as most of the
earlier studies measured delinquency using official records as an indicator of such behavior.
The more recent studies have documented that
social class tends to be a selective factor and
influences whether or not a youngster is booked
(Gold, 1963), referred to a juvenile court
(Bodine, 1963), receives an official or unofficial
hearing (Reiss and Rhodes, 1959), and the type
of disposition recommended (Cohen, 1963). As
a consequence of this observation, many investigators have turned to the use of self-report
techniques to measure a respondent's past delinquent behavior in order to minimize bias associated with the screening process (Clark and
Wenninger, 1962; Dentler and Monroe, 1961;
Hardt, 1968).

On the other side of the issue, some social
researchers have shown concern about the validity of self-reported behavior. Deutscher (1966)
cites a number of studies which suggest the relationship between reported behavior and overt
behavior is far from strong, thus it is important
to be critical about the problems involved in relying on self-report as a measure of behavior.

A number of investigators have in fact been
concerned with the problem of inaccurate reporting. Various checks such as the use of peers
as informants (Gold, 1966), use of detached
workers for confirmation (Short and
Strodtbeck, 1965), and use of a polygraph test to
check validity (Clark and Tifft, 1966), have all
been used to determine reporting accuracy.

It is the purpose of this selection to examine
the question of the quality of the self-report
technique as a method to measure delinquent
behavior and determine the degree of accuracy
that may be obtained in using this method.

At a conference on the use of self-report surveys, a number of ways have been suggested that
might be found useful in appraising the quality
of self-reported behaviors (Hardt and Bodine,
1965). These included:

1. Checking self-reports of events with
other reports of the event, utilizing either reliable records or other observers.

2. Use of distinctive criterion groups, the
"known group" approach.

3. Use of a "lie scale" or "social desirability
scale" to measure individual tendencies to give
an overly favorable self-image.

▶SOURCE: *"On Determining the Quality of the Delinquency
Self-Report Method," Journal of Research in Crime and Delin-
quency (July 1977), 14:247–261. Reprinted with permission of the
National Council on Crime and Delinquency.*

4. Measures of internal consistency, or interlocking items.

We shall, then, examine the findings in one large scale self-report survey with respect to each of these four checks. Such an inspection should provide some indication as to whether the self-report questionnaire is a sufficiently refined instrument to be employed on a large scale in delinquency studies.

PROCEDURES

The present analysis is based on one segment of data collected within a community embarking upon the development of a neighborhood-based delinquency prevention program. The city has a population of slightly under 250,000 and is the center of one of the major metropolitan areas in a Middle Atlantic state.

Initially, census tracts were selected for intensive study which, during a recent period, consistently had shown the highest delinquency and school drop-out rates. A total of seven tracts were identified; all had low income populations and high proportions of renter-occupied dwellings. The tracts were concentrated in three distinct but contiguous geographic areas. One area consisted of three predominantly non-white tracts; the other two areas, each of two census tracts, were pre-dominantly white (93-98%) and are combined for this analysis. For purposes of contrast with these areas, a middle-ranking income area of the community was identified which had low delinquency and drop-out rates. In this area consisting of two tracts, four out of five dwellings were owner-occupied and fewer than one percent of the residents were non-white.[1]

[1]Interviews conducted with random samples of parents confirmed the substantial differences in socio-economic status of these areas. In the area selected to represent a middle ranking income neighborhood, half of the fathers were employed in white-collar occupations and three-fourths of the mothers had at least a high school diploma. The highest comparable figures for any other area revealed

Public schools were identified which served the seventh through ninth grade pupils of the three areas. Since in one of the low income white areas, a substantial minority of pupils attended a local parochial school, this school was also included in the study. While the survey was administered to all pupils in the selected schools, this data analysis is restricted to the 914 boy respondents; 191 from the school in the Negro area, 386 from the white low income area, and 337 from the middle income area.

Within a school, questionnaires were administered simultaneously in all classrooms by pairs of trained monitors, most of whom were college graduate students. In almost all cases, teachers left the classroom after introductions were completed. The monitors stressed that the questionnaire was not a test but an opinion poll to find out "how young people are getting along and what young people are thinking about things." Pupils were informed that "your answers are private with us. No one else is going to see your answers." and instructed not to put their names on the questionnaire.[2] In general, two successive classroom periods (approximately 100 minutes) were allotted to the completion of the "Youth

that fewer than one-eighth of the fathers were in white-collar jobs and fewer than one-third of the mothers completed high school.

[2]The responses were confidential, but identities were actually established from biographic data in order to match pupil responses against data from official records and parental interviews. Advocates of a full and free informed consent position might object that the instructions were misleading since they may have been interpreted as implying total anonymity. The researchers believed that signed questionnaires would provide less valid information and were concerned with establishing whether even unsigned questionnaires were a relatively valid data source.

While the totally anonymous questionnaire is a versatile and relatively inexpensive technique for obtaining reports of juvenile behaviors on an aggregate level, if the answers are to be taken seriously either by policy makers or social theorists, it was regarded as essential to determine whether the responses were more than capricious check marks on a piece of paper. These data were obtained prior to the passage of the Buckley amendment which limits researchers' access to public school populations.

Opinion Poll." The self-report questions followed sections in which the pupils had an opportunity to express their personal evaluations of schools, teachers, and education. For a description of the major sections of the poll, see Appendix A.

The nineteen items included in the general self-report scale are reproduced in Appendix B along with the introductory statement that preceded the scale.[3] Fourteen items deal with delinquent or disapproved activities, eleven of which were used to form sub-scales and an omnibus scale. Some of these items were selected from previous inventories, others were developed to represent delinquent acts of local concern. Two other items were designed as "good boy" items to help break the tendency to a particular response set. The other three items deal with reports of contact with the police and courts.

In responding to each self-report item, pupils were asked to check "the last time that you did each of the following things" with four alternatives listed:

—in the last seven days

—in the last 12 months

—over a year ago

—never

Official data on the arrest or ticketing history of pupils in the five schools were obtained from the files of county central registry of juvenile offenders (Cary and Hardt, 1965). This registry contains standard reports of police contacts with juveniles obtained from 19 separate police agencies serving the county. These data are believed to be virtually complete for at least six years prior to the survey.

[3] Also included in Appendix B are twelve self-report items which were divided into three groups of four items, and incorporated in the three alternate sections which concluded the poll. Questionnaires containing each of the three alternate sections were distributed randomly to approximately one-third of the pupils within a classroom.

FINDINGS

In Table I, responses made to the entire set of items are summarized. Two sets of percentages are presented; the first column represents lifetime incidence, and the second indicates involvement during the last year.

The first grouping of 25 items consists of the delinquent or "disapproved behaviors" listed in order from those acts most frequently admitted. The following single item, 4Z, is an attempt to obtain reports of being a victim. The next pair of items are approved or positively valued behaviors, e.g., helping parents and loaning money to friends. The last three items refer to involvement with police and court agencies.

Some evidence of the "face validity" of the aggregated responses is suggested by the findings of Table II. It should be noted that the two "good boy" items receive the highest endorsement, e.g., "helping parents" was reported by 96 per cent of the boys. Also, the ordering of items of "disapproved behavior" reveals that two relatively trivial items, fist fighting and smoking, head the list. Nearly nine out of ten boys admit fist fighting. Vandalism and public nuisance behaviors also rank high, while theft and assaultive items rank low. The two least frequently reported behaviors involve the relatively serious acts of joy-riding in a "borrowed" car and experimenting "to get kicks."

Let us turn to the first procedure, that of checking self-reports against other reports of the event. It is difficult to envision any direct check on the validity of such an extensive series of reports on juvenile misbehaviors. However, some of these misbehaviors are detected and recorded. One of the potential community responses is a police contact leading to the issuance of a ticket. An estimate of both the gross and net amount of reporting errors can be obtained by comparing self-reports of police ticketing with official police records. It may be seen in Table I that 22 per cent of the boys report having received a ticket. Our search of the central registry files revealed that only 19 per cent of

Table I. Reported Behavior, Incidence for Lifetime and
Last Year, Boys Only

Item Number	Item Description	Per Cent Reporting Behavior in:	
		Lifetime	Last Year
1X	Fist fight	87	57
1	Smoking	73	55
3Z	Sneak in	53	31
4Y	Street noise	53	34
2Z	Yard damage	52	26
2	Broke lights	50	22
14	Bad friends	47	27
4X	Thrown out	44	23
9	Drinking	44	34
2Y	Threaten	42	28
3X	Personal theft	41	22
4	Store theft	40	17
3Y	Enter building	38	21
6	School damage	38	24
15	Stole $2+	33	17
11	Group fight	30	18
7	Out all night	23	17
2X	Drive illegally	19	12
8	Meter theft	18	5
12	Assault	17	10
1Z	Purse snatch	16	12
16	Knife fight	15	9
1Y	Coin machine	15	10
18	Auto theft	10	7
13	Got kicks	6	4
4Z	Was threatened	45	31
5	Helped parents	96	93
19	Loaned money	88	83
10	Police warning	58	36
17	Police ticketing	22	11
3	Court appearance	19	9

A total of 914 questionnaires were returned. For individual items designated by numeral only, N values range from 897-914. For item numbers followed by X, Y, or Z, a split form distribution was employed with N = 309 for X items, N = 311 for Y items, and N = 294 for Z items.

the boys had an officially recorded police contact. Thus, our self-report does not minimize but slightly over-estimates the rate of police ticketing. This, however, is only an indication of the net amount of error. The gross amount including compensating errors of over-reporting and underreporting could be much larger. In order to determine this gross error, summary or aggregate data do not suffice, but data on individual misreporting are needed. The use of biographic data on the questionnaire compared with other records of pupils from a given classroom made it possible to match all but 27 of the 914 questionnaires; another ten boys did not reply to the question on a prior police record.

In Table II, responses to the self-report item on ticketing or arrest during the boy's lifetime (Item 27) are matched against recorded police contacts obtained prior to the survey. The relationship between the two measures is very high (gamma = .95). Among boys with a police record, 78 per cent acknowledge that fact; in contrast, fewer than one out of ten without a record claims to have been ticketed. When the relationship is examined from the standpoint of self-report status, the findings reveal that among boys who report never having received a ticket (N = 672), 94 per cent do not have a police record. On the other hand, among the 190 boys who claim to have been ticketed during their lifetime, 71 per cent were found to possess a police record.

Despite this general association between the two sources, there are 95 cases (or 11 per cent of the total number) in which a discrepancy occurs. Perhaps the most surprising feature in this analysis is that the number of over-reporters (N = 56) exceeds that of under-reporters (N = 39). By "over-reporters," we refer to boys who do not have an official record but claim to have received a ticket at some prior time; while the term "under-reporters" refers to boys with official records who deny the fact that they "ever" received a ticket. Are the two types of dis-

crepancies to be explained by deliberate falsification, memory failures, by carelessness in reporting, or are there other identifiable factors related to inaccurate reporting?

One of the factors which might lead to an over-reporting discrepancy stems from the fact that our criterion of a recorded contact in the central registry is not perfectly isomorphic with the "ticketing or arrest" information requested in the questionnaire. A minority of the junior high school boys have already reached their sixteenth birthday; tickets received after that age would not be considered "juvenile delinquencies" and therefore would not be included in the registry. A second source of an over-reporting type of discrepancy would occur if the boy had previously been ticketed but only in some other county.

In order to determine whether such factors might account for some of the discrepancies, the over-reporting rate was calculated for two subgroups. The first sub-group, subsequently referred to as the "purified group," consists of boys under 16 years of age who had lived in the county for at least three years. The second, or "residual" sub-group, consists of all other boys. The incidence of over-reporting within the purified group (7.0 per cent) is less than half of that of the residual group (14.9 per cent). This finding suggests that perhaps half of the over-reporting is due to the lack of a common reference for the question and the record system.

Table II. Self-Reports of Ticketing by Official Record States[a]

Self-Report of Ticketing[b]	Official Record					
	No		Yes		Total	
	%	(N)	%	(N)	%	(N)
Yes	8.1	(56)	77.5	(134)	22.0	(190)
No	91.9	(633)	22.5	(30)	78.0	(672)
Total	100.0	(689)	100.0	(173)	100.0	(862)

Gamma = .95

[a] Excludes 27 unidentifiable cases, and 10 "no responses" to ticketing question.
[b] Refers to report of ticketing over *lifetime* period.

The under-reporters were also examined to determine what factors were linked to their "reporting-errors." It was reasoned that while a boy who had received one ticket in his lifetime may have been somewhat confused about the official nature of the proceedings, it would not be as likely that a boy with two tickets would have much doubt about having an official record. Among the boys who had received only one ticket, 31 per cent were "under-reporters" but among those with more than one ticket, only 13 per cent denied *ever* having received a ticket. Among the 29 boys who received a single ticket but denied ever having been arrested, 19 were willing to admit that sometime they had received a police warning (Item 10). Thus, we do not believe that deliberate falsification accounts for the major part of the "under-reporting" errors.

A second procedure suggested for validating responses to a self-report scale is that of utilizing "known groups" or groups believed to be substantially different on the study criterion. Sometimes reformatory groups have been used to define a highly delinquent group, but the conditions of test administration to such a segregated group are far different than the administration of tests in a high school. In this study, we have used the history of recorded police contacts to define a group that it is anticipated will tend to have higher self-reported violation scores than other juveniles.

The self-reported violation score is derived from an omnibus scale consisting of the eleven items designated by an asterisk in Appendix B. Scores ranging from 0 through 11 were obtained by totalling the number of items on which boys admitted involvement "ever." (The mean score was 3.5 with a standard deviation of 2.9; the internal consistency reliability of the scale was .82 as obtained by Kuder-Richardson formula #20).

In Table III we see that our anticipation is confirmed. Boys with official police tickets are more likely to have high violation scores than boys without tickets (gamma = .55). Nearly 60 per cent of boys with two or more tickets are high violators compared to an incidence rate of only 15 per cent for boys without a ticket. Boys with only one ticket are in an intermediate position; 37 per cent are high violators.

Thus, using amount of official ticketing as a criterion to define "known groups," we see that the self-reported violation status corresponds to these known groups.

In Table IV, the same basic data as in Table III are presented, but this time percentages are run in the opposite direction to determine what percentage of boys of a specific violation status have received police tickets. These findings illustrate the contribution which the self-report approach can make in the location of subgroups of boys with extensive involvement in delinquent

Table III. Self-Reported Violation Scores by Number of Officially Recorded Police Contacts

Self-Report Score	Number of Police Tickets		
	0	1	2+
	%	%	%
High (6–11)	15.3	36.7	57.8
Medium (3–5)	33.2	39.8	23.9
Low (0–2)	51.5	23.5	18.3
	100.0	100.0	100.0
	N = (662)	(98)	(71)

**Table IV. Number of Officially Recorded
Police Contacts by Self-Reported Violation Status**

Self-Report Violation Status		Number of Police Contacts			
		0	1	2+	Total
	No.	%	%	%	%
High (6–11)	(178)	56.7	20.2	23.1	100.0
Medium (3–5)	(276)	79.7	14.1	6.2	100.0
Low (0–2)	(377)	90.5	6.1	3.4	100.0

activity. *A majority of boys ranking high on the self-report scale do not have an offically recorded police contact.* Thus this general approach reveals that while boys who have police contacts tend to be highly delinquent in behavior, most boys admitting extensive delinquent involvement do not have a police record.

A more indirect method utilizing the general procedure of known groups relied upon sociometric data. Each boy was asked to name his four best friends within the school. In most cases (N = 700), it was possible to determine the official delinquency status of these friends. Boys who had two or more friends who were officially delinquent had a mean self-report violation score of 4.5, boys with one delinquent friend had a mean score of 3.7, and boys with no delinquent friends had a mean score of 2.8. This general relationship persisted within each social area.[4]

Turning to the third approach, what is the relationship between self-reported delinquency status and the respondent's tendency to give "socially desirable" answers? A specially constructed scale was designed to measure social desirability; similar types of "lie scales" have been incorporated in the MMPI and other personality tests. The five items incorporated in the

[4]For example, in the Negro low income area, the rate of boys who were high self-reported violators (last year's activity) was 29% among those with 2 or more delinquent friends and only 8% among those with no delinquent friends. Rates of high self-reported violations for comparable groups in the white middle income area were 42% and 12%.

social desirability scale are included in Appendix C. The per cent endorsing individual items ranged from 5 to 17 per cent. Scores were based on the number of key answers which were endorsed. Scores of 2 or more were considered "High" on social desirability; all other scores were considered "Low."

No linear relationship exists between self-reported delinquency and social desirability (gamma = −.06). The rate of high social desirability scores was 19 per cent among high violators, 14 percent among medium violators, and 23 per cent among low violators. The possibility of a curvilinear relationship may warrant further examination.

In addition, high social desirability scores were found to be more frequent among inaccurate responders. Using the categorization of respondents employed in Table II, the rate of high social desirability scorers was found to be only 17 per cent among accurate non-delinquents and 18 per cent among accurate delinquents, while it was 29 per cent among "over-reporters" and 39 per cent among "under-reporters." While the initial analysis did not suggest that the social desirability response set introduced a strong overall biasing effect on self-reports, it would seem desirable to include such a scale so that controls or adjustments for social desirability may be introduced in making the key comparisons within a study.

The fourth procedure for assessing the quality of responses is basically an internal consistency approach using either interlocking items or the repetition of identical items. If the replies showed a large proportion of discrepant answers, serious questions could be raised not only about the reliability but also about the practical validity of replies.

The single check of this nature which we used involved two items believed to be logically inter-related. In item 10 of the self-report scale, boys were asked whether they had ever been warned or questioned by a policeman. Seven items later they were asked to indicate whether they had ever been ticketed or arrested. It was assumed that boys who admitted ticketing should also have previously admitted that they had been questioned. An examination of the responses to the two items revealed that only 18 boys (2.0 per cent of the sample) made an inconsistent response, viz., having been ticketed but never questioned or warned.

As was mentioned in our description of the population, three very distinct types of neighborhoods were included in the survey. To what extent can we have a similar degree of confidence in replies from the three areas?

In Table V, two measures of accuracy are presented for the three neighborhoods. The first measure is the percentage of boys with low scores on the "lie" scale. The second measure is the percentage of boys with recorded police contacts who admit having been ticketed. On both measures, we note that the white middle-class area shows the highest percentage of accurate responders. There is relatively little difference between the Negro and white low income areas. This finding suggests that middle income boys are more careful and accurate respondents, and that a greater degree of carelessness or deliberate falsification may be found in low income boys. Thus, in making area comparisons, it would be desirable to compare boys with similar degrees of reporting accuracy.

Overall these findings suggest that the self-report instrument yields accurate responses and can make an important contribution to etiological studies of delinquent behavior, but now we turn to the question, is the instrument sufficiently sensitive to be employed in evaluation studies?

One piece of evidence garnered from our study suggests that the items are sufficiently sensitive to reflect behavioral change. For several years, the city had been plagued with an increasing loss of parking meter revenues as a result of theft from and destruction of meters. In certain sections of the city, the technology for "cracking meters" was becoming widespread among teenagers and even younger children. As a result of growing concern with this problem, the city replaced the older meters with more expensive, theft-proof meters. The old meters were replaced shortly over a year prior to the survey. Meter revenues have sharply increased, and theft and breakage have markedly declined.

The efficacy of this step as one delinquency control device is attested to by the reports of the boys themselves. It may be noted in Table 1 that on almost all of the items, a majority of the boys who report a specific behavior indicate that their most recent commission of the act was within the last year. A striking exception to this general

Table V. Response Accuracy of Boys from Three Neighborhoods

Neighborhood	% Low on Lie Scale	% of Ticketed Admitting Record
Middle income—white	88	88
Lower income—white	77	72
Lower income—non-white	76	73

pattern is provided by the item (8) dealing with parking meter theft. Of those boys *ever* involved in thefts from other types of coin machines (1Y), 67 per cent admit involvement during the last year.

IMPLICATIONS AND SUMMARY

With the increasing use of self-report techniques in delinquency studies, critical appraisals of the validity of the technique are needed (Wyner, 1976). Measurement techniques inextricably shape as well as reflect the conceptualization of the phenomena under study, and thus impact on the theoretical formulations which appear viable. The original questioning of class-linked theories of delinquency was based in part on a lack of confidence in measuring delinquency solely through official record data.[5] Cohen pointed out that, "We can never lay to rest the ghost of unrepresentativeness as long as our statistical base of operations is delinquencies known to the courts, the police, or even the schools and social agencies." (Cohen, 1960). As a result, in turning to the use of self-report, "hidden" delinquencies were uncovered with somewhat different patterns of distribution, and new theories had to be formulated to account for behaviors that were now shown to be less strongly associated with social class.

While critics of the self-report technique can no longer ignore the limitations of the earlier approach, some of their continuing skepticism may be based on the belief that self-reported behaviors are also contaminated or distorted by certain attitudes or self-concepts held by some respondents. Certainly, their contention warrants exploration, and Gould (1969) for one attempts to distinguish between subjective and objective characteristics of the delinquency pro-

cess. However, if the focus of interest is on delinquent acts committed by the respondent, the findings of this paper suggest that the self-report technique yields reasonably valid data for most respondents, and suggest as Liska (1974:263) points out, "the strong criticism leveled against the use of questionnaire items as a measure of overt behavior (cf. Deutscher, 1966) is not empirically substantiated."

Several types of evidence having a bearing on the relatively high validity of delinquency self-report questionnaires were drawn from a large survey of junior high school pupils. Besides the apparent face validity the evidence included:

1. A close correspondence between self-reports of police ticketing and official records. The net discrepancy in total rates was three percentage points, with the gross rate of inaccurate respondents being eleven per cent. However, evidence was advanced that not all of these inaccurate respondents should be considered deliberate falsifiers.

2. Differences in self-reported violation between two "known groups"—those apprehended by police and those without a record.

3. The lack of any widespread tendency to endorse a set of "lie" items and the minimal relation between the lie scale and delinquency involvement.

4. A close correspondence in replies obtained to a pair of interlocking items.

Some of our findings suggest that lower class youngsters may tend to be less accurate reporters and that boys who fail to make accurate reports of their arrest status may consist of overexaggerators as well as overly defensive boys. In any investigation, whether of the etiological or evaluative type, analyses should be made separately for groups of accurate and inaccurate responders or with controls introduced for the "social desirability" response set.

If accuracy of reporting behavior is due to the

---

[5] Another technique developed in the last decade which has yielded valuable data for the epidemiological study of crime patterns has been the household victimization surveys (Hindelang, 1976). Since the age of the perpetrator is frequently unknown, this approach does not appear to be as appropriate for the study of juvenile delinquency patterns.

fact that behavior questions are viewed as "threatening," the use of the self-report technique, guaranteeing anonymity, is probably the best method for overcoming this problem. In their discussion of such problems, Sudman and Bradburn (1974: 142–3) conclude:

"The best and most widely used method for reducing response effects for threatening questions is the use of self-administered questionnaires, which in some cases, insure anonymity, and which remove the threat of direct disclosure to another person of what may be considered socially unacceptable behavior . . ."

Thus, despite the minor problems which may be encountered in using the self-report instrument, evidence was presented which suggests there is a high degree of validity in the responses obtained and that the instrument is sufficiently sensitive to be considered in the evaluation of delinquency prevention and control studies.

REFERENCES

Bodine, George E.
1963 "Factors related to police referrals to Juvenile Court," Syracuse University, Youth Development Center, unpuplished paper.

Cary, Lee J. and Robert H. Hardt
1965 The Central Registry: An Index of Juveniles Who Have Contact with Law Enforcement Agencies. Syracuse: Syracuse University Youth Development Center.

Clark, John P. and Larry L. Tifft
1966 "Polygraph and interview validation of self-reported deviant behavior." American Sociological Review 31 (August): 516–23.

Clark, John P. and Eugene P. Wenninger
1962 "Socio-economic class and area as correlated of illegal behavior among juveniles." American Sociological Review 27 (December): 826–34.

Cohen, Albert K.
1960 Delinquent Boys: The Culture of the Gang. Glencoe: The Free Press.

Cohen, Yona
1963 "Criteria for the probation officer's recommendations to the juvenile court judge." Crime and Delinquency 9 (July): 265–70.

Dentler, Robert and Lawrence J. Monroe
1961 "Early adolescent theft." American Sociological Review 26 (October): 733–45.

Deutscher, Irwin
1966 "Words and deeds: social science and social policy." Social Problems 13 (Winter): 235–65.

Gold, Martin
1963 Status Forces in Delinquent Boys. Ann Arbor: University of Michigan.
1966 "Undetected delinquent behavior." Journal of Research in Crime and Delinquency 3 (January): 27–46.
1970 Delinquent Behavior in an American City. Belmont, California: Brooks/Cole Publishing Company.

Gould, Leroy C.
1969 "Who defines delinquency: a comparison of self-reported and officially reported indices for three racial groups." Social Problems 16 (Winter): 325–36.

Hardt, Robert H.
1968 "Bad kids or good cops" in Irwin Deutscher and Elizabeth J. Thompson, Among the People: Encounters with the Poor. New York: Basic Books.

Hardt, Robert H. and George E. Bodine
1965 Development of Self-Report Instruments in Delinquency Research: A Conference Report. Syracuse: Syracuse University Youth Development Center.

Hardt, Robert H. and Sandra J. Peterson
1968 "Neighborhood status and delinquency activity as indexed by police records and a self-report survey." Criminologica 6 (May): 37–47.

Hindelang, Michael J.
1976 Criminal victimization in eight American cities: a descriptive analysis of common theft and assault. Cambridge, Massachusetts: Ballinger.

Hirschi, Travis
1969   Causes of Delinquency. Berkeley: University of California Press.

Kvaraceus, William C.
1944   "Juvenile Delinquency and Social Class," Journal of Educational Sociology 18 (September): 51–4.

Liska, Allen E.
1974   "Emergent issues in the attitude-behavior consistency controversy," American Sociological Review 39 (April): 261–72.

Reiss, Albert J. and Albert L. Rhodes
1959   A Socio-Psychological Study of Conforming and Deviating Behavior Among Adolescents. Iowa City: State University of Iowa.

Shaw, Clifford and Henry D. McKay
1942   Juvenile Delinquency in Urban Areas. Chicago: University of Chicago Press.

Short, James F. and Strodtbeck, Fred L.
1965   Group Process and Gang Delinquency. Chicago: University of Chicago Press.

Sudman, Seymour and Norman M. Bradburn
1974   Response Effects in Surveys: A Review and Synthesis. Chicago: Aldine Publishing Company.

Wyner, Gordon A.
1976   Sources of Response Error in Self-Reports of Behavior. Unpublished Ph.D. Dissertation, University of Pennsylvania.

Appendix A

Appendix B

Self-Reported Behavior Items

YOUNG PEOPLE DO LOTS OF THINGS THAT ARE GOOD—BUT ONCE IN A WHILE THEY BREAK SOME RULES. SOME OF OUR MOST FAMOUS PEOPLE SAID THEY BROKE QUITE A FEW RULES WHEN THEY WERE GROWING UP.

WE WANT TO GET A CLEAR PICTURE OF THE THINGS YOUNG PEOPLE DO. THE WAY YOU CAN HELP IS BY GIVING A TRUE PICTURE OF HOW YOUNG PEOPLE ACT.

DON'T WORRY ABOUT LOOKING GOOD—OR LOOKING BAD.

WHEN WAS THE LAST TIME THAT YOU DID EACH OF THE FOLLOWING THINGS?

CHECK ONLY THE *LAST TIME* THIS HAPPENED.

[a]1 I SMOKED A CIGARETTE.
[a]2 I BROKE STREET LIGHTS OR WINDOWS IN A BUILDING.
3 I WAS SENT TO COURT.
[a]4 I TOOK SOMETHING WORTH MORE THAN 50¢ FROM A STORE.
5 I HELPED MY PARENTS AROUND THE HOUSE.
[a]6 I DAMAGED OR MESSED UP SOMETHING IN A SCHOOL OR SOME OTHER BUILDING.
[a]7 I STAYED OUT ALL NIGHT AND DIDN'T TELL MY PARENTS WHERE I WAS.
[a]8 I BROKE INTO A PARKING METER.
[a]9 I DRANK SOME BEER, WINE, OR LIQUOR WITHOUT MY PARENTS KNOWING ABOUT IT.
10 I WAS WARNED OR QUESTIONED BY A POLICEMAN.
[a]11 I TOOK PART IN A FIGHT WHERE OUT GROUP OF KIDS FOUGHT A DIFFERENT GROUP.
[a]12 I HELPED TO JUMP SOMEBODY AND BEAT THEM UP.
13 I TRIED TO GET KICKS FROM SMOKING REEFER CIGARETTES, TAKING PEP PILLS OR SNIFFING GLUE.
14 I RAN AROUND WITH SOME KIDS WHO HAD A BAD REPUTATION.
15 I TOOK SOMETHING WHICH DIDN'T BELONG TO ME WHICH WAS WORTH MORE THAN $2.
[a]16 I TOOK PART IN A FIGHT WHERE KNIVES OR OTHER WEAPONS WERE USED.
17 I WAS GIVEN A TICKET OR WAS ARRESTED BY THE POLICE.
[a]18 I WENT FOR A RIDE IN A CAR TAKEN WITHOUT THE OWNER'S PERMISSION.
19 I LET A FRIEND BORROW A LITTLE OF MY OWN MONEY.

Appendix B. Self-Reported Behavior Items *(continued)*

SUPPLEMENTAL ALTERNATE FORMS

1X   I HAD A FIST FIGHT WITH SOMEBODY.

2X   I DROVE A CAR AROUND THE STREETS WITHOUT A LICENSE OR PERMIT.

3X   I TOOK SOMETHING WORTH MORE THAN 50¢ WHICH BELONGED TO ANOTHER KID OR PERSON.

4X   I GOT THROWN OUT OF SOME PLACE FOR MAKING NOISE AND ACTING UP.

1Y   I BROKE OPEN A CANDY OR CIGARETTE MACHINE OR PAY PHONE.

2Y   I TOLD ANOTHER KID I WOULD GET THEM IF THEY DIDN'T DO WHAT I TOLD THEM.

3Y   I WENT INTO SOMEONE'S BUILDING WHEN NO ONE WAS THERE AND LOOKED OR PLAYED AROUND.

4Y   I MADE SO MUCH NOISE ON THE STREET THAT SOMEBODY COMPLAINED.

1Z   I SNATCHED SOMEONE'S PURSE OR WALLET FROM THEM BUT DIDN'T HURT THEM.

2Z   I DAMAGED OR MESSED UP SOMETHING IN SOMEBODY'S YARD OR IN THE PARK.

3Z   I TRIED TO SNEAK INTO A MOVIE OR BALL GAME WITHOUT PAYING.

4Z   I HAD OTHER KIDS TELL ME THEY WOULD GET ME IF I DIDN'T DO WHAT THEY TOLD ME.

[a]Items included in eleven-item omnibus scale.

Appendix C

Social Desirability Response Set Scale

ITEM NUMBER	ITEM	KEY ANSWER	PER CENT WITH KEY ANSWER
20P	ALWAYS I HAVE TOLD THE COMPLETE TRUTH	AGREE	15
38P	EVERY SINGLE THING I'VE EVER DONE HAS BEEN RIGHT AND GOOD AND KIND.	AGREE	17
18P	ONCE IN AWHILE I'VE GOTTEN ANGRY.	DISAGREE	5
29P	THERE ARE TIMES I'VE FELT SAD.	DISAGREE	7
60P	SOMETIMES I'VE DONE THINGS I'VE BEEN TOLD NOT TO DO.	DISAGREE	12

10. A Critique of Criminal Victimization Surveys

JAMES P. LEVINE

THE CRIMINAL VICTIMIZATION SURVEY IS BEING used increasingly as an alternative or supplement to reported crime data in assessing the seriousness of crime in various localities (U.S. Department of Justice, 1975) and in evaluating the effectiveness of particular crime prevention programs and policies (Kelling et al., 1974). Although this procedure for measuring crime is rather costly, it has several properties which have made it quite attractive to those engaged in criminal justice research. The most obvious advantage of this method is that it detects the apparently substantial number of crimes that are not reported to the police—what has been called "the dark figure of crime" (Biderman and Reiss, 1967). Indeed, national and city crime rates projected from survey data are roughly twice as high as those based on reported crimes which are summarized annually by the FBI in the Uniform Crime Reports (U.S. Department of Justice, 1974a).

Not only do reported crime rates omit many crimes actually committed, but since the degree of underreporting can fluctuate both geographically and temporally, it is hazardous to make comparisons between areas or to discern trends within areas on the basis of police reports (Kamisar, 1972). Many factors may cause this variation: the efficiency of police in discovering crime (Greenwood and Wadycki, 1973), the sophistication of police crime-reporting procedures, political and administrative pressure put on police officers to distort the true amount of crime by failing to record some crimes and misclassifying others (Seidman and Couzens, 1974; Milakovich and Weis, 1975), the amount of public confidence in the police, the varying legal definitions of crimes in different jurisdictions, and the extent to which victims of crime are insured and therefore specifically motivated to report crimes. Although Skogan's (1974) comparison of reported crime data and survey data in then large cities shows a moderate correspondence between the two measures, the study reaffirms that the magnitudes of crime yielded by both methods vary considerably.

Because survey research is constrained by a commonly accepted set of methodological rules and considerable administrative supervision (in the more sophisticated studies), it seems less likely that the amount of errors that do occur will change much from one survey to another. The reliability of properly conducted criminal victimization surveys is fairly high, so they are useful instruments with which to compare the crime rates of various communities and to assess the utility of alternative crime prevention programs.

UNDUE FAITH IN VICTIMIZATION SURVEYS

As valuable as crime surveys are, they present certain validity problems which proponents

▶SOURCE: *"The Potential for Crime Overreporting in Criminal Victimization Surveys," Criminology (November 1976), 14:307–330. Reprinted by permission.*

have tended to overlook. Just as unjustified faith is often placed in questionable economic indicators like the gross national product (Morgenstern, 1963) and the consumer price index (Samuelson, 1974), the victimization surveys have emerged as a kind of talisman—a foolproof way of telling the *actual* amount of crime that is committed.

Although surveys of a socially complex phenomenon like crime are plagued by sampling difficulties and the intrusion of "response errors" arising out of the artificiality of the interview situation, the accuracy of results is rarely challenged. The language of research reports is infrequently qualified, and the findings have been uncritically accepted by both professionals dealing with law enforcement and the lay public.

Thus, a Law Enforcement Assistant Administration study reports on the basis of about 10,000 personal interviews that "250,000 incidents of rape, assault, robbery, burglary, or larceny *occurred* in San Jose during 1970; 140,000 *occurred* in Dayton" (italics added; U.S. Department of Justice, 1974b). Likewise, an earlier study conducted under the auspices of the President's Commission on Law Enforcement and the Administration of Justice was said to "show that the *actual amount* of crime in the United States is several times that reported in the Uniform Crime Reports" (italics added; President's Commission . . ., 1967:21).

Even less cautious are the words of two legal scholars who state that "these [victimization] studies *unanimously agree* that *the actual rate* [of crime] *is* several times greater than that shown in the *Uniform Crime Reports*" (italics added; Center and Smith, 1973: 1045). Ironically, this comment is included in an analysis of the value of the Uniform Crime Reports entitled "Criminal Statistics—Can They Be Trusted?" The question is a good one, but it must be directed at the new methods of crime measurement as well as the old.

The so-called unreported crime uncovered in the surveys may well include many "crimes" that never took place at all, and the "gap" between reported and unreported crime may be more aptly interpreted as the difference between two fallible measurement techniques rather than a showing of a massive failure of victims to notify police. Whereas Thompson (1971: 457), in characterizing survey findings, asserts "that there is at least twice as much crime than is ever reported to police," it is equally logical to reach the opposite conclusion that only half as much crime ever occurs as is reported to interviewers. In reality, neither of these statements is probably correct: while police reports no doubt suffer from crime underreporting, surveys may be flawed by crime overreporting which leads to inflated crime rates.

Methodological evaluations of victimization surveys have emphasized factors that lead to omission of crimes, such as sampling biases (e.g., leaving out commuters in city surveys), "memory fading" (the inability of victims to recall crimes), and communications barriers between respondents and interviewers that inhibit free expression about personal matters such as crime. For example, "known victims" (i.e., those in police files) have been interviewed to ascertain what percentage revealed the crimes that have apparently been committed against them (U.S. Department of Justice, 1972).

There has been less attention paid to the reverse problem of overreporting—the inclusion in survey results of non-criminal events that have been misrepresented as crimes.[1] There are three central participants in surveys whose actions may distort results—the respondents themselves, the interviewers, and the coders of the data. How each of them may contribute to excessively high crime figures will now be discussed.

[1]Thus, a recent 270-page report of the Law Enforcement Assistance Administration analyzing surveys of the "National Crime Panel" conducted in 13 cities treats the problem of response error in a total of two sentences (U.S. Department of Justice, 1975: 257).

FALSE REPORTING BY RESPONDENTS

Response invalidity is a persistent problem in survey research. Not only do respondents often conceal real opinions and attitudes, but they frequently give incorrect information when asked for seemingly innocuous factual information. Indeed, two social psychologists who are authorities on interviewing reach the following sobering conclusion (Cannel and Kahn, 1968: 548):

"We believe that the generalization to be made with the greatest confidence is that significant problems of invalidity and unreliability are common in interview data, even for apparently simple questions asked under conditions of obvious legitimacy."

Numerous studies have shown high levels of error when attempts are made to verify survey responses by the use of behavioral indicators. Table I is a compilation of research findings demonstrating significant deviation between facts articulated by respondents and independent measures of the same phenomena. The wide range of topics concerning which incorrect responses were given raises questions about the authenticity of crimes described to interviewers. If people are not trustworthy in talking about their voting behavior, financial position, business practices, sex lives, and the academic progress of their children, then surely we should not take for granted their reporting of crime.

There are specific attributes of the victimization survey which render reports of crime particularly suspect. Not only may respondents purposely fabricate incidents, but they may unintentionally provide false information by wrongfully interpreting misfortunes that befall them as crimes, by misunderstanding the legal definition of crimes, or by forgetting exactly when crimes occurred. Each of these processes may artificially inflate crime data and it is therefore important that they be understood.

Mistaken Interpretation of Incidents as Crimes

Epistemologists have gone to great lengths to explain that all human observations entail the making of inferences. Hanson (1958: 7) expresses this idea glibly, but accurately: "There is more to see than meets the eyeball." The shapes, sounds, colors, and textures we perceive are interpreted according to our theories and intuitions about how the world functions.

The subjectivity of perceptions surely affects whether certain harms that are experienced are conceived of as criminal in nature or are thought to result from less malevolent forces, like bad luck or personal negligence. Of course some events, like armed bank robberies, leave little room for varying hypotheses—they are clearly crimes. On the other hand, many occurrences are more mysterious in nature, requiring the victim to use his own judgment to figure out what happened. Many incidents which are honestly thought of as crimes by respondents may well have been misconstrued because the victim either lacks sufficient information to understand the situation correctly or jumps to improper conclusions in assessing the evidence available to him.

Examples of this type of error abound. A broken house window may be thought of as evidence of an attempted burglary when the damage was really caused by a baseball thrown by children playing in the street. The wallet presumed to have been stolen by a pickpocket may have been accidentally left on a store counter. A woman may perceive sexual advances as an attempted rape when in fact the man involved had every intention of stopping if the woman seriously objected. Respondents may report all of these matters as crimes when something quite different has really transpired.

There are various reasons why people might make such mistakes. A generalized fear of crime may lead some to paranoid interpretations of unsettling experiences. If criminals are thought to be lurking everywhere, it is only natural to blame them when something goes awry.

Even relatively calm people are capable of serious misperceptions when they are in dis-

Table I. Invalid Factual Information Given by Respondents in Various Social Surveys

Study	Factual Item	Verification Source	Sample Size	Percent of Respondents Giving Incorrect Information
Hyman (1944)	Whether grocers put up government posters they received	Visual observation premesis	221	42
Parry & Crossley (1950)	Whether Denver residents voted in all six recent elections	Official voting records	Unclear	46[a]
Goddard, Broder, Wenar (1961)	When children of clinic users were vaccinated	Clinic records	20	80
Lansing, Ginsburg, Braaten (1961:64)	Amount of money in savings account	Bank records	109	47[b]
Lansing, Ginsburg, Braaten (1961:97)	Whether debtors had outstanding cash loan	Creditors' records	94	61
David (1962)	Amount of money given to welfare recipients	Official records	46	63[c]
Udry & Morris (1967)	Whether women had sexual intercourse on previous day	Urine analysis (check for semen)	15	20
Tittle & Hill (1967)	Whether students voted in student elections	Actual voting records	301	9
Hagburg (1968)	Number of class sessions attended by adult students	Instructors' attendance records	227	64
Weiss (1968)	Whether children of welfare mothers had failed grades	School records	680	37

[a]For each election, incorrect responses ranged from 14 percent to 29 percent.

[b]Answers were considered incorrect if respondents failed to mention an existing account or failed to state the correct amount in the account within $1,000 of the true balance.

[c]Answers were considered incorrect if respondents failed to admit receiving welfare or there was more than a 10 percent discrepancy between the amount given and the amount reported.

tress. The accuracy of observations is diminished under conditions of high emotion (Cannel and Kahn, 1968: 543), so it is quite possible that someone who is upset about a loss or injury or who feels uncomfortable in an alien environment may have his perceptions impaired. This blurring of perception was most tragically demonstrated during the Detroit riots in 1967 when police and national guardsmen wound up shooting each other because the panic which seized them lessened their ability to discriminate law-breakers from law-enforcers; "snipers" often turned out to be colleagues (National Advisory Commission on Civil Disorders, 1968: 97–104). This was an extreme situation, but even in less dire circumstances people who are searching for an explanation of otherwise inexplicable events may well distort, embellish, or completely imagine facets to convince themselves and others that they have been victims of crimes.

Incorrect Classification of Incidents as Crimes

It is virtually impossible to construct survey instruments that communicate the same specific meaning of questions to each and every respondent. Asking the seemingly simple question, "Which magazines have you read in the past seven days?" can evoke a variety of ideas because the verb "read" can be understood to mean glanced at, skimmed, thoroughly perused, or studied in detail. Likewise, an Englishman asked how often he has tea might think of the beverage, or a late afternoon snack, or the main evening meal, or an elegant Sunday repast. No amount of care and qualification in question-wording can totally eliminate the ambiguities of human speech.

Consequently, questions asked in crime surveys may elicit quite different recollections from different people. Because of misunderstanding, respondents may volunteer incidents that fall *outside* the category of events intended to be covered by the questions. Even when complex legal definitions of crimes are painstakingly translated into laymen's language, there remains ample room for confusion. This is demonstrated by studies showing that even the slightest changes in the wording or ordering of questions on victimization can affect the nature of responses (Reiss, 1967: 148–149).

For example, one question used on the Census Bureau interview schedule asks: "Did anyone beat you up, attack you, or hit you with something such as a rock or a bottle?" This attempt to determine whether the respondent has been assaulted may bring forth many noncriminal events because "attack" can be broadly construed to mean being chased, cursed, nudged, jostled, bumped, or impeded. Those who are hypersensitive to victimization might relate all kinds of encounters which fail to satisfy the legal requirements of assault.

Moreover, certain responses that are given presume a knowledge of legal nuances which may be lacking. One of the Census Bureau crime incident questions asks: "How did the person(s) attack you?" and one of the choices is "raped" or "tried to rape." To accept the alleged victim's designation of her experience as a rape ignored the fact that this crime is fraught with complexities—requiring the presence of several elements (force or the threat of it, penetration, and so on) and permitting a host of legal defenses (consent, mistake, and the like). Many women who think and say that they are raped are wrong because they have a mistaken understanding of the law. In many cases they may have been offended, insulted, mistreated, or abused; but legally they have not been raped and it is erroneous to include their misfortunes when measuring crime.

The extent of popular misconceptions about what constitutes a crime is indicated by Ennis's (1967: 90–93) study in which trained evaluators scrutinized the reports of 3296 cases of alleged criminal victimization mentioned by respondents in a national survey. Over one-third (34.9%) of all the events initially recorded as crimes were disqualified because the facts averred by respondents were insufficient to meet the criteria defining a criminal act. This is a problem which continuously confronts and frustrates police who are frequently asked by distraught people to intervene in disputes or disorders where no infraction of criminal law has occurred and police action is inappropriate. Laymen who are untutored in law are simply not competent to make conclusive judgments about whether they have been criminally victimized.

Respondent ignorance about the law may result in bona fide crimes being classified as more serious than they really are. Thus, the definition of aggravated assault used in the Law Enforcement Administration surveys requires that victims be injured from a weapon or "seriously" injured from a weaponless attacker (U.S. Department of Justice, 1974b: 74). A person who discovers some ugly bruises the day after being hit may truly think he was quite badly hurt and therefore describe his injury as serious, but the damage inflicted upon him may have been insufficient for labeling the assault as aggravated.

All of this reflects an even more profound taxonomy problem. What is called criminal behavior is partially the result of social norms defining deviant behavior, and in practice communities regularly modify the criminal law "on the books" tolerating certain kinds of conduct which are technically illegal (Wheeler, 1967). Victimization surveys, on the other hand, are designed to produce a recitation of a broad spectrum of crime-related life experiences many of which were not originally very disturbing to those affected and therefore of questionable relevance to crime statistics.

Thus, while almost any nonaccidental, unprovoked shove is an assault, there are innumerable such infractions which are shrugged off as minor annoyances by those who are victimized (such as the aggressiveness of rush-hour subway riders competing for empty seats). Likewise, if neighborhood children abscond with odd change left on a table after an afternoon of play, most people sustaining the loss would hesitate to identify their actions as lar-

ceny. Many of these kinds of matters may be recounted as crimes in response to the thorough cross-examination of interviewers even though they were conceived of as minor irritations when they first happened.

In fact, the most common reason given by respondents for not reporting crimes to police is that they were not very important or the damage done was negligible (U.S. Department of Justice, 1974a: 5). More than half of the unreported crimes detected in the San Jose and Dayton surveys involved larcenies of less than $50.00 (U.S. Department of Justice, 1974b: 24). What this implies is that many trivial grievances which stay out of police records because people are not very upset are elevated to criminal status by the aggressive probing and searching of interviewers.

As Lejins (1966: 1018) correctly notes, regarding such minor incidents as crimes runs contrary to a fundamental juridical precept—*de minimus non curat lex* (i.e., the law does not concern itself with trifles). The legal system itself routinely countenances many criminal acts that are deemed insignificant: citizens refuse to sign complaints, police fail to intervent, prosecutors dismiss charges, and juries acquit defendants whose guilt seems undeniable. If the commission of many offenses does not warrant judicial interest and disapproval, it is questionable whether these acts deserve to be counted as crimes at all. Since survey findings seem to include many of these trivial occurrences, the results are highly skewed and give an unrealistically grim portrayal of the crime problem.

Memory Failures About When Crimes Occurred

It is commonplace for people who have experienced some dreadful event to say that it seems like "just yesterday" when it happened. Traumatic crimes are no doubt imprinted in victims' minds and there may well be a convergence of the *immediate* recollection of what took place and the *past* occurrence of the incident. This may result in a tendency to erroneously remember the crime as having taken place more recently than was actually the case. The potential for this kind of mistake is small if respondents were asked whether they were victimized in the last 24 hours or even the past week, but in order to keep the numbers in the sample of respondents down to an economically feasible size, most surveys use a time period of 12 months, which seems too long to expect reliable recall about the date when a crime transpired.

Memory fallibility about the timing of events is indicated by a study in which husbands and wives were separately asked when they moved into the local community and considerable disparity emerged in their answers even though they were reporting the same event (Asher, 1974: 476). More direct evidence of the forward telescoping of earlier crimes into a more recent time frame was adduced in a Washington, D.C. study in which it was estimated that 17% of crimes recalled by respondents actually took place before the six-month cutoff point (Skogan, 1975: 27).

An additional test of this phenomenon is provided by the Dayton-San Jose crime surveys conducted in January and February 1971. The number of incidents identified as having occurred in the first half of 1970 was much lower than the number alleged to have taken place in the last half of the year (U.S. Department of Justice, 1974b: 37). Some of this difference may be explained by the failure of victims to remember crimes in the first six months ("memory fading"), but no doubt some of the crimes placed by respondents in the last six months actually occurred earlier.

These temporal errors can significantly increase the crime rates based on survey data. Surely some crimes that took place prior to the time period under consideration are inaccurately moved ahead by respondents and therefore improperly recorded. For the few months immediately preceding the time period of the survey, the number of such mistakes may be quite high. Indeed, Biderman (1970: 2) points

out that those interviewed may unconsciously shift earlier crimes into the time period under study to avoid the uneasy experience of giving a long series of negative answers to questions about victimization (which are thought to be disturbing to the interviewer).

Since there is no very feasible way of detecting these errors, many are wrongly included in the calculation of annual crime rates. Official crime data, in contrast, is not subject to this kind of error because most reports to police are made very soon after crimes actually happen.

Lying

It is obvious that some victims may intentionally conceal crimes when interrogated by interviews for the same reasons that they sometimes do not file reports with police (embarrassment, fear of repercussions, and the like). What is less clear is the opposite possibility—deliberate fabrication of crimes that never occurred or lying about the gravity of genuine crimes. Just as the self-serving lies and evasions of businessmen often make a mockery of economic data based on information garnered from them (Morgenstern, 1963: 17–28), the respondents in victimization surveys may have good reasons for concocting false stories about crime.

The very characteristics of the survey method which enable it to uncover some crimes that victims do not report to the police can operate to encourage falsification of crimes. Guarantees of anonymity and the unofficial nature of responses may encourage some victims to talk who would otherwise remain silent, but by the same token these factors provide conditions of impunity for those who dishonestly manufacture or exaggerate incidents. Whereas falsely reporting a crime to police or knowingly giving false information about crimes is a criminal offense in most jurisdictions that can result in imprisonment, no such consequences face those who lie to interviewers.

Various motivations might inspire such lying. A number of respondents may pervert the truth in an attempt to justify false insurance claims or illegitimate income tax deductions. Some may overstate the seriousness of the crime in order to gain the sympathy of the interviewer. Others may think of themselves as performing a social service by dramatizing the crime problem, perhaps feeling that it is unjust that lucky people like themselves who have managed to escape crime were selected for the survey while so many less fortunate acquaintances who *were* victimized were left out.

Role expectations may prompt falsification. Respondents may feel obligated to give the interviewer what they think he is seeking—a showing of as much crime as possible. Such sentiments are likely to be accentuated among those included in the National Crime Panel, a national probability sample being reinterviewed by the Law Enforcement Assistance Administration every six months about victimization. Panel members may think that they are failing to do the job for which they were chosen if they regularly fail to report any crime. This kind of "panel conditioning" affects many long-term surveys in which respondents who are periodically reinterviewed wind up reporting things as they think they should rather than as they are (Moser and Kalton, 1972: 142).

Thus, there is good reason to doubt the authenticity of many allegations of victimization made in surveys. It has been estimated that as many as one-third of the complaints made to the police are "unfounded," i.e., without sufficient basis in fact or law to constitute crime (Cameron, 1972: 317; Center and Smith, 1973: 1078). In the less revealing context of the survey, we would a fortiori expect an even greater number of wrongful reports. Response error in crime surveys is a formidable problem.

INTERVIEWER BIASES

Interviewers are another source of errors in surveys. It is well documented that survey responses are affected by the characteristics of the interviewers and the nature of their interactions with respondents (Kish, 1962; Phillips and Clancy, 1972; Cosper, 1972; Williams, 1968). The demeanor of the interviewer, his rapport with respondents, the way he phrases questions, and the manner in which he clarifies ambiguities are all potentially biasing factors. The fact that the identical survey instrument is used by all interviewers in no way precludes them from wittingly or unwittingly cuing respondents to answer in a particular way.

Moreover, there is always the possibility that the interviewer will blatantly tamper with the findings by recording answers incorrectly or making up the answers to questions they do not ask. This has been aptly referred to as "the cheater problem in polling" (Crespi, 1945).

These problems could be discounted if it could be assumed that biases in one direction caused by some interviewers were simply cancelled out by the opposite kind of bias introduced by other interviewers. If an equal amount of overreporting and underreporting is encouraged by interviewers, the net result would not grossly distort reality. However, it is more plausible that interviewer bias in victimization surveys is unevenly balanced in its impact and systematically tends to engender abnormally high levels of crime reporting.

The major reason is interviewer self-interest. As Roth (1966) has so trenchantly argued, paid employees who engage in social research are, like many other workers, most concerned with keeping their jobs, avoiding work that is unpleasant, and giving the boss what he wants. Interviewers who must engage in the same repetitive task on a daily basis and who presumably receive relatively little intrinsic job satisfaction are unlikely to be intensely committed to the canons of scientific objectivity. On the contrary, they may act in a fashion designed to please their superiors by producing results in keeping with what they think is most advantageous to the organization for which they are working.

Prodding respondents to mention crimes or distorting their responses to registering crimes can accomplish two self-serving purposes. It reduces the tedium of a steady stream of negative answers which makes the interview session itself rather dull, and it promotes results that are consonant with the ultimate purpose of the study. Since the development of victimization surveys has been predicated on the assumption that a vast number of crimes go unreported, it is essential to find evidence of such crimes in order to justify continuance of this costly method of crime accounting. If official crime data were nearly equivalent to that reported in surveys, there would be little sense in expending substantial funds merely to replicate statistics already gathered by police in the course of their normal duties.

In a practical sense, thousands of jobs are dependent on a showing of more crime than has been previously reported. The National Crime Panel of the Law Enforcement Assistance Administration is composed of literally tens of thousands of respondents and therefore creates a huge number of interviewing jobs. Discovery of high crime rates well above those based on police data confirms the importance of these interviews, while contrary findings may raise doubts about the wisdom of continuing such endeavors and the organizations which carry them out. From academicians who direct and analyze crime surveys to the rank-in-file workers in the "field," all those benefiting from such projects have a stake in the framing of favorable results. While rigor and impartiality compose one set of norms governing any polling organization, "the more crime, the better" is likely to become a countervailing institutional ethos.

Consequently, it is not surprising that interviewers who were required in a 1967 National Opinion Research Center survey to judge the accuracy of respondents' statements on the basis of intangible factors such as facial expression and speech hesitancy found very few of the crime anecdotes told to them to be questionable. The fact that interviewers had reservations about the authenticity or exactitude of fewer than one-half of 1% of the crimes reported (Biderman, 1967: 36) suggests that the presumed interest of those in charge to boost the amount of crime detected is well appreciated by those responsible for collecting the data.

Even if interviewers are scrupulously dedicated to the professional norm of neutrality, they are still bound to be subconsciously affected by the "expectation bias" that to a greater or lesser extent affects all kinds of behavioral research. Some of the most rigorously controlled experiments on both humans and animals in which the discretion of the researcher would seem to be insignificant have been shown to be influenced by a priori predictions about results (Rosenthal, 1966). Since the post hoc nature of surveys makes them an intrinsically sloppier method of data collection, the opportunity for interviewer expectations to distort outcomes would seem to be even greater, and several studies have indeed demonstrated the intrusion of this kind of error (Smith and Hyman, 1950; Wyatt and Campbell, 1950).

A striking manifestion of this phenomenon occurred in the 1948 preelection polling done by the American Institute of Public Opinion which indicated a Dewey landslide in the Presidential race. In a subsequent post mortem to determine where the survey went wrong, some interviewers revealed that they anticipated a Dewey sweep and therefore created an informal "quota" system for themselves according to which they would try to bring in a relatively high proportion of pro-Dewey answers each day. When they failed to meet their daily target, they felt as if somehow they were doing their job in an unsatisfactory manner (Hyman, 1954: 35–36).

The high amount of unrecorded crime commonly acknowledged and discovered in previous surveys is surely well known to interviewers. They may inadvertently strive to meet these levels by subtly ferreting out crimes from respondents who otherwise would have given negative answers. In all good conscience, interviewers may encourage more crime reporting than is warranted in order to produce outcomes consistent with past research and current hypotheses.

CODING UNRELIABILITY

Surveys evoke descriptions of harmful incidents experienced by respondents which must be assessed as to possible criminality and classified into various crime categories. It has been shown that even relatively simple coding tasks are characterized by low levels of intercoder reliability and therefore high degrees of measurement error (Crittenden and Hill, 1971). Where complex judgments are required, as is the case in coding victimization data, scientifically desired objectivity ought not to be presumed. Because coders must make decisions solely on the basis of the unclear, incomplete accounts of respondents as filtered secondhand by interviewers, they inevitably play a role in determining the amount and kinds of crime ultimately extracted from interviews.

The unreliable quality of the coding process was demonstrated by one study in which the judgments of National Opinion Research Center coders was compared with that of detectives and lawyers who used the same interview data to decide whether respondents were criminally victimized. A great deal of dissensus emerged, with NORC coders disagreeing with the lawyers in 36% of the cases and with the police in 35% of the cases (Ennis, 1967: 93).

This variation means that the crime designations made by coders are subject to the same biases that contaminate the interview stage of data collection. Like interviewers, coders also stand to gain if higher crime levels are found. Since there are many marginal cases of criminality that are reported and few precise coding guidelines, many "crimes" that emanate from the surveys may be artifacts of the coding process rather than legally recognizable criminal events.

MEASURING RESPONSE ERROR

Although response error is a thorny problem in the victimization survey, the overreporting biases discussed above are mainly conjectural. It is necessary to undertake research which confirms or rejects these hypotheses about the nature of errors so that crime rates based on survey results can be adjusted accordingly.

To measure response error, a sample of alleged victimizations could be thoroughly investigated for corroborating evidence about what happened, just as insurance companies try to verify claims made by policy holders who contend they were robbed or burglarized. Specifically, some respondents could be questioned in much greater detail than is ordinarily done in an attempt to expose incongruities or suspicious lapses of information. Also, relatives and associates of those claiming to have been victimized could be contacted to obtain validating information. While many minor crimes are not discussed much by victims, it would seem normal for news of serious offenses to be communicated within the victim's circle of acquaintances, unless it is an embarrassing crime like rape where a great indignity was suffered.

Various checks can be made on interviewers to assess and control the quality of their work. Simply analyzing the variation in crime reporting among respondents questioned by different interviewers will determine whether individual propensities of interviewers are affecting outcomes, but it will not show whether there are biases common to all interviewers. Utilizing persons outside the polling organization to conduct some of the interviews and comparing the data which they amass with that produced by employees of the organization might bring forth evidence of systematic bias introduced by the entire regular interviewing contingent. Another monitoring technique is to use outsiders to revisit some respondents and repeat the interview to determine whether the same tale of crime is forthcoming.

The subjectivity of coders should also be evaluated. To detect variation in coders' inclinations, not only can different individuals be assigned to code some of the same interviews, but the aggregate results emerging from various coders can be compared. To check for nonrandom skewing of the data in the same direction by all employed coders, a subsample of completed questionnaires could be independently coded by personnel unaffiliated with victimization surveys who would seemingly have less incentive to prejudice outcomes.

CONCLUSION

Users of victimization surveys have been careless in reporting results without due regard for the many methodological weaknesses of survey research. It is not the occasional faux pas that is the problem but a range of distortions generated by all those involved in surveys which cumulatively may produce overblown crime rates out of proportion to the real level of crime.

In an area of research as fraught with measurement difficulties as the enumeration of crimes, it behooves us to use multiple indicators in an effort to get a best estimate of the "true" amount of crime. As Chilton and Spielberger (1972: 74) remark, "any single measure of crime will have serious disadvantages if it is used alone." In light of the underreporting of crime in official records and the apparent overcounting of surveys, a prudent course may be to average crime rates based on the two data sets to derive a reasonable approximation of the actual incidence of crime. Only an omniscient deity would be capable of providing an exact tabulation of crime, and in lieu of such an authoritative accounting it is probably most sensible to develop a crime index based on various admittedly faulty measures rather than to pretend that any single source of data provides a perfect image of reality.

Certainly skepticism is in order concerning the central finding of victimization surveys that massive amounts of crime go unreported to police. Uncritical acceptance of these dubious results has many untoward consequences which ought to be avoided. Not only is an already unnerved public likely to be further distraught about physical security, but unwise government policies may be adopted in response to these findings which purport to show so many more crimes than were previously thought to exist. In particular, additional funds may be allocated to law enforcement agencies to fight crime which might be spent better elsewhere, and civil liberties may be sacrificed on the basis of an exaggerated view of the crime peril. Finally, the growth of knowledge in the field of criminology will be retarded if unsound data is used to learn about the characteristics of victims, perpetrators, and crimes.

REFERENCES

Asher, H. (1974) "Some consequences of measurement error in survey data." Amer. J. of Pol. Sci. 18 (May): 469–485.

Biderman, A. (1970) Time Distortions of Victimization Data and Mnemonic Effects. Washington, D.C.: Bureau of Social Research.

—— (1967) "Surveys of population samples for estimating crime incidence." Annals of the Amer. Academy of Pol. and Social Sci. 374 (November): 16–33.

—— and A. Reiss (1967) "On exploring the 'dark figure' of crime." Annals of the Amer. Academy of Pol. and Social Sci. 374 (November): 1–15.

Cameron, N. (1972) "Lies, damned lies, and statistics." Victoria University of Wellington Law Rev. 6 (August): 310–321.

Cannell, C. and R. Kahn (1968) "Interviewing," in G. Lindzey and E. Aronson (eds.) The Handbook of Social Psychology, II. Reading, Mass.: Addison-Wesley.

Center, L. and T. Smith (1973) "Criminal statistics—can they be trusted?" Amer. Criminal Law Rev. 11 (Summer): 1045–1086.

Chilton, R. and A. Spielberger (1972) "Increases in crime: the utility of alternative measures," J. of Criminal Law, Criminology, and Police Sci. 63: (March) 68–74.

Cosper, R. (1972) "Interviewing effects in a survey of drinking practices." Soc. Q. 13 (Spring): 228–236.

Crespi, L. (1945) "The cheater problem in polling." Public Opinion Q. 9 (Winter): 432–445.

Crittenden, K. and R. Hill (1971) "Coding reliability and validity of interview data." Amer. Soc. Rev. 36 (December): 1073–1080.

David, M. (1962) "The validity of income reported by a sample of families who received welfare assistance during 1959." J. of the Amer. Statistical Association 57 (March): 680–685.

Ennis, P. (1967) Criminal Victimization in the United States: A Report of a National Survey. Chicago: National Opinion Research Center.

Goddard, K., G. Broder, and C. Wenar (1961) "Reliability of pediatric histories: a preliminary study." Pediatrics 28 (December): 1011–1018.

Greenwood, M. and W. Wadycki (1973) "Crime rates and public expenditures for police protection: their interaction." Rev. of Social Economy 31 (October): 138–151.

Hagburg, E. (1968) "Validity of questionnaire data: reported and observed attendance in an adult education program." Public Opinion Q. 32 (Fall): 453–455.

Hanson, N. R. (1958) Patterns of Discovery. England: Cambridge Univ. Press.

Hyman, H. (1954) Interviewing in Social Research. Chicago: Univ. of Chicago Press.

——— (1944) "Do they tell the truth?" Public Opinion Q. 8 (Winter): 557–559.

Kamisar, Y. (1972) "How to use, abuse—and fight back with—crime statistics." Oklahoma Law Rev. 25 (May): 239–258.

Kelling, G., T. Pate, D. Dieckman, and C. Brown (1974) The Kansas City Preventative Patrol Experiment: A Summary Report, Washington, D.C.: Police Foundation.

Kish, L. (1962) "Studies of interviewer variance on attitudinal variables." J. of Amer. Statistical Association 57 (March): 92–115.

Lansing, J., G. Ginsburg, and K. Braaten (1961) An investigation of Response Error. Urbana: University of Illinois Bureau of Economic and Business Research.

Lejins, P. (1966) "Uniform crime reports." Michigan Law Rev. 64 (April): 1011–1030.

Milakovich, M. and K. Weis (1975) "Politics and measures of success in the war on crime," Crime and Delinquency 21 (January): 1–10.

Morgenstern, O. (1963) On the Accuracy of Economic Observations. Princeton, N.J.: Princeton Univ. Press.

Moser, C. A. and G. Kalton (1972) Survey Methods in Social Investigation. New York: Basic Books.

National Advisory Commission on Civil Disorders (1968) Report. New York: Basic Books.

Parry, H. and H. Crossley (1950) "Validity of responses to survey questions." Public Opinion Q. 14 (Spring): 61–80.

Phillips, D. and K. Clancy (1972) " 'Modeling effects' in survey research." Public Opinion Q. 34 (Summer): 246–253.

President's Commission on Law Enforcement and Administration of Justice (1967) The Challenge of Crime in a Free Society. Washington, D.C.: Government Printing Office.

Reiss, A. (1967) "Measurement of the nature and amount of crime," in President's Commission on Law Enforcement and Administration of Justice, Studies in Crime and Law Enforcement in Major Metropolitan Areas: Field Surveys III, Volume I. Washington, D.C.: Government Printing Office.

Rosenthal, R. (1966) Experimenter Effects in Behavioral Research. New York: Appleton-Century-Crofts.

Roth, J. (1966) "Hired hand research." Amer. Sociologist 1 (August): 190–196.

Samuelson, R. (1974) "Riding the monthly escalator: the consumer price index." New York Times Magazine (December 8): 34–35.

Seidman, D. and M. Couzens (1974) "Getting the crime rate down: political pressure and crime reporting." Law and Society Rev. 8 (Spring): 457–494.

Skogan, W. (1975) "Measurement problems in official and survey crime rates." J. of Criminal Justice 3 (Spring): 17–31.

——— (1974) "The validity of official crime statistics: an empirical investigation." Social Sci. Q. 55 (June): 25–38.

Smith, H. and H. Hyman (1950) "The biasing effect of interviewer expectations on survey results." Public Opinion Q. 14 (Fall): 491–506.

Thompson, C. (1971) "Computerization of criminal law: phase one—criminal statistics." Indiana Legal Forum 4 (Spring): 446–470.

Tittle, C. and R. Hill (1967) "The accuracy of self-reported data and prediction of Political activity." Public Opinion Q. 31 (Spring): 103–106.

Udry, J. and N. Morris (1967) "A method for validation of reported sexual data." J. of Marriage and Family Living 29 (August): 442–446.

U.S. Department of Justice (1975) Criminal Victimization Surveys in Thirteen American Cities. Washington, D.C.: Law Enforcement Assistance Administration.

———— (1974a) Crime in the Nation's Five Largest Cities. Washington, D.C.: Law Enforcement Assistance Administration.

———— (1974b) Crimes and Victims: A Report on the Dayton-San Jose Pilot Survey of Victimization. Washington, D.C.: Law Enforcement Assistance Administration.

———— (1972) San Jose Methods Test of Known Crime Victims. Washington, D.C.: National Institute of Law Enforcement and Criminal Justice, Statistics Division.

Weiss, C. (1968) "Validity of welfare mothers' interview responses." Public Opinion Q. 32 (Winter): 622–633.

Wheeler, S. (1967) "Criminal statistics: a reformulation of the problem." J. of Criminal Law, Criminology, and Police Sci. 58 (September): 317–324.

Williams, J. A. (1968) "Interviewer role performance: a further note on bias in the information interview." Public Opinion Q. 32 (Summer): 287–294.

Wyatt, D. and D. Campbell (1950) "A study of interviewer bias as related to interviewers' expectations and own opinions." Int'l J. of Opinion and Attitude Research 4: 77–83

11. Mythical Numbers and the Cost of Crime

MAX SINGER

IT IS GENERALLY ASSUMED THAT HEROIN ADDICTS in New York City steal some two to five billion dollars worth of property a year, and commit approximately half of all the property crimes. Such estimates of addict crime are used by an organization like RAND, by a political figure like Howard Samuels, and even by the Attorney General of the United States.[1] The estimate that half the property crimes are committed by addicts was originally attributed to a police official and has been used so often that it is now part of the common wisdom.

The amount of property stolen by addicts is usually estimated in something like the following manner:

There are 100,000 addicts with an average habit of $30.00 per day. This means addicts must have some $1.1 billion a year to pay for their heroin (100,000 × 365 × $30.00). Because the addict must sell the property he steals to a fence for only about a quarter of its value, or less, addicts must steal some $4 to $5 billion a year to pay for their heroin.

These calculations can be made with more or less sophistication. One can allow for the fact that the kind of addicts who make their living illegally typically spend upwards of a quarter of their time in jail, which would reduce the amount of crime by a quarter. (*The New York Times* recently reported on the death of William "Donkey" Reilly. A 74 year old ex-addict who had been addicted for 54 years, he had spent 30 of those years in prison.) Some of what the addict steals is cash, none of which has to go to a fence. A large part of the cost of heroin is paid for by dealing in the heroin business, rather than stealing from society, and another large part by prostitution, including male addicts living off prostitutes. But no matter how carefully you slice it, if one tries to estimate the value of property stolen by addicts by assuming that there are 100,000 addicts and estimating what is the minimum amount they would have to steal to support themselves and their habits (after making generous estimates for legal income), one comes up with a number in the neighborhood of $1 billion a year for New York City.

But what happens if you approach the question from the other side? Suppose we ask, "How much property is stolen—by addicts or anyone else?" Addict theft must be less than total theft. What is the value of property stolen in New York City in any year? Somewhat surprisingly to me when I first asked, this turned out to be a difficult question to answer, even approximately. No one had any estimates that they had even the faintest confidence in, and the question doesn't seem to have been much asked. The amount of officially reported theft in New York

▶SOURCE: *"The Vitality of Mythical Numbers," The Public Interest (Spring 1971), 23:3–9. Reprinted with permission of Max Singer from The Public Interest. Copyright 1971 by National Affairs, Inc.*

[1] New York RAND Issue Paper on Drug Addiction Control in New York, 1968; Howard Samuels, Position Paper on Narcotics, 1970; Speech by Attorney General Mitchell, October 6, 1969.

City is approximately $300 million a year, of which about $100 million is the value of automobile theft (a crime that is rarely committed by addicts). But it is clear that there is a very large volume of crime that is not reported; for example, shoplifting is not normally reported to the police. (Much property loss to thieves is not reported to insurance companies either, and the insurance industry had no good estimate for total theft.)

It turns out, however, that if one is only asking a question like, "Is it possible that addicts stole $1 billion worth of property in New York City last year?" it is relatively simple to estimate the amount of property stolen. It is clear that the two biggest components of addict theft are shoplifting and burglary. What *could* the value of property shoplifted by addicts be? All retail sales in New York City are on the order of $15 billion a year. This includes automobiles, carpets, diamond rings, and other items not usually available to shoplifters. A reasonable number for inventory loss to retail establishments is 2 per cent. This number includes management embezzlements, stealing by clerks, shipping departments, truckers, etc. (Department stores, particularly, have reported a large increase in shoplifting in recent years, but they are among the most vulnerable of retail establishments and not important enough to bring the overall rate much above 2 per cent.) It is generally agreed that substantially more than half of the property missing from retail establishments is taken by employees, the remainder being lost to outside shoplifters. But let us credit shoplifters with stealing one per cent of all the property sold at retail in New York City—this would be about $150 million a year.

What about burglary? There are something like two and one-half million households in New York City. Suppose that on the average one out of five of them is robbed or burglarized every year. This takes into account that in some areas burglary is even more commonplace, and that some households are burglarized more than once a year. This would mean 500,000

burglaries a year. The average value of property taken in a burglary might be on the order of $200. In some burglaries, of course, much larger amounts of property are taken, but these higher value burglaries are much rarer, and often are committed by non-addict professional thieves. If we use the number of $200 × 500,000 burglaries, we get $100 million of property stolen from people's homes in a year in New York City.

Obviously, none of these estimated values is either sacred or substantiated. You can make your own estimate. The estimates here have the character that it would be very surprising if they were wrong by a factor of 10, and not very important for the conclusion if they were wrong by a factor of two. (This is a good position for an estimator to be in.)

Obviously not all addict theft is property taken from stores or from people's home. One of the most feared types of addict crime is property taken from the persons of New Yorkers in muggings, and other forms of robbery. We can estimate this, too. Suppose that on the average, one person in 10 has property taken from his person by muggers or robbers each year. That would be 800,000 such robberies, and if the average one produced $100 (which it is very unlikely to do), $8 million a year would be taken in this form of theft.

So we can see that if we credit addicts with *all* of the shoplifting, *all* of the theft from homes, and *all* of the theft from persons, total property stolen by addicts in a year in New York City amounts to some $330 million. You can throw in all the "fudge factors" you want, add all the other miscellaneous crimes that addicts commit, but no matter what you do, it is difficult to find a basis for estimating that addicts steal over a half billion dollars a year, and a quarter billion looks like a better estimate, although perhaps on the high side. After all, there must be some thieves who are not addicts.

Thus, I believe we have shown that whereas it is widely assumed that addicts steal from $2-$5 billion a year in New York City, the actual number is *ten* times smaller, and that this can be demonstrated by five minutes of thought.[2] So what? A quarter billion dollars' worth of property is still a lot of property. It exceeds the amount of money spent annually on addict rehabilitation and other programs to prevent and control addiction. Furthermore, the value of the property stolen by addicts is a small part of the total cost to society of addict theft. A much larger cost is paid in fear, changed neighborhood atmosphere, the cost of precautions, and other echoing and re-echoing reactions to theft and its danger.

One point in this exercise in estimating the value of property stolen by addicts is to shed some light on people's attitudes toward numbers. People feel that there is a lot of addict crime, and that $2 billion is a large number, so they are inclined to believe that there is $2 billion worth of addict theft. But $250 million is a large number, too, and if our sense of perspective were not distorted by daily consciousness of federal expenditures, most people would be quite content to accept $250 million a year as a lot of theft.

Along the same lines, this exercise is another reminder that even responsible officials, responsible newspapers, and responsible research groups pick up and pass on as gospel numbers that have no real basis in fact. We are reminded by this experience that because an estimate has been used widely by a variety of people who should know what they are talking about, one cannot assume that the estimate is even approximately correct.

But there is a much more important implication of the fact that there cannot be nearly so much addict theft as people believe. This implication is that there probably cannot be as many addicts as many people believe. Most of the money paid for heroin bought at retail comes from stealing, and most addicts buy at retail. Therefore, the number of addicts is basically—although imprecisely—limited by the amount of theft. (The estimate developed in a Hudson Institute study was that close to half of the volume of heroin consumed is used by people in the heroin distribution system who do not buy at retail, and do not pay with stolen property but with their "services" in the distribution system.[3]) But while the people in the business (at lower levels) consume close to half the heroin, they are only some one-sixth or one-seventh of the total number of addicts. They are the ones who can afford big habits.

The most popular, informal estimate of addicts in New York City is 100,000-plus (usually with an emphasis on the "plus"). The federal register in Washington lists some 30,000 addicts in New York City, and the New York City Department of Health's register of addicts' names lists some 70,000. While all the people on those lists are not still active addicts—many of them are dead or in prison—most people believe that there are many addicts who are not on any list. It is common to regard the estimate of 100,000 addicts in New York City as a very conservative one. Dr. Judianne Densen-Gerber was widely quoted early in 1970 for her estimate that there would be over 100,000 teenage addicts by the

[2]Mythical numbers may be more mythical and have more vitality in the area of crime than in most areas. In the early 1950's the Kefauver Committee published a $20 billion estimate for the annual "take" of gambling in the United States. The figure actually was "picked from a hat." One staff member said: "We had no real idea of the money spent. The California Crime Commission said $12 billion. Virgil Petersen of Chicago said $30 billion. We picked $20 billion as the balance of the two."

An unusual example of a mythical number that had a vigorous life—the assertion that 28 Black Panthers had been murdered by police—is given a careful biography by Edward Jay Epstein in the February 13, 1971, *New Yorker*. (It turned out that there were 19 Panthers killed, ten of them by the police, and eight of these in situations where it seems likely that the Panthers took the initiative.)

[3]A parallel datum was developed in a later study by St. Luke's Hospital of 81 addicts—average age 34. More than one-half of the heroin consumed by these addicts, over a year, had been paid for by the sale of heroin. Incidentally, these 81 addicts had stolen an average of $9,000 worth of property in the previous year.

end of the summer. And there are obviously many addicts of 20 years of age and more.[4]

In discussing the number of addicts in this article, we will be talking about the kind of person one thinks of when the term "addict" is used.[5] A better term might be "street addict." This is a person who normally uses heroin every day. He is the kind of person who looks and acts like the normal picture of an addict. We exclude here the people in the medical profession who are frequent users of heroin occasionally, wealthy people who are addicted but do not need to steal and do not frequent the normal addict hangouts, etc. When we are addressing the "addict problem," it is much less important that we include these cases; while they are undoubtedly problems in varying degrees, they are a very different type of problem than that posed by the typical street addict.

The amount of property stolen by addicts suggests that the number of New York City street addicts may be more like 70,000 than 100,000, and almost certainly cannot be anything like the 200,000 number that is sometimes used. Several other simple ways of estimating

[4]Among other recent estimators we may note a Marxist, Sol Yurick, who gives us "500,000 junkies" (*Monthly Review,* December 1970), and William R. Corson, who contends, in the December 1970 *Penthouse,* that "today at least 2,500,000 black Americans are hooked on heroin."

[5]There is an interesting anomaly about the word "addict." Most people, if pressed for a definition of an "addict," would say he is a person who reguarly takes heroin (or some such drug) and who, if he fails to get his regular dose of heroin, will have unpleasant or painful withdrawal symptoms. But this definition would not apply to a large part of what is generally recognized as the "addict population." In fact, it would not apply to most certified addicts. An addict who has been detoxified or who has been imprisoned and kept away from drugs for a week or so would not fit the normal definition of "addict." He no longer has any physical symptoms resulting from not taking heroin. "Donkey" Reilly would certainly fulfill most people's ideas of an addict, but for 30 of the 54 years he was an "addict" he was in prison, and he was certainly not actively addicted to heroin during most of the time he spent in prison, which was more than half of his "addict" career (although a certain amount of drugs are available in prison).

the number of street addicts lead to a similar conclusion.

Experience with the addict population has led observers to estimate that the average street addict spends a quarter to a third of his time in prison. (Some students of the subject, such as Edward Preble and John J. Casey, Jr., believe the average to be over 40 per cent.) This would imply that at any one time, one-quarter to one-third of the addict population is in prison, and that the total addict population can be estimated by multiplying the number of addicts who are in prison by three of four. Of course the number of addicts who are in prison is not a known quantity (and, in fact, as we have indicated above, not even a very precise concept). However, one can make reasonable estimates of the number of addicts in prison (and for this purpose we can include the addicts in various involuntary treatment centers). This number is approximately 14,000-17,000 which is quite compatible with an estimate of 70,000 total New York City street addicts.

Another way of estimating the total number of street addicts in New York City is to use the demographic information that is available about the addict population. For example, we can be reasonably certain that some 25 percent of the street addict population in New York City is Puerto Rican, and some 50 per cent are Negroes. We know that approximately five out of six street addicts are male, and that 50 per cent of the street addicts are between the ages of 16 and 25. This would mean that 20 per cent of the total number of addicts are male Negroes between the age of 16 and 25. If there were 70,000 addicts, this would mean that 14,000 Negro boys between the ages of 16 and 25 are addicts. But altogether there are only about 140,000 Negro boys between the ages of 16 and 25 in the city—perhaps half of them living in poverty areas. This means that if there are 70,000 addicts in the city, one in 10 Negro youths are addicts, and if there are 100,000 addicts, nearly one in six are, and if there are 200,000 addicts, one in three. You can decide for yourself which of these degrees of penetration of the young Negro male group is most believable, but it is rather clear that the number of 200,000 addicts is implausible. Similarly, the total of 70,000 street addicts would imply 7,000 young Puerto Rican males are addicted, and the total number of Puerto Rican boys between the ages of 16 and 25 in New York City is about 70,000.

None of the above calculations are meant in any way to downplay the importance of the problem of heroin addiction. Heroin is a terrible curse. When you think of the individual tragedy involved, 70,000 is an awfully large number of addicts. And if you have to work for a living, $250 million is an awful lot of money to have stolen from the citizens of the city to be transferred through the hands of addicts and fences into the pockets of those who import and distribute heroin, and those who take bribes or perform other services for the heroin industry.

The main point of this selection may well be to illustrate how far one can go in bounding a problem by taking numbers seriously, seeing what they imply, checking various implications against each other and against general knowledge (such as the number of persons or households in the city). Small efforts in this direction can go a long way to help ordinary people and responsible officials to cope with experts of various kinds.

Theory and Criminology

THIS SECTION CONTAINS SEVERAL CURRENTLY RELEVANT AND WIDELY DISCUSSED theoretical explanations of delinquent and criminal behavior. Robert K. Merton's article on "Social Structure and Anomie" has become a sociological classic. In it he describes the disproportionate relationship between two basic elements of the social structure: culturally approved goals and institutionalized means to these goals. In one mode of adjustment, innovation, lower-class boys are said to reject conventional means to success while, at the same time, accepting and desiring conventional economic goals and rewards; delinquency becomes a solution to otherwise insoluable problems. Cloward and Ohlin's "Opportunity Theory" remains, after 16 years, one of the more widely accepted models of delinquent behavior. Their theory focuses on the unequal availability of conventional and even nonconventional and illegal routes to success. There is, they argue, differential access to both legitimate and illegitimate opportunities. A three-fold typology of gangs is predicated: the Criminal, the Conflict, and the Retreatist. There have been, over the years, a number of empirical tests of Opportunity Theory. One of the more interesting, by Quicker, involves a causal analysis of crucial Cloward and Ohlin variables that are said to lead to delinquency. By the use of data derived from a cohort of high school boys, and by positing two different forms of goal discrepancies, the research concludes that long-range goal discrepancies do not seem to be associated with delinquency, whereas short-term goal discrepancies are strongly related to delinquent behavior.

Another major theoretical view of crime has come to be known as the "Subculture of Violence." Wolfgang and Ferracuti argue that in heterogenous populations, there exist variations in crucial attitudes toward, and the use of, force or violence, and these differences are related to one's social status. Overt physical violence may become a common, subculturally expected, and even demanded, response to specified stimului, with penalties accruing to those who deviate from these violence norms. Erlanger's test of this thesis reviews major pertinent literature and then deals with the results of a special analysis of attitudinal survey data acquired by the President's Commission on the Causes and Prevention of Violence, in addition to his own research in Milwaukee, Wisconsin. He concludes that the bulk of available data does not support the

Subculture of Violence theory, while admitting that, at the present time, the full model has not been definitively tested.

The major focal concerns of the lower class, as analyzed by Miller, are: trouble, toughness, smartness, excitement, fate, and autonomy. He suggests that lower-class adolescent delinquents are not truly deviant from the underlying values of the stratum of society in which they find themselves. Wellford's article deals with perhaps the most widely regarded current theoretical perspective, labelling theory. He contends that one version of labelling theory is based on nine basic assumptions. Each of these are examined in terms of recent evidence, and Wellford concludes that, within this particular framework, the labelling perspective is not a useful model to pursue.

The section concludes with two controversial views of criminality. Unquestionably the most influential criminological model in recent years has been that of "radical criminology" offering, as it does, a socialist-Marxist explication of crime. The most preeminent and prolific proponent of this view is Richard Quinney, who in his selection deals with the political economy of the capitalist system which, he holds, is characterized by dominance and repression. Quite the opposite view is offered by van den Haag who attacks, with some force, liberal sentiments that favor the criminal instead of the victim or society. This view is less a systematic explanation of crime than an ideological onslaught on the radical perspective.

12. Social Structure and Anomie

ROBERT K. MERTON

THERE PERSISTS A NOTABLE TENDENCY IN sociological theory to attribute the malfunctioning of social structure primarily to those of man's imperious biological drives which are not adequately restrained by social control. In this view, the social order is solely a device for "impulse management" and the "social processing" of tensions. These impulses which break through social control, be it noted, are held to be biologically derived. Nonconformity is assumed to be rooted in original nature.[1] Conformity is by implication the result of an utilitarian calculus or unreasoned conditioning. This point of view, whatever its other deficiencies, clearly begs one question. It provides no basis for determining the nonbiological conditions which induce deviations from prescribed patterns of conduct. In this paper, it will be suggested that certain phases of social structure generate the cricumstances in which infringement of social codes constitute a "normal" response.[2]

▶SOURCE: *"Social Structure and Anomie," American Sociological Review, (October 1938), 3:672–682. Reprinted with permission.*

[1]*E.g.,* Ernest Jones, *Social Aspects of Psychoanalysis,* 28, London, 1924. If the Freudian notion is a variety of the "original sin" dogma, then the interpretation advanced in this selection may be called the doctrine of "socially derived sin."

[2]"Normal" in the sense of a culturally oriented, if not approved, response. The statement does not deny the relevance of biological and personality differences which may be significantly involved in the *incidence* of deviate conduct. Our focus of interest is the social and cultural matrix; hence we abstract from other factors. It is in this sense, I take it, that James S. Plant speaks of the "normal reaction of normal people to abnormal conditions." See his *Personality and the Cultural Pattern,* 248, New York, 1937.

The conceptual scheme to be outlined is designed to provide a coherrent, systematic approach to the study of socio-cultural sources of deviate behavior. Our primary aim lies in discovering how some social structures *exert a definite pressure* upon certain persons in the society to engage in nonconformist rather than conformist conduct. The many ramifications of the scheme cannot all be discussed; the problems mentioned outnumber those explicitly treated.

Among the elements of social and cultural structure, two are important for our purposes. These are analytically separable although they merge imperceptibly in concrete situations. The first consists of culturally defined goals, purposes, and interests. It comprises a frame of aspirational reference. These goals are more or less integrated and involve varying degrees of prestige and sentiment. They constitute a basic, but not the exclusive, component of what Linton aptly has called "designs for group living." Some of these cultural aspirations are related to the original drives of man, but they are not determined by them. The second phase of the social structure defines, regulates, and controls the acceptable modes of achieving these goals. Every social group invariably couples its scale of desired ends with moral or institutional regulation of permissible and required procedures for attaining these ends. These regulatory norms and moral imperatives do not necessarily coincide with technical or efficiency norms. Many procedures which form the standpoint of *particular individuals* would be most efficient in securing desired values, e.g., illicit oil-stock schemes, theft, fraud, are ruled out of the institutional area of permitted conduct. The choice of expedients is limited by the institutional norms.

To say that these two elements, culture goals and institutional norms, operate jointly is not to say that the ranges of alternative behaviors and aims bear some constant relation to one another. The emphasis upon certain goals may vary independently of the degree of emphasis upon institutional means. There may develop a disproportionate, at times, a virtually exclusive, stress upon the value of specific goals, involving relatively slight concern with the institutionally appropriate modes of attaining these goals. The limiting case in this direction is reached when the range of alternative procedures is limited only by the technical rather than institutional considerations. Any and all devices which promise attainment of the all important goal would be permitted in this hypothetical polar case.[3] This constitutes one type of cultural malintegration. A second polar type is found in groups where activities originally conceived as instrumental are transmuted into ends in themselves. The original purposes are forgotten and ritualistic adherence to institutionally prescribed conduct becomes virtually obsessive.[4] Stability is largely ensured while change is flouted. The range of alternative behaviors is severely limited. There develops a tradition-bound, sacred society characterized by neophobia. The occupational psychosis of the bureaucrat may be cited as a case in point. Finally, there are the intermediate types of groups where a balance between culture goals and institutional means is maintained. These are the significantly integrated and relatively stable, though changing, groups.

An effective equilibrium between the two phases of the social structure is maintained as long as satisfactions accrue to individuals who conform to both constraints, viz., satisfactions from the achievement of the goals and satisfactions emerging directly from the institutionally canalized modes of striving to attain these ends. Success, in such equilibrated cases, is twofold. Success is reckoned in terms of the product and in terms of the process, in terms of the outcome and in terms of activities. Continuing satisfactions must derive from sheer *participation* in a competitive order as well as from eclipsing one's competitors if the order itself is to be sustained. The occasional sacrifices involved in institutionalized conduct must be compensated by socialized rewards. The distribution of statuses and roles through competition must be so organized that positive incentives for conformity to roles and adherence to status obligations are provided *for every position* within the distributive order. Aberrant conduct, therefore, may be viewed as a symptom of dissociation between culturally defined aspirations and socially structured means.

Of the types of groups which result from the

---

[3] Contemporary American culture has been said to tend in this direction. See André Siegfried, *America Comes of Age,* 26–37, New York, 1927. The alleged extreme (?) emphasis on the goals of monetary success and material prosperity leads to dominant concern with technological and social instruments designed to produced the desired result, inasmuch as institutional controls become of secondary importance. In such a situation, innovation flourishes as the *range of means* employed is broadened. In a sense, then, there occurs the paradoxical emergence of "materialists" from an "idealistic" orientation. Cf. Durkheim's analysis of the cultural conditions which predispose toward crime and innovation, both of which are aimed toward efficiency, not moral norms. Durkheim was one of the first to see that "contrairement aux idées courantes le criminel n' apparait plus comme un être radicalement insociable, comme une sorte d'élément parasitaire, de corps étranger et inassimilable, introduit au sein de la société; c'est un agent régulier de la view sociale." See *Les Régles de la Méthode Sociologique,* 86–89, Paris, 1927.

[4] Such ritualism may be associated with a mythology which rationalizes these actions so that they appear to retain their status as means, but the dominant pressure is in the direction of strict ritualistic conformity, irrespective of such rationalizations. In this sense, ritual has proceeded farthest when such rationalizations are not even called forth.

independent variation of the two phases of the social structure, we shall be primarily concerned with the first, namely, that involving a disproportionate accent on goals. This statement must be recast in a proper perspective. In no group is there an absence of regulatory codes governing conduct, yet groups do vary in the degree to which these folkways, mores, and institutional controls are effectively integrated with the more diffuse goals which are part of the culture matrix. Emotional convictions may cluster about the complex of socially acclaimed ends, meanwhile shifting their support from the culturally defined implementation of these ends. As we shall see, certain aspects of the social structure may generate countermores and antisocial behavior precisely because of differential emphases on goals and regulations. In the extreme case, the latter may be so vitiated by the goal-emphasis that the range of behavior is limited only be considerations of technical expediency. The sole significant question then becomes, which available means is most efficient in netting the socially approved value?[5] The technically most feasible procedure, whether legitimate or not, is preferred to the institutionally prescribed conduct. As this process continues, the integration of the society becomes tenuous and anomie ensues.

Thus, in competitive athletics, when the aim of victory is shorn of its institutional trappings and success in contests becomes construed as "winning the game" rather than "winning through circumscribed modes of activity," a premium is implicitly set upon the use of illegitimate but technically efficient means. The star of the opposing football team is surreptitiously slugged; the wrestler furtively incapacitates his opponent through ingenious but illicit techniques; university alumni covertly subsidize "students" whose talents are largely confined to the athletic field. The emphasis on the goal has so attenuated the satisfactions deriving from sheer participation in the competitive activity that these satisfactions are virtually confined to a successful outcome. Through the same process, tension generated by the desire to win in a poker game is relieved by successfully dealing oneself four aces, or when the cult of success has become completely dominant, by sagaciously shuffling the cards in a game of solitaire. The faint twinge of uneasiness in the last instance and the surreptitous nature of public delicts indicate clearly that the institutional rules of the game *are known* to those who evade them, but that the emotional supports of these rules are largely vitiated by cultural exaggeration of the success-goal.[6] They are microcosmic images of the social macrocosm.

Of course, this process is not restricted to the realm of sport. The process whereby exaltation of the end generates a *literal demoralization*, i.e., a deinstitutionalization, of the means is one which characterizes many[7] groups in which the two phases of the social structure are not highly integrated. The extreme emphasis upon the accumulation of wealth as a symbol of success[8] in

[5]In this connection, one may see the relevance of Elton Mayo's paraphrase of the title of Tawney's well known book. "Actually the problem *is not that of the sickness of an acquisitive society; it is that of the acquisitiveness of a sick society.*" *Human Problems of an Industrial Civilization*, 153, New York, 1933. Mayo deals with the process through which wealth comes to be a symbol of social achievement. He sees this as arising from a state of anomie. We are considering the unintegrated monetary-success goals as an element in producing anomie. A complete analysis would involve both phases of this system of interdependent variables.

[6]It is unlikely that interiorized norms are completely eliminated. Whatever residuum persists will induce personality tensions and conflict. The process involves a certain degree of ambivalence. A manifest rejection of the institutional norms is coupled with some latent retention of their emotional correlates. "Guilt feelings," "sense of sin," "pangs of conscience" are obvious manifestations of this unrelieved tension; symbolic adherence to the nominally repudiated values or rationalizations constitute a more subtle variety of tensional release.

[7]"Many," and not all, unintegrated groups, for the reason already mentioned. In groups where the primary emphasis shifts to institutional means, i.e., when the range of alternatives is very limited, the outcome is a type of ritualism rather than anomie.

[8]Money has several peculiarities which render it particularly apt to become a symbol of prestige divorced from in-

our own society militates against the completely effective control of institutionally regulated modes of acquiring a fortune.[9] Fraud, corruption, vice, crime, in short, the entire catalogue of proscribed behavior, becomes increasingly common when the emphasis on the *culturally induced* success-goal becomes divorced from a coordinated institutional emphasis. This observation is of crucial theoretical importance in examining the doctrine that antisocial behavior most frequently derives from biological drives breaking through the restraints imposed by society. The difference is one between a strictly utilitarian interpretation which conceives man's ends as random and an analysis which finds these ends deriving from the basic values of the culture.[10]

Our analysis can scarcely stop at this juncture. We must turn to other aspects of the social structure if we are to deal with the social genesis of the varying rates and types of deviate behavior characteristic of different societies. Thus far, we have sketched three ideal types of social orders constituted by distinctive patterns of relations between culture ends and means. Turning from these types of *culture patterning,* we find five logically possible, alternative modes of adjustment or adaptation *by individuals* within the culture-bearing society or group.[11] These are schemati-

cally presented in the following table, where (+) signifies "acceptance," (−) signifies "elimination" and (±) signifies "rejection and substitution of new goals and standards."

	Culture Goals	Institutionalized Means
I. Conformity	+	+
II. Innovation	+	−
III. Ritualism	−	+
VI. Retreatism	−	−
V. Rebellion[12]	±	±

Our discussion of the relation between these alternative responses and other phases of the social structure must be prefaced by the observation that persons may shift from one alternative to another as they engage in different social activities. These categories refer to role adjustments in specific situations, not to personality *in toto.* To treat the development of this process in various spheres of conduct would introduce a complexity unmanageable within the confines of this paper. For this reason, we shall be concerned primarily with economic activity in the broad sense, "the production, exchange, distribution and consumption of goods and services" in our competitive society, wherein wealth has taken on a highly symbolic cast. Our task is to search out some of the factors which exert pressure upon individuals to engage in certain of these logically possible alternative responses. This choice, as we shall see, is far from random.

In every society, Adaptation I (conformity to

---

stitutional controls. As Simmel emphasized, money is highly abstract and impersonal. However acquired, through fraud or institutionally, it can be used to purchase the same goods and services. The anonymity of metropolitan culture, in conjunction with this peculiarity of money, permits wealth, the sources of which may be unknown to the community in which the plutocrat lives, to serve as a symbol of status.

[9]The emphasis upon wealth as a success-symbol is possibly reflected in the use of the term "fortune" to refer to a stock of accumulated wealth. This meaning becomes common in the late sixteenth century (Spencer and Shakespeare). A similar usage of the Latin *fortuna* comes into prominence during the first century B.C. Both these periods were marked by the rise to prestige and power of the "bourgeoisie."

[10]See Kingsley Davis, "Mental Hygiene and the Class Structure," *Psychiatry,* 1928, I, esp. 62-63; Talcott Parsons, *The Structure of Social Action,* 59-60, New York, 1937.

[11]This is a level intermediate between the two planes distinguished by Edward Sapir; namely, culture patterns and

personal habit systems. See his "Contribution of Psychiatry to an Understanding of Behavior in Society," *Amer. J. Social.,* 1937, 42:862-70.

[12]This fifth alternative is on a plane clearly different from that of the others. It represents a *transitional* response which seeks to *institutionalize* new procedures oriented toward revamped cultural goals shared by the members of the society. It thus involves efforts to *change* the existing structure rather than to perform accommodative actions *within* this structure, and introduces additional problems with which we are not at the moment concerned.

both culture goals and means) is the most common and widely diffused. Were this not so, the stability and continuity of the society could not be maintained. The mesh of expectancies which constitutes every social order is sustained by the modal behavior of its members falling within the first category. Conventional role behavior oriented toward the basic values of the group is the rule rather than the exception. It is this fact alone which permits us to speak of a human aggregate as comprising a group or society.

Conversely, Adaptation IV (rejection of goals and means) is the least common. Persons who adjust" (or maladjust) in this fashion are, strictly speaking, *in* the society but not *of* it. Sociologically, these constitute the true "aliens." Not sharing the common frame of orientation, they can be included within the societal population merely in a functional sense. In this category are *some* of the activities of psychotics, psychoneurotics, chronic autists, pariahs, outcasts, vagrants, vagabonds, tramps, chronic drunkards and drug addicts.[13] These have relinquished, in certain spheres of activity, the culturally defined goals, involving complete aim-inhibition in the polar case, and their adjustments are not in accord with institutional norms. This is not to say that in some cases the source of their behavioral adjustments is not in part the very social structure which they have in effect repudiated nor that their very existence within a social area does not constitute a problem for the socialized population.

This mode of "adjustment" occurs, as far as structural sources are concerned, when both the culture goals and institutionalized procedures have been assimilated thoroughly by the individual and imbued with affect and high positive value, but where those institutionalized procedures which promise a measure of successful attainment of the goals are not available to the individual. In such instances, there results a twofold mental conflict insofar as the moral obligation for adopting institutional means conflict with the pressure to resort to illegitimate means (which may attain the goal) and inasmuch as the individual is shut off from means which are both legitimate *and* effective. The competitive order is maintained, but the frustrated and handicapped individual who cannot cope with this order drops out. Defeatism, quietism and resignation are manifested in escape mechanisms which ultimately lead the individual to "escape" from the requirements of the society. It is an expedient which arises from continued failure to attain the goal by legitimate measures and from an inability to adopt the illegitimate route because of internalized prohibitions and institutionalized compulsives, *during which process the supreme value of the success-goal has as yet not been renounced.* The conflict is resolved by eliminating *both* precipitating elements, the goals and means. The escape is complete, the conflict is eliminated and the individual is socialized.

Be it noted that where frustration derives from the inaccessibility of effective institutional means for attaining economic or any other type of highly valued "success," that Adaptations II, III and V (innovation, ritualism and rebellion) are also possible. The result will be determined by the particular personality, and thus, the *particular* cultural background, involved. Inadequate socialization will result in the innovation response whereby the conflict and frustration are eliminated by relinquishing the institutional means and retaining the success-aspiration; an extreme assimilation of institutional demands will lead to ritualism wherein the goal is dropped as beyond one's reach but conformity to the mores persists; and rebellion occurs when emancipation from the reigning standards, due to frustration or to marginalist perspectives, leads to the attempt to introduce a "new social order."

Our major concern is with the illegitimacy ad-

[13]Obviously, this is an elliptical statement. These individuals may maintain some orientation to the values of their particular differentiated groupings within the larger society or, in part, of the conventional society itself. Insofar as they do so, their conduct cannot be classified in the "passive rejection" category (IV). Nels Anderson's description of the behavior and attitudes of the bum, for example, can readily be recast in terms of our analytical scheme. See *The Hobo,* 93-98, *et passim,* Chicago, 1923.

justment. This involves the use of coventionally proscribed but frequently effective means of attaining at least the simulacrum of culturally defined success,—wealth, power, and the like. As we have seen, this adjustment occurs when the individual has assimilated the cultural emphasis on success without equally internalizing the morally prescribed norms governing means for its attainment. The question arises, Which phases of our social structure predispose toward this mode of adjustment? We may examine a concrete instance, effectively analyzed by Lohman,[14] which provides a clue to the answer. Lohman has shown that specialized areas of vice in the near north side of Chicago constitute a "normal" response to a situation where the cultural emphasis upon pecuniary success has been absorbed, but where there is little access to conventional and legitimate means for attaining such success. The conventional occupational opportunities of persons in this area are almost completely limited to manual labor. Given our cultural stigmatization of manual labor, and its correlate, the prestige of white collar work, it is clear that the result is a stain toward innovational practices. The limitation of opportunity to unskilled labor and the resultant low income can not compete *in terms of conventional standards of achievement* with the high income from organized vice.

For our purposes, this situation involves two important features. First, such antisocial behavior is in a sense "called forth" by certain conventional values of the culture *and* by the class structure involving differential access to the approved opportunities for legitimate, prestige-bearing pursuit of the culture goals. The lack of high integration between the means-and-end elements of the cultural pattern and the particular class structure combine to favor a heightened frequency of antisocial conduct in such groups. The second consideration is of equal significance. Recourse to the first of the alternative

responses, legitimate effort, is limited by the fact that actual advance toward desired success-symbols through conventional channels is, despite our persisting open-class ideology,[15] relatively rare and difficult for those handicapped by little formal education and few economic resources. The dominant pressure of group standards of success is, therefore, on the gradual attenuation of legitimate, but by and large ineffective, strivings and the increasing use of illegitimate, but more or less effective, expedients of vice and crime. The cultural demands made on persons in this situation are incompatible. On the one hand, they are asked to orient their conduct toward the prospect of accumulating wealth and on the other, they are largely denied effective opportunities to do so institutionally. The consequences of such structural inconsistency are psychopathological personality, and/or antisocial conduct, and/or revolutionary activities. The equilibrium between culturally designated means and ends becomes highly unstable with the progressive emphasis on attaining the prestige-laden ends by any means whatsoever. Within this context, Capone represents the triumph of amoral intelligence over morally prescribed "failure," when the channels of vertical mobility are closed or narrowed[16] *in a society*

---

[14]Joseph D. Lohman, "The Participant Observer in Community Studies," *Amer. Sociol. Rev.,* 1937, 2:890-98.

[15]The shifting historical role of this ideology is a profitable subject for exploration. The "office-boy-to-president" stereotype was once in approximate accord with the facts. Such vertical mobility was probably more common then than now, when the class structure is more rigid. (See the following note.) The ideology largely persists, however, possibly because it still performs a useful function for maintaining the *status quo*. For insofar as it is accepted by the "masses," it constitutes a useful sop for those who might rebel against the entire structure, were this consoling hope removed. This ideology now serves to lessen the probability of Adaptation V. In short, the role of this notion has changed from that of an approximately valid empirical theorem to that of an ideology, in Mannheim's sense.

[16]There is a growing body of evidence, though none of it is clearly conclusive, to the effect that our class structure is becoming rigidified and that vertical mobility is declining. Taussig and Joslyn found that American business leaders are being *increasingly* recruited from the upper ranks of our society. The Lynds have also found a "diminished chance to

which places a high premium on economic affluence and social ascent for all its members.[17]

This last qualification is of primary importance. It suggests that other phases of the social structure besides the extreme emphasis on pecuniary success, must be considered if we are to understand the social sources of antisocial behavior. A high frequency of deviate behavior is not generated simply by "lack of opportunity" or by this exaggerated pecuniary emphasis. A comparatively rigidified class structure, a feudalistic or caste order, may limit such opportunities far beyond the point which obtains in our society today. It is only when a system of cultural values extols, virtually above all else, certain *common* symbols of success *for the population at large* while its social structure rigorously restricts or completely eliminates access to approved modes of acquiring these symbols *for a considerable part of the same population,* that antisocial behavior ensues on a considerable scale. In other words, our egalitarian ideology denies by

implication the existence of noncompeting groups and individuals in the pursuit of pecuniary success. The same body of success-symbols is held to be desirable for all. These goals are held to *transcend class lines,* not to be bounded by them, yet the actual social organization is such that there exist class differentials in the accessibility of these *common* success-symbols. Frustration and thwarted aspiration lead to the search for avenues of escape from a culturally induced intolerable situation; or unrelieved ambition may eventuate in illicit attempts to acquire the dominant values.[18] The American stress on pecuniary success and ambitiousness for all thus invites exaggerated anxieties, hostilities, neuroses and antisocial behavior.

This theoretical analysis may go far toward explaining the varying correlations between crime and poverty.[19] Poverty is not an isolated variable. It is one of a complex and interdependent social and cultural variables. When viewed in such a context, it represents quite different states of affairs Poverty as such, and consequent limitation of opportunity, are not sufficient to induce a conspicuously high rate of criminal behavior. Even the often mentioned "poverty in

get ahead" for the working classes in Middletown. Manifestly, these objective changes are not alone significant; the individual's subjective evaluation of the situation is a major determinant of the response. The extent to which this change in opportunity for social mobility has been recognized by the least advantaged classes is still conjectural, although the Lynds present some suggestive materials. The writer suggests that a case in point is the increasing frequency of cartoons which observe in a tragi-comic vein that "my old man says everybody can't be President. He says if ya can get three days a week steady on W.P.A. work ya ain't doin' so bad either." See F. W. Taussig and C. S. Joslyn, *American Business Leaders,* New York, 1932; R. S. and H. M. Lynd, *Middletown in Transition,* 67 ff., chap. 12, New York, 1937.

[17]The role of the Negro in this respect is of considerable theoretical interest. Certain elements of the Negro population have assimilated the dominant caste's values of pecuniary success and social advancement, but they also recognize that social ascent is at present restricted to their own caste almost exclusively. The pressures upon the Negro which would otherwise derive from the structural inconsistencies we have noticed are hence not identical with those upon lower class whites. See Kingsley Davis, *op. cit.,* 63; John Dollard, *Caste and Class in a Southern Town,* 66 ff., New Haven, 1936; Donald Young, *American Minority Peoples,* 581, New York, 1932.

[18]The psychical coordinates of these processes have been partly established by the experimental evidence concerning *Anspruchsniveaus* and levels of performance. See Kurt Lewin, *Vorsatz, Wille und Bedurfnis,* Berlin, 1926; N. F. Hoppe, "Erfolg und Misserfolg," *Psychol. Forschung,* 1930, 14:1-63; Jerome D. Frank, "Individual Differences in Certain Aspects of the Level of Aspiration," *Amer. J. Psychol.,* 1935, 47:119-28.

[19]Standard criminology texts summarize the data in this field. Our scheme of analysis may serve to resolve some of the theoretical contradictions which P. A. Sorokin indicates. For example, "not everywhere nor always do the poor show a greater proportion of crime . . . many poorer countries have had less crime than the richer countries . . . The [economic] improvement in the second half of the nineteenth century, and the beginning of the twentieth, has not been followed by a decrease of crime." See his *Contemporary Sociological Theories,* 560-61, New York, 1928. The crucial point is, however, that poverty has varying social significance in different social structures, as we shall see. Hence, one would not expect a linear correlation between crime and poverty.

the midst of plenty" will not necessarily lead to this result. Only insofar as poverty and associated disadvantages in competition for the culture values approved for *all* members of the society is linked with the assimilation of a cultural emphasis on momentary accumulation as a symbol of success is antisocial conduct a "normal" outcome. Thus, poverty is less highly correlated with crime in southeastern Europe than in the United States. The possibilities of vertical mobility in these European areas would seem to be fewer than in this country, so that neither poverty *per se* nor its association with limited opportunity is sufficient to account for the varying correlations. It is only when the full configuration is considered, poverty, limited opportunity and a commonly shared system of success symbols, that we can explain the higher association between poverty and crime in our society than in others where rigidified class structure is coupled with *differential class symbols of achievement.*

In societies such as our own, then, the pressure of prestige-bearing success tends to eliminate the effective social constraint over means employed to this end. "The-end-justifies-the-means" doctrine becomes a guiding tenet for action when the cultural structure unduly exalts the end and the social organization unduly limits possible recourse to approved means. Otherwise put, this notion and associated behavior reflect a lack of cultural coordination. In international relations, the effects of this lack of integration are notoriously apparent. An emphasis upon national power is not readily coordinated with an inept organization of legitimate, i.e., internationally defined and accepted, means for attaining this goal. The result is a tendency toward the abrogation of international law, treaties becomes scraps of paper, "undeclared warfare" serves as a technical evasion, the bombing of civilian populations is rationalized,[20] just

as the same societal situation induces the same sway of illegitimacy among individuals.

The social order we have described necessarily produces this "strain toward dissolution." The pressure of such an order is upon outdoing one's competitors. The choice of means within the ambit of institutional control will persist as long as the sentiments supporting a competitive system, i.e., deriving from the possibility of outranking competitors and hence enjoying the favorable response of others, are distributed throughout the entire system of activities and are not confined merely to the final result. A stable social structure demands a balanced distribution of affect among it various segments. When there occurs a shift of emphasis from the satisfactions deriving from competition itself to almost exclusive concern with successful competition, the resultant stress leads to the breakdown of the regulatory structure.[21] With the resulting attenuation of the institutional imperatives, there occurs an approximation of the situation erroneously held by utilitarians to be typical of society generally wherein calculations of advantage and fear of punishment are the sole regulating agencies. In such situations, as Hobbes observed, force and fraud come to constitute the sole virtues in view of their relative efficiency in attaining goals,—which were for him, of course, not culturally derived.

It should be apparent that the foregoing discussion is not pitched on a moralistic plane. Whatever the sentiments of the writer or reader concerning the ethical desirability of coordinating the means-and-goals phases of the social structure, one must agree that lack of such coordination leads to anomie. Insofar as one of the most general functions of social organizations is to provide a basis for calculability and regularity of behavior, it is increasingly limited

---

[20]See M. W. Royse, *Aerial Bombardment and the International Regulation of War,* New York, 1928.

[21]Since our primary concern is with the sociocultural aspects of this problem, the psychological correlates have been only implicitly considered. See Karen Horney, *The Neurotic Personality of Our Time,* New York, 1937, for a psychological discussion of this process.

in effectiveness as these elements of the structure become dissociated. At the extreme, predictability virtually disappears and what may be properly termed cultural chaos or anomie intervenes.

This statement, being brief, is also incomplete. It has not included an exhaustive treatment of the various structural elements which predispose toward one rather than another of the alternative responses open to individuals; it has neglected, but not denied the relevance of, the factors determining the specific incidence of these responses; it has not enumerated the various concrete responses which are constituted by combinations of specific values of the analytical variables; it has omitted, or includes only by implication, any consideration of the social functions performed by illicit responses; it has not tested the full explanatory power of the analytical scheme by examining a large number of group variations in the frequency of deviate and conformist behavior; it has not adequately dealt with rebellious conduct which seeks to refashion the social framework radically; it has not examined the relevance of cultural conflict for an analysis of culture-goal and institutional-means malintegration. It is suggested that these and related problems may be profitably analyzed by this scheme.

13. Opportunity Theory

RICHARD A. CLOWARD
LLOYD E. OHLIN

THE AVAILABILITY OF ILLEGITIMATE MEANS

SOCIAL NORMS ARE TWO-SIDED. A PRESCRIPTION implies the existence of a prohibition, and *vice versa*. To advocate honesty is to demarcate and condemn a set of actions which are dishonest. In other words, norms that define legitimate practices also implicitly define illegitimate practices. One purpose of norms, in fact, is to delineate the boundary between legitimate and illegitimate practices. In setting the boundary, in segregating and classifying various types of behavior, they make us aware not only of behavior that is regarded as right and proper but also of behavior that is said to be wrong and improper. Thus the criminal who engages in theft or fraud does not invent a new way of life; the possibility of employing alternative means is acknowledged, tacitly at least, by the norms of the culture.

This tendency for proscribed alternatives to be implicit in every prescription, and *vice versa*, although widely recognized, is nevertheless a reef upon which many a theory of delinquency has foundered. Much of the criminological literature assumes, for example, that one may explain a criminal act simply by accounting for the individual's readiness to employ illegal alternatives of which his culture, through its norms, has already made him generally aware. Such explanations are quite unsatisfactory, however, for they ignore a host of questions regarding the *relative availability* of illegal alternatives to various potential criminals. The aspiration to be a physician is hardly enough to explain the fact of becoming a physician; there is much that transpires between the aspiration and the achievement. This is no less true of the person who wants to be a successful criminal. Having decided that he "can't make it legitimately," he cannot simply choose among an array of illegitimate means, all equally available to him. As we have noted earlier, it is assumed in the theory of anomie that access to conventional means is differentially distributed, that some individuals, because of their social class, enjoy certain advantages that are denied to those elsewhere in the class structure. For example, there are variations in the degree to which members of various classes are fully exposed to and thus acquire the values, knowledge, and skills that facilitate upward mobility. It should not be startling, therefore, to suggest that there are socially structured variations in the availability of illegitimate means as well. In connection with delinquent subcultures, we shall be concerned principally with differentials in access to illegitimate means within the lower class.

Many sociologists have alluded to differentials in access to illegitimate means without explicitly incorporating this variable into a

▶SOURCE: *Delinquency and Opportunity*, Glencoe, Ill.: The Free Press, 1961, pp. 145–152, 161–186. Reprinted by permission.

theory of deviant behavior. This is particularly true of scholars in the "Chicago tradition" of criminology. Two closely related theoretical perspectives emerged from this school. The theory of "cultural transmission," advanced by Clifford R. Shaw and Henry D. McKay, focuses on the development in some urban neighborhoods of a criminal tradition that persists from one generation to another despite constant changes in population.[1] In the theory of "differential association," Edwin H. Sutherland described the processes by which criminal values are taken over by the individual.[2] He asserted that criminal behavior is learned, and that it is learned in interaction with others who have already incorporated criminal values. Thus the first theory stresses the value systems of different areas; the second, the systems of social relationships that facilitate or impede the acquisition of these values.

Scholars in the Chicago tradition, who emphasized the processes involved in learning to be criminal, were actually pointing to differentials in the availability of illegal means—although they did not explicitly recognize this variable in their analysis. This can perhaps best be seen by examining Sutherland's classic work, *The Professional Thief.* "An inclination to steal," according to Sutherland, "is not a sufficient explanation to the genesis of the professional thief."[3] The "self-made" thief, lacking knowledge of the ways of securing immunity from prosecution and similar techniques of defense, "would quickly land in prison; . . . a person can be a professional thief only if he is recognized and received as such by other professional thieves." But recognition is not freely accorded: "Selection and tutelage are the two necessary elements in the process of acquiring recognition as a professional thief. . . . A person cannot acquire recognition as a professional thief until he has had tutelage in professional theft, *and tutelage is given only a few persons selected from the total population.*" For one thing, "the person must be appreciated by the professional thieves. He must be appraised as having an adequate equipment of wits, front, talking-ability, honesty, reliability, nerve and determination." Furthermore, the aspirant is judged by high standards of performance, for only "a very small percentage of those who start on this process ever reach the stage of professional thief. . . ." Thus motivation and pressures toward deviance do not fully account for deviant behavior any more than motivation and pressures toward conformity account for conforming behavior. The individual must have access to a learning environment and, once having been trained, must be allowed to perform his role. Roles, whether conforming or deviant in content, are not necessarily freely available; access to them depends upon a variety of factors, such as one's socioeconomic position, age, sex, ethnic affiliation, personality characteristics, and the like. The potential thief, like the potential physician, finds that access to his goal is governed by many criteria other than merit and motivation.

What we are asserting is that access to illegitimate roles is not freely available to all, as is commonly assumed. Only those neighborhoods in which crime flourishes as a stable, indigenous institution are fertile criminal learning environments for the young. Because these environments afford integration of different age-levels of offender, selected young people are exposed to "differential association" through which tutelage is provided and criminal values and skills are acquired. To be prepared for the role may not, however, ensure that the individual will ever discharge it. One important limitation is that more youngsters are recruited into

[1] See esp. C.R. Shaw, *The Jack-Roller* (Chicago: University of Chicago Press, 1930); Shaw, *The Natural History of a Delinquent Career* (Chicago: University of Chicago Press, 1931); Shaw *et al., Delinquency Areas* (Chicago: University of Chicago Press, 1940); and Shaw and H. D. McKay, *Juvenile Delinquency and Urban Areas* (Chicago: University of Chicago Press, 1942).

[2] E. H. Sutherland, ed., *The Professional Thief* (Chicago:. University of Chicago Press, 1937); and Sutherland, *Principles of Criminology,* 4th Ed. (Philadelphia: Lippincott, 1947).

[3] All quotations on this page are from *The Professional Thief,* pp. 211–13. Emphasis added.

these patterns of differential associations than the adult criminal structure can possibly absorb. Since there is a surplus of contenders for these elite positions, criteria and mechanisms of selection must be evolved. Hence a certain proportion of those who aspire may not be permitted to engage in the behavior for which they have prepared themselves.

Thus we conclude that access to illegitimate roles, no less than access to legitimate roles, is limited by both social and psychological factors. We shall here be concerned primarily with socially structured differentials in illegitimate opportunities. Such differentials, we contend, have much to do with the type of delinquent subculture that develops.

LEARNING AND PERFORMANCE STRUCTURES

Our use of the term "opportunities," legitimate or illegitimate, implies access to both learning and performance structures. That is, the individual must have access to appropriate environments for the acquisition of the values and skills associated with the performance of a particular role, and he must be supported in the performance of the role once he has learned it.

Tannenbaum, several decades ago, vividly expressed the point that criminal role performance, no less than conventional role performance, presupposes a patterned set of relationships through which the requisite values and skills are transmitted by established practitioners to aspiring youth:

"It takes a long time to make a good criminal, many years of specialized training and much preparation. But training is something that is given to people. People learn in a community where the materials and the knowledge are to be had. A craft needs an atmosphere saturated with purpose and promise. The community provides the attitudes, the point of view, the philosophy of life, the example, the motive, the contacts, the friendships, the incentives. No child brings those into the world. He finds them here and available for use and elaboration. The community

gives the criminal his materials and habits, just as it gives the doctor, the lawyer, the teacher, and the candlestock-maker theirs."[4]

Sutherland systematized this general point of view, asserting that opportunity consists, at least in part, of learning structures. Thus "criminal behavior is learned" and, furthermore, it is learned "in interaction with other persons in a process of communication." However, he conceded that the differential-association theory does not constitute a full explanation of criminal behavior. In a papar circulated in 1944, he noted that "criminal behavior is partially a function of opportunities to commit [*i.e.*, to perform] specific classes of crime, such as embezzlement, bank burglary, or illicit heterosexual intercourse." Therefore, "while opportunity may be partially a function of association with criminal patterns and of the specialized techniques thus acquired, it is not determined entirely in that manner, and consequently differential association is not the sufficient cause of criminal behavior."[5]

To Sutherland, then, illegitimate opportunity included conditions favorable to the performance of a criminal role as well as conditions favorable to the learning of such a role (differential associations). These conditions, we suggest, depend upon certain features of the social structure of the community in which delinquency arises.

DIFFERENTIAL OPPORTUNITY: A HYPOTHESIS

We believe that each individual occupies a position in both legitimate and illegitimate opportunity structures. This is a new way of defining the situation. The theory of anomie views the individual primarily in terms of the legitimate opportunity structure. It poses questions re-

[4]Frank Tannenbaum, "The Professional Criminal," *The Century*, Vol. 110 (May-Oct. 1925), p. 577.

[5]See A. K. Cohen, Alfred Lindesmith, and Karl Schuessler, eds., *The Sutherland Papers* (Bloomington, Ind.: Indiana University Press, 1956), pp. 31–35.

garding differentials in access to legitimates routes to success-goals; at the same time it assumes either that illegitimate avenues to success-goals are freely available or that differentials in their availability are of little significance. This tendency may be seen in the following statement by Merton:

"Several researchers have shown that specialized areas of vice and crime constitute a "normal" response to a situation where the cultural emphasis upon pecuniary success has been absorbed, but where there is little access to conventional and legitimate means for becoming successful. The occupational opportunities of people in these areas are largely confined to manual labor and the lesser white-collar jobs. Given the American stigmatization of manual labor *which has been found to hold rather uniformly for all social classes,* and the absence of realistic opportunities for advancement beyond this level, the result is a marked tendency toward deviant behavior. The status of unskilled labor and the consequent low income cannot readily compete *in terms of established standards of worth* with the promises of power and high income from organized vice, rackets and crime. . . . [Such a situation] leads toward the gradual attenuation of legitimate, but by and large ineffectual, strivings and the increasing use of illegitimate, but more or less effective, expedients."[6]

The cultural-transmission and differential-association tradition, on the other hand, assumes that access to illegitimate means is variable, but it does not recognize the significance of comparable differentials in access to legitimate means. Sutherland's "ninth proposition" in the theory of differential association states:

"Though criminal behavior is an expression of general needs and values, it is not explained by those general needs and values since noncriminal behavior is an expression of the same needs and values. Thieves generally steal in order to secure money, but likewise honest laborers work in order to secure money. The attempts by many scholars to explain criminal behavior by general drives and values, such as the happiness principle, striving for social status, the money motive, or frust-

ration, have been and must continue to be futile since they explain lawful behavior as completely as they explain criminal behavior."[7]

In this statement, Sutherland appears to assume that people have equal and free access to legitimate means regardless of their social position. At the very least, he does not treat access to legitimate means as variable. It is, of course, perfectly true that "striving for social status," "the money motive," and other socially approved drives do not fully account for either deviant or conforming behavior. But if goal-oriented behavior occurs under conditions in which there are socially structured obstacles to the satisfaction of these drives by legitimate means, the resulting pressures, we contend, might lead to deviance.

The concept of differential opportunity structures permit us to unite the theory of anomie, which recognizes the concept of differentials in access to legitimate means, and the "Chicago tradition," in which the concept of differentials in access to illegitimate means is implicit. We can now look at the individual, not simply in relation to one or the other system of means, but in relation to both legitimate and illegitimate systems. This approach permits us to ask, for example, how the relative availability of illegitimate opportunities affects the resolution of adjustment problems leading to deviant behavior. We believe that the way in which these problems are resolved may depend upon the kind of support for one or another type of illegitimate activity that is given at different points in the social structure. If, in a given social location, illegal or criminal means are not readily available, then we should not expect a criminal subculture to develop among adolescents. By the same logic, we should expect the manipulation of violence to become a primary avenue to higher status only in areas where the means of violence are not denied to the young. To give a third example, drug addiction and participation in subcultures organized around the consump-

---

[6]R. K. Merton, *Social Theory and Social Structure,* Rev. and Enl. Ed. (Glencoe, Ill.: Free Press, 1957), pp. 145–46.

[7]*Principles of Criminology, op. cit.,* pp. 7–8.

tion of drugs presuppose that persons can secure access to drugs and knowledge about how to use them. In some parts of the social structure, this would be very difficult; in others, very easy. In short, there are marked differences from one part of the social structure to another in the types of illegitimate adaptation that are available to persons in search of solutions to problems of adjustment arising from the restricted availability of legitimate means.[8] In this sense, then, we can think of individuals as being located in two opportunity structures—one legitimate, the other illegitimate. Given limited access to success-goals by legitimate means, the nature of the delinquent response that may result will vary according to the availability of various illegitimate means. . . .[9]

We come now to the question of the specific social conditions that make for the emergence of distinctive delinquent subcultures. Throughout this analysis, we shall make extensive use of the concepts of social organization developed in the preceding chapter: namely, integration of different age-levels of offenders, and integration of carriers of conventional and deviant values. Delinquent responses vary from one neighborhood to another, we believe, according to the articulation of these structures in the nieghborhood.

[8] For an example of restrictions on access to illegitimate roles, note the impact of racial definitions in the following case: "I was greeted by two prisoners who were to be my cell buddies. Ernest was a first offender, charged with being a 'holdup' man. Bill, the other buddy, was an old offender, going through the machinery of becoming a habitual criminal, in and out of jail. . . . The first thing they asked me was, 'What are you in for?' I said, 'Jack-rolling.' The hardened one (Bill) looked at me with a superior air and said, 'A hoodlum, eh? An ordinary sneak thief. Not willing to leave jack-rolling to the niggers, eh? That's all they're good for. Kid, jack-rolling's not a white man's job.' I could see that he was disgusted with me, and I was too scared to say anything." (Shaw, *The Jack-Roller, op. cit.,* p. 101).

[9] For a discussion of the way in which the availability of illegitimate means influences the adaptations of inmates to prison life, see R. A. Cloward, "Social Control in the Prison," *Theoretical Studies in Social Organization of the Prison,* Bulletin No. 15 (New York: Social Science Research Council, March 1960), pp. 20–48.

Our object here is to show more precisely how various forms of neighborhood integration affect the development of subcultural content.

THE CRIMINAL SUBCULTURE

The criminal subculture, like the conflict and retreatist adaptations, requires a specialized environment if it is to flourish. Among the environmental supports of a criminal style of life are integration of offenders at various age-levels and close integration of the carriers of conventional and illegitimate values.

Integration of Age-Levels

Nowhere in the criminological literature is the concept of integration between different age-levels of offender made more explicit than in discussions of criminal learning. Most criminologists agree that criminal behavior presupposes patterned sets of relationships through which the requisite values and skills are communicated or transmitted from one age-level to another. What, then, are some of the specific components of systems organized for the socialization of potential criminals?

Criminal Role-Models

The lower class is not without its own distinctive and indigenous illegitimate success-models. Many accounts in the literature suggest that lower-class adults who have achieved success by illegitimate means not only are highly visible to young people in slum areas but often are willing to establish relationships with these youth.

"Every boy has some ideal he looks up to and admires. His ideal may be Babe Ruth, Jack Dempsey, or Al Capone. When I was twelve, we moved into a neighborhood with a lot of gangsters. They were all swell dressers and had big cars and carried 'gats.' Us kids saw these swell guys and mingled with them in the cigar store on the corner. Jack Gurney was the one in the mob that I had a fancy to. He used to take my sis out and that way I saw him often. He was in the stick-up rackets before he was in the beer rackets, and he was a swell dresser and had lots of dough. . . . I liked to be near and felt stuck up over the other guys because he came to my home to see my sis."[10]

Just as the middle-class youth, as a consequence of intimate relationships with, say, a banker or a businessman, may aspire to *become* a banker or a businessman, so the lower-class youth may be associated with and aspire to become a "policy king": " 'I want to be a big shot. ... Have all the guys look up to me. Have a couple of Lincolns, lots of broads, and all the coppers licking my shoes.' "[11] The crucial point here is that success-goals are not equally available to persons in different positions in the social structure. To the extent that social-class lines act as barriers to interaction between persons in different social strata, conventional success-models may not be salient for lower-class youth. The successful criminal, on the other hand, may be an intimate, personal figure in the fabric of the lower-class area. Hence one of the forces leading to rational, disciplined, crime-oriented delinquency may be the availability of criminal success-models.

Age-Grading of Criminal Learning and Performance

The process by which the young acquire the values and skills prerequisite for a stable criminal career has been described in many studies. The central mechanism in the learning process is integration of different age-levels of offender. In an extensive study of a criminal gang on the Lower East Side of New York City, Bloch and Niederhoffer found that

"... the Pirates [a group of young adults] was actually the central organizing committee, the party headquarters for the youthful delinquents in the area. They held regular conferences with the delegates from outlying districts to outline strategy. ... The younger Corner Boys [a gang of adolescents in the same vicinity] who ... were trying to join with the older Pirates ... were on a probationary status. If they showed signs of promise, a couple of them were allowed to accompany the Pirates on tours of exploration to look over the terrain around the next job."[12]

At the pinnacle of this age-graded system stood an adult, Paulie.

"Paulie had real prestige in the gang. His was the final say in all important decisions. Older than the other members [of the Pirates] by seven or eight years, he maintained a certain air of mystery. ... From talks with more garrulous members, it was learned that Paulie was the mastermind behind some of the gang's most impressive coups."[13]

The basis of Paulie's prestige in the gang is apparent in the following account of his relationship with the full-fledged adult criminal world:

"From his contacts, information was obtained as to the most inviting locations to burglarize. It was he who developed the strategy and outlined the major stages of each campaign of burglary or robbery. ... Another vital duty which he performed was to get rid of the considerable loot, which might consist of jewelry, clothing, tools, or currency in large denominations. His contact with professional gangsters, fences, bookies, made him an ideal choice for this function."[14]

Learning alone, as we have said, does not ensure that the individual can or will perform the role for which he has been prepared. The social structure must also support the actual performance of the role. To say that the individual must have the opportunity to discharge a stable criminal role as well as to prepare for it does not mean that role-preparation necessarily takes place in one stage and role-performance in a succeeding stage. The apprentice may be afforded opportunities to play out a particular role at various points in the learning process.

[10]C. R. Shaw, "Juvenile Delinquency—A Group Tradition," *Bulletin of the State University of Iowa*, No. 23, N. S. No. 700, 1933, p. 8.
[11]*Ibid.*, p. 9.

[12]H. H. Bloch and Arthur Niederhoffer, *The Gang: A Study in Adolescent Behavior* (New York: Philosophical Library, 1958), pp. 198–99.
[13]*Ibid.*, p. 201.
[14]*Ibid.*

"When we were shoplifting we always made a game of it. For example, we might gamble on who could steal the most caps in a day, or who could steal in the presence of a detective and then get away. This was the best part of the game. I would go into a store to steal a cap, by trying one on when the clerk was not watching, walk out of the store, leaving the old cap. With the new cap on my head I would go into another store, do the same thing as in the other store, getting a new hat and leaving the one I had taken from the other place. I might do this all day. . . . It was the fun I wanted, not the hat. I kept this up for months and *then began to sell the things to a man on the West Side. It was at this time that I began to steal for gain.*"[15]

This quotation illustrates how delinquent role-preparation and role-performance may be integrated even at the "play-group" stage of illegitimate learning. The child has an opportunity to actually perform illegitimate roles because such activity finds support in his immediate neighborhood milieu. The rewards—monetary and other—of successful learning and performance are immediate and gratifying at each age level.

Integration of Values
Unless the carriers of criminal and conventional values are closely bound to one another, stable criminal roles cannot develop. The criminal, like the occupant of a controversial role, must establish relationships with other categories of persons, all of whom contribute in one way or another to the successful performance of criminal activity. As Tannenbaum says, "The development of the criminal career requires and finds in the immediate environment other supporting elements in addition to the active 'criminal gangs'; to develop the career requires the support of middlemen. These may be junk men, fences, lawyers, bondsmen, 'backers,' as they are called."[16] The intricate systems of relationship between these legitimate and illegitimate persons constitute the type of environment in which

the juvenile criminal subculture can come into being.[17]

An excellent example of the way in which the content of a delinquent subculture is affected by its location in a particular milieu is afforded by the "fence," a dealer in stolen goods who is found in some but not all lower-class neighborhoods. Relationships between such middlemen and criminals are not confined to adult offenders; numerous accounts of lower-class life suggest not only that relationships form between fences and youngsters but also that the fence is a crucial element in the structure of illegitimate opportunity. He often caters to and encourages delinquent activities among the young. He may even exert controls leading the young to orient their stealing in the most lucrative and least risky directions. The same point may be made of junk dealers in some areas, racketeers who permit minors to run errands, and other occupants of illegitimate or semilegitimate roles.

As the apprentice criminal passes from one status to another in the illegitimate opportunity system, we should expect him to develop an ever-widening set of relationships with members of the semilegitimate and legitimate world. For example, a delinquent who is rising in the structure might begin to come into contact with mature criminals, law-enforcement officials, politicians, bail bondsmen, "fixers," and the like. As his activities become integrated with the activities of these persons, his knowledge of the illegitimate world is deepened, new skills are acquired, and the opportunity to engage in new types of illegitimate activity enhanced. Unless he can form these relationships, the possibility of a stable, protected criminal style of life is effectively precluded.

The type of environment that encourages a criminal orientation among delinquents is, then,

---

[15]Shaw, *op. cit.*, p. 3. Emphasis added.

[16]Frank Tannenbaum, *Crime and the Community* (New York: Columbia University Press, 1938), p. 60.

[17]In this connection, see R. A. Cloward, "Social Control in the Prison," *Theoretical Studies of the Social Organization of the Prison*, Bulletin No. 15 (New York: Social Science Research Council, March 1960), pp. 20–48, which illustrates similar forms of integration in a penal setting.

characterized by close integration of the carriers of conventional and illegitimate values. The *content* of the delinquent subculture is a more or less direct response to the local milieu in which it emerges. And it is the "integrated" neighborhood, we suggest, that produces the criminal type of delinquent subculture.

Structural Integration and Social Control

Delinquent behavior generally exhibits a component of aggressiveness. Even youth in neighborhoods that are favorable learning environments for criminal careers are likely to engage in some "bopping" and other forms of violence. Hence one feature of delinquency that must be explained is its tendency toward aggressive behavior. However, aggressiveness is not the primary component of all delinquent behavior; it is much more characteristic of some delinquent groups than of others. Therefore, we must also concern ourselves with the conditions under which the aggressive component becomes ascendant.

The importance of assessing the relative dominance of expressive and instrumental components in delinquent patterns is often overlooked. Cohen, for example, stresses the aggressive or expressive aspect of delinquent behavior, remarking that "it is non-utilitarian, malicious and negativistic," although he also asserts that these traits may not characterize all delinquency. Cohen's tendency to neglect relatively non-aggressive aspects of delinquency is related to his failure to take into account the relationships between delinquent behavior and adult criminality. However, *depending upon the presence or absence of those integrative relationships,* behavior that appears to be "non-utilitarian" in achieving access to conventional roles may possess considerable utility for securing access to criminal roles. Furthermore, these integrated systems may have important consequences for social control.

To the extent that delinquents take as their primary reference group older and more sophisticated gang boys, or even fully accultu-rated criminals or racketeers, dramatic instances of "malicious, negativistic" behavior may represent efforts to express solidarity with the norms of the criminal world. Delinquents who so behave in an attempt to win acceptance by older criminals may be engaging in a familiar sociological process; namely, overconformity to the norms of a group to which they aspire but do not belong. By such overconformity to the norms of the criminal world, delinquents seek to dramatize their eligibility for membership. To an observer oriented toward conventional values, aggressive behavior of this kind might appear to be purposeless. However, from the perspective of the carriers of deviant values, conspicuous defiance of conventional values may validate the "rightness" of the aspirant. Once he has been defined as "right," he may then be selected for further socialization and preparation for mature criminal activity.

Once the delinquent has successfully demonstrated his eligibility for acceptance by persons higher in the criminal structure, social controls are exerted to suppress undisciplined, expressive behavior; there is no place in organized crime for the impulsive, unpredictable individual. A dramatic illustration of the emphasis upon instrumental performance is offered by the case of Murder, Inc. Abe Reles, a former member of the syndicate who turned state's evidence, made certain comments about Murder, Inc., which illustrate perfectly Max Weber's famous characterization of the norms governing role performance and interpersonal relationships in bureaucratic organizations: *"Sine ira et studio"* ("without anger or passion").

"The crime trust, Reles insists, never commits murder out of passion, excitement, jealousy, personal revenge, or any of the usual motives which prompt private, unorganized murder. It kills impersonally, and solely for business considerations. Even business rivalry, he adds, is not the usual motive, unless 'somebody gets too balky or somebody steps right on top of you.' No gangster may kill on his own initiative; every murder must be ordered by the leaders at the top, and it must serve the welfare of the organization. . . .

The crime trust insists that that murder must be a business matter, organized by the chiefs in conference and carried out in a disciplined way. 'It's a real business all the way through,' Reles explains. 'It just happens to be that kind of business, but nobody is allowed to kill from personal grievance. There's got to be a good business reason, and top men of the combination must give their okay.'"[18]

The pressure for rational role performance in the adult criminal world is exerted downward, we suggest, through interconnected systems of age-graded statuses. At each point in this illegitimate hierarchy, instrumental rather than expressive behavior is emphasized. In their description of the Pirates, for example, Bloch and Niederhoffer observe that Paulie, the adult mastermind of the gang, avoided expressive behavior: "The younger Pirates might indulge in wild adolescent antics. Paulie remained aloof."[19] Paulie symbolized a mode of life in which reason, discipline, and foresight were uppermost. To the extent that younger members of the gang identified with him, they were constrained to adopt a similar posture. Rico, the leader of a gang described in a recent book by Harrison Salisbury, can be characterized in much the same way:

"This youngster was the most successful kid in the neighborhood. He was a dope pusher. Some weeks he made as much as $200. He used his influence in some surprising ways. He persuaded the gang members to stop bopping because he was afraid it would bring on police intervention and interfere with his drug sales. He flatly refused to sell dope to boys and kicked out of the gang any kid who started to use drugs. He sold only to adults. With his money he bought jackets for the gang, took care of hospital bills of members, paid for the rent on his mother's flat, paid most of the family expenses and sometimes spent sixty dollars to buy a coat as a present for one of his boys."[20]

The same analysis helps to explain a puzzling aspect of delinquent behavior; namely, the apparent disregard delinquents sometimes exhibit for stolen objects. Some theorists have concluded from this that the ends of stealing are not utilitarian, that delinquents do not steal because they need or want the objects in question or for any other rational reason. Cohen, for example, asserts that "were the participant in the delinquent subculture merely employing illicit means to the end of acquiring economic goods, he would show more respect for the goods he has thus acquired."[21] Hence, Cohen concludes, the bulk of stealing among delinquents is "for the hell of it" rather than for economic gain. Whether stealing is expressive or instrumental may depend, however, on the social context in which it occurs. Where criminal opportunities exist, it may be argued that stealing is a way of expressing solidarity with the carriers of criminal values and, further, that it is a way of acquiring the various concrete skills necessary before the potential criminal can gain full acceptance in the group to which he aspires. That is, a certain amount of stealing may be motivated less by immediate need for the objects in question than by a need to acquire skill in the arts of theft. When practice in theft is the implicit purpose, the manner of disposing of stolen goods is unimportant. Similarly, the status accruing to the pickpocket who can negotiate a "left-front-breech" derives not so much from the immediate profit attaching to this maneuver as from the fact that it marks the individual as a master craftsman. In other words, where criminal learning environments and opportunity structures exist, stealing beyond immediate economic needs may constitute anticipatory socialization. But where these structures do not exist, such stealing may be simply an expressive act of defiance of conventional values.

Shaw pointed to a related aspect of the social control of delinquent behavior. Noting the pre-

[18]Joseph Freeman, "Murder Monopoly: The Inside Story of a Crime Trust," *The Nation*, Vol. 150, No. 21 (May 25, 1940), p. 648. This is but one of many sources in which the bureaucratization of crime is discussed.

[19]Bloch and Niederhoffer, *op. cit.*, p. 201.

[20]H. E. Salisbury, *The Shook-up Generation* (New York: Harper & Bros., 1958), p. 176.

[21]A. K. Cohen, *Delinquent Boys: The Culture of the Gang* (Glencoe, Ill.: Free Press, 1955), p. 36.

stige ordering of criminal activities, he commented on the way in which such definitions once internalized, tend to regulate the behavior of delinquents:

"It is a matter of significance to note . . . that there is a general tendency among older delinquents and criminals to look with contempt upon the person who specializes in any form of petty stealing. The common thief is not distinguished for manual dexterity and accomplishment, like the pickpocket or mobsman, nor for courage, ingenuity and skill, like the burglar, but is characterized by low cunning and stealth—hence the term 'sneak thief.' . . . It is possible that the stigma attaching to petty stealing among members of older delinquent groups is one factor which gives impetus to the young delinquent's desire to abandon such forms of petty delinquency as stealing junk, vegetables, breaking into freight cars . . . and to become identified with older groups engaged in such crimes as larceny of automobiles and robbery with a gun, both of which are accredited 'rackets' among older delinquents. . . ."[22]

To the extent that an area has an age-graded criminal structure in which juvenile delinquents can become enmeshed, we suggest that the norms governing adult criminal-role performance filter down, becoming significant principles in the life-organization of the young. The youngster who has come into contact with such an age-graded structure and who has won initial acceptance by older and more sophisticated delinquents will be less likely to engage in malicious, destructive behavior than in disciplined, instrumental, career-oriented behavior. In this way the adult criminal system exerts controls over the behavior of delinquents. Referring to urban areas characterized by integration of different age-levels of offender, Kobrin makes an observation that tends to bear out our theoretical scheme:

". . . delinquency tends to occur within a partial framework of social controls, insofar as delinquent activity in these areas represents a tolerated means for the acquisition of an approved role and status. Thus,

while delinquent activity here possesses the usual characteristics of violence and destructiveness, there tend to develop effective limits of permissible activity in this direction. Delinquency is, in other words, encompassed and contained within a local structure, and is marginally but palpably related to that structure."[23]

In summary, the criminal subculture is likely to arise in a neighborhood milieu characterized by close bonds between different age-levels of offender, and between criminal and conventional elements. As a consequence of these integrative relationships, a new opportunity structure emerges which provides alternative avenues to success-goals. Hence the pressures generated by restrictions on legitimate access to success-goals are drained off. Social controls over the conduct of the young are effectively exercised, limiting expressive behavior and constraining the discontented to adopt instrumental, if criminalistic styles of life.

THE CONFLICT SUBCULTURE

Because youngsters caught up in the conflict subculture often endanger their own lives and the lives of others and cause considerable property damage, the conflict form of delinquency is a source of great public concern. Its prevalence, therefore, is probably exaggerated. There is no evidence to suggest that the conflict subculture is more widespread than the other subcultures, but the nature of its activities makes it more visible and thus attracts public attention. As a consequence, many people erroneously equate "delinquency" and "conflict behavior." But whatever its prevalence, the conflict subculture is of both theoretical and social importance, and calls for explanation.

Earlier in this book, we questioned the common belief that slum areas, because they are slums, are necessarily disorganized. We pointed

[22]Shaw, *op. cit.*, p. 10.

[23]Solomon Kobrin, "The Conflict of Values in Delinquency areas." *American Sociological Review*, Vol. 16 (Oct. 1951), p. 657.

to forms of integration which give some slum areas unity and cohesion. Areas in which these integrative structures are found, we suggested, tend to be characterized by criminal rather than conflict or retreatist subcultures. But not all slums are integrated. Some lower-class urban neighborhoods lack unity and cohesivensss. Because the prerequisities for the emergence of stable systems of social relations are not present, a state of social disorganization prevails.

The many forces making for instability in the social organization of some slum areas include high rates of vertical and geographic mobility; massive housing projects in which "site tenants" are not accorded priority in occupancy, so that traditional residents are dispersed and "strangers" re-assembled; and changing land use, as in the case of residential areas that are encroached upon by the expansion of adjacent commercial or industrial areas. Forces of this kind keep a community off balance, for tentative efforts to develop social organization are quickly checked. Transiency and instability become the overriding features of social life.

Transiency and instability, in combination, produce powerful pressures for violent behavior among the young in these areas. First, an unorganized community cannot provide access to legitimate channels to success-goals, and thus discontent among the young with their life-chances is heightened. Secondly, access to stable criminal opportunity systems is also restricted, for disorganized neighborhoods do not develop integration of different age-levels of offender or integration of carriers of criminal and conventional values. The young in short, are relatively deprived of *both* conventional and criminal opportunity. Finally, social controls are weak in such communities. These conditions, we believe, lead to the emergence of conflict subcultures.

Social Disorganization and Opportunity

Communities that are unable to develop conventional forms of social organization are also unable to provide legitimate modes of access to culturally valued success-goals. The disor-

ganized slum is a world populated with failures, with the outcasts of the larger society. Here families orient themselves not toward the future but toward the present, not toward social advancement but toward survival. The adult community, being disorganized, cannot provide the resources and opportunities that are required if the young are to move upward in the social order.

Just as the unintegrated slum cannot mobilize legitimate resources for the young, neither can it provide them with access to stable criminal careers, for illegitimate learning and opportunity structures do not develop. The disorganized slum, populated in part by failures in the conventional world, also contains the outcasts of the criminal world. This is not to say that crime is nonexistent in such areas, but what crime there is tends to be individualistic, unorganized, petty, poorly paid, and unprotected. This is the haunt of the small-time thief, the grifter, the pimp, the jackroller, the unsophisticated "con" man, the pickpocket who is all thumbs, and others who cannot graduate beyond "heisting" candy stores or "busting" gas stations. Since they are unorganized and without financial resources, criminals in these areas cannot purchase immunity from prosecution; they have neither the money nor the political contacts to "put in the fix." Hence they are harassed by the police, and many of them spend the better part of their lives in prison. The organized criminal world is generally able to protect itself against such harassment, prosecution, and imprisonment. But professional crime and organized rackets, like any business enterprise, can thrive only in a stable, predictable, and integrated environment. In this sense, then, the unintegrated area does not constitute a promising launching site for lucrative and protected criminal careers. Because such areas fail to develop criminal learning environments and opportunity structures, stable criminal subcultures cannot emerge.

Social Disorganization and Social Control

As we have noted, social controls originate in

both the conventional and the illegitimate sectors of the stable slum area. But this is apparently not the case in the disorganized slum. The basic disorganization of the conventional institutional structure makes it impossible for controls to originate there. At the same time, Kobrin asserts, "Because adult crime in this type of area is itself unorganized, its value system remains implicit and hence incapable of generating norms which function effectively on a groupwide basis." Hence juvenile violators readily escape not merely the controls of conventional persons in the community but those of adult violators as well." Under such conditions,

". . . [the] delinquencies of juveniles tend to acquire a wild, untrammelled character. Delinquents in this kind of situation more frequently exhibit the personality traits of the social type sometimes referred to as the hoodlum. Both individually and in groups, violent physical combat is engaged in for its own sake, almost as a form of recreation. Here groups of delinquents may be seen as excluded, isolated conflict groups dedicated to an unending battle against all forms of constraint. The escape from controls orignating in any social structure, other than that provided by unstable groupings of the delinquents themselves, is here complete."[24]

Unlike Kobrin, we do not attribute conflict behavior in unorganized urban areas to the absence of controls alone. The young in such areas are also exposed to acute frustrations, arising from conditions in which access to success-goals is blocked by the absence of any institutionalized channels, legitimate or illegitimate. They are deprived not only of conventional opportunity but also of criminal routes to the "big money." In other words, precisely when frustrations are maximized, social controls are weakened. Social controls and channels are to success-goals are generally related: where opportunities exist, patterns of control will be found; where opportunities are absent, patterns of social control are likely to be absent too. The association of these two features of social organization is a logical implication.

Social Disorganization and Violence

Those adolescents in disorganized urban areas who are oriented toward achieving higher position but are cut off from institutionalized channels, criminal as well as legitimate, must rely upon their own resources for solving this problem of adjustment. Under these conditions, tendencies toward aberrant behavior become intensified and magnified. The adolescents seize upon the manipulation of violence as a route to status not only because it provides a way of expressing pent-up angers and frustrations but also because they are not cut off from access to violent means by vicissitudes of birth. In the world of violence, such attributes as race, socioeconomic position, age, and the like are irrelevant; personal worth is judged on the basis of qualities that are available to all who would cultivate them. The principal prerequisites for success are "guts" and the capacity to endure pain. One doesn't need "connections," "pull," or elaborate technical skills in order to achieve "rep." The essence of the warrior adjustment is an expressed feeling-state: "heart." The acquisition of status is not simply a consequence of skill in the use of violence or of physical strength but depends, rather, on one's willingness to risk injury or death in the search for "rep." A physically immature boy may find a place among the warrior elite if, when provoked, he will run such risks, thus demonstrating "heart."

As long as conventional and criminal opportunity structures remain closed, violence continues unchecked. The bulk of aggressive behavior appears to be channeled into gang warfare; success in street combat assures the group that its "turf" will not be invaded, that its girls will not be molested, that its members will otherwise be treated deferentially by young and old in the local community. *If new opportunity structures are opened, however, violence tends to be relinquished.* Indeed, the success of certain efforts to discourage violent aggressive behavior

[24]*Ibid.*, p. 658.

among warrior gangs has resulted precisely from the fact that some powerful group has responded deferentially to these gangs. (The group is powerful because it can provide, or at least hold out the promise of providing, channels to higher position, such as jobs, education, and the like.) The most dramatic illustration of this process may be seen in programs conducted by social group workers who attach themselves to street gangs. Several points should be noted about the results of these programs.

First, violent behavior among street gangs appears to diminish rapidly once a social worker establishes liaison with them. Reporting on the outcome of detached-worker programs in Boston, for example, Miller notes, "One of the earliest and most evident changes . . . was that groups worked with directly [by social workers] relinquished active participation in the [established] network of conflict groups. . . ."[25] The reduction in conflict may reflect the skill of the social workers, but another explanation may be that *the advent of the street-gang worker symbolized the end of social rejection and the beginning of social accommodation.* To the extent that violence represents an effort to win deference, one would logically expect it to diminish once that end has been achieved.

Secondly, a detached-worker program, once initiated, tends to give rise to increased violence among groups to which workers have *not* been provided. In the Boston experience, to the extent that they interpreted having a street-club worker as an act of social deference, gangs came to compete for this prestige symbol. As Miller notes, "During later phases of the Program [there was] an upsurge in gang fights involving Program groups. . . . These conflicts did not involve Program groups fighting one another but represented for the most part attacks on Program groups by corner groups in adjacent areas which did not have an area worker." Miller suggests that such attacks took place in part be-

cause "the outside groups knew that Program groups were given a social worker in the first place because they were trouble-some; so they reasoned. 'They were bad, and they got a social worker; if we're bad enough now, we'll get a social worker, too.' " An attack by an outside gang on a Program gang was not, therefore, simply an expression of the traditional hostility of one gang toward another but an attempt on the part of the non-Program gang to win "rep." Thus Miller is led to observe, "A program aiming to 'clean up' the gang situation in a single section of the city cannot count on limiting its influence to that section but must anticipate the fact that its very success in its home district may increase difficulties in adjacent areas." This suggests that programs aimed at curbing violence constitute a new opportunity structure in which gangs compete for social deference from the conventional world.

Finally, a resurgence of violent behavior may be observed when the liaison between the street worker and the gang is terminated if the members of the gang have not been successfully incorporated in a conventional opportunity system. Continuing to lack conventional economic opportunity, the gang fears the loss of the one form of recognition it has achieved from conventional society, symbolized by the street worker. Hence the group may reassert the old patterns of violence in order to retain the social worker. Under these conditions, the conventional society will continue to accommodate to the group for fear that to do otherwise would result in renewed violence, as indeed it so often does. A successful street-gang program, in short, is one in which detached workers can create channels to legitimate opportunity; where such channels cannot be opened up, the gang will temporize with violence only as long as a street worker maintains liaison with them.

In summary, severe limitations on both conventional and criminal opportunity intensify frustrations and position discontent. Discontent is heightened further under conditions in which social control is relaxed, for the area lacking integration between age-levels of offender and be-

[25]This quotation and those that follow are from W. B. Miller, "The Impact of a Community Group Work Program on Delinquent Corner Groups," *Social Service Review*, Vol. 31, No. 4 (Dec. 1957), pp. 390–406.

tween carriers of conventional and criminal values cannot generate pressures to contain frustrations among the young. These are the circumstances, we suggest, in which adolescents turn to violence in search of status. Violence comes to be ascendant, in short, under conditions of relative detachment from all institutionalized systems of opportunity and social control.

THE RETREATIST SUBCULTURE

The consumption of drugs—one of the most serious forms of retreatist behavior—has become a severe problem among adolescents and young adults, particularly in lower-class urban areas. By and large, drug use in these areas has been attributed to rapid geographic mobility, inadequate social controls, and other manifestations of social disorganization. In this section, we shall suggest a hypothesis that may open up new avenues of inquiry in regard to the growing problem of drug use among the young.

Pressures Leading to Retreatist Subcultures

Retreatism is often conceived as an isolated adaptation, characterized by a breakdown in relationships with other persons. Indeed, this is frequently true, as in the case of psychotics. The drug-user, however, must become affiliated with others, if only to secure access to a steady supply of drugs. Just as stable criminal activity cannot be explained by reference to motivation alone, neither can stable drug use be fully explained in this way. Opportunity to use drugs must also be present. But such opportunities are restricted. As Becker notes, the illegal distribution of drugs is limited to "sources which are not available to the ordinary person. In order for a person to begin marihuana use, he must begin participation in some group through which these sources of supply become available to him."[26]

Because of these restrictions on the availability of drugs, new users must become affiliated with old users. They must learn the lore of drug use, the skills required in making appropriate "connections," the controls which govern the purchase of drugs (*e.g.,* drugs will not generally be made available to anyone until he is "defined as a person who can safely be trusted to buy drugs without endangering anyone else"), and the like. As this process of socialization proceeds, the individual "is considered more trustworthy, [and] the necessary knowledge and introductions to dealers [then become] available to him." According to Becker, the "processes by which people are emancipated from the larger set of controls *and become responsive to those of the subculture*" are "important factors in the genesis of deviant behavior."[27] The drug-user, in other words, must be understood not only in terms of his personality and the social structure, which create a readiness to engage in drug use, but also in terms of the new patterns of associations and values to which he is exposed as he seeks access to drugs. The more the individual is caught in this web of associations, the more likely that he will persist in drug use, for he has become incorporated in a subculture that exerts control over his behavior.

Despite these pressures toward subcultural formation, it is probably also true that the resulting ties among addicts are not so solidary as those among participants in criminal and conflict subcultures. Addiction is in many ways an individualistic adaptation, for the "kick" is essentially a private experience. The compelling need for the drug is also a divisive force, for it leads to intense competition among addicts for money. Forces of this kind thus limit the relative cohesion which can develop among users.

"Double Failure" and Drug Use

We turn now to a discussion of the social conditions which give rise to retreatist reactions such as drug use among adolescents. According to Merton,

"Retreatism arises from continued failure to near the goal by legitimate measures and from an inability

---

[26]H. S. Becker, "Marihuana Use and Social Control," *Social Problems*, Vol. 3, No. 1 (July 1955), pp. 36–37.

[27]*Ibid., p. 35.* Emphasis added.

to use the illegitimate route because of internalized prohibitions, this process occurring while the supreme value of the success-goal has not yet been renounced. The conflict is resolved by abandoning both precipitating elements, the goals and the norms. The escape is complete, the conflict is eliminated and the individual is asocialized."[28]

Thus he identifies two principal factors in the emergence of retreatist adaptations: (1) continued failure to reach culturally approved goals by legitimate means, and (2) inability to employ illegitimate alternatives because of internalized prohibitions. We take it that "internalized prohibitions" have to do with the individual's attitudes toward norms. Retreatists, according to Merton, do not call into question the legitimacy of existing institutional arrangements—a process which might then be followed by the use of illegitimate alternatives. Rather, they call into question their own adequacy, locating blame for their dilemma in personal deficiencies. One way of resolving the intense anxiety and guilt which ensue is to withdraw, to retreat, to abandon the struggle.

This definition of the processes giving rise to retreatist behavior is useful in connnection with some types of retreatism, but it does not, we believe, fit the facts of drug use among lower-class adolescents. It is true that some youthful addicts appear to experience strong constraints on the use of illegitimate means; the great majority of drug-users, however, had a history of delinquency before becoming addicted. In

these cases, unfavorable attitudes toward conventional norms are evident. Hence we conclude that internalized prohibitions, or favorable attitudes toward conventional norms, may not be a necessary condition for the emergence of retreatist behavior.

If internalized prohibitions are not a necessary component of the process by which retreatism is generated, then how are we to account for such behavior? We have noted that there are differentials in access both to illegitimate means; not all of those who seek to attain success-goals by prohibited routes are permitted to proceed. There are probably many lower-class adolescents oriented toward success in the criminal world who fail; similarly, many who would like to acquire proficiency in the use of violence also fail. We might ask, therefore, what the response would be among those faced with failure in the use of *both* legitimate and illegitimate means. We suggest that persons who experience this "double failure" are likely to move into a retreatist pattern of behavior. That is, retreatist behavior may arise as a consequence of limitations on the use of illegitimate means, whether the limitations are internalized prohibitions or socially structured barriers. For our purpose, the two types of restriction are functional equivalents. Thus we may amend Merton's statement as follows:

"Retreatism arises from continued failure to near the goal by legitimate measures and from an inability to use the illegitimate route because of internalized prohibitions *or socially structured barriers*, this process occurring while the supreme value of the success-goal has not yet been renounced."

This hypothesis permits us to define two general classes of restreatist: those who are subject to internalized prohibitions on the use of illegitimate means, and those who seek success-goals by prohibited routes but do not succeed. If we now introduce a distinction between illegitimate opportunity structures based on the manipulative use of violence and those based on es-

---

[28]R. K. Merton, *Social Theory and Social Structure*, Rev. and Enl. Ed. (Glencoe, Ill.: Free Press, 1957), pp. 153–54. For discussion of drug use among juveniles, see D. L. Gerard and Conon Kornetsky, "Adolescent Opiate Addiction—A Study of Control and Addict Subjects," *Psychiatric Quarterly*, Vol. 29 (April 1955), pp. 457–86; Isidor Chein *et al.*, *Studies of Narcotics Use Among Juveniles* (New York University, Research Center for Human Relations, mimeographed, Jan. 1956); Harold Finestone, "Cats, Kicks, and Color," *Social Problems*, Vol. 5, No. 1 (July 1957), pp. 3–13; and D. M. Wilmer, Eva Rosenfeld, R. S. Lee, D. L. Gerard, and Isidor Chein, "Heroin Use and Street Gangs," *Criminal Law, Criminology and Police Science*, Vol. 48, No. 4 (Nov.–Dec. 1957), pp. 399–409.

sentially criminal means, such as fraud, theft, and extortion, we can identify four classes of retreatist.

Types I and II both arise in the manner described by Merton—that is, as a consequence of internalized restrictions on the use of illegitimate means. The two types differ only with respect to the content of the internalized restraints. In type II, it is the use of criminal means that is precluded; in type I, it is the use of violence. Resort to illegitimate means, violent or criminal, apparently evokes extreme guilt and anxiety among persons in these categories; such persons are therefore effectively cut off from criminal or violent routes to higher status. For persons of types III and IV, access to illegitimate routes is limited by socially structured barriers. They are not restrained by internal prohibitions; they would employ illegitimate means if these were available to them.

Generally speaking, it has been found that most drug addicts have a history of delinquent activity prior to becoming addicted. In Kobrin's research, conducted in Chicago, "Persons who become heroin users were found to have engaged in delinquency *in a group-supported and habitual form* either prior to their use of drugs or simultaneously with their developing interest in drugs.[29] And from a study of drug addicts in California, "A very significant tentative conclusion [was reached]: namely, that the use of drugs follows criminal activity and criminal association rather than the other way around, which is often thought to be the case."[30] In other words, adolescents who are engaged in group-

Retreatist Adaptations

Basis of Illegitimate Opportunity Structure	Restrictions on Use of Illegitimate Means	
	Internalized Prohibitions	Socially Structured Barriers
Violence	I	III
Criminal Means	II	IV

supported delinquency of the criminal or conflict type may eventually turn to drug use. Indeed, entire gangs sometimes shift from either criminal or conflict to retreatist adaptations.

We view these shifts in adaptations as responses to restrictions on the use of illegitimate means. Such restrictions, as we have seen, are always operative; not all who would acquire success by violence or criminal means are permitted to do so. It is our contention that retreatist behavior emerges among some lower-class adolescents because they have failed to find a place for themselves in criminal or conflict subcultures. Consider the case of competition for membership in conflict gangs. To the extent that conflict activity—"bopping," street-fighting, "rumbling," and the like—is tolerated, it represents an alternative means by which adolescents in many relatively disorganized urban areas may acquire status. Those who excel in the manipulation of violence may acquire "rep" within the group to which they belong and respect from other adolescent groups in the vicinity and from the adult world. In areas which do not offer criminal opportunities, the use of violence may be the only available avenue to prestige. But prestige is, by definition, scarce—just as scarce among adolescents who seek to acquire it by violence as it is elsewhere in the society. Not only do juvenile gangs compete vigorously with one another, but within each gang there is a continual struggle for prestigeful positions. Thus some gangs will acquire "rep" and others will fail; some persons

---

[29]Solomon Kobrin, *Drug Addiction Among Young Persons in Chicago* (Illinois Institute for Juvenile Research, Oct. 1953), p. 6. Harold Finestone, in a study of the relationship between addicts and criminal status, comments: "The impression gained from interviewing . . . was that these addicts were petty thieves and petty 'operators' who, status-wise, were at the bottom of the criminal population of the underworld." "Narcotics and Criminality," *Law and Contemporary Problems*, Vol. 22, No. 1 [Winter 1957]. pp. 69–85).

[30]*Narcotics in California* (Board of Corrections, State of California, Feb. 18, 1959), p. 9.

will become upwardly mobile in conflict groups and others will remain on the periphery.

If the adolescent "failure" then turns to drugs as a solution to his status dilemma, his relationships with his peers become all the more attenuated. Habitual drug use is not generally a valued activity among juvenile gangs. Ordinarily the drug-user, if he persists in such behavior, tends to become completely disassociated from the group. Once disassociated, he may develop an even greater reliance upon drugs as a solution to status deprivations. Thus adolescent drug-users may be "double failures" who are restrained from participating in other delinquent modes of adaptation because access to these illegitimate structures is limited.

Our hypothesis states that adolescents who are double failures are more vulnerable than others to retreatist behavior; it does not imply that *all* double failures will subsequently become retreatists. Some will respond to failure by adopting a law-abiding lower-class style of life—the "corner boy" adaptation. It may be that those who become retreatists are incapable of revising their aspirations downward to correspond to reality. Some of those who shift to a corner-boy adaptation may not have held high aspirations initially. It has frequently been observed that some adolescents affiliate with delinquent groups simply for protection in gang-ridden areas; they are motivated not by frustration so much as by the "instinct of self-preservation." In a less hostile environment, they might simply have made a corner-boy adjustment in the first place. But for those who continue to exhibit high aspirations under conditions of double failure, retreatism is the expected result.

Sequences of Adaptation

Access to success-goals by illegitimate means diminishes as the lower-class adolescent approaches adulthood. Illegitimate avenues to higher status that were available during early adolescence become more restricted in later adolescence. These new limitations intensify frustration and so create pressures toward withdrawal or retreatist reactions.

With regard to criminal means, late adolescence is a crucial turning point, for it is during this period that the selection of candidates for stable adult criminal roles takes place. It is probably true that more youngsters are exposed to criminal learning environments during adolescence than can possibly be absorbed by the adult criminal structure. Because of variations in personality characteristics, criminal proficiency, and capacity to make "the right connections," or simply because of luck, some persons will find this avenue to higher status open and some will find it closed off. In effect, the latter face a dead end. Some delinquents, therefore, must cope with abrupt discontinuity in role-preparation and role-performance which may lead to retreatist responses.

In the case of conflict patterns, a similar process takes place. As adolescents near adulthood, excellence in the manipulation of violence no longer brings high status. Quite the contrary, it generally evokes extreme negative sanctions. What was defined as permissible or tolerable behavior during adolescence tends to be sharply proscribed in adulthood. New expectations are imposed, expectations of "growing up," of taking on adult responsibilities in the economic, familial, and community spheres. The effectiveness with which these definitions are imposed is attested by the tendency among fighting gangs to decide that conflict is, in the final analysis, simply "kid stuff":

"As the group grows older, two things happen. Sports, hell raising, and gang fights become 'kid stuff' and are given up. In the normal course of events, the youthful preoccupations are replaced with the more individual concerns about work, future, a steady girl, and the like."[31]

In other words, powerful community expectations emerge which have the consequence of closing off access to previously useful means of

[31]Wilmer *et al., op. cit.,* p. 409.

overcoming status deprivations. Strains are experienced, and retreatist behavior may result.

As we have noted, adolescents who experience pressures leading to retreatist reactions are often restrained by their peers. Adolescent gangs usually devalue drug use (except on an experimental basis or for the sake of novelty) and impose negative sanctions upon those who become "hooked." The very existence of the gang discourages the potential user:

> "The activities of the gang offer a measure of shared status, a measure of security and a sense of belonging. The boys do not have to face life alone—the group protects them. Escape into drugs is not necessary as yet."[32]

In the post-adolescent period, however, the cohesiveness of the peer group usually weakens. Those who have the requisite skills and opportunities begin to make the transition to adulthood, assuming conventional occupational and kinship roles. As the solidarity of the group declines, it can no longer satisfy the needs or control the behavior of those who continue to rely upon it. These members may try to reverse the trend toward disintegration and, failing this, turn to drugs:

[32]*Ibid.*

> "This group organized five years ago for self-protection against other fighting groups in the area. Recently, as the majority grew cool to bopping, a group of three boys broke off in open conflict with the president; *soon after, these three started using heroin and acting 'down with the cats.'* They continue making efforts to get the gang back to fights. . . . The three users are still out and it is unlikely that they will be readmitted."[33]

For some adolescents, the peer group is the primary avenue to status as well as the primary source of constraints on behavior. For these youngsters, the post-adolescent period, during which the group may disintegrate or shift its orientation, is one in which social controls are weakened precisely when tensions are heightened.

Whether the sequence of adaptations is from criminal to retreatist or from conflict to retreatist, we suggest that limitations on legitimate and illegitimate opportunity combine to produce intense pressures toward retreatist behavior. When both systems of means are simultaneously restricted, it is not strange that some persons become detached from the social structure, abandoning cultural goals and efforts to achieve them by any means.

[33]*Ibid.*, p. 405. Emphasis added.

14. Goal Discrepancy and Delinquency

JOHN C. QUICKER

THE PRIMARY IMPETUS FOR INVOLVEMENT IN DE-linquency according to Cloward and Ohlin (1960:105) stems from the pressure resulting from a discrepancy between high aspirations and limited legitimate opportunities, which forces lower-class adolescents to seek alternative—often deviant—means to realize these aspirations. More completely, these adolescents are conditioned by the culture to aspire to relatively lofty goals without having the appropriate cultural or pragmatic support to achieve them. Frustrated by repeated failures to reach these goals and unable to lower their aspirations, these boys will seek the technically most efficient way—whether legitimate or not—to realize these goals. The pressure resulting from this discrepancy between cultural goals and socially sanctioned means is then the cause for most delinquency in our society.

THE IDEA OF GOALS

In their analysis of the consequences of goal discrepancy for adolescents, Cloward and Ohlin (1960:94–106) focus on the one essential goal, the occupational goal. Their theory involves the notion that having the appropriate occupation is the main determinant of success in our society. Not only does it provide one with an invidious distinction, but it also provides the necessary

▶SOURCE: *"The Effect of Goal Discrepancy on Delinquency," Social Problems (October 1974, 22(1):76–86. Reprinted by permission.*

material and economic indicators of success.

Clearly, Cloward and Ohlin's theory is concerned with a temporal sequence of events leading to delinquency: the boy first experiences the discrepancy, becomes frustrated, and in desperation turns to delinquency. What is clear in a causal theory and what indeed happens in reality may be incongruent. It may be that the experience of involvement in delinquency occurs prior to any discrepancy and that this experience reduces one's expectations of getting an appropriate job. As Bordua (1961:134) states, "Participation in gang delinquency in itself diminishes the fitness of many boys for effective functioning in the conventional world." A number of researchers have demonstrated that delinquency does indeed have profound effects on an adolescent's perception of his chances for success (Short, *et al.*, 1965; Spergel, 1967; Rivera and Short, 1967). Boys who are involved in delinquency generally perceive less chances for success than boys who have not been involved. As Rivera and Short (1967:76) state, "The fact of gang membership appears to be associated with a relative reduction of occupational goal levels."

In short, we have two confounding arguments. The theory argues for goal discrepancy occuring prior to involvement in delinquency and as the primary cause for involvement. Studies conducted subsequent to the theory have shown that the delinquency itself may be causing the goal discrepancy, thereby, confounding the causal nexus of the theory; thus it appears as if the actual causal sequence is problematic. Is the anticipated failure of these goals a cause or an effect of delinquency? Clearly an answer to this question must involve an analysis of behavior over time.

Cloward and Ohlin seem to be making the assumption that delinquent adolescents are in a sense miniature adults, since it is the frustrated occupational goals that are the prime contributors to delinquency, and not any other goals which may be more immediate in the juvenile's life than a concern for the occupation he may want. Especially here, they have reduced the importance frustrated educational goals may have on the adolescent's life. Their perception is that these "goals" are a means to the future occupational goals, rather than goals themselves (Cloward & Ohlin, 1960:97–103). They suggest that unlike occupational goals, the youth are able to "scale down" their educational goals to a "realistic" level from which they are able to operate without the frustration of unmitigated occupational goals. These boys, while being cognizant of the value of education, cannot "afford" to acquire it, realize this, and instead of developing a pejorative frustration reaction as they do with occupational goals, get in touch with reality and accept it.

While Cloward and Ohlin have de-emphasized the importance that frustrated educational goals play in an adolescent's life, I believe that has been an oversight on their part. The argument here is that unrealizable major life goals, when they occur, are powerful sources of frustration. To be frustrated by inability to achieve occupational goals can produce strain which can lead to delinquency, as Cloward and Ohlin argue, but to be frustrated from achieving more immediate goals, such as educational goals, can also produce strain which can lead to delinquency as well.

The literature in general supports the contention that delinquent boys are the least successful educationally (Elliott, 1962; Short, 1964; Short, 1965; Spergel, 1967; Wendling & Elliott, 1968). However, in the same sense that the causal

sequence was confounded when occupational goals were considered, so it is here that again the temporal sequence is unclear. That is, did the frustration stemming from unrealizable educational aspirations cause the boys to become involved in delinquency, or did the involvement in delinquency cause the educational goal discrepancy? Once again an analysis that considers boys' educational aspirations and expectations prior to their involvement in delinquency is necessary to determine the effect this educational goal discrepancy can have had in producing delinquency.

STATEMENT OF THE PROBLEM

This study is an attempt to clarify some of the basic issues Cloward and Ohlin raise concerning the temporal sequence of events that cause delinquency. Previous studies dealing with these causal issues could be interpreted as having offered general support for the theory, though they have left unexplained the actual causal sequence. This study will expand Cloward and Ohlin's original theoretical framework by considering not only the occupational goals they emphasize, but in addition will also consider more immediate educational goals. Using panel data, it will attempt to unravel the temporal sequence by showing the effect these frustrated goals have on non-delinquent youth in producing delinquency.

RESEARCH PROCEDURES

1. The Sample and Variables

The population used for this study consisted of the total male population of eight high schools in California, a total of 1,338 boys. The design included considerable variation in the ethnicity and social class of the students. This cohort of boys was followed over a four-year period, beginning in 1963, by distribution of a questionnaire each of the four years. In addition, at these yearly intervals, the records of the school authorities and police were used to add official data to the collection. Since each boy was followed as a unit over this period, the data represent a panel and are, therefore, able to reflect changes in status and behavior.[1]

Conceptualization of the notion "goals" involved two distinct types: long range and short range goals. These were in turn operationalized so that a discrepancy score for each of the boys on each of the goals could be determined. For the long range goals, a discrepancy score was computed between a boy's occupational aspirations and expectations, called occupational goal discrepancy. For the short range goals, a discrepancy score was computed between a boy's educational aspirations and expectations, called educational goal discrepancy.

The dependent variable in this study, delinquency, was measured behaviorally by utilizing the Nye and Short (1957) scale for determining self-reported delinquent behavior.[2] Unfortunately these measures were not taken every year of the study, but only in the first year and again in the last. Instead of having time lagged data every year then, the lags involve longer periods, which, on the positive side, allow more time for the effect variables to influence the affected ones.[3]

This delinquency measure was differentiated into two variables by severity of the act. If a reported act was in violation of a felony statute, it was considered a serious self-reported act. If, on the other hand, the act was in violation of a misdemeanor statute, it was then considered to be a non-serious self-reported act. The primary

rationale behind this differentiation was to establish categories of offenders based on a behavioral indicator of seriousness in an effort to determine if these categories were differentially affected by the independent variables.

The purpose of this study, then, was to test the tenability of two hypotheses derived from the causal postulations of delinquency suggested by Cloward and Ohlin:

1.   Delinquency varies directly with perceived occupational goal discrepancy.

2.   Delinquency varies directly with perceived educational goal discrepancy.

2. *Methods of Analysis*

The analysis utilized a procedure that combined the methods developed by Campbell (1963a, 1963b) and Lazarsfeld (1948) as reported in Lipset, *et al.* (1954) for estimating the direction and source of causal influence from panel data. Initially all five variables were correlated with one another in a matrix using a Pearsonian r. Then by using Campbell's cross-lagged Panel Correlation Technique, a series of lagged and cross-lagged correlations were developed and analyzed. Following this technique, a modified version of Lazarsfeld's Sixteen-fold Table Analysis was applied to the data to determine the direction and strength of the final relationship.[4]

Basically, the Campbell Technique served three important functions: (a) to determine whether there was any association between the various measures of the variables (b) to determine whether the predominant direction of this association was lagged or simultaneous, and (c) to determine, if the association was lagged, the dominant direction of the lag. Of these functions, (a) and (b) are relatively clear, while (c) requires some explanation.

The Campbell Technique was designed to de-

[1]A comprehensive description of the study population is given in Elliott & Voss (1971), Chapter 3, pp. 6–13.

[2]An official measure of delinquency was also used but is not reported here because the results, while generally directionally similar, were, nevertheless, much weaker. Since official data are subject to so much bias themselves, the weaker results are difficult to analyze.

[3]At this point it does not seem to be appropriate to debate the relative merits of this particular lag period. It seems sufficient to show that lagging did in fact occur, and that we were able to measure variable effects over this lagged period. Any other arguments are academic since we in essence have no way of determining their empirical validity.

[4]A more comprehensive analysis of the relationship of these two procedures is given in Yee and Gage (1968).

termine which of two variables, A and B, correlated with one another, is the cause and which is the effect. A time lagged analysis assumed that if $rA_1 B_2 > B_1 A_2$, then A existed prior to B and caused it. Conversely, if $rB_1 A_2 > A_1 B_2$, then B existed prior to A and caused it. As Pelz and Andrews (1964:837) state, if A caused B, then "the state of A at time t should be more strongly associated with the state of B at time t + k, then the state of B at time t is associated with the state of A at time t + k." However, Pelz and Andrews incorrectly assume that there are only two hypotheses involved, either A caused B or B caused A. Each lagged correlation itself produces two sets of hypotheses so that there is a total of four sets involved. These are as follows: When $A_1 B_2 > B_1 A_2$ then,

1. Increases in A increase B, and decreases in A decrease B.

2. Increases in B decrease A, and decreases in B increase A.

When $B_1 A_2 > A_1 B_2$ then,

3. Increases in B increase A, and decreases in B decrease A.

4. Increases in A decrease B, and decreases in A increase B.

If A is causally prior to B, then it may be that A is increasing B and producing the larger correlation. However, it may also be true that given the presence of A and B, with A assumed to have occurred first, the introduction of B may now be decreasing A, so that the *relative* correlation is still larger. Both variables are presented in this technique so that two cross-lagged correlations are indicated, one of which may be larger than the other. If A is actually increasing B, the change is said to be congruous; but if B is decreasing A, then the change is incongruous. The cause of the inequality may be an increase in congruity produced by A increasing B, or actually a loss of congruity by B decreasing A. How-

ever, Yee and Gage (1968:120) observe, ". . . it is impossible to ascertain this possibility from the cross-lagged r's because the latter (incongruous change) confound, or prevent us from distinguishing between, the source and direction of the influence of the two correlated variables."

Consequently, the Campbell Technique allowed us to eliminate one of two sets of hypotheses and to accept the other set as tenable. But the problem now is to discover which hypothesis of the remaining set of two is the most tenable. For this, the Lazarsfeld Analysis was used.

This analysis enabled us to discern whether the change which occurred was predominantly congruous or incongruous. The number of changes toward congruity was compared to those toward incongruity, with the largest number taken to be indicative of the most tenable hypothesis. A phi coefficient was then calculated to determine the relative strength of this relationship.[5]

For purposes of this study, only half of the Lazarsfeld Analysis is reported. That is, the total analysis indicates both how the juveniles responded before they were delinquent and after or as a result of the delinquency. Since this research is only concerned with the postulated causes of delinquency and the influence these have on generating delinquency, the consequences of having been a delinquent are not considered. In short, adolescents who at time one were not delinquent, will be analyzed at time two, to determine how many are now delinquent after exposure to the "causes of delinquency," while the effect of delinquency on an adolescent's perception of goals is not reported.

FINDINGS AND ANALYSIS

The first of the operational hypotheses is that the more one experiences occupational goal dis-

[5]In effect then, we are calculating non-delinquent transition rates for subjects stratified with respect to the independent variables (Davis; 1963). The transition rate simply indicates the probability of a non-delinquent becoming delinquent for each stratum of the independent variable.

Table I. Cross-Lagged Analysis of Delinquency by Occupational Goal Discrepancy (OGD)

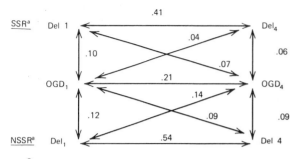

[a]SSR = Serious self-reported delinquency; NSSR = non-serious self-reported delinquency.

crepancy (OGD), the more likely is he to be involved in delinquency. Table I gives the Campbell analysis for considering the relationship of delinquency to this type of discrepancy. As can be seen from these data, it is apparent that irrespective of which measure of the dependent variable is used, serious or non-serious self-reported delinquency, the correlations are all very low, the implication of which is that the delinquency is not related to occupational goal discrepancy, either as a cause or as an effect.[6]

To end the analysis of these variables at this stage would not be in order given their priority in the theory. That is, this is the relationship explicitly outlined in the theory; a rejection of it should not occur lightly. Consequently, if the theory had been supported here, the following would have been most tenable:

---

[6]However, there is one relatively strong cross-lagged relationship which should be noted. The relationship between Del₁ OGD₄ with NSSR is .14, the strongest relationship of this analysis. This is probably due to chance, though its implications suggest further inconsistency with the research hypothesis. That is, this relationship implies the following hypotheses as most tenable:

1. Increases in delinquency produce increases in occupational goal discrepancy.

2. Increases in occupational goal discrepancy produce decreases in delinquency.

Since these hypotheses are both weak and inconsistent with the theory, further analysis was not pursued.

---

1. Increases in occupational goal discrepancy produce increases in delinquency.

2. Increases in delinquency produce decreases in occupational goal discrepancy.

Hypothesis (1) is predicted by the theory, while hypothesis (2) could be true and not inconsistent with the theory.

The next step is then to determine which of these hypotheses is most tenable in a Lazarsfeld Analysis. Since these relationships were found to be weak initially, this latter analysis should support our earlier contentions of no relationship; and this is precisely what it does. The Lazarsfeld Analysis, while indicating that the greatest change is toward congruity, suggesting that hypothesis (1) would be the most tenable, shows the differences between the changes to be very small.

Table II indicates the relative proportions of juveniles becoming delinquent on high and low measures of the independent variable. Examination of these data confirms our initial notion that OGD is not related to delinquency. Clearly, on both measures of delinquency, those experiencing high OGD are no more likely to be involved in delinquency than those experiencing low OGD. Thus, both of these analyses suggest that occupational goal discrepancy is not causally related to delinquency as predicted by the theory.

It is of interest to note here that these findings are supported in a recent study by Hirschi (1969:182–183). From an analysis of the effect that high occupational aspirations coupled with low occupational expectations have on an adolescent's involvement in delinquency, he concludes, "Frustrated occupational ambition cannot be an important cause of delinquency in the present sample . . . the higher the aspiration, the lower the rate of delinquency, regardless of the student's expectations." In short, then, neither the findings from this study nor those from Hirschi's are able to support the Cloward and Ohlin basic causal tenet that frustrated occupa-

Table II. Delinquency Rates by Occupational Goal Discrepancy

		Rate (per 1,000)	ϕ
SSR	Hi OGD	250	−.002
	Lo OGD	254	
NSSR	Hi OGD	271	−.001
	Lo OGD	273	

tional goals are responsible for delinquency. When they are related, the delinquency could be producing the frustrated goals, but not vice-versa.

The next part of this analysis involves consideration of a more immediate frustrated goal in the adolescent's life, educational goal discrepancy (EGD). To reiterate this hypothesis, as educational goal discrepancy increases, so will delinquency.

Table III indicates that the strongest relationships are cross-lagged relationships for both cases of the dependent variable, −.26 for the serious measure and −.27 for the non-serious measure. The strength of these correlations is consistent, r Del_1 EGD_4 > EGD_1 Del_4. However, these correlations are negative, suggesting a reversal in the order of the tenable hypotheses. These are then as follows:

1. Increases in delinquency produce decreases in educational goal discrepancy.

2. Increases in educational goal discrepancy produce increases in delinquency.

Taken together, these hypotheses are not inconsistent with our extension of the theory, though it is hypothesis (2) which is explicitly

predicted. Hypothesis (1) could be tenable if we consider delinquency a successful solution to the frustration stemming from this discrepancy. That is, if adolescents are turning to delinquency as a solution to the problems of educational goal discrepancy, then we would expect the most educational goal discrepancy to produce the most delinquency, i.e., hypothesis (2). Now if delinquency successfully resolves the problem of educational goal discrepancy, then we could expect that the more one is involved in delinquency, the more his educational goal discrepancy would be reduced, i.e., hypothesis (1). Since our concern again is not with the consequ-

Table III. Cross-Lagged Analysis of Delinquency by Educational Goal Discrepancy (EGD)

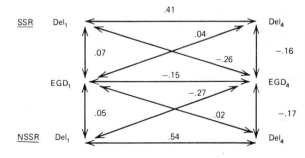

ences of delinquency, but rather with its cause, further discussion of this point is not in order here. However, the Lazarsfeld Analysis must now be considered to determine which of these hypotheses is most tenable: is the observed interaction toward congruity or incongruity?

The Lazarsfeld Analysis indicates that the change is indeed a congruous change, in the direction predicted by hypothesis (2). Table IV indicates the rate of that change and strength of the relationship. For both the serious and nonserious delinquency measures, it is evident that those who experience high EGD are much more likely to become delinquent than those who experience low EGD; the relationships are quite strong. For the serious delinquency, 345 out of 1,000 boys who experienced high EGD became delinquent, while only 30 out of 1,000 with the low EGD became delinquent. The non-serious delinquency rates are slightly more impressive, 407 to 29. These data then, very strongly suggest the acceptance of hypothesis (2) as most tenable.

CONCLUSION

The results of this study have interesting implications for the Cloward and Ohlin opportunity theory. The study corroborates earlier specula-tion by Bordua and the empirical findings of Hirschi that frustrated occupational goals do not seem to be influential in producing delinquency. Those who perceive frustration are no more likely to get involved in delinquency than those who do not. However, the concept of goal frustration is more involved than Cloward and Ohlin theorized. There do seem to be other goals more immediate than occupational goals, which can be influential in producing delinquency. Specifically, this study has shown that one of these goals, educational goals, will produce delinquency when they are frustrated. Additional research should explore the effect that other frustrated immediate goals have on delinquency.

This study, while critical of the initial theory, has also expanded it. The Cloward and Ohlin concept of goal frustration seems to be too narrow, though the idea of frustrated goals leading to delinquency seems viable. Adolescents live in an adolescent world, dominated by their peer culture. Their perception of what they "want to be when they grow up," is by no means entirely precise. Most seem to have vague ideas of what is desirable, or what their parents might like them to be, but the thought of not achieving is not a very influential life force. Certainly the thought of not making it is not—in itself—

Table IV. Delinquency Rates by Educational Goal Discrepancy

		Rate (per 1,000)	ϕ
SSR	HI EGD	345	.356
	Lo EGD	30	
NSSR	Hi EGD	407	.377
	Lo EGD	29	

serious enough to cause sufficient pressure to violate the internalized normative structure. Planning far ahead, worrying about the very distant future, is, in this rapidly changing world, just not a powerful cause of much frustration.

However, the above discussion should not be taken to minimize the consequences that real frustration may have on an adolescent's life. Indeed, adolescents experience many situations that produce intense frustrations, sufficiently intense to produce the delinquency with which Cloward and Ohlin are concerned. But these frustrations stem from more immediate circumstances; they stem from what is happening now, tomorrow, not what may happen in the more distant future, if it ever comes. School is important; how popular one is in one's peer group is important; how one is getting along with one's parents is important; how one is getting along with members of the opposite sex is important—the *now* is important. As one young person told me, "Man, I can't worry about what kind of job I'm gonna have when I grow up, I may never get there. The world may not be here that long."

REFERENCES

Bordua, David J.
  1961   "Delinquent subcultures: Sociological interpretations of gang delinquency." The Annals of the American Academy of Political and Social Science 338 (November): 120–136.

Campbell, Donald T. and J. C. Stanley
  1963   "Experimental and quasi-experimental designs for research on teaching," in Handbook of Research on Teaching. Chicago: Rand-McNally.

Campbell, Donald T.
  1963   "From description to experimentation: Interpreting trends as quasi-experiments," in C. W. Harris (ed.), Problems in Measuring Change. University of Wisconsin Press.

Cloward, Richard A. and Lloyd E. Ohlin
  1960   Delinquency and Opportunity: A Theory of Delinquent Gangs. New York: Free Press.

Davis, James A.
  1963   "Panel analysis: Techniques and concepts in the interpretation of repeated measurements." National Opinion Research Center. Preliminary draft (November) University of Chicago.

Elliott, Delbert S. and Harwin L. Voss
  1971   Delinquency and Dropout, A Summary Report to the National Institutes of Mental Health, Grant Numbers MH-170173 and RG1 MH 15285. (November).

Elliott, Delbert S.
  1962   "Delinquency and perceived opportunity." Sociological Inquiry 32, 1(Winter): 216–227.

Hirschi, Travis
  1969   Causes of Delinquency, Berkeley: University of California Press.

Lipset, Seymour, M., P. F. Lazarsfeld, A. H. Barton, and J. Linz
  1954   "The psychology of voting: An analysis of political behavior," in G. Lindzey, ed., Handbook of Social Psychology V.2. Massachusetts: Addison-Wesley, 1124–1175.

Nye, Ivan F. and James F. Short Jr.
  1957   "Scaling delinquent behavior." American Sociological Review 22:326–331.

Pelz, Donald C. and Frank M. Andrews
  1964   "Detecting causal priorities in panel study data." American Sociological Review 29:836–848.

Rivera, Ramon J. and James F. Short, Jr.
  1967   "Occupational goals: A comparative analysis," in Malcolm W. Klein, ed., Juvenile Gangs in Context: Theory, Research and Action. New Jersey: Prentice-Hall.

Short, James F. Jr.
  1964   "Gang delinquency and anomie," in Marshall B. Clinard, ed., Anomie and Deviant Behavior. New York: Free Press. 98–127.

Short, James, F. Jr., Ramon J. Rivera, and Ray A. Tennyson

1965   "Perceived opportunity, gang membership and delinquency." American Sociological Review 30–1. 56–67.

Spergel, Irving
1967   "Deviant patterns and opportunities of pre-adolescent negro boys in three Chicago neighborhoods," in Malcolm W. Klein, ed. Juvenile Gangs in Context: Theory, Research and Action. New Jersey: Prentice-Hall Inc. 38–54.

Wendling, Aubrey and Delbert S. Elliott
1968   "Class and race differentials in parental aspirations and expectations." Pacific Sociological Review 11–2(Fall): 123–133.

Yee, A. H. and N. L. Gage
1968   "Techniques for estimating the source and direction of causal influence in panel data." Psychological Bulletin 70:115–126.

15. The Subculture of Violence

MARVIN E. WOLFGANG
FRANCO FERRACUTI

THE CULTURAL CONTEXT

LIKE ALL HUMAN BEHAVIOR, HOMICIDE AND OTHER violent assaultive crimes must be viewed in terms of the cultural context from which they spring. De Champneuf, Guerry, Quetelet early in the nineteenth century, and Durkheim later, led the way toward emphasizing the necessity to examine the *physique sociale,* or social phenomena characterized by "externality," if the scientist is to understand or interpret crime, suicide, prostitution, and other deviant behavior. Without promulgating a sociological fatalism, analysis of broad macroscopic correlates in this way may obscure the dynamic elements of the phenomenon and result in the empirical hiatus and fallacious association to which Selvin refers (1). Yet, because of wide individual variations, the clinical, idiosyncratic approach does not necessarily aid in arriving at Weber's *Verstehen,* or meaningful adequate understanding of regularities, uniformities, or patterns of interaction. And it is this kind of understanding we seek when we examine either deviation from, or conformity to, a normative social system.

Sociological contributions have made almost commonplace, since Durkheim, the fact that deviant conduct is not evenly distributed throughout the social structure. There is much empirical evidence that class position, ethnicity, occupa-

▶SOURCE: *The Subculture of Violence, London: Tavistock, 1967, pp. 150–163. Reprinted by permission.*

tional status, and other social variables are effective indicators for predicting rates of different kinds of deviance. Studies in ecology perform a valuable service for examining the phenomenology and distribution of aggression, but only inferentially point to the importance of the system of norms. Anomie, whether defined as the absence of norms (which is a doubtful conceptualization) or the conflict of norms (either normative goals or means) (2), or whether redefined by Power (3) as "meaningless," does not coincide with most empirical evidence on homicide. Acceptance of the concept of anomie would imply that marginal individuals who harbor psychic anomie that reflects (or causes) social anomie have the highest rates of homicides. Available data seem to reject this contention.

Anomie as culture conflict, or conflict of norms, suggests, as we have in the last section, that there is one segment (the prevailing middle-class value system) of a given culture whose value system is the antithesis of, or in conflict with, another, smaller, segment of the same culture. This conceptualism of anomie is a useful tool for referring to subcultures as ideal types, or mental constructs. But to transfer this norm-conflict approach from the social to the individual level, theoretically making the individual a repository of culture conflict, again does not conform to the patterns of known psychological and sociological data. This latter approach would be forced to hypothesize that socially mobile individuals and families would be

151

most frequently involved in homicide, or that persons moving from a formerly embraced sub-value system to the predominant communal value system would commit this form of violent deviation in the greatest numbers. There are no homicide data that show high rates of homicides among persons manifesting higher social aspirations in terms of mobility. It should also be mentioned that anomie, as a concept, does not easily lend itself to psychological study (4).

That there is a conflict of value systems, we agree. That is, there is a conflict between a prevailing culture value and some subcultural entity. But commission of homicide by actors from the subculture at variance with the prevailing culture cannot be adequately explained in terms of frustration due to failure to attain normative-goals of the latter, in terms of inability to succeed with normative-procedures (means) for attaining those goals, nor in terms of an individual psychological condition of anomie. Homicide is most prevalent, or the highest rates of homicide occur, among a relatively homogeneous subcultural group in any large urban community. Similar prevalent rates can be found in some rural areas. The value system of this group, we are contending, constitutes a subculture of violence. From a psychological viewpoint, we might hypothesize that the greater the degree of integration of the individual into this subculture, the higher the probability that his behavior will be violent in a variety of situations. From the sociological side, there should be a direct relationship between rates of homicide and the extent to which the subculture of violence represents a cluster of values around the theme of violence.

Except for war, probably the most highly reportable, socially visible, and serious form of violence is expressed in criminal homicide. Data show that in the United States rates are highest among males, non-whites, and the young adult ages. Rates for most serious crimes, particularly against the person, are highest in these same groups. In a Philadelphia study of 588 criminal homicides (5), for example, non-white males

aged 20–24 had a rate of 92 per 100,000 compared with 3.4 for white males of the same ages. Females consistently had lower rates than males in their respective race groups (non-white females, 9.3; white females, 0.4, in the same study), although it should be noted, as we shall discuss later, that non-white females have higher rates than white males.

It is possible to multiply these specific findings in any variety of ways; and although a subcultural affinity to violence appears to be principally present in large urban communities and increasingly in the adolescent population, some typical evidence of this phenomenon can be found, for example, in rural areas and among other adult groups. For example, a particular, very structured, subculture of this kind can be found in Sardinia, in the central mountain area of the island. Pigliaru has conducted a brilliant analysis of the people from this area and their criminal behavior, commonly known as the *vendetta barbaricina* (6).

In Colombia, the well known *violencia* has been raging for the last 15 years, causing deaths of a total estimated between 200,000 and 300,000 (7). The homicide rate in several areas has been among the highest in the world, and homicide has been the leading cause of death for Colombian males aged between 15 and 45. Several causes, some political, initially associated with the rise of this phenomenon continue to exist, and, among them, a subcultural transmission of violence is believed to play an important role. More will be said later about the subcultural traditions of violence in Sardinia, Columbia, and elsewhere.

We suggest that, by identifying the groups with the highest rates of homicide, we should find in the most intense degree a subculture of violence; and, having focused on these groups, we should subsequently examine the value system of their subculture, the importance of human life in the scale of values, the kinds of expected reaction to certain types of stimulus, perceptual differences in the evaluation of stimuli, and the general personality structure of the subcultural actors. In the Philadelphia study it was pointed out that:

". . . the significance of a jostle, a slightly derogatory remark, or the appearance of a weapon in the hands of an adversary are stimuli differentially perceived and interpreted by Negroes and whites, males and females. Social expectations of response in particular types of social interaction result in differential 'definitions of the situation.' A male is usually expected to defend the name and honor of his mother, the virtue of womanhood . . . and to accept no derogation about his race (even from a member of his own race), his age, or his masculinity. Quick resort to physical combat as a measure of daring, courage, or defense of status appears to be a cultural expression, especially for lower socio-economic class males of both races. When such a culture norm response is elicited from an individual engaged in social interplay with others who harbor the same response mechanism, physical assaults, altercations, and violent domestic quarrels that result in homicide are likely to be common. The upper-middle and upper social class value system defines subcultural mores, and considers many of the social and personal stimuli that evoke a combative reaction in the lower classes as 'trivial.' Thus, there exists a cultural antipathy between many folk rationalizations of the lower class, and of males of both races, on the one hand, and the middle-class legal norms under which they live, on the other (8)."

This kind of analysis, combined with other data about delinquency, the lower-class social structure, its value system, and its emphasis on aggression, suggest the thesis of a violent subculture, or by pushing the normative aspects a little further, a *subculture of violence*. Among many juvenile gangs, as has repeatedly been pointed out, there are violent feuds, meetings, territorial fights, and the use of violence to prove "heart," to maintain or to acquire "rep" (9).

Physical aggression is often seen as a demonstration of masculinity and toughness. We might argue that this emphasis on showing masculinity through aggression is not always supported by data. If homicide is any index at all of physical aggression, we must remember that in the Philadelphia data non-white females have rates often two to four times higher than the rates of white males. Violent behavior appears more dependent on cultural differences than on sex differences, traditionally considered of paramount importance in the expression of aggression. It could be argued, of course, that in a more matriarchal role than that of her white counterpart, the Negro female both enjoys and suffers more of the male role as head of the household, as parental authority and supervisor; that this imposed role makes her more aggressive, more male-like, more willing and more likely to respond violently. Because most of the victims of Negro female homicide offenders are Negro males, the Negro female may be striking out aggressively against the inadequate male protector whom she desperately wants but often cannot find or hold (10).

It appears valid to suggest that there are, in a heterogeneous population, differences in ideas and attitudes toward the use of violence and that these differences can be observed through variables related to social class and possibly through psychological correlates. There is evidence that modes of control of expressions of aggression in children vary among the social classes (11). Lower-class boys, for example, appear more likely to be oriented toward direct expression of aggression than are middle-class boys. The type of punishment meted out by parents to misbehaving children is related to this class orientation toward aggression. Lower-class mothers report that they or their husbands are likely to strike their children or threaten to strike them, whereas middle-class mothers report that their type of punishment is psychological rather than physical; and boys who are punished physically express aggression more directly than those who are punished psychologically. As Martin Gold (12) has suggested, the middle-class child is more likely to turn his aggression inward; in the extreme and as an adult he will commit suicide. But the lower-class child is more accustomed to a parent-child relationship which during punishment is for the moment that of attacker and attacked. The target for aggression, then, is external; aggression is directed toward others (13).

The existence of a subculture of violence is partly demonstrated by examination of the social groups and individuals who experience the highest rates of manifest violence. This examination need not be confined to the study of one national or ethnic group. On the contrary, the existence of a subculture of violence could perhaps receive even cross-cultural confirmation. Criminal homicide is the most acute and highly reportable example of this type of violence, but some circularity of thought is obvious in the effort to specify the dependent variable (homicide), and also to infer the independent variable (the existence of a subculture of violence). The highest rates of rape, aggravated assaults, persistency in arrests for assaults (recidivism) among these groups with high rates of homicide are, however, empirical addenda to the postulation of a subculture of violence. Residential propinquity of these same groups reinforces the sociopsychological impact which the integration of this subculture engenders. Sutherland's thesis of "differential association," or a psychological reformulation of the same theory in terms of learning process, could effectively be employed to describe more fully this impact in its intensity, duration, repetition, and frequency. The more thoroughly integrated the individual is into this subculture, the more intensely he embraces its prescriptions of behavior, its conduct norms, and integrates them into his personality structure. The degree of integration may be measured partly and crudely by public records of contact with the law, so high arrest rates, particularly high rates of assault crimes and high rates of recidivism for assault crimes among groups that form the subculture of violence, may indicate allegiance to the values of violence.

We have said that overt physical violence often becomes a common subculturally expected response to certain stimuli. However, it is not merely rigid conformity to the demands and expectations of other persons, as Henry and Short (14) seem to suggest, that results in the high probability of homicide. Excessive, compulsive, or apathetic conformity of middle-class individuals to the value system of their social group is a widely recognized cultural malady. Our concern is with the value elements of violence as an integral component of the subculture which experiences high rates of homicide. It is conformity to *this* set of values, and not rigid conformity *per se,* that gives important meaning to the subculture of violence.

If violence is a common subcultural response to certain stimuli, penalties should exist for deviation from *this* norm. The comparatively nonviolent individual may be ostracized (15), but if social interaction must occur because of residential propinquity to others sharing in a subculture of violence, he is most likely to be treated with disdain or indifference. One who previously was considered a member of the ingroup, but who has rebelled or retreated from the subculture, is now an out-group member, a possible threat, and one for the group to avoid. Alienation or avoidance takes him out of the normal reach of most homicide attacks, which are highly personal among friends, relatives, and associates. If social interaction continues, however, the deviant from the subculture of violence who fails to respond to a potentially violent situation, may find himself a victim of an adversary who continues to conform to the violence values.

It is not far-fetched to suggest that a whole culture may accept a value set dependent upon violence, demand or encourage adherence to violence, and penalize deviation. During periods of war the whole nation accepts the principle of violence against the enemy. The nonviolent citizen drafted into military service may adopt values associated with violence as an intimately internalized re-enforcement for his newly acquired rationalization to kill. War involves selective killing of an out-group enemy, and in this respect may be viewed as different from most forms of homicide. Criminal homicide may be either "selective" or non-discriminate slaying, although the literature on homicide consistently reveals its intragroup nature. However, as in wartime combat between opposing individuals when an "it-was-either-him-or-me" situation arises, similar attitudes and reactions occur among participants in homicide. It may be relevant to point out that in the Philadelphia study of criminal homicide, 65 per cent of the offenders and 47 percent of the victims had previous arrest records. Homicide, it appears, is often a situation not unlike that of confrontations in wartime combat, in which two individuals committed to the value of violence came together, and in which chance, prowess, or possession of a particular weapon dictates the identity of the slayer and of the slain. The peaceful noncombatant in both sets of circumstances is penalized, because of the allelomimetic behavior of the group supporting violence, by his being ostracized as an outgroup member, and he is thereby segregated (imprisoned, in wartime, as a conscientious objector) from his original group. If he is not segregated, but continues to interact with his original group in the public street or on the front line that represents the culture of violence, he may fall victim to the shot or stab from one of the group who still embraces the value of violence.

An internal need for aggression and a readiness to use violence by the individual who belongs to a subculture of violence should find their psychological foundation in personality traits and in attitudes which can, through careful studies, be assessed in such a way as to lead to a differential psychology of these subjects. Psychological tests have been repeatedly employed to study the differential characteristics of criminals; and if a theoretical frame of reference involving a subculture of violence is used, it should be possible to sharpen the discriminatory power of these tests. The fact that a subject belongs to a specific subculture (in our case, a deviant one), defined by the ready use of violence, should, among other consequences, cause the subject to adopt a differential perception of his environment and its stimuli. Variations in the surrounding world, the continuous

challenges and daily frustrations which are faced and solved by the adaptive mechanism of the individual, have a greater chance of being perceived and reacted upon, in a subculture of violence, as menacing, aggressive stimuli which call for immediate defense and counter-aggression. This hypothesis lends itself to objective study through appropriate psychological methodologies. The word of Stagner (16) on industrial conflict exemplifies a similar approach in a different field. This perceptual approach is of great importance in view of studies on the physiology of aggression, which seem to show the need of outside stimulation in order to elicit aggressive behavior (17).

Confronted with many descriptive and test statistics, with some validated hypotheses and some confirmed replications of propositions regarding aggressive crime in psychological and sociological studies, interpretative analysis leading to the building of a theory is a normal functional aspect of the scientific method.

But there are two common and inherent dangers of an interpretative analysis that yields a thesis in an early stage of formulation, such as our thesis of a subculture of violence. These are: (a) the danger of going beyond the confines of empirical data which have been collected in response to some stated hypothesis; and (b) the danger of interpretation that produces generalizations emerging inductively from the data and that results in tautologous reasoning. Relative to the first type of danger, the social scientist incurs the risk of "impressionistic," "speculative" thinking, or of using previous peripheral research and trying to link it to his own data by theoretical ties that often result in knotted confusion typically calling for further research, the caveat of both "good" and "poor" analyses. Relative to the second danger, the limitations and problems of tautologies are too well known to be elaborated here. We hope that these two approaches to interpretation are herein combined in degrees that avoid compounding the fallacies of both, but that unite the benefits of each. We have made an effort to stay within the limits imposed by known empirical facts and not to become lost in speculative reasoning that combines accumulated, but unrelated, facts for which there is no empirically supportive link.

We have said that overt use of force or violence, either in interpersonal relationships or in group interaction, is generally viewed as a reflection of basic values that stand apart from the dominant, the central, or the parent culture. Our hypothesis is that this overt (and often illicit) expression of violence (of which homicide is only the most extreme) is part of a subcultural normative system, and that this system is reflected in the psychological traits of the subculture participants. In the light of our discussion of the caution to be exercised in interpretative analysis, in order to tighten the logic of this analysis, and to support the thesis of a subculture of violence, we offer the following corollary propositions:

1. *No subculture can be totally different from or totally in conflict with the society of which it is a part.* A subculture of violence is not entirely an expression of violence, for there must be interlocking value elements shared with the dominant culture. It should not be necessary to contend that violent aggression is the predominant mode of expression in order to show that the value system is set apart as subcultural. When violence occurs in the dominant culture, it is usually legitimized, but most often is vicarious and a part of phantasy. Moreover, subcultural variations, we have earlier suggested, may be viewed as quantitative and relative. The extent of difference from the larger culture and the degree of intensity, which violence as a subcultural theme may possess, are variables that could and should be measured by known sociopsychological techniques (18). At present, we are required to rely almost entirely upon expressions of violence in conduct of various forms—parent-child relationships, parental discipline, domestic quarrels, street fights, delinquent conflict gangs, criminal records of assaultive behavior, criminal homicide, etc.—but the

number of psychometrically oriented studies in criminology is steadily increasing in both quantity and sophistication, and from them a reliable differential psychology of homicides should emerge to match current sociological research.

2. *To establish the existence of a subculture of violence does not require that the actors sharing in these basic value elements should express violence in all situations.* The normative system designates that in some types of social interaction a violent and physically aggressive response is either expected or required of all members sharing in that system of values. That the actors' behavior expectations occur in more than one situation is obvious. There is a variety of circumstances in which homicide occurs, and the history of past aggressive crimes in high proportions, both in the victims and in the offenders, attests to the multisituational character of the use of violence and to its interpersonal characteristics (19). But, obviously, persons living in a subcultural milieu designated as a subculture of violence cannot and do not engage in violence continuously, otherwise normal social functioning would be virtually impossible. We are merely suggesting, for example, that ready access to weapons in this milieu may become essential for protection against others who respond in similarly violent ways in certain situations, and that the carrying of knives or other protective devices becomes a common symbol of willingness to participate in violence, to expect violence, and to be ready for its retaliation (20).

3. *The potential resort or willingness to resort to violence in a variety of situations emphasizes the penetrating and diffusive character of this culture theme.* The number and kinds of situations in which an individual uses violence may be viewed as an index of the extent to which he has assimilated the values associated with violence. This index should also be reflected by quantitative differences in a variety of psychological dimensions, from differential perception of violent stimuli to different value expressions in questionnaire-type instruments. The range of violence from minor assault to fatal injury, or certainly the maximum of violence expected, is rarely made explicit for all situations to which an individual may be exposed. Overt violence may even occasionally be a chance result of events. But clearly this range and variability of behavioral expressions of aggression suggest the importance of psychological dimensions in measuring adherence to a subculture of violence.

4. *The subcultural ethos of violence may be shared by all ages in a sub-society, but this ethos is most prominent in a limited age group, ranging from late adolescence to middle age.* We are not suggesting that a particular ethnic, sex, or age group all share in common the use of potential threats of violence. We are contending merely that the known empirical distribution of conduct, which expresses the sharing of this violence, theme, shows greatest localization, incidence, and frequency in limited sub-groups and reflects differences in learning about violence as a problem-solving mechanism.

5. *The counter-norm is nonviolence.* Violation of expected and required violence is most likely to result in ostracism from the group. Alienation of some kind, depending on the range of violence expectations that are unmet, seems to be a form of punitive action most feasible to this subculture. The juvenile who fails to live up to the conflict gang's requirements is pushed outside the group. The adult male who does not defend his honor or his female companion will be socially emasculated. The "coward" is forced to move out of the territory, to find new friends and make new alliances. Membership is lost in the subsociety sharing the cluster of attitudes positively associated with violence. If forced withdrawal or voluntary retreat are not acceptable modes of response to engaging in the counter-norm, then execution, as is reputed to occur in organized crime, may be the extreme punitive measure.

6. *The development of favorable attitudes toward, and the use of, violence in a subculture usually involve learned behavior and a process of differential learning* (21), *association* (22), *or identification* (23). Not all persons exposed—even equally exposed—to the presence of a subculture of violence absorb and share in the values in equal portions. Differential personality variables must be considered in an integrated social-psychological approach to an understanding of the subcultural aspects of violence. We have taken the position that aggression is a learned response, socially facilitated and integrated, as a habit, in more or less permanent form, among the personality characteristics of the aggressor. Aggression, from a psychological standpoint, has been defined by Buss as "the delivery of noxious stimuli in an interpersonal context" (24). Aggression seems to possess two major classes of reinforcers: the pain and injury inflicted upon the victim and its extrinsic rewards (25). Both are present in a subculture of violence, and their mechanism of action is facilitated by the social support that the aggressor receives in his group. The relationship between aggression, anger, and hostility is complicated by the habit characteristics of the first, the drive state of the second, and the attitudinal interpretative nature of the third. Obviously, the immediacy and the short temporal sequence of anger with its autonomic components make it difficult to study a criminal population that is some distance removed from the anger-provoked event. Hostility, although amenable to easier assessment, does not give a clear indication or measure of physical attack because of its predominantly verbal aspects. However, it may dispose to or prepare for aggression (26).

Aggression, in its physical manifest form, remains the most criminologically relevant aspect in a study of violent assaultive behavior. If violent aggression is a habit and possesses permanent or quasi-permanent personality trait characteristics, it should be amenable to psychological assessment through appropriate diagnostic techniques. Among the several alternative diagnostic methodologies, those based on a perceptual approach seem to be able, according to the existing literature (27), to elicit signs and symptoms of behavioral aggression, demonstrating the existence of this "habit" and/or trait in the personality of the subject being tested. Obviously, the same set of techniques being used to diagnose the trait of aggression can be used to assess the presence of major psychopathology, which might, in a restricted number of cases, have caused "aggressive behavior" outside, or in spite of, any cultural or subcultural allegiance.

7. *The use of violence in a subculture is not necessarily viewed as illicit conduct and the users therefore do not have to deal with feelings of guilt about their aggression.* Violence can become a part of the life style, the theme of solving difficult problems or problem situations. It should be stressed that the problems and situations to which we refer arise mostly within the subculture, for violence is used mostly between persons and groups who themselves rely upon the same supportive values and norms. A carrier and user of violence will not be burdened by conscious guilt, then, because generally he is not attacking the representatives of the non-violent culture, and because the recipient of this violence may be described by similar class status, occupational, residential, age, and other attribute categories which characterize the subuniverse of the collectivity sharing in the subculture of violence. Even law-abiding members of the local subculture area may not view various expressions of violence as menacing or immoral. Furthermore, when the attacked see their assaulters as agents of the same kind of aggression they themselves represent, violent retaliation is readily legitimized by a situationally specific rationale, as well as by the generally normative supports for violence.

Probably no single theory will ever explain the variety of observable violent behavior. However, the subculture-of-violence approach offers, we believe, the advantage of bringing together psychological and sociological constructs to aid in the explanation of the concentration of violence in specific socio-economic groups and ecological areas.

Some questions may arise about the genesis of an assumed subculture of violence. The theoretical formulation describes what is believed to be a condition that may exist in varying manifestations from organized crime, delinquent gangs, political subdivisions, and subsets of a lower-class culture. How these variations arise and from what base, are issues that have not been raised and that would require research to describe. Moreover, the literature on the sociology of conflict, derived principally from Simmel (28), on the social psychology of conflict (29), and on the more specific topic of the sociology of violence (30) would have to be carefully examined. That there may be some universal derivatives is neither asserted nor denied. One could argue (1) that there is a biological base for aggressive behavior which may, unless conditioned against it, manifest itself in physical violence; (2) that, in Hegelian terms, each culture thesis contains its contraculture antithesis, that to develop into a central culture, nonviolence within must be a dominant theme, and that therefore a subtheme of violence in some form is an invariable consequence. We do not find either of these propositions tenable, and there is considerable evidence to contradict both.

Even without returning philosophically to a discussion of man's pre-political or pre-societal state, a more temporally localized question of genesis may be raised. The descriptions current in subcultural theorizing in general sociology or sociological criminology are limited principally to a modern urban setting, although applications of these theories could conceivably be made to the criminal machinations in such culture periods as Renaissance Florence. At present, we create no new statement of the genesis of a subculture of violence, nor do we find it necessary to adopt a single position. The beginning could be a Cohen-like negative reaction that turned into regularized, institutionalized patterns of prescription. Sufficient communication of dominant culture values, norms, goals, and means is, of course, implicitly assumed if some subset of the population is to react negatively. The existence of violent (illegitimate) means also requires that some of the goals (or symbols of goals) of the dominant culture shall have been communicated to subcultural groups in sufficient strength for them to introject and to desire them and, if thwarted in their pursuit of them, to seek them by whatever illegal means are available. The Cloward-Ohlin formulation is, in this context, an equally useful hypothesis for the genesis of a subculture of violence. Miller's idea of a "generating milieu" does not assume—or perhaps even denies—the communication of most middle-class values to the lower class. gespecially relevant to our present interest would be communication of attitudes toward the use of violence. Communication should, perhaps, be distinguished from absorption or introjection of culture values. Communication seems to imply transmission cognitively, to suggest that the recipients have conscious awareness of the existence of things. Absorption, or introjection, refers to conative aspects and goes beyond communication in its power to affect personalities. A value becomes part of the individual's attitudinal set or predisposition to act, and must be more than communicated to be an integral element in a prepotent tendency to respond to stimuli. It might be said that, both in Cohen's and in Cloward-Ohlin's conceptualizations, middle-class values are communicated but not absorbed as part of the personality or idioverse of those individuals who deviate. In Miller's schema, communication from middle to lower class is not required. A considerable degree of isolation of the latter class is even inferred, suggesting that the lower-class ethic has a developmental history and continuity of its own.

We are not prepared to assert how a subculture of violence arises. Perhaps there are several ways in different cultural settings. It may be that even within the same culture a collective conscience and allegiance to the use of violence develop into a subculture from the combination of more than one birth process, i.e. as a negative reaction to the communication of goals from the parent culture, as a positive reaction to this communication coupled with a willingness to use negative means, and as a positive absorption of an indigenous set of subcultural values that, as a system of interlocking values, are the antithesis of the main culture themes.

Whatever may be the circumstances creating any subculture at variance, the problems before us at present are those requiring more precision in defining a subculture, fuller descriptions and measurements of normative systems, and research designed to test hypotheses about subcultures through psychological, sociological, and other disciplinary methods. In the present selection we have tried to provide an outline of how some of these problems might be resolved. We have used the conceptualization of a subculture of violence as a point of theoretical departure for an integrated sociological and psychological approach to definition, description, and measurement. It now seems appropriate to examine in more detail some of the relevant theory and data on homicide and other assaultive offenses in order to show how these formulations and empirical facts may lead into and be embraced or rejected by the thesis of a subculture of violence.

REFERENCES

1. Hanan C. Selvin, 'Durkheim's *Suicide* and Problems of Empirical Research', *American Journal of Sociology* (1958) **63**:607–619.

2. Robert K. Merton, *Social Theory and Social Structure*, Glencoe, Ill.: The Free Press, 1949, pp. 131–194.

3. E. H. Powell, 'Occupational Status and Suicide: Toward a Redefinition of Anomie', *American Sociological Review* (1958) **23**:131–139. See also the latest book publication which discusses the major notions, research, and inferences of anomie: Marshall Clinard (ed.) *Anomie and Deviant Behavior: A Discussion and Critique*, New York: The Free Press of Glencoe, 1964.

4. What is meant by psychological anomie can be a number of different constructs. For example, MacIver gives a psychological definition of anomie which describes psychopathological syndromes resulting from loss of sense of social cohesion [R. M. MacIver, *The Ramparts We Guard,* New York: Macmillan, 1950]. Ansbacher (H. L. Ansbacher, 'Anomie, the Sociologist's Conception of Lack of Social Interest', *Ind. Psychol. Newsletter* (1959) **5:**11–12, 3–5) has equated this to Adler's lack of social interest [A. Adler, *Social Interest,* New York: Putnam, 1939]. Merton defines psychological anomie as a counterpart of, and not a substitute for, sociological anomie [Merton, *op. cit.*], and, indeed, it would be difficult to exclude a psychological correlate to such a pervading concept as sociological anomie. The difficulty rests with its integration into other meaningful personality constructs and with its reliable measurement. Srole's scale [L. Srole, 'Anomie, Authoritarianism and Prejudice', *American Journal of Sociology* (1959) **62:**63–67; L. Srole, 'Social Integration and Certain Corollaries: An Exploratory Study', *American Sociological Review* (1959) **21:**709–716] has had so far a very limited application and its use is difficult in groups characterized by low educational level.

For an expository analysis of anomie as a psychological concept, see Stephen H. Davol and Gunars Reimanis, 'The Role of Anomie as a Psychological Concept', *Journal of Individual Psychology* (1959) **15:**215–225.

5. Marvin E. Wolfgang, *Patterns in Criminal Homicide,* Philadelphia, Pennsylvania: University of Pennsylvania Press, 1958.

6. A Pigliaru, *La vendetta barbaricina come ordinamento giuridico,* Milano: Giuffrè, 1959.

For an amazing report on the whole small town, Albanova, near Rome, that is devoted to the use of violence, see Giulio Frisoli, 'La pistola regalo di battesimo', *Epoca* (February 27, 1965), and Giulio Frisoli and Pietro Zullino, 'Il segreto di Albanova, *Epoca* (March 7, 1965).

7. G. Guzman Campos, O. Fals Borda, and E. Umaña Luna, *'La Violencia en Colombia: Estudio de un proceso social',* Bogotá: Tercer Mundo, 1962.

8. Wolfgang, *Patterns in Criminal Homicide,* pp. 188–189.

9. We have elsewhere, referred to the many studies of delinquency that discuss these matters. For recent items, see especially Lewis Yablonsky, *The Violent Gang,* New York: Macmillan, 1962; also, Dorothy Hayes and Russell Hogrefe, 'Group Sanction and Restraints Related to Use of Violence in Teenagers', paper read at the 41st annual meeting of the American Orthopsychiatric Association, Chicago, Illinois, March 20, 1964.

10. For an especially insightful comment that aided our thinking on this topic, see Otto Pollak, 'Our Social Values and Juvenile Delinquency', *The Quarterly of the Pennsylvania Association on Probation, Parole and Correction* (September, 1964) **21:**12–22.

11. There is an abundant literature on the combined topics of child-rearing practices, physical aggression, and social class. Among the earlier works, particularly useful are R. R. Sears, *Survey of Objective Studies of Psychoanalytical Concepts,* Bulletin 51, New York: Social Science Research Council, 1943; A. Davis and R. J. Havighurst, 'Racial Class and Color Difference in Child Rearing', *American Sociological Review* (1946) **11:**698–710; J. H. S. Bossard, *The Sociology of Child Development,* New York: Harper and Brothers, 1948.

Several specific references of special use in our concern with the transmission of values related to violence or physical aggression include:

Charles McArthur, 'Personality Differences Between Middle and Upper Classes', *Journal of Abnormal and Social Psychology* (1955) **50:**247–254.

Clyde R. White, 'Social Class Differences in the Use of Leisure', *American Journal of Sociology* (1955) **61:**145–151.

O. G. Brim, 'Parent-Child Relations as a Social System: I. Parent and Child Roles', *Child Development* (1957) **28:**342–364.

Joel B. Montague and Edgar G. Epps, 'Attitudes Toward Social Mobility as Revealed by Samples of Negro and White Boys', *Pacific Sociological Review* (1958) **1:**81–84.

Lawrence Kohlberg, 'Status as Perspective on Society: An Interpretation of Class Differences in Children's Moral Judgments', paper delivered at the Society for Research in Child Development Symposium on Moral Process, Bethesda, Maryland, March 21, 1959.

Melvin L. Kohn, 'Social Class and Parent-Child Relationships: An Interpretation', *American Journal of Sociology* (1963) **68:**471–480.

Louis Kriesberg, 'The Relationship Between Socio-Economic Rank and Behavior', *Social Problems* (1963) **10**:334–353.

Hyman Rodman, 'The Lower-Class Value Stretch', *Social Forces* (1963) **42**:205–215.

John C. Leggett, 'Uprootedness and Working Class Consciousness', *American Journal of Sociology* (1963) **68**:682–692.

C. R. Roger, 'Toward a Modern Approach to Values: The Valuing Process in the Mature Person', *Journal of Abnormal and Social Psychology* (1964), **68**:160–167.

Leigh Minturn and William W. Lamberts, *Mothers of Six Cultures*, New York: Wiley, 1964, especially Chapter 7, 'Aggression Training: Mother-Directed Aggression', pp. 136–162.

Kathryn P. Johnson and Gerald R. Leslie, 'Methodological Notes on Research in Childrearing and Social Class', paper presented to the annual meeting of the American Sociological Association, Montreal, August, 1964.

Excellent summaries of the literature in current works are found in Paul Henry Mussen (ed.) *Handbook of Research Methods in Child Development,* New York: Wiley, 1960; in Martin L. Holffman and Lois W. Hoffman, *Review of Child Development Research,* Vol. I, New York: Russell Sage Foundation, 1964; and in the rich bibliography noted in John J. Honigmann and Richard J. Preston, 'Recent Developments in Culture and Personality', Supplement to *The Annals of the American Academy of Political and Social Science* (July, 1964) **354**:153–162.

All of the recent literature we have been able to examine from anthropology, psychology, and sociology buttressed the general position of our thesis regarding class, punishment, and aggression.

12. Martin Gold, 'Suicide, Homicide and the Socialization of Aggression', *American Journal of Sociology* (May, 1958) **63**:651–661.

13. *Ibid.*

14. This is different from the 'strength of the relational system' discussed by Henry and Short in their provocative analysis (Andrew F. Henry and James F. Short, Jr., *Suicide and Homicide,* Glencoe, Ill.: The Free Press, 1954, pp. 16–18, 91–92, 124–125). Relative to the Henry and Short suggestion, see Wolfgang, *Patterns in Criminal Homicide,* pp. 278–279. The attempt of Gibbs and Martin to measure Durkheim's reference to 'degree of integration' is a competent analysis of the problem, but a subculture of violence integrated around a given value item or value system may require quite different indices of integration than those to which these authors refer (Jack P. Gibbs and Walter T. Martin, 'A Theory of Status Integration and Its Relationship to Suicide, *American Sociological Review* (April, 1958) **23**:140–147.

15. Robert J. Smith, 'The Japanese World Community: Norms, Sanctions, and Ostracism', *American Anthropologist* (1961) **63**:522–533. Withdrawal from the group may be by the deviant's own design and desire, or by response to the reaction of the group, Cf. Robert A. Dentler and Kai T. Erikson, 'The Functions of Deviance in Groups', *Social Problems* (Fall 1959) **7**:98–107.

16. Ross Stagner, *Psychology of Industrial Conflict,* New York: Wiley, 1956.

17. See, for example, John Paul Scott, *Aggression,* Chicago: University of Chicago Press, 1958, pp. 44–64.

18. For the concept of subculture to have psychological validity, psychologically meaningful differences should, of course, be evident in subjects belonging to the subculture of violence. From a diagnostic point of view, a number of signs and indicators, of both psychometric and projective type, can be used. The differential perception of violent stimuli can be used as an indicator. Partial studies in this direction are those of Shelley and Toch (E. L. V. Shelley and H. Toch, 'The Perception of Violence As an Indicator of Adjustment in Institutionalized Offenders', *Journal of Criminal Law, Criminology and Police Science,* (1962) **53**:463–469).

19. The Philadelphia study (Wolfgang, *Patterns in Criminal Homicide*) showed that 65 percent of the offenders and 47 percent of the victims had a previous police record of arrests and that 75 percent of these arrests were for aggravated assaults. Here, then, is a situation in homicide often not unlike that of combat in which two persons committed to the value of violence come together and in which chance often dictates the identity of the slayer and of the slain.

20. A recent study (L. G. Schultz, 'Why the Negro Carries Weapons', *Journal of Criminal Law, Criminol-*

ogy and Police Science (1962) **53**:476–483) on weapon-carrying suggests that this habit is related, within the colored population, to lower-class status, rural origin from the South, and prior criminal record.

21.   As previously mentioned, differential reactions to conditioning may be the cause of differential adherence to the subculture by equally exposed subjects.

22.   Alternative hypotheses make use of the concept of differential association (Edwin H. Sutherland and Donald E. Cressey, *Principles of Criminology,* Philadelphia: Lippincott, 1955).

23.   Differential identification has been presented as a more psychologically meaningful alternative to simple association (Daniel Glaser, 'Criminality Theories and Behavioral Images', *American Journal of Sociology* (1956) **5**:433–444).

24.   A. H. Buss, *The Psychology of Aggression,* New York: Wiley, 1961, pp. 1–2.

25.   *Ibid.,* pp. 2–4.

26.   *Ibid.,* Chapter I, *passim.*

27.   For an analysis of relevant literature on diagnostic psychological instruments, see Buss, *op. cit.,* Chapters VIII and IX. For discussion of a preventive psychiatric system, see Leon D. Hankoff, 'Prevention of Violence', paper read at the annual meeting of the Association for the Psychiatric Treatment of Offenders, New York, May 7, 1964.

28.   *The Sociology of Georg Simmel* (translated, edited, and with an introduction by Kurt H. Wolff), Glencoe, Ill.: The Free Press, 1950; *Georg Simmel, 1858–1918* (edited by Kurt H. Wolff), Columbus, Ohio: Ohio State University Press, 1959; Georg Simmel. *Conflict and the Web of Group Affiliations* (translated by Kurt H. Wolff and Reinhard Bendix), New York: The Free Press of Glencoe, 1964 paperback edition; Lewis Coser, *The Functions of Social Conflict,* Glencoe, Ill.: The Free Press, 1956; *The Nature of Human Conflict,* (edited by Elton B. McNeil) Englewood Cliffs, N.J.: Prentice-Hall, 1965.

29.   The issues of *The Journal of Conflict Resolution* are, of course, pertinent. Relative to our main concern with violence, see especially Rolf Dahrendorf, 'Toward a Theory of Social Conflict', *Journal of Conflict Resolution* (1958) **2**:170–183; the entire issue entitled 'The Anthropology of Conflict', *Journal of Conflict Resolution* (1961), Volume V, Number 1.

30.   For an early provocative discussion of violence from a sociological viewpoint and as a tool of social protest against the Establishment, as a proletarian technique to threaten the existing institutions of society, see Georges Sorel, *Reflections on Violence* (the original French text appeared in 1906).

For recent general references to the sociology of violence, see:

Joseph S. Roucek, 'The Sociology of Violence', *Journal of Human Relations* (1957) **5**:9–21.

David Marlowe, 'Commitment, Contract, Group Boundaries and Conflict', reprinted from *Science and Psychoanalysis* (Masserman), New York: Grune & Stratton, 1963, pp. 43–55.

E. V. Walter, 'Violence and the Process of Terror', *American Sociological Review* (1964) **29**:248–257.

Jessie Bernard, 'Some Current Conceptualizations in the Field of Conflict', *American Journal of Sociology* (1965) **70**:442–454.

Austin L. Porterfield, *Cultures of Violence,* Fort Worth, Texas: Leo Potishman, 1965.

There is a growing concern in peace research with what has been called 'the sociology of nonviolence'. For a review of these ideas, see Martin Oppenheimer, 'Towards a Sociology of Nonviolence', paper read at the Eastern Sociological Society meeting, Boston, April 11, 1964.

16. The Empirical Status of the Subculture of Violence Thesis

HOWARD S. ERLANGER

IN THE STUDY OF ADULT INTERPERSONAL VIO-
lence (which may be defined as acts of physical
aggression directed at persons, excluding acts
under the aegis of, or directed against, political,
parental, or other authority), one of the most
important and most often cited theoretical
statements has been the "subculture of violence"
thesis (Wolfgang, 1958; Wolfgang and Ferracuti, 1967). According to Wolfgang and Ferracuti, violence results from adherence to a set
of values which supports and encourages its expression. These values are seen as being in
conflict with but not totally in opposition to
those of the dominant culture. It is said that
within the subculture, various stimuli such as a
jostle, a slightly derogatory remark, or the appearance of a weapon in the hands of an adversary are perceived differently than in the dominant culture; in the subculture they evoke a
combative reaction.

Although violence obviously is not and cannot
be used continuously, Wolfgang and Ferracuti
see the requirement to be violent as a norm governing a wide variety of situations. They judge
the subcultural theme to be "penetrating and
diffuse" and argue that violations of the subcultural norm are punished within the subculture.
Adherence to the norm is not necessarily viewed
as illicit conduct, and "a carrier and user of violence will [generally] not be burdened by con-

scious guilt . . . [and] even law-abiding members
of the local subcultural area may not view various expressions of violence as menacing or immoral" (Wolfgang and Ferracuti, 1967:161).

When preparing the 1967 volume, Wolfgang
and Ferracuti could locate no data on the distribution of values regarding violence, so they
were forced to rely on inferences from available
data on criminal acts of interpersonal violence.
Since criminal statistics indicate that the groups
with the highest rates of homicide are males,
nonwhites, lower- and working-class whites, and
young adults, it is, therefore, among these
groups that "we should find in most intense degree a subculture of violence" (Wolfgang and
Ferracuti, 1967:153). They acknowledge that
their reasoning here is circular, and they agree
that individual data on values are necessary for
an adequate test of the theory.

In the years since the subculture of violence
thesis was first introduced, there have been a
variety of studies which directly or indirectly
bring data to bear on the thesis. In the study of
juvenile delinquency, for example, there has
been a related controversy over the value system
of adolescent gangs. W. Miller (1958) has argued that these gangs reflect the "focal concerns" of lower-class culture, which he sees as
including "toughness" and "excitement." However, the analysis of gang values by Short and
Strodtbeck (1965) failed to confirm the existence of these focal concerns, and a study by
Lerman (1968) has questioned the existence of a
distinctive lower-class culture reflected in gangs.

▶SOURCE: "The Empirical Status of the Subculture of Violence
Thesis," Social Problems (1974), 22(2):280–292. Reprinted by
permission.

In addition, various studies (e.g., Short and Strodtbeck, 1965; Jansyn, 1966) have concluded that gang activity is related more to group processes than to a violence oriented subculture,[1] and later work by Miller and his colleagues does not indicate that physical aggression is an important part of lower-class gang life (Miller *et al.*, 1961; Miller, 1966).

Some studies, such as those of Kobrin *et al.* (1967) and Yablonsky (1962) have found that status within the gang is at least in part based on the criteria outlined by Wolfgang and Ferracuti, but Yablonsky has also emphasized the fluid nature of group membership and the limited ability of leaders to sanction members who do not conform (see also Matza, 1964; Short and Strodtbeck, 1965). Moreover, it is important to remember that the existence of violence as a criterion of status in gangs in low-income neighborhoods is insufficient to establish the existence of such norms among nongang juveniles in those neighborhoods, especially since it is generally the most extreme gangs that have been studied. When the whole juvenile population is studied, the patterns can be quite different (Hirschi, 1969).

In the study of adult interpersonal violence, research has been much more limited. Various studies and texts in sociology (e.g., Amir, 1971; Clinard, 1973; Schur, 1969) and social psychology (e.g., Akers, 1973; Toch, 1969) have stressed the subcultural view, but they have not used individual data to support their arguments. The idea of a subculture of violence is conspicuous by its *absence* in various well known ethnographic studies of adult lower-class communities (e.g., Liebow, 1967; Suttles, 1968;

Whyte, 1955). Since these writers are not explicitly concerned with the issue, the absence of discussion is not definitive evidence against the thesis. It does, however, suggest that violence is not a major theme in the groups studied.[2]

Few systematic studies of class differences in values or attitudes among adults have been reported in the literature, and some of the most often cited are quite dated. Most studies that do exist do not specifically deal with low-income groups; the lower class is either omitted or combined with the working class for analysis.[3] Insofar as the present author can determine, until the late 1960s no survey data on the values or attitudes of adults toward violence were available.

In a recent paper, Ball-Rokeach (1973) analyzes responses to the Rokeach Value Survey given by males with various degrees of participation in violence. She finds no important differences in the ranking of 18 "terminal values" or of 18 "instrumental values" by men classified as having no, a "moderate," or a "high" degree of participation in violence at any time in their life. She reports that controls for education and income, which are crucial for the examination of a subculture which is said to be class-based, do not affect the findings. A comparison of prisoners convicted of violent crimes and persons con-

---

[1]Some critics of this manuscript have held that the group process material in the Short and Strodtbeck work supports the subculture of violence thesis. Although the material may be open to varying interpretations, Short reports that he "never felt that our data were supportive of the subculture of violence thesis" (personal communication). Short feels that the group process mechanisms are related to subcultural variations, but that the subculture of violence thesis is not particularly helpful in explaining the outcomes they observed.

[2]One anthropological study that does recount many violent incidents is Lewis's biography of the Rios family in Puerto Rico and New York. But although a degree of machismo is clearly present, violence is often criticized by the family. Most of the family members feel hurt by the violence and deprivation they experienced as children, and many resolve to do better with their children. In an earlier discussion of poverty in Mexico, Lewis (1961) lists "frequent resort to violence" as an element of the culture of poverty, while in *La Vida* (1966) he talks more generally of lack of impulse control. In neither case does he say that the culture requires acts of violence.

[3]One relevant study which combines class data in this way is Schneider and Lysgaard's (1953) work on the "deferred gratification pattern." Although the findings of class differences are open to criticism (see Miller, 1965), note that at any rate the differences in the use of physical violence were small and were considered unimpressive by the authors.

victed of non-violent crimes also found no important differences in the ranking of values. Although there are some difficulties with the data used in these studies,[4] they are the only recent materials which attempt to measure directly value hierarchies; and they yield findings incompatible with the subculture of violence thesis.

Attitudinal data collected for the President's Commission on the Causes and Prevention of Violence in 1968 also call the subcultural thesis into question. In a national survey, for which questionnaire construction was supervised by Ball-Rokeach, respondents were asked about their general approval of the use of physical aggression in certain kinds of interpersonal interactions; those who gave this general approval were then asked about four or five more specific situations. The general approval questions asked whether there were "any situations that you can imagine" in which the respondent would approve of such acts as a husband slapping his wife's face; a husband shooting his wife; a man punching (or choking) an adult male stranger; one teenage boy punching (or knifing) another. Because these items and their follow-ups are so general, acceptance of them does not imply membership in a subculture of violence. But conversely, it seems reasonable to assume that persons who are in such a subculture would find it quite easy to support many of the items, especially those dealing with relatively minor forms of violence. If levels of support in low-status groups are relatively low, then the finding can be taken as suggestive evidence contrary to the thesis.[5]

Preliminary analysis of these data has been reported elsewhere (Baker and Ball, 1969; Stark and McEvoy, 1970). The present author has undertaken a detailed analysis of these data, using cross tabulation and multiple regression. My analysis does not alter the basic preliminary findings, which showed an absence of major differences by race or class[6] in approval of interpersonal violence, and in general a low rate of approval. For example, marital fighting is often thought to be a characteristic of the "subculture of violence," but when approval of a husband slapping his wife's face is examined, only 25 percent of white and 37 percent of black married men aged 18–60 say that they can imagine *any* situation in which they would approve, with no systematic variation by income or education. (There is an age effect, with men over 40 being sharply lower in approval, but it is independent of race, education, or income.) Moreover, both the level of support and the variation by race decrease markedly when follow-up items are examined. A similar pattern is found for items relating to approval of a man choking an adult male stranger; while on items relating to punching an adult male stranger, approval by whites is higher than that by black.

Attitudes toward machismo can be gauged by an index made up of items relating to approval of teenage fighting. The items on this index seem to be very easy to support—"Are there any situations you can imagine in which you would approve of a teenage boy punching another teenage boy?" If yes, or not sure, "would you approve if he didn't like the other boy?" . . . "if

[4]On the dependent variable, there are weaknesses in the indicators of the values supporting violence. "An Exciting Life," "Pleasure," "Social Recognition," and being "Courageous" are examples of the indicators of the machismo concept; yet the phrases accompanying these and each of the other value choices suggest a very broad interpretation, e.g., "a stimulating and active life;" "an enjoyable, leisurely life;" "respect, admiration;" "standing up for your beliefs." On the independent variable, in the national study, the "degree of participation in violence" includes both aggression and victimization, is based on the variety rather than the extent of experience, and weighs childhood incidents equally with any recent ones. Even if a respondent's aggression were being estimated with some accuracy, the violence may have occurred long before the contemporary value patterns were established. Also the studies apparently do not control for age or race.

[5]Of course, this does not mean that a person's response to the general item directly indicates his attitude or action in some actual instance in which he may become (or have been) involved in.

[6]Social class is indicated by income and education. Occupational data were not coded.

he had been ridiculed and picked on by the other boy?" . . . "if he had been challenged by the other boy to a fist fight?" . . . "if he had been hit by the other boy?" The index was constructed by scoring a yes response to each of the five items as 2, a not sure as 1, and a no as 0. The range is thus 0–10.

Whites tend to score higher than blacks on this index; and when parents with at least one teenage child are analyzed separately, only 12 percent of black parents, compared to 38 percent of white parents, score above six on the ten point index. Among whites, parents with low-income score lower than those with high-income.

If a subculture of violence existed among low-status adults, or if low-status adults valued the expression of violence among their children, the general trend on this index would be expected to be the reverse of that found, and the rate of support at the high end of the index would have been much higher. The data and conclusions say nothing about the extent of fighting among lower-class or black teenagers; and the questions of unintentional socialization through the latent effects of parental behavior, or of socialization to violence by teenage peers, remain open. It may well be that lower-class or black teenagers are involved in a disproportionate number of fights, and the lower rate of approval by their parents could be a result of the frequency or seriousness of these fights. But such a situation would only support the conclusion that lower-class parents in general, and black parents in particular, do not especially like the idea of their children fighting and that teenage fighting is probably not a product of an adult value system emphasizing violence.

SOME NEW DATA: PEER ESTEEM AND PSYCHOLOGICAL CORRELATES OF FIGHTING

In addition to the investigation of verbal support for a "subculture of violence," support and sanction in peer interactions can be examined.

Wolfgang and Ferracuti (1967:160) argue that nonviolent members of a subcultural group are subject to great pressure to conform, that sanction is an integral part of the existence of a norm, and that "alienation of some kind . . . seems to be a form of punitive action most feasible to this subculture." It seems to follow that, conversely, persons who adhere to the values would be more likely than those who do not to be liked, respected, and accorded high status in the group. Data from a 1969 survey of black and white males aged 21–64 in Milwaukee, Wisconsin, give some evidence on this point.[7] Physical aggression is indicated by the item "How often do you get in angry fist fights with other men?" (never, almost never, sometimes, often); perceived esteem accorded by others is indicated by two items, "How do you compare with most men you know on being respected and listened to by other people?" (five point code, from much worse to much better) and "How do you compare with most men you know on being well liked by other people and having lots of friends?" (same code). Since the esteem items are doublebarreled, they are less precise than desirable. However they are useful for exploratory purposes.

Because the subcultural hypothesis posits statistical interaction, separate analyses were made for the "lower class" (income less than $5,000) and "nonpoor" (income over $5,000), and for blacks and whites. As a result, low-income whites have a small sample size and detailed analysis cannot be carried out for this subsample.

The bottom row of Table I shows that the pattern of fighting by race and income group is consistent with the subcultural thesis; blacks are

[7]The data are from an ongoing study of correlates of self-esteem directed by Russell Middleton (sponsored by the National Science Foundation); I am grateful to him for permission to analyze and report the relationships presented here. The interviews were conducted by the Wisconsin Survey Research Laboratory and respondents and interviewers were matched by race. An area probability sample for the Milwaukee city limits was used.

Table I. Effect of Fighting on Feeling "Respected and Listened to by Others"

	White			Black		
	< $5,000	≥ $5,000	Total	< $5,000	≥ $5,000	Total
Hypothesized Relation	Positive	Strong Neg.		Strong Pos.	Positive	
Zero order r	−.15	.02		−.25	−.18[b]	
Beta, net of social desirability index (SDI)	−.05	.02		−.22	−.18[b]	
Beta, net of SDI, occupation and age	a	.08		.02	−.14	
(N)	(15)	(207)	(222)	(51)	(184)	(235)
% who fight	47%	19%	21%	39%	29%	31%

[a] Because of small sample size, this coefficient cannot be computed.
[b] Indicates beta significant at .05 or better.

more likely to fight than whites, and the poor are more likely to fight than the nonpoor.[8] (Contrary to expectations, poor whites are more likely to fight than poor blacks, but the percentage for whites is unreliable because of the low N.) However, this pattern is also consistent with several other non-subcultural theories, such as those of Henry and Short (1954), Coser (1963), Gold (1958), or Cloward and Ohlin (1960). The important question here is whether men who fight are accorded (or at least see themselves as being accorded) more esteem by others.

Although the subculture of violence thesis does not make a prediction about the overall association between race or economic status and peer respect or high status among peers, it predicts that the basis of the respect of status will be different in different groups. Subcultural theory would seem to predict a relatively strong positive correlation between the peer esteem

item and fighting for low-income blacks, a somewhat smaller (but at least statistically significant) positive correlation for low-income whites and nonpoor blacks,[9] and a relatively strong negative correlation for nonpoor whites.

Table I shows the relationship between fighting and perceiving "respect by others," in terms of zero order correlations and as the net effect (beta) of fighting on perceived esteem by others, controlling first for social desirability bias[10] and then for social desirability bias, occu-

[8] The differences by class and race reported for the samples here are larger than those found on items in the Violence Commission survey, which asked retrospectively about acts of physical aggression. See Baker and Ball (1969) or Stark and McEvoy (1980).

[9] An alternative prediction would be that, because of strong norms against violence among the "black bourgeoisie," the correlation between violence and esteem would be negative at least for those nonpoor blacks in white-collar jobs.

[10] "Social desirability bias" is indicated by a five item adaptation of Crowne and Marlow's (1964) scale, which includes items which are either socially desirable but probably untrue or probably true but socially undesirable. (For example, True or False: "I never hesitate to go out of my way to help someone in trouble.") Of the five items, three were worded such that agreement was socially desirable, and two worded such that disagreement was socially desirable. Respondents scoring high on this scale are somewhat more likely to report that they do not get in fights and that they are held in high esteem by others.

Table II. Effect of Fighting on Feeling "Well Liked by Other People and Having Lots of Friends"
By race and income, with controls Milwaukee men, aged 21-64, 1969

	White		Black	
	< $5,000	≥ $5,000	< $5,000	≥ $5,000
Hypothesized Relation	Positive	Strong Neg.	Strong Pos.	Positive
Zero order r	.22	−.01	−.12	−.01
Beta, net of social desirability index (SDI)	.21	−.01	−.09	−.01
Beta, net of SDI, occupation and age	a	−.03	.16	−.04
(N)	(15)	(207)	(51)	(184)

[a]Because of small sample size this coefficient cannot be computed.

NB: None of the coefficients in the table are significant at .05 or better.

pation, and age.[11] The findings are inconsistent with the predictions outlined, with the betas and zero order correlations being either very close to zero or having a sign opposite that predicted.[12] Table II shows the relationship between fighting and perceptions of being "liked by others," in terms of zero order correlations and the net effect of fighting on perceived esteem. Here the findings are somewhat as predicted by subcultural theory, with low-income blacks and low-income whites showing a positive net effect of fighting on perceived esteem. But the former beta is rather small; and although the latter is larger, neither of them is statistically significant. Moreover, for nonpoor white men, the predicted strong negative correlation does not appear.

[11]Both occupation and age were indicated by sets of dummy variables. For occupation, the categories were white collar, blue collar, farm; for age they were 21–25, 26–30, 31–35, 36–45, 46–55, 56–64.

[12]A competing interpretation of the zero and near zero relationships in Tables 1 and 2 is that they mask a strong reciprocal causality. The possibility of such reciprocal causality, which would be consistent with the subcultural thesis, has been explored for blacks using two stage least squares analysis (Erlanger and Winsborough, 1975). The results of that analysis support the conclusion in the text.

Although the findings here do not refute the subculture of violence thesis, taken as a whole they cast doubt on it. To the extent that violence is important to low-income or black men, and to the extent that a subcultural norm is being enforced through ostracism or peer rebuke, we would expect to find a relatively strong positive relationship between fighting and perceived general esteem. Similarly, if a counternorm of nonviolence is important in the white middle class, a strong negative relationship should have been found. Overall the data here are not consistent with this predicted pattern; and if we take statistical significance as a minimal criteria of support, none of the predictions of subcultural theory is supported. It is possible, of course, that the available indicators mask the relationships predicted. For example, perhaps responses to fighting draw approval or rebuke as predicted, but these responses do not affect the overall evaluation perceived by the violent person. In this case, however, we would have to conclude that violence is not as important to the subculture as hypothesized, for as the sanction gets stronger—e.g., ostracism—consequences for general esteem should follow.

As a corollary to the analysis of violence and

Table III. Relationship Between Fighting and Happiness
Milwaukee men, aged 21-64, 1969

	White		Black	
	< $5,000	≥ $5,000	< $5,000	≥ $5,000
Hypothesized Relation	Positive	Strong Neg.	Strong Pos.	Positive
Zero order r	−.09	−.07	−.36*	−.19*
Partial r, net of social desirability index (SDI)	.08	−.07	−.33*	−.19*
Partial r, net of SDI, occupation and age	a	−.09	−.30*	−.18*
(N)	(15)	(207)	(51)	(184)

ᵃBecause of small sample size this coefficient cannot be computed.
*Indicates partial r significant at .05 or better.

esteem, the relationship between violence and feeling of well being can be examined. The subcultural thesis holds that violence is normal behavior and is the product of normal group processes. Similarly, it posits that violent people do not feel guilty about their actions. An empirical inquiry could examine psychiatric records or administer various personality tests (see, e.g., Ferracuti, Lazzari, and Wolfgang, 1970); alternatively, various measures of psychological adjustment can be included in an interview schedule or questionnaire. One such measure is an index of happiness which can be constructed from items in the Milwaukee survey.[13] It would seem that outside the subculture men who are violent would be less likely to be happy than would non-violent men, both because they were receiving negative sanctions for their violence and because in this group it would be the more marginal men who would be violent. By contrast, within the subculture, happiness would be positively correlated with violence, since vio-

lence is posited as not being a pathological condition and since non-violent men are hypothesized to be negatively sanctioned. Table III shows that fighting is negatively correlated with happiness for all four subgroups, and (statistically) significantly so for blacks. Except for nonpoor whites, these findings run directly counter to the predictions of the subcultural thesis. And even for nonpoor whites, the finding of a correlation even less negative than for blacks can also be considered evidence contrary to the thesis.[14]

DISCUSSION

Although much suggestive evidence on the subculture of violence exists, there is a clear need for further research in this area. Methodologically, this research should be designed so that there is adequate representation of minorities and of poor whites for analysis; and it should make some attempt to cover both "streetcorner men" and more traditional householders (cf.

[13]The items were these: "On the whole, how happy would you say you are now?" "On the whole, how happy would you say you are now compared with other men you know?" "How often do you feel very discouraged and depressed?" "How often do you get the feeling that life is not worth living?" Each item had four possible responses.

[14]Because of the uncertain direction of causation, partial correlation coefficients may be a more appropriate measure of association here than regression coefficients. However, use of partial r's would not have changed the findings.

Hannerz, 1969). A major limitation of existing survey data is that they are based only on persons in households (cf. Parsons, 1972). Another is that the surveys do not have concentrated samples in a given neighborhood. These difficulties are alleviated, but not erased, by the data from the field studies.

Substantively, work needs to be done on establishing the pervasiveness of a subculture. At least three quite different degrees of pervasiveness may exist. In the most extreme case, a large majority of the demographic group presumed to have the subcultural trait would exhibit it in some way, as opposed to a minority of members of other demographic groups. In this case, one could characterize the demographic group as subcultural. A more limited pervasiveness exists when the trait is exhibited by a minority of a particular demographic group, as compared to a virtual absence in other groups; this would constitute a subculture *within* a demographic group. Finally, some analysts would consider a small but statistically significant difference between demographic groups as evidence of a subculture. However, it seems incorrect to characterize such a subculture as being located in the demographic group with greater support for the value, or to characterize that demographic group as a subculture. Rather, the subculture would have to be defined as the group of people who hold the value, irrespective of their demographic group.[15]

These differences in the pervasiveness of subcultures have important implications for the public imagery of social groups. In the case of the subculture of violence, if class or racial groups can in fact be characterized as being different (or if findings are presented as though they could), popular conceptions of widespread

pathology among non-whites and low-income whites would be supported. By contrast the exisence of a subculture within a class or racial group, or of value differences that are statistically significant but not large, would be more consonant with the view that there is wide variation in the values, needs, and problems of the poor and of nonwhites.

Future research should also focus more closely on the precise content of supposed subcultural differences.[16] It is possible, for example, that rather than a "subculture of violence," something like a "subculture of masculinity" exists, with violence being only one of many possible outlets, and not necessarily the preferred one. In this case, violence may result from the blocking of alternative opportunities to exhibit "machismo" (cf. Miller, 1966). Another possibility is that the use of liquor may be part of a broader social configuration which generates situations conducive to violence. A value system which sanctions or even encourages either drunken brawls or wild behavior on certain special occasions would not necessarily be the same as one which requires "quick resort to physical combat as a measure of daring, courage, or defense of status" in everyday interaction.[17]

Finally, the origins, permanence, and relationship to social structure must also be given careful consideration in future research. These considerations are especially important in the

---

[15]Also, as Rodman (1963) suggests, this case might be better understood as one of a variation on a common cultural theme, not as a tension between the values of a dominant culture and a subculture. Of course, even if such a difference is not considered subcultural, it may still be descriptively interesting and important in the explanation of violence.

[16]This can probably best be done by beginning with relatively unstructured in-depth interviews with informants. A move in this direction is made by Toch (1969), who conducted intensive interviews with both convicts and policemen who had frequently engaged in assault. But even here the subcultural thesis is drawn from the literature rather than grounded in the accounts of those interviewed.

[17]Similar considerations hold for the question of the existence of a subculture of violence in the American South. Many writers have noted the quite disproportionately high rate of homicide in the South, and recently Gastil (1971), Hackney (1969), and Reed (1972) have argued that this divergence can be explained by regional differences in the acceptability of violence. But again, the exact content of the hypothesized subculture is generally unclear, and data do not support the application of the subculture of violence thesis to the South (Erlanger, 1975).

formation of social policy (cf. Banfield, 1968; Lewis *et al.*, 1969; Liebow, 1971; Valentine, 1968).

CONCLUSION

Although the subculture of violence thesis has received a certain measure of acceptance in the field, a wide variety of evidence suggests that it is questionable. All of the data available have limitations of various sorts, and the thesis cannot be said to have been definitively tested. On balance, however, more of available evidence is inconsistent with the thesis than consistent with it.

At this time we do not know how important a deviant value system is in explaining violence in the United States;[18] and, if it exists, we do not know whether such a value system can be said to be found predominantly within the black or low-income white communities or whether it can be said to be relatively independent of social structure. But there is enough evidence to conclude that these groups are not *characteristically* different from the dominant society in their rate of approval of the use of physical aggression. This conclusion, along with a growing empirical literature on other aspects of the lives of poor and black (and other minority) persons in the United States, is compatible with the view that the social and economic deprivations experienced by members of these groups are primarily the result of social structural factors, rather than the product of group pathology (cf. Goodwin, 1972; Institute for Social Research, 1974; Kriesberg, 1970; Shiller, 1973).

---

[18]This analysis does not address Wolfgang and Ferracuti's contention that a subculture of violence exists in Colombia, Sardinia, Mexico, Albania, and Albanova, Italy. The case of Sardinia is explored in more detail in Ferracuti *et al.* (1970), who find some evidence in support of the hypothesis but concludes that "the subculture of violence in Sardinia is limited to violent offenders" (1970:110). This suggests that although it may be that violent offenders in Sardinia receive support for their actions from a limited group, Sardinia itself cannot be characterized as embracing a subculture of violence.

REFERENCES

Akers, Ronald L.
1973   Deviant Behavior. A Social Learning Approach. Belmont: Wadsworth Publishing

Amir, Menachem
1971   Patterns in Forcible Rape. Chicago: University of Chicago Press.

Baker, Robert K. and Sandra J. Ball
1969   Mass Media and Violence; Report to the National Commission on Causes and Prevention of Violence. Washington, D.C.: U.S. Government Printing Office.

Ball-Rokeach, Sandra J.
1973   Values and Violence: A Test of the Subculture of Violence Thesis. American Sociological Review 38:6 (December) pp. 736–49.

Banfield, Edward C.
1968   The Unheavenly City. Boston: Little, Brown.

Clinard, Marshall B.
1973   Sociology of Deviant Behavior. New York: Holt, Rinehard, and Winston.

Cloward, Richard A. and Lloyd Ohlin
1960   Delinquency and Opportunity. New York: The Free Press.

Coser, Lewis A.
1963   "Violence and the social structure." Science and Psychoanalysis 6:30–42. Reprinted in Shalom Endleman (ed.), Violence in the Streets. Chicago: Quadrangle (1969).

Crain, Robert L. and Carol Sachs Weisman
1972   Discrimination, Personality, and Achievement. New York: Seminar Press.

Crowne, Douglas P. and David Marlowe
1964   The Approval Motive. New York: John Wiley.

Ferracuti, Franco, Renato Lazzari, and Marvin E. Wolfgang
1970   "A Study of the Subculture of Violence Thesis," in Ferracuti *et al.*, Violence in Sardinia. Rome: Mario Bulzoni, editor.

Gastil, Raymond D.
1971   "Homicide and a regional culture of violence." American Sociological Review 36 (June): 412–27.

Gold, Martin
1958   "Suicide, homicide, and socialization of aggression." American Journal of Sociology 63(May): 651–61.

Goodwin, Leonard
1972   Do the Poor Want to Work? Washington, D.C.: Brookings Institution.

Hackney, Sheldon
1969   "Southern Violence," in Hugh Davis Graham and Ted Robert Gurr (eds.), History of Violence in America. Report of the Task Force of the President's Commission on Causes and Prevention of Violence. New York: Bantam Books. 505–28.

Hannerz, Ulf
1969   Soulside: Inquiries into Ghetto Culture and Community. New York: Columbia University Press.

Henry, Andrew and James F. Short
1954   Suicide and Homicide. New York: The Free Press.

Hirschi, Travis
1969   Causes of Delinquency. Berkeley and Loss Angeles: The University of California Press.

Institute for Social Research
1974   The Changing Status of Five Thousand American Families: Highlights from the Panel Study of Income Dynamics. Mimeo. Ann Arbor: The University of Michigan.

Jansyn, Leon R., Jr.
1966   "Solidarity and delinquency in a street corner group." American Sociological Review 31(October): 600–14.

Kobrin, Solomon, Joseph Puntil, and Emil Peluso
1967   "Criteria of status among street groups." Journal of Research in Crime and Delinquency 4(January).

Kriesberg, Louis
1970   Mothers in Poverty: A Study of Fatherless Families. Chicago: Aldine.

Lerman, Paul
1968   "Individual values, peer values, and subcultural delinquency." American Sociological Review 33(April): 219–35.

Lewis, Oscar
1961   Children of Sanchez. New York: Vintage.
1966   La Vida: A Puerto Rican Family in the Culture of Poverty. San Juan and New York: Random House.
1969   et al., Review Symposium: Culture and Poverty (Charles A. Valentine). Current Anthropology 10(April, June): 189–201.

Liebow, Elliot
1967   Talley's Corner. Boston: Little, Brown.
1971   "Comment on Miller's Paper," pp. 131–36 in J. Alan Winter (ed.), The Poor. Grand Rapids, Michigan: W. B. Eerdmans.

Matza, David
1964   Delinquency and Drift. New York: John Wiley.

Miller, S. M., Arthur Seagull, and Frank Riessman
1965   "The Deferred Gratification Pattern: A Critical Appraisal," in Louis Ferman et al., Poverty in America. Ann Arbor: University of Michigan Press.

Miller, Walter B.
1958   "Lower class culture as a generating milieu of gang delinquency." Journal of Social Issues 14(Summer): 5–19.
1961   et al., "Aggression in a boy's street-corner group." Psychiatry 24(November): 283–98.
1966   "Violent crimes in city gangs." Annals of American Academy of Political and Social Science 364(March): 96–112.

Mulvihill, Donald J. and Melvin Tumin
1969   Crimes of Violence. Staff Report to the National Commission on Causes and Prevention of Violence. Vols. 11, 12, and 13. Washington, D.C.: U.S. Government Printing Office.

Parsons, Carole W. (ed.)
1972   America's Uncounted People. Washington, D.C.: National Academy of Sciences.

Reed, John S.
1972   The Enduring South: Subcultural Persistence in Mass Society. Lexington, Massachusetts: D. C. Heath.

Rodman, Hyman
1963   "The lower class value stretch." Social Forces 42(December): 205–15.

Schneider, Louis and Sverre Lysgaard
  1953   "The deferred gratification pattern: A preliminary study." American Sociological Review 18(April): 142–49.

Schur, Edwin
  1969   Our Criminal Society. Englewood Cliffs, New Jersey: Prentice-Hall.

Schiller, Bradley R.
  1973   "Empirical studies of welfare dependency: A survey." Journal of Human Resources 8(Supplement): 19–32.

Short, James F. and Fred L. Strodtbeck
  1965   Group Process and Gang Delinquency. Chicago: University of Chicago Press.

Stark, Rodney and James McEvoy III
  1970   "Middle class violence," Psychology Today 4(November): 52–4, 110–12.

Suttles, Gerald D.
  1968   The Social Order of the Slum. Chicago: University of Chicago Press.

Toch, Hans H.
  1969   Violent Men. Chicago: Aldine.

Valentine, Charles A.
  1968   Culture and Poverty—Critique and Counter-Proposals. Chicago: University of Chicago Press.

Whyte, William F.
  1955   Street Corner Society, Chicago: University of Chicago Press.

Wolfgang, Marvin E.
  1958   Patterns of Criminal Homicide. Philadelphia: University of Pennsylvania Press.
  1967   and Franco Ferracuti. The Subculture of Violence, Towards an Integrated Theory in Criminology. London: Tavistock-Social Science Paperbacks.

Yablonsky, Lewis
  1962   The Violent Gang. New York: Macmillan.

17. Lower Class Culture and Gang Delinquency

WALTER B. MILLER

THE ETIOLOGY OF DELINQUENCY HAS LONG BEEN A controversial issue, and is particularly so at present. As new frames of reference for explaining human behavior have been added to traditional theories, some authors have adopted the practice of citing the major postulates of each school of thought as they pertain to delinquency, and going on to state that causality must be conceived in terms of the dynamic interaction of a complex combination of variables on many levels. The major sets of etiological factors currently adduced to explain delinquency are, in simplified terms, the physiological (delinquency results from organic pathology), the psychodynamic (delinquency is a "behavioral disorder" resulting primarily from emotional disturbance generated by a defective mother-child relationship), and the environmental (delinquency is the producer of disruptive forces, "disorganization," in the actor's physical or social environment).

This paper selects one particular kind of "delinquency"[1]–law-violating acts committed by members of adolescent street corner groups in lower class communities—and attempts to show that the dominant component of motivation underlying these acts consists in a directed attempt by the actor to adhere to forms of behavior, and to achieve standards of value as they are defined within that community. It takes as a premise that the motivation of behavior in this situation can be approached most productively by attempting to understand the nature of cultural forces impinging on the acting individual as they are perceived *by the actor himself*—although by no means only that segment of these forces of which the actor is consciously aware—rather than as they are perceived and evaluated from the reference position of another cultural system. In the case of "gang" delinquency, the cultural system which exerts the most direct influence on behavior is that of the lower class community itself—a long-established, distinctively patterned tradition with an integrity of its own—rather than a so-called "delinquent subculture" which has arisen through conflict with middle class culture and is oriented to the deliberate violation of middle class norms.

The bulk of the substantive data on which the following material is based was collected in connection with a service-research project in the control of gang delinquency. During the service aspect of the project, which lasted for three years, seven trained social workers maintained contact with twenty-one corner group units in a "slum" district of a large eastern city for periods of time ranging from ten to thirty months.

▶SOURCE: *"Lower Class Culture as a Generating Milieu of Gang Delinquency," Journal of Social Issues* (1958), 14:5–19. Reprinted by permission.

[1]The complex issues involved in deriving a definition of "delinquency" cannot be discussed here. The term "delinquent" is used in this paper to characterize behavior or acts committed by individuals within specified age limits which if known to official authorities could result in legal action. The concept of a "delinquent" individual has little or no utility in the approach used here; rather, specified types of *acts* which may be committed rarely or frequently by few or many individuals are characterized as "delinquent."

Groups were Negro and white, male and female, and in early, middle, and late adolescence. Over eight thousand pages of direct observational data on behavior patterns of group members and other community residents were collected; almost daily contact was maintained for a total time period of about thirteen worker years. Data include workers' contact reports, participant observation reports by the writer—a cultural anthropologist—and direct tape recordings of group activities and discussions.[2]

FOCAL CONCERNS OF LOWER CLASS CULTURE

There is a substantial segment of present-day American society whose way of life, values, and characteristic patterns of behavior are the product of a distinctive cultural system which may be termed "lower class." Evidence indicates that this cultural system is becoming increasingly distinctive, and that the size of the group which shares this tradition is increasing.[3] The lower

[2]A three year research project is being financed under National Institutes of Health Grant M-1414, and administered through the Boston University School of Social Work. The primary research effort has subjected all collected material to a uniform data-coding process. All information bearing on some seventy areas of behavior (behavior in reference to school, police, theft, assault, sex, collective athletics, etc.) is extracted from the records, recorded on coded data cards, and filed under relevant categories. Analysis of these data aims to ascertain the actual nature of customary behavior in these areas, and the extent to which the social work effort was able to effect behavioral changes.

[3]Between 40 and 60 percent of all Americans are directly influenced by lower class culture, with about 15 percent, or twenty-five million, comprising the "hard core" lower class group—defined primarily by its use of the "female-based" household as the basic form of child-rearing unit and of the "serial monogamy" mating pattern as the primary form of marriage. The term "lower class culture" as used here refers most specifically to the way of life of the "hard core" group; systematic research in this area would probably reveal at least four to six major subtypes of lower class culture, for some of which the "concerns" presented here would be differently weighted, especially for those subtypes in which "law-abiding" behavior has a high overt valuation. It is impossible within the compass of this short paper to make the finer intracultural distinctions which a more accurate presentation would require.

class way of life, in common with that of all distinctive cultural groups, is characterized by a set of focal concerns—areas or issues which command widespread and persistent attention and a high degree of emotional involvement. The specific concerns cited here, while by no means confined to the American lower classes, constitute a distinctive *patterning* of concerns which differs significantly, both in rank order and weighting from that of American middle class culture. Table I presents a highly schematic and simplified listing of six of the major concerns of lower class culture. Each is conceived as a "dimension" within which a fairly wide and varied range of alternative behavior patterns may be followed by different individuals under different situations. They are listed roughly in order of the degree of *explicit* attention accorded each, and, in this sense represent a weighted ranking of concerns. The "perceived alternatives" represent polar positions which define certain parameters within each dimension. As will be explained in more detail, it is necessary in relating the influence of these "concerns" to the motivation of delinquent behavior to specify *which* of its aspects is oriented to, whether orientation is *overt* or *covert, positive* (conforming to or seeking the aspect), or *negative* (rejecting or seeking to avoid the aspect).

The concept "focal concern" is used here in preference to the concept "value" for several interrelated reasons: (1) It is more readily derivable from direct field observation. (2) It is descriptively neutral—permitting independent consideration of positive and negative valences as varying under difficult conditions, whereas "value" carries a built-in positive valence. (3) It makes possible more refined analysis of subcultural differences, since it reflects actual behavior, whereas "value" tends to wash out intracultural differences since it is colored by notions of the "official" ideal.

Trouble

Concern over "trouble" is a dominant feature of lower class culture. The concept has various shades of meaning; "trouble" in one of its as-

Table I. Focal Concerns of Lower Class Culture

Area		Perceived Alternatives (state, quality, condition)
1. Trouble:	law-abiding behavior	law-violating behavior
2. Toughness:	physical prowess, skill; "masculinity"; fearlessness, bravery, daring	weakness, ineptitude; effeminacy; timidity, cowardice, caution
3. Smartness:	ability to outsmart, dupe, "con"; gaining money by "wits"; shrewdness, adroitness in repartee	gullibility, "con-ability"; gaining money by hard work; slowness, dull-wittedness, verbal maladroitness
4. Excitement:	thrill; risk, danger; change, activity	boredom; "deadness," safeness; sameness, passivity
5. Fate:	favored by fortune, being "lucky"	ill-omened, being "unlucky"
6. Autonomy:	freedom from external constraint; freedom from superordinate authority; independence	presence of external constraint; presence of strong authority; dependency, being "cared for"

pects represents a situation or a kind of behavior which results in unwelcome or complicating involvement with official authorities or agencies of middle class society. "Getting into trouble" and "staying out of trouble" represent major issues for male and female, adults and children. For men, "trouble" frequently involves fighting or sexual adventures while drinking; for women, sexual involvement with disadvantageous consequences. Expressed desire to avoid behavior which violates moral or legal norms is often based less on an explicit commitment to "official" moral or legal standards than on a desire to avoid "getting into trouble," e.g., the complicating consequences of the action.

The dominant concern over "trouble" involves a distinction of critical importance for the lower class community—that between "law-abiding" and "non-law-abiding" behavior. There is a high degree of sensitivity as to where each person stands in relation to these two classes of activity. Whereas in the middle class community a major dimension for evaluating a person's status is "achievement" and its external

symbols, in the lower class, personal status is very frequently gauged along the law-abiding-non-law-abiding dimension. A mother will evaluate the suitability of her daughter's boyfriend less on the basis of his achievement potential than on the basis of his innate "trouble" potential. This sensitive awareness of the opposition of "trouble-producing" and "non-trouble-producing" behavior represents both a major basis for deriving status distinctions, and an internalized conflict potential for the individual.

As in the case of other focal concerns, which of two perceived alternatives—"law-abiding" or "non-law-abiding"—is valued varies according to the individual and the circumstances; in many instances there is an overt commitment to the "law-abiding" alternative, but a covert commitment to the "non-law-abiding." In certain situations, "getting into trouble" is overtly recognized as prestige-conferring; for example, membership in certain adult and adolescent primary groupings ("gangs") is contingent on having demonstrated an explicit commitment to the law-violating alternative. It is most important to note that the choice between "law-abiding" and "non-law-abiding" behavior is still a choice *within* lower class culture; the distinction between the policeman and the criminal, the outlaw and the sheriff, involves primarily this one dimension; in other respects they have a high community of interests. Not infrequently brothers raised in an identical cultural milieu will become police and criminals respectively.

For a substantial segment of the lower class population "getting into trouble" is not in itself overtly defined as prestige-conferring, but is implicitly recognized as a means to other valued ends, e.g., the covertly valued desire to be "cared for" and subject to external constraint, or the overtly valued state of excitement or risk. Very frequently "getting into trouble" is multi-functional, and achieves several sets of valued ends.

Toughness

The concept of "toughness" in lower class culture represents a compound combination of qualities or states. Among its most important components are physical prowess, evidenced both by demonstrated possession of strength and endurance and athletic skill; "masculinity," symbolized by a distinctive complex of acts and avoidances (bodily tatooing; absence of sentimentality; non-concern with "art," "literature," conceptualization of women as conquest objects, etc.); and bravery in the face of physical threat. The model for the "tough guy"—hard, fearless, undemonstrative, skilled in physical combat—is represented by the movie gangster of the thirties, the "private eye," and the movie cowboy.

The genesis of the intense concern over "toughness" in lower class culture is probably related to the fact that a significant proportion of lower class males are reared in a predominantly female household, and lack a consistently present male figure with whom to identify and from whom to learn essential components of a "male" role. Since women serve as a primary object of identification during pre-adolescent years, the almost obsessive lower class concern with "masculinity" probably resembles a type of compulsive reaction-formation. A concern over homosexuality runs like a persistent thread through lower class culture. This is manifested by the institutionalized practice of baiting "queers," often accompanied by violent physical attacks, an expressed contempt for "softness" or frills, and the use of the local term for "homosexual" as a generalized pejorative epithet (e.g., higher class individuals or upwardly mobile peers are frequently characterized as "fags" or "queers"). The distinction between "overt" and "covert" orientation to aspects of an area of concern is especially important in regard to "toughness." A positive overt evaluation of behavior defined as "effeminate" would be out of the question for a lower class male; however, built into lower class culture is a range of devices which permit men to adopt behaviors and concerns which in other cultural milieux fall within the province of women, and at the same time to be defined as "tough" and manly. For example, lower class men can be professional short-order cooks in a diner and still be regarded as "tough." The highly intimate circumstances of the street corner gang involve the recurrent expression of strongly affectionate feelings towards other men. Such expressions, however, are disguised as their opposite, taking the form of ostensibly aggressive verbal and physical interaction (kidding, "ranking," roughhousing, etc.).

Smartness

"Smartness," as conceptualized in lower class culture, involves the capacity to outsmart, outfox, outwit, dupe, "take," "con" another or others, and the concomitant capacity to avoid being outwitted, "taken," or duped oneself. In its essence, smartness involves the capacity to achieve a valued entity—material goods, personal status—through a maximum use of mental agility and a minimum use of physical effort. This capacity has an extremely long tradition in lower class culture, and is highly valued. Lower class culture can be characterized as "non-intellectual" only if intellectualism is defined specifically in terms of control over a particular body of formally learned knowledge involving "culture" (art, literature, "good" music, etc.), a generalized perspective on the past and present conditions of our own and other societies, and other areas of knowledge imparted by formal educational institutions. This particular type of mental attainment is, in general, overtly disvalued and frequently associated with effeminacy; "smartness" in the lower class sense, however, is highly valued.

The lower class child learns and practices the use of this skill in the street corner situation. Individuals continually practice duping and outwitting one another through recurrent card games and other forms of gambling, mutual exchanges of insults, and "testing" for mutual "conability." Those who demonstrate competence in this skill are accorded considerable prestige. Leadership roles in the corner group are frequently allocated according to demonstrated capacity in the two areas of "smartness" and "toughness"; the ideal leader is often accorded more prestige than the "tough" one— reflecting a general lower class respect for "brain" in the "smartness" sense.[4]

The model of the "smart" person is represented in popular media by the card shark, the professional gambler, the "con" artist, the promoter. A conceptual distinction is made between two kinds of people: "Suckers," easy marks, "lushes," dupes, who work for their money and are legitimate targets of exploitation; and sharp operators, the "brainy" ones, who live by their wits and "getting" from the suckers by mental adroitness.

Involved in the syndrome of capacities related to "smartness" is a dominant emphasis in lower class culture on ingenious aggressive repartee. This skill, learned and practiced in the context of the corner group, ranges in form

[4] The "brains-brawn" set of capacities are often paired in lower class folk lore or accounts of lower class life, e.g., "Brer Fox" and "Brer Bear" in the Uncle Remus stories, or George and Lennie in "Of Mice and Men."

from the widely prevalent semi-ritualized teasing, kidding, razzing "ranking," so characteristic of male peer group interaction, to the highly ritualized type of mutual insult interchange known as "the dirty dozens," "the dozens," "playing house," and other terms. This highly patterned cultural form is practiced on its most advanced level in adult male Negro society, but less polished variants are found throughout lower class culture—practiced, for example, by white children, male and female, as young as four or five. In essence, "doin' the dozens" involves two antagonists who vie with each other in the exchange of increasingly inflammatory insults, with incestuous and perverted sexual relations with the mother a dominant theme. In this form of insult interchange, as well as on other less ritualized occasions for joking, semi-serious, and serious mutual invective, a very high premium is placed on ingenuity, hair-trigger responsiveness, inventiveness, and the acute exercise of mental faculties.

Excitement

For many lower class individuals the rhythm of life fluctuates between periods of relatively routine or repetitive activity and sought situations of great emotional stimulation. Many of the most characteristic features of lower class life are related to the search for excitement or "thrill." Involved here are the highly prevalent use of alcohol by both sexes and the widespread use of gambling of all kinds—playing the numbers, betting on horse races, dice, cards. The quest for excitement finds what is perhaps its most vivid expression in the highly patterned practice of the recurrent "night on the town." This practice, designated by various terms in different areas ("honky-tonkin'"; "goin' out on the town"; "bar hoppin'"), involves a patterned set of activities in which alcohol, music, and sexual adventuring are major components. A group or individual sets out to "make the rounds" of various bars or night clubs. Drinking continues progressively throughout the evening. Men seek to "pick up" women, and women play the risky game of entertaining sexual advances. Fights between men involving women, gambling, and claims of physical prowess, in various combinations, are frequent consequences of a night of making the rounds. The explosive potential of this type of adventuring with sex and aggression, frequently leading to "trouble," is semi-explicitly sought by the individual. Since there is always a good likelihood that being out on the town will eventuate in fights, etc., the practice involves elements of sought risk and desired danger.

Counterbalancing the "flirting with danger" aspect of the "excitement" concern is the prevalence in lower class culture of other well established patterns of activity which involve long periods of relative inaction, or passivity. The term "hanging out" in lower class culture refers to extended periods of standing around, often with peer mates, doing what is defined as "nothing," "shooting the breeze," etc. A definite periodicity exists in the pattern of activity relating to the two aspects of the "excitement" dimension. For many lower class individuals the venture into the high risk world of alcohol, sex, and fighting occurs regularly once a week, with interim periods devoted to accommodating to possible consequences of these periods, along with recurrent resolves not to become so involved again.

Fate

Related to the quest for excitement is the concern with fate, fortune, or luck. Here also a distinction is made between two states—being "lucky" or "in luck," and being unlucky or jinxed. Many lower class individuals feel that their lives are subject to a set of forces over which they have relatively little control. These are not directly equated with the supernatural forces of formally organized religion, but relate more to a concept of "destiny," or man as a pawn of magical powers. Not infrequently this often implicit world view is associated with a conception of the ultimate futility of directed effort towards a goal: if the cards are right, or

the dice good to you, or if your lucky number comes up, things will go your way; if luck is against you, it's not worth trying. The concept of performing semi-magical rituals so that one's "luck will change" is prevalent; one hopes that as a result he will move from the state of being "unlucky" to that of being "lucky." The element of fantasy plays an important part in this area. Related to and complementing the notion that "only suckers work" (Smartness) is the idea that once things start going your way, relatively independent of your own effort, all good things will come to you. Achieving great material rewards (big cars, big houses, a roll of cash to flash in a fancy night club), valued in lower class as well as in other parts of American culture, is a recurrent theme in lower class fantasy and folk lore; the cocaine dreams of Willie the Weeper or Minnie the Moocher present the components of this fantasy in vivid detail.

The prevalence in the lower class community of many forms of gambling, mentioned in connection with the "excitement" dimension, is also relevant here. Through cards and pool which involve skill, and thus both "toughness" and "smartness"; or through race horse betting, involving "smartness"; or through playing the numbers, involving predominantly "luck," one may make a big killing with a minimum of directed and persistent effort within conventional occupational channels. Gambling in its many forms illustrates the fact that many of the persistent features of lower class culture are multifunctional—serving a range of desired ends at the same time. Describing some of the incentives behind gambling has involved mention of all the focal concerns cited so far—Toughness, Smartness, and Excitement, in addition to Fate.

Autonomy

The extent and nature of control over the behavior of the individual—an important concern in most cultures—has a special significance and is distinctively patterned in lower class culture. The discrepancy between what is overtly valued and what is covertly sought is particularly striking in this area. On the overt level there is a strong and frequently expressed resentment of the idea of external controls, restrictions on behavior, and unjust or coercive authority. "No one's gonna push *me* around," or "I'm gonna tell him he can take the job and shove it. . . ." are commonly expressed sentiments. Similar explicit attitudes are maintained to systems of behavior-restricting rules, insofar as these are perceived as representing the injunctions, and bearing the sanctions of superordinate authority. In addition, in lower class culture a close conceptual connection is made between "authority" and "nurturance." To be restrictively or firmly controlled is to be cared for. Thus the overtly negative evaluation of superordinate authority frequently extends as well to nuturance, care, or protection. The desire for personal independence is often expressed in such terms as "I don't need *nobody* to take care of me. I can take care of myself!" Actual patterns of behavior, however, reveal a marked discrepancy between expressed sentiment and what is covertly valued. Many lower class people appear to seek out highly restrictive social environments wherein stringent external controls are maintained over their behavior. Such institutions as the armed forces, the mental hospital, the disciplinary school, the prison or correctional institution, provide environments which incorporate a strict and detailed set of rules defining and limiting behavior, and enforced by an authority system which controls and applies coercive sanctions for deviances from these rules. While under the jurisdiction of such systems, the lower class person generally expresses to his peers continual resentment of the coercive, unjust, and arbitrary exercise of authority. Having been released, or having escaped from these milieux, however, he will often act in such a way as to insure recommitment, or choose recommitment voluntarily after a temporary period of "freedom."

Lower class patients in mental hospitals will exercise considerable ingenuity to insure continued commitment while voicing the desire to get out; delinquent boys will frequently "run" from a correctional institution to activate efforts to return them; to be caught and returned means that one is cared for. Since "being controlled" is equated with "being cared for," attempts are frequently made to "test" the severity or strictness of superordinate authority to see if it remains firm. If intended or executed rebellion produces swift and firm punitive sanctions, the individual is reassured, at the same time that he is complaining bitterly at the injustice of being caught and punished. Some environmental milieux, having been tested in this fashion for the "firmness" of their coercive sanctions, are rejected, ostensibly for being too strict, actually for not being strict enough. This is frequently so in the case of "problematic" behavior by lower class youngsters in the public schools, which generally cannot command the coercive controls implicitly sought by the individual.

A similar discrepancy between what is overtly and covertly desired is found in the area of dependence-independence. The pose of tough rebellious independence often assumed by the lower class person frequently conceals powerful dependency cravings. These are manifested primarily by obliquely expressed resentment when "care" is not forthcoming rather than by expressed satisfaction when it is. The concern over autonomy-dependency is related both to "trouble" and "fate." Insofar as the lower class individual feels that his behavior is controlled by forces which often propel him into "trouble" in the face of an explicit determination to avoid it, there is an implied appeal to "save me from myself." A solution appears to lie in arranging things so that his behavior will be coercively restricted by an externally imposed set of controls strong enough to forcibly restrain his inexplicable inclination to get in trouble. The periodicity observed in connection with the "excitement" dimension is also relevant here; after involvement in trouble-producing behavior (assault, sexual adventure, a "drunk"), the individual will actively seek a locus of imposed control (his wife, prison, a restrictive job); after a given period of subjection to this control, resentment against it mounts, leading to a "break away" and a search for involvement in further "trouble."

FOCAL CONCERNS OF THE LOWER CLASS ADOLESCENT STREET CORNER GROUP

The one-sex peer group is a highly prevalent and significant structural form in the lower class community. There is a strong probability that the prevalence and stability of this type of unit is directly related to the prevalence of a stabilized type of lower class child-rearing unit—the "female-based" household. This is a nuclear kin unit in which a male parent is either absent from the household, present only sporadically, or, when present, only minimally or inconsistently involved in the support and rearing of children. This unit usually consists of one or more females of child-bearing age and their offspring. The females are frequently related to one another by blood or marriage ties, and the unit often includes two or more generations of women, e.g., the mother and/or aunt of the principal child-bearing female.

The nature of social groupings in the lower class community may be clarified if we make the assumption that it is the *one-sex peer unit* rather than the two-parent family unit which represents the most significant relational unit for both sexes in lower class communities. Lower class society may be pictured as comprising a set of age-graded one-sex groups which constitute the major psychic focus and reference group for those over twelve or thirteen. Men and women of mating age leave these groups periodically to form temporary marital alliances, but these lack stability, and after varying periods of "trying out" the two-sex family arrangement, gravitate back to the more "comfortable" one-sex grouping, whose members exert strong pressure on the individual *not* to disrupt the group by adopting a two-sex household pattern of life.[5] Membership in a stable and solidary peer unit is vital to the lower class individual precisely to the extent to which a range of essential functions—psychological, educational, and others, are not provided by the "family" unit.

The adolescent street corner group represents the adolescent variant of this lower class structural form. What has been called the "delinquent gang" is one subtype of this form, defined on the basis of frequency of participation in law-violating activity; this subtype should not be considered a legitimate unit of study per se, but rather as one particular variant of the adolescent street corner group. The "hanging" peer group is a unit of particular importance for the adolescent male. In many cases it is the most stable and solidary primary group he has ever belonged to; for boys reared in female-based households the corner group provides the first real opportunity to learn essential aspects of the male role in the context of peers facing similar problems of sex-role identification.

The form and function of the adolescent corner group operate as a selective mechanism in recruiting members. The activity patterns of the group require a high level of intra-group solidarity; individual members must possess a good capacity for subordinating individual desires to general group interests as well as the capacity for intimate and persisting interaction. Thus highly "disturbed" individuals, or those who cannot tolerate consistently imposed sanctions on "deviant" behavior cannot remain accepted members; the group itself will extrude those whose behavior exceeds limits defined as "normal." This selective process produces a type of group whose members possess to an unusually high degree both the *capacity* and *motivation* to conform to perceived cultural norms, so that the nature of the system of norms and values oriented to is a particularly influential component of motivation.

Focal concerns of the male adolescent corner group are those of the general cultural milieu in

[5]Further data on the female-based household unit (estimated as comprising about 15 per cent of all American "families") and the role of one-sex groupings in lower class culture are contained in Walter B. Miller, Implications of Urban Lower Class Culture for Social Work. *Social Service Review*, 1959, *33*, No. 3.

which it functions. As would be expected, the relative weighting and importance of these concerns pattern somewhat differently for adolescents than for adults. The nature of this patterning centers around two additional "concerns" of particular importance to this group—concern with "belonging," and with "status." These may be conceptualized as being on a higher level of abstraction than concerns previously cited, since "status" and "belonging" are achieved *via* cited concern areas of Toughness, etc.

Belonging

Since the corner group fulfills essential functions for the individual, being a member in good standing of the group is of vital importance for its members. A continuing concern over who is "in" and who is not involves the citation and detailed discussion of highly refined criteria for "in-group" membership. The phrase "he hangs with us" means "he is accepted as a member in good standing by current consensus"; conversely, "he don't hang with us" means he is not so accepted. One achieves "belonging" primarily by demonstrating knowledge of and a determination to adhere to the system of standards and valued qualities defined by the group. One maintains membership by acting in conformity with valued aspects of Toughness, Smartness, Autonomy, etc. In those instances where conforming to norms of this reference group at the same time violates norms of other reference groups (e.g., middle class adults, institutional "officials"), immediate reference group norms are much more compelling since violation risks involving the group's most powerful sanction: exclusion.

Status

In common with most adolescents in American society, the lower class corner group manifests a dominant concern with status. What differentiates this type of group from others, however, is the particular set of criteria and weighting thereof by which "status" is defined. In general, status is achieved and maintained by demonstrated possession of the valued qualities of lower class culture—Toughness, Smartness, expressed resistance to authority, daring, etc. It is important to stress once more that the individual orients to these concerns *as they are defined within lower class society;* e.g., the status-conferring potential of "smartness" in the sense of scholastic achievement generally ranges from negligible to negative.

The concern with "status" is manifested in a variety of ways. Intragroup status is a continued concern, and is derived and tested constantly by means of a set of status-ranking activities; the intra-group "pecking order" is constantly at issue. One gains status within the group by demonstrated superiority in Toughness (physical prowess, bravery, skill in athletics and games such as pool and cards), Smartness (skill in repartee, capacity to "dupe" fellow group members), and the like. The term "ranking," used to refer to the pattern of intra-group aggressive repartee, indicates awareness of the fact that this is one device for establishing the intra-group status hierarchy.

The concern over status in the adolescent corner group involves in particular the component of "adultness," the intense desire to be seen as "grown up," and a corresponding aversion to "kid stuff." "Adult" status is defined less in terms of the assumption of "adult" responsibility than in terms of certain external symbols of adult status—a car, ready cash, and, in particular, a perceived "freedom" to drink, smoke, and gamble as one wishes and to come and go without restrictions. The desire to be seen as "adult" is often a more significant component of much involvement in illegal drinking, gambling, and automobile driving than the explicit enjoyment of the acts as such.

The intensity of the corner group member's desire to be seen as "adult" is sufficiently great that he feels called upon to demonstrate qualities associated with adultness (Toughness, Smartness, Autonomy) to a much greater degree than a lower class adult. This means that he will seek out and utilize those avenues to these qualities which he perceives as available with greater intensity than an adult and less regard for their "legitimacy." In this sense the adolescent variant of lower class culture represents a maximization of an intensified manifestation of many of its most characteristic features.

Concern over status is also manifested in reference to other street corner groups. The term "rep" used in this regard is especially significant, and has broad connotations. In its most frequent and explicit connotation, "rep" refers to the "toughness" of the corner group as a whole relative to that of other groups; a "pecking order" also exists among the several corner groups in a given interactional area, and there is a common perception that the safety or security of the group and all its members depends on maintaining a solid "rep" for toughness vis-a-vis other groups. This motive is most frequently advanced as a reason for involvement in gang fights: "We *can't* chicken out on this fight; our rep would be shot!"; this implies that the group would be relegated to the bottom of the status ladder and become a helpless and recurrent target of external attack.

On the other hand, there is implicit in the concept of "rep" the recognition that "rep" has or may have a dual basis—corresponding to the two aspects of the "trouble" dimension. It is recognized that group as well as individual status can be based on both "law-abiding" and "law-violating" behavior. The situational resolution of the persisting conflict between the "law-abiding" and "law-violating" bases of status comprises a vital set of dynamics in determining whether a "delinquent" mode of behavior will be adopted by a group, under what circumstances, and how persistently. The determinants of this choice are evidently highly complex and fluid, and rest on a range of factors including the presence and perceptual immediacy of different community reference-group loci (e.g., professional criminals, police, clergy, teachers, settlement house workers), the personality structures and "needs" of group members, the presence in the community of social work, recreation, or

educational programs which can facilitate utilization of the "law-abiding" basis of status, and so on.

What remains constant is the critical importance of "status" both for the members of the group as individuals and for the group as a whole insofar as members perceive their individual destinies as linked to the destiny of the group, and the fact that action geared to attain status is much more acutely oriented to the fact of status itself than to the legality or illegality, morality or immorality of the means used to achieve it.

LOWER CLASS CULTURE AND THE MOTIVATION OF DELINQUENT BEHAVIOR

The customary set of activities of the adolescent street corner group includes activities which are in violation of laws and ordinances of the legal code. Most of these center around assault and theft of various types (the gang fight; auto theft; assault on an individual; petty pilfering and shoplifting; "mugging"; pocket-book theft). Members of street corner gangs are well aware of the law-violating nature of these acts; they are not psychopaths, nor physically or mentally "defective"; in fact, since the corner group supports and enforces a rigorous set of standards which demand a high degree of fitness and personal competence, it tends to recruit from the most "able" members of the community.

Why, then, is the commission of crimes a customary feature of gang activity? The most general answer is that the commission of crimes by members of adolescent street corner groups is motivated primarily by the attempt to achieve ends, states, or conditions, which are valued, and to avoid those that are disvalued within their most meaningful cultural milieu, through those culturally available avenues which appear as the most feasible means of attaining those ends.

The operation of these influences is well illustrated by the gang fight—a prevalent and characteristic type of corner group delinquency. This type of activity comprises a highly stylized and culturally patterned set of sequences. Although details vary under different circumstances, the following events are generally included. A member or several members of group A "trespass" on the claimed territory of group B. While there they commit an act or acts which group B defines as a violation of its rightful privileges, an affront to their honor, or a challenge to their "rep." Frequently this act involves advances to a girl associated with group B; it may occur at a dance or party; sometimes the mere act of "trespass" is seen as deliberate provocation. Members of group B then assaults members of group A, if they are caught while still in B's territory. Assaulted members of group A return to their "home" territory and recount to members of their group details of the incident, stressing the insufficient nature of the provocation ("I just *looked* at her! Hardly even said anything!"), and the unfair circumstances of the assault ("About *twenty* guys jumped just the *two* of us!"). The highly colored account is acutely inflammatory; group A, perceiving its honor violated and its "rep" threatened, feels obligated to retaliate in force. Sessions of detailed planning now occur; allies are recruited if the size of group A and its potential allies appears to necessitate larger numbers; strategy is plotted, and messengers dispatched. Since the prospect of a gang fight is frightening to even the "toughest" group members, a constant rehearsal of the provocative incident or incidents and the essentially evil nature of the opponents accompanies the planning process to bolster possibly weakening motivation to fight. The excursion into "enemy" territory sometimes results in a full scale fight; more often group B cannot be found, or the police appear and stop the fight, "tipped off" by an anonymous informant. When this occurs, group members express disgust and disappointment; secretly there is much relief; their honor has been avenged without incurring injury; often the anonymous tipster is a member of one of the involved groups.

The basic elements of this type of delinquency are sufficiently stabilized and recurrent as to constitute an essentially ritualized pattern, resembling both in structure and expressed motives for action classic forms such as the European "duel," the American Indian tribal war, and the Celtic clan feud. Although the arousing and "acting out" of individual aggressive emotions are inevitably involved in the gang fight, neither its form nor motivational dynamics can be adequately handled within a predominantly personality-focused frame of reference.

It would be possible to develop in considerable detail the processes by which the commission of a range of illegal acts is either explicitly supported by, implicitly demanded by, or not materially inhibited by factors relating to the focal concerns of lower class culture. In place of such a development, the following three statements condense in general terms the operation of these processes:

1. Following cultural practices which comprise essential elements of the total life pattern of lower class culture automatically violates certain legal norms.

2. In instances where alternate avenues to similar objectives are available, the non-law-abiding avenue frequently provides a relatively greater and more immediate return for a relatively smaller investment of energy.

3. The "demanded" response to certain situations recurrently engendered within lower class culture involves the commission of illegal acts.

The primary thesis of this paper is that the dominant component of the motivation of "delinquent" behavior engaged in by members of lower class corner groups involves a positive effort to achieve states, conditions, or qualities valued within the actor's most significant cultural milieu. If "conformity to immediate reference group values" is the major component of motivation of "delinquent" behavior by gang members, why is such behavior frequently referred to as negativistic, malicious, or rebellious? Albert Cohen, for example, in *Delinquent Boys* (Glencoe: Free Press, 1955) describes behavior which violates school rules as comprising elements of "active challenge and defiance." He ascribes to the gang "keen delight in terrorizing 'good' children, and in general making themselves obnoxious to the virtuous." A recent national conference on social work with "hard-to-reach" groups characterized lower class corner groups as "youth groups in conflict with the culture of their (*sic*) communities." Such characterizations are obviously the result of taking the middle class community and its institutions as an implicit point of reference.

A large body of systematically interrelated attitudes, practices, behaviors, and values characteristic of lower class culture are designed to support and maintain the basic features of the lower class way of life. In areas where these differ from features of middle class culture, action oriented to the achievement and maintenance of the lower class system may violate norms of middle class culture and be perceived as deliberately non-conforming or malicious by an observer strongly cathected to middle class norms. This does not mean, however, that violation of the middle class norm is the dominant component of motivation; it is a by-product of action primarily oriented to the lower class system. The standards of lower class culture cannot be seen merely as a reverse function of middle class culture—as middle class standards "turned upside down"; lower class culture is a distinctive tradition many centuries old with an integrity of its own.

From the viewpoint of the acting individual, functioning within a field of well-structured cultural forces, the relative impact of "conforming" and "rejective" elements in the motivation of gang delinquency is weighted preponderantly on the conforming side. Rejective or rebellious elements are inevitably involved, but their influence during the actual commission of delinquent acts is relatively small compared to the influence of pressures to achieve what is valued by the actor's most immediate reference groups. Expressed awareness by the actor of the element of rebellion often represents only that aspect of motivation of which he is explicitly conscious; the deepest and most compelling components of motivation—adherence to highly meaningful group standards of Toughness, Smartness, Excitement, etc.—are often unconsciously patterned. No cultural pattern as well-established as the practice of illegal acts by members of lower class corner groups could persist if buttressed primarily by negative, hostile, or rejective motives; its principal motivational support, as in the case of any persisting cultural tradition, derives from a positive effort to achieve what is valued within that tradition, and to conform to its explicit and implicit norms.

18. Labelling Theory

CHARLES WELLFORD

INTRODUCTION

IN RECENT YEARS CRIMINOLOGISTS HAVE BEGUN to emphasize the importance of society's reaction to crime, as an important ingredient in the perpetuation and intensification of criminal and delinquent careers. Basically, this perspective has provided a theoretical model by which criminologists could reassert their interest in the study of the criminal justice system, after decades of focusing on the characteristics of the offender. In this respect, the reemergence of the sociology of law and the theoretical and empirical analysis of the police, courts, and corrections (an important reemergence in the field of criminology) has been significantly advanced by labelling theorists. While there has yet to energe the "crucial experiment" to evaluate the adequacy of labelling theory for criminology, it is suggested here that we are able to consider basic characteristic of this perspective and offer an evaluation of those characteristics as a guide for further development in theoretical criminology. While some have rejected the perspective without a convincing demonstration of the inadequacy of the theory, and others have suggested it is not testable, I suggest that one can estimate the validity of the theory for criminology by asses-

▶SOURCE: *"Labelling Theory and Criminology; An Assessment," Social Problems (February 1975) 23(3): 332–345. Reprinted by permission.*

sing the assumptions on which the theory is based.[1]

Before beginning the analysis, it is important to note that labelling theory itself has been modified by some of the early contributors to this perspective, in particular, by a move to what is generally described as the conflict perspective.[2] Some have suggested that labelling theory was only a necessary stage in the development of a radical criminological theory (e.g., Quinney, 1973). However, this analyis will be restricted to a consideration of labelling theory and not conflict theory; but since these cannot be completely separated, the most relevant implications for the conflict perspective will be noted.

LABELLING THEORY ASSUMPTIONS

The present analysis of labelling theory is drawn from the recent discussion of this perspective by

[1]Gove (1970; 1974) has provided a consideration of the value of labelling theory for the study of mental illness. He suggests, on the basis of the reanalysis of existing data, that the theory does not account for the selection, treatment, and perpetuation of mental illness. Recently Scheff (1974) has offered a rebuttal of Gove's analysis. Although not convincing, it will undoubtedly be taken as evidence of inconclusiveness in this area. The Gove analysis and Scheff reply consider only mental illness and the evaluation of two of the assumptions to be discussed here. I will provide a more extensive consideration of the elements of labelling theory as used by criminologists and restrict my analysis to the issues of interest to criminologists.

[2]For elaboration of this point, see Davis (1972).

Schrag (1971). Following a consideration of the works of Tannenbaum (1938), Lemert (1951), Becker (1963), Turk (1969), and Quinney (1970), Schrag identifies what he considers the basic assumptions that distinguish labelling theory from other theoretical perspectives. The assumptions identified are: 1) no act is intrinsically criminal; 2) criminal definitions are enforced in the interest of the powerful; 3) a person does not become a criminal by violation of the law but only by the designation of criminality by authorities; 4) due to the fact that everyone conforms and deviates, people should not be dichotomized into criminal and non-criminal categories; 5) the act of "getting caught" begins the labelling process; 6) "getting caught" and the decision-making in the criminal justice system are a function of offender as opposed to offense characteristics; 7) age, socioeconomic class, and race are the major offender characteristics that establish patterns of differential criminal justice decision-making; 8) the criminal justice system is established on a freewill perspective that allows for the condemnation and rejection of the identified offender; and, 9) labelling is a process that produces, eventually, identification with a deviant image and subculture, and a resulting "rejection of the rejectors" (Schrag 1971: 89–91). While one might extent or modify these assumptions, it is suggested that they represent comprehensive analysis of the theory as it is generally presented and used in criminological theory, research and policy. In the remainder of this analysis these assumptions will be considered, and the literature pertinent to each will be reviewed.

It is clear that in a formal sense the above do not all qualify as assumptions, but rather they are hypotheses which we would suggest labelling theorists would contend have been demonstrated to be true (i.e., "facts"). Elements one, three, and eight of Schrag's analysis should be considered assumptions, while the other represents statements assumed to be established by empirical observations. Thus, although I shall consider each of the points raised by Schrag,

nominally accepting his identification of each as an assumption, I would suggest that elements one, six, and nine represent the basis of the labelling perspective.

THE EVALUATION OF THE ASSUMPTIONS

Assumption 1: No Act Is Intrinsically Criminal

Basic to the labelling perspective is the assumption that legally proscribed behavior varies considerably from culture to culture, thus demonstrating the relative character of defiance (Schur: 1971, 14). This notion of relativism is applied to all forms of deviant behavior and establishes the assumption that crime is a form of behavior defined by the powerful to control the less powerful and to direct the benefits of society to those controlling economic and political power (Assumption 2)—an issue to be discussed in the next section with regard to the benefit of insulation from control by the criminal justice system. While this position may have some validity in the analysis of acts of deviant behavior such as stuttering, certain sexual behaviors, etc., I contend that the assumption has little import for Criminology as it attempts to explain those acts that have traditionally occupied criminologists.

Murder, forcible rape, aggravated assault, robbery, burglary, larceny, and auto theft represent one operationalization of crime characteristically considered important by citizens and criminologists (i.e., violations of the criminal law that involve elements of injury, theft, or damage).[3] Serious violations of the criminal law rep-

[3]It is possible within the related conflict perspective to interpret this focus by Criminology as an indication of the allegiances of criminologists to the dominant order. While we do not accept that explanation, we note from both our perspective and that of the conflict theorists, criminology and the public are viewed as primarily concerned with these forms of criminal behavior. Since its inception, criminology has encouraged the development of a society and a system of criminal law that controls violations of property and person by others. Self-inflicted or moralistic crimes have been the

resent the behavioral units that criminologists have attempted to explain. Addressing this notion of crime, it is important to note the similarity and consistency with which these acts are proscribed cross-culturally and through time. Lemert (1972: 22), for example, notes that:

"the extreme relevance in some statements of labelling theory leaves the unfortunate impression that almost any meaning can be assigned to human attributes in action. To the contrary, human interaction always occurs within limits: biological, psychological, ecological, technological, and organizational. These explain why certain general kinds of behavior are more likely to be deemed as undesirable than others. Practically all societies in varying degrees and ways disapprove of incest, adultery, promiscuity, cruelty to children, laziness, disrespect for parents and elders, murder, rape, theft, lying, and cheating. Perhaps the point to make is that certain kinds of actions are likely to be judged deleterious in any context—willfully causing the death of others, consuming large amounts of alcohol for long periods of time, spreading infectious disease, or losing one's eyesight. It is not so much that these violate rules, it is that they destroy, downgrade, or jeopardize values universal in nature."

Similarly, Linton (1952: 660) observes, following a review of anthropological literature on ethical norms, that "the resemblances in ethical concepts so far outweigh the differences that a sound basis for mutual understanding between groups and different cultures is already in existence." Hoebel's (1954: 286–287) analysis of primitive law led him to identify certain "legal universals" including homicide, rape, and the right to private property. Finally Matza (1964: 155–156) observes that "one need not succumb to rampant relativism—the frivolous view that law is completely arbitrary."

Major cross-cultural differences can be observed with regard to the procedures by which society enforces its norms; however, this should not lead to the conclusion that criminal behaviors of the type described are not uniformly proscribed. This position need not be interpreted, as one that emphasizes the existence or importance of "natural law." The evidence is that all societies have found it functional to control certain kinds of behavior. The fact that the acts described above are proscribed in all societies clearly indicates the weakness of Assumption One for criminology. Serious violations of the law are universally understood and *are,* therefore, *in that sense,* intrinsically criminal. The acceptance of this assumption in labelling theory by supporters and critics has been without reference to any data relevant to serious crime.[4] Juvenile status offenses, crimes without victims, etc., may exhibit crosscultural variations but not those criminal behaviors of primary concern to criminologists.

This fact is recognized by Schur (1971: 14) when he observes:[5]

"Some forms of deviation may, it is true, lend themselves less readily to labelling analysis than do others . . . The value of labelling analysis in explaining a particular form of deviance may be related to the degree of consensus on its social definition . . . borderline forms of deviance seem to be especially good candidates for labelling analysis and those de-

---

objects of decriminalization efforts at least since Beccaria. Our use of "serious crime" reflects this consistent theme in criminology, the focus on "true criminal law." Following Calhoun (1927), true criminal law, in contrast to primitive law and tort, "recognizes the principle that attacks upon the persons or property of individuals, or rights thereto annexed, as well as offenses that affect the state directly, may be violations of the peace and good order." In the remainder of this paper, it is to this conception of the unit of analysis of criminology to which I will refer as serious crime.

[4]Schur (1971) states the "empirical evidence tends to support the relativistic stance," but does not make reference to or discuss this evidence. Gibbs (1972) asserts that today "no specific type of act (for example, sexual intercourse between siblings) is deviant or criminal in all social units." It is important to note the example Gibbs uses, and the fact that he also fails to reference empirical support for the position.

[5]The use of quotes from Lemert and Schur, both of whom are identified with the development of labelling theory, is to draw attention to the recognition by such theorists of the limited scope of labelling theory and their explicit rejection of this assumption. In fact, this assumption is more critical to conflict theory and may reflect the changes in labelling theory that have occurred during the transition of labelling theory for many to a structural-conflict orientation.

viations on which widespread consensus exists less promising candidates.

As noted earlier, Criminology has long recognized the undesirability of over-legalization and the necesity for criminology to address serious criminal law violations. To the degree that the acceptance of this designation of the unit of analysis for criminologists prevails in the discipline, the labelling theory "holds less promise" of providing a viable model on which to build a theory of criminal behavior.

The issue of consensus on the serious criminal violations can be observed not only with regard to the uniformity of proscriptions but also in the recent research on perception of offense seriousness. The scale of seriousness observed by Sellin and Wolfgang (1964) for the United States has been found to be highly correlated with scales generated from samples in Canada (Akman and Normandeau, 1968), Taiwan (Hsu, 1969), the Belgian Congo (DeBoeck, A. and G. Houchou, 1968), Puerto Rico (Valez-Diaz and Megargee: 1971), and among United States prisoners (Figlio, 1972). Consequently, similar behaviors are ranked and weighted in very similar ways by vastly different national and subnational samples.

In sum, if intrinsic is taken to mean nonrelative and consensual, then the presence of "intrinsically criminal acts" is clearly demonstrated. Similar behaviors are proscribed cross-culturally and are assessed in terms of seriousness by different national samples. On those criminal behaviors that have been the focus of criminology, there is social consensus. Whether that consensus is determined by value consensus, false consciousness or some other set of explanatory concepts is not our concern at this time. Our observation is simply that the labelling model may not be useful to Criminology when it addresses such consensually (intrinsically) defined deviant acts.

Assumption One has also been challenged by Gibbs (1966; 1972) on logical-definitional grounds. He observes that the notion that deviant acts are only known by the reaction they receive raises the issue of defining the reaction—what type of reaction is necessary to define an act as deviant. Can it be a self-reaction or an informal reaction? If not, why not? How are these logically different from "public" or "outsider" reactions? If self or informal reactions are possible "definers" of deviance, what is their source? Gibbs suggests that the defining of deviance must involve a normative commitment and acceptance of *behavior* as deviant. The consideration of the source and cause of the reaction takes, Gibbs suggests, the labelling theorist towards normative theories,[6] and thus the implicit acceptance of the intrinsic (for that social system) nature of the deviance.

In summary, both empirically (for serious criminal behavior) and logically (for all instances of deviance), the assumption of extreme relativism is seriously questioned. To the degree this assumption is crucial, criminologists should be reluctant to accept the labelling perspective.

Assumptions 2, 3, 5, 6, and 7

All of these assumptions relate to the operation of the criminal justice system. They propose that the person does not become criminal by violating the law (Assumption 3) but by being labelled as a violator of the law (an acceptable but trivial issue in the operationalization of the concept criminal); that the labelling of violations of the law is done in the interest of the powerful (Assumption 2); that the condition of power relates mainly to the conditions of sex, race, social class, and age (Assumptions 5 and 6); that the applications of criminal sanction by the criminal justice system is similarly dependent on sex, race, age, and social class (Assumption 7).

While it is true, as some contend in reviewing the literature on criminal justice decision-making, that differences can be observed in decision-making with regard to certain basic

---

[6]Obviously the alternative is towards conflict theory, a progression noted earlier in this paper. However, as noted above, it should be clear that the assumption under discussion and those discussed in the next section are also important ingredients in the conflict formula as it applies to criminal behavior.

characteristics of the offender as they affect police and court disposition, I contend that the overwhelming evidence is in the direction of minimal differential law enforcement, determination of guilt, and application of sanction. In the area of law enforcement it now seems clear that for juvenile offenses the variables of complainant behavior and offense type are considerably more important than class, race, demeanor, etc., as variables affecting the decision to arrest (Hohenstein: 1969; Black and Reiss: 1970; Terry: 1967; Ferdinand and Luchterhand: 1970; Williams and Gold: 1972). This is not to imply that offender characteristics are of no consequence, but that in terms of the explanation of variance in criminal justice disposition, offense-related variables are far more important.[7] The primary examples to the contrary (Piliavin and Briar: 1964; Cicourel: 1968; Goldman: 1963) represent studies of questionable rigor which do not control for offense seriousness and focus on non-citizen initiated police behavior, a minor portion of formal sanctioning.[8]

The recent work of Thornberry (1973) presents evidence from a large scale longitudinal study of juveniles that purports to indicate a class and race effect on arrest, disposition, and sanctions for juveniles. Acknowledging that research reported to date does not support that contention that blacks and those from lower socioeconomic statuses are more severely treated by the juvenile justice system, the author proposes to re-examine this finding with data from a cohort originally studied by Wolfgang *et al.* (1972). Using percentage analysis, he observes that when seriousness of offense and number of previous offenses are controlled, the relationship between race and disposition and

the relationship between SES and dispositions remains for police, intake and court decision-making (1973: 96–97). While recognizing the need for the consideration of other variables Thornberry (1973: 97–98) concludes:

"We have noted that a number of earlier studies found that racial and social class disparities in dispositions could generally be explained by legal variables such as the seriousness of the offense and the number of previous offenses committed. . . . An analysis of comparable data for the Philadelphia birth cohort, however, yields findings that are quite different. With the earlier studies, we found that both the legal and nonlegal variables are related to dispositions. But unlike the previous studies, the present study shows that when the two legal variables were held constant, the racial and SES differences did not disappear. . . . The most important finding, however, in relation to the previous research done in this area, is that the nonlegal variables are still related to the severity of the disposition received, even when the legal variables are held constant."

Since this represents the only rigorous study to reach this conclusion, I will consider it in some detail.

First, it should be noted that the measurement procedures used in this study do not consider, as Thornberry observes, relevant control variables. There is no consideration of complainant behavior, victim-offender relations, or most importantly, offense seriousness, or type. The latter is most crucial because Thornberry *purports* to control for this by use of the Sellin-Wolfgang (1964) seriousness score. However, the control is in terms of only two categories, high or low seriousness, where low equals a seriousness score on the Sellin-Wolfgang scale of one (essentially all juvenile status offenses) and "high" equals a seriousness score of greater than one (i.e., the remainder of the range of the seriousness scale—the entire scale as described in the original publication (Sellin and Wolfgang: 1964)). Furthermore, socioeconomic status is measured by the median income of the area in which the subject resided, an obvious example of the ecological fallacy. Thus, one would not expect, on the basis of their measurement, seri-

---

[7]Some conception of justice could properly argue that such characteristics should not explain any of the variance. Such a moral position can be accepted while recognizing the inappropriateness of this assumption as a basis for the development of a scientific theory.

[8]For a detailed critical analysis of these works that demonstrates their methodological problems, see Ward (1971) and Hagan (1972).

ousness and SES to affect relationships to the degree suggested by research using more appropriate measurement techniques.

Even if one accepts the measures presented by Thornberry, the data can be analyzed to assess the specific impact of race on disposition. By demonstrating that percentage differences remain between blacks and whites or low and high socioeconomic status groups after controlling for offense related characteristics, Thornberry concludes that his results are different from previous empirical research and, therefore, must be weighed on the side of confirming the assumption under consideration. If, however, one measures the extent of the relationships, the data come closer to supporting rather than challenging previous rigorous research. For example, we measured the strength of the association in Thornberry's tables of racial effects on disposition using ϕ^2. The bivariate relationships between race and disposition are associated at .04 for police, .002 for intake, and .03 for court disposition. The relationship between race and disposition under varying conditions of control is reported in Table I.

The measures of association (or a careful reading of the percentage differences) indicate a substantial reduction in the association between race and severity of disposition. Furthermore, where seriousness is in fact controlled (i.e., the condition of low seriousness), the relationship is almost reduced to zero for police intake and court disposition; conversely, where seriousness is not controlled (i.e., the highly variable category of high seriousness), the relationships are not unfiormly changed for police. The importance of the inadequate control for seriousness is reflected in these data. Similar results were obtained for the analysis of socioeconomic status.

In sum, due to problems of variables that were not included in the study and the measurement of the key control variable of seriousness and the type of analysis, Thornberry reached conclusions not justified. In fact, the data reflect the minimal contribution of race and SES to criminal justice decision-making—the consistent fidning of empirical research on this issue.

Despite the above data the issue of differential court decision-making, cannot be as conclusively answered. Hood and Sparks (1970) conclude, following an exhaustive review of the literature, that the definitive studies of sentencing demonstrate the importance of offense characteristics and criminal histories and the relative unimportance of "personal factors" (sex, age, and race). There are, however, areas where offender characteristics are considered significant. The application of the death penalty (Bedau,

Table I. Association Between Race and Disposition Under Varying Conditions of Control (from Thornberry Data)*

Seriousness	Number of Prior Offenses	ϕ^2 (Police)	ϕ^2 (Intake)	ϕ^2 (Court)
Lo	None	.004	.01	.003
Lo	1 or 2	.008	.004	.03
Lo	3+	.01	.01	.04
Hi	None	.05	.002	.002
Hi	1 or 2	.02	.0004	.007
Hi	3+	.008	.00004	.02

*It is well known that measures of association on nominal and ordinal data are difficult to interpret and vary in magnitude depending upon cell ratios, marginal distributions, etc. The use of ϕ^2 is based on Blalock's (1972:299) observation that when independent and dependent marginals do not coincide, ϕ^2 should be selected rather than Q, since it will generate the conservative estimate.

1964) and the length of the penalties for minor offenses have been suggested as more significantly associated with race and socioeconomic status. Williams and Gold (1972) (although acknowledging the inadequacy of their sample of court cases) also suggest a severe racial effect on juvenile court disposition. Again, however, the weight of evidence would support a conclusion that non-crime related, offender characteristics should be relegated to a low position in the hierarchy of variables explaining the variance in court decision-making for juveniles, as is reflected in the above analysis of Thornberry's data.

In summary, one would conclude that the evaluation of this assumption leads to a generally negative conclusion with regards to the effectiveness of labelling theory to account for the data reflecting an absence of differential criminal justice decision-making based predominantly on offender characteristics. However, it should be observed that if criminal laws are enforced in the interest of the powerful, the powerful must be relatively evenly distributed throughout the racial and social composition of the population; or the powerful have selected laws for uniform enforcement that are only committed by the less powerful and are only considered law violations by the more powerful. While neither of these possible defenses of Assumption Two seem plausible for serious crime, they will be explored in another paper specifically on conflict theory.[9]

Assumption 4

This assumption, based on self-report data, deals with the universality of deviant behavior. The assumption is that since deviant behavior is

distributed evenly throughout the population and is, therefore, behavior engaged in by both those designated as criminals and non-criminals, the differentials with regard to the proportion of the population arrested and incarcerated cannot reflect variation in behavioral distributions. The evidence on this is from the self-report studies which indicate a general absence of association between social class and delinquency and a rather wide-spread involvement in delinquent behavior. However, it must be remembered, the extensiveness or universality of delinquency is primarily a function of the items included in self-report studies. For example, in Clark and Wenninger's (1962) study of delinquency those items in which 50 percent or more of the sample indicated involvement were: did things my parents told me not to do; minor theft; told lie to my family, principal, or friends; used swear words or dirty words out loud in school, in church, or on the streets so other people could hear me; showed or gave someone a dirty picture, a dirty story, or something like that; been out at night just fooling around after I was supposed to be home; hung around other people who I knew had broken the law a lot of times or who were known as bad people; and, threw rocks, cans, sticks, and other things at passing cars, bicycles, or persons. On more serious delinquency items (i.e., attack someone with the idea of killing them, beat up on kids who had not done anything to me, carried a razor, switchblade, or gun to be used against other people), the percentage of respondents indicating their involvement in these behaviors was less than ten percent (Clark and Wenninger, 1962: 829–830). Thus, again as in the case of Assumption One, the consideration of minor delinquencies (those that would least likely develop into a situation where labels would be applied) lends support to the assumption of labelling theory concerning the universality or predominant distribution of delinquent behavior. However, when one considered behavioral measures of more serious kinds of delinquency the restricted kinds of delinquency the restricted nature of

---

[9]The observation that, for example, race is minimally associated with decision-making is not inconsistent with the observation that a disproportionate number of incarnated offenders are black (a frequently cited indicator of the differential law enforcement). The associations reported in the Thornberry data would generate 654 institutional commitments, 82 percent of which would be black. This is accounted for by the accumulation of minimal associations and the distribution of blacks in the control variables.

those behaviors becomes perhaps more evident.

This should not be taken to imply that the deviant or delinquent is to be understood as one entirely different from the general population; for in fact he does engage, in most instances, in conforming behavior. It should, however, raise some questions about the assumption underlying labelling theory concerning the universality of the behavior and allow us to recognize that with regard to serious crime, as previously defined, there is a relatively minor portion of the population that becomes engaged in these behaviors with varying degrees of frequency and commitment, even thought his proportion may be generally constant across social class levels for juvenile populations. Again, I would suggest that one would have to conclude that the validity of this assumption for criminology is questionable in terms of the existing data and that, therefore, the strength of the perspective on which this assumption is based is similarly weakened.

Assumption 8

The assumption that behavior is willed as the underlying dimension of the criminal justice system seems neither testable nor of crucial significance for labelling theory. The assumption may well be true as frequent analyses of the historical emergence of the criminal justice system would attest; however, it is difficult to see its importance for the perspective in question. The labelling perspective could equally (and perhaps more forcefully) apply to a system that denied will, emphasized causation, recognized the need for rehabilitation, and stressed diversion, decriminalization, and deinstitutionalization. Unless the system ignored in all significant ways instances of deviant behavior, there would be the potential for labelling. As Schur (1969) has observed, perhaps our system is more unworkable than others; however, it would not appear that any system would avoid problems of labelling and social disapproval. In that sense the assumption is not an important one to the theory, although it may in fact be correct.

Assumption 9

It is contended that being labelled and the subsequent social disapproval contingent upon that label will produce a condition of "rejecting one's rejectors." It is in this assumption that one understands the dynamic aspect of labelling theory; where labels produce hostility, which produce behavior, which produce labels, which produce more hostility, which produce more intensive behavior, etc., etc. The process of creating secondary deviance becomes the focal concern of labelling theory. In this respect, one might wish to modify the assumption to reflect the secondary nature of the labelling effect. That is, the impact of labelling by the criminal justice system is mediated through, in most expositions of labelling theory, the effects this labelling has on areas such as employment, education, community acceptance, etc., and not the direct effect on the subject. This is particularly important in the consideration of the area of delinquency, since juveniles would be most responsive to the impact of primary socializing agencies. The issue then in assessing this assumption is the impact of criminal justice labelling on other segments on one's social environment and the subsequent impact on the actor. The studies of the effects of legal stigma by Schwartz and Skolnick (1964) are frequently cited to support this area, as are the reviews of the legal consequences of conviction for felonies. It is in this area that one can consider the central elements of labelling theory.

Labelling theory represents in its consideration of the relationships between self-concept, attitudes, etc. and behavior that Warner and DeFleur (1968) have described as the postulate of consistency. This postulate assumes that attitudes directly cause behavior, and that one can understand behavioral dimensions simply by understanding the subject's attitudes. Therefore, in labelling theory one assumes that degradation effects self-concept (a logical but not empirically demonstrated assumption), and that the change in self-concept produces a necessary change in behavior (a not logical and not empirically demonstrated occurrence). In the social psychological literature Warner and DeFleur observe that the postulate of consistency was challenged early in the work on racial relations by the postulate of independent variation, i.e., that attitudes and behavior vary independently and need not, and in fact should not, be considered as causally related. The work of Merton (1949) is recognized as a significant statement of the need to consider those factors other than attitudes that might account for discriminatory behavior. This led to the postulate of contingent consistency, a postulate which suggests that attitudes and behavior will be isomorphic only under certain kinds of social and environmental conditions and that for most behaviors the social or situational determinants can alter the intensity and direction of the relationship between attitudes and behavior.

Similarly the assumption in labelling theory that implies a consistent relationship between such entities as self-concept, attitude, and behavior may well represent a gross oversimplification of the determinants of behavior and draws one's attention again to the subject as opposed to the situation in which behavior occurs. While again the assumption may be deemed to be correct to the degree to which it is addressing only attitudinal change, the evidence from other areas of analysis suggest that it would need to be significantly modified before one could use this as a way of understanding the effect of the labelling process on behavior.[10] Behavior would still

be understood as situationally determined with labelling effects being primarily related to attitudinal changes which then would have to be studied to determine if in fact they are involved in the protion of subsequent behavior changes. In this sense, then, the theoretical position of labelling theory is challenged by the notion that it has presented a simplistic view of behavior causation, one that stresses the explanation of intellectual as opposed to the behavioral characteristics of the subject.

The work of Lofland (1969) is frequently cited as an effort to enlarge the conceptual structure of labelling theory. He identifies four primary sources of deviance facilitants: place; hardware; other; and actor. The social (pivotally) deviant is most likely when others are united in imputing deviance, normal hardware is removed, deviant hardware is provided, place rounds are integrated, and actor becomes disoriented and attached to the deviant identity. The apparent complexity of Lofland's theory would suggest that the above criticism of the simpler labelling model could not be applied to his analysis. Unfortunately, it is not clear that Lofland intended to or in fact produced a theory of deviance. Rather he generated an analysis of the impact of uncorrelated, independent variables (i.e., place, hardware, actor, and other) and has not systematically considered their interaction. His work is less a theory of deviance than it is a listing of elements to be considered in a theory. As he notes:

"Although Tannenbaum noted the components of others, places, hardware and actor and alluded to the more specific operation of more specific elements, he did not, as others have not, bring them to specific and *separate* (emphasis added) consideration. If it is now even remotely more possible directly to address the analytic task posed by him and others before and after him, then my aim has been accomplished (1969: 203–204)."

Despite the richness of his examples, Lofland does not address the task identified above of establishing the relative importance and strength of these explanatory sets. Again, our suggestion,

---

[10]I cannot here fully expand on this position. In addition to Warner and DeFleur, Deutscher (1966) has provided an extensive review of this literature. In the delinquency research, recent related statements are to be found in Short and Strodtbecks (1965) analysis of the values of gang delinquents and similar work by Empey and Lubeck (1968). Although not as conclusive, the prisonization literature indicates some support for the independence of commitment to inmate codes and behavioral conformity, e.g., Garabedian (1963) and Wellford (1967; 1973). Increasingly situational constraints and determinants as opposed to (or preferably in interaction with) self-concepts, beliefs or attitudes are gaining recognition as important components of an adequate causal model for human behavior.

following the more general social psychological research, would be that while the research suggested by Lofland's conceptual development must be done, the results will most likely demonstrate the importance of place *vis-à-vis* actor and other. Labelling *theory* is not advanced by Lofland's analysis—rather, as he observes, the analytical tools are developed from which a theory could emerge. Thus, labelling theory remains at the less complex level reflected in Assumption Nine—an assumption that is easily rejected.

LABELLING THEORY ASSUMPTIONS: A SUMMARY

The assumptions of labelling theory as presented by Schrag have been submitted to a review based upon existing empirical evidence in criminology and related disciplines. In each instance my conclusion is that the assumptions underlying the theory are at significant variance with the data as we now understand it, or are not crucial to the labelling perspective. Labels are distributed and labels may affect attitudes. The assumption that labels are differentially distributed, and that differential labelling affects behavior is not supported by the existing criminological research. In sum, one should conclude that to the degree that these assumptions can be taken to be basic to the labelling perspective, the perspective must be seriously questioned; and criminologists should be encouraged to explore other ways to conceptualize the causal process of the creation, perpetuation, and intensification of criminal and delinquent behavior—most obviously the analysis of situational determinants. At the same time we can recognize the potential value of labelling theory for other forms of deviant behavior, and as a component of a more comprehensive theory (Davis, 1972).

REFERENCES

Akman, Dogan and A. Normandeau
 1968 "Towards the measurement of criminality in Canada: A replication study." Acta Criminological 1:135–260.

Becker, Howard S.
 1963 Outsiders: Studies in the Sociology of Deviance, Glencoe, Illinois: Free Press.

Bedau, Hugo
 1964 The Death Penalty in America. Chicago: Aldine.

Blalock, Hubert
 1972 Social Statistics. New York: McGraw-Hill. Sociological Review 35:63–77.

Blalock, Hubert
 1972 Social Statistics. New York: McGraw-Hill.

Calhoun, George M.
 1927 The Growth of Criminal Law in Ancient Greece. Berkeley: University of California Press.

Cicourel, Aaron
 1968 The Social Organization of Juvenile Justice New York: John Wiley

Clark, John and Eugene Wenniger
 1962 "Socio-economic class and area as correlates of illegal behavior among juveniles." American Sociological Review 27:826–834.

Davis, Nanette J.
 1972 "Labeling theory in deviance research: A critique and reconsideration." Sociological Quarterly 13:447–474.

DeBoeck, A. and G. Houschou
 1969 "Prodegomenes a une statistique criminelle congolaise." Cahiers Economiques et Society 6.

Deutscher, Irwin
 1966 "Words and deeds: Social science and social policy." Social Problems 13:235–354.

Empey, Lamar and Steven Lubeck
 1968 "Conformity and deviance in the situation of company." American Sociological Review 33:760–774.

Ferdinand, Theodore and Elmer Luchterhand
 1962 "Inner city youth, the police, the juvenile court and justice." Social Problems 18:510–527.

Figlio, Robert
1972   The Seriousness of Offenses: An Evaluation by Offenders and Nonoffenders, Ph.D. Dissertation, University of Pennsylvania.

Garabedian, Peter
1963   "Social roles and processes of socialization in the prison community." Social Problems 11:139–152.

Gibbs, Jack
1966   "Conceptions of deviant behavior: The old and the new." Pacific Sociological Review 9:9–14.
1972   "Issues in defining deviant behavior," in Theoretical Perspectives on Deviance (ed.) R. Scott and J. Douglas. New York: Basic Books.

Goldman, Nathan
1963   The Differential Selection of Juvenile Offenders for Court Appearance. National Council on Crime and Delinquency.

Gove, Walter
1970   "Societal reaction as an explanation of mental illness: An evaluation." American Sociological Review 35:873–884.

Gove, Walter and Patrick Howell
1974   "Individual resources and mental hospitalization: A comparison and evaluation of the societal reaction and psychiatric perspective." American Sociological Review 39:86–100.

Hagan, John L.
1972   "The labelling perspective, the delinquent, and the police." Canadian Journal of Criminology and Corrections 14:150–165.

Hoebel, E. A.
1954   The Law of Primitive Man. Cambridge: Harvard University Press.

Hohenstein, William
1969   "Factors influencing the police disposition of juvenile offenders," in Delinquency: Selected Studies Zed.) M. Wolfgang and T. Sellin. New York: John Wiley.

Hood, Roger and Richard Sparks
1970   Key Issues in Criminology. London: Weidenfield and Nicolson.

Hsu, Marlene
1969   "A study of the differential response to the Sellin-Wolfgang index of delinquency." Sociological Commentator Spring: 41–50.

Lemert, Edwin
1972   Human Deviance, Social Problems and Social Control (2nd Edition). Englewood-Cliffs: Prentice-Hall.

Linton, Ralph
1952   "Universal ethical principles: An anthropological view," in Moral Principles of Action (ed.) R. Anshen, New York: Harper and Bros.

Lofland, John
1969   Deviance and Identity. Englewood Cliffs: Prentice-Hall.

Matza, David
1964   Delinquency and Drift. New York: John Wiley.

Merton, Robert
1949   "Discrimination and the American Creed," in Discrimination and National Welfare (ed.) R. MacIver. New York: Institute for Religious and Social Studies.

Piliavin, Irving and Scott Briar
1964   "Police encounters with juveniles." American Journal of Sociology 70:206–214.

Quinney, Richard
1970   Social Reality of Crime. Boston: Little, Brown, Co.

Quinney, Richard
1973   "Crime control in capitalist society: A critical philosophy of legal order." Issues in Criminology 8:75–99.

Scheff, T. J.
1974   "The labelling theory of mental illness." American Sociological Review 39:444–452.

Schrag, Clarence
1971   Crime and Justice: American Style. Washington, D.C.: G.P.O.

Schur, Edwin
1969   Our Criminal Society. Englewood-Cliffs: Prentice-Hall.

Schur, Edwin
  1971   Labelling Deviant Behavior. Englewood-Cliffs: Prentice-Hall.

Schwartz, Richard and Jerome Skolnick
  1964   "Two studies of legal stigma," in The Other Side (ed.) H. Becker. Glencoe, Illinois: Free Press.

Sellin, Thorsten and Marvin Wolfgang
  1964   The Measurement of Delinquency. New York: John Wiley.

Tannenbaum, Frank
  1938   Crime and the Community. Boston: Ginn.

Terry, Robert
  1967   "Discrimination in the handing of juvenile offenders by social control agencies." Journal of Research in Crime and Delinquency 4:218–230.

Thornberry, Terrence
  1973   "Race, socio-economic status and sentencing in the juvenile justice system." Journal of Criminal Law and Criminology 64:90–98.

Turk, Austin
  1969   Criminality and the Legal Order. New York: Rand McNally.

Valez-Diaz, A. and Edward Megaree
  1971   "An investigation of differences in value judgments between youthful offenders and nonoffenders in Puerto Rico." Journal of Criminal Law, Criminology and Police Science 61:549–556.

Ward, Richard
  1971   "The labelling theory: A critical analysis." Criminology 9:268–290.

Warner, Lyle and Melvin DeFleur
  1960   "Attitude as an interactional concept: Social constraint and social distance as intervening variables between attitudes and actions." American Sociological Review 34:153–169.

Wellford, Charles
  1967   "Factors associated with adoption of the inmate code: A study in normative socialization." Journal of Criminal Law, Criminology and Police Science 58:197–203.

Wellford, Charles
  1973   "Contact and commitment in a correctional community." British Journal of Criminology 13:108–121.

Williams, Jay and Martin Gold
  1972   "From delinquent behaviors to official delinquency." Social Problems 20:209–227.

Wolfgang, Marvin and Thorsten Sellin
  1964   The Measurement of Delinquency. Glencoe, Illinois: Free Press.

Wolfgang, Marvin, Robert Figlio, and Thorsten Sellin
  1972   Delinquency in a Birth Cohort. Chicago: University of Chicago Press.

19. Capitalism and Criminal Justice

RICHARD QUINNEY

DEVELOPMENT OF CAPITALIST ECONOMY

CRIME IS A MANIFESTATION OF THE MATERIAL conditions of society. The failure of conventional criminology is to ignore, by design, the material conditions of capitalism. Since the phenomena of crime are products of the substructure—are themselves part of the superstructure—any explanation of crime in terms of other elements of the superstructure is no explanation at all. Our need is to develop a general materialist framework for understanding crime, beginning with the underlying historical processes of social existence.

*

Any investigation of the meaning (and changing meanings) of crime in America, requires a delineation of the periods of economic development in the United States. A few attempts at such delineation already exist, but for other than the study of crime. For example, Douglas Dowd in his book *The Twisted Dream* notes briefly three different periods of American development, with particular reference to the role of the state in American economic life: (1) American mercantilism, up to Jackson's Presidency; (2) laissez-faire capitalism, coming to a climax in the decades after the Civil War; and (3) maturing

industrial capitalism, up to the present.[1] Similarly, in another treatment, William A. Williams in his book *The Contours of American History* arranges American history according to the following periods: (1) the age of mercantilism, 1740–1828; (2) the age of laissez nous faire, 1819–96; and (3) the age of corporate capitalism, 1882 to the present.[2] To this scheme, others add that American capitalism is now in the stage of either "monopoly capital" or "finance capital."[3]

It is debatable, nevertheless, in our study of crime in the United States, whether America was capitalist from the beginning, with capitalism merely imported from the Old to the New World. Or whether, as James O'Connor has recently argued, capitalist development has occurred in only fairly recent times.[4] For the first hundred years of nationhood the United States resisted large-scale capitalist production. Independent commodity production predomi-

[1] Douglas F. Dowd, *The Twisted Dream: Capitalist Development in the United States Since 1776* (Cambridge, Mass.: Winthrop, 1974), pp. 42–48.

[2] William Appleman Williams, *The Contours of American History* (New York: World, 1961).

[3] Paul A. Baran and Paul M. Sweezy, *Monopoly Capital: An Essay on the American Economic and Social Order* (New York: Monthly Review Press, 1966). Robert Fitch and Mary Oppenheimer, "Who Rules the Corporations," *Socialist Revolution*, no. 4 (July-August 1970): 73–107; no. 5 (September-October 1970): 61–114; no. 6 (November-December 1970):33–94.

[4] James O'Connor, "The Twisted Dream," *Monthly Review* 26 (March 1975): 46–53.

▶SOURCE: *Class, State and Crime. New York: David McKay Co., Inc, 1977, pp. 35, 42–44, 45–46, 50–52, 57–59, 60–62, 93–94, 98–100. (Editorial adaptations.) Reprinted by permission.*

nated; farmers, artisans, small manufacturers and other petty producers were the mainstay of the economy. Only as northern capitalists acquired land from the farmers (thus appropriating their labor power) and as immigrant labor power was imported from Europe did capitalism finally emerge in the United States. American capitalism emerged when capitalists won the battle as to who was to control labor power. Surplus labor was now in the hands of a capitalist ruling class. Workers could be exploited.

For certain, we are today in a stage of late, advanced capitalism in the United States. The current meaning of crime in America can be understood only in relation to the character of capitalism in the present era. Similarly, the meanings of crime at various times in the past have to be understood according to the particular stage of development. Only in the investigation of crime in the development of capitalism do we truly understand the meaning of crime. Concrete research will provide us with knowledge about the role of crime in the development of capitalism.

DOMINATION AND REPRESSION

The capitalist system must be continuously reproduced. This is accomplished in a variety of ways, ranging from the establishment of ideological hegemony to the further exploitation of labor, from the creation of public policy to the coercive repression of the population. Most explicitly, the *state* secures the capitalist order. Through various schemes and mechanisms, then, the capitalist class is able to dominate. And in the course of this domination, crimes are carried out. These crimes, committed by the capitalist class, the state, and the agents of the capitalist class and state, are the crimes of domination.

*

The coercive force of the state, embodied in law and legal repression, is the traditional means of maintaining the social and economic order. Contrary to conventional wisdom, law instead of representing community custom is an instrument of the state that serves the interests of the developing capitalist ruling class. Law emerged with the rise of capitalism, as Stanley Diamond writes: "Law arises in the breach of a prior customary order and increases in force with the conflicts that divide political societies internally and among themselves. Law *and* order is the historical illusion; law versus order is the historical reality."[5] Law and legal repression are, and continue to serve as, the means of enforcing the interests of the dominant class in the capitalist state.

Through the legal system, then, the state forcefully protects its interests and those of the capitalist ruling class. Crime control becomes the coercive means of checking threats to the existing social and economic order, threats that result from a system of oppression and exploitation. As a means of controlling the behavior of the exploited population, crime control is accomplished by a variety of methods, strategies, and institutions.[6] The state, especially through its legislative bodies, establishes official policies of crime control. The administrative branch of the state establishes and enforces crime-control policies, usually setting the design for the whole nation. Specific agencies of law enforcement, such as the Federal Bureau of Investigation and the recent Law Enforcement Assistance Administration, determine the nature of crime control. And the state is able through its Department of Justice officially to repress the "dangerous" and "subversive" elements of the population. Altogether, these state institutions attempt to rationalize the legal system of employing the advanced methods of science and technology. And whenever any changes are to

[5]Stanley Diamond, "The Rule of Law Versus the Order of Custom," *Social Research* 38 (Spring 1971): 71.

[6]See Richard Quinney, *Critique of Legal Order: Crime Control in Capitalist Society* (Boston: Little, Brown, 1974), pp. 95–135.

be attempted to reduce the incidence of crime, rehabilitation of the individual or reform within the existing institutions is suggested.[7] Drastically to alter the society and the crime-control establishment would be to alter beyond recognition the capitalist system.

*

Although the capitalist state creates and manages the institutions of control (employing physical force *and* manipulation of consciousness), the basic contradictions of the capitalist order are such that this control is not absolute and, in the long run, is subject to defeat. Because of the contradictions of capitalism, the capitalist state is more weak than strong.[8] Eventually the capitalist state loses its legitimacy, no longer being able to perpetuate the ideology that capital accumulation for capitalists (at the expense of workers) is good for the nation or for human interests. The ability of the capitalist economic order to exist according to its own interests is eventually weakened.[9] The problem becomes especially acute in periods of economic crisis, periods that are unavoidable under capitalism.

In the course of reproducing the capitalist system crimes are committed. It is a contradiction of capitalism that some of its laws must be violated in order to secure the existing system.[10] The contradictions of capitalism produce their own sources of crime. Not only are these contradictions heightened during times of crisis, making for increased crimes of domination, but the nature of these crimes changes with the further development of capitalism.

The crimes of domination most characteristic of capitalist domination are those that occur in the course of state control. These are the *crimes of control.* They include the felonies and misdemeanors that law-enforcement agents, especially the police, carry out in the name of the law, usually against persons accused of other violations. Violence and brutality have become a recognized part of police work. In addition to these crimes of control, there are the crimes of more subtle nature in which agents of the law violate the civil liberties of citizens, as in the various forms of surveillance, the use of provocateurs, and the illegal denial of due process.

Then there are the *crimes of government,* committed by the elected and appointed officials of the capitalist state. The Watergate crimes, carried out to perpetuate a particular governmental administration, are the most publicized instances of these crimes. There are also those offenses committed by the government against persons and groups who would seemingly threaten national security. Included here are the crimes of warfare and the political assassination of foreign and domestic leaders.

Crimes of domination also consist of those crimes that occur in the capitalist class for the purpose of securing the existing economic order. These *crimes of economic domination* include the crimes committed by corporations, ranging from price fixing to pollution of the environment in order to protect and further capital accumulation. Also included are the economic crimes of individual businessmen and professionals. In addition, the crimes of the capitalist class and the capitalist state are joined in organized crime. The more conventional criminal operations of organized crime are linked to the state in the present stage of capitalist development. The operations of organized crime and the criminal operations of the state are united in the attempt to assure the survival of the capitalist system.

[7]Alexander Liazos, "Class Oppression: The Functions of Juvenile Justice," *Insurgent Sociologist 5* (Fall 1974): 2–24.

[8]Wolfe, "New Directions in the Marxist Theory of Politics." p. 155.

[9]See Stanley Aronowitz, "Law, Breakdown of Order, and Revolution," in *Law Against the People: Essay to Demystify Law, Order and the Courts,* ed. Robert Lefcourt (New York: Random House, 1971), pp. 150–82; and John H. Schaar, "Legitimacy in the Modern State," in *Power and Community: Dissenting Essays in Political Science,* ed. Philip Green and Sanford Levinson (New York: Random House, 1979), pp. 276–327.

[10]See Richard Quinney, *Criminology: Analysis and Critique of Crime in America* (Boston: Little, Brown, 1975), pp. 131–61.

Finally, many *social injuries* are committed by the capitalist class and the capitalist state that are not usually defined as criminal in the legal codes of the state.[11] These systematic actions, involving the denial of basic human rights (resulting in sexism, racism, and economic exploitation) are an integral part of capitalism and are important to its survival.

Underlying all the capitalist crimes is the appropriation of the surplus value created by labor. The working class has the right to possess the whole of this value. The worker creates a value several times greater than the labor power purchased by the capitalist. The excess value created by the worker over and above the value of labor power is the surplus value which is appropriated by the capitalist. Surplus value, as exploitation, is essential to capitalism, being the source of accumulation of capital and expansion of production.

Domination and repression are a basic part of class struggle in the development of capitalism. The capitalist class and state protect and promote the capitalist order by controlling those who do not own the means of production. The labor supply and the conditions for labor must be secured. Crime control and the crimes of domination are thus necessary features and the natural products of capitalist political economy.

*

For the unemployed, as well as for those who are always uncertain about their employment, the life condition has its personal and social consequences. Basic human needs are thwarted when the life-giving activity of work is lost or curtailed. This form of alienation gives rise to a multiplicity of psycho-social maladjustments and psychic disorders.[12] In addition, unemployment means the loss of personal and family income. Choices, opportunities, and even life maintenance are jeopardized. For many people, the appropriate reaction consists not only of mental disturbance but also of outright acts of personal and social destruction.

Although the statistical evidence can never show conclusively the relation between unemployment and crime, largely because such statistics are politically constructed in the beginning to obscure the failings of a capitalist economy, there is sufficient observation to recognize the obvious fact that unemployment produces criminality. Crimes of economic gain increase whenever the jobless seek ways to maintain themselves and their families. Crimes of violence rise when the problems of life are further exacerbated by the loss of life-supporting activity. Anger and frustration at a world that punishes rather than supports produce their own forms of destruction. Permanent unemployment—and the acceptance of that condition—can result in a form of life where criminality is an appropriate and consistent response.

Hence, crime under capitalism has become a response to the material conditions of life.[13] Nearly all crimes among the working class in capitalist society are actually a means of *survival*, an attempt to exist in a society where survival is not assured by other, collective means. Crime is inevitable under capitalist conditions.

Yet, understanding crime as a reaction to capitalist conditions, whether as acts of frustration or means of survival, is only one side of the picture. The other side involves the problematics of the *consciousness* of criminality in capitalist society.[14] The history of the working class is in large part one of rebellion against the conditions of capitalist production, as well as against the

[11]Tony Platt, "Prospects for a Radical Criminology in the United States," *Crime and Social Justice* 1 (Spring-Summer, 1974): 2–10; Herman and Julia Schwendinger, "Defenders of Order or Guardians of Huamn Rights?" *Issues in Criminology* 5 (Summer 1970): 123–57.

[12]K. William Kapp, "Socio-Economic Effects of Law and High Employment," *Annals of the American Academy of Political and Social Science* 418 (March 1975): 60–71.

[13]David M. Gordon, "Capitalism, Class, and Crime in America," *Crime and Delinquency* 19 (April 1973): 163–86.

[14]Taylor, Walton, and Young, *New Criminology*, pp. 220–21.

conditions of life resulting from work under capitalism. Class struggle involves, after all, a continuous war between two dialectically opposed interests: capital accumulation for the benefit of a nonworking minority class that owns and controls the means of production and, on the other hand, control and ownership of production by those who actually labor. Since the capitalist state regulates this struggle, the institutions and laws of the social order are intended to assure the victory of the capitalist class over the working class. Yet the working class constantly struggles against the capitalist class, as shown in the long history of labor battles against the conditions of capitalist production.[15] The resistance continues as long as there is need for class struggle, that is, as long as capitalism exists.

With the instruments of force and coercion on the side of the capitalist class, much of the activity in the working-class struggle is defined as criminal. Indeed, according to the legal codes, whether in simply acting to relieve the injustices of capitalism or in taking action against the existence of class oppression, actions against the interest of the state are crimes. With an emerging consciousness that the state represses those who attempt to tip the scales in favor of the working class, working-class people engage in actions against the state and the capitalist class. This is crime that is politically conscious.

Crimes of accommodation and resistance thus range from unconscious reactions to exploitation, to conscious acts of survival within the capitalist system, to politically conscious acts of rebellion. These criminal actions, moreover, not only cover the range of meaning but actually evolve or progress from *unconscious reaction to political rebellion*. Finally, the crimes may eventually reach the ultimate state of conscious political action—*revolt*. In revolt, criminal actions are not only against the system but are also an attempt to overthrow it.

*

THE MEANING OF CRIME

A Marxist understanding of crime, as developed here, begins with an analysis of the political economy of capitalism. The class struggle endemic to capitalism is characterized by a dialectic between domination and accommodation. Those who own and control the means of production, the capitalist class, attempt to secure the existing order through various forms of domination, especially crime control by the iapitalist state. Those who do not own and control the means of production, especially the working class, accommodate and resist in various ways to capitalist domination.

Crime is related to this process. Crime control and criminality (consisting of the crimes of domination and the crimes of accommodation) are understood in terms of the conditions resulting from the capitalist appropriation of labor. Variations in the nature and amount of crime occur in the course of developing capitalism. Each stage in the development of capitalism is characterized by a particular pattern of crime. The meaning and changing meanings of crime are found in the development of capitalism.

What can be expected in the further development of capitalism? The contradictions and related crises of capitalist political economy are now a permanent feature of advanced capitalism. Further economic development along capitalist lines will solve none of the internal contradictions of the capitalist mode of production.[16] The capitalist state must, therefore, increasingly utilize its resources—its various control and repressive mechanisms—to maintain the capitalist order. The dialectic between oppression by the capitalist class and the daily struggle of survival by the oppressed will continue—and at an increasing pace.

[15]Sidney Lens, *The Labor Wars: From the Molly Maguires to the Sitdowns* (New York: Doubleday, 1973); Jeremy Brecher, *Strike!* (Greenwich, Conn.: Fawcett, 1972); Samuel Yellin, *American Labor Struggles* (New York: S. A. Russell, 1936); Richard O. Boyer and Herbert M. Morais, *Labor's Untold Story* (New York: Cameron Associates, 1955).

[16]Ernest Mandel, "The Industrial Cycle in Late Capitalism," *New Left Review* 90 (March-April 1975): 3–25.

The only lasting solution to the crisis of capitalism is, of course, socialism. Under late, advanced capitalism, socialism will be achieved only in the struggle of all people who are oppressed by the capitalist mode of production, namely, the workers and all elements of the surplus population. An alliance of the oppressed must take place.[17] Given the objective conditions of a crisis in advanced capitalism, and the conditions for an alliance of the oppressed, a mass socialist movement can be formed, cutting across all divisions within the working class.

The objective of Marxist analysis is to lead to further questioning of the capitalist system, leading to an improved understanding of the consequences of capitalist development. The *ultimate meaning* of crime in the development of capitalism is the need for a socialist society. And as the preceding discussion indicates, in moving toward the socialist alternative, our study of crime is necessarily based on an economic analysis of capitalist society. Crime is essentially a product of the contradictions of capitalism. Crime is sometimes a force in social development: when it becomes a part of the class struggle, increasing political consciousness. But our real attention must continue to be on the capitalist system itself. Our understanding is furthered as we investigate the nature, sources, and consequences of the development of capitalism. As we engage in this work, the development of socialism becomes more evident.

*

CRIME AND CONSCIOUSNESS

Is crime more than a by-product of capitalism? If more than a by-product, when and how does crime become a *force* in the class struggle? The question is crucial to a Marxist analysis of crime; the answer determines whether (or better, in what instances) criminality is to be considered as an active part in structuring social life and in the dynamics of social change. It is thus the consciousness of criminal behavior that becomes important in our investigation. For it is consciousness that gives behavior a rational purpose in human history.

For the working class there are several possibilities for breaking through the conditions of capitalism: "One possibility involves conscious, organized efforts aimed at the goal of eliminating capitalist society itself as the historical manifestation of the class contradiction. The other possibility involves crude, unconscious reactions against the social position of working class people in the form of evading bourgeois laws through criminal acts."[18] Actions thus range from unconscious reactions to exploitation, to conscious acts of survival, to politically conscious acts of rebellion.

The problem regarding criminality, therefore, becomes that of the consciousness of the working class. The problem is stated precisely as follows:

"This means that the questions must be pursued as to how to determine the concrete causes of behavior which in the social setting of the proletariat lead either to conscious class struggle on the one hand, or to conforming behavior or delinquent behavior on the other. In pursuing this question, it would be necessary to characterize the general conditions which under capitalist conditions contribute to the evolution of proletarian class consciousness and organized political praxis, and which contain as well, in their contradiction, the delusion of individuals and the hindering of the development of class struggle. Besides these general conditions, it would be necessary to characterize the specific circumstances which lead to the development of criminal behavior patterns within the proletariat. This implies that the intellectual interests of such an analysis must be measured against a critical understanding of science which is fundamentally oriented toward the principal necessity of the overthrow of capitalist ruling apparatus."[19]

---

[17]O'Connor, *Fiscal Crisis of the State*, pp. 221–56.

[18]Falco Werkentin, Michael Hofferbert, and Michael Baurmann, "Criminology as Police Science or: 'How Old Is the New Criminology?'" *Crime and Social Justice* 2 (Fall-Winter 1974): 27.

[19]Ibid.

In theoretically considering the problematics of consciousness of criminality we assist in the transformation of unconscious criminality into conscious political activity. The development of class consciousness and struggle is the goal of a Marxist analysis of crime.

*

The revolutionary character of the working class, in relation to urban crime, was noted by Engels in his study of the conditions of the working class in mid-nineteenth-century England.[20] Engels saw in crime, at this stage in the capitalist development of England, all of its contradictory nature. Generally, criminality represents a response to the oppression of the working class. Engels describes much of this behavior as being committed by an underclass of the surplus population that includes people who have lost all hope of ever returning to work, vagabonds, beggers, paupers, and prostitutes. Yet from this mass of suffering Engels sees a kind of person emerging who, provoked by intense distress, revolts openly against society.

Throughout Engels' discussion there is the recognition that criminality is a primitive form of insurrection, a response to deprivation and oppression. Criminality in itself is not a satisfactory form of politics. As Steven Marcus notes in his study of Engels' writing on crime:

"Crime is a primitive form of insurrection, driven by need and deprivations, an incomplete but not altogether mistaken response to a bad situation, and coming into active existence only by overcoming the resistance of inherited values and internalized sanctions. . . . Nevertheless, an inescapable part of the meaning of crime is its essential failure. It is insufficiently rational and excessively, or too purely, symbolic and symptomatic. Most of all, in it the criminal remains socially untransformed: he is still an isolated individual pursuing activities in an underground and alternate marketplace; if he is successful, he is a small-time entrepreneur; at best, he is the member or leader of a gang. In no instance is he capable of organizing a movement to withstand the institutional forces that are arrayed against him. He lives in a parallel and parasitic world whose horizon is bounded and obscured by the larger society upon which it depends."[21]

This is crime, as Engels recognized, in its early phase of development, before becoming a political force.

The initial failure of crime is contradicted by the fact that for some people criminality is the beginning of a conscious rebellion against capitalist conditions. In the larger context, as Engels realized, criminality is transitional, an action against brutalizing conditions, a possible stage in the development of political consciousness.[22] *If* criminally defined behavior becomes a conscious activity in the organization of workers, including the organization of those who are unemployed (in the surplus population), then crime attains a political and revolutionary character. In conscious response to social and economic oppression, action that is defined by the state as criminal could become a part of the revolutionary process.

[20]Frederick Engels, *The Condition of the Working Class in England in 1844,* trans. Florence Kelley Wischnewetzky (New York: J. W. Lovell, 1887).

[21]Steven Marcus, *Engels, Manchester, and the Working Class* (New York: Random House, 1974), pp. 223–24.

[22]Ibid., pp. 224–26.

20. No Excuse for Crime

ERNEST VAN DEN HAAG

"ENVIRONMENT IS THE ROOT OF ALL EVIL—AND NOthing else! A favourite phrase. And the direct consequence of it is that if society is organized on normal lines, all crimes will vanish at once, for there will be nothing to protest against, and all men will become, righteous in the twinkling of an eye."[1]

Except in narrowly specifiable conditions, the law does not see offenders as victims of conditions beyond their control. But criminologists often do.[2] Paul Bator describes views shared by many:

"... that the criminal law's notion of just condemnation is a cruel hypocrisy visited by a smug society on the psychologically and economically crippled; that its premise of a morally autonomous will with at least some measure of choice whether to comply with the values expressed in a penal code is unscientific and outmoded; that its reliance on punishment as an educational and deterrent agent is misplaced, particularly in the case of the very members of society most likely to engage in criminal conduct; and that its failure to provide for individualized and humane rehabilitation of offenders is inhuman and wasteful."[3]

GHETTOES AND "POLITICAL PRISONERS"

Most criminologists are not quite so explicit. But some are. Consider two. S. I. Shuman, Professor of Law and Psychiatry at Wayne State University goes farther than Bator. Shuman maintains that "if the ghetto victim does what for many such persons is inevitable and is then incarcerated ... he is in a real sense a political prisoner," because he is punished for "the inevitable consequences of a certain socio-political status."[4] If these consequences were indeed "inevitable," the punishment would be unjust, as Professor Shuman argues. Why, however, would the (unjustly) punished offender become a "political prisoner," as Professor Shuman also claims?

All punishments are imposed, or sanctioned, by the political order which the law articulates. Are all convicts, then, political prisoners? or all

▶SOURCE: *"No Excuse for Crime,"* Annals, American Academy of Political and Social Sciences (January 1966) 423:133–141. Reprinted by permission.

[1]Fedor Dostoevski, *Crime and Punishment* (1866). Dostoevski's novel is directed against this notion, which he puts in the mouth of one of Raskolnikov's friends. The notion itself is still around. Thus, Alex Thio in *The American Sociologist*, vol. 9, no. 1 (February 1974), p. 48: "... laws benefit the powerful, for it is much easier and less costly for them to punish the powerless criminals than to eradicate the cause of the crimes by changing the basic structure of society ... laws, by virtue of enabling the powerful to perpetuate the social-structural causes of murder, rape, arson and burglary, ensure the perpetuation of those crimes."

[2]To legally excuse an offense, it must be shown that external conditions were such that a reasonable person, acting with normal diligence could not have avoided his act—unless it is shown that the offender lacked the mental competence to know what he was doing or that what he was doing was wrong.

[3]Paul Bator, "Finality in Criminal Law and Federal *Habeas Corpus* for State Prisoners," *Harvard Law Review* 76 (1963).

[4]S. I. Shuman, *Wayne Law Review*, March 1973, pp. 853–4. Professor Shuman's argument is more intelligent than most, but otherwise prototypical.

those unjustly punished? or all convicts who come from disadvantaged groups? If such a definition were adopted, every confict, all disadvantaged convicts, or everyone unjustly punished wouod be a political prisoner. "Political prisoner" would become a synonym for "convicted," for "disadvantaged," or for "unjustly punished."

If we want to distinquish between political and other prisoners, a "political prisoner" must be defined as someone imprisoned because he tried to change the political system. The aim of his crime determines whether or not the criminal is political; the offender who intended personal enrichment cannot become a political criminal independently of his actual intent, simply because a penalty is imposed for "the inevitable consequences of a socio-political status," which led him to enrich himself illegally. If any unlawful attempt to improve one's personal situation within the existing order "because of the inevitable consequences of a certain socio-political status" is a political crime, then all crimes committed by severely deprived persons are political. But is the ghetto dweller who becomes a pimp, heroin dealer, or mugger a political criminal just as the one who becomes a violent revolutionary? Ordinarily, an offender who did not address the political order is not regarded as a political criminal, whether he is a victim of politics or not, whereas an offender whose crime did address the political order is a political criminal, even if he is not a victim of politics. This usage permits a meaningful distinction, which Professor Shuman obliterates by making "political" refer to presumptive causes rather than to overt intentions.

INEVITABLE CRIMES?

Professor Shuman goes on to claim that

"arguing that inevitability is too strong a connection between crime and poverty or ghetto existence because not all such persons commit crimes, is rather like arguing that epilepsy or heart attack ought not to excuse because not all epileptics or persons with weak hearts are involved in a chain of events which results in injury."

He adds that "those poverty or ghetto victims who do not commit crimes are extraordinary."

Surely "extraordinary" is wrong here as a statistical generalization: most poor people do not commit crimes;[5] those who do are extraordinary, not those who don't. Perhaps Professor Shuman means that it takes more resistance within than it does outside the "ghetto" not to commit crimes, which is quite likely. But "inevitabilty"? Here, the analogy with epilepsy or heart diseases is unpersuasive. Such conditions serve as legal excuses only because they produce seizures beyond the control of the person affected. These seizures are legal excuses only when they are the cause of the crime or injury or of the failure to control it. Otherwise a "weak heart" or an epileptic condition is not an excuse. Thus, poverty could not be an excuse, unless it can be shown to produce seizures beyond their control which cause the poor to commit crimes.

Poverty does not produce such seizures. Nor would poverty deprive the victim, if he were to experience a seizure (of criminality?), of control in the way an epileptic seizure does the epileptic. Poverty affects motivation and increases temptation, as does sexual frustration or, sometimes, marriage—hardly an uncontrollable seizure. To have little or no money makes it tempting to steal; the poverty-stricken person is more tempted than the rich. But a poor person is not shorn of his ability to control temptation. Indeed it is to him that the legal threat is addressed. He is able to respond to it unless he suffers from a specific individual defect or disease which makes him incompetent.

There is a generous and strong moral bias in Shuman's arguments, although he does not seem fully aware of it. The bias was already

[5]Perhaps they do—if questionnaires rather than conviction records are followed. (The reliability of questionnaire data is as questionable as that of police records.) It seems likely that about theee times as many crimes are committed as are recorded. If so, the statement "most poor people do not commit crimes" remains correct.

noted by Friedrich Nietzche when he wrote in *Beyond Good and Evil*: "[writers] are in the habit of taking the side of criminals." States in undisguised moral terms, the argument goes: the poor are entitled to rob or rape because of the injustice they suffer—poverty. The moral nature of the argument is concealed by an erroneous factual claim: poor offenders can't help committing crimes and, therefore, should not be held responsible.

The nonfactual, moral nature or bias of the argument is easily revealed if "power" is substituted for "poverty." Suppose one were to credit fully Lord Acton's famous saying: "Power tends to corrupt and absolute power corrupts absolutely." Those who hold power, then, could be held responsible for criminal acts only to some degree, since they live in conditions which tend to corrupt them. Those who hold "absolute power" can not be held responsible for criminal acts at all. They would be "power victims," as ghetto dwellers are "ghetto victims." Their rapes would be political acts, and they would be political prisoners when punished for them. Power would become a legal excuse. "Absolute power" would be an absolute excuse.

This does not appear to be what Shuman advocates. Yet he urges that poverty (or slums) should be an excuse since—like power—it leads to crime. Shuman wants to excuse the poor and not the wealthy and powerful, not because, as he suggests, poverty is causally more related to crime than wealth; rather, he sees deprivation as morally unjust and painful, and power and wealth as morally undeserved and pleasant, wherefore he wants to excuse the poor and punish the wealthy.[6] He is morally prejudiced against those corrupted by undeserved wealth—whom he gives no sign of excusing—and in favor of those corrupted by unjust deprivation.

The generosity of his prejudice leads Shuman to overlook a logical error in his argument. In some sense, everybody is what he is, and does what he does, as a result of his genetic inheritance and the influence of his environment—poverty or wealth or power—that interacted with his genetic inheritance and produced him and his conduct. This is no more the case for the poor than for the rich, for criminals than for noncriminals. However, there is no reason to believe that, except in individual cases (which require specific demonstration), genetics, or the environment, so compel actions that the actor must be excused because he could not be expected to control them.

Unless none of us is responsible for what he does, it would have to be shown why criminals, or why poor criminals, are less able to control their conduct and therefore less responsible than others. This cannot be shown by saying that they are a product of the conditions they live in. We all are. Nor can nonresponsibility be claimed by showing that their living conditions are more criminogenic than others. Greater temptation does not excuse from responsibility or make punishment unjust. The law, in attempting to mete out equal punishment, does not assume equal temptation.

When it is used to excuse crime in the way advocated by Shuman, moral indignation about squalor, however well justified, may have the paradoxical effect of contributing to high crime rates. Crime becomes less odious if moral disapproval of poverty, slums, or ghettoes becomes intense, pervasive, and exculpatory enough to suggest to the "underprivileged" that they are entitled to take revenge through crime and, when they do, to be spared punishment. Those inclined to offenses will perceive the reduced certainty and severity of punishment in such a moral climate as a failure of society to defend its social order. Offenders, not unreasonably, will attribute this failure to doubts about the jus-

[6]What are the psychological reasons (the scientific or causal as distinguished from the moral ones they rationalize) for excusing the slum-dwelling robber (who wishes to support his habit, or girl friend) and not the embezzler (who wishes to take his girl friend to Acapulco)? Wherein is the embezzler's ambition, greed, wish for prestige, sexual desire less strong, less excusable, or less predetermined by his character and experience than the slum dweller's?

tification of the social order and to guilt feelings about those deprived by it, who are believed to be "driven to crime" and, when caught, to be unjustly punished "political prisoners."

In my opinion, Shuman is wrong, but Richard Quinney[7] is embarrassing. After explaining "critical philosophy" (the Frankfurt pseudonym of Marxism) at remarkable length by means of pronouncements such as, "a critical philosophy is radically critical," and "Marx held that only under the appropriate conditions can human possibilities be realized," Quinney concludes that "criminal law is an instrument . . . to maintain and perpetuate the existing social and economic order," as though revealing something interesting, or linked to the capitalist order. Yet the criminal law always defends the existing order and those who hold power in it by penalizing those who violate it; and the legal order never can do less than articulate the "social and economic order," capitalist or socialist. How could it be otherwise? If, within a given social order, some people lawfully are richer or more powerful than others, the criminal law must *inter alia* defend their advantages.

Further, in any social order those who are not affluent and powerful are more tempted to rebel, or to take what is not theirs, than those who are—who need not take what they already have. Hence, the burden of the law falls most heavily on the least privileged: the threats and punishments of the criminal law are meant to discourage those who are tempted to violate it, not those who are not. Marxists are as right in saying that the criminal law is addressed disproportionately to the poor as Anatole France was in his witticism: "the law in its majestic equality forbids rich and poor alike . . . to steal bread." However, that discovery is about as interesting as the disclosure that the prohibition law was meant to restrain drinkers rather than the teetotalers who imposed it. The criminal law would be redundant if it did not address those

tempted—by taste or social position—to break it.

Quinney also asserts that with socialism "law as we know it" will disappear, for "the crime problem" will be solved "once society has removed all possibility of hatred" (August Bebel). Trotsky held similar views: under socialism

"man will be incomparably stronger, more intelligent, more subtle. His body will be more harmonious, his movements more rhythmical, his voice more musical; his style of life will acquire a dynamic beauty. The average type of man will rise to the level of an Aristotle, Goethe, Marx. From this mountain crest, the new peaks will rise."[8]

Bebel and Trotsky had no experience of socialism when they wrote. Richard Quinney must be congratulated for managing to preserve or regain his innocence, untainted by the available theoretical and practical experience. Bereft of Quinney's innocence, I do not foresee a society—socialist or otherwise—in which men will not quarrel and envy each other, wherefore the criminal law will have to restrain them and protect the social order against those who are, or feel, disadvantaged by it. At present the societies which claim to be socialist seem to use legal punishments more than others.[9] I see no reason for maintaining that future socialist societies—whatever form of socialism they adopt—will need criminal law any less.

BLACK CRIME RATES

Crime among blacks occurs at a rate about 10 times higher than among whites, when blacks and whites are compared as groups. Most crimes are intraracial. The victims of violent crimes are almost as often black as the criminals. (The victims of property crimes committed by blacks and of assaultive crimes concerned with property, such as robbery, are more often white.) Some figures may give an idea of the gross dif-

---

[7]Richard Quinney, *Critique of Legal Order: Crime Control in a Capitalist Society* (Boston: Little Brown & Co., 1974).

[8]Leon Trotsky, *Literature and Revolution,* (New York: Russell & Russell, 1957).

[9]Solzhenitsyn's *Gulag Archipelago* is only the latest illustration of this well-known phenomenon.

ference. In 1970 blacks in the United States accounted for about 60 percent of all arrests for murder and, according to the FBI's figures, for 65 percent of the arrests for robbery.[10] (Blacks constitute 12 percent of the population.) The difference between black and white crime rates may well be explained by different environments. What has been said in the preceeding section should prevent confusion of such an explanation with a justification for individual offenders.

However, simple comparisons of black and white crime rates are misleading. They ignore the fact that a greater proportion of blacks are young and poor, and the young and poor of any race display the highest crime rates. In other words, the age- and income-related variances must not be attributed to race. The age-specific crime rates of blacks are only slightly higher than those of whites on the same socio-economic level.[11] The remaining difference cannot be attributed to racially discriminating law enforcement.[12] What discrimination there is may lead in the opposite direction. Crime is less often reported in black communities, and police are less inclined to arrest blacks for crimes against blacks then they are to arrest whites for crimes against whites.

The difference in crime rates should not come as a surprise. Blacks have been oppressed for a long time. Many are recent migrants from rural to urban areas who have the usual difficulties of acculturation faced by most immigrants.

Their access to the labor market was, and still is, limited because of lack of training due to past discrimination. All this has some effect on the legitimate opportunities available to them and, as importantly perhaps, on the ability of individuals to utilize what opportunities there are.

Thus, we should expect a somewhat higher crime rate for blacks, and no explanation in *current* economic terms is needed. Such an explanation would not be supported by the available data. Between 1960 and 1970, the medium income of white families went up 69 percent; that of black families doubled. Whereas only 3 percent of black families earned more than $10,000 a year in 1951, 13 percent did so in 1971.[13] Thus disparity between the income (and the social status) of blacks and whites, though it remains considerable, has been diminished even faster than the difference between white poor and nonpoor. The difference between black and white crime rates has not decreased. Clearly the crude economic explanation—poverty—won't do. Possibly resentment of the remaining disparities has not decreased as these disparities have become fewer and less considerable. Resentment, then, could have prevented the black crime rates from falling as blacks become less deprived and the black-white difference in economic and social status become smaller.[14]

Continuing cultural differences, created by

---

[10]F. B. Graham, "Black Crime: The Lawless Image," *Harper's Magazine*, September 1970, p. 64.

[11]See M. A. Forslund, "A Comparison of Negro and White Crime Rates," *Journal of Criminal Law, Criminology and Police Science* 61 (June 1970); E. R. Moses, "Negro and White Crime Rates," in M. E. Wolfgang et al., eds., *The Sociology of Crime and Delinquency* (New York: John Wiley & Sons, 1970); R. M. Stephenson and F. R. Scarpitti, "Negro-White Differentials in Delinquency," *Journal of Research in Crime and Delinquency* 5 (July 1968).

[12]See D. J. Black and A. J. Reiss, Jr., "Police Control of Juveniles," *American Sociological Review* 35 (January 1970); E. Green, "Race, Social Status and Criminal Arrest," *American Sociological Review* 35 (June 1970).

[13]The figures used are in dollars of constant purchasing power, that is, they exclude the effects of inflation; they are taken from Ben J. Wattenberg and Richard M. Scammon, "Black Progress and Liberal Rhetoric," *Commentary*, April 1973, p. 35.

[14]For teenagers, the economic picture is darker. And teenagers account for much crime. One-third of black teenagers were unemployed in 1971, against 15 percent of white teenagers. The high unemployment rate probably contributed to high crime rates in both cases, and the difference in the unemployment rate of white and black teenagers contributed to the difference in crime rates. The high teenage unemployment rates may be causes at least in part by minimum wage legislation, which requires that teenagers be paid a minimum, which often exceeds what their production is worth to employers. (The minimum wage rate for most other workers rarely is above what they are worth to employers.)

historical circumstances, probably contribute to the difference in crime rates of blacks and whites as well; but we know too little as yet to usefully describe, let alone explain, these cultural differences. Phrases such as "the culture of violence" merely describe what is yet to be understood.[15] Surely crime is largely produced by the life styles generated by the subcultures characteristic of those who commit it. But does this tell us more than that crime is produced by a crime-producing subculture?

ENVIRONMENT AND PERSONALITY

What are we to conclude? Many people, black and white, living under the conditions ordinarily associated with high crime rates—such as poverty or inequality—do not commit crimes, while many people not living under these conditions do. It follows that these conditions are neither necessary nor sufficient to cause crime. Crime rates have risen as poverty and inequality have declined. It follows that high crime rates need not depend on more poverty or inequality and are not remedied by less. More resentment may increase crime rates even when there is less poverty—but resentment is hard to measure and may increase with improving conditions, as was pointed out by Alexis de Tocqueville.[16]

Since the incidence of crime among the poor is higher than among the nonpoor, it is quite likely that when combined with other ingredients—not always easily discerned—poverty and inequality do produce high crime

rates, probably by affecting motivations and temptations. Thus, poverty may be an important element—though neither indispensable nor sufficient by itself—in the combination that produces high crime rates and explains the variance among groups. But recognition of the importance of poverty as a criminogenic condition should not lead us to neglect individual differences. Enrico Ferri, unlike some of his latter-day followers, did not neglect them. He wrote:

"If you regard the general condition of misery as the sole source of criminality, then you cannot get around the difficulty that out of the one thousand individuals living in misery from the day of their birth to that of their death, only one hundred or two hundred become criminals. . . . If poverty were the sole determining cause, one thousand out of one thousand poor ought to become criminals. If only two hundred become criminals, while one hundred commit suicide, one hundred end as maniacs, the other six hundred remain honest in their social condition, then poverty alone is not sufficient to explain criminality.[17]

THE LEGAL AND THE SOCIAL APPROACH

Surely it is futile to contrast environmental (social) with individual (psychological) causation, as though they were mutually exclusive alternatives. Instead, we might ask in quantitative terms:

1.   How much of the variance in crime rates—among social groups, or between two time periods—is controlled by specific differences in social conditions?

2.   Which of these (*a*) can be changed; (*b*) at what cost, monetary or otherwise?

3.   At what cost can we then reduce the crime rate in general, or the variance, by changing social conditions? What specific social

---

[15]Ghettoization does not explain much, for, except for black ghettoes, the incidence of crime in ghettoes (ethnically segregated slums) is low. In Chinese or Jewish ghettoes there was little crime. On the other hand, variances in crime rates everywhere are associated with ethnic differences.

[16]Democracy in America. For example:

"It is natural that the love of equality should constantly increase together with equality itself, and that it should grow by what it feeds on. . . ."

". . . The mere fact that certain abuses have been remedied draws attention to the others and they now appear more galling; people may suffer less, but their sensibility is exacerbated. . . ."

[17]Enrico Ferri, *The Positive School of Criminology,* ed. Stanley E. Grupp (Pittsburgh: University of Pittsburgh, Press, 1968), p. 60.

change in likely to bring about what specific change in crime rates and in variances?

To illustrate: if we assume that X percent of the variance between black and white crime rates is explained by the lower employment rates of black males, then we might be able to predict that a rise of X percent in the employment rate of black males would lead to a decline of X percent in the crime rate or in the variance. There are all kinds of pitfalls in such a simplified model. Employment rates, for instance, are determined by a variety of factors. Richard Cloward came to grief by assuming that employment rates are determined exclusively by employment opportunities.[18]

Still, in the apt words of Enrico Ferri: "Certain discreet shelters arranged in convenient places contribute more to the cleanliness of cities than fines or arrests."[19] Ferri meant public urinals. But the principle applies to any change in the social or physical environment, and the questions it poses are always: (1) What is the ratio of the cost of the change in social conditions to the benefit (the reduction in crime rates) compared to the ratio of a change in other variables (for example, expenditures on police; higher or more regular punishments) to the benefit (the reduction in crime rates)? (2) Given these ratios, which change is preferable in view of other merits or demerits?

Parking violations can be reduced by better policing, higher fines, and more public garages. Very high fines would help, but may not be tolerable. More public garages will help, but may be too costly. Without some punishment for violation, there would be no incentive to use public garages, and without some legitimate opportunity, it is likely that the law will be violated unless punishments are extremely severe and certain. The alternatives—"improve social conditions" and "increase punishment"—are not mutually exclusive. They are cumulative. The question is, which combination promises the greatest benefits at the least cost.

[18]See Daniel Patrick Moynihan's *Maximum Feasible Misunderstanding* (New York; The Free Press, 1969) for an analysis of these pitfalls.

[19]Enrico Ferri, *Criminal Sociology* (New York: Agathon Press, Inc., 1917), p. 24.

The Causes of Crime:
Causation and Prediction

THE ULTIMATE CONCERN OF ANY SCIENTIST MUST BE THE DETECTION OF CAUSAL patterns. If this is difficult in the physical sciences, it seems incredibly complex in the social sciences. The first two selections address themselves to certain problems encountered in this quest. MacIver's short statement on social causation reveals several difficulties that are inevitably met in attempting to ascertain basic causes of a relativistic phenomenon such as crime. Hirschi and Selvin, in a frequently reprinted article, affirm that statements as to causation can be made only when three conditions are present; an appropriate statistical analysis is made based on an observed association between dependent and independent variables; the latter is causally prior to the former; and there is no spurious relationship. The authors then proceed to cite a number of false criteria of causality that tend to assert instead of prove the manner in which some sociological factor "causes" crime.

Prediction, as distinguished from causation, does not attempt to ascertain true causal linkages but, instead, utilizes any combination of predictor items that will indicate relative risks of the occurence of future behavior for members of a group or population. Wilkins deals with the serious objection to the use of any prediction device because each individual is unique, and even the most efficient and valid prediction cannot state with certitude that a particular person will do. A good prediction instrument need not produce meaningful results, but it should produce powerful (accurate) results. Simon's selection claims that the function of prediction is to identify in a group those who are at risk of committing crimes and to determine the relative degrees of risk.

21. Social Causation

ROBERT MACIVER

IT IS VAIN TO SEEK THE CAUSES OF CRIME AS such, of crime anywhere and everywhere. Crime is a legal category. The only thing that is alike in all crimes is that they are alike violations of law. In that sense the only cause of crime as such is the law itself. What is a crime in one country is no crime in another; what is a crime at one time is no crime at another. The law is forever changing, adding new crimes to the catalogue and cancelling former ones. It may even, as not infrequently happens in times of crisis or revolution, designate as the most heinous of crimes certain forms of behavior that were previously counted highly honorable. Since, then, crime varies with the law, the conditions that evoke it are equally variant. Moreover, the social conditions that increase the frequency of some categories of crime may diminish the frequency of others. Crime, then, is essentially relative. It has no inherent quality or property attaching to it as such, attaching to crime of all categories under all conditions. If indeed we do raise the question: Why crime? we are asking merely why people are so constituted that they violate laws under any conditions whatever. The question has no more specific significance than the question: Why human nature?

Since crime, as a category of social action, has no inherent universal property, we cannot expect to find, in the variety of persons who are convicted of crimes, any one psychological or physiological type, any character trait whatever that differentiates them all from other persons. The crime committer may be a maniac or a genius, a scoundrel or a patriot, a man without scruple or a man who puts his scruples above the law, a reckless exploiter or a man in desperate need. All attempts to find a physiognomy of crime have failed.[1] The vaguer attempts to find a particular mentality associated with law-breaking are without warrant. The endless vicissitudes of circumstance, opportunity, and personal history preclude the expectation of any simple inclusive formula. There are, of course, criminal groups, gangs, habitual offenders who make a profession of crime under similar conditions, and these may well develop, like any other social or professional groups, their own distinctive traits.

These considerations reinforce the position we have already stated and which we shall develop more fully later on, that the only effective quest for causes is that which enquires into a specific difference between two or more comparable situations. The more determinate the difference and the more clearly comparable the situations, the more promising is the quest. If, for example, certain crimes are more in evidence during depressions than in better times,

[1]The most recent and most elaborate attempt is that of E. A. Hooton, *The American Criminal*, Cambridge, Massachusetts, 1939. See the searching criticism by Robert Merton and M. F. Ashley-Montagu, "Crime and the Antropologist," *American Anthropologist* (July-September, 1940), Vol. 42, pp. 384–408.

under the same social system, and if these crimes have a relative economic aspect, the problem is specific and easily attacked. But if there is a greater frequency of crime or of certain crimes among business people, the problem is not yet demarcated, since many other conditions besides the mode of occupation distinquish the social groups to which laborers predominantly belong from the social groups to which business people predominantly belong. Or again, if there is a greater frequency of crime among bachelors than among married men, we cannot at once proceed to the question: Why does the marital condition act as a deterrent of crime? For there may very well be other factors than the married state distinguishing the unmarried, as a broad social category, from the married. First we must analyze our difference-revealing groups and situations to discover the grounds of their comparability, relative to the phenomenon under investigation. It is only when we have discovered in this way specific relations between crime and situation that we can hope to throw much light on any larger issues regarding the incidence of crime.

It is not unusual for writers on the subject of crime to be preoccupied with some types of crime and to explain crime in general by considerations drawn from the study of these types. We find this tendency in some authors who have made a particular study of gangs, and who consequently are apt to identify the gangster with the criminal. We should observe also that the expression "the criminal" has certain connotations that limit its application. A great number of those who commit crimes are not "criminals," as that term is usually understood. Hence even if we could explain why men become criminals, or habitual offenders within a certain range of crime, we would not have thereby explained why men commit crimes.

The opposite error, but one invoking a more flagrant confusion, is attributable to those who, in dealing with the causes of crime, are mainly concerned with moral explanations. Often they write as though crime itself were almost equivialent to wrong-doing or "immortality." We find this tendency in a number of writers who are content to refer crime to "bad homes," "vicious neighborhoods," "the weakening of the moral sense," "bad heredity," "lack of social control," "individualism," "egocentricity," "the decay of religious life," "the decline of social standards," and so forth. Such explanations are in the first instance vague and inconclusive. They introduce indeterminate principles as though they were determinate causes. If these principles explain anything—though they themselves require more definition and explanation than the phenomena to which they are applied—they explain a host of other things as much, and therefore as badly. But our objection at this point is that they fail to recognize the distinction between a moral category and a legal category. No one would deny that moral attitudes are involved in violations of the legal code. But we cannot assume that there is one characteristic type of moral attitude, describable as individualsim, egocentricity, and so forth, that is peculiarly associated with the commission of crime. A crime is an infraction of a legal code that is not identical with any of the diverse moral codes of groups or individuals. The numerous conjectures of occasion, opportunity, personal experience, and socio-economic situation, to which acts of crime are responsive, make the appeal to any universal moral principle at best an inadequate and unilluminating explanation.

A simple correlation predicates no nexus between the correlated variables. It merely directs our enquiry in a particular direction. Where there is causation there is also correlation, but where there is correlation there may be no corresponding causation. Many things are happening and many things are changing at the same time. Some are causally independent, some are interdependent, some are alike dependent on the same larger causal scheme but not on one another. A correlation is a clue or a question mark. Its significance is what we can infer from it or what we may learn by following the lead it provides. Sometimes we can draw no inference, sometimes the lead peters out. Correlation techniques are extremely useful in many areas of investigation, both in the physical and in the social sciences, but their heuristic value is small where the correlated variables do not fall within or cannot be brought within a single coherent order. An illustration or two may suffice.

"If bales of heavy dark wood and equally heavy bales of light colored aspen wood are compared (as to the relationship between weight and volume), then an influence of coloring on the weight might be disclosed which actually does not exist. The statistics of Russian compulsory fire insurance discloses a striking relationship between the average number of buildings destroyed in one conflagration in the country and the use or non-use of fire engines for its extinction: fires extinguished by a fire brigade furnished with a fire engine are, on the average, more destructive than others. To conclude from this that the destruction of fire engines constitutes the best means of reducing damage from fire would be . . . absurd".[2]

Why is this conclusion absurd? Not because it is inconsistent with other correlations. Established correlations cannot contradict one another, because they assert nothing regarding the relationship of the correlated variables. The conclusion is absurd because it is inconsistent with all the causal knowledge we already possess regarding the relationship of fire engines and fires. This illustration brings out the principle that the discovery of a correlation can serve only as the starting point for further investigation and analysis. This principle has a particular significance for the social sciences. We discover, for example, various correlations of social phenomena and physical phenomena. We discover, say, that the frequency of homicide is positively correlated with the summer rise of temperature. We cannot stop there. We certainly cannot conclude forthwith that summer heat is a caause of homicide. Nor again can we conclude that wintry weather is a cause of crimes against property. The nexus between summer heat and homicide, if one exists, is not immediate. We must seek for a more direct relation between homicide and certain ways of living, certain modes of behaving, that are associated, under certain conditions of civilization, with the season of hot weather. We may thus find a nexus that is not only more direct but also more understandable, more coherent with what knowledge we already possess regarding the responses of human beings to the conditions under which they live.[3]

The fallacy of this assumption is so simple that it ought to be immediately obvious, but it is committed rather frequently in studies of social causation. When a number of diverse factors are interactive and when a particular phenomenon is the result of their interactivity, we cannot treat them as though they were independent, homogeneous units each of which produces a measurable portion of their joint product. This crudely mechanistic assumption vitiates those investigations that seek to assess, often in precise quantitative terms, the role of the various components of a causal complex. It is present when writers list in order of priority or of importance the *diverse* causes they postulate for crime, unemployment, divorce, and other phenomena, the prevalence of which is subject to statistical measurement.

We have called this fallacy "mechanistic," meaning thereby it treats the various components of a social situation, or of any organized system, as though they were detachable, isolable, homogeneous, independently operative, and therefore susceptible of being added to or subtracted from the causal complex, increasing or decreasing the result by that amount. But even a slight acquaintance with mechanism itself should teach us to avoid this fallacy. We find writers who tell us that juvenile delinquency is due so much to this factor and so much to that and so much to this other. But no mechanic would make the mistake of saying that the car-

---

[2]A. A. Tschuprow, *Principles of the Mathematical Theory of Correlation* (London, 1939), p. 21.

[3]On this subject we see the writer's book, *Society: A Textbook of Sociology* (New York, 1973), Chap. V.

buretor contributed so much and the ignition system so much and the gasoline so much to the speed of the car.[4] If a car is an organization of parts and materials that interdependently determine its functioning, at least no less so is a society. Moreover, the conditions to which social phenomena are responsive belong to a variety of different orders, so as to make the comparative rating of factors within the causal complex even more incongruous. When we are faced with the problem of multiple order causation we must proceed upon entirely different lines. In due course we shall deal with it. For the present a simple illustration may suffice. Various studies have been made of fatigue as a cause of industrial accidents.[5] These have led in turn to researches into the cause of fatigue in industrial operations. Evidences have been adduced to show that, besides the physical factors lying in the nature of the work itself and of the working conditions and besides the physiological factors of the health and strength of the workers, there are also psycho-sociological factors, described in such terms as "morale," "emotional adjustment," "co-operative and non-co-operative attitudes," and so on.[6] The issue here raised is that the valuations and attitudes of the workers are *interactive* with the physical conditions in the causation of fatigue and that therefore neither set of factors can be independently assessed. If this is so for a localized physiological phenomenon such as industrial fatigue, how much more should we pause before attempting to attach any independent or absolute rating to the numerous factors involved in the wide-ranging social phenomenon of crime!

---

[4]It is of course another matter altogether to attribute to a change in any one factor, given the other factors as before, a difference, under stipulated conditions, in the result, say in the speed of the car. An important distinction between a mechanical unity and an organic or a social unity is that we can often change one factor in the former while keeping all the others wholly or practically unchanged.

[5]For example, Emery S. Bogardus, *The Relation of Fatigue to Industrial Accidents,* Chicago, 1912.

[6]An account of the conclusions to this effect of the Committee on Elimination of Fatigue in Industry is given by Donald A. Laird, "Work and Fatigue," *Scientific American* (1930), Vol. 143, pp. 24–26.

22. False Criteria of Causality

TRAVIS HIRSCHI
HANAN C. SELVIN

"SMOKING PER SE IS NOT A CAUSE OF LUNG CANCER. Evidence for this statement comes from the thousands of people who smoke and yet live normal, healthy lives. Lung cancer is simply unknown to the vast majority of smokers, even among those who smoke two or more packs a day. Whether smoking is a cause of lung cancer, then, depends upon the reaction of the lung tissues to the smoke inhaled. The important thing is not whether a person smokes, but how his lungs react to the smoke inhaled. These facts point to the danger of imputing causal significance to superficial variables. In essence, it is not smoking as such, but the carcinogenic elements in tobacco smoke that are the real causes of lung cancer."[1]

The task of determining whether such variables as broken homes, gang membership, or anomie are "causes" of delinquency benefits from a comparison with the more familiar problem of deciding whether cigarette smoking "causes" cancer. In both fields many statistical studies have shown strong relations between these presumed causes and the observed effects, but the critics of these studies often attack them as "merely statistical." This phrase has two meanings. To some critics it stands for the belief that only with experimental manipulation of the independent variables is a satisfactory causal inference possible. To others it is a brief way of saying that observing a statistical association between two phenomena is only the first step in plausibly inferring causality. Since no one proposes trying to give people cancer or to make them delinquent, the fruitful way toward better causal analyses in these two fields is to concentrate on improving the statistical approach.

In setting this task for ourselves we can begin with one area of agreement: all statistical analyses of causal relations in delinquency rest on observed associations between the independent and dependent variables. Beyond this there is less agreement. Following Hyman's reasoning,[2] we believe that these two additional criteria are the minimum requirements for an adequate causal analysis: (1) the independent variable is causally prior to the dependent variable (we shall refer to this as the criterion of "causal order"), and (2) the original association does not disappear when the influences of other variables causally prior to both of the original variables are removed ("lack of spuriousness").[3]

▶SOURCE: *False Criteria of Causality in Delinquency," Social Problems* (Winter 1966), 13(3):254–268. Reprinted by permission.

[1]This is a manufactured "quotation"; its source will become obvious shortly.

[2]Herbert H. Hyman, *Survey Design and Analysis.* Glencoe, Illinois: The Free Press, 1955, chs. 5–7.

[3]Hyman appears to advocate another criterion as well: that a chain of intervening variables must link the independent and dependent variables of the original relation. We regard this as psychologically or theoretically desirable but

The investigator who tries to meet these criteria does not have an easy time of it.[4] Our examination of statistical research on the causes of delinquency shows, however, that many investigators do not try to meet these criteria but instead invent one or another new criterion of causality—or, more often, of noncausality, perhaps because noncausality is easier to demonstrate. To establish causality one must forge a chain of three links (association, causal order, and lack of spuriousness), and the possibility that an antecedent variable not yet considered may account for the observed relation makes the third link inherently weak. To establish noncausality, one has only to break any one of these links.[5]

Despite the greater ease with which noncausality may be demonstrated, many assertions of noncausality in the delinquency literature turn out to be invalid. Some are invalid because the authors misuse statistical tools or misinterpret their findings. But many more are invalid because the authors invoke one or another false criterion of noncausality. Perhaps because assertions of noncausality are so easy to demonstrate, these invalid assertions have received a great deal of attention.

A clear assertion that certain variables long considered causes of delinquency are not really causes come from a 1960 *Report to the Congress:*

"Many factors frequently cited as causes of delinquency are really only concomitants. They are not causes in the sense that if they were removed delinquency would decline. Among these factors are:
Broken homes.
Poverty.
Poor housing.
Lack of recreational facilities.
Poor physical health.
Race.
Working mothers."[6]

According to this report, all of these variables are statistically associated with delinquency, i.e., they are all "concomitants." To prove that they are not causes of delinquency it is necessary either to show that their relations with delinquency are spurious or that they are effects of delinquency rather than causes. Since all of these presumptive causes appear to precede delinquency, the only legitimate way to prove noncausality is to find an antecedent variable that accounts for the observed relations. None of the studies cited in the *Report* does this.[7] Instead, the assertion that broken homes, poverty, lack of recreational facilities, race, and working mothers are not causes of delinquency appears to be based on one or more of the following false "criteria":[8]

---

not as part of the minimum methodological requirements for demonstrating causality in nonexperimental research.

[4]Hirschi and Selvin, *op. cit.*

[5]Popper calls this the asymmetry of verifiability and falsifiability. Karl R. Popper, *The Logic of Scientific Discovery*, New York: Basic Books, 1959, esp. pp. 27–48. For a fresh view of the verification-falsification controversey, see Thomas S. Kuhn, *The Structure of Scientific Revolutions*, Chicago: University of Chicago Press, 1962. Kuhn discusses Popper's views on pp. 145–146. Actually, it is harder to establish noncausality than our statement suggests, because of the possibility of "spurious independence." This problem is discussed in Hirschi and Selvin, *op. cit.*, pp. 38–45, as "elaboration of a zero relation."

[6]U.S. Department of Health, Education, and Welfare, *Report to The Congress on Juvenile Delinquency*, United States Government Printing Office, 1960, p. 21. The conclusion that "poor housing" is not a cause of delinquency is based on Mildred Hartsough, *The Relation Between Housing and Delinquency*, Federal Emergency Administration of Public Works, Housing Division, 1936. The conclusion that "poor physical health" is not a cause is based on Edward Piper's "unpublished Children's Bureau manuscript summarizing the findings of numerous investigators on this subject." Since we have not examined these two works, the following conclusions do not apply to them.

[7]The works cited are: broken homes, Negly K. Teeters and John Otto Reinemann, *The Challenge of Delinquency*, New York: Prentice-Hall, 1950, pp. 149–154; poverty, Bernard Lander, *Toward an Understanding of Juvenile Delinquency*, New York: Columbia University Press, 1954; recreational facilities, Ethel Shanas and Catherine E. Dunning, *Recreation and Delinquency*, Chicago: Chicago Recreation Commission, 1942; race, Lander, *op cit.*, working mothers, Eleanor E. Maccoby, "Children and Working Mothers," *Children,* 5 (May-June, 1958), pp. 83–89.

[8]It is not clear in every case that the researcher himself reached the conclusion of noncausality or, if he did, that this

1. Insofar as a relation between two variables is not *perfect,* the relation is not causal.

(a) Insofar as a factor is not a *necessary condition* for delinquency, it is not a cause of delinquency.

(b) Insofar as a factor is not a *sufficient condition* for delinquency, it is not a cause of delinquency.

2. Insofar as a factor is not *"characteristic"* of delinquents, it is not a cause of delinquency.

3. If a relation between an independent variable and delinquency is found for a *single value of a situational or contextual factor,* then the situational or contextual factor cannot be a cause of delinquency.[9]

4. If a relation is observed between an independent variable and delinquency and if a psychological variable is suggested as *intervening* between these two variables, then the origianl relation is not causal.

5. *Measurable* variables are not causes.

6. If a relation between an independent variable and delinquency is *conditional* upon the

conclusion was based on the false criteria discussed below. Maccoby's article, for example, contains a "conjectural explanation" of the relation between mother's employment and delinquency (i.e., without presenting any statistical evidence she suggests that the original relation came about through some antecedent variable), but it appears that the conclusion of noncausality in the *Report* is based on other statements in her work.

[9] All of the foregoing criteria are related to the "perfect relation" criterion in that they all require variation in delinquency that is unexplained by the "noncausal" variable. A more general statement of criterion 3 would be: "if variable X is related to delinquency when there is no variation in variable T, then variable T is not a cause of delinquency." In order for this criterion to be applicable, there must be some residual variation in delinquency after T has had its effect. Although both forms of this criterion fairly represent the reasoning involved in some claims of non-causality, and although both are false, the less explicit version in the text is superficially more plausible. This inverse relation between explicitness and plausibility is one reason for the kind of methodological explication presented here.

value of other variables, the independent variable is not a cause of delinquency.

In our opinion, all of these criteria of noncausality are illegitimate. If they were systematically applied to any field of research, no relation would survive the test. Some of them, however, have a superficial plausibility, both as stated or implied in the original works and as reformulated here. It will therefore be useful to consider in some detail just why these criteria are illegitimate and to see how they reappear in delinquency research.

False Criterion 1. Insofar as a relation between two variables is not perfect, the relation is not causal.

"Despite the preponderance of Negro delinquency, one must beware of imputing any causal significance to race per se. There is no *necessary* concomitance between the presence of Negroes and delinquency. In Census Tracts 9-1 and 20-2, with populations of 124 and 75 Negro juveniles, there were no recorded cases of delinquency during the study period. The rates of Negro delinquency also vary as widely as do the white rates indicating large differences in behavior patterns that are not a function or effect of race per se. It is also of interest to note that in at least 10% of the districts with substantial Negro juvenile populations, the Negro delinquency rate is lower than the corresponding white rate."[10]

There are three facts here (1) not all Negroes are delinquents; (2) the rates of Negro delinquency vary from place to place; (3) in some circumstances, Negroes are less likely than whites to be delinquent. These facts lead Lander to conclude that race has no causal significance in delinquency.

In each case the reasoning is the same: each fact is another way of saying that the statistical relation between race and delinquency is not perfect, and this apparently is enough to dis-

[10] Bernard Lander, *Towards an Understanding of Juvenile Delinquency,* New York: Columbia University Press, p. 32. Italics in original. An alternative interpretation of the assumptions implicit in this quotation is presented in the discussion of criterion 6, below.

qualify race as a cause. To see why this reasoning is invalid one has only to ask for the conductions under which race *could be* a cause of delinquency if this criterion were accepted. Suppose that the contrary of the first fact were true, that *all* Negroes are delinquent. It would then follow necessarily that Negro delinquency rates would not vary from place to place (fact 2) and that the white rate would never be greater than the Negro rate (fact 3). Thus in order for race to have "any" causal significance, all Negroes must be delinquents (or all whites non-delinquents). In short, race must be perfectly related to delinquency.[11]

Now if an independent variable and a dependent variable are perfectly associated,[12] no other independent variable is needed: that is, perfect association implies single causation, and less-than-perfect association implies multiple causation. Rejecting as causes of delinquency those variables whose association with delinquency is less than perfect thus implies rejecting the principle of multiple-causation. Although there is nothing sacred about this principle, at least at the level of empirical research it is more viable than the principal of single causation. All studies show that more than one independent variable is needed to account for delinquency. In this field, as in others, perfect relations are virtually unknown. The researcher who finds a less-than-perfect relation between variable X and delinquency should not conclude that X is not a cause of delinquency, but merely that it is not the *only* cause.[13]

For example, suppose that tables like the following have been found for variables A, B, C, and D as well as for X (Table I). The researcher using the perfect relation criterion would have to conclude that none of the causes of delinquency has yet been discovered. Indeed, this criterion would force him to conclude that there are *no causes* of delinquency except *the* cause. The far-from-perfect relation between variable X and delinquency in the table above leads him to reject variable X as a cause of delinquency. Since variables, A, B, C, and D are also far from perfectly related to delinquency, he must likewise reject them. Since it is unlikely that *the* cause of delinquency will ever be discovered by quantitative research, the researcher who accepts the perfect relation criterion should come to believe that such research is useless: all it can show is that there are *no* causes of delinquency.

[11]Strictly speaking, in this quotation Lander does not demand that race be perfectly related to delinquency, but only that all Negroes be delinquents (the sufficient conditions of criterion 1-b). Precedent for the "perfect relation" criterion of causality appears in a generally excellent critique of crime and delinquency research by Jerome Michael and Mortimer J. Adler published in 1933: "There is still another way of saying that none of the statistical findings derived from the quantitative data yields answers to etiological questions. The findings themselves show that every factor which can be seen to be in some way associated with criminality is also associated with non-criminality, and also that criminality is found in the absence of every factor with which it is also seen to be associated. In other words, what has been found is merely additional evidence of what we either knew or could have suspected, namely, that there is a plurality of related factors in this field." *Crime, Law and Social Science,* New York: Harcourt Brace, p. 53.

[12]"Perfect association" here means that all of the cases fall into the main diagonal of the table, that (in the 2 × 2 table) the independent variable is both a necessary and a sufficient cause of the dependent variable. Less stringent definitions of perfect association are considered in the following paragraphs. Since Lander deals with ecological correlations, he could reject race as a cause of delinquency even if it were perfectly related to delinquency at the census tract level, since the ecological and the individual correlations are not identical.

Table I. Delinquency by X, Where X Is Neither a Necessary Nor a Sufficient Condition for Delinquency, but May Be One of Several Causes

	X	Not X
Delinquent	40	20
Nondelinquent	60	80

[13]We are assuming that the causal order and lack of spuriousness criteria are satisfied.

False Criterion 1-a. Insofar as a factor is not a necessary condition for delinquency, it is not a cause of delinquency.

The "not necessary" (and of course the "not sufficient") argument against causation is a variant of the "perfect relation" criterion. A factor is a necessary condition for delinquency if it must be present for delinquency to occur—e.g., knowledge of the operation of an automobile is a necessary condition for auto theft (although all individuals charged with auto theft need not know how to drive a car). In the following table the independent variable X is a necessary (but not sufficient[14]) condition for delinquency (Table II).

The strongest statement we can find in the work cited by the Children's Bureau in support of the contention that the broken home is not a cause of delinquency is the following:

"We can leave this phase of the subject by stating that the phenomenon of the physically broken home is a cause of delinquent behavior is, in itself, not so important as was once believed. In essence, it is not that the home is broken, but rather that the home is inadequate, that really matters."[15]

This statement suggests that the broken home is not a necessary condition for delinquency (de-

Table II. Delinquency by X, Where X Is a Necessary but Not Sufficient Condition for Delinquency

	X	Not X
Delinquent	67	0
Nondelinquent	33	100

[14]To say that X is a necessary condition for delinquency means that all delinquents are X (i.e., that the cell in the upper right of this table is zero); to say that X is a sufficient condition for delinquency implies that all X's are delinquent (i.e., that the cell in the lower left is zero); to say that X is a necessary and sufficient condition for delinquency means that all X's and no other persons are delinquent (i.e., that both cells in the minor diagonal of this table are zero).

[15]Teeters and Reinemann, *op. cit.,* p. 154.

linquents may come from intact but "inadequate" homes). The variable with which the broken home is compared, inadequacy, has all the attributes of a necessary condition for delinquency: a home that is "adequate" with respect to the prevention of delinquency will obviously produce no delinquent children. If, as appears to be the case, the relation between inadequacy and delinquency is a matter of definition, the comparison of this relation with the relation between the broken home and delinquency is simply an application of the illegitimate "necessary conditions" criterion. Compared to a necessary condition, the broken home is "not so important." Compared to some (or some *other) measure* of inadequacy, however, the broken home may be very important. For that matter, once "inadequacy" is empirically defined, the broken home may turn out to be one of its important causes. Thus the fact that the broken home is not a necessary condition for delinquency does not justify the statement that the broken home is "not [a cause of delinquency] in the sense that if [it] were removed delinquency would decline."[16]

False Criterion 1-b. Insofar as a factor is not a sufficient condition for delinquency, it is not a cause of delinquency.

A factor is a sufficient condition for delinquency if its presence is invariably followed by delinquency. Examples of sufficient conditions are hard to find in empirical research.[17] The

[16]*Report to The Congress,* p. 21. Two additional illegitimate criteria of causality listed above are implicit in the quotation from Teeters and Reinemann. "Inadequacy of the home" could be treated as an intervening variable which interprets the relation between the broken home and delinquency (criterion 4) or as a theoretical variable of which the broken home is an indicator (criterion 5). These criteria are discussed below.

[17]In his *Theory of Collective Behavior* (New York: The Free Press of Glencoe, 1963) Neil J. Smelser suggests sets of necessary conditions for riots, panics, and other forms of collective behavior; in this theory the entire set of necessary conditions for any one form of behavior is a sufficient condition for that form to occur.

nearest one comes to such conditions in delinquency research is in the use of predictive devices in which several factors taken together are virtually sufficient for delinquency.[18] (The fact that several variables are required even to approach sufficiency is of course one of the strongest arguments in favor of multiple causation.) Since sufficient conditions are rare, this unrealistic standard can be used against almost any imputation of causality.

"First, however, let us make our position clear on the question. Poverty per se is not a cause of delinquency or criminal behavior; this statement is evidenced by the courage, fortitude, honesty, and moral stamina of thousands of parents who would rather starve than steal and who inculcate this attitude in their children. Even in the blighted neighborhoods of poverty and wretched housing conditions, crime and delinquency are simply nonexistent among residents."[19]

"Many mothers, and some fathers, who have lost their mates through separation, divorce, or death, are doing a splendid job of rearing their children."[20]

"Our point of view is that the structure of the family *itself* does not cause delinquency. For example, the fact that a home is broken does not cause delinquency, but it is more difficult for a single parent to provide material needs, direct controls, and other important elements of family life."[21]

The error here lies in equating "not sufficient" with "not *a* cause." Even if every delinquent child were from an impoverished (or broken) home—that is, even if this factor were a necessary condition for delinquency—it would still be possible to show that poverty is not a sufficient condition for delinquency.

In order for the researcher to conclude that poverty is a cause of delinquency, it is not necessary that all or most of those who are poor become delinquent.[22] If it were, causal variables would be virtually impossible to find. From the standpoint of social action, this criterion can be particularly unfortunate. Suppose that poverty were a necessary but not sufficient condition for delinquency, as in the table. Advocates of the "not sufficient" criterion would be forced to conclude that, if poverty were removed, delinquency would not decline. As the table clearly shows, however, removal of poverty under these hypothetical conditions would *eliminate* delinquency!

To take another example, Wootton reports Carr-Saunders as finding that 28% of his delinquents and 16% of his controls came from broken homes and that this difference held in both London and the provinces. She quotes Carr-Saunders' "cautious" conclusion:

"We can only point out that the broken home may have some influence on delinquency, though since we get control cases coming from broken homes, we cannot assert that there is a direct link between this factor and delinquency."[23]

Carr-Saunders' caution apparently stems from the "not sufficient" criterion, for unless the broken home is a sufficient condition for delinquency, there must be control cases (nondelinquents) from broken homes.

In each of these examples the attack on causality rests on the numbers in a single table. Since all of these tables show a non-zero relation, it seems to us that these researchers have misinterpreted the platitude "correlation is not cau-

[18]In the Gluecks' prediction table, those with scores of 400 or more have a 98.1% chance of delinquency. However, as Reiss has pointed out, the Gluecks *start* with a sample that is 50% delinquent. Had they started with a sample in which only 10% were delinquent, it would obviously have been more difficult to approach sufficiency. Sheldon Glueck and Eleanor Glueck, *Unraveling Juvenile Delinquency,* Cambridge: Harvard University Press, 1950, pp. 260–262; Albert J. Reiss, Jr., "Unraveling Juvenile Delinquency. II. An Appraisal of the Research Methods," *American Journal of Sociology,* 57:2, 1951, pp. 115–120.

[19]Teeters and Reinemann, *op cit.,* p. 127.

[20]*Ibid.,* p. 154.

[21]F. Ivan Nye, *Family Relationships and Delinquent Behavior,* New York: John Wiley, 1958, p. 34. Italics in original.

[22]We are of course assuming throughout this discussion that the variables in question meet what we consider to be legitimate criteria of causality.

[23]Barbara Wootton, *Social Science and Social Pathology,* New York: Macmillan, 1959, p. 118.

sation." To us, this platitude means that one must go beyond the observed fact of association in order to demonstrate causality. To those who employ one or another variant of the perfect relation criterion, it appears to mean that there is something suspect in any numerical demonstration of association. Instead of being the first evidence for causality, an observed association becomes evidence against causality.

False Criterion 2. Insofar as a factor is not "characteristic" of delinquents, it not a cause of delinquency.

"Many correlation studies in delinquency may conquer all these hurdles and still fail to satisfy the vigorous demands of scientific causation. Frequently a group of delinquents is found to differ in a statistically significant way from a nondelinquent control group with which it is compared. Nevertheless, the differentiating trait may not be at all characteristic of the delinquent group. Suppose, for example, that a researcher compares 100 delinquent girls with 100 nondelinquent girls with respect to broken homes. He finds, let us say, that 10% of the nondelinquents come from broken homes, whereas this is true of 30% of the delinquent girls. Although the difference between the two groups is significant, the researcher has not demonstrated that the broken home is characteristic of delinquents. The fact is that 70% of them come from unbroken homes. Again, ecological studies showing a high correlation between residence in interstitial areas and delinquency, as compared with lower rates of delinquency in other areas, overlook the fact that even in the most marked interstitial area nine tenths of the children do not become delinquent."[24]

This argument is superficially plausible. If a factor is not characteristic, then it is apparently not important. But does "characteristic" mean "important"? No. Importance refers to the variation accounted for, to the size of the association, while "being characteristic" refers to only one of the conditional distributions (rows or columns) in the table (in the table on page 223,

[24]Milton L. Barron, *The Juvenile in Delinquent Society,* New York: Knopf, 1954, pp. 86–87.

X is characteristic of delinquents because more than half of the delinquents are X). This is not enough to infer association, any more than the statement that 95% of the Negroes in some sample are illiterate can be taken to say anything about the association between race and illiteracy in that sample without a corresponding statement about the whites. In the following table, although Negroes are predominantly ("characteristically") illiterate, race has no effect on literacy, for the whites are equally likely to be illiterate.

	Race	
	Negro	*White*
Literate	5	5
Illiterate	95	95

More generally, even if a trait characterizes a large proportion of delinquents and also characterizes a large proportion of nondelinquents, it may be less important as a cause of delinquency than a trait that characterizes a much smaller proportion of delinquents. The strength of the relation is what matters—that is, the *difference* between delinquents and nondelinquents in the proportion having the trait (in other words, the difference between the conditional distributions of the dependent variable). In the quotation from Barron at the beginning of this section, would it make any difference for the imputation of causality if the proportions coming from broken homes had been 40% for the nondelinquents and 60% for the delinquents, instead of 10 and 30%? Although broken homes would now be "characteristic" of delinquents, the percentage difference is the same as before. And the percentage difference would still be the same if the figures were 60 and 80%, but now broken homes would be characteristic of *both* nondelinquents and delinquents!

The "characteristic" criterion is thus statistically irrelevant to the task of assessing causality. It also appears to be inconsistent with the principle of multiple causation, to which Barron elsewhere subscribes.[25] If delinquency is really traceable to a plurality of causes," then some of these causes may well "characterize" a minority of delinquents. Furthermore, this "inconsistency" is empirical as well as logical: in survey data taken from ordinary populations it is rare to find that any group defined by more than three traits includes a majority of the cases.[26]

False Criterion 3. If a relation between an independent variable and delinquency is found for a single value of a situational or contextual factor, that situational or contextual factor cannot be a cause of delinquency.

No investigation can establish the causal importance of variables that do not vary. This obvious fact should be even more obvious when the design of the study restricts it to single values of certain variables. Thus the researcher who restricts his sample to white Mormon boys cannot use his data to determine the importance of race, religious affiliation, or sex as causes of delinquency. Nevertheless, students of delinquency who discover either from research or logical analysis that an independent variable is related to delinquency in certain situations or contexts often conclude that these situational or contextual variables are not important causes of

delinquency. Since personality or perceptual variables are related to delinquency in most kinds of social situations, social variables have suffered most from the application of this criterion:

"Let the reader assume that a boy is returning home from school and sees an unexpected group of people at his doorstep, including a policeman, several neighbors, and some strangers. He may suppose that they have gathered to welcome him and congratulate him as the winner of a nationwide contest he entered several months ago. On the other hand, his supposition may be that they have discovered that he was one of several boys who broke some windows in the neighborhood on Halloween. If his interpretation is that they are a welcoming group he will respond one way; but if he feels that they have come to 'get' him, his response is likely to be quite different. In either case he may be entirely wrong in his interpretation. *The important point, however, is that the external situation is relatively unimportant.* Rather, what the boy himself thinks of them [it] and how he interprets them [it] is the crucial factor in his response."[27]

There are at least three independent "variables" in this illustration: (1) the external situation—the group at the doorstep; (2) the boy's past behavior—entering a contest, breaking windows, etc.; (3) the boy's interpretation of the group's purpose. As Barron notes, variable (3) is obviously important in determining the boy's response. It does not follow from this, however, that variables (1) and (2) are unimportant. As a matter of fact, it is easy to see how variable (2), the boy's past behavior, could influence his interpretation of the group's purpose and thus affect his response. If he had not broken any windows in the neighborhood, for example, it is less likely that he would think that the group had come to "get" him, and it is therefore less likely that his response would be one of fear. Since Barron does not examine the relation between this situational variable and the response, he cannot make a legitimate statement about its causal importance.

[25]*Ibid.*, pp. 81–83.

[26]There are two reasons for this: the less-than-perfect association between individual traits and the fact that few traits are simple dichotomies. Of course, it is always possible to take the logical complement of a set of traits describing a minority and thus arrive at a set of traits that does "characterize" a group, but such artificial combinations have too much internal heterogeneity to be meaningful. What, for example, can one say of the delinquents who share the following set of traits: not Catholic, not middle class, not of average intelligence?

The problem of "characteristic" traits arises only when the dependent variable is inherently categorical (Democratic; member of a gang, an athletic club, or neither) or is treated as one (performs none, a few, or many delinquent acts). In other words, this criterion arises only in tabular analysis, not where some summary measure is used to describe the association between variables.

[27]Barron, *op. cit.*, pp. 87–88. Italics added.

Within the context of this illustration it is impossible to relate variable (1), the group at the doorstep, to the response. The reason for this is simple: this "variable" does not vary—it is fixed, given, constant. In order to assess the influence of a group at the doorstep (the external situation) on the response, it would be necessary to compare the effects of groups varying in size or composition. Suppose that there was no group at the doorstep. Presumably, if this were the case, the boy would feel neither fear nor joy. Barron restricts his examination of the relation between interpretation and response to a single situation, and on this basis concludes that what appears to be a necessary condition for the response is *relatively unimportant!*

In our opinion, it is sometimes better to say nothing about the effects of a variable whose range is restricted than to attempt to reach some idea of its importance with inadequate data. The first paragraph of the following statement suggests that its authors are completely aware of this problem. Nevertheless, the concluding paragraphs are misleading:

"We recognized that the Cambridge-Somerville area represented a fairly restricted socio-economic region. Although the bitter wave of the depression had passed, it had left in its wake large numbers of unemployed. Ten years after its onset, Cambridge and Somerville still showed the effects of the depression. Even the best neighborhoods in this study were lower middle class. Consequently, our results represent only a section of the class structure.

"In our sample, however [*therefore*], there is not a *highly* significant relation between 'delinquency areas,' or subcultures, and crime. If we had predicted that every child who lived in the poorer Cambridge-Somerville areas would have committed a crime, we would have been more often wrong than right. Thus, current sociological theory, by itself, cannot explain why the majority of children, even those from the 'worst' areas, never became delinquent."

Social factors, in our sample, were not strongly related to criminality. The fact that a child's neighborhood did not, by itself, exert an independently important influence may [*should not*] surprise social scientists. Undeniably, a slum neighborhood can mold a

child's personality—but apparently only if other factors in his background make him susceptible to the sub-culture that surrounds him."[28]

False Criterion 4. If a relation is observed between an independent variable and delinquency and if a psychological variable is suggested as intervening between these two variables, then the original relation is not causal.

There appear to be two elements in this causal reasoning. One is the procedure of *conjectural interpretation.*[29] The other is the confusion between *explanation,* in which an antecedent variable "explains away" an observed relation, and *interpretation,* in which an intervening variable links more tightly the two variables of the origianl relation. In short, the vanishing of the partial relations is assumed, not demonstrated, and this assumed statistical configuration is misconstrued.

This criterion is often encountered in a subtle form suggestive of social psychological theory:

"The appropriate inference from the available data, on the basis of our present understanding of the nature of cause, is that whether poverty, broken homes, or working mothers are factors which cause

[28]William McCord and Joan McCord, *Origins of Crime,* New York: Columbia University Press, 1959, pp. 71 and 167.

In a study restricted to "known *offenders*" in which the dependent variable is the *seriousness* of the *first offense* Richard S. Sterne concludes: "Delinquency cannot be fruitfully controlled through broad programs to prevent divorce or other breaks in family life. The prevention of these would certainly decrease unhappiness, but it would not help to relieve the problem of delinquency." Since the range of the dependent variable, delinquency, is seriously reduced in a study restricted to *offenders,* such conclusions can not follow from the data. *Delinquent Conduct and Broken Homes,* New Haven: College and University Press, 1964, p. 96.

[29]Like conjectural explanation, this is an argument, unsupported by statistical data, that the relation between two variables would vanish if the effects of a third variable were removed; here however, the third variable "intervenes" causally between the original independent and dependent variables.

delinquency depends upon the meaning the situation has for the child."[30]

"It now appears that neither of these factors [the broken home and parental discipline] is so important in itself as is the child's reaction to them."[31]

"A factor, whether personal or situational, does not become a cause unless and until it first becomes a motive."[32]

The appropriate inference about whether some factor is a cause of delinquency depends on the relation between that factor and delinquency (and possibly on other factors causally prior to both of these). All that can be determined about meanings, motives, or reactions that *follow from* the factor and *precede* delinquency can only strengthen the conclusion that the factor is a cause of delinquency, not weaken it.

A different example may make our argument clearer. *Given* the bombing of Pearl Harbor, the crucial factor in America's response to this situation was its interpretation of the meaning of this event. Is one to conclude, therefore, that the bombing of Pearl Harbor was relatively unimportant as a cause of America's entry into World War II? Intervening variables of this type are no less mportant than variables further removed from the dependent variable, but to limit analysis to them, to deny the importance of objective conditions, is to distort reality as much as do those who ignore intervening subjective states.[33]

This kind of mistaken causal inference can occur long after the original analysis of the data. A case in point is the inference in the *Report to The Congress*[34] that irregular employment of the mother does not cause delinquency. This inference appears to come from misreading Maccoby's reanalysis of the Gluecks' results.

Maccoby begins by noting that "the association between irregular employment and delinquency suggests at the outset that it may not be the mother's absence from home per se which creates adjustment problems for the children. Rather, the cause may be found in the conditions of the mother's employment or the family characteristics leading a mother to undertake outside employment."[35] She then lists several characteristics of the sporadically working mothers that might account for the greater likelihood of their children becoming delinquent. For example, many had a history of delinquency themselves. In our opinion, such conjectural "explanations" are legitimate guides to further study but, as Maccoby says, they leave the causal problem unsettled:

"It is a moot question, therefore, whether it is the mother's sporadic employment as such which conduced to delinquency in the sons; equally tenable is the interpretation that the emotionally disturbed and antisocial characteristics of the parents produced both a sporadic work pattern on the part of the mother and delinquent tendencies in the son."[36]

Maccoby's final step, and the one of greatest interest here, is to examine simultaneously the effects of mother's employment and mother's supervision on delinquency. From this examination she concludes:

"It can be seen that, whether the mother is working or not, the quality of the supervision her child re-

[30]Sophia Robison, *Juvenile Delinquency*, New York: Holt, Rinehart and Winston, 1961, p. 116.

[31]Paul W. Tappan, *Juvenile Delinquency*, New York: McGraw-Hill, 1949, p. 135.

[32]Sheldon and Eleanor Glueck, *Family Environment and Delinquency*, Boston: Houghton-Mifflin, 1962, p. 153. This statement is attributed to Bernard Glueck. No specific reference is provided.

[33]Write your own life history, showing the factors *really* operative in you coming to college, contrasted with the external social and cultural factors of your situation." Barron, *op. cit.*, p. 89.

[34]*Op. cit.*, p. 21.

[35]Eleanor E. Maccoby, "Effects upon Children of Their Mothers' Outside Employment," in Norman W. Bell and Ezra F. Vogel (eds.), *A Modern Introduction to The Family*, Glencoe, Illinois: The Free Press, 1960, p. 523. In fairness to the Children's Bureau report, it should be mentioned that Maccoby's argument against the causality of the relation between mother's employment and delinquency has a stronger tone in the article cited there (see footnote 7) than in the version we have used as a source of quotations.

[36]*Ibid.*

ceives is paramount. If the mother remains at home but does not keep track of where her child is and what he is doing, he is far more likely to become a delinquent (within this highly selected sample), than if he is closely watched. Furthermore, if a mother who works does arrange adequate care for the child in her absence, he is no more likely to be delinquent . . . than the adequately supervised child of a mother who does not work. But there is one more lesson to be learned from the data: among the working mothers, a majority did not in fact arrange adequate supervision for their children in their absence."[37]

It is clear, then, that regardless of the mother's employment status, supervision is related to delinquency. According to criterion 3, employment status is therefore not a cause of delinquency. It is also clear that when supervision is held relatively constant, the relation between employment status and delinquency disappears. According to criterion 4, employment status is therefore *not* a cause of delinquency. This appears to be the reasoning by which the authors of the *Report to The Congress* reject mother's employment as a cause of delinquency. But criterion 3 ignores the association between employment status and delinquency and is thus irrelevant. And criterion 4 treats what is probably best seen as an intervening variable as an antecedent variable and is thus a misconstruction of a legitimate criterion. Actually, the evidence that allows the user of criterion 4 to reach a conclusion of noncausality is, at least psychologically, evidence of *causality*. The disappearance of the relation between mother's employment and delinquency when supervision is held relatively constant makes the "How?" of the original relation clear: working mothers are less likely to provide adequate supervision for their children, and inadequately supervised children are more likely to become delinquent.

False Criterion 5. Measurable variables are not causes.

"In tract 11-1, and to a lesser extent to tract 11-2, the actual rate [of delinquency] is lower than the pre-

dicted rate. We suggest that these deviations [of the actual delinquency rate from the rate predicted from home ownership] point up the danger of imputing a causal significance to an index, per se, despite its statistical significance in a prediction formula. It is fallacious to impute causal significance to home ownership as such. In the present study, the author hypothesizes that the extent of home-ownership is probably highly correlated with, and hence constitutes a measure of community anomie."[38]

"As a preventive, 'keeping youth busy,' whether through compulsory education, drafting for service in the armed forces, providing fun through recreation or early employment, can, at best, only temporary postpone behavior that is symptomatic of more deep-seated or culturally oriented factors. . . . Merely 'keeping idle hands occupied' touches only surface symptoms and overlooks underlying factors known to generate norm-violating behavior patterns."[39]

The criterion of causation that, in effect, denies causal status to measurable variables occurs frequently in delinquency research. In the passages above, home ownership, compulsory education, military service, recreation, and early employment are all called into question as causes of delinquency. In their stead one finds as causes anomie and "deepseated or culturally oriented factors." The appeal to abstract as opposed to more directly measurable variables appears to be especially persuasive. Broad general concepts embrace such a variety of directly measurable variables that their causal efficacy becomes almost self evident. The broken home, for example, is no match for the "inadequate" home:

"[T]he physically broken home as a cause of delinquent behavior is, in itself, not so important as was once believed. In essence, it is not that the home is broken, but rather that the home is inadequate, that really matters."[40]

---

[37]*Ibid.*, p. 524.

[38]Lander, *op. cit.*, p. 71.
[39]William C. Kvaraceus and Walter B. Miller, *Delinquent Behavior: Culture and the Individual,* National Education Association, 1959, p. 39.
[40]Teeters and Reinemann, *op. cit.*, p. 154.

The persuasiveness of these arguments against the causal efficacy of measurable variables has two additional sources: (1) their logical form resembles that of legitimate criterion "lack of spuriousness"; (2) they are based on the seemingly obvious fact that "operational indices" (measures) do not *cause* the variations in other operational indices. Both of the following arguments can thus be brought against the assertion that, for example, home ownership causes delinquency.

Anomie causes delinquency. Home ownership is a measure of anomie. Anomie is thus the "source of variation" in both home ownership and delinquency. If the effects of anomie were removed, the observed relation between home ownership and delinquency would disappear. This observed relation is thus causally spurious.

Home ownership is used as an indicator of anomie, just as responses to questionnaire items are used as indicators of such things as "authoritarianism," "achievement motivation," and "religiosity." No one will argue that the responses to items on a questionnaire *cause* race hatred, long years of self-denial, or attendance at religious services. For the same reason, it is erroneous to think that home ownership "causes" delinquency.

Both of these arguments beg the question. As mentioned earlier, conjectural explanations, although legitimate guides to further study, leave the causal problem unsettled. The proposed "antecedent variable" may or *may not* actually account for the observed relation.

Our argument assumes that the proposed antecedent variable is directly measurable. In the cases cited here it is not. If the antecedent variable logic is accepted as appropriate in these cases, all relations between measurable variables and delinquency may be said to be causally spurious. If anomie can "explain away" the relation between *one* of its indicators and delinquency, it can explain away the relations between *all* of its indicators and delinquency.[41] No

matter how closely a given indicator measures anomie, the indicator is not anomie, and thus not a cause of delinquency. The difficulty with these conjectural explanations is thus not that they may be false, but that they are *non-falsifiable*.[42]

The second argument against the causality of measurable variables over-looks the following point: it is one thing to use a measurable variable as an indicator of another, not directly measurable, variable; it is something else again to assume that the measurable variable is *only* an indicator. Not owning one's home may indeed be a useful indicator of anomie; it may, at the same time, be a potent cause of delinquency in its own right.

The user of the "measurable variables are not causes" criterion treats measurable variables as epiphenomena. He strips these variables of all their causal efficacy (and of all their meaning) by treating them merely as indexes, and by using such words as *per se, as such,* and *in itself.*[43] In so doing, he begs rather than answers the important question: Are these measurable variables causes of delinquency?

False Criterion 6. If the relation between an independent variable and delinquency is conditional upon the value of other variables, the independent variable is not a cause of delinquency.

"The rates of Negro delinquency also vary as widely as do the white rates indicating large differences in behavior patterns that are not a function or effect of race per se. It is also of interest to note that in at least 10 percent of the districts with substantial

---

[41]As would be expected, Lander succeeds in disposing of all the variables in his study as causes of delinquency—even

those he says at some points are *"fundamentally"* related to delinquency."

[42]While Lander throws out his measurable independent variables in favor of anomie, Kvaraceus and Miller through out their measurable dependent variable in favor of "something else." "Series of normviolating behaviors, which run counter to legal codes and which are engaged in by youngsters [delinquency], are [is] only symptomatic of something else in the personal make-up of the individual, in his home and family, or in his cultural milieu." *Op. Cit.,* p. 34. The result is the same, as the quotations suggest.

[43]The appearance of these terms in the literature on delinquency almost invariably signals a logical difficulty.

Negro juvenile populations, the Negro delinquency rate is lower than the corresponding white rate."[44]

"The appropriate inference from the available data, on the basis of our present understanding of the nature of cause, is that whether poverty, broken homes, or working mothers are factors which cause delinquency depends upon the meaning the situation has for the child."[45]

Both of these quotations make the same point: the association between an independent variable and delinquency depends on the value of a third variable. The original two-variable relation thus becomes a three-variable conditional relation. In the first quotation, the relation between race and delinquency is shown to depend on some (unspecified) property of census tracts. In the second quotation, each of three variables is said to "interact" with "the meaning of the situation" to cause delinquency.

One consequence of showing that certain variables are only conditionally related to delinquency is to invalidate what Albert K. Cohen has aptly named "the assumption of intrinsic pathogenic qualities"—the assumption that the causal efficacy of a variable is, or can be, independent of the value of other causal variables.[46] Invalidating this assumption, which Cohen shows to be widespread in the literature on delinquency, is a step in the right direction. As many of the quotations in this paper suggest, however, the discovery that a variable has no *intrinsic* pathogenic qualities has often led to the conclusion that it has no pathogenic qualities at all. The consequences of accepting this conclusion can be shown for delinquency research and theory.

Cloward and Ohlin's theory that delinquency is the product of lack of access to legitimate means *and* the availability of illegitimate means assumes, as Palmore and Hammond have

shown,[47] that each of these states is a necessary condition for the other—i.e., that lack of access to legitimate and access to illegitimate means "interact" to produce delinquency. Now, if "conditional relations" are non-causal, neither lack of access to legitimate nor the availability of illegitimate means is a cause of delinquency, and one could manipulate either without affecting the delinquency rate.

Similarly absurd conclusions could be drawn from the results of empirical research in delinquency, since all relations between independent variables and delinquency are at least conceivably conditional (the paucity of empirical generalizations produced by delinquency research as a whole shows that most of these relations have already actually been found to be conditional).[48]

Any one of the criteria of causality discussed in this paper makes it possible to question the causality of most of the relations that have been or could be revealed by quantitative research. Some of these criteria stem from perfectionistic interpretations of legitimate criteria, others from misapplication of these legitimate criteria. Still others, especially the argument that a cause must be "characteristic" of delinquents, appear to result from practical considerations. (It would indeed be valuable to the practitioner if he could point to some easily identifiable trait as the "hallmark" of the delinquent.) Finally, one of these criteria is based on a mistaken notion of the relation between abstract concepts and measurable variable—a notion that only the former can be the causes of anything.

The implications of these standards of causality for practical efforts to reduce delinquency

---

[44]Lander, *op. cit.,* p. 32. This statement is quoted more fully above (see footnote 10).

[45]See footnote 30.

[46]"Multiple Factor Approaches," in Marvin E. Wolfgang *et al.* (eds.), *The Sociology of Crime and Delinquency,* New York: John Wiley, 1962, pp. 78–79.

[47]Erdman B. Palmore and Phillip E. Hammond, "Interacting Factors in Juvenile Delinquency," *American Sociological Review,* 29 (December, 1964), pp. 848–854.

[48]After reviewing the findings of twenty-one studies as they bear on the relations between twelve commonly used independent variables and delinquency, Barbara Wootton concludes: "All in all, therefore, this collection of studies, although chosen for its comparative methodological merit, produces only the most meager, and dubiously supported generalizations," *Op. cit.,* p. 134.

are devastating. Since nothing that can be pointed to in the practical world is a cause of delinquency (e.g., poverty, broken homes, lack of recreational facilities, working mothers), the practitioner is left with the task of combatting a nebulous "anomie" or an unmeasured "inadequacy of the home"; or else he must change the adolescent's interpretation of the "meaning" of events without at the same time changing the events themselves or the context in which they occur.

Mills has suggested that accepting the principle of multiple causation implies denying the possibility of radical change in the social structure.[49] Our analysis suggests that rejecting the principle of multiple causation implies denying the possibility of *any* change in the social structure—since, in this view, nothing causes anything.

[49]C. Wright Mills, "The Professional Ideology of Social Pathologists," *American Journal of Sociology,* 44 (September, 1942), pp. 165–180, esp. pp. 171–172.

23. The Unique Individual

LESLIE WILKINS

THE OBJECTION STATES THAT PREDICTION IS USE-less (or dangerous?) because the individual is unique. Prediction is said to be either (or both) impossible or undesirable, and this argument rests on the complexity of human relationships. That the social and psychological make-up of man is complex is not denied. Nor is the argument that "only certain items matter" advanced from the statistical standpoint. While prediction methods lead to the simplification of the problem they do not approach by this route. Let us begin to show how this procedure is based by accepting the point that every individual is unique when we consider the complex of factors in his circumstances and make-up. Let us go further and claim that if we could measure any *one thing with sufficient accuracy* the individual would be unique, as we have already argued for height or weight. Since the "complexity" concept and the "accuracy" concept both lead to the concept of the unique individual, we will commence our discussion from the latter case because of its greater simplicity.

Our assumption of uniqueness from one accurate measurement may be related to the theorem of Dedekind which states that number is infinite—between any two numbers of which we can conceive there is always another number

▶SOURCE: *"What is Prediction and is it Necessary in Evaluating Treatment?" Report of a Conference on Research and Potential Application of Research in Probation, Parole and Delinquency Prediction, sponsored by the Citizens' Committee for Children of New York Inc. and Research Center, New York School of Social Work, Columbia University (mimeo), pp. 23–34. (Editorial adaptations.)*

which may also be conceived. Now this is true, but the fact does not worry us. We operate with number sufficient for the purpose. For example we estimate circumferences of circles from their diameters using π, but we could raise the objection that the true value of π was unknown and also object that we could not exactly measure diameters. No one would regard this argument as of much value. We would use a value of π which, *having regard to the accuracy* with which we measured the diameter, would give results sufficiently accurate for estimating the circumference. This is our solution in physical problems. It might be claimed that our measuring instruments in this field are obviously highly accurate but the analogy cannot be rejected on these grounds. Not a hundred years ago the accuracy of measurement was often a limiting factor in the physical sciences, and at the frontiers of knowledge may be so today. If measurement is rejected outright there is little likelihood of it being improved; if it is accepted and its possibilities appreciated it is likely that advance will be made in the techniques of measurement. *This joint interplay of improvement in measurement techniques and the use of measurement is important in the social sciences also.* What we can do is limited by what we know and what we know is also limited by what we can do. With this point in mind let us look further into our analogue.

If we measure persons to the nearest inch we shall find many who are alike and can be classified together. This accuracy is sufficient for many purposes and inadequate for others. In

233

general, if we are to take one characteristic at a time and to classify individuals into broad groups we shall find many alike. We cannot reject the utility of this principle, but it seems that this is what the critics of prediction are trying to do. They are claming that the measurement is too coarse and that they could measure or describe much more accurately than the degree of accuracy we are utilizing. They claim, in fact, that they know (can show?) that they can describe individuals with such precision that they are seen to be unique, and go on to suggest that because we do not utilize this information our methods are incorrect. Logically they should surely also argue—number is infinite—I will not agree to use number which I know to be inaccurate! Clearly the concept of sufficient accuracy for utility must be accepted. This involves immediately the concept of use for a purpose. Our next point follows from this. Not only are different degrees of accuracy required for different purposes, but information which is useful for one purpose is not required for another. The number of measurements required as well as their accuracy depends on the complexity of the task.

This may seem obvious, but what follows from an acceptance of this obvious assessment of reasonable behavior is often rejected. Let us assume the acceptance of this argument insofar as we have stated:

1.   Measurement is always approximate.

2.   The number and accuracy of measurements should depend on purpose.

Then it seems to follow that there is no point in demonstrating that individuals are unique nor that prediction methods use only a fraction of the information, or information which is inaccurate, without also showing that the omitted measurements of the items not accurately measured were (a) relevant, (b) not sufficiently accurate where both (a) and (b) apply *to a specific and limited purpose*. This should provide a dilemma for

those opposing prediction on "uniqueness" grounds or on grounds of complexity which are similar. The proof of relevance and of the degree of accuracy with respect to a purpose can, it seems, only be found by the use of prediction methods. But there is a little more to it than that.

In prediction methods we do not necessarily seek a "meaningful" result (a subjectively satisfying explanation?) but a "powerful" result; we do not expect one classification to simple categories to suffice. There is a rationale behind the "small number of elements" to which the critics refer. The number is derived in two ways—one the trivial case which was appropriate to the Borstal study,[1] and the other, more general. In the Borstal study *all* the information which could be used was in fact used, and the resulting small number of elements condensed all the useful information available, where *"use"* was defined by the specification of the criteria. In the nontrivial case the procedure is one of balance. Let us again suppose that there is an infinity of "useful" facts; then each must contribute an infinitely small amount of information such that no method could be found of using it. More realistically we wish to find systems which could be used and which are found to apply in practice. Let us suppose we begin by finding one element which helps our purpose; we are better able to predict if we use this element and do not reject it. Then we wish to find others which will *not do again* the work already done by our first element, and *only* that part of the work.

In our search for more information we have the hard test of *use-for-purpose*. We wish to add categories and classifications or measurements that are useful, but we must also stop adding before the system breaks down. Similarly, we may wish to increase our accuracy of measurement, but there will come a point where increased accuracy becomes unnecessary—where the increase does not result in any significant increase in our control. Again, it must be stres-

[1]Mannheim and L. T. Wilkins, *Prediction Methods in Relation to Borstal Training*, London: H.M.S.O., 1955.

sed, for our single specific and unidimensional purpose.

That is not to say that we shall at that time have sufficient information for our purposes, but merely that the items of information which are candidates for inclusion cannot justify their claim to be included in terms of the work they will do towards the end purpose. We shall reject such information and seek other information *as a continuous process,* so that the area of our ignorance is gradually reduced. Any item may be a candidate for inclusion, irrespective of its "face validity." We shall not accept any abstract theory because it is convincing in itself; we shall decide to accept or reject it after we have investigated those concrete and practical consequences which can be directly tested by the contribution each item makes to the specific problem of specification or decision.

The process of finding items for test is related to problems in strategy. Each item may be considered in two dimensions which may be regarded as having a "cost" or "penalty" rating:

1. The cost of testing the item if false.

2. The cost (loss) of not testing the item if true.

If an item is likely to have a low rating on (2) and a low rating on (1) we may test it, but if we assess (2) as small and (1) as large, we shall not. It is here that social theory can help; it is here that we may seek a division of labor in the work—the grinding routine work—which is the major part of any science. The problem normally reduces to an evaluation of (2) since (1) is usually known with precision. Of course electronic computers have helped in reducing part of the cost of (1), but only for one aspect of cost; at some point we shall find our sample sizes are inadequate to test the data, and the cost of increased sample size is usually considerable. If we accept the selection procedure for equations which uses the most efficient solution (not necessarily the most "meaningful") we can operate more success-

fully, because we shall be rejecting items as new ones are added according to a simple arithmetical routine and the computer can make our decisions for us. If the item explains a significant amount of variance it will retain it; if not, our sample size is not greatly reduced[2] by the mere test and reject process. At some point[3] the contribution of further information will become so small *relative to our sample* size that we shall not be able to test its significance. Such items cannot be accepted on the grounds that (a) they are not tested and (b) their contribution could only be small. If we do not accept these limiting conditions we shall find no grounds for rejecting any item and will reduce the whole procedure to absurdity by being able to specify each case uniquely. In the scientific meaning of the word we cannot "explain" any unique case or once-for-all event, since any event which is unique or once-for-all can be no guide to future action.

One further point should, perhaps, be made before we proceed to deal briefly with the second part of the objection. The simplification process we have described above is possible only because we work to one specific purpose. We may, of course, select many objectives *one at a time* to extract different information from different or similar classifications. This piece-meal approach is essential to this method, indeed perhaps to all scientific method.[4] Thus items of information which might help to make an individual unique but which do not help any particular purpose *when that purpose is considered* may be *rejected,* but *accepted* when tested by their utility *for another purpose* or another criterion. We

[2]Degrees of freedom in test and rejection procedures of this kind are lost, but the variance of the item is not a factor.

[3]The "stopping" procedure is the point of "efficiency" which we described elsewhere, but is only a part of the concept of efficiency. It is, however, the only part which concerns the objections to prediction methods on the grounds of complexity or uniqueness of case material.

[4]But theory has a very important role in the scientific method. The writer has gone into this aspect elsewhere. The omission from this discussion does not mean that theory is rejected—it too, is a useful tool.

cannot set out to solve general problems by the scientific method—general solutions or "omnibus" laws can be made only when the necessary piece-by-piece research has proceeded far enough, and a genius of sufficient status is found to state the general law. A *completely general* solution should not be sought directly—indeed the information necessary would be so vast that we should reach again the concept of the unique individual. But this seems to involve a contradiction within itself. Prediction methods seek not *the* explanation, but *an* explanation which is operationally defined by the specification of a limited purpose and one purpose at a time in each "explanation." They *must*, therefore, use only a small number of elements and indeed, solutions which require a large number *cannot* be based on more than mere speculation. This is a hard fact of scientific life as we know it today.

Objectivity and Subjectivity

The objection has now, perhaps, lost much of its point, and we shall deal very briefly with the remaining statements. The objection continues, "through the necessity to employ objective factors prediction procedures lose touch with many significant intangible and dynamic features of personality frequently observed in the clinical situation. Successful prediction requires an understanding and assessment of the uniqueness of the individual."*

The last sentence contains its own refutation. If a case is unique what experience can the clinician use to guide him? If experience of the past is of any value at all then it can be applied only by observation of *similarities* not differences. It is not the uniqueness that concerns the clinician but the similarities between the particular case and prior cases in his or other people's experience. If this is so, then this is exactly the same as with the statistical procedures in the prediction

*[Reference is here made to criticisms summarized by L. Ohlin, Paper prepared for the Third International Congress of Criminology, London, 1955, Preparatory Papers.—Editors].

method where experience is derived from the past and is analyzed and condensed systematically by known procedures rather than subjectively. Moreover statistical experience can be based on samples of the population which we know to be unbiased. A clinician has only his own sample to guide him with no guarantee of its lack of bias.

Is this critcism reduceable to a claim that a biased sample assessed subjectively provides better guidance than the procedures of the statistical method? If so, there is no denying the clinician's right to make such a claim in the name of faith and hope but not in the name of science or technology. It is certainly not acceptable to claim in the same breath that the past is no guide ("the case is unique") and that it is experience that counts.

But perhaps it may be conceded that when facts are being considered, statistical methods are acceptable, and stress might be laid on the importance of the "significant intangible features of personality frequently observed in the clinical situation." If these features are "intangible" how can we know that they exist? How in fact does the clinician take them into account? Can they not be described in words? If not, are they more than the prejudices of the observer? If they are describable they may be dealt with statistically (although the statistician would reserve his right to introduce the *describer* as well as the *described* as a possible source of variance.) How do we know that these intangible features (if they exist) do not so overlap with observable, objective features that there would be no point in including them? Indeed we cannot test this until those who maintain that they can deal with these intangible features can reduce their claim to a set of hypotheses of a kind which can be tested.

Faith in intangibles, if coupled with a scientific attitude, is an essential challenge to further development. There is no wish to discourage faith but only to indicate that it is not a substitute for nor an answer to analytical methods. It might indicate where the next step forward in the scientific method might be made, and should stimulate effort towards further scientific endeavor, but not be used as a criticism of such endeavor. Science acknowledges the partial nature of knowledge and looks always for newer, better explanations, but cannot reduce its rigor.

Invention and Examination

In research we are concerned both with the formulation and testing of hypotheses. In the main the scientific method can say much about the latter aspect of research designs, but very little is known about the processes involved in the former operation. Indeed, apart from indicating the types of hypotheses which may be the more efficiently tested, research methods leave the matter of hypothesis formulation to the individual and provide no certain guidance. *Up to the point where a hypothesis is formed,* it is imagination and experience that count. Each research worker should know himself and his ways of thinking and recognize that source or sources of stimulation to invention which are for him the most fruitful.

Once hypotheses are formed, we have entered a world of communication and we can discuss techniques and share our experiences so that the concept of a body of scientific thought is meaningful. Accordingly, we do not criticize clinical approaches, intuitive approaches or any other approach *to hypothesis formation.* Hypotheses should be plentiful, but their mortality rate should also be high. A hypothesis should not be allowed to live beyond the point where it can be phrased in a way subject to test. If it survives the test its life should be extended until a better explanation—a more general or more powerful hypothesis—succeeds in passing appropriate tests. It follows that all informed persons should be able to agree upon the rigor of the tests and should also agree to accept the results so that the failed hypothesis is interred by agreement and does not appear again to waste research time.

From this also follows that *communication of research findings is a part of the research method.* If

research workers are unaware that certain theories have been tested, effort will be wasted not only in redundant testing but in the misdirection of thought processes. Unless such misdirection is part of a national defense system (where it is presumably desired to waste research effort of potential enemies) communication of both positive and negative results is an integral part of science.

Symbols and Semantics

This brings us to consider the second point. Those who do not favour the statistical or mathematical approach quite often object that the replacement of living individuals by mathematical symbols is essentially wrong. But such persons are prepared to read case papers which they believe are more "human" and more realistic. Clearly if a case is to be communicated from one case worker to another, then words must be used. Only in this way can one case worker learn from another. If this verbal communication of information is ignored, then each case worker must be assumed to begin from scratch and to act solely upon his own personal experience unmodified by the experience of others. The egoistic approach must, of course, be rejected. But the translation of events or emotional experiences into words represents a replacement of the real things by symbols, namely words. It is then the claim that words are more effective systems of symbols than mathematical symbols. This is a hypothesis but it has not been demonstrated to be true. There is obviously no difference of kind if I write a description of an emotional experience in words in English or Latin, nor is there any difference of kind if I write the description as x, y or any other symbol. Words mean what by convention they have come to mean and the majority of words may be defined in other words. The effectiveness of words might be assessed by two criteria:

a. How they convey meaning—are they effective for communication?

b.   How they allow of manipulation by the processes of logic—do they assist the thought processes?

A system of words with all (a) qualities and no (b) would be deficient over-all. The use of jargon which grows around any specialist study is an indication that normal language has been found to be deficient in either (a) or (b)—usually (a)—quality. The development of symbolic logic is an indication that some persons (not usually mathematicians) have found the redundancy and uncertainty of normal language inadequate for purpose (b). The use of mathematical models is another way of improving the efficiency of words for (b) purposes. It will be clear, however, that there is no fundamental difference between the use of word-symbols to describe things and the use of abstract symbols. The difference exists mainly in that all persons have some knowledge of the use of words, for communication purposes and in general have found it possible to use the same system of symbols for (b) purposes also. The number of persons who "speak the language" is reduced when math-ematical models are used and the coverage of communication is reduced, but nothing else need be lost. On the other hand, much is gained in that systems of operations built up over many centuries may be pressed into service once we can translate problems into this language.

If we require to *communicate* most effectively we should use the most common language consistent with the required degree of accuracy in communication. If we require to *use thought processes,* we should use any system of symbols which proves most effective. Some may choose one and others another. Eventually all researchers must submit to the trial by publication; they must be able to communicate their results so that a sufficient number of other qualified persons may examine their work. If we choose a system of symbolic logic to describe our thought processes we would be advised to use a system already in existence; if we choose mathematical models, we have chosen perhaps the most developed system of symbols where the largest number of persons will be able to follow our work without excessive background explanation of our system.

24. Criminological Prediction and Its Purposes

FRANCES H. SIMON

INTRODUCTION TO PREDICTION STUDIES

EFFORTS TO ESTIMATE THE VARYING DEGREES TO which people are at risk of committing offences, and to identify those who are most likely to begin, or to continue in, careers of crime have absorbed a good deal of energy in criminological research. Such investigations have become commonly known as prediction studies. The word "prediction" may be used generally to mean the estimation of one phenomenon from a knowledge of others to which it is related, and criminological prediction includes such large scale studies as the forecasting of future national crime rates and patterns from population trends and other social data.[1] "Prediction" will be employed here, however, mainly to refer to research aimed at identifying, among selected groups of persons, those who are at risk of committing crimes or delinquencies.

A glance at a few of the best-known prediction studies is enough to show their variety of subject matter. The Gluecks, authors of much prediction research (8), are perhaps best noted for their attempts to identify children who are at risk of becoming delinquent when older. Their

▶SOURCE: *Prediction Methods in Criminology. Home Office Research Studies No. 7, London: Her Majesty's Stationery Office, 1971, pp. 3–11, 14–15. (Editorial adaptations.) Reprinted by permission of the Controller of Her Brittanic Majesty's Stationery Office.*

---

[1]See, for instance, the paper *Predicting the Volume and Structure of Future Criminality* by Jepsen and Pal (15).

5-factor Social Prediction Table (7) allots to each child a score, based on data concerning parental affection, discipline, supervision, and family cohesion; this score is said to show the child's chances of developing into a delinquent. Mannheim and Wilkins (17), combined certain social history data taken from the case records of borstal boys to form a score, alternatively presented as a five-category table, which indicated for each boy the probability of his avoiding serious reconviction for about three and a half years after being released from borstal. Stott used information on children's school behaviour, supplied by teachers, to construct a 'maladjustment score' which he then suggested could be used to predict delinquency (26) and which he showed to be related to the probability of further offending in a group of boys on probation (25). And of the numerous American studies designed to predict which prisoners are likely to be good risks for release on parole, one of the most thorough is that of Ohlin (21), who combined items from case records with personality ratings by prison staff to form a score showing the chances of parole violation for men released from Illinois penitentiaries.

In the present context, then, a prediction instrument is one which uses certain information applying to a person at one time in order to estimate the probability of his becoming, or remaining, criminal (or delinquent) at some later time. The criterion of criminality must be defined; often it comprises the conviction of an offence (perhaps of more than a given degree of seriousness) within a stated follow-up period. The instrument must distinguish between different risks; it uses the information on which it is based to classify persons according to their different probabilities of being criminal, and it must separate the low risks from the high ones. It may take various forms: a table showing risk groups, or a score or equation which gives individual probabilities of risk.

A prediction instrument may be used to estimate risks of criminality which are genuinely in the future; for example, one may try to identify children with a high probability of becoming delinquent when older so as to give them preventive treatment now. But such instruments may also be used for persons whose criminality is actually already known, in order to estimate their "expected risk" on the basis of information applicable at an earlier stage; for example, released borstal boys whose later careers are already known may be divided into "good" and "bad" risks according to their personal histories up to the moment of the borstal sentence. This latter use of prediction methods is frequent in research on the effectiveness of treatment; if persons given various treatments (whose outcomes may already be established) are classified according to the risks that would have been expected before treatment began, a baseline is formed against which the outcomes of the treatments can be judged. (This is not as straightforward as it sounds). In the U.S.A. prediction devices are called base expectancy instruments. ...

Prediction instruments are made for defined classes of persons: for example, parolees, schoolchildren, borstal boys, or young men on probation. From now on, such a class will be referred to as a "population."

The information on which attempts at prediction are based may be of several kinds. Psychological test results may be used: Hathaway, Monachesi and others (11), for example, have investigated the extent to which the Minnesota Multiphasic Personality Inventory can be used to predict juvenile delinquency. Stott's data on children's behaviour at school were collected on special forms designed for the purpose and filled in by teachers (26). Mannheim and Wilkins are among several writers who have compared the predictive value of statistical tables based on data from case records with subjective assessments made by institution staff; in the course of their borstal study they examined the prognostic utility of governors' and housemasters' reports (17). The question of whether individual clinical assessment results in more successful prediction than is achieved by the use of actuarial[2] tables has been most notably examined by Meehl (19) and Sawyer (22). ... A great many prediction studies have adopted an empirical approach, examining a large number of items of information (which may be of more than one kind) for their prognostic value, and then selecting the best of these for combining into a prediction score or table.

This selection and combination of predictive items may be done by a variety of mathematical techniques, ranging from a simple totting up of points for "good" and "bad" factors to more complex methods which take account not only of the association of each factor with subsequent criminality but also of the relationships between the factors themselves. Of these latter the standard technique is multiple regression, but alternatives such as predictive attribute analysis and other procedures presented by Macnaughton-Smith (16) have recently been developed. Part of the purpose of our probation prediction study ... was to apply several of these methods to the same data and compare the results. The essential feature common to all of them is that they afford a means of selecting from a large

[2]An actuarial prediction (in the sense in which the phrase is used here) for an individual is made by consulting a statistical table and reading off from it the probability shown for persons of his class. As Meehl says, this is essentially a clerical operation, though the construction of the table itself, which involves analysing data on a large number of other individuals and deciding on the definitions of the risk classes, is research. In a clinical prediction the clinician makes a personal diagnosis and judgment about the individual, using whatever information he considers appropriate.

number of items those which have the most predictive value, and of combining these with the aim of making the combination a more powerful predictor than any of the individual items alone.

THE NEED FOR VALIDATION

In constructing an instrument to predict criminality among a certain population of persons, the first stage is usually to examine information on a sample of cases among whom it is already known which ones became criminal. Items seen to be related to criminality can then be selected and combined by any of the methods referred to above. At this stage the table (if it is a table) is an experience table, since it summarises the experience of the particular sample of cases on which it is based; it cannot properly be called a prediction table until its predictive validity has been tested by applying it to another sample.

This validation is necessary for several reasons. The first is a statistical one, and relates to the nature of the method used in constructing the experience table.

When for a sample of cases a number of variables is examined and a selection is made not according to any prior hypothesis but simply on the basis of which ones show the highest correlations with a certain criterion, a few of these apparently high associations will be due to chance, and would not be expected to recur in another sample. The larger the original number of variables, the more likely it is (other things being equal) that chance associations will be included in the selection. An experience table based on this selection will rely in part on relationships that appear to be strong for that particular sample but are not so strong in the population: it will be biased. Further bias is introduced if the selected variables are then combined in a way which takes advantage of the various relationships between them, for some of these may be present by chance in the sample and will not occur in the same patterns in the population. Tests of significance can reduce the danger but

not eliminate it. The result is that the experience table is tailored too closely to the sample on which it was built and its power of estimating the criterion in that sample is misleadingly high; it has been overfitted, and when it is applied to another sample its predictive power is liable to shrink.

Several of the methods available for building a combination of selected variables are subject to shrinkage. This need not be regarded as a problem, however, provided that a validation test is done. Multiple regression, for instance, is theoretically one of the most efficient ways of making use of the relationships existing between a number of variables;[3] the fact that a few of them may be over-estimated (and a few others, indeed, under-estimated) in the construction sample need not deter the researcher from employing the method, as long as it is realised that the resulting equation may be biased, and that the application of the equation to another sample is necessary to obtain an unbiased estimate of its predictive power for the population. If strong predictive relationships exist in the population they should be present in both samples (if these have been properly chosen) and the multiple regression will take them into account; but the validation will show up the bias resulting from the incorporation of chance effects present in the first sample. The predictive power of the regression equation, artificially high for the first sample, will shrink to an unbiased estimate of its true level. Validation is thus an essential step in the making of a predictor.

The amount of shrinkage can be reduced by using a large number of cases for the construction sample, since in a large sample there is less risk of chance effects obscuring real ones. Shrinkage will also be less where the original number of variables from which selection is made for the predictor is small, or where a high

---

[3] Provided, of course, that its underlying assumptions are met by the data; in criminology this may not be so. See the discussion by Grygier.

proportion of the original number is included in the selection, for in both situations there is less risk of giving undue weight to associations which appear high by chance in the construction sample. Quantifying the variables in ways which are not too sensitive to the peculiarities of the construction sample will also help. If these various steps to reduce shrinkage are taken, they will have the effect of making the predictive power of the initial experience table lower than it otherwise would be; it will now be nearer to its true level for the population, and will contract less on validation.

Some methods of constructing a predictor are not liable to shrinkage in this way. If variables are selected not as the best-appearing out of a large number in the construction sample but on the basis of a prior hypothesis, and the associations are tested for significance, the risk of chance inflation will be very slight. Bias could still enter if the selected variables were combined with a view to optimising the relationships existing in the construction sample. But if there is no bias in the selection, or alternatively if all of a given set of variables are used without selection, and if the method of combining them does not play on the relationships between them which appear in the construction sample, shrinkage should not occur. The technique developed by Lance is an example. Where an already existing instrument, such as a psychological inventory, is used as a predictor without alteration, the question of shrinkage does not arise.

Apart from the statistical fact of shrinkage, a second point in connection with validation is that the predictive usefulness of some factors may change with time. Items which for a certain population appear highly predictive of delinquency at one time may not be so a few years later; changes in courts' sentencing policies and in penal treatments are among the many influences, known and unknown, which may alter people's patterns of behaviour. Even the ways in which case records are kept can affect the prognostic value of information collected.

The population for whom the table was designed may itself change through selection or other causes: Goodman (9), for instance, has shown that the very use of a prediction table as a selector may in time alter the structure of the population to whom it is being applied and thus tend to invalidate the predictions. In order to ensure its continuing validity, a prediction table in use should be periodically retested and brought up to date. And it goes without saying that a table constructed for use on one population cannot be assumed suitable for another until its validity for the latter has been tested.

This leads to a third point: the importance of the base rate, i.e. the frequency with which the cases to be identified occur in the population to whom the prediction table is applied. Take as an example the prediction of delinquency among a population of children. If the actual proportion of delinquents is small, it may be convenient in the first stage of constructing an experience table to use a sample which is not drawn randomly from the population, but is selected so that the ratio of delinquents to non-delinquents is larger; having adequate numbers of both will facilitate a study of the links between variables. However, probabilities of delinquency for the various risk groups derived from this sample must be recalculated before being applied to the population in which the delinquency rate is lower, or else the experience table must be validated on a new sample with a representative delinquency rate. The problem is that of false positives: where a test is being used to try to pick out certain members of a population, the greater the extent to which the minority whom it is desired to identify are swamped by the majority, some of whom also give a positive response to the test, the greater will be the number of false positives picked up.

This point is one on which much of the Gluecks' prediction work has been repeatedly criticised. The problem is not overcome by "validation" studies in which the experience table is applied to fresh groups of delinquents and non-delinquents separately (as, for instance, in some of the projects reported by Glueck) for these do not make any allowance for the relative proportions in the real population. However, when the distributions of predictive score classes or risk categories have been determined among delinquents and non-delinquents separately, it is quite easy to calculate what would be the probability of a person in a particular category being a delinquent, taking into account the overall delinquency rate. . . . Alternatively, the predictor should be validated on a fresh sample drawn randomly from the population.

For populations in which the cases to be identified form a sizeable proportion of the total, the experience table can be based on a random sample, and no recalculation is required. Validation, however, may be necessary for any other of the reasons discussed above. In nearly all prediction studies, validation should be regarded as an essential step.

Validation may be retrospective, where the experience table is tested on another sample of persons for whom it is already known which ones became delinquent, or it may be prospective, where the table is applied to a fresh group at an early stage in their careers, and the researcher then waits for a "follow-up" period, which may be several years, to see in which persons delinquency develops. If the information used to build the experience table is of a kind which can be gathered by the researcher from records just as well after the event as at the time (such as, for example, the number of previous convictions occurring up to a certain date) a retrospective study is feasible and there is no reason why it should not be done; it will save research time since all the necessary data are already available. If, however, the table is based on information which is specially gathered for the purpose and which cannot be reliably deduced later from other records, a prospective study will be necessary. Sometimes a predictor is constructed by first using judgments about a person which may be contemporaneous with his criminality, and then inferring that they would have applied earlier; an example is Stott's

maladjustment score which is based on teachers' descriptions of their pupils (24,26). If there is any possibility of the original judgments having been biased by a knowledge of criminality, a prospective validation is essential.

PURPOSES OF PREDICTION STUDIES

A prediction table, whether based on clinical prognoses or constructed statistically, is a classification of persons into risk groups. (The probabilities expressed by a prediction equation are individual estimates of risk; they can, if desired, be grouped to form a table.) Such a classification may in theory be used in various ways.

Research

If a risk classification of offenders is based on certain of their characteristics which are known before they are allocated to different kinds of penal treatment, then the estimate of prior risk is a baseline against which the outcome of any particular treatment can be measured. (For example: prisoners might be sent to institutions with different regimes; or probationers might be allocated to officers who used different methods of supervision.) It can then be seen which forms of treatment appear to reduce the reconviction rate (or other criterion of outcome) below the expected risk, and which to increase it. The allocation to treatment could be done in terms of the risk groups themselves, or alternatively the offenders may be classified and allocated to treatments on some quite independent system; the prior risk for each treatment group can then be worked out by combining the individual risk estimates for all persons in the group, and the actual outcome for the group can be compared with the expectation. Either way, the risk classification provided by the prediction table is being used as a tool to help in the evaluation of treatment.

There are, however, snags. The prediction table itself has necessarily been constructed from a sample of offenders who were receiving some kind of "treatment" (any form of disposal used by the courts can be regarded as a way of treating people) and so the term "prior risk" is not strictly accurate; it is not "pre-treatment" risk but "risk for the average of all given treatments" that prediction tables based on pre-treatment characteristics will show. One cannot have a treatment-free predictor.[4] This means that as patterns of treatment change, prediction tables based on them will become out of date; a base expectancy worked out five years ago will be unreliable for use in research comparisons now. Revalidation is necessary.

Another caution is that, although a certain type of treatment may appear, for any one risk group, to produce a significant change in the reconviction rate (or other measure of outcome) when comparison is made with the expected value, there is always the possibility that the change may have been caused, not by the treatment itself, but by something else, unmeasured, that was present at the same time and that may or may not occur again. This points to the necessity of designing the research so as to specify as clearly as possible what are the important constituents of treatment and how they are being measured. The problem is of course not peculiar to investigations which use prediction tables, and discussion of it need not be expanded here.

A further difficulty is that if the research is done on an already existing system of allocation to treatment, there may be selection processes at work for which the prediction table is unable to allow. Certain offender-type/treatment combinations may occur too rarely in practice to be evaluated. Or, even if it appears that people in the same risk group are being allocated to a variety of treatments, so that the outcomes of different treatments for the same risks can be compared, there may be covert selection factors at work which actually alter the risk in a way the prediction table does not show. Morrison (20) discusses this point very clearly, casting doubt on the finding by Mannheim and Wilkins (17) that open borstals achieve better success rates than closed ones when allowance is made (in terms of their prediction table) for the types of risk sent to either. If the officials allocating boys to different borstals judge the lads, not only in terms of the information which is systematically recorded in their case-histories (and which was therefore available for inclusion in the prediction table), but on other characteristics which may or may not be explicitly stated but which also influence the risk, and if these characteristics are at all independent of the factors which were available to the prediction table, then the extent to which boys sent to open borstals actually are better risks may be much greater than is revealed by the risk groups of the table. Cockett (4) presents some evidence that this may in fact happen. A proper comparison of different treatments given to cases classified by the table as equal risks will then be difficult.

It is to be expected that in a system of allocation to different regimes or types of treatment such as is used for borstal lads, these selection processes will occur. They are less likely to be present when the normal basis of the allocation procedure is, for example, geographical, as happens in many probation areas where one officer is alloted all, or most, of the probation cases in a particular locality. Here the conditions approximate more to a "natural experiment" in so far as the one officer will be dealing with a range of different risks;[5] but, of course, he may vary his methods of treatment to match the risks as he perceives them, and this amounts to selec-

---

[4]"Treatment" here is used to mean any way in which the court deals with a convicted offender, including simply discharging him; the point is that it is impossible to separate out the strict "poor risk." However, if "treatment" is used in a more specific sense, to mean, say, an institutional sentence or a supervision order, one can of course work out base expectancies for persons who did not receive such treatment, and compare them with the outcomes for otherwise similar persons who did.

[5]Though an officer working in a "high delinquency" locality may have a different, and possibly shorter, range of risks than his colleagues elsewhere.

tion. One of the main aims of the probation research programme[6] . . . was to construct a classification of types of probation treatment whose outcomes for different types of offender could be assessed with the help of a prediction table; but the accomplishment of this aim depends, among other things, on there being a sufficient variety of risk/treatment combinations for comparisons to be made, and on having a prediction table which accurately describes the risks.

The best solution, from the research worker's point of view, to the problems posed by selection is to allocate cases to different types of treatment according to a research design, i.e. as a planned experiment. Persons judged to fall in the same category of an offender classification would be sent, at random, to different types of treatment, whose outcomes could then be evaluated. But experimental allocation raises both administrative and ethical difficulties. In practice, choice as to forms of treatment may be limited by considerations like high caseloads or institutional overcrowding, and the need to minimise escapes from prison. The pressures on penal administrators to keep the system functioning smoothly may limit freedom to experiment. And a proposal to experiment on convicted persons with different forms of treatment raises ethical questions. It is not intended to discuss these here, but the interested reader is referred to Bradford Hill's presentation (12) of the case for experiments in medicine, where the issues are to some extent parallel.[7]

[6]For an outline of the probation research programme currently being carried out by the Home Office Research Unit see Folkard and others (6) and also Chapter 7 of the *Report of the Work of the Probation and After-Care Department,* 1966–68 (Home Office) (13).

[7]Arguing the case for the controlled clinical trial, Bradford Hill points out that, in the absence of organised knowledge of the effectiveness of any treatment, the continued use of such treatment may itself be an experiment, but an unscientific one which does little to advance knowledge further. To continue in this state of ignorance, instead of taking planned steps to reduce it, is the less ethical course. Bradford Hill sets out very clearly, however, the difficulties of designing controlled experiments and the fact that ethical

Wilkins (28) suggested that the difficulties of setting up direct experiments to compare treatments could be got round by using predictive methods to study already existing systems. In many situations this may be the best practicable approach, but the possible presence of uncontrolled selection factors should not be overlooked.

The problems associated with the use of prediction tables as a research tool may partly explain why their employment in this way seems so far to have been rather limited. Selected examples can be given, however, of the use of tables to help evaluate different types of treatment, both in a "natural" setting (i.e. where an already existing allocation practice is being examined) and in a planned experiment. As has already been mentioned, Mannheim and Wilkins used their borstal prediction table to compare the success rates achieved by open and closed borstals (17). Benson used it in comparison of borstal inmates with young prisoners (1). More recently, Cockett (4) has employed the Mannheim-Wilkins risk categories to match samples of trainees released from seven borstals in an attempt to compare their results. Beverly and Guttmann (2,3) compared the different institutions from which California Youth Authority wards were released in terms of parole violation rates, allowing for the various risks by using base expectancy tables. The development and use of prediction tables has played a large part in correctional research in California; a concise account of it up to 1962 is given by Gottfredson and Beverly (10). Similar work has been started in Wisconsin (30). Among instances of experimental designs for evaluating treatment which include the use of base expectancies are the Community Treatment Project sponsored by the California Youth Authority and the National Institute of Mental Health (U.S.A.) (27), where direct release and special supervision in the community are being compared with institu-

issues may often prevent what from the research point of view would be the ideal design.

tional treatment for C.Y.A. wards, and the use of a modified version of the Glueck social prediction table by the New York City Youth Board to test the effectiveness of child guidance therapy in preventing delinquency.

For further reading on the use of prediction instruments in evaluating treatment, and some of the associated problems, the reader is referred to Hood's paper *Research on the Effectiveness of Punishments and Treatments* (1964) (14) and Wilkins' book *Evaluation of Penal Measures* (1969 (29). Sparks' paper *Types of Treatment for Types of Offenders* (1967) (23) is a review and discussion of research using typologies of offenders and treatment, with and without base expectancies.

*

SUMMARY

In the present context, a "prediction" or "base expectancy" study is one which aims at estimating, for a defined group of persons, the various degrees to which they are at risk of committing crimes or delinquencies.

The information on which the prediction is based may be of various kinds: for example, psychological tests, biographical data, or direct observations of behaviour. Predictions may be made by individual clinical assessment, or actuarially by using a statistical formula in which several predictive items of information have been mathematically combined and probabilities calculated from a sample of cases.

Various methods exist for constructing a statistical prediction instrument; their common feature is that they offer a means of selecting the best predictive factors from a larger number, and then combining them with the aim of making the combination more powerful than any of the factors alone. The usual procedure is to examine data on a sample of cases for whom the outcome (reconviction, or whatever is to be predicted) is already known, to combine selected items, and to relate the combination to the outcome probabilities in the sample.

With nearly all methods, the instrument *must* be validated, i.e. tested on a sample other than the one from which it was constructed. This is necessary to correct for any exploitation of chance relationships which may occur during the selection or combination of variables. Predictive power is liable to shrink between the construction and validation samples, but its value for the latter is an unbiased estimate of its value for the population. Revalidation from time to time is also necessary, to allow for changes in the predictive power of the factors used, or in the population itself. A prediction instrument constructed for use on one population cannot be assumed valid for another without being tested.

If the cases which the instrument is designed to identify occur only rarely in the population, it may be advantageous in construction to use not a random sample but one in which they occur more frequently. But probabilities derived from this sample must be re-calculated for the population unless for a validation run a random sample is used. This is the problem of the base rate.

The purposes to which prediction instruments may be put can be considered under the two heads of research and administration. A prediction table which estimates the expected risk of success or failure on the basis of pretreatment information may be used as a research tool in the evaluation of different treatments: their results can be compared with expectation. There are difficulties, however. The predictor is not "treatment-free," but implies a comparison with the average of all the treatments given to the sample on which it was based. If an existing system of allocation to treatment is being studied, covert selection factors may alter the risks so that the expectancies shown by the table are not accurate. Some offender/treatment combinations may occur too rarely to be evaluated. The best design from the researcher's point of view is experimental allocation to different treatments, but this may pose ethical and practical problems. Nevertheless, examples can be given of research using prediction tables as a tool, in both experimental and other systems of allocation to treatment.

For administrators and penal practitioners, prediction tables could in theory be used at various stages: delinquency prevention, sentencing, treatment, release (from institutions) and after-care. In practice there are difficulties here too. Labelling persons as good or bad risks may have undesirable effects. To help courts in sentencing, a prediction table would need to show the likely outcomes of various sentences for comparable offenders, but so far not a great deal has been done on "all-sentence" prediction, and instruments constructed on separate sentenced groups (such as probationers or borstal boys) do not meet the need. A predictive classification may be of use when administrators are deciding on treatment within any one type of sentence, e.g. the degree of supervision that a probationer should receive, though if based only on pre-sentence information is will not necessarily indicate the individual's treatment needs.

Much has been written, mostly in the U.S.A., about the use of prediction tables as aids to selecting prisoners for release on parole. Though many tables have been constructed by research workers, their actual use by administrators seems so far to have been fairly limited. Less has been said about after-care, though there are projects where parolees in different risk groups have been given different degrees of supervision. One reason why prediction tables have been comparatively little used may be that for practical purposes their power is generally rather low.

REFERENCES

1. Benson, Sir George. 1959. Prediction methods and young prisoners. *British Journal of Delinquency*. London. Vol. IX, no. 3.

2. Beverly, R. F. 1965. *An Analysis of Parole Performance by Institution of Release* (1959–1962). Research Report no. 40 of the California Youth Authority, Sacramento.

3. Beverly, R. F. and Guttmann, E. S. 1962. *An Analysis of Parole Performance by Institution of Release* (1956–1960). Research Report no. 31 of the California Youth Authority, Sacramento.

4. Cockett, R. 1967. Borstal training: a follow-up study. *British Journal of Criminology*. London. Vol. VII, no. 2.

5. Craig, M. M. and Furst, P. W. 1965. What happens after treatment? A study of potentially delinquent boys. *Social Service Review*. Chicago. Vol. XXXIX, no. 2.

6. Folkard S., Lyon, K., Carver, M. M. and O'Leary, E. 1966. *Probation Research: A Preliminary Report*. H.M.S.O., London.

7. Glueck, S. and E. 1950. *Unraveling Juvenile Delinquency*. The Commonwealth Fund, New York. Table XX-3, pp. 261–262.

8. Glueck, S. and E. 1960. *Predicting Delinquency and Crime*. Harvard University Press, Cambridge, Massachusetts.

9. Goodman, L. A. 1953. The use and validity of a prediction instrument. *American Journal of Sociology*. Chicago. Vol. LVIII, no. 5.

10. Gottfredson, D. M. and Beverly, R. F. 1962. Development and operational use of prediction methods in correctional work. *Proceedings of the Social Statistics Section,* American Statistical Association, Washington, D.C.

11. Hathaway, S. R. and Monachesi, E. D. (eds). (1953). *Analysing and Predicting Juvenile Delinquency with the M.M.P.I.* University of Minnesota Press, Minneapolis.

12. Hill, Sir Austin Bradford. 1962. *Statistical Methods in Clinical and Preventive Medicine.* E. & S. Livingstone Ltd., Edinburgh and London. See especially pages 175–188, 'The Problems of Experiments in Man'.

13. Home Office. 1969. *Report on the Work of the Probation and After-Care Department, 1966–68.* H.M.S.O., London.

14. Hood, R. 1964. Research on the effectiveness of punishments and treatments. Report presented to the Second European Conference of Directors of Criminological Research Institutes, October 1964, and published in *Collected Studies in Criminological Research*. Vol. I, 1967. Council of Europe, Strasbourg.

15.   Jepsen, J. and Pal, L. 1966. *Predicting the Volume and Structure of Future Criminality*. Paper prepared for the Fourth European Conference of Directors of Criminological Research Institutes. Council of Europe, Strasbourg.

16.   Macnaughton-Smith, P. 1965. *Some Statistical and other Numerical Techniques for Classifying Individuals*. H.M.S.O., London.

17.   Mannheim, H. and Wilkins, L. T. 1955. *Prediction Methods in Relation to Borstal Training*. H.M.S.O., London. P 170 and Appendix V.

18.   *Ibid.*, page 220.

19.   Meehl, P. E. 1954. *Clinical versus Statistical Prediction: a theoretical analysis and a review of the evidence.* University of Minnesota Press, Minneapolis.

20.   Morrison, R. L. 1955. Predictive research: a critical assessment of its practical applications. *British Journal of Delinquency.* London. Vol. VI, no. 2.

21.   Ohlin, L. E. 1951. *Selection for Parole.* Russell Sage Foundation, New York.

22.   Sawyer, J. 1966. Measurement *and* prediction, clinical *and* statistical. *Psychological Bulletin.* Washington, D.C. Vol. LXVI, no. 3.

23.   Sparks, R. F. 1967. Types of treatment for types of offenders. Report presented to the Fifth Conference of Directors of Criminological Research Institutes, 1967, and published in *Collected Studies in Criminological Research*. Vol. III, 1968. Council of Europe, Strasbourg.

24.   Stott, D. H. 1960. The prediction of delinquency from non-delinquent behaviour. *British Journal of Delinquency.* London. Vol. X, no. 3.

25.   Stott, D. H. 1964. Prediction of success or failure on probation: a follow-up study. *International Journal of Social Psychiatry.* London. Vol. X, no. 1, pages 27–29.

26.   Stott, D. H. and Sykes, E. G. 1956. *The British Social Adjustment Guides.* University of London Press, London.

27.   Warren, M. Q. and Palmer, T. B. 1965. *Community Treatment Project: Research Report no. 6.* Appendix O. California Youth Authority, Sacramento.

28.   Wilkins, L. T. 1955. Symposium on predictive methods in the treatment of delinquency. *British Journal of Delinquency.* London. Vol. VI, no. 2.

29.   Wilkins, L. T. 1969. *Evaluation of Penal Measures.* Random House, New York.

30.   Wisconsin State Department of Public Welfare, Madison. Several of the research bulletins published since 1962 by the Bureau of Research describe prediction tables constructed for various groups of offenders.

The Causes of Crime:
Biological Factors

IN RECENT YEARS IT HAS BECOME UNFASHIONABLE TO ENTERTAIN SERIOUSLY THE idea that genetic or biological factors may be significantly associated with criminal behavior. Yet biological explanations of crime have been developed, with considerable force, for almost 200 years.

The selections in this section deal with disparate physiological and genetic elements, ranging from physical attractiveness and menses to sophisticated investigations of XYY chromosomes and identical hereditary makeup, in the form of "twin studies". Cavior and Howard found that for both blacks and whites, juvenile delinquents are significantly less attractive than a nondelinquent control group of high school students. This suggests to them that unattractiveness may be either a contributing factor in antisocial behavior or that it alters the risk of being arrested or receiving a lengthy sentence. Dalton produces data indicating a positive relationship between menstrual and premenstrual tension and the commission of crime, as measured by the activities of a number of institutionalized females.

As a serious test of the role of heredity in antisocial behavior, Crowe examines a population of female offenders' children who were put up for adoption, compared to an equal number of control adoptees. The results seem to confirm a significantly higher rate of antisocial personalities among the experimental subjects than the controls, but lingering methodological problems still remain.

The major investigation that has thus far taken place concerning genetic composition and the presence or absence of the XYY chromosome is by Witkin et al. Using a number of Copenhagen males, the authors find the XYY condition to be rare (less than 3 per 100) and, although persons with such a genetic composition are slightly higher in criminality, there is no serious evidence that the sex chromosome complement contributes heavily to aggressive crime. Dalgard and Kringlen's study of a sample of identical and fraternal twins born in Norway who reach the ages of 40 to 50 concludes that there are negligible differences with regard to "concordant" crimes.

25. Attractiveness and Juvenile Delinquency

NORMAN CAVIOR
L. RAMONA HOWARD

SEVERAL RECENT INVESTIGATIONS HAVE YIELDED high, positive correlations between physical attractiveness and *(a)* popularity among children (Cavior, 1970; Pope, 1953; Staffieri, 1967), *(b)* popularity and dating preferences among adolescents (Cavior, 1970; Cavior & Miller, 1972), *(c)* acceptance into college sororities and fraternities (Roff & Brody, 1953), *(d)* popularity and dating preferences among college students (Berscheid, Dion, Walster, E., & Walster, G.M., 1971; Brislin & Lewis, 1968; Byrne, Ervin, & Lamberth, 1970; Coombs & Kenkel, 1966; Perrin, 1921; Stroebe, Insko, Thompson, & Layton, 1971; Walster, Aronson, Abrahams, & Rottman, 1966), *(e)* actual dating partners (Murstein, 1972; Silverman, 1971), and *(f)* actual marriage partners (Cavior & Boblett, 1972). These and other studies indicate the importance of physical attractiveness in various dyadic and group processes and suggest the possibility that unattractive people may be rejected by others. Such rejection may lead to retaliatory antisocial behavior.

It has long been suggested that the somatotype of the male juvenile offender is characterized by a predominance of mesomorphy and an absence of ectomorphy and endomorphy as compared with youths not labeled as delinquent (Glueck, S., & Glueck, E., 1950;

▶SOURCE: *"Facial Attractiveness and Juvenile Delinquency Among Black and White Offenders," Journal of Abnormal Child Psychology* (1973), 1(2):202–213. Reprinted by permission.

Sheldon, 1949). Research by Staffieri (1967) and Cavior (1970) has indicated that in the general population high ratings of physical attractiveness are associated with mesomorphy and low ratings with ectomorphy and endomorphy. If the same relations were found among delinquents, it would seem that physical attractiveness does not play a contributory role to delinquency. An experimental study with adults in the New York City Department of Corrections, however, showed that cosmetic and reconstructive plastic surgery significantly reduced the recidivism rate among nonaddict criminals with facial deformities, as compared with a control group of criminals with similar facial problems who did not receive surgery (Kurtzberg, Safar, & Cavior, 1968). In addition, informal observations of white delinquents, made by Cavior in the New York City correctional system and at the Kennedy Youth Center, also suggested that there was a greater proportion of unattractive faces among prison immates than among the general population outside of prison. These findings and observations suggested the two hypotheses tested in the first study of the present report:

1. There is a positive relationship between facial appearance and delinquent behavior; i.e., juvenile delinquents are less facially attractive than nondelinquents.

2. There are significant differences in the degree of facial physical attractiveness among

Quay's four behavior dimensions of juvenile offenders (Quay, 1972; Quay & Parsons, 1971; U.S. Department of Justice, 1970)

The classification system at the Kennedy Youth Center is based on the use of three instruments developed in an extensive program of research into the dimensions of deviant behavior in adolescents and children. Data from the instruments are transformed into scores for each behavior dimension and the delinquent is assigned to the dimension on which he obtained the highest composite score. The four dimensions are inadequate-immature, neurotic-disturbed, unsocialized-psychopathic, and socialized-subcultural. Research has shown that the delinquents selected as extremes on the dimensions systematically vary along a number of psychologically relevant dimensions (e.g., Borkovec, 1970; Orris, 1969; Skrzypek, 1969).

The first study of this report dealt with white delinquents; the second study, black delinquents. At the time Study I was initiated there were very few black raters available to rate the pictures of the black students at the Kennedy Youth Center. Later the investigators were able to secure the help of black raters to replicate this study with the black offenders.

STUDY I

Method

Subjects   The Kennedy Youth Center furnished facial photographs of the inmates as well as their behavior dimension classification. The pictures had been taken on the photographic vending machines found in many stores and amusement parks. There were 103 inmates, all white males, who ranged in age from 16 to 21 with a median of 18. The facial pictures of 78 white nondelinquents were obtained from the yearbook of a high school in Morgantown, West Virginia. The 78 nondelinquents comprised the entire male graduating class for that year, and ranged in age from 17 to 19 with a median age of 18.

The pictures of the high school students were

approximately the same size as the delinquents' pictures (2 × 1½ in.), but they were printed on different paper. Everything below the neck was covered with tape to prevent judgements from being affected by ties, shirt styles, or other clothing. It was not possible to control for factors such as smiling, although in our experience factors such as clothing styles and smiling do not seem to make major differences in judging physical attractiveness; structural characteristics and hair styles seem to be more important. The hair styles in the delinquent and high school groups were similarly short.

The pictures were judged by freshmen and sophomores in introductory psychology classes at West Virginia University. There were two groups of judges, each consisting of 30 males and 30 females, all white, with a median age of 18. One group of males and females judged the Kennedy Youth Center pictures and the other group judged the high school pictures. (The data on the high school students were originally gathered for another study.)

Procedures   The pictures were placed on 3 × 5 in. index cards, coded on the back. The judges sorted the pictures into five physical-attractiveness categories, from very unattractive (1) to very attractive (5). Cavior and Dokecki (1973) have found that this rating procedure yields results extremely similar to those obtained by a ranking procedure tested for significance by the Kendall Coefficient of Concordance, and that both types of measures are reliable. The deck of pictures was shuffled before each judge sorted them. The persons who collected the data on the delinquents and the judges who rated them knew nothing of the purposes or hypotheses of the study, and the judges did not know the pictures were of delinquents. The person who collected the data with the pictures of the nondelinquents knew that they were of high school students although the judges who rated them did not. Neither of the persons who collected the data in the two parts of this study had any knowledge that the data would be compared with each other since this was not originally planned.

Results

Interrater reliability was extremely high as indicated by very low standard deviations of the ratings; for the pictures of the delinquents the mean standard deviation was .53, and of the high school group .46. In addition, the correlation between male and female ratings of the delinquent pictures was .92 $(p < .001)$, and of the nondelinquent pictures .94 $(p < .001)$. Only the results of the combined ratings of male and female judges are presented since separate analyses yielded identical results.

A one-way analysis of variance with five levels (four behavior dimensions plus the high school students) was used to analyze the facial-attractiveness ratings and yielded an F ratio of 4.78 $(df = 4/176; p < .01)$, which indicated that there were significant differences among the mean facial attractiveness ratings assigned to the five groups of pictures. Duncan's New Multiple Range Test indicated that each group differed significantly from every other group $(p < .05)$, with one exception. The one exception was that there was no significant difference between the high school group and the delinquent socialized-subcultural group; however, the difference between these two groups reached a significance level of .10. In descending order, the means of the facial attractiveness ratings for each of the five groups of subjects were: high school students, 2.73 $(SD = .46, N = 78)$; socialized-subcultural, 2.46 $(SD = .61, N = 26)$; neurotic-disturbed, 2.28 $(SD = .48, N = 40)$; inadequate-immature, 2.05 $(SD = .43, N = 28)$; and unsocialized-psychopathic, 1.90 $(SD = .56, N = 9)$. In terms of the overlap of the ratings, 9% of the delinquents' pictures received mean ratings of 3 or higher (3 = average) as compared to 37% of the high school pictures.

STUDY II

After the first study was completed, the second study was begun with black inmates at the Kennedy Youth Center.

In addition to the two hypotheses examined in Study I, it was hypothesized that

1.   Black inmates are darker in skin color than black high school students.

2.   Lightness of skin color is positively correlated with physical attractiveness, rated by both black and white raters.

3.   White raters give higher physical attractiveness ratings than black raters.

The hypothesis that black delinquents are darker in skin color than black high school students was suggested by research findings such as those obtained by Ransford (1970), who interviewed 312 black males shortly after the Watts riot. Dark blacks were found to be in lower occupational and income positions that light blacks, even when education (as a measure of skill) was held constant. Moreover, blacks who had moved to the periphery or completely out of the ghetto and those in more prestigeful white-collar jobs tended to be lighter than those in the ghetto or at the bottom of the class structure. Similar results have been obtained by Edwards (1959), Drake and Cayton (1962), Frazier (1962), and Bullough (1969).

The hypotheses that physical attractiveness and lightness of skin color are positively correlated and that white raters would give higher physical attractiveness ratings than black raters were based on the following considerations. Until very recently, with the increased emphasis on black identity and the consequent beauty of blackness, a dark color had been devalued within the black community; blacks were socialized to accept the white world and white standards of beauty (e.g., Stevenson & Stewart, 1958). There developed among blacks a color stratification system in which light skin color was valued and dark skin color was viewed as an unfortunate disability (Brody, 1963; Brown, 1969; Lincoln, 1967). Similarly, Cavior and Dokecki (1970) found a high positive correlation between lightness of skin color and peer-rated physical attractiveness among Mexican children in Monterrey, Mexico; and Cavior (1970) found a positive correlation between lightness of skin color and peer-rated physical attractiveness among white fifth- and eleventh-grade children.

Not only are blacks now being taught to think that black is beautiful, but so are whites, although neither group seems to be learning and behaving accordingly. Whites, in particular, would likely find it very difficult, especially in the presence of a black person, to describe blacks as less than average in attractiveness. In other words, white raters' responses might in large part be determined by their defensiveness, in the presence of a black experimenter, against stating that they find blacks generally unattractive.

Method

Subjects   Facial pictures and behavior dimension ratings of 56 black residents were obtained from the Kennedy Youth Center. These were all the pictures available at the time study was initiated. The residents, all black males, ranged in age from 16 to 21 with the median age of 18. Pictures of 56 black, nondelinquent high school seniors were randomly selected from a yearbook of a high school in Atlanta, Georgia. These subjects ranged in age from 17 to 19 with a median age of 18. The two groups of pictures were the same size as those in Study I, and the same precautions were taken to minimize effects that might result from the differences in quality between them.

Raters   The pictures were rated by three groups of raters. One group included 30 black males and 30 black females, average age 19, who were students at West Virginia University. This group of raters rated the pictures on physical attractiveness. Another group of raters consisted of 15 white females, average age 25, and 15 white males, average age 31. The females in this group were primarily graduate students at West Virginia University; the males were psychology department faculty and graduate students. This group of raters also rated the pictures on physical attractiveness. The third group of raters consisted of 15 black females, average age 30, and 15 black males, average age 23, who rated the pictures for skin color. The

females in this group were teachers in an elementary school in Atlanta, Georgia; the males consisted of five teachers in the same school and 10 undergraduate students from West Virginia University. None of the raters knew the purpose of the study.

Procedure   The two sets of pictures (delinquent and nondelinquent) were combined into a single group of 112 pictures, which were rated on physical attractiveness with the same scale as in Study I. The ratings of skin color were also on a 5-point scale from very dark (1) to very light (5).

Results

Interrater reliability within each of the three groups of raters was high as indicated by low standard deviations on almost all the pictures: for the attractiveness ratings of the high school and delinquent pictures, respectively, the mean standard deviations among the black raters were .48 and .51, and among the white raters .52 and .57. The standard deviations of the skin-color ratings were similar in magnitude. The between-sex correlations were .90 ($p < .001$) for blacks judging physical attractiveness, .88 ($p < .001$) for whites judging physical attractiveness, and .98 ($p < .001$) for blacks judging skin color. Therefore, only the combined ratings of the male and female raters are reported; results were identical when analyzed separately for each sex.

Three one-way analyses of variance with five levels (four behavior dimensions from Kennedy Youth Center, plus high school subjects) were used to examine the facial attractiveness and skin-color ratings. The results indicated that there were significant differences among the five groups for blacks judging skin color ($F = 23.397$, $df = 4/107$, $p < .001$), and for blacks judging physical attractiveness ($F = 4.357$, $df = 4/107$, $p < .003$), but not for whites judging physical attractiveness ($F = .949$, $df = 4/107$, $p > .05$).

The mean physical attractiveness and skin-color ratings, and the results of Duncan's New Multiple Range Tests, are shown in Table I. For

Table I. Mean Physical Attractiveness (PA) and Skin Color (SC)
Ratings in Study II

Race of Raters	Dimension Judged	Group									
		High School (N = 78)		Inadequate-Immature (N = 15)		Neurotic-Disturbed (N = 7)		Unsocialized-Psychopathic (N = 13)		Socialized-Subcultural (N = 21)	
		M	SD	M	SD	M	SD	M	SD	M	SD
Black	PA	2.40	.48	2.16[a]	.63	1.79[a]	.33	2.01[a]	.44	2.09[a]	.44
White	PA	2.90[a]	.52	2.98[a]	.49	2.52[a]	.66	2.88[a]	.44	2.90[a]	.60
Black	SC	3.24	.67	2.11[a]	.95	1.71[a]	.51	1.76[a]	.58	2.03[a]	.77

[a]Means which did not differ significantly from each other according to Duncan's New Multiple Range Test.

blacks judging physical attractiveness and skin color there were no significant differences among the four dimensions of delinquency, but the subjects representing each of the four dimensions were rated as significantly less attractive and darker in skin color than the high school students. Results support the hypotheses that black delinquents are less attractive and darker in skin color than black high school students, but failed to confirm the finding obtained in Study I that there are significant differences in physical attractiveness among the four dimensions. In terms of the overlap of the ratings of attractiveness made by the black raters, 45% of the delinquent pictures received mean ratings of 2 or higher (2 = less than average) as compared to 77% of the high school pictures. There was very little overlap in the skin-color ratings: 83% of the high school pictures were rated as light as compared to 17% of the delinquents' pictures. The results shown in Table I also support the hypothesis that white raters assign higher physical-attractiveness scores to black pictures than do black raters. Furthermore, even though interrater reliabilities were extremely high in both studies, the white judges assigned substantially higher physical-attractiveness ratings to black pictures (Study II) than to the white pictures (Study I). This result lends further support the hypothesis that whites may be rating the black pictures from a position of defensiveness.

The correlations between the lightness of skin color and physical attractiveness ratings were .53 ($p < .001$) for the black raters and .72 ($p < .001$) for the white raters. The difference between these two correlation values was significant ($Z = 1.77, p < .05$, one-tailed test), indicating that white raters respond more to skin color in judging the attractiveness of blacks than do black raters.

DISCUSSION

The data from both studies can be interpreted as supporting the hypothesis that both black and white delinquents are significantly lower in facial attractiveness than nondelinquents. This finding suggests that there is a relationship between facial attractiveness and delinquency, and is congruent with the findings of Kurtzberg et al. (1968) on the effectiveness of facial plastic surgery in reducing recidivism. Although, strictly speaking, pictures were judged rather than persons, Cavior and Dokecki (1973) found high, postive correlations between ratings of pictures made by persons who knew and others who did not know the persons judged. Presumably the raters who knew the persons depicted were ranking the actual persons when they were ranking the pictures.

The comparison of ratings between Kennedy Youth Center offenders and the high school students suggests that a lack of facial attractiveness may play a contributory role in the development of antisocial behavior and/or reduce the probability that the offender will receive a suspended sentence, or even that he will be arrested. A recent study by Dion (1972) on physical attractiveness and evaluation of children's transgressions indicated that adults display differential treatment toward attractive and unattractive children in circumstances in which their behavior is identical, and further that the severe transgression of an attractive child is less likely to be seen as reflecting an enduring disposition toward antisocial behavior than that of an unattractive child. In addition, the transgression itself tends to be less negatively evaluated when committed by an attractive child. Finally, research by Miller (1970) and Dion, Berscheid, and Walster (1972) indicated that positive personality descriptions and predictions regarding future behavior are assigned to attractive individuals, while negative personality descriptions and predictions are assigned to unattractive individuals.

The finding in Study I, with white offenders, that physical attractiveness varies among the four dimensions of delinquent behavior described by Quay, suggests the possibility that different behaviors or different perceptions of similar behaviors are associated with different levels of physical attractiveness. This would follow Dion's (1972) finding that for the same transgression, children of different levels of physical attractiveness are treated differently. Whether the absence of a relationship between physical attractiveness and Quay's dimensions among the black delinquents resulted from the relatively small sample size, methodological problems, the positive correlation between lightness of skin color and physical attractiveness, or whether no relationship exists, cannot be determined at this time.

The results of Study II also confirmed the hypotheses that black delinquents are significantly darker in skin color than black high school students and that there is a positive correlation between lightness of skin color and physi-

cal attractiveness rated by both black and white raters. These findings suggest that dark-skinned blacks may receive different treatment even within the black culture, in addition to being treated differently by the white culture. This may be due to an internalization by both cultures of the concept that the color white symbolized and connotes positive adjectives such as purity, cleanliness, and godliness, while black symbolizes and connotes such things as dirt, evil, and death; good cowboys wear white hats and the outlaws, black hats.

From a theoretical viewpoint, either the stimulus value of the person to the observer or attribution, self-concept, or reinforcement theory, among others, can be invoked to account for the results, either alone or in combination. In addition, attitude-similarity research tends to suggest that liking (and therefore acceptance) is dependent on the extent of either perceived attitude similarity or actual attitude similarity (e.g., Byrne, 1969; Cavior & Miller, 1972). One could therefore speculate that the apparent visibility of the black skin, coupled with stereotyped expectancies, would necessarily establish barriers to perceived attitude similarity and subsequent liking as well as subsequent handling in various aspects of the legal process.

It is important to note that there were some qualitative differences between the photographs of the delinquent and high school groups, and that different rating methods were used in the two studies. These differences might also explain some of the present findings; consequently, the results and conclusions should be considered as suggestive of the possible contribution of physical appearance to social deviance. These differences cannot account for the difference in physical attractiveness ratings among the four dimensions of delinquency in Study I, nor the finding, in Study II, that white raters assigned significantly higher ratings to the pictures of blacks than did the black raters. In addition, the issue of the defensiveness of the white raters, in Study II, is difficult to evaluate since the effects due to the presence of a black experimenter cannot be separated from the effects due to the photographs of the black subjects.

Future research in this area might benefit from nonreactive (unobtrusive) research strategies. For example, it should be possible to observe directly actual courtroom situations in which blacks and whites of different levels of physical attractiveness and skin coloration are tried for similar offences.

REFERENCES

Berscheid, E., Dion, K., Walster, E., & Walster, G. M. Physical attractiveness and dating choice: A test of the matching hypothesis. *Journal of Experimental Social Psychology,* 1971, 7, 173–189.

Borkovec, T. D. Autonomic reactivity to sensory stimulation in psychopathic, neurotic and normal delinquents. *Journal of Consulting and Clinical Psychology,* 1970, **35,** 217–222.

Brislin, R. W., & Lewis, S. A. Dating and physical attractiveness: Replication. *Psychological Reports,* 1968, **22,** 976.

Brody, E. B. Color and identity conflict in young boys. *Psychiatry,* 1963, **26,** 188–200.

Brown, H. R. *Die nigger die.* New York: The Dial Press, 1969.

Bullough, B. *Social psychological barriers to housing desegration.* University of California: The Center for Real Estate and Urban Economics, 1969.

Bryne, D. Attitudes and attraction. In L. Berkowitz (Ed.), *Advances in experimental social psychology,* Vol. 4. New York: Academic Press, 1969.

Byrne, D., Ervin, C. R., & Lamberth, J. C. Continuity between the experimental study of attraction and "real life" computer dating. *Journal of Personality and Social Psychology,* 1970, **16,** 157–165.

Cavior, N. Physical attractiveness, perceived attitude similarity, and interpersonal attraction among the fifth and eleventh grade boys and girls. Unpublished doctoral dissertation, University of Houston, 1970.

Cavior, N., & Boblett, P. J. Physical attractiveness of dating versus married couples. *Proceedings of the 80th Annual Convention of the American Psychological Association,* 1972, **7,** 175–176.

Cavior, N., & Dokecki, P. R. Physical attractiveness and interpersonal attraction among fifth grade boys: A replication with Mexican children. Paper presented at the meeting of the Southwestern Psychological Association: St. Louis, Mo.: Apr. 25, 1970.

Cavior, N., & Dokecki, P. R. Physical attractiveness, perceived attitude similarily, and academic achievement as contributors to interpersonal attraction among adolescents. *Development Psychology,* 1973, **8,** in press.

Cavior, N., & Miller, K. Physical attractiveness, attitude similarity, and length of acquaintance as contributors to interpersonal attraction among adolescents. Unpublished manuscript, West Virginia University, 1972.

Coombs, R. H., & Kenkel, W. F. Sex differences in dating aspirations and satisfaction with computer-selected partners. *Journal of Marriage and the Family,* 1966, **28,** 62–66.

Dion, K. Physical attractiveness and evaluations of children's transgressions. *Journal of Personality and Social Psychology,* 1972, **24,** 207–213.

Dion, K., Berscheid, E., & Walster, E. What is beautiful is good. *Journal of Personality and Social Psychology,* 1972, **24,** 285–290.

Drake, S. C., & Cayton, H. R. *Black metropolis.* New York: Harper & Row, 1962.

Edwards, F. *The Negro professional class.* Glencoe, Ill.: The Free Press, 1959.

Frazier, E. F. *Black bourgeoisie: The rise of a new middle class in the United States.* New York: Collier Books, 1962.

Glueck, S., & Glueck, E. *Unraveling juvenile delinquency.* New York: Harper, 1950.

Kurtzberg, R. L., Safar, H., & Cavior, N. Surgical and social rehabilitation of adult offenders. *Proceedings of the 76th Annual Convention of the American Psychological Association,* 1968, **3,** 649–650.

Lincoln, C. Color and group identity in the United States. *Daedalus,* 1967, **96,** 527–541.

Miller, A. G. Role of physical attractiveness in impression formation. *Psychonomic Science,* 1970, **19,** 241–243.

Murstein, B. I. Physical attractiveness and marital choice. *Journal of Personality and Social Psychology,* 1972, **22,** 8–12.

Orris, J. B. Visual monitoring performance in three subgroups of male delinquents. *Journal of Abnormal Psychology,* 1969, **74,** 227–237.

Perrin, F. A. C. Physical attractiveness and repulsiveness. *Journal of Experimental Psychology,* 1921, **4,** 203–217.

Pope, B. Socioeconomic contrasts in children's peer culture prestige values. *Genetic Psychology Monographs,* 1953, **48,** 157–220.

Quay, H. C. Patterns of aggression, withdrawal and immaturity. In H. C. Quay & J. S. Werry (Eds.), *Psychopathological disorders of childhood.* New York: Wiley, 1972.

Quay, H. C., & Parsons, L. B. The differential behavioral classification of the juvenile offender (Federal Bureau of Prisons, Department of Justice) Washington, D.C.: U.S. Government Printing Office, 1971.

Ransford, H. E. Skin color, life chances and antiwhite attitudes. *Social Problems,* 1970, **18,** 164–179.

Roff, M., & Brody, D. S. Appearance and choice status during adolescence. *Journal of Personality,* 1953, **36,** 347–356.

Sheldon, W. H. *Varieties of delinquent youth: An introduction to constitutional psychiatry.* New York: Harper, 1949.

Silverman, I. Physical attractiveness and courtship. *Sexual Behavior,* Sept. 1971, 22–25.

Skrzypek, G. J. Effect of perceptual isolation and arousal on anxiety, complexity preference and novelty preference in psychopathic and neurotic delinquents. *Journal of Abnormal Psychology,* 1969, **74,** 321–329.

Staffieri, J. R. A study of social stereotype of body image in children. *Journal of Personality and Social Psychology,* 1967, **1,** 101–104.

Stevenson, H. W., & Stewart, E. C. A developmental study of racial awareness in young children. *Child Development,* 1958, **29,** 399–409.

Stroebe, W., Insko, C. A., Thompson, V. D., & Layton, B. D. Effects of physical attractiveness, attitude similarity and sex on various aspects of interpersonal attraction. *Journal of Personality and Social Psychology,* 1971, **18,** 79–91.

U.S. Department of Justice, Federal Bureau of Prisons, Robert F. Kennedy Youth Center. Differential treatment . . . A way to begin. Washington, D.C.: U.S. Government Printing Office, 1970.

Walster, E., Aronson, V., Abrahams, D., & Rottman, L. Importance of physical attractiveness in dating behavior. *Journal of Personality and Social Psychology,* 1966, **4,** 508–516.

26. Menstruation and Crime

KATHARINA DALTON

IT HAS BEEN SHOWN THAT DURING MENSTRUATION a deterioration occurs both in a schoolgirl's work and in her behaviour (Dalton, 1960a, 1960c), and it is also at this time that women are most liable to be involved in accidents (Dalton, 1960b) or to be admitted to hospital with an acute psychiatric illness (Dalton, 1959). This gradual recognition of the social significance of menstruation in the various aspects of a woman's life has led to an investigation of the importance of the menstrual factor in crime.

Over a period of six months in one of H.M. Prisons I interviewed all newly convicted women below the age of 55 on the first weekday after their sentence. The prisoners were asked their age, parity, duration of menstruation, length of cycle, date of last menstruation, and whether they observed any symptoms before or during menstruation. A similar interview was arranged for all prisoners who had been reported to the governor for bad behaviour while serving their sentence.

RESULTS

Of the 386 newly convicted prisoners, 284 (74%) were menstruating regularly and 156 (41%) had committed their offence during the previous 28 days. Table I shows the distribution of the menstrual history of the newly convicted prisoners.

▶SOURCE: *"Menstruation and Crime," British Medical Journal (December 30, 1961), 2:1752–1753. Reprinted by permission of the author and the editor of the British Medical Journal.*

Table I. Menstrual History of 386 Criminal Women

Regular menstruation		284
Offence committed within 28 days	156	
More than 28 days since offence	102	
Unable to recall date of last menses	26	
Amenorrhoea		38
Probably pubertal	6	
Probably pregnant	28	
Puerperal	4	
Menopause		64
Natural	48	
Artificial	16	

In analysing the results, the method used was that described in previous surveys into the relationship of menstruation to acute psychiatric illness (Dalton, 1959) and accidents (Dalton, 1960b). The menstrual cycle was divided into seven four-day periods, in which Days 1–4 represented menstruation and Days 25–28 the premenstruum. The relationship of the date of offence to menstrual cycle in the 156 women who committed their offences during the previous 28 days is shown in Table II.

Nearly half of all crimes (49%) were committed by women during menstruation or in the premenstruum. On a normal distribution, only two-sevenths (29%) of all crimes would be expected during this period of eight days. The probability of a distribution, such as has been found, occurring by chance is less than one in a thousand ($\chi^2 = 12.7$ on 1 d.f.) and therefore

Table II. Time of Crime of 156 Regularly
Menstruating Women

Day of Cycle	No.	%
1-4	41	26-3
5-8	13	8-3
9-12	20	12-8
13-16	21	13-5
17-20	19	12-2
21-24	7	4-5
25-28	35	22-4
Total	156	100

suggests that the association between menstruation and crime is highly significant.

Menstruation seems of greater importance in crimes of theft: 56% of such crimes occurred during menstruation and the premenstruum, whereas for prostitution the figure was 44% (Table III). Seven of the 13 (54%) alcoholics were sentenced at this time. "Theft" is used here to include all offences against another's property—for example, shoplifting, burglary, embezzlement, forgery. "Prostitution" covers those convicted under the Street Offences Act, 1959. "Alcoholism" covers those found drunk and disorderly in public places and refusing, or unable, to pay the fine. Menstruation is also of greater importance among first offenders than among those with more than three previous convictions. It was noted that nulliparous women were most liable to commit their of-fences during the premenstruum and the parous women during menstruation; this is similar to the difference in accident proneness among nulliparous and parous women (Dalton, 1960b).

The dates of conviction of those 102 women who menstruated regularly and whose crime had been committed more than 28 days previously were evenly distributed throughout the menstrual cycle. It would appear, therefore, that menstruation had no prejudicial effect on those women during their appearance in court.

"Premenstrual tension" was defined as mood changes, headaches, tiredness, bloatedness, or mastitis during the premenstruum and "dysmenorrhoea" was defined as pain during menstruation. Premenstrual tension was present among 43 (27%) of the 156 prisoners whose offences had occurred during the previous menstrual cycle, and 27 (63%) of these 43 women had committed their crime during the time of their symptoms. Premenstrual tension was more common among those sentenced for theft (29%) than among the prostitutes (19%); in fact, the incidence of premenstrual tension among prostitutes is probably below that for women generally. Dysmenorrhoea was present in only 22 of the 156 prisoners (14%) who had committed their crime during the previous menstrual cycle, and these 22 prisoners had a normal distribution of crime throughout the menstrual cycle.

Table III. Crimes Committed During Menstruation and Premenstruum

Type	Crimes during Menstruation and Premenstruum		Total Crimes	x^2 on 1 D.P.	Probability
	No.	%			
All crimes	76	48.7	156	30-9	< 0.001
Theft	36	56.3	64	18.5	< 0.001
Prostitution	34	43.6	78	8.6	< 0.01
Alcoholism	7	53.8	13	*	*
First offence	21	51-2	41	10.3	< 0.001
2nd and 3rd offences	25	49	51	10.4	< 0.001
4 or more offences	19	47.5	40	7.0	< 0.05

*Too few to determine probability.

Among the prisoners reported for bad behaviour were 94 who were menstruating regularly, and 51 (54%) of these were disorderly during menstruation or the premenstruum. Among the 54 prisoners reported only once, 43% were associated with menstruation, whereas among the 40 prisoners reported more than once, 70% were associated with menstruation. This is similar to the observation among schoolgirls that the adverse effect of menstruation was greatest among those with most offences (Dalton, 1960c).

In cases where the reported prisoner suffered from premenstrual tension and had been disorderly during this time, the prisoner was offered the opportunity of treatment for premenstrual tension.

DISCUSSION

The marked similarity of the effect of menstruation on naughty schoolgirls, newly convicted women, and disorderly prisoners is shown in the Chart. The offences for which the naughty schoolgirls were punished were petty and might be committed by any law-abiding citizen—for example, talking when silence is requested, lateness, forgetfulness—and would appear to be an altogether different type from those crimes for which a prison sentence is passed, or the offences for which a prisoner is reported to the governor. The hormonal changes of menstruation probably make the individual less amenable to discipline.

The analysis shows that there is a highly significant relationship between menstruation and crime. This could mean that the hormonal changes cause women to commit crime during menstruation and the premenstruum and/or that women are more liable to be detected in their criminal acts during this time. The adverse effect of menstruation was greatest among sufferers of premenstrual tension, with its concomitant symptoms of lethargy, slower reaction time, and mental dullness; and these factors would lead to easier detection during certain days of the menstrual cycle, especially among habitual law-breakers—for example, prostitutes

Times of Offences during Menstrual Cycle

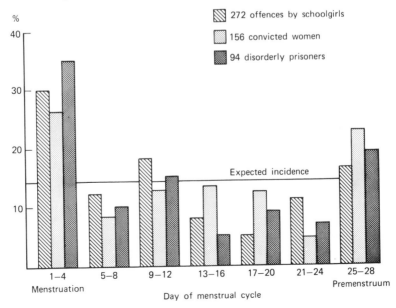

and shoplifters. Premenstrual tension is also accompanied by irritability, lethargy, depression, and water retention, and these symptoms alone may be responsible for certain crimes—for example, irritability and loss of temper may lead to violence and assault, lethargy may lead to child neglect, and depression to suicide (still a crime at the time of investigation). If water retention is present in an alcoholic, then alcohol retention tends to occur, increasing the liability for the woman to become drunk and disorderly.

One alcoholic aged 45 years, with numerous previous sentences, described how she usually started menstruating during her stay in the police cell or first day in prison and also how alcohol had a more deleterious effect on her during this time, yet she sought solace in alcohol when she became depressed.

These findings again emphasize the need for a simple test for the presence of premenstrual tension. Unfortunately, the severity and type of symptom may vary from month to month and symptoms increase at times of stress, thereby adding to the difficulties of diagnosis. Premenstrual tension responds to treatment, but such treatment would need to be continued after the expiration of the prison sentence if any improvement in criminal tendency is to be expected; this suggests the need for such women being placed on probation subject to regular medical supervision.

SUMMARY

An investigation carried out in a women's prison revealed that almost half the women committed their crime during menstruation or the premenstruum. Premenstrual tension appears to be an important factor, and 63% of the sufferers committed their crime at the time of their symptoms.

REFERENCES

Dalton K. (1959), *Brit. med. J.,* **1,** 148.

——— (1960a). Ibid., **1,** 326.

——— (1960b). Ibid., **2,** 1425.

——— (1960c). Ibid., **2,** 1647.

27. Adoption and Antisocial Personality

RAYMOND R. CROWE

THE POSSIBILITY THAT HEREDITY MAY PLAY SOME role in the etiology of psychopathy was first investigated by means of twin studies. The literature now contains eight studies of criminal twins.[1,2] Concordance between monozygotic twins has always been high, ranging from 36% to 100%, but concordance between dizygotic twins can also be high, ranging up to 54%. Furthermore, in the studies that separated the sexes, concordance between same-sex twins was higher than between opposite-sex twins. These findings are compatible with a hereditary liability but they also suggest a substantial environmental influence.

On the environmental side, a considerable body of work on delinquents, criminals, and antisocials has implicated a number of factors as being associated with an antisocial outcome. The more important of these are early environmental or emotional deprivation,[3] parental rejection,[4] a broken family unit,[5] parental psychopathology or deviance,[6] and low socioeconomic status.[7]

Additional evidence for a hereditary factor has come from two recent adoption studies.[8,9] The first examined psychiatric records of biological relatives of psychopathic adoptees and found a significantly higher rate of psychopathy than among the adoptive relatives

▶SOURCE: *"An Adoption Study of Antisocial Personality," Archives of General Psychiatry (December 1974), 31:785–791. Copyright 1974, American Medical Association. Reprinted by permission.*

or among the biological and adoptive relatives of control adoptees. In a similar study based on criminal records, biological relatives of criminal adoptees were found to have a higher rate of criminality than either the adoptive relatives or the biological and adoptive relatives of control adoptees. The unique finding in the latter study was that a criminal outcome in an adoptee correlated independently with criminality in either a biological or an adoptive paent. Thus, the adoption research has provided strong evidence for a genetic factor leading to psychopathy as well as providing further evidence that the environment is also important.

In another adoption study, on 10- and 11-year-old adopted children, no association was found between criminality in the biological fathers and typical juvenile antisocial behavior such as truancy, lying, and stealing.[10] However, the children had not passed the age of risk for developing antisocial personality and, therefore, a conclusion cannot be drawn at this time. The only deviant behavior of note found among the children was strongly suggestive of the hyperkinetic syndrome, a disorder that may be related to antisocial personality in adulthood.[11]

In view of the above findings based on records, there is need for a comparable adoption study based on a complete follow-up and personal data collection. This article reports such a study. It has entailed the follow-up of a group of persons born to incarcerated female offenders and given up for adoption in infancy. The assumption is made that the majority of the mothers were antisocial personalities which is supported by Cloninger's finding of sociopathy in 65% of a comparable group of female offenders.[12] The null hypothesis tested states that the offspring of antisocial mothers, if reared apart from their mothers, are not more likely to become antisocial than a control group of adoptees. The follow-up has consisted of obtaining pertinent records on the adoptees plus interviews with the adult subjects.

METHODS

Selection of Subjects

A proband group was obtained consisting of 52 adoptees born to a group of 41 female offenders; 38 from the Women's Reformatory and three from the State Training School who subsequently committed adult offenses. The probands were born between 1925 and 1956 and were thus in or through the period of risk for developing the disorder. Cases were obtained by searching records at the institutions for evidence that an inmate had given a baby up for adoption and by checking names of consecutive admissions to the reformatory through the state index of adoptions. Two sources were used because the index of adoptions was not sufficiently complete prior to 1945 to make its use alone feasible.

Ninety percent of these 41 mothers were felons. The most frequent offenses were check felonies (15 women convicted), prostitution (five), larceny (four), desertion (three), adultery (three), breaking and entering (two), lewdness (two), and one each convicted of assault, conspiracy, aiding prisoners to escape, bigamy, transmitting a venereal disease, contributing to the delinquency of a minor, and exposing a dead body. The last offense stemmed from the abandonment of a baby who subsequently died. The mother was first charged with murder but the charge was reduced. All of the mothers were felons except four who were convicted of lewdness, transmitting a venereal disease and contributing to the delinquency of a minor.

The proband group consisted of 52 white subjects, 27 men and 25 women. The mean age at the beginning of the follow-up was 25.6 years (SD 7.9 yr, range 15 to 45). They were adopted by unrelated persons with the exceptions of one adoption by a paternal aunt, one by a maternal great aunt, and two by maternal cousins. Not enough information was available on the biological fathers to provide descriptive data on them and information on the biological mothers was limited to data obtained from the institution records that often gave little more than legal data.

A group of control adoptees was selected from the state index of adoptions by selecting the nearest entry to each proband's that matched for age, sex, race, and approximate age at the time of the adoptive decree. Due to a scarcity of index cards on the earlier adoptions, probands born prior to 1945 were matched with controls born within five years of the proband, and those born between 1945 and 1950 were matched with controls born within 24 months of the proband. One proband born in 1925 was matched with a control born seven years later. Nevertheless, the mean age of the controls of 24.6 yr (SD 6.5 yr) fell within one year of that of the probands. No information was available on the biological parents of the control group.

At the time of the matching process, sufficient information for matching was not available on many important variables that might be expected to influence the outcome of the adoptees. Fortunately, sufficient information was gathered during the follow-up to compare a substantial subsample of the probands and controls on the more important variables. The comparison is shown in Table I. Data on the adoption were obtained by sending requests for information to the major adoption agencies in the state plus information obtained from the interviews. The age at maternal separation, age at final adoptive placement, and thus length of time spent in orphanages and temporary placement was known for 38 probands and 32 controls, 67% of the subjects overall. Because the distributions were heavily skewed toward younger ages they were converted to cumulative frequency distributions and tested for differ-

Table I. Adoption Data

	Probands, N=38	Controls, N=32
Early environment		
Mean age at maternal separation	3.9 mo	3.7 mo
Range	0-18	0-48 (.10<P<.20)[a]
SD	5.0	9.5
Mean age at adoptive placement	9.5 mo	7.1 mo
Range	0-26	0-48 (.10<P<.20)
SD	8.5	12.3
Mean time in orphanage	5.6 mo	3.4 mo
Range	0-24	0-24 (.20<P<.30)
SD	6.4	5.6

	Probands, N=40	Controls, N=35
Adoptive homes		
Mean socioeconomic status[b]	4.0	3.9
Broken homes, permanent	18%	20%
Broken homes, temporary	0	6%
Broken by divorce	5%	6%
Psychopathology in adoptive parents (alcoholism, drug dependence or psychopathy)	18%	11%

[a]Probabilities are based on the Kolmogorov-Smirnov two-sample test of the difference between culumative distributions.

[b]Using a 7-point scale based on occupational status of the adoptive father.

ences with the Kolmogorov-Smirnov two-sample test. The greater ranges and standard deviations for the controls were due to two subjects who were separated and three who were placed at a considerably later age than the others (a problem that arose from lack of information during the matching process). The controls tended to be separated and placed at earlier ages than the probands but the difference did not approach statistical significance. The possibility that this difference, though not statistically significant, could have been psychologically important will be dealt with later in analyzing the results.

Data on the adoptive homes was obtained from the interviews and was available on 40 probands and 35 controls, 72% of the subjects overall. Socioeconomic status was scored on a 7-point scale based on the adoptive father's occupation and was pratically identical for the two groups. Likewise, the groups were closely matched for broken homes, divorce, and parental psychopathology, with none of the differences approaching statistical significance.

One environmental variable that could not be controlled was the degree of deprivation or rejection that could have occurred while the probands were living with their biological parents. This will be dealt with in analyzing the results. Based on the environmental variables examined here, however, it appears that the proband and control groups were comparable.

FOLLOW-UP PROCEDURE

The initial follow-up was limited to searching for records on the subjects in Iowa. Records obtained from the State Bureau of Criminal Investigation and from the state psychiatric hospitals were the subject of two previous communications,[13,14] but the data will be summarized again for completeness. It was estimated that 42 probands and 42 controls reached the age of 15 while living in the state and were, therefore, considered to be at risk; 37 probands and 37 controls were adults. These figure are estimates only and not the exact number of persons at risk but are undoubtedly closer to the true numbers than the original number of 52 subjects in each group.

The final follow-up was restricted to subjects over 18 years old by the end of the follow-up period. The subject of adoption was not broached unless the interviewees raised it themselves. One control was not interviewed because he had been adopted out of state and no suitable reason for the interview, aside from adoption, could be given. The other follow-up statistics are given in Table II and are similar for the two groups. Follow-up information was obtained on 40 probands and 35 controls, an overall follow-up rate of 82%. Of the 75 subjects followed up, I interviewed 67 (three by telephone) and information on an additional five was obtained through interviews with parents. The mean age of the probands followed up was 27.4 yr (SD 6.6 yr) and that of the controls was 26.1 yr (SD 5.1 yr). Twenty-one of the probands were men and 15 women compared with 20 male controls and 15 women. Although information was not ob-

Table II. Follow-Up Statistics

	Probands	Controls
Unlocated	5	5
Refused	1	5
Not contacted	0	1
Records only	3	0
Interviewed	37	35
Totals	46	46

Menninger Health Sickness Rating Scores (MHSRS)

tained on all subjects, the records searches were carried out on the original groups. Therefore, tabulations were based on the total number of 46 probands and 46 controls rather than the somewhat smaller numbers actually followed up.

All subjects were administered a standard structure psychiatric interview that lasted about one hour. The interview consisted of a medical history, psychiatric history, family history, and finally a social history covering schooling, adolescence, occupation, military history, legal difficulties, and social behavior. After the interview the subject was given the Minnesota Multiphasic Personality Inventory (MMPI) to be self-administered and returned by mail. Twenty-four probands and 16 controls returned the test, and out of these one in each group was eliminated because the validity scales indicated that they could not be interpreted with confidence.

The follow-up information was transcribed into case histories and submitted to three experienced clinicians who reviewed them independently and blindly made diagnoses. The judges were Dr. Paul Huston, Dr. Ming Tsuang, and Dr. Irving Gottesman, and the classifications used were *DSM-II* and ICD-8. A final diagnosis was made when two of the three judges agreed. Complete disagreement (no judge agreeing with another) was considered an undiagnosed disorder and further broken down into undiagnosed personality disorder and other undiagnosed disorder. In addition, Dr. Tsuang made diagnoses based on the research criteria described by Feighner et al.[15] Two judges (P.E.H. and I.I.G.) rated each case on the

Menninger Health Sickness Rating Scores (MHSRS)

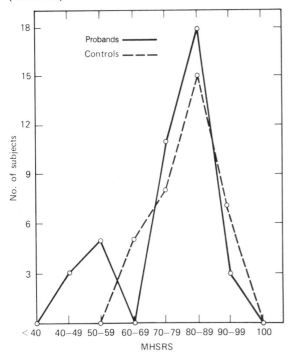

Menninger Health Sickness Rating Scale (MHSRS), a global rating of psychiatric impairment that is suitable for arriving at a quantitative estimate of psychopathology.[16]

RESULTS

Records

The data from the records follow-up are presented in Table III. Of the 37 probands at risk, seven had arrest records as adults, all seven had at least one conviction, four had multiple arrests, two had multiple convictions, and three were felons. Two controls had adult arrests but only one was convicted. Six probands had spent time in penal or correctional institutions; three as juveniles, four as adults, and one was incarcerated both as a juvenile and as an adult. None of the controls had been incarcerated for an offense.

An estimated 42 probands and 42 controls reached the age of 15 in the state and were at risk for referral to a psychiatric facility. Seven

Table III. Records Follow-Up

	Probands, N=37	Controls N=37
Arrest records		
Adult arrest	7	2
Adult conviction	7	1 P=.03[a]
	N=42	N=42
Incarceration		
Juvenile[b]	3	0
Adult	4	0
Either	6	0 P=.01
	N=42	N=42
Psychiatric hospital records		
Number hospitalized	7	1
Outpatient only	1	1
Total number seen	8	2 P=.04
Number with both psychiatric and arrest records	6	0 P=.01

[a]Probabilities are Fisher's exact, one-tailed.
[b]One juvenile was actually ascertained through hospital records and was sent to the training school shortly thereafter.

probands were hospitalized and one was seen as an outpatient. Seven of the eight were seen for behavior of an antisocial nature and six of the examinations were court ordered. Two controls were seen, one as an inpatient and one as an outpatient. Both were seen for antisocial behavior but neither examination was court ordered. Six of the eight probands with hospital records also had arrest records but neither of the two controls had arrest records. Thus, the results of the records follow-up indicated that a substantial minority of the probands had exhibited antisocial behavior of a serious nature.

Diagnoses

Forty-six probands and 46 controls were included in the final follow-up and at risk for a psychiatric diagnosis. Diagnoses of antisocial personality were considered separately and are shown in Table IV. Six probands received a definite diagnosis of antisocial personality, four of these made by all three judges and two by two of the three. None of the controls received a

Table IV. Diagnoses of Antisocial Personality

Diagnosis	No. of Subjects With Diagnosis	
	Probands, N=46	Controls, N=46
Definite antisocial personality[a]	6	0
Probable antisocial personality	0	1
Total†	6	1
Borderline antisocial[b]	0	3
Research criteria diagnosis[a]	6	0

[a]Probabilities are Fisher's exact, one tailed: * $P = .01$; † $P = .06$.
[b]Diagnosis made by only one judge.

definite diagnosis of antisocial personality although one received a diagnosis of probable antisocial personality by two judges. Combining definite and probable cases, six probands and one control were diagnosed as antisocial personalities. Three controls with undiagnosed personality disorders were tabulated here as borderline cases since they were regarded as anti-social personalities by one of the judges (two by one judge and the third by another). Six probands but no controls were diagnosed as antisocial personalities by research criteria. Thus, the stricter the criteria, the better was the discrimination between the two groups. If the borderline case was included the difference between groups was not significant; if only definite or probable cases were included the difference bordered on significance $(P = .055)$, and if the comparison was restricted to definite or research criteria diagnoses the difference was significant at the .01 probability level. Therefore, the data support the conclusion that there were significantly more antisocial personalities among the probands than among the controls. Furthermore, there is considerable overlap between the probands diagnosed as antisocial personalities and those ascertained through records since all six antisocial probands had arrest records and five of the six also had records at one of the state psychiatric institutions.

Table V gives the complete diagnostic breakdown of the two groups. Two judges agreed on either a diagnosis or on "no psychiatric disor-

der" in 85% of the cases. The undiagnosed cases (complete disagreement between judges) were subdivided into undiagnosed personality disorder, when two judges agreed on this category, and into other undiagnosed illness. The only

Table V. Diagnoses

Diagnosis	% With Diagnosis[a]	
	Probands, N=46	Controls, N=46
No mental disorder	39	48
Antisocial personality	13[b]	2[c]
Alcohol or drug dependence	2[d]	4
Schizoid personality	2	0
Inadequate personality	2	2
Passive-aggressive personality	2	0
Hysterical personality	2	0
Explosive personality	2	0
Undiagnosed personality disorder	7	9
Depression (by history)	9[e]	7[e]
Psychophysiological reaction	7	2
Neurosis	4	4
Homosexuality	0	4
Borderline intelligence	2	2
Undiagnosed illness (not personality disorder)	7	2
Lost to follow-up	13	24

[a]Totals exceed 100% due to diagnostic overlap.
[b]One antisocial was also diagnosed borderline intelligence.
[c]Diagnosed "probable antisocial personality."
[d]Also diagnosed "explosive personlity."
[e]Included both endogenous and reactive.

significant difference between the two groups was the frequency of the diagnosis of antisocial personality. Alcoholism, drug dependence, and personality disorders other than antisocial personality were equally distributed between probands and controls. Likewise, the number of probands receiving any diagnosis was not significantly different from the controls. Thus, the probands differed from the controls on the diagnosis of antisocial personality and on no other diagnosis.

The diagnoses based on research criteria are presented in Table VI. Again, the only significant difference between probands and controls was that of antisocial personality. The research criteria diagnoses agreed reasonably well with the other diagnoses on total number of subjects receiving a diagnosis. The chief difference lay in the number with "undiagnosed illness" by research criteria, a category that included the previous diagnoses of "undiagnosed illness" plus many of the personality disorders. Subjects diagnosed as alcohol or drug dependent by research criteria were more likely to be diagnosed as personality disorders by *DSM-II* or ICD-8. There were no diagnoses of either hysteria or probable hysteria. One of the female antisocial

probands had a history of medical symptoms strongly suggestive of hysteria in addition to antisocial personality. However, as she was not located for interview and data were from records, this diagnosis could not be made.

Menninger Health Sickness Rating
The MHSRS scores are shown in the Figure. Kendall's rank correlation coefficient between raters was 0.63 for the probands and 0.36 for the controls *(P < .01* in both cases). Therefore, the mean rating of the two judges was used as the final score. Eight probands were clearly separated due to their low scores from the other probands as well as from the controls. These were the six with antisocial personalities plus two other probands diagnosed inadequate personality and schizoid personality, respectively. With these eight subjects excluded, the remainder of the probands did not differ from the controls on their MHSRS scores *(t = .73, 65 df, .40 < P < .50).* Therefore, the data on severity of psychopathology support the conclusion that the difference between probands and controls is accounted for largely by the six probands diagnosed as antisocial personalities.

Minnesota Multiphasic Personality Inventory
Although only limited confidence can be placed in the MMPI data due to the relatively small number of tests returned, the results are consistent with the conclusion that the nonantisocial probands did not differ appreciably from the controls. Profiles were not obtained on the eight probands with the low MHSRS scores. The mean profile of the remaining probands was practically identical to that of the controls and both were within normal limits. (Welch codes: probands 4-2 *36890 571*/FKL, controls 4-*290 78 51 36*/FKL).

Interview Results
Another indicator of adjustment is level of social functioning. The structured interview utilized objective criteria to assess social functioning in childhood, adolescence, schooling, military experience, marriage, occupation, and social be-

Table VI. Research Criteria Diagnoses

Diagnosis	% With Diagnosis[a]	
	Probands, N=46	Controls, N=46
No mental disorder	35	35
Antisocial peronality	13[b]	0
Alcoholism, definite	0	7
Alcoholism, probable	2	0
Drug dependence	2	7
Total alcohol and drug dependence	4	9
Borderline mental retardation	2	2
Homosexuality	0	4
Primary depression	7	4
Undiagnosed illness	30	26
Lost to follow-up	13	25

[a]See footnote for Table 5.

[b]Includes one subject also diagnosed borderline mental retardation.

havior. The antisocials had behavior disorders involving a number of these areas, but when the probands as a whole were compared with the controls they did not differ significantly from the controls on any of the criteria.

Environmental Influences

Based on the above evidence the six antisocial probands appear to constitute a dichotomous subgroup within the probands and the greater part of the difference between probands and controls lies within this subgroup. Therefore, this subgroup was compared with the nonantisocial probands and with the controls to determine whether the subgroup differed in other important respects from the other subjects. The comparison is shown in Table VII for the environmental variables. Four of the antisocial probands were men and two women. Unexpectedly, outcome was independent of the length of time the probands remained with their natural mothers. Therefore, whatever deprivation or rejection might have occurred during that time did not influence the outcome and can be dismissed as a confounding influence.

However, age at adoptive placement and length of time spent in temporary care (orphanages and temporary foster homes) showed a clear association with an antisocial outcome. Five of the six antisocial probands spent over 12 months in temporary care and were, therefore, placed for adoption when they were over a year of age (the sixth was placed at 4½ months). The antisocial probands differed significantly from the others in this respect ($\chi^2 = 15$, 1 df, $P < .001$). Further, antisocial outcome was found to be associated with length of time spent in temporary care and not simply with a late age of final placement. This was supported by the fact that five of seven probands placed late due to time spent in temporary care became antisocial but none of the ten placed late due to late separation from their natural mothers became antisocial ($\chi^2 < 6.97$, 1 df, $P < .01$).

The next question to be answered was whether the proband and control groups were comparable with respect to the number of subjects in each group spending 12 months or longer in temporary care. Seven probands (18.4%) and four controls (12.5%) fell into this category; the difference was not significant. Further, these seven probands were closely

Table VII. Comparison of Antisocial Probands With Nonantisocial Probands and Controls

	Antisocial Probands	Nonantisocial Probands	Controls
Early environment	N=6	N=32	N=32
Mean age at separation	4.6 mo	3.6 mo	3.7 mo
Range	1-12	0-18	0-48
SD	4.4	5.2	9.5
Mean age at plcement	18.8 mo	7.7 mo	7.1 mo
Range	4½-26	0-24	0-48
SD	9.4	7.6	12.3
Months in orphanage	14.2	4.0	3.4
Range	5-21	0-24	0-24
SD	5.7	5.1	5.6
Adoptive homes	N=6	N=34	N=35
Mean SES	4.0	4.0	3.9
	range 3-6		
Broken homes, permanent	33%	15%	20%
Divorce	17%	3%	6%
Parental psychopathology	17%	18%	11%

comparable with the four controls in spending a mean of 16.7 months and range of 12 to 24 months in temporary care compared with the controls' mean of 16.5 months and range of 13 to 24 months. Therefore, the probands did not differ from the controls on this variable that was so strongly associated with an antisocial outcome. However, five of the seven probands became antisocial compared with none of the four controls. The numbers are small for statistical comparison but nevertheless a two-tailed exact probability of .09 was reached suggesting that the interaction of genetic and environmental factors was more important in leading to an antisocial outcome than either alone. This is further supported by the fact that the antisocial proband who was placed early in life was placed in a home that was broken by divorce when she was 3. The control diagnosed as probable antisocial personality was placed at six weeks.

The orphanage records of the six antisocial probands did not reveal any reason for their remaining in the orphanage longer than the others. Two were cared for in foster homes for the greater part of the time and their care there was considered quite good. Three spent over one year in the state orphanage. The nursery there was adequately staffed, the quality of physical care was good and, although personal attention was lacking, the babies were not subjected to the degree of deprivation that has been described in some orphanages of that day. Therefore, it does not appear that the antisocial probands were subjected to extraordinary circumstances in infancy that the other probands and controls were not subjected to.

The nature of the adoptive homes is shown in the lower half of Table VII. Socioeconomic status of the adoptive homes did not correlate with outcome. However, of the six homes in which the antisocial probands were placed, two were broken; one by divorce when the proband was 3 and the other by the accidental death of both parents when the proband was eight. Of seven broken homes in the proband group, two were associated with an antisocial outcome and

of two broken by divorce, one was associated with an antisocial result. One of the seven probands placed in a home characterized as having a deviant parent became antisocial. The four probands reared by distant biological relatives did not become antisocial. The control diagnosed as probable antisocial personality was placed in a home in which the father was described as having a drinking problem.

Biological Parents

The biological parents of the six antisocial probands were investigated as far as available information permitted. Five of the six mothers were felons, convicted of larceny (2), desertion, prostitution, and assault. The proband born to the mother who deserted her family was placed in the orphanage in the first month of life and, therefore, this factor should not have influenced his outcome. The misdemeanant was convicted of contributing to the delinquency of a minor. Five of the six had records for other offenses compared with 37% of the mothers of the nonantisocial probands who had records of multiple offenses, a nonsignificant difference. In reviewing the orphanage records of the antisocial probands it was noted that five of the six alleged natural fathers were said to have had records of offenses too. Similar data were not available on the other probands for comparison. However, the reformatory's records on the mothers indicated that nine (26%) of the mothers had husbands who were either serving or had served time in a penitentiary. This is undoubtedly an underestimate of the true situation because only serious offenders were mentioned and those were probably not consistently recorded. Nevertheless, it is clear that positive assortative mating occurred, especially among the biological parents of the antisocials.

COMMENT

The first conclusion to be drawn from the results is that the probands have developed a high rate of antisocial personality. Thirteen percent

(± SE 5%) have developed antisocial personalities, a significantly higher rate than was found for the controls. An estimate of the expected rate of antisocial personality among adoptees can be derived from the control group of this study plus two other studies in which a control group of adoptees was followed up and given diagnoses in a comparable manner.[17,18] Among a group of 172 adoptees an estimate of 2.3% ± 1.1% definite antisocial personality was obtained, or 4.0% ± 1.5% if probable cases are included. Thus, the finding of one probable case among the controls is not out of line with expectation but 13% ± 5% among the probands is considerably higher than expected. These findings reject the null hypothesis and indicate that heredity plays some role in the development of antisocial personality.

A number of influences on both the genetic and environmental side probably affected the 13% estimate of antisocial personality. The first of these is the number of the probands' mothers who were themselves antisocial personalities. Certainly not all were and this factor would tend to reduce the number of offspring expected to become antisocial. On the other hand, the severity of the disorder in the mothers might influence the likelihood of the disorder being transmitted to their offspring. Multiple offenses, as an indicator of severity, pointed in the expected direction but the difference was not statistically significant.

Of more importance from a genetic standpoint is the positive assortative mating that was clearly demonstrated by the probands' natural parents. Five of the six antisocial probands were offspring of such unions. It is unknown to what extent this occurred among the mothers of the probands but the fact that it was discovered fortuitously in 14 (34%) of the mothers indicates that the true rate must have been quite high. This factor could increase considerably the rate of the disorder in the offspring over the expected rate with only one parent affected.

Another factor to be considered is whether the adoptive parents knew of the natural mother's criminal record and the effect this may have had on the adoptees. This question could not be answered for the proband group as a whole since the study covered many years and multiple adoption agencies thus making it impossible to determine whether a consistent policy was followed as to what the adoptive parents were told. However, considerable information was available on the antisocial probands due to their frequent contacts with authorities. This included psychiatric and social histories, and in five of the six cases, included a history from the adoptive parents. In no case was there an indication that the adoptive parents knew. Furthermore, the other probands did not evidence more delinquency, criminality, or behavior disorder than the controls as might be expected if this influence were operative. Although the question cannot be answered definitively the available evidence does not indicate that this was an important influence in determining the probands' outcome.

One last source of potential bias that deserves comment is the lack of blindness of the study. Although the judges were blind, the interviewer knew which subjects were probands and could have influenced the decision of the judges through the case histories. However, the fact that the records, which were not influenced by the investigator, turned up virtually the same findings as the interview diagnoses strongly supports the validity of the interview diagnoses.

The second conclusion to be drawn is that the nonantisocial probands did not demonstrate more antisocial behavior, or other psychopathology, than did the controls. This finding was supported by both the diagnoses and the other indexes of psychopathology. It was originally anticipated that if the genetic hypothesis was confirmed, the probands would evidence a high rate of alcoholism, drug dependence, and hysteria since these disorders are frequently found in relatives of criminals and a similar group of disorders was found in biological relatives of psychopathic adoptees.[8,19,20] It was also anticipated that the probands might be more deviant as a group than the controls but that the difference might be too small to be reflected in the diagnoses. The data provide no support for either hypothesis. Another interesting point about the data is the sharp dichotomy between the antisocial and nonantisocial probands that is so well demonstrated by the MHSRS ratings. One might expect a smoother gradation from deviant to normal with some borderline cases lying in between. However, the only cases that might be considered borderline were among the controls.

The third conclusion is that certain unfavorable environmental factors were associated with the development of antisocial personality in the probands but not in the controls. The most convincing of these was length of time in orphanages and temporary placement. This is consistment with the findings of two studies of adopted children referred for psychiatric consultation that found that antisocial behavior in the children was related to the age at which they had been placed for adoption.[21,22] Data on the adoption were not known but the late placement probably represented time spent in orphanages prior to final placement. Both studies found that six months was the best arbitrary cut-off point beyond which antisocial behavior was likely to result. Although this differs from the present finding of 12 months the difference is one of degree rather than kind.

The unique finding in the present study is that the unfavorable environmental influences were associated with the development of antisocial personality in the probands but not in the controls, although the groups were comparable with respect to their exposure to these influences. This suggests that the two groups responded differently to the same environmental conditions and that the probands may have been more susceptible. The data were suggestive of this but fell short of statistical significance.

This raises the question of what is inherited and how it is inherited. Until a better grasp can be obtained on what the inherited predisposition is, little can be said about how it may be inherited. It is now apparent that any theory of inheritance will have to take environmental factors into account. One genetic theory that could account for a number of the findings of the present study is the threshold model proposed by Gottesman and Shields[23] for schizophrenia. The essence of the model is that a polygenically inherited predisposition interacts with the environment and this determines whether a given individual will exceed a hypothetical threshold for manifestation of the disorder. Persons below the threshold appear phenotypically normal and those above it are affected. This model could account for the sharp dichotomy between antisocial and nonantisocial probands as well as for the fact that so few probands were affected vis-à-vis the high rate of positive assortative mating. It could also account for the failure to find the expected rates of alcoholism, drug dependence, and hysteria among the probands since these disorders would be more prevalent among subjects reared by their natural parents as was the case in the studies that found this spectrum of disorders.

Although the adoption study is not usually thought of as a tool for studying the environment, it is particularly well suited for this purpose because genetic variables can be largely accounted for. Thus, the present study has turned up several environmental conditions that have previously been linked to antisocial personality. The results have also corroborated the genetic findings of other adoption studies on psychopathy that were based on records. Thus, the evidence at this time points to the importance of both genetic and environmental influences in the development of antisocial personality.

REFERENCES

1. Slater E, Cowie V: *The Genetics of Mental Disorders.* London, Oxford University Press, 1971, p 114.

2. Christiansen KO: Crime in a Danish twin population. *Acta. Genet Med Gemellol (Roma)* 19:323–326, 1970.

3. Rutter M: *Maternal Deprivation Reassessed.* Harmondsworth, England, Books Ltd, 1972, pp 53–119.

4.   Jenkins RL: Psychiatric syndromes in children and their relations to family background. *Am J Orthopsychiatry* 36:450–457, 1966.

5.   Rutter M: Parent-child separation: Psychological effects on the children. *Am J Child Psychol Psychiatry* 12:233–260, 1971.

6.   O'Neal P, et al: Parental deviance and the genesis of sociopathic personality. *Am J Psychiatry* 118:1114–1124, 1962.

7.   McCord W, McCord J: *The Psychopath: An Essay on The Criminal Mind*. New York, Van Nostrand, 1964, pp 88–89.

8.   Schulsinger F: Psychopathy, heredity, and environment. *Int J Ment Health* 1:190–206, 1972.

9.   Hutchings B, Mednick S: Registered criminality in the adoptive and biological parents of registered male criminnal adoptees, in Fieve RR, Brill H, Rosenthal D (eds): *Genetic Research in Psychiatry*. Baltimore, Johns Hopkins University Press, to be published.

10.   Bohman M: A study of adopted children, their back-ground, environment and adjustment. *Acta Paediat Scand* 61:90–97, 1972.

11.   Morrison J, Stewart MA: A family study of the hyperactive child syndrome. *Biol Psychiatry* 3:189–195, 1971.

12.   Cloninger CR, Guze SB: Psychiatric illness and female criminality: The role of sociopathy and hysteria in the antisocial woman. *Am J Psychiatry* 127:303–311, 1970.

13.   Crowe RR: The adopted offspring of women criminal offenders: A study of their arrest records. *Arch Gen Psychiatry* 27:600–603, 1972.

14.   Crowe RR: An adoptive study of psychopathy: Preliminary results from arrest records and psychiatric hospital records, in Fieve RR, Brill H, Rosenthal D (eds): *Genetic Research in Psychiatry*. Baltimore, Johns Hopkins University Press, to be published.

15.   Feighner JP, et al: Diagnostic criteria for use in psychiatric research. *Arch Gen Psychiatry* 26:57–63, 1972.

16.   Luborsky L: Clinician's judgements of mental health: A proposed scale. *Arch Gen Psychiatry* 7:407–417, 1962.

17.   Heston LL, Denney D: Interactions between early life experience and biological factors in schizophrenia, in Rosenthal D, Kety S (eds): *The Transmission of Schizophrenia*. Oxford, England, Pergamon Press, 1968, pp 363–376.

18.   Goodwin DW, et al: Alcohol problems in adoptees raised apart from alcoholic biological parents. *Arch Gen Psychiatry* 28:238–243, 1973.

19.   Guze SB, et al: Psychiatric illness in the families of convicted criminals: A study of 519 first degree relatives. *Dis Nerv Syst* 28:651–659, 1967.

20.   Cloninger CR, Guze SB: Psychiatric illness in the families of female criminals: A study of 288 first-degree relatives. *Br J Psychiatry* 122:697–703, 1973.

21.   Humphrey M, Ounsted C: Adoptive families referred for psychiatric advice: The children. *Br J Psychiatry* 109:599–608, 1962.

22.   Offord DR, et al: Presenting symptomatology in adopted children. *Arch Gen Psychiatry* 20:110–116, 1969.

23.   Gottesman II, Shields J: A polygenic theory of schizophrenia. *Proc Natl Acad Sci* 58:199–205, 1967.

28. XYY And Criminality

HERMAN A. WITKIN
SARNOFF A. NEDNICK
FINI SCHULSINGER
ESKILD BAKKESTRØM
KARL O. CHRISTIANSEN
DONALD R. GOODENOUGH
KURT HIRSCHHORN
CLAES LUNDSTEEN
DAVID R. OWEN
JOHN PHILIP
DONALD B. RUBIN
MARTHA STOCKING

FEW ISSUES IN BEHAVIOR GENETICS HAVE RECEIVED more public and scientific attention than that given to the possible role of an extra Y chromosome in human aggression. Soon after the literature began to suggest an elevated frequency of the XYY genotype among inmates of institutions for criminals and delinquents, interest in this issue had a meteoric rise; and it has been sustained ever since. This happened for several reasons. Stories about a few men who had or were presumed to have an extra Y chromosome and who had committed serious crimes were given prominent attention in the press, suggesting the intriguing idea that the single Y chromosome normally found in males contributes to "aggressive tendencies" in that sex and that an extra Y carries these tendencies beyond their usual bounds. Reports of antisocial behavior in XYY men, often based on a single case, soon

▶SOURCE: "Criminality in XYY and XXY Men," *Science* (August 13, 1976), 193:547–555. Copyright 1976 by the American Association for the Advancement of Science. Reprinted by permission.

began to appear in the scientific literature (1) and were taken as evidence of an XYY-aggression linkage. The serious moral and legal implications of such a linkage attracted the interest of social scientists and legal groups to the XYY phenomenon (2), and students of genetics and psychology saw in it, as Lederberg (3) has said, "one of the most tangible leads for connecting genetic constitution with behavior in man."

A number of studies have supported the earlier finding of an elevated frequency of cases with an XYY complement among men in institutions, particularly in penal-mental institutions (4–8). At the same time, these studies have not provided clear evidence of whether or not there exists an "XYY syndrome" of which antisocial behavior is a prominent component. Neither have they provided a definitive answer to the question of why men with an extra Y chromosome are at higher risk for institutionalization than XY men. For the sake of identifying the kind of research that is needed to clarify these issues, it is worth reviewing the main limitations of the studies on which our present information about XYY men is based, and also the lacunae in our knowledge.

First, the search for XYY men has often been conducted in selected groups presumed to be likely to contain them, such as institutionalized men and tall men. Second, a number of reports now in the literature are based on observations of a single case or just a few cases (1). Third, many studies of XYY's have not included control XY's; and in those that did, comparisons were often made with knowledge of the genotype of the individuals being evaluated (5). The control groups used have varied in nature, and comparison of results from different studies has therefore been difficult. There has been a dearth of psychological, somatic, and social data obtained for the same individual XYY men. Finally, there do not yet exist adequate prevalence data for the XYY genotype in the general adult population with which the XYY yield of any particular study may be compared. Though incidence data on neonates are available for a fairly large number of subjects, incidence studies of neonates are still few, and there are potential problems in the practice of pooling highly variable incidence findings from studies with populations that are quite different from each other or whose characteristics have not been adequately specified.

With the evidence in its present state, it is not surprising to find divergent views about the support it provides for a link between XYY and aggression, as for example in the contradictory conclusions reached in recent reviews on the XYY literature (4–7). Whatever the interpretation of the available evidence, however, most investigators concerned with the XYY problem are agreed on the research that is now required to determine whether the XYY complement has any behavioral or social consequences. What is needed, ideally, is an ascertainment study of a large population unselected with regard to institutionalization or height, and a comparison of the XYY cases identified with control XY's in

psychological, somatic, social, and developmental characteristics, the evaluation of these characteristics in the two groups being made according to a double-blind procedure.

The study we undertook, done in Denmark because of the excellent social records kept there, was designed to meet as many of these specifications as our financial resources allowed. It was already evident at the time we undertook the study that XYY's tend to be very tall (9). As a way of maximizing the chances of obtaining a sufficient sample of XYY's for intensive individual study, we decided to do chromosomal determinations of all men in the top 15 percent of the height distribution of our Danish male population. A sampling of men in the bottom 85 percent would also have been desirable, but the probability of finding XYY's among shorter men is so small as to make an effective study of shorter XYY's too expensive to conduct.

A first aim of this research project was to determine whether XYY's from the total general population have an elevated crime rate. A second aim, if an elevated crime rate appeared, was to identify intervening variables that may mediate the relation between an extra Y chromosome and increased antisocial behavior. Three variables of particular interest are aggressiveness, intelligence, and height.

A common interpretation of the finding that XYY's tend to be overrepresented in criminal institutions is that aggressiveness is an intervening variable. In this view, an extra Y chromosome increases aggressive tendencies and these, in turn, lead to increased criminal behavior. If this interpretation is correct, we may expect crimes committed by XYY men to be aggressive in nature, involving assaultive actions against other persons. We designate this the aggression hypothesis.

Concerning intelligence the reasoning is as follows: In common with most genetic aberrations, an extra Y in the male chromosomal complement is likely to have an adverse effect on development. Among possible dysfunctions, of particular interest for the XYY question is dysfunction in the intellectual domain. There is some evidence, although it is hardly consistent, of an intellectual impairment in XYY men *(7, 10, 11)*. Intellectual impairment may contribute to antisocial behavior. It seems plausible also that when individuals with impaired intellectual functioning commit crimes, they are more likely to be apprehended than are criminals of normal intelligence. This conception of intelligence as an intervening variable, mediating the relation between the presence of an extra Y chromosome and antisocial behavior, may be designated the intellectual-dysfunction hypothesis.

The extreme height of XYY's may facilitate aggressive acts on their part. In addition, it may cause them to be perceived by others as dangerous, with the possible consequence that they are more likely than shorter men to be suspected of crimes, to be pursued and apprehended, and, when tried, to be convicted. The view that tallness may serve as an intervening variable we designate the height hypothesis.

Because XXY's (Klinefelter males) also tend to be tall, we could expect our case-finding effort in the top 15 percent height group to identify a number of XXY's as well as XYY's. Most studies of XXY's have suffered from essentially the same limitations as those mentioned earlier for studies of XYY's; a study of XXY's is therefore of value in its own right. In addition, there is some evidence that XXY's also appear in institutions with disproportinate frequency. This raises the possibility that any sex chromosome aberration in males, and not particularly an extra Y, may be associated with increased risk of institutionalization *(5)*. Comparison of XYY's and XXY's may help to assess this possibility.

This article deals with the results of the case-finding study among tall men and with the evidence obtained to this point from the social records available for the XYY and XXY men who were found. An intensive individual study is now being conducted with these men and their controls *(12)*.

CASE-FINDING PROCEDURE

The population from which we sampled consisted of all male Danish citizens born to women who were residents of the municipality of Copenhagen, Denmark, between 1 January 1944 and 31 December 1947, inclusive. Not only did Copenhagen afford a very large source population, but available demographic data indicated that most men born in the city at that time would still be living there. The parish records, in which all births are registered, were used to identify the males born there in the chosen period. They numbered 31,436. The *folkeregister* (the Danish national register) provided current addresses and other information.

Information about the height of these men was obtained from draft board records where possible. The use of the 4-year period between 1944 and 1947 to define the target population provided us with a group of men who were at least 26 years old, the age by which Danish men are required to report to their draft boards for a physical examination, at which time their heights are recorded. For the small group of men who for some reason had never visited their draft boards, height data were obtained from other sources, such as institutions and the civil defense. In the very few cases where such sources were not available, cards were addressed directly to the men themselves requesting that they send us their heights.

By these methods, a group was composed consisting of 28,884 men who were still alive when the study began and for whom height information could be obtained. This group numbered 2552 fewer cases than the target population of 31,436 Copenhagen-born men. Of these 2552 cases 1791 were dead; 37 could not be traced for height determination; 21 could not be located at all in the *folkeregister* (probably for such reasons as name changes, death at birth, address change at birth), and 703 had emigrated and no record of their height was available. Of the 664 emigrants for whom we were able to determine age at emigration, 85.2 percent had emigrated before age 18, so that it is probable that in many of those cases the decisions about emigration were made by parents.

A cutoff point of 184 centimeters was used in composing the tall group in which the search for sex chromosome anomalies was to be conducted. The resulting group consisted of 4591 men, the top 15.9 percent of the height distribution in the total group of 28,884. Deaths reduced the tall group by 33 during the case-finding period, leaving a total of 4558 men to be searched for sex chromosome anomalies. An attempt was made to visit the homes of all 4558 for the purpose of obtaining blood samples and buccal smears to be used in determing chromosomal constitution.

Before home visiting began, members of the study staff were interviewed by the news media. These interviews provided an opportunity to publicize the purpose and nature of the study, with the result that most of the men who were asked to participate in the study had already heard of it when first approached. The initial individual contact was made by a letter, which mentioned the nature of the study and indicated that someone from the study staff would visit at a specified time. If the subject expected not to be at home at that time, he was asked to return a card on which he could suggest an alternative time. Men not found at home, and who had not asked for an alternative date, were subsequently revisited, up to a total of 14 times in the most extreme instance.

When the subject was seen, he was shown a newspaper clipping reporting the interview with our staff members and any questions he had were answered. The subject was also assured that his anonymity would be maintained. He was then asked whether he would be willing to give a buccal smear and, if he agreed, whether he would be willing to give a few drops of blood from an earlobe as well. The home visitor also asked the subject to fill out a questionnaire, and told him that at a later time he might be asked to participate further in the study. As the case-finding effort progressed, various methods were adopted to facilitate and encourage participation, such as setting up a station at one of the centrally located hospitals in Copenhagen to which the men were invited to come during a wide range of daytime and evening hours, and offering small financial inducements.

The 4139 men for whom sex chromosome determinations were made constituted 90.8 percent of the starting group of 4558 living tall men (13). Of the 419 unexamined cases, 174 men declined to participate; 138 men emigrated in the course of the study or were sailors and away from Denmark; 25 were destitute men without identifiable homes; and 82 men, on repeated visits, were not found at the official addresses listed for them in the *folkeregister (14)*. Some characteristics of these cases, and of the 174 men who declined to take part, are given below.

The buccal smears and blood samples were taken to the Chromosomal Laboratory of Rigshospitalet, in Copenhagen, for analysis. The buccal smears were stained with hematoxylin for the detection of X chromatin (15) and with quinacrine dihydrochloride for the detection of Y chromatin (16). The peripheral blood was treated by a micromethod modification (17) of the method of Moorhead *et al.* (18). Chromosome preparations were stained conventionally with orcein and by the method of Seabright (19) for G-banding and the method of Caspersson *et al.* (20) for Q-banding and identification of the Y chromosome (21).

DOCUMENTARY DATA

A variety of records were available for almost all the men in the study. The present report is limited to data from these records for five variables: height, convictions for criminal offenses, level of intellectual functioning as indicated by scores on an army selection test and by educational attainment, and parental social class at the time of the subject's birth.

The sources of information about height have already been described.

The source of data on convictions for criminal offenses was penal certificates *(straffeattest)* obtained from penal registers *(strafferegistrene)* maintained in the offices of local police chiefs. These certificates are extracts of court records of trials and cover all violations of the penal code that resulted in convictions. Offenses in the Danish penal code include such acts as these, among others: forgery, intentional arson, sexual offenses, premeditated homicide, attempted homicide, manslaughter, assault and battery, housebreaking, larceny, receiving stolen goods, and damage to property belonging to others. The penal certificates contain highly reliable information concerning the section of the penal law violated and the penalty imposed. A subject was considered to have a criminal record if he was convicted of one or more criminal offenses.

For evaluation of level of intellectual functioning, two kinds of measures were used. One was scores from the test employed in screening army recruits for intelligence, the *Børge Priens Prøver* (BPP), available from the draft-board records. Because the BPP was constructed as a screening device, it covers only a limited number of cognitive dimensions. The BPP scores are accordingly only rough indicators of intellectual level. The scores could not be obtained for some men; most frequent in this group were men who had never taken the test and men whose records were not available because they were in the army.

The second measure of intellectual functioning was educational level achieved. In Denmark examinations are given at the end of the 9th, 10th, and 13th years of schooling. From the available social records it was possible to determine which, if any, of these examinations was passed. For our "educational index" subjects who passed no examination were given a score of 0. and those who passed the first-, second-, and third-level examinations were given scores of 1, 2, and 3, respectively. It should be noted that the maximum rating assigned was 3 regardless of how many additional years of education the individual may have had *(22)*. In a very small

number of cases information needed for determining the educational index could not be obtained.

Parental socioeconomic status (SES) was classified primarily according to father's occupation at the time of the subject's birth. In a small number of cases the father or his occupation was not known; in some of these instances mother's occupation was known and was used instead. A seven-point SES classification was used, modified from a nine-point classification devised by Svalastoga *(23)*.

FREQUENCY OF XYY'S AND XXY'S AND OF CRIMINALS AMONG THEM

Among the 4139 men for whom sex chromosome determinations were made, 12 XYY's and 16 XXY's were identified. These frequencies represent prevalence rates of 2.9/1000 and 3.9/1000, respectively. Thirteen men were identified as XY's with other chromosomal anomalies. The remainder, all identified as having the normal XY complement, constituted the control group *(13)*.

A search in the penal registers showed that 41.7 percent of the XYY's (5 of 12 cases). 18.8 percent of the XXY's (3 of 16 cases), and 9.3 percent of the XY controls had been convicted of one or more criminal offenses (Table I). The difference between the percentages for the XYY's and the XY controls is statistically significant *(P < .01*, exact binominal test). The rate for the XXY's is somewhat higher than the rate for the XY controls but that difference is not significant; neither is the difference in rates between the XYY's and XXY's.

A first approach to evaluation of the aggression hypothesis was to examine the nature of the crimes of which the five XYY's had been convicted (Table II). Their offenses were not particularly acts of aggression against people. Only in case 2 do we find an instance of such an act. The difference between the XYY's and XY's in percentage of cases with one or more convictions for crimes of violence against another

Table I. Crime rates and mean values for background variables of XY's, XYY's, and XXY's. Significance level pertains to comparison with the control group (XY) using a two-sided test. For criminality rate an exact binomial test was used; for all other variables a *t*-test was used.

Group	Criminality		Army selection test (BPP)			Educational Index			Parental SES			Height		
	Rate (%)	N	Mean	S.D.	N	Mean	S.D.	N	Mean	S.D.	N	Mean	S.D.	N
XY	9.3	4096	43.7	11.4	3759	1.55	1.18	4084	3.7	1.7	4058	187.1	3.0	4096
XYY	41.7[a]	12	29.7[b]	8.2	12	0.58[a]	0.86	12	3.2	1.5	12	190.8[b]	4.6	12
XXY	18.8	16	28.4[b]	14.1	16	0.81[c]	0.88	16	4.2	1.8	16	189.8[b]	3.6	16

[a] P < .01.
[b] P < .001.
[c] P < .05.

Table 2. Nature of offenses of XYY's convicted on one or more criminal charges.

Case No. 2

This man is a chronic criminal who, since early adolescence, has spent 9 of 15 years in youth prisons and regular prisons. By far his most frequent criminal offense, especially in his youth, has been theft or attempted theft of a motor vehicle. Other charges included burglary, embezzlement, and procuring for prostitution. On a single occasion he committed a mild form of violence against an unoffending person; for this together with one case of burglary he received a sentence of around three-quarters of a year. This aggressive act was an isolated incident in a long period of chronic criminality. Except for this act, and the charge of procuring, all his nearly 50 offenses were against property, predominantly larceny and burglary. His single most severe penalty was somewhat less than a year in prison. Most of his crimes were committed in the company of other persons (BPP. 27).

Case No. 3

This man committed two thefts, one in late adolescence, the second in his early 20's. The penalties for both were mild—a small fine for the first, and less than 3 months in prison for the second. His last offense was 7 years ago (BPP. 37).

Case No. 5

This man committed two petty offenses as a young adult, within a short time of each other (one the theft of a motor-assisted cycle the other, a petty civil offense), for which the penalties were detentions of approximately 2 weeks and less than 2 weeks, respectively. His last offense was committed 10 years ago (BPP, 28).

Case No. 7

This man committed his only criminal offenses in his 20's, within a short period of time: falsely reporting a traffic accident to the police and causing a small fire. On both occasions he was intoxicated. The penalty was probation. His last offense was committed 5 years ago (BPP. 25).

Case No. 12

This man was under welfare care as a child and has spent only three to four of the last 20 years outside of institutions for the retarded. He is an episodic criminal. When very young he committed arson. Later his crimes included theft of motor vehicles, burglary, larceny, and embezzlement. His more than 90 registered offenses were all against property, mostly theft and burglary. For crimes committed while he was out of an institution, the penalty imposed was placement in an institution for the mentally retarded. For crimes committed while he was in such an institution—once theft of a bicycle, another time theft of a quantity of beverage—he was continued in the institution (BPP. 18).*

*Since this man was mentally retarded and spent many years in an institution for the retarded, he was not given a BPP at the draft board. The BPP of 18 was estimated by a stepwise linear regression, using a double cross-validity design, from the correlation between BPP scores and scores for the Wechsler Adult Intelligence Scale for the men in the individual case study.

person—8.4 percent (one man out of the 12) versus 1.8 percent (71 out of 4096)—is not statistically significant (one-tailed exact binomial test.) If we compare only those who had criminal convictions, the XYY's and XY's are again very similar in percentage of convictions that involved crimes of violence against a person (20.0 and 19.4 percent, respectively). These data provide no evidence that XYY's are more likely to commit crimes of violence than XY's (24).

The generally mild penalties imposed on the convicted XYY's (Table II) indicate that their crimes were not extremely serious. By far the most severe sentence was imprisonment for somewhat less that a year (25), imposed on case 2. Also suggesting that the XYY's with records of criminal convictions are not serious criminals is the fact that for one (case 5) the last conviction was 10 years ago, for another (case 3) 5 years ago, and for a third (case 7) 5 years ago. Of the remaining two XYY's both of whom had extensive criminal records, one (case 12) is mentally retarded. In fact, all five of these XYY's have BPP's below the average of 43.7 (Table I) for the XY controls, all but one of them well below that average.

There is a suggestion in our data that several of the crimes of XYY's were committed under circumstances which made detection of the crime and apprehension of the perpetrator particularly likely. Thus, one man sent in a false alarm directly to the police about a presumably serious traffic accident. Another man committed many burglaries of homes while the owners were on the premises.

Turning to the three XXY's with criminal records (Table III), we find that one, in the single crime he committed, assaulted his wife in an extremely brutal way, while under the influence of alcohol. The other two had short periods of juvenile delinquency, and the penalties imposed on them were slight. The last conviction of one was 7 years ago, of the other 10 years ago. All three have BPP scores well below the XY average. Finally, in percentage of cases with one or more convictions for crimes of violence against another person, the difference between the XXY's and the XY controls (6.2 percent versus 1.8 percent) was not statistically significant (one-tailed exact binomial test) (26).

As a first step toward evaluating the intellectual-dysfunction hypothesis, the intellectual level of each of the two proband groups was compared to that of the XY controls, scores on the army selection test (BPP) and the educational index being used for this purpose. For both kinds of measures the mean for the control group (Table I) is significantly higher than the means for either the XYY or the XXY group ($P < .05$ in each instance, t-test). The means for the two proband groups are not significantly different from each other. (It should be noted that the two indicators of intellectual level we used are highly related: for the control group the correlation between BPP scores and educational index is .59 [$P < .00005$. t-test].)

Having established that the proband groups are significantly lower than the XY controls on

Table 3. Nature of offenses of XXY's convicted on one or more criminal charges.

Case No. 17

This man's only criminal offense, committed when he was well into his 20's, was that he attacked his wife in an exceptionally brutal way, without any provocation from her. This happened twice, within a very short interval, while he was under the influence of liquor. For this he was imprisoned for somewhat more than a year (BPP. 26).

Case No. 25

The criminal career of this man consisted of two offenses: the first, in late adolescence, a theft of edibles from a food store, for which he was placed on probation, the second the theft of a motor vehicle, for which he was given less than 3 weeks of simple detention. Both crimes were committed in company with others. The last occurred 7 years ago (BPP. 11).

Case No. 27

This man had a short period of juvenile delinquency. His offenses included attempted theft and theft of a motor vehicle and a bicycle, burglary, and theft from a vending machine. On his first offense, in early adolescence, the charge was withdrawn and he was put under the care of child welfare authorities. His two other penalties consisted of withdrawal of charge on payment of a fine. Several of his offenses were committed in company with another person. The last occurred 10 years ago (BPP. 16).

both measures of intellectual level, we next examine the relation of these measures to criminality. Our data show, first, that BPP scores are significantly related to frequency of occurrence of registered crimes leading to convictions. In the control group, men with no record of such crimes had a mean BPP of 44.5, whereas those with one or more such crimes had a mean BPP of 35.5 ($P < .00001$, t-test). The educational index showed a similar relation to criminality (means of 1.62 for noncriminals and 0.74 for criminals [$P < .00001$, t-test]).

Overall, then, the pattern of results on intellectual functioning provides support for the intellectual-dysfunction hypothesis.

Both proband groups are significantly taller than the XY control groups (Table I). Within the restricted height range of the XY's, however, noncriminals (mean height 187.1 centimeters) were slightly taller ($P = .0013$, t-test) than criminals (mean height, 186.7 centimeters), a finding contrary to the hypothesis that tallness may mediate the relation between the extra Y chromosome and the likelihood of criminal convictions.

In neither proband group is parental SES significantly different from that of the XY control group (Table I). As expected, parental SES was significantly higher ($P < .0001$, t-test) for noncriminals (mean = 3.71) than for criminals (mean = 3.02).

CRIMINAL RATES AFTER ADJUSTMENT FOR BACKGROUND VARIABLES

We next compare the criminal rates of XYY's and XXY's with that of XY's equivalent to them in level of intellectual functioning, height, and parental SES. Only subjects for whom complete data were available are included (all 12 XYY's all 16 XXY's, and 3738 XY's). The analysis consists of three stages: the first step establishes the probability that an XY with a particular set of values for the background variables is a criminal; the second step establishes for each XYY or XXY the probability that he would be a criminal

if he were an XY with his background-variable values; the third step compares the observed frequency of criminals in the proband group with the frequency predicted in the second step.

To permit use of existing programs for the log-linear analysis we employed, it was necessary to make the two continuous variables, BPP and height, categorical. Past work (27) with simpler problems suggests that five or six categories often provide a very good representation of a continuous variable. Because height showed a very low relation to criminality in our sample of tall men, we used only five categories for height. The finding that BPP is strongly related to criminality, particularly within the restricted range of low BPP scores, made it advisable to use more categories for BPP. Accordingly, seven categories were employed for this variable.

In the 980-cell contingency table representing all combinations of the $5 \times 7 \times 4 \times 7$ categories for height, BPP, educational index, and parental SES, respectively, let us consider a particular cell. If $n_1 + n_2$ of the 3738 XY's (n_1 being criminals and n_2 noncriminals) fall in that cell, the proportion $n_1/(n_1 + n_2)$ gives a good estimate of the probability that a new XY in that cell will be a criminal, provided the value of $n_1 + n_2$ is large. In many of the 980 cells, however, both n_1 and n_2 are small; in fact in 376 cells both n_1 and n_2 are zero. But it is not necessary to consider each cell independently. Instead, a model may be built for these probabilities which lets us "borrow strength" from similar cells. Critical in building such a model is the definition of similarity. The method we used in constructing a model for our contingency table has been described by Bishop, Fienberg, and Holland (28). This method is based on log-linear models that are analogous to the usual linear models (that is, regression and analysis of variance). The difference between them is that log-linear models are appropriate for categorical dependent variables (such as criminal/noncriminal), whereas linear models are appropriate for continuous dependent variables. For those familiar with linear models, it is appropriate to think of the analyses performed here as if they were regressions, with criminality taken as the dependent variable and BPP, height, parental SES, and educational index as independent variables, even though in fact the computations required for the log-linear analyses are quite different. We present here only the final results of our analyses.

For the 3738 tall XY's used in the analyses, the proportion of criminals in each of the 980 cells of the contingency table can be very accurately predicted from a model with only six parameters: a grand mean parameter, reflecting the overall level of criminality in the population; one regression parameter reflecting the tendency of criminality to increase as parental SES decreases; two regression parameters (for linear and quadratic components) reflecting the tendency of criminality to increase more and more rapidly as educational index decreases; and two regression parameters (for linear and quadratic components) reflecting the tendency of criminality to increase more and more rapidly as BPP parameters relating criminality to height, indicating that the presence of the components for parental SES, BPP, and educational index there is no additional effect attributable to height. Also, there are no parameters reflecting interactions among these variables, because their effects on criminality are independent.

The fit of this six-parameter model to the full contingency table is extremely good. Globally, the adequecy of the fit is indicated by the log-likelihood ratio criterion divided by its degrees of freedom. (In fact, this corresponds to an F test in the analysis of variance or multiple regression. Under the null hypothesis that the model reflects the true state of nature the ratio should be about unity, and it should be larger than unity if the model does not fit.) This criterion for the six-parameter model and our four-way table is $491.65/(980-376-6)$ or 0.82. The significance test of the adequacy of the model follows from the fact that under the six-parameter model the log-likelihood criterion is distributed as χ^2 with 598 degrees of freedom. Hence, the significance level for the test of the adequacy of

the six-parameter model, as opposed to the alternative one-parameter-per-cell model, is $P < .99$. The six-parameter model thus cannot be rejected.

Locally, the fit of the six-parameter model is also very good. In individual cells with reasonably large $n_1 + n_2$ values, the estimated probability is close to the observed proportion; and in collections of cells in which the total $n_1 + n_2$ is large, the estimated probability is also close to the observed proportion.

We now apply this model to the XYY and XXY probands. Tables IV and V show the educational index, parental SES, BPP, and height of each proband and whether or not he had a criminal record. Also shown is the probability, predicted from the six-parameter model, that he would be a criminal if he were an XY. The last column gives the estimated standard errors of the estimated proportions. Since the sample size for the model (3738) is very large compared to the number of parameters used, these estimated standard errors are probably very accurate. It should be noted that for both XYY's and XXY's, the standard error is less than 16 percent of the estimated proportion except in one case (an XXY), in which it is 19 percent. Hence, the predicted probabilities are very accurate, particularly for the XYY's and may be considered exact for our purposes.

The number of criminals to be expected in each of the proband groups if their crime rate was the same as that of XY's equivalent in parental SES, educational index, BPP, and height is given by the sum of the predicted probabilities (column 7 of each table); the observed number of criminals is given by the sum of the 0 and 1 values (column 6).

The result of adjustments for BPP, parental SES, and educational index indicates that these variables account for some of the raw difference in criminality between the XYY and XY groups. However, an elevation in crime rate among the XYY's remains ($P = .037$; one sided exact binomial test) even after these adjustments are made, the observed and the predicted number

Table IV. Individual XYY's. Values of background variables, observed criminality (1 = record of one or more convictions, 0 = no record), and probability of criminality predicted from the XY model.

Case No.	Educational index	Parental SES	BPP	Height (cm)	Criminality Observed	Criminality Predicted Probability	Criminality Predicted Standard error
1	0	2	41	201	0	.14	.013
2	0	1	27	188	1	.21	.018
3	2	6	37	194	1	.05	.008
4	1	3	23	188	0	.22	.026
5	0	3	28	191	1	.18	.012
6	0	3	19	191	0	.27	.022
7	0	4	25	193	1	.16	.013
8	2	4	44	192	0	.05	.005
9	0	4	24	187	0	.25	.024
10	2	2	37	184	0	.07	.009
11	0	5	33	196	0	.15	.016
12	0	1	18[a]	185	1	.31	.027
					$N = 5$	$N = 2.06$	

[a]Estimated (see Table 2, footnote).

Table V. Individual XXY's. Values of background variables, observed criminality (1 = record of one or more convictions, 0 = no record), and probability of criminality predicted from the XY model.

Case No.	Educational index	Parental SES	BPP	Height (cm)	Criminality Observed	Criminality Predicted Probability	Criminality Predicted Standard error
13	1	4	27	188	0	.13	.014
14	2	5	47	185	0	.04	.005
15	0	4	35	191	0	.16	.013
16	0	3	23	184	0	.27	.022
17	1	3	26	187	1	.14	.014
18	2	4	50	195	0	.05	.005
19	0	5	14	192	0	.37	.058
20	2	7	49	186	0	.04	.006
21	0	3	14	188	0	.41	.054
22	0	5	9	197	0	.37	.057
23	1	1	39	191	0	.12	.015
24	2	7	33	188	0	.07	.013
25	0	4	11	190	1	.39	.055
26	0	1	15	195	0	.31	.027
27	0	4	16	190	1	.25	.024
28	2	7	46	189	0	.04	.006
					$N = 3$	$N = 3.16$	

of criminals in the XYY group being 5 and 2.06, respectively. The XYY's are not significantly different in criminality from the XY group ($P =$ .41) after the adjustment for background variables is made, as is shown by the agreement between observed and predicted number of criminals (3 versus 3.16).

DISCUSSION AND CONCLUSIONS

A first question to consider is the validity of the ascertainment data of 2.9/1000 XYY's and 3.9/1000 XXY's among the tall men sampled in the study.

For XYY's other prevalence data are available from two recent large-scale studies of tall men, but comparison with ours is made difficult by differences in source populations and in the heights taken as cutoff points. In one of these studies (29) the prevalence rate for the tall normal men sampled appears to be a good deal higher than our own, whereas in the other (11) it seems not very different.

Studies of the incidence of XYY in neonates are still few in number and their results variable. Two recent reviews have tentatively suggested an incidence rate of about 1/1000 live-born males (6, 7), another (5) a rate in the range of 1/1500 to 1/3000. On the basis of these values the expected number of XYY's in our total population at birth would be about 9 to about 29. For several reasons it is difficult to determine the proportion of these who would be likely to be present in the tall segment we sampled in adulthood. There are uncertainties about the rate of attrition through death among XYY's (30). There are also uncertainties about how many XYY's there might be among the unexamined tall men in our study (those who refused to participate, who emigrated, or who could not be located) (31) and among the shorter men we did not examine. Though our obtained frequency falls well within the range estimated from neonatal studies, given all the limitations and uncertainties involved in generating those estimates the correspondence must be in-

terpreted with caution. At the same time, there seem to be no grounds in these figures for suspecting a bias in our prevalence findings.

An evaluation of our XXY prevalence figure of 3.9/1000 presents the same problems as our XYY data: there are no satisfactory prevalence data for comparison, and incidence data are not yet adequate.

As to the rate of criminality, our finding is consistent with past findings from studies of institutionalized populations, in that the XYY's we identified had a higher mean rate of criminal convictions than the XY controls.

With regard to the possible correlates of the elevated XYY crime rate, the hypothesis we considered that height may be an intervening variable was not confirmed. In fact, within our tall XY group height showed a small but statistically significant negative relation to criminality.

On the other hand, the evidence from this study is consistent with a second hypothesis we considered, the intellectual-dysfunction hypothesis. The XYY's had an appreciably lower mean on the BPP, the army selection intelligence test, than did the XY's, and they also had a substantially lower mean on the related index of educational level attained, although some of the XYY's were within or not far out of the normal range on these variables. Moreover, in our XY sample criminality showed a substantial relation to both measures of level of intellectual functioning.

While intellectual functioning is thus clearly implicated as an important mediating variable, we cannot at this time say whether it is the only factor involved. When the two intelligence indicators were controlled, along with parental SES and height, in order to determine how these variables account for the observed XYY-XY difference in crime rate, an elevation in the XYY crime rate remained, though the difference was reduced. However, the BPP is not a comprehensive test of intelligence. It is possible that there are areas of cognitive dysfunction in XYY's that it does not tap and that a more comprehensive battery of cognitive tests would increase the explanatory power of the intellectual-dysfunction hypothesis (32).

In evaluating that hypothesis it is important to recall that the crime data we used were derived from records of individuals who were actually apprehended. People of lower intelligence may be less adept at escaping detection and so be likely to have a higher representation in a classificatory system based on registered crimes. The elevated crime rate found in our XYY group may therefore reflect a higher detection rate rather than simply a higher rate of commission of crimes.

It should be stressed that finding a relation between the presence of an extra Y chromosome and impaired intellectual functioning does not mean that the Y chromosome is ordinarily implicated in intellectual functioning and that a specific genetic basis for intelligence has thereby been established. That is no more true than would be the conclusion that, because trisomy 21 is associated with the markedly impaired intellectual functioning found in Down's syndrome, autosome 21 must make a direct genetic contribution to ordinary intellectual development. Chromosomes and genes exert their influence on development in concert; altering any one of them may accordingly affect the overall organization of the individual's genetic material, with consequences beyond the specific contribution each component may make individually. The potentially serious consequences of altering the organization of genetic material is reflected in the finding that chromosomal abnormalities are evident in about half of all spontaneous abortions in the first trimester of pregnancy, the period when such abortions are most frequent (33). In the case of the XYY complement, as in the case of Down's syndrome, it seems more plausible that the intellectual deficit found is one manifestation of altered ontogenetic development, resulting from a change in overall organization of genetic material, than that the particular chromosome involved (the Y chromosome or autosome 21) is directly implicated in ordinary intellectual functioning. A finding that has already emerged from the individual case studies we are conducting of the XYY's and the XY controls seems consistent with the view that the aberrant XYY complement may have broad adverse developmental consequences. In waking electroencephalograms (EEG's) the XYY's showed a significantly lower average frequency of alpha rhythm than matched XY controls (34). Slower EEG frequencies are normally predominant at an earlier age (35); our finding can therefore be viewed as suggesting a developmental lag.

The third hypothesis we examined, the aggression hypothesis, received little support in an examination of the criminal records of the XYY's. Among all offenses committed by XYY's there was only a single instance of an aggressive act against another person; and in that case the aggression was not severe. Thus the frequency of crimes of violence against another person was not statistically significantly higher in the XYY's than in the XY's. The elevated crime rate in our XYY sample reflects an elevated rate of property offenses. This picture is in keeping with results of previous studies, most of which have also found that XYY's are not more likely to commit crimes against people than are XY's (5). The infrequency of violent criminal acts among our XYY's is in line as well with the observation that XYY's show less aggressive behavior while in prison than do XY prisoners (36). Also consistent is our finding that XYY's were no more likely to decline to participate in this study than XY's. The aggression hypothesis cannot be ruled out by the analyses done thus far, but the evidence from the personality evaluations and the social-developmental histories in the individual case studies now being analyzed will allow a further and more direct assessment of that hypothesis.

We did not examine shorter XYY's in this study, but such men appear to be uncommon in institutions, even when ascertainment has been done with men unselected for height. Further, a recent study by Owen (37), based on the entire group of approximately 28,000 men who served as the source population for this study, has shown a slight inverse relation between height and criminal offenses. Thus height differences would not explain why short XYY's should appear less frequently in institutions than tall ones. Whether they do not appear because they are uncommon or because they do not commit detectable crimes, with regard to aggression shorter XYY's need be of no greater concern to society than the general run of men.

In addition to the variables of height, intellectual functioning, and aggression thus far examined as possible mediators in the relation between the XYY complement and an elevated crime rate, other variables are being considered in the individual case studies. These include characteristics of endocrine, neurological, and neuropsychological functioning.

The picture of the XXY's that has emerged to this point is in most ways similar to that of the XYY's. The XXY's showed a somewhat elevated crime rate compared to the XY's, but below that of the XYY's. The difference in crime rate between the XXY's and XYY's was not statistically significant. Though the XXY crime rate was slightly higher than that of the XY's, the difference was not statistically significant and the elevation disappeared when background variables were controlled. As to aggression, only one of the XXY's was convicted for an act of aggression, which was severe in nature. The XXY's were not significantly different from the XY's in frequency of crimes of violence against other persons. The XXY evidence thus does not provide any more impressive support for the aggression hypothesis than the XYY evidence does. With regard to intelligence, the XXY's, like the XYY's, had a substantially lower mean BPP and mean intellectual index than XY's did. The similarities between the XYY's and the XXY's suggest that, with regard to the characteristics considered thus far, the consequences of an extra Y chromosome may not be specific to that chromosome aberration but may result from an extra X chromosome as well.

The data from the documentary records we

have examined speak on society's legitimate concern about aggression among XYY and XXY men. No evidence has been found that men with either of these sex chromosome complements are especially aggressive. Because such men do not appear to contribute particularly to society's problem with aggressive crimes, their identification would not serve to ameliorate this problem.

REFERENCES AND NOTES

1. See, for example, H. Forssman, *Lancet* **1967-I.** 1389 (1967); R. M. Goodman, W. S. Smith, C. J. Migeon, *Nature (London)* **216,** 942 (1967); S. Kelly, R. Almy, M. Bernard, *ibid.* **215,** 405 (1967); T. Persson, *J. Ment. Defic. Res.* **11,** 239 (1967); B. W. Richards and A. Stewart, *Lancet* **1966-I,** 984 (1966).

2. S. A. Shah, *Report on the XYY Chromosomal Abnormality,* Public Health Services publication No. 2103 (1970).

3. J. Lederberg, *Soc. Res.* **43,** 387 (1973).

4. For recent comprehensive reviews of this evidence see *(5–7)*. See also L. F. Jarvik, V. Klodin, S. S. Matsuyama, *Am. Psychol.* **28,** 674 (1973); S. A. Shah and D. S. Borgaonkar, *ibid.* **29,** 357 (1974).

5. D. S. Borgaonkar and S. A. Shah, in *Progress in Medical Genetics,* A. G. Steinberg and A. G. Bearn, Eds. (Grune & Stratton, New York, 1974), vol. 10.

6. E. B. Hook, *Science* **179,** 139 (1973).

7. D. R. Owen, *Psychol. Bull.* **78,** 209 (1972).

8. In view of institutional variations in admissions policies, not always clearly specified in the published reports, it is difficult to judge whether the tendency of XYY men to appear more frequently in penal-mental than in straight penal institutions reflects the involvement of a mental aspect as well as a penal aspect. No clear tendency toward higher representation of XYY's in mental institutions has been found; however, studies of such institutions have been few.

9. This has been shown both by height data from XYY ascertainment studies of unselected male populations [for example, D. J. Bartlett, W. P. Hurley, C. R. Brand, E. W. Poole, *Nature (London)* **219,** 351 (1968); B. F. Crandall, R. E. Carrel, R. S. Sparkes, *J. Pediat.* **80,** 62 (1972); L. E. DeBault, E. Johnston, P.

Abnormalities. D. J. West, Ed. (Cropwood Round-Table Coinference. Institute of Criminology. Univ. of Cambridge, 1969), pp. 61–67.

37.   D. R. Owen, in preparation.

38.   This review was supported by grants MH 23975 and MH 628 from the National Institute of Mental Health. For advice at different points in the conception and conduct of the study, in analyses of the data, and in the preparation of this article we are grateful to L. L. Cavalli-Sforza, P. Holland, J. Lederberg, R. Schiavi, S. A. Shah, and A. Theilgaard. We are indebted to the Danish Ministry of Justice for making available the criminal records that were used in this article.

29. Criminal Behavior in Twins

ODD STEFFEN DALGARD
EINAR KRINGLEN

PARTICULARLY IN THE PSYCHIATRIC LITERATURE it has been maintained that genetic factors play a central role in the etiology of crime, but during the last 20 to 30 years, with increasing delinquency and violence in the Western countries, there has been a weakening of the genetic hypothesis in criminology. A significant number of investigations have shown how delinquency and criminal behaviour are related to psychological, social and cultural factors. However, even though today one is apt to stress psycho-social factors in the etiology of crime, it is nevertheless common to suppose that hereditary factors play a role, at least in certain types of criminal behaviour. For instance, it is reasonable to assume that typical juvenile crime, which varies in accordance with social conditions, is largely environmentally determined, whereas more serious crime, such as grave violence and sexual assaults, is more individually determined and perhaps even genetic in origin. Crime is a cultural and legal concept and accordingly what is considered crime varies to some extent from country to country. In order to entertain the idea that crime could have a genetic origin, one has, of course, to assume that crime is linked to certain personality characteristics, such as aggressive tendencies or deficient ego control.

▶SOURCE: *"A Norwegian Twin Study of Criminality,"* The *British Journal of Criminology* (July 1976), 16:213–232. Reprinted by permission.

THE TWIN METHOD

The study of the relative contributions of genetic and environmental factors in human behaviour can best be carried out by the classic twin method. This method is based on the existence of two types of twins: *monozygotics* (MZ) and *dizygotics* (DZ). Whereas MZ twins are supposed to be identical in hereditary endowment, DZ twins are no more alike genetically than common sibs. Thus all differences in MZ have to be attributed to the environment in the widest sense of that term, whereas differences in DZ, on the other hand, may be due to both hereditary and environmental factors.

Through a comparison of concordance figures in MZ and DZ with regard to certain traits, one might arrive at an impression of the relative significance of hereditary and environment for the trait in question. A pair is called *concordant* if both twins in a twin-pair harbour the same trait or illness, *discordant* if they are dissimilar, for instance if one twin is criminal and the other is not. Significantly higher concordance figures in the group of identical twins have usually been regarded as evidence in support of a hereditary background of the traits concerned. Conversely, if a characteristic is chiefly environmentally determined, one would expect similar concordance rates in MZ and DZ. In the case of epidemics where genetic differences are far less important than environmental ones, one would expect clustering in families but no marked difference in concordance rates for MZ and DZ. The same would be true for criminality in the case of environmentally causative origin.

GENERAL METHODOLOGICAL PROBLEMS

We shall not here discuss methodological problems but we would like to draw attention to a few common sources of error in twin research and make some general statements with regard to interpretation of data.

The results of twin studies are debatable if the following requirements are not fulfilled:

(a) The sampling must be based upon complete series of twins. *Cf.* Rosenthal's (1962) theoretical discussion and Kringlen's (1967) empirical research in the field of schizophrenia.

(b) The separation of MZ and DZ same-sexed twins must be reliably carried out. Particularly in small samples is blood- and serum-typing necessary.

(c) The concept of concordance must be clearly defined and the method of computing concordance given, since there are different measures of concordance (Allen *et al.*, 1967).

Higher concordance figures in MZ than in DZ have usually been regarded as proof of hereditary disposition for the trait concerned. Such an interpretation is, however, based on the following assumptions:

(a) The environmental conditions are in general similar for MZ and DZ pairs. This assumption is obviously not true. Zazzo (1960) and others have shown that the environment of MZ pairs is more likely to be closely similar than the environment of DZ pairs.

(b) The frequency of the trait concerned is not higher in MZ than in DZ pairs. Christiansen's (1968) data throw doubt on this assumption with regard to criminality since he found that MZ twins were more frequently imprisoned for crime than DZ twins.

PREVIOUS CRIMINOLOGICAL TWIN STUDIES

Table I gives a summary of previous twin studies, along with the present one, with regard to concordance in crime.

Lange (1929) studied 30 pairs of same-sexed (male) twins and observed that 10 of 13 MZ were concordant, whereas only 2 of 17 DZ displayed concordance. Concordance was defined as offences which lead to imprisonment. Lange obtained his sample of criminal same-sexed twins from prisons, from registered convicted psychopaths, and from his own psychiatric hospital. In addition to the 13 MZ and the 17 DZ of the same sex he learned by chance of ten opposite-sexed twin pairs. The zygosity—monozygotic or dizygotic—was determined by means of somatic measurements, photographs and fingerprints. As a rule the author himself examined personally both twins in a pair. In his monograph Lange gives a fairly detailed description of all the MZ pairs. He concluded his famous study by stating that heredity plays a major role in crime under contemporary conditions.

LeGras (1933) found that all four of his MZ were concordant whereas the five DZ were discordant with regard to criminality. He investigated both psychotic and criminal twins and collected his sample by writing to heads of asylums, prisons, state working colonies and correctional institutions as well as by a search of the university psychiatric-neurological department in Utrecht. Where the twin pairs were similar in appearance they were investigated by means of the Siemens' method (Siemens, 1924), whereas in cases of dissimilarity they were considered dizygotic and investigated further by mail only.

Rosanoff *et al.* (1934) obtained their relatively

Table I. Pairwise Concordance for Criminality in Previous and Present Twin Studies[a]

	MZ		DZ — same sex		DZ — opposite sex	
	No. of Pairs	Per cent. Concordance	No. of Pairs	Per Cent. Concordance	No. of Pairs	Per Cent. Concordance
Lange 1929, Germany	13	76.9	17	11.8	10	10.0
LeGras 1933, Holland	4	100.0	5	0.0	—	—
Rosanoff et al. 1934, U.S.A.	37	67.6	28	17.9	32	3.1
Kranz 1936, Germany	31	64.5	43	53.5	50	14.0
Stumpfl 1936, Germany	18	61.1	19	36.8	28	7.1
Borgstrom 1039, Finland	4	75.0	5	40.0	10	20.0
Yoshimasu 1961, Japan	28	60.7	18	11.1	—	—
Tienari 1963, Finland	5	60.0	—	—	—	—
Christiansen 1968, Denmark	81	33.3	137	10.9	226	3.5
Dalgard and Kringlen 1976, Norway[b]	49	22.4	89	18.0	—	—
	31	25.8	54	14.9	—	—

[a]Only concordance rates for adult criminals are included in the table. Some studies include female same sex twin pairs, i.e. Rosanoff, Kranz, Stumpfl, and Christiansen.

[b]Broad and strict concepts of crime, respectively.

large sample of twins both from mental and penal institutions. The sample was divided into three groups: criminal adults, i.e. persons 18 years or over who had been sentenced by a criminal court; juvenile delinquents, i.e. boys and girls who had been placed on probation or had been committed to a correctional institution; and children with behaviour disorders who had not been in conflict with the law. It is unclear to what degree the twins were personally seen by the research team. Concordance for the adult group was 67.6 per cent. in MZ and 17.9 per cent. in same-sexed DZ, whereas only 3.1 per cent. of the opposite-sexed DZ were concordant. Concordance rates in juvenile delinquents were 93 per cent. in MZ, and 80 per cent. in DZ of the same sex, and 20 per cent. in DZ opposite-sexed. Concordance in children was 87 per cent. in MZ, 43 per cent. in same-sexed DZ and 28 per cent. in opposite-sexed DZ.

Kranz (1936) sampled from several prisons and thus obtained 552 pairs of twins. However, the majority had to be excluded, 127 pairs because they were in fact not twins, 202 pairs because one of the partners had died, and 97 pairs because of uncertain zygosity diagnosis or un-

certain concordance. The author combined Siemen's similarity method with blood testing in determining the zygosity of the remaining same-sex subject twin-pairs and Kranz himself investigated most of the twins personally. Concordance in MZ and DZ of the same sex was 64.5 per cent. and 53.5 per cent. respectively, whereas the concordance figure for opposite-sexed DZ was considerably lower, namely 14 per cent. In his comprehensive monograph Kranz discusses the zygosity diagnosis of several pairs in detail, and he gives a thorough description of the life histories of both MZ and DZ pairs.

Stumpfl (1936) collected his sample from several prisons as well as from the register of "biological criminals." Zygosity was determined by photographs and physical measurements. The author investigated most of the twins personally and supplemented his data by information from relatives and official sources. The concordance rates of this study fall into the same pattern as we have observed for the Rosanoff and Kranz studies, concordance figures being highest in MZ and lowest in opposite-sexed DZ with the same-sexed DZ falling in between (61.1–36.8–7.1 per cent.).

Borgstrom (1939) reported that three of his four MZ pairs were concordant compared with two out of five DZ same-sexed pairs. Only two out of ten opposite-sexed DZ pairs were concordant.

Yoshimasu (1961) studied 46 same-sexed (male) twin pairs and observed that 17 of 28 MZ and two of 18 DZ were concordant. The author was aware of the significance of representative sampling but could not obtain a complete series because of no access to a twin register. Zygosity was based on various measures, and on blood-typing. We have not been able to obtain Yoshimasu's original report.

Tienari (1963) in his large-scale twin study of various types of psychopathology reported that six of 15 MZ pairs were concordant with regard to psychopathic behaviour, and three of five MZ were concordant with respect to manifest criminal behaviour.

Christiansen (1968) based his study on the Danish twin register, which includes virtually all twins born in Denmark between 1870 and 1910. Nearly 6,000 pairs of twins where both twins had survived the age of 15 were checked against the central police register and/or the local police registers. Zygosity diagnosis was based on a modified similarity test which previously had been controlled by a thorough blood and serum testing. In his 1968 paper the author reported that 35.8 per cent. of the 67 male MZ pairs were concordant, *i.e.* both twins had been recorded in the official penal register, in contrast to 12.3 per cent. concordance in 114 male DZ pairs. In the female group the concordances were 21.4 per cent. in 14 MZ pairs and 4.4 per cent. in 23 DZ pairs. In the group of opposite-sexed DZ pairs the concordance was 3.5 per cent.

The studies reviewed above consistently show a higher concordance for MZ than for DZ twins, a finding which supports the genetic hypothesis. However, the differences in concordance figures in MZ and DZ are in some studies slight and statistically not significant. Furthermore one also observes a difference in concordance between same-sexed DZ and opposite-sexed DZ, a finding which indeed emphasises the significance of environmental factors. Finally, the 1968 study and the results of the present one deviate considerably from the general pattern previously reported. Not only is the difference in concordance for MZ and DZ small in these last studies but the concordance in MZ is considerably lower than reported earlier. In fact discordance is more pronounced than concordance.

We shall now present some findings from our own study, reverting later on to these other studies. We shall then try to explain the observed differences in concordance figures and will argue that the recent studies which show that genetic factors play a minimal role in the etiology of crime are more reliable, essentially due to improved sampling.

THE PRESENT INVESTIGATION

The aim of this investigation was first of all to arrive at "true" or representative concordance figures for MZ and DZ twins with regard to criminality in order to elucidate the relative contributions of heredity and environment in anti-social behaviour. In addition, we wanted to study in more detail the developmental histories of MZ twin-pairs discordant for crime in order to throw light on individual predisposing factors. Finally, our aim was to study nosological aspects of behaviour. Given an MZ criminal twin, what spectrum of behaviour can one observe in the MZ co-twin?

In order to reach our aim, the investigation was from the start planned in two steps. To begin with, we wanted to study the total sample of twins in a crude manner. Afterwards we intended to carry out a more intensive study of a sub-sample focusing attention on discordance. In this selection we shall report our methods and findings regarding the first part of the study and accordingly address ourselves to the problem of concordance figures.

Sample

A twin register comprising all twins born in Norway between 1900 and 1935 had previously been compiled by one of the authors (Kringlen, 1967). This register contains the names and dates of birth of approximately 66,000 twins, *i.e.* 33,000 pairs. In the present investigation the names of all male twins born in the period 1921 to 1930 were checked against the national criminal register at December 31, 1966. We thus obtained a sample of 205 pairs of twins who had passed the main risk period for serious crime; 42 pairs where one twin had died before age 15 were excluded from the sample. In addition, 24 pairs were excluded for other reasons (*cf.* Table II). Female twin-pairs and opposite-sexed twins were not included in the investigation because the low frequency of reported crime for women would have required an unusually large basic twin population to afford a sufficient sample, and hence considerable secretarial work. Thus we are left with a sample of 139 twin-pairs where according to the national criminal register one or both of the twins had been convicted. Local directories enabled us to ascertain the addresses of the subjects, whereupon the twins were approached personally for blood test and interview.

Zygosity Diagnosis

The zygosity diagnoses were in most cases based on blood and serum typing. The following systems were employed: ABO, MN, CDEce, Hp, Gc, PGM, K, SP, and C_3. Identicalness on all these systems was considered evidence of monozygosity. The dizygotics were classified as

such when dissimilar on at least two factors. All pairs were thus not tested on all systems. By such a thorough testing, the zygosity diagnosis is rendered almost 100 per cent. correct (Juel-Nielsen *et al.*, 1958). In case it was not practically possible to have blood samples taken from both twins, the zygosity diagnosis was determined by comparing the twins with regard to such physical categories as similarity of external appearance, colour of eyes and hair, shape of face, and height. Finally, in all cases we obtained information with respect to identity confusion as children. Research has shown that simple questions such as "Were you mixed up as children? Were you considered alike as two drops of water?" can determine the zygosity correctly in over 90 per cent. of cases (Cederlöf *et al.*, 1961). Accordingly, even though blood tests were not available in all cases, there is no reason to believe that many if any twin pairs have been misclassified.

Table III gives the zygosity diagnosis of the sample.

Interview and Supplementary Information

The main part of the personal investigation was carried out in 1969–71. The twins were, of course, geographically distributed throughout the country so the home visits had to be made by private car, airplane, and sometimes boat to reach remote places.

Information about the life history of the twins was obtained through a semi-structured interview which lasted one to one-half-a-half hours. Each twin was usually interviewed once either by an advanced medical student or by the authors.

Table II. Survey of the Sample

Number of original twin pairs		205
Excluded from original sample due to		
death of one twin prior to age 15	42	
unknown address	10	
other reasons	14[a]	66
Number of pairs in final sample		139

[a]Six pairs by death of both twins, two pairs due to their living in the most northern part of the country, two pairs were in fact not twins, two pairs could not be located, two pairs were living abroad.

Table III. Zygosity Determination of Same-Sexed (Male) Twin Pairs

Zygosity Diagnosis	Blood-Tested	Not Blood-Tested	Total
MZ	33 pairs	16 pairs	49 pairs
DZ	49 pairs	40 pairs	89 pairs
Unknown	–	1 pair	1 pair
Total	82 pairs	57 pairs	139 pairs

The interview covered such items as childhood and adult biography, and included present social background, somatic and mental health status, as well as criminal career. In addition each twin was asked to describe his co-twin. Sometimes it was possible to obtain information from siblings and/or parents as well, so that the data could be constantly corrected and supplemented. In some cases, interviews with both twins could not be obtained, because one of the twins was dead, lived in an inaccessible location, was at sea or abroad. Table IV shows the extent of personal interviewing. In close to 70 per cent. of cases both twins in a pair were interviewed. In only four pairs did we not obtain a personal interview with either twin.

In most instances we were able to study the legal case material of convicted twins. This was crucial in order to arrive at an objective picture with regard to criminal life. Usually the interviewer studied the legal case material before he interviewed the twin so as to facilitate discussing the case with the subject. In case of so-called judicial observation, we were permitted to study the psychiatric documents. We would also like to add that the total sample has been checked against the psychosis register and, in case of medical treatment or hospitalisation, additional information has been obtained.

RESULTS

Survey of the Sample

First we shall give a description of the sample by

Table IV. Extent of Personal Interviewing

	MZ Pairs	DZ Pairs	Total Pairs
Both twins	35	58	93
Only one twin	12	29	41
Neither	2	2	4
Total	49	89	138[a]

[a]One pair with unknown zygosity diagnosis excluded.

age, civil status, social class, mental health, and crime committed (omitting one pair with uncertain zygosity diagnosis). Then we shall report the concordance figures for various types of crimes, and finally some data with regard to discordance.

Of the 276 twins, *i.e.* 138 pairs, 248 were alive at the time of investigation; 11 had died of accidents, ten of somatic diseases, three by suicide, and four could not be traced. All subjects were men in the age group 40–50 years at the time of investigation, with a mean age of 44.9 years (44.8 years in MZ and 45.0 in DZ).

Table V, on social class, shows some overrepresentation of classes V and VI compared to the general population. More than 50 per cent. work as factory workers, small-holders and fishermen, and only 5.4 per cent. belong to the upper social strata. On the other hand, most of the people have an occupation, only 3.3 per cent. being without durable jobs or on social security. There is no significant difference in social class distribution for MZ and DZ.

As to civil status there is a slight overrepresentation of never-married in the sample compared to the general population (17 per

Table V. Distribution According to Social Strata

	No.	Per cent.
I. Professionals in high positions, executive, managerial	3	1.1
II. Professionals in lower positions, higher employees, businessmen	12	4.3
III. School-teachers, technicians, employees	23	8.3
IV. Skilled workers, lower employees, farmers	66	23.9
V. Unskilled workers, small-holders, fishermen	158	57.3
VI. Day labourers, others without a stable job	9	3.3
Unknown	5	1.8
Total	276	100.0

cent. versus 13.5 per cent.), and the rate of divorce is somewhat increased.

Of the subjects 65 per cent. had elementary schooling as the only formal education, which corresponds closely to Christie's (1960) figures for a 1933 cohort of Norwegian criminal males. The corresponding figure for the general population of that cohort was lower, namely 48 per cent. with only elementary school.

Table VI gives an impression of the mental health status of the subjects. A rather conservative classification has been employed based on a global evaluation of subjective and objective symptoms as well as social functioning. We were able to evaluate 262 subjects of whom the majority were functioning satisfactorily, socially, and most of the subjects were without marked neurotic symptoms, such as pain, tensions, irritability, anxiety or depression. 15 per cent. had moderate but clear-cut neurotic or psychopathic traits and some did not function adequately socially, *i.e.* did not work or were hospitalised or imprisoned. Only 7.6 per cent. had serious symptoms such as psychotic symptoms or severe alcohol or drug problems, some of these combined with grave social dysfunction. In other words, in this male population, age 40–50 years, 20–25 per cent. could be said to have been seriously disturbed mentally, a figure which is commonly reported in investigation on the general population.

With regard to alcohol consumption, we obtained reliable information on 262 subjects. Of these, 33 per cent. had an alcohol problem and drank too much according to rather liberal standards, but only 13 per cent. could be considered chronic alcoholics. According to various studies, the risk of developing alcoholism in the male Norwegian population is around 8 per cent.

Table VII shows the types of crime committed by the group. As one can see, theft/burglary is the most common crime, followed by traffic law violation. Crime involving violence is, for instance, rather uncommon, constituting barely 10 per cent.

Thus, this sample of male twin pairs where the index twin is in the Criminal Register does differ slightly from the general population with regard to certain epidemiological variables. They seem to have a lower social class distribution; they seem to have received a less-than-

Table VI. Global Evaluation of Mental Health

	No.	Per cent.
1. No symptoms, adequate social functioning	129	77.5
2. Slight symptoms, adequate social functioning	74	
3. Moderate symptoms, adequate social functioning	15	14.9
4. Moderate symptoms, some social impairment	24	
5. Serious symptoms, some social impairment	9	7.6
6. Serious symptoms, grave social impairment	11	
Total	262	100.0

Table VII. Type of Crime Committed[a]

Reason for conviction	No. of persons	Percentage
Theft, burglary	70	32.6
Violation of motor vehicle law	53	24.7
Violation of vagrancy law	18	8.4
Violence	17	7.9
Treason during world War II	17	7.9
Sexual assault on children	11	5.1
Deceit, fraud	11	5.1
Violation of military criminal law	7	3.3
Indecent exposure	3	1.4
Threats of bodily harm	2	0.9
Intoxication	2	0.9
Incest	2	0.9
Rape	2	0.9
Robbery	1	0.5
Total	215	100.5

[a]Some persons were convicted for several types of crime.

normal degree of education; they are to a lesser degree married; and frequency of alcoholism seems higher in this group than in the general population. However, these differences are by and large of a minor nature.

CONCORDANCE FIGURES IN TWIN STUDIES

Concordance is usually defined as persistent manifestation of similar traits in both twins. A pair is labelled concordant if both twins have the same illness or same behaviour, for instance if both are criminals, discordant if one twin is criminal and the co-twin is not. The concept of concordance implies a dichotomy which is not always acceptable. Accordingly, in the case of measurable traits, concordance is usually expressed as the average intra-pair difference. In psychiatry the view has gained ground that there is no qualitative distinction between mental health and illness in general. Therefore dichotomies are often drawn arbitrarily or the reference is, for instance, to partial concordance, as when one twin is schizophrenic and the co-twin is borderline schizophrenic.

There are different ways of computing concordance rates (Allen *et al.,* 1967). The *direct pairwise method* is simple and most used when comparing concordance in MZ and DZ. By this method one simply calculates the percentage of concordant pairs in the sample. The *proband method* is more useful when one also wishes to compare incidences (concordances) in siblings.

(Proband is the name given to index cases in a genetic investigation.) The proband concordance is the proportion of afflicted twins or sibs who have an afflicted partner. In other words it is the morbidity rate of the partners of affected twins. By this method each affected pair doubly ascertained counts twice. Concordance is not a correlation in the usual sense since the number of twin pairs in which neither is a criminal is usually not accessible.

Direct pairwise concordance is obtained according to the formula $\frac{c}{c+d}$ where c is the number of concordant pairs and d is the number of discordant pairs. The proband concordance is ascertained by this formula: $\frac{c+x}{c+x+d}$ where x is the number of pairs represented by two independently ascertained cases, and c and d as defined above.

Table VIII gives concordance rates for MZ and DZ when a broad concept of crime is employed. Crime is here defined as legally punishable behaviour reported to the Criminal Register. As the table shows, the figures yield high rates for proband concordance in both MZ and DZ, but the pairwise concordance shows the higher ratio MZ/DZ, namely 1.24 against 1.20. The concordance rates in MZ are higher than in DZ, but the difference is slight and statistically not significant. (The 95 per cent. confidence interval for the difference between concordance rates included 0; See Dixon and Massey, 1969, p. 249.)

Table IX gives concordance rates when a more strict concept of crime is employed. Crime

Table VIII. Concordance with Respect to Criminality, Employing a Broad Concept of Crime[a]

Zygosity	Total Pairs	Concordant Pairs	Discordant Pairs	Pairwise Concordance	Proband Concordnace
MZ	49	11	38	22.4%	36.7%
DZ	89	16	73	18.0%	30.5%
MZ/DZ				1.24	1.20

[a]Including, for instance, crime according to the motor vehicle law, the military law, and cases of treason during World War II.

Table IX. Concordance with Respect to Criminality, Employing a Strict Concept of Crime[a]

Zygosity	Total Pairs	Concordant Pairs	Discordant Pairs	Pairwise Concordance	Proband Concordance
MZ	31	8	23	25.8%	41.0%
DZ	54	8	46	14.9%	25.8%

[a]According to the criminal law, including: violence, sexual assault, theft and robbery.

here is defined as anti-social acts which would be considered crimes in most countries, such as crimes of violence, crimes involving sexual norms, crimes against property. Here the difference in concordance rates between MZ and DZ increases, although the difference is still not statistically significant ($p > 0.05$).

In Table X the sample is split up according to various types of crime. For crimes related to theft and burglary which have the highest incidence, the pairwise concordance is 19.1 per cent. in MZ and 18.5 per cent. in DZ, pratically no difference at all. With regard to other types of crimes the numbers are so small that no conclusion is indicated with regard to concordance, except that the general pattern seems to be that of discordance in both MZ and DZ.

Thus the data do show higher concordance figures in MZ and DZ with regard to criminal behaviour. However, the differences reported are of a minor character, and statistically not significant. The natural conclusion would appear to be that, if there does exist a genetic disposition to criminal behaviour, the disposition is a weak one. Even such a modest conclusion, however, is based on the underlying assumption that the environmental conditions for MZ pairs do not differ from those of DZ pairs, an assumption which today cannot be accepted. MZ twins receive, in fact, more similar external environmental influence than do DZ, because they are treated more often as a unit and are seen together more. Consequently higher concordance figures in MZ may not be the result of heredity only. Table XI shows clearly that the MZ pairs have been treated more frequently as a unit and have experienced more extreme closeness and interdependence than the DZ pairs. In the MZ group, for instance, 92 per cent. of the pairs felt they had been brought up as a unit as against 77 per cent. of the dizygotic group. In the MZ group 94 per cent. had been dressed alike in

Table X. Concordance for Similar Type of Crime in Monozygotic and Dizygotic Twins

	MZ		DZ	
Type of crime	Concordant Pairs	Discordant Pairs	Concordant Pairs	Discordant Pairs
Theft, burglary	4	17	7	31
Violence, robbery with menace	1	4	1	12
Deceit, fraud	0	5	0	6
Sexual offence against children	2	2	0	5
Exhibitionism	0	1	0	2
Rape	0	0	0	1
Incest	0	1	0	1
Total	7	30	8	58

Table XI. Twin Relationship and External Environment in MZ and DZ Twins

Twin relationship as children and as adolescents	MZ pairs	DZ pairs	Total pairs
Brought up as a unit	45	67	112
Brought up differently	4	20	24
Unknown	0	2	2
Dressed alike	46	64	110
Dressed differently	3	23	26
Unknown	0	2	2
Extremely strong closeness	14	5	19
Strong closeness	28	27	55
Slight closeness, as "sibs"	7	57	64

childhood as against 74 per cent. of the DZ pairs. A still clearer difference is revealed when one compares the subjective feeling of emotional closeness and mutual identity. Most of the MZ pairs, namely 86 per cent., had felt an extreme or strong interdependence compared with 36 per cent., of the DZ. Expressed another way, only 13 per cent. of the MZ group felt that in childhood and adolescence they had been no more close than non-twins sibs, whereas 64 per cent. of the DZ pairs had felt so.

Let us examine the implications of these findings with regard to concordance figures. In Table XII we have compared the concordance figures in MZ and DZ according to degree of psychological closeness, i.e. strong or weak intra-pair interdependence. The table shows that the previously observed difference in concordance between MZ and DZ now almost disappears in the group of twins who have experienced a close relationship. Thus when one compares MZ and DZ who have more or less experienced the same environmental influences the difference in concordance figures vanishes. The second row in the table speaks against this hypothesis. However, one is inclined to de-emphasise this observation since the numbers concerned are very small.

How then can these factors influence the concordance rates? Most likely, similar external milieu and mutual identification lead to similarities in personality, including the shared criminal tendencies. For the same reason, the twins in a pair, as adults, operate together as a unit, and accordingly carry out criminal acts together. However, the significance of these factors must not be exaggerated. One has to bear in mind that, even in MZ and DZ with rather similar external environment, discordance is more conspicuous than concordance.

Table XII. Concordance for Crime in the Strict Sense in Twins with Respect to Intra-pair Interdependence

Degree of Closeness	MZ		DZ	
	Concordance	Per Cent.	Concordance	Per Cent.
Extreme or strong	6/26	23.2	3/14	21.4
Moderate or weak	2/5	40.0	5/40	12.5
Total group	8/31	25.8	8/54	14.9

Table XIII shows that twins of MZ and DZ concordant pairs to a large extent operate together in criminal acts. We have also data showing that a relatively larger number of twin pairs who work together during acts of crime have been closely connected in childhood. This applies particularly to MZ pairs; however, the numbers are small and not statistically significant.

DISCORDANCE

We have shown in this study that the difference between MZ and DZ with regard to concordance rates in crime is negligible. Even in MZ discordance is more conspicuous than concordance. But why the discordance? Our information is as yet not sufficient to throw much light on this question. We will therefore just give a few conclusions based on our preliminary findings and revert to this problem in a later paper.

First, one observes that the criminal twin has belonged as an adult to a lower social class and has been more often somatically and mentally ill, and more often classified as an alcoholic, than his co-twin. Furthermore, one finds differences in personality characteristics in both MZ and DZ, *e.g.* the criminal twin in discordant pairs has been the more suspicious or sceptical by nature, the more restless and anxious, the more dominant and self-assertive. If these differences occurred only in the DZ but not the MZ group they might be ascribed to genetic factors. However, since the differences are present in both MZ and DZ pairs they have to be ascribed to environmental influences in the broadest sense of that term, *i.e.* they could be due to organic perinatal factors or to psycho-social factors after birth. But since there is no correlation between criminal behaviour in adult life and birth order, birth weight and physical condition in infancy, such differences in personality and life outcomes as alcoholism and criminality must be psycho-social in origin.

Finally a reservation: one should bear in mind that the figures on which we based our observations are small, and in many cases the actual

Table XIII. Degree of Contact with Co-Twin During Criminal Act in Concordant Pairs

Degree of Togetherness	MZ	DZ	Total
Always together in the same act	7	3	10
Partly together in the same act	1	9	10
Never together in the same act	8	4	12
Total	16	16	32

extent of intra-pair differences has not been fully explored and tabulated. The differences reported here are statistically significant in only a few cases, and accordingly one should at this time regard them as hypothetical, interesting observations which will have to be more carefully investigated.

GENERAL DISCUSSION

In a sample obtained from the Norwegian criminal register we have observed very slight differences in concordance rates in MZ and DZ twins with regard to crime. Since MZ twins experience a more similar upbringing and an identity with each other stronger than that of DZ twins, we have compared groups of monozygotic with dizygotic twin pairs who by and large have experienced this same close twin relationship and report the same type of upbringing with regard to dressing and treatment by the parents. In such a comparison the difference in concordance between MZ and DZ practically disappears altogether. These findings lead us to conclude that *the significance of hereditary factors in registered crime is non-existent.*

One could, of course, object that by focusing attention only on registered crime one misses the unreported and unconvicted crime. Could it not be that several of the co-twins of registered criminals in fact are also criminals and accordingly the reported concordance figures are minimum figures? Obviously our figures are minimum figures in this respect. However, in our interviews we tried to obtain information with regard to criminal behaviour in the co-twin, and furthermore there is no reason to believe that we should have missed disproportionately more MZ co-twins than DZ co-twins with criminal records. Thus even if one accepts the possibility that the real figures should be higher, there is no reason to believe that the relative difference in concordance rates between MZ and DZ is affected by this source of error.

Our results are clearly at variance with most of the twin literature on crime. In several of the more comprehensive earlier studies the concordance rates found are considerably higher for MZ than for DZ twins. Table XIV shows the results of the major studies, excluding investigations with smaller samples. As one can observe, the figures for DZ vary considerably, with a range of 11–53 per cent. In MZ there is a more uniform pattern, with concordance in the range of 61–77 per cent. However, in all the previous studies, except Kranz, there is a clear-cut difference between MZ and DZ.

Why then do the more recent studies from Scandinavia, by Christiansen and ourselves, de-

viate? To answer this question we have to examine the crucial factors related to sampling and zygosity diagnosis. It is evident that sampling is important in concordance studies of twins. If the sampling is unsystematic and uncontrolled the likelihood of obtaining disproportionately more concordant than discordant pairs is increased.

It goes without saying that the probability of being brought to the attention of investigators is greater for concordant pairs than for the less conspicuous discordant cases. If the probability of finding a twin in an institutional population is p and the members of concordant pairs are discovered independently, the probability of catching a discordant pair is p and the probability of finding a concordant pair is: $p + p - (p \times p)$. For instance, if p is 0.6, then the probability of finding a discordant pair is 0.6 and 0.6 + 0.6 − (0.6 × 0.6) = 0.84 for a concordant pair. In reality the difference in probability is most likely greater because the twins in concordant pairs are often not reported independently.

It is also obvious that the establishment of correct zygosity diagnosis is of importance, par-

Table XIV. Pairwise Concordance Figures for Criminality in MZ and DZ in Relation to Two Critical Variables*

Investigator	MZ Concordance %	DZ Concordance %	Sampling Complete unselected sample	Zygosity diagnosis Blood and serum typing**
Lange 1929	76.9	11.8	No	No
Rosanoff et al. 1934	67.6	17.9	No	No
Kranz 1936	64.5	53.5	No	Yes
Stumpfl 1936	61.1	36.8	No	No
Yoshimasu 1961	60.7	11.1	No	Yes
Christiansen 1968	33.3	10.9	Yes	Yes
Dalgard and Kringlen 1975	25.8	14.9	Yes	Yes

*LeGras, Borgstrøm and Tienari have been excluded because of small samples, cf. Table I.

**Kranz employed a limited number of blood groups; Christiansen based his zygosity diagnosis on a modified similarity test based on a questionnaire, but this method had previously been controlled by thorough blood and serum testing.

ticularly when one is dealing with small samples as one usually does in twin research. Recent experimental studies have shown that there is a tendency to diagnose MZ as DZ when blood-testing is not employed. As there are more discordant than concordant DZ in the various studies, this source of error will have the effect of inflating the concordance rate in MZ.

Why, then, is the proportion of MZ considerably higher than expected in earlier studies, namely 45 per cent. in the Lange study, 57 per cent. in Rosanoff's, 42 per cent. in Kranz's, and 49 per cent. in the study by Stumpfl? (The Japanese study is a special case since the twin population of Asia differs from the European one.) In the Christiansen study the proportion of MZ in same-sex twins is 37 per cent. and in the present study 36 per cent., numbers which correspond fairly well with expected frequencies for the normal population of twins. We have no satisfactory explanation to offer. Could it be that an uncontrolled sampling without access to a regional or national twin register will automatically obtain relatively more MZ than DZ same-sexed twins since the first group are considered by most people to be more interesting subjects?

In reviewing the major twin studies with respect to crime one notes that Lange, Rosanoff, Kranz, Stumpfl and Yoshimasu did not obtain unselected complete series of criminal twins as Christiansen and the present authors did. Neither did they secure their zygosity diagnosis through blood tests to the same degree as did the Scandinavian investigators. Let us, however, examine the various studies in more detail.

Sampling

Lange obtained twins from resident populations of both a prison and a mental hospital, and he also included in his sample convicted psychopathic probands registered by a research institution, twins resident in prisons in Bavaria on a certain day, as well as any other twin-pairs in the convict's family. By such a method he was theoretically likely to obtain relatively more concordant than discordant pairs because concor-

dant pairs have a greater chance of being found. However, since Lange does not give figures for the original population of inmates it is difficult to know how successful his sampling was.

Rosanoff and co-workers sampled a series of institutions, such as psychiatric hospitals and clinics and penal and correctional institutions. The investigators do not give a detailed account of the sampling technique. It is, however, evident that the sampling was uncontrolled and unsystematic, and accordingly one would expect to find relatively more concordant than discordant pairs.

Kranz obtained the major part of his sample from Prussian prisons. Every inmate of all the jails in that region had been asked on a certain day if he was a twin. The author supplemented his original sample by inquiring of every recently-admitted prisoner in six penal institutions in a specific area over a one-year period whether he was a twin. According to the author this last series had not been obtained by continual registration. Nevertheless, most likely Kranz by his sample secured from the outset a rather unselected group of criminal twins. However, because of later exclusion of a large number of pairs, the representativeness of his final sample might be questioned. Whereas his original material consisted of 552 pairs of twins, after excluding 427 of them for a variety of reasons, he was left with only 125 pairs. It is noteworthy that he left out a total of 97 pairs because of uncertain zygosity diagnosis or uncertain concordance. Since we are not given more detailed information concerning this group it is difficult to evaluate its impact on the final sample.

Stumpfl also seems to have obtained, at the outset, a rather unselected sample of twins by collecting 550 twin-pairs from consecutively admitted convicts of German prisons and from the files of a research institute in Bavaria. However, the author states that he investigated only 65 of these pairs more thoroughly, and the reason for selection was "availability," which of course is a dubious criterion with regard to sampling. Thus it is impossible to have any idea how this selectivity might affect concordance figures in MZ and DZ.

Yoshimasu tried to obtain a complete unselected series of criminal twins, but according to himself he did not succeed. His sample most likely would contain a preponderance of concordant cases.

Christiansen, in contrast to earlier investigators, had access to a national twin register and thus an unselected sample of criminal twins could be located. By such a sampling method the probability of identifying more concordant than discordant cases is negligible.

Our own investigation followed, in principle, the Danish method. All male twins of the national twin register born 1920–29 were checked against the central criminal register. Thus a complete and representative sample of criminal twins was obtained.

In summary, then, *from a sampling point of view we might conclude that previous studies, due to possible sampling errors, most likely obtained a preponderance of concordant pairs, which would render too high concordance figures in MZ and DZ twins.* Any real difference in concordance figures between MZ and DZ will accordingly be artificially increased due to deficient sampling. The Danish and Norwegian studies, however, were able to avoid these sampling problems and thus the results of these studies are more reliable.

Zygosity

Lange relied on physical measurements, photographs and fingerprints, but for part of his sample he only obtained superficial information due to uncooperativeness of the twins. Accordingly there is a risk that some of his MZ twins have been classified as DZ.

Rosanoff *et al.* investigated the largest sample, but methodologically their study is far from satisfactory. Not only was the sampling unsystematic but it is quite unclear how the zygosity diagnoses were established. Most likely a sort of similarity method was employed and, as noted before, this will lead to misclassification of some MZ.

Kranz is the only one of the earlier investigators who, to some extent, employed blood grouping. The blood groups most used were the ABO and MN systems, which today are considered very reliable. If twins in a pair differ on any of these systems, they are without doubt dizygotic. The opposite is, however, not true since same-sexed DZ may in fact both have blood group A in 10 per cent. He also used the similarity method of Siemen and in some cases he had access to photographs of the twins. Thus there is no reason to believe that many same-sex twin pairs were misclassified.

Stumpfl employed only the similarity method and thus one would assume that some of his MZ might have been classified as DZ. The proportion of MZ is, however, considerably higher than one would expect. This could of course be due to the fact that he studied twins who were "available," and one might then infer that MZ were more available than DZ.

Yoshimasu seems to have employed both the similarity method and blood tests and thus the zygosity diagnosis of his sample is likely to be reliable. The proportion of MZ in his sample seems very high but according to vital statistics corresponds rather well with the expectation for Japan.

Christiansen studied a sample where zygosity had been established by a modified similarity test. The method had been tested out previously by comparing a group of same-sexed twins where thorough blood and serum typing had been performed. By this method probably not more than 5 per cent. of the sample falls into the dubious group, so only a couple of the basic MZ pairs might theoretically have been incorrectly classified as DZ.

With respect to our own study we shall refer the reader to our previous account. Suffice it to say that interview questions concerning identity confusion in childhood, photographs and blood tests were all used to establish zygosity. In fact 60 per cent. of the sample were blood-tested. In case of misclassification this applies most likely to some MZ who might have been wrongly diagnosed as DZ. Table III might support such an assumption since 40 per cent. of the blood-tested pairs are MZ whereas only 30 per cent. of the non-blood-tested pairs have been so classified. These reservations should, however, not affect the concordance figures to a significant degree.

CONCLUSION

Our data and review of the literature suggest that previous studies of criminal twins probably observed too great a difference in concordance rates between MZ and DZ due to sampling errors and unreliable zygosity diagnosis. Here we would like to emphasise the fact that the number of twin pairs of different zygosity is in most previous studies relatively small and, accordingly, a shift of two or three cases from one group to the other would produce different concordance rates. An unsystematic, uncontrolled sampling procedure will include disproportionately more concordant than discordant cases, and zygosity determination without blood and serum grouping tends to classify MZ pairs as DZ.

Compared with previous investigations the present study and Christiansen's study have been able to collect large samples and avoid sources of error due to deficient sampling and zygosity diagnosis. Accordingly the results of these studies probably give a better picture of the relative significance of heredity and environment in crime than did previous studies.

The concordance rates in the Christiansen study were 33.3 per cent in MZ and 10.9 per cent. in DZ of the same sex. In our study the difference between MZ and DZ is still smaller, namely 22.4 per cent. in MZ and 18.0 per cent. in DZ, when a broader concept of crime is employed, and 25.8 per cent. and 14.9 per cent. when a more strict concept of crime is used. These differences between MZ and DZ are not impressive compared with previous twin studies,

but are still clear-cut. Since MZ pairs usually are brought up more similarly than DZ, this slight difference in concordance rates could be partly explained on these grounds. In our study we have been able to show that the difference in fact disappears almost completely when this "twin relationship factor" is controlled for. In other words, the difference in concordance rates between MZ and DZ is partly due to environmental factors. The consistent difference in concordance rates between same-sexed and opposite-sexed DZ also supports this conclusion (cf. Table I).

SUMMARY

In an unselected sample of 138 pairs of same-sexed male twins, age 40–50 years, who were obtained through the national twin and criminal registers of Norway, concordance with respect to registered crime was slightly higher in monozygotic (MZ) than in dizygotic (DZ) twins. Employing a broad concept of crime—including violation of the motor vehicle law and treason during World War II—concordance was 11/49 or 22.4 per cent. in MZ and 16/89 or 18.0 per cent. in DZ. With a more strict concept of crime, concordance was 8/31 or 25.8 per cent. in MZ and 8/54 or 14.9 per cent. in DZ.

However, since MZ pairs experience a more similar upbringing than DZ pairs, we compared groups of MZ and DZ who by and large had been exposed to the same type of environmental influences in childhood and adolescence. In such a comparison the difference in concordance almost completely disappears. These findings support the view that *hereditary factors are of no significant importance in the etiology of common crime*.

These observations and conclusions are at variance with most of the earlier twin studies in criminality. However, it has been demonstrated by a review of the older literature that previous studies in this field, owing to various sources of error, gave results in which the genetic factor was over-estimated. The present study seems to have avoided the pitfalls of unrepresentative sampling and uncertain zygosity diagnosis and has therefore arrived at considerably lower concordance figures in MZ with respect to crime.

REFERENCES

Allen, G., Harvald, B. and Shields, J. (1967). "Measures of twin concordance." *Acta genet.* (Basel), **17**, 475–481.

Borgstrøm, C. (1939). "Eine Serie von Kriminellen Zwillingen." *Arch. Rass. ges. Biol.,* **33**, 334–343.

Cederlöf, R., Friberg, L., Jonsson, E. and Kaij, L. (1961). "Studies on similarity diagnosis in twins with the aid of mailed questionnaires." *Acta genet.* (Basel), **11**, 338–62.

Christiansen, K. (1968). "Threshold of tolerance in various population groups illustrated by results from Danish criminological twin study." In: de Reuck, A. V. S. (ed.), *The Mentally Abnormal Offender.* Boston: Little, Brown & Co.

Christie, N. (1960). *Unge Norske Lovovertiedere.* Oslo: Universitetsforlaget.

Dixon, W. J. and Massey, F. J. (1969). *Introduction to Statistical Analysis.* New York: McGraw-Hill.

Gottesman, I. I. and Shields, J. (1972). *Schizophrenia and Genetics.* New York: Academic Press.

Juel-Nielsen, A. and Hauge, M. (1958). "On the diagnosis of zygosity in twins and the value of blood groups." *Acta genet.* (Basel), **8**, 256–273.

Kranz, N. (1936). *Lebensschicksale Krimineller Zwillinge.* Berlin: Springer.

Kringlen, E. (1967). *Heredity and Environment in the Functional Psychoses.* Oslo: Universitetsforlaget and London: Heinemann, 1968.

Lange, J. (1929). *Verbrechen als Schicksal. Studien an Kriminellen Zwillingen.* Leipzig: Thieme.

LeGras, A. M. (1933). "Psychose und Kriminalität bei Zwillingen." *Z. ges. Neurol. Psychiat.,* **144**, 198–222.

Rosanoff, A. J., Handy, L. M. and Plesset, I. R. (1934). "Criminality and delinquency in twins." *J. Crim. Law Criminol.,* **24**, 923–934.

Rosenthal, D. (1962). "Problems of sampling and diagnosis in the major twin studies of schizophrenic twins." *J. Psychiat. Res.,* **2**, 116–134.

Siemens, H. W. (1924). *Die Zwillingpathologie, Ihre Bedeutung, ihre Methodik, ihre bisherigen Ergebnisse.* Berlin: Springer.

Stumpfl, F. (1936). *Die Ursprünge des Verbrechens, dargestellt am Lebenslauf von Zwillingen.* Leipzig: Thieme.

Tienari, P. (1963). "Psychiatric illness in idential twins." *Acta Psychiat. Scand.,* **39**, suppl. 171.

Yoshimasu, S. (1961). "The criminological significance of the family in the light of the studies of criminal twins." *Acta Criminol. Med. leg. jap.,* **27**, 117–141. Cited after *Excerpta Criminologica,* **2**, 723–724, 1962.

Zazzo, R. (1960). *Les Jumeaux, Le Couple et la Personne.* Paris: University of France Press.

The Causes of Crime:
Psychological Factors

THERE CAN BE LITTLE QUESTION THAT A LARGE SEGMENT OF ANY COMMUNITY strongly holds to the belief that, in some murky manner, criminals and delinquents are psychologically distinctive from law-abiding, conventional persons. In the past an appreciable proportion of professionals who deal with criminals have evinced similar ideas. The evidence that has been produced does not confirm such comforting beliefs. New, more carefully designed and carried out research does make some modest claims regarding psychological variations. In this section, intelligence, learning disabilities, extroversion and neuroticism, and "compulsive" masculinity, among others, are examined in so far as they may be associated with criminality.

Despite an imposing body of research, both current and past, regarding the crucial association of intelligence ("IQ") and delinquency, many (and perhaps most) sociologists sharply discount the importance of intelligence in preference for more "fashionable" variables. The selection by Hirschi and Hindelang places this issue within a historical perspective and indicate the several reasons why this neglect has, in fact, occurred.

The next selection is an analysis of the evidence as to whether or not learning disabilities, by resulting in decreased effectiveness of social rewards, may lead some children to engage in delinquency. Lieber and Sherin next investigate the romantic and ancient folk belief that lunar synodic cycles may cause human emotional disturbances. They find a pattern of lunar periodicity for homicides in Florida over a 15-year period, but admit no significant periodicity for parallel Ohio data. Testing Eysenck's theory that delinquents are more likely to be extroverted and neurotic than nonoffenders, Hindelang used a population of high school male students and found some evidence for an association between extroversion and delinquency, but no evidence linking neuroticism to delinquency.

Silverman and Dinitz examine the manner in which compulsive masculinity, race, and matriarchal family structures may be associated. They conclude that black delinquents rate themselves as more manly than white delinquents do, and that delinquents from female-based homes are more hypermasculine than delinquents from other types of households.

Tennenbaum, essentially updating earlier work by Schuessler and Cressey, and Waldo and Dinitz, find some psychological studies that differentiate criminal from noncriminal groups, as do several psychological instruments, particularly one scale of the MMPI and one scale of the CPI.

Does the continuous viewing of pornography cause some males to rape and others to engage in heterosexual or homosexual child molestation? In research initiated by the Presidential Commission on Obscenity and Pornography, Kant and Goldstein compare the exposure to erotic material in the backgrounds of sexual criminals and a group of nonsex offenders. They conclude that there are no serious grounds for assuming that contact with pornography leads to sex crimes.

30. Intelligence and Delinquency

TRAVIS HIRSCHI
MICHAEL J. HINDELANG

FEW GROUPS IN AMERICAN SOCIETY HAVE BEEN defended more diligently by sociologists against allegations of difference than ordinary delinquents. From the beginning, the thrust of sociological theory has been to deny the relevance of individual differences to an explanation of delinquency, and the thrust of sociological criticism has been to discount research findings apparently to the contrary. "Devastating" reviews of the research literature typically meet with uncritical acceptance or even applause, and new theories and "new criminologies" are constructed in a research vacuum, a vacuum that may itself claim research support.

A major source of this stance toward individual differences is the notion widely held in the field of deviance that "kinds of people" theories are non- or even antisociological. Most of the major theorists in the area (Sutherland, Merton, Cohen, Becker) have more or less explicitly argued this point, and efforts to bring criminology "up-to-date" with the rest of sociology frequently imply that interest in individual differences is an outmoded relic of the field's positivistic past (e.g., Matza, 1964; Taylor et al, 1973). Another source of this stance toward difference is frankly moral. According to Liazos (1972), who provides extensive documentation, sociologists repeatedly assert that deviants are "at least as good as anyone else." If Liazos'

▶SOURCE: *American Sociological Review, Vol. 42, No. 4, August 1977, pp. 571–587.*

analysis is any guide, we may assume it is easy to confuse the moral-evaluative "as good as" with the empirical "the same as." For example, Liazos goes on to argue that the repeated assertion that ' "deviants' are *not different* may raise the very doubts we want to dispel." Sociologists have observed for some time that, "always and everywhere, *difference* is the occasion and excuse for ignoring the equal claims of others" (Ross, 1901:25). They therefore feel duty-bound, it seems, to protect delinquents from those who would justify abusing them on these grounds.

Among the many possible individual differences between delinquents and non-delinquents, none is apparently more threatening to the integrity of the field and to its moral commitments than IQ. To the standard list of scientific and moral arguments against IQ, the sociological student of crime and delinquency can add the weight of a half-century struggle against biological theories, and the predatory social ethic they are alleged to foster. In fact, the single argument against IQ developed within criminology is sufficiently simple and persuasive that the standard list need not be invoked. At the time criminology became a subfield of sociology, marked differences in IQ between delinquents and nondelinquents were pretty much taken for granted, and a major task confronting those wishing to claim the field for the sociological perspective was to call these alleged differences into question. This task was successfully accomplished. IQ, it was confidently suggested, doesn't matter (see Sutherland, 1924:108). Today, textbooks in crime and delinquency ignore IQ or impatiently explain to the reader that IQ is no longer taken seriously by knowledgeable students simply because no differences worth considering have been revealed by research.

As we shall show, the textbooks are wrong.[1] IQ is an important correlate of delinquency. It is at least as important as social class or race. This fact has straightforward implications for sociological theorizing and research, most of which has taken place within the context of official denial of IQ differences. Its implications for social policy are variably straightforward and are, in any event, strictly irrelevant to questions of the current impact of IQ on delinquency: the actual relation between IQ and delinquency must be the standard against which all arguments, including our own, are judged.

THE CURRENT TEXTBOOK VIEW

Many textbooks do not even mention IQ (e.g., Gibbons, 1970; Bloch and Geis, 1962). Most, however, introduce the subject and then argue against its significance. The basic position is that there are no differences in IQ between delinquents and nondelinquents. The research and reviews most frequently cited in support of this conclusion are now over forty years old (e.g., Murchison, 1926; Sutherland, 1931; Zeleny, 1933). The tendency to rely on summaries provided by other textbooks, especially, in this case, those written by psychologists, is much in evidence.

Despite the selectivity of textbook summaries of the evidence, most of them leave the reader with the distinct impression that IQ may be a very important cause of delinquency after all. Few textbook writers seem able to resist additional arguments that have the effect of undercutting their basic position:

[1] In a more general treatment of the measurement and correlates of delinquency, Gordon (1976) independently reaches conclusions about the importance of IQ that are very close to those reported here.

"It is now generally recognized that so-called intelligence tests tend to measure the degree to which the individual has assimilated and internalized middle-class values rather than intelligence.

We could anticipate that a feeble-minded individual would be more readily incarcerated than other individuals." (Haskell and Yablonsky, 1974:216)

"It is not mental deficiency per se which results in crime; rather the inability of a mentally deficient person to make adequate social adjustments. ..." (Johnson, 1968:173)

"Although a higher percentage of delinquent children come from the ranks of the mental defective, particularly from those of borderline intelligence, it is not the mental deficiency per se but the inability of the child to make adequate school or social adjustments that usually results in delinquency." (Sutherland and Cressey, 1974:174, quoting Coleman, 1950)

"The great proportion of persons with low intelligence scores undoubtedly are nondeviants, whereas there are large numbers of persons with above normal intelligence who are."(Clinard, 1968:170)

All of these arguments take for granted a negative correlation between IQ and delinquency. The "middle-class values" interpretation of IQ tests suggests that scores of these tests may well be the strongest predictor of delinquency available. The "not per se" argument asserts that the relation is, in fact, causal in the usual meaning of the term—i.e., nonspurious. The "more readily incarcerated" view contradicts the "not per se" argument by suggesting a direct link between IQ and, at least, official delinquency. And the "great proportion" argument asserts only that the relation is not perfect. Still, the current view, simply stated, is that IQ makes no difference. This view is not supported by the results of research.

RECENT RESEARCH ON OFFICIAL DELINQUENCY

At least half a dozen recent studies permit examination of the effects of IQ on official delinquency. These studies have been conducted in diverse settings, they rely on a variety of measures of IQ and of delinquency, and they all employ some measure of control for the effects of such variables as social class and race. All of them show IQ to be an important predictor of official delinquency.[2]

How strong is this effect? Since social class and race are considered important correlates of official delinquency by almost everyone, they should provide a sufficiently stringent criterion and be available for comparison. Further, since both class and race are frequently used to discount the effects of IQ, this comparison will provide evidence relative to the common argument that IQ effects are merely a by-product of race and class effects.

IQ, SOCIAL CLASS AND OFFICIAL DELINQUENCY

Reiss and Rhodes (1961) examined the juvenile court records of more than 9,200 in-school *white* boys in Davidson County, Tennessee. Using three-category divisions on occupational status of the head of household and on IQ, they found that the rate (per 100) of court adjudication ranged from 5.7 in the high to 9.6 in the low status groups, and from 4.8 in the high to 10.3 in the low IQ groups. In other words, the rate of adjudication in the lowest occupational group was 1.7 times that of the highest occupational group, while the rate of the adjudication in the lowest IQ group was 2.1 times that of the highest IQ group.[3] Since the distributions of occupational status and IQ were roughly comparable, in the Davidson County data IQ is more important than social class as a predictor of official delinquency among white boys.

[2]Unless otherwise noted, all references to "the relation between IQ and delinquency" assume an inverse correlation.

[3]When father's occupational status was dichotomized and IQ trichotomized, the two variables were shown to have independent effects, with some tendency toward interaction: the effects of occupational status were more marked as IQ decreased, which also says that the effects of IQ were more marked for blue-collar than for white-collar boys.

Hirschi (1969) examined the police records of over 3,600 boys in Contra Costa County, California. Since previously published analyses do not directly compare the effects of social class and IQ, we have reanalyzed these data, with the results shown in Tables I and II (for details of data collection, see Hirschi, 1969:35–46).

In these data, the effect of IQ on official delinquency is stronger than that of father's education. Among whites, the gamma for the relationship between IQ and delinquency is −.31, while the comparable gamma for father's education is −.20; among blacks, the gammas are −.16 and −.05, respectively. Although the data are not shown, a composite measure of family status which includes employment and welfare status, presence of the father, and education and occupation of the parents shows results comparable to those for father's education in both racial categories. For whites, the gamma is −.18; for blacks, it is −.09. When the effects of this measure of family status and IQ are examined *simultaneously* within racial groups, the results are consistent with the zero-order relations. Both family status and IQ are independently related to official delinquency; the superiority of IQ in comparison with family status, however measured, is especially noticeable among blacks.

Wolfgang et al. (1972) obtained IQ scores on 8,700 of the 10,000 boys in their Philadelphia cohort. They do not present measures of associ-

Table I. Percent Committing Two or More Official Delinquent Acts by IQ (Stanford Binet) and Race[a]

	IQ				
	0-19	20-39	40-59	60-79	80-99
White males	22.6 (204)	25.6 (282)	14.6 (309)	8.4 (341)	6.2 (403)
Black males	38.2 (429)	36.2 (273)	26.2 (153)	19.7 (71)	19.0 (42)

[a] IQ scores are shown as percentiles. Gammas, calculated on the entire range of delinquency scores (0-4), are −.31 for whites and −.16 for blacks.

Table II. Percent Committing Two or More Official Delinquent Acts by Father's Education and Race[a]

Race	Father's Education				
	Less than High School Grad.	High School Graduate	Trade or Business	Some College	College graduate
White males	17.7 (356)	14.3 (485)	13.4 (82)	8.0 (201)	7.8 (306)
Black males	33.8 (343)	34.4 (209)	42.1 (57)	30.8 (123)	19.1 (84)

[a]Gammas, calculated on the entire range of delinquency scores (0-4), are −.20 for whites and −.05 for blacks.

ation for these IQ scores and delinquency, nor do they show tabular material in which IQ is treated as an independent variable. They do however, present average IQ scores by number of contacts with the police in groups homogeneous on class and race. The differences in average scores between chronic offenders and nondelinquents range from nine IQ points among high socioeconomic status nonwhites to fourteen IQ points among low socioeconomic status whites (Wolfgang et al., 1972:62, 93). Again, although no direct comparison with social class is possible, the Philadelphia data reveal a strong relation between IQ and delinquency independent of class.[4]

West (1973:84) followed 411 London boys over a ten-year period and "compared the delinquent and non-delinquent groups on the prevalence of low IQ in just the same way [he] compared them on other factors such as poverty, large families, or criminal parents." The relation between IQ and delinquency in West's data is substantial. While one-quarter of those with IQ scores of 110 or more had a police record, the same was true of one-half of those with IQ scores of 90 or less. Even more impressively, while only one in fifty boys with an IQ of 110 or more was a recidivist, one in five of those with an IQ of 90 or less fell in this category. West (1973:84–5) concludes from his thorough analysis that "low IQ was a significant precursor

[4]Wolfgang et al. used the Philadelphia Verbal Ability Test. The typical IQ test has a standard deviation of 15.

of delinquency to much the same extent as other major factors." Although he reports a stronger relation between family income and delinquency than that typically reported in American studies, IQ was able to compete with it on equal terms and to survive when family income and several other measures of family culture were controlled by a matching procedure.

It should be noted that the striking differences in delinquency produced by IQ in West's data reflect a difference in IQ of about 12 points between nondelinquents and recidivists—a difference that falls within the range of the race- and SES-specific differences calculated from the Wolfgang et al. data. West's data agree with those of Wolfgang et al. that the IQ effect is largely attributable to multiple offenders (recidivists), which may explain the relatively weak performance of IQ in studies of self-reported delinquency.

IQ, RACE AND OFFICIAL DELINQUENCY

Comparison of the effects of race and IQ is more difficult than the class-IQ comparison because of a greater paucity of data or, at least, of appropriately analyzed data. There can be no doubt that IQ is related to delinquency within race categories. All of the studies mentioned are consistent on this point. The relative strength of the two variables is, however, open to question.

The multiple regression analysis using number of offenses as the dependent variable presented by Wolfgang et al. (1972:275–9) includes both race and IQ. Unfortunately for present purposes, it also includes highest grade completed and number of school moves, variables which account for the bulk of the explained variance in this measure of delinquency. Thus, the fact that race places third behind these school variables and IQ accounts for virtually nothing cannot be taken as direct evidence of their relative importance. We know that IQ is strongly related to delinquency in the Wolfgang data independent of race. We know, too, that IQ is strongly related to the school variables ($r = .468$ for highest grade completed) that, in variance terms, do most of the work. Therefore, we know that if these intervening variables were excluded from the analysis, the proportion of variance accounted for by IQ would increase substantially.

In the Contra Costa data, IQ and race have virtually identical effects on official delinquency. For illustration, we compare a dichotomous measure of IQ with the two categories of race in Table III.

Measures of association between IQ and delinquency and between race and delinquency reflect the percentage differences in Table III: race and IQ are virtually identical in their ability to predict delinquency. For race, $r = .26$; for IQ, $r = .27$.

The findings of McCord and McCord (1959:66, 203) from the Cambridge-Sommerville Youth Study are sometimes cited (e.g., West, 1973:91) as showing "no connection between low IQ and delinquency." Although in the McCords' data those in the lowest IQ group (80 or below) did have an intermediate rate of conviction during the follow-up period,[5] within the normal range of IQ scores (above 80) there was a monotonic decrease in rates of conviction from almost one-half in the 81–90 IQ group to one-quarter in the 110 or more IQ group. Because those in the lowest IQ group are only ten percent of the sample, the McCords' data, too, show an inverse relation between IQ and official misconduct.

Such problems of interpretation do not arise in Short and Strodtbeck's (1965) study of gang delinquency in Chicago. They report that gang boys scored lower on "all six intelligence measures" than non-gang boys in the same (lower) class; this difference held for white and black respondents alike.

Toby and Toby (1961) found "intellectual status" to be a significant forerunner of delinquency independent of socioeconomic status. And Reckless and Dinitz (1972) found that their teacher-nominated "good" boys had IQs from 8 to 12 points higher than their teacher-nominated "bad" boys in a class-homogeneous area.[6]

All in all, it seems reasonable to conclude on the basis of currently available data that IQ is related to official delinquency and that, in fact, it is as important in predicting official delinquency as social class or race. We know of no current research findings contrary to this conclusion.

SELF-REPORTED DELINQUENCY

A significant consequence of the no-IQ-difference position was that it helped set the

Table III. Percent Committing Two or More Official Delinquent Acts by IQ and Race[a]

	IQ	
Race	Low	High
White males	24.3	9.4
	(486)	(1053)
Black males	37.6	23.3
	(702)	(266)

[a]IQ scores dichotomized at the 40th percentile.

[5]Our figures are for the experimental and control groups combined (McCord and McCord, 1959:66, 203). Strictly speaking, the McCord data apply to adult criminality as well as juvenile delinquency, since the average age of their subjects was 27 at the time data on convictions were obtained.

[6]The Toby-Toby and Reckless-Dinitz studies may be marginal to the question of IQ effects. However, this concern would carry greater weight if their results were contrary to research focusing directly on the IQ question.

stage for extensive use of self-report methods of measuring delinquent behavior. This position explicitly asserts that delinquents are as likely as others to possess the various skills reflected by IQ tests. If, however, the assumption of equal ability is unfounded, the measurement of delinquent behavior by the self-report method may be confounded with IQ, i.e., those most likely to commit delinquent acts may be least able to report adequately on their behavior. The self-report method, especially questionnaires,[7] therefore does not provide an unambiguous test of the hypothesis that IQ is related to delinquent behavior.

In any event, most studies do find a relation between IQ and self-reported delinquency, but this relation is less robust than that found in official data. At one extreme, West (1973:158) found that 28.4 percent of the worst quarter of his sample on self-reported delinquency had low IQs, as compared to 16.6 percent in the remaining three-quarters—a difference only slightly smaller than his finding for official delinquency.

Weis (1973), too, found differences as strong as those typically reported when delinquency is measured by official data. In his study in a white upper-middle-class community near San Francisco, Weis collected Wechsler-Bellevue IQ scores and self-reports of delinquency for 255 male and female eleventh-grade students. One of the clusters emerging from his analysis was a property deviance scale that included items on theft, burglary, shoplifting and vandalism. When these scores were trichotomized, Weis found that 27 percent of those with IQ scores of less than 110, and 49 percent of those with IQ scores of 110 or more, had low scores on the property deviance scale. He found a similar difference (23% versus 41%) on a social deviance scale that included items on marijuana, alcohol and gambling.[8]

More typical of self-report studies, however, are the relations from the Contra Costa data shown in Table IV. Among white males, twice the proportion in the lowest as in the highest IQ group report involvement in two or more of a possible six delinquent acts; among black males the comparable ratio is 3:2.

Whatever the strength of the relations in Table IV, we believe they should be evaluated by comparison with social class and race. As Table IV shows, race has no impact on self-reported delinquency—a finding consistent with much of the self-report literature (e.g., Williams and Gold, 1972). The same literature has consistently revealed a weaker relation of social class (e.g., Nye et al., 1958; Akers, 1964) to self-reported delinquency than that found in Table IV. The weight of the evidence is that IQ is more important than race and social class. The voluminous criticisms advanced against self-report delinquency research—with an eye to rescuing social class—presumably would have the same or even greater consequences for IQ. For example, the heavy reliance on in-school populations, the overabundance of minor offenders, and the dependence on subject cooperation may work to attenuate the relationship between social class and delinquency. If so, there is reason to believe that these factors would also depress the relation between self-reported delinquency and IQ. In fact, Hirschi (1969:46) reports that among those with the highest grades in English who had no police records, 79 percent cooper-

Table IV. Percent Committing Two or More Self-Reported Delinquent Acts by IQ and Race[a]

Race	Low IQ				High IQ
White males	24 (196)	26 (270)	20 (302)	19 (336)	12 (396)
Black males	27 (393)	26 (257)	19 (149)	19 (68)	18 (30)

[a]IQ scores are grouped in percentiles as in Table I. Gammas, calculated on the entire range of delinquency scores (0-6), are −.15 for whites and −.07 for blacks.

[7]Early warnings that the questionnaire method is especially limited by the high rates of illiteracy among delinquents (Erickson and Empey, 1963) have gone essentially unheeded.

[8]For details of data collection, see Weis (1973). The data reported in the text cannot be found in Weis' dissertation. We are grateful to him for making them available to us.

ated with the self-report survey, while among those with the lowest grades in English who had police records, only 38 percent cooperated. More importantly, not only did grades in English and official delinquency substantially affect cooperation with the self-report survey, the two factors were found to interact: low ability boys with police records were disproportionately unlikely to appear in the self-report sample. Since official delinquents are likely to be "self-report" delinquents (if sampled), the number of self-reported delinquents in the sample is considerably depressed, especially at the low end of the ability scale.

In short, however delinquency is measured, IQ is able to compete on at least equal terms with class and race, the major bases of most sociological theories of delinquency. At the same time, a relation between IQ and delinquency is routinely denied in sociological textbooks.

IMPLICATIONS FOR THEORY

Our original purpose in introducing theory was frankly argumentive: we expected to find theorists struggling with a conflict between their own logic and the erroneous "results of research" on IQ. In short, we expected to find that they had often been led astray by the anti-IQ climate of criminology.

Actual examination of currently influential theories required revision of our plans. In most cases, theorists were not paying all that much attention to the "results of research." *We* had been led astray by the naive textbook assumption that theory organizes research and research tests and modifies theory. In the case of IQ, however, it would be more accurate to say that theory opposes research and research ignores theory.

Theories from the period (Merton, 1938; Sutherland and Cressey, 1974) when most researchers considered low IQ a strong correlate of delinquency ignore this variable,[9] while theories from the period when IQ was almost universally considered irrelevant predict either very strong negative (Cohen, 1955) or weak but important positive relations (Cloward and Ohlin, 1960) with delinquency. And a theoretical tradition (labeling) spanning both periods has managed to take a position opposite to research in both of them. Although all of these theories have been heavily researched, investigators have paid little or no attention to their views regarding IQ.

Since it is difficult to argue with those who agree, we will briefly show that resistance to consideration or inclusion of IQ does not characterize any current theory; that, on the contrary, several important theories require a relation between IQ and delinquency. Explicit recognition of this fact would only increase their scope, the plausibility of their claims, and their consistency with research findings.

The best example is Cohen's (1955) effort to relate social class to delinquency by way of differential experience in the educational system. In Cohen's theory, children differentially prepared or qualified encounter a school system that treats all comers alike. Children inadequately "prepared" for success in school find the experience painful and are likely, as a consequence, to turn to delinquency. The place of IQ in this process would seem obvious and, in fact, Cohen (1955:102–3) could not be more explicit on this question:

"It may be taken as established that ability, as measured by performance in conventional tests of intelligence, varies directly with social class. . . . The conventional tests do test for abilities that are highly prized by middle-class people, that are fostered by middle-class socialization, and that are especially important for further achievement in the academic world and in middle-class society. In short, *the results of these tests are one important index of the ability of the child to meet middle-class expectations,* to do the kinds of things that bring rewards in the middle-class world." (emphasis added)

In Cohen's theory, intelligence intervenes between social class and delinquency or it is at least an important indicator of the social class of the

---

[9]The Gluecks reported periodically throughout the thirties that their delinquents were "burdened with feeblemindedness" (e.g., Glueck and Glueck, 1934).

child. In either case, IQ should be more strongly related to delinquency than such indirect measures of the ability of the child to meet middle-class expectations as *"father's* occupation."

Cohen's views on the interchangeability of IQ and class illustrate how the former could have been used to extend the scope of his theory beyond the confines of "lower-class delinquency." The situation facing the middle-class child with low IQ may not be all that different from the situation facing the lower-class child and, if such a situation explains the delinquency of one of them, it may explain the delinquency of the other as well. If both lower and middle-class delinquency can be explained by the same mechanism, Cohen's reliance on a separate mechanism for middle-class boys (Cohen, 1955:162–9) is inexplicable or is, at the very least, theoretically and empirically inelegant.

If a zero relation between IQ and delinquency would falsify Cohen's theory, it would virtually falsify the theory of Cloward and Ohlin (1960) as well, but for quite different reasons. Cloward and Ohlin (1960:111) suggest a positive relation between intelligence and delinquency:

"Some persons who have experienced a marked discrepancy between aspirations and achievements may look outward, attributing their failure to the existence of unjust or arbitrary institutional arrangements which keep men of ability and ambition from rising in the social structure. Such persons do not view their failure as a reflection of personal inadequacy but instead blame a cultural and social system that encourages everyone to reach for success-goals. In contrast to this group there are individuals who attribute failure to their own inadequacies—to a lack of discipline, zeal, intelligence, persistence, or other personal quality."

In other words, the lower-class boy with a high IQ whose talents go unrecognized and unrewarded is a prime candidate for delinquency.

On the basis of available evidence, Cloward and Ohlin are wrong. For present purposes, however, the point is that their theory requires research on the IQ of juvenile offenders and is

enduring testimony to the dangers in the view that IQ need be "no longer seriously considered" by criminologists.[10]

At first glance, labeling theory would seem to be an exception to our argument that IQ is important, since this theory puts no stock in the notion that individual differences may act as causes of delinquent behavior. In one of the first efforts by a labeling theorist to neutralize individual difference research, Tannenbaum (1938:6) focused special attention on IQ, arguing that "whatever 'intelligence' is, it has no demonstrated relationship to crime." As labeling theory has "progressed," however, as it has become more closely associated with the conflict perspective according to which "society organizes itself for the protection of the ruling classes against the socially inferior" (Doleschal and Klapmuts, 1973:622), it has tended more and more to recognize that it too is dependent on individual differences. The generally low IQ of official delinquents is now accepted by labeling theorists and is used as evidence *for* their view that the system discriminates against or creates the disadvantaged (Doleschal and Klapmuts, 1973:612, 616; Polk and Schafer, 1972:34–54).

If labeling theorists argue that discrimination produces the relation between IQ and delinquency, then the mechanism that connects IQ to delinquency is the bone of contention between labeling and conventional theories —not the fact of a relation itself. We will return to the mechanism question.

Perhaps the only major theory strictly silent on the question of IQ is Sutherland's "differential association" (Sutherland and Cressey, 1974:75–7). Sutherland (1931) played a major role in constructing the current position of criminology on IQ. He rejoiced in its alleged failure to discriminate between delinquents and nondelinquents, and his influential text con-

---

[10]Although Merton (1938) ignores IQ and its "success" implications, IQ is obviously relevant to any opportunity theory.

tinues to belittle "mental testers" to the present day. Even so, differential association has nothing to fear from intelligence. This theory faintly suggests a positive association among those exposed to the delinquent culture (as does any theory that emphasizes the need to learn crime), but it really cannot be used to predict even the sign of the relation in the general population. If the theory cannot predict the sign of this relation, it is, nonetheless, capable of accounting for any relation between IQ and delinquency that might be revealed by research.

A final set of theories might be grouped under the heading of "social control" (for a convenient summary, see Nettler, 1974). These theories focus on a broad range of causal variables, and they are relatively open to individual differences, to the idea that "in learning to conduct ourselves, some of us need more lessons that others" (Nettler, 1974:232). Although none of them may now consider IQ of central importance, most suggest a negative association, and none would have difficulty absorbing this variable. In fact, for those sociologically-oriented control theories that emphasize "stakes in conformity" (e.g., Toby, 1957), IQ is of obvious importance.

Most sociological theories, then, have been saying for some time that IQ should be related to delinquency for the same reason that social class is, or should be related to it. Given the theoretical overlap of IQ and social class, the contrast in how the research community has reacted to their varying fates would be hard for an outsider to understand.

The finding that social class was unrelated to self-reported delinquency produced a large volume of follow-up reasearch. The "finding" that IQ was unrelated to any measure of delinquency was, in contrast, accepted without so much as a murmur of protest. The literature on IQ contains none of the "what may have gone wrong" kinds of methodological critiques so often encountered in efforts to save social class. Instead, it is marked by considerable speculative ingenuity directed against an established relation.

The extent to which this relation has been established may be revealed by a review of the history of IQ testing as it applies to delinquency and crime.

HISTORY

As a cause of delinquency, IQ got off to a very strong start in the first years of this century. The notion that "imbeciles" and "idiots" would be unable to resist criminal impulses or, for that matter, even to distinquish right from wrong, was a straightforward extension of Lombroso's then prestigious theory of the born or biologically defective criminal. Initial research did nothing to dampen enthusiasm for this idea. Goring (1972:255) in Great Britain reported that criminals "as a class, are highly differentiated mentally from the law abiding classes," and Goddard (1914:7) in the United States concluded that "probably from 25% to 50% of the people in our prisons are mentally defective and incapable of managing their affairs with ordinary prudence." In the period 1910–1914, the "percentage feebleminded" in fifty studies of institutionalized delinquents had a median value of 51 (Sutherland, 1931:358). Since it was then assumed that the proportion feebleminded in the general population was less than one percent (Goring used an estimate of .46 percent), the conclusion that faulty intelligence was the "single most important cause of crime" followed, or at least seemed to follow directly from the evidence.

If we follow the fate of IQ through mainstream criminology, we discover that its day was very brief. Less than two decades after Goring estimated .6553 as a "minimum value" for the correlation between mental defectiveness and crime, Sutherland (1931) was poking fun at the absurdities of the "mental testers."[11]

[11]Sutherland summarized about 350 studies conducted between 1910 and 1928 noting downward trends in the proportion feebleminded in delinquent and criminal groups, as well as inconsistencies in the results. "In those early days of mental testing the influence of Goddard was very great; he had

His negative review of their research was so influential that the "modern" or "recent" position on IQ described by today's textbooks appears to have been firmly established at that time, i.e., forty-five years ago.

Sutherland's stance is not difficult to understand. As Savitz (1972:xviii) has reminded us, the medical profession seized power in criminology before the end of the nineteenth century and still maintained a preeminent position in the early days of intelligence testing—both Goring and Goddard were physicians. A short time later, however, criminology had become a subfield of sociology. Given this shift in disciplinary dominance, an equivalent paradigm shift is now pretty much accepted as a logical necessity. "Intelligence" was a central element of the "old" paradigm. It just had to go. And go it did.

The history of IQ in research findings is not so quickly or easily told. The initial claims about the proportion of feebleminded delinquents were excessively high because—as Merrill (1947:159) has pointed out—researchers were basing their cutting point on children in institutions for the mentally deficient. The logic of this procedure went something like this: if no child in an institution for the feebleminded has a mental age in excess of twelve, then a mental age of twelve or less is sufficient to classify a person feebleminded. There was nothing especially silly about this procedure, it merely made the mistake of assuming that the same procedure would not also classify a large portion of the general population feebleminded. As it became appa-

---

asserted that the more expert the mental tester the larger the proportion of delinquents he would find to be feebleminded. Many of the testers attempted to demonstrate their superiority in that manner." "Consequently a report regarding the proportion of a delinquent group feebleminded is of primary significance in locating the mental tester upon a scale of mental testing methods. In this sense the psychometric tests of delinquents throw more light upon the intelligence of the mental testers than upon the intelligence of delinquents." (Sutherland, 1931:358–62).

rent that a too-large portion of the general population would be classified feebleminded, the mental age requirement was first abruptly and then gradually lowered, with the result that the proportion feebleminded among delinquents also first abruptly and then gradually declined. Sutherland (1931) called attention to this twenty-year trend—which, in fact, continued for another 30 years (Woodward, 1955; Caplan, 1965)—and allowed his readers to conclude that it would continue until the initial claims of difference between delinquents and nondelinquents had no foundation in fact.

The most direct evidence against an IQ difference resulted from the extensive testing of the draft army in World War I. Murchison (1926) and Tulchin (1939) reported that the distribution of intelligence in the draft army was virtually identical to the distribution among adult prisoners. Without including details of the investigation, Murchison also reported that the prisoners in a certain midwestern institution were more intelligent than the guards, an anecdotal fact even now more widely quoted than the results of many carefully conducted studies showing important differences in favor of the intelligence hypothesis. Although Sutherland (1931:364) acknowledged that "serious questions have been raised regarding the validity of these tests and the validity of using the draft army as a sample of the general population," he carefully noted that "the consistency in results is a fact that cannot be overlooked."

By the late 1920s and early 1930s, the evidence was sufficiently mixed that summaries of the research literature were arriving at variant conclusions. Thomas and Thomas (1928:365) concluded from their review of the same literature examined by Sutherland that important differences between delinquents and nondelinquents on IQ were "beyond question." They reached this conclusion by focusing on the many studies reporting such differences and by discounting the draft-army research as being so clearly out of line as to be suspect. In 1935,

Chassell published an extensive review of research on this question. Her general conclusion, based on nearly 300 studies:

"Undoubtedly the relation between morality and intellect in the general population is considerably higher than usually found in restricted groups. Nevertheless, it is hardly probable that this relation is high. Expressed in correlational terms, the relation in the general population may therefore be expected to fall below .70" (Chassell, 1935:470)[12]

As IQ tests improved, the average score of samples of delinquents also improved until, with the advent of the Revised Stanford Binet and the Wechsler-Bellevue scales in the late 1930s, they were obtaining an average IQ of about 92 (Merrill, 1947; Woodward, 1955; Caplan, 1965). With the advent of these improved tests about 35 years ago, the marked trends and occasional fluctuations of earlier research apparently came to an end. Since that time, it has been reasonable to expect that samples of delinquents would differ from the general population by about eight IQ points. This conclusion has been accepted by Woodward (1955) and Caplan (1965) in major reviews of the literature and is generally consistent with the more recent research reviewed in this paper.

The question, then, is how a reliable eight IQ point difference was converted to the no-difference conclusion of the textbooks. One possibility is that an eight IQ point difference was not seen as theoretically or practically important. This possibility is easily disputed: no modern reviewer has questioned the importance of a difference of this magnitude.[13] As-suming that ten percent of the population is delinquent, this difference would produce a correlation (Yule's Q) between IQ and delinquency of about $-.4$.

The neglect of IQ after a reliable and important difference had been established may be traced to the initial plausibility of an unusual number of counter-arguments. These arguments are so numerous and diverse that we can hope to deal with them only generally and briefly.

THE SPURIOUSNESS ARGUMENT

Scholarly reviews of the literature have made such of the hypothesis that the low IQs of delinquents are a spurious consequence of differences in class or culture. Against the estimated eight IQ point difference between delinquents and nondelinquents, Woodward (1955) assembles a good deal of material suggesting the possibility that cultural factors are at work: the children of professionals differ from those of unskilled manual workers by about 20 IQ points; average IQ scores are low in *areas* with high delinquency rates;[14] children in large families have low IQ scores and are more likely to be delinquent; overcrowding is related both to low IQ and delinquency; finally, studies based on sib-sib comparisons (such as Healy and Bronner, 1936) and on other methods of control for cultural factors "tend to support the contention that complete control *would* eliminate the difference between delinquents and nondelinquents" (Woodward, 1955:289; emphasis added).[15] As

---

[12]Present-day researchers would not be so modest about a correlation of .70! Chassell's caution may be indicative of the standards against which empirical relations were judged in the early days of quantitative research. These standards may account for the ease with which reviewers were able to reject IQ as a "significant" causal variable (see also footnote 1).

[13]Caplan (1965:104) refers to this eight-point difference as a "first class" relationship. As noted below, however, he cautions the reader that cultural factors be taken into account before it is accepted as genuine.

[14]This is an example of what might be called the reverse ecological fallacy: because IQ and delinquency are related at the ecological level, it is *unlikely* that they are related at the individual level.

[15]Healy and Bronner (1936) controlled cultural factors by matching 105 delinquents with their same sex, nondelinquent sib nearest in age and then comparing IQ test scores. Although they found an IQ difference in favor of the nondelinquents, this difference was not statistically significant and was not interpreted as practically or theoretically sig-

we have seen, the evidence says otherwise. Differences by class and race do not account for IQ differences between delinquents and nondelinquents. These differences remain pronounced within groups homogeneous on these variables. If there exists a cultural correlate on both IQ and delinquency strong enough to account for the relation between them, it has not yet been identified.

Ten years after Woodward's influential review (see Wootten, 1959:302), Caplan (1965) was unable to find additional research material bearing directly on her cultural hypothesis. His conclusions about the effects on IQ are, however, if anything, more skeptical than Woodward's, because he is able to cite an additional source of concern.

ARGUMENTS FOCUSING ON THE MEASUREMENT OF DELINQUENCY

The advent of the self-report method helped Caplan (1965:120-1) call into question the measures of delinquency upon which the original findings of IQ differences were based. Once again, the evidence against IQ was inferential rather than direct: if official data measure delinquency imperfectly, then imperfections in measurement rather than the phenomenon itself may account for the observed relation. And,

---

nificant by them. (Thirty-four percent of the delinquents and 26 percent of the nondelinquents had IQs under 90.)

The difficulty with this widely cited study (e.g., Wootton, 1959) is that its design makes the outcome a statistical necessity. Pushing the logic of Healy and Bronner's matching procedure one step further, we would compare identical twins raised together, only one of whom was delinquent. Since the correlation between the IQs of identical twins raised together is about .87, a figure "nearly as high . . . the correlation between two parallel tests for the same individual" (Eckland, 1967:177), we would be asking whether errors in IQ measurement are related to delinquency. By the same token, knowing that the "control" is a brother or sister reared in the same household tells us a good deal about what to expect in the way of IQ (in most studies the sib-sib correlation is in the neighborhood of .55), and there is little reason to expect the original relation to survive with anything like its "natural" magnitude.

indeed, few have been able to resist ascribing IQ differences between officially identified delinquents and nondelinquents to the ability of the bright delinquent to avoid detection or to differential response of officials to high and low IQ adolescents (e.g., Sutherland, 1931; Doleschal and Klapmuts, 1973; Stark, 1975).

Both the differential detection and differential reaction hypotheses require that IQ have a direct or independent effect on official delinquency.[16] Such direct effect hypotheses compete with intervening variable hypotheses and may be directly tested when the latter are available. A competing hypothesis widely mentioned in the literature (e.g., Short and Strodtbeck, 1965:238; West, 1973:44) is that IQ affects delinquency through school performance. If IQ has the direct effect suggested by the differential detection and reaction hypotheses, nothing consequent to IQ can explain the zero order relation. Two studies bear on this question. When Wolfgang et al. removed by statistical adjustment the effects of such intervening variables as highest grade completed, the relation between IQ and such "detection" measures as number of offenses virtually vanished (Wolfgang et al., 1972:275–9). (We have replicated this finding with the Contra Costa County data.) Taking a somewhat different approach, West (1973:217) also was able to reduce the relation between IQ and official delinquency below the significant level by matching on peer and teacher ratings on "troublesomeness." These ratings were made at ages eight and ten, well before the delinquent acts recorded by officials. Once again, then, *the differential ability to avoid detection and the differential official reaction on the basis of IQ arguments are not supported by available evidence.* (The tests of the official reaction hypothesis are limited by available data to reactions by the police.)

Tests of these and related direct effect

---

[16]Contrary to the "intelligence per se is not a cause . . ." arguments with which it is often paired, the differential detection argument suggests that, in fact, intelligence per se *is* a cause of delinquency—when delinquency is measured by official records.

hypotheses[17] at the same time identify the mechanism linking IQ to delinquency. This mechanism, the data suggest, is performance in and attitudes toward the school. That school variables are strong enough to account for the impact of IQ should come as no surprise. Their significance for delinquency is nowhere in dispute and is, in fact, one of the oldest and most consistent findings of delinquency research (e.g., Thrasher, 1963; Gold, 1970; Hindelang, 1973; Weis, 1973). What should come as a surprise is the easy acceptance of the no-difference-on-IQ conclusion, since the consequences of IQ differences are generally accepted as major predictors of delinquency. This brings us to the most troublesome of the arguments against IQ effects.

ARGUMENTS FOCUSING ON THE MEASUREMENT OR MEANING OF IQ

The facts we have presented compete with a wide variety of counter-arguments that focus on the meaning or measurement of IQ: "anybody can learn anything" (Eckland, 1967:174–5, quoting Faris, 1961:838), "it is impossible to make intelligence part of any respectable theory" (ASR referee, 1975), "so-called intelligence tests measure only 'test intelligence' and not innate intelligence" (Clinard, 1968:170), and "mainly they [IQ tests] measure the socioeconomic status of the respondent" (Chambliss and Ryther, 1975:373). Excellent discussions of many of these issues are available in the sociological literature (Eckland, 1967; Gordon, 1975). We will deal only with those counter-hypotheses that have a direct bearing on the relation between IQ and delinquency and

that can be addressed to some extent using data already presented.

The Cultural Bias of IQ Tests
The argument against IQ tests most frequently encountered in the sociological literature is that these tests are biased against low-income and minority group children. Specific test items (e.g., "What color are rubies?") are often presented to show the obviousness of this bias (Chambliss and Ryther, 1975:373). Since the groups said to be discriminated against by IQ tests are the same groups with high rates of delinquency, the cultural bias hypothesis is certainly plausible. In form, it is identical to the traditional cultural hypothesis previously encountered and may be tested using the same data. These data show that the bias hypothesis is inadequate: important differences in IQ between delinquents and nondelinquents *within* race and class categories cannot be explained by argument or evidence that these tests are biased in favor of middle-class whites.

The Stability of Test Scores
To the extent that IQ test scores are unstable and subject to subtle social influence; the meaning of a correlation between IQ and delinquency is open to question. It may be that reaction to the misbehavior of the child influences his IQ, that the low IQ child today may be the high IQ child tomorrow, and so on. These possibilities are summarized in assertions that "the scores are highly unstable through time" (Polk and Schafer, 1972:195). Unfortunately for such assertions, they are not consistent with the evidence: the IQs of children at four or five years of age have a correlation of about .7 with their IQs at age 17 (Bloom, 1964); after age ten, test-retest correlations (regardless of the number of years between the tests) fall between the test's reliability and the square of its reliability (Jensen, 1969:18). For that matter, the ability of IQ tests to predict delinquency at some period far removed from their administration is inconsis-

---

[17]Other very old direct effect hypotheses are that IQ differences stem from (1) the inability of the unintelligent to understand distinctions between right and wrong or (2) their inability to foresee and appreciate the consequences of their acts. These hypotheses assume that low IQ children are more likely to be delinquent, regardless of the social consequences (e.g., school difficulties) of their lack of IQ. Again, current data do not appear to support hypotheses of this form.

tent with the gross implications of the instability argument.

A fall-back position for those who would argue instability is that these scores *could be* manipulated by simple and straightforward shifts in the environment of the child:

"We may treat people differently out of ignorance or prejudice, but the result is the same as if the supposed differences were real. Studies have shown that school children seen as liable to be educationally backward become educationally backward and that, vice versa, children seen as educationally capable become educationally capable." (Taylor et al., 1973:142; see also Polk and Schafer, 1972:46; Schur, 1973:164)

The study cited in support of such arguments is Rosenthal and Jacobson, *Pygmalion in the Classroom* (1968). In this study, students in grades K through 5 in one elementary school were given group-administered IQ tests at the end of the 1964 academic year. The following fall, a random 20 percent of the students were identified to their teachers as students expected to show unusual intellectual gains during the academic year. In May, 1964, all students were re-tested on the same IQ test. Although both the experimental and the control subjects showed IQ gains, the experimental and control subjects showed a 3.8 point greater gain, with the bulk of this gain coming in the first and second grades. On the basis of these results, Rosenthal and Jacobson (1968:98) conclude that favorable expectations of teachers "can be responsible for gains in their pupils' IQ's and, for the lower grades, that these gains can be quite dramatic."

Unfortunately, *Pygmalion* has problems. Snow (1969:197) asserts that the study "stands as a casebook example of many of Darrell Huff's *(How to Lie with Statistics)* admonitions to data analysis" and that it "fails to come close to providing an adequate demonstration of the phenomenon" (the effects of teacher expectations on IQ scores). Thorndike (1968:708) begins his similarly negative review with what has turned out to be a prophetic statement:

"In spite of anything I can say, I am sure it *(Pygmalion in the Classroom)* will become a classic—widely referred to and rarely examined critically. Alas, it is so

defective technically that one can only regret that it ever got beyond the eyes of the original investigators!"

Thorndike concludes that "the basic data . . . are so untrustworthy that any conclusions based upon them must be suspect." And, indeed, this too was prophetic. Elashoff and Snow (1971) report that *none of nine attempts to replicate the effects of teacher expectations on IQ scores has been successful.* One would think that this would be enough to put an end to the "Rosenthal effect." However, Beeghley and Butler (1974:750) still maintain that the effects of teacher expectations on IQ "have been forcefully demonstrated by Rosenthal and Jacobson," and they muddy the waters by citing two "replications" of *Pygmalion.* In the first, "changes in intellectual functioning were not expected" by the investigators themselves (Meichenbaum et al., 1969:307) and in fact, as far as we can determine, IQ was not even a variable in the study. In the second, the author summarizes a variety of research results and concludes the findings do not "provide any direct proof that teacher expectations can influence pupil performance" (Pidgeon, 1970:126). Ironically—for a study which Beeghley and Butler purport to be a replication of *Pygmalion*—Pidgeon (1970:126) notes that the Rosenthal and Jacobson study "would bear repetition, providing conditions could be found for employing a more satisfactory research design." As of now, it is clear that no labeling or expectation effects of the sort alleged by Rosenthal and Jacobson (and widely cited in the crime and delinquency literature) have been established.

CONCLUSIONS

The assertion that IQ affects the likelihood of delinquent behavior through its effect on school performance is consistent with available data. The corollary descriptive assertion that delinquents have lower IQs than nondelinquents is firmly established. Both of these assertions are inconsistent with the "no-IQ-difference" view of the textbooks. They are clearly inconsistent with the image of the delinquent in much sociological writing on the subject, and those planning prevention and treatment programs would do well to take them into account.[18]

Interestingly enough, most modern theories of delinquency assume (and some explicitly state) that IQ affects delinquency. That their views have been ignored by researchers testing them speaks to the depth of the concern that individual differences are both non-sociological and positively dangerous. In this sense, IQ is doubly significant in that it represents an entire class of variables traditionally ignored by sociological students of crime and delinquency. Variables in this large residual category (virtually everything beyond class culture, and official processing) will not lose their status as alternative hypotheses simply by being ignored, and they will continue to restrict and even embarrass sociological theory until some effort is made to incorporate them.

For that matter, IQ is a poor example of a variable that may require modification of sociological perspectives. As of now, there is no evidence that IQ has a direct impact on delinquency. The police bias, differential ability to avoid detection, and inability to appreciate moral distinctions hypotheses are not consistent with current data. If the mechanism linking IQ to delinquency is school performance and adjustment, then IQ does not lead away from the arena in which sociological theories have focused their quest for the antecedents of delinquency; rather, it helps illuminate the social processes occuring there.

REFERENCES

Akers, Ronald L.
1964   "Socio-economic status and delinquent behavior: a retest." Journal on Crime and Delinquency 1:38–46.

[18]See Nettler (1974:162–5). The range of treatment programs affected by these differences is considerably broader than is usually imagined: "The frequent mental dullness . . . and reading and writing disabilities of a larger proportion of delinquents *make them poor risks for industrial training*" (Shulman, 1951:781, emphasis added).

Beeghley, Leonard and Edgar W. Butler
1974   "The consequences of intelligence testing in public schools before and after desegregation." Social Problems 21:740–54.

Bloch, Herbert A. and Gilbert Geis
1962   Man, Crime and Society. New York: Random House.

Bloom, B.A.
1964   Stability and Change in Human Characteristics. New York: Wiley.

Caplan, Nathan S.
1965   "Intellectual functioning" Pp. 100–38 in Herbert C. Quay (ed.), Juvenile Delinquency. Princeton: Van Nostrand.

Chambliss, William J. and Thomas E. Ryther
1975   Sociology: The Discipline and Its Direction. New York: McGraw-Hill.

Chassell, Clara F.
1935   The Relation between Morality and Intellect. New York: Teachers College, Columbia University.

Clinard, Marshall B.
1968   Sociology of Deviant Behavior. New York: Holt, Rinehart and Winston.

Cloward, Richard E. and Lloyd E. Ohlin
1960   Delinquency and Opportunity. New York: Free Press.

Cohen, Albert K.
1955   Delinquent Boys: The Culture of the Gang. New York: Free Press.

Coleman, James C.
1950   Abnormal Psychology and Modern Life, Glenview, Il.: Scott, Foresman.

Doleschal, Eugene and Nora Klapmuts
1973   "Toward a new criminology." Crime and Delinquency Literature: 607–26.

Eckland, Bruce K.
1967   "Genetics and sociology: a reconsideration." American Sociological Review 32:193–4.

Elashoff, J. and R. Snow
1971   *Pygmalion* Reconsidered. Worthington, Oh.: Jones.

Erickson, Maynard L. and La Mar T. Empey
1963   "Court records, undetected delinquency and decision-making." Journal of Criminal Law, Criminology and Police Science 54:456–69.

Faris, Robert E. L.
1961   "The ability dimension in human society." American Sociological Review 26:835–43.

Gibbons, Don C.
1970   Delinquent Behavior. Englewood Cliffs, N.J.: Prentice-Hall.

Glueck, Sheldon and Eleanor Glueck
1934   Five Hundred Delinquent Women. New York: Knopf.

Goddard, Henry H.
1914   Feeble-Mindedness: Its Causes and Consequences. New York: Macmillan.

Gold, Martin
1970   Delinquent Behavior in an American City. Belmont, Ca.: Brooks/Cole.

Gordon, Robert A.
1975   "Examining labeling theory: the case of mental retardation." Pp, 83–146 in Walter Gove (ed.), The Labelling of Deviance. New York: Wiley.
1976   "Prevalence: the rare datum in delinquency measurement and its implications for the theory of delinquency." Pp. 201–84 in Malcolm W. Klein (ed.), The Juvenile Justice System. Beverly Hills, Ca.: Sage.

Goring, Charles
[1913] The English Convict. Montclair, N.J.:
1972   Paterson Smith.

Haskell, Martin R. and Lewis Yablonsky
1974   Crime and Delinquency. Chicago: Rand McNally.

Healy, William and Augusta F. Bronner
1936   New Light on Delinquency and Its Treatment. New Haven: Yale University Press.

Hindelang, Michael J.
1973   "Causes of delinquency: a partial replication and extention." Social Problems 20:471–87.

Hirschi, Travis
1969   Causes of Delinquency. Berkeley: University of California Press.

Jensen, A. R.
1969   "How much can we boost I.Q. and scholastic achievement?" Harvard Educational Review 39:1–123.

Johnson, Elmer
1968   Crime, Correction and Society. Homewood, Il.: Dorsey Press.

Liazos, Alexander
1972   "The poverty of the sociology of deviance: nuts, sluts, and perverts." Social Problems 20:103–20.

McCord, William and Joan McCord
1959   Origins of Crime: A New Evaluation of the Cambridge-Somerville Study. New York: Columbia Press.

Matza, David
1964   Delinquency and Drift. New York: Wiley.

Meichanbaum, Donald H., Kenneth S. Bowers and Robert R. Ross
1969   "A behavioral analysis of teacher expectancy effect." Journal of Personality and Social Psychology 13:306–16.

Merrill, Maud A.
1947   Problems of Child Delinquency. Boston: Houghton Mifflin.

Merton, Robert K.
1938   "Social structure and anomie." American Sociological Review 3:672–16.

Murchison, Carl
1926   Criminal Intelligence. Worcester, Ma.: Clark University Press.

Nettler, Gwynn
1974   Explaining Crime. New York: McGraw-Hill.

Nye, F. Ivan, James F. Short, Jr. and Virgil J. Olson
1958   "Socio-economic status and delinquent behavior." American Journal of Sociology 63:381–9.

Pidgeon, Douglas
1970   Expectation and Pupil Performance. London: National Foundation for Educational Research in England and Wales.

Polk, Kenneth and Walter E. Schafer
1972   Schools and Delinquency. Englewood Cliffs, N.J.: Prentice-Hall.

Reckless, Walter C. and Simon Dinitz
1972   The Prevention of Delinquency. Columbus: Ohio State University Press.

Reiss, Albert J. and Albert L. Rhodes
1961 "The distribution of juvenile delinquency in the social class structure." American Sociological Review 26:720–32.

Rosenthal, R. and Lenore Jacobson
1968 Pygmalion in the Classroom. New York: Holt, Rinehart and Winston.

Ross, Edward A.
1901 Social Control. New York: Macmillan.

Savitz, Leonard D.
1972 "Introduction." Pp. v–xx in Gina Lombroso-Ferrero, Criminal Man. Montclair, N.J.: Patterson Smith.

Schur, Edwin M.
1973 Radical Non-Intervention: Rethinking the Delinquency Problem. Englewood Cliffs, N.J.: Prentice-Hall.

Short, James F., Jr. and Fred L. Strodtbeck
1965 Group Process and Gang Delinquency. Chicago: University of Chicago Press.

Shulman, Harry M.
1951 "Intelligence and delinquency." Journal of Criminal Law and Criminology 41:763–81.

Snow, R.
1969 "Unfinished Pygmalion." Contemporary Psychology 14:197–9.

Stark, Rodney
1975 Social Problems. New York: CRM/Random House.

Sutherland, Edwin H.
1924 Criminology. Philadelphia: Lippincott.
1931 "Mental deficiency and crime," Pp. 357–75 in Kimball Young (ed.), Social Attitudes. New York: Holt, Rinehart and Winston.

Sutherland, Edwin H. and Donald R. Cressey
[1939] Principles of Criminology. Philadelphia:
1974 Lippencott.

Tannenbaum, Frank
1938 Crime and the Community. Boston: Ginn.

Taylor, Ian, Paul Walton and Jock Young
1973 The New Criminology. New York: Harper.

Thomas, William I. and Dorothy Swaine Thomas
1928 The Child in America. New York: Knopf.

Thorndike, R. L.
1968 "Review of R. Rosenthal and L. Jacobson, 'Pygmalion in the Classroom.'" American Educational Research Journal 5:708–11.

Thrasher, F.
[1927] The Gang. Chicago: University of Chicago
1963 press.

Toby, Jackson
1957 "Social disorganization and stake in conformity: complementary factors in the predatory behavior of hoodlums." Journal of Criminal Law, Criminology and Police Science 48:12–7.

Toby, Jackson and Marcia L. Toby
1961 Low School Status as a Predisposing Factor in Subcultural Delinquency. New Brunswick, N.J.: Rutgers University. Mimeo.

Tulchin, Simon H.
1939 Intelligence and Crime. Chicago: University of Chicago Press.

Weis, Joseph
1973 Delinquency among the Well-to-Do. Unpublished dissertation. University of California, Berkeley.

West, D. J.
1973 Who Becomes Delinquent? London: Heinemann.

Williams, Jay and Martin Gold
1972 "From delinquent behavior to official delinquency." Social Problems 20:209–29.

Wolfgang, Marvin, Robert M. Figlio and Thorsten Sellin
1972 Delinquency as a Birth Cohort. Chicago: University of Chicago Press.

Woodward, Mary
1955 "The role of low intelligence in delinquency." British Journal of Delinquency 5:281–303.

Wootton, Barbara
1959 Social Science and Social Pathology. New York: Macmillan.

Zeleny, Leslie D.
1933 "Feeblemindedness and criminal conduct." American Journal of Sociology 38:564–78.

31. Learning Disabilities and Juvenile Delinquency

CHARLES A. MURRAY

CONCEPTUALLY, WE SHALL APPLY A RECENT FORmulation reached collaboratively by several leading authorities in the LD field: a learning disability will be used to refer to "those children of any age who demonstrate a *substantial deficiency in a particular aspect of academic achievement because of perceptual or perceptual-motor handicaps, regardless of etiology or other contribution factors.*" (Wepman et al., 1975, p. 306. Emphasis added).[1]

▶SOURCE: *The Link Between Learning Disabilities and Juvenile Delinquency. Washington D.C.: National Institute of Juvenile Justice and Delinquency Prevention Law Enforcement Assistance Administration, U.S. Department of Justice (April 1976) pp. 21, 23–41, 42–64, F 1–3. (Editorial adaptations.)*

---

[1]The advantages of using these established terms are judged to outweigh the advantages of greater specificity. For the record, this study generally subscribes to the discussion of operational characteristics which follows the conceptual definition in Wepman et al. It is worth quoting at length: "The term *perceptual* as used here relates to those mental (neurological) processes through which the child acquires his basic alphabets of sounds and forms. The term *perceptual handicap* refers to inadequate ability in such areas as the following: recognizing fine differences between auditory and visual discriminating features underlying the sounds used in speech and the orthographic forms used in reading; retaining and recalling those discriminated sounds and forms sequentially, both in sensory and motor acts . . .; distinguishing figure-ground relationships . . .; recognizing spatial and temporal orientations; obtaining closure . . .; integrating intersensory information . . .; relating what is perceived to specific motor functions. . . . Behavior disturbances, severe mental retardation, poverty, lessened educational opportunity, visual impairment, hearing loss, or muscular paralysis all may produce educational problems but do not fall into the classification of specific learning disabilities.

Operationally, we include as learning disabilities the perceptual and perceptual-motor handicaps which are often labeled as dyslexia, aphasia, or hyperkinesis. . . .

It is not intuitively obvious that a learning disability will cause delinquency. A causal chain is implied: The LD produces effects which in turn produce other effects which in turn produce other effects which ultimately produce delinquency. Diagrammatically, the general form is as follows:

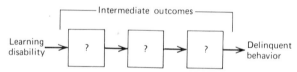

The chain—we will call it the "rationale"—is only occasionally spelled out when a causal argument is presented in the social sciences. But implicit or explicit, it is a crucial part of the evidence. A statistical relationship between the

For example, a child who is deficient in learning because of an emotional disturbance, but who shows no perceptual or perceptual-motor problem, would not be classified as having a learning disability. On the other hand, a child who is deficient in learning because of a nutritional problem, and who also shows a specific perceptual or perceptual-motor deficiency preceded by a nutritional problem, would properly be classified as having a learning disability. . . ." (Wepman et al., 1975, pp. 306–307. Emphasis in the original) The major question we would raise about this approach is whether it is operationally possible to disentangle the relative contribution of various problems to learning deficiencies.

states of "being learning disabled" and "being delinquent" has to make sense causally as well as pass the statistical litmus test. The more detailed the specification of the intermediate steps, the easier it is to examine the dynamics which will make a correlation coefficient or a t statistic meaningful. In this section we will review the causal rationale under three headings: its basic logic, the evidence presented for that logic, and how the rationale fits into the broader context of what is known about delinquency.

A. The Hypothesized Causal Sequence

Discussions with proponents of the LD/JD link and a review of the literature reveal two routes by which LD is thought to produce delinquency.

The first of these is a familiar one which links LD to school failure, to dropout, and to delinquency—the "School Failure rationale," for convenience.

The most graphic description of it is found in this passage by Berman:

"The cycle begins with early problems at home. The child was showing perceptual and attention problems even prior to school, but the behavior was written off as 'ornery' or 'uncooperative' personality. The child enters the early grades of school already accustomed to the fact that he won't be able to do things as well as expected of him, that he will fail and be humiliated continually. This prophecy is fulfilled in school as teachers, considering the child 'a behavior problem,' punish and ridicule him for failures or for

behaviors that he cannot control. The child begins to think of himself as a loser, as someone who can never hope to live up to what people expect of him.

"Rather than face the embarrassment of continual failure in front of friends and teachers, the behavioral signs become even more pronounced. Clowning around and general disruptiveness become the ways which best insulate this youngster from having to face continual and repeated failure. He becomes much more successful as a clown or troublemaker than he ever could be as a student.

"Teachers now are completely diverted away from any learning problems and concentrate solely on how to deal with the child's behavior. He gets further and further behind, becomes more and more of a problem. Eventually he's suspended, drops out or is thrown out of school to roam the streets, and the inevitable road to delinquency is well under way. The original problems have never been dealt with; the child is thought of as incorrigible. His problems are seen as psychogenic, not as the result of deflated self-esteem and fears of inadequacy, all of which have been generated by disability. His prophecy of himself as a loser has been fulfilled" (Berman, 1975, pp. 45–46).

This rationale refers to three immediate effects on the learning disability (or set of disabilities): adults perceive the child as being a disciplinary problem; the child is inherently handicapped in achieving academically (apart from the effects of the self-fulfilling prophecy that Berman mentions); and his peers perceive him as socially awkward and generally unattractive except as an object of ridicule. Diagrammatically:

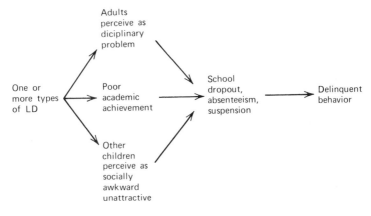

It is useful to further elaborate on the mechanism which is thought to be involved in the process leading to dropout; namely, the *labeling process*, whereby a student who has a prior record or who is a behavior problem (or both) tends to be labeled as a problem student. Perhaps he is informally labeled; perhaps he is grouped in classes with other problem students. As a result of labeling, it is argued, the child's negative self-image is reinforced by adults as well as by his peers; and, further, he is thrown into contact with other "problem" children, many of whom are likely to be considered problems *because* they are hostile to school and prone to engage in delinquency. The result is to encourage the LD child to be socialized by the children who are most likely to drop out or to become delinquent. The School Failure rationale now looks roughly like this:

second motive could plausibly be inferred from the dropout's lack of marketable skills—committing thefts is the most available way of making a living. And a separate sequence is added, which does not depend on dropout or school failure: the fact of continual failure itself is hypothesized to produce needs for compensation, which in turn increase the reinforcement value of acts which defy authority.

This rationale linking LD and delinquency is shown in Figure 1 below. It is not a complete set of links—a full-scale rationale would require variables and interactions and feedback loops of terrific complexity—but it does set down the essential events of one common line of argument linking LD and delinquency.

The second line of argument linking LD and delinquency is briefer and much more direct, at least in taking the chain to the point of increased

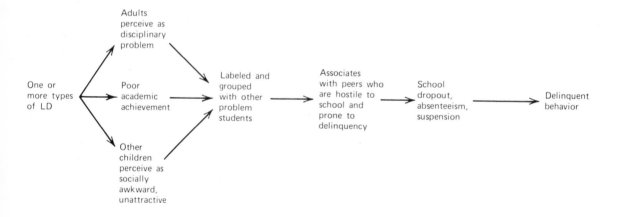

Finally, it is important to specify the mechanisms hypothesized to produce delinquent behavior. These are least often made explicit, since the contribution of dropout to delinquency is often taken for granted. There appear to be two main mechanisms for that linkage. First, the dropout simply has more time on his hands—as Elliott and Voss put it (without endorsing it), " 'idle hands are the devil's workshop' has been translated into a simple scientific proposition" (Elliott & Voss, 1974, p. 110). A

susceptibility to delinquent behavior. In effect, this rationale—call it the Susceptibility rationale—argues that certain types and combinations of LD are accompanied by a variety of socially troublesome personality characteristics. These go beyond the physical and social awkwardness which was discussed earlier. General impulsiveness is one of these characteristics: many LD children are said to be quicker than normal children to act on a sudden whim. Closely related to this is an apparent poor ability

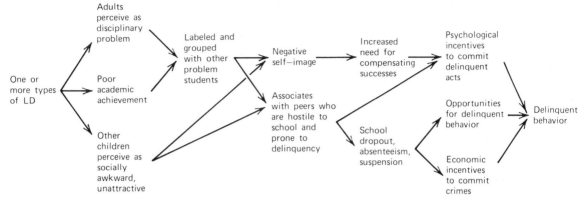

Figure 1. The school failure rationale linking LD and delinquency.

to learn from experience. The LD child is often said to have more than usual difficulty in accepting (or absorbing) the probability that if an act was accompanied by unpleasant consequences the last time, it will be accompanied by them this time too. The third commonly discussed characteristic which fits into this rationale is poor reception of social cues. As one observer of LD children put it, ". . . he does not appreciate the 'weight' of what is said or the 'toughness' of social danger signs" (Peters, 1974, p. 2). He can back himself into a confrontation without knowing how he got there.

Together, characteristics like these point to a child who is said to be less than ordinarily sensitive to the usual social sanctions and rewards. The problem is not initially callousness or street toughness on the part of the child. He might, on the contrary, be extremely receptive to rewards and sanctions. But the messages do not get

through in quite the way they were intended, with the result that some of the factors which might restrain a normal child from committing a delinquent act might not restrain the LD child. The Susceptibility rationale for linking LD to delinquency is, then, just that: a causal chain suggesting that *ceteris paribus*, the LD child starts out with a strike against him when exposed to opportunities for committing delinquent acts. The basic steps are recapitulated in Figure 2 below.

The two chains of reasoning summarized above capture the major arguments used to link LD with delinquency. The ultimate test of the arguments is simple—at least in theory. If the link exists, a population of learning disabled children will show higher rates of "delinquency" (however defined) than a matched set of children who are not learning disabled. But such a test has not been conducted; and one is not

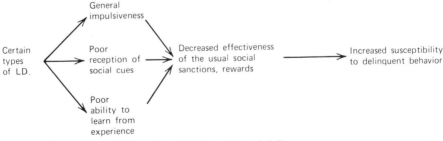

Figure 2. The susceptibility rationale linking LD and delinquency.

likely to be completed in the near future. There are a number of very difficult obstacles. A major one is time: to test whether LD *causes* delinquency, it is (among other things) essential to know that the LD exists prior to the delinquency. This implies the need to identify samples of LD and "normal" children at an early age, and to follow them through adolescence—the kind of longitudinal study that is so badly needed in so many aspects of the effort to understand and prevent delinquency. Lacking that, the evidence for and against the LD/JD link must take other forms. In the remainder of this section, we attempt to describe the overall state of the evidence.

B. The Case for a Link

With rare exception, the impetus for discussing LD as a cause of delinquency has originated not among the academic specialists on either delinquency or LD, but among practitioners: counselors for schools and juvenile courts, staffs in correctional facilities for juveniles, and clinical psychologists who work with disturbed youth.

*

The evidence which the proponents offer in support of the LD/JD link takes two forms: the observational evidence of these professionals who work with delinquents, and some quantitative studies.

1. *The Observational Record.* Of the types, the observational data are at the same time less systematic and more persuasive. In effect, the counselors, correctional staff members, and psychologists whom we consulted were reporting case studies of the sequences of events we have outlined. The children they see in the course of their work *are* in the process of being labeled as problem children; they *are* experiencing school failures and contemporaneously committing delinquent acts; they *are* showing up in juvenile courts just following dropout from school. Moreover, these practitioners report that their client youth give self-reports of "reasons why" which fit the rationales: children who say that their sets of friends have changed

because they are isolated by academic and social failure; who say they are dropping out of school because of failures; and who convey their sense of getting even with their school failures by committing delinquent acts.

That these observers are practitioners has also sometimes meant that they are not specially trained in observing and diagnosing learning problems or disabilities. But among the most active proponents of the LD/JD link have been some who do have the specialist's credentials. One, for example, began as a clinical psychologist specializing in treatment of children with known brain insult and inferred minimal brain damage. Subsequently, he was hired as a psychologist for a municipal juvenile court. As he relates it, ". . . my first year in the juvenile court was really a living hell. Because most of the kids I was seeing I was sure were like those kids whom we call minimally brain damaged. . . . I felt that I had some kind of hang-up on this, that I was seeing minimal brain damage in everybody" (Poremba, 1974, p. 3). He, like other psychologists with whom we talked, became convinced that his clinical judgment had not deserted him; that in fact he was observing minimal brain damage in an unusually high proportion of the delinquents he met. Other practitioners have come to the rationale from an educational or a legal specialty.

The common bond among them is a wealth of day-to-day personal experiences with delinquents and disturbed youth which exemplify the nodes outlined in the rationales. Throughout our interviews with them, it was apparent that they were able to give as many examples as we were prepared to hear.

There are a few examples of summarization of these kinds of observations, or ongoing attempts to summarize them. One of them is pragmatic observation of one senior staff member of a state correctional office that summer is a slack time for the intake and diagnostic people. This may mean simply that surveillance and apprehension of delinquents is lower when school is in summer recess; but it is also plausible, and supportive of the School Failure rationale, that "inability to cope with school, whether academically or emotionally, increases a kid's chances of getting in trouble and getting committed" (Hursch, 1976).

Another source of information to support the causal argument is the retrospective analysis of school records. Compton argues that analysis of records of learning disabled children reveals that "In a generalization of all of these patterns, [grades] two through six, there are at least two significant items common to all—a sudden drop in achievement coupled with truancy" (Compton, 1974, pp. 50–51). The report was based on preliminary results, and detailed analysis of these patterns is not available; but there is clearly a potential means of investigation through school records of this sort.

These examples of attempts to summarize the observational evidence also serve to illustrate the difficulties of the task. Much of the most provocative information is nearly intractable to systematic examination. Each account is a story in itself, about a single case, and to be persuasive it must be told in some detail. And if the professional who works with delinquents tries to summarize years of experience, he or she has to do it in subjective terms, regardless of the validity of the judgment. There is no way (that we can find) of doing justice in a summary report to the evidence accumulated by these observers.

The intractability of the anecdotal evidence to the formal requirements of "data" should not obscure its latent authority. The persons whom we interviewed had dealt with thousands of delinquents: a "sample size" and representation which, if it were applied to a systematic survey, would be formidable. On a practical level, this should add weight to the conclusions of many of the practitioners we interviewed. When, for example, a psychologist in a juvenile facility generalizes that there is a subgroup of delinquents which is different from the rest, in ways which indicate that learning disabilities are a primary variable, her description warrants attention no matter how different it is to convert her perception into a bundle of data suitable for quantitative assessment.

2. *The Quantitative Record.* If it is true that many experienced, perceptive observers report that the phenomena supporting an LD/JD link characterize large groups of delinquents, it is also true that other, equally experienced and perceptive observers believe that these phenomena are rare. This is not a new observation. In response to it, several studies of the LD/JD link have been conducted which purport to demonstrate that, statistically an unusually high proportion of delinquents are learning disabled.[2] And the claims are increasing in

[2]From a research standpoint, measuring incidence of LD among delinquent populations is a poor second-best to the ideal test of following the development of delinquency longitudinally among a pre-identified LD population. There are statistical reasons—*ex post facto* analyses must work around several statistical constraints which tend to decrease confidence in causal interpretations. There is the major, very practical consideration of accurate data collection: researchers can document what is happening in the present much more accurately than they can reconstruct what happened in the past. There is the objectivity problem: once one *knows* that the child is both LD and delinquent, it is a struggle to keep from selectively fixing on those data which support a link between the two phenomena. And finally, even ignoring these problems, the measurement of LD among an already-delinquent population and an "already-nondelinquent" population is measuring LD in the adolescent, not in the child who preceded him. Even with careful diagnosis, estimation of the incidence of LD prior to the occurrence of delinquency would tend to *falsely exclude* (1) all spontaneous remissions among children who once were LD, and (2) children who have learned to compensate for their LD. It would tend to *falsely include* (3) all children with minor perceptual deficits who are underachieving primarily for other reasons, and (4) some non-LD-like symptoms which did not exist in childhood. The degree of error introduced by these false-positive and false-negative diagnoses is unknown. But it can be concluded that there is high potential for mistaken estimates of childhood LD, when the diagnoses are based on testing of the children as adolescents. And to make matters even more confused, it is plausible that the false omissions and inclusions will vary systematically: on inspection of the four categories above, the best bet would appear to be that more false *exclusions* will be found among the non-delinquent population; more false *inclusions* among the delinquent population. Or in other words: the difference in LD incidence rates will look greater than it really

speeches, at conferences, and in the press that these studies are proof of the LD/JD link; accusations are heard that the relationship is being "studied to death" rather than being made the target of practical programs.

. . . For this overview of the case for the link, it should be stated frankly that the extensive examination we devote to the studies is out of proportion to their weight as evidence. If the topic were not the LD/JD link, but some less highly-charged research question, they would have been summarized in a few sentences: There have been a few reports, most of them using very small samples, most of them informally designed, which have tried to draw conclusions about LD among delinquents. The studies do generally support the notion that delinquents in institutions suffer widely from learning handicaps, ranging from retardation to ocular problems to emotional disturbance to perceptual-motor problems. A few of the more carefully designed studies offer solid if small-sample ($N = 15$, $N = 46$) evidence that there is a statistically significant difference between the incidence of perceptual and perceptual-motor deficits in a population of institutionalized delinquents and a population of secondary school students. This evidence is worth noting, and it warrants further exploration. It cannot be interpreted in terms of LD incidence among delinquents, nor for estimating difference of incidence between delinquents and nondelinquents. As evidence of LD's causal relationship to delinquency, it is much less provocative than the observational, qualitative accounts. . . .

Overall, the evidence which was cited in direct support of the rationales may be summarized as follows. It is abundant, particularly in describing the importance of learning handicaps in general, but it exists in a highly qualitative, anecdotal form. Some of it was provided by persons whose commitment to persuading us seemed stronger than their concern with a balanced report of their experiences. But most of it came from people who appeared to be perceptive observers with a rich practical knowledge of delinquents and delinquency. The quantitative evidence adds little to their observations.

C. THE CASE AGAINST A LINK

The proponents and opponents of the LD/JD link tended to break along practitioner/academician lines. This is not entirely accurate—many of the practitioners also hold teaching positions or perhaps conduct some research; many of the academicians work with youth in clinics and correctional facilities. But as a rule, it can be said that none of the leading proponents of the consultants who specialize in delinquency were unanimously skeptical that a significant causal relationship exists. Their skepticism was based on two types of objection: *the general state of causal explanations* for delinquency, and some more *specific existing evidence* which casts doubt on some of the causal links between LD and delinquency.

1. LD and Causal Explanations in General. The single point of consensus was that the rationales for the link between LD and delinquency comprise one very small segment of a very large causal map. The diagrammed relationships shown in the School Failure rationale (Figure 1), for example, are nested within a series of larger causal networks. LD is only one of many causes of school failure; school failure is only one of the many ways in which the school experience might cause delinquency; and the school is only one of many settings in which delinquency is thought to be nurtured. A parallel illustration could be drawn about the Susceptibility rationale: LD is only one of many sources of the psychological attributes said to increase susceptibility to delinquency; this set of attributes is only one of many psychological configurations which can conduce

---

was, falsely encouraging the conclusion that delinquents more often suffer from LD than non-delinquents.

These issues are not raised in the critiques of the specific articles—we lack any way of estimating the degree of error they introduce. But it remains true that all of them begin with these crippling, inescapable constraints of *ex post facto* analysis against them.

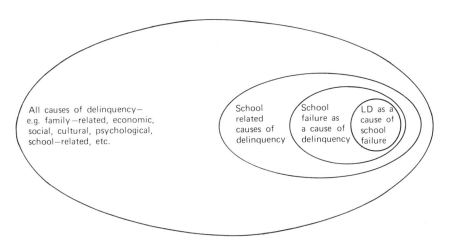

to delinquency; and psychological attributes are only one of many other factors which contribute to delinquent behavior.

These "other factors," it was frequently emphasized, are of major and documented importance. Given what is already known about the importance of poverty, the broken home, social disadvantagement, cultural alienation, emotional disorders, socialization by delinquent peers, or any of a number of other variables, the argument that LD is a primary cause of a major part of the delinquency problem is extremely dubious on its face—we are accumulating more "primary causes" than the number of delinquents will bear.

To get around this objection, it was argued, the proponents of the LD/JD link are driven toward one of two alternatives. The first is to argue that LD can be a critical *catalyst* of delinquent behavior, interacting with other potential causes. The second alternative is to argue that the socioeconomic factors which are said to cause delinquency actually cause LD, which in turn causes the delinquency. Either alternative produces the same question: how much of the variance can be attributed to the causal influence of the LD? Or less formally, to what extent are LD and delinquency symptoms of the same disease? Even if it is assumed for the sake of argument that (for example) pre-school en-

vironmental disadvantages can cause genuine LD, and that LD can increase the likelihood of delinquency, it is also an odds-on bet that the same home is having many other deleterious effects on the child. So, it was asked, even if the child is treated for his learning disability, how much difference will it make?

Variations on this argument were common among the specialists on delinquency, cutting across theoretical schools of thought. It reduced to a single theme: the notion that a significant proportion of delinquent behavior can be *causally* explained by a single variable, LD, goes against the grain of the scholarship on delinquency. One of the few things known for sure about delinquency is that its causes are multivariate and complex.

2. *The Rationales and Existing Evidence.* In general, the many explanations for delinquency and their supporting data do not either contradict or confirm the causal logic linking LD with delinquency. They simply do not intersect. But there are aspects of delinquency research which are relevant. They are summarized below, for each of the rationales.

(a) *The School Failure Rationale.* Most specialists in delinquency must keep in touch with educational developments as well; similarly, most specialists in the education of exceptional children deal with issues relating to delinquents and predelinquents. So nearly all of the consultants, whether they came from a delinquency or education specialty, had things to say about the school/delinquency relationship. . . .

The Association between School Failure and Delinquency   On one point underlying the School Failure rationale there was no argument: delinquents characteristically do have poor school records. This relationship was one of the first to be documented in the study of delinquency and it has been observed repeatedly. A recent example, by no means the most dramatic one, is the finding in the Philadelphia cohort study that more than half (54.6%) of the delinquent boys were below average in school achievement, compared to only 27.4% of the non-delinquent boys (Wolfgang et al., 1972, p. 63). The *association* between poor school performance and delinquency was not disputed by any of the consultants. But there was no consensus on the strength of the *causal* relationship.

Direct Critique of the Causal Linkages   By far the most direct critical commentary on the logic of the School Failure rationale is found in a study by a British specialist on learning disabilities, E.M.R. Critchley (see Critchley, 1968). Using demanding operational definitions of reading retardation and dyslexia, the author analyzed the records of 371 institutionalized delinquent boys. The interpretation of his findings is obscured by his inclusion of dyslexic boys with the much larger sample of reading retarded,[3] and his findings are by no means "definitive." But he does appear to stay well within his data when he concludes as follows:

"In the past, many have speculated upon a causal connection between reading retardation, truancy, and delinquency, . . . but few people have attempted an investigation of this linkage. The present attempt . . . including (i) examination of the aetiology of read-

ing disability as seen among delinquent children, (ii) review of the emotional and scholastic background of the retarded readers and comparison of their background with that of other delinquents not retarded in reading, and (iii) scrutiny of the life-history of the more intelligent of the retarded readers to trace the relationship between early schooling, disruptive events and behavioral disorders, did not reveal the manner whereby a dyslexic child may drift into delinquency." (Critchley, 1968, p. 1546)

With this exception, the studies which directly address the LD/JD link have concluded that their data supported its existence. Criticism of the linkages comes from more indirect sources.

The effects of labeling. An important part of the School Failure logic is that LD children are mistakenly "labeled" as slow learners or behavior problems, which sets up a destructive cycle whereby the child does in fact become a behavior problem or a failure in school. Consultant opinion on this topic diverged widely.

Some consultants were convinced that labeling's causal role is substantial and proven: children do tend to become what they are told they are. The more powerful the labeling ritual (e.g., the process of becoming an adjudicated delinquent), the more powerful the effects. Within the school, being labeled "dumb" by peers or a "slow learner" by adults might produce less dramatic immediate effects than being labeled "delinquent," but it does escalate the frustration which can motivate delinquent behavior. By the same logic, being labeled "LD" can have its own debilitating effects on a child's development. At this point in the argument, opinion divided radically. Some consultants criticized the labels as being artificial and harmful props of our educational system, and stressed the need for fundamental reform. Others adopted a more limited stance, criticizing inaccurate labeling rather than the process itself, or criticizng failure to follow up the label with remedial programs.

Others had reached generally skeptical conclusions about the causal role of labeling. One source of skepticism was the many logical prob-

---

[3]Though his definition of "dyslexia" was so stringent that, as he points out, "it may have been that the number of developmental dyslexics in the sample was seriously underestimated" (p. 1545).

lems of demonstrating the relationship. To the extent that labeling reflects reality, it will in fact *predict* certain behaviors. The temporal sequence—labeling, followed by predicted result—has a spuriously causal appearance. Other skepticism was expressed about the plausibility of the argument. Children are labeled in dozens of ways simultaneously, with labels of mixed valence: the class brain who is clumsy at athletics; the star athlete who barely passes his courses; the able underachiever in the classroom who is a social leader among his peers. Neither the socialization nor the psychological development of the child is likely to be governed by any one label. And finally, the most general source of skepticism was the state of the data. A number of studies have attempted to demonstrate the effects of labeling; there appeared to be widespread dissatisfaction with the quality of them.

School Dropout and Delinquency Proponents of LD's causal role repeatedly portray dropout as a key event bridging LD and delinquency, and it would appear to be one of the most obvious, least arguable links in the chain. But there is increasing doubt that the "obvious" causal role of dropout actually exists. A recent and major longitudinal study of dropout and delinquency (Elliott and Voss, 1974) raises serious doubts about the extent to which dropout contributes to delinquency. Elliott and Voss, like others before them, found that dropouts have much higher rates of official and self-reported delinquency than non-dropouts. But the longitudinal analysis reveals that the highest rates occurred *prior* to dropping out of school. Once they were no longer in school, "the findings based on the two measures of delinquency [police records and self-reported delinquency] are consistent—there is decreasing involvement in delinquency after dropout" (Elliott & Voss, 1974, p. 119). This is not a decisive criticism of the School Failure rationale—the essential event is school failure; dropout is only one alternative route to subsequent delinquency. But this can be viewed in light of the additional finding that "educationally handicapped" dropouts had only slightly, non-significantly higher mean delinquency rates than "intellectually capable" dropouts (Elliott & Voss, 1974, p. 115). Put conservatively, these findings, using a large, multi-school sample and what appears to be a carefully executed methodology, are at least not supportive of arguments for the disability → failure → delinquency chain as a dominant source of delinquency.

Much the same conclusion could serve as a summary about the relationship of the existing theory and data to the School Failure rationale: They are not supportive of a major role for LD as a cause of school failure leading then to delinquency; neither do they eliminate the possibility that LD plays this major role.

(b) *The Susceptibility Rationale.* The consultants who deal with LD children emphasized how ordinary these children are in general personality, when the disabilities are mild. The milder the disability, the more the LD child is indistinguishable from his non-LD peers. And by the same logic, the milder the disability, the less likely that it is a cause of subsequent delinquency. But many of those who argue for a closer look at the LD/JD link did so out of observation of a personality type characteristic of the severely learning disabled child who has reached early adolescence without diagnosis or treatment. A constellation of personality traits is said to be at work: impulsiveness, poor receptivity of social cues, and poor ability to learn from experience. The pattern of traits was summarized in various ways. The most evocative was provided by Dr. Helen Hursch, a supervisor of daignostic services in the Colorado system. "I think of them as large pre-schoolers," she said of the residents in a cottage set aside for delinquents diagnosed as severely learning disabled; and that conveys the overall image suggested by other sources: of LD delinquents who are not essentially hostile, who often try hard to please without being sure how to do it, who are impulsive in childlike ways; generally immature; often very dependent. The question asked here is: to what extent have these traits been found to characterize delinquents as a group?

Classification of Delinquents   One source of information on this issue is the results of personality classification programs which have been applied operationally by juvenile corrections services. The most widely used of these is the "Interpersonal Maturity Level Classification" system first developed in the 1950's (see Sullivan, Grant, & Grant, 1957) and since expanded and applied in California, New York, and many other states. The system defines seven successive stages of interpersonal maturity, ranging from the level of a newborn infant to that of a socially mature adult. For all practical purposes, levels 2 through 4 have been found to include almost all juvenile delinquents who have undergone the classification process. A total of nine delinquent subtypes have been defined within those three levels.

Which of these levels include the severely disabled child who is characterized in the Susceptibility rationale? Two were proposed. One was the "I-2" level, applied to a child whose interpersonal standing and behavior are integrated in ways that conceive and react to others primarily as "givers" or "withholders." He has no conception of interpersonal refinement beyond this. He is unable to explain, understand, or predict the behavior or reactions of others. The child is not interested in things outside himself except as a source of supply. He behaves impulsively, unaware of the effects of his behavior on others. Since the child is a simple perceiver, "a receiver of life's impact," and has difficulty understanding structure, he has many problems in school, and typically needs small classes and specially trained teachers (Warren et al., 1966). According to Marguerite Q. Warren, who was one of the leading figures in the development of the system, extensive classification experience in California and New York indicates that only about five percent of all delinquents fall in the I-2 classification.

A second level in which LD delinquents tend to cluster was argued to be "I-3 cfm," the "im-

mature conformist." This child may generally be described as immature, dependent, extremely eager for social approval, and with low self-esteem. About 26% of juvenile delinquents in New York are classified as I-3 cfm. Referring specifically to institutionalized delinquents, Hursch estimates that I-3 cfm's constitute half to two-thirds of the intake for Colorado.

Neither of these groups should be seen as learning disabled by another name. It is argued simply that those delinquents who *are* severely LD tend to cluster within them. The problem is estimating the proportions. Warren (who disclaimed expertise in LD *per se*) speculates that most LD would fall in I-2. And on a more general level, her experience with classification results of the Interpersonal Maturity system and other systems left her very skeptical that LD can explain much of the variance in delinquency.

Another view was posed by Hursch. In her experience, the I-3 cfm group contains the bulk of the LD delinquents; specifically, "the 'low' end, in the interpersonal sense, are my 'large preschoolers'. . . . The extreme high end of the group usually, like the I-4's, are not LD, [while those in] the low end almost all are either retarded or LD." She describes the relevant symptoms as follows: "The most important area of difficulty usually is language. They have auditory reception problems (difficulty distinguishing the stimuli to which they are trying to attend from the background noise), sequencing, memory span, discrimination, etc., poor inner language to use in thinking, difficulty retrieving words and facts they obviously know, plus small vocabularies and confused grammar. . . ." (Hursch, 1976).

Whether the results of the experiences in classifying delinquents are inconsistent with the logic of the Susceptibility chain depends very much on the assumptions which are chosen. If the subset of LD children within the I-2 and I-3 cfm levels is assumed to be large, a nontrivial overall proportion of LD delinquents can be inferred. If the subset is assumed to be small, some very modest overall proportion of LD "susceptible" delinquents is implied. In either case, however, it appears most reasonable to assume that a clear minority of the total delinquent population is involved.

Personality Characteristics

Herbert C. Quay approached the topic of delinquent personality from a quantitative and behavioral perspective, asking this question: can the deviant behaviors of children and adolescents be grouped into a few basic syndromes that are 1) *internally consistent* (if a child exhibits behaviors, A, B, and C, chances are high that he will also exhibit behavior D), 2) *independent* (mixes of behavior across syndromes are limited), 3) *replicable* (the same patterns are found to occur across a variety of youth populations, 4) *valid* (the same patterns persist across measurement procedures, and 5) *inclusive* (the syndromes effectively encompass the universe of deviant behaviors in children). His synthesis of the literature and several studies of his own, lead him to the conclusion that these conditions can be met by use of only four syndromes, labeled "conduct disorder," "personality disorder," "immaturity," and "socialized delinquency" (Quay, 1972).

The relevance of this to the LD/JD issue parallels the relevance of the Interpersonal Maturity system: one of the syndromes—immaturity—roughly corresponds to the personality characteristics which are often ascribed to severely learning disabled children. Among the most common behavior traits in the immaturity subgroup have been preoccupation, short attention span, and clumsiness; in the life histories of children in this classification, key characteristics cited by Quay are truancy from home and inability to cope with complex world. Again, it must be emphasized that the immaturity syndrome does not coincide with the characteristics of the severely learning disabled; it is an imperfect superset which plausibily encompasses most of the severely LD children, plus many others who exhibit correlate personality traits without suffering from the learning disability. Quay's summary is worth quoting at length:

"Although the third major pattern [immaturity] has not been as pervasive and prominent as the previous two patterns, it has nevertheless appeared in a number of studies. . . . As with conduct and personality disorder, immaturity has been found in samples of children and adolescent studies in public schools, child-guidance clinics, and institutions for the delinquent. . . . With the notable exception of a study of emotionally disturbed children in special classes, . . . it is generally less prominent than either conduct disorder or personality disorder. . . . Since most of the behaviors [in the immaturity pattern] seem appropriate to all children at some state in their development, this pattern seems to represent a persistence of these behaviors when they are inappropriate to the chronological age of the child and society's expectations of him. At the same time, regression to an earlier form of behavior could also be involved. Again, this pattern occurs in all settings where deviant children are found. It seems especially prominent in public school classes for the emotionally disturbed . . . and the learning disabled. . . ." (Quay, 1972)

The point to emphasize is that the set of delinquents characterized by the behaviors of the "immaturity" pattern has consistently accounted for a smaller proportion of delinquents than any of the other three patterns; presumably, the severely LD are only a portion of even that population. Quay's impromptu estimate (not to be confused with the quantitative evidence just cited) of the proportion of the delinquents who were learning disabled in the sense of "a clearly demonstrable perceptual or integrative disorder" was very small—less than one percent.

Many other personality classification schemes have been employed for describing delinquents. They have broad overlap—a 1966 NIMH conference on typologies attended by the progenitors of most of the major ones was able to reach substantial consensus on commonalities (Warren, 1971, p. 249). And in most of them, there is a category which roughly corresponds to the configuration suggested by the Susceptibility rationale. A delinquent subtype exists which shares many of the personality characteristics of the learning disabled. But the evidence in the literature on personality and delinquency suggests that this subtype comprises a minority, perhaps a small minority, of the overall delinquent population. This does not argue decisively against the School Failure rationale, whereby academic failures alone could be the critical trigger regardless of personality characteristics. But the Susceptibility rationale does hinge on personality traits. The evidence on the delinquent personality cited above does raise a number of doubts about how widely the rationale can be applied to explain delinquency.

THE QUANTITATIVE EVIDENCE

During the past seven years, several studies have sought to measure the incidence of LD among delinquent populations. Many of them have reported startlingly high proportions. Half, three-quarters, even 90 percent of the members of the delinquent samples have been diagnosed as suffering from one or more learning disabilities. And, as the introductory quotations indicate, one school of thought holds that the evidence has already demonstrated the basic relationship.

A. A Note on the General Approach to Proof

The following is a technical critique. It deals with problems of operational definition, sample selection, tests, procedures, and data analysis. The value of the final results are often discounted because of defects in these areas; failures which sometimes may seem minor at first glance. Given this approach, it may rightly be asked whether methodological hair-splitting is obstructing the effort to appraise the overall sense of the data. What is, finally, "enough" evidence? Since this appraisal has been based on certain points of view about the meaning of enough, it is appropriate to state them explicitly.

The first assumption is that in reaching program decisions, *an agency . . . should not as a matter of course demand the same standards of proof that are applied by the scientific community.* If program deci-

sions have to wait for a precise calibration of what kinds of learning disability lead to what kinds of delinquency under what circumstances, nothing is going to be done for years, if ever. A rougher determination has to be made: based on the evidence at hand and the problem that has to be addressed, what is a reasonable use of tax dollars? Often, the issues are such that hard data cannot be obtained, and decisions to go ahead must be based on qualitative or ambiguous evidence.

But the argument for the LD/JD link has embedded in it a straightforward statement of statistical association: delinquent behavior occurs among LD children more often than would be expected by chance. This is a statement which can be rigorously tested with methods already at hand. Its truth is a necessary condition for sustaining the argument that LD causes delinquency. So in this case it seems not only reasonable but essential to take a hard look at the statistical evidence. In doing so, we apply a second assumption:

When one of the critical variables (LD) has no objective operational definition and no objective metrics for measuring the degree of its presence or absence, the technical aspects of instrumentation, testing procedures, and data analysis become critical factors in assessing not just the precision of conclusions, but whether they mean anything at all.

Assessing incidence of LD among delinquents is a fundamentally different research problem than, say, assessing incidence of myopia or hearing loss. Questions that can be trivial for some other types of associational research take on central importance.

Operational definition offers an excellent illustration. One of the studies which will be discussed in this section found that 90.4% of the delinquents examined were learning disabled. There was no control group, but on the face of it there are good reasons for asking why one would be needed: nobody argues that 90% of nondelinquent children—or any figure approaching it—are learning disabled. And even supposing that as many as a third of the diagnoses were false-positives, that would still leave more than half of the delinquents "genuinely" LD—a very large proportion. In short, the initial reported incidence is so high that apparently no amount of haggling over methodology will lower the percentage to a point that there is any question whether delinquents are disproportionately learning disabled.

But the meaning of "90.4%" changes radically when one notes the author's statement that "our philosophy [is] that a learning disability or dysfunction is *anything which prevents a child from achieving successfully in a normal educational setting*," including sociological and psychological "dysfunctions" and (apparently) visual and hearing handicaps (Compton, 1974, p. 49. Emphasis added). The interpretation of "90.4%" becomes further confused when it is realized that it includes learning disabilities which were classified as "mild." How mild can LD be and still be a plausible cause of the delinquency?

For purposes of this study, these problems of operational definition make "90.4%" and uninterpretable number. For it is entirely compatible to accept as fact that (a) 90.4% of children whose behavior problems are so great that they have to be institutionalized also have some sort of learning difficulty; and that (b) this is not a relevant datum in assessing the proportion of those youth who have significantly disabling perceptual or integrative disorders. The issue is not one of methodological nuance, but a basic problem of using one label for two very different constructs.

Much the same introductory comments could be made about the importance of examining the *diagnostic tests*, in terms of both their content and their intended uses. A "good test" is a valid, reliable instrument for measuring what it is supposed to measure. When the thing-to-be-measured is an uncomplicated construct like spelling ability, a statement that the subject has a spelling problem because he did poorly on the spelling test has a common-sense meaning. As the thing-to-be-measured becomes less concrete, the test must measure a construct *which is defined by the test itself*—exemplified by the famous dictum that intelligence is that which is measured by an IQ test. When, as in the case of LD, there are no tests for which LD is the construct, it is mandatory that the diagnostic procedures be subjected to special scrutiny: the diagnostician is not working with self-evident test results, but with results which he then *infers* to be evidence that the subject is learning disabled. Thus, any statement to the effect that the subjects were administered tests A, B, and C, and that the results showed that X percent of the subjects were learning disabled has to be seen as a red flag: what are those tests, and what are they intended to test for? Again, this is not a technical issue, such as arguing the relative merits of the Wechsler or the Stanford-Binet IQ tests. It is a variation on the Fallacy of the Tool which occurs chronically in quantitative social science: use of the wrong tools, because they are the only ones available. An "abnormal" score on a test is evidence for the LD/JD association only if the test measures constructs related to perceptual or integrative disorders.

Finally, *testing procedures and analytic techniques* takes on added importance when the topic is LD. Given that a substantial portion of personal judgment is inescapable in arriving at a diagnosis of LD—LD consultants of all schools agreed on this point—the question is also inescapable: has the researcher protected himself from the consequences of his own biases? This is not an indictment of the integrity of the researchers whose work we shall be reviewing. Arriving at consistent, unbiased judgments is much more complicated than simply being honest. Every researcher who has tried to apply a qualitative rating scheme over a large number of cases is familiar with the subtle ways in which judgments can be skewed, despite the most conscientious efforts to apply the same criteria to each case. When the topics under investigation are as highly charged as those of learning disabilities and juvenile delinquency, the potential for distortions is multiplied, and procedural precautions become correspondingly more significant.

B. The State of the Evidence

With the above remarks in mind, we turn to the review of the available evidence. Three types are examined: (1) evidence of *simple association* between the conditions of being delinquent and learning disabled; (2) evidence specifying the *magnitude of the difference* in LD incidence among delinquents and non-delinquent populations; and (3) evidence of *incidence of LD among delinquents,* without reference to a non-delinquent group.

Category 1: Simple Association *(Do delinquents and non-delinquents show significant differences on tests for learning disabilities?)*

Summary: The evidence is limited and equivocal, but the existence of a difference is supported.

Discussion: Despite all the studies comparing delinquent and non-delinquent children, very few have compared both populations on perceptual and integrative deficits. We found only two: Berman's (1975) unpublished article, "A neuropsychological approach to the etiology, prevention, and treatment of juvenile delinquency" and an article entitled "Neuropsychological function of normal boys, delinquent boys, and boys with learning problems," coauthored by Hurwitz, Bibace, Wolff, and Rowbotham (1972).

... Briefly, the Berman study compared 45 boys in the Rhode Island Training School with 45 non-delinquent boys in an inner-city Providence secondary school adapting the Halstead-Reitan battery of tests which is customarily used to test for organic brain damage. The Hurwitz group conducted two separate small sample studies (both reported in the same 1972 article). One compared 15 delinquent boys in a training school, 15 in a school for learning disabled children, and 15 public school students on a test of motor development. The second, with delinquent and non-delinquent samples of 13, sought to build on a hypothesis suggested by the first study, by administering tests which would dis-criminate "sequencing" or "temporal" skills from "spatial" or "non-sequencing" skills.

A summary of our assessment is that *both studies are valid tests of whether a clinical sample and a normal sample differed on the tests being administered.* That is, we are satisfied that differences in scores cannot readily be attributed to incomparabilities in testing conditions and procedures or to experimenter bias, and that the statistical tests of significance were appropriate for the data.

Interpretation of the test scores poses a different problem. In one case (Hurwitz et al., 1972), the author's interpretations appears to be an extremely precise reflection of the data. In the other case (Berman, 1975), the interpretation is more speculative, and the test results admit of other explanations.

The summary conclusions of the Hurwitz study are that

• The delinquent sample was "significantly retarded on a broad spectrum test of motor development."

• The delinquent sample "had specific difficulties in tasks demanding the sequential ordering of sensori-motor and verbal elements."

• Overall, "the neuropsychological deficits of delinquent boys and boys with learning disabilities are manifested more clearly in tasks of temporal sequencing than in tasks of perceptual restructuring" (Hurwitz et al., 1972, p. 392).

The summary conclusions of the Berman study are that

• The delinquent sample was *not* retarded in "motor skills, attentional abilities, and gross sensory functioning."

• The deficits of the delinquent sample were found in "verbal, perceptual, and non-verbal conceptual spheres" (Berman, 1975, p. 40).

Converting these findings into statements about learning disabilities is difficult. Eighteen separate tests (plus general intelligence tests) were administered to the boys in the studies. Their terminology overlaps without being synonymous, and the constructs tested overlap without being identical. A starting point, however, is an inventory of the individual tests and the comparison of delinquent/non-delinquent performance, as shown in Table I on the following page.

It will be remembered that the critical features of LD as we are operationally using that term are:

- General I.Q. of "normal" or better ($\geq$80).

- Distinguishable from emotional disturbance or physical handicaps (e.g., poor hearing).

- Not *directly* attributable to environmental disadvantage.

- Existence of deficits in academic achievement relative to ability.

- Evidence of perceptual or perceptual-motor disorder.

We shall examine the studies in terms of each of these stipulations.

1. *Can the results be explained by deficits of general intelligence.*

Our judgment is that *the Hurwitz results as reported are not explainable by deficits of general intelligence* among the Ss. In absolute terms, all of the boys in Study I (motor development) were in the normal range (mean IQ, 101; range, 96–117; S.D. 22.5). All but an estimated 2 of the 13 boys in Study II (temporal and spatial tasks) were in the normal range (our interpolation from the reported mean IQ of 96 with a range from 73 to 108 and an S.D. of 14.8). In Study II, group IQ differences were significant at the .05 level, but "the correlation between IQs and spatial and temporal tasks within each population was not significant. . . ." (Hurwitz 1972, p. 392). More to the point, an analysis of covariance with intelligence as the control factor was carried out, and it showed that for only one test (the Raven Matrices Test) did IQ differences contribute to observed differences between the means of the two groups—and still the difference was not statistically significant.

In contrast, *it appears that for the Berman study, general intelligence could account for some of the between-group differences.* The analyses which could resolve this question have not yet been carried out. These observations seem pertinent: The mean full-scale IQ (WAIS) of the delinquent sample was only 90.6. This is lower than the mean for other surveys of delinquents in training schools, and raises the possibility that Berman had to work with a sample of boys with unusually low intelligence. Also, the standard deviation was 11.4, which, with the assumption of a normal distribution, suggests that roughly eight out of the 45 delinquents were below the 80-point score often used to demarcate the bottom edge of the normal range. And finally, the difference between the means of the delinquent and control samples was 12.5 points, significant at the .001 level. As an absolute difference, it is less than those reported in the two sets of Hurwitz samples; but two factors make the problem an acute one for interpreting the Berman findings.

First, failure to take lower delinquent IQ into account would have tended to falsely *disconfirm* the Hurwitz argument that neuropsychological deficits among delinquents divide along the temporal/spatial dimensions. The influence of general intelligence differences would have been to obscure evidence for the Hurwitz study's explanation, not to enhance it. In contrast, *the failure to take lower delinquent IQ into account could tend to falsely confirm the Berman study's argument* that delinquents suffer from an impoverishment of neuropsychological adaptive abilities which is negligible for the less complex abilities and progressively more severe for more complex abilities. A rival hypothesis appears to be equally consistent with the data, that the delinquents' scores differ from a control group's in proportion to the test's correlation with the WAIS results. Conceptually, Berman's use of

Table I. Summary of LD-Related Test Results Comparing Delinquent and Control Samples

Primary Modalities		Test	Study	Findings		
				Better Mean Score	Significant difference?	$P \leq$
Motor	Gross and fine motor opment: repetitive tasks	Six items of the Lincoln-Oseretsky Test	Hurwitz	control	yes	.01
	Fine motor development	Halstead-Reitan Finger Oscillation Test	Berman	delinquent	no	
	Sensorimotor rhythm (variability of peak-to-peak)	Tapping tests	Hurwitz	control	yes	.01
	Gross and fine motor development: nonrepetitive	27 items of the Lincoln-Oseretsky Test	Hurwitz	control	no	
Auditory	Auditory discrimination	Rhythm subtest of the Seashore Test of Musical Talent	Berman	$\cong$	no	
Visual	Visual discrimination of colors (repetitive)	Three subtests of the Stroop Test	Hurwitz	control	yes	.01, .05, .05
	Visual discrimination of objects (repetitive)	Naming repeated objects	Hurwitz	control	yes	.05
	Perceptual discrimination of embedded figures	Children's Embedded-Figures Test	Hurwitz	control	no	
Visual-motor	Visual-motor integration	Beery-Buktenica visual-motor Integration Test	Hurwitz	$\cong$	no	
	Visual-motor integration, memory	Graham-Kendall Memory-for-Designs Test	Hurwitz	control	no	
	Visual-motor integration (spatial organization)	Reitan Trailmaking Test, Parts A and B	Berman	control	yes	.01, .001
Visual-auditory	Auditory-visual integration	Halstead-Reitan Speech Sounds Perception Test	Berman	control	yes	.05
Tactile-other	Tactile discrimination, fine motor development	Halstead-Reitan Tactual Performance Test: Time	Berman	control	yes	.05
	Tactile-visual integration, fine motor	Halstead-Reitan Tactual Performance Test: Memory	Berman	control	yes	.01
	Tactile-visualization of spatial configurations	Halstead-Reitan Tactual Performance Test: Localization	Berman	control	yes	.01
General	Sensory-perceptual disturbances	Six subtests of Reitan Sensory-Perceptual Disturbances Test	Berman	$\cong$	no	
	Spatial relationships	Standard Raven Progressive Matrices	Hurwitz	control	no	
	Concept formation	Halstead-Reitan Categories Test	Berman	control	yes	.001

"complex adaptive abilities" is difficult to distinguish from a descriptor of general intelligence.

The second reason why the IQ difference confounds interpretation of the Berman study and not the Hurwitz study is, of course, that the Hurwitz study tested for its relevance while the Berman study did not. It *may be* that the IQ influence can legitimately be discounted in the Berman study, but the analyses necessary to demonstrate that were not performed.

On the other side of the argument, studies applying the Halstead-Reitan battery indicate that, with the exception of the Category Test, the test scores are not substantially correlated with IQ scores. Insofar as this independence may have held true for Berman's sample, the importance of differences in IQ are diminished.

2. *Can the results be explained by emotional disturbance or physical handicaps?*

The Hurwitz study used as a criterion of selection that no Ss suffer from major neurological or other organic illnesses, or from obvious psychotic symptoms. Berman's article does not specify procedures on this point. Berman reports that standard admissions tests did not reveal obvious physical or emotional handicaps (Berman, 1976).

Berman took his control group from the same inner-city Providence High School that is reported to contribute roughly 80% of the Training School's population. It is plausible to assume that differences in SES background were relatively small. In addition, delinquents and controls were matched pairwise for race as well as age. *Differential environmental disadvantage does not readily explain between-group differences in the Berman study.*

In Hurwitz, both Study I and Study II used delinquent Ss which were uniformly from families at lower socioeconomic levels, while control Ss were from families at lower-middle or middle class socio-economic levels. If it were true that the tests of temporal/sequencing abilities differed from the tests of spatial/perceptual restructuring abilities in their degree of culture-specific grounding, this distinction in the Ss' SES background would presumably bias the statistical results. We are unable to determine any basis for assuming this to be the case, and conclude that *environmental disadvantage is probably not an important factor in the Hurwitz findings. . . .*

Before leaving this question, however, we should note the Hurwitz study's own speculation:

"While we have no evidence to support the claim, the skewed distribution of social class membership in one of the two clinical populations together with the similarity of their deficits on tasks of voluntary sequencing raises the possibility that children with delayed or disturbed neuromuscular development are more likely to be identified as delinquents when they grow up in a lower-class context and to be identified as children with learning disabilities when they come from a middle-class environment" (Hurwitz, 1972, p. 393).

3. *Are the purported neuropsychological deficits accompanied by school achievement deficits relative to ability?*

Neither of the articles contains any information on the delinquent Ss' academic status. Berman did collect data on grade-levels using the Wide Range Achievement Test but did not include them in the article because of what he sees as the subjectivity of the grade level concept and its vulnerability to confounding through environmental factors. His data do indicate that the delinquent sample was lagging significantly behind the control group on reading, spelling, and arithmetic (Berman, 1976). Whether this is a reflection of generally lower *ability* among the delinquent rather than the disabling effects of LD remains an open question (and one for which it is difficult to conceive of a satisfactory procedure).

4. *Are the neuropsychological deficits measured by the tests comparable to those perceptual and perceptual-motor disorders which are defined as being learning disabilities?*

In answering this question, it seems appropriate to avoid as much semantic nit-picking as possible. We shall approach it from this perspective: Do any of the tests appear to *not* involve significant perceptual processes? Are there any which appear to involve complex concept formation which is predominantly a function of general intelligence?

We judge the Lincoln-Oseretsky Test (Hurwitz, which divided it into two subtests) and the Finger Oscillation Test (Berman) to be tests of motor development which would fall outside all but a very wide definition of perceptual or perceptual-motor processes. At the other end of the spectrum, it appears that at least two tests—the Category Test and the Raven Progressive Matrices Test—overlap well into the domains of concept formation, and a third—Trailmaking Part B—is grounded in an academically learned skill.

The first of these, the Halstead-Reitan Category Test (in Berman's study), is said by Reitan to be

"a relatively complex concept formation test which requires fairly sophisticated ability in noting similarities and differences in stimulus material, postulating hypotheses, . . . testing these hypotheses, . . . and the ability to adapt hypotheses. . . . While the test is not especially difficult for most normal [lesion-free] subjects, it seems to require competence in abstraction to postulate in a structured rather than permissive context" (Reitan, 1966, p. 166).

The Raven Progressive Matrices Test (Hurwitz) is commonly used as a proxy measure of general intelligence. Even though there seems to be agreement that it does indeed measure "perceptual adequacy," it is said to do so at an advanced level.

Finally, Part B of the Trailmaking Test appears to be extremely sensitive to how fast the S can remember which letter comes after which, in the Roman alphabet. If many of the Berman delinquents were school dropouts or reading retarded, it is plausible that the sequence of the ABCs had been differentially ingrained in the clinical and control samples. The Trailmaking Test Part B, scored as it is in elapsed time to completion, would be sensitive to such differences (Reitan, 1976).

The results of this recasting of the tests (remembering the borderline nature of some of the decisions) may be summarized as follows:

The control samples performed significantly better ($p \leq .05$) than the delinquent samples on . . .

    1 out of 3 motor tasks

    1 out of 2 IQ-related tasks

    1 out of 1 achievement-related task

    7 out of 12 perceptual and perceptual-motor tasks

The delinquent sample did not perform significantly better than the control sample on any of the tasks.

These 18 test results were obtained from samples of 15, 13, and 45. Overall, they do comprise evidence that delinquents who have reached the point of being institutionalized tend to be outperformed on a variety of tests, including perceptual ones, by a comparable sample of "normal" youth who have never been arrested. This is a modest conclusion; it seems also a fair one. The evidence is too slender, from samples of too few, to justify much more.

Category 2: Magnitudes of Difference (*How great is the difference in incidence of LD, comparing delinquents with non-delinquents?*)

Summary: Only one study has reported incidence of LD among a sample of delinquents and a sample of non-delinquent controls. "LD" was diagnosed if the S scored in the impaired range on at least one subtest of a battery used to diagnose brain lesions.

Discussion: A truism bears repeating here: a statistically significant difference is not necessarily a substantively significant one. The preceding pages have dealt exclusively with the most elementary of the issues: when researchers have compared test scores of delinquent and non-delinquent samples, were the groups' scores different? Is there reason to believe that these differences would occur by chance at least less than five times in 100 trials?

Now we are asking the much more direct (and policy-related question: *How do differences in mean test scores translate into percentage of non-delinquents who are learning disabled?*

The Hurwitz article does not address this question in detail. It does point out that all 15 delinquent boys in Study I scored below the 5th percentile on the Lincoln-Oseretsky Test or Motor Development, while only one of the normal boys obtained a score below the 70th percentile. Beyond that, no assessment of incidence rates was attempted. We would add as a general rule, however, that the fact that a statistically significant difference is obtained from a sample of 15 or 13 tends to indicate a "large" difference. The Hurwitz samples were so small that minor differences would usually be obscured.

The Berman study does make statements about incidence. After presenting the statistical results which were discussed earlier, the study presents the results of diagnoses which were made from the tests. Berman concludes that 56% of the delinquent sample showed at least one major disability "significant enough to warrant professional attention," compared to 23% among a control population. (Berman, 1975, pp. 44–45).

The diagnosis was based on a simple criterion: all of the Halstead-Reitan subtests have a cutoff score to distinguish impaired from non-impaired. A subject was classified as LD if he scored in the impaired range on any subtest of that battery. We shall not try to address the validity of this procedure. The Halstead-Reitan battery is just that: a battery of subtests, a critical feature of which is a summary "impairment index" based on the combined test results. It was designed to be used in conjunction with the subtest scores to diagnose brain lesions. It is of proven validity for that purpose in applying it to diagnosis of LD, Berman breaks new ground. Questions of validity have yet to be tackled. Compared to standards used in popular discussions of the LD/JD link, the criterion is relatively conservative. In terms of the standards which were generally urged by the LD consultants for this study, use of a single subtest score to diagnose a specific learning disability is unacceptable. Berman's results show that more than twice as many institutionalized delinquents as non-delinquents scored in the impaired range on at least one subtest of a battery otherwise used to diagnose brain lesions. This finding is unquestionably intriguing. But it is a major leap from that datum to a conclusion by the reader that more than twice as many delinquents as non-delinquents are learning disabled.

We were unable to discover any other studies which directly compared incidence of LD among delinquent and non-delinquent samples. Instead, a number of studies were found which attempted to measure LD incidence in a delinquent population. We now turn to those studies.

Category 3: Incidence Among Delinquents
(How commonly do delinquents suffer from LD?)

Summary: As of the end of 1975, no usable estimate was available. Different studies have applied widely disparate definitions of LD and have reached widely disparate results. Nor can it be deduced which is closest to the mark. All of them fall far short of a thorough, widely acceptable survey of incidence of LD among delinquents—some, because the objectives were limited; some, because of very severe problems in the conduct and presentation of the work.

Discussion: Of the many titles which suggest a study of LD among delinquents, only a few present incidence data. Of the many titles which suggest a study of learning problems and delinquency, only a handful deal with learning disabilities as such. The nature of the collateral evidence—the studies of reading retardation among delinquent youth, the anecdotal articles on LD among delinquents, the literature reviews—can be seen in the collection of titles in Appendix E. Here, the purpose is more limited: *When proponents of the LD/JD link claim, as in the quotations heading this chapter, that the high incidence of LD among delinquents has been proved, what evidence are they talking about?*

We identified six studies for which it is reasonable to critique an estimate of incidence. By that, we mean that the studies explicitly sought to diagnose LD among a delinquent sample which was not preselected on the basis of learning problems, and which sought to draw some conclusions about the incidence of LD. The studies are: Berman (1975), Compton (1974), Critchley (1968), Duling et al. (1970), Mulligan (1969), and Stenger (1975). . . .

*

First, only two of the six studies (Critchley, 1968 and Stenger, 1975) were written for a scientific or academic audience. It is therefore quite possible that procedures in the other four were not fully reported. A lengthly account of, say, diagnostic techniques is not appropriate for a presentation to an ACLD conference. Sometimes we have been able to clarify issues through interviews with the authors; sometimes that has not been possible. Overall, it should be remembered that we are assessing these studies by standards that most of them never pretended to meet.

This, however, leads to the second, extremely important point made at the outset of this section and reiterated here: the technical issues we raise are fundamental ones. *We are not assessing whether the estimates of incidence are off-base by a few percentage points, but whether they mean anything at all.* In the discussion which follows, we have deliberately tried to avoid pointing to technical errors which are only peripherally relevant.

Tables II and III summarize some facts about the studies: the populations from which the samples were drawn, sample sizes, reported incidence of LD, and the operational criteria which led to the diagnoses. . . .

Populations   The use of institutionalized male delinquents in four of the six studies has the advantage of finessing at least some of the definitional questions surrounding delinquency. As a rule, institutionalization in a training school has been increasingly reserved for juveniles who have been adjudicated for offenses which would be crimes if committed by an adult. Increasingly, it has been reserved for juveniles who have been apprehended for more than one offense. So the populations in these four studies can plausibly be assumed to include few borderline cases. The *dis*advantage of using institutionalized delin-

Table II. Summary of LD Incidence Findings in the Existing Literature

			Diagnosed as LD	
Study	*Population*	*N*	*N*	*Percent*
Berman	Institutionalized male delinquents	46	26	56
Critchley	Institutionalized male delinquents	106	not reported	
Compton	Institutionalized male delinquents	444	?	90.4
Duling	Institutionalized male delinquents	59	19	32
Mulligan	Adjudicated delinquents and children referred by schools for delinquent tendencies	32	4[a]	n.a.
Stengel	Males and females, non-institutionalized adjudicated delinquents	67	15	22

[a]19 others showed some similar symptoms of varying severity, but funds did not permit full-scale diagnosis.

Table III. Operational Criteria for Diagnosis of LD Applied by the Incidence Studies

Study	Criterion for diagnosis of LD	Comments
Berman	Subject scores in impaired range on at least one subtest of the Halstead-Reitan Battery	The Halstead-Reitan tests were developed for use as a battery in diagnosis of brain lesions. Reliability of separate subtests for diagnosis of LD is unknown.
Compton	not specified	An extensive battery of established tests was used. "Mild", "moderate" and "severe" levels were specified. Bases for these classifications are not known.
Critchley	(dyslexia only) Reading retardation of 3 or more years if IQ $\geqslant$ 90, 5 or more if IQ < 90; plus indications based on test batteries for dyslexia. Ocular, other medical and psychological explanations were checked.	Author assumes underdiagnosis of dyslexics because of stringency of the criteria.
Duling	Criterion cannot be reconstructed. Probably based on scoring beyond cut-off points on at least one of 3 or 4 tests.	Text is ambiguous and contradictory about tests used and scoring procedures.
Mulligan	(dyslexia only) Reading retardation of more than 2 years, plus indications based on batteries for dyslexia and medical history.	Funds were available for only four full-scale diagnoses.
Stenger	(1) Subject has academic difficulties, (2) WRAT more than 10 points below FSIQ, (3) difference between VIQ and PIQ more than 15 points or "significant" scattering of subtest scores.	VIQ/PIQ difference as indicator of LD has extensive and controversial literature. Widely seen as useful screening device; not adequate alone.

quents is their unrepresentativeness. If the question is whether delinquent acts in general tend to be committed disproportionately by learning disabled youth, testing institutionalized delinquents for LD is likely to yield inferences based on very skewed samples. It should be assumed that status offenders are underrepresented and that one-time offenders are underrepresented. Most significantly, it should be assumed that out of the set of delinquents who *could* be committed to an institution because of their offense histories, the ones who actually *are* committed also tend to be those who are not getting along at school. The child who is "seriously" delinquent but also attending school regularly and not acting out in the classroom is more likely to stay out of the institution. In short, we suggest that an institutionalized delinquent population is selected in ways which will drive up the incidence of all kinds of learning problems even beyond the high levels of learning problems among delinquents in general.

Incidence Estimates   The range of the estimates is impressive: from 90.4% to 56% to 32% to 22%. The disparity of estimates fairly reflects the disparity of definitions, procedures, and analyses in the studies.

Criterion for Diagnosis of LD   Of the six studies, only two (Critchley and Mulligan) use an approximation of the operational definition which has been proposed; that is, one which requires evidence of underachievement relative to ability and consistent, multiple indicators of perceptual disorder. One of the two (Critchley) concluded on balance that the high rates of reading retardation did not indicate comparably high rates of dyslexia; but he did not eliminate the possibility. The other study (Mulligan) was truncated for lack of funds; the author believes that continuation of the study would have produced an unusually high number of diagnoses of dyslexia.

The Compton study deserves special mention with regard to diagnosis. Conceptually, Compton's approach to LD was very broad— "anything which prevents a child from achieving successfully in a normal educational setting" (Compton, 1974, p. 49). But actual diagnosis of the delinquents was conducted by use of an extensive set of established tests. The data referenced by Compton are potentially very rich, despite the obstacles to interpreting them from the published record.

The operational criterion used in Duling et al. is indecipherable. The sum of the criticisms is that the more closely the article is read, the more difficult it is to understand how a subject was tagged "LD."

Stenger's criterion is attractive insofar as it demands evidence of underachievement relative to ability; but her reliance on the analysis of IQ scores and subtests as evidence of perceptual disorder raises a number of difficulties: the significance of VIQ/PIQ differences and the scattering of subtest scores is the subject of an active

debate. There seems to be reasonably broad agreement that the procedure is a useful screening device.

*

Methodological Considerations   Overall, how do the studies match up against normal standards of data analysis and interpretations?

Berman   This study represents a generally careful, competent administration of the tests in question. The two main issues about the LD incidence rates are: 1) How many of the delinquent sample (mean IQ = 90.6, standard deviation = 11.4) who were diagnosed LD were also mentally retarded? 2) Does a score on a single subtest constitute a meaningful definition of "disability?" With a sample size of only 46, even relatively small changes in numbers of LD diagnoses would produce large changes in the percentage estimates of incidence.

Compton   The raw data which Compton was using could well be an invaluable source of information about LD among delinquents. But the published record, meant for a nontechnical audience and using tabulations compiled for planning treatment needs, is unusable for estimating incidence of LD. An examination of the matrix in the article indicates that a narrower definition of LD would cut the 90.4% figure drastically. When, for example, the reader asks about the subset of the Compton sample most likely to have met a strict definition of LD—"severe" cases of auditory, visual, and language processing disabilities—the percentage is less than 20%. It is probably *much* less, because the percentage is computed from diagnoses, not individuals (mean = 2.6 diagnoses per handicapped child) and the definitions of even these areas are very broad (including in language processing, for example, bilingual children who do not decode equally well in both languages). This does not mean that only the "severe" cases would have met a strict definition of LD (we have no way of knowing); the point is simply that the reader cannot work backwards from the published record into an estimate of what the data imply about learning disabilities among delinquent children.

Critchley   This article is by far the most scholarly, painstaking available discussion of dyslexia among a delinquent population. The discussion of method is precise and the interpretation of results is restrained. Critchley's is also the only study that fails to support the LD/JD link. This does not disprove the link, but it does raise the question: If the other studies had used a comparably rigorous approach to the clinical phenomena and the evidence of disability in learning, how deeply would their estimates of LD incidence have been cut?

Duling et al.   Whether the problem is simply trying to decide what tests were used (one of them is given five different labels), or for what purposes, or the results of the analysis, this article fails to give the reader consistent answers. A close examination of the text does not resolve confusion; it adds new questions.

Mulligan   This study, conducted at the Sonoma County Probation Department, is a potentially valuable study cut short. Diagnostic procedures appear to have been thorough, and Mulligan's presentation of case-by-case data is extremely helpful in interpreting the findings. But the case-by-case data also reveal that the sample of 32 children who were to be tested for dyslexia was very different—perhaps drawn from a completely different population—than the "total caseload" of 60 adjudicated, committable delinquents referred to the Special Supervision Unit of the Department for which reading-level data are initially presented (Mulligan, 1969, pp. 177–179). In particular, the smaller sample suffered from substantially more severe learning problems than the total caseload of the Special Supervision Unit. Insofar as we can reconstruct the procedure, it seems that the 32 were drawn from overall referrals to the probation department, not just from among adjudicated delinquents. The 32 included children referred under California's compulsory education laws for truancy or for acting out behavior in the classroom, even though they had committed no delinquent act. For some (unknown) proportion of the 32, then, the question was not "Do adjudicated delinquents tend to have dyslexia?" but "Do children with severe school problems tend to have dyslexia?"—two very different questions. This helps to account for the inference which could be drawn from the Mulligan data, that the adjudicated, committable delinquents had *fewer* learning problems than the borderline cases. In any event, the four children who mainfested the most severe reading retardation, or who were already in classes for the educationally handicapped, were diagnosed and found to be dyslexic. Funds were exhausted before another 19 reading retarded children in the sample of 32 could be diagnosed.

Stenger   Within the limits set for itself, this appears to have been a carefully conducted survey. The author's attempt to distinguish between underachievement because of LD from problems of generally low mental capacity is especially welcome. The validity of the PIQ/VIQ approach to the diagnosis of perceptual disorders is a major question mark in interpreting the results.

Adding up the pieces of evidence and the obstacles to interpreting them, what can be said about the incidence of LD among delinquents? When a draft of this discussion was shown to reviewers of varying perspectives, the answers varied predictably. At one extreme, some argued simply that the studies had been subjected to a hatchet job. Another, sometimes related argument was that so much smoke must mean some fire. From another extreme, it was argued that the existing evidence that delinquents are disproportionately learning disabled is too slipshod to warrant serious attention. We obviously do not share the first of these views. But we do share some common ground with each of the other reactions, when the quantitative studies are seen in the perspective of the other, less formal evidence which was obtained.

REFERENCES

Berman, A. Personal communication, 1976.

Berman, A., Siegal, A. A neurological approach to the etiology, prevention and treatment of juvenile delinquency. Unpublished document, 1975.

Compton, R. The learning disabled adolescent. In B. Kratoville (Ed.), *Youth in trouble.* Proceedings of a symposium, Dallas-Fort Worth Regional Airport, May 1974. San Rafael, Calif.: Academic Therapy Publications, 1974.

Critchley, E. Reading retardation, dyslexia and delinquency. *British Journal of Psychiatry,* 1968, 114, 1537–1547.

Duling, F., Eddy, S., & Risko, V. *Learning disabilities and juvenile delinquency.* Unpublished paper prepared at the Robert F. Kennedy Youth Center, Morgantown, W. Va., 1970.

Elliott, D. S., & Voss, H. L. *Delinquency and dropout.* Lexington, Mass.: Heath and Company, 1974.

Hursch, H. Personal communication, 1976.

Hurwitz, I., Bibace, R. M., Wolff, P. H., & Rowbotham, B. M. Neuropsychological function of normal boys, delinquent boys, and boys with learning problems. *Perceptual and Motor Skills,* 1972, 35(2), 387–394.

Jacobson, F. N. Learning disabilities and juvenile delinquency: A demonstrated relationship. In R. E. Weber (Ed.), *Handbook of learning disabilities: A prognosis for the child, the adolescent, the adult.* Englewood Cliffs, N. J.: Prentice-Hall, 1974. Pp. 189–216.

Mulligan, W. A study of dyslexia and delinquency. *Academic Therapy Quarterly,* 1969, 4(3), 177–187.

Peters, J. E. Speech before the Symposium on the Relationship of Delinquency to Learning Disabilities Among Youth, Little Rock, Arkansas, December 1974. Pp. 1–6.

Poremba, C. D. Speech before the Symposium on the Relationship of Delinquency to Learning Disabilities Among Youth, Little Rock, Arkansas, December 1974. Pp. 1–11.

Poremba, C. D. Learning disabilities, youth and delinquency: Programs for intervention. In H. R. Myklebust (Ed.), *Progress in learning disabilities.* Vol. 3. New York: Grune & Stratton, 1975. Pp. 123–149.

Quay, H. C., & Werry, J. S. (Ed.) *Psychopathological disorders of childhood.* New York: John Wiley & Sons, 1972.

Reitan, R. M. A research program on the psychological effects of brain lesions in human beings. In N. R. Ellis (Ed.), *Internatonal review of research in mental retardation.* Vol. I. New York: Academic Press Inc., 1966. Pp. 153–218.

Reitan, R.M. Personal communication, 1976.

Silberberg, N. E., & Silberberg, M. C. School achievement and delinquency. *Review of Educational Research,* 1971, 41(1), 17–33.

Stenger, M. *Frequency of learning disabilities in adjudicated delinquents.* Masters thesis at the University of Missious-Kansas City. Kansas City, Missiouri, 1975.

Sullivan, Grant, & Grant. The development of interpersonal maturity: Applications to delinquency. *Psychiatry,* 1971, 20, 373–385.

Wacker, J. A. *The reduction of crime through the prevention and treatment of learning disabilities.* Report to the National Institute of Law Enforcement and Criminal Justice, Law Enforcement Assistance Administration, September 1974.

Warren, M. Q. et al. Interpersonal maturity level classification: juvenile diagnosis and treatment of low, middle, and high maturity delinquents. Community Treatment Project, California Youth Authority, 1966.

Wepman, J. M., Cruickshank, W. M., Deutsch, C. P., Morency, A., Strother, C. R. Learning disabilities. In Nicholas Hobbs (Ed.), *Issues in the classification of children.* Vol. I. San Francisco: Jossey-Bass, 1975. Pp. 300–317.

Wolfgang, M. E., Figlio, R. M., & Sellin, T. *Delinquency in a birth cohort.* University of Chicago Press, 1972.

32. Lunar Cycles and Homicides

ARNOLD L. LIEBER
CAROLYN R. SHERIN

THE CONCEPT OF LUNAR INFLUENCE ON HUMAN and animal behavior has intrigued mankind for thousands of years. Observers in almost every age known to man have attempted to correlate the positions of the moon in relation to the Earth and sun with various terrestrial phenomena, but scientific evidence has been lacking (1). Today it is well known that the moon, through the effects of its gravitational forces on the Earth, is the major regulator of tidal changes in our great bodies of water. Recent meteorological evidence (2–10) suggests that a tidal effect exists in certain atmospheric phenomena of the Earth as well.

If one considers the human organism as a microcosm comprised of essentially the same elements as and in similar proportions to those of the Earth's surface (approximately 80 percent water and 20 percent organic and inorganic minerals), one could speculate that the gravitational forces of the moon might exert a similar influence upon the water mass of the human microcosm. One of us (A.L.L.), drawing on evidence from various medical and nonmedical scientific disciplines, theorizes that the moon, via the effects of its gravitational forces on the human organism, causes cyclic changes in water flow among the fluid compartments of the body (intracellular, extracellular, intravascular, and intraluminal), as well as changes in total body water, resulting in what might be termed "biological tides" (11). These changes, together with associated electrolyte and hormonal shifts, may set the stage for differential thresholds of neural triggering and/or altered levels of neuromuscular irritability, thus giving rise to "normal" variations in emotional tone and, in certain constitutionally predisposed individuals, to more or less severe emotional disturbance.

In order to explore this theory two preliminary hypotheses have been formulated: 1) that a relationship exists between the lunar synodic cycle and human emotional disturbance, and 2) that any measurable disturbance would be directly proportional to the magnitude of gravitational force exerted upon the Earth at that point in time. The purpose of this study was to test these two hypotheses, using homicides as a quantifiable reflection of massive emotional upheavals in members of the general population. If a lunar effect on homicides does exist, we postulated that it would resemble a tidal periodicity, with the greatest frequency of occurrence falling around new and full moon. If gravity is the main determinant of such an effect, then the greatest frequency in homicides would be expected to occur at times of maximum tidal force, i.e., coincidence of new moon and/or full moon with lunar perigee.

▶SOURCE: *"Homicides and the Luna Cycles: Toward a Theory of Lunar Influence on Human Emotional Disturbance," American Journal of Psychiatry* (July 1972) 129:101–106. Copyright 1972, the American Psychiatric Association. Reprinted by permission.

METHOD

Data on all homicides committed in Dade County, Fla., during the 15-year period 1956–1970 (a total of 1,949 cases) were collected from the office of the Dade County Medical Examiner. The case number and time of injury (month, day, year, and hour) for each homicide were keypunched onto individual data cards. Data on all homicides that occurred in Cuyahoga County, Ohio, during the 13-year period 1958–1970 (a total of 2,033 cases) were collected in a similar manner from the Cuyahoga County Coroner's office in Cleveland. For homicides in which the day of injury but not the precise hour was known, the hour 12 (noon) was punched in the appropriate card columns. Homicides for which the exact date of injury was not known were eliminated from the data samples. The final usable data samples consisted of 1,887 cases for Dade County and 2,008 cases for Cuyahoga County. Two computer programs were prepared for the IBM 1130 computer to handle the data.

Generation of Lunar Phase Interval Program

A lunar synodic decimal scale is used by meteorologists at the National Oceanic and Atmospheric Administration (NOAA) for measuring lunar influences on atmospheric phenomena. In keeping with the fluctuating nature of astronomical phenomena, the time intervals used in constructing this scale are not necessarily equal; in fact, they are revised every ten years. In order to measure the number of homicides per unit of time, however, it is necessary for the time intervals to be of equal length. For this reason a new system was designed called the "lunar phase interval scale." All dates designated on the homicide cards were converted to number of minutes, using as a base an arbitrary date in the distant past. This time was divided into equal periods of 29.53 days (the average number of days in the lunar synodic cycle over any long period of time; the exact synodic cycle may vary by almost a day in any given year).

These 29.53-day periods were subdivided into 30 equal time intervals; the number 30 was an arbitrary choice, although in choosing it we took into consideration the number of homicides in the data samples.

The subdivisions, called lunar phase intervals, were numbered from 1 to 30. The number of homicides falling into all subdivisions (lunar phase intervals) numbered 1 were counted; the number of homicides falling into all subdivisions numbered 2 were counted, and so on, yielding a total of 30 counts. These counts encompassed the total number of cases in the data sample being run. In order to determine which of the subdivisions represented each of the four phases of the synodic cycle (new moon, first quarter, full moon, or last quarter) test cases that occurred on dates in which there was a new moon (12) were run. The lunar phase interval in which these fell was designated as new moon. This was repeated for each of the other three phases. The plots produced by this program were used for qualitative inspection of the data; no test of significance was involved.

Generation of the Program for Statistical Comparisons

Lunar phase instants (12) for each phase during the 15-year period 1956–1970 were keypunched onto data cards and stored by the computer. Instants of each lunar apogee and perigee for the same period were keypunched and stored as were the dates when a full moon and/or a new moon coincided with perigee to within 24 hours (13). Each homicide data sample, corrected for periods of Daylight Saving Time, was converted to Universal Time. All dates and times in each of the data files were converted to minutes beginning with 12 a.m. on January 1, 1956. Time windows of 72, 48, and 24 hours before and after each phase were examined for the number of homicides occurring over the 15-year span. Unilateral time periods of varying length on either side of an index phase could also be examined. The test of significance between binomial proportions was used to determine whether the actual number of homicides that occurred within the various windows differed significantly from the number expected, based strictly on the fraction of the total time covered by the windows.

The Dade County homicide sample was run using the first program and the homicide counts were plotted for each lunar phase interval. For the sake of clarity and conformity to existing conventions in lunar phase plotting, our interval number 19, which corresponds to the new moon, was plotted first on our graphs (see Figure 1). The Dade sample was then run using the second program. The number of homicides found in the various time windows around each phase, as well as around apogee, perigee, etc., together with the number of minutes in each window were tabulated. A one-tailed test was used to determine whether the results were significant in the predicted direction. The significant findings are recorded in Table I. This procedure was repeated using the homicide sample for Cuyahoga County.

RESULTS

Homicides in Dade County, plotted for lunar phase intervals, showed an apparent lunar periodicity (see Figure 1). The homicides peaked at full moon and showed a trough leading up to new moon, followed by a secondary peak just after new moon. These homicides showed statistically significant groupings around full moon and new moon (table 1). The number of cases occurring within the 24 hours before and after full moon over the 15-year period was significantly greater (p < .03) than the expected values. Starting 24 hours after new moon, the homicides committed in the next 24-hour period showed a significant increase (p = .003). Cases occurring around apogee and perigee did not differ significantly from expected values, nor did cases occurring around coincidences of full moon and perigee and/or new moon and perigee differ significantly from expected values.

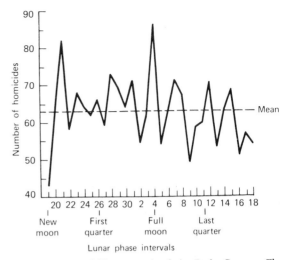

Figure 1. Homicides committed in Dade County, Fla. (1956-1970). Plotted in relation to the lunar synodic cycle.

In the Cuyahoga sample (Figure 2) homicides peaked at three intervals after full moon. There was a secondary peak one interval after last quarter and another secondary peak two intervals after new moon. The two curves present a similar configuration but the peaks in the Cuyahoga data are shifted to the right. Starting 24 hours after new moon, the cases in the next 24-hour period approached significance (p = .07); and starting 48 hours after full moon, the cases in the next 24-hour period also approached significance (p = .07). As in the Dade sample, there was no significant increase in the frequency of homicides relative to the apogee-perigee cycle.

DISCUSSION

Our findings suggest that a lunar influence on the frequency of homicides may exist. Studies of this type, aimed at delineating small effects, require large samples of accurate data collected over a long period of time. Ideally such studies should be replicated using an independent data sample from a different geographical area. Previously reported studies on the relationship of moon phase and mental illness (14–22) have

Table I. Homicides in Dade County (1956-1970): Tests that Reached Statistical Significance[a]

| Index Phase (IP) | Time Window Examined | | Minutes in time window | Homicides in time window | Level of significance[b] |
	Hours before IP	Hours after IP			
New moon	0	24 to 48	267,840	86	p = .003
New moon	0	24 to 72	535,680	149	p = .018
Full moon	0	48	532,800	145	p = .054
Full moon	24	24	532,800	148	p = .029

[a]Complete data tables for both Dade and Cuyahoga Counties in which all time windows tested for each phase are shown are available from the authors upon request.

[b]In determining the statistical significance of each result, two values remained constant -the total time of the study, which was 7,889,760 minutes, and the total number of homicides, which was 1,887.

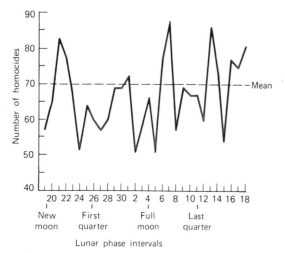

Figure 2. Homicides committed in Cuyahoga County, Ohio (1958–1970), plotted in Relation to the Lunar Synodic Cycle.

usually failed to consider one or more of these essentials and their results have been equivocal. The present study shows a statistically significant lunar periodicity for homicides occurring in Dade County, Fla., over a 15-year period. A similar periodicity was found in the sample for Cuyahoga County, Ohio, although the peaks were shifted to the right and did not quite reach significance. This suggests that geographic location may be a significant variable, as it often is for geophysical and meteorological phenomena.

Support for this interesting possibility is provided by the studies of Brown and Park. Studying the metabolic activity of hamsters in Evanston, Ill., Brown and Park (23) were able to demonstrate a lunar periodicity in running activity in hamsters over a one-year period. Figure 3 shows a comparison of their curve of hamster activity with the curve of homicides in Cuyahoga County (Cleveland) (Figure 3). Cleveland and Evanston are in almost identical locations with respect to geographical latitude, and the similarity between the two periodicities relative to the lunar synodic cycle is striking.

To explore the second hypothesis, the role of gravitation was assessed by testing the data on homicides for significance relative to the anomalistic or apogee-perigee cycle of the moon. No relationship was found between frequency of homicides and position of the moon in its anomalistic cycle. Times of maximum lunar gravitational influence occur at the coincidence of new moon or full moon with lunar perigee; at these times the ocean tides are unusually high. During our 15-year study period, coincidence of new or full moon with perigee (to within 24 hours) occurred 29 times, and time-window analysis of these periods showed no significant increase in the frequency of homicides. However, informal observations suggest that times of maximum gravitational force may be related to *qualitative* differences in individual

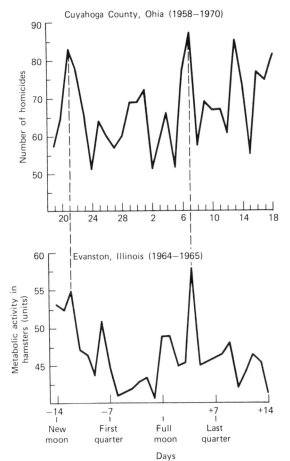

Figure 3. Comparison of curve of homicides in Cuyahoga County with curve of activity in hamsters. (Cleveland, Ohio, is at latitude 41.30 N and longitude 81.41 W; Evanston, Ill., is at latitude 42.02 N and longitude 87.41 W. Note the striking coincidence of peaks relative to the lunar synodic cycle.)

acts of violence. Perusal of the official narratives on individual incidents of homicide indicates that homicides occurring during these periods are often of a particular bizarre or ruthless nature. A considerable number of crimes committed at these times appear to be provoked by irrational actions on the part of the victims.

It must be emphasized that these observations are subjective and would be difficult to quantify. Yet meteorologists have reported analogous findings. Carpenter and associates (10), in demonstrating a lunar influence on hurricane formation, showed that the apogee-perigee cycle plays no role in the timing of storm formation (this is strictly a function of the synodic cycle) but may affect the amplitude of the peaks that occur in relation to the synodic cycle. Since the frequency of homicides does not increase in direct proportion to the forces of gravity, the second hypothesis was not supported by our study. Our observations suggest that the possible role of gravitational forces on human behavior is a complex problem requiring further study.

In anticipation of certain inevitable questions, we recognize that this study in no way implies cause-and-effect relationships. Although we specifically examined our data in relation to the lunar cycle, the possibility exists that other (nonlunar) periodicities could account for the observed effect. Some might attribute to moon lore (suggestion) the effect of a self-fulfilling prophecy in that unusual behavior has been associated historically with times of full moon. We would like to point out, however, that this hardly explains the effect demonstrated around new moon, which has little anecdotal significance with regard to moon lore.

We consider that the findings documented here support the first of our hypotheses in that a relationship between the lunar synodic cycle and crimes of violence, as reflected by homicides, appears to exist. This relationship, if confirmed in independent data samples, would be compatible with Lieber's theory of biological tides. Aggravated assault, which is essentially the same criminal act as homicide, differing only in that the victim survives, represents such an independent data sample; we are currently in the process of examining this.

The methodology developed for this study should prove useful in assessing the possible influence of lunar cycles on any quantifiable variable that occurs over a known period of time. Further, it appears that geographical location is a significant factor in determining the timing of such occurrences as homicide peaks in relation to the synodic cycle. Confirmation of this effect awaits a replication in Dade County, Fla., of

Brown and Park's studies of metabolic activity in hamsters.

REFERENCES

1. McDaniel WB: The moon, werewolves and medicine. Trans Coll Physicians Phila 18:113–122, 1950

2. Bjerknes J: Atmospheric tides. Journal of Marine Research 7:157–162, 1948

3. Stolov HL: Tidal wind fields in the atmosphere. Journal of Meteorology 12:117–140, 1955

4. Jordan CL: Tidal forces and the formation of hurricanes. Nature 175:38–39, 1955

5. Bradley DA, Woodbury MA, Brier GW: Lunar synodical period and widespread precipitation. Science 137:748–749, 1962

6. Kiser WL, Carpenter TH, Brier GW: The atmospheric tides at Wake Island. Monthly Weather Review 91:566–572, 1963

7. Brier GW, Bradley DA: The lunar synodical period and precipitation in the United States. Journal of Atmospheric Science 21:386–395, 1964

8. Brier GW: Diurnal and semidiurnal atmospheric tides in relation to precipitation variations. Monthly Weather Review 93:93–100, 1965

9. Brier GW, Simpson J: Tropical cloudiness and rainfall related to the tidal and pressure variations. Quarterly Journal of the Royal Meteorological Society 95:120–147, 1969

10. Carpenter TH, Holle RL, Fernandez-Partagas JJ: Observed relationships between lunar tidal cycles and formation of hurricanes and tropical storms. Monthly Weather Review (to be published)

11. Lieber AL: Moon, myth and mental illness: a research proposal. Presented to the Research Coordinating Committee, University of Miami School of Medicine, Miami, Fla, June 1970

12. American Ephemeris and Nautical Almanac, annual eds. Washington, DC, US Government Printing Office, 1956–1970

13. Carpenter TH: Decimal Ephemeris of the Sun and Moon, 1848 to 1974. Washington, DC, US Weather Bureau Library, 1970 (microfilm)

14. Kelley DM: Mania and the moon. Psychoanal Rev 29:406–426, 1942

15. Oliven JF: Moonlight and nervous disorders. Amer J Psychiat 99:579–584, 1943

16. Pokorny AD: Moon phases, suicide, and homicide. Amer J Psychiat 121:66–67, 1964

17. Osborn RD: The moon and the mental hospital. Journal of Psychiatric Nursing 6:88–93, 1968

18. Pokorny AD: Moon phases and mental admissions. Journal of Psychiatric Nursing 6:325–327, 1968

19. Bauer SF, Hornick EJ: Lunar effect on mental illness. Amer J Psychiat 125:696–697, 1968

20. Lilienfeld DM: Lunar effect on mental illness. Amer J Psychiat 125:1454, 1969

21. Lester D, Brockopp GW, Priebe K: Association between full moon and completed suicide. Psychol Rep 25:598, 1969

22. Shapiro JL, Streiner DL, Gray AL, et al: The moon and mental illness. Percept Motor Skills 30:827–830, 1970

23. Brown FA, Park YH: Synodic monthly modulation of the diurnal rhythm of hamsters. Proc Soc Exp Biol Med 125:712–715, 1967

33. Extroversion, Neuroticism, and Delinquency

MICHAEL J. HINDELANG

IN CRIME AND PERSONALITY, EYSENCK[1] HAS applied his general theory of personality[2] to the problem of criminal behavior in great detail. His theoretical argument is that personality is made up of two orthogonal components—extroversion-introversion and emotional stability-instability. Eysenck defines the extrovert as one who is more outgoing, active, and sociable than the introvert, who keeps more to himself and is less active. The emotionally unstable (neurotic) person is characterized by excessive anxiety and worry, while the emotionally stable person exhibits less anxiety and worry. It is Eysenck's contention that offenders are more extroverted and neurotic than nonoffenders.

Eysenck's argument that criminals should be extroverted is much more elaborate than his argument that criminals should be more neurotic than controls. Briefly,[3] he suggests that there is a relationship between the personality attribute of extroversion and Pavlov's notion of cortical fatigue (cortical inhibition)—something which builds up, for example, during conditioning trials and dissipates with rest. Eysenck believes that extroverts build up cortical fatigue more quickly than introverts, and in fact, he presents evidence which supports this proposition.[4]

This relationship between extroversion and cortical fatigue implies several behavioral consequences. For instance, the conditioning of extroverts will be more difficult than will the conditioning of introverts; in the former case, cortical fatigue builds up quickly during conditioning trials and thus, conditioning occurs more slowly. This in turn means that extroverts and introverts who come from similar environments will be differently socialized—introverts internalizing the norms to a greater extent than extroverts, since the internalization of norms can be thought of as a conditioning process. Furthermore, since cortical fatigue builds up more quickly in extroverts than in introverts, when individuals are exposed to sustained stimulation, cortical fatigue will build up more quickly in the extroverted subjects than in the introverted subjects. This will reduce the effective amount of stimulation experienced by the extroverts.[5] The implication of this is that extroverts are relatively stimulus-seeking and introverts are relatively stimulus-avoiding; since stimulation has less of

▶SOURCE: *"Extroversion, Neroticism and Self-Reported Delinquent Involvement," Journal of Research in Crime and Delinquency (January 1971), 8(1): 23–31.* Reprinted with permission of the National Council on Crime and Delinquency.

[1]H. Eysenck, *Crime and Personality,* (London: Pergamon Press, 1964).

[2]H. Eysenck, *Dimensions of Personality,* (London: Routedge and Kegan Paul, 1947); H. Eysenck, *The Structure of Human Personality,* (London: Routledge and Kegan Paul, 1953); H. Eysenck, *The Dynamics of Anxiety and Hysteria,* (London: Routledge and Kegan Paul, 1957).

[3]Space does not permit an adequate presentation of Eysenck's theoretical rationale and the empirical evidence supporting his position. The reader unfamiliar with his theory is encouraged to see Eysenck (1964) for a complete explication.

[4]Eysenck, 1964, *op cit., supra* note 1, pp. 64–94.

[5]Eysenck, 1964, *op cit., supra* note 1, p. 97.

an effect on extroverts than on introverts, time passes more slowly for the former than for the latter.

Thus, Eysenck's position is that the internalization of norms is a conditioned reflex and since extroverts condition poorly due to their tendency to build up cortical fatigue quickly, they have not been adequately socialized. In addition, since time passes more slowly for extroverts, they become easily bored and their seeking of stimulation (including excitement) often brings them outside the law. Finally, high emotional instability (neuroticism) acts as a driving force which further propels individuals to action.

Several researchers have conducted investigations which bear directly on Eysenck's contentions that criminals and delinquents are more extroverted and neurotic than controls. Michael[6] has found that extroverts who were referred to her clinic as children were more likely to become delinquents and criminals known to the police than were introverts and ambiverts who were referred to her clinic. Bartholomew[7] has found institutionalized criminals to be more extroverted and neurotic than noncriminals. Likewise, Price[8] has found institutionalized delinquent girls to be more extroverted and neurotic than controls. Becker,[9] Knapp,[10] Jurjevich,[11] and Siegman[12] have found offenders to exhibit neuroticism and anxiety to a greater extent than nonoffenders.

All of the studies cited above (with the exception of Siegman's) have defined the delinquent and criminal populations as being composed of those individuals who have official police records and/or who are institutionalized at the time of the study. These "official" criminals are most probably not representative of those engaging in illegal activities. When the criminal sample is biased, some of the same factors that bias it may be the very cause that the variable under study shows up more frequently than in a control sample. For example, some of the studies referred to above have found institutionalized criminals and delinquents to be more extroverted than controls.[13] However, there is also evidence which indicates that extroverts tend to be less cautious than introverts.[14] It is possible then, that those criminals who are caught and successfully prosecuted are less cautious than those criminals who operate undetected and continue to commit crimes. Since carelessness is correlated with extroversion, institutionalized criminals may be more extroverted than controls—not because criminals in general are more extroverted than noncriminals, but because institutionalized criminals are more careless (and hence more extroverted) than noninstitutionalized criminals. In addition, most of the studies cited above have obtained extroversion and neuroticism scores during incarceration. It is possible that the institutionalization experience or testing within an institutional setting may have resulted in elevated extroversion and neuroticism scores. Finally, none of the studies referred to above has examined the relationship of extroversion and neuroticism to types of illegal behavior such as theft, drug use, etc.

[6]C. Michael, "Follow-Up Studies of Introverted Children, Part III: Relative Incidence of Criminal Behavior," *Journal of Criminal Law, Criminology, and Police Science*, 47:414–422, (1957).

[7]A. Bartholomew, "Some Comparative Australian Data for the MPI," *Australian Journal of Psychology*, 15:46–51, (1963).

[8]J. B. Price, "Some Results on the Maudsley Personality Inventory from a Sample of Girls in Borstal," *British Journal of Criminology*, 8:383–401, (1968).

[9]P. Becker, "Some Correlates of Delinquency and Validity of Questionnaire Assessment Methods," *Psychological Reports*, 16:271–277, (1965).

[10]R. Knapp, "Delinquency and Objective Personality Test Factors," *Journal of Applied Psychology*, 49:8–10, (1965).

[11]R. Jurjevich, "Normative Data for the Clinical and Additional MMPI Scales for a Population of Delinquent Girls," *Journal of General Psychology*, 69:143–146, (1963).

[12]A. Siegman, "Personality Variables Associated with Admitted Criminal Behavior," *Journal of Consulting Psychology*, 26:199, (1962).

[13]C. Michael, *op cit.*, *supra* note 6, pp. 412–422; A. Bartholomew, *op cit.*, *supra* note 7, pp. 46–51.

[14]Eysenck, 1964, *op cit.*, *supra* note 1, pp. 64–94.

In an attempt to circumvent these three methodological difficulties, a battery of tests including Eysenck's Maudsley Personality Inventory (which measures extroversion and neuroticism) and a self-report index of delinquent involvement were administered to a middle-class sample of 234 boys (mean number of years of father's education = 12.9, standard deviation = 2.6 years) from a Catholic high school in Oakland, California. The sample consists of those boys from the school population (N = 280) who were present and willing to cooperate on the day of testing. The author was introduced to the respondents as a researcher from the University of California who was interested in finding out about the attitudes and activities of high school students. The subjects were asked to respond anonymously and were assured that their responses would be considered confidential.

The twenty-six delinquent activities[15] in Table I made up the self-report delinquency questionnaire. The respondents were asked to indicate the number of times in the last year they had engaged in each activity. For each activity, if the number of times that the activity had been engaged in was between zero and eight, inclusive, the respondent was given a score equal to that number; if the respondent indicated that he had engaged in the activity nine or more times, he was given a score of nine.

By first using extroversion and then using neuroticism scores, subjects were trichotomized into high, medium, and low groups. Those with scores of .6 of a standard deviation or more above the mean were placed in the high group; those with scores of .6 of a standard deviation or more below the mean were placed in the low group; and the remaining subjects were placed in the middle group.

[15]It is recognized that some of the 26 activities are quite trivial and some of them (e.g., cheating on school exams) are not even prohibited by law. However, Eysenck's theory purports to encompass a wide variety of norm-violating behaviors; this accounts for the diversity of behaviors included among the 26 items. The term "delinquent activities" is used throughout the text for ease in communication since the vast majority of activities are in fact illegal for juveniles.

Using the 26 delinquent activities separately as dependent variables, and extroversion and neuroticism as independent variables, Table I presents the results of Kruskal-Wallis H-tests. According to Eysenck's theory, with *other things being equal*, one would expect delinquent involvement to increase monotonically as a function of both extroversion and neuroticism. With respect to extroversion, this relation is evident for theft of more than \$10 ($p < .003$), getting drunk ($p < .04$), individual fist fights ($p < .02$), group fist fights ($p < .008$), carrying weapons ($p < .02$), individual weapon fights ($p < .04$), marijuana use ($p < .03$), forcing one's sexual attentions on a girl ($p < .02$), promiscuous sexual activity ($p < .001$), drag racing ($p < .007$), driving under the influence of alcohol or drugs ($p < .02$), cheating on school exams ($p < .008$), using false identification ($p < .05$), as well as for overall delinquent involvement[16] ($p < .04$); there is a trend toward such a relationship for theft less than \$10 ($p < .07$), gambling ($p < .08$), shaking down others for money ($p < .10$), and involvement in hit and run accidents ($p < .06$).

Turning to the neuroticism variable in Table I, it is seen that the relationships between neuroticism and the delinquent activities are not linear, but tend generally toward curvilinear patterns. In nearly all cases the middle neurotic group (i.e., the most "normal" group) is the most delinquent, and the low neurotic group is the least delinquent, with the high neurotic group falling between the other two. The curvilinear relationships that reach or approach statistical significance are those between neuroticism and minor theft ($p < .03$), drinking ($p < .03$), marijuana use ($p < .02$), cheating on school exams ($p < .004$), using false identification ($p < .05$), cutting school ($p < .004$), as well as overall delinquent involvement ($p < .06$). The exceptions to the curvilinear pattern that reach or approach statistical significance are the monotonically increasing relationship between

[16]The score for overall delinquent involvement is arrived at by taking a simple sum across the 26 delinquent activities.

Table I. H-Test Results Comparing the Mean Ranked Delinquent Involvement of Extroversion and Neuroticism Groups

Activity	Extroversion					Neuroticism				
	Low	Medium	High	w^a	p	Low	Medium	High	w	p
Theft less than $10	103.2	118.0	128.8	.15	.07	103.4	129.3	114.0	.17	.03
Theft greater than $10	96.6	123.6	127.6	.22	.003	115.2	119.0	117.7	.03	.91
Property Destruction causing less than $10 damage	110.3	116.2	126.9	.10	.32	100.9	123.4	125.5	.17	.04
Property destruction causing greater than $10 damage	110.1	118.2	122.7	.08	.43	106.9	117.6	125.9	.13	.13
Drinking alcohol	106.8	116.1	126.5	.11	.22	101.2	127.8	116.2	.17	.03
Getting drunk	110.3	111.5	130.8	.17	.04	107.4	122.0	117.9	.11	.24
Engaging in fist-fights with an individual	99.8	118.8	132.2	.18	.02	109.1	122.9	118.4	.08	.43
Engaging in gang fist-fights	101.4	119.3	132.0	.20	.008	116.4	118.7	118.7	.02	.96
Carrying a concealed weapon	101.7	118.4	130.0	.18	.02	120.6	118.6	111.6	.06	.63
Engaging in fights with an individual with a weapon	113.7	114.4	127.1	.16	.04	115.8	120.5	115.2	.07	.57
Engaging in gang fights with weapon	112.4	119.9	118.3	.09	.40	123.8	117.0	110.7	.15	.08
Engaging in illegal gambling	113.4	121.7	112.9	.15	.08	121.1	115.2	113.9	.11	.28
Using marijuana	109.6	110.9	132.0	.17	.03	99.6	124.9	121.6	.19	.02
Sniffing glue	112.4	116.9	121.2	.09	.39	109.3	120.2	118.4	.13	.15
Using LSD, methedrine, or mescaline	115.1	113.6	122.2	.10	.30	109.6	120.3	116.3	.12	.19
Using heroin	116.0	117.1	117.7	.06	.67	115.5	118.0	115.5	.11	.23
Shaking down others for money	108.3	120.4	119.2	.14	.10	114.7	118.7	115.3	.05	.75
Visiting a prostitute	111.4	120.3	117.0	.10	.29	112.0	121.2	114.2	.12	.22
Forcing sexual attention on girl against her will	108.2	116.6	126.7	.19	.02	112.9	120.7	116.0	.09	.39
Engaging in promiscuous sexual activity	94.0	114.2	129.0	.25	.001	111.5	116.2	110.4	.05	.74
Drag racing on street in excess of speed limit by 20 MPH	101.2	115.0	131.9	.21	.007	114.3	118.2	114.8	.03	.89
Driving while strongly under influence of alcohol or drugs	106.5	115.9	126.0	.18	.02	112.1	118.4	116.5	.06	.61
Being involved in hit and run accidents	109.4	116.5	112.6	.16	.06	120.8	115.7	111.9	.11	.24
Cheating on exams	97.3	117.4	132.3	.21	.008	95.2	126.4	123.2	.22	.004
Using false ID to pose as older person	102.4	120.8	116.9	.16	.05	109.1	123.9	107.5	.16	.05
Cutting school	88.6	105.6	101.3	.13	.19	84.5	113.6	95.2	.24	.004
Total delinquent involvement	82.2	100.0	110.6	.18	.04	87.6	109.8	95.9	.17	.06
Number in each group	59	105	70			68	94	72		

[a]This is the square root of the ratio of the explained to the total variance.

neuroticism and minor destruction of property ($p < .04$), and the montonically decreasing relationship between neuroticism and group weapon fighting ($p < .08$).

By using a cluster analysis technique (Tryon, 1958) it was possible to examine six clusters of delinquent activities made up of 17 separate acts. The clusters are composed of the following delinquent behaviors. *Cluster One, Theft:* thefts of less than $10 and thefts of more than $10; *Cluster Two, Malicious Destruction:* property destruction doing less than $10 damage, property destruction doing more than $10 damage; *Cluster Three, Aggressiveness:* engaging in individual fist fights, engaging in group fist fights, engaging in individual weapon fights, and carrying a dangerous weapon; *Cluster Four, Soft Drug Use:* drinking alcohol, getting drunk, using marijuana, driving under the influence of alcohol or drugs; *Cluster Five, Hard Drug Use:* using heroin, sniffing glue, using LSD, methedrine, or mescaline; *Cluster Six, School Misconduct:* cheating on school exams and cutting classes.

Using the six clusters of delinquent and the overall delinquent involvement score as dependent variables and extroversion and neuroticism as independent variables, Table II presents the results of the nonparametric H-tests. From Table II it can be seen that with respect to extroversion, the monotonic relation hypothesized by Eysenck reaches statistical significance for theft ($p < .005$), aggressiveness ($p < .001$), activities associated with the use of "soft" drugs ($p < .04$), school misconduct ($p < .04$), and total delinquent involvement ($p < .04$).

It can be seen from Table II that the relationships between neuroticism and the delinquent clusters are not linear as Eysenck has hypothesized but rather, as did the individual delinquency items, tend generally toward curvilinear patterns. In most cases the middle neurotic group is, again, the most delinquent; the low neurotic group is the least delinquent; with the high neurotic group falling between the other two. The curvilinear relationships that reach or approach statistical significance are those between neuroticism and "soft" drug use

($p < .02$), school misconduct ($p < .003$), and total delinquent involvement ($p < .06$); the exception to the curvilinear pattern is the trend toward significance for the monotonically increasing relationship between neuroticism and malicious destruction ($p < .06$).

Although the relations are weak, the data in the present study are generally consonant with Eysenck's theoretical formulations concerning the relation between extroversion and delinquent involvement. Interestingly, this relationship is persistent across a wide variety of activities. As extroversion increases, involvement in property theft, soft drug use, fighting offenses, school misconduct, total delinquency, malicious destruction of property, and hard drug use also increase; only in the last two areas does the relationship between extroversion and the clusters of delinquent activities fail to attain statistical significance.

The relationships between neuroticism and the delinquent activities are, however, even weaker and less uniform than the relationships between extroversion and the delinquent activities. Only for malicious destruction of property is there evidence ($p < .06$) of the linear relation between neuroticism and illegal behavior which Eysenck predicts. For the remaining illegal activities the tendency is for those respondents with average levels of neuroticism to be the most delinquent, while those at the low and high extremes are less delinquent. This is not the linear pattern that one would expect if Eysenck's theoretical formulations with respect to neuroticism were correct. Instead, the data are characterized by a curvilinear pattern. This Yerkes-Dodson (inverted-U) pattern has often been used to describe the relationship between drive level and performance.[17]

[17]P. Broadhurst, "The Interaction of Task Difficulty and Motivation: The Yerkes-Dodson Law Revived," *Acta Psychologia*, 16:321–338, (1959); J. Taylor, "The Relationship of Anxiety to the Conditioned Eyelid Response," *Journal of Experimental Psychology*, 41:81–92, (1951). Eysenck (1964:142–161), in fact, discusses this curvilinear pattern in another discussion of drive level; but he does not apply it to the relationship between neuroticism and criminality.

Table II. H-Test Results Comparing Mean Ranked Involvement in Clusters of Delinquent Behaviors of Low, Medium, and High Extroversion and Neuroticism Groups

	Extroversion					Neuroticism				
	Low	Medium	High	w^a	p	Low	Medium	High	w	p
Cluster 1: Theft (.74)[b]	96.0	127.7	134.0	.22	.005	107.9	127.6	116.9	.12	.18
Cluster 2: Malicious Destruction (.73)	108.0	117.4	128.9	.12	.19	102.7	121.3	128.3	.17	.06
Cluster 3: Aggressiveness (.70)	94.1	120.5	138.6	.25	.001	115.3	123.9	116.3	.06	.67
Cluster 4: Soft Drug Use (.79)	106.7	113.3	134.3	.16	.04	99.2	129.2	119.6	.19	.02
Cluster 5: Hard Drug Use (.70)	116.3	120.4	129.3	.10	.29	116.9	126.3	119.9	.08	.45
Cluster 6: School Misconduct (.83)	99.7	121.8	127.9	.16	.04	96.2	132.7	119.0	.22	.003
Total Delinquent Involvement	82.2	100.0	110.6	.16	.04	87.6	109.8	95.9	.17	.06
n Per Group	59	105	70			68	94	72		

[a]This is the square root of the ratio of the explained to the total variance.

[b]Numbers appearing in parentheses represent the reliability coefficients of the cluster scores on the full sets of delinquent activities defining each cluster.

Eysenck argues that offenders should be more neurotic than nonoffenders. This is comparable to saying that a group of high neurotic subjects should be more delinquent than a group of low neurotic subjects. In the present study, if one ignores the middle neurotic subjects, there is a general trend for the high neurotic group to be more delinquent than the low neurotic group. In order to test Eysenck's hypothesis exactly for each delinquent activity, the neuroticism scores for those engaging in the activity were compared with the neuroticism scores for those not engaging in the activity. In only three of the 26 cases (malicious destruction of property doing more than $10 damage, malicious destruction of property doing less than $10 damage, and cheating on exams in school) were the offenders significantly ($p < .05$) more neurotic than the nonoffenders; in the case of group weapon fighting, the offenders were significantly ($p < .05$) less neurotic than the nonoffenders. When all 26 activities are consi-

dered, the mean probability that the difference between the neuroticism scores of the offenders and nonoffenders is due to chance alone is .42.[18] It can, therefore, be said that Eysenck's formulations with respect to the neurotic proclivities of offenders are not generally supported by the present data.

One reason why past research has not found nonlinear relationships between neuroticism and illegal behavior (if indeed the curvilinearity exists in the populations previously studied) is certainly because past researchers have relied almost exclusively upon dichotomies between offenders and nonoffenders. Such procedures would, of course, quite effectively mask curvilinearity. However, the fact that even when the

[18]A similar analysis was carried out with the extroversion scores and it was found that in 19 out of 26 activities the offenders were significantly more extroverted than the nonoffenders. For all 26 activities, the mean probability that the difference between the extroversion scores for the offenders and nonoffenders is due to chance alone is .03.

offender/nonoffender dichotomy technique was used (see the paragraph above), poor discrimination was found, indicating that more than merely analytical differences between the present and past findings exist.

In *Crime and Personality,* Eysenck reports the findings of several researchers who have compared the extroversion and neuroticism scores of offenders and nonoffenders. It is interesting to note that across a variety of studies, in terms of standard scores, the mean differences between the institutionalized offenders and the nonoffenders were about 2.5 units and 4.6 units for extroversion and neuroticism, respectively. When the findings of these studies which used institutionalized offenders are contrasted with the finding of the present study which used noninstitutionalized offenders, the question arises as to why the neuroticism scores should be such a powerful discriminator in the previous studies and a relatively poor discriminator in the present study. In most previous studies there have been at least three apparent differences between members of the offender and nonoffender groups: (1) members of the offender group had been convicted of some violation of the law while members of the nonoffender group, in general, had not; (2) members of the offender group had been institutionalized while members of the nonoffender group, in general, had not been institutionalized; and (3) members of the offender group had responded to their personality questionnaires in the institution while members of the nonoffender group had responded to their questionnaires outside of the institution. In the present study, the only apparent difference between the offenders and nonoffenders was that the former reported having engaged in a delinquent act and the latter reported not having engaged in a delinquent act.[19] Since the larger difference in neuroticism scores that previous researchers have found has not been replicated in the present study, it is possible that the results in the earlier studies can be accounted for by any or all of the three factors noted above. That is the most neurotic offenders may be most likely to be convicted; institutionalization may cause neuroticism; an institutional environment may influence respondents to answer in a more neurotic direction. On the other hand, it may be that when a self-report technique is used, the moderately neurotic respondents are more inclined to disclose their delinquent involvement than those with extreme levels of anxiety.[20]

In any event, since the present self-report technique has produced results substantially discrepant from those of earlier studies, it would seem that greater reliance on multimethod approaches is warranted. That is, if self-reported offenders as well as "official" offender are used as subjects, incongruous results may provide clues not only to etiology, but also to the effects of the official sifting mechanisms and/or to the effects of the incarceration process itself; congruous results, on the other hand, will increase our confidence that we have uncovered differences of etiological significance.

[19]Offenders and nonoffenders were found, in the main, not to differ in social class, race, age, or education.

[20]Likewise, it is possible that the fact that the respondents are juveniles (most of the previous work has been done on adults), that the infractions are generally not very serious, or that the respondents were from a Catholic School may have influenced the results.

34. Compulsive Masculinity and Delinquency

IRA J. SILVERMAN
SIMON DINITZ

ALTHOUGH THE SOCIOLOGICAL, PSYCHOLOGICAL, psychiatric, and particularly the psychoanalytic literatures are replete with references to the relationship between compulsive masculinity and delinquency, there are no definitive, and few empirical studies of this concept.

The introduction of the concept of compulsive masculinity into the sociological literature is generally attributed to the work of Talcott Parsons. Parsons (1947) specifically related the occurrence of compulsive masculinity to the emergence of the mother-dominated household as an increasingly characteristic type of familial organization. The primacy of the instrumental role of the father as breadwinner compelled the mother to assume the principal responsibility for the socialization of the children. Thus, boys initially identify with and depend upon their mothers as primary role models. However, at adolescence, boys must repudiate their feminine identification because they are destined to become adult males, not females. Parsons considers the behavior that results from the boy's repudiation of this feminine identification to be marked by a kind of reaction formation involving compulsive masculinity.

In summary, Parons argues that the female-dominated household has negative consequences for male development because it creates anxiety about maleness; this anxiety, in turn, is transformed into compulsive masculinity. The latter, it should be added, tends to promote antisocial and aggressive conduct.

Taking the work of Parsons as his point of departure, Toby (1966) has further elaborated the concept of compulsive masculinity. Toby (1966: 20–21) believes that the compulsive masculinity hypothesis can explain violent behavior among certain types of adolescent boys. He hypothesizes that violent behavior would be more prevalent among boys (a) from matriarchial homes (especially black boys), (b) who grow up in households in which it is relatively difficult to identify with a father figure, (c) whose physical and social development toward adult masculinity is slower than their peers, (d) of working-class rather than middle-class background.

Rosen (1969) has reviewed the clinical literature to determine whether there is any empirical basis for the Parsonian conceptualization. Although he found some evidence for the development of sexual anxiety and compensatory masculinity among boys from female-based households, no link between this behavior and delinquency was demonstrated.

One recent study, omitted in Rosen's review of the clinical literature, lends considerable empirical support to the Parsonian formulation. This study, which investigated the relationship between masculinity and father presence or absence from the home, was conducted by Barclay and Cusumano (1967). Using more subtle per-

▶SOURCE: *"Compulsive Masculinity and Delinquency: An Empirical Investigation, Criminology (February 1974), 11:498–515. Reprinted by permission of the publisher, Sage Publications, Inc.*

ceptual measures of masculinity, these researchers were able to get beneath the "he-man" facade of their subjects and tap their basic orientation. They found that boys from father-absent homes made higher, more field dependent, and hence, by definition, more feminine scores than boys with fathers. Barclay and Cusumano suggest that this finding provides evidence of the existence of a compensatory drive toward hypermasculinity among boys from father-absent homes. Moreover, they contend that this drive results in the development of exaggerated masculine interest and characteristics.

Rosen (1969) has also reviewed the sociological literature on matricentric families and fatherless homes. Based on his examination of the literature, he concluded that the absence of a father fails to account for a significant portion of male delinquency.

Recent emphasis on compulsive masculinity has focused chiefly on nonwhite boys and is tied to the research on the lower-class black matriarchial family. In fact, the lower-class black family structure is normally cited as an illustration not only of the emergence of the female-based household, but also of the consequences of this household organization for problems of masculine identification.

Moynihan (1968), in particular, has called attention to the "pathological" nature of the black matriarchal family. From his point of view, the female-based black family is highly generative of much aberrant, inadequate, and antisocial behavior frequently observed in the lower-class black community (Rainwater and Yancy, 1967: 67).

Kenneth Clark has also spent considerable time studying the lower-class black family structure. He feels that the dominance of the black family by the female, in conjunction with the society's relegation of the black male to a menial and subservient position, has had profound influence on the means available to the black male for maintaining self-esteem. Denied the opportunity for achievement in business, politics, and in industry, the black male feels compelled to base his self-esteem on the kind of behavior that tends to support a stereotyped picture of the black male—sexual impulsiveness, irresponsibility, verbal bombast, posturing, and compensatory achievement in entertainment and athletics (Clark, 1965: 70).

Moreover, the all-too-frequent absence of the black male from the home has had especially profound implications for the male children; the black boy has no strong male role figure to emulate. As a result, males come to regard the maintenance of stable family life as unmasculine. In fact, Clark (1965: 71) points out, the young black man comes to gauge his masculinity by the number of girls he can attract and conquer.

Liebow's (1967) recent study of a group of lower-class black males lends some empirical support to Clark's thesis. Based on his street corner research as a participant-observer, Liebow concludes that lower-class, female-based households have resulted from the black male's failure to be able to carry out his duties and responsibilities as husband and father. Liebow (1967: 216) also found evidence to support the contention of Clark and others that black males validate their manliness through sexual conquest.

Hannerz (1969) has also developed a thesis of the black male's conception of self by observing life in a black neighborhood. Based on his observations, Hannerz takes issue with those who hold that the black matriarchal homes cause young boys to be deficient or uncertain about their masculinity because their fathers are absent or peripheral in household affairs. He contends that black boys can and do learn the nature of the male role from (a) observing the behavior of their mothers' more or less steady boyfriends; (b) the reactions of adult females in the home to their behavior; (c) peer-group reinforcement of the images of masculinity gleaned from the home.

Based on his research, Hannerz (1969: 17) concludes that "the behavior of the street corner male is a natural pattern of masculinity with which ghetto dwellers grow up and which to some extent they grow into."

Although there has been a great deal of discussion about the role played by the black matriarchal family in juvenile delinquency, only Rosen (1969) has actually examined this relationship empirically. Rosen examined the relationship between the factors of father absence, sex of main wage earner, main decision-making, and most influential adult on the one hand and delinquency on the other for a sample of 921 black males aged 13–15 who resided in lower-class, high-delinquency areas. He concluded (1969: 175) that "the factor of matriarchy may be only one of numerous 'original causes' which 'push' a lower class Negro male into delinquency, thus accounting for the small association for matriarchy and delinquency."

While Moynihan and others have considered how the life situation of the black boy generates problems of masculinity, othere have related the life situation of the lower-class boy—regardless of color—to problems of masculinity.

Miller (1966) has studied lower-class life and found that an exaggerated emphasis on masculinity, which he calls toughness, represents only one of several concerns of lower-class culture. Miller (1966: 140) considers the toughness component to include the following characteristics:

"Physical prowess, evidenced both by demonstrated possession of strength and endurance and by athletic skill; 'masculinity,' symbolized by a distinctive complex of acts and avoidances (bodily tatooing, absence of sentimentality, non-concern with 'art', 'literature,' conceptualization of women as conquest objects, etc.); and bravery in the face of physical threat."

From Miller's point of view, this emphasis has emerged because a significant proportion of lower-class males are reared in predominantly female households and lack a consistent male figure with whom to identify and from whom to learn essential components of a "male" role. He concludes (1966: 140) that "since women serve as primary objects of identification during pre-

adolescent years, the almost obsessive lower class concern with masculinity probably resembles a type of compulsive reaction formation." Moreover, Miller considers this focal concern of toughness, along with the other focal concerns of lower-class culture—trouble, fate, autonomy, and smartness—to account for much of lower-class delinquency.

Fannin and Clinard (1965) investigated the differences between lower- and lower-middle-class white delinquents in conception of self as a male, and behavioral correlates of such differences. They found that lower-class boys conceived of themselves as being tougher, more fearless, powerful, fierce, and dangerous than the middle-class delinquents, who, on the other hand, saw themselves as being more loyal, clever, smart, smooth, and bad. Moreover, these self-conceptions were found to be related to specific types of behavior. The "tough guys" significantly more often committed violent offenses, fought more often, carried weapons, had lower occupational aspirations, viewed dating primarily as a means to sexual intercourse which was achieved by conquest, and stressed physical prowess and callousness.

Fannin and Clinard (1965: 213) feel that their data suggest that "a significant proportion of offenses involving physical violence may be committed by delinquents who stress certain masculine traits in their self-conceptions as males which help to channel and legitimate such violence." Moreover, they feel that "self conception may act as a closure factor restricting the possibilities of behavior to a narrowed universe."

In addition to examining the etiology of compulsive masculinity, special concern has been devoted to the relationship between compulsive masculinity and violent behavior.

Wolfgang and Ferracuti (1967: 259) posited the existence of a subculture of violence in which masculinity is a focal concern. This subculture is not restricted to the United States, nor to the Latin American countries where the concept of machismo is a dominant cultural theme. "Machismo," as defined by Wolfgang and Ferracuti (1967), involves the equation of maleness with overt physical aggression.

Furthermore, based on a thorough analysis of the research on violence both here and abroad, these authors conclude that most violent behavior can be explained by the existence of this subculture of violence. They define the subculture of violence as a complex of values, attitudes, and material traits that have violence as their central theme. Violence is evident in the life style, socialization processes, and interpersonal relations of groups that possess this value cluster (Wolfgang and Ferracuti, 1967: 140). Moreover, the subcultural ethos of violence is most prominent among males in the limited age groups ranging from middle to late adolescence (1967: 158–159).

Finally, concern with compulsive masculinity and the violence that results from it is certainly more than an academic concern, as evidenced by the establishment of the National Commission on the Causes of and Prevention of Violence (1969).

This paper will report on one part of a study undertaken to examine some of the hypothesized aspects of compulsive masculinity. The particular contributions of this paper will be in examining how the factors of family situation and race relate to some of the hypothesized aspects of compulsive masculinity.

METHOD

In order to examine the relationship between compulsive masculinity, race, and matriarchal home, a study was conducted of a representative cross-section of the population at the Fairfield School for Boys, the largest Ohio Youth Commission operated facility for delinquent boys.

The sample for this study was drawn from five of the fifteen cottages at Fairfield. These particular cottages were chosen because they represent a cross-section of the institutional population.

Each of the boys in these cottages was administered a questionnaire which included a compulsive masculinity index, the Lykken Scale, and the Zuckerman Scale.

The compulsive masculinity index was used to measure the boys' self-identification with tough behavior (e.g., weapon-carrying maintaining a reputation as a tough guy) and sexual athleticism.[1]

The Lykken Scale was included to measure impulsiveness and proneness to activities that are high risk in nature and excitement oriented. It also measures general hostility (for a detailed description of the Lykken Scale, see Lykken, 1957).

The Zuckerman Scale was included in this study to measure field dependency—tendency to be effected by environmental influences including peer pressures—a variable Barclay and Cusumano (1967:35) found to be highly correlated with compulsive masculinity (for a detailed description of this scale, see Zuckerman, 1964).

Finally, each respondent was also asked to rate himself and all the other boys in his cottage according to how manly he considered himself and each other boy to be. The ratings for himself and each of the others involved circling a number on a continuum from one to ten (least to most). The second part required the respondent to rate himself and each boy in the cottage according to how tough he considered each one (including himself) to be. Again, these ratings for himself and each of the others involved circling a number on a continuum from one to ten (least to most).

Furthermore, the cottage supervisor, two cottage officers, and the cottage social worker were also asked to rate each boy on a continuum from one to ten, according to how tough and how manly they considered each boy to be. The purpose of these ratings was to obtain a measure of the consistency or discrepancy between a boy's conception of his own masculinity and toughness, and the conceptions of his masculinity by

[1]This scale was developed by the researcher because there was no measure of "compulsive masculinity." For detailed discussion of the development of this scale, see Silverman (1970).

all other boys in the group, and by the cottage staff.

Some 284 boys ranging in age from fourteen to nineteen with the median at seventeen were studied and evaluated. Of these 53.9% of the boys were white. Moreover, institutional records showed that the mother-based home was the modal type of household (34.9%) for this sample with natural parent families (24.3%) ranking second and biological and stepparent families (2.89%) ranking third.

FINDINGS

Race

A comparison of the white and black delinquents' self-ratings on manliness showed that the black boys rated themselves significantly higher (more manly) than the white boys. The mean self-rating of the black delinquents was 7.0 as compared to the white delinquents whose mean self-rating score was 6.4 (based on a range of 0–9). Also, on the toughness self-ratings, the black delinquent boys rated themselves higher (tougher) than the white boys. The means were 6.0 and 5.6 respectively. A similar pattern was found on the compulsive masculinity index. The

black delinquents had a higher mean score on this index than the white delinquents. The mean scores were 15.3 and 14.1 respectively (based on a range of 0–32; see Table I).

Moreover on manliness, the black delinquent boys were rated significantly higher by their cottage mates than the white delinquents. The mean scores were 4.8 and 4.3, respectively. This pattern was also evident on the group toughness rating (see Table I).

An examination of the discrepancy scores on the manliness rating scale revealed that black delinquent boys held perceptions of their own manliness that were slightly closer to those of the other evaluators. On both boy-group and boy-social worker comparisons, the white delinquents had slightly lower mean manliness discrepancy scores.

On the other hand, the pattern of discrepancy scores on the toughness rating scale was exactly the opposite. On toughness, the black delinquents' perceptions of their own toughness were more consistent with those held by their cottage mates, the cottage staff, and their social workers than were those of the white delinquent boys (see Table I).

Table I. Mean Scores on Manliness and Toughness Ratings and the Compulsive Masculinity Index, and Discrepancies in Self and other Ratings, by Race

Race	Mean Scores		Discrepancy Scores		
	Self-Rating	Group Rating	Boy-Group	Boy-Cottage Staff	Boy-Social Worker
Manliness					
White	6.4 } a	4.3 } b	2.1	2.0	1.2
Black	7.0	4.8	2.2	1.7	1.1
Toughness					
White	5.6	3.4	2.2	1.8	1.0
Black	6.0	4.0	2.0	1.3	.9

Compulsive masculinity index

	Mean Ratings
White	14.1
Black	15.3

$^a p < .05.$
$^b p < .001.$

Table II. Mean Scores on the Lykken Scale and the Zuckerman Scale, by Race

Race	Mean Lykken Scale Score	Mean Zuckerman Scale Score
White	13.6	13.5 ⎫
Black	14.3	11.0 ⎭ a

[a]p < .001.

Finally, all three groups of evaluators rated the delinquent boys lower on both manliness and toughness than they perceived themselves to be, with the social worker more closely approximating the delinquent boys' self-perceptions than the other two sets of evaluators.

Data from this study also supported the hypothesized differences in black and white proneness for excitement-oriented, high-risk activities, hostility, impulsiveness, and field dependency.

The black delinquent boys had higher mean Lykken scores than the white delinquents, indicating greater impulsiveness, hostility, and proneness to engage in excitement-oriented high-risk activity than white delinquent boys.

An examination of the Zuckerman Scale scores by race revealed that the white delinquents had significantly higher mean scores than the black delinquents, suggesting greater black field dependence. (Zuckerman found field dependence to be negatively correlated with his scale.) Moreover, since Barclay and Cusumano (1967) have indicated that field dependence is related to "compulsive masculinity," this finding provides additional evidence for the hypothesis concerning race and "compulsive masculinity."

Type of Household

An examination of the delinquents' self-ratings on the manliness index revealed that delinquents coming from female-based homes had a mean manliness score of 6.8, which ranked high compared with delinquents from other types of households. On the toughness variable, delin-

quent boys from mother-based homes rated themselves significantly higher than delinquents from other types of family situations (see Table III). Similarly, the mean scores of delinquents from mother-based homes on the compulsive masculinity scale disclosed that these delinquents had high mean scores (14.4) compared to delinquents from other types of households.

Moreover, the group rated the delinquent boys from mother-based households the highest on both manliness and toughness. On manliness the mother-based delinquents received a mean high rating of 4.7, which was significnatly higher than that received by the father-based delinquents who had a low mean group rating of 4.0. This same pattern also prevailed on the toughness ratings. However, here, mother-based delinquents received a mean rating that was significantly higher than the delinquents coming from father-based and surrogate-parent homes. The mean group rating for the mother-based delinquents was 3.9, as compared with 3.3 received by both the father-based and surrogate-parent delinquents.

Table III shows that delinquent boys from mother-based homes had mean manliness discrepancy scores—boy-group, boy-staff, boy-social worker—that were generally low compared with delinquents from other types of households. Thus, of the six household types examined, delinquent boys from mother-based homes held perceptions of their manliness that were relatively consistent with those of their evaluators. On the toughness discrepancy scores, delinquents from mother-based homes had perceptions of their toughness that were relatively discrepant from those held by their evaluators.

It is interesting to note that on both the manliness and toughness dimensions, delinquents from natural-parent homes had conceptions of themselves that were the most consistent with those of their cottage mates, the cottage staff, and their social worker.

Data from this study also provided some support for the hypothesized differences in hostil-

Table III. Mean Scores on Manliness and Toughness Ratings and the Compulsive Masculinity Index, and Discrepancies in Self and Other Ratings by Type of Household

| Type of Household | Mean Scores | | Discrepancy Scores | | |
	Self-Rating	Group Rating	Boy-Group	Boy-Cottage Staff	Boy-Social Worker
Manliness					
Natural parents	6.5	4.6	1.9	1.5	.8
Parent and stepparent	7.0	4.6	2.3	2.3	1.6
Mother-based	6.8	4.7 ⎫	2.1	1.7	1.2
Father-based	6.1	4.0 ⎬ a	2.1	1.9	1.3
Surrogate	6.7	4.1 ⎭	2.6	2.3	1.2
Toughness					
Natural parents	5.1 ⎫	3.6	1.5	1.0	.2
Parent and stepparent	5.7 ⎬ a	3.6	2.1	1.6	1.0
Mother-based	6.2	3.9	2.3	1.7	1.2
Father-based	5.7	3.3	2.4	1.7	1.7
Surrogate	5.6	3.3	2.3	1.3	.8

Compulsive masculinity index

	Mean Ratings
Natural parents	14.2
Parent and stepparent	16.0
Mother-based	14.4
Father-based	13.9
Surrogate	13.8

a p > .05.

ity, impulsivity, proneness to engage in excitement-oriented, high-risk activities, and field dependence of delinquent boys from matriarchal homes and from other types of households.

Delinquents from mother-based homes did not have appreciably different mean Lykken scores as compared with delinquent boys from other types of households. On the Zuckerman Scale, however, delinquents from mother-based homes had the lowest mean score when compared with delinquents from other types of households. There is thus some support for Barclay and Cusumano's (1967) findings that delinquents from mother-based homes were

more field dependent than delinquents from father-present homes.

Following the explanation of field dependency provided by Barclay and Cusumano (1967), this finding indicates that delinquent boys from mother-based homes are more likely to be susceptible to situational, including peer-group, pressures and to be more hypermasculine in orientation than boys from other types of households.

Moreover, further evidence of the role played by mother-based homes in generating problems of compulsive masculinity is provided by the fact that on the Zuckerman Scale, delinquent boys from father-based homes had the highest mean scores when compared with delinquents from other households, while it will be recalled that mother-based delinquents had the lowest scores on this scale. Thus, father-based delinquents are theoretically least field dependent, while mother-based boys are the most field dependent. One explanation for this finding is that when mothers are absent from the home, fathers spend more time with their sons, allowing the boys to observe them in a wider variety of situations. Thus, these boys may develop more accurate conceptions of manliness than boys from other types of households, who have limited or no interaction with their fathers.

DISCUSSION

The Female-based Household

Data from this study clearly suggested that delinquent boys from female-based households were more hyper-masculine than delinquents from other types of households. That is, the self-ratings of the mother-based-household boys on the three direct measures of compulsive masculinity showed that these delinquent boys (a) had the most exaggerated perceptions of their own manliness and toughness; (b) placed great emphasis on tough behavior—drinking, weapon-carrying, kicking a fallen opponent, maintaining a reputation as a tough guy (compulsive masculinity index); (c) emphasized sexual athleticism—conceptualization of women as conquest objects (compulsive masculinity index); (d) were more impulsive (Lykken Scale); (e) were more hostile (Lykken Scale): (f) were more predisposed to engage in excitement-oriented, high-risk activities (Lykken Scale); and (g) were overly predisposed to peer pressures (Zuckerman Scale). These findings lend support to the Parsonian thesis that the mother-based home generates problems of compulsive masculinity, which in turn promote antisocial and aggressive conduct.

As Parsons and his interpreters have suggested, the development of problems of compulsive masculinity among boys from female-based homes can be traced to the period of adolescent development when boys must adopt masculine self-definitions and roles. Two factors probably interact to make this transition difficult. First, since these boys have no father in the home, their mothers have to play both roles—a most difficult assignment. Second, these boys have had no stable male model from whom they could learn the socially acceptable attributes of manliness. What develops when these boys realize that they must repudiate their earlier identification with their mothers is a type of reaction formation. In other words, boys from female-based households may tend to become preoccupied with appearing to be "real men" in their own eyes as well as in the eyes of others. In the absence of a consistent and middle-class male model, these boys come to believe that being a "real man" involves stressing aggressive masculine traits such as toughness, sexual athleticism, and daring, and they seek to convince both themselves and others of their superior manliness and toughness.

These data may imply that an exaggerated male self-concept may act as a closure factor, restricting the possibilities of behavior to a narrowed universe, as suggested by Fannin and Clinard (1965). In other words, delinquent boys may come to regard antisocial and aggressive conduct as the only means by which to maintain an image of being a "real man." The argument set forth here represents one possible explanation for the seemingly greater "compulsive masculinity" among delinquent boys from female-based households than delinquents from other types of households. However, much more research is necessary before this Parsonian conception can be accepted as more than a sensitizing theme for viewing the delinquency problems of boys from mother-based homes. It is suggested that future research explore (a) the consequences of the female-based household for male development—e.g., between delinquent boys and nondelinquent boys; and (b) the role of the masculine self-concept in delinquency.

The Black Boy

Data presented in this study have also shown that black delinquents as a group define themselves as being more manly and tough than white delinquents in the same training school. It will be recalled that on the various instruments and scales, black as compared with white delinquents (a) considered themselves to be more manly and tough, (b) placed more emphasis on tough behavior, (c) emphasized sexual athleticism, (d) were more impulsive, (e) were more hostile, (f) were more predisposed to engage in excitement-oriented, high-risk activities, and (g) were more predisposed to peer pressures for deviant behavior, based on the various scales and measures used.

The Parsonian interpretation of compulsive masculinity among boys from female-based homes certainly applies to black boys from matriarchal families. In fact, the lower-class black family structure is normally cited as an illustration, not only of the emergence of the female-based household, but also of the consequences of this household organization for problems of masculine identification.

However, in addition to the mother-based home, the black male's menial and more subservient status in American society has done much to foster a male definition which centers around toughness, sexual athleticism, and antisocial and retreatist behavior. The fact that the black male has been denied the opportunity for achievement in business, politics, and industry has compelled him, as well as other disadvantaged males generally, to base his self-esteem on contracultural norms, including those subsumed under the heading of compulsive masculinity.

It may well be that disadvantaged males become preoccupied with maintaining an image of themselves as real men through antisocial and aggressive behavior since the alternative to this facade is an acceptance of oneself as a failure. Certainly, if this is the case, the hypermasculinity of the black delinquents represents a normative subcultural definition of manliness.

This study has shown, as predicted, that black delinquents rate themselves as being more masculine than white delinquents. It is suggested that future research involve two interrelated studies. Research should be conducted on the impact of subservient social position on self-concept as a male. In addition, it is necessary to study the coping behavior techniques of the majority of black boys from matriarchal families who do not become delinquent.

CONCLUSION

In general the data from this study have provided some empirical support for the theoretically posited relationship between the factors of race, matriarchy, and compulsive masculinity.

However, this study has not been able to address itself to various issues that are of great importance in evaluating the etiologic significance of compulsive masculinity in delinquent behavior. For example, is compulsive masculinity endemic to low socioeconomic adolescents as such (Miller, 1966; Toby, 1966), or only to those of lower-class background who become delinquent? How are boys able to maintain exaggerated self-concepts of their manliness and toughness in the face of interaction with "significant others" who judge them far less masculine and tough? To what extent are the self and other definitions of masculinity derived from and related to the various physique types and to such other "hard" measures as physical strength, maturational status, and agility? If machismo or compulsive masculinity are learned life styles, how might these styles be converted into more socially acceptable channels? Finally, is it possible to develop a treatment program for delinquents which capitalizes on these self-perceptions and life style definitions?

Much, obviously, remains to be done.

REFERENCES

Allen, H. (1969) "Bio-social correlates of two types of anti-social sociopaths." Ph.D. dissertation. Ohio State University.

Barclay A. G. and D. R. Cusumano (1967) "Testing masculinity in boys without fathers." Trans-Action 5 (December): 33–35.

Clark, K. (1965) Dark Ghetto: Dilemmas of Social Power. New York: Harper & Row.

Fannin, L. F. and M. Clinard (1965) "Differences in the conception of self as a male among lower and middle class delinquents." Social Problems 13 (Fall): 205–214.

Hannerz, A. (1969) "Roots of Black manhood." Trans-Action 6 (October): 112–21.

Hardt, R. H. and G. E. Bodine (1965) "Development of self-report instruments in delinquency research: a conference report." Syracuse, N.Y.: Syracuse Univ. Press.

Liebow, E. (1967) Tally's Corner: A Study of Negro Street-Corner Men. Boston: Little, Brown.

Lykken, D. T. "A study of anxiety in sociopathic personality." J. of Abnormal and Social Psychology 55:6–10.

Miller, W. B. (1966) "Lower class culture as a generating milieu of gang delinquency," pp. 137–150 in R. Giallombardo (ed.) Juvenile Delinquency: A Book of Readings. New York: John Wiley.

Moynihan, D. P. (1968) "The president and the Negro: the moment lost," pp. 431–460 in R. Perracci and M. Pilisuk (eds.) The Triple Revolution: Social Problems in Depth. Boston: Little, Brown.

National Commission on the Causes and Prevention of Violence (1969) To Establish Justice. To Insure Domestic Tranquility. Washington, D.C.: Government Printing Office.

Parsons, T. (1947) "Certain primary sources and patterns of aggression in the social structure of the Western world." Psychiatry 10 (May): 167–181.

Rainwater, L. and L. Yancy (1967) The Moynihan Report and the Politics of Controversy. Cambridge: MIT Press.

Rosen, L. (1969) "Matriarchy and lower class Negro male delinquency." Social Problems 17 (Fall): 175–189.

Silverman, I. J. (1970). "Compulsive masculinity and delinquency." Ph.D. dissertation. Ohio State University.

Toby, J. (1966) "Violence and the masculine ideal: some qualitative data." Annals of the Amer. Society of Pol. and Social Sci. 364 (March): 19–27.

Wolfgang, M. E. and F. Ferracuti (1967) The Subculture of Violence: Toward an Integrated Theory of Criminology. London: Associated Book Publishers.

Zuckerman, M. (1964) "Development of a sensation-seeking scale." J. of Consulting Psychology 6:477–482.

35. Personality and Criminality

DAVID J. TENNENBAUM

VARIOUS PSYCHOLOGICAL TESTS HAVE BEEN DE-
veloped to assess different aspects of personality
in recent years. An increasing number of new
scales, and subscales developed from other tests,
have been described in the literature in attempts
to correlate criminality and personality.

Schuessler and Cressey (1950) first reviewed
personality characteristics of criminals. Later,
Waldo and Dinitz (1967) updated the earlier
summary. The present work is an attempt to
update their findings, and to comment on recent trends noted in the literature from 1966 to
1975.

The initial study of Schuessler and Cressey
found only 42 percent of 113 reported studies
to show a significant difference between criminal (delinquent) and noncriminal (nondelinquent) groups. Waldo and Dinitz seem to do an
admirable job of explicating the Schuessler-
Cressey work. In Schuessler and Cressey's
studies, thirty different personality tests were
used.

In the Waldo-Dinitz paper, of the ninety-four
studies cited, 81 percent were shown to differentiate criminals and noncriminals. This, of
course, is nearly twice as many as were seen to
differentiate between these two populations
some fifteen years earlier.

▶SOURCE: *"Research Studies of Personality and Criminality: A Summary and Implications of the Literature," Journal of Criminal Justice, Vol. 5, No. 3, 1977, pp. 1–19. Reprinted by permission Pergamon Press Ltd.*

METHOD

To examine as much of the appropriate literature as feasible, the Mechanized Information
Center of the Ohio State University Library was
contacted to draw from the computer-indexed
literature of *Psychological Abstracts* for the appropriate years. However, this became fruitless,
as a computer search showed that this type of
literature was encoded in so many disparate
terms that a significant number of them would
have been ignored. Therefore, the primary
sources used were *Psychological Abstracts* and
Crime and Delinquency Abstracts for articles published from 1966 to 1975.

For each article that appeared to potentially
fit the strict guidelines described below, the original article was consulted. In an attempt to use
only data that compared a sample of a delinquent or criminal population to a control (noncriminal) population, the following criteria all
had to be met prior to inclusion in the study:

1.   A study completed in the United States[1],
having a sample of clearly defined criminals or
delinquents had to be compared with a control
group matched for at least minimal demographic qualities (e.g., age, socioeconomic status,

[1]As was noted in the Waldo-Dinitz work, inclusion of articles completed outside the United States would not have
altered findings significantly; there would have been an unfair representation should only some have been included.

race or sex). Samples selected from a limiting population, such as a group of psychopathic versus normal Army draftees, were excluded because of the limitations of the population pool itself (in recent years, many men do not enter the Army).

2. A standard personality test, a set of defined tasks proposed to measure aspects of personality, or a projective instrument defined as such in the study, had to be incorporated into the test situation.

3. A sample size large enough conducive to allow statistical analysis had to be used, i.e., case studies were omitted.

Essentially, only studies describing matched samples and tested on some specific dimension of personality were used. Although each study was consulted to test it for inclusion, it was impossible to find every article since the library service either did not have a subscription, or it declared specific issues of journals "snagged." The seven articles not obtained may have added to the summary; however, even if some of these articles would have been applicable for inclusion, it is quite unlikely that the appearance of the overall data would be significantly altered.

RESULTS

Table I shows a composite of the Schuessler-Cressey and the Waldo-Dinitz summaries, as these compare to the present study. Examination of Table I highlights several observations:

1. In comparison with the finding by Schuessler-Cressey that 42 percent of their studies showed a significant difference in the two populations, the present study is remarkably similar to the results cited by Waldo and Dinitz—that study showing 81 percent of studies reviewed to differentiate between a criminal and noncriminal sample, the present study finding thirty-five of forty-four, or 80 percent, of the studies to have at least one test showing what the

authors conclude is a difference between the populations.

The discrepancy between the 42 percent noted above and the 39.8 percent noted in Table I is the result of a miscalculation of the pre-1950 data (cf. Waldo and Dinitz, 1967:189) in which, although 42 percent of the *studies* are noted as differentiating the populations, since some studies used more than one instrument, a significant finding in any one test was cited as a significant difference for the respective study; hence the contrast of 80 percent of the present *studies* showing a difference, and 62.5 percent of the respective *tests* reflecting this difference.

2. Use of specific personality tests has changed markedly over the years, as may easily be seen by noting that only two, the Minnesota Multiphasic Personality Inventory and the Rorschach, have been reported as being used during all three time periods examined. In fact, table I shows that in the pre-1950 time period, twenty-nine different tests were used; in the 1950-1965 time span, again twenty-nine different tests were used; however, in the present review, fifty-two different personality tests were used. To look at this in a different light, Schuessler and Cressey cited twenty-nine tests in 113 studies; Waldo and Dinitz cited twenty-nine different tests used in 94 studies; the present summary shows 52 tests being used in only 44 different studies. Possibly the uniqueness of many tests devised by the authors, though often not replicated, accounts for this dramatic inversion. Across all studies, 101 different tests were used.

3. Table I also points toward the lack of any one test being used in many studies; that is, even though various scales of the MMPI were used in twenty-nine of the ninety-four Waldo-Dinitz studies (31 percent), particular scales of the MMPI (especially the *Pd* scale) still allow the MMPI to be the most frequently cited test, even though it was used here in only eight of the forty-four studies (18 percent).

Table I. Composite of Results Found by Each Study

	Schuessler-Cressey		Waldo-Dinitz		Present Study	
	Times Used	Times Different	Times Used	Times Different	Times Used	Times Different
Activity Vector Analysis	—	—	—	—	1	1
Authoritarian Scale	—	—	2	1	—	—
B. P. C.	1	0	—	—	—	—
Barron Ego Strength Scale	—	—	—	—	1	1
Bell Adjustment Inventory	4	0	—	—	—	—
Bender-Gestalt	—	—	5	4	—	—
Bernreuter Personality Inventory	7	0	—	—	—	—
Bipolar Psychological Inventory	—	—	—	—	1	1
Brown Personality Inventory	1	1	—	—	—	—
Burks' Behavior Rating Scale	—	—	—	—	1	0
Butler-Haigh	—	—	—	—	1	1
California Behavior Preference Record	—	—	—	—	1	1
California Psychological Inventory	—	—	8	8	6	4
California Test of Personality	1	0	1	1[a]	—	—
Cassel Group Level of Aspiration Test	—	—	3	3[a]	—	—
Cattel Character-Temperament Test	1	1	—	—	—	—
Character Tests	13	6	—	—	—	—
Conservatism Scale	—	—	—	—	1	1
Death Anxiety Scale	—	—	—	—	1	0
Dogmatism Scale	—	—	—	—	1	0
Downey Will-Temperament Tests	3	0	—	—	—	—
Edwards Personal Preference Schedule	—	—	2	1	1	1
Embedded Figures Test	—	—	—	—	1	0
Famous Sayings Test	—	—	2	1	—	—
Fear of Death Scale	—	—	—	—	1	0
Furfey Developmental Age Test	3	2	—	—	—	—
Future Events Test	—	—	—	—	1	1
Goodenough Drawing Test	1	1	—	—	—	—
Gordon's Conformity Scale	—	—	2	2	—	—
Guilford Martin Inventory	1	0	—	—	—	—
Holtzman Inkblot Technique	—	—	1	1	—	—
House-Tree-Person Test	—	—	1	0	—	—
Howard's Maze Test	—	—	—	—	1	0
Humm-Wadsworth Temperament Scale	1	0	—	—	—	—
IES Arrow Dot Test	—	—	1	1	—	—
IES Test	—	—	—	—	1	0
Internal-External Scale	—	—	—	—	3	1
Interpersonal Trust Scale (Rotter)	—	—	—	—	2	0
Junior Eysenck Personality Inventory	—	—	—	—	2	2
Juvenile Attitude/Interest List	—	—	—	—	1	1
Kent-Rosanoff Word Association Test	3	2	—	—	—	—
Laslett Word Association Test	3	2	—	—	—	—
LeShan Story Method	—	—	—	—	1	0

Table I. Composite of Results Found by Each Study (*continued*)

	Schuessler-Cressey		Waldo-Dinitz		Present Study	
	Times Used	*Times Different*	*Times Used*	*Times Different*	*Times Used*	*Times Different*
M-B History Record	—	—	—	—	1	1
Machover Draw-A-Person Test	—	—	2	1	—	—
Maller Case Inventory	1	0	—	—	—	—
Manifest Anxiety Scale	—	—	—	—	3	2
Mental Health Analysis Test	—	—	1	0	—	—
Miniature Situations Test	—	—	—	—	1	1
Minnesota Counseling Inventory	—	—	—	—	1	1
Minnesota Multiphasic Personality Inventory	4	2	29	28	8	7[a]
Minnesota Tests of Creative Thinking	—	—	—	—	1	1
Mirror Drawing Test	1	0	—	—	—	—
Mosher Guilt Scale	—	—	—	—	1	1
Murray Psychoneurotic Inventory	2	2	—	—	—	—
New Junior Maudsley Inventory	—	—	—	—	1	1
Neyman-Kohlstedt Introversion-Extraversion	3	0	—	—	—	—
Objective-Analytic Personality Test	—	—	1	1	—	—
Parental Authority-Love Statements	—	—	—	—	1	0
Personal Opinion Inventory	—	—	1	1	—	—
Personal Space	—	—	—	—	1	1
Petrie, McCulloch, and Kazdin Tasks	—	—	—	—	1	1
Petrie's Kinesthetic Task	—	—	—	—	1	0
Picture Arrangement Test (from WISC)	—	—	—	—	1	1
Picture Identification Test	—	—	1	1	—	—
Porteus Maze Test	4	4	3	3	—	—
Pressey Interest-Attitude Test	4	2	—	—	—	—
Pressey X-O Test	8	2	—	—	—	—
Protestant Ethic Scale	—	—	—	—	1	0
Psychomotor Test II	—	—	1	1	1	1
Rathus Assertiveness Schedule	—	—	—	—	1	0
Reaction-Time Tasks	—	—	—	—	1	1
Rogers Test of Personality Adjustment	2	0	—	—	—	—
Rorschach Test	3	0	5	2	1	1
Rosenzweig Picture-Frustration Test	—	—	6	3	1	1
Sensation Seeking Scale	—	—	—	—	2	0
Sentence Completion Test	—	—	2	2	—	—
Situational Interpretation Test	—	—	1	1	—	—
Standard Raven Progressive Matrices	—	—	—	—	1	0
Stein-Sarbin Checklist	—	—	—	—	1	1
Street Gestalt Completion Test	—	—	1	1	—	—
Sweet Personal Attitudes Test	6	3	—	—	—	—
Symonds Picture Story Test	—	—	2	1[a]	—	—
Szondi	—	—	3	2	—	—

Table I. Composite of Results Found by Each Study (continued)

	Schuessler-Cressey		Waldo-Dinitz		Present Study	
	Times Used	Times Different	Times Used	Times Different	Times Used	Times Different
Telenomic Trends Instrument	—	—	—	—	1	1
Tennessee Self-Concept Scale	—	—	—	—	1	0
Thematic Apperception Test	—	—	3	1	—	—
Thorndike Dimensions of Temperament	—	—	—	—	3	1
Thorne's Integration Level Test Series	—	—	—	—	2	2
Thurstone Personality Schedule	3	2	—	—	—	—
Time Apperception Test	—	—	—	—	1	0
Time Estimation	—	—	—	—	1	0
Twenty-Statements Test	—	—	—	—	1	1
Values Inventory for Children	—	—	—	—	1	1
Vineland Social Maturity Scale	3	1	—	—	—	—
Washburn Social Adjustment Inventory	2	1	—	—	—	—
Ways of Living Test	—	—	—	—	1	1
Woodworth Personal Data Sheet	19	9	—	—	—	—
WTAT	—	—	—	—	1	0
Other objective tests	—	—	3	3	—	—
Other projective tests	—	—	1	1	—	—
Totals	108	43	94	76	72	45
		(39.8%)		(80.8%)		(62.5%)

[a] These numbers represent a significant result in the opposite direction from that hypothesized.

Table II points to another transition noted in the present summary. In contrast with the findings of Waldo-Dinitz—that there was an increase in the number of objective and performance tests used—there is now a decrease in the number of projective tests used in the various studies. Specifically, of the fifty-nine times in which objective personality tests were used, in thirty-nine cases differences were found (66 percent). This percentage of times found different versus times used is significantly less than the 91 percent cited by Waldo and Dinitz. In studies using performance tests, of eight tests used (one per study), three were found to differentiate between the samples (37.5 percent). This again is markedly lower; in fact, it is exactly 50 percent lower. For the studies using projective tests, of the five different tests used (again, one test per study), four were found to significantly differentiate between criminal and noncriminal groups (80 percent). This result is not significantly different from the 63 percent figure found by Waldo and Dinitz.

DISCUSSION

Looking at the full range of personality testing on criminal versus noncriminal groups through 1975, the overall conclusion surfaces that, whereas early investigators (pre-1950) were exploring various psychological tests, the middle investigators (1950–65) narrowed the field by concentrating on the Minnesota Multiphasic Personality Inventory and the California Psychological Inventory, while more recent authors (1966–75) investigated many new and different instruments in an attempt to find a test that could adequately differentiate criminals from noncriminals. Yet, the two scales that were validated on *known* groups of criminals—the

Table II. Tests Used and Frequency of Significant Differences Shown between Criminal and Noncriminal Samples

	Times Used	Times Different
Objective personality tests		
Activity Vector Analysis [5] [a]	1	1
Barron Ego Strength Scale [28]	1	1
Bipolar Psychological Inventory [29]	1	1
Burks' Behavior Rating Scale [22]	1	0
Butler-Haigh [12]	1	1
California Behavior Preference Record [44]	1	1
California Psychological Inventory [16] [22] [24] [36] [44]	5	4
Conservatism Scale [43]	1	1
Death Anxiety Scale [1]	1	0
Dogmatism Scale [1]	1	0
Edwards Personal Preference Schedule [25]	1	1
Fear of Death Scale [1]	1	0
Future Events Test [37]	1	1
IES Test (Impulse-Ego-Superego) [38]	1	0
Internal-External Scale [1] [22] [24]	3	1
Interpersonal Trust Scale [13] [17]	2	0
Junior Eysenck Personality Inventory [34] [43]	2	2
Juvenile Attitude/Interest List [14]	1	1
M-B History Record [2]	1	1
Manifest Anxiety Scale [10] [23] [30]	3	2
Miniature Situations Test [31]	1	1
Minnesota Counseling Inventory [32]	1	1
Minnesota Multiphasic Personality Inventory [1] [11] [15] [16] [23] [26] [29] [39]	8	7
Minnesota Tests of Creative Thinking [21]	1	1
Mosher Guilt Scale [26¼	1	1
New Junior Maudsley Inventory [34]	1	1
Parental Authority-Love Statements [35]	1	0
Protestant Ethic Scale [1]	1	0
Rathus Assertiveness Schedule [17]	1	0
Rosenzweig Picture-Frustration Test [40]	1	1
Sensation Seeking Scale [3] [17]	2	0
Standard Raven Progressive Matrices [43]	1	0
Stein-Sarbin Checklist [20]	1	1
Telenomic Trends Instrument [41]	1	1
Tennessee Self-Concept Scale [1]	1	0
Thorndike Dimensions of Temperament [4]	1	1
Thorne's Integration Level Test Series [8] [9]	2	2
Values Inventory for Children [14]	1	1
Ways of Living Test [42]	1	1
WTAT [28]	1	0
	59	39 (66%)

Table II. Tests Used and Frequency of Significant Differences Shown between Criminal and Noncriminal Samples (*continued*)

	Times Used	Times Different
Performance tests		
Embedded Figures Test [22]	1	0
Howard's Maze Test [3]	1	0
Personal Space [7]	1	1
Petrie, McCulloch, and Kazdin Tasks [6]	1	1
Petrie's Kinesthetic Task [3]	1	0
Reaction-Time Tasks [27]	1	1
Time Apperception Test [18]	1	0
Time Estimation (27)	1	0
	8	3
		(37.5%)
Projective tests		
Happiness Test [33]	1	1
LeShan Story Method [23]	1	0
Picture Arrangement (from WISC) [23]	1	1
Rorschach [23]	1	1
Twenty-Statements Test [10]	1	1
	5	4
		(80%)

[a]Numbers in brackets refer to numbered references in which the tests were used; e.g., [5] refers to the reference to Clark and Hasler (1967).

Psychopathic deviate (*Pd*) scale of the MMPI and the Socialization (*So*) scale of the CPI—continue to most often differentiate criminal from noncriminal populations. This is to be expected: known groups should imply predictive validity.

As was detailed in the Waldo-Dinitz review, both the MMPI and the CPI are self-reported, objectively scored inventories based on empirical criterion keying. As the most widely used personality inventory, the MMPI consists of 550 statements to which the subject is asked to respond "true," "false," or "cannot say." The ten standard scales, designed to measure various psychologically abnormal or unusual traits are supplemented by three validity scales and a fourth scale noting the number of omissions or "cannot say" responses. The MMPI scale most often cited in the research on criminality, however, is the *Pd* scale. Although the scale has indeed been able to identify criminal and noncriminal samples, this is to be expected by the item content, which includes such statements as "I have never been in trouble with the law."

Similarly, the CPI, with about half of its items drawn from the MMPI, includes 480 true-false items and yields eighteen clinical scales and three validity scales. The important difference between the CPI and the MMPI is that the CPI is designed to describe normal populations, whereas the MMPI was validated on psychiatric samples. Yet, here again the scale found commonly used in the literature is the *So* scale, a scale validated on delinquents (i.e., patients diagnostically seen as psychopaths). As is effectively pointed out in the Waldo-Dinitz summary, this creates an argument by tautology, the scale development insures surface validity, but in practice, provides no information not obtainable simply by procuring a list of offenders.

Besides the MMPI, the only test used within all three time periods was the Rorschach, still the most popular projective psychological instrument. Scores are based on the subject's spontaneous, visual associations to ambiguous stimuli, ten bilaterally symmetrical inkblots. It is assumed that the individual's handling of the inkblots parallels his or her interpersonal percepts. But, even though traditional psychological testing procedures stress the use of projective techniques, the data in table 1 show their relatively infrequent use in such studies.

CONCLUSION

In comparing studies reviewed from 1966 to 1975 with those of the earlier time periods, the present study, using more stringent criteria for inclusion, shows remarkably similar results to Waldo and Dinitz' overall finding of approximately 80 percent of the studies showing differences in criminal and noncriminal groups. With the attempt in the 1966–75 time period to try many new and different tests, it is disconcerting to find that personality tests, per se, are no better predictors of criminal personalities now than were those of ten years ago. Indeed, as some practitioners are now suggesting, there may be a "criminal personality," but this may be such a complex entity that our current testing procedures are not reflecting the multidimensional differences *between* criminals and noncriminals; the majority of current testing allows for more differences to be found *within* groups of criminals and noncriminals than between the two groups. Essentially, the data do not reveal any significant differences between criminal and noncriminal psychology because most results are based on tautological argument. The conclusion remains that cursory personality testing has not differentiated criminals from noncrimrinals.

REFERENCES

Brown, D. J. (1972). The fear of death and the western-protestant ethic personality identity. *Dissertation abstracts*, 32 (12-B):7302–03. [1]

Barden, D. M. F. (1972). A comparison of the histories of delinquent boys and girls. *Dissertation abstracts*, 30 (8-B):3860–61. [2]

Brodsky, A. M. (1971). The effect of environmental stimulation on sensation seeking behavior of criminals and noncriminals. *Dissertation abstracts, 31 (7-B): 4327.* [3]

Christensen, L. and LeUnes, A. (1973). Personality differences of offenders and nonoffenders. *Psychological reports*, 32:242–42. [4]

Clarke, W. V., and Hasler, K. R. (1967). Differentiation of criminals and noncriminals with a self-concept measure. *Psychological reports*, 20:623–32. [5]

Compton, N. H. (1967). Perceptual characteristics of delinquent girls. *Perceptual and motor skills*, 24:596–98. [6]

Dabbs, J. M., Fuller, J. P., and Carr, T. S. (1973). Personal space when "cornered": College students and prison inmates. *Proceedings of the 81st Annual Convention of the American Psychological Association*, 8:213–14. [7]

Davis, C. (1971). A relationship of self-identification to role-playing. Unpublished master's thesis, North Carolina Central University. [8]

Davis, C., and Panton, J. H. (1972). A delinquency predictive scale for Thorne's integration level test series. *Journal of clinical psychology*, 28:186–89. [9]

Dorn, D. S,. (1968). Self-concept, alienation, and anxiety in a contraculture and subculture: A research report. *Journal of criminal law, criminology, and police science*, 59:531–35. [10]

Elion, V. H., and Megargee, E. I. (1975). Validity of the MMPI Pd scale among black males. *Journal of consulting and clinical psychology*, 43:166–72. [11]

Fichtler, H., Zimmerman, R. R., and Moore, R. T. (1973). Comparison of self-esteem of prison and non-prison groups. *Perceptual and motor skills*, 36:39–44. [12]

Fitzgerald, B. J. Pasewark, R. A., and Noah, S. J. (1970). Validity of Rotter's interpersonal trust scale: A study of delinquent adolescents. *Psychological reports*, 26:163–66. [13]

Goldberg, L., and Guilford, J. S. (1972). Delinquent values: It's fun to break the rules. *Proceedings of the 80th Annual Convention of the American Psychological Association*, 7:237–38. [14]

Hawk, S. S., and Peterson, R. A. (1974). Do MMPI psychopathic deviancy scores reflect psychopathic deviancy or just deviance? *Journal of personality assessment*, 38:362–68. [15]

Hindelang, M. J. (1972). The relationship of self-reported delinquency to scales of the CPI and the MMPI. *Journal of criminal law, criminology, and police science*, 63:75–81. [16]

Karoly, P. (1975). Comparison of "psychological styles" in delinquent and nondelinquent females. *Psychological reports*, 36:567–70. [17]

Kroth, R. L. (1969). A study of three aspects of time among normal and delinquent school age males in Costa Rica and the United States. *Dissertation abstracts*, 29 (7-A):2094. [18]

Kuenstler, W. H. (1970). Differential effects of positive and negative social reinforcement on juvenile delinquents and Sunday school students. *Dissertation abstracts*, 31 (3-B):1541–42. [19]

Kulik, J. A., Stein, K. B., and Sarbin, T. R. (1968). Dimensions and patterns of adolescent antisocial behavior. *Journal of consulting and clinical psychology*, 32:375–82. [20]

Kuo, Y. Y. (1967). A comparative study of creative thinking between delinquent boys and non-delinquent boys. *Dissertation abstracts*, 28 (3-B):1166. [21]

Levy, V. (1972). Field independence and typologies of delinquency. *Dissertation abstracts*, 32 (12-A):6810. [22]

Matulef, N. J. (1967). Future time perspective and personality characteristics of male adolescent delinquents and non-delinquents. *Dissertation abstracts*, 28 (3-B):1204–05. [23]

Miller, R. E. (1969). Impulsivity and locus of control among juvenile delinquents. *Dissertation abstracts*, 30 (6-A):2340–41. [24]

Pasewark, R. A., Fitzgerald, B. J., and Watson, R. L. (1971). Associated personality differences in delinquents and non-delinquents. *Journal of personality assessment*, 35:159–61. [25]

Parsons, R. W. (1970). The Mosher guilt scale: Theoretical formulative research review and normative data. *Journal of projective techniques and personality assessment*, 34:266–70. [26]

Pfeiffer, K., and Maltzman, I. (1974). Warned reaction times of sociopaths. *Journal of research in personality*, 8:64–75. [27]

Polk, F. F., (1967). Toward a typology of the delinquent personality. *Dissertation abstracts*, 28 (4–B): 1968. [28]

Pryor, A. B. (1972). Relationships of the Minnesota Multiphasic Personality Inventory and the Bipolar Psychological Inventory to each other and to incarceration. *Dissertation abstracts*, 32 (7-A):3798–99. [29]

Royala, R. E. (1968). Delay of gratification and time estimation in normal and maladjusted boys. *Dissertation abstracts*, 29 (4–B): 1509–10. [30]

Santostefano, S., and Wilson, G. (1968). Construct validity of the Miniature Situations Test: II. The Performance of institutionalized delinquents and public school adolescents. *Journal of clinical psychology*, 24:355–58. [31]

Sasek, J. (1975). Differences between felons and students on the Minnesota Counseling Inventory. *Psychological reports*, 236:774. [32]

Schuessler, K. F., and Cressey, D. B. (1950). Personality characteristics of criminals. *American journal of sociology*, 476–84.

Scott, E. M. (1967). Happiness: A comparison between delinquent and non-delinquent girls. *Psychotherapy: Theory, research, and practice*, 4:78–80. [33]

Shamberg, N. S. (1968). An experimental investigation of Eysenck's theory with respect to four adolescent groups. *Dissertation abstracts*, 29 (2-B):760–61. [34]

Silver, A. W., and Derr, J. (1966). A comparison of selected personality variables between delinquent and non-delinquent adolescents. *Journal of clinical psychology*, 22:49–50. [35]

Stein, K. B., Gough, H., and Sarbin, T. R. (1966). The dimensionality of the CPI socialization scale and an empirically derived typology among delinquent and non-delinquent boys. *Multivariate behavioral research*, 1:197–208. [36]

————Sarbin, T., and Kulik, J. A. (1968). Future time perspective: Its relation to the socialization process and the delinquent role. *Journal of consulting and clinical psychology*, 32:257–64. [37]

Sterling, E. S. (1970). The comparative personality integration of lower class and middle class delinquent and non-delinquent males. *Dissertation abstracts, 30* (9-B):4383–84. [38]

Suther, P. B., and Allain, A. N. (1973). Incarcerated and street heroin addicts: A personality of comparison. *Psychological reports,* 32:243–46. [39]

Teichman, M. (1971). Ego defense, self-concept and image ascribed to parents by delinquent boys. *Perceptual and motor skills,* 32:819–23. [40]

Thompson, G. C., and Gardner, E. F. (1969). Adolescents' perceptions of happy-successful living. *Journal of genetic psychology,* 115:107–120. [41]

Trabont, J. L. (1969). A study of values ascribed to self and "significant other persons" by delinquents and non-delinquent adolescent youth. *Dissertation abstracts,* 30 (2-A):595–96. [42]

Waldo, G. P., and Dinitz, S. (1967). Personality attributes of the criminal: An analysis of research studies, 1950–1965. *Journal of research in crime and delinquency,* 4:185–202.

Wilson, G. D., and MacLean, A. (1974). Personality, attitudes, and human preferences of prisoners and controls. *Psychological reports,* 4 (3, part I):847–54. [43]

Winters, A. W. (1967). Identification of early delinquent tendencies in preadolescent children in Umatilla and Oregon counties of Oregon. *Dissertation abstracts,* 27 (11-A):3645–46. [44]

36. Pornography and Its Effect

HAROLD S. KANT
MICHAEL J. GOLDSTEIN

THE PORTRAYAL OF SEX IN ALL MEDIA SEEMS TO increase exponentially. Books that had to be smuggled into the country 10 years ago can be borrowed from most public libraries, and films that formerly were seen only at stag shows now play at the neighborhood movie theater. Many parents, educators and clergymen have become alarmed; they fear that this increasing exposure to erotic materials will twist young minds, lead to depravity and encourage sex crimes.

We recently completed a research project that strongly indicates that these fears are groundless, and that some exposure to pornography may be salutary. We found, for example, that a sample of rapists had seen less pornography as teen-agers than a comparable group of normal adults had. The same was true for child molesters. Steady customers of an adult bookstore also had seen less erotica as adolescents than our control group had.

In fact, the normal adults in our sample reported more experience with pornography as teen-agers than any deviant group we studied and, as adults, they continue to see more erotica than sex offenders do.

In all of these groups masturbation had been the most common adolescent response to pornography. Both the deviants and the pornography users say that, as adults, they continue to masturbate when they are stimulated by erotica.

Only the normal group reports that heterosexual activity is their most common release when they are aroused by pornography.

In general we found that pornography cannot be shown to trigger any identifiable, specific form of sexual activity. One's family background and his current attitudes—and his access to partners—seem much more likely to determine his sexual behavior.

LINK

These findings grew out of studies done for the Commission on Obscenity and Pornography by the Legal and Behavioral Institute, and were reported by us in recent papers before the American Sociological and Psychological Associations. With collaborators, psychiatrists Lewis Judd of the University of California, San Diego, and Richard Green of University of California, Los Angeles, we attempted to find out if there is a relationship between experience with pornography and the development of normal or abnormal sexual behavior.

The 60 deviants we studied were recently admitted patients at the Atascadero State Hospital in California. They were Caucasian males, each of whom was either charged with or convicted of rape or child molestation. The child molesters were separated into those who sought out boys as sex objects and those who chose girls. The 52 users of pornography were customers of an adult bookstore in Los Angeles.

▶SOURCE: *"Pornography" Psychology Today* (1976), *4(7): 61–64. Reprinted by permission.*

For our control group, the UCLA survey research center selected 133 Caucasian males from the Los Angeles area whose ages and educational backgrounds matched those of our sex offenders. Sixty-three of this group agreed to take part in the study.

A trained interviewer spent two hours with each subject questioning him on 276 items that covered demographics, sex attitudes, sex history, fantasies, and exposure and reaction to pornographic books, photographs, movies and live shows. Questioning followed a systematic order, from the most probable stimulus that one might encounter (partial nudity) to the least likely stimulus (sadomasochistic activity). We asked the subject to recall the number of times he had seen each type of stimulus during his adolescence, and during the year prior to the interview.

We studied other groups as well—including homosexuals, lesbians, transsexuals, normal blacks and female pornography users, but will not include them in this report.

TEENS

As we expected, most persons in all groups had seen examples of partial nudity as teen-agers, and few had seen examples of sadomasochistic activity. Generally, the rapists and the child molesters had seen less pornography of all kinds than normals had. The rapists differed less from controls than the two pedophile groups did, but even here there were significant differences. Rapists were significantly less likely than normals to have seen representations of fully nude women, of normal intercourse, of mouth-genital contact or of sadomasochistic activity.

The child molesters had seen less pornography of every kind than our normal group did. Only 62 per cent of these sex offenders who prefer immature partners had seen representations of heterosexual intercourse, while 85 per cent of the control group had encountered this kind of pornography as teen-agers.

Persons who are avid buyers and consumers of commercial pornography show a pattern closer to the deviate samples than to the normal group. As teen-agers they had seen less pornography of every kind than normals did. It appears that sex deviates and users are markedly lacking in adolescent experience with stimuli that represents the culture's definition of a normal sex act.

GAP

During the year before they were confined, the sex offenders had seen less pornography than controls had. The gap between rapists and normals was more striking than it had been during adolescence, especially for photography and films of heterosexual intercourse, male nudity and oral-genital relations. Child molesters who chose boys as sex objects had seen less heterosexual stimuli than normals had, but about the same amount of homosexual pornography that the normals had seen. Child molesters who chose girls had seen less pornography of every kind than normals had. In short, our normal adults had seen more pornography when they were teen-agers than the sex criminals had and they see it even more often as adults.

Users, on the other hand, saw far more pornography of every kind as adults than our control group did. The change from low exposure to pornography when they were adolescents to a markedly increased exposure to erotic stimuli in the adult years suggests some sort of compensatory-interest pattern.

The questions we asked our subjects about their reactions to erotic materials were designed to elicit data that might explain the role that pornography plays in peoples' lives as adolescents and as adults. More sex offenders and users than normals told us they masturbated in response to erotic materials. But only the users said they masturbated significantly more frequently with pornography than without it, indicating that this kind of stimuli still played a meaningful role in their sex lives.

It appears that the pattern of self-stimulation and release, common for all groups as teen-agers, fails to disappear from the behavior of sexual deviants and pornography users as they grow older. Child molesters masturbated less frequently when they were teen-agers than did rapists, users or normals, and there is little change in their pattern of self-stimulation from adolescence to adulthood.

ACTS

Each subject chose one peak adolescent experience and one peak adult experience with erotica to discuss with the questioner. All groups reported that the desire to imitate this vivid experience declined from adolescence to adulthood. We found the least decline among users, 58 per cent of whom said that they still desired to imitate the acts they had encountered in the peak experience with pornography. Few in any group had ever attempted to enact the peak stimuli and generally there were fewer adult than adolescent attempts to imitate the acts.

Users and the molesters of girls reported most acting out of peak pornographic stimuli. Twenty per cent of these groups have tried to duplicate the most exciting postures or acts they have seen or read about as compared to 13 per cent of the normal group. This suggests that pornography does not generally stimulate to di-

rect imitation, but tends toward general sexual arousal and masturbation.

When they were asked if these intense experiences made them want to engage in other kinds of sexual activity, the groups showed no sharp differences. Forty per cent of the molesters of boys reported that they actually had carried out other sexual activities, while only 15 per cent of the molesters of girls and 20 per cent of the rapists said they had done so. Users and normals fell between these groups, with 32 per cent of the users and 35 per cent of the normals engaging in other sexual activities when they were aroused by the peak erotic stimuli.

In the hope that their backgrounds might help to explain the role of pornography in the lives of our subjects, we looked for differences among the childhoods of our subjects. No group reported any substantial amount of erotic material in their childhood homes.

The rapists, who found it very difficult to talk about sex, said that there was little nudity in their homes while they were growing up and that sex was never discussed. Only 18 per cent of the rapists said their parents had caught them with erotic materials; in those instances the parents had become angry and had punished them. (In the control group, 37 per cent reported that their parents knew they read erotic materials, but only seven per cent reported being punished. Most reported that their pa-

Response to Pornography (in percentages)

	Controls (n=46)	Rapists (n=20)	Child Molester (male target) (n=20)	Child Molester (female target) (n=20)	Pornography Users (n=50)
Masturbation	37 (87)[a]	80 (90)	60 (65)	45 (60)	78 (86)
Masturbation while looking at it	11	35	25	10	46
Sexual relations with another person	48	55	60	55	56
Recollection of it during sexual relations	19	20	30	30	28
[Masturbation without pornographic stimulus]	30	75	70	60	68

[a]Figures in parentheses are for activities as teen-agers — others are adult figures.

Percentages of Pornography Users and Control-group Members Who Were Exposed to Pornography When They Were Teen-agers

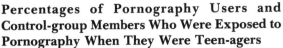

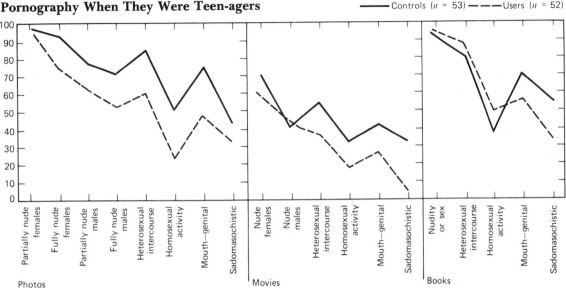

rents had been indifferent, and some said their parents had explained the materials to them—an occurrence not reported by any other group.)

Rapists tended to oppose premarital sex, and many of them relied on their wives for a great deal of their sex information. This may indicate late learning, a supposition supported by an Atascadero staff member who told us that sex offenders frequently display great ignorance of sexual matters. He said that at least one rapist in the hospital, when he was first admitted, had had no idea where babies come from.

Rapists told us of extensive extramartial intercourse and of a high frequency of sexual relations, but they also reported less enjoyment of sex than the controls. They reported more homosexual experience than controls.

SOURCE

Child molesters who seek out boys found talking about sex more uncomfortable than any other group did. There had been little tolerance of

nudity in their childhood homes and no discussion of sex. Male friends were the main sources of their sex information.

Most had never married and they were opposed to premarital sex. As we had expected, they were more tolerant of homosexuality than controls were. Fifty per cent of this group had had their first homosexual experiences before they were 14, and had learned about masturbation from friends rather than through self-discovery. They rarely reported steady sex partners, and they said that when they did have intercourse, it tended to be unsatisfying.

Child molesters who chose girls reported little discussion of sex in their childhood homes. Male friends gave them little of their sex information, and they had learned significantly more about sex from clergymen than controls had. They, too, were uncomfortable in talking about sex, and were the least permissive of all groups on premarital and extramarital intercourse. Most had been married. A relatively high number in this group (31 per cent) had had their first sexual experiences with prostitutes.

EASE

Users asserted greater comfort when they were talking about sex than the sex-offender group did. Their parents had taken permissive attitudes toward nudity in the home while they were children, although as they had reached adolescence parental attitudes had become less tolerant. When their parents became aware of their children's interest in erotic materials, they showed little concern and did not punish them.

Users had liberal sexual attitudes: over 75 per cent approved of premarital sex and took a tolerant view of homosexuality. They tended to have had first intercourse later than most other groups, and a considerable number had had sexual intercourse first with prostitutes. Adultery was more common in this group, and many members had had more than seven extramarital affairs. Their frequencies of intercourse were close to those reported by controls, but they used a wider variety of means to reach orgasm (petting, oral stimulation, oral-genital stimulation) than controls did. Users of pornography report that they enjoy sex greatly.

NAY

For the rapists, the data suggest very repressive family backgrounds regarding sexuality. The pattern of inhibition and punitiveness found in their families appears to be consistent with rapists' reports of extensive heterosexual and homosexual activity with little enjoyment. They give "fear of sex" as the reason that pornography does not stimulate them to engage in or even to desire sexual activity. Rapists are less likely than normals to encounter sadomasochistic pornography, so the idea for the aggressive sexual act does not appear to derive from pornography. A high percentage of rapists report frequent homosexual activity, which suggests that the aggressive sex act can sometimes represent an attempt to cover homosexual tendencies.

Molesters of boys tend to be sexually immature at the time of their first homosexual contacts. Their low exposure to erotica suggests that their sexual development more likely was influenced by actual childhood sexual contacts than by erotica.

Molesters of girls appear to have developed

Percentage of Rapists, Child Molesters and Control-group Members Who Were Exposed to Pornography When They Were Teen-agers

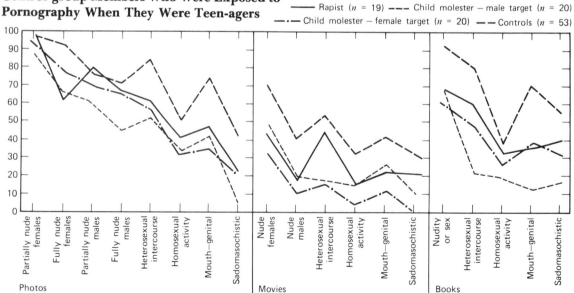

——— Rapist (n = 19) – – – Child molester – male target (n = 20)
—·— Child molester – female target (n = 20) —— Controls (n = 53)

highly restrictive attitudes that interfere with their ability to obtain or to enjoy mutual sexual relations. Given their restrictive and their intolerant attitudes toward premarital sex, it seems reasonable to suppose that they associate sex with sin and with dirtiness. Perhaps their choice of immature girls represents a search for sex partners who are innocent and free from the connotation of sin.

ACCESS

Users seem to be motivated to experience heterosexual relations in all possible ways, either symbolically through pornography or realistically through sexual contacts. While the childhood sexual interest and curiosity of users had been tolerated, they had had limited access to erotica and were late to experience heterosexual intercourse. Thus, their extensive interest in all varieties of sexuality could represent an attempt to make up for lost time. In addition, their childhood experience of high parental toleration and low actual contact could permit infantile fantasies about sex to flourish unchecked by actual experience. These fantasies may persist into adulthood and color their sexual activities. The erotica-masturbation cycle may be a part of their effort to compensate for lost social sexual opportunities through fantasies and self-stimulation.

It appears that all groups of sexual deviates, no matter what their ages, education or occupations, share one common characteristic: they had little exposure to erotica when they were adolescents. This suggests that a reasonable exposure to erotica, particularly during adolescence, reflects a high degree of sexual interest and curiosity that correlates with adult patterns of acceptable heterosexual interest and practice. Less than average adolescent exposure to pornography reflects either avoidance of heterosexual stimuli or development in a restrictive and punitive atmosphere. It appears that the amount of exposure to pornography is a surface manifestation of the total pattern of sexual development. If sexual development proceeds along a deviant track, then deviant sexual behavior will correlate with either under-exposure to pornography or obsessive interest in it.

It appears that unresolved adolescent sexual conflicts relate to adult sexual patterns that require erotica as a necessary stimulus to gratification. In the normally developed male, the adolescent use of erotica declines and the sexual partner becomes the primary source of arousal and gratification.

The Causes of Crime:
Sociological Factors

THE PURSUIT OF THE CAUSES OF CRIME BY RESEARCHERS OF VARIOUS DISCIPLINES shows interesting variability in prominence, growth, and "fashion" over the years. Early in the twentieth century, biological studies seemed to be most prevalent and to have offered the greatest promise. In the period from about the 1920s through the 1940s, psychological and psychiatric investigators were both abundant and comparatively prestigious. Although there has been a recent resurgence of biological studies, research into the causes of adult criminality and juvenile delinquency seem to have been made within a sociological frame of reference in recent decades. It is, therefore, a much more abundant literature from which we have drawn examples for the selections in this section.

One dominant, inordinately important aspect of modern American society is the obsession with winning or "being Number One," with unwanted as well as desirable consequences. One tragic result of this mania is depicted in Woodley's selection on the American Soap Box Derby. As American as apple pie, the desire to win the annual race at Akron, Ohio, by use of Yankee ingenuity has lead to rather sophisticated skullduggery and dishonest manipulation of car specifications and help from unauthorized adults.

Rosen and Nielsen in their selection specially written for this volume survey in great depth the major sociological variable of family structure, as previous research has related it to juvenile delinquency. They summarize, and more crucially, recalculate some existing data produced by several major studies of broken homes. They conclude that a broken home, no matter how operationalized, had a very weak relationship with little explanatory value to juvenile delinquency. The element of gender differences in crime arising, not out of biological distinctiveness, but the manner in which society socializes males differently from females is dealt with by Rita Simon. She considers female criminals and their changing pattern of criminality in recent years, particularly as regards the increasing percentage of women involved in serious (Index) crimes. The sociological variable of race, as represented by black-white arrest differentials over 20 years in a northern industrial community is traced by Green. He attributes the excessive black crime rates to a larger percentage of blacks being in the lower class, being more unskilled and more heavily migrant than whites. Racially repressive law enforcement acts are, once more, not found to be significant.

The next two items focus on the rather central social institution of education. Kelly's investigation of status origins and track position within a school system concludes that track position is more important than social class and it is the strongest predictor of (self-reported) delinquency. Elliott, in a major study of delinquency and school dropouts, finds that dropouts have both higher official delinquency rates and higher self-reported rates of delinquency.

The institution of religion and its effect on criminal behavior, for inexplicable reasons, have not been given much attention by sociologists. In one of the few studies of its kind, Hirschi and Stark attempt to measure the relationship between religious training, as measured by the single criterion of church attendance, and delinquency. They find that while religious adherents accept socially ethical values and often believe in a Heaven and Hell, such attitudes seem quite unrelated to actual behavior, specifically the commission of delinquent acts.

Perhaps the most mesmerizing force of our time is the mass media, particularly in its most dazzling form, television. Public and legislative concern over the corrupting influence of television, particularly Saturday morning cartoon shows, has resulted in a series of studies under the aegis of the U.S. Surgeon-General, examining television and its relationship to juvenile misconduct. What the public and legislators hoped for, of course, was an inexpensive, obvious, common-sensical, simple-to-manipulate, single factor that could be identified and eliminated because it instigated violent behavior. This particular selection does not confirm the hoped-for relationship between TV violence and violence in young, impressionable children; but it does, in passing, mention other sources of arousal to aggression, beyond the mere viewing of violence.

The next three selections deal with the theme of group or gang behavior. In a massive survey of violent gangs in 12 large American cities, Walter Miller identifies types of gang assaultive encounters, the property destruction they wreak, victims of their violence, weaponry used, and motives for such gang behavior. Chambliss investigates a white middle-class gang's behavior and the extent to which they are not perceived of as delinquent by school authorities and police, compared to the more visible and more reacted-to working-class Roughnecks. Until recently, girls rarely formed gangs, but were content to be peripheral members of all-male adolescent gangs. This no longer seems to be the case. Just as females account for an increasing proportion of all offenses, girl gangs have also become more common. An article by Miller, "The Molls", describes an adolescent lower-class urban gang of "corner girls," who engage in crime, truancy, and vandalism and who were, in the author's words, "wise before their time."

The final selection, by Roncek, critically examines previous literature on population density and its debilitating effect, particularly regarding crime. The evidence, he finds, tends to support a positive relationship between overcrowding and crime, and population density is suggested as an important variable in predicting area criminality.

37. How To Win the Soap Box Derby

RICHARD WOODLEY

THE ALL-AMERICAN SOAP BOX DERBY WILL ONCE again be run in Akron, Ohio, in August. But it will be a smaller, cheaper, surely more honest shadow of its former self. The thirty-seven-year-old Derby lost its virginity in a sinful caper last year and almost fell apart.

It will be remembered that last year's winner, fourteen-year-old Jimmy Gronen, was disqualified when an electromagnet was discovered in his racer. The magnet, mounted in the nose, drew the nose against the metal starting gate and caused the car to be yanked ahead when the gate flopped down to start the race.

That incident, and subsequent evidence of rampant skullduggery over the years, caused the Akron Chamber of Commerce to withdraw its sponsorship, asserting that the Derby had become a victim of "cheating, fraud, and hoax."

The befouling of the venerable Derby was not, to be sure, the idea of the children who aspired to its crown, but of the adults who guided the innocents in the childhood game of coasting downhill in a homemade wagon. The proclaimed villain in this case was Jimmy Gronen's guardian uncle, Robert B. Lange, Sr., who was earlier known for his development of the admired plastic-shell ski boot bearing his name. For violating the sanctity of the Derby ("It's like discovering that your Ivory Snow girl has made

a blue movie," commented a prosecutor), Lange, forty-eight, of Boulder, Colorado, was ordered by a Colorado court in a "nonjudicial" bargain to pay $2,000 to a boys' club. The judge said Lange owed an apology to the youth of the nation.

But Lange admits only a "serious mistake in judgment," and avers that cheating has been so rife that all he did was to even his nephew's odds in a dirty system. In fact, when I talked to him not long ago, he was inclined to sue those responsible for disqualifying his nephew without banishing others who had cheated in the same race.

If mores may be defined as the accepted mode of behavior which does not threaten the stability of the community, it is more important to define the community than the mores. The withdrawal of the Chamber of Commerce, combined with information from many others involved with the Derby for many years, confirms that Lange, however wrong in his actions, is right in his assessments. The sponsor of the first thirty-five championships was Chevrolet, which deftly and without substantive explanation withdrew its sponsorship before the 1973 race. It is widely inferred that Chevrolet, while probably not condoning the growing wickedness in the competition, at least turned a deaf ear and blind eye to the problem.

And so the scandal blew, with its fallout, and the Derby, for which children aged eleven to fifteen supposedly build their own $75 racers that supposedly conform to construction rules

▶SOURCE: *"How to Win in the Soap Box Derby," Harper's Magazine (August 1974), 249: 62–66, 67–69. Copyright © 1974 by Richard Woodley. Reprinted by permission of Paul R. Reynolds, Inc.*

and supposedly coast unaided down the 954-foot macadam track called Derby Downs, fell prey to what seemed to be a national malaise: winning, being everything, is worth doing anything to achieve. The Derby, like the Presidency, will likely survive, because enough people want it to. At the last minute, the Akron Jaycees picked up the interim sponsorship, and the Derby is scheduled to run in Akron on August 17, with a new rule book and tighter controls. The intention is to return the Derby—which had become sophisticated and expensive, with fiberglass racers, adult engineering, and meddling old grads—to the kids. Such a retreat to morality is publicly welcomed by all; whether such a basic Derby might be too mundane to attract sustaining interest remains to be seen.

A FAMILY EVENT

Lange's son, Bobby, Jr., won the race in 1972, the same year that Jimmy Gronen, because of the lengthy hospitalization of his widowed mother, joined the Lange family. Jimmy won the 1973 race in a car almost identical to Bobby's. Bobby's car disappeared mysteriously from the Lange basement shortly after the scandal about Jimmy's magnet broke. Lange figures that somebody must have just swiped it but insists that it contained no magnet. He admits, however, that it was an illegal car in other ways, as was Jimmy's.

No scandal was hinted at prior to Jimmy's championship race. The pre-race week had gone smoothly; the 138 local race winners—including 19 girls, and entrants from Venezuela, West Germany, and Canada, were greeted with customary hoopla by Akron. There was a police escort into town, welcoming kisses, and ritualistic donning of Derby T-shirts and beanies. The contestants were then deposited at the YMCA's Camp Y-Noah for four days of fun before the championships. Their racers had been impounded for safekeeping at Derby Downs.

Akron was a good host, as it has been for the American Golf Classic, the Firestone-PBA Tournament of Champions for bowlers, big-time spelling bees, and other events which have made the "Rubber Capital of the World" (Firestone, General Tire, B. F. Goodrich, Goodyear Tire) a hub of all-American activities, of which the All-American Soap Box Derby—the "World's Gravity Grand Prix"—was just about the grandest family event of the year. There was a giant parade with bands and Marines and celebrities.

Prior to and during the race heats, contestants milled nervously around their racers in the paddock area. The cars were nothing like what the children's parents had made in earlier years. They were smooth racers, so slender and streamlined that drivers who had grown a bit between their local races in June and July and these finals in August had to wedge themselves in slowly. Many of the models were designed in "layback" style: the drivers were almost lying down, their eyes just visible over the cockpit.

There were differences in design—such as between the high-tailed layback and the "sit-up" models—and they were painted all manner of colors, with the sponsors' names professionally lettered on the sides, along with the drivers' names and car numbers. But beyond that, there was an enforced similarity. Their overall length could not exceed 80 inches, their height no more than 28 inches, their width no more than 34¾ inches, and the wheelbase could not be less than 48 inches. Total weight of car and driver could not exceed 250 pounds. Any metal in the car was to be a functional part of the construction; no welded parts were permitted.

All entrants had been issued a brand-new set of computer-matched official gold Soap Box Derby championship wheels to replace the red ones on which they had won in their local towns. They were to be placed on official Soap Box Derby axles, and neither wheels nor axles were to be tampered with in any way.

The rule book stated the whole reason for the Derby to the contestants: "The Soap Box Derby is for YOU. You must build your own car. You

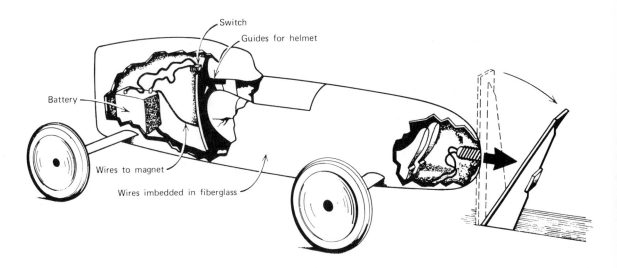

Switch

Guides for helmet

Battery

Wires to magnet

Wires imbedded in fiberglass

must not let adults or anyone else work on your car. You may accept advice and counsel from adults in the design and construction of your car . . ."

James H. Gronen first raced in the forty-sixth two-car heat. (The official records: "Fourteen-year-old Jim, who is called 'Big Jim' by his friends, is 4-feet, 11-inches tall and weighs 68 pounds. He lost in the first round of the double-elimination Boulder race when a broken steering cable caused him to hit a curb. The damage was repaired and he raced on to victory. He likes skiing, sailing, and motorcycles.") His green fiberglass layback number 12 was carefully walked down the hill to the starting line and set in position in Lane 2 beside the entry from Nashville. The noses of both cars, angled downhill, rested against the spring-loaded steel flaps which rose out of the shimmering macadam.

On signal, the starting flaps dropped forward and the cars rolled, gathering speed to between thirty and thirty-five miles per hour by the time they crossed the finish line. Jimmy Gronen won in a time of 27.48 seconds. On subsequent heats through the afternoon, Jimmy beat cars from Lancaster, Ohio; Appleton, Wisconsin; Columbus, Georgia; and Winston-Salem, North Carolina. In the semifinal, Jimmy beat the Ossining, New York, car with a 27.63 time. In the

final, he beat Bret Allen Yarborough of Elk Grove, California, though with his slowest time yet, 27.68.

When Jimmy was presented the trophy, his long, wispy blond hair tossing beneath his helmet edge in the breeze, the braces on his teeth sparkling in the sun, he said simply with a smile, "I was hoping that I'd win." He was also given a gold ring and a $7,500 college scholarship.

When Jimmy received his trophy, there was, amid the cheering, a solidly audible round of boos. Spectators were curious about why Jimmy's times had strangely worsened with each heat. People were showing the officials pictures they had taken of the starts, claiming they showed the Gronen car leaping head. And during the heats, it was said, officials had caught Jimmy cheating by buffing his tires on the pavement, and had made him substitute a new set. They had drilled in his car to remove excess weight. And what was this about some cars having been disqualified before the race, and then somehow reinstated? People wondered whether Jimmy's car was in fact Bobby's car from the year before. It was rumored that the Lange cars had cost over $20,000 to build, that they were constructed by experts at the Lange ski factory and were tested in a wind tunnel.

Derby officials began looking over the Gronen car. An inspector found a small button in the headrest, drilled through the headrest, and found wires and a battery. The car was taken to Goodyear Aerospace, near Derby Downs, and X-rayed. That was how the hunk of metal, the magnet, was discovered in the nose. To activate it, Jimmy would have leaned his helmet back against the switch in the headrest. Officials later found a second switch, formed by two supports under the cowling which covered the steering wheel, turned on by Jimmy pulling them together with his thumbs.

On Monday, Chamber of Commerce officials called in the press and announced news of the magnet and Jimmy's disqualification. Bret Yarborough was declared the new champion, and each of the following eight finishers was moved up a notch. The press leaped on the story, spreading the scandal across the nation in a mix of chuckles and pronouncements. In Putnam County, New York, Derby Director Ronald Mills, whose daughter, Diane, had been moved up to second place, said, "It's just unbelievable that anyone would want that ego trip that bad." Andy Noyes, father of now-third-place winner Chris, said, "Let's give the Derby back to the kids, where it belongs."

CHARGES OF CORRUPTION

Gronen's car was immediately locked in a bank storage room (as evidence, should there be lawsuits or criminal charges), and the Chamber of Commerce clammed up. Prosecutors in Akron and Boulder quickly began hearing from people from all over, some anonymously, who described other cheating. Akron Prosecutor Stephen Gabalac said, "If the Chamber doesn't come out swinging now, even the golfers won't want to come here. The whole town is besmirched."

And then Lange issued a statement admitting responsibility for sanctioning the magnet, which Jimmy had installed. He asserted that both Jimmy and Bobby had built their own cars and

that no significant expense went into them except in the permissible "area of advice and counsel." He admitted that Bobby's car had been tested in a wind tunnel, which, he said, was neither uncommon nor illegal.

Then he leveled his charges: "Anyone participating in derby races with eyes and ears open would soon learn, as I did, that . . . the Derby rules have been consistently and notoriously violated by some participants without censure or disqualification." He said it was "common knowledge" that eleven-year-olds cannot build winning racers, and that "it is all that some mechanically inclined and dexterous fourteen- or fifteen-year-old boy can do to carry out the superfine mechanical construction and machine work required." That was why, he said, there were adult professional builders who "build cars for sale to participants or race the cars themselves with young, lightweight drivers, who are known as chauffeurs. Early in my experience one of the professional builders offered to build a car for my son for $2,500, which I promptly refused because I felt the true value of the derby would come from my son's own efforts."

"After seeing my nephew work hundreds of hours to build his own car," Lange said, "knowing that he would be competing in Akron against professionally built cars, and against cars that would be in violation of the official rules, and having heard and believing that some fast cars in Akron would be equipped with a magnetic nose, I determined that he should build and install a magnetic nose so as to be competitive. I knew that this was a violation of the official Derby rules and consider it now to be a serious mistake in judgment."

As prosecutors continued to receive information of violations, at year's end the Chamber abandoned the race with its "cheating, fraud, and hoax" statement. Later on, I went to see Lange in Boulder.

Lange is a convivial, hospitable man with a smooth manner and modish style, with a moustache, and hair down over his ears. He still carries athletic leanness (he was a swimmer at Harvard and skis and surfs often now). His wife, Vidie, a graphic artist, is similarly lean and friendly and modish, with long blond hair. We sat in the living room of their spacious, ranch-style house, where we could look out through the glass wall upon the sparsely grassed, yellow foothills of the Rockies. From time to time, their son Bobby, grown tall and gangly, and their nephew Jimmy Gronen, shorter and stockier, stopped by for bits of chat. But at Lange's request, to protect the boys from any further involvement, they were not included in the general Derby discussion.

Lange's ski and ski-boot company was bought in 1972 by the Garcia Corporation. Last summer Lange became inactive as president of his division, though he remains a consultant and draws a $90,000 salary. The Lange factory is in nearby Broomfield, and it is there and in a machine shop in Boulder, as well as in the Lange garage, that the boys built their racers.

"I'm sure that not one Derby official in Akron believes for a second that they built their cars," Lange said, "but they did. Most people violate that rule, but I think the most important thing of all, the most exciting thing for the boys, was the thrill of building their cars and running them down the hill."

Lange's involvement with the Derby, aside from a brief try as a boy, goes back to 1970, with Bobby. "He built a car and lost right here in Boulder. He worked hard on it, but we didn't know anything, and he didn't have a chance."

He went to Akron to visit that year's championship, and then to Detroit, where Chevrolet had the winning cars on display. Through casual conversations and careful examination and measurement and photography of the cars, he began to learn about the technology, aerodynamics, and mechanics. Good alignment, he decided was it. Also, it seemed to him that wooden cars, such as Bobby's first, built in the dry climate of Boulder, would be slowed by absorbing moisture in the dampness of Akron. At

a special Soap Box rally in Detroit, he also began to learn of the dark side of the Derby.

"A bunch of us got together and just got to talking, and I began to realize that a lot of these cars just weren't built by kids. These men were building them. One guy said, 'Well, there are drivers and there are builders.' I learned about souping up wheels. They use all kinds of solvents to expand the tires, then when they come back down they're faster. I don't know the full technology about the tires, but they have to be resilient, so that when you go over a tiny bump, the tire kind of pushes back. The flex on the wheels sets up vibrations, and if the car vibrates properly, it goes a lot faster. And there are ways of working on bearings. I also learned that most people do not win with official Derby axles. One guy, a production-line worker, was building axles in his spare time and selling them all over the country. He was bragging about it."

"Were these guys telling you how to cheat?" I asked.

"They were telling me how to *win*," Lange said. "They were just doing me a favor. They don't feel it's cheating; it's so common it's just part of the game. These are ordinary guys, lots of engineers, not rich or anything. It's their life. They just live and die Derby. They probably thought, 'We'll give Lange a little bit of help, but he's never going to be any real problem.' Because I was coming out of nowhere, you know. They knew I wasn't a builder."

DESIGNED TO WIN

Lange's first step along the trail toward scandal occurred four years ago in Detroit, when he paid about $20 for a set of illegal axles for Bobby's second car. That car was made of fiberglass, which wouldn't absorb moisture, and had a metal T strip down the mid-bottom to which the axles could be bolted for sure and precise alignment. Lange made a "female" fiberglass mold from which the fiberglass top and bottom halves, which were identical, could be shaped.

"But we didn't work on vibrations that year," Lange said. "We didn't realize how important that was." The second car was a great improvement, but it was beaten in Boulder.

Now, however, Derby was deep in Lange's blood; his competitive nerves were alive. He took Bobby to Anderson, Indiana, where one of the biggest wildcats is held annually after Akron, and Bobby's car was second fastest of about 130 cars. At first he thought they might just make some minor alterations for the coming season, but they actually needed a whole new car for the 1972 derby, which would be Bobby's third try.

"I didn't work on constructing Bobby's car, but I spent a lot of time designing. Bobby was too far back in that car. Having your weight where you want it is probably one of the most important things in the race. Live weight is high in the center of gravity, whereas dead weight you can put where you want it, which is in the back. Since the car is running at a tilt most of the way, weight in the rear has more drop, so you have more energy in your car. The whole principle is to add dead weight back up the hill, and to balance that you slide the boy forward. Ideally, from an energy standpoint, you would put all your weight over the rear wheels. But that advantage would be overcome by friction when you get down on the flat, friction on the tires and the bearings that takes the resiliency out. So you have to have a balance. I have four slide scales, like doctors' scales, and you put one wheel on each scale so you get it just right,"

Also, the car was not aerodynamically correct. "A friend of mine who works at Cal Tech said that what we had was fine in water but was not fine in air doing under fifty miles an hour. The nose has to be rounded, like a tear drop. So when we got the car ready, we shipped it out to California, and my friend put it in the Cal Tech wind tunnel. You mount it up on pins and put fine pieces of thread all over the sides so you can see the airflow, what the laminar flow is and so forth. Computers measure the drag. Aerodynamics is only a small percentage in impor-

tance, but at the finish line you're looking for inches."

Lange also applied his ski knowledge. "I had come up with a new theory of the vibration in the car that really made it go fast, just like a downhill ski. If it gets too much oscillation up and down, it goes slow. Even a smooth surface has very slight undulations. Get a ski trip that's too stiff, and it doesn't undulate right. In the suspension of a derby car, the rear is solid, but if the front gets too solid, or too floppy, it goes slow. The oscillations load and unload the bearings as it goes downhill. You want that action in there, but it has to be just right. We worked on the vibrations by moving the attachment points back and forth, so that all of a sudden we had the right oscillations, and the car just kind of took off.

"And, of course, I was a super-expert in fiberglass, and a super-expert in machining things so they stay in line. I designed a jig just like an engine-block jig, to hold the car while you work on it, where you can lock it in and spin it all around, where the spindles of the axles are kept absolutely square and parallel all the time, and you don't knock it out of line in assembly."

Bobby milled a square end on the T alignment bar, pushed an axle against it, drilled and tapped, and put the dowel pins in. Then he slid the T into the length of the body and assembled the car in the jig, then look it out and balanced it on the scales, making it about ten pounds heavier in the rear. Following the guidance from the wind tunnel, he worked out subtleties in the shape with automobile-body putty.

"The molding was done here in our garage," Lange said, "but all the metalwork and assembly were done in the factory, right out in front of everybody, by Bobby. He learned to run all the machines, and somebody there would just check the setups. Bobby would go down there at 3:30 and work till 10:00 almost every night for three straight months. He loved it."

In order to accommodate the added deadweight without exceeding the 250-pound limit, Bobby was dieting and exercising. "He trained down from 123 to 106," Lange said. "I had him running three miles a day."

With everything honed, shaped, balanced, squared, light, firm, and quick, Bobby won the 1972 Boulder race easily ("There isn't much derby knowledge here, compared with some places where it's really hot and heavy. If you can't win the Boulder race easily, you won't do anything in Akron"), and went on to Akron.

In the course of watching Bobby win the championship, Lange lost whatever faith he had in the honesty of the Derby. "I still didn't know all the things that were really going on until Bobby got into the zoo. I learned right away that a kid can't leave his car for a minute, because of the sabotage there. You don't have to do much—just put a little linseed oil in a guy's bearings, and he's out of the race. And then Bobby had all these stories about guys not building their cars. Guys had illegal welded parts, double-drilled axles, they were juicing wheels—just putting some kind of stuff on their hands, like a spitball pitcher, to rub 'quickies' on their tires.

"And the big talk about the magnets was around. There was supposed to be a car in that race with a magnet, faster than Bobby's, but he cracked up. The whole thing made me sick. After Bobby won, Vidie and I were both glad we were through with that mess."

When Chevrolet dropped its sponsorship, a special Organizational Board of the Derby was set up, to seek a sponsor and perhaps develop new rules. Lange served on it. "I was through, but I wanted to see the place cleaned up, an entirely different kind of race. But I think in everybody's mind at that point was not to rock the boat, not to do something that would cause the whole race to collapse."

Then the Akron Chamber of Commerce took over, and there were no rule changes for 1973.

That same summer, Jimmy Gronen moved from his home in Dubuque, Iowa, to live with the Langes. Jimmy had never built a racer, and through the following fall and winter showed no interest. "Then in March," Lange said, "Jimmy

suddenly asked if he could build a car. I was absolutely shocked."

It was a time, Mr. and Mrs. Lange agreed, for soul-searching. "I was fighting with myself," Vidie Lange said. "The boys enjoyed it so much, building the cars. It's a terrible turmoil in your house, all this sanding, all this fiberglass everywhere. I wondered whether the race was as bad as I thought it was, or whether I was just angry because of the turmoil."

In the end, it was Vidie who encouraged the building of yet one more racer. "When you introduce another person into your house," she said, "you try very hard to make him a part of your family and do the things for him you're doing for your other children."

"So finally we decided to do it," Bob Lange said. "I think it did a great thing for my relationship with Jimmy. But time was so short—just three months before the local race, and you really need about six. So we said we'll design a car that Jimmy can build, but the only way we could get it done in time was to use Bobby's mold—which was not illegal—and built one that was essentially the same. Even so, it would be nip and tuck. Bobby had had three years' experience working in a machine shop. I told Jimmy he just couldn't be a machinist in such a short time. We had to take shortcuts, everything was simplified. Where Bobby used five bolts, Jimmy used three—stuff like that. There was nothing much new we tried to do, just tried to get in the damn race. The only thing we did, since he was so much smaller than Bobby, was to move him further forward in the car. And where Bobby's car was about ten pounds heavy in the rear, we made Jimmy's about forty. He weighed about ninety pounds, but he was chubby, so he started his diet right away."

They made axles, and for weight in the rear Lange used epoxy mixed with buckshot. "Technically the axles were illegal. I knew they couldn't pass a hardness test. But they had never done anything about that anyway. I don't call the buckshot and epoxy illegal; I designed it so they couldn't call it illegal."

Since the car was virtually the same as Bobby's, there was no wind-tunnel test. They assumed they would get to Akron with it. As expected, despite an accident in an early heat, Jimmy won the Boulder race as easily as Bobby had. And, as they had done with Bobby's car after the Boulder race, they brought Jimmy's car home to paint and letter it for Akron. (It is technically illegal to bring a car home after winning the local race, but the practice is common. Lange didn't want the car touched by "some yokel" who might somehow jar the car out of alignment.)

Then came the magnet. "We had done everything," Lange said. "I had Jimmy down to weight, the car balanced the way I wanted. I knew we had a fast car. But we also knew what we were up against. I had files on other cars. A guy from Michigan told me he had a car that was a whole car-length faster than Bobby's, for example. And we knew the Elk Grove car was going to be superfast. So we said, 'What else can we do? How can you make a car faster? Have we done everything?' We discussed theory. Jimmy came up with some ideas, Bobby with some."

The idea that recurred, although Lange doesn't recall who brought it up first, was a magnet. "Vidie probably would have shot us if she had known we were kicking that around. The year before at Akron, all the builders I talked with knew all about magnets. It wasn't anything new at all. It certainly wasn't *my* idea. I had heard a story about one guy who had a magnet, and somebody turned it on and left it on so it wore down before the race. I'd heard about an insepctor measuring a car with a steel tape measure when, bang! it stuck to the thing. They made the driver remove the magnet, but they let him run. We knew Jimmy would be running against all those chauffeurs in professionally built cars, and maybe other cars that had magnets, so we figured that in order to be competitive we would probably try one. It was the only thing we could think of. I figured even if they detected it they wouldn't throw him out, just make him disconnect it."

NO MORAL CRISIS

Given the situation at Akron, Lange did not consider the immorality of using a magnet. "These boys had sat in on meetings with builders. They knew what was in those cars. Our attitude toward the Akron race was that it was one big wildcat, and we were in it. There was no moral crisis for Jimmy. He had been around all these super-illegal cars and saw the whole business. The scene was there, he didn't create it. Jimmy wanted to win the race."

Moreover, he said, he wasn't even sure it would work. And if it did, it would be no greater advantage than good axles, wheels, balance, and all the rest. "There's a lot of things I'd rather have than a magnet. What's more of an advantage than having a guy that's been building racers for eighteen years? Who's kidding who about advantage? You call a magnet a secret motor? You're pulling a secret motor in if you add a pound, because your weight is your motor. I don't go along with the magnet being a different type of thing from the other things that are just commonly being done. Sure, I take full responsibility for it because I'm the one that should say yes or no. But I had never seen a magnet, or how they were designed. The kids designed it, and Jimmy put it in. They learn all that stuff in science class in school. All you need is a little ingenuity."

And so Jimmy put the battery in the tail fin, and ran copper wires on either side along the inside seam, where the top and bottom halves were joined. Using a stick to reach the recesses of the fuselage, he glued strips of fiberglass over the wire. He cut a hole in the nose. He bolted together four small pieces of iron, totaling about three inches in length, wrapped them with the wires, laid them in the hole, filled in around them with fiberglass resin and body putty, sanded the metal head smooth to the nose, and painted it over so that there was no visible seam or metal. The entire inside of the car was coated with black primer, which obscured any view. Lange said his only contribution was to suggest the second fail-safe thumb switch under the cowling to protect against the battery running down if one switch was turned on by accident, say, in shipping.

They tested the magnet once, by putting an I beam across the nose and trying to putt the car forward. "You could feel it," Lange said, "but it wouldn't make the car move. And the battery's got to sit for a month, so there's no point in wearing it down by testing it. It's either going to work, or it's not going to work. Anyway, nothing would substitute for a bad car. Jimmy's was a super car without it. As it turned out, he would have won anyway, but at the time I didn't think he could win without the magnet."

And then they went to Akron, where Jimmy was to win. They were attended by controversy from the beginning. Before the races, several cars, including Jimmy's, were listed for disqualification for having illegally hard axles, but officials backed down and allowed all the cars to run, just as Lange had supposed they would. During the races, officials took Jimmy's first set of wheels away because he had been working on them with his hands, and buffing them. Then they drilled in his car to remove some of the buckshot weight, while Jimmy wept in frustration. "Friends kept running up to me," Lange said, "and saying how much the officials were hassling Jimmy. I said, 'He's all right, he's a big boy, you know.' "

And finally Jimmy won it all, just before losing it all, and he said he didn't even have a chance to turn on the thumb switch for the last championship run.

Lange believes that part of the reason for singling out Jimmy for harsh treatment was jealousy from other builders they beat. Also, the Akron Chamber of Commerce, he felt, "wouldn't have made such a big issue over the thing" if it had been aware of what had been going on for years. "As a matter of fact," Lange said, "since Jimmy won about five guys have called me and said they used magnets."

The swirl of claims, charges, rumors, and denials continues. This year at Akron, the contestants will have to demonstrate their skills by duplicating "selected steps in the construction of their car"; "female" fiberglass molds of the Lange type, which can be reused, are prohibited (next year fiberglass may be banned altogether); the insides of the cars, from nose to tail, must be accessible to permit inspection for such things as magnets.

The case of the Soap Box Derby scandal is closed, more or less. Jimmy has not returned his trophy or accepted his disqualification. Lange says his nephew has been quite philosophical. "Sure, he was upset. He said, 'Here they're calling me a cheater, when these other guys are more cheaters than I am.' " But, he said, Jimmy's friends have been "super," and people in general have been sympathetic because "they know what was going on."

I agreed with Lange that to discuss all this with Jimmy would exacerbate old wounds and expose him to further painful publicity, and I wished not to do that. I came away with a sense of charm and spirit within the Lange household, and warmth in the relationships with their children, and I prefer to trust that sense.

But I cannot shake a certain melancholy. Perhaps Jimmy Gronen did not adapt to cheating as easily as all that. When he sat poised in his racer at the top of Derby Downs, with the knowledge of what he was doing, the fear of detection, the hope of winning, the faith in his guardian uncle, and the memories of the past year, he must have felt at least a transient pang of utter loneliness. And I wonder how often that stab has recurred, and will, at odd times, to different stimuli, with varying intensities, and whether winning was worth so scarred a heritage from the age of fourteen.

38. The Broken Home and Delinquency

LAWRENCE ROSEN
KATHLEEN NEILSON

CONSIDERABLE ATTENTION HAS BEEN FOCUSED ON the family as a contributing factor in delinquency. Three major approaches have been utilized to explicate the relationship between familial factors and delinquency. Respectively, these orientations emphasize: (1) deviant structural configurations, (2) deviant familial relationships, and (3) the transfer of deviant norms.

The "deviant structure" orientation focuses on delinquency as a result of the child being nurtured in a household that has deviated from the "ideal" or normative family structure in a given society. According to this perspective, one would expect that in American society, a child living in a "broken home" would, for a variety of related reasons, tend to become delinquent, since this is a departure from the predominant and ideal arrangement of a nuclear family with both parents present. The second approach that emphasized deviant familial relationships assumes that the type of familial interaction will have an effect on the subsequent behavior of the child. Factors such as too much love or lack of love, too harsh or too lax discipline, lack of familial solidarity, emotional inconsistency, etc., will often result in rebellion, psychological difficulties, and personality problems, with a subsequent increased probability of delinquency. The final orientation—the transfer of deviant norms—focuses on the differential socialization of children and their resultant tendencies to-

ward either conforming or delinquent behavior. According to this perspective, delinquents would be taught to favor violation of societal norms and juvenile statutes, whereas nondelinquents would internalize respect for societal norms and juvenile statutes.

This selection evaluates the empirical evidence that addresses itself to the effect of one aspect of the family structure—the presence of a "broken" or "intact" home—on delinquency.

CONCEPT OF A BROKEN HOME

The definition of a broken home that is most commonly employed in the delinquency literature refers to a home that is characterized by the absence of at least one natural parent because of death, desertion, divorce, or separation. However, some variations can be found, such as the absence of either a natural *or* a stepparent or even absences that may be temporary in nature (e.g., absences resulting from institutional commitment or occupational opportunities away from the home). The definition of a broken home can also be restricted so that only divorce, desertion, and/or separation are utilized as reasons for the break.

All conceptions of a broken home, however, include two major dimensions: (1) the absence of a parent or parents, and (2) the reason for the absence. Thus the variability in the definition of broken home is a consequence of the extension or restriction of the concept in terms of which

▶SOURCE: *Selection especially written for this volume.*

parent or parents are absent or the reasons for the absence. In order to evaluate the literature systematically on this dimension, it seems appropriate to avoid the more restrictive definitions of broken homes and to employ a more general one. For purposes of this study, a broken home simply refers to a family that is characterized by the absence of at least one parent (natural or step).

REVIEW OF THE LITERATURE

The literature in delinquency exhibits a considerable amount of controversy concerning the relative importance of the broken home as a contributing factor of delinquency. Peterson and Becker (1965), for example, argue strongly for its importance:

"... the substantial relationship between delinquency and broken homes remains as one of the overriding facts any conception of delinquency must take into account." (p. 69)

On the other hand, a harsh criticism of this position is posited by Mannheim (1965):

"No other term in the history of criminological thought has been so much overworked, misused, and discredited as this. For many years universally proclaimed as the most obvious explanation of both juvenile delinquency and adult crime, it is now often regarded as the 'black sheep' in the otherwise respected family of criminological theories, and most writers shamefacedly turn their backs to it." (p. 618)

A perusal of the literature indicates that the once popular position that broken homes are instrumental in the development of delinquent behavior has waned somewhat in recent years. The predominant position among contemporary criminologists seems to be that broken homes are of *secondary* importance for understanding juvenile delinquency.

Despite this view among the professionals, it seems that the public tends to believe that the broken home is a major cause of delinquency. This is an understandable concern, considering that the prevalance of broken homes has in-

creased substantially since the middle of the 1960s. In 1974 there were approximately 2.5 million more children (below the age of 18) living in households with at least one parent absent than in 1965. In 1974 it was estimated that approximately 11.8 million children were residing in broken homes (U.S. Bureau of the Census, 1974:111–112). Thus, if the broken home is a major cause of delinquency, a sizable number of the youths in the United States could be adversely effected.

Because the studies have varied widely in terms of defining delinquency and broken homes, sampling procedures, research design, and data analysis, it is somewhat difficult to find an adequate base for comparison. Although it is nearly impossible to consider all the conditions of research, we decided to invoke the following criteria for inclusion of eligible studies for review:

1. A comparison group of nondelinquents must have been included in their research design.

2. The data must have been presented in sufficient detail so that a ϕ^2 (phi square) could be computed.

3. The delinquent group did not consist solely of institutionalized youths. (There is evidence that family structure is a factor in the judicial decision to commit a juvenile to a correctional institution. By using only an institutional population, there is a decided possibility that the proportion of broken homes would be somewhat inflated.)[1]

In addition to these requirements we also decided to use the same statistical measure of strength of association, namely ϕ^2. This was deemed necessary to provide a common base of comparison. Most studies have relied either on

[1] Richard S. Sterne (1964), P.M. Smith (1955). The Gluecks' (1950) study, although utilizing an institutional population of delinquents, was included because it is widely cited.

percentage differences of χ^2 (chi square). Each is inadequate for our purposes. Percent differences do not adequately measure strength of association. In addition, exclusive reliance on χ^2 (or other inferential tests of association/no association) are inappropriate because of the variable sample sizes between studies. Thus, all the studies were reanalyzed by computing a ϕ^2 as well as χ^2 for purposes of assessing inferential probability. Since almost all of the studies meeting this criteria were conducted on males, the findings for Table I relate only to males (females are discussed in a subsequent section).

Despite the variation in time, locale, sample size, nature of population, definitions of both delinquency and broken home, and in basic research design, the conclusion is clear: the strength of the relationship is very small (even though in nine studies a significant level of at least 0.05 was reached).

A word is in order concerning the two studies (the Gluecks and the Browning), which seem to have a typically high ϕ^2 value (although both values were below 0.10). The Glueck's study, using 500 institutionalized boys as its delinquents, may well have involved an administra-

Table I. Summary of Studies Investigating "Broken Home" and Male Delinquency

Researcher	Year Published	N	Association	
			ϕ^2	χ^{2} [a]
Shaw and McKay[b]	1932	8953	0.004	40.28
Weeks and Smith[c]	1939	2449	0.012	24.49
Carr-Saunders, et al.[d]	1944	3925	0.019	74.57
Glueck and Glueck[e]	1950	1000	0.078	78.50
Nye[f]	1958	1160	0.005	5.80
Browning[g]	1960	164	0.096	15.69
Morris[h]	1964	112	0.014	1.57
Hardt[i]	1965	164	0.022	3.66
Hardt[j]	1965	191	0.015	2.92
Tennyson[k]	1967	320	0.007	2.21
Tennyson[l]	1967	217	0.009	1.87
Koval and Polk[m]	1967	873	0.009	7.60
Rosen[n]	1968	866	0.012	10.13
Rosen, Lalli, and Savitz[o]	1975	532	0.025	12.66
Rosen, Lalli, and Savitz[p]	1975	502	0.004	1.78

[a] All χ^2 values are for one degree of freedom. Significant Values are: for 0.001 level, 10.83; for 0.01 level, 6.64; and for 0.05 level, 384.

[b] Clifford Shaw and H.D. McKay (1932). Delinquents are from Juvenile Court in Chicago, 1929-1930. The nondelinquents, ages 10 to 17, were sampled from public schools in Chicago. The delinquency rate of the control group was not checked; therefore it is not known how many delinquents were in the control group. "Broken home" defined as at least one parent absent because of death, desertion, divorce, separation, or confinement in an institution.

[c] H.A. Weeks and Margaret G. Smith (1939). Delinquents are from Juvenile Court in Spokane, Washington. The nondelinquents are a random sample of public secondary school students, Spokane Washington, 1937, having no court record. The age of delinquency is 7 to 18 years. Definition of "broken home" same as that given by Shaw and McKay (footnote 2).

[d] A.M. Carr-Saunders, H. Mannheim, and E. Rhodes (1944). Delinquents (ages 7 to 17) are taken from those appearing before court in 1938 in selected cities in England (including London). The nondelinquents were chosen by asking the head teacher at the school at which the delinquent attended for a youth who would be similar to the delinquent youth. The matching variables were age and residence. "Broken home" defined as at least one natural parent absent because of death, separation, or divorce.

tive bias of disproportionate commitments from broken homes to juvenile institutions. A second possible reason for the relatively high association stems from the matching design employed by the researchers (thus giving them an equal number of delinquents and nondelinquents). ϕ^2 is affected by the marginals in such a manner that its values are maximized when there is a 50-50 split. A reordering of the Glueck's data to give a split of 30 percent delinquents and 70 percent nondelinquents (which is closer to the other studies listed in Table I) yields a ϕ^2 of

0.018 (still significant at the 0.0001 level).[2] The Browning study seemed to employ the least systematic procedure of all studies used. The nondelinquents were not selected on a probability basis, and the delinquents chosen were only those who had either committed a truancy (a

[2]A similar reordering for all the other studies in Table I not having approximately a 30–70 split on the dependent variable, although producing some changes in the ϕ^2 failed to effect the conclusion of a very weak relationship between the two variables. (Not a single recomputed ϕ^2 value exceeded 0.025.)

---

e Sheldon Glueck and Eleanor Glueck (1950). The sample of delinquents was taken from correctional schools and the nondelinquents from Boston public schools in 1939. The delinquents and nondelinquents were matched for age, intelligence, and ethnicity. "Broken home" is one "broken by separation, divorce, or prolonged absence of a parent."

f F. Ivan Nye (1958). The sample was selected from high school students in three "medium-sized" towns in Washington in 1955. The measurements of delinquent group being those scoring highest on the delinquency scale. The association values noted include stepparents in the intact family; a reconstruction of the broken home definition to exclude stepparents yields a ϕ^2 of less than 0.001 and χ^2 of 1.16.

g Charles J. Browning (1960). The youths were chosen from a population that was white, at least third generation Americans, Protestant, Catholic or no religion, enrolled in public schools, and living in a common court jurisdiction within Los Angeles (no date given). The mean age of the youths in the sample was 15. The delinquents were defined as those having a court record and whose most serious offense was auto theft or truancy (the analysis divided delinquency into most serious and least serious). The nondelinquents were those who had no record or truancy for the year of the study. The proportion of delinquents was 66.5%. "Broken home" defined as a "boy not living with both of his natural parents."

h Ruth Morris (1964). Very little information is given concerning the selection of both delinquents and nondelinquents, other than the fact that they were selected as a match for white female delinquents with two or more police contacts in Flint, Michigan. The matching variables were social class, intelligence, grade in school, and age. Broken home defined as at least one parent absent.

i Robert H. Hardt (1965). The study was conducted in 1963 in a city of 250,000 located in "the center of one of the major metropolitan areas in a Middle Atlantic state." Delinquents were defined as having a record or a "suspected" or "alleged" delinquent in the Central Registry of Juvenile Police Contacts. Both the delinquents and nondelinquents were seventh-, eighth- and nith-grade students attending parochial and public schools. Broken home defined as father absent.

j Ibid. The sample is the same as noted in footnote except that delinquency was defined as self-report.

k Ray A. Tennyson (1967). Delinquency was membership in a gang defined as "troublesome" by the "Program for Detached Workers of the YMCA of Chicago." (This sample was not a random one.). The nongang members were suggested by the YMCA workers. An intact home was a response by the youth of either "both parents continuously" or "mostly both parents" to the question, "Whom did you live with when growing up?"

l Ibid. Same as footnote k, but the sample was white boys.

m John P. Koval and Kenneth Polk (1967). Sample taken from one high school and a nonprobability selection of "dropouts" residing in a "small city" in Lane County, Oregon (no date given). Delinquency was defined as a court or police record, with family structure being characterized only as "natural family intact."

n Lawrence Rosen (1968). Sample of black youths, 13 to 15 years old, drawn by an area sampling technique, residing in a low-income, high-delinquent, predominantly black area of Philadelphia in the summer of 1963. Delinquency was defined as at least one apprehension by the juvenile authorities. "Broken home" was simply the absence of at least one parent.

o Lawrence Rosen, M. Lalli, and L. Savitz (1975). Sample of black youths attending public schools in Philadelphia in 1970, age 13. Delinquency was defined at least one official contact with police or juvenile court. Broken home was defined as the absence of at least one parent.

p Ibid. A sample of white youths, age 14, attending public school or a ninth grade in Catholic school in 1971. Delinquency and broken home same as in footnote o.

"less serious" offense) or auto theft (a "serious" offense).

To a limited extent, other issues have been researched. The major ones are sex, social class, race, and age. (In analyzing these issues we have referred to studies that do not meet the criteria given above. This was necessary because, for the most part, these studies contain the only available empirical evidence on these issues.)

SEX

As already indicated, the major portion of studies meeting our criteria for inclusion in this review have researched male subjects. There are a few studies of females but, for the most part, they have simply compared broken home rates of male and female delinquents. (Weeks, 1940; Monahan, 1957; Chilton and Markle, 1972; Datesman and Scarpitti, 1975.) All of these studies have found that the proportion of broken homes was greater for female delinquents than male delinquents. This has, of course, led all the authors to conclude that the broken home is of greater importance in the etiology of delinquency for females. (The usual theoretical argument is that the family is of greater salience for females in terms of affectional needs, status, role definition, and control. Therefore any disruption or problem in the family would have greater consequence for the behavior of females.) However, reaching such a conclusion on the basis of this kind of evidence is hazardous because of the unequal delinquency rates of males and females. (The implicit assumption of the kind of data analysis employed in these studies is that the delinquency rates are equal.)

We are aware of at least two studies that meet our criteria. Using a sample of delinquent white girls in Flint, Michigan with two or more police contacts and a group of nondelinquents matched for age, intelligence, social class, and school grade,[3] Morris (1964) found a relatively

[3]No information was given on how the nondelinquents were selected.

large difference in delinquency rates between girls residing in broken homes and those coming from intact homes ($\phi^2 = .279$; $\chi^2 = 31.75$). The second study by Nye (1958), used a self-report measure of delinquency and also found sizable differences in delinquency rates ($\phi^2 = 0.037$; $\chi^2 = 42.81$). Both studies exhibited stronger associations for females than for males in their sample (see Table I).

There is also some evidence on the effect of type of offense. Weeks (1940), when controlling for type of offense and source of referral to juvenile court, found that the difference in broken home rates between male and female delinquents was appreciably reduced. He thus argued that the reason for the higher rates of broken homes for female delinquents was due both to the larger incidence of juvenile status offenses (runaway, truancy, ungovernability) for females, and the greater likelihood of parents referring their daughters to juvenile court for these types of offenses. Datesman and Scarpitti (1975) also found some important differences between black and white delinquents in this regard. For the black delinquents the incidence of broken homes was greater for females, for person and property offenses; the reverse was true for juvenile status offenders (although this difference was not statistically different). For the white delinquents the broken home rates was greater for females, for the person and juvenile status offenders, but about equal for property offenders.

As we will argue shortly, these differences between males and females may be more a consequence of the differential likelihood of delinquency in the general population for these groups instead of a differential impact of broken homes.

RACE

Both Toby (1957) and Chilton and Markle (1972) have, on the basis of general juvenile court statistics, argued that the broken home has a stronger association with delinquency for whites than for blacks. However, the two studies [by Tennyson (1967) and Rosen et al. (1975)] that have data for blacks and whites show very little if any difference between whites and blacks in this regard (see Table I). In fact, the one study (Rosen et al., 1975) with a representative sample of youths exhibits a slightly higher relationship for blacks than for whites.

AGE

Two studies have investigated the issue of age. Toby (1957), in reexamining the Shaw and McKay data, has argued that the broken home is more important for the younger males. However, our reanalysis of the same data does not support this conclusion. The ϕ^2 values for the 10 to 12-year-olds[4] was exactly the same as 13 to 17-year-olds.[5]

Chilton and Markle (1972) found a slightly higher incidence of broken homes for the 10 to 13-year-old delinquents than those aged 14 to 17 years.

SOCIAL CLASS

The evidence for this area is extremely sparse. Chilton and Markle (1972) report a higher

proportion of broken homes for the children from the low-income families. The major difficulty in interpreting this finding is that the broken home rates in the general population also decrease as family income increases.

Weeks and Smith (1939), using fathers' occupations as a measure of social class, found a slightly higher relationship between the two variables for professional and white collar boys ($\phi^2 = 0.025$; $\chi^2 = 7.0$) than the boys with laborer and unemployed fathers ($\phi^2 = 0.016$; $\chi^2 = 7.21$). Utilizing the Warner I.S.C. scale as measure of social class, Rosen, Lalli, and Savitz (1975) researched this issue separately for whites and blacks. The data are presented in Table II. For the white youths all associations were nonsignificant. However, the ϕ^2 values would indicate that the broken home has more impact for the lowest social class group. The findings for the black youths are somewhat more mixed. The χ^2 values show that relationship is only significant for the lowest social class. The ϕ^2 values, on the other hand, would lead us to conclude that the relationship is of some importance for the highest income level.

---

[4]This age group is, one assumes, what Toby meant by preadolescent (he never actually defined the age range) when he characterized the association between "broken homes" and delinquency as "considerable" for "preadolescents." A computation of ϕ^2 for the 10 to 11-year-old group would have been unfeasible because of the extremely small proportion (2.7%) of delinquents in that group.

[5]This generalization is true only for the Shaw and McKay data with its given age distribution and differential delinquency rates by age. (The rates were about 5% for the 10 to 12-year-olds and 32% for the 13 to 17-year-olds.) One may well ask what the relationship between delinquency and "broken home" would be if the delinquency rates were the same for both age groups. Reconstructing the data for the 10 to 12-year-olds to yield an identical delinquency rate as the 13 to 17-year-old group (the effect is similar to standardizing the age distribution of the delinquents on the basis of the nondelinquents, a procedure that Toby argues Shaw and McKay should have followed) gives a ϕ^2 of 0.019. Although this finding now supports Toby's assertion of a differential age effect, the value of ϕ^2 for the younger group is still quite less than the "considerable association" claimed by Toby.

Table II. Relationship Between Broken Home and Delinquency for Social Class Level (Warner I.S.C.) for White and Black Males

Social Class (Warner)	N	ϕ^2	χ^2
		Blacks	
Low	249	0.019	4.86
Middle	171	0.011	1.87
High	112	0.027	3.03
		Whites	
Low	78	0.028	2.22
Middle	155	0.008	1.26
High	269	0.006	1.50

Source: Rosen, Lalli, and Savitz (1975).

DISCUSSION

As we have already indicated, there are major problems in reaching any firm conclusions on the basis of such a review because of the variability in research design and sampling strategies. Most studies that have used comparative non-delinquent groups have not used representative samples. Some studies have looked at total juvenile court populations and contrasted them with total population statistics (Monahan, 1958; Chilton and Markle, 1972). Consequently, it is possible that the findings (especially with respect to age, race, and sex) are artifacts of artificial sampling constraints and reversed dependent probabilities (i.e., the likelihood of family status for a delinquent rather than the reverse of delinquency status for family types). The primary interest should focus be on the relationship between family structure and delinquency in the total population with whatever proportion of delinquency and broken homes naturally occur in that population. It is clear that many of the studies reviewed do not allow for any reasonable conclusion in this regard. This is especially true of those studies that use only delinquents as their research population (e.g., Chilton and Markle, 1972).

As a way of attempting to gain a more adequate approach to this problem, we simulated what the relationship between delinquency and family structure might be in the total U.S. population by utilizing data provided by Chilton and Markle (1972). In their study they used data from all youths having contact with juvenile and county courts of Florida in the first four months of 1969. As a comparison, they utilized data for the total U.S. population of 10 to 17-year-olds for 1968. Utilizing this same data, it is possible to compute ϕ^2 values for different assumed general delinquency rates. The simulated data are presented in Table III and can be viewed as holding true for the total United States if one is willing to assume that delinquents processed in Florida and for whom information on family structure was available (such information was not available for 40% of the delinquents) are representative of all delinquents in the United States.

The data in Table III are given for two conditions of delinquency likelihood: a value of 3%[6] and 10%. For each condition, both a ϕ^2 value and a set of dependent probabilities are computed. The first two columns in Table III give the probability of finding a broken home for delinquents and nondelinquents, respectively.

The $Pr\ (B/D)$ is the usual statement made when one is simply using a delinquent population. (This is what, for example, can be found in the Chilton and Markle study.) Since family structure is seen as the cause of delinquency, the more appropriate dependent probabilities are those given in the last two columns, namely $Pr\ (D/B)$ and $Pr\ (D/I)$.

Several kinds of issues can be examined in this table. First we examine the table for the delinquency rate of 3% (i.e., every group listed in the table would have a 3% delinquency rate). The relationship for broken home and delinquency is very weak for all children ($\phi^2 = 0.012$) and consistent with the majority of studies listed in Table I. As the general delinquency rate increases, the strength of the relationship increases. Thus the ϕ^2 value for the total group for a 10% delinquency rate increases to 0.042. If one looks at the $Pr\ (D/B)$ and $Pr\ (D/I)$ columns for both delinquency levels, one can clearly see that delinquents are more likely to come from broken homes than they are from intact homes for all demographic groups. And, among the broken home group, females, whites, and the very young have slightly higher likelihoods of delinquency rates. These are some conclusions as reached by most researchers, but it is quite

[6]The rate of 3% is the usual incidence rate cited nationally for all youths 7 to 17 years of age. The usual prevalence figure is 10 to 15%. Since the Chilton and Markle study is using incidence of delinquency, the more appropriate reference is the 3% value.

Table III. Simulation of Broken Home Delinquency Relationships for Selected Demographic Groups for Assumed General Delinquency Rates of 0.03 and 0.10

| | Pr (D) = 0.03 | | | | | Pr (D) = 0.10 | | | | |
| | | Pr | | | | | Pr | | | |
	ϕ^2	B/D	B/N	E/B	D/I	ϕ^2	B/D	B/N	D/B	D/I
Total	0.012	0.40	0.16	0.07	0.02	0.042	0.40	0.14	0.24	0.07
Male	0.012	0.40	0.16	0.07	0.02	0.042	0.40	0.14	0.24	0.07
Female	0.015	0.44	0.16	0.08	0.02	0.057	0.44	0.14	0.26	0.07
Black	0.002	0.58	0.43	0.04	0.02	0.010	0.58	0.41	0.14	0.07
White	0.008	0.30	0.12	0.07	0.02	0.028	0.30	0.11	0.23	0.08
Black male	0.002	0.58	0.43	0.04	0.02	0.010	0.58	0.41	0.14	0.07
White male	0.008	0.30	0.12	0.07	0.02	0.028	0.30	0.11	0.23	0.08
Black Female	0.004	0.60	0.42	0.04	0.02	0.013	0.60	0.41	0.14	0.07
White female	0.015	0.38	0.12	0.08	0.02	0.061	0.38	0.10	0.29	0.07
Age 10-13	0.023	0.45	0.14	0.09	0.02	0.077	0.45	0.12	0.30	0.06
Age 14-17	0.006	0.38	0.18	0.06	0.02	0.026	0.38	0.17	0.20	0.08

Key: D = Delinquent
        N = Nondelinquent
        B = Broken home
        I = Intact home
        Pr = Probability

Source: Analysis based on data presented in Chilton and Markle (1972)

clear that they are contingent on the assumption that the groups being compared have the same general delinquency rate. This is, of course, not a viable assumption: females have higher rates than males, blacks have higher rates than whites, and the older delinquents have higher rates than the younger ones. Therefore, a more appropriate comparison can be made by comparing across both general delinquency levels in Table III. In comparing males with females, for example, it is more realistic to consider the values for females at the 3% delinquency level with the values for males at the 10% level. In that comparison, one can see that the broken home is of greater relevance to males than females. In other words, males from broken homes have a higher delinquency rate than females from broken homes. The ϕ^2 values also support the same conclusion. The conclusions are similar for race and age: broken homes seem more strongly related to delinquency for blacks and for the older age group. These findings with respect to sex, race and age are the opposite from those reached by Toby (1957) and Chilton and Markle (1972).

Once more we should stress, however, that broken homes are weakly related to delinquency for all groups. (Not a single ϕ^2 value was above 0.1 in Table III.)

Of course, the actual values of ϕ^2 and the dependent probabilities will be contingent on the actual delinquency rates in the population;

however, the usefulness of this type of simulation does indicate that conclusions based on artificial constraints on sampling and inappropriate dependent probabilities can possibly lead to faulty generalizations about the relationship between delinquency and broken homes in the general population.

CONCLUSION

A variety of possible explanations can be forwarded to account for the lack of a strong relationship between broken homes and delinquency. The most obvious explanation for this fact is that the family may not be a major contributing factor in terms of delinquency. Social structural or social process variables (delinquent value systems, opportunity structures, subcultures, etc.) may be the main determinants. Another possibility allows for the importance of the family as an independent variable for delinquency, but emphasizes the "quality of family interaction" instead of the family structure per se as causative. Finally, the crude research designs and statistical measures employed in almost all of the studies of broken homes and delinquency may have combined to offer conclusions that are at best questionable.

In conclusion, the information compiled in this report illustrates that the concept of broken homes, no matter how it is defined or measured, has little explanatory power in terms of delinquency. Since, for the most part, the studies included here have had difficulties both in conceptualizing and measuring the broken home concept and in controlling for significant variables, such as age at the time of the break and subsequent arrangements after the break, it is impossible to rule out completely the factor of broken homes as contributing to the etiology of delinquent tendencies. Until these problems are resolved, the relevance of broken homes for delinquency is not totally disproven. The most one can say at present is that the empirical evidence does not support the thesis that the broken home is a significant factor in the development of delinquent tendencies.

REFERENCES

Browning, C.J.
1960   "Differential Impact of Family Disorganization on Male Adolescents." *Social Problems* 8:37–44.

Carr-Saunders, A.M., H. Mannheim, and E. Rhodes
1944   Young Offenders. New York: MacMillan.

Chilton, R.J., and G.E. Markle
1972   "Family Disruption, Delinquent Conduct and the Effect of Subclassification." *American Sociological Review, 37:33–55*

Datesman, S.K., and F.R. Scarpitti
1975   "Female Delinquency and Broken Homes." *Criminology, 13:33–55*

Glueck, S., and E. Glueck
1950   *Unravelling Juvenile Delinquency.* New York: Commonwealth Fund.

Hardt, R.H.
1965   "Delinquency and Social Class: Studies of Juvenile Deviations or Police Disposition." Unpublished paper presented at Eastern Sociological Meetings, New York.

Koval, J.P., and K. Polk
1967   "Problem Youth in a Small City," pp. 123–138 in Malcolm W. Klein (Ed.). *Juvenile Gangs in Context.* Englewood Cliffs, N.J.: Prentice-Hall.

Mannheim H.
1965   *Comparative Criminology,* Boston: Houghton-Mifflin Company.

Monahan, T.P.
1957   "Family Status and the Delinquent Child: A Reappraisal and Some New Findings." *Social Forces, 35:250–258.*

Morris, R.R.
1964   "Female Delinquency and Relational Problems." *Social Forces, 43:82–89.*

Nye, F.I.
1958   *Family Relationships and Delinquent Behavior.* New York: John Wiley and Sons.

Peterson, D.R., and W.C. Becker
1965   "Family Interaction and Delinquency," p. 69 in Herbert C. Quay (Ed.). *Juvenile Delinquency.* Princeton, N.J.: D. Van Nostrand pp. 63–99.

Rosen, L.
1968   The Delinquent and Non-Delinquent in a High Delinquent Area. Unpublished doctoral dissertation, Temple University.

Rosen, L., M. Lalli, and L. Savitz
1975   "City Life and Delinquency: The Family and Delinquency." Report submitted to National Institute for Juvenile Justice and Delinquency Prevention. Law Enforcement Assistance Administration. Unpublished.

Shaw, C., and H.D. McKay
1932   "Are Broken Homes a Causative Factor in Juvenile Delinquency?" *Social Forces,* *10:*514–524

Smith, P.M.
1955   "Broken Homes and Juvenile Delinquency." *Sociology and Social Research,* *39:*307–311

Sterne, R.S.
1964   *Delinquent Conduct and Broken Homes.* New Haven, Conn.: College and University Press.

Tennyson, R.A.
1967   "Family Structure and Delinquent Behavior," pp. 57–69 in Malcolm W. Klein (Ed.), *Juvenile Gangs in Context.* Englewood Cliffs, N.J.: Prentice-Hall.

Toby, J.
1957   "The Differential Impact of Family Disorganization." *American Sociological Review,* *22:*402–412.

U.S. Bureau of the Census
1974   Current Population Reports; Special Studies, p. 23, No. 54: Social and Economic States of the Black Population in the United States.

Weeks, H.A.
1940   "Male and Female Broken Home Rates by Types of Delinquency." *American Sociological Review, 5:*601–609.

Weeks, H.A., and M.G. Smith
1939   "Juvenile Delinquency and Broken Homes in Spokane, Washington." *Social Forces, 18:*48–59.

39. American Women and Crime

RITA J. SIMON

ON THE OCCASION OF THE HAMLYN LECTURES AT Sheffield University, in 1963, Lady Barbara Wooton observed:

"It is perhaps rather curious that no serious attempt has yet been made to explain the remarkable facts of the sex ratio in detected criminality; for the scale of the sex differential far outranks all the other tracts (except that of age in the case of indictable offenses) which have been supposed to distinguish the delinquent from the nondelinquent population. It seems to be one of those facts which escape notice by virtue of its very conspicuousness. It is surely, to say the least, very odd that half the population should be apparently immune to the criminogenic factors which lead to the downfall of so significant a proportion of the other half. Equally odd is it, too, that although the criminological experience of different countries varies considerably, nevertheless the sex differential remains."[1]

Much has happened in the dozen or so years since Lady Wooton made these remarks. The main thrust of this article will be to describe those changes, to explain why they have occurred, and to make some prognosis about their implications for the future.

The topic, women and crime, is currently enjoying a wave of interest unknown at any previous time. Interest in the female offender is, I believe, a specific manifestation of the increased general interest and attention that women have been receiving since the latter part of the 1960s. Women themselves have been largely responsible for their increased notoriety. Having organized into a visible and vocal social movement, whose objectives are the attainment of greater freedom and more responsibility, they have also succeeded in drawing attention to themselves. One of the consequences of this attention has been to question and to research many aspects of women's roles that have hitherto been of little interest or concern to social scientists, clinicians, and law enforcement officials.

The movement for woman's liberation has changed a lot of things about women's reality; and it has been at least partially responsible for changes in women's behavior vis-à-vis criminal activities, as well as scholars' perceptions of the types of women who are likely to engage in crime. In 1966, Rose Giallombardo characterized the image of the woman offender as follows:

"Women who commit criminal offenses tend to be regarded as erring and misguided creatures who need protection and help rather than as dangerous criminals from whom members of society should be protected."[2]

How similar that sounds to the observations of the Gluecks, who wrote, in 1934:

▶SOURCE: "American Women and Crime," Annals, American Academy of Political and Social Sciences (January 1976), 423:31–46. Reprinted by permission.

[1]Lady Barbara Wooton, "A Magistrate in Search of the Causes of Crimes," Crime and the Criminal Law, 1963, pp. 6–8.

[2]Rose Giallombardo, Society of Women: A Study of a Women's Prison (New York: John Wiley & Son, Inc., 1966), p. 7.

"The women are themselves on the whole a sorry lot. The major problem involved in the delinquency and criminality of our girls is their lack of control of their sexual impulses."[3]

How strange these observations sound when one notes that, in 1970, four of the FBI's ten most wanted fugitives were women. Daniel Green, writing a few months ago in the *National Observer,* commented:

"Before the advent of militant feminism, female radicals were little more than groupies in the amorphous conglomeration of revolutionary and anti-war groups that came to be known collectively in the '60s as The Movement. Like camp followers of old, they functioned principally as cooks, flunkies, and sex objects.

"Sexual equality came to the Movement in the gas-polluted streets of Chicago during the '68 Democratic Convention. Enraged by the tactics of Mayor Daley's police, Middle American daughters raised for gentler things shrieked obscenities and hurled rocks as ferociously as veteran street fighters. From then on, guerrilla women were dominant figures in the splintered Movement, particularly the defiantly militant Weatherman faction, which they purged of "*macho*" sexism" and renamed the Weather Underground."[4]

What role has the woman's liberation movement played in changing both the image of the female offender and the types of criminal activities that she is likely to commit? The rhetoric of the woman's movement has emphasized similarity between the sexes. Kate Millet, for example, argues that all of the significant behavioral differences between the sexes are those that have been developed by culture, environment, and sexist training.[5] Others in the movement have emphasized that women are no more moral, conforming, or law-abiding than men.

They have urged their sisters to neither bask in feelings of superiority nor entrap themselves into wearing masks of morality and goodness.

In their contacts with law enforcement officials, women in the movement are prepared to trade preferential and paternalistic treatment for due process in civil and criminal procedures. Movement lawyers have claimed that women defendants pay for judges' beliefs that it is more in man's nature to commit crimes than it is in woman's. Thus, they argue that when a judge is convinced that the woman before him has committed a crime, he is more likely to overreact and punish her, not only for the specific offense, but also for transgressing against his expectations of womanly behavior.

The existence of such statutes as the "indeterminate sentence" for women, or the sanctioning of a procedure whereby only convicted male defendants have their minimum sentences determined by a judge at an open hearing and in the presence of counsel, while the woman's minimum sentence is decided by a parole board in a closed session in which she is not represented by counsel, are cited as evidence of the unfair, punitive treatment that is accorded to women in the court.[6]

The position that some supporters of the Equal Rights Amendment (ERA) have taken vis-à-vis prisons also illustrates the willingness of the woman's movement to accept the responsibilities of equality. The movement recognizes that the stereotypes that are held of women in the larger society provide some advantages to female inmates. For example, physically, penal institutions for women are usually more attractive and more pleasant than the security-oriented institutions for men. The institutions tend to be located in more pastoral settings and they are not as likely to have the gun towers, the concrete walls, and the barbed wire that so often

---

[3]Sheldon Glueck and Eleanor Glueck, *Five Hundred Delinquent Women)* New York: Alfred A. Knopf, Inc., 1934), p. 96.

[4]Daniel A. Green, "The Dark Side of Women's Liberation: Crime Takes a Female Turn," *National Observer,* September 1974, p. 2.

[5]Ibid., p. 2.

[6]For a more detailed discussion of how the indeterminate sentence is applied to women, see: Linda Temen, "Discriminatory Sentencing of Women Offenders," *Criminal Law Review* 11 (winter 1973), p. 355.

characterize institutions for men. Women inmates usually have more privacy than men. They tend to have single rooms; they may wear street clothes rather than prison uniforms; they may decorate their rooms with such things as bedspreads and curtains, that are provided by the prison. Toilet and shower facilities also reflect a greater concern for women's privacy. Advocates of ERA have written that they would eliminate these differentials by subjecting both men and women to the same physical surroundings in sexually integrated institutions. "Ideally, the equalization would be up to the level presently enjoyed by the women. But, if a State faces an economic roadblock to equalizing up, the ERA would tolerate equalization down to a lower, more economically feasible level."[7]

One of the major goals of the contemporary woman's movement is equal opportunities with men for positions and jobs that carry prestige and authority. While the objectives of the woman's movement of the 1920s were to get women out of their homes and into factories and offices, today success is more likely to be measured by the proportion of women in managerial and professional positions, by the proportion of women who have completed college and university, and by the absence of lower salary scales for women who hold the same types of jobs as men.

A review of census data indicates that the gap between men and women who occupy management and professional positions is as great today as it was 25 years ago. In 1948, for example, 29 percent of the women employed in white-collar positions occupied professional and managerial slots; in 1971 the percentage was 33. Among men, in 1948, the proportion of white-collar positions represented in the managerial and professional subcategories was 61 percent; in 1971 it was 70 percent. Between 1950 and 1970, the proportion of women who graduated from college increased by 70 percent; but as of 1971

there were still almost six men for every four women who completed four years of college. On the matter of income, the annual earnings of women between 1956 and 1970 decreased in comparison to those of men (1956: women—$3,619, men—$5,716; 1970: women—$4,794, men—$8,845).

Notable changes have occurred, however, in the proportion of married women employed on a full-time basis between 1950 and 1970—a shift from 24.8 percent to 41.1 percent—and especially among married women with children of school age (6–17 years), where there has been an increase from 28.3 percent to 49.2 percent.

There is still much to be done before the woman's movement can claim success in achieving equality between men and women in jobs involving occupational prestige and high incomes. But the increase in the proportion of women who hold full-time jobs, the consciousness that the movement's rhetoric has succeeded in raising, along with the changes that have occurred in women's legal rights in such areas as personal property, abortion, and divorce laws, have all contributed to altering women's overall status as well as increasing opportunities and propensities that women have for committing crimes. What changes have already occurred in the area of crime will be described in some detail in the following pages.

WOMEN AS CRIMINALS

Table I describes the proportion of women who have been arrested for all crimes, for all serious crimes, and for serious violent and property crimes from 1932 to 1972.[8] The average rates of change in the proportion of women arrested between 1953 and 1972, between 1958 and 1972,

---

[7]R. R. Arditi et al., "The Sexual Segregation of American Prisoners," *Yale Law Journal* 82 (November-May 1973), p. 1266.

[8]It may appear that this discussion uses arrest statistics as proxies for describing crime rates among men and women without regard for the hazards of doing so. While the hazards are recognized, unfortunately there are no other data prior to these statistics that provide information about the characteristics of the suspect as well as the offense he or she is believed to have committed. Criminologists usually prefer to use statistics for determining crime rates that are

and between 1967 and 1972 are also shown here. The last period is particularly crucial, because we would expect that during this period the rate of change would be marked by the greatest increase.

The average increase in the proportion of women arrested for serious crimes is greater than the average increase in the proportion of women arrested for all crimes. The data also show that the average rate of increase was greatest in the period from 1967 to 1972—.52 for all crimes and .84 for serious offenses. Note also that from 1961 onward the percentage of women arrested for serious crimes was greater than the percentage of women arrested for all offenses.

The popular impression that in recent years women have been committing crimes of violence at a much higher rate than they have in the past is disputed by the statistics in Table I. In fact, the increase in the proportion of arrests of women for serious crimes is due almost wholly to the increase in property offenses. Indeed, the percentage of women arrested for crimes of violence shows neither an upward nor a downward trend. The news item that, in 1970, four out of the FBI's most wanted fugitives were women must be juxtaposed against those statistics, which tell quite a different story.

The percentages for property offenses, however, show that big changes have occurred. In 1932, about one in every 19 persons arrested was a woman. In 1972, one in 4.7 persons arrested was a woman. Not only has there been a consistent increase in the percentage of women who have been arrested for property offenses, but also the biggest increases have occurred in the period beginning in 1967. This last finding is most congruent with our major hypothesis—that women's participation in selective crimes will increase as their employment opportunities

computed on the basis of crimes known to the police, but those statistics do not identify the suspect in any way. It is also recognized that the proportions of arrests vary considerably from one type of offense to another. Arrest rates are more accurate proxies for behavior in violent types of crimes than they are for crimes against property.

expand and as their interests, desires, and definitions of self shift from a more traditional to a more liberated view. The crimes that are considered most salient for this hypothesis are various types of property, financial, and white-collar offenses.

Table II describes the percentage of female and male arrests, for serious crimes and for serious property and violent offenses within the total male and female arrests for all crimes.

In 1953, one out of 12.8 female arrests was for serious crimes as opposed to one out of slightly less than 10.9 male arrests. But two decades later, more women were arrested for serious offenses (about one out of four) than were males (about one out of five). The average rate of change among the women was greater during each of the three time periods than it was for the men. But the time span from 1967 to 1972 does not show a greater increase when compared with time periods that extend farther back. The percentage increase of men who have been arrested for violent offenses over the two decades is almost four times the percentage increase for women. For property offenses, it is the percentage increase for women who have been arrested that is three times the percentage increase for men.

Table III describes women's participation in the specific offense categories that are included in the index of serious offenses from 1932 to 1972 (type I offenses). Note that among all six offenses, only one shows a marked increase over time. After 1960, the proportion of women who have been charged with larceny or theft in any given year is much greater than is the proportion in any of the other offense categories, property as well as violent. It is interesting to note that until about 1960 the proportions of women who were arrested for homicide and aggravated assault were similar to those arrested for larceny, but in 1972 the percentage in the larceny category had almost doubled the 1960 percentage; whereas from 1960 on, the proportions have remained roughly the same for the homicide and aggravated assault offenses.

Table IV describes trends in the proportion

Table I. Percentage of Females Arrested for all Crimes, for Serious Crimes, and for Serious Violent and Property Crimes: 1932-1972

Year[a]	All Crimes	Serious Crimes[b]	Violent Crimes	Property Crimes
1932	7.4	5.8	6.5	5.3
1933	7.2	5.9	7.1	5.2
—	—	—	—	—
1935	6.9	6.0	7.3	5.3
1936	7.3	6.4	8.0	5.7
—	—	—	—	—
1938	6.8	5.4	7.0	4.6
—	—	—	—	—
1942	12.0	8.9	9.8	8.3
1943	16.1	10.1	10.5	9.9
—	—	—	—	—
1946	10.7	7.7	7.7	7.7
1947	10.3	8.0	8.3	7.8
—	—	—	—	—
1949	9.9	8.0	9.9	7.3
1950	9.6	8.1	9.4	7.2
—	—	—	—	—
1953	10.8	9.4	11.9	8.5
1954	10.9	8.9	11.6	8.2
1955	11.0	9.1	12.0	8.4
1956	10.9	9.0	13.5	8.0
1957	10.6	9.3	13.1	8.5
1958	10.6	9.7	11.9	9.3
1959	10.7	10.5	12.7	10.0
1960	11.0	10.9	11.8	10.8
1961	11.3	11.5	11.6	11.4
1962	11.5	12.4	11.5	12.6
1963	11.7	12.7	11.6	12.9
1964	11.9	13.5	11.6	13.9
1965	12.1	14.4	11.4	14.9
1966	12.3	14.8	11.3	15.6
1967	12.7	15.0	10.8	16.0
1968	13.1	15.0	10.3	16.1
1969	13.8	16.6	10.6	17.9
1970	14.6	18.0	10.5	19.7
1971	15.0	18.3	10.9	20.1
1972	15.3	19.3	11.0	21.4
Average rate of change (per year) 1953-72	+0.23	+0.52	−0.05	+0.68
Average rate of change 1958-72	+0.35	+0.68	−0.07	+0.86
Avergae rate of change 1967-72	+0.52	+0.84	+0.04	1.07

Source: For the data in tables 1-4, *Uniform Crime Reports* (Washington D.C.: U.S. Department of Justice, Federal Bureau of Investigation).

[a] Not all of the years between 1933 and 1953 are included; but the periods of the depression, the Second World War, and the

Table II. Females and Males Arrested for Cirmes of Violence and Property and for Serious Crimes Combined, as Percentages of All Arrests in Their Respective Sex Cohorts: 1953-1972

Year	Violent Crimes		Property Crimes		Serious Crimes	
	Females	Males	Females	Males	Females	Males
1953	2.2	2.0	5.6	7.2	7.8	9.2
1954	2.2	2.1	6.0	8.2	8.2	10.3
1955	2.3	2.1	6.2	8.3	8.5	10.4
1956	2.3	1.9	5.9	8.4	8.2	10.3
1957	2.2	1.8	7.1	9.0	9.3	10.8
1958	2.1	1.9	7.8	9.0	9.9	10.9
1959	2.3	1.9	8.3	8.9	10.6	10.8
1960	2.5	2.4	9.9	10.2	12.4	12.6
1961	2.5	2.4	10.9	10.8	13.4	13.2
1962	2.4	2.4	12.2	10.9	14.6	13.3
1963	2.5	2.4	13.4	12.0	15.9	14.4
1964	2.6	2.6	15.4	13.0	18.0	15.6
1965	2.6	2.7	16.3	12.8	18.9	15.5
1966	2.8	3.0	17.3	13.1	20.1	16.1
1967	2.8	3.2	18.0	13.7	20.8	16.9
1968	2.5	3.5	18.2	14.3	20.7	17.8
1969	2.6	3.6	19.6	14.3	22.2	17.9
1970	2.5	3.6	21.3	14.8	23.8	18.4
1971	2.7	3.2	21.5	15.3	24.2	19.2
1972	2.9	4.4	22.3	14.8	25.2	19.2
Average rate of change, 1953-72	+0.04	+0.13	+0.88	+0.40	+0.92	+0.53
Average rate of change, 1958-72	+0.06	+0.18	+1.04	+0.41	+1.11	+0.59
Average rate of change, 1967-72	+0.02	+0.24	+0.82	+0.22	+0.90	+0.46

Note: When the data are examined in this way, only the years in which all arrests have been recorded are included.

immediate postwar years are included in the sample. Between 1955 and 1953, the data reported in tables 1-5 are based on fingerprint records received from local law-enforcement officials throughout the United States. They are limited to arrests for violations of state laws and local ordinances. But not all persons arrested are fingerprinted. Beginning in 1953, the system was changed, and the figures from 1953 through 1972 describe all arrests in cities with a population of more than 2,500. While recognizing that the sources for the pre-1953 data are different than those collected later, I think that for purposes of comparison—for example, male versus female arrests—they are worth presenting.

b Serious crimes, according to the *Uniform Crime Reports* published by the FBI, are criminal homicide (murder, nonnegligent manslaughter, and manslaughter by negligence), forcible rape, robbery, aggravated assault, burglary, larceny, and auto theft. We have omitted forcible rape from our calculations because women are never charged with such an offense.

Table III. Females Arrested as Percentage of All Arrests for Type I Offenses, 1932-1972

Year	Criminal Homicide	Robbery	Aggravated Assault	Burglary	Larceny/ Theft	Auto Theft
1932	8.7	3.3	8.6	1.7	9.3	1.6
1933	9.7	4.4	8.3	1.9	8.4	1.4
1935	9.9	4.6	8.0	1.7	8.3	1.7
1936	10.0	4.8	8.7	1.9	8.5	1.8
1938	9.6	3.9	7.9	1.5	7.1	1.5
1942	13.2	5.0	10.8	2.2	12.6	2.3
1943	13.2	5.3	11.7	3.1	15.5	2.2
1946	10.8	4.6	8.5	2.5	12.9	2.1
1947	11.3	4.5	9.4	2.7	12.4	2.2
1949	12.8	4.5	10.6	2.5	11.9	2.4
1950	13.5	4.3	10.6	2.5	11.5	2.7
1953	14.1	4.3	15.9	2.0	13.9	2.6
1954	14.2	4.2	15.9	2.2	13.0	2.5
1955	14.2	4.2	16.0	2.3	13.3	2.6
1956	14.8	4.3	17.6	2.3	12.6	2.5
1957	14.7	3.9	17.5	2.0	13.2	2.7
1958	16.4	4.5	15.7	2.4	14.3	3.2
1959	16.8	4.6	16.4	2.7	15.4	3.2
1960	16.1	4.6	15.3	2.8	16.8	3.6
1961	15.9	4.9	15.2	3.2	18.0	3.7
1962	17.2	5.1	14.7	3.6	19.6	3.9
1963	15.9	4.9	14.9	3.3	20.1	3.7
1964	16.6	5.3	14.4	3.7	21.4	4.3
1965	16.3	5.3	14.4	3.8	23.2	4.2
1966	15.9	5.1	14.0	3.8	24.0	4.1
1967	15.4	5.2	13.6	4.1	24.8	4.3
1968	15.4	5.5	13.1	4.1	25.2	4.9
1969	14.8	6.3	13.2	4.3	27.2	5.1
1970	14.8	6.2	13.3	4.6	29.0	5.0
1971	16.0	6.4	13.9	4.8	29.1	6.0
1972	15.6	6.6	13.9	5.1	30.8	5.7
Average rate of change, 1953-72	+0.08	+0.12	−0.10	+0.16	+0.89	+0.16
Average rate of change, 1958-72	−0.06	+0.14	−0.13	+0.19	+1.18	+0.18
Average rate of change, 1967-72	+0.04	+0.28	+0.06	+0.20	+1.20	+0.28

of women arrested for selected offenses in the type II category.[9] The figures show that in 1972

[9]The type II offenses shown in Table IV have been included because there has been a change in the arrest pattern for women or because they are offenses for which arrest rates for women are consistently high.

approximately one in four persons arrested for forgery was a woman and one in 3.5 arrests for embezzlement and fraud involved a woman. If present trends in these crimes persist, approximately equal numbers of men and women will be arrested for fraud and embezzlement by the

Table IV. Other Crimes, Females Arrested as Percentage of All People Arrested
for Various Crimes: 1953-1972

Year	Embezzlement and Fraud	Forgery and Counter-feiting	Offenses Against Family and Children	Narcotic Drug Laws	Prostitution and Commercialized Vice
1953	18.3	14.0	9.3	15.7	73.1
1954	14.4	13.4	9.6	17.5	70.1
1955	15.6	15.2	9.8	17.1	68.8
1956	15.5	16.6	9.1	16.3	62.9
1957	14.4	14.8	9.0	15.6	69.2
1958	14.3	15.1	8.6	16.4	69.0
1959	14.9	16.2	8.9	16.2	65.2
1960	15.7	16.8	9.7	14.6	73.5
1961	15.7	17.5	11.2	15.4	71.8
1962	17.6	18.1	11.0	15.1	76.1
1963	18.3	18.7	11.5	14.2	77.0
1964	19.5	19.3	11.3	14.1	81.2
1965	20.7	19.2	11.0	13.4	77.6
1966	21.8	20.9	12.1	13.8	79.3
1967	23.4	21.4	11.4	13.7	77.2
1968	24.4	22.3	10.9	15.0	78.0
1969	26.3	23.2	11.4	15.5	79.5
1970	27.8	24.4	11.3	15.7	79.1
1971	27.4	24.8	11.6	16.3	77.4
1972	29.7	25.4	12.3	15.7	73.5
Average rate of change, 1953-72	+0.60	0.60	0.16	0	+0.02
Average rate of change, 1958-72	+1.10	+0.74	+0.26	−0.05	+0.32
Average rate of change, 1967-72	+1.26	+0.80	+0.18	+0.40	−0.74

1990s, and for forgery and counterfeiting the proportions should be equal by the 2010s. The prediction made for embezzlement and fraud can be extended to larceny as well. On the other hand, if trends from 1958 to 1972 continue, fewer women will be arrested for criminal homicide and aggravated assault.

In summary, the data on arrests indicate the following about women's participation in crime: (1) The proportion of women arrested in 1972 was greater than the proportion arrested one, two, or three decades earlier. (2) The increase was greater for serious offenses than it was for all type I and type II offenses combined. (3) The increase in female arrest rates among the serious offenses was caused almost entirely by women's greater participation in property offenses, especially in larceny.

The data show that, contrary to impressions that might have been gleaned from the mass media, the proportion of females arrested for violent crimes has changed hardly at all over the past three decades. Female arrest rates for homicide, for example, have been the most stable of all violent offenses. Further probing of female arrest rates in the type II offenses revealed that the offenses that showed the greatest increases were embezzlement and fraud and forgery and counterfeiting. The increases were especially marked for the period from 1967 to 1972. None of the other offenses included in either type I or type II, save larceny, showed as big a shift as did these two white-collar offenses. Should the average rate of change that occurred between 1967 and 1972 continue, female arrest rates for larceny/theft, embezzlement, and fraud will be commensurate to women's representation in the society, or, in other words, roughly equal to male arrest rates. There are no other offenses among those contained in the uniform crime reports, save prostitution, in which females are so highly represented.

Two final observations: (1) it is plausible to assume that the police are becoming less "chivalrous" to women suspects and that the police are beginning to treat women more like equals; (2) police behavior alone cannot account for both the large increases in larceny, fraud, embezzlement, and forgery arrests over the past six years and for the lack of increase in arrests for homicide, aggravated assault, and other violent crimes.

The more parsimonious explanation is that as women increase their participation in the labor force their opportunity to commit certain types of crime also increases. As women feel more liberated physically, emotionally, and legally, and less subjected to male power, their frustrations and anger decrease. This explanation assumes that women have no greater store of morality or decency than do men. Their propensities to commit crimes do not differ, but, in the past, their opportunities have been much more limited. As women's opportunities increase, so will the likelihood that they will commit crimes. But women will be most likely to commit property, economic, and financial types of offenses. Their greater freedom and independence will result in a decline in their desire to kill the usual objects of their anger or frustration: their husbands, lovers, and other men upon whom they are dependent, but insecure about.

CROSS NATIONAL ARREST STATISTICS

A brief comparison of female arrest statistics in the United States with those collected by the International Criminal Police Organization for 25 countries all over the world in 1963, 1968, and 1970 shows that the United States moved from eighth place in 1963 to fourth place in 1968 to third place in 1970.

But the heterogeneity of the countries that rank directly above and directly below the United States makes it difficult to draw any conclusions about the types of societies that are conducive to high female arrest rates. Among those countries closest to the United States, there is, on the one hand, the West Indies, Thailand, and Burma; and, on the other hand, Portugal, West Germany, Luxembourg, France, Austria and Great Britain.

Perhaps more sense can be made of the rankings when they are broken by types of offenses. The offense categories that are included in the International Criminal Statistics and their definitions are listed in footnote 10. Table V compares the United States' female arrest statistics with other countries for offense categories I, III (A and B), IV, and VI.[10]

---

[10]I. Murder: Any act performed with the purpose of taking human life, no matter under what circumstances. This definition excludes manslaughter and abortion, but not infanticide.
II. Sex offenses: Each country uses the definitions of its own laws for determining whether or not an act is a sex crime; rape and trafficking in women are also included.
III. Larceny: Any act of intentionally and unlawfully removing property belonging to another person. This category includes such a wide variety of offenses, that it was subdivided into:
    A. major larceny: robbery with dangerous aggravating circumstances (for example, armed robbery, burglary, housebreaking)
    B. minor larceny: all other kinds of larceny (for example, theft, receiving stolen goods)
IV. Fraud: Any act of gaining unlawful possession of another person's property other than by larceny. This category includes embezzlement, misappropriation, forgery, false pretenses, trickery, deliberate misrepresentation, swindle in general.
V. Counterfeit currency offenses: This includes any viola-

Table V. Ranking of Countries by Percentage of Women Arrested for Various Crimes: 1963, 1968, 1970

Country	All Crimes		Murder		Major Larceny		Minor Larceny		Fraud		Drugs	
	Rank	Percent	Rank	Percent	Rank	Percent	Rank	Percent	Rank	Percent	Rank	Percent
West Indies	1	28.9	11	13.3	13	3.4	11	16.3	5.5	15.4	—	—
New Zealand	2	25.3	4	16.9	8	4.2	6	19.6	5.5	15.4	5	14.2
Thailand	3	17.3	19	4.2	15	3.0	14	14.4	13	10.1	11	4.6
West Germany	4	16.4	8	15.0	10	3.8	1	25.5	2	21.8	3	14.6
Luxembourg	5	16.2	—	—	2.5	8.7	13	15.4	14	9.5	—	—
United States	6	15.2	6.5	15.4	7	5.3	2	24.8	1	23.5	7	11.1
Austria	7.5	13.8	3	22.0	2.5	8.7	4	22.6	3	20.8	4	14.3
France	7.5	13.8	12	12.8	1	8.8	8.5	16.6	4	18.7	—	—
England and Wales	9	13.5	6.5	15.4	16	2.6	7	18.5	8	14.4	—	—
Tunisia	10	12.8	1	27.0	4	8.5	18	7.3	20	4.6	12	3.5
Israel	11	12.1	22	2.8	17	2.5	19	6.8	17	6.6	8	7.7
Korea	12	11.5	2	22.4	9	4.0	16	10.0	15	8.2	2	23.1
Scotland	13	10.9	10	13.4	11	3.7	8.5	16.6	7	14.5	—	—
Netherlands	14	10.4	15	8.1	13	3.4	3	23.5	9	13.1	—	—
Ireland	15	10.1	13	12.5	5	6.5	10	16.5	11	10.6	—	—
Monaco	16	7.5	—	—	—	—	—	—	—	—	—	—
Tanzania	17	6.9	9	14.1	19	2.2	21	4.2	21	2.1	—	—
Cyprus	18	6.7	17	6.5	18	2.4	17	7.7	19	4.7	9	6.8
Finland	19	6.6	16	6.9	13	3.4	12	15.9	12	10.3	—	—
Japan	20	4.6	5	16.5	20	1.2	5	20.5	16	7.0	1	24.1
Malawi	21	4.2	20.5	4.0	22	.9	23	2.6	22	1.7	14	1.0
Hong Kong	22	3.0	20.5	4.0	21	1.0	22	4.1	18	5.5	13	2.2
Fiji	23.5	1.9	18	4.5	23	.3	20	5.1	23	.8	—	—
Brunei	23.5	1.9	—	—	—	—	—	—	—	—	10	4.8
Canada	—	—	17	10.0	0	5.5	15	13.4	10	11.8	6	13.9

For property and financial crimes—such as larceny, as defined by the FBI statistics, and fraud—the United States ranks second and first, respectively. Countries that rank directly above and below are those of Western Europe such as West Germany, Austria, and the Netherlands. For crimes of violence and drugs, American women rank sixth and seventh and are surrounded by a heterogeneous collection of countries that include the West Indies, New Zealand, West Germany, Scotland, and Canada. The pos-

itions of the United States and the countries of Western Europe in the larceny and fraud rankings are consistent with the hypothesis that, in those societies in which women are more likely to be employed in commercial and white-collar positions and to enjoy legal and social rights, they are also more likely to engage in property and economic types of crimes.

CONVICTIONS AND SENTENCES

Examination of convictions and sentencing patterns between men and women over time is difficult because of the absence of judicial statistics at the level of state courts. The federal statistics that are available from 1963 to 1971 are con-

tion in connection with manufacture, issuing, altering, smuggling, or traffic in counterfeit currency.
VI. Drug offenses: This category covers any violation involving illicit manufacture of, traffic in, transportation of, and use of narcotic drugs.

sistent with the arrest data in that they show that over the eight-year time span, the highest proportion of women have been convicted for fraud, embezzlement, and forgery. These same offenses also show the greatest increase in the proportion of females who have been convicted between 1963 and 1971.

California statistics from 1960 through 1972 do not show that the increase in convictions has followed the increase in arrests for the same types of offenses.[11] Although there has been an increase of 31 percent in the proportion of women convicted for all types of crimes from 1962 to 1972, that increase has been due solely to the higher conviction rates for violent offenses.

New York State statistics on the proportion of female commitments to correctional institutions by type of offenses from 1963 to 1971 reveal an overall decline and no significant changes within any of the offense categories.

The proportion of female commitments to all state penal institutions declined between 1950 and 1970 from 5.1 percent to 4.7 percent.

On the whole, using the rather meager statistics that are available, it appears that the courts have not been adapting their behavior to meet the changing roles that women, and perhaps the police in their interactions with women, are performing. In interviews that were conducted with about 30 criminal trial court judges in the Midwest in the winter of 1974, we found that most of the judges had not observed, and did not anticipate, any changes either in the numbers or types of women or in the types of offenses that women were likely to be charged with in the immediate future. Most of the respondents said that they expected to continue to be easier on women than on men, when it came to passing sentence.

WOMEN AS VICTIMS OF CRIMES

This section shifts the focus of this article and turns the issue on its head by examining the role of women as victims of criminal acts. One of the issues to which the woman's movement has directed much of its efforts has been the treatment of women who are victims of rape. The movement has been critical of the legal system and has demanded changes in the standards of proof and identification that are required. It has pointed to the police and demanded that they behave more humanely. It has insisted that medical and psychological facilities be made available and has called for changes in the manner and circumstances under which women who claimed they had been raped are examined. It has also demanded that the services of a therapist be made available to the victim as soon as possible after she has reported the attack. The movement itself has been instrumental in setting up "rape hot lines" in many communities.

For all the attention that has been devoted to the female as "rape victim," it is interesting to note the proportions of men and women who have been victims of all types of criminal acts. For example, Wolfgang reported the characteristics of victims of criminal homicide from 1948 to 1952 and found that 76.4 percent were men and 23.6 percent were women. In 1972, the FBI reported that 22.2 percent of all murder victims were women.

In 1971, under the auspices of the Law Enforcement Assistance Administration, the Bureau of the Census conducted victimization surveys in Montgomery County, Ohio (Dayton), and in Santa Clara County, California (San Jose). In Dayton, 16,000 persons over the age of 16 and in San Jose, 28,000 persons over the age of 16 were victims of assault, robbery, or personal larceny at least once during 1970. The proportion of female victims in each city is shown below:

	Dayton	San Jose
Women as a percent of:		
Assault victims*	31	34
Robbery victims	36	34
Personal larceny victims	49	30

[11]The state of California maintains the most comprehensive crime and judicial statistics in the 50 states.

*Includes persons who reported they were raped.

It is obvious that the percentage of women victims is less than their representation in each of the communities. Even when rape victims are included in the assault categories, the proportion of assault victims is less than the 50 percent that one might expect simply on the basis of female representation in the community.

The following statistics allow for comparison between women and other categories in the two communities by showing rates of victimization per 100 population.

Victimization Rates

	Dayton	San Jose
Persons victimized by:		
Assault*	3.2	3.3
Robbery	0.8	0.8
Personal larceny	0.4	0.2
Women victimized by:		
Assault*	1.9	2.1
Robbery	0.6	0.5
Personal larceny	0.4	0.2

*Includes persons who reported they were raped.

Victimization Rates

	Dayton	San Jose
Young men between 16 and 24 victimized by:		
Assault	11.7	9.2
Robbery	1.7	2.4
Personal larceny	0.8	1.0
Minority group members*		
Assault	3.1	3.9
Robbery	1.6	1.0
Personal larceny	0.8	0.3

*Dayton figures are for black persons; San Jose figures are for persons of Spanish origin or descent.

These figures, along with the national data on homicide, indicate that women are *less* likely to be victims of crimes than are men, and especially young men. Of course, one might argue that the relevant comparison is not the proportion of female victims by their representation in the society, but the proportion of female victims by the proportion of female offenders. If it is men— and especially men between the ages of 16 and 24—who commit the highest proportion of criminal acts, then perhaps one should expect persons in that category to also account for the highest proportion of victims.

In their report to the *National Commission on the Causes and Prevention of Violence,* Mulvihill and Tumin described the results of a survey of victim and offender patterns for four major violent crimes in 17 large American cities. The crimes were: criminal homicide, aggravated assault, forcible rape, and robbery (armed and unarmed).[12] Table VI describes the sex of the offender and the sex of victim for one of those types of offenses.

The Mulvihill-Tumin data also show the following characteristics:

1. For all four offense categories, at least two-thirds of both the victims and the offenders are men. Armed robbery is almost exclusively a male situation: 90 percent of the victims and 95 percent of the offenders are men.

2. In the case of criminal homicide, 34 percent of the interactions are intersexual, and the roles performed by the men and women are divided almost equally—16.4 percent female offender/male victim, 17.5 percent male offender/female victim. There is a greater likelihood that the victim of a homicide perpetrated by a women will be a family member (most likely her spouse) than when the homicide is committed by a man. Women are also more likely to kill members of their family than are men. White and black women share that propensity almost equally.

[12]They obtained a 10 percent random sample of 1967 offense and arrest reports from the following cities: Atlanta, Boston, Chicago, Cleveland, Dallas, Denver, Detroit, Los Angeles, Miami, Minneapolis, New Orleans, New York, Philadelphia, St. Louis, San Francisco, Seattle, and Washington.

Table VI. Sex of Victim and Offender for Aggravated
Assault Arrests, 17 Cities, 1967

| | Sex of Victim | | |
Sex of Offender	Male	Female	Total
Male	56.6	27.0	83.6 (727)
Female	9.3	7.1	16.4 (142)
Total	65.9 (573)	34.1 (296)	100 (869)

Note: The figures represent percentages; those in parentheses are numbers of offenses.

3. In the other offense categories, when the situation is intersexual, there is a much greater likelihood that the male will be the offender and the female the victim. For aggravated assault cases, the ratio of male-female victims is 3:1, in armed robbery, 2.5:1; and in unarmed robbery, 13:1.

These 1967 data are consistent with those obtained in the 1971 victimization surveys of Dayton and San Jose in that they also portray the male as being the victim much more frequently than the female. These data serve the additional function of dramatizing the extent to which violent crime is still very largely a male enterprise (males are both the perpetrators and the victims). Only 3.8 percent of all the criminal homicides, 7.1 percent of all the aggravated assaults, and .9 and 2.9 percents of all the armed and unarmed robberies were acts perpetrated by females against females. Finally, the 1967 data also show that, when violent offenses are intersexual, the woman's role is much more likely to be that of the victim and the male's that of the offender. Homicide is the exception.

CONCLUDING REMARKS

In the last three or four years, all of the mass media—films, newspapers, television, magazines, and radio—have agreed upon a common theme vis-à-vis women and crime. They have claimed that more women are engaging in more acts of violence than have been engaged in by American women at any time in the past. And they have attributed much of the females' greater propensities for violence to the woman's movement. The fact that, in 1970, four women made the FBI list for the ten most wanted criminals served as prima facie evidence of the accuracy of their perceptions. The Patty Hearst scenario also did much to convince the mass media that the image they were projecting about the increased propensities for violence by American women was indeed an accurate one.

40. Race, Social Status, and Arrest

EDWARD GREEN

THE RECURRENTLY HIGHER OFFICIAL ARREST RATE of Negroes over whites poses a persistent issue in the study of deviance relative to ethnicity. Although it is well established that criminogenic conditions such as poverty, family instability, slum residence, and migration are much more concentrated among Negroes than whites, the extent to which the differential accounts for the racial variance in crime rates remains problematical (Sellin, 1928:64). One point of view holds out the prospect that under comparable circumstances the white and Negro crime rates would not differ substantially (Wolfgang, 1964:61), a presumption which finds some support in the historical experience of lower class white migrant groups who as recent arrivals on the American urban scene also incurred high arrest rates which later declined in relation to their upward social movement and cultural assimilation. A less sanguine view holds that the circumstances of whites and Negroes are not fully comparable, that the experience of the Negro in America differs not only in degree but in kind from that of lower class white ethnic minorities (Johnson, 1941:94; Moses 1947:420). Thus even under equivalent socioeconomic conditions, racial crime rates would materially differ: the disabilities produced by discrimination add to the incidence of Negro crime by engendering frustrations which find expression in exp-

losive assaults or repeated acts of predatory crime (Pettigrew, 1964:150–156); racial discrimination in law enforcement exaggerates the official record of Negro crime by artificially inflating Negro rates of arrest and conviction (Johnson, 1941).

The latter point of view is supported by the results of Moses' (1947) controlled investigation. He approached the problem by means of a comparison of arrest rates in two pairs of contiguous white and Negro neighborhoods in Baltimore partially equated with respect to selected socioeconomic characteristics of the inhabitants. The white and Negro neighborhoods were alike in regard to the racial homogeneity of their populations, the dominance of lower occupational and educational levels, and the average size of households. They differed greatly, however, in the percentage of home owners—whites exceeding Negroes 7 to 1 in one pair of neighborhoods, and 10 to 1 in the other. The results show that Negroes exceeded whites in arrest rates for felonies by a ratio of 6 to 1, a disparity which Moses attributes to racial proscriptions accentuating the burden of low socioeconomic status. It does not appear, however, that the social and economic differences between the two racial groups are sufficiently controlled to justify this conclusion. Although there was a dominance of blue collar workers among both races, whites predominated as foremen, craftsmen, and kindred workers, whereas Negroes predominated as laborers. Further, the employment data do not take ac-

▶SOURCE: *"Race, Social Status and Criminal Arrest," American Sociological Review (June 1970), 35:476–490. Reprinted by permission.*

count of the distribution of the unemployed which in all likelihood was greater among Negroes than whites. Perhaps more significantly, the whites were largely of eastern European extraction and the Negroes, of southern native American origin. Hence, it is hardly likely that the populations in the white and Negro neighborhoods were nearly alike in all analytically significant respects save race. Rather the comparison involves two culturally disparate groups whose relatively low economic status confers upon them only a superficial resemblance.

This study will reexamine the connection between race and crime in the light of racial differences in status characteristics related to variations in crime rates. Instead of comparing the crime rates of two racially distinct subcommunities like in the frequency distribution of the social traits of their inhabitants, as Moses attempted to do, we directly compare the arrest rates of whites and Negroes equated with respect to the variables of sex, age, and especially, occupation, employment status, and nativity as indices of social status.

RESEARCH SETTING

The locus of the study, Ypsilanti, is a small industrial city lying close to the boundaries of the Detroit and Ann Arbor metropolitan areas in southeastern Michigan. With an estimated population of 25,000 in 1968, residing in an incorporated area of only four square miles, Ypsilanti reproduces in microcosm many of the features of urban transition—the trends of demographic and ecological changes and, particularly, the rapidly rising official rates of crime—characteristic of large northern industrial cities during the past quarter of a century.

War-time and post-war economic development, attracting migrants to the area, and rising birth rates swelled the city's population from 12,121 in 1940 to 18,312 by 1950 and 20,957 by 1960, a net increase of 73% over 1940, and to an estimated 23,000 in 1965. Ypsilanti Township bounding the city on the east, west, and south

provides the city with a suburban fringe whose population increased more than six-fold between 1940 and 1960, from 4,153 to 26,000, surpassing in size the population within the city of Ypsilanti. In 1960, the first census year for which data on the state of birth of residents were published for individual communities, 42% of Ypsilanti's inhabitants were born outside of the state. Slightly more than 20%, or 4,671, of the city's population in 1960 consisted of Negroes of whom 2,471 or 52.9% were not native to the state. Nearly half of the white majority migrated from other states, a very large percentage originating in the Appalachian region. The high percentage of southern migrants in both races and the virtual absence of foreign-born among the whites heighten the cultural equivalency of two racial groups, thus facilitating a rigorously controlled analysis of racial crime rates.

Official records of the Ypsilanti police show a pronounced increase in crime rates between the period just prior to the United States' entry into World War II and 1966. Official reports for 1941 list a total of 227 arrests for assorted crimes, a rate of 1,870 per hundred thousand of population. The number of arrests skyrocketed during the war years, 1942–1945, to an average of 1,653 per year, a fantastic rate of 10,804 per hundred thousand, as the community received an influx of migrants seeking jobs in local war industries. The average annual arrest rate declined during the post-war period of 1946–1955 to 4,764, owing in part to the departure of many temporary war-time residents. But many of the migrants remained, and by 1956 the crime index had resumed an upward trend, rising to such an extent that by 1966 Ypsilanti's arrest rate of 6,428.5 for all offenses exceeded by 32% the average rate of 4,884.7 for the 51 largest American cities over 250,000 in population with the highest average arrest rate of all classes of cities (U.S. Department of Justice, 1966, 110). The arrest rate of 163.4 for crimes against the person—felonious homicide, forcible rape, aggravated assault, and robbery—fell between the average of 228.7 for cities over 250,000 in population, and the average of 134.0 for cities 100,000 to 250,000 in population, and was two and one-half times higher than the average rate of 61.0 for cities in its own size class.

Ypsilanti's rate (4,902 per hundred thousand in 1966) of serious crimes known to the police (criminal homicide, including manslaughter by negligence, forcible rape, robbery, aggravated assault, burglary and breaking or entering, all cases of larceny, and auto theft) was twice as great as the average of other cities in its size class and even greater than the average (4,554.6) of the 55 largest cities in the nation with populations of over 250,000[1] (U.S. Department of Justice, 1966:96).

THE SAMPLE

The data comprise two bodies of materials. The first consists of the personal and legal information given in the records of all arrests, exclusive of juvenile detentions, in 1942, the first year that systematic records of all arrests were kept, the census years of 1950, and 1960, and 1965. The cases are classified by the seriousness of the offense under two categories: (1) *Index crimes,* arrests for serious offenses constituting the crime index of the Federal Bureau of Investigation—murder and nonnegligent manslaughter, forcible rape, robbery, burglary, larceny over $50, and auto theft; and (2) *other crimes,* preponderantly arrests for minor offenses. Since arrests for Index crimes make up only one-tenth of the cases, in order to have a broader basis for inference concerning racial arrest rates for the more serious offenses, an additional body of data on all arrests for high misdemeanors and felonies in 1950–1959 and 1961–1964 has been combined with the cases of felonies and high misdemeanors for 1960 and 1965. These cases are classified by the character of the offense into (1) crimes against the person,

(2) crimes against property, and (3) "others," predominantly crimes against the public welfare. The distinction between felonies and high misdemeanors on the one hand and ordinary misdemeanors on the other is legally crucial. The latter are tried in the municipal court, a lower trial court of limited criminal jurisdiction, and are punishable by prison sentences of no more than 90 days. The former are heard in the circuit court, a tribunal of county-wide criminal jurisdiction, and are subject to prison terms as high as life imprisonment.

Rates of arrest are computed per hundred thousand of population, even though Ypsilanti's population did not exceed 25,000 by 1966, in order to render them comparable to the rates given in official statistics of crime published by the Justice Department.

RESULTS

Criminal statistics published annually in the *Uniform Crime Reports* perennially demonstrate the powerful effect of *age, sex,* and *race* on crime rates. Males constituting half of the population make up about 90% of the persons arrested for serious crimes; young people age 11–25, comprising less than 25% of the population, account for almost 75% of the persons arrested for serious crimes; and Negroes, only 11% of the population, contribute 30% of the arrestees for serious crimes. Very similar results emerge locally. Table 1 records a disproportionately high number of arrests for Negroes compared with whites, men compared with women, and youths 17 to 24 years of age compared with persons age 25 and over. It also shows a much greater likelihood of arrest for persons in low status occupations and the unemployed, compared with those in high status occupations, and for persons born out-of-state, compared with those born in Michigan.

The trend of Negro arrest rates during the 25-year period covered by this study strongly suggests the acculturation, quantitatively and qualitatively, of the Negro to the white man's

---

[1] A very large portion of the remarkable increase in crime rates in Ypsilanti derives demonstrably from improved police procedures for recording and labelling crimes.

criminal behavior pattern. The percentage of Negroes among those arrested for Index crimes fluctuated downward from 53.2 in 1942 to 48.4 in 1950, 39.7 in 1960, and 44.7 in 1965. The percentage of Negroes among those arrested for lesser crimes fluctuated upward from 22.4 in 1942 to 34.1 in 1950, 28.7 in 1960, and 33.7 in 1965. For all offenses combined, the percentage of Negroes arrested increased from 24.2% in 1942 to 34.5% in 1965, a 42% increase over the 25-year period. But the Negro arrest figures did not keep pace proportionately with the growth

Table I. A Comparison of Persons Arrested in Ypsilanti, by Type of Offense, with the Population of Ypsilanti According to the Percentage Distribution of Selected Characteristics in Sample Years

	Arrests (1942)		Population (1940)	Arrests (1950)		Population (1950)
	Index	Other		Index	Other	
Sex						
Total	100.0	100.0	100.0	100.0	100.0	100.0
	(N=47)	(N=759)	(N=12,121)	(N=31)	(N=498)	(N=18,302)
Male	93.6	92.5	49.2	90.3	90.8	48.8
Female	6.4	8.1	50.8	9.7	8.6	51.1
Not ascertained	0.0	0.0	—	0.0	0.0	—
Age						
Total	100.0	100.0	100.0	100.0	100.0	100.0
	(N=47)	(N=759)	(N=10,144)	(N=31)	(N=498)	(N=13,634)
17-24	66.0	27.3	19.7	35.5	25.3	26.7
25 and over	34.0	72.3	80.3	64.5	72.9	73.3
Not ascertained	0.0	0.4	—	0.0	1.8	—
Race						
Total	100.0	100.0	100.0	100.0	100.0	100.0
	(N=47)	(N=759)	(N=12,121)	(N=31)	(N=498)	(N=18,320)
White	46.8	77.2	86.1	51.6	64.1	80.3
Negro	53.2	22.4	13.9	48.4	34.1	19.7
Not ascertained	0.0	0.4	—	0.0	1.8	—
Occupation (persons in labor force)						
Total	100.0	100.0	100.0	100.0	100.0	100.0
	(N=45)	(N=737)	(N=5,269)	(N=23)	(N=416)	(N=7,547)
White collar and skil.	2.2	12.8	47.6	4.3	9.4	55.0
S-skil. and unskil.	75.6	77.3	42.9	65.2	79.3	39.2
Unemployed	15.6	7.1	8.2	30.4	10.6	4.8
Not ascertained	6.7	2.8	1.2	0.0	0.7	1.0
Nativity						
Total	100.0	100.0	100.0	100.0	100.0	100.0
	(N=47)	(N=750)	—	(N=31)	(N=498)	—
Michigan	51.1	42.2	—	25.8	27.7	—
Elsewhere						
South	27.7	20.9	—	38.7	45.2	—
Other states	19.1	33.9	—	29.0	25.5	—
Not ascertained	2.1	3.0	—	6.5	1.6	—

Table I. (Continued)

	1960			1965		
	Arrests		Population	Arrests		Population
	Index	Other		Index	Other	
Sex						
Total	100.0	100.0	100.0	100.0	100.0	100.0
	(N=68)	(N=762)	(N=20,957)	(N=76)	(N=915)	(N=23,000)[a]
Male	95.6	91.3	47.7	86.8	92.7	47.7
Female	2.9	7.2	52.3	11.8	6.9	52.3
Not ascertained	1.5	1.4	—	1.3	0.4	—
Age						
Total	100.0	100.0	100.0	100.0	100.0	100.0
	(N=68)	(N=762)	(N=14,789)	(N=76)	(N=915)	(N=16,237)[a]
17-24	63.2	33.3	31.2	65.8	37.2	31.2
25 and over	35.3	64.3	68.8	32.9	62.1	68.8
Not ascertained	1.5	2.4	—	1.3	0.8	—
Race						
Total	100.0	100.0	100.0	100.0	100.0	100.0
	(N=68)	(N=762)	(N=20,957)	(N=76)	(N=915)	(N=23,000)[a]
White	58.8	69.7	77.4	53.9	65.6	77.4
Negro	39.7	28.7	22.6	44.7	33.7	22.6
Not ascertained	1.5	1.6	—	1.3	0.8	—
Occupation (persons in labor force)						
Total	100.0	100.0	100.0	100.0	100.0	100.0
	(N=62)	(N=724)	(N=9,666)	(N=60)	(N=869)	(N=10,609)[a]
White collar and skil.	6.5	9.3	48.7	3.3	6.6	48.7
S-skil and unskil.	38.7	57.6	39.2	51.7	70.0	39.2
Unemployed	38.7	16.6	8.5	33.3	15.5	8.5
Not ascertained	16.1	16.6	3.5	11.7	7.9	3.5
Nativity						
Total	100.0	100.0	100.0	100.0	100.0	100.0
	(N=68)	(N=762)	(N=20,957)	(N=76)	(N=915)	(N=23,000)[a]
Michigan	36.8	28.5	56.5	46.1	27.8	56.5
Elsewhere	—	—	41.7	—	—	41.7
South	47.1	54.3	—	38.2	55.0	—
Other states	13.2	13.0	—	14.5	13.6	—
Not ascertained	2.9	4.2	1.8	1.3	3.7	1.8

[a]Estimated.

in Negro population, which increased by 60% between 1940 and 1960—from 13.9% in 1940 to 19.7% in 1950, to 22.6% in 1960, and undoubtedly, to an even higher level in 1965.

Males in each sample year of the study constitute slightly less than half of the population but regularly produce over nine-tenths of the arrests for Index and non-Index crimes.

The percentage of persons age 17 to 24 and over 24, respectively, arrested for non-Index crimes in each sample year closely approximates the percentage distribution of these two age categories in the population of an age of criminal responsibility which begins at 17 in Michigan. With respect to Index crimes, youths age 17 to 24 comprising from one-fifth to one-third of the population over 16 years of age consistently account for two-thirds of the arrests. In view, however, of the steady increase in the percentage of youths by more than half, from 19.7 in 1940 to 31.2 in 1960, and an estimated 34.0 in 1965, the findings signify an actual decline in the youth arrest rate for serious crimes.

We cannot compare Ypsilanti to similar urban settings with respect to the effect of socio-economic variables on arrest rates since the *Uniform Crime Reports* do not contain pertinent data. In each sample year the labor force constitutes just over one-half of the population 14 years of years of age. The lower occupational strata comprising semiskilled and unskilled workers—operatives, service workers, and laborers—and the unemployed make up almost half of the labor force, but are arrested for non-Index offenses in the various sample years from 7–13 times as frequently as the white collar workers—professionals, managers, entrepreneurs, sales and clerical personnel—and craftsmen who, combined, make up slightly more than one-half of the labor force. The disparity between the upper and lower occupational groupings is even greater in the proportion of arrests for Index crimes, the latter exceeding the former by about 40 times in 1942; 22, in 1950; 12, in 1960; and 26, in 1965.

During the period surveyed, the percentage of arrests contributed by the employed, particularly the white-collar and skilled category, declined in relation to the proportion of the employed in the labor force; conversely, the percentage of all arrests contributed by the unemployed more than doubled from 7.5% in 1942 to 10% in 1950, 18.3% in 1960, and 16.7% in 1965 (see Table I).

The criminogenic effect of migration has been challenged by a Philadelphia study (Savitz, 1962), which found that Negro youths native to Philadelphia became delinquent more frequently than those born elsewhere. The results in Ypsilanti show, to the contrary, that migrants, defined as persons born outside of Michigan, and particularly those who originate in the rural South, are much more likely to be arrested than natives. Between 1940 and 1960 the migrant population increased to two-fifths of the total population. Concomitantly, as Table I shows, in each sample year migrants accounted for the bulk of arrests for Index and non-Index crimes, the percentage climbing, for all cases, from 54.3 in 1942 to 70.5 in 1950, and leveling at 66.7 in 1960 and 67.3 in 1965. There is no indication, and no reason to assume, that between 1940 and 1965 the proportion of migrant arrests increased more than the proportion of migrants in the population.

The 1960 census data permit a direct assessment of the effect of migration on arrests. Table 1 shows that migrants accounted for 41.7% of the population of Ypsilanti, 67.3% of persons arrested for non-Index crimes, and 60.3% of those arrested for Index crimes. Southerners predominate among migrant arrestees, comprising four-fifths of those arrested for non-Index crimes and two-thirds of those arrested for Index crimes.

Thus, of all of the above criteria of demographic classification—age, sex, race, occupation, and nativity—only one grouping, namely, the occupational category of the unemployed, increased its arrest rate more rapidly than its rate of growth during the period studied. Certain elements of the population with a high susceptibility to criminal arrest—Negroes, youths, and migrants—increased in size proportionately more than groups with a relatively low likelihood of arrest—whites, older persons, and natives. Such trends in population composition, locally and in other highly urbanized areas, have contributed to a rise in general arrest rates but not necessarily to a rise in arrest rates for specific elements of the population.

Turning to the effect of sex, age, occupation, and nativity on racial arrest rates, we find that we may not attribute the racial disparity in arrests to a dissimilarity between white and Negro in sex ratio inasmuch as the census reports for 1940, 1950, and 1960 show that the races are virtually equal in this regard.[2] Neither may we impute the disparity to differences between the races in age distribution since in each of the three census years, the white population, with a lower arrest rate than the Negro population, consists of a smaller proportion of persons under 17, a larger proportion of persons in the high arrest rate age category of 17 to 24, and about an equal proportion of persons over 24.[3]

A strong presumption arises, however, that sociocultural differences, measured by the indices of occupation and nativity, account for much of the racial variance in arrest rates. United States Census data for Ypsilanti confirm that a much higher proportion of Negroes than whites is found in the high crime rate categories at the lower end of the occupational scale, among the unemployed and the migrants. In the 1940 Census whites are represented proportionately twice as frequently as Negroes in the white collar and skilled occupations, 51.3% to 24.1%; and in the

1950 and 1960 census, respectively, about three times as frequently, 62.5% to 22.4% and 57.5% to 17%. The percentage of whites in the semiskilled and unskilled occupations declined between 1940 and 1960 from 42.6 to 32.9, while the percentage of Negroes at that level increased from 44.7 to 61.9. The proportion of Negro unemployed greatly exceeded the proportion of white unemployed in each census year: 28.3% to 5.1% in 1940, 12.2% to 3.1% in 1950, and 16.5% to 6.3% in 1960.

The data on nativity provided in the 1960 census indicate that a much larger proportion of Negroes compared with whites were born outside of Michigan, 53.5% to 38.3%.

Holding constant the effect of *occupation* or *nativity* as shown in Table II sharply reduces the racial variance in arrest rates. At the level of the white-collar and skilled workers, both the number and rate of arrests per hundred thousand of population for Index crimes are small for both races; in the four sample years combined, there were only eight cases, six white and two Negro. For non-Index offenses the difference between whites and Negroes in the white-collar and skilled occupations was practically nil in 1942, 3,780 to 3,600; and in 1950, 920 to 960; in 1960 and 1965, respectively, Negroes pulled ahead of whites, 4,200 to 1,190 and 3,750 to 850.

At the semiskilled and unskilled occupational level in 1942, Negroes exceeded whites by six times in rates of Index crimes, 5,440 to 890, and by two times in rates of non-Index crimes, 44,880 to 22,580. In the ensuing sample years the differential markedly declined. The Negro rate of arrests for Index crimes approximately doubled the white rate in each sample year: 770 to 380 in 1950, 980 to 400 in 1960, and 1,140 to 560 in 1965. The racial arrest rates for non-Index crimes more nearly approached parity: Negroes exceeded whites in 1950—13,300 to 9,860, but yielded to whites in 1960—8,620 to 11,960 and very closely approximated them in 1965—15,000 to 14,700. In view of the depth of the occupational stratum denoted by the cate-

[2] The ratio of male to female arrests is more or less greater for whites than for Negroes in each sample year (see Table 2).

[3] There is no clear trend of racial difference in the ratio of younger persons to older persons arrested for Index crimes. In 1942 the variation in arrest rates for Index crimes between persons age 17 to 24 and those 25 and over, respectively, was somewhat greater for Negroes, 7,790 to 750, than whites, 840 to 140. In 1950, however, the relative standing of the two races in this regard was reversed, due as much to changes in enforcement activities and recording policies as to any change in the rate of miscreancy of the racial-age groupings. Among whites the Index crime arrest rate for persons age 17 to 24 was more than twice as great as for those age 25 and over, 260 to 100, whereas among Negroes the two age groups were nearly equal, 550 to 660. In 1960 and 1965, under improved uniform crime reporting procedures, the ratio of younger offenders to older offenders with respect to arrest rates for Index crimes was about the same for the two races—in 1960, 720 to 140 for whites and 2,430 to 570 for Negroes, and in 1965, 720 to 100 for whites and 2,830 to 640 for Negroes (see Table II).

Age differences in arrest rates for non-Index crimes are more or less greater for Negroes than for whites in every sample year.

Table II. Rates of Arrest per 100,000 of Population by Race, Type of Offense, and Selected Characteristics in Sample Years

| | 1942[a] | | | | 1950 | | | |
| | Index | | Other | | Index | | Other | |
	White	Negro	White	Negro	White	Negro	White	Negro
Total	210	1,470	5,630	10,000	110	420	2,190	4,750
N	22	25	586	170	16	15	322	171
Sex								
Male	430	1,830	10,880	12,080	200	780	4,070	8,398
Female	0	250	580	2,080	30	60	310	1,000
Age								
17-24	840	7,790	9,770	24,240	260	550	2,720	7,640
25 & over	180	750	6,850	12,190	100	660	2,870	7,040
Occupation								
White collar & skil.	0	600	3,780	3,600	30	0	920	960
Semiskil. & unskil.	890	5,440	22,580	44,880	380	770	9,860	13,300
Unemployed	330	3,060	12,210	7,650	2,120	1,740	15,370	8,700
Not in labor force	30	180	440	9,900	0	0	200	1,000
Nativity								
Michigan	b	b	b	b	b	b	b	b
N	14	10	271	49	3	5	89	47
Elsewhere	b	b	b	b	b	b	b	b
South (N)	2	11	73	86	4	8	126	99
Other states (N)	6	3	227	30	7	2	101	23
Not ascertained (N)	0	1	15	5	2	0	6	2

[a]1942 rates based on 1940 Census data.
[b]Census data on nativity unavailable for 1940 and 1950.

gory semiskilled and unskilled—which includes at the top "affluent" blue-collar factory operatives with seniority, steady work, and high wages, and at the bottom, the marginally employed—it is likely that the results tend to overstate the amount of Negro criminality relative to the criminality of whites in the same occupational class inasmuch as whites tend to predominate at the higher levels of blue-collar work, and Negroes, at the lower levels.

However, in the white-Negro comparison on the level of unemployment, all other things are nearly equal, since in a period of economic expansion and prosperity the unemployed of both races are likely to be equated at the bottom of the socioeconomic scale. In 1942 unemployed Negroes scored substantially higher than unemployed whites in arrest rates for Index crimes, 3,060 to 330, although the actual number of cases involved was insignificant, six Negroes and one white,[4] but arrests for non-Index offenses, totaling 52, were proportionately much higher for whites than Negroes yielding rates of 12,210 to 7,650. In 1950 whites exceeded Negroes in arrest rates for Index crimes, 2,120 to 1,740, and non-Index crimes, 15,370 to 8,700. In 1960, the white rate barely exceeded the Negro rate for Index crimes, 2,940 to 2,900 but decidedly surpassed the Negro rate for non-Index crimes 16,590 to

[4]The inconsequential number of index crimes reflects imprecision in official police recording procedures in 1942 rather than civil tranquillity, a matter to be treated in a subsequent report.

(continued)

| | 1960 | | | | 1965 | | | |
| | Index | | Other | | Index | | Other | |
White	Negro	White	Negro	White	Negro	White	Negro
250	570	3,280	4,660	230	650	3,370	5,940
40	*27*	*531*	*219*	*41*	*34*	*600*	*309*
510	1,130	6,360	8,700	410	1,240	6,600	11.200
10	40	440	680	60	110	370	1,040
720	2,430	4,690	11,270	720	2,830	5,300	16,540
140	570	4,270	6,710	100	640	4,200	8,170
90	0	1,190	4,200	20	250	850	3,750
400	980	11,960	8,620	560	1,140	14,700	15,000
2,940	2,900	16,590	11,600	2,090	2,250	17,860	10,000
120	0	550	1,000	204	448	518	1,613
190	290	1,850	1,710	220	420	1,680	3,220
19	*6*	*181*	*36*	*24*	*11*	*180*	*74*
340	740	6,040	6,840	390	960	7,950	9,700
13	18	270	140	10	18	313	190
6	3	68	31	7	4	86	36
2	0	12	12	0	1	21	9

11,600. In 1965 the Negro rate for Index crimes slightly surpassed the white rate, 2,250 to 2,090, but for non-Index crimes trailed considerably behind, 17,860 to 10,000. It is doubtful, however, that at the lowest socioeconomic level Negroes are less prone to commit minor (non-Index) crimes than whites. As most crime is intraracial in the offender-victim relationship and in the neighborhood setting, it is likely that Negro victims of Negro offenders or Negroes adversely affected by the crimes of Negroes are less apt to complain to the police than whites victimized by whites, due possibly to a greater tolerance of neighborhood disturbances, a distrust of police, or a lesser likelihood that the property loss of Negroes is covered by insurance.

The frequency of arrests of persons not in the labor force is relatively small in each sample year, although the Negro rate generally exceeds the white rate. Since this category does not, however, represent a social class level but rather a cross-section of the class structure of each group—the retired, homemakers, students, and the like—the higher Negro rate likely reflects the comparatively lower socioeconomic level of the Negro population.

The racial difference in nativity inflates the general arrest rate of the Negro much more than that of the white. In 1960, the first census year for which data on the nativity of residents of Ypsilanti were published, 44.1% of the Negro population compared with a somewhat larger 60.1% of the white population of Ypsilanti were

Table III. Average Annual Arrest Rate per Hundred Thousand of Population for High Misdemeanors and Felonies by Type of Offense, Race and Selected Social Characteristics in 1950-1965[a]

| | Person | | | | Property | | | | Other | | | |
| | White | | Negro | | White | | Negro | | White | | Negro | |
	N	R	N	R	N	R	N	R	N	R	N	R
Total	49	18.8	89	117.5	221	85.0	102	134.4	226	86.9	179	236.3
Sex												
Male	41	33.1	81	220.0	199	161.3	86	233.8	220	178.8	158	429.4
Female	8	5.6	8	20.0	22	16.3	16	40.0	6	4.4	21	52.5
Age												
17-24	24	37.5	35	364.4	129	201.9	55	573.1	57	89.4	37	385.6
25 and over	25	20.0	54	146.9	92	72.5	47	127.5	169	133.8	142	385.9
Occupation												
W.C. and skil.	2	3.1	2	35.6	17	24.4	2	35.0	26	37.5	7	122.5
Semiskil. and unskil.	25	62.5	53	255.0	93	232.5	47	226.3	135	337.5	123	591.3
Unemployed	14	183.8	17	308.1	76	997.5	41	743.1	38	498.8	26	471.3
Not in labor force	5	6.3	7	43.1	14	18.1	4	25.0	11	13.8	7	43.1
Nativity												
Michigan	16	10.0	14	41.9	104	66.3	42	125.0	101	64.4	31	92.5
Elsewhere	33	36.9	75	187.5	117	130.6	60	150.0	125	139.4	148	370.0

[a]Using 1960 population data as base to compute rates.

born in Michigan. Since migrants contribute more heavily to crime rates than nonmigrants, and Negroes include a higher proportion of migrants than whites, holding constant the factor of migrant status effects a reduction in the racial difference in arrest rates (see Table II). In 1960 the Negro superiority over whites in arrest rates for Index crimes declines from a ratio of 2.25 to 1, uncontrolled, (570 to 250) to 1.50 to 1 for the Michigan born (290 to 190), and remains slightly more than twice as high as the white rate (740 to 340) for those born out-of-state. The racial difference in rates of non-Index crimes declines from a ratio of 4 to 3 in favor of the Negro (4,660 to 3,280) to near parity, a slightly higher white rate among the native born—1,850 to 1,710, and a moderately higher Negro rate among those born elsewhere—6,840 to 6,040.

The data on arrests for felonies and high misdemeanors in 1950–1965 add another dimension to the analysis showing, in Table III, the effect of the type of offense—personal, property, or *other* (mainly crimes against the "public")—singly and interactively with each of the demographic variables of sex, age, occupation, and nativity on racial diferences in the average annual arrest rate. The racial variance in arrest rates differs widely among the different types of offenses. Crimes against the person display a ratio of Negro to white arrest rates of about 6 to 1 (117.5 to 18.8); "other" crimes, a ratio of nearly 3 to 1 (236.3 to 86.9); and crimes against property, about 1.5 to 1.0 (134.4 to 85.0). Differences in racial arrest rates, expectedly, persist at a high level within each sex and age category. The control of the variables of occupation and nativity as shown in Table III, however, markedly reduces the racial arrest rate differential. During the 16-year period the average annual rate per hundred thousand of population for crimes against the person is much higher in all occupational categories for Negroes than for whites. The racial differential for property crimes is negligible at all levels of occupational status among the employed; among the unemployed the white rate is higher, 997.5 to 743.1. For "other" offenses, Negroes show a much higher rate at the white collar and skilled level, 122.5 to 37.5; and semi-skilled and unskilled level, 591.3 to 337.5. Among the unemployed, whites slightly exceed Negroes, 498.8 to 471.3.

The control of the effect of nativity somewhat reduces the excess of Negro over white arrest rates in all offense categories, except cases of property crimes committed by natives, wherein the Negro superiority increases slightly.

Since *race, occupation,* and *nativity,* each displays a close association with arrest rates and since a much higher proportion of Negroes than whites is found at low status occupational levels including the unemployed and among migrants, we proceed to an investigation of the joint effects of *occupation* and *nativity* on racial differences in arrest rates. As already noted, the census did not issue figures on State of birth by individual communities until 1960. Hence the analysis is restricted to the cases of arrest in 1960 and 1965. In calculating the 1965 rates, proportional increases were made in the 1960 figures to reflect the general growth of the population, although no adjustments were made to express estimated changes during the five-year period in the racial-occupational-nativity distribution. In computing the average annual rates for the high misdemeanor and felony arrests in 1950–1965, the census figures for 1960 were used, inasmuch as the 1960 population data very closely approximate the average of the 1950 census data and the estimates for 1965.

The 1960 census report does not supply data on the number of persons native to the State of residence and elsewhere, respectively, in each occupational category. Hence we have devised estimates by applying the percentage distribution of occupations for each race uniformly to those born in the State of arrest and those born elsewhere. The resulting figures are used as bases for the computation of arrest rates for each racial-occupational-nativity group. Since the natives of each race are more likely to be found in greater proportion at the upper occupational level than the non-natives, this procedure may have the effect of slightly overestimating the arrest rate of the natives at the upper occupational level (white collar and craftsmen) and the migrants at the lower occupational level (semiskilled, unskilled, and unemployed), and slightly underestimating the arrest rate of the natives at the lower occupational level and the migrants at the upper occupational level because it reduces the size of the base used in calculating rates for the former categories and enlarges it for the latter categories.

The results, as shown in Table IV, indicate that among groupings of persons more or less homogeneous with respect to *occupation* and *nativity* there is no consistent trend of racial difference in arrest rates. Considering first the arrests of the native-born persons for Index crimes in 1960, we observe that at each occupational level whites incur higher arrest rates than Negroes, although the total number of cases (N = 20) is too small to justify any firm inference. For non-Index crimes, the white arrest rate substantially exceeds the Negro rate at the level of semiskilled and unskilled occupations, 6,060 to 3,000, and at the level of the unemployed, 8,670 to 6,000, but falls somewhat short of the Negro rate, 810 to 1,250, among white collar and skilled workers. Among persons born out-of-state, white rates for Index crimes exceed Negro rates slightly at the level of the white collar and skilled, and rather markedly at the level of the unemployed, 5,500 to 3,890. In turn, Negro rates greatly exceed white rates among the semiskilled and unskilled, 1,710 to 440. With respect to rates of arrest for non-Index crimes, whites yield to Negroes, 1,710 to 6,840, in the category of the white collar and skilled workers, but greatly surpass Negroes in the categories of the semiskilled and unskilled workers, 22,890 to 12,710, and the unemployed, 28,890 to 15,560.

The summary of the statistical analysis of the 1960 data (with Index and non-Index crimes consolidated) shows a high degree of interaction among the three independent variables of race, occupation, and migration, and a marked reduction in the racial imbalance in arrest rates when this interaction is taken into account. The

racial difference for persons born in the state is not statistically significant in three out of the four occupational categories—white collar and skilled, the unemployed, and those not in the labor force—but is significantly higher for whites than for Negroes among the semiskilled and unskilled. For persons born out-of-state, the white rate significantly surpasses the Negro rate among the semiskilled and unskilled workers and the unemployed, but falls significantly short of the Negro rate at the level of white collar and skilled workers and persons not in the labor force.

The results of the analysis of the 1965 data, also given in Table IV, closely follow the results for the 1960 data. Among the native-born people the racial difference in arrest rates at each occupational level fails to achieve significance. The racial difference is more pronounced in the migrant population: Negroes significantly exceed whites at the level of white collar workers and craftsmen, and among persons not in the labor force, but fall significantly short of the whites at the level of the unemployed. Among the semi-skilled and unskilled, the white rate surpasses the Negro rate, though not significantly.

The data on the high misdemeanor and felony cases given in Table V yield similar findings concerning the interrelationships among the variables of occupation, migration, and racial arrest rates. Arrest rates are highest for the miscellaneous category of other offenses, predominantly victimless crimes, followed in descending order by property crimes and crimes against the person. Within each offense category, taking each demographic variable singly, arrest rates are decidely higher for the migrant than for the native, the lower occupational levels than for the higher occupational levels, the unemployed than for the employed, and the Negro than for the white. Controlling simultaneously for *occupation* and *nativity*, however, markedly reduces the racial differential, although not equally in all offense categories.

In crimes against the person, the number of

arrests at the white collar and skilled level for those native to the state of residence and those born elsewhere is negligible, two whites and two Negroes. In the category of semiskilled and unskilled workers, Negroes have much higher arrest rates than whites both among the natives, 93.8 to 29.4, and the migrants, 392.5 to 125.0. The rate of arrest for personal crimes differs little by race for the native born unemployed, 86.3 for whites and 83.1 for Negroes, and is low in comparison with the rate for the unemployed with out-of-state origins who exhibit a statistically nonsignificant excess of Negro over white arrest rates, 571.9 to 341.3.

The effect of the racial factor on arrest rates for property crimes is astonishingly low. At the white collar and skilled level the racial difference in arrest rates is negligible for native and migrant. At the semiskilled and unskilled level the white rate is higher than the Negro rate both for natives and migrants, 166.9 to 145.6 and 367.5 to 294.4, respectively. Among the native unemployed, Negroes slightly exceed whites, 916.9 to 861.9; among the nonnative unemployed the Negro arrest rate is little more than half the white arrest rate, 629.4 to 1,228.8.

In cases of "other" crimes the racial factor is significant only for the employed born out-of-state, with Negroes exceeding whites 197.5 to 47.5 among the migrant white collar and skilled, and 955.6 to 541.9 among the migrant semiskilled and unskilled. Among the native-born persons at all occupational levels and the out-of-state unemployed, the differences are slight.

The statistical summary of the data in Table V condenses the occupational classification, excluding those not in the labor force, into two categories, *employed* and *unemployed*. The results support, generally, the statistical hypothesis of no significant difference in crime rates between the races, showing that in only three comparisons out of twelve do arrest rates differ significantly: the Negro arrest rate exceeds the white arrest rate among the native-born employed and the nonnative employed suspected of crimes against the person and the

nonnative employed suspected of "other" crimes. In the other nine comparisons whites display the higher rate in five instances and Negroes, in four instances, but the differences are neither statistically nor analytically significant.

SUMMARY AND CONCLUSIONS

This investigation confirms the hypothesis that the higher official rate of crime for Negroes compared with whites results predominantly from the wider distribution among Negroes of lower social class characteristics associated with crime. The findings, based on an analysis of official police records, spanning the period 1941–1965 in a small industrial community in the Great Lakes region, show, for both white and Negro, disproportionately high arrest rates for males, youths age 17 to 24, persons in low income occupations (semiskilled and unskilled workers), the unemployed, and persons not native to the State, predominantly Southerners. The racial variance in arrest rates does not reflect differences between the races in the distribution of the sexes or age groups since the races are about equal in sex ratio and whites have a somewhat higher proportion of persons in the age category most vulnerable to arrest, youths 17 to 24. The races differ greatly, however, in the distribution of occupational and natal characteristics; with these variables controlled, the arrest rates of the races tend toward parity and in several instances a higher rate for whites.

Even for serious crimes of violence including robbery, with a greater preponderance of Negro over white arrests than any other major category of crimes, migrant whites incur substantially higher arrest rates than native-born (Michigan) Negroes at each occupational level. This difference reflects the effect of the southern regional culture pattern which the southern migrant transplants to his new abode in the urban industrial center. Rates of felonious assault and homicide have been regularly higher

Table IV. Arrest Rates per 100,000 of Population by Type of Offense, Race, Occupation, and Nativity in 1960 and 1965

Nativity	Occupation	Index White N	Index White R	Index Negro N	Index Negro R	Other White N	Other White R	Other Negro N	Other Negro R	Total White N	Total White R	Total Negro N	Total Negro R	p
Michigan	white collar and skill	1	40	0	0	21	810	2	1,250	22	850	2	1,250	=1.00
,,	s. skil and unskil.	6	400	2	330	91	6,060	18	3,000	97	6,460	20	3,330	< .02
,,	unemployed	4	1,330	3	200	26	8,670	9	6,000	30	10,000	12	6,200	> .30
,,	not in labor force	4	130	0	0	17	5,300	2	410	21	600	2	410	=1.00
Else-where	white collar and skil.	2	120	0	0	29	1,710	13	6,840	31	1,830	13	6,840	< .001
,,	s. skill and unskil.	4	440	12	1,710	206	22,890	89	12,710	210	23,330	101	14,420	< .001
"	unemployed	10	5,550	7	3,890	52	28,890	28	15,560	62	34,440	35	19,450	< .01
,,	not in labor force	2	100	0	0	9	430	9	1,450	11	530	9	1,450	> .05

1965

													p
Michigan white collar and skil.	1	20	0	0	12	250	2	1,160	13	270	2	1,160	> .30
,, s. skil. and unskil.	9	540	4	630	117	7,120	42	6,660	126	7,660	46	7,290	> .99
,, unemployed	5	1,590	3	1,780	22	7,000	16	9,520	27	8,590	19	11,300	> .30
,, not in labor force	7	1,960	3	550	14	3,920	3	550	21	5,880	6	1,100	> .20
Else-where white collar and skil.	0	0	1	470	29	1,580	13	6,220	29	1,580	14	6,690	< .001
,, s. skil. and unskil	6	570	11	1,430	267	25,520	163	21,300	273	26,090	174	22,730	> .10
,, unemployed	6	3,000	6	2,940	72	36,000	25	12,250	78	39,000	31	15,190	< .001
,, not in labor force	4	170	2	300	14	600	14	2,100	18	770	16	2,400	< .01

Interaction Effects[a]

	1960			1965		
	x^2	df	p	x^2	df	p
Race × Nativity	9.1	1	< .01	34.5	1	< .001
Race × Occupation	71.3	3	< .001	98.4	3	< .001
Nativity × Occupation	1,678.3	3	< .001	416.5	3	< .001
Race × Nativity × Occupation	38.5	3	< .001	128.1	3	< .001

[a] Based on chi square of the racial difference in the proportion arrested for Index and Other Offenses combined in each occupational category. The statistical test for interaction is given in Kellog V. Wilson, "A Distribution-Free Test of Analysis of Variance Hypotheses," *Psychological Bulletin*, Vol. 53, No. 1, 1956, 96-101.

Table V. Average Annual Arrest Rate per 100,000 of Population, 1950-1965, for High Misdemeanors and Felonies, by Type of Offense, Race, Occupation, and Nativity

		Person				Property				Other			
		White		Negro		White		Negro		White		Negro	
Nativity	Occupation	N	R	N	R	N	R	N	R	N	R	N	R
In state of arrest	white collar and skil.	1	2.5	0	0.0	7	16.9	0	0.0	13	31.3	1	39.4
"	semiskil. and unskilled	7	29.4	9	93.8	40	166.9	14	145.6	57	237.5	16	166.3
		X^2 (all employed) = 18.7; p < .001				X^2 = 2.9; p > .10				X^2 = 1.3; p > .30			
"	unemployed	4	86.3^a	2	83.1	40	861.9	22	916.9	18	388.1	10	416.9
						X^2 = .07; p > .70				X^2 = .06; p > .80			
"	not in labor force	3	5.6	1	12.5	8	15.6	1	12.5	8	15.6	2	25.0
Out of state	white collar and skil.	1	3.8	2	65.6	10	36.9	2	65.6	13	47.5	6	197.5
"	semiskil. and unskilled	13	125.0	44	392.5	53	367.5	33	294.4	78	541.9	107	955.6
		X^2 (all employed) = 69.0; p < .001				X^2 = 4.3; p > .05				X^2 = 94.3; p < .001			
"	unemployed	10	341.3	17	571.9	36	1,228.8	19	629.4	20	683.1	21	706.3
		X^2 = 1.31; p > .30				X^2 = 2.4; p > .10				X^2 = .008; p > .95			
"	not in labor force	2	6.3	6	51.9	6	18.1	3	31.3	3	8.8	5	51.9

^{a}Too few cases for analysis.

in the South than elsewhere in the nation and express a heritage which southerners of both races share in common (Pettigrew and Spier, 1962).

The findings lend no credence to the explanation of the Negro white crime rate differential in terms of some distinctive aspect of Negro culture or in terms of racial conflict, whether viewed as the Negro's reaction to the frustrations resulting from racial discrimination or the expression of racial bias by the police. To be sure, we cannot ignore the interdependence between the depressed socioeconomic status and the racial discrimination endured by the Negro. The effect of socioeconomic status on arrest rates, however, appears to operate independently of race. Likewise we cannot surmise that police officers are innocent of racial prejudice or that the victims of racial prejudice endure their burden without rancor. Nevertheless, there is no indication here, or systematic evidence elsewhere, of the transformation of racial prejudice into racial discrimination in the enforcement of the law (Green, 1961:56–62; 1964; Black and Reiss, 1967:115) or of the transformation of the frustrations produced by racial inequality into criminal behavior. Indeed, the data suggest the converse: during the period 1940 to 1965, certainly a period of rising expectations and militancy on the part of Negro Americans, the proportion of Negroes in the total population of the community increased to a greater extent than the proportion of Negroes among persons arrested for all offenses while the proportion of Negroes among persons arrested for Index crimes actually decreased.

REFERENCES

Black, Donald J. and Albert J. Reiss, Jr.
1967   Patterns of Behavior in Police and Citizen Transactions. Ann Arbor, Michigan: Mimeographed.

Green, Edward
1961   Judicial Attitudes in Sentencing. New York: St. Martin's Press.
1964   "Inter and intra-racial crime relative to sentencing." Journal of Criminal Law Criminology and Police Science 55 (September):348–358.

Johnson, Guy B.
1941   "The Negro and Crime." The Annals of the American Academy of Political and Social Science 271 (September):93–104.

Moses, Earl
1947   "Differentials in crime rates between Negroes and whites based on comparisons of four socio-economically equated areas." American Sociological Review 12 (August):411–420.

Pettigrew, Thomas F.
1964   A Profile of the American Negro. Princeton, New Jersey: D. Van Nostrand Co., Inc.

Pettigrew, Thomas F. and Rosalind B. Spier
1962   "The ecological structure of Negro homicide." American Journal of Sociology 67 (May):621–629.

Savitz, Leonard
1962   "Delinquency and migration." Pp. 199–205 in Marvin E. Wolfgang, Leonard Savitz and Norman Johnston, The Sociology of Crime and Delinquency. New York, John Wiley and Sons, Inc.

Sellin, Thorsten
1928   "The Negro criminal, a statistical note." The Annals of the American Academy of Political and Social Science 140 (November):52–64.

U.S. Department of Justice
1966   Uniform Crime Reports.

Wilson, Kellogg V.
1956   "A distribution-free test of analysis of variance hypotheses." Psychological Bulletin 53 (January):96–101.

Wolfgang, Marvin E.
1964   Crime and Race: Conceptions and Misconceptions. New York: Institute of Human Relations Press.

41. Status Origins, Track Position, and Delinquency

DELOS H. KELLY

TRADITIONALLY, SOCIAL SCIENTISTS HAVE RE-
ported an inverse relationship between status
origins and youth deviance, particularly delinquent activity (e.g., Havighurst et al., 1962; Hollingshead, 1949; Shaw and McKay, 1942;
Thrasher, 1936). Numerous class-based theories
have been advanced (e.g., Cloward and Ohlin,
1960; Cohen, 1955; Merton, 1968) to give
meaning to this observation. Recently, however,
and commencing primarily with the use of self-
report instruments by Nye et al. (1958), investigators have concluded that status origins are a
relatively weak predictor of youth deviance (Akers, 1964; Haney and Gold, 1973; Voss, 1966;
Winslow, 1967). Other researchers, utilizing
official measures of delinquency, have reported
similar findings (Kelly and Balch, 1971; Polk
and Halferty, 1966; Rhodes and Reiss, 1969).

Failure to detect a strong linkage between
status origins and deviance has prompted much
theoretical speculation (Kelly, 1971; Kelly,
1972; Kelly and Balch, 1971; Polk, 1969;
Rhodes and Reiss). For example, in a recent article, we have argued that a "school status"
theory of delinquency requires further development (Kelly and Balch, 1971). What this
means in effect is "... *that one's location in the
reward structure of the school is a far more important
determinant of nonconfirming behavior than one's so-*

cial class background (Schafer and Polk, 1967)"
[italics mine] (Kelly and Balch, 1971:426). This
particular argument was based primarily upon
the pioneering works of Hargreaves (1967) and
Schafer et al. (1970). To be more specific, Hargreaves, in his yearlong study of an English secondary school for boys, noted that his low
stream (track) boys, when compared with the
high stream, exhibited the highest rates of
school misconduct and delinquent involvement.
Schafer et al. (1970) produced similar findings
from their study of male and female sophomores attending two midwestern high schools.
Their low track students, when compared with
the high, were more likely to possess a history of
school misconduct and delinquency. These observations, it was noted, persisted when such
background and selection factors as IQ, father's
occupation, and past performance were controlled. Hargreaves, it was additionally noted,
failed to conduct any comparable controls and
thus it was pointed out that his findings might be
subject to alternative explanations. Overall, however, it was argued that track position, independent of such factors as status origins, should be
inversely related to delinquency and delinquent
involvement (Kelly and Balch, 1971:426–427).

Although the studies of Hargreaves and particularly Schafer et al. (1970) are most provocative and insightful, it should be noted that they
do suffer from several possible limitations. Most
significantly, Hargreaves, although utilizing a
clearly defined measure of stream (track) posi-

▶SOURCE: *"Status Origins, Track Position, and Delinquent Involvement," The Sociological Quarterly (Spring 1975), 16:264–
271. Reprinted by permission.*

tion (i.e., whether a student was assigned to stream A, B, C, D, or E), did not control status origins, a potentially important selection factor for student placement in streams (Kelly, 1973). On the other hand, even though several control variables were considered and introduced, Schafer et al.'s measure of track position (i.e., whether a sophomore took English with the college prep or non-college prep section during the first semester) appears somewhat questionable. If, by way of illustration, a student took English with a college prep section and math with a non-college prep section, then how should he be classified with respect to track position? No doubt a pupil who takes English with a college prep section will also take math, science, and history with a college prep section (Tanner, 1965). No doubt, too, exceptions exist with respect to this general principle. Failure to make clearcut distinctions of this nature, therefore, may have partially contaminated their measure of track position.

In spite of these potential limitations, it should be stressed that the works of especially Hargreaves and Schafer et al. represent a shift of focus in two important directions. First, given the recent evidence suggesting that status origins may not be an especially powerful predictor of such behavioral outcomes as youth rebellion and deviance, then these researchers have examined the relative predictive power of additional variables, most notably stream (track) position. Second, and associated closely with the first trend, instead of focusing rather exclusively on positive outcomes, these investigators have examined some apparent, *negative* effects of tracking or student stratification systems.

In this paper, I attempt to assess these trends empirically. Initially, by utilizing selected measures of delinquent involvement, I examine the relative predictive power of status origins as opposed to track position. Thereafter, I discuss the major theoretical and policy implications of the findings, particularly as they relate to our present knowledge about youth deviance and delinquent involvement.

PROCEDURES

In December of 1971 a survey questionnaire containing a range of demographic, school, and peer variables was designed and administered to all male and female seniors (180) attending two high schools in western New York State.[1] These students were drawn primarily from rural towns and villages. The schools, themselves, were situated in two small towns (January, 1972 populations of 3,619 and 3,260. respectively for each school setting).[2]

In terms of actual variable concerns, status origins were determined through use of Hollingshead's Index of Social Position, together with an Oregon supplement.[3] Subjects were classified as middle- and working-class according to their father's occupation. Middle-class occupations included executive, professional, sales, and clerical positions. Skilled, semi-skilled, and unskilled jobs made up the working-class category. Out of the initial population of 180, 173 seniors could be classified in terms of status origins. Fifty-nine percent of these were placed

[1] The questionnaire was administered to all seniors present on the appointed day. A same day check of records for both schools indicated that a total of six students were absent. Given this small number, no attempt was made to contact them.

[2] For the purposes of this study, these two populations will be combined. Separate analyses prior to combination produced virtually identical results, particularly with respect to the relationship between track position and those measures selected for examination in this study

[3] It should be noted that the Oregon supplement has been used in much of my previous research. This classificatory scheme was developed in an attempt to handle the relatively large number of farming and logging occupations encountered during the coding of our Oregon data. Such a scheme has proven useful in the classification of the present data, particularly with regard to the farming occupations.

Although we are using dichotomies, it should be pointed out that each respondent was initially classified in terms of his or her father's occupation. Thereafter, the various distributions were examined for such phenomena as skewness, curvilinearity, and the like. Such statistical checks conducted prior to collapsing indicate that no information is being masked or lost. It should be additionally noted that the attenuation of cell frequencies during the standardization process necessitated the use of dichotomies.

in the working-class category, while the remaining 41 percent were categorized as being middle-class. For selected reasons (e.g., missing data), the remaining seven questionnaires could not be used in the data analysis.[4]

Track position, the second major independent variable, was measured by the question: "Which curriculum are you currently enrolled in?" Pupils who indicated that they were located specifically in a college-prep program were placed in the college-bound track. Students who responded that they were taking a vocational or general program were placed in the non-college-bound track.[5] The majority of the subjects (58 percent) were pursuing a non-college-prep curriculum.

This measure of track position would appear to be valid. For instance, by the time they are seniors most students know, without error, their location within the academic hierarchy of the school. That is, they know whether they are college or non-college material.[6] Furthermore, by focusing on seniors in the second half of their school year, we can guard against the potentially contaminating effect that student mobility (or the movement of pupils between various tracks) might have upon the measure of track position (Hargreaves; Jones et al., 1972; Schafer et al., 1970; Schafer and Olexa, 1971).[7] Since the peak years for delinquent activity generally range from 15 to 17 years of age, at least in terms of official arrest rates (Perlman, 1964; President's Commission on Law Enforcement and Administration of Justice, 1967), then this focus on seniors should also give us a better "feel" for the total history of delinquent involvement for our subjects (Sellin and Wolfgang, 1964). This may be an inaccurate assumption, particularly when one considers the noted biases that exist with respect to official statistics (Gibbons, 1970; Short and Nye, 1958). There is evidence, however, of an association between extensiveness of involvement and the probability of being arrested (Sellin and Wolfgang).[8]

The actual measures of delinquent involvement were obtained through use of a refined, self-report checklist containing thirty-six acts. These acts were drawn primarily from the works of Kelly and Winslow (1970), Sellin and Wolfgang (1964), and Short and Nye (1958). Of the thirty-six offense categories selected, the respondents reported involvement with thirty-five. For exploratory purposes, however, nine

[4]Initially, I had planned on constructing a two-factor index of status origins. The information on income, however, was incomplete. When queried about this, the majority of students indicated that they had no idea about how much their fathers or mothers earned. During the spot checking of additional background information, it also was found that several subjects had failed to record their father's occupation, and when asked about this most displayed a reluctance to discuss the subject.

[5]Analyses conducted prior to combining indicate that no information was lost. In terms of the outcomes selected for examination in this study, the patterns for the vocational and general track students were much the same.

[6]In these two schools, as is the case with most New York schools, whether rural or urban, track or student stratification systems have a long history. As far as actual assignment to tracks, a combination of selection factors (previous academic achievement, IQ scores, achievement test scores) are used. The specific criteria employed, however, are unstandardized. It is also interesting to note that the students themselves have relatively little choice in this matter. Furthermore, once a student is assigned to a particular curriculum, he usually stays there. That is, there is little movement between tracks. Such observations, it can be noted, support my recent review of the tracking literature concerning not only track assignment procedures but also student mobility patterns (Kelly, 1973).

[7]As indicated previously, as well as demonstrated in terms of past research (e.g., Jones et al., 1972; Schafer and Olexa, 1971), there is some movement of students between tracks after their initial assignment. By grade twelve, however, the rate of change drops virtually to zero. Such an observation thus gives us a degree of confidence that, in terms of the measure of track position, non-college-bound students have not been mixed with the college-bound.

[8]There is also evident an association between sex and delinquent behavior. Evidence, both official and self-report in nature (e.g., Perlman, Short and Nye), indicates that males, when compared with females, not only are more likely to possess a history of delinquency or delinquent involvement but that they also commit qualitatively different acts. In this study, therefore, the patterns for both males and females are examined.

Table I. Reported Delinquent Involvement, by Selected Predictor Variables and Controls (Yule's Q)

	Zero-Order			First-Order[a]	
	(1)	(2)	(3)	(4)	(5)
				Track Position With Sex Controlled	Track Position With Status Origins Controlled
Self-Report Act	Sex Status	Origins	Track Position		
1. Expelled from School	−.60	−.10	−.66	−.70	−.67
2. Placed on School Probation	−.07	+.07	−.52	−.69	−.49
3. Skipped School	−.24	−.24	−.45	−.41	−.41
4. Stole Book from Library	−.21	+.08	−.39	−.36	−.43
5. Involved in Gang Fighting	−.57	+.08	−.61	−.58	−.60
6. Smoked Cigarettes	+.06	−.02	−.57	−.57	−.60
7. Smoked Marijuana	−.09	+.22	−.39	−.37	−.46
8. Shoplifted	−.14	+.07	−.46	−.44	−.50
9. Drank Alcohol	−.14	+.13	−.45	−.43	−.48

[a]To obtain the first-order partials, a weighting system known as direct standardization was used (Anderson and Zelditch, 1968:175-179). For an alternative method, see, particularly, Davis.

acts were deemed especially appropriate. The first four acts were selected because they are specifically school-related, whereas the remaining five were chosen because they are acts that are often used as general indicators of youth deviance and delinquency (e.g., Polk). Students who indicated that they had committed any of these acts at least once were characterized as exhibiting delinquent involvement.

FINDINGS

According to the data in Table I, sex is the best predictor of delinquent involvement. With one exception (smoked cigarettes, a negligible positive association of +.06), it is negatively associated with each dependent measure (Column 1). The magnitude of association, moreover, is substantial for some acts.[9] In particular, males, when compared with the females, are more likely to report having been expelled from

[9]The guidelines used to assess the strength of an association are contained in Davis (1971:39).

school and involved in fighting. These data also exhibit a low negative association between sex and skipping school, stealing, drinking, and shoplifting. The overall impact of status origins, by contrast, is not only generally weaker but also somewhat more inconsistent (Column 2).

Although middle-class respondents, when contrasted with the working-class, do report a higher level of involvement for a majority (six) of the nine acts, only three acts (drinking, smoking marijuana, and shoplifting) bear a low positive association with status origins. Of the remaining three acts which are negatively associated with class, two (school expulsion and skipping school) exhibit a low negative association with the measure of status origins.

At the zero-order level, track position is inversely related to each measure of delinquent involvement (Column 3). The magnitude of association ranges from moderate to substantial for all acts. For these measures, then, the non-college-bound students, when compared with the college-bound, are more likely to report involvement. In fact, it should be noted that track position, relative to both sex and status origins, emerges as the strongest predictor of our dependent measures.

Given the nature of both past and present findings, it is possible that sex and/or status origins might confound the demonstrated relationship between track position and self-report delinquent involvement. These data, however, offer little support for such a possibility.

In examining the effect of track position with sex controlled (Column 4), it can be noted that the original relationships generally hold at about the same level. This is apparent from the observation that the differences between the zero-order and first-order Q's are, for the most part, negligible (a comparison of the coefficients in Column 3 with Column 4). For school probation, sex appears to be operating as a suppressor variable (Davis, 1971:95–96). That is, when sex is controlled, the relationship between track position and probation becomes stronger. Examination of each partial table indicates, however, that the frequencies for two cells fall below an expected frequency of five (the actual observed frequencies are 1 each for college-bound males and females). Thus the strengthened relationship is probably a statistical artifact (Davis).

A similar pattern emerges when status origins are introduced as a control (Column 5). The original relationships are virtually unaffected (a comparison of the coefficients in Column 3 with Column 5). Track position again emerges as the strongest predictor of delinquent involvement.

DISCUSSION

Generally speaking, these results offer little encouragement for the class-based theories of delinquency and deviance. The overall impact of status origins was both weak and inconsistent.[10]

[10]This does not mean that status origins are unimportant. As I have argued elsewhere (Kelly, 1973), social class and race are often systematically used as a basis for *assignment* to tracks; however, these selection factors appear to play a relatively unimportant role in accounting for the *outcomes* attri-

The track data, by contrast, exhibited not only more consistent but also more pronounced patterns.

Overall, then, these findings provide general support for the hypothesis that, relative to one's *background,* one's *location* in the academic hierarchy is the strongest and most consistent predictor of self-report, delinquent involvement. What, then, are the major theoretical and policy implications of this observation?

Theoretically, these findings underscore the need to develop further a "school status" theory of delinquency or delinquent involvement. These findings and others (e.g., Kelly and Pink, 1973; Polk and Schafer, 1972; Rosenthal and Jacobson, 1968; Schafer and Polk, 1967) would seem to suggest further that such a formulation should incorporate a major concern for the nature of the school experience, particularly in terms of the typing processes and ceremonies that take place between, for example, student-teacher, and student-administrator. We must also begin to realize and understand more fully that the term or label "delinquent," like any other status, is a status conferred upon selected social actors. An excellent illustration of this status conferring or labeling ceremony can be noted in Cicourel and Kitsuse's (1963) research. In this particular study, guidance counselors, in an effort to justify their own position in the academic hierarchy, began to identify emotional and behavioral problems among the students that previously went unnoticed. Over time this initial identifying and subsequent typing pro-

buted to tracking (e.g., dropout and delinquency). Analysis of the data in this study, as well as additional analyses of the complete list of delinquent acts, supports this observation, particularly in terms of how the class variable operated. We should add also that race or ethnic origin cannot confound our findings; there was only one non-white included within our population frame. It can perhaps be argued that a population homogeneous with respect to race may limit our findings. Perhaps this is the case. It can be noted in Shafer and Olexa's study, however, that even though race was systematically used as a criterion for track placement, it was relatively unimportant in accounting for the outcomes they noted.

duced an exclusionary process whereby specific students were shunted into the deviant career lines (i.e., the emotional and delinquent careers) that existed within this high school. These very typing, sorting, and segregating processes, it might be added, have been reported in our recent study of 105 ninth graders attending school in the state of Oregon (Balch and Kelly, 1974).

The preceding results and observations would seem to suggest clearly that educators could play a major role in reducing selected forms of school misconduct and delinquency. As a start, the social typing and screening processes that take place within the school need to be systematically analyzed. Deliberate attempts must be made to find out how students are identified and subsequently assigned to the various tracks that exist in most schools. Finally, and as the results of this study also indicate, the negative effects of student stratification systems need to be examined in greater detail (Kelly, 1974).

REFERENCES

Akers, R. L.
1964   "Socio-economic status and delinquent behavior: a retest." Journal of Research in Crime and Delinquency 1 (January):38–46.

Anderson, Theodore R. and Morris Zelditch, Jr.
1968   A Basic Course in Statistics. Second Edition. New York: Holt, Rinehart and Winston.

Balch, R. W. and D. H. Kelly
1974   "Reactions to deviance in a junior high school: student views of the labeling process." Instructional Psychology 1 (Winter):25–38.

Cicourel, Aaron V. and John I. Kitsuse
1963   The Educational Decision-Makers. New York; Free Press.

Cloward, Richard A. and Lloyd E. Ohlin
1960   Delinquency and Opportunity: A Theory of Delinquent Gangs. New York: Free Press.

Cohen, Albert K.
1955   Delinquent Boys: The Culture of the Gang. New York: Free Press.

Davis, James A.
1971   Elementary Survey Analysis. Englewood Cliffs (New Jersey): Prentice-Hall.

Gibbons, Don C.
1970   Delinquent Behavior. Englewood Cliffs (New Jersey): Prentice-Hall.

Haney, B. and M. Gold
1973   "The juvenile delinquent nobody knows." Psychology Today 7 (September):49–52, 55.

Hargreaves, David
1967   Social Relations in a Secondary School. New York: Humanities Press.

Havighurst, Robert J., Paul Hoover Bowman, Gordon P. Liddle, Charles V. Matthew, and James W. Pierce
1962   Growing Up in River City. New York: John Wiley.

Hollingshead, August B.
1949   Elmtown's Youth. New York: John Wiley.

Jones, J. D., E. L., Erickson, and R. Crowell
1972   "Increasing the gap between whites and blacks: tracking as a contributory source." Education and Urban Society 4 (May):339–349.

Kelly, Delos H.
1974   "Student perceptions, self-concept, and curriculum assignment." Urban Education 9 (October):257–269.
1973   "Track assignment and student mobility patterns as barriers to equality of educational opportunity: a review of recent research." Contemporary Education 45 (Fall):27–30.
1972   "Social origins and adolescent success patterns." Education and Urban Society 4 (May):351–365.
1971   "School failure, academic self-evaluation, and school avoidance and deviant behavior." Youth and Society 2 (June):489–503.

———and R. W. Balch
1971   "Social origins and school failure: a reexamination of Cohen's theory of working class delinquency." Pacific Sociological Review 14 (October):413–430.

————and W. T. Pink
1973   "Social origins, school status, and the learning experience: a theoretical and empirical examination of two competing viewpoints." Pacific Sociological Review 16 (January):121–134.

————and R. W. Winslow
1970   "Seriousness of delinquent behavior: an alternative perspective." British Journal of Criminology 10 (April):124–135.

Merton, Robert K.
1968   Social Theory and Social Structure. Enlarged Edition. New York: Free Press.

Nye, F. I., J. F. Short, Jr., and V. J. Olson
1958   "Socio-economic status and delinquent behavior." American Journal of Sociology 63 (January):381–389.

Perlman, I. R.
1964   "Antisocial behavior of the minor in the U.S." Federal Probation 28 (December):23–30

Polk, K.
1969   "Class, strain and rebellion among adolescents." Social Problems 17 (Fall):214–224.

————and D. S. Halferty
1966   "Adolescence, commitment, and delinquency." Journal of Research in Crime and Delinquency 3 (July):82–96.

Polk, Kenneth and Walter E. Shafer (eds.)
1972   Schools and Delinquency. Englewood Cliffs, New Jersey: Prentice-Hall.

President's Commission on Law Enforcement and Administration of Justice
1967   The Challenge of Crime in a Free Society. Washington, D.C.: U.S. Government Printing Office.

Rhodes, A. L. and A. J. Reiss, Jr.
1969   "Apathy, truancy and delinquency as adaptations to school failure." Social Forces 48 (September):12–22.

Rosenthal, Robert and Lenore Jacobson
1968   Pygmalion in the Classroom. New York: Holt, Rinehart and Winston.

Schafer, Walter E. and Carol Olexa
1971   Tracking and Opportunity: The Locking-Out Process and Beyond. Scranton: Chandler.

Schafer, W. E., C. Olexa and K. Polk
1970   "Programmed for social class: tracking in high school." Transaction 7 (October):39–46, 63.

Schafer, Walter E. and Kenneth Polk
1967   "Delinquency and the schools." Pp. 222–277 in Task Force Report: Juvenile Delinquency and Youth Crime. Washington, D.C.: U.S. Government Printing Office.

Sellin, Thorsten and Marvin E. Wolfgang
1964   The Measurement of Delinquency. New York: John Wiley.

Shaw, Clifford R. and Henry D. McKay
1942   Juvenile Delinquency and Urban Areas. Chicago: University of Chicago Press.

Short, J. F. Jr., and F. I. Nye
1958   "Extent of unrecorded delinquency, tentative conclusions." Journal of Criminal Law, Criminology and Police Science 49 (November-December):296–302.

Tanner, Daniel
1965   School For Youth: Change and Challenge in Secondary Education. New York: Macmillan.

Thrasher, Frederick M.
1936   The Gang. Chicago: University of Chicago Press.

Voss, H. L.
1966   "Socio-economic status and reported delinquent behavior." Social Problems 13 (Winter): 314–324.

Winslow, R. W.
1967   "Anomie and its alternatives: a self-report study of delinquency." The Sociological Quarterly 8 (Autumn):468–480

42. Delinquency and School Dropout

DELBERT S. ELLIOTT

INTRODUCTION

THE FOCUS OF THIS SELECTION[1] IS ON THE RELA-tionship between delinquency and dropout. Our concern over this relationship grew out of a larger study testing a general theoretical explanation of the causes of delinquent behavior and dropout, which viewed these two behaviors as alternative responses to failure experiences at school. This postulated relationship between school failure and delinquency or dropout led to an expected relationship between delinquency and dropout that appeared to be at odds with the current view that dropout leads to an increasing likelihood of delinquency.

Relying heavily on Cloward and Ohlin's work in *Delinquency and Opportunity* (1960), we propose that the crucial conditions for delinquency are goal blockage or failure to achieve personal goals, extrapunitiveness, normlessness, and exposure to delinquent persons or groups. A similar set of variables and casual sequences provide a parallel explanation of high school dropout: dropout involves failure to achieve personally valued goals, intrapunitiveness, social isolation, and exposure to dropouts or pro-dropout

influences. Because of the central place occupied by the school in the lives of young people, we argue that it is the most important context in the generation of delinquent behavior, and we thus postulate that delinquency and dropout are alternative responses to limited opportunities and goal failure experienced primarily in the social context of the school.[2]

While both delinquency and dropout are considered responses to failure experiences encountered at school, they are postulated to involve different explanations or rationalizations for failure, and different forms of personal alienation. The way in which an individual explains his or her failure basically determines what that person will do about it (Cloward and Ohlin, 1960). Those who attribute the blame for their difficulties to unjust or artibrary institutional arrangements, discriminatory practices on the part of teachers, administrators, or other students, or some other external feature of the school context are most likely to adopt a delin-

▶SOURCE: *Selection especially written for this volume.*

[1]This selection is an adaptation from D. S. Elliott and H. L. Voss, *Delinquency and Dropout* (Lexington, Mass.: Lexington Books, D. C. Heath and Company, 1974, Chapter 5) and is reprinted here by permission of the publisher. The larger study was supported by grants MH 07173 and MH 15285 from the Center for Studies in Crime and Delinquency, NIMH.

[2]The findings from the larger study confirmed this hypothesis. For males in particular, the school was the critical social context in the generation of delinquency and dropout; for females, both the school and home were important contexts for delinquency. Utilizing the theoretical variables identified here, the multiple correlation of the postulated variables and self-reported delinquency frequency scores was 0.54 for males and 0.50 for females. R values for gains in delinquency across the study period were 0.44 and 0.40. R values for dropout were 0.41 for both males and females. In all of these analyses, the temporal order of predictor and criterion variables were maintained (i.e., they were genuine predictive analyses).

quent response to their failure. Their explanation for failure provides a justification for criticizing, attacking, and ultimately withdrawing their sense of moral commitment from the normative system. Extrapunitiveness is thus postulated to be a conditional variable in the relationship between school failure and delinquency. It explains why some youths experiencing difficulties at school become alienated from conventional norms and adopt delinquent means for achieving their goals while others do not.

Not all persons experiencing goal failure at school attribute their problem to the policies, practices, and situations encountered in this setting. If personal inadequacy—lack of discipline, effort, or intelligence—is considered the source of failure, then the outcome is pressure either to change oneself or to develop techniques to protect oneself from a feeling of personal inadequacy. An intrapunitive or impunitive explanation of failure implies acceptance of the legitimacy of conventional norms, not alienation from them. Apart from developing greater personal competence, there are two possible adaptations for persons who attribute blame to themselves: the individual may lower his or her aspirations and engage in a form of passive compliance to the norms, or withdraw from efforts to achieve presumably unattainable goals. In the context of the school, students who adopt the first solution are referred to as "low achievers" or "poorly motivated" students; students who adopt the latter solution are referred to as truants and dropouts. Dropping out of school is one alternative for youths who are failing to achieve valued goals and who assume personal responsibility for this problem.[3] We thus postulate that dropouts tend to be intrapunitive or impunitive and develop feelings of social isolation and/or powerlessness in response to their failure at school.

In summary, delinquency and dropout are viewed as alternatives available to those ex-periencing failure and frustration at school. On the one hand, they may remain in school and attempt to deal with their failure by attacking the system of norms that they believe to be the cause of their difficulties, expressing their resentment and rejection of this system and those who attempt to enforce its norms. On the other hand, they may leave school, retreating from the situation that produces the failure and frustration. Once out of this context, there is little or no need to attack the school or the normative system it represents.

Several hypotheses concerning the relationship between delinquency and dropout follow logically from this explanation. First, the act of leaving school should reduce school-related frustrations and alienation and thereby lower the motivational stimulus for delinquency. To the extent that perceived failure in school provides a motivational stimulus for delinquency, dropout should lead to a decreasing probability of delinquency. While this expectation is consistent with our theoretical position, it is important to note several complicating factors. A youth's prior involvement in the delinquent subculture or the experience of official labeling as a delinquent may provide continuing motivation for delinquency. In this case, the hypothesized relationship would hold only for those dropouts who were not subcultural delinquents and were not labeled, either formally or informally, as delinquent persons prior to leaving school. In addition, failure in school may be repeated in the dropout's out-of-school experience; he or she may trade failure in school for failure in the economic context. In essence, the same motivational stimulus is involved, but failure is experienced in a different social context from that postulated here as the most relevant for delinquency. It is also possible that the school is an effective agent of social control because it regulates and supervises so much of the normal activity of adolescents. If there is a constant level of motivation for delinquency among juveniles attending school and out-of-school, then the absence of the restraints imposed on youths by the

---

[3]There is some evidence that dropouts lower their aspirations immediately prior to leaving school (Krane, 1976).

school will result in a higher rate of delinquent behavior among dropouts. The absence of restraints may compensate for a lower motivational stimulus for delinquency among dropouts with the result that in- and out-of-school delinquency rates for dropouts would be comparable. Writers who adopt a control perspective argue that this one factor should produce higher rates of delinquency among dropouts (Cervantes, 1965; Haskell and Yablonsky, 1970; Schafer and Knudten, 1970; Simpson and Van Arsdol, 1967; Havinghurst, 1963). Control theorists generally avoid the issue of instigation to delinquency, whereas we have postulated variables that may positively motivate youths toward delinquent behavior, whether restraints are present or absent. Although we argue on theoretical grounds that departure from school should reduce the motivational stimulus for delinquency, it may not follow that the rate of delinquency will diminish with dropout if any of the above factors are operative. Nevertheless, even in the presence of these possible complicating factors, we would not expect an *increasing* delinquency rate to be a consequence of dropout.

Second, we postulate that while dropout should not lead to an increasing probability of delinquency, a high involvement in delinquency should lead to an increased likelihood of dropout. If we assume that delinquency is a response to frustrations encountered in the school context, then those frustrated students who remain in school and attempt to deal with their frustration by attacking the school's system or norms and values should encounter increasing conflict with school authorities and an increasing risk of suspension or expulsion. Not all of the students' depredations will occur within the school. However, we assume that adolescents involved in serious and frequent delinquent behavior outside the context of the school will rarely be models of propriety in school. Nor does the school operate in a vacuum; students labeled delinquent by the police or courts are likely to be considered troublemakers by school personnel. Although their withdrawal from school may often be in-

voluntary, adolescents who are disruptive in school or are involved in delinquent acts should have a relatively high probability of being classified as dropouts. In essence, we are arguing that dropout provides a satisfactory resolution of the school failure problem, whereas delinquency does not; a delinquent response to school failure complicates the difficulty and increases the likelihood of some type of exit from the school system.

PRIOR RESEARCH

Consistently higher rates of official delinquency among high school dropouts in comparison with the general youth population or high school graduates have been reported—dropouts have three to four times more police contacts than graduates (Cervantes, 1965; Elliott, 1961, 1966; Shafer and Polk, 1967; Schreiber, 1963a, 1963b; Simpson and Van Arsdol, 1967; Jeffery and Jeffery, 1970; Bachman et al., 1971; Hathaway and Monachesi, 1963; Hathaway, Reynolds, and Monachesi, 1969). In fact, Schreiber (1963b) found the delinquency rate for dropouts to be ten times higher than the rate in the total youth population or among high school graduates. Clearly, these studies have established an association between official delinquency rates and dropout. However, the temporal order of this relationship has not been determined, nor has a causal relationship been demonstrated. In all but one of the studies cited, police arrests or court contacts were employed to measure delinquency, and we are concerned about the appropriateness of official records as a measure of delinquent behavior (Kitsuse and Cicourel, 1963; Gold, 1963; Short, 1958). Furthermore, with three noteworthy exceptions, the temporal sequence between delinquency and dropout was not examined or controlled in these studies; instead, the investigators employed *ex post facto* designs and failed to note the relative frequency of arrest or court appearance before and after the point of dropout. Nor have juveniles who differ with respect to their involvement in delinquent behavior at some point in time been compared in terms of subsequent rates of dropout. Schreiber (1963b) and Jeffery and Jeffery (1970) have been careful to note that existence of a correlation or an association between dropout and delinquency is not sufficient grounds to argue for a specific causal relationship. Unfortunately, most writers have assumed that dropout causes greater involvement in delinquency; the folk adage, "idle hands are the devil's workshop," has been translated into a simple scientific proposition.

The only known studies in which rates of delinquency before and after dropout are compared are those of Elliott (1966), Jeffrey and Jeffery (1970), and Bachman et al., (1971). Elliott reports that delinquents who dropped out had a higher official referral rate while in school than after dropout. He also notes that male dropouts had a lower police contact rate than males in school. Elliott's study was retrospective and involved a small sample. Because the study was exploratory, a substantial number of subjects who left the area during the study period were excluded from his analysis. Consequently, his conclusions must be considered tentative. Furthermore, the measure of delinquency that Elliott employed was based exclusively on official police records. Nevertheless, Elliott's study casts doubt on the common assumption that dropping out of school leads to greater involvement in delinquency.

Jeffery and Jeffery (1970) employed a rather unique research design insofar as the temporal sequence of dropout and delinquency is concerned. They compared the rates of delinquency of dropouts before and after entry into a special school program. The investigators' primary purpose was evaluation of a special educational program designed to help dropouts pass the GED, but they included a comparison of the dropouts' official delinquency contacts before and after entering the program. They conclude: "The number of weeks a student (dropout) was in the project did not deter him from delinquent conduct; in fact, the longer a student was in the project the higher the chances of delinquency" (Jeffery and Jeffery, 1970:8). The exact nature of the comparison they made is not clear, nor do they discuss the types of controls utilized for variable lengths of time in the program. If dropouts who return to school differ from all dropouts or the general population of youth, Jeffery and Jeffery's results cannot be generalized beyond the universe of dropouts who subsequently return to school. Such limitations suggest, that we view their conclusion with caution, but it is consistent with Elliott's finding that higher rates of delinquency are associated with school attendance, not dropout. The study by Bachman et al. (1971) provides more compelling evidence. This study involved a representative national sample of tenth-grade boys and a longitudinal design following these boys through their normal years of high school to graduation. For dropouts in this study, measures of delinquent behavior were obtained before and after dropping out. The results indicate that the boy who is likely to drop out of school is involved in far above average levels of delinquency before dropping out. In fact, level of involvement in delinquency was found to be the strongest predictor of future dropout. An examination of delinquency rates after dropout indicated a continuing involvement in delinquency, but there was ". . . no evidence whatever that dropping out *increased* their rate of delinquency" (Bachman et al., 1971:123). Unfortunately, the self-reported measures of delinquency employed in this study involved different "periods of risk," and the pre-post comparisons involved different time periods, rendering it difficult to determine if the actual *rate* of delinquency changed. It was clear, however, that dropouts showed no *relative* increase in delinquency after they dropped out.

Although the above evidence is limited, it appears consistent with the expectations derived from our theoretical scheme. A more detailed analysis of the relationship is clearly needed: one that utilizes both official and self-reported measures of delinquency, controls for the temporal order of delinquency and dropout, and considers out-of-school conditions such as unemployment and marriage.

DESCRIPTION OF THE STUDY

In this research, a type of cluster sample was used in which the basic sampling unit was a school instead of a person. We sampled only in the purposive selection of eight schools to guarantee inclusion of students with a wide range of social, economic, and racial or ethnic characteristics. All of the schools were located within two metropolitan areas; seven of the schools were located in southern California, and the other was in the northern part of the state. All students who entered these schools as ninth graders in September 1963 comprised the target population. From the available pool of 2663 students, we encountered five student refusals and did not obtain parental permission to interview 41 others. Thus, the study population consisted of 2617 students.

The research design was longitudinal. Initial observations were obtained when the study population entered the ninth grade, and additional observations were obtained annually until the usual date for graduation from high school for the cohort. Limitation of the study population to a single academic class "controls" the effects of age or maturation. We attempted to make personal contact with each respondent in the original cohort during each of the four annual data-gathering phases. Included in this effort were those students who dropped out as well as those who transferred to another school. In addition to the annual students questionnaires or interviews, a parent of each subject was interviewed in the first year of the study, and relevant information from school, police, and court records was also obtained for each subject.

Even though completion of a longitudinal study involves considerable expense and presents a number of special data-gathering problems, the nature of our problem required use of this type of design if we were to assess pos-

tulated cause-effect relationships. The first observations were calculated to precede dropout and extensive involvement in delinquent behavior in order to permit accurate determination of the temporal order of events. As is often the case with research in the behavioral sciences, neither the independent nor dependent variables could be manipulated artificially; it was essential to take repeated measurements through time and to relate previous measurements to subsequent differences while controlling for those factors known to be relevant. A longitudinal design permits a more adequate test of expected relationships than a cross-sectional design. On the other hand, a fundamental problem in longitudinal studies involves the loss of subjects over the course of the project. To minimize case attrition because of residential mobility, we developed elaborate tracking techniques. As a result, the attrition over the four-year study period was less than 10 percent.

MEASURES OF DELINQUENCY AND DROPOUT

A self-reported measure of delinquent behavior similar to that utilized by Short and Nye (1957) and Bachman et al. (1971) was employed as the basic measure of delinquent behavior. The study population reported an average of ten delinquent offenses over the study period on this scale (male $\overline{X} = 12$; female $\overline{X} = 7$). Considering the total study period, no significant race or class differentials in frequency of offense were found on the self-report measure, although there was an indication that those with lower social-class backgrounds or minority group statuses had a relatively higher involvement in delinquent behavior during the junior high school years and a relatively lower involvement during the high school years than did Anglos and those from higher SES backgrounds.

A second measure of delinquent behavior involved the number of police contacts (investigation reports) for persons in the study. A total of 1486 police contacts were recorded for the study population prior to June 1967 (end of twelfth grade). This resulted in a mean of 0.869 contacts for males and 0.253 for females. The analysis of police contact reports revealed the expected race, sex, and class differentials with minority groups, males, and those with lower socioeconomic statuses having disproportionately high police contact rates. With respect to these characteristics, the study population appears quite similar to other populations studied.

A comparison of self-reported offenses and police contact reports (limited to ten offenses on the self-report measure) revealed that overall there were fewer than five police contacts for every 100 self-reported offenses. The ratio of police contacts to self-reported offenses varied by sex, race, and social class with males, minority groups (particularly blacks), and lower-class subjects encountering a relatively greater risk of a police contact for each self-reported act.

Three separate dropout measures were developed: dropout status, attendance status, and graduate status. The dropout was defined as a person who left school for one or more consecutive months without transferring to another school. By the end of the study, 558 (21 percent) persons were classified as dropouts. Since dropouts were in school for some part of the study and frequently returned to school at some later point (there were 130 reentries), attendance status referred to the subject's presence or absence from school during each specific year of the study. The graduate status measure reflected the final educational outcome (at the termination of the study) classifying subjects as graduates and nongraduates. Graduates comprised 79 percent of the original cohort. Nongraduates included 2 percent who were still attending school and 19 percent who were out of school at the termination of the study. Approximately 10 percent of those classified as dropouts were also classified as graduates.

FINDINGS

Persons classified as dropouts at the end of the study had a substantially greater number of re-

corded police contacts and reported considerably more delinquent behavior than did the graduates. The mean number of police contacts for dropouts was approximately four times higher than the average for graduates. A similar pattern exists with respect to police contacts for serious offenses, although the dropout-graduate ratio for females is somewhat lower, (3:1).

The police contact rates for dropouts and graduates appear to be consistent with the findings of previous research. Using juvenile court records, which are less inclusive than police contact reports, Schreiber (1963b) reported a 10:1 dropout-graduate ratio. For comparative purposes the proportion of graduates adjudicated delinquent was 0.03; the comparable figure for dropouts was 0.17. Restricting the analysis to adjudicated delinquents, we still observe differences between dropouts and graduates substantially lower than the ratio reported by Schreiber.

Involvement in delinquent behavior was also measured by self-reported delinquency, and differences between graduates and dropouts were statistically significant and substantial. Male dropouts reported a mean of 16.82 offenses; in comparison, male graduates reported an average of 10.59 delinquent acts. Comparable figures for females were 8.74 and 6.33. Although the means for dropouts were consistently higher than those for graduates, in no case did the mean for dropouts exceed the mean for graduates by a factor of 2. The relative differences in dropout-graduate ratios suggest that there is, given a constant number of delinquent acts, a higher risk of official action for dropouts than graduates.[4]

Both the official and self-report measures of delinquent behavior support the conclusion that dropouts have been involved in more delinquent behavior than graduates, although the

---

[4]This finding is consistent with the observation that dropouts are disproportionately drawn from among lower-class and minority youths. See Chapter IV, *Delinquency and Dropout.*

differences on the self-report measure are not nearly as dramatic as those based on official police contacts. Dropouts are also more likely to have been adjudicated delinquent.

Having established the association between delinquency and dropout, we turn now to a consideration of the nature of this relationship. There are four alternative, although not mutually exclusive, ways in which delinquency and dropout could be associated. If dropout is treated as the causal variable, then it is possible that dropout increases or decreases the probability of delinquent behavior. On the other hand, if delinquency is considered as the causal variable, then delinquency may increase or decrease the probability of dropout. The effect of dropout on delinquency can be determined by comparing the dropouts' in- and out-of-school delinquency rates; in this way support may be provided for either the first or second hypothesis. In a similar manner, we compare the dropout rates of subjects with high and low rates of delinquency to ascertain the effect of delinquency on dropout; this approach may provide evidence in support of either the third or fourth alternative. The hypotheses within each of the pairs are mutually exclusive. However, the alternatives in the first set are not necessarily inconsistent with the hypotheses in the second set; for example, delinquency could lead to dropout which, in turn, could produce increasing or decreasing rates of delinquency.

THE EFFECT OF DROPOUT ON DELINQUENCY

If dropping out of school leads to increased delinquent activity, a comparison of delinquency rates while dropouts are in and out of school should provide evidence in support of such a causal sequence. In- and out-of-school rates of police contact during each study period[5] are

[5]The study was divided into five time periods: Period I—prior to the first annual questionnaire; Period II—between first and second annual questionnaires (early ninth to mid-tenth grades); Period III—between second and third questionnaires (mid-tenth to mid-eleventh; Period IV—

presented in Table I. In this table dropouts are categorized according to the period in which they left school. Dropouts in Period II (hereafter cited as DO IIs) left school sometime during the second period (early ninth to mid-tenth grade), and the number of days in and out of school during this period had to be calculated for each dropout, as did the number of police contacts prior to and subsequent to his or her leaving school. Individually, DO IIs contributed a variable amount of time and number of police contacts to the in-school and out-of-school rates during Period II. Similarly, dropouts in Periods III, IV, and V (hereinafter cited as DO IIIs, IVs, and Vs, respectively) have in-school and out-of-school rates for the period in which they left school. The vertical line in Table I represents the point of dropout; values on the left side of the table are in-school rates, and those to the right are out-of-school rates. Because the dropouts are categorized according to the period in which they left school, a comparison of the dropouts' rate of police contact within any particular time period requires examination of the diagonal cells. For comparative purposes, police contact rates by study period are also shown in the first row of Table I for graduates who were in school throughout the study.

Comparison of police contact rates of dropouts and graduates in Period I clearly demonstrates that, with the exception of those dropping out late in their junior or senior year (DO Vs), dropouts had substantially higher contact rates prior to the start of the study. In Period I the rate for respondents who were to drop out in the follow year (DO IIs) was five times higher than the rate of eventual graduates. Only one category of dropouts, the DO Vs, had a rate lower than the graduates, and this category, which contained 65 subjects, included 13 dropout reentries and 52 respondents who tenaciously remained in school almost to the date of graduation. Furthermore, dropouts consistently had higher police contact rates than

between third and last questionnaires (mid-eleventh to late twelfth grades); and Period V—after the last questionnaire.

Table I. Total Police Contact Rates,[a] by Subjects In and Out of School

	In School					Out-of-School			
Periods:	I	II	III	IV	V				
Graduates (N = 2142)	0.19	0.19	0.27	0.20	0.19				
Periods:	I	II	III	IV	V	V			
DO V (N = 65)	0.10	0.47	0.60	0.68	1.12	0.43			
Periods:		I	II	III	IV	IV	V		
DO IV (N = 195)		0.55	0.48	0.74	0.81	0.41	0.00		
Periods:			I	II	III	III	IV	V	
DO III (N = 106)			0.71	0.71	1.64	0.30	0.01	0.00	
Periods:				I	II	II	III	IV	V
DO II (N = 109)				1.00	1.70	0.94	0.32	0.10	0.00

[a]Mean number of police contacts per 1000 days. The summer period from June 15 to September 15 is excluded For this analysis Period I was assumed to have started in September 1959, when the cohort's mean age was 10 years.

graduates for every period they were in school; the rates for dropouts were never less than twice the rate of graduates in any single time period. The case of the DO IIs was particularly impressive. While in school during Period II, their rate was nine times higher than the police contact rate of graduates. These data are consistent with the findings reported by Elliott (1966); they demonstrate forcefully that dropouts have higher in-school rates of police contact than graduates.

For each category of dropouts the police contact rates increase with time while they are in school. Furthermore, the highest rate for each category is observed in the period in which dropout occurs. The pattern is similar regardless of when the subjects dropped out; that is, the rate of police contact increases steadily and peaks in the last period the subjects are in school. In contrast, among graduates the rate increases somewhat from Period II to Period III, but then declines to the earlier level in Periods IV and V. Among the graduates the magnitude of the rate changes with time is slight, particularly in comparison with the changes observed in each dropout category. The dropouts' increasing involvement with the police while they are in school is not accounted for by the general trend observed in the total population. The higher initial or prestudy police contact rates and the accelerating rates through time are also observed for serious police contacts.

The out-of-school rates for dropouts indicate a dramatic reversal of the in-school trend. In the period in which dropout occurs, the rate for out-of-school police contacts is approximately one-half the magnitude of the in-school rate for DO IIs and IVs; the out-of-school rate declines even more sharply among DO IIIs and Vs. For each category of dropouts the rate systematically declines in the period after which dropout occurred, and it continues to decline in subsequent time periods. In the later periods the police contact rates are substantially lower than the comparable rates for graduates. In Periods IV and V, the out-of-school police contact rates for dropouts are close to 0. The figures for Period V must be treated as tentative approximations, because this was a short time period. Nevertheless, these data support the conclusion that dropping out of school is associated with decreasing, instead of increasing out-of-school rates of police contact. Dropouts who have been out of school for a relatively short time have higher rates of police contact than prospective graduates who are still in school. It is not until Period IV that the official delinquency rates of DO IIs and IIIs reach a level lower than the rates of future graduates. From the standpoint of a causal argument, the most important finding is that dropping out of school is associated with a decreasing involvement with the police.

Use of the self-measure instead of police contacts produces similar findings, as shown in Table II. This analysis is limited to a comparison of graduates with DO IIs who did not return to school, because these dropouts were in school during nearly all of their junior high school years, but were out of school for all of their senior high school years.[6] Thus, the first self-report measure covers the period these dropouts were in school, while the second coincides with the period they were out of school. On the other hand, graduates were in school continuously throughout the junior and senior high school years. Because the length of the two periods is identical, means are used instead of rates.

In Table II, males and females are considered separately to control for the established differences in delinquency rates by sex. It is also assumed that the effect of dropping out might be different for males than for females. During the junior high school years, male dropouts report a mean of 8.57 offenses in comparison with 3.88 for graduates; female dropouts and graduates report 4.40 and 2.47 offenses, respectively. Even greater differences are observed for serious offenses during the junior high school years. Male dropouts report more than three times as many serious offenses as graduates. These differences are all significant statistically. These data are consistent with the findings

based on police contacts and indicate that, while in school, dropouts have substantially greater involvement in delinquent activity than graduates.

A comparison of the means for male dropouts reveals a decline from 8.57 self-reported offenses while in school to 8.13 after dropping out of school. This represents a 5 percent average decrease in raw scores. The comparable rate of change for female dropouts is a decrease of 4 percent. Substantially greater decreases are observed in the means for serious offenses, -28 percent for male and -57 percent for female dropouts.[7] While the decrease in the total number of offenses is slight, it is, nevertheless, clear that the high rates of delinquency among the dropouts cannot be attributed to their dropping out of school. The dropouts reach a high level of involvement in delinquency prior to leaving school, but once they are out of school, their total offense rates decline slightly, and their involvement in serious offenses declines substantially.

While the dropouts' involvement in delinquent behavior decreased from the junior to the senior high school years, graduates reported an increasing number of delinquent acts. The change from a mean of 3.88 total offenses for males in junior high school to 6.76 delinquent acts in senior high school represents a 74 percent average increase in raw scores. A similar increase is observed for serious offenses. Female graduates also report substantially more delinquent acts in senior high school than in junior high school; their average increase exceeds 55 percent for the total number of offenses as well as for serious offenses. Given the sizable increases in delinquent behavior among graduates, the declining rates for dropouts as-

[6]In Period II (early ninth to mid-tenth grade) 109 subjects dropped out of school. Fifty percent ($N = 55$) of these dropouts failed to complete the fourth annual questionnaire and thus had missing data for the second self-reported delinquency measure. The means in Table II for senior high school and the residual gain means in the text are based on an N of 54. A check for possible selectivity in this loss provided no evidence of a selective loss with respect to prior delinquency scores. This loss did not affect the police contact measures, as official records were searched in the appropriate geographical areas for all dropouts and graduates whether or not they completed each of the annual questionnaires; except for eight cases, the whereabouts of all subjects were known, even if interviews were not completed.

[7]Unfortunately, year-by-year changes are not reflected in the self-reported delinquency measure, and the systematic decline observed in police contacts for each year out of school cannot be replicated with these data. Nevertheless, the findings based on the two measures of delinquency are consistent—there is a decreasing involvement in delinquency after dropout.

Table II. Mean Number of Self-Reported Delinquent Acts and Percentage Change Scores for Dropouts in Period II and Graduates During Junior and Senior High School, by Sex

	Males						Females					
	Junior High		Senior High		Percentage Change		Junior High		Senior High		Percentage Change	
	Total Means	Serious	Total Means	Serious	Total Percentages	Serious	Total Means	Serious	Total Means	Serious	Total Percentages	Serious
Dropouts	8.57	3.59	8.13	2.60	−5.1	−17.6	4.40	1.17	4.21	0.50	−4.3	−57.3
Graduates	3.88	0.99	6.76	1.71	+74.2	+72.7	2.47	0.43	3.83	0.67	+55.1	+55.8
t test	3.90[a]	3.71[a]	0.85	1.00			2.74[a]	2.31[b]	0.61	−0.54		

[a] $p < 0.01$.
[b] $p < 0.05$

sume even greater importance, because they represent a trend counter to the one occurring in the general population.

In terms of raw scores the dropouts' self-reported delinquency declined slightly after they left school. With the exception of serious offenses among females, in the senior high school period the dropouts' mean self-report scores were slightly greater than the means for graduates, although the differences were not significant. In view of the dropouts' significantly more extensive involvement in delinquency while in school, we would have predicted higher rates of delinquency for the dropouts during the high school years, even if they had not dropped out of school. The use of residual gain scores allows for a comparison of dropouts and graduates in terms of self-reported delinquency scores in which the effects of prior delinquency have been partialled out. The residual gain score for dropouts represents the difference between their out-of-school delinquency score and an expected score based on their prior delinquency level. Similarly, the residual gain score for graduates reflects the difference between their high school score and a predicted score based on their prior delinquency in junior high school.

A comparison of mean residual gain scores indicated that dropouts reported fewer offenses than expected while graduates reported slightly more than expected.[8] Both male and female dropouts reported an average of approximately one less offense than expected, given their prior self-reported delinquency scores. The slightly higher self-reported means for dropouts than graduates in the high school years are thus explained by the dropouts' initially higher involvement in delinquency. Once they leave school, dropouts commit fewer offenses than students in school with similar levels of prior delinquency.

Whether delinquency is measured in terms of police contacts or self-reports, similar patterns are revealed: (1) dropouts show a high level of involvement in delinquency while they are in school, and their involvement declines after they leave school; (2) there is limited initial involvement in delinquency on the part of graduates, but it generally increases in the high school years; and, finally, (3) the rates of delinquency for subjects out of school are no greater—and possibly slightly lower—than the rates for students in school. Because these findings are contrary to the widely accepted belief that dropout leads to an increasing risk of delinquent activity, it is necessary to consider the possibility that the relationship is spurious. The findings we have presented on the relationship between delinquency and dropout are consistent with the results of earlier research; in this study the dropouts' involvement in delinquency is substantially greater than the participation of graduates in delinquency. The fact that these data also confirm a higher in-school and a lower out-of-school delinquency rate makes it unlikely that this finding is due to some unique feature of the study population.

With respect to the measure of delinquency based on police contacts, it might be argued that the lower out-of-school rate is simply a consequence of a decrease in visibility, which accompanies dropout. We do not deny that dropout may affect the visibility of delinquent acts, but it is unlikely that this could explain the decrease in delinquency among out-of-school youths, in view of the fact that a similar finding was produced when a self-report measure, unaffected by visibility to the police, was employed. Furthermore, the finding that lower-class and minority-group youths have a higher risk of police contact contradicts this possibility, because these youths contribute disproportionately to the dropout categories. If operative, the effect of police bias would be to exaggerate estimates of delinquency among dropouts in comparison with graduates. Another possibility is that if school officials frequently initiate police

---

[8]Mean residual gain scores were as follows: dropout males, -1.37; dropout females, -0.70; graduate males, $+0.06$; graduate females, $+0.04$.

action, then those in school are more visible. However, school-related offenses such as truancy are not included in this analysis, and in less than one-half of 1 percent of the police departments' investigation reports are school personnel identified as the source of the complaint. This corroborates Elliott's (1966) finding that the school is rarely the agency that initiates action resulting in a police contact. It does not appear that differential visibility can account for the decreasing police contact rate among dropouts.

While the problem of spuriousness can never be resolved, the observed relationship between delinquency and dropout cannot be explained by class or sex differences among dropouts and graduates or by differential visibility. Two additional facts support the conclusion that the relationship is not spurious—the police contact and the self-report measures produce consistent findings, and the overall rates are similar to those reported in earlier studies.

THE EFFECT OF DELINQUENCY ON DROPOUT

The observation that dropouts have significantly higher police contact and self-reported delinquency rates while in school than graduates appears to be consistent with our expectation that delinquency increases the probability of dropout. However, it does not demonstrate that subjects who were highly involved in delinquency at the beginning of the study or in a particular time period have a greater likelihood of dropping out than respondents with limited involvement in delinquency. To ascertain the effect of delinquency on dropout, we compared the in-school to out-of-school transition rates of subjects stratified according to prior involvement in delinquency (Davis, 1963). Comparison between the strata indicates the relative probability of dropout during a given period for subjects with and without police contact at the beginning of that period; in this analysis the size of each stratum is held constant, as are differences in initial marginal frequencies. The in-school to out-of-school transition rates for subjects with no police contacts and juveniles with one or more police contacts at the beginning of each period are presented in Table III. For convenience of reading the rates are stated in percentages.

The transition rates for respondents who experienced police contact are consistently higher than for juveniles with no official record. For

Table III. In-School to Out-of-School Transition Rates, by Time Period, Stratified by Police Contact (Percentages)

	Period							
	II		III		IV		V	
Police Contact[a]	Rate	N	Rate	N	Rate	N	Rate	N
One or more police contacts	0.8	308	1.0	418	2.1	464	1.0	464
No police contacts	0.3	2307	0.4	2082	0.7	1876	0.4	1652
t value	4.55[b]		5.45[b]		8.75[b]		5.26[b]	

[a]Persons were classified as being in one or the other of these strata at the beginning of each successive time period. Subjects with no police contact at the beginning of Period II could be in either strata at the beginning of Period III. However, respondents who entered the "one or more" strata at any given point remained in it in subsequent time periods.

[b]$p < 0.01$.

each study period the probability of dropout is more than two times greater for those who experienced police contact than for respondents with no police contact. In Period IV, these probabilities differ by a factor of 3. These data offer strong support for the hypothesis that official contact with the police increases the likelihood of dropout.

In-school to out-of-school transition rates for respondents with high, moderate, and low levels of self-reported delinquency at the beginning of the study are presented in Table IV. These transition rates reflect the probability of dropout over the entire study period. The data confirm that extensive involvement in delinquent behavior, whether or not it leads to official action, increases the probability of dropout. The transition rates of subjects with high initial self-reported delinquency scores are more than double the rates of respondents with low scores; more than one-third of the respondents with high initial self-report scores dropped out of school prior to graduation. The direction and magnitude of the differences in Table IV are similar to those in Table III. Together, these data offer impressive support for the hypothesis that delinquency leads to dropout.

The expected relationship between delinquency and dropout is not a simple one: delinquency increases the probability of dropout, which in turn decreases the probability of delinquency. Measures of delinquency based on police contacts and self-reports provide evidence in support of this causal sequence. These relationships were postulated in our theoretical scheme and support the basic proposition that the school is the critical social context for the generation of delinquent behavior.

DELINQUENCY AND POST-DROPOUT EXPERIENCES

Earlier, we suggested that dropouts' decreasing involvement in delinquency would depend on several contingencies in their out-of-school experiences, particularly employment and marriage. Dropout should reduce the motivation for delinquency to the extent that the dropout makes a satisfactory adjustment in the adult, working community. Should he or she en-

Table IV. In-School to Out-of-School Transition Rates, by Sex, Stratified by Self-Reported Delinquency in Period I (Percentages)

Self-reported delinquency 1[a]	Males	Females	Total	N
High	3.5	3.3	3.3	775
Moderate	1.6	2.4	2.0	804
Low	1.1	1.4	1.3	1038
t values				
High versus moderate	6.55[b]	2.57[b]	6.36[b]	
High versus low	8.57[b]	6.55[b]	10.77[b]	
Moderate versus low	2.13[c]	4.08[b]	4.22[b]	

[a]The membership in each strata was determined at the beginning of the study on the basis of total self-reported delinquency scores for Period I and could not be readjusted for each period, as was the case with police contacts. For both sexes, those with less than two offenses were considered low; those with two to four offenses, moderate; and those with five or more offenses, high. These cutting points were used to trichotomize the initial self-report scores for each sex.

[b]$p < 0.01$.

[c]$p < 0.05$.

counter difficulty in obtaining a job, establishing new friendships, and making the transition into an adult role, one type of failure has simply been traded one for another, and we would not anticipate any dramatic decrease in motivation for delinquent behavior.

The circumstances of youths after they have dropped out of school vary widely. The unemployed, unmarried, out-of-school teenager probably comes closest to fitting the popular conception of the aimless, drifting high school dropout. On the other hand, males who are steadily employed and married, as well as females who are married, are viewed as having successfully entered conventional adult roles in the community, and we would not expect continued involvement in delinquent behavior. It was therefore hypothesized that dropouts who were employed and married should be less delinquent than unmarried and unemployed dropouts.

In Table V the rate of police contact for out-of-school dropouts by sex, marital status, and employment status is presented. For Periods II, III, and IV, subjects who were out of school were jointly classified with respect to marriage and employment; the rate of police contact during each period was determined for respondents in each category. Subjects who were employed or married for the major part of a given time period were classified as employed or married for that period. Respondents who were married or employed for less than one-half of the period and subjects unmarried or unemployed for the entire period were classified as unmarried and unemployed.[9]

[9]The rates do not accurately reflect relatively short shifts from one marriage-employment category to another *within* a given time period, as all offenses in a particular time period are attributed to the single category that characterized the subject for the majorty of the time involved. The rates in Table V reflect the total experience of dropouts in various marriage-employment categories through time; a given dropout may have contributed to the unmarried-unemployed rate for Period II, the unmarried-employed rate for Period III, and the married-employed rate for Period IV.

Table V. Police Contact Rates[a] for Out-of-School Dropouts, by Sex, Marital Status, and Employment Status

	Married	Unmarried	Total
Males			
Employed	6.1	14.9	11.8
Unemployed	0.0	17.5	15.9
Total	5.1	15.4	13.3
Females			
Employed	4.0	2.4	3.0
Unemployed	1.8	6.2	3.1
Total	2.1	4.7	3.0
Total			
Employed	5.2	10.2	8.6
Unemployed	1.8	11.7	6.0
Total	2.6	10.9	7.0

[a]The number of police contacts per 100 dropouts in each marriage-employment category. The number of dropouts involved by period are as follows: Period II, 80; III, 136; IV, 484.

While out of school, male dropouts had 25 official police contacts, and female dropouts had 8 contacts. Thus, this analysis involves only 33 offenses. An examination of the rates reveals that for males marital status is the variable most highly associated with police contact. The police contact rate for unmarried males is more than three times the rate for married males. The rate for unemployed dropouts is also greater than for employed dropouts, but the difference is small. As expected, males who were unmarried and unemployed had the highest rate of police contacts, whereas married and unemployed males had the lowest rate. The finding must be viewed with caution, because there were very few cases of this type; most of the married male dropouts were also employed. Nevertheless, it is clear that marriage and not employment is the critical variable.

In general, the same conclusions apply to female dropouts, but the limited number of police contacts they experienced forces us to view these findings as highly tentative. Again, the highest rate is found in the unemployed-unmarried category. The rate for unmarried females is more than twice the rate for married females, but there is no difference in the rates according to employment status. The lowest rates are found in the married-unemployed and the employed-unmarried categories. The first of these presumably describes the typical house-wife; the second depicts the career woman. Either marriage or employment presumably is a deterrent to delinquency, but marriage and employment apparently do not work together to deter delinquency for female dropouts. Drop-outs who do not marry or obtain employment appear to have the greatest risk of police contact.

Combining the males and females, we confirm the importance of marital status—the delinquency rate of unmarried dropouts is four times higher than the rate of married dropouts. The rate of police contact for all employed dropouts is higher than for unemployed drop-outs; however, this is due primarily to the large number of married and unemployed females who have very limited involvements with the police.

An analysis employing self-reported delin-quent behavior revealed relationships similar to the ones observed with the police contact mea-sure. Marriage again appeared to be a more im-portant variable than employment; the mean self-reported delinquency score of those in the unmarried category was more than two and one-half times the score of married dropouts. This difference was found for both male and female dropouts. It also appears that un-employment is associated with higher levels of self-reported delinquency for married and un-married males, as well as for unmarried females. In no case are these employment differences as large as the ones observed for married and un-married dropouts. The number of cases is small, but the relationships are similar whether self-report or police contact data are employed, and

this consistency lends credence to the general finding.

SUMMARY

Analyzing the effect of dropout on delinquency, we find that dropouts consistently have higher police contact rates; than graduates for every period they are in school, and these rates in-crease with time while they are in school. How-ever, the police contact rate systematically de-clines in the period after which dropout occurs, and it continues to decline in subsequent time periods. In the later periods the rates are sub-stantially lower than the rates for graduates. Use of the self-report measure produces similar findings. The dropouts reach a high level of in-volvement in delinquency prior to leaving school, but once they are out of school, their involvement in serious offenses declines sub-stantially, and the total number of offenses re-ported declines slightly. In comparison, graduates report an increasing number of de-linquent acts, as well as serious offenses, with time. Whether delinquency is measured in terms of police contacts or self-reports, similar patterns are revealed. The rates of delinquency for those out of school are no greater—and pos-sibly lower—than the rates for students in school. The relationship between delinquency and dropout cannot be explained by class or sex differences among dropouts and graduates or by differential visibility.

The expected relationship between delin-quency and dropout is observed; delinquency increases the probability of dropout, which in turn decreases the probability of delinquency. This causal sequence is supported with mea-sures of delinquency based on police contacts and self reports. For each study period the probability of dropout is more than two times higher for those who experienced police contact than for subjects with no police contact. Exten-sive involvement in delinquent behavior, whether or not it leads to official action, in-creases the probability of dropout.

The dropouts' out-of-school experiences with respect to marriage and employment are related to their involvement in delinquency. With marriage and employment, the dropout makes the transition from adolescence into conventional adult roles. It is this factor, we suggest, that accounts for the general decline in the dropouts' rates of delinquent behavior. This interpretation is consistent with the finding that marriage is a more significant deterrent for delinquency than employment, since marriage is a less ambiguous indicator of adult status than employment, particularly when sporadic and part-time employment to some extent characterize student roles.

The employment-delinquency relationship is more complex than the association between marriage and delinquency. Unemployed males and unmarried females have consistently higher police contact and self-reported rates of delinquency. For married females, the opposite is true, girls with jobs have higher rates than unemployed females. In part, then, the lower rates of delinquency observed among dropouts may be attributed to changes in marital and employment status that follow dropout.

REFERENCES

Bachman, J. G., S. Green, and I. D. Wirtanen
1971   *Youth in Transition, Volume III: Dropping Out—Problem or Symptom.* Ann Arbor, Mich.: Institute for Social Research.

Cervantes, L. F.
1965   *The Dropout.* Ann Arbor, Mich.: University of Michigan Press.

Cloward R., and L. E. Ohlin
1960   *Delinquency and Opportunity: A Theory of Delinquent Gangs.* Glencoe, Ill.: Free Press.

Davis, J. A.
1963   Panel analysis: Techniques and concepts in the interpretation of repeated measurements. Unpublished monograph. Chicago: University of Chicago National Opinion Research.

Elliott, D. S.
1961   Delinquency, opportunity and patterns of orientations. Unpublished Ph.D. dissertation. Seattle: University of Washington.
1966   "Delinquency, school attendance and dropout." *Social Problems, 13:* 307–314.

Gold, M.
1963   *Status Forces in Delinquent Boys.* Ann Arbor, Mich.: University of Michigan.

Haskell, M. R., and L. Yablonsky
1970   *Crime and Delinquency.* Chicago: Rand McNally and Company.

Hathaway, S. R., and E. D. Monachesi
1963   *Adolescent Personality and Behavior.* Minneapolis: University of Minnesota Press.

Hathaway, S. R., P. Reynolds, and E. D. Monachesi
1969   "Follow-up of the later careers and lives of 1,000 boys who dropped out of high school." *Journal of Consulting and Clinical Psychology, 33:*370–380.

Havighurst, R. J.
1963   "Research on the school work-study program in the prevention of juvenile delinquency." In William R. Carriker (Ed.). Washington, D.C.: U.S. Government Printing Office.

Jeffery, C. R., and I. A. Jeffery
1970   "Delinquents and dropouts: An experimental program in behavior change." *Canadian Journal of Corrections, 12:*47–58.

Kitsuse, J. I., and A. V. Cicourel
1963   "A note on the use of official statistics." *Social Problems, 11* (Fall):131–139.

Krane, S.
1976   School dropout: A response to aspiration opportunity discrepancy? Unpublished monograph. Boulder: University of Colorado (June).

Schafer, W. E., and K. Polk
1967   "Delinquency and the schools." In President's Commission on Law Enforcement and Administration of Justice, Juvenile Delinquency and Youth Crime. Washington, D.C.: U.S. Government Printing Office, pp. 222–277.

Schafer, W. F., and R. D. Knudten
  1970   *Juvenile Delinquency.* New York: Random House.

Schreiber, D.
  1963a   "The dropout and the delinquency." *Phi Delta Kappa, 44:*215–221.
  1963b   "Juvenile delinquency and the school dropout problem." *Federal Probation, 27:*15–19.

Short, J. F., Jr., and F. I. Nye
  1957–58   "Reported behavior as a criterion of deviant behavior." *Social Problems, 5:*207–213.

Short, J. F.
  1958   "Extent of unrecorded juvenile delinquency: Tentative Conclusions." *Journal of Criminal Law, Criminology, and Police Science, 49:*296–302.

Simpson, J. E., and M. D. Van Arsdol, Jr.
  1957   "Residential history and educational status of delinquents and non-delinquents." *Social Problems, 15:*25–40.

43. Hellfire and Delinquency

TRAVIS HIRSCHI
RODNEY STARK

FROM TIME TO TIME JUDGES ADVISE JUVENILE OF-
fenders to attend church for periods of months
or years. Such "sentences" are not intended as
punishment.[1] Because the judge assumes that
religious training and commitment produce
moral character, he assumes such attendance
may lead to repentance and reform. This view is
widespread in law enforcement circles. As J.
Edgar Hoover tells us:

"Invariably when you analyze the reasons for such
[criminal] actions, certain facts stand out stark and
revealing—the faith of our fathers, the love of God,
and the observance of His Commandments have
either been thrust aside or they never existed in the
heart of the individual transgressor . . ." (Coogan,
1954).

It is hardly surprising that this position is
supported by clergymen. Religious leaders traditionally blame "rising crime and immorality" on
a decline in religious conviction, and many
argue that religious commitment is the *only* secure basis for moral behavior. In the writings of
religious scholars, again and again we encounter
the same syllogism:

"Most acts of delinquency are amoral, and the roots
of morality are either principally or exclusively religious. Delinquents, therefore, should be lower than
nondelinquents in religiosity or religiousness"
(Cortes, 1965:122).

Such notions are congruent with the social
scientific view that religious sanctioning systems
play an important role in ensuring and maintaining conformity to social norms (Davis,
1948:73–74, 371–373). Drawing heavily on the
work of Emile Durkheim, the way in which religion performs this role is usually summarized as
follows (Yinger, 1957): (1) through its belief system values; (2) through its rituals it reinforces
commitment to these values; (3) through its system religion legitimates social and individual
values; (2) through its rituals it reinforces commitment to these values; (3) through its system
of eternal rewards and punishment, religion
helps to insure the embodiment of values in actual behavior.

It is hard to challenge the idea that persons
often do have internalized ethics which sometimes govern their actions. But does religion, at
least in contemporary society, have much to do
with developing or sustaining such personal
ethics? Indeed, is the Christian sanctioning system of hellfire for sinners and heavenly glory
for the just, able to deter unlawful behavior
even among those who are firm believers?

By implication these questions bear on present concerns over the relevance of religion in
modern life. Many clergymen have come to
doubt the ability of the faith to move men on

▶SOURCE: *"Hellfire and Delinquency," Social Problems (Fall
1969), 17(2): 202–213. Reprinted by permission.*

[1]However, Hager (1957) reports that the judge's advice
may in effect become a requirement and nonattendance
considered a violation of probation or parole.

moral questions. These doubts have arisen mainly around such matters as prejudice, peace, poverty, and various political abominations. However, the relation between religiousness and delinquency seems to offer an especially critical test of the relevance of religion. For if religion proves immaterial here, in an area where it has always concentrated its efforts to influence the ways in which men act, then its failure would seem acute. Evidence on this question is mixed. Against the pronouncements of the theoretical sociologists, the lawman, the layman, and the clergy, a few criminologists have stood firm. In their view, the allegedly intimate connection between religiosity and noncriminality is not obvious. Teeters (1952:41) only slightly overstates the position of this group when he writes:

"If there are any studies whatsoever that show up the value of religious training as a deterrent to crime, delinquency, immorality, or unethical conduct, this writer has never seen them."[2]

But there is by no means unanimity on this point among criminologists, and the usual problems arise when one attempts to reach a firm conclusion from past research. Much of this research does not meet minimum standards of adequacy: for example, many of the studies cited in typical review articles do not even have comparison groups (see Powers, 1967). But there is a further and somewhat unusual problem: interestingly enough, accusations of bias, either for or against religion, are common.[3] And, indeed, there does seem to be a relation between the findings and the religiosity of the researcher. While most studies conducted by criminologists suggest that religion has little or no effect, research by re-

ligionists tends to indicate that religion is just what it has always been thought to be, a powerful "aid to the sword" in the maintenance of conformity, a factor in delinquency at least equal to the variables traditionally considered important by criminologists.[4]

Given these conflicting claims, given the sociological view of the functions of religious institutions, and given the more narrowly practical question of the relevance of religion to man's day-to-day behavior, we propose to examine again the question of the relation between religiosity and delinquency.

SAMPLE AND DATA

The sample on which our study is based was drawn from students entering the public junior and senior high schools of Western Contra Costa County, California, in the Fall of 1964. This population was stratified by race, sex, school, and grade, and random samples drawn from each substratum.[5] Of the 5,545 students drawn in the original sample, 4,077 or 74 percent eventually completed a lengthy questionnaire.[6] School records on the entire original

---

[2]Teeters is replying to Coogan (1952) who takes criminologists to task for ignoring the impact of religion.

[3]"There seems to be a bias in favor of religious influence as an aid to good behavior whenever the investigator is a religious leader" (Powers, 1967:196). Compare: "Many research persons are . . . definitely anti-religious in their approach to the crime problem" (Elliott, 1952:835). For expansion of the latter view, see Coogan (1952).

[4]". . . the difference in religiosity was extremely significant. There was no other variable which discriminated better between (delinquents and nondelinquents); (Cortes 1965:123). See also Travers and Davis (1961).

[5]Sampling was disproportionate by race and sex: 85 percent of Negro boys, 60 percent of Negro girls, 30 percent of white boys, and 12 percent of white girls were selected. These percentages were selected in each grade in all schools except where the sampling fraction would not produce at least 25 students in each school, in which case the entire population of the school was included. When race and sex are held constant, as in the present analysis, the original sample is therefore unbiased—except for a very slight overrepresentation of Negroes from predominantly white schools.

[6]In previous analyses of these data, adjustment has been made for differences among the substrata in the proportion actually completing the questionnaire. Such weighting procedures were not available for the present analysis. In most cases, however, comparison with previous results is possible, and the conclusions do not differ from one procedure to the other.

sample, and police records on all boys in the original sample are also available.[7]

Measures of Delinquency

Delinquency was measured both by self-reports and by examination of police records. The self report index of delinquency was constructed from these items:

1. Have you ever taken little things (worth less than $2) that did not belong to you?

2. Have you ever taken things of some value (between $2 and $50) that did not belong to you?

3. Have you ever taken things of large value (worth over $50) that did not belong to you?

4. Have you ever taken a car for a ride without the owner's permission?

5. Have you ever banged up something that did not belong to you on purpose?

6. Not counting fights you may have had with a brother or sister, have you ever beaten up on anyone or hurt anyone on purpose?

All of these acts are violations of law. In legal terms, they represent petty and grand larceny, auto theft, vandalism, and assault. Since the students reported when they had committed each of the acts listed, index scores were constructed simply by counting the number of separate offenses the student had committed in the year prior to administration of the questionnaire. The measure of official delinquency is a count of the number of offenses known to the police over the period of about three years prior to examination of police records. Among white boys, the correlation between the self-report and official measures is .27. Rather than concern ourselves with the relative validity of these

measures, we shall conduct parallel analyses using both the self-report and official measures of delinquency.

Measures of Religiosity

If delinquency research is subject to dismissal on the ground that its findings bear only tangentially on the real phenomenon of delinquency, research on religiosity is doubly vulnerable to this charge. We shall not here be concerned with what religiosity really is. Instead, we shall take for granted the view that religiosity is many things; that these things should not be inextricably bound to each other by definition, but may be linked to each other by conjecture and hypothesis (Stark and Glock, 1968:11–21).

The usual beginning point in studies of the effects of religion on delinquency is a measure of church attendance. In our opinion, this is as it should be. The view that church attendance should reduce delinquency is accepted by sociologists, layman, and the clergy, not because it keeps the child off the streets for a few hours each week, but because participation in religious activities is believed to promote: (1) the internalization and/or acceptance of moral values, the belief that one's fellows deserve fair and just treatment; (2) acceptance of the legitimacy of legal authority, of the law and its agents; (3) belief in the literal existence of a supernatural world, and therefore the belief that one may be punished in the world to come for violations in the here and now.

We begin by examining the effects of church attendance on the attitudes and beliefs that in this view *link* such attendance to conformity with conventional codes of conduct.

RELIGION AND MORAL VALUES

Sociological theorists have been generally unwilling to see in delinquency evidence of immorality. In fact, sociologists have become so leery of "morality" as a concept that they are likely to stress the view that "illegality" and "immorality" are not the same thing, and, by extension, have

---

[7]All of which gives unusually detailed information on the extent of non-response bias in the questionnaire sample. For analysis of the extent and effect of nonresponse bias, see Wilson (1965:3–21) and Hirschi (1969:41–46).

little to do with one another. The clergyman, in contrast, has remained steadfast in the belief that morality and delinquency are intimately related, that most illegal acts are also immoral, and that the church has therefore an important role to play in the prevention of delinquency. Therefore, we must first ask: Is church attendance related to morality as the latter is traditionally defined by the church?

Two items on the questionnaire seem particularly appropriate as measures of morality. The students were asked whether they agreed or disagreed with these statements:

To get ahead, you have to do some things that are not right.

Suckers deserve to be taken advantage of.

Table I shows the relations between these items and church attendance. Although seven of the eight relations are in the direction favoring the view that attendance at religious services promotes acceptance of moral values, in all cases but one the relations are miniscule. For all intents and purposes, then, church attendance does not affect acceptance of the moral values assumed to be important deterrents of delinquency. Stu-

Table I. Percent Accepting Amoral Statements, by Church Attendance, Race, and Sex

Suckers deserve to be taken advantage of

| | Church Attendance | | | | | |
	Once a Week	2-3 Times a Month	Once Month— Holidays	Hardly Ever	Never	Gamma[a]
White boys	25 (610)	29 (187)	30 (220)	27 (360)	32 (211)	−.04
Negro boys	43 (525)	41 (191)	43 (121)	53 (124)	40 (40)	−.03
White girls	16 (363)	17 (82)	23 (79)	19 (115)	19 (36)	−.03
Negro girls	36 (541)	37 (147)	46 (46)	25 (60)	32 (19)	.01

To get ahead, you have to do some things that are not right

White boys	26 (610)	30 (187)	35 (220)	28 (360)	35 (211)	−.08
Negro boys	49 (525)	48 (191)	60 (121)	50 (124)	52 (40)	−.04
White girls	20 (363)	18 (82)	16 (79)	24 (115)	31 (36)	−.09
Negro girls	31 (541)	38 (147)	28 (46)	57 (60)	58 (19)	−.14[b]

[a]In all tables presented, gamma was computed before the table was collapsed to its present form. For example, there were originally three categories of response to "Suckers deserve to be taken advantage of"—agree, undecided, disagree. The double- and triple-negative problems make straightforward interpretation of the sign of the relation difficult. In the tables on this page, the minus sign means literally that as non-attendance increases agreement with the statement declines.

[b]χ^2 significant at one percent level.

dents who attend church are as likely as nonattenders to believe that those unable to defend themselves from exploitation deserve such exploitation; they are as likely to believe that success in worldly terms requires, and by implication justifies, the breaking of the moral law.

RELIGION AND ACCEPTANCE OF WORLDLY AUTHORITY

Sutherland has said that persons become criminal because of an excess of definitions favorable to violation of law (Sutherland and Cressey, 1960:78). Although Sutherland did not specify the content of these attitudes and values conducive to law violation, attitudes toward the law itself and toward the agents of the legal system, especially the police, are obviously relevant. Once again, then, we are led to expect a relation between religiosity and non-criminality, for the religious-moral laws advocated by the churches are largely incorporated in legal restraints. Most crimes, in other words, are also violations of the teachings of the church (Elliott, 1952:364). Furthermore, the churches strongly encourage respect for the law and cooperation with legal authorities.

The items used to determine the efficacy of the church in promoting such respect are straightforward. Students were asked to respond to the following statements:

It is all right to get around the law if you can get away with it.

I have a lot of respect for the (local) police.

Table II shows that students who attend church frequently are very slightly more likely than infrequent attenders to express respect for the police, and are slightly less likely to agree

Table II. Respect for Law and Respect for the Police by Church Attendance, Race, and Sex

Percent Agreeing All Right To Get Around The Law	Church Attendance					
	Once a Week	2-3 Times a Month	Once Month— Holidays	Hardly Ever	Never	Gamma
White boys	10	8	18	9	17	−.13[a]
	(542)	(179)	(211)	(343)	(207)	
Negro boys	21	20	28	32	28	−.10
	(407)	(169)	(105)	(102)	(36)	
White girls	6	6	7	5	3	−.09
	(333)	(78)	(75)	(112)	(31)	
Negro girls	18	20	35	20	47	−.22[a]
Percent expressing Respect for the Police						
White boys	65	63	62	60	49	.09[a]
	(610)	(187)	(220)	(360)	(211)	
Negro boys	62	65	56	49	37	.09[a]
	(525)	(191)	(121)	(124)	(40)	
White girls	73	76	62	69	56	.08
	(363)	(82)	(79)	(115)	(36)	
Negro girls	65	62	67	62	52	.05
	(541)	(147)	(46)	(60)	(19)	

[a]Significant at the five percent level (χ^2).

that law violation is okay if you don't get caught. Seven of the eight relations are in the direction predicted from the assumption that exposure to religious teachings fosters acceptance of the legitimacy of worldly authority. In this case, four of the seven relations are statistically significant. We would conclude, then, on the basis of these data, that church attendance has some, very weak, effect on the development of attitudes apparently favorable to obedience to law.[8]

RELIGION AND SUPERNATURAL SANCTIONS

Sociologists are as likely as churchmen to stress the fear of supernatural sanctions in the maintenance of conformity. According to Ross (1920:131), for example, Christianity has made the doctrine of a future life "a deterrent influence of the strongest kind." The idea is simple: In the life beyond death, the lot of each man will be at least in part determined by his thoughts and actions during his worldly existence. Since crimes unseen by worldly authorities are seen by watchers in another world, the fear of hell operates silently and efficiently to assure conformity to conventional, worldly norms.

It would appear obvious that participation in organized religious activities contributes to belief in the existence of a life beyond death populated by spirits or persons capable of punishing one for wrongdoings while on earth. Since we have already seen cases where obvious relations were nonexistent, however, in Table III we show the relation between church attendance and an index of belief in supernatural sanctions. The index was constructed from responses to two items: "There is a life beyond death," and, "The devil actually exists." Among all groups

except Negro girls (where belief in the devil and a life beyond death is common even among those who do not attend church) differences by church attendance are marked. Those attending church with some frequency are much more likely to believe in the literal existence of a supernatural realm than those only rarely attending church.

To this point we have examined three presumed consequences or correlates of religious activity thought by many to be important in the prevention of delinquency. One of the three routes by which religion might affect delinquency has been to all intents and purposes closed: those attending church are no more likely than those not attending church to accept moral and ethical principles opposed to the commission of illegal acts.[9] A second possible route from religiosity to nondelinquency remains only partially open: students attending church are only slightly more likely to have attitudes favorable to law and the police. If religiosity does affect delinquency, its major path of influence must be through its effect on belief in the existence of other-worldly sanctions, for it is only here that differences by church attendance are in any way pronounced.

We have seen the effect of church attendance on the variables through which it presumably affects delinquency. Are those variables themselves actually related to delinquency? According to Table IV, that set of variables unrelated to church attendance, which we have called measures of acceptance of moral values, *is* indeed related to delinquency. Students agreeing that suckers deserve what they get, that in order to achieve success in life one must occasionally sacrifice what one considers right, are much more likely than students disagreeing with these

---

[8]Other analysis shows that respect for the law and for the police decline rather markedly with age in the present sample. Although church attendance also declines with age, the relations in Table II survive when age is held relatively constant.

[9]The lack of relationship between church attendance and moral and ethical principles in these data is supported by the more general finding that commitment to the tenets of Christian ethicalism, such as "Love thy neighbor" or "Do good unto others," is not related to commitment to Christian orthodoxy, or to church attendance, praying, or participation in church activities. See: Stark and Glock (1968) Ch. 9.

Table III. Percent High on Index of Belief in Supernatural Sanctions by Church Attendance, Race, and Sex

| | Church Attendance | | | | | |
	Once a Week	2-3 Times a Month	Once Month— Holidays	Hardly Ever	Never	Gamma
White boys	49 (505)	28 (162)	23 (194)	19 (334)	12 (187)	−.40
Negro boys	50 (357)	34 (149)	30 (98)	21 (94)	32 (31)	−.30
White girls	49 (327)	34 (79)	23 (74)	19 (108)	31 (32)	−.34
Negro girls	42 (447)	40 (126)	36 (39)	42 (50)	53 (15)	−.07

statements to have committed delinquent acts, by both self-report and by official measures.

According to Table V, respect for the law and for the police, while only weakly related to church attendance, are both strongly negatively related to the commission of delinquent acts, again by both the self-report and official measures, and within all race-sex categories.

But when we turn to the one intervening variable strongly influenced by church attendance, the pattern reverses: *Students who believe in the Devil and in a life after death are just as likely to commit delinquent acts as are students who do not believe in a supernatural world* (as Table VI shows).

On the basis of what we know, then, there is very little reason to expect a relation between religious activity and delinquency. The beliefs such activity affects are essentially unrelated to delinquency; the beliefs and attitudes the church has been traditionally assumed to affect are in fact strongly related to delinquency, but, alas for the church, it does not influence these beliefs and attitudes. And, indeed, Table VII shows that church attendance is essentially unrelated to delinquency. *Students who attend church every week are as likely to have committed delinquent acts as students who attend church only rarely or not at all.* None of the relations in Table VII approaches statistical significance. None of the dif-

ferences is of theoretical or practical significance, nor were they affected by denominational controls. Participation in religious activities and belief in a supernatural sanctioning system have no effect on delinquent activity.

Further evidence for the same conclusion is provided by the lack of a relation between the mother's church attendance and delinquency, by the absence of important differences between those students who belong to a church and those who do not, and by the fact that the several measures of religiosity are unrelated to yet another form of unethical conduct, cheating on tests— thus replicating a finding that goes back almost forty years (Hartshorne and May, 1930:357–362).

DISCUSSION

There are, of course, studies showing weak relations between church attendance and nondelinquency. In fact, two of the most respected pieces of research in the field, those of Nye (1958:35–36) and of the Gluecks (1950:166–167) show that children who attend church regularly are somewhat less likely than nonattenders to be delinquent. If we grant that Nye's and the Gluecks' data are as good as our own, it may appear that we have contributed merely to the inconsistency and inconclusiveness

Table IV. Percent Committing Two or More Delinquent Acts by Acceptance of Moral Values

Suckers deserve to be taken advantage of

	Agree	Undecided	Disagree	Gamma
White boys (SR)[a]	30	22	12	−.27
	(440)	(324)	(824)	
Negro boys (SR)	26	28	17	−.12
	(230)	(217)	(319)	
White girls (SR)	11	3	5	−.03
	(74)	(131)	(411)	
Negro girls (SR)	14	6	7	−.21
	(174)	(179)	(328)	
White boys (Off)[b]	12	10	6	−.20
	(440)	(324)	(824)	
Negro boys (Off)	23	23	15	−.17
	(240)	(231)	(330)	

To get ahead, you have to do some things that are not right

	Agree	Undecided	Disagree	Gamma
White boys (SR)[a]	27	26	13	−.26
	(468)	(264)	(856)	
Negro boys (SR)	26	28	17	−.12
	(254)	(159)	(327)	
White girls (SR)	11	11	3	−.29
	(71)	(103)	(429)	
Negro girls (SR)	10	10	6	−.14
	(154)	(135)	(388)	
White boys (Off)[b]	12	11	7	−.18
	(468)	(264)	(856)	
Negro boys (Off)	22	22	18	−.09
	(259)	(162)	(333)	

[a]Self-reported delinquent acts.
[b]Official delinquent acts. The police records of girls were not available.

of delinquency research. In our opinion such a conclusion is not warranted. Neither Nye nor the Gluecks report anything beyond the fact of a small relation. Had they attempted to determine why church attendance is or is not related to delinquency in their samples, as we have done, they might very well have concluded that church attendance is not in fact *causally* related to delinquency. The fact that there are many reasons to expect a causal relation between church attendance and delinquency is not sufficient reason to accept an observed relation without further analysis.

This touches on a problem endemic in evaluations of social science research. Had our investigation shown that religion is a deterrent to delinquency, we would have been accused of demonstrating the obvious. But the point in testing

Table V. Percent Committing Two or More Delinquent Acts
by Respect for the Police and Respect for Law

It is all right to get around the law if you can get away with it

	Agree	Undecided	Disagree	Gamma
White boys (SR)	44	29	13	−.41
	(177)	(259)	(1081)	
Negro boys (SR)	33	27	16	−.18
	(208)	(181)	(477)	
White girls (SR)	18	12	4	−.42
	(38)	(76)	(528)	
Negro girls (SR)	15	9	5	−.25
	(154)	(136)	(458)	
White boys (Off)	16	12	7	−.33
	(183)	(264)	(1089)	
Negro boys (Off)	27	19	17	−.22
	(212)	(187)	(482)	

I have a lot of respect for the Richmond police

	Agree	Undecided	Disagree	Gamma
White boys (SR)	13	23	39	.34
	(969)	(396)	(223)	
Negro boys (SR)	15	32	33	.26
	(463)	(219)	(183)	
White girls (SR)	4	9	14	.32
	(450)	(156)	(42)	
Negro girls (SR)	6	7	15	.16
	(460)	(152)	(137)	
White boys (Off)	5	10	22	.33
	(969)	(396)	(223)	
Negro boys (Off)	17	19	30	.19
	(472)	(222)	(187)	

common sense notions is demonstrated by the fact that this one, as with many others, is simply wrong. Unfortunately, when social science reports against common sense, it is too often accused of falsehood, inadequate methods, or plain stupidity. Whenever one does research on religion this problem becomes especially acute. A common response from religionists to findings they dislike is to dismiss them by redefining relgiousness in a way that excludes all culpability (Stark and Glock, 1968: Ch. 1). Thus, some will be prompted to respond that delin-

quency *is* irreligiosity, and that no *truly* religious youths commit delinquent acts. Such assertions are irrefutable, for they are true by definition. But, if one grants that religiousness has several components, and that they are capable of varying to some extent independently of each other, then we may conclude on the basis of these data that such central aspects of religiosity as attendance at religious services and belief in the existence of a supernatural world are unrelated to the legality or, for that matter, the morality of behavior.

Table VI. Percent Committing Two or More Delinquent Acts, by Belief in Existence of Other-worldly Sanctions, Race, and Sex

	Index of Belief in Supernatural Sanctions			
	Low	*Medium*	*High*	*Gamma*
White boys (SR)	19 (320)	20 (641)	16 (425)	−.03
Negro boys (SR)	19 (91)	21 (363)	25 (300)	.09
White girls (SR)	7 (127)	5 (257)	5 (234)	.11
Negro girls (SR)	11 (81)	8 (314)	8 (275)	−.07
White boys (Off)	8 (329)	9 (660)	8 (433)	.02
Negro boys (Off)	16 (99)	22 (379)	17 (312)	−.07

Table VII. Percent Committing Two or More Delinquent Acts by Church Attendance, Race, and Sex

	Church Attendance					
	Once a Week	*2-3 Times a Month*	*Once Month— Holidays*	*Hardly Ever*	*Never*	*Gamma*
White boys (SR)	17 (545)	21 (186)	23 (210)	20 (346)	22 (206)	.02
Negro boys (SR)	22 (424)	24 (172)	21 (112)	25 (114)	40 (38)	.10
White girls (SR)	5 (337)	5 (79)	8 (79)	4 (112)	15 (34)	.01
Negro girls (SR)	7 (488)	10 (137)	19 (43)	10 (59)	6 (18)	.11
White boys (Off)	7 (554)	6 (187)	13 (220)	9 (360)	11 (211)	.06
Negro boys (Off)	19 (445)	22 (191)	18 (121)	24 (124)	25 (40)	.08

This, of course, does not say anything about the prevailing level of law-abiding behavior or morality in American society. On the contrary, the roots of morality, of law-abiding conduct are probably much the same as they have always been: attachment to, or, if you will, love for one's neighbor and awareness of and concern for the real-life costs of crime. The church is irrelevant to delinquency because it fails to instill in its members love for their neighbors and because belief in the possibility of pleasure and pain in another world cannot now, and perhaps never could, compete with the pleasures and pains of everyday life.

REFERENCES

Coogan, John E.
1952   " 'The Myth Mind' in an engineer's world."
        Federal Probation 16 (March): 26–30.
1954   "Religion a preventive of delinquency."
        Federal Probation 18 (December): 25–29.

Cortes, Juan B.
1965   "Juvenile delinquency: A biosocial ap-
        proach." Pp. 114–155 in Angelo D'Agos-
        tino (ed.), Family, Church, and Commun-
        ity. New York: P. J. Kenedy.

Davis, Kingsley
1948   Human Society. New York: Macmillan.

Elliott, Mable A.
1952   Crime in Modern Society. New York:
        Harper.

Glueck, Sheldon, and Eleanor
1950   Unraveling Juvenile Delinquency. Cam-
        bridge: Harvard, University Press.

Hager, Don J.
1957   "Religion, delinquency, and Society." Social
        Work 2 (July): 16–21.

Hartshorne, Hugh, and Mark A. May
1930   Studies in Deceit. New York: Macmillan.

Hirschi, Travis
1969   Causes of Delinquency. Berkeley: Univer-
        sity of California Press

Nye, F. Ivan
1958   Family Relationships and Delinquent Be-
        havior. New York: Wiley

Powers, George Edward
1967   "Prevention through religion." Pp. 99–127
        in William E. Amos and Charles F. Wellford
        (eds), Delinquency Prevention: Theory and
        Practice. New York: Prentice Hall.

Ross, Edward A.
1920   Social Control. New York: Macmillan.

Stark, Rodney, and Charles Y. Glock
1968   American Piety: The Nature of Religious
        Commitment. Berkeley: University of
        California Press.

Sutherland, Edwin H., and Donald R. Cressey
1960   Principles of Criminology. Philadelphia: J.
        B. Lippincott.

Teeters, Negley K.
1952   "Reply": Federal Probation 16 (September):
        41.

Travers, John F., and Russel G. Davis
1961   "A study of religious motivation and delin-
        quency." Journal of Educational Sociology
        34 (January): 205–220.

Wilson, Alan B. et al.
1965   Technical Report #1: Secondary School
        Survey. Berkeley: Survey Research Center.

Yinger, J. Milton
1957   Religion, Society and the Individual. New
        York: Macmillan.

44. Television Violence and Children

SURGEON-GENERAL'S SCIENTIFIC ADVISORY COMMITTEE ON TELEVISION AND SOCIAL BEHAVIOR

THE FACT THAT YOUNG CHILDREN EXTENSIVELY view television raises important questions about the role this medium plays in the child's life. Television can be a major force in teaching the child about the complexities of the world around him. Indeed, some producers of television drama claim that they attempt to depict many aspects of life—its problems, happiness and joy, sadness and violence. However, while most people recognize television's potential for providing the child with a broad range of experiences, there is much public concern about the possible harmful effects of television entertainment. This concern focuses on the possibility that particular aspects of television viewing will overstimulate the child, lead to disturbed sleep and nightmares, or incite the child to aggressive behavior. For example, the National Center for Health Statistics reports that a survey of the parents of approximately 7,000 children between the ages of six and 11 years indicates that the sleep disturbances of more than one out of four children are considered by the parents to be related to television and radio programs (Roberts and Baird, 1971).

In addition, many teachers of young children, especially at the nursery school level, suggest that television viewing may have negative as well as positive aspects. While recognizing its poten-

tial for entertainment and cultural enrichment, they feel that television viewing may be a "cop-out on learning." Their view is consonant with early beliefs on the parts of some researchers that television may reduce creative or productive activities (Maccoby, 1951). Later studies indicate that the relationship between very heavy viewing and low interest in other activities may be a manifestation of preexisting personality and familial factors in the heavy viewer, and may constitute "a vicious circle" in which these factors lead to heavy viewing which in turn reduces the child's contacts with others (Himmelweit et al., 1958).

For convenience, one can differentiate between the general effects television may have on the child's intellectual and emotional life and television's more specific impact on the child's aggressive behavior. This chapter attempts to summarize and interpret the available experimental evidence on the impact of televised violence on children.

If viewing televised violence leads to an increase in the viewer's aggressive behavior, it may do so either by "teaching" novel aggressive acts which can be learned and *imitated* or by *instigating* aggressive behaviors which have previously been learned. Studies on the imitation of aggressive behavior usually focus on identifying the stimulus conditions under which a child will mimic or copy the behavior that he has just observed on television or in real life. Research on the instigation of aggressive behavior assesses

▶SOURCE: *Television and Growing Up: The Impact of Televised Violence. Washington, D.C.: National Institute of Mental Health*, 1971, pp. 61–73, 211–230. (*Editorial adaptations.*)

the postviewing incidence of any aggressive behaviors, not just those which mimic the behavior the child has previously viewed.

IMITATION OF MEDIA VIOLENCE

A child may acquire a new item of behavior through attentive observation. Rehearsal or practice of this new skill increases his competence. If the initial attempts are rewarded or encouraged, the child is likely to continue to perform the newly acquired behavior. If they are punished, he is less likely to persist, especially while he is under the surveillance of the punisher. Observation, imitation, then practice is a common sequence through which new behaviors enter the child's repertoire.

Throughout human history, very young children have been able to learn from imitating the behavior of others in their presence. These others might be members of the household, friends of the family, neighbors, playmates, teachers, priests, etc. With the advent of the modern pictorial media of communication, children can now also see the behavior of individuals who are not personally present but whose images are conveyed via film or television. We use the term "models" for individuals whose behavior children can observe and thus imitate, whether these individuals are personally in the child's presence or are observed by him through the media.

The child with a television set in his own home has the opportunity to observe the behavior of many diverse models. In forming impressions of how adult males normally behave, for example, the young boy of today may rely not only on observing the behavior of his father and his uncles, the repairman and deliveryman who come to his house, his doctor, and other men in his life, but also on observing television newscasters, comedians, actors, musicians, and cowboys in westerns, and so forth. The very young child today is exposed to more different models of masculine behavior than any child in human history, in part because of the television set in his home.

Because psychologists have been concerned with the amount of aggression and violence available to children in the mass media (and particularly on television) and with the possibility that youngsters will imitate this aggression in their own behavior, many experiments have studied children's copying of aggressive behavior. Typically in these experiments, one film shows distinctive and novel aggressive behaviors, while another film—similar in length, use of color, identity of the actors, and the character of the situation—does not feature aggressive behavior. The different children who watch the two films are then compared for their aggressive behaviors in sessions conducted after the showing of the films. Careful records are made of the acts which do or do not mimic the distinctive aggressive behaviors just displayed in one of the films but not the other.

Albert Bandura pioneered studies of this sort over ten years ago. Since the publication of his original work (e.g., Bandura and Walters, 1963; Bandura, Ross, and Ross, 1961), many psychologists in the United States and abroad have conducted similar experiments. There are now about 20 different published experiments concerned with children's imitation of filmed aggression shown on a movie or television screen. All of these studies demonstrate that young children can, and under some circumstances do, imitate what they observe on television or in films. Whether they actually do imitate depends on many factors, including inhibition, social pressures, and socially approved role models. The fact that children can mimic film-mediated aggressive behavior is perhaps the best-documented finding in the research literature on the effects of the pictorial media.

Many other experiments show children's imitation of other kinds of behavior. Some of these show copying of film-mediated behavior, while others show mimicking of a live person. These experiments buttress the findings of the many studies directly concerned with aggression. Psychologists generally consider quite convincing the evidence that children can readily learn many kinds of behavior, including aggressive actions, by attentively watching those behaviors being modeled by persons in their presence, on film, or on television. In this vein, after reviewing the literature, Weiss (1969) pointed out that "there is little doubt that, by displaying forms of aggression or modes of criminal and violent behavior, the media are 'teaching' and people are 'learning.'"

MEDIA INSTIGATION OF AGGRESSIVE BEHAVIOR

The distinction between imitation and instigation is crucial to a precise understanding of the influence television may exert on the behavior of the viewer. In the previous section we summarized prior research on the imitation of acts portrayed on television or in films.

The new research in this program was commissioned after the phenomenon of imitation of aggressive behavior portrayed on film had been well demonstrated. These new studies do not concentrate on adducing additional evidence for it, though other new studies will undoubtedly provide further documentation of this phenomenon. Rather, current research focuses on the conditions under which children *will* carry out the aggressive behavior we already know they *can* imitate. Given that children can imitate the aggressive behavior they observe, what are the inhibiting or disinhibiting factors that make it more or less likely they will do so? In this section we will review the findings of recent research which bear on the issue of television's role in stimulating or instigating antisocial aggressive behavior in children.

During the past decade, a large number of studies have examined television's role in facilitating or encouraging aggressive behavior. Many of these studies deal with aggression in children; another sizable group focuses on the aggressive behavior of older youth and adults. The results of approximately 30 previously published experiments have been widely interpreted as supporting the thesis that children or adults who view violence in either films or television programs are more likely to behave in an aggressive or violent manner than those who do not view such fare (Baker and Ball, 1969). However, some reviewers have questioned this interpretation and suggest that additional research is needed before the question of the impact of televised violence can be answered (Singer, 1971; Weiss, 1969).

Five reports in this research program focus on television's role in the instigation of aggressive behavior: Stein and Friedrich (1971); Feshbach (1971); Liebert and Baron (1971); Ekman et al. (1971); and Leifer and Roberts (1971). The ten separate studies reported by these authors differ in terms of the subjects and specific research procedures. However, the general research paradigm is similar in each study. The typical procedure is to show one group of children films or television programs that contain a number of violent episodes, while another group views relatively nonviolent material. Subsequently, each child is placed in a setting where his behavior may be observed. The specific types of aggressive behavior differed from one study to another, and were not restricted to the mimicking or copying of what had just been observed. The child's aggressive behavior after watching the television program can be quite different in quality and character from the aggressive or violent behavior displayed in the television program.

Virtually none of the prior research dealt with effects of actual television programs. The earlier investigations typically employed a several-minute violent excerpt from a motion picture, severed from its original context. In contrast, much of the new research discussed in this chapter has made use of actual television programs so that what has been presented as television has not been unlike television programs seen in the home. These studies are perhaps more cogent than the prior research for determining the effects of content as it is presented on home television screens.

Most of the prior studies on the instigating effects of filmed violence had used college students as subjects and had assessed each viewer's electric shocks administered to an ostensible victim (e.g., Berkowitz and Rawlings, 1963; Berkowitz, Corwin, and Heironimus, 1963; and Geen, 1968). In the series of new studies, a wide range of other measures of aggression (including multiple measures within each study) were employed. These measures varied from the administration of painful noise or heat to an ostensible victim to self-report willingness to use physical or verbal force as a means of conflict resolution. In addition, one study obtained naturalistic observations of the physical and verbal interpersonal aggression occurring in the child's daily life.

The likelihood that a viewer—either child or adult—will behave more aggressively after watching aggressive behavior portrayed on film or television has been suggested by the results of a number of prior studies. In a review by Atkin, Murray, and Nayman (1971), the majority of studies, covering various age levels, share the conclusion that viewing violence increases the likelihood that some viewers will behave aggressively immediately or shortly thereafter.

Some reviewers (Hartley, 1964; Klapper, 1968; Weiss, 1969; Singer, 1971) have disagreed with this interpretation. These writers have questioned whether the behavior observed can be regarded as "aggression" in a socially meaningful sense. They note that the subjects are *directed* to administer shocks and that the index of aggression is an extremely small increment in the number, duration, or intensity of the shocks supposedly given. They note also that the subject gets no feedback from his supposed victim, who is unseen and unheard, and that the subjects are in some instances explicitly told that the shocks are mild. These reviewers contend that this behavior, which they see as explicitly authorized, very limited, and involving no violation of social norms, cannot be equated with real interpersonal aggression in the consensual sense of the term, nor regarded as necessarily predictive of such behavior.

Catharsis

Some reviewers and researchers have expressed different views regarding the general effects of televised violence. Feshbach and Singer (1971) have in fact suggested that viewing televised violence provides an opportunity for the discharge (catharsis) of aggressive feelings and thus *reduces* the likelihood that the viewer will engage in aggressive or violent behavior. The same prediction follows from an inhibition hypothesis, which holds that exposure to violent content leads to anxiety, guilt, or the greater salience of norms and taboos in regard to aggression, with consequent reduced aggressive behavior.

The theory underlying the catharis hypothesis (Feshbach, 1961; Feshbach, 1969) stipulates that the child who views violence on television vicariously experiences the violence and thereby harmlessly discharges his pent-up anger, hostility, and frustration.

The Feshbach and Singer (1971) study provides the most comprehensive test of the "catharsis" hypothesis to be published to date. The investigators presented institutionalized adolescent and preadolescent boys with a "diet" of either aggressive or nonaggressive television programming over a six-week period and concurrently measured the day-to-day aggressive behavior of these boys. The results indicated that, in some cases, the children who viewed the nonviolent television programs were more aggressive than the boys who viewed the aggressive programs.

These conclusions deviate from the bulk of research findings in this area. The accumulated experimental investigations sponsored by this program, fail to support Feshbach's theory and conclusions. This type of disagreement can be resolved only when other investigators have repeated the experiment with appropriate methodological refinements designed to control possible sources of error.

Such a replication has recently been undertaken by Wells (1971), and the preliminary analysis indicates that the findings do not confirm those of Feshbach and Singer in reference to physical aggressiveness, although certain other findings are confirmed. Specifically, in both studies, the behavioral differences attributed to television were detected only in the lower socioeconomic level schools. Both studies also demonstrated greater *verbal* aggressiveness among boys who viewed the less violent programs. But—in a direct reversal of Feshbach and Singer—Wells found significantly greater *physical* aggressiveness among boys who viewed the more violent television programs. Moreover, the differences he found, in regard to both verbal and physical aggression, were limited to boys who were above average in aggression before the study began. Wells attributes the greater verbal aggression elicited by the less violent program diet to dissatisfaction with the banning of action-adventure programs. He interprets the greater physical aggression elicited by the more violent program diet as a tendency for the action-adventure content to stimulate aggressive behavior. He found no evidence that would support a catharsis interpretation, unless the difference in regard to verbal aggressiveness were so interpreted.

As matters now stand, the weight of the experimental evidence from the present series of studies, as well as from prior research, suggests that viewing filmed violence has an observable effect on some children in the direction of increasing their aggressive behavior. Many of the findings, however, fail to show any statistically significant effects in either direction.

New Evidence from the Present Studies

In the present series of studies, the research that bears most directly on aggressive behavior in the daily life of the child is a controlled experiment by Stein and Friedrich (1971). These investigators observed the daily behavior of three-and-one-half to five-and-one-half-years old (52 boys and 45 girls) who had been exposed to a diet of either aggressive, prosocial, or neutral programming. The general design of this study provided for a three-week baseline period during which observers recorded the child's usual patterns of social behavior. During the following four weeks, the children viewed 12 20-minute episodes in one of three "diets" of television or film programming. The *aggressive* programming consisted of 12 installments of *Batman* or *Super-*

man cartoons; the *neutral* programming consisted of children's films on "nature" or travelogues; the *prosocial* program consisted of 20-minute segments of *Misterogers Neighborhood*, which stressed the themes of sharing, cooperative behavior, and adaptive coping with frustrations. Each child's daily interpersonal behavior was observed throughout the four-week period and continued to be monitored during a two-week follow-up. All observations were conducted in a nursery school (initially a new setting for the child) during normal interaction with other children.

The investigators used several combined measures of aggression, two of which —physical and verbal—were combined into an interpersonal aggression score. No significant differences were found among the overall effects of the three types of television treatment. Moreover, exposure to the diet of televised violence was found to have no consistent effect on children who had initially displayed a low level of aggressive behavior. Among children who were initially high in aggressive behavior, the difference in the changes that occurred is plausibly interpreted as indicating greater stimulation of aggressive behavior among those who viewed the violent diet than among those who viewed the neutral diet.[1] On each of the two component

[1]This conclusion requires some explanation. When subjects are divided into those with high and low initial levels on any measure and when that measure (or a very similar one) is repeated, it is frequently found that the "initially high scorers" obtain slightly lower scores the second time and the initially low scorers obtain slightly-scores the second time, as a result of a general tendency for imperfectly reliable scores to regress toward the mean. In the presence of the regression effect, it is difficult to assess the amount and direction of changes attributable to an experimental variable. The type of regression effect just described seems to run through the data in the Stein and Friedrich study: the children rated as low in initial level of aggressive behavior showed an increase in aggressive behavior while those rated as initially high showed a decrease in aggressive behavior following exposure to television, regardless of which television program they saw. The main finding bearing on the effects of televised violence is that among those children who were initially high in aggressive behavior, those given the diet of televised violence showed little decrease, whereas the children who

measures of aggression, the corresponding differences were in the same direction, but not large enough to be statistically significant.[2]

The most striking finding was an increase in prosocial behavior among the children who viewed the prosocial programs (e.g., *Misterogers Neighborhood*). This increase was limited to those young viewers who came from families of low socioeconomic status. These children tended to become more cooperative, helpful, and sharing in their daily relations with others; the children from families of high socioeconomic status did not. Rather, the high-status children showed an increase in prosocial interpersonal behavior after viewing aggressive programming. An analysis of variance revealed a significant interaction between type of program viewed and socioeconomic status ($p < .05$). The main implications of the Stein and Friedrich research are

---

were given the neutral diet showed much more decrease (enough to be a significantly greater decrease) on one of the combined measures of aggressive behavior (interpersonal aggression). In view of the overall regression effect, this finding is tantamount to finding that exposure to the diet of televised violence gave rise to *relatively* more change in the direction of interpersonal aggressive behavior than exposure to the neutral diet.

There was no corresponding significant difference between those initially high in aggressive behavior who received the *prosocial* diet and those who received either the neutral or the violent diet.

For subjects who were initially low in aggressive behavior, there were no significant differences attributable to variations in television diet.

[2]In another field study, Cameron and Janky reported similar findings. In their study, parents were asked to restrict their child's television viewing to a diet of programs which were either aggressive or passive and then observe his daily behavior. Although serious methodological problems are inherent in this procedure, the results suggest that the child's behavior tended to change in the direction of the type of program content viewed: children who viewed "pacific" programs were adjudged by their parents to become less aggressive, while those who viewed the aggressive programs were adjudged to become more aggressive. Because of the strong possibility of biased judgments by the parents, we cannot give as much weight to this evidence as to the findings from controlled experiments which rely on trained observers who are "blind" about which type of program each child had seen.

that even relatively short repeated exposure (20 minutes) to the types of television programs available to children can exert positive or negative effects on the daily life behavior of nursery school children, but that the effects vary for different types of children.

In the Stein and Friedrich study, the age of the children was held constant. In other studies which compared younger with older children, age was an important predispositional factor associated with responsiveness to aggressive television fare. Liebert and Baron (1971) presented children with an opportunity to either help or hurt another child after they had viewed either an aggressive or a nonaggressive segment of television programming. The experiment was carried out with 68 boys and 68 girls at two age levels: five and six years old and eight and nine years old. Each child individually viewed a six-and-one-half minute "program." The "aggressive" program included three and one-half minutes of *The Untouchables,* preceded and followed by commercials; the "control" program included three and one-half minutes of a track race film with the same commercials. Then, so that aggressive behavior could be measured, each viewer was told that a child was playing a game in another room and that he could either help the other child or hurt him and prevent him from winning the game. The hurtful act consisted of pressing a button which the subject was told would make the handle of a game that the "other" child was playing become very hot and hard to turn. The helpful act consisted of pressing another button which he was told would make the handle very easy to turn and allow the other child to win more prizes. The experimenter emphasized that the longer the child pushed on the "help" button the more the other child was helped, and that the longer the child pushed the "hurt" button the more he hurt the other child. This procedure provided several measures of interpersonal aggression in terms of duration, frequency, and latency of hurting responses. An additional measure of postviewing behavior was the amount of aggression observed in a free play situation— specifically, play with nonaggressive or aggressive toys.

The results indicate that, in both age groups, children who viewed the televised aggressive episode demonstrated a greater willingness to engage in interpersonal aggression against an ostensible child victim. The five- and six-year-old children who viewed the *Untouchables* episode aggressed sooner and for a longer time than those who viewed the track race episode. For the older children (eight and none years old), those who viewed *The Untouchables* also showed significantly longer duration of aggressive responses than the equivalent controls, but they did not aggress any sooner. With regard to the child's spontaneous aggressive play behavior, it can again be noted that the children who viewed the televised violence episode subsequently showed more aggressive play than those children in the control condition. In this instance, younger boys were the most likely to behave aggressively.

Additional analyses of the behavior of these same children (Ekman et al., 1971) suggested that subsequent aggressive behavior is related to the child's reaction during viewing. Boys aged five and six whose facial expressions were judged to display such positive emotions as pleasure, happiness, interest, or involvement while viewing televised violence were more likely to make hurting responses than boys whose facial expressions indicated displeasure or disinterest in such fare. In addition, reactions judged to display happiness while viewing violence were positively related to aggressive play. However, this relationship between emotional reactions while viewing and subsequent aggressive behavior was not found for girls at ages five and six.

Additional evidence bearing on age differences comes from a study by Leifer and Roberts (1971). These investigators compared children of three different age groups, ranging from four to 16 years old, on their understanding of the ostensibly subtle motivations and conse-

quences that surround violent acts depicted on television. They asked each child about his own aggressive tendencies on a questionnaire given immediately after the child viewed televised violence. Aggressive reactions were measured in terms of the child's answers to a series of questions about conflict situations (e.g., "You are walking down the street. Some kid is mad at you and comes up and hits you. What do you do?" Possible answers are: "Hit them"; "Call them 'stupid' "; "Leave them"; "Tell a grownup"). One form of the questionnaire was developed for children four to ten years old, and another was developed for ten- to 16-year-olds.

In one experiment, 271 children (40 kindergarteners, 54 third, 56 sixth, 51 ninth, and 70 twelfth graders) were presented with a standard commercial television program that contained numerous episodes of violence. (A panel of adult judges had initially rated two programs, *Rocket Robin Hood* and *Batman,* as comprehensible by children four to five years old; two westerns, *Have Gun Will Travel* and *Rifleman,* as comprehensible by ten- to 12-year-olds; and two crime shows, *Felony Squad* and *Adam 12,* as appropriate for teenagers.) Each child was randomly assigned to view one of the appropriate programs. Immediately after the viewing, each child was questioned about his understanding of the motivations for and the immediate and final consequences of each of the violent episodes in the program. In addition, each child indicated the likelihood that he would behave aggressively by his choice of behavioral options in the hypothetical conflict situations described in the questionnaire.

The results showed that, as expected, there were consistent increases in understanding across the age range: kindergarteners could answer accurately only about one-third of the questions about either motivations or consequences; third graders could answer about one-half, and twelfth graders could answer about 95 percent. The majority of the kindergarten children did not understand very much about the settings of televised violence. Leifer and Robert's findings suggest that for most young children, a violent act depicted on television is a singular event devoid of its context. For the young television viewers, violence evidently is often perceived in discrete punches.

The results suggest that both age and sex were important in predicting subsequent aggressive behavior: boys were consistently more aggressive than girls and aggressiveness tended to increase with age. However, among the variables studied, one of the best predictors of the subsequent aggressive score was the amount of violence portrayed in the television program: children who viewed the more violent programs gave more aggressive responses, on the average, than those who viewed less violence ($p < .05$).

Additional studies by the same investigators bear out the conclusion that adolescents comprehend the depicted motivations for and consequences of aggression better than younger children. However, there was little evidence in these studies that motivations or consequences had any influence on the effect of televised violence on aggressiveness. On the whole, the findings strongly suggest the importance of further investigation in this area, since it is often claimed that the context in which violence is portrayed modifies any effect such portrayals may have.

Feshbach (1971) provides evidence that an effective moderating influence may arise from the way televised violence is labeled. His findings support the hypothesis that being told about the reality or fantasy character of acts depicted on television will influence the subsequent behavior of viewers. Forty boys and girls, between nine and 11 years of age, viewed a six-minute film of a campus riot; the film was composed of both newsreel clips and segments of a Hollywood movie. On a random basis, half the children were told that the film was an NBC newsreel; the other children were informed that this was a film made in a Hollywood studio. After viewing this film, each child was required to play a guessing game with an adult, responding to the adult's errors by pressing buttons which al-

legedly caused noises of various degrees of loudness in the earphones that the adult was wearing.

The results indicate that, among the children who saw the riot film, those who were told that the violence was real subsequently produced louder noises in the laboratory game than those who were told that the violence was make-believe ($p < .01$). On the other hand, the response level of children who viewed the fantasy aggressive program was actually lower than that of children who did not view an aggressive program ($p < .05$). The latter finding provides one of the rare bits of support for the catharsis or inhibition hypothesis.

If positive findings are confirmed in subsequent studies, one would expect that when a program is clearly labeled as fiction, young viewers will react to it in a different way than if they are led to believe that the program is showing real events. However, it should be noted that Feshbach's results pertain to the behavior of children at an age when the labeling of a program (as fiction or as reality) can be clearly understood. It is not clear that the young child consistently perceives television entertainment programs to be fantasy. A considerable research literature on the thought processes of children (e.g., Piaget, 1954 and 1962) suggests that a distinction between what is "real" and what is "make-believe" in standard dramatic television programs is probably nearly impossible for the young child below the age of six years. For older children, however, labels might reduce the tendency to display overt aggressive behavior among those who are disposed to be adversely stimulated by televised violence.

A full assessment of the impact of televised violence on children must, of course, include other forms of emotional reactions besides aggression. We have mentioned parents' complaints that many television programs stimulate anxiety reactions and produce sleep disturbances and nightmares in young children (e.g., Hess and Goldman, 1968; Lyle and Hoffman, 1971a and 1971b; Roberts and Baird, 1971).

Very little systematic research has checked on these allegations; consequently, we simply do not know whether any types of television programs are likely to create sustained anxiety reactions in a sizable proportion of children.

Some pertinent findings bearing on children's dreams have been reported by Foulkes and his collaborators. Foulkes and Rechtschaffen (1964) have reported some evidence that viewing televised violence produced more vivid and emotional dreams in children. However, a more recent systematic followup study by Foulkes, Belvedere, and Brubaker (1971) assessed the impact of televised violence in a western program on the child's dream content (including manifestations of hostility, guilt, and anxiety) and found little or no measurable effect. This study was limited, however, to preadolescent boys (aged ten to 12). Whether younger children exposed to televised violence show any noticeable change in the degree to which their dreams are characterized by hostility, guilt, or anxiety remains an open question. In the absence of dependable evidence, we can draw no conclusions about the likelihood of sleep disturbances or other manifestations of anxiety in younger children.

General Arousal as a Source of Instigation

All of the research discussed so far has been concerned with the effects of the portrayal of violence or aggression in communication content on subsequent behavior or attitudes. A radically different approach is presented in the progress report of Tannenbaum (1971).

In a program of research that began before this committee was formed and that will continue into the future, Tannenbaum has been investigating the hypothesis that the emotional arousal elicited by a communication affects the level or intensity of whatever subsequent behavior may occur. Arousal, then, is conceived of as independent of content as a predictor of effects.

Preliminary findings, based on college students, support the corollary proposition that content other than violent or aggressive material may instigate aggressiveness. With aggressive behavior measured by willingness either to administer electric shocks or to give negative ratings that might hurt another's career, the effects of videotapes or films judged to be erotic, humorous, aggressive, or neutral in content were assessed in several experiments. The viewing of erotic and of humorous materials was followed by greater aggressiveness than the viewing of neutral material, and the viewing of erotic material was followed by greater aggressiveness than the viewing of aggressive material. The nature of the subsequent behavior, then, is conceived of as independent of content, as is the arousal.

However, Tannenbaum also has provided support for the proposition that violent or aggressive content can instigate aggressiveness. In these same experiments, the viewing of aggressive material was followed by greater aggressiveness than the viewing of neutral or humorous material.

Tannenbaum's preliminary findings also support a second corollary proposition—that aggressive content may instigate behavior which is nonaggressive, and in fact prosocial. In experiments designed to test this hypothesis, "humor reactions" of equal magnitude were found to follow a humorous film and an aggressive film. In addition, "rewarding behavior" (presentation to another person of tokens presumably redeemable for cash) was found to occur after both aggressive and nonaggressive stimulus films. Whether "aggressive" or "rewarding" behavior occurred appeared to be less a product of the film than of attitudes earlier engendered in the subjects regarding the recipient of the behavior.

It remains a matter of speculation whether general arousal should be taken as a complete explanation of any effects, with violent content having an effect on aggressiveness only through a special power to arouse, or whether specific content and consequent cognitive processes have an independent influence. The crucial test would involve comparison of the effects of aggressive content with and without the capacity to elicit emotional arousal. Unfortunately, such a test has not so far been made because aggressive content devoid of arousing capabilities is difficult—and, in fact, may be impossible—to devise.

The preliminary nature of this research suggests extreme caution in advancing any conclusions. If generalized arousal is verified either as the single or as a contributing factor, the interpretation of many findings as reflecting exclusively the instigating effects of aggressive content would have to be modified. However, what can now be said specifically about the capacity of violent or aggressive content to instigate aggressiveness would *not* be greatly affected. Instead, such effects of such content to a greater or lesser degree would become a special case of a more general phenomenon capable of more varied effects.

*

CONCLUSIONS

The available experimental evidence bearing on the effects of aggressive television entertainment content on children supports certain conclusions. First, violence depicted on television can immediately or shortly thereafter induce mimicking or copying by children. Second, under certain circumstances television violence can instigate an increase in aggressive acts. The accumulated evidence, however, does not warrant the conclusion that it has an adverse effect on the majority of children. It cannot even be said that the majority of the children in the various studies we have reviewed showed an increase in aggressive behavior in response to the violent fare to which they were exposed. The evidence does indicate that televised violence may lead to increased aggressive behavior in certain subgroups of children, who might constitute a small portion or a substantial proportion of the total population of young television viewers. We cannot estimate the size of the frac-

tion, however, since the available evidence does not come from cross-section samples of the entire American population of children.

The research studies . . . tell us something about the characteristics of those children who are most likely to display an increase in aggressive behavior after exposure to televised violence. There is evidence that among young children (ages four to six) those most responsive to television violence are those who are highly aggressive to start with—who are prone to engage in spontaneous aggressive actions against their playmates and, in the case of boys, who display pleasure in viewing violence being inflicted upon others.

The very young have difficulty comprehending the contextual setting in which violent acts are depicted and do not grasp the meaning of cues or labels concerning the make-believe character of violence episodes in fictional programs. For older children, one study has found that labeling of violence on a television program as make-believe rather than as real reduces the incidence of induced aggressive behavior. Contextual cues to the motivation of the aggressor and to the consequences of acts of violence might also modify the impact of televised violence, but evidence on this topic is inconclusive.

Since a considerable number of experimental studies on the effects of televised violence have now been carried out, it seems improbable that the next generation of studies will bring many great surprises, particularly with regard to broad generalizations not supported by the evidence currently at hand. It does not seem worthwhile to continue to carry out studies designed primarily to test the broad generalization that most or all children react to televised violence in a uniform way. The lack of uniformity in the extensive data now at hand is much too impressive to warrant the expectation that better measures of aggression or other methodological refinements will suddenly allow us to see a uniform effect.

Several specific directions for subsequent inquiry are repeatedly suggested by the most recent studies. First, identify the predispositional characteristics of those subgroups of children who display an increase in aggressive behavior in response to televised violence. Second, ascertain at what ages different reactions occur. Third, check on the moderating influence of labeling, contextual cues, and other factors under the control of television producers which may reduce the likelihood that predisposed children will react adversely to televised violence. Fourth, further investigate the possibility that content other than violent content may increase the likelihood of subsequent aggressiveness, that violent content may instigate other behavior besides aggressiveness, and the applicability of such findings to preschool children, elementary school children, and adolescents. Finally, we must call attention once again to the gap in longitudinal research on the effects of television programs on children. This gap needs to be filled before we can learn something dependable about the long-term effects of repeated exposure to standard television fare on the personality development of the child.

REFERENCES

Atkin, C. K., Murray, J. P., and Nayman, O. B. (Eds.) *Television and Social Behavior* Vol. 6. *The effects of television on children and youth: A review of theory and research.* (Rev. ed.) Washington, D.C.: Government Printing Office, 1971.

Baker, R. K., and Ball, S. J. *Mass media and violence: A staff report to the National Commission on the Causes and Prevention of Violence.* Washington, D.C.: Government Printing Office, 1969.

Bandura, A., Ross, D., and Ross, S. A. Transmission of aggression through imitation of aggressive models. *Journal of Abnormal and Social Psychology,* 1961, 63, 575–582.

Bandura, A. and Walters, R. H. *Social learning and personality development.* New York: Holt, Rinehart, and Winston, 1963.

Berkowitz, L., (Ed.) *Roots of aggression: a re-examination of the frustration-aggression hypothesis.* New York: Atherton Press, 1969.

Berkowitz, L., Corwin, R., and Heironimus, M. Film violence and subsequent aggressive tendencies. *Public Opinion Quarterly,* 1963, 27, 217–229.

Berkowitz, L., and Rawlings, E. Effects of film violence on inhibitions against subsequent aggression. *Journal of Abnormal and Social Psychology,* 1963, 66(3), 405–412.

Clark, C. Race, identification, and television violence. In G. A. Comstock, E. A. Rubinstein, and J. P. Murray (Eds.), *Television and Social Behavior.* Vol. 5. *Television's Effects: Further Explorations.* Washington, D.C.: Government Printing Office, 1971.

Clark, D. G., and Blankenburg, W. B. Trends in violent content in selected mass media. In G. A. Comstock and E. A. Rubinstein (Eds.), *Television and Social Behavior.* Vol. 1. *Content and Control.* Washington, D.C.: Government Printing Office, 1971.

Feshbach, S. Reality and fantasy in filmed violence. In J. P. Murray, E. A. Rubinstein, and G. A. Comstock (Eds.) *Television and Social Behavior.* Vol. 2. *Television and Social Learning.* Washington, D.C.: Government Printing Office, 1971.

Feshbach, S., and Singer, R. *Television and aggression.* San Francisco: Jossey-Bass, 1971.

Foulkes, D. and Rechtschaffen, A. Presleep determinants of dream content: Effects of two films. *Perceptual and Motor Skills,* 1964, (3), 983–1005.

Foulkes, D., Belvedere, E., and Brubaker, T. Televised violence and dream content. In G. A. Comstock, E. A. Rubinstein, and J. P. Murray (Eds.), *Television and Social Behavior.* Vol. 5. *Television's Effects: Further Explorations.* Washington, D.C.: Government Printing Office, 1971.

Hartley, R. L. *The impact of viewing "aggression": Studies and problems of extrapolation.* New York: Columbia Broadcasting System, 1964.

Hess, R. D. and Goldman, H. Parent's views of the effects of television on their children. *Child Development,* 1962, *33,* 411–426.

Himmelweit, H. T., Oppenheim, A. N., and Vince, P. *Television and the child: an empirical study of the effects of television on the young.* London: Oxford University Press, 1958.

Klapper, H. L. "Did anyone do anything that would be wrong for you to do?": Children's perceptions and moral evaluations of television programs. Paper presented at the American Association for Public Opinion Research, Bolton's Landing, New York, May 1969.

Klapper, J. T. Statement of Dr. Joseph T. Klapper, Director, Office of Social Research, Columbia Broadcasting System, before the National Commission on the Causes and Prevention of Violence, Oct. 16, 1968.

Leifer, A. D., and Roberts, D. F. Children's responses to television violence. In J. P. Murray, E. A. Rubinstein, and G. A. Comstock (Eds), *Television and Social Behavior.* Vol. 2. *Television and Social Learning.* Washington, D.C.: Government Printing Office, 1971.

Liebert, R. M. and Baron, R. A. Short-term effects of televised aggression on children's aggressive behavior. In J. P. Murray, E. A. Rubinstein, and G. A. Comstock (Eds), *Television and Social Behavior.* Vol. 2. *Television and Social Learning.* Washington, D.C.: Government Printing Office, 1971.

Lyle, J. and Hoffman, H. R. Children's use of television and other media. In E. A. Rubinstein, G. A. Comstock, and J. P. Murray (Eds), *Television and Social Behavior.* Vol. 4. *Television in Day-to-Day Life: Patterns of Use.* Washington, D.C.: Government Printing Office, 1971. (a)

Lyle, J. and Hoffman, H. R. Explorations in patterns of television viewing by preschool-age children. In E. A. Rubinstein, G. A. Comstock and J. P. Murray (Eds), *Television and Social Behavior.* Vol. 4. *Television in Day-to-Day Life: Patterns of Use.* Washington, D.C.: Government Printing Office, 1971 (b)

Maccoby, E. E. Television: Its impact on school children. *Public Opinion Quarterly,* 1951, *15,* 421–444.

Piaget, J. *The construction of reality in the child.* New York: Basic Books, 1954.

Piaget, J. *Play, dreams and imitation in childhood.* New York: Norton, 1962.

Roberts, J. and Baird, J. T. Parent ratings of behavior patterns of children, United States. *Vital and Health Statistics, National Center for Health Statistics,* Series 11, No. 108, PHS No. 1000. Washington, D.C. Government Printing Office, 1971.

Singer, J. L. (Ed.) *The control of aggression and violence.* New York Academic Press, 1971.

Stein, A. H. and Friedrich, L. K., Television content and young children's behavior. In J. P. Murray, E. A. Rubinstein, and G. A. Comstock (Eds.), *Television and Social Behavior.* Vol. 2. *Television and Social Learning.* Washington, D.C.: Government Printing Office, 1971.

Tannenbaum, P. H. Studies in film-and television-mediated arousal and aggression: A progress report. In G. A. Comstock, E. A. Rubinstein, and J. P. Murray (Eds.), *Television and Social Behavior.* Vol. 5. *Television's Effects: Further Exploration.* Washington, D.C.: Government Printing Office, 1971.

Weiss, W. Effects of the mass media of communication. In G. Lindzey and E. Aronson (Eds.) *The handbook of social psychology.* (2nd ed.) Reading, Mass.: Addison-Wesley, 1969. Pp. 77–195.

Wells, W. D. Television and aggression: A replication of an experimental field study. (In preparation.)

45. Gang Violence

WALTER B. MILLER

GANGS AND INFORMATION. THE TASK OF OBTAIN-
ing and presenting accurate, balanced, and current information concerning youth gangs and
related phenomena presents unusual difficulties. These have several sources. First, although
gangs and their illegal activities are far more
visible than illegalities involved in corporate
crime, syndicate crime, and various forms of
consumer fraud, all of which may involve intricate and ingenious methods of deliberate concealment, there are still elements of concealment,
duplicity, and deliberate deception in the activity of gang members which can be brought to
light only by trusted persons who maintain close
and continued contact with gang members. A
second reason is that gang activities through the
years have provided a highly marketable basis
for media pieces which are often sensationalized
or exaggerated, and which represent as typical
the most extreme forms of current gang manifestations. This is one aspect of the relation between youth gangs and adult agencies which has
remained virtually unchanged throughout the
years. A third reason is that information released by many of the agencies dealing with
gang problems—police, courts, probation,
municipal authorities, public service agencies,
private agencies, and others—are frequently
presented in such a way as to best serve the organizational interests of the particular agency
rather than the interests of accuracy. This aspect
of the relation between gangs and adult agencies
has also showed remarkable stability over time.

But probably the single most significant obstacle to obtaining reliable information is the fact,
already noted, that there does not exist, anywhere in the United States, one single agency
which takes as a continuing responsibility the
collection of information based on *explicit* and
uniformly applied data collection categories which
would permit comparability from city to city and
between different periods of time. Data-
collection operations such as the routine collection of unemployment data by the Bureau of
Labor Statistics or of arrest data by the Federal
Bureau of Investigation have never been seriously considered, let alone implemented. This
striking omission has a variety of detrimental
consequences, and is a major reason why authorities are caught off guard by what appears
as a periodic waxing and waning of youth gang
violence, and for the generally low effectiveness
of efforts to cope with it.

Methods of the Twelve-City Survey

For purposes of gathering information capable
of providing preliminary answers to the question of the degree to which the activities of
youth gangs and groups constitute a crime problem on a nation-wide basis, site visits were made
to 12 of the nation's largest cities. The major
criterion for selection of cities was population
size, but also considered were the nature of av-

▶SOURCE: *Violence by Youth Gangs and Youth Groups as a
Crime Problem in Major American Cities. Washington, D.C.: Law
Enforcement Assistance Administration, U.S. Department of Justice*
(1975), pp. 2–4, 8–11, 35–44. (Editorial adaptations.)

ailable information as to gang problems, achieving some order of regional representation, and other factors. The 12 cities were as follows: New York, Chicago, Los Angeles, Philadelphia, Houston, Detroit, Baltimore, Washington, Cleveland, San Francisco, St. Louis and New Orleans.[1] Site visits ranged from two to five days per city. An "interview guide" was prepared to serve as a basis of information gathering; this was not intended as a formal questionnaire, but was used rather to provide a set of questions which could be asked, as appropriate, in the several cities, in order to cover informational areas which could be examined on a comparative basis for all cities. Most interviews lasted between one and four hours, depending on scheduling circumstances and the time available to respondents. Staff members representing 81 different agencies participated in 64 interviews, with a total of 159 respondents contributing information. Agencies are categorizable according to 18 types. Types of agencies and numbers of respondents are indicated in Table I.

Selection of respondents was based on several criteria. Highest priority was given to those whose professional activities brought them into the most direct contact with youth in the community. Thus, for service agencies, preferred respondents were those engaged in "outreach," "area work," or "gang/group work" programs, and for police agencies, personnel specializing in gang work on the level of intelligence, operations, or both. In addition, the commanding officer of the youth/juvenile bureau/division in each of the 12 cities were interviewed, often in conjunction with line personnel familiar with particular districts, precincts, or neighborhoods. Members of police research or data analysis divisions were also preferred respondents.

Initially, probation personnel were not seen as priority respondents, but contacts during earlier itineraries showed that most probation workers were closely familiar with the commun-

[1]In a thirteenth city, San Diego, a single interview was conducted.

Table 1. Number and Agency-affiliations of Survey Respondents

Agency	No. Persons Interviewed
1. Police dept: juvenile/yth div'n/bureau	37
2. Police dept: youth gang div'n/specialists	7
3. Police dept., other: (e.g., crime analysis, community rels.)	6
4. Municipal/county gang/ group work. "Outreach"	28
5. Municipal/county youth service	13
6. Municipal/county criminal justice council, planning agency	8
7. Municipal/county, other	10
8. Private agency gang/group work, "Outreach"	14
9. Private youth service	4
10. Private service, other	3
11. Judicial	8
12. Probation, court	7
13. Probation, other	3
14. Prosecution	2
15. Youth corrections: parole	1
16. Youth corrections: other	5
17. Public schools	2
18. Academic research	1
	159

ity situation, and thus were interviewed more extensively in later itineraries. The low representation of academic researchers among respondents does not reflect a low selection priority but rather the extreme rarity of academicians conducting gang-related research. The paucity of school personnel in Table I reflects the fact that the importance of the schools as an arena for gang activity did not become clear until initial data analyses. Telephone interviews with selected school personnel were conducted, and such respondents will be utilized more extensively during the second phase of the survey.

A "full" interview involved responses to approximately 65 items of judgment or information: however, in few cases was it possible to obtain responses to all items, and selections were made on the basis of type of agency, time available, local circumstances, detail offered by respondents, and other factors. As the table shows, interviews often involved more than one respondent—particularly in cases where adequate city-wide information required persons familiar with often contrasting crime situations of different intra-urban areas. Of 68 full or partial interviews, 32, or 47 percent, involved multiple respondents. Often there was consensus with respect to particular items; frequently there was not. For this reason the "respondent" rather than the "agency" is the unit in some of the following tables.[2]

*

Definition of "Gang"   Before presenting the respondents' answers to these questions, it is necessary to examine the meaning they ascribed to the term "gang." Low consensus among respondents in their conceptions of the nature of a gang would necessarily introduce considerable ambiguity into their appraisals of the nature of gang problems. If, for example, some significant number of respondents were to consider as a "gang" any ad hoc assemblage of youths such as civil-disturbance looters or anti-school-integration demonstrators, or to apply the term to any sporadic assemblage of street-corner loungers, judgments that their city faced serious gang problems would have to be interpreted with considerable caution.[3]

Following the questions as to the existence and seriousness of gang problems, each respondent was asked "Just how do *you* define the term "gang?" Two kinds of probes followed the replies. The first queried specifically as to ele-

ments omitted from the definitions (e.g., "Is it necessary for a group to engage regularly in illegal activity for you to consider it a gang?" "Does a group have to have a name in order to be a gang?" "Can a group be a gang without making special claim to a particular turf of territory?"). The second was intended to find out whether respondents made a distinction between "gangs" and "law-violating youth groups." A typical "hanging group" or "street group" was described in some detail (congregate around park, housing project, store; engage in noisy disturbance; commit minor offenses such as petty shoplifting, smoke marijuana, drunkenness, vandalism), and respondents were asked whether they considered such groups to be "gangs."

Results of these queries for the six cities designated in Table III as "gang problem" cities are shown in Table II.[4] Of initial significance is the fact that of 24 respondents providing codable answers to the "gang vs. group" question, 18, or three-quarters, denied the status of "gang" to "hanging" or "street corner" groups. Thus the majority of respondents in the six largest metropolitan areas reserved the use of the term "gang" for associational units which were both more formalized and more seriously criminal than the more common type of street group. What characteristics *did* respondents cite as major defining criteria of a "gang?"

Table II lists in rank order the five criteria most frequently cited, along with the percentage of respondents citing or accepting the specified criterion as an essential feature of a "gang."

The criteria most frequently cited were: violent or criminal behavior as a major activity of group members; group organized, with func-

---

[2]In addition to interview data, approximately 225 pages of reports, statistical data, and other documents were obtained from agency representatives in the 12 cities.

[3]An extended discussion of definitional issues is contained in W. B. Miller, "American Youth Gangs: Past and Present" in A. Blumberg, *Current Perspectives on Criminal Behavior,* 1974, pp. 213–221.

[4]Analyses of responses for the six "group-problem" cities of the present survey, including comparisons of these with "gang problem" city responses, will be presented in a future report. The small number of cases on which present conclusions are based will be increased by the planned addition to the analysis of responses from eight additional gang- and group-problem cities in addition to the six for which data has been collected but not analyzed.

Table II. Five Most Frequently Cited Criteria for Defining a Gang:
Six Gang-Problem Cities (N Respondents = 57 : N Responses = 158

	No. Responses Specifying as Defining Criterion	No. Responses Specifying Criterion Not Necessary	% Responses Specifying as Defining Criterion
Violent or criminal behavior a major activity of group members	30	11	73.2
Group organized, with functional role-division, chain-of-command	21	2	91.3
Identifiable leadership	20	0	100.0
Group members in continuing recurrent interaction	19	1	95.0
Group identified with, claims control over, identifiable community territory	17	0	100.0
	107	14	88.4

tional role-division and chain-of-command authority; identifiable leadership; continuing and recurrent interaction or association among group members; identification with and/or claims of control over, some identifiable community territory or territories. Citations of these five represented 77 percent (121:158) of all cited criteria.

Rephrasing these separately cited criteria in more formal terms produces the following definition:

A gang is a group of recurrently associating individuals with identifiable leadership and internal organization, identifying with or claiming control over territory in the community, and engaging either individually or collectively in violent or other forms of illegal behavior.

Several considerations are relevant to the general utility of this respondent-based definition. One concerns those criteria which a minority of respondents asserted were *not* essential to the definition; a second concerns six less-frequently cited criteria not included in Table III; and a third concerns intercity variation in definitional conceptions.

Results presented in Table II indicate a high degree of consensus in definitional conceptions among respondents representing a variety of professional pursuits in six different cities. Ninety percent or more were in agreement as to four of the five criteria, with the remaining criterion (illegality/violence) showing an agreement level of 73 percent. It is of interest that the criterion with the lowest level of general acceptance was also the one most frequently cited.

No systematic attempt was made to find out why some respondents felt that involvement in illegal behavior was not an essential criterion of a gang, and in some cases no reasons were offered. Reasons that were given varied considerably. The most common was that the major influence behind the formation of gangs is the natural tendency of similar-aged peers to form themselves into groups for a variety of purposes—including companionship, seeking collective solutions to common problems, and self-protection--and that while illegal behavior might often accompany this process, it was not *per se* an essential condition of gang formation (this position contradicts that of others who maintained that the commission of violent or il-

Table III. Respondents' Estimates as to Existence and Seriousness of Problems with Youth Groups Specifically Designated as "Gangs" (N Cities = 12; N Respondents = 67)

Proportion Reporting Group Problems		Estimate of Seriousness relative to most serious crime problems			
		High	Medium	Low	No Estimate
All, or all but one: $\frac{37}{39}$ (95%)		Los Angeles Philadelphia Detroit	New York Chicago	San Francisco	
Majority: $\frac{5}{8}$ (63%)			Cleveland	Washington	
Minority: $\frac{4}{16}$ (25%)				St. Louis Baltimore New Orleans	
None: $\frac{0}{4}$ (0%)					Houston
12 Cities: $\frac{46}{67}$ (69%)					

legal acts was in fact the central purpose behind the formation of gangs).

Other reasons were: gangs are sufficiently frightening that they can achieve their ends merely by threatening violence without having to engage in it; the gang to which the respondent belonged as a youth did not engage in illegality; conceiving a gang primarily in terms of illegal behavior overlooks the fact that much of what gangs do is not illegal; once a community perceives a group as a "gang" they will be so defined whether or not they are involved in illegality.

The five criteria of Table II represent 77 percent of all criteria cited by the 57 respondents. The remaining 33 percent (51 responses) include a number of additional criteria relating to age, sex, group size, and others. Of these, the age factor is probably most important to definitional specificity. Eight of 12 respondents (two-thirds) who cited age specified that in their minds the term "gang" applies to youth or juveniles. The remaining four felt that groups containing adults could properly be designated gangs. Some of these had in mind units such as motorcycle gangs, whose members often include persons in their twenties and thirties. No respondent cited maleness as a criterion of gang membership, and several stated specifically that members could be either male or female.

Few respondents explicitly addressed the issue of size, apparently being satisfied with the size implication of the term "group". Different respondents used the numbers three, four, and five as the bottom size limit for a "gang." One respondent put the upper limit at three or four thousand. Also cited were: having a name and/or identifying dress or insignia; a clubhouse or other meeting place; having multiple units (age-level subdivisions, branches); and periodic combat with rival gangs. A final category included a set of diverse criteria such as maintaining a distinctive subculture or counterculture, being bound by mutual loyalty, using the group to achieve status superior to that which one could achieve as an individual, and maintaining clandestine and/or ritualistic practices.

It is also important to know, in evaluating respondents' judgments as to the character of gang problems, to what degree conceptions of gangs may have varied by city. Comparing definitional criteria offered by local respondents shows little intercity variation. While the total number of responses is much too small to support statistically sound conclusions,[5] what evidence is available fails to show that the definitional criteria cited by respondents in any city differed significantly from those cited in others.

With regard to the distinction between a "gang" and a "group," all respondents in four of the six cities made the distinction, and in the two cities where some failed to do so, (Chicago, Detroit), a majority did. With regard to the five major defining criteria, the highest proportion of respondents in any city not accepting any of the criteria was one-third, and this degree of non-acceptance occurred in only two of 30 possible cases. (In Detroit, one-third of the respondents felt that illegal behavior and organization were not essential to the definition of a gang). In 19 of the 30 possible instances, no respondent disagreed with the inclusion of the criterion under consideration.

Thus, although to provide cases would be needed to provide respectable statistical underpinning to these conclusions, preliminary data indicate that the definition presented earlier based on 158 definitional criteria cited by 57 respondents, corresponds quite closely with conceptions shared by a substantial majority of respondents in six major cities. The definition thus indicates quite specifically the kind of unit referred to in respondents' evaluations of gang problems in their cities.

*

GANG-MEMBER VIOLENCE

Statistical data as to the numbers of gangs, gang members, and arrests for various types of of-

fenses are of direct value in approximating the size and scope of contemporary gang problems, but they do not convey much of the "flavor" of gang violence and other problematic activities. Following sections will deal briefly with major forms of gang activity primarily on a "qualitative" rather than a quantitative level, so as to provide a clearer picture of the character of certain current gang activities.[6]

The present section discusses assaultive behavior and other forms of violent crime engaged in by gang members either collectively or as individuals. Violent crime by gang members plays a central role in whether youth gangs are perceived as a "problem" in a particular community, and how serious that problem is seen to be.

As noted earlier, and discussed elsewhere[7] the bulk of activities engaged in by gang members are non-criminal, and the bulk of criminal behavior engaged in by members of most gangs is of the less serious kind. While the kinds of disorderly congregation, public drinking, and similar activities that are characteristic of so many gangs are often seen as "problematic" in smaller and/or wealthier communities, such behavior would scarcely give rise to the "high seriousness" estimates ascribed to gang problems by respondents in the largest cities.

It is the practice by youth gangs of *violence*, and particularly lethal violence, that provides the most crucial element in perceptions by city officials that youth gangs present a "problem." On a very gross level, one can distinguish four kinds of gang-member violence; these will be cited in order of their increasing capacity to engender perceptions that gangs pose a serious problem.

---

[6]Information was gathered with respect to 24 different forms of gang activity. Partial data derived from some of these forms has been reported in earlier sections, (e.g., ethnic status, age-levels). This report thus includes analyses based on eight of these 24 forms, leaving approximately 16 forms yet to be reported on.

[7]Miller, Walter B., "Violent Crimes in City Gangs," *Annals of the American Academy of Political and Social Science*, Vol. 364, March 1966, pp. 96–112.

[5]The descriptive matrix distributes 107 responses over 30 cells (five major criteria, six cities).

The first is often regarded as "normal" gang violence—attacks in which both assailants and victims are gang members. With the partial exception of unusually bloody, large-scale, or protracted intergang conflict, this type has the lowest capacity to engender a sense of problem. This is documented by the fact that continuing intergang violence during the 1960's in Chicago, Los Angeles and Philadelphia (150 reported gang-related killings in Chicago in 1967) went almost totally unremarked by the New York and Washington-based media. Some secretly or openly espouse the cynical position that such violence is a solution rather than a problem; the more gang members kill one another off, the fewer will be left to present problems. This sentiment was forwarded openly by one respondent.

A somewhat higher degree of concern may be engendered when gang members victimize non-gang members with social characteristics similar to their own. Insofar as such non-gang members are seen as "innocent victims" of gang violence (not infrequently gang members will wrongly identify a target of retaliation), concern is aroused, but to the degree that victims share the same age, sex, ethnic and neighborhood characteristics as gang members, a similar kind of "let them kill each other off" element may affect judgments. Respondents working in slum communities frequently complain that gang violence is seen as problematic only when outsiders are victimized. Official concern is more likely to be aroused when gang member crime is directed against the property of the general public—in house burglaries, store robberies, arson, vandalism of homes, schools, public facilities, and the like. Finally, the highest sense of "problem" is engendered when there is a real or perceived increase in victimization by gang members of persons with different social characteristics— young children, females, the elderly, non-community members—through mugging, robbery, rape, murder. In the mid-1970's public and edititorial concern over gang violence was heightened when gang members in some cities began to pursue a pattern of systematically victimizing elderly persons—accosting them on the street or in their dwellings, stealing their social security checks and other possessions, and frequently beating them, sometimes fatally.

Assuming that it is this latter type of gang violence which has the greatest capacity to create a sense of "problem," it is significant that informants in several cities cited as a major new development of the 1970's the increasing tendency of gang members to victimize non-gang adults and children, wuth some claiming that this had become the dominant form of gang violence. New Yorkers and Los Angelenos in particular cited this development.

What does the survey evidence show? Following sections will examine the issue of gang violence under four headings: forms of gang-member engagement, victims of gang violence, weaponry, and motives for violence.

Forms of Assaultive Encounters: Gang Members

There is a common misconception that the predominant form of hostile encounter between or among gangs is the "gang fight" or rumble— conceived as a massed encounter between rival forces, arranged in advance by mutual consent. Paralleling the notion that if there is no gang fighting there are no "true" gangs is the notion that if there are no "rumbles there is no "true" gang conflict. The widespread attention accorded the prearranged rumble as a form of encounter in the 1950's reinforced the notion that it was the major or even exclusive form of gang conflict. In fact, gang members in the past have commonly engaged one another in hostile encounters in a wide variety of ways, and the gangs of the 1970's are no exception.

Information gathered during the survey with respect to assaultive behavior involving gang members (behavior involving non-gang-members is discussed in the next section) was originally categorized according to approximately 15 different types. These were collapsed into a categorization delineating 8 forms, as presented in Table IV. These are here designated the "planned rumble," the "rumble," "warfare,"

Table IV. Major Forms of Assaultive Encounters: Gang Member Participants 1973-1975

Form	Existence Reported						No. Cities Reporting
	N.Y.C.	Chi.	L.A.	Phil.	Detr.	S. Fr.	
"Planned rumble": prearranged encounter between sizable rival groups	R	R	R	O	R	—	5
"Rumble": encounter between rival groups, generally sizable	O	R	R	R	R	R	6
"Warfare": continuing pattern of retaliatory engagements by members of rival groups; various forms	O	R	O	R	O	R	6
"Foray": smaller bands engage rival bands	R	R	R	R	O	O	6
"Hit": smaller bands attack one or two gang rivals	O	R	R	R	R	O	6
"Fair fight"/"Execution": single gang member engages single rival	—	R	R	R	R	O	5
"Punitive assault": gang members assault or kill present or potential members of own gang	O	O	O	R	—	—	4
No. forms reported per city	6	7	7	7	6	5	

R = Reported by respondent
O = Reported by other source.

the "foray," the "hit," the "fair fight," the "execution," and "punitive assault." Table IV provides no information as to the prevalence or frequency of the several forms; it indicates simply that the existence of the designated form in one of the six gang-problem cities was reported either by a respondent during interviews or by another source (newspaper accounts, special reports, etc.) between January 1973 and June 1974. The 1973 cutoff date was adopted in order to insure that reported forms represent the most current manifestations.

Table IV indicates the existence in all cites of most of the designated forms, thus showing that currently, as in the past, violent encounters among gang members take a variety of different forms rather than one or a few. If all forms had been reported for all cities, a total of 42 would have appeared in the Table. As it is, the existence of the designated form is indicated in 38 of 42 possible cases. The planned rumble was not reported for San Francisco; no "execution" or "fair fight" was reported for New York; "punitive assault" was not reported for Detroit and San Francisco. This does not necessarily mean that these forms are absent in these cities, but rather that available information did not indicate their presence.

The eight forms of encounter of Table IV do not represent mutually exclusive categories, as will be shown, but rather elements or episodes which can combine in many ways under varying circumstances. The fairly widespread notion that the "planned rumble" was the dominant form of gang conflict in the 1950's but disappeared in the '70's is contradicted by the fact that its existence was reported in five of the six gang-problem cities. Detailed accounts of classic, full-scale mass engagements (called "jitterbugging," "jamming," and other terms in the '50's) were recorded for all five cities during 1974 and 1975. However, the notion that the planned rumble is relatively uncommon as a form of gang confrontation (rather than having disappeared) is given support by the fact that respondents in three cities (New York, Los Angeles, Detroit) reported this type as extant but rare, and one city, San Francisco, did not report it at all.[8] In Chicago, respondents said that the planned rumble type of engagement was fairly common among Latin gangs, but not among others.

The "rumble"—an engagement between gangs resulting from unplanned encounters between fairly large numbers of rival gang members (20 to 50) or from raids by one large group into rival territory, was reported for six cities. There is no uniformly accepted terminology for the several forms of gang engagement cited here, but there is some overlap among cities in terms used for either or both planned and unplanned rumbles. The term "rumble" is used in New York, Chicago, and Detroit: "gang-banging" in Chicago and Los Angeles; "gang warring" in Philadelphia. The term "gang warfare," to refer either to specific engagements or a continuing series of engagements is used in Chicago, Los Angeles, Chicago, and San Francisco. Terms such as "jitterbugging," "jamming," and others used during the 1950's are not currently in use. The term "warfare" as used here applies only to a continuing series of engagements between rival gangs or among coalitions of gangs. In some cities this term (e.g., "gang-warring," in Philadelphia) is applied to

particular encounters as well. The actual kinds of engagements comprising "warfare" can include any combination of rumbles, planned rumbles, forays, hits, fair fights, and executions, often in logical sequences ("foray" produces retaliatory "hit" leads to "rumble" leads to retaliatory execution, and so on). The essential element of warfare is that of retaliation and/or revenge, with an initiating incident leading to a series of retaliations, counter-retaliations and so on (among New Guinea tribes, this type of engagement is known as the "pay-back" pattern). In several cities gangs or sets of gang names become paired with each other as enemies, with enmity sometimes brief, sometimes lasting. Some of these are: Latin Kings and Gaylords (Chicago); Bishops and Chains, "warfare" between 1972 and 1974, when the two gangs merged into a single gang called the "Brotherhood" (Detroit); Savage Skulls and Roman Kings (Bronx); Crips and Piru, Sangra and Lomas (Los Angeles); Hwa Ching and Chung Ching Yee (San Francisco).

The "foray" was represented by a number of respondents as the currently dominant form of gang engagement. This pattern, locally called "guerilla warfare," and by other terms, involves relatively small (five to 10) raiding parties, frequently motorized, reconnoitering in search of rivals, and engaging in combat if contact is made. Forays are seldom announced, and count on surprise for their success. Raiding parties are almost always armed, and tactics are mobile, fluid, and often intricate. Since the raiding parties almost always carry firearms, such engagements frequently involve serious injuries and sometimes death. The "hit" resembles the foray in that it involves a small band of gang members generally in automobiles, scouting out individual members of rival gangs, finding one or two, and blasting away at them with shotguns, rifles, or other firearms. In a variant of a hit, members of the marauding band leave the auto once a rival is located and engage him on foot.

One pattern of engagement which combines several of the forms just cited was reported, with

[8]The "rumble," in either its pre-arranged or "spontaneous" manifestations, was in all probability not nearly as common in the 1950's as a generally supposed. One study that reported prevalence data on forms of gang engagement in the '50's states that "The most common forms (of gang-member assault) was the collective engagement between members of different gangs; . . . (but) few of these were full-scale massed-encounter gang fights; most were brief strike-and-fallback forays by small guerrilla bands." (W. B. Miller, *Ibid.,* 1966, p. 107.)

high consensus as to details, by a majority of Chicago respondents. A carful of gang members cruises the area of a rival gang, looking for rival gang members. If one is found, he will be attacked in one of several ways; gang members will remain in the car and shoot the victim, or will leave the car and beat or stab him. If the victim is wearing a gang sweater, this will be taken as a trophy, and in fact this kind of coup-counting is often given as the reason for the "hit" expedition. This type of initiatory incident (called a "preemptive strike" by one respondent) is followed by a retaliatory attack in numbers by the gangmates of the "strike" victim, generally in the form of an unannounced excursion into rival gang territory, although in some instances retaliation may take the form of a planned rumble. The latter form was stated to be more common for conflict occurring in school-environments, and among Latino gangs.

One respondent stated that while motorized forays and/or hits are common in Chicago, its consequences are less lethal than in Philadelphia, since the major type of weapons used, .22 pistols or rifles, are less likely to produce death or serious injury than the sawed-off shotguns characteristically employed in the latter city. A Philadelphia respondent reported that local gang members often conduct an initial recon-noitering excursion on bicycles, and return with cars once gang rivals have been located.

The "fair fight" and "execution" share in common only the fact that they involve only two antagonists. The former type involves two rival gang members who engage in one-to-one combat as representatives of their respective gangs. While never particularly common in the past, this form appears to have become virtually extinct in the 1970's, although its presence was reported in one instance. One respondent explained the demise of the fair fight on the grounds that today's gangs have abandoned the traditional sense of gang honor, which required that rival gangs accept as binding the victory or defeat achieved by their designated champion. Today, he said, a defeat in a "fair fight" would at

once be followed by an attack by the losing side, dishonorably refusing to accept its outcome. In Detroit, a respondent said that one-to-one fights between members of rival gangs most often serve as the initiatory incident which triggers a series of larger scale retaliatory engagements.

In the "execution," a particular member of a rival gang is selected for assassination on the basis of behavior for which he is seen to have been responsible as an individual or as a representative of his gang—for example, making advances to a girl associated with the offended gang. A single gang member acts as a "hit" man, seeks out the target, and attempts to kill him, generally by shooting. A "punitive assault" involves actual or potential members of the same gang. A gang member may be subject to a disciplinary beating or in rare instances killed for violating gang rules; in some cases local youth who refuse to join a gang, or having joined wish to leave, are subject to attack on these grounds. Evidence as to the prevalence of punitive assault is unavailable, but it is in all probability the least prevalent of the forms noted here; it has rarely been reported for previous periods, and may represent one of the newer developments of the 1970's.

Property Destruction   In an earlier paper on gang violence,[9] damage inflicted on property was included as one form of violent crime. The present report does not include a discussion of this form. It should be noted, however, that destruction of property constitutes a very serious form of gang crime in some areas. With respect to vandalism per se, gangs in certain suburban and/or outer-city communities are actively engaged in inflicting damage on automobiles and other property, with damage costs totalling hundreds of thousands of dollars. In some slum communities, gangs have effected almost complete destruction of community recreational facilities and have participated in extensive destruction of school facilities. Another extremely serious manifestation of property damage ac-

[9]W. B. Miller, 1966, *Ibid.*

tivities is gang involvement in arson. The burning of hundreds of structures—residential and business, abandoned or occupied, has become increasingly prevalent in slum-area communities throughout the nation, and in many instances gang members are the agents of these conflagrations—sometimes accidentally, more often, deliberately.[10]

Victims of Gang Violence

Findings just presented convey some notion of the present character of gang-member violence in major American cities, but do not include information on two important related issues; what is the relative *prevalence* of the various forms cited, and what categories of persons are the primary victims of gang violence? The latter question, as already noted, is of particular importance in light of widespread claims that it is now *non*-gang members who are the primary victims—particularly adults. As is the case in other sections of this report, the kinds of data necessary to provide accurate and reliable answers to these questions are unavailable. However, to an even greater extent than in other sections, and partially with respect to the latter questions, it is important to attempt some sort of approximation, however rough and tentative, because respondents' estimates of the proportion of non-gang victims varies so widely. One stated, for example, that over 80 percent of victims were non-gang members, while another claimed that non-gang victims comprised only a small minority, and even here victimization was accidental. Not only were these two respondents referring to the same city, but they were both members of the same police department.

One of the few available sources of routine identification as to the identity of victims which is amenable to quantitative treatment are incidents of gang violence described in the daily

press in sufficient detail as to permit analytic categorization. Methodologically, the use of newspaper reports involves obvious problems, particularly with respect to issues of representativeness and selection criteria. However, the importance of analyzing some fairly large population of events to derive numerical findings as to what categories of persons are most frequently victimized serves to counter-balance to some degree the obvious limitations of the data source. Moreover, as will be seen, a surprising degree of regularity in the results obtained seems to indicate a higher level of adequacy for these data than one might expect.

Table V is based on an analysis of 301 incidents of gang violence reported in the press of the four largest cities between January 1973 and June 1975. The 1973 cutoff date was used to insure that reported victimization patterns be as current as possible. Two major categories of victim are distinguished—gang members and non-gang member, as well as two sub-categories of each; for gang members, whether victimization occurred in the context of larger-scale rumbles/warfare, or smaller-scale band/individual assaults; for non-gang members these are two subcategories of victim—peers—generally males of similar age, and non-peers—mostly male or female adults, but sometimes children.

One surprising feature of the table is the degree of similarity among the four cities in the proportions of reported victims in the several categories. Four-city totals show that just about 60 percent of reported victims were gang-members, and 40 percent non-gang members. None of the four cities varies by more than 10 percentage points from these figures. These findings would appear to weaken assertions that the majority of victims of gang violence in the 1970's are non-gang-members. It should be noted that in addition to estimates reported earlier which diverge sharply from these figures, figures given by other respondents, sometimes in the same cities, were very close to those shown here. A probation worker in the city where

---

[10]See, for example, F. C. Shapiro "Raking the Ashes of the Epidemic Flame," *New York Times Magazine,* July 13, 1975, p. 16—"We know it's the work of a juvenile gang. They're waiting for (the firemen) when we get there, all wearing their uniform jackets."

Table V. Victims of Gang Violence: Four Cities
(N Incidents = 301: 1973-'75)[a]

	City				
Type of Victim	N.Y.C. N=80	Chi. N=58	L.A. N=108	Phil. N=55	Four Cities N=301
Gang Member	51.2[b]	56.9	66.7	65.5	60.5
Via rumble, warfare	36.2	22.4	35.2	28.2	31.9
Via band, ind'l assault	15.0	34.5	31.5	36.2	28.6
Non-Gang Member	48.8	43.1	33.3	34.6	39.5
Peers	11.5	8.6	11.1	18.2	11.9
Children, Adults	37.5	34.5	22.2	16.4	27.6
	100.0	100.0	100.0	100.0	100.0

[a] First 6 months
[b] All figures in table are percentages

police officials gave diametrically opposed estimates reckoned that "about 60 percent of gang victims are other gang members."

Of the four victim subcategories, the gang-members involved in rumbles and "warfare" ranked highest as victims, gang members assaulted in the course of individual or smaller band encounters, second highest, adults or children not affiliated with gangs ranked third, and non-gang peers, fourth.

While these figures would appear to weaken assertions that the primary victims of 1970's gangs are uninvolved "outsiders" rather than other gang members or local peers, they provide no basis for determining whether the proportions shown here differ substantially from those of the past. The 28 percent four-city figure for non-gang, non-peer victims might represent a major development if equivalent percentages in the past were, say, in the neighborhood of 5 percent. Directly comparable data for past periods are not available. However, there are data which permit an indirect comparison. These were gathered in the course of a three-year gang study in Boston in the 1950's, in the course of which all known incidents of gang assault involving members of seven gangs in one

city district were recorded by field workers, analyzed, and reported.[11]

Table VI compares proportions of three categories of victim obtained through the current four-city analysis and the single-community study 20 years earlier. In the face of differences of time, methods and locations, proportions are surprisingly similar. Gang members were victims in 60 percent of reported incidents in the '70's compared to 57 percent in the '50's. Non-gang adults and children were victims in 28 percent of current incidents, 22 percent in the past. The non-gang-peer category showed less similarity, with such persons being victimized by gangs only about half as often as during the recent period. Even so, the proportions fall within 10 percent of each other.

Comparing victimization figures by category for the four major cities clarifies the issue of non-gang member victimization. The four-city average of victimization of children and adults—28 percent—is somewhat, but not much higher than the 22 percent figure of the earlier study. On this basis, such victimization does not appear as a particular distinctive practice of con-

[11] Walter B. Miller, *Ibid.,* 1966, Table 5, p. 109.

Table VI. Three Categories of Gang Member Victims
Two Studies Compared: 1955-57, 1973-75

Type of Victim	301 Press-Reported Incidents, Four Cities, 1973-75	77 Field Recorded Incidents, One Community, 1955-57[a]
Gang member	60.5	57.1
Non-gang child, adult	27.6	22.0
Non-gang peer	11.9	20.8
Three categories	100.0	99.9

[a]Violent Crimes in City Gangs, 1966, Table 5, p. 109

temporary gangs. However, looking at city-by-city percentages, it is apparent that the children and adult victimization figures in the two largest cities (New York 38 percent, Chicago 35 percent) are substantially higher than those for the next largest (Los Angeles 22 percent, Philadelphia 16 percent) as well as the 1950's figure (21 percent). This suggests that there is considerable substance to claims by New Yorkers and Chicagoans that increasing victimization of children and adults represents a significant development, but that similar claims by Los Angelenos and Philadelphians be regarded with some caution.

Weaponry

How lethal is the violence of contemporary gangs? Data just presented concerning the forms and victims of gang violence provide no direct information as to the consequences of such violence. No examination of injuries, maiming, intimidation, property destruction, and other consequences of actual or threatened violence is included in this report. However, the discussion of gang member violence in the 1970's requires at the very least some attention to the role of weaponry—a primary instrument of violent victimization.[12]

On October 27, 1919, a Chicago newspaper ran a story on the killing of a member of the Elston youth gang by a 15-year-old member of the Belmonts—a North Side gang—in the course of a continuing "turf war" between the two gangs. The story used these words: "(The Elston gang member) was killed by a bullet from a .22-caliber rifle. In the past two years, when the two gangs realized the impotency of using bare knuckles and ragged stones, each turned to firearms."[13]

This statement, incorporating the basic notion that gangs until recently have engaged in violence by means other than guns but that today have turned to guns, has been forwarded repeatedly in almost identical form during every decade of the 55 years since the Belmont-Elston killing. Most often the time period cited for the reported resort to guns is "two or three years ago;" a less frequent version of the statement uses the period "15 or 20 years ago"—often corresponding to the gang-member age-period of the reporter's life.

[12]Information concerning use, prevalence, and types of weapons was solicited in each of the 12 survey cities as one of the 24 "gang information topics" mentioned earlier. However, this report does not present an analysis of this topic with the degree of detail used, for example, in the analysis of the "operating philosophies" item of the survey guide (W.B. Miller, "Operating Philosophies of Criminal Justice and Youth Survey Professionals in Twelve Major American Cities" Op. cit.). The present treatment of weaponry is based on a partial and non-systematic examination of selected materials for six of the 12 cities.

[13]Frederick M. Thrasher, The Gang, University of Chicago Press, 1927, p. 180.

Given the almost ritualized nature of the claim that gangs of the past used fists, clubs, missiles, and the like, but have "only recently" turned to guns, claims of increasing use and prevalence of guns must be approached with particular caution. Statements regarding guns made both by survey respondents and in other sources have thus been subject to particularly careful appraisal. Approaching the factual accuracy of such statements with an attitude of scepticism, one conclusion nonetheless seems inescapable. The prevalence, use, quality, and sophistication of weaponry in the gangs of the 1970's far surpasses anything known in the past, and is probably the single most significant characteristic distinguishing today's gangs from their predecessors.

Why has information as to gang-related killings not been reported on a routine basis in past studies of youth gangs? Very probably a major reason is that in the past actual killings were relatively rare as an outcome of assaultive activities by gangs. Admitting the dangers of generalizations in the absence of reliable information from the past, the weight of evidence would seem to support the conclusion that the consequences of assaultive activities by contemporary gangs are markedly more lethal than during any previous period. Data just presented respecting the forms and victims of gang violence show some departures from the practices of previous periods, but by and large these differences are not of sufficient magnitude to account for marked differences in the degree of lethality currently observed. It would appear that the major differentiating factor is that of weaponry. This raises several questions: how prevalent are firearms, what is the character of gang weaponry, and how can one account for increases in its prevalence and quality?

Questions as to the use of firearms in the several cities typically elicited answers such as "*Everybody's* got them; they have them either on their persons or in their homes" (New York); "Guns are now available all over; they are a prime target of burglaries" (Chicago); "In this city a gang is judged by the number and quality of weapons they have; the most heavily armed gang is the most feared; for our gangs, firepower is the name of the game" (Los Angeles); "The most dramatic change in the gang situation here lies in the use of firearms" (Philadelphia).

There is little doubt that such statements involve elements of exaggeration; when pressed, some of these who claimed that "everybody" now has guns said that in a typical gang of 40 persons, perhaps 20 own guns, compared to two or three in the past. Others stated that the gangs did not actually possess all the guns they used, but borrowed or rented arms from other gangs or persons. In the absence of more careful analysis of the weaponry data, the possibility of such exaggeration remains. Even so, there was virtually unanimous agreement by respondents in all cities that guns of a variety of kinds were extremely prevalent in the community, easy to obtain, and used extensively by gang members.

A very rough notion of the prevalence of weapons is furnished by the kinds of arrest figures presented in the previous section. New York police reported approximately 1,500 arrests of gang members for "possession of dangerous weapons" between 1972 and 1974 (all "dangerous weapons" are not firearms, but most are); Chicago recorded 700 gang member arrests for "possession of firearms" in 1974 alone; in the same year Los Angeles reported 1,100 gang-member arrests for "assault with a deadly weapon," and 115 more for "shooting at inhabited dwellings." Philadelphia reported about 500 shooting incidents involving gang members between 1971 and '73. These figures substantially under-represent the actual number of guns in circulation, since they record only gun use or possession that comes to official notice.[14]

Probably the most careful accounting of gang

---

[14] A discussion of reasons for the increased availability of weapons in the 1970's will be included in the expanded version of this report.

weaponry in major cities is that of the Bronx Division of the New York City Police Department's Gang Intelligence Unit. Lists compiled in 1973 and '74 included 25 categories of weapon used by gang members. Of these, weapons in 17 of the categories utilize gunpowder or some other explosive. The categories include: "Rifles, all calibers;" "Shotguns, all calibers (sawed-off);" Handguns (revolvers, automatics) 22, 25, 32, 38, 45 caliber;" "Semi-automatic rifles converted to automatic;" "Home-made mortars;" "Home-made bazookas;" "Molotov Cocktails;" "Pipe Bombs." In only one of the six cities, San Francisco, was the "Saturday night special" (a cheap, short-barrelled .22 revolver) cited as the major kind of gang weapon; in all other cities respondents claimed that the majority of guns used were at the level of high-quality police weapons; the Smith and Wesson .38, one common type of police weapon, was mentioned several times. Home-made "zip guns," reported as prevalent in the 1950's, were mentioned as still used by some younger gang members, but several informants said that such crude weaponry was held in contempt by most gang members.

Accurate information concerning the role of weaponry is important not only because of its obvious bearing on the capacity of gang members to pose a lethal threat to one another and to non-gang victims, but because such information bears directly on the issue of the "causes" or origins of contemporary patterns of gang violence.[15] One of the most common elements of current efforts to account for increased gang violence is the notion, particularly favored by the media, that today's gang member, in common with other violent youthful offenders, simply lacks the capacity to conceive the taking of human life as wrongful. This position, frequently forwarded in the past in connection with conceptions of "psychopathic" or "sociopathic" personalities, is given substance in

current media images through televised or quoted statements by youthful killers such as "What do I feel when I kill somebody? Nothing at all. It's nothing more to me than brushing off a fly."

These images serve to symbolize a theory that basic changes have occurred in the moral capacity of many youth whereby the act of killing is seen simply as a means to an end, unaccompanied by any sense of moral wrongness, and that the spread of such a morality underlies increases in lethal violence by gang members and others.

Without exploring the plausibility, character of supportive evidence, or other implications of this position, it is appropriate simply to note at this point that of two posited factors for explaining increases in violence—a basic personality change in American youth and an increased availability of firearms, the latter appears far more likely to exert a significant influence. The fact that guns are readily available, far more prevalent, and far more widely used than in the past seems well established, while the postulated changes in basic moral conceptions remain highly conjectural.

This would suggest that theories based on changes in technologies or social arrangements show a more obvious relationship to changes in patterns of gang violence than theories based on changes in human nature. This point may also be illustrated in connection with a development noted earlier.

Data just presented indicates that the motorized foray has become more prevalent relative to the rumble as a form of intergang conflict. One reason clearly involves technology. The classic rumble could be and can be executed with combatants proceeding by foot to the battle site and there engaging each other with fists, clubs, chains, and possibly knives—logistical and technological means available to combatants throughout recorded history. By contrast, the foray, in one of its major forms, requires two technological devices—the automobile and the gun. While both have been in existence for some

---

[15] A fuller and more systematic treatment of the causes or origins of current manifestations of youth gang violence will be included in the expanded version of this report.

time, neither has been readily available in large numbers to urban adolescents until relatively recently. In the 1970's, for reasons not well understood, the conjoint use of guns and cars has increased substantially. Those technological and economic factors which govern the availability to adolescents of firearms and automobiles have thus played a major role in changing the character of major forms of gang violence.

Motives for Gang Violence

Consideration of the reasons behind acts of violence by gang members is part of the larger issue of the motivation for gang behavior in general, and as such is not treated in the present report. However, one aspect of this issue is relevant to the present discussion. Of four distinguishable motives for engaging in gang violence—honor, local turf-defense, control, and gain, all four have been operative in the past, and all four continue to be operative in the present. However, it would appear that violent acts in the service of the latter two—control and gain, have been increasing in frequency at the expense of the former. Much of the information concerning forms of gang violence—intimidation of possible court witnesses, claims of control over the facilities and educational/disciplinary policies of the schools, claims of complete hegemoy over parks and other recreational areas—reflects an increased use of violence for purposes of control.

Similarly, reports of the extension of extortion or "shakedown" operations from peers to adult merchants, robbery of "easy" victims such as elderly people, predatory excursions by smaller bands for mugging or otherwise robbing the general citizenry, appear to reflect greater stress on the use of violence as a means to the acquisition of money and salable goods. All these issues—the nature of motives for violence, possible changes in the character of such motives, and possible reasons for such changes, call for additional information and analysis.

Summary   A common propensity to exaggerate and sensationalize the prevalence and severity of gang violence makes it particularly important to approach this topic with care, caution, and scepticism. Claims that "gangs of today" are far more violent than their predecessors must be regarded with particular caution, since such claims have been made so often in the past. In reviewing academic studies of gang problems in the 1950's and '60's, it would appear that the more careful and scholarly the study, the less emphasis was placed by the authors on the centrality and gravity of violence as a basic form of gang activity. One of the foremost scholars of gangs of the '50's and '60's, Malcolm Klein, in a comprehensive view of gang studies of this period, consistently played down the saliency and seriousness of violence as a form of gang behavior, and concluded his review with the statement "Gang violence, it must be admitted, is *not* now a major social problem."[16]

Starting from the assumption that gang violence during the past several decades was less severe than represented by most contemporary reporters, and recognizing that the tendency to exaggerate such severity is equally characteristic of the present period, the following conclusions as to gang violence in the 1970's seem warranted.

Violent acts committed by members of youth gangs in six major cities in the 1970's, as in the past, encompass a wide range of different forms and manifestations. Of these, violence which takes as its victims persons outside the immediate orbit of gang members—primarily adults and children in similar or different communities—has the greatest capacity to arouse public fear, and to engender perceptions that youth gangs pose a serious crime problem. Eight forms of inter-and intra-gang conflict may be distinguished—the planned rumble, the rumble, warfare, the foray, the hit, the fair fight, the execution, and punitive assault. While there is some evidence of "specializations" in different cities, most of the above forms were reported as

---

[16]M. Klein, "Violence in American Juvenile Gangs," *Op cit.,* p. 1,457.

present in all six cities. The notion that the "rumble," in either its "planned" or "spontaneous" form has disappeared was not supported by available evidence; however, it does appear that the "foray"—an excursion by smaller bands, generally armed and often motorized—has increased in prevalence relative to the rumble. With respect to victimization, the notion that non-gang adults and children have become the primary victims of gang violence was not supported; of three categories of victim identifiable through press reports, other gang members comprised about 60 percent, adults and children about 28 percent, and non-gang peers about 12 percent. The 60 percent gang, 40 percent non-gang ratios based on four city averages do not differ substantially from figures recorded in the past. However, when figures are differentiated by city, considerable substance is granted the notion of increased non-gang-member victimization in the nation's two largest cities, where non-gang-members appear as victims in almost half of the reported incidents, and non-gang children and adults in well over one-third.

A major development of the 1970's appears to lie in a very substantial increase in the availability, sophistication, and use of firearms as an instrument of gang violence. This may well be the single most significant feature of today's gang activity in evaluating its seriousness as a crime problem. The increased use of firearms to effect violent crimes (often in concert with motorized transport) has substantially increased the likelihood that violence directed both to other gang members and the general citizenry will have lethal consequences.

Participation in destructive acts by gang members involving property destruction also appears to be on the rise. Major manifestations are extensive vandalism of school facilities, destruction of parks, recreational and other public facilities, and the destruction of buildings through arson.

Related to changes in forms and victims of gang-member violence noted above appear to be changes in motives for violence. Insofar as gang violence is played out in an arena of inter-gang conflict, motives arising out of "honor" ("rep," "heart" in the past), and defense of local turf play a major role; as muggings, robberies, and extortion of community residents have become relatively more prevalent, and as efforts to intimidate witnesses, determine school policies, and dominate public facilities have become more widespread, the motives of "gain," and "control" can be seen as playing a larger role.

In sum, taking into account tendencies to exaggerate the scope and seriousness of gang violence, and to represent the "gang of today" as far more violent than its predecessors, evidence currently available indicates with considerable clarity that the amount of lethal violence currently directed by youth gangs in major cities both against one another and against the general public is without precedent. It is not unlikely that contemporary young gangs pose a greater threat to the public order, and greater danger to the safety of the citizenry, than at any time during the past.

46. The Saints and The Roughnecks

WILLIAM J. CHAMBLISS

EIGHT PROMISING YOUNG MEN—CHILDREN OF good, stable, white upper-middle-class families, active in school affairs, good pre-college students—were some of the most delinquent boys at Hanibal High School. While community residents and parents knew that these boys occasionally sowed a few wild oats, they were totally unaware that sowing wild oats completely occupied the daily routine of these young men. The Saints were constantly occupied with truancy, drinking, wild driving, petty theft and vandalism. Yet not one was officially arrested for any misdeed during the two years I observed.

This record was particularly surprising in light of my observations during the same two years of another gang of Hanibal High School students, six lower-class white boys known as the Roughnecks. The Roughnecks were constantly in trouble with police and community even though their rate of delinquency was about equal with that of the Saints. What was the cause of this disparity? the result? The following consideration of the activities, social class and community perceptions of both gangs may provide some answers.

▶SOURCE: *"The Saints and the Roughnecks," Society (November/December 1973) 11(1):24–31. Reprinted by permission of Transaction, Inc., from Society Vol. 11. Copyright © 1973 by Transaction, Inc.*

THE SAINTS FROM MONDAY TO FRIDAY

The Saints' principal daily concern was with getting out of school as early as possible. The boys managed to get out of school with minimum danger that they would be accused of playing hookey through an elaborate procedure for obtaining "legitimate" release from class. The most common procedure was for one boy to obtain the release of another by fabricating a meeting of some committee, program or recognized club. Charles might raise his hand in his 9:00 chemistry class and asked to be excused—a euphemism for going to the bathroom. Charles would go to Ed's math class and inform the teacher that Ed was needed for a 9:30 rehearsal of the drama club play. The math teacher would recognize Ed and Charles as "good students" involved in numerous school activities and would permit Ed to leave at 9:30. Charles would return to his class, and Ed would go to Tom's English class to obtain his release. Tom would engineer Charles' escape. The strategy would continue until as many of the Saints as possible were freed. After a stealthy trip to the car (which had been parked in a strategic spot), the boys were off for a day of fun.

Over the two years I observed the Saints, this pattern was repeated nearly every day. There were variations on the theme, but in one form or another, the boys used this procedure for getting out of class and then off the school grounds. Rarely did all eight of the Saints manage to leave school at the same time. The average number avoiding school on the days I observed them was five.

Having escaped from the concrete corridors the boys usually went either to a pool hall on the other (lower-class) side of town or to a cafe in the suburbs. Both places were out of the way of people the boys were likely to know (family or school officials), and both provided a source of entertainment. The pool hall entertainment was the generally rough atmosphere, the occasional hustler, the sometimes drunk proprietor and, of course, the game of pool. The cafe's entertainment was provided by the owner. The boys would "accidently" knock a glass on the floor or spill cola on the counter—not all the time, but enough to be sporting. They would also bend spoons, put salt in sugar bowls and generally tease whoever was working in the cafe. The owner had opened the cafe recently and was dependent on the boys' business which was, in fact, substantial since between the horsing around and the teasing they bought food and drinks.

THE SAINTS ON WEEKENDS

On weekends the automobile was even more critical than during the week, for on weekends the Saints went to Big Town—a large city with a population of over a million 25 miles from Hanibal. Every Friday and Saturday night most of the Saints would meet between 8:00 and 8:30 and would go into Big Town. Big Town activities included drinking heavily in taverns or nightclubs, driving drunkenly through the streets, and committing acts of vandalism and playing pranks.

By midnight on Fridays and Saturdays the Saints were usually thoroughly high, and one or two of them were often so drunk they had to be carried to the cars. Then the boys drove around town, calling obscenities to women and girls; oc-

casionally trying (unsuccessfully so far as I could tell) to pick girls up; and driving recklessly through red lights and at high speeds with their lights out. Occasionally they played "chicken." One boy would climb out the back window of the car and across the roof to the driver's side of the car while the car was moving at high speed (between 40 and 50 miles an hour); then the driver would move over and the boy who had just crawled across the car roof would take the driver's seat.

Searching for "fair game" for a prank was the boys' principal activity after they left the tavern. The boys would drive alongside a foot patrolman and ask directions to some street. If the policeman leaned on the car in the course of answering the question, the driver would speed away, causing him to lose his balance. The Saints were careful to play this prank only in an area where they wre not going to spend much time and where they could quickly disappear around a corner to avoid having their license plate number taken.

Construction sites and road repair areas were the special province of the Saints' mischief. A soon-to-be-repaired hole in the road inevitably invited the Saints to remove lanterns and wooden barricades and put them in the car, leaving the hole unprotected. The boys would find a safe vantage point and wait for an unsuspecting motorist to drive into the hole. Often, though not always, the boys would go up to the motorist and commiserate with him about the dreadful way the city protected its citizenry.

Leaving the scene of the open hole and the motorist, the boys would then go searching for an appropriate place to erect the stolen barricade. An "appropriate place" was often a spot on a highway near a curve in the road where the barricade would not be seen by an oncoming motorist. The boys would wait to watch an unsuspecting motorist attempt to stop and (usually) crash into the wooden barricade. With saintly bearing the boys might offer help and understanding.

A stolen lantern might well find its way onto the back of a police car or hang from a street lamp. Once a lantern served as a prop for a reenactment of the "midnight ride of Paul Revere" until the "play," which was taking place at 2:00 AM in the center of a main street of Big Town, was interrupted by a police car several blocks away. The boys ran, leaving the lanterns on the street, and managed to avoid being apprehended.

Abandoned houses, especially if they were located in out-of-the-way places, were fair game for destruction and spontaneous vandalism. The boys would break windows, remove furniture to the yard and tear it apart, urinate on the walls and scrawl obscenities inside.

Through all the pranks, drinking and reckless driving the boys managed miraculously to avoid being stopped by police. Only twice in two years was I aware that they had been stopped by a Big City policeman. Once was for speeding (which they did every time they drove whether they were drunk or sober), and the driver managed to convince the policeman that it was simply an error. The second time they were stopped they had just left a nightclub and were walking through an alley. Aaron stopped to urinate and the boys began making obscene remarks. A foot patrolman came into the alley, lectured the boys and sent them home. Before the boys got to the car one began talking in a loud voice again. The policeman, who had followed them down the alley, arrested this boy for disturbing the peace and took him to the police station where the other Saints gathered. After paying a $5.00 fine, and with the assurance that there would be no permanent record of the arrest, the boy was released.

The boys had a spirit of frivolity and fun about their escapades. They did not view what they were engaged in as "delinquency," though it surely was by any reasonable definition of that word. They simply viewed themselves as having a little fun and who, they would ask, was really hurt by it? The answer had to be no one, although this fact remains one of the most difficult things to explain about the gang's behavior. Unlikely though it seems, in two years of drinking, driving, carousing and vandalism no one was seriously injured as a result of the Saints' activities.

THE SAINTS IN SCHOOL

The Saints were highly successful in school. The average grade for the group was "B," with two of the boys having close to a straight "A" average. Almost all of the boys were popular and many of them held offices in the school. One of the boys was vice-president of the student body one year. Six of the boys played on athletic teams.

At the end of their senior year, the student body selected ten seniors for special recognition as the "school wheels"; four of the ten were Saints. Teachers and school officials saw no problem with any of these boys and anticipated that they would all "make something of themselves."

How the boys managed to maintain this impression is surprising in view of their actual behavior while in school. Their technique for covering truancy was so successful that teachers did not even realize that the boys were absent from school much of the time. Occasionally, of course, the system would backfire and then the boy was on his own. A boy who was caught would be most contrite, would plead guilty and ask for mercy. He inevitably got the mercy he sought.

Cheating on examinations was rampant, even to the point of orally communicating answers to exams as well as looking at one another's papers. Since none of the group studied, and since they were primarily dependent on one another for help, it is surprising that grades were so high. Teachers contributed to the deception in their admitted inclination to give these boys (and presumably others like them) the benefit of the doubt. When asked how the boys did in school, and when pressed on specific examinations, teachers might admit that they were disappointed in John's performance, but would quickly add that they "knew that he was capable of doing better," so John was given a higher grade than he had actually earned. How often this happened is impossible to know. During the time that I observed the group, I never saw any of the boys take homework home. Teachers may have been "understanding" very regularly.

One exception to the gang's generally good performance was Jerry, who had a "C" average in his junior year, experienced disaster the next year and failed to graduate. Jerry had always been a little more nonchalant than the others about the liberties he took in school. Rather than wait for someone to come get him from class, he would offer his own excuse and leave. Although he probably did not miss any more classes than most of the others in the group, he did not take the requisite pains to cover his absences. Jerry was the only Saint whom I ever heard talk back to a teacher. Although teachers often called him a "cut up" or a "smart kid," they never referred to him as a troublemaker or as a kid headed for trouble. It seems likely, then, that Jerry's failure his senior year and his mediocre performance his junior year were consequences of his not playing the game the proper way (possibly because he was disturbed by his parents' divorce). His teachers regarded him as "immature" and not quite ready to get out of high school.

THE POLICE AND THE SAINTS

The local police saw the Saints as good boys who were among the leaders of the youth in the community. Rarely, the boys might be stopped in town for speeding or for running a stop sign. When this happened the boys were always polite, contrite and pled for mercy. As in school, they received the mercy they asked for. None ever received a ticket or was taken into the precinct by the local police.

The situation in Big City, where the boys engaged in most of their delinquency, was only slightly different. The police there did not know the boys at all, although occasionally the boys were stopped by a patrolman. Once they were caught taking a lantern from a construction site. Another time they were stopped for running a stop sign, and on several occasions they were stopped for speeding. Their behavior was as before: contrite, polite and penitent. The urban police, like the local police, accepted their demeanor as sincere. More important, the urban police were convinced that these were good boys just out for a lark.

THE ROUGHNECKS

Hanibal townspeople never perceived the Saints' high level of delinquency. The Saints were good boys who just went in for an occasional prank. After all, they were well dressed, well mannered and had nice cars. The Roughnecks were a different story. Although the two gangs of boys were the same age, and both groups engaged in an equal amount of wild-oat sowing, everyone agreed that the not-so-well-dressed, not-so-well-mannered, not-so-rich boys were heading for trouble. Townspeople would say, "You can see the gang members at the drugstore, night after night, leaning against the storefront (sometimes drunk) or slouching around inside buying cokes, reading magazines, and probably stealing old Mr. Wall blind. When they are outside and girls walk by, even respectable girls, these boys make suggestive remarks. Sometimes their remarks are downright lewd."

From the community's viewpoint, the real indication that these kids were in for trouble was that they were constantly involved with the police. Some of them had been picked up for stealing, mostly small stuff, of course, "but still it's stealing small stuff that leads to big time crimes." "Too bad," people said. "Too bad that these boys couldn't behave like the other kids in town; stay out of trouble, be polite to adults, and look to their future."

The community's impression of the degree to which this group of six boys (ranging in age from 16 to 19) engaged in delinquency was somewhat distorted. In some ways the gang was more delinquent than the community thought; in other ways they were less.

The fighting activities of the group were fairly readily and accurately perceived by almost everyone. At least once a month, the boys would get into some sort of fight, although most fights were scraps between members of the group or involved only one member of the group and some peripheral hanger-on. Only three times in the period of observation did the group fight together; once against a gang from across town, once against two blacks and once against a group of boys from another school. For the first two fights the group went out "looking for trouble"—and they found it both times. The third fight followed a football game and began spontaneously with an argument on the football field between one of the Roughnecks and a member of the opposition's football team.

Jack had a particular propensity for fighting and was involved in most of the brawls. He was a prime mover of the escalation of arguments into fights.

More serious than fighting, had the community been aware of it, was theft. Although almost everyone was aware that the boys occasionally stole things, they did not realize the extent of the activity. Petty stealing was a frequent event for the Roughnecks. Sometimes they stole as a group and coordinated their efforts; other times they stole in pairs. Rarely did they steal alone.

The thefts ranged from very small things like paperback books, comics and ballpoint pens to expensive items like watches. The nature of the thefts varied from time to time. The gang would go through a period of systematically shoplifting items from automobiles or school lockers. Types of thievery varied with the whim of the gang. Some forms of thievery were more profitable than others, but all thefts were for profit, not just thrills.

Roughnecks siphoned gasoline from cars as often as they had access to an automobile, which was not very often. Unlike the Saints, who owned their own cars, the Roughnecks would have to borrow their parents' cars, an event which occurred only eight or nine times a year. The boys claimed to have stolen cars for joy rides from time to time.

Ron committed the most serious of the group's offenses. With an unidentified associate the boy attempted to burglarize a gasoline station. Although this station had been robbed twice previously in the same month, Ron denied any involvement in either of the other thefts. When Ron and his accomplice approached the station, the owner was hiding in the bushes beside the station. He fired both barrels of a double-barreled shotgun at the boys. Ron was severely injured; the other boy ran away and was never caught. Though he remained in critical condition for several months, Ron finally recovered and served six months of the following year in reform school. Upon release from reform school, Ron was put back a grade in school, and began running around with a different gang of boys. The Roughnecks considered the new gang less delinquent than themselves, and during the following year Ron had no more trouble with the police.

The Roughnecks, then, engaged mainly in three types of delinquency; theft, drinking and fighting. Although community members perceived that this gang of kids was delinquent, they mistakenly believed that their illegal activities were primarily drinking, fighting and being a nuisance to passersby. Drinking was limited among the gang members, although it did occur, and theft was much more prevalent than anyone realized.

Drinking would doubtless have been more prevalent had the boys had ready access to liquor. Since they rarely had automobiles at their disposal, they could not travel very far, and the bars in town would not serve them. Most of the boys had little money, and this, too, inhibited their purchase of alcohol. Their major source of liquor was a local drunk who would buy them a fifth if they would give him enough extra to buy himself a pint of whiskey or a bottle of wine.

The community's perception of drinking as prevalent stemmed from the fact that it was the most obvious delinquency the boys engaged in. When one of the boys had been drinking, even a casual observer seeing him on the corner would suspect that he was high.

There was a high level of mutual distrust and dislike between the Roughnecks and the police. The boys felt very strongly that the police were unfair and corrupt. Some evidence existed that the boys were correct in their perception.

The main source of the boys' dislike for the police undoubtedly stemmed from the fact that the police would sporadically harass the group. From the standpoint of the boys, these acts of occasional enforcement of the law were whimsical and uncalled for. It made no sense to them, for example, that the police would come to the corner occasionally and threaten them with arrest for loitering when the night before the boys had been out siphoning gasoline from cars and the police had been nowhere in sight. To the boys, the police were stupid on the one hand, for not being where they should have been and catching the boys in a serious offense, and unfair on the other hand, for trumping up "loitering" charges against them.

From the viewpoint of the police, the situation was quite different. They knew, with all the confidence necessary to be a policeman, that these boys were engaged in criminal activities. They knew this partly from occasionally catching them, mostly from circumstantial evidence ("the boys were around when those tires were slashed"), and partly because the police shared the view of the community in general that this was a bad bunch of boys. The best the police could hope to do was to be sensitive to the fact that these boys were engaged in illegal acts and arrest them whenever there was some evidence that they had been involved. Whether or not the boys had in fact committed a particular act in a particular way was not especially important. The police had a broader view: their job was to stamp out these kids' crimes; the tactics were not as important as the end result.

Over the period that the group was under observation, each member was arrested at least once. Several of the boys were arrested a number of times and spent at least one night in jail. While most were never taken to court, two of the boys were sentenced to six months' incarceration in boys' schools.

THE ROUGHNECKS IN SCHOOL

The Roughnecks' behavior in school was not particularly disruptive. During school hours they did not all hang around together, but tended instead to spend most of their time with one or two other members of the gang who were their special buddies. Although every member of the gang attempted to avoid school as much as possible, they were not particularly successful and most of them attended school with surprising regularity. They considered school a burden—something to be gotten through with a minimum of conflict. If they were "bugged" by a particular teacher, it could lead to trouble. One of the boys, Al, once threatened to beat up a teacher and, according to the other boys, the teacher hid under a desk to escape him.

Teachers saw the boys the way the general community did, as heading for trouble, as being uninterested in making something of themselves. Some were also seen as being incapable of meeting the academic standards of the school. Most of the teachers expressed concern for this group of boys and were willing to pass them despite poor performance, in the belief that failing them would only aggravate problem.

The group of boys had a grade point average just slightly above "C." No one in the group failed either grade, and no one had better than a "C" average. They were very consistent in their achievement or, at least, the teachers were consistent in their perception of the boys' achievement.

Two of the boys were good football players. Herb was acknowledged to be the best player in the school and Jack was almost as good. Both boys were criticized for their failure to abide by training rules, for refusing to come to practice as often as they should, and for not playing their best during practice. What they lacked in sportsmanship they made up for in skill, apparently, and played every game no matter how poorly they had performed in practice or how many practice sessions they had missed.

TWO QUESTIONS

Why did the community, the school and the police react to the Saints as though they were good, upstanding, nondelinquent youths with bright futures but to the Roughnecks as though they were tough, young criminals who were headed for trouble? Why did the Roughnecks and the Saints in fact have quite different careers after high school—careers which, by and large, lived up to the expectations of the community?

The most obvious explanation for the differences in the community's and law enforcement agencies' reactions to the two gangs is that one group of boys was "more delinquent" than the other. Which group *was* more delinquent? The answer to this question will determine in part how we explain the differential responses to these groups by the members of the community and, particularly, by law enforcement and school officials.

In sheer number of illegal acts, the Saints were the more delinquent. They were truant from school for at least part of the day almost every day of the week. In addition, their drinking and vandalism occurred with surprising regularity. The Roughnecks, in contrast, engaged sporadically in delinquent episodes. While these episodes were frequent, they certainly did not occur on a daily or even a weekly basis.

The difference in frequency of offenses was probably caused by the Roughnecks' inability to obtain liquor and to manipulate legitimate excuses from school. Since the Roughnecks had less money than the Saints, and teachers carefully supervised their school activities, the Roughnecks' hearts may have been as black as the Saints', but their misdeeds were not nearly as frequent.

There are really no clear-cut criteria by which to measure qualitative differences in antisocial behavior. The most important dimension of the difference is generally referred to as the "seriousness" of the offenses.

If seriousness encompasses the relative economic costs of delinquent acts, then some assessment can be made. The Roughnecks probably stole an average of about $5.00 worth of goods a week. Some weeks the figure was considerably higher, but these times must be balanced against long periods when almost nothing was stolen.

The Saints were more continuously engaged in delinquency but their acts were not for the most part costly to property. Only their vandalism and occasional theft of gasoline would so qualify. Perhaps once or twice a month they would siphon a tankful of gas. The other costly items were street signs, construction lanterns and the like. All of these combined probably did not quite average $5.00 a week, partly because much of the stolen equipment was abandoned and presumably could be recovered. The difference in cost of stolen property between the two groups was trivial, but the Roughnecks probably had a slightly more expensive set of activities than did the Saints.

Another meaning of seriousness is the potential threat of physical harm to members of the community and to the boys themselves. The Roughnecks were more prone to physical violence; they not only welcomed an opportunity to fight; they went seeking it. In addition, they fought among themselves frequently. Although the fighting never included deadly weapons, it was still a menace, however minor, to the physical safety of those involved.

The Saints never fought. They avoided physical conflict both inside and outside the group. At the same time, though, the Saints frequently endangered their own and other people's lives. They did so almost every time they drove a car, especially if they had been drinking. Sober, their driving was risky; under the influence of alcohol it was horrendous. In addition, the Saints endangered the lives of others with their pranks. Street excavations left unmarked were a very serious hazard.

Evaluating the relative seriousness of the two gangs' activities is difficult. The community reacted as though the behavior of the Roughnecks was a problem, and they reacted as though the behavior of the Saints was not. But the members of the community were ignorant of the array of delinquent acts that characterized the Saints' behavior. Although concerned citizens were unaware of much of the Roughnecks' behavior as well, they were much better informed about the Roughnecks' involvement in delinquency than they were about the Saints'.

VISIBILITY

Differential treatment of the two gangs resulted in part because one gang was infinitely more visible than the other. This differential visibility was a direct function of the economic standing of the families. The Saints had access to automobiles and were able to remove themselves from the sight of the community. In as routine a decision as to where to go to have a milkshake after school, the Saints stayed away from the mainstream of community life. Lacking transportation, the Roughnecks could not make it to the edge of town. The center of town was the only practical place for them to meet since their homes were scattered throughou the town and any noncentral meeting place put an undue hardship on some members. Through necessity the Roughnecks congregated in a crowded area where everyone in the community passed frequently, including teachers and law enforcement officers. They could easily see the Roughnecks hanging around the drugstore.

The Roughnecks, of course, made themselves even more visible by making remarks to passersby and by occasionally getting into fights on the corner. Meanwhile, just as regularly, the Saints were either at the cafe on one edge of town or in the pool hall at the other edge of town. Without any particular realization that they were making themselves inconspicuous, the Saints were able to hide their time-wasting. Not only were they removed from the mainstream of traffic, but they were almost always inside a building.

On their escapades the Saints were also relatively invisible, since they left Hanibal and traveled to Big City. Here, too, they were mobile, roaming the city, rarely going to the same area twice.

DEMEANOR

To the notion of visibility must be added the difference in the responses of group members to outside intervention with their activities. If one of the Saints was confronted with an accusing policeman, even if he felt he was truly innocent of a wrongdoing, his demeanor was apologetic and penitent. A Roughneck's attitude was almost the polar opposite. When confronted with a threatening adult authority, even one who tried to be pleasant, the Roughneck's hostility and disdain were clearly observable. Sometimes he might attempt to put up a veneer of respect, but it was thin and was not accepted as sincere by the authority.

School was no different from the community at large. The Saints could manipulate the system by feigning compliance with the school norms. The availability of cars at school meant that once free from the immediate sight of the teacher, the boys could disappear rapidly. And this escape was well enough planned that no administrator or teacher was nearby when the boys left. A Roughneck who wished to escape for a few hours was in a bind. If it were possible to get free from class, downtown was still a mile away, and even if he arrived there, he was still very visible. Truancy for the Roughnecks meant almost certain detection, while the Saints enjoyed almost complete immunity from sanctions.

BIAS

Community members were not aware of the transgressions of the Saints. Even if the Saints had been less discreet, their favorite delinquencies would have been perceived as less serious than those of the Roughnecks.

In the eyes of the police and school officials, a boy who drinks in an alley and stands intoxicated on the street corner is committing a more serious offense than is a boy who drinks to inebriation in a nightclub or a tavern and drives around afterwards in a car. Similarly, a boy who steals a wallet from a store will be viewed as having committed a more serious offense than a boy who steals a lantern from a construction site.

Perceptual bias also operates with respect to the demeanor of the boys in the two groups when they are confronted by adults. It is not simply that adults dislike the posture affected by boys of the Roughneck ilk; more important is the conviction that the posture adopted by the Roughnecks is an indication of their devotion and commitment to deviance as a way of life. The posture becomes a cue, just as the type of the offense is a cue, to the degree to which the known transgressions are indicators of the youths' potential for other problems.

Visibility, demeanor and bias are surface variables which explain the day-to-day operations of the police. Why do these surface variables operate as they do? Why did the police choose to disregard the Saints' delinquencies while breathing down the backs of the Roughnecks?

The answer lies in the class structure of American society and the control of legal institutions by those at the top of the class structure. Obviously, no representative of the upper class drew up the operational chart for the police which led them to look in the ghettos and on streetcorners—which led them to see the demeanor of lower-class youth as troublesome and that of upper-middle-class youth as tolerable. Rather, the procedures simply developed from experience—experience with irate and influential upper-middle-class parents insisting that their son's vandalism was simply a prank and his drunkenness only a momentary "sowing of wild oats"—experience with cooperative or indifferent, powerless, lower-class parents who acquiesced to the laws' definition of their son's behavior.

ADULT CAREERS OF THE SAINTS AND THE ROUGHNECKS

The community's confidence in the potential of the Saints and the Roughnecks apparently was justified. If anything, the community members underestimated the degree to which these youngsters would turn out "good" or "bad."

Seven of the eight members of the Saints went on to college immediately after high school. Five of the boys graduated from college in four years. The sixth one finished college after two years in the army, and the seventh spent four years in the air force before returning to college and receiving a B.A. degree. Of these seven college graduates, three went on for advanced degrees. One finished law school and is now active in state politics, one finished medical school and is practicing near Hanibal, and one boy is now working for a Ph.D. The other four college graduates entered submanagerial, managerial or executive training positions with larger firms.

The only Saint who did not complete college was Jerry. Jerry had failed to graduate from high school with the other Saints. During his second senior year, after the other Saints had gone on to college, Jerry began to hang around with what several teachers described as a "rough crowd"—the gang that was heir apparent to the Roughnecks. At the end of his second senior year, when he did graduate from high school, Jerry took a job as a used-car salesman, got married and quickly had a child. Although he made several abortive attempts to go to college by attending night school, when I last saw him (ten years after high school) Jerry was unemployed and had been living on unemployment for almost a year. His wife worked as a waitress.

Some of the Roughnecks have lived up to

community expectations. A number of them were headed for trouble. A few were not.

Jack and Herb were the athletes among the Roughnecks and their athletic prowess paid off handsomely. Both boys received unsolicited athletic scholarships to college. After Herb received his scholarship (near the end of his senior year), he apparently did an about-face. His demeanor became very similar to that of the Saints. Although he remained a member in good standing of the Roughnecks, he stopped participating in most activities and did not hang on the corner as often.

Jack did not change. If anything, he became more prone to fighting. He even made excuses for accepting the scholarship. He told the other gang members that the school had guaranteed him a "C" average if he would come to play football—an idea that seems far-fetched, even in this day of highly competitive recruiting.

During the summer after graduation from high school, Jack attempted suicide by jumping from a tall building. The jump would certainly have killed most people trying it, but Jack survived. He entered college in the fall and played four years of football. He and Herb graduated in four years, and both are teaching and coaching in high schools. They are married and have stable families. If anything, Jack appears to have a more prestigious position in the community than does Herb, though both are well respected and secure in their positions.

Two of the boys never finished high school. Tommy left at the end of his junior year and went to another state. That summer he was arrested and placed on probation on a manslaughter charge. Three years later he was arrested for murder; he pleaded guilty to second degree murder and is serving a 30-year sentence in the state penitentiary.

Al, the other boy who did not finish high school, also left the state in his senior year. He is serving a life sentence in a state penitentiary for first degree murder.

Wes is a small-time gambler. He finished high school and "bummed around." After several years he made contact with a bookmaker who employed him as a runner. Later he acquired his own area and has been working it ever since. His position among the bookmakers is almost identical to the position he had in the gang; he is always around but no one is really aware of him. He makes no trouble and he does not get into any. Steady, reliable, capable of keeping his mouth closed, he plays the game by the rules, even though the game is an illegal one.

That leaves only Ron. Some of his former friends reported that they had heard he was "driving a truck up north," but no one could provide any concrete information.

REINFORCEMENT

The community responded to the Roughnecks as boys in trouble, and the boys agreed with that perception. Their pattern of deviancy was reinforced, and breaking away from it became increasingly unlikely. Once the boys acquired an image of themselves as deviants, they selected new friends who affirmed that self-image. As that self-conception became more firmly entrenched, they also became willing to try new and more extreme deviances. With their growing alienation came freer expression of disrespect and hostility for representatives of the legitimate society. This disrespect increased the community's negativism, perpetuating the entire process of commitment to deviance. Lack of a commitment to deviance works the same way. In either case, the process will perpetuate itself unless some event (like a scholarship to college or a sudden failure) external to the established relationship intervenes. For two of the Roughnecks (Herb and Jack), receiving college athletic scholarships created new relations and culminated in a break with the established pattern of deviance. In the case of one of the Saints (Jerry), his parents' divorce and his failing to graduate from high school changed some of his other relations. Being held back in school for a year and losing his place among the Saints had sufficient impact on Jerry to alter his self-image and virtually to assure that he would not go on to college as his peers did. Although the experiments of life can rarely be reversed, it seems likely in view of the behavior of the other boys who did not enjoy this special treatment by the school that Jerry, too, would have "become something" had he graduated as anticipated. For Herb and Jack outside intervention worked to their advantage; for Jerry it was his undoing.

Selective perception and labelling—finding, processing and punishing some kinds of criminality and not others—means that visible, poor, nonmobile, outspoken, undiplomatic "tough" kids will be noticed, whether their actions are seriously delinquent or not. Other kids, who have established a reputation for being bright (even though underachieving), disciplined and involved in respectable activities, who are mobile and monied, will be invisible when they deviate from sanctioned activities. They'll sow their wild oats—perhaps even wider and thicker than their lower-class cohorts—but they won't be noticed. When it's time to leave adolescence most will follow the expected path, settling into the ways of the middle class, remembering fondly the delinquent but unnoticed fling of their youth. The Roughnecks and others like them may turn around, too. It is more likely that their noticeable deviance will have been so reinforced by police and community that their lives will be effectively channelled into careers consistent with their adolescent background.

47. The Molls

WALTER B. MILLER

YOU'VE SEEN THE CORNER GANG GIRLS ON THE streets of the inner city, talking tough, showing off, looking more menacing than "nice young girls" should. In association with "brother gangs" or by themselves, many of these gang girls (some as young as 12 or 13 years old) hang out at night, use obscene language, insult and play pranks on passersby, drink alcoholic beverages in public, mock social workers and "good kids."

As part of our research on the gangs of Midcity (an inner-city district of an eastern seaport) we studied the Molls, one group of corner gang girls. Although girls' gangs have received little attention during the current wave of concern over gangs and gang violence, the Molls have their counterparts in most major American cities—for example, the Ghetto Sisters and female Savage Nomads of New York. A female field worker maintained continuing contact with the Molls for 30 months. At the start of the contact period the average Moll was 13.5 years old, and at the end, 16 years old. Although the size of the group varied according to the season and changing individual circumstances, the Molls could say of about 11 girls, "She hangs with us."

The Molls were white and Catholic—mostly Irish, with one set of sisters of Irish-German background. Fathers who were known and employed worked at jobs as signhanger, plate

▶SOURCE: *"The Molls," Society (November/December 1973) 11(1): 32–35. Published by permission of Transaction, Inc., from Society Vol. 11 #1. Copyright © by Transaction, Inc.*

glass cutter and factory laborer. Most of the girls' mothers were employed outside the home, holding low-skilled jobs such as housemaid, laundry-press operator, machine operator in a shoe factory and kitchen worker in a hospital. All eight of the Molls' families were known to have received some form of assistance from public welfare agencies. All of their families had been on welfare.

As 14 years olds, the Molls were known in the neighborhood as "bad girls," and in one sense the girls shared this appraisal. The principal leader of the Molls once said of herself, "I'm a real gang girl!" In another sense, they felt this reputation to be unfair. To most neighborhood adults, it was axiomatic that girls who were "bad" after the fashion of the Molls must also be sexually "bad." The Molls resented the lumping together of sexual immorality and what they regarded as conventional illegal behavior. The same girl who boasted of being a real gang girl, fondly reminiscing at 16 of her gang's misbehavior at 14, said, "But we never was really *bad*—not in *that* [sexual] way. . . ."

CRIMINAL BEHAVIOR

What, in fact, was the character of the Molls' criminal behavior? By the time they were 17, all 11 of the Molls were known to have engaged in some form of illegal behavior. Five of the girls had been arrested, four had appeared in court, and two had been confined to correctional institutions. The Molls thus equalled the record of the Midcity boys' gang with the highest percentage of members known to have been arrested. Involvement in illegal acts ranked them well above two male gangs from the same city. Contrast their arrest rate of 45 percent with an 8 percent figure for the other female gang, a group of upwardly mobile black girls, the Queens. The Molls' six most frequent offenses were: truancy (15 involvements per ten girls per ten-month period); theft (4.7); drinking violations (3.3); property damage (2.8); sex offenses (1.3); assault (0.7).

PLAYING HOOKEY

Truancy, failure to attend school for a day, several days or extended periods, was the Molls' most frequent offense. Seven of the 11 girls were known to have truanted, with 44 instances of truancy having been recorded during the contact period. One girl deliberately stayed out of school for three weeks in hopes of being expelled from one school so she could enter another. While out of school the girls often stayed home, sometimes to perform household duties, sometimes to play records and gossip. Mothers' reactions to truancy varied, both among mothers and by the same mother at different times. In some instances daughters stayed home to care for younger siblings or do other household chores at the request of their mothers (especially those who worked during the day). In such cases mothers would write fraudulent excuse notes for the girls. Other mothers were opposed to truancy and punished their daughters for skipping school. The girls themselves gave a variety of reasons for truancy, ranging from home obligations to boredom with studies. Whatever their reasons, the Molls' pattern of irregular school attendance between the ages of 14 and 16 represented an advance manifestation of their ultimate permanent discontinuation of schooling.

In accordance with compulsory education laws, all 11 girls were attending school (some irregularly) at age 14 but as the girls approached the age when leaving school was permitted, they truanted with increasing frequency. Once past age 16, all but two dropped out; none entered college. The Moll's drop-out rate was about 80 percent.

STEALING

Theft was the Moll's second most frequent offense, and as many girls were known to have stolen as to have truanted. Moll theft was generally quite minor in comparison with some of the boy's gangs. Girls stole postcards, magazines, popcorn and fountain pens from local stores. Three of the girls engaged in shoplifting from downtown stores, and one was put on probation when caught. In one instance three girls stole $31 from the aunt of one of them and bought clothes with the money. The Molls themselves considered this theft their most serious, and they later made some attempts at restitution.

DRINKING

Illegal drinking was the third most frequent offense, with six girls known to have been involved. The girls drank beer, wine and liquor at home, on the corner, at school, by themselves and with their brother gang, the Hoods. Most Moll drinking was relatively light, resulting primarily in boisterous behavior. Occasionally they drank more heavily and got drunk. One girl who had been drinking quite heavily made a game of darting into the street to see how closely she could avoid being hit by cars. Several times the Molls were caught in illegal possession of liquor. Once two girls brought a bottle of whiskey to school and in another instance police caught the Molls and Hoods drinking beer in the park. None of these apprehensions resulted in official action. In the school incident the girls told authorities they had mistaken the bottle of liquor for a bottle of perfume.

VANDALISM

Property damage or vandalism, the Molls' fourth most frequent offense, ranked high in its capacity to disturb neighborhood residents. Two rough categories of property damage could be distinguished: acts undertaken primarily for excitement and amusement, and those undertaken primarily out of hostility. Some destructive acts appeared to be motivated primarily by a desire for "fun"—such as burning rubbish barrels in the Molls' hanging alley, burning the name "Molls" on the ceiling of the housing project recreation room and breaking windows in abandoned houses. The Molls also directed destructive acts against persons who had aroused their anger. They broke housing project windows after the project manager denied the girls permission to use the recreation room they had marked, and they smashed windows at the house of a neighborhood woman whom the Molls believed to be spreading untrue stories about them. The clearest instance of hostility-motivated vandalism occurred when the Molls' principal leader was committed to a correctional institution on the complaint of her mother. The mother told authorities that the girls had attacked her brand-new automobile with nails and glass and scratched it so extensively that it had to be completely repainted.

SEX OFFENSES

While much of the Molls' sexual behavior violated the moral standards of many middle-class adults, their involvement in sexual activities which violated legal statutes was low relative to other offenses. While indirect evidence (pregnancy) indicated that three of the Molls had engaged in sexual intercourse by age 16, the girls were very discreet about nonmarital sexual activity. This contrasts with their involvement in offenses such as truancy and vandalism, which they talked about quite freely and even boasted about, under appropriate circumstances.

ASSAULT

Direct involvement by the Molls in assaultive offenses was rare. Only one clearly illegal incident was recorded during the contact period; from their perch on the roof of the housing project Molls threw rocks at a customer leaving the delicatessen below. The rarity of assaultive offenses cannot by attributed simply to the fact that the Molls were female, since the other female gang, the Queens, showed 18 involvements in assaultive acts during the observation period, besting one of the male gangs in this respect.

The Molls also engaged in a number of offenses during the observation period which do not fall readily under the above categories. One summer they spent their time killing neighborhood cats. Several times they provided hideouts for prison escapees. At other times they carried knives and other weapons for Hoods who were involved in gang fighting.

The Molls' major offenses, then, were truancy, theft, alcohol violations and vandalism. (Truancy was no longer illegal after the age of 16, at which point many of the Molls dropped out of school, anyway.) The remaining three major violations approximate the crimes characteristic of lower-class adolescent males; the patterns differ only in that "property damage" appears in place of "assault." Much of the Molls' vandalism represented direct expressions of hostility against particular persons; the Molls attempted to hurt a person by hurting something he owned. Vandalism apparently served the Molls as a vehicle for expressing hostility, in much the same way as did assault for other groups.

FOLLOWING THE BOYS

One reason that the Molls' pattern of criminal involvement so closely resembled that of the males was that they had engaged in a serious attempt, particularly between the ages of 13 and 15, to find favor in the eyes of the Hoods, and to become recognized as *their* girls. Since the Hoods were among the most criminal of the male gangs whose court experience was examined, the Molls' campaign to gain their trust and affection involved showing that they shared a general orientation to law violation.

One way of doing this was to approve, support and abet their criminal activities; another was to themselves commit, if only in attenuated form, the same kinds of offenses. The Molls themselves, while recognizing their desire to emulate the boys as only one of several motives, were aware that the wish to gain acceptance by the Hoods was an important reason for committing crimes. One used these words: "Ya know, if ya been hangin' with them *every night,* ya wanna do the same things as they do. Ya don't wanna be an *outcast!* When the boys hooked pickles, *we* hooked pickles. . . . During this period failure to engage in male-type criminality invoked male-type sanctions. A Moll who refused to go along on a property-destruction venture was taunted with the words, "Fairy! fairy!" This accusation of non-masculinity was deserved, one of the girls explained, "because she won't do vandalism with us no more."

The Molls' attempt to emulate and be accepted by the boys also influenced their sexual behavior. Although one popular image of girls in gangs pictures them as freely available concubines, and much writing on female delinquency stresses the centrality of sexual offenses, the behavior of the Molls; particularly during early adolescence, appeared to be predicated on the assumption that the way to get boys to like you was to be *like* them rather than accessible to them. As already noted, the Molls did not flaunt their sexual exploits in order to win esteem, as they did in the case of other offenses; on the contrary, they were quite secretive about the sexual misbehavior they did engage in.

HOW BAD IS BAD?

A further aspect of the Molls' pattern of illegal behavior concerns their reputation as "bad girls." It has frequently been observed that standards applied to female behavior are stricter than those applied to male comportment, and that a degree of criminal involvement which might appear rather modest for boys is seen as quite serious for girls. How "bad" the Molls are

judged to be depends a great deal on the basis of comparison one uses. Compared with male gangs of the same social status the Molls were not very criminal. Their rate of involvement in all forms of illegal behavior, including truancy, was approximately 25 offenses for each ten girls per ten-month period—less than one-tenth the rate of the male gangs of the same socioeconomic status. On the other hand, their rate was approximately the same as that of one of the higher status boys' gangs and, compared to middle-class girls, or even with the Queens, whose comparable rate was 6.8, the Molls appear quite criminal. Acts such as nightly public drinking by 13 year olds, carrying knives for gang fighters, chronic and parent-abetted truancy—while scarcely unheard of among higher-status girls—are generally infrequent.

LEADERSHIP HIERARCHY

The leadership and clique situation among the Molls reflected the fact that their gang was small relative to those of the boys, that they were female rather than male, and that criminal involvement was an important aspect of gang activities. Moll members fell into two cagegories—more active and less active. The more active clique was comprised of six girls who hung out frequently and participated regularly in gang activities. The less active clique was made up of five girls who hung out less frequently and participated less often in gang activities. The more active clique was clearly dominant; it set the tone for the gang and provided its leadership.

There were two leaders—a principal leader, whose authority was clearly recognized, and a secondary leader. Both girls were members of the more active clique. The secondary leader served as a standby who assumed leadership when the principal leader was institutionalized, and relinquished it when she returned.

The more active clique was unequivocally the more criminal. Although all the girls were known to have engaged in illegal activity, the rate of involvement in illegal acts for the active clique was 23.7 involvements for each ten girls per ten-month period, compared to a rate of only 1.3 for the less active girls. Active members accounted for 43 of the gang's 44 recorded truancies; all had been arrested at least once; two had been sentenced in court. None of the less active girls had gone to court; and only one was known to have truanted. The two girls who finished high school both belonged to the less active clique.

It is clear that the more criminal clique represented the dominant orientation of the gang as a whole. Further, the principal leader showed the highest rate of illegal involvement of all 11 girls, and the secondary leader the second highest. There was little direct conflict between the two leaders. Instead, like parallel leaders of some of the boys' gangs, they competed for prestige by striving to excel in illegal accomplishments.

BEST FRIENDS

Aside from associational patterns which resembled those of the boys' gangs, there were other patterns which reflected the fact that the Molls were female. Prominent was a "best friend" pattern which cross-cut the two major cliques. Two girls would develop crushes on one another and spend much of their time together. They were then known as "best friends," and shared secrets and confidences until some violation of trust or competition over a boyfriend dissolved their special intimacy into the ordinary ties between gang members. Best-friend pairings were generally of limited duration, with different pairings and repairings succeeding each other during the contact period. The relative instability of the best-friend sets served to protect the solidarity of the larger group. The best-friend pattern, generally involving two girls but sometimes three, was more prevalent during the summer months, when jobs, visits and other pursuits reduced the size and stability of the hanging group, and during the later part of the contact

period, as an increase in the tempo of mating and a divergence of life paths weakened ties to the larger gang.

FEMINISM AND THE MOLLS

The Molls' life-style is a product of the subcultures to which these girls belong—particularly those of females, adolescents, urban dwellers and lower status persons. Of particular interest in a day of expanding female consciousness is the question of the degree to which the Molls' way of life reflects the interests, concerns and customary behavior patterns of other women.

Two objectives of contemporary American feminism are particularly relevant to the lifeways of the Molls: first, that females should have free and equal opportunities to participate in the full range of life enterprises to which they may aspire, including those occupations and pursuits traditionally seen as male; and second, that women should be characterized and judged as individuals in their own right rather than being seen simply as reflecting the status achieved by those males with whom they may be affiliated.

The Molls and similar young girls' gangs appear to have ample opportunity to follow the same adolescent pursuits as the boys in their peer group—nightly street-corner congregation, public outdoor drinking, extensive use of profanity and, in particular, a classic set of offenses traditionally associated with male juvenile delinquency—stealing, vandalism, drunkenness and, to a lesser degree, fighting. Equal opportunity may not be available in adult activities, although the Molls will be called upon, at least as often as their male peers, to be breadwinners and heads of households.

Despite their freedom to act like the boys, the Molls do not seek to be judged for themselves. The evidence is clear that the Molls and other young women like them not only did not resent the fact that their status was directly dependent on that of the boys, but actively sought this condition and gloried in it. The Molls accepted without question a declaration by one of the Hoods that "they ain't nuthin' without us, and they know it." Jackets of female gang members in New York bear the legend, "Property of the Savage Nomads."

The Molls and many of their sisters are either not yet aware of or attracted to the tenets of Women's Liberation. The set of objectives espoused by the adult, middle-class mainstream of contemporary feminism has, so far, passed them by. Gang girls may, as they grow older, develop different perceptions of themselves and may no longer be satisfied with reflected status. Or, they may find that their present life-style and assumptions prepare them adequately for the reality of their ultimate social position.

48. Density and Crime

DENNIS W. RONCEK

THIS SELECTION EXAMINES THE SOUNDNESS OF THE available evidence for and against the importance of urban density and housing overcrowding in explaining the spatial distribution of crime. Recent research into the effects of these variables has received widespread attention in major scientific journals. Yet it is questionable whether the methodological quality of the research warrants this and whether the conclusions of these studies are based upon strong enough evidence to be scientifically acceptable. This selection contends that the answer must be negative in both cases for most of this research. If there is to be adequate scientific knowledge for theory and public policy, then it is necessary to be cognizant of the relative strengths and weaknesses of the research and the inferences from it. This paper, therefore, is intended to offer a detailed methodological critique of research to date and, in conclusion, recommendations for improving the quality of research so that it can contribute to scientific knowledge and wise policy decisons.

The evidence relating density (population per unit area) and housing unit crowding (persons per room) to crime are both examined, since it is not clear which, if either, is more important. I will draw from a set of criminological studies of juvenile delinquency as well as research in which

▶SOURCE: *"Density and Crime: A Methodological Critique," American Behavioral Scientist (July/August 1975), 18(6): 843–860. Reprinted by permission of the publisher, Sage Publications, Inc.*

the central interest was on the effects of density. There are remarkable similarities between the two sets of studies, despite the fact that they were designed for different theoretical purposes. In the criminological studies, the area distribution of delinquency was carefully examined, and overcrowding and density were studied; but the methods and findings of this research have not been systematically used to address the density problem. Only occasionally has some of the delinquency literature been cited in density-pathology studies.

Recent popular interest in the effects of density and crowding appear to have been stimulated by the work of Calhoun (1962) and other ethologists and by their popularizers (Morris, 1967; Ardrey, 1966). Prior to this, there existed only one study examining the direct effects of density upon urban crime rates (Schmitt, 1957). Neither Wirth (1938) nor Simmel (1970) linked density to crime, while Shaw and McKay (1942) were more concerned with the propositions of ecological theory derived from Park. In the latter's conceptions, the processes of invasion, succession, segregation, and competition involved in the process of city growth were seen to be the essential dynamics contributing the social instability which produced high juvenile delinquency rates (Shaw and McKay, 1942: 18–22). Shaw and McKay (1942: 154–155, 439) only mentioned poor housing as relating to high delinquency rates in conjunction with low economic status. This is clearly different from the concerns of modern "density researchers," who focus on a static conception of density or overcrowding as an existing characteristic which is related to high crime and juvenile delinquency rates.

The lack of specific arguments linking density to aggression and crime by the early theorists plus the more global perspective present in delinquency research combined to inhibit the development of a large volume of research on density. Delinquency studies failed to comment significantly upon the effect of such environmental factors on the incidence of crime. Although research focused on juvenile delinquency out of concern for understanding the etiology of later criminal behavior, an examination of this work is still useful in assessing evidence for the effects of overcrowding and density.

RESEARCH FOCUSING ON DENSITY

Seven intracity studies of density have included crime or delinquency as a dependent variable. The primary methodological defects of the studies are (1) excessive aggregation of data, (2) poorly chosen indicators or variables, and (3) lack of statistical control and improper use or reporting of statistics.

Excessive Aggregation

Most studies attempting to relate density or overcrowding to crime have attempted to make inferences about the effects on the individual from areal data. While it is valid to make inferences to areas from data which are also from similar units, often the areas used were not meaningful units and were so large as to make inferences to individuals untenable. Even when researchers attempted to hedge their conclusions because of the nature of the data used, the focus of their studies was not ecological. While Schmitt (1957) used census tracts in his study of juvenile delinquency and prison rates, he aggravated the degree of aggregation by collapsing the tracts, which contained an average of 8,533 persons (Choldin and Roncek, 1975: 2), into only three areas: low, medium, and high den-

sity. In his later study he used tracts as the units of analysis. Galle et al. (1972) used 74 of the 75 community areas in Chicago in an attempt to measure the effect of density and crowding on juvenile delinquency rates; these areas averaged over 47,000 persons in a mean of 11.6 tracts in 1960 (Choldin and Roncek, 1975). Although Freedman (1972) did not reveal the year of origin of his data, he used the 334 health areas of New York City which probably had an average population of 23,000 (Choldin and Roncek, 1975: 2). Gillis (1974) neither reported the average population of his tracts nor indicated which of Edmonton's tracts were included in his ad hoc sample.

The basic problem is that, as the degree of aggregation increases, so does the magnitude of the correlations and the poorer they are as a measure of individual-level relationships (Yule and Kendall, 1942; Robinson, 1950; Duncan and Davis, 1953; Goodman, 1953; 1959; Slatin, 1969; Hannan, 1971; Hammond, 1973). This is due to the heterogeneity of land uses and densities within each area which are then combined to obtain an average density. It may be that crimes are committed or criminals reside in the low-density or uncrowded parts of these areas or the area may contain high-density, high-crime pockets, but this cannot be discovered by using large areas. Further complications arise since the type of area used varies across studies, so that the results are not directly comparable.

The use of density, i.e., total population over total area, for units as large as cities introduces similar distortions. If it is the prevalence of dense areas within cities which accounts for differential crime rates across cities, then a measure such as the average density may be insensitive to the existence of high-density pockets. The inclusion of totally nonresidential areas in the total area of the city is crucial in this regard. If a great deal of land is so used, the average density may be a misleading estimate of the actual living conditions. The percentage of high-density neighborhoods or the percentage of persons living in high-density areas is the correct index to use. From this viewpoint, I find the inferences to individuals made by Booth and Welch (1973) and the implications in Momeni (1974) to be unsound.

Indicators of Variables

The choice of indicators, especially the dependent variable, is also crucial. Most intracity studies have used juvenile delinquency rates (Schmitt, 1957; 1966; Galle et al., 1972; Freedman, 1972; Factor and Waldron, 1973; Gillis, 1974). The rationale for doing so is often not clear. Criminologists have criticized the use of such offender rates, since offenders who are not apprehended are not counted. Rates of imprisonment used by Schmitt (1957; 1966) are even worse indicators of the incidence of crime, since they are affected by the results of the judicial process as well.

Another basic question is the extent to which the residential location of offenders correlates with the location of offenses. Unfortunately, this topic is not well researched. Schmid and Schmid (1972), studying one larger city, found high correlations between offender and offense rates for most but not all types of crime. They also found that both types of rates correlate similarly with a housing-type variable similar to density. However, the discrepancies between rates are not so small as to be negligible. Therefore, it would not seem advisable to substitute one measure for the other.

The special offender rate types of interest here are juvenile delinquency rates, and offense rates in relation to density and overcrowding. The evidence here is even sketchier than above. Phillips (1974) argued that arrest rates for juveniles did not resemble the distribution of occurrence of any crime. Unfortunately, he did not report the correlations, so the degree to which the distributions diverge cannot be assessed; he also did not report their respective relationships to density or overcrowding. Schmitt (1957: 376) found that the population per net residential acre and the percentage of

units containing 1.51 or more persons per room were both positively related to both the juvenile delinquency and prison rates, but their relationships to other measures of crowding were not so similar. Unfortunately, Schmitt did not relate either to offense rates. Thus, the degree to which the juvenile delinquency rate is an adequate indicator of crime is open to question, and the biases inherent in any arrest rate would seem to preclude any sound conclusion as to the effects of density or overcrowding on the relative incidence of crime or on the propensity to criminality.

Victimization data may be slightly better, but the reliance on the respondent's memory is still questionable (Skogan, 1974; 28). Furthermore, adequate sampling would be necessary, and it is not clear that the procedures now in use would provide an adequate basis for examining intracity density effects.

Offense rates may differ depending on what variable is used as the denominator. While Boggs (1965) argued strongly for risk-related rates, Schmid and Schmid (1972; 154) found that alternative bases also have unsatisfactory characteristics. Phillips (1973) and Boggs (1965) found that risk-related rates lowered the relative position of heavily commercialized tracts with respect to other tracts on the incidence of crime. Whether this is desirable or not is questionable. Both authors agree that the volume of crime in commercialized tracts is high. This is an important fact which becomes obscured by offense rates with bases other than the residential population. If population-based rates are interpreted only as indices controlled for population size rather than as indicators of risk, the identification of the variables which predict this volume of crime is important and the use of such rates is sound.

Problems with the independent variables seem to be less serious than those with the dependent variable or the unit of analysis. Gordon (1967) and Ward (1974) have raised questions as to the effect of using summary measures, such as medians or means, to indicate the level of a particular variable for an area. Since these measures are not as sensitive to the tails of the distribution as the percentage of the population which is above or below some specified level, these two researchers have suggested that the correlations will be lower than if more sensitive measures had been used. This issue has arisen in attempts to discern the effects of socioeconomic variables as compared to housing variables. If crime is a function of some level of absolute poverty, then the percentage of residents below the poverty level is likely to be a more valid measure of the influence of socioeconomic position on crime. If, however, the incidence of crime depends on income inequality, then it is possible that the summary measures may represent the relative position of urban subareas better.

Another general issue is whether gross density or net residential density should be used. Ideally, separate analyses for each should be done, but the unavailability of information may preclude this. This rationale is not adequate for units of analysis as large as community areas, since more refined data have been available for some time.

Another specific problem is the use of artificial measures of the independent variables— e.g., Galle et al.'s index of household crowding which was derived by dividing the resident population by the number of rooms in each area (Galle et al., 1972: 30). A measure based on the percentage of the population living in units with a particular minimum number of persons per room or one based on the percentage of housing units containing a specified level of persons per room should have been used. This type of averaging may not represent the degree of housing-unit crowding of any segment of the population nor of any portion of the housing units. Another instance is Galle et al.'s construction of a social class index through regression on each dependent variable. This is a conservative strategy, since it maximizes the relationships of the composite index to the dependent variable, but valuable information may be lost as to the effect of each of the components. Furthermore,

it may lead to underestimating the effect of other independent variables since this index has had its predictive power optimized.

Two other serious defects are present in Gillis (1974). First, Gillis' data for the independent variables are not from the same year as the information on the dependent variable. Second, only 30 of the 45 tracts in the city studies were used for convenience, and no comparison of the omitted and included tracts was presented. Both of these difficulties leave the validity of the results open to serous question.

Use of Statistics

The frequency of serious mistakes in statistical analysis made in density research is beginning to decline. Nevertheless, many of the procedures used are still open to question. Fortunately, studies such as Schmitt's (1957) article which do not use multivariate procedures have almost disappeared from the literature, with the exception of Factor and Waldron (1973), who used simple rank-order correlations, ignoring the higher level of measurement of their variables.

The basic difficulties in other studies involve the uses of partial correlation and multiple regression. Schmitt (1966) presented only partial correlations and these often did not control for socioeconomic and density/overcrowding variables simultaneously. Since partials are only correlations between residuals, they only indicate the amount of variance which could be explained after all other variables explain as much variance as possible. They are only useful in examining whether or not the amount of nonredundant variance is significant and do not indicate adequately the relationships among different variables vis-à-vis the dependent variable. The lack of simultaneous control is a serious deficiency, since one of the basic questions in both the research on density and on crime is the extent to which social-structural factors such as socioeconomic status account for the incidence of crime apart from other variables. Galle et al. (1972) have similar problems, although they rely primarily on the multiple partial correlation.

While multiple regression has become an increasingly popular technique, the use of it and reporting of results is often inadequate. Often neither regression coefficients nor significance tests for the coefficients were reported (Galle et al., 1972; Freedman, 1972; Gillis, 1974). Stepwise regression is used by Freedman (1972) without even reporting the variables used nor whether he had allowed all the variables in his implicit model to enter the analysis. The objection to this is that stepwise regression admits the variable with the largest zero-order correlation into the equation first and admits other variables into the equation on the basis of subsequent partial correlations. Thus, the contribution each variable makes to the variance explained is partially a result of the order of entry. If regression coefficients are reported, then the relative importance of each variable can be ascertained apart from the order. Furthermore, the relative importance may change with a different set of variables; hence, it is necessary to state the model specifically (Gordon, 1968).

There are also problems in the attempted use of path analysis by Gillis (1974), even apart from his somewhat misleading references to the beta weights of straightforward multiple regression as path coefficients. Since the data for juvenile delinquency and social allowance (welfare rate) are from the same year, the positing of a one-way causal relationship from the welfare rate to the delinquency rate must either be justified or other procedures should be used. More serious are the omissions from the path analysis of internal density as a predictor of social allowance and national origin as a predictor of juvenile delinquency. Their relatively large beta weights of .30 and .24 should have been tested for significance before a decision was made to omit them. No test of the adequacy of the path diagram with these variables first included and then excluded was performed, so that one cannot tell from the article whether the elimination of these variables could be justified. Even though it may be possible to claim that significance tests would not be relevant (since Gillis' ad hoc sample can

perhaps be treated as a population), this cannot justify the omission of these variables. If the latter argument is used, the variables would have to be retained since they do have a small effect, and the model is misspecified if they are omitted. If significance tests on the entire regression equation are made (Gillis, 1974: 311), then no excuse is available for not testing both the coefficients and the models. The low number of cases may result in the failure to find significance, but Gillis does not comment on these issues; hence, the validity of Gillis' work must be seriously questioned.

DELINQUENCY RESEARCH IN CRIMINOLOGY

The studies in this tradition have attempted to identify factors indicating social instability, which was posited to permit the existence of conflicting value systems in the areas. While the inferences from demographic data to the types of value systems held by residents of subareas of the city are basically unwarranted, the search for general factors associated with delinquency is basically sound and the quality of the research is generally high.

Lander (1954) first explicitly uses overcrowding to predict juvenile delinquency. His work on Baltimore was replicated by Bordua (1958) and Chilton (1964) for Detroit and Indianapolis, respectively. Other studies also in this tradition, although they take a slightly different approach, will be considered. The examination of the methodological procedures of the studies will proceed along the same lines as that for the density studies.

Excessive Aggregation

Of the six studies considered here, only Cartwright and Howard (1966) used units larger than census tracts, since they created special areas they called "gang neighborhoods." They compared the medians and percentage values of a long list of variables to the corresponding measures for the white and nonwhite populations of the entire city of Chicago. The problem here is that the same types of units are not being compared. Any conclusion to the effect that gang neighborhoods differ from non-gang neighborhoods is not justifiable. All other delinquency researchers examined tracts, which represented the best available data.

Indicators of Variables

In Lander (1954), Bordua (1958), Chilton (1964), Bloom (1966), and Rosen and Turner (1967), juvenile delinquency offender rates were used. Any criticism must be tempered since these researchers attempted to predict juvenile delinquency and not to explore the effects of density/overcrowding. While the measure was far from ideal, these were the only data available.

Only Rosen and Turner (1967) deviated from the five other studies in lowering the level of measurement from a ratio scale to a nominal scale dichotomized at the city mean which destroyed information. If there is a high probability of error in the exact value of the rate, the lower level of measurement will be a more stable indicator. Dichotomizing at the mean is also questionable, since the mean is affected by extreme values which may make the resulting classification of tracts into high or low delinquency tracts less reliable than if the median were used.

The Cartwright and Howard (1966) study refers to only sixteen gangs. Therefore, it is essentially a large case study which may not be generalized. Since probability sampling was not used to select gangs or gang neighborhoods, there is no valid procedure by which the residential neighborhood of the gangs can be compared to nongang neighborhoods. Yet the authors claimed to find that overcrowding was not relevant to the presence of gangs (Cartwright and Howard, 1967: 358). These methodological weaknesses cast doubt on the validity of their conclusions.

The quality of the measures of the independent variables in the delinquency studies is acceptable, but there is excessive use of median-based measures, except by Rosen and Turner

(1967). All the others used median measures for such variables as education, rent, income, and overcrowding. Gordon (1967: 941) found that, by using percentage variables for Lander's data, the correlations of both education and rent with delinquency rose dramatically. However, he did not recompute the regression coefficient for overcrowding.

Rosen and Turner (1967) also destroyed the intervality of their independent variables. However, some variables were dichotomized, others trichotomized, and one divided into four categories. They offered no rationale for the number and placement of cutting points. Although the work in criminology seems on the whole to be slightly more rigorous and better specified than in the density research, great caution must be used in inferring from the results.

Use of Statistics

The delinquency studies, with the exceptions of Bloom (1966) and Cartwright and Howard (1966), employ better statistical procedures than those in most of the density research.

Multiple regression and factor analysis were used by Lander (1954) at roughly the same time as research on density was being done on the basis of sight comparisons of rates. Standardized regression coefficients were reported for all variables used in each of the three studies (Lander, 1954; Bordua, 1958; Chilton, 1964). Tests of significance for the coefficients were performed and reported by Bordua (1958) and Chilton (1964). Unfortunately Lander (1954) reports tests of significance only for the partial correlation for the variables used in the linear regression, indicating an attempt to test for the significance of the controlled relationships. Furthermore, these studies permitted all the variables to enter the equations simultaneously, rather than relying solely on stepwise methods. While Lander's attempt to test for curvilinearity appears to be affected by extreme multicollinearity, his use of regression is still sound. Gordon raised a number of issues about the relationships among the sets of variables included in the equations, but these do not pertain to the overcrowding variable. Therefore, there is a basis for confidence in the results of these studies, provided generalizations are restricted to the ecological level.

Although the use of factor analysis by these three researchers has drawn much criticism and comment (Gordon, 1967; Borgatta, 1968; Chilton, 1968; Lander, 1968), the reexamination of the data of these three studies by Gordon (1967) seems to be adequate.

More serious statistical problems are present in the work of Bloom (1966), Cartwright and Howard (1966), and Rosen and Turner (1967). These include composite variable construction and lack of statistical controls (Bloom, 1966), and lack of tests of differences of proportions (Cartwright and Howard, 1966).

The primary problems in Rosen and Turner (1967) center on their use of the technique of predictive attribute analysis. While the technique permits the atheoretical empirical discovery of interaction, it is affected by the number of levels of each variable and is severely limited by the number of tracts used. While both limitations prevent the technique from handling large numbers of variables, the dependence on the number of levels implies that the reliable use of this method requires theoretical specification. The technique indicates neither the strength of controlled relationships nor the significance of particular relationships, since it has no sampling theory base such as the central limit theorem.

In summary, the delinquency research has been, with exceptions, more rigorous than density research and, even in the weaker study, the consideration given to interaction is interesting.

OPTIMAL METHODS

Given that previous methodology has been heavily criticized, it is mandatory that the critic also give guides for better procedures. This section draws heavily upon the methodology presented at length in Choldin and Roncek (1975).

Of primary importance is the use of meaningful units of analysis. In studying the effect of density on the distribution of crime, block-level statistics will be most appropriate. The advantages of this unit are that it is small, so that the values that variables take are not affected seriously by aggregation; the population and housing there are very homogeneous; and the block is a basic ecological unit of the city—it represents the immediate residential environment. In the one study which used blocks, the average block population was 77 persons (Choldin and Roncek, 1975). When this is compared with the average population of tracts, community areas, and health areas, the gain in precision is obvious. This gain in accuracy will be reflected in a much more accurate estimate of the effect of density upon the occurrence of crime. Even in multicity studies, a measure of density based upon the proportion of dense blocks will reflect the differential residential concentration across cities. One drawback is that the density of a block does not take into account the density of the area surrounding it. For this the variable population potential can be used (Choldin and Roncek, 1975: 7–9). In multicity studies, the proportion of blocks which have a population potential above a certain value can be used as a variable to test for such effects. The perspective here is thoroughly ecological and is concerned with the question of what types of residential environments are associated with the location of crimes.

For measuring the dependent variable, the primary data should be drawn from "offenses known to the police," which does not depend on the processes of apprehension or conviction or a victim's memory. Since juvenile delinquency rates have been used so often in the past, it seems wise to use population-based rates for total crime and specific types of crime, e.g., violent crime. Such rates would provide baselines against which other results, perhaps using different denominators, could be compared. Also interesting might be investigation of the relationships of major variables to the absolute number of crimes per block.

For the independent variables, Gordon's critique of the use of measures of central tendency should be kept in mind. Finally, researchers should exert the effort to use measures which are not crude artifacts—especially when actual data are available.

Further use of multiple regression techniques, with adequate reporting of procedures and the use of normal conventions of testing coefficients and reporting them, is advised. This is not to imply that testing or reporting partial or multiple partial correlations is not also useful; but without the structural coefficients, they are not sufficient.

An ideal study on the relationships between crime and density would use "offenses known to the police," small areas, precise measures of independent variables when available, and employ multivariate techniques properly and report results fully.

WHAT IS LEFT OR WHAT IS RIGHT?

Clearly the quality of the scientific knowledge of the effects of density or overcrowding is not high, but the findings to this point must be evaluated.

In the studies reviewed here which used density and employed relatively sophisticated multivariate techniques (Galle et al., 1972; Freedman, 1972; Gillis, 1974; Rosen and Turner, 1967), only Rosen and Turner found a significant effect for density on the juvenile delinquency rates. In fact, most of the studies demonstrating strong relationships for density were those which relied on zero-order correlations or less rigorous techniques (Schmitt, 1957; Bloom, 1966; Factor and Waldron, 1973; Schmid and Schmid, 1972). Only Schmitt (1966) indicated strong effects for density, after controlling for relevant independent variables. Unfortunately, the drawbacks and defects of these studies prevent the conclusion that density has no independent effect when other variables are controlled, but the evidence to date indicates that this is probably true. In two studies which were not reviewed here, but which have fewer methodological defects (Newman, 1973; Choldin and Roncek, 1975), the evidence does indicate that density has little or no positive independent effect on crime rates.

The evidence tends to indicate that there is a positive relationship between overcrowding and crime. Schmitt (1957; 1966), Galle et al. (1972), Choldin and Roncek (1975), Bordua (1958), and Chilton (1964) all found relatively strong effects for overcrowding. Lander (1954) also shows some effects, if Gordon's (1967) criticisms are accepted. Only Freedman (1972) and Cartwright and Howard (1966) find little or no effect, but both of these have such serious weaknesses that their negative findings are not to be trusted. It is impressive that across cities, over time, and with different units of analysis, the regression coefficient for overcrowding has been sizable and significant. This was true for violent crime rates, although not the general crime rate in Peoria (Choldin and Roncek, 1975: 33). Even in Gordon's (1967) recomputation of the factor analyses of the data of Bordua and Chilton, overcrowding loads highest on the same factor as juvenile delinquency. In the case of Lander, the loadings of juvenile delinquency on the SES and anomie factors are so similar after the reanalyses that the fact that overcrowding's highest loading is not on the same factor as the highest loading for delinquency is not significant.

In conclusion, the evidence points toward overcrowding being the more important variable in predicting both the occurrence of crime and the residential location of juvenile delinquents; however, its effects appear to be smaller than those of social-structural variables. Nevertheless, definitive conclusions must await the results of future research conducted on large cities using block data. The process by which overcrowding leads to crime has not yet been clarified. Hopefully, further research will lead to the discovery of how overcrowding is related to the distribution of crime.

REFERENCES

Ardrey, R. (1966) The Territorial Imperative. New York: Atheneum.

Bloom, B. L. (1966) "A census tract analysis of socially deviant behaviors." Multivariate Behavior Research 1 (July): 307–320.

Boggs, S. L. (1965) "Urban crime patterns." Amer. Soc. Rev. 30 (December) 6: 899–908.

Booth, A. and S. Welch (n.d.) "Crowding and urban crime rates." (unpublished)

Bordua, D. J. (1958) "Juvenile delinquency and 'anomie'; an attempt at replication." Social Problems 6 (Winter): 230–238.

Borgatta, E. F. (1968) "On the existence of Thurstone's oblique reference solution." Amer. Soc. Rev. 33 (August): 598–600.

Calhoun, J. B. (1962) "Population density and social pathology." Sci. Amer. 206 (February): 139–148.

Cartwright, D. S. and K. I. Howard (1966) "Multivariate analysis of gang delinquency. I: ecologic influences." Multivariate Behavioral Research 1 (July): 321–371.

Chilton, R. J. (1968) "Another response to Gordon." Amer. Soc. Rev. 33 (August): 600–601.

———(1964) "Continuity in delinquency area research: a comparison of studies for Baltimore, Detroit, and Indianapolis." Amer. Soc. Rev. 29 (February): 71–83.

Choldin, H. M. and D. W. Roncek (1975) "Density and pathology: the issue expanded." Presented at the annual meeting of the Population Association of America, Seattle, Washington.

Duncan, O. D. and B. Davis (1953) "An alternative to ecological correlation." Amer. Soc. Rev. 18 (December): 665–666.

Factor, R. M. and I. Waldron (1973) "Contemporary population densities and human health." Nature 243 (June 16): 381–384.

Freedman, J. L. (1972) "Population density, juvenile delinquency and mental illness in New York City," pp. 512–523 in S. M. Mazie (ed.), Commission on Population Growth and the American Future, Research Reports. Volume V: Population Distribution and Policy. Washington, D.C.: Government Printing Office.

Galle, O. R. W. Gove, and J. M. McPherson (1972) "Population density and pathology." Science 176 (April 7): 23–30.

Gillis, A. R. (1974) "Population density and social pathology: the case of building type, social allowance and juvenile delinquency." Social Forces 53 (December): 306–314.

Goodman, L. (1959) "Some alternatives to ecological correlation." Amer. J. of Sociology 64 (May): 610–625.

———(1953) "Ecological regressions and behavior of individuals." Amer. Soc. Rev. 18 (December): 663–664.

Gordon, R. A. (1968) "Issues in multiple regression." Amer. J. of Sociology 73 (March): 592–616.

———(1967) "Issues in the ecological study of delinquency." Amer. Soc. Rev. 32 (December): 927–944.

Hammond, J. L. (1973) "Two sources of error in ecological correlations." Amer. Soc. Rev. 38 (December): 754–777.

Hannan, M. T. (1971) Aggregation and Disaggregation in Sociology. Lexington, Mass.: D. C. Heath.

Lander, B. J. (1968) "Ecological studies of delinquency: a rejoinder to Robert A. Gordon." Amer. Soc. Rev. 33 (August): 594–597.

———(1954) Towards an Understanding of Juvenile Delinquency. New York: Columbia Univ. Press.

Momeni, J. A. (1974) "The effect of population density on serious crime and hospital admission rates." Presented at the annual meeting of the American Sociological Association, Montreal, Canada.

Morris, D. (1969) The Human Zoo. New York: McGraw-Hill.

Nettler, G. (1974) Explaining Crime. New York: McGraw-Hill.

Newman, O. (1973) Defensible Space. New York: Collier.

Phillips, P. D. (1974) "Intraurban crime patterns," Presented at the annual meeting of the Canadian Association of Geographers.

———(1973) "Risk-related crime rates and crime patterns." Proceedings of the Association of American Geographers 5:221–224.

Robinson, W. S. (1950) "Ecological correlations and the behavior of individuals." Amer. Soc. Rev. 15 (June): 351–357.

Rosen, L. and S. H. Turner (1967) "An evaluation of the Lander approach to the ecology of delinquency." Social Problems 15 (Fall): 189–200.

Schmid, C. F. and S. E. Schmid (1972) Crime in the State of Washington. Olympia, Wash.: Washington State Planning & Community Affairs Agency.

Schmitt, R. C. (1966) "Density, health, and social disorganization." J. of the Amer. Institute of Planners 32 (Jaunary) 1: 38–40.

———(1957) "Density, delinquency and crime in Honolulu." Sociology & Social Research 41 (March-April): 274–276.

Shaw, C. R. and H. D. McKay (1942) Juvenile Delinquency and Urban Areas. Chicago: Univ. of Chicago Press.

Simmel, G. (1970) "The metropolis and mental life," pp. 777–787 in R. Gutman and D. Popenoe (eds.), Neighborhood, City, and Metropolis. New York: Random House.

Skogan, W. S. (1974) "The validity of official crime statistics: an empirical investigation." Social Sci. Q. 55 (June): 25–38.

Slatin, G. T. (1969) "Ecological analysis of delinquency: aggregation effects." Amer. Soc. Rev. 34 (December): 894–907.

U.S. Bureau of the Census (1971) Census of Housing: 1970 Block Statistics Final Report, HC(3)-71. Peoria, Illinois Urbanized Area. Washington, D.C.: Government Printing Office.

Ward, S. K. (1974) "Overcrowding and social pathology: a re-examination of the implications for the human population." Master's thesis, Brown University Department of Sociology. (unpublished)

Wirth, L. (1938) "Urbanism as a way of life." Amer. J. of Sociology 44 (July): 1–24.

Yule, G. U. and M. G. Kendall (1947) An Introduction to the Theory of Statistics. London: Charles Griffin.

The Causes of Crime:
Economic Factors

ONE MAJOR RECENT TREND OF SIGNIFICANCE IN THE FIELD OF CRIMINOLOGY HAS been the introduction of serious economic and econometric analyses of criminal behavior and criminogenic conditions. The first selection by Cobb is an illuminating example of the manner in which an economic hypothesis (as contrasted to a "sickness" hypothesis) is articulated, formulated into a mathematical equation, and from this, various economic costs constructed. Following that, there are two sociological rejoinders by Bailey and by Logan who take Cobb to task for what they regard as sociologically naive assumptions on human behavior. The several selections together represent the quite contrasting economic and sociological estimates of basic motivational features of criminality. The final selection is an extensive comparison of the state of the economy and crime rates in five countries over a 70-year period. Brenner examines trends in crime rates as related to such vital economic concerns as cyclic variations in employment, economic growth, and inflation.

49. An Economic Hypothesis of Crime

WILLIAM E. COBB

AN IMPORTANT ISSUE HAS ARISEN CONCERNING the basic motivational characteristics of the criminal element in our society. The two approaches which seem to be receiving most attention have been characterized as the "economic hypothesis" and the "sickness hypothesis."[1] We will summarize here the arguments of those endorsing the two points of view and then make an attempt to merge the two into one hypothesis, acceptable to both sides and consistent with the basic behavior postulate of economic theory—utility maximization. This analysis will not resolve all areas of disagreement between the two factions, but will correctly define those areas of conflict. In the final section of the paper we will summarize some empirical work.[2]

I. THE TWO HYPOTHESES

The Economic Hypothesis

The economic hypothesis is founded on the principle that crime is just like any other enterprise: *the potential criminal evaluates all possibilities within the limits of all information which he possesses and chooses that activity which maximizes his utility.* This hypothesis has become entrapped in that maze of misconception which accompanies most attempts to explain "utility-inspired" motivation to the lay economist. There is apparent difficulty in differentiating between utility gain and monetary return. Economists have become infamous through their attempts to convert nonpecuniary costs and benefits into dollar equivalents. These attempts, however, do seem to have logical foundations. If an individual voluntarily trades some nonpecuniary property right—be it physical or psychological—for a pecuniary income, then it would seem logical to conclude (and impossible to disprove) that he expects his net utility change to be a positive one *at the time of the trade.* Few, if any, economists argue that receipt of dollars is the only motivating factor in any decision process. The basic argument in an economic (or utility maximization) approach is that an individual decision maker explicitly or implicitly considers *all* benefits and costs which he expects to result from a decision.

Of course the decision maker is allowed to miscalculate. Decisions are made with limited knowledge and may prove to be incorrect, an ex post revelation. Sociologists have coined a useful phrase with their creation of the term "bounded rationality."[3] The essence of this notion is that

▶SOURCE: *"Theft and Two Hypotheses,"* in Rottenberg, Simon (Ed.), *The Economics of Crime and Punishment.* Washington, *American Enterprise Institute for Public Policy Research, 1973, pp. 19–30.* © *American Enterprise Institute for Public Policy Research 1973, reprinted by permission.*

[1]A good survey article is Gordon Tullock's "Two Hypotheses" which will appear in Gordon Tullock, ed., *The Economics of Crime* (Blacksburg, Va.: Center for Study of Public Choice, forthcoming).

[2]The empirical work was made possible by a National Science Foundation grant. Institutional interest in such projects is an important facet of research into, and reform of, the law enforcement system.

[3]H. A. Simon, "Bounded Rationality," *Administrative Behavior.* (New York: The Free Press, 1957), pp. 33–41.

individuals have perceptual as well as information-processing limits, and even though they may intend to act rationally, they can do so only in a limited fashion."[4]

Gary Becker has written, "Some persons become 'criminals,' therefore, not because their basic motivation differs from that of other persons, but because their benefits and costs differ."[5] Advocates of the economic hypothesis accept this proposition and argue that criminal activities can be altered by a change in the expected net utilities of individual decision makers. That is, in order to reduce crime we must lower the expected benefits, raise the expected costs, or effect some combination thereof which insures that crime has an expected negative influence on the utility of most potential criminals.

The Sickness Hypothesis

The sickness hypothesis attacks the problem of crime from a different perspective. Many sociologists adhere to this approach and vehemently attack the economic formulation:

"This misplaced faith in punishment may rest upon the unrealistic assumption that people *consciously decide* whether to be criminal—that they consider a criminal career, rationally balance its dangers against its rewards, and arrive at a decision based upon such pleasure-pain calculation. It supposedly follows that if the pain element is increased by severe punishments, people will turn from crime to righteousness. A little reflection reveals the absurdity of this notion."[6]

The same sociologists present empirical data which allegedly show that punishment has no deterrent effect whatever on crime.[7] Propo-

nents argue that the expected payoff of crime may be negative (negative net utility) and that the criminal is sick because he disregards this negative effect. Since the potential criminal does not act within the realm of even bounded rationality, adjustments of the expected benefits and costs of crime will in no way alter his decision to commit a crime.[8] Advocates of the sickness hypothesis conclude that rehabilitation is the only solution to the control of criminal behavior.

II. A RESOLUTION OF THE CONTROVERSY

Extensive discussions with proponents of each of the two hypotheses reveals a basic communication gap between them. Few sociologists believe that punishment, in general, does not deter. To hold to such a position would be to reject scientific evidence which indicates that most, if not all, living organisms react to pleasure-pain stimuli. Common sense, as well as Pavlov, tells us that we do react to punishment. Would you ever illegally park your automobile if the penalty were raised from the present small fine to twenty years of imprisonment? On the other hand, would you illegally park more than you do now if the only punishment were a note on your windshield saying, "Shame on you"? Clearly punishment does have a deterrent effect on this type of crime.

The actual argument that sociologists are making is not that punishment does not deter, but rather that our current system of punishment is not effective. Almost invariably, one can eventually persuade advocates of the sickness approach to concede this point. As Gibbs has said:

"Sociologists have participated in the controversy between the classical and positivist schools, and many of them have clearly questioned the deterrent efficacy

[4]K. E. Weick, *The Social Psychology of Organizing.* (Reading, Mass.: Addison-Wesley Publishing Company, 1968), p. 9.

[5]Gary Becker, "Crime and Punishment: An Economic Approach," *Journal of Political Economy,* vol. 76 (March-April 1968). p. 176.

[6]Paul B. Horton and Gerald R. Leslie, *The Sociology of Social Problems,* 4th ed. (New York: Appleton Century-Crofts, 1970), p. 167.

[7]See R. G. Caldwell, "The Deterrent Influence of Corporal Punishment upon Prisoners Who Have Been Whipped," *American Sociological Review,* vol. 9 (April 1944), pp. 171–177.

[8]This position is not limited to sociologists. A former criminal lawyer with whom this topic was discussed adamantly argued for this viewpoint.

of punitive reactions to crime, capital punishment in particular. The pronouncements of some sociologists on capital punishment are questionable and unfortunate. In particular, the general question of the deterrent efficacy of punishment cannot be answered by research on the death penalty alone. Execution is, after all, only one type of punitive reaction to crime; but sociologists tend to extend their opinions on the death penalty to punitive reactions generally. *The point is that some sociologists do not treat the general question of deterrence as an open one.*[9] [Italics mine.]

Punishment does function as a deterrent. The problem with our system of criminal justice is that no one has attempted to determine the utility that a criminal loses as a result of various penalties. A year of imprisonment does not affect everyone in the same manner. A preacher convicted of petit larceny and given a suspended sentence might suffer greater utility loss than a vagrant incarcerated for 90 days for the same crime. As Charles R. Tittle has pointed out, "The crucial question is not simply whether negative sanctions deter, but rather under what conditions are negative sanctions likely to be effective."[10] Negative sanctions are effective only if the negative utility which the potential criminal expects to result from their imposition is greater than the positive utility he expects to gain from the crime.

In his oft-cited article on crime, Gary Becker says of the economic hypothesis:

"This approach implies that there is a function relating the number of offenses by any person to his probability of conviction, to his punishment if convicted, and to other variables, such as the income available to him in legal and other illegal activities, the frequency of nuisance arrests, and his willingness to commit an illegal act. This can be represented as

$$O_j = O_j (p_j, f_j, u_j), \qquad (1)$$

where O_j is the number of offenses he would commit during a particular period, p_j his probability of convic-

tion per offense, f_j his punishment per offense, and u_j a portmanteau variable representing all these other influences."[11]

If sociologists were arguing that punishments do not deter crime, they would be arguing that

$$\partial O_j / \partial f_j = O. \qquad (2)$$

Clearly, this is not the case! They are, in fact, arguing that the change in committed offenses resulting from a change in punishments is very small and hence,

$$\partial O_j / \partial f_j < \partial O_j / \partial u_j, \qquad (3)$$

or as is argued in some cases,

$$\partial O_j / \partial f_j < \partial O_j / \partial p_j. \qquad (4)$$

Equation (3) represents the view that, although increases in punishment may deter, changes in the variables in u_j—income available to the potential criminal in legal activities, his willingness to commit an illegal act (moral code), et cetera—more effectively reduce the level of crime.

Equation (4) represents a similar argument that changes in the probability of apprehension reduce criminal offenses more than changes in the punishment per offense.

The formulation of the sickness hypothesis as seen in equations (3) and (4) does not run counter to the utility maximization approach used by economists. However, as elementary students of economics recognize, within a budget constraint, **B**, the relevant decision model requires:

$$\frac{\partial O_j / \partial p_j}{P_{p_j}} = \frac{\partial O_j / \partial f_j}{P_{f_j}} = \frac{\partial O_j / \partial u_j}{P_{u_j}}, \qquad (5)$$

and

$$(p_j \cdot P_{p_j}) + (f_j \cdot P_{f_j}) + (u_j \cdot P_{u_j}) = B, \qquad (6)$$

vhere P_{p_j}, P_{f_j}, and P_{u_j} represent the prices of apprehension, punishment, and "rehabilitation,"

[9]Jack P. Gibbs, "Crime Punishment, and Deterrence," *Social Science Quarterly,* March 1968, p. 515.

[10]Charles R. Tittle, "Crime Rates and Legal Sanctions," *Social Problems,* vol. 16 (Spring 1969), p. 411.

[11]Becker, "Crime and Punishment," p. 117.

respectively. (Henceforth, ∂u_j will be called "re-habilitation.") That is, in order to minimize crime within a given budget, expenditures on crime prevention should be divided so that the above equalities hold.

The disagreement between proponents of each of the two hypothesis is one that can be empirically decided: Will a dollar of expenditures on crime reduction be more effectively spent on altering the probability of apprehension, on altering punishments per offense, or on altering factors included in the portmanteau variable, which we are calling rehabilitation?

III. ECONOMICS OF THEFT

Within the framework of the model just discussed, reduction in the level of criminal activity might be accomplished in three ways: (1) redistributing expenditures among the three variables p_j, f_j, and u_j, (2) increasing total expenditures (budget, B) while holding constant the distribution of expenditures, and (3) a combination of increasing or redistributing the budget.

These methods depend pivotally on the assumption that criminals are rational decision makers in the sense that they do not make decisions on a random basis. If criminal acts were random (irrational), they would not be a function of *any* decision variables, including p_j, f_j, and B.

It does seem plausible, however, that a person *always* seeks to maximize his *expected* net benefits and that acts in which ex ante costs exceed benefits will never be perpetrated. The problem which exists in all decision-making processes is that ex ante costs and benefits seldom are equivalent to ex post costs and benefits. Stated more simply, people have imperfect knowledge.

In most discussions "irrationality" usually is limited to the realm of bounded rationality. An irrational action is implicitly defined as one for which, due to imperfect knowledge, ex ante net benefits are positive but ex post net benefits are negative. As psychologists have noted, "rational-

ity seems better understood as a post-decision rather than a pre-decision occurrence."[12]

Within this framework, the proposition that criminals act irrationally is identical to one that states that crime does not pay. If crime does not pay, one method of reducing the level of crime is to convince (educate) potential criminals that they are making incorrect calculations. If crime does pay, this method would convert to convincing (indoctrinating) potential thieves that they are incorrect in their calculations, when, in fact, they are making the correct choices. Equations (1), (5), and (6) will then convert to

$$O_j = O_j (P_j, f_j, u_j, k_j), \qquad (7)$$

$$\frac{\partial O_j/\partial p_j}{P_{p_j}} = \frac{\partial O_j/\partial f_j}{P_{f_j}} = \frac{\partial O_j/\partial u_j}{P_{u_j}} = \frac{\partial O_j/\partial k_j}{P_{k_j}}, \qquad (8)$$

and

$$(p_j \cdot P_{p_j}) + (f_j \cdot P_{f_j}) + (u_j \cdot P_{u_j}) + k_j(P_{k_j}) = B, \qquad (9)$$

where k_j represents the "knowledge" possessed by individual j, P_{k_j} represents the price of providing that knowledge, and $\partial O_j/\partial k_j$ represents the change in the number of offenses committed by him which result from a change in the "knowledge" which he possesses.[13]

The following empirical analysis examines only one small facet of the problem which this model encompasses. It is an attempt to determine whether education or indoctrination, as defined above, is the more viable method of reducing one type of crime—theft. That is, it is an attempt to measure some of the ex post costs and benefits of thieves in order to determine whether or not thieves are, as a group, making the "correct" choices.

Method and Scope

The method employed is a "simple" benefit-cost

[12]Weick, *Social Psychology of Organizing*, p. 38.
[13]"Knowledge" here refers to what an individual believes to be true, not to an actual state of the world. In effect k_j is included in u_j of equation (1).

technique. The costs associated with the actual acts of committing theft, along with the costs of capture, conviction, and imprisonment, are compared to the benefits from these thefts. I have confined my analysis to those crimes classified as either grand larceny or burglary by the Federal Bureau of Investigation, in only one locality, Norfolk, Virginia, for the two years 1964 and 1966.

The first problem concerned what to include as the benefits of theft. After I obtained estimates of the market value of stolen merchandise, I made adjustments to find the value of this merchandise *to the thief*, this being somewhat less than the market value because of problems in disposing of stolen materials. It is this value of stolen property to the thief which best approximates the benefit he receives.

Costs to thieves are most difficult to evaluate. There are positive physical costs such as the actual work involved in committing thefts, the disposable income lost while incarcerated, and the fines which are levied in addition to incarcerations. There are negative physical costs (benefits) which accrue to thieves while they are incarcerated: free room and board, free medical and dental care, welfare payments to dependents, and wages earned within the prison.

To be added to the physical costs just mentioned are psychic costs, such as loss of freedom, and attainment of a "bad reputation," which may prove to be a negative cost.

Temporarily ignoring both psychic and negative costs, we find that the cost decision is narrowed to three variables: (1) the work involved in theft, (2) lost disposable income, and (3) fines. The first of these—the work or time involved in committing thefts—seems to be relatively negligible. It simply takes very little time to commit the average theft. For convenience, this cost will be assumed to be zero.

The cost side of the analysis now centers on two factors—lost disposable income as a result of incarceration and fines levied on convicted thieves.

The Benefits: 1964

In 1964 there were 2,388 reported cases of burglary and 1,867 reported cases of grand larceny in the city of Norfolk.[14] These 1964 thefts may be divided into five categories as shown in Table I.

The figures exhibited in the table show values for reported stolen property only. If we desire an examination of benefits to the criminal, an attempt must be made to place a value on property stolen but *not reported stolen*. The President's Commission on Law Enforcement and Administration of Justice has issued a report indicating that total unreported thefts might well exceed the total number of reported thefts.[15] The commission cites a figure for the cash value of unreported crimes which indicates that 50 percent of total dollars stolen is unreported.[16] Using this 50 percent figure, values in Table I are doubled to those shown in Table II.

As shown in each of these two tables the Norfolk Police Department made significant recovery of stolen property in the period being investigated. Benefits to the criminal do not include recovered property, as it is assumed that the property was recovered from the thief and not from the individual to whom it was given or sold. The important figure is the difference between total property stolen and property recovered. Table II shows the net value of each of the categories.

The figures in Table III need one final adjustment before they suit our purposes. The values shown are those placed on the property by its owner. The value of stolen property to the thief is considerably less than this. Through in-

[14]Norfolk Police Department, *Annual Police Report,* Norfolk, Virginia, 1964.

[15]President's Commission on Law Enforcement and Administration of Justice, *The Challenge of Crime in a Free Society* (Washington, D.C.: Government Printing Office, 1967), pp. 20–21.

[16]U.S. Task Force on Assessment of Crime, *Task Force Report: Crime and Its Impact, An Assessment* (Washington, D.C.: Government Printing Office, 1967), pp. 46–47.

Table I. Total Reported Thefts Excluding Robbery and Petit Larceny, City of Norfolk, 1964

Category	Stolen	Recovered
Currency	$ 83,773	$ 9,988
Jewelry	187,744	35,462
Furs	8,149	32
Clothing	75,726	11,132
Miscellaneous	300,109	59,053
Total	$655,501	$115,667

Source: Norfolk Police Department, *Annual Police Report,* Norfolk, Virginia, 1964.

Table II. Total Reported and Unreported Thefts Excluding Robbery and Petit Larceny, City of Norfolk, 1964

Category	Stolen		Recovered
Currency	$ 83,773 × 2 =	$ 167,546	$ 9,988
Jewelry	187,774 × 2 =	375,548	35,462
Furs	8,149 × 2 =	16,298	32
Clothing	75,726 × 2 =	151,452	11,132
Miscellaneous	300,109 × 2 =	600,218	59,053
Total		$1,311,062	$115,667

Table III. Net Take from Total Reported and Unreported Thefts, City of Norfolk, 1964

Category	Net Take
Currency	$ 157,558
Jewelry	340,086
Furs	16,266
Clothing	140,320
Miscellaneous	541,165
Total	$1,195,395

Table IV. Adjusted Net Take from Total Reported and Unreported Thefts, City of Norfolk, 1964

Category	Net Take		
Currency	$157,558 × 1.00 =	$157,558
Jewelry	340,086 × 0.20 =	68,017
Furs	16,266 × 0.20 =	3,253
Clothing	140,320 × 0.12 =	16,838
Miscellaneous	541,165 × 0.20 =	108,233
Total		$353,899

terviews within the Norfolk Police Department and in an interview with a professional "fence" in the Norfolk area, it was determined that, on the average, thieves can sell stolen merchandise for only approximately 20 percent of its market value. For certain types of merchandise this figure is still lower—wearing apparel, for instance. The professional thief may receive greater percentages than these because he will normally have his own selling outlets. However, professionalism appears to be a rather rare exception in the area under study.

The consensus among those interviewed indicates that, for stolen property, 20 percent of the market value would approximate the value to the thief—cash and clothing being the two exceptions. Cash obviously retains its entire value, while clothing is almost valueless to the thief. In the case of clothing, most of the value to the thief involves that clothing which he retains for his own use. The fence who was interviewed suggested that, to the thief, stolen clothing would realistically be worth approximately 12 percent of its market value. Upon agreement by police officials, this figure was adopted.

Applying these percentages to Table III, the figures for net benefits shown in Table IV are obtained, totaling $353,899. Of the 1,867 reported cases of grand larceny, 193 (10.3 percent) resulted in arrests. Of the 2,388 reported cases of burglary, 335 (14 percent) resulted in arrests.

Of those convicted, 195 were adults and these adults stole 82.04 percent of the total amount stolen by those arrested. Since the present study is concerned only with adults, this figure was used to adjust net benefits, attempting to exclude that portion of the total stolen by juveniles. Assuming that adults steal 82.04 percent of all merchandise stolen, total benefits to adults become $290,339.

The Costs: 1964

Of the 195 adults arrested, 31 served time in prison on felony convictions (both burglary and grand larceny are considered to be felonies), while 29 served time on a less serious misdemeanor charge. Investigation revealed that these 29 were probably guilty of the more serious charge, but that the court found it expedient, as it so often does, to reduce the charge. We have assumed that these individuals were guilty of committing one of the crimes being investigated.

Of the 31 convicted felons, 25 served 52.09 years in prison. The remaining six were convicted of multiple offenses. The average of the first 25 was used to approximate the length of time in prison for these six which resulted from crimes of burglary or grand larceny. Adding this approximation yields a total of 64.57 years served in prison.

A misdemeanor conviction involves a sentence of one year or less. An approximation of the time served by the 29 so convicted was 13.77 years. This is an approximation because records for some individuals could not be found. They were tried, convicted, and sentenced, but if they served the sentences, no one seems to know where they served them. Averages for those whose records were available were used for the seven individuals who "disappeared."

Total time served in jail for the 1964 thefts was 78.34 years. Along with these years of imprisonment went fines totaling $2,460 levied on misdemeanants.

Since our cost measure is essentially alternative income available to the convicted thief in legal occupations, an estimate of this income was obtained by approximating the average yearly income—prior to arrest—of the sixty men and women convicted for the 1964 thefts.

Employment records revealed the type of job most frequently held by these individuals. We then used studies by the Bureau of Statistics of the Department of Labor to obtain average hourly wages for each type of job—specifically in the Norfolk area. Results show that the sixty individuals imprisoned in 1964 could have earned, on the average, $1.62 per hour in legitimate jobs had they not gone to prison.

Table V. Income Lost as Result of Incarceration, 1964

Weeks Worked Per Year, Assumed	Gross Income Per Year, Average	Total Income Lost[a]	Total Income Lost, Plus Fines[a]
30	$1,932	$151,353	$153,813
40	$2,576	$201,804	$204,264
50	$3,220	$252,255	$254,715

[a]For the 78.34 years served.

Records further indicated frequent periods of unemployment for these persons, and led us to a seemingly reasonable assumption that, on the average, each person worked only approximately thirty weeks per year. Assuming a forty hour work-week, we found that the average yearly gross income per person was $1,932. For the 78.34 years served, $151,353 was lost in addition to the $2,460 in fines. Total lost income as a result of incarceration was $153,813.

We also made our calculations on the bases of forty and fifty weeks worked per year, respectively, and these results are shown in Table V.

The Benefits: 1966

Identical procedures were used to obtain an estimate of benefits from 1966 thefts.[17] These benefits were significantly higher than those of 1964: $460,121 compared to $290,339. Examination of the data revealed several possible explanations for this gap. Of some importance was the fact that a greater amount was stolen in 1966: $1,915,603 compared to $1,203,806. Possibly more significant was the fact that only 61 individuals served time for these thefts and their total sentences were only 67.45 years as compared to 78.34 years served for the 1964 thefts. The 1965 change in the Virginia State Code

[17]Norfolk Police Department, *Annual Police Report*, Norfolk, Virginia, 1966.

which raised from $50 to $100 the minimum theft classified as grand larceny must be considered significant here. (For the purpose of comparison, we continued to use $50 as the lower limit to crimes classified as grand larceny.)

The Costs: 1966

We determined the average hourly wage for the 61 individuals incarcerated in 1966 to be $1.55. Fines totaling $2,615 were levied. The calculation for each of the three assumptions concerning weeks worked per year are shown in Table VI.

The Benefits and Costs: 1964, 1966 Combined

We have added together the figures used in each of the individual calculations to give a broader base to our results. Table VII compares and combines the results for 1964 and 1966.

Conclusions to Empirical Analysis

We must now ask if, indeed, those factors affecting cost which we "temporarily" disregarded can be ignored. Psychic costs present the major roadblock in our analysis. The bad reputation aspect can reasonably be omitted. Superficial investigation points to the fact that a criminal record may be of some benefit to the convict. In numerous cases, especially in the ghetto, the criminal is held in esteem when he returns to his community upon release from prison.

The real problem arises in consideration of

Table VI. Income Lost as Result of Incarceration, 1966

Weeks Worked Per Year, Assumed	Gross Income Per Year, Average	Total Income Lost[a]	Total Income Lost, Plus Fines[a]
30	$1,860	$125,457	$128,072
40	$2,480	$167,276	$169,891
50	$3,000	$202,350	$204,965

[a]For the 67.45 years served.

Table VII. Benefits and Costs of Theft, City of Norfolk, 1964 and 1966

Year	Total Income			Total Benefits from Theft
	Weeks Worked Per Year			
	30	40	50	
1964	$153,813	$204,264	$254,715	$290,339
1966	128,072	169,891	204,965	460,121
1964 and 1966	$281,885	$374,155	$459,680	$750,989[a]

[a]Total of *unrounded* data for both years.

the psychic costs of the loss of freedom. Until a realistic estimate can be made for this cost, our conclusions must be considerably weaker than we would like. Examining Table VII for the two years combined and making the most likely assumption that the convicted criminals would have worked thirty weeks per year, the benefits from theft are more than double the costs, with a net difference of $469,104.[18] We find that, for the total 145.79 years served in prison, benefits exceed costs by this amount. For the individuals who served these sentences, the average evaluation of the cost of "loss of freedom" would have to be greater than $3,225 per year in prison before one could say that theft is not profitable.

Several studies have been proposed to determine the true cost of this loss of freedom aspect. In one preliminary report, James P. Gunning revealed that prisoners he worked with would pay only an average of $1,500 per year in return for freedom.[19] This would seem to be a close approximation to the cost associated with loss of freedom, but the sample size and procedure

[18]This figure would be increased if the benefits and costs were discounted over the lifetime of the thieves involved—benefits from theft, on the average, accrue several months before costs are "levied." A further increase in the gap between benefits and costs would result if one considered the fact that "legitimate" income is taxable while income from crime is "tax exempt."

[19]James P. Gunning, "A Report on the Study of the Costs of Incarceration," Virginia Polytechnic Institute and State University, 1970 (mimeographed).

used to arrive at this figure make the result of little significance.

Finally, we have ignored the negative costs associated with incarceration. These costs would seem definitely to be determinable, but as yet little work has been performed here.[20]

[20]Paul Nobblett, "Economics of Crime," Virginia Polytechnic Institute and State University. 1969 (unpublished).

What *do* these results show? Ignoring the psychic costs of the loss of freedom, thieves in Norfolk did make a net profit. Using Gunning's approximation, theft continues to be profitable with inclusion of this loss of freedom cost. Further study is needed but these conclusions indicate that thieves, as a group, are making the "correct" choices.

50. Two Responses to "Cobb"

WILLIAM C. BAILEY
CHARLES H. LOGAN

THE TWO HYPOTHESES

IN MR. COBB'S VIEW, THERE IS A WIDE GAP BEtween the economists' and sociologists' assessments of "the basic motivational characteristics of the criminal element in this country." The economic hypothesis of crime "is founded on the principle that crime is just like any other enterprise: *The potential criminal evaluates all possibilities within the limits of all information which he possesses and chooses that activity which maximizes his utility.*" Here, man is viewed as a rational being who chooses those behavioral alternatives—criminal or conventional—which he expects to result in maximum reward and miminum cost, or in other words, maximum profit. This model of behavior, of course, permits miscalculation of anticipated costs and benefits (imperfect knowledge) and variation among individuals in the cost and benefit contingencies associated with any given action and consequence.

Proponents of the economic hypothesis, according to Cobb, believe that criminal activities can be altered by changes in the net utility of individual decision makers, or, in other words, by putting into the "red" the net gain potential criminals might expect.

In contrast, Cobb sees sociologists typically adhering to what he calls the sickness

hypothesis. Unfortunately, he does not bother to inform us of the major principles of this hypothesis, nor am I quite sure what theoretical model of crime he believes most sociologists commonly accept. What he does say is that proponents of the sickness hypothesis argue that the threat of punishment has no deterrent effect whatever on crime because, even though the expected payoff of crime may be negative (negative net utility), "the criminal is sick because he disregards this negative effect." Mr. Cobb goes on to say that proponents of this model conclude that "rehabilitation is the only solution to the control of criminal behavior."

I must say that I am somewhat bewildered by Cobb's discussion of sociologists and the sickness hypothesis. First, in his discussion of this hypothesis he fails to mention one sociological theory of crime or to name a single theorist in sociology who fits this model. And, I might add, from his description of the sickness hypothesis I can think of no example myself. I know of no major theory of crime in sociology that views the criminal as *sick* because he disregards negative sanctions. Nor am I completely sure whether to interpret Cobb as saying that sociologists view criminals as sick because they disregard the expectation of negative net utility, or because they are sick they disregard negative net utility.

Furthermore, I know of no major theory of crime in sociology that views rehabilitation as "the only solution to the control of criminal behavior." What about preventive measures? Are

►SOURCE: *"Comments. . ."* in Rottenberg, Simon (Ed.), *The Economics of Crime and Punishment.* Washington, D.C.: American Enterprise Institute for Public Policy Research, 1973. Pp. 49–56. *(Editorial adaptations.) Reprinted by permission.*

they not another approach to crime control? In fact, do not most sociological discussions of crime control clearly suggest a preference for prevention over rehabilitation? I submit that an examination of any text in criminology or juvenile delinquency will reveal this to be the case.

What Cobb seems to be saying by introducing the economic and sickness hypothesis is that economists and sociologists differ in the relative importance they would assign the threat of legal sanctions as a deterrent to crime. I must emphasize relative importance here for it would be a serious mistake to view all sociologists as of one opinion on this question, and the same probably applies for economists as well. Clearly a casual survey of the recent sociological literature on crime will reveal a wide variety of opinions on the question of crime and deterrence. Furthermore, such a survey will reveal no careful scholar citing any empirical evidence presently available as conclusive proof "that punishment has no deterrent effect whatever on crime."

In sum, I must take strong exception to Cobb's assessment of current thinking of sociologists on the question of crime and deterrence. The position of Paul B. Horton and Gerald R. Leslie, whose discussion of this issue in 1960 is cited by Cobb, should not be construed to reflect the views of all sociologists nor even most sociologists, as Cobb would lead us to believe. In short, I can only conclude that Cobb's lack of familiarity with the current criminological literature is responsible for many of the conclusions he draws.

A RESOLUTION OF THE CONTROVERSY?

Having presented the economic and sickness hypotheses, Cobb moves on to the task of resolving the controversy he sees between these two models. A communication gap is suggested as the major factor separating proponents of the two hypotheses. Sociologists, he concludes, "do not really believe that punishment in general does not deter." The actual argument that

sociologists are making, he says, "is not that punishment does not deter, but rather that our current system of punishment is not effective."

Again, I must take issue with Mr. Cobb for I do not see a gap in communication lying at the heart of the difficulty here. I agree with his view that few sociologists would deny a role to "punishment in general" in influencing social behavior, crime included. To do so would be to disregard completely the accomplishments in behavioral psychology. But more importantly, such denial would reject a sizeable body of theory and research in nearly every subfield of sociology. Here I refer to the influence of the theoretical works of George C. Homans in 1961, John W. Thibaut and Harold H. Kelley in 1959, Paul F. Secord and Carl W. Backman in 1964 and others who attempt to explain social behavior in terms of rewards exchanged and costs incurred in interaction.[1]

For most sociologists, the question of "punishment in general" is not the question of importance here. Rather, the real issue is the role that one class of negative sanctions—legal sanctions—do play, and can play, in the prevention and control of crime. As Cobb points out, many sociologists in the past have seriously questioned the role of legal sanctions as deterrents. Some have even gone so far as to conclude that there is no hope whatsoever of legally punishing persons into conformity. Fortunately, most criminologists have come to view the issue of deterrence as an open question, and one not yet resolved.

It is of interest to note here that Cobb is critical of sociologists for their unwillingness to view the issue of deterrence as an open question. I might level the same criticism against Cobb. After recognizing, as Charles R. Tittle suggests, that we should now be asking "under what con-

[1]George C. Homans, *Social Behavior: Its Elementary Forms* (New York: Harcourt, Brace and World, 1961); John W. Thibaut and Harold H. Kelley, *The Social Psychology of Groups* (New York: John Wiley and Sons, 1959); and Paul F. Secord and Carl W. Backman, *Social Psychology* (New York: McGraw-Hill Book Co., 1964).

ditions are negative sanctions likely to be effective," he repeatedly concludes that "punishment does function as a deterrent."

After concluding that sociologists really do believe that punishment in general does deter crime, Cobb next attempts to merge the economic and sickness hypotheses through using Becker's interpretation of the economic hypothesis. Becker argues essentially that the number of crimes committed by a person is a function of five factors: (1) the probability of conviction (punishment), (2) the nature and severity of the punishment, (3) the income available to the actor from alternative legal and illegal activities, (4) the frequency of nuisance arrests, and (5) the actor's willingness to commit an illegal act.[2]

I seriously question if Becker's hypothesis and Cobb's discussion of it add significantly to our understanding of crime. All Becker and Cobb suggest is that the number of offenses a person would commit is influenced by the threat of legal sanctions, income available from other sources, and one's willingness to commit an offense in the first place, whatever that means. I do not take issue with the probable importance of the first four factors Becker enumerates. All of these considerations, in one form or another, have long been recognized by deterrence theorists since the writings of Cesare Beccaria in 1809, Jeremy Bentham in 1843, and others on the etiology of crime and its control. I might also add to this list, Adam Smith's 1896 *Lecture on Justice, Police, Revenue and Arms* which would appear to be of some relevance here.[3]

What particularly bothers me about Becker's scheme, and I see Cobb adding nothing to it, is

his inclusion of the catchall variable, a person's willingness to commit an illegal act in the first place, without specifying the importance of this factor alone and in comparison to the factors that he does enumerate, and without discussing the important factors that influence one's willingness to commit illegal acts. It is precisely these questions that have provided the major source of debate between classical and positivist criminologists over the last century and a half.

It is of interest to note that in Becker's lengthy essay, "Crime and Punishment: An Economic Approach," he mentions Beccaria and Bentham only in passing in the last paragraph of his paper. Cobb does not mention these writers nor the classical school of criminology in his theoretical discussion.

SOME METHODOLOGICAL COMMENTS

In the empirical section of his selection, Cobb presents a very interesting analysis of the ex post costs and benefits to thieves, as a group, for two years in Norfolk, Virginia. The method employed is a "simple" benefit-cost technique. In discussing this section of the selection I would like to confine myself to some methodological comments and to the conclusions he draws from his investigation.

The Benefits of Theft

Cobb first attacks the problem of determining the benefits of two types of theft: burglary and grand larceny. In assessing benefits he recognized three important considerations. First, not all thefts are reported to the authorities. Accordingly, Cobb makes the appropriate adjustments in the police figures by using the estimate of the President's Commission that reported costs of theft underestimate the true value by half.

Second, Cobb recognized that the market value of stolen goods to the thief is considerably less than the value placed on stolen goods by theft victims. Excluding stolen cash and clothing, he puts the estimated value of stolen

[2]Gary Becker, "Crime and Punishment: An Economic Approach" *Journal of Political Economy,* vol. 76 (March-April 1968), pp. 169–217.

[3]Cesare Beccaria, *Essay on Crimes and Punishment* (New York: Gould Press, 1809; Bobbs-Merrill edition, 1963, New York); Jeremy Bentham, *Principles of Penal Law,* 1st ed. (Edinburgh: W. Tait, 1943); and Adam Smith, *Lecture on Justice, Police, Revenue, and Arms* (Oxford: Clarendon Press, 1896).

goods to the thief at 20 percent. Finally, Cobb adjusts the total benefit to thieves by the value of stolen goods recovered by the police.

I suggest that a few additional benefit considerations and questions might have been examined, even though adjustments for some of these would not have been possible in his analysis. First, it should be recognized that not all victims of theft recognize their loss. This would appear particularly true for theft from businesses. Norman Jaspan and Hillel Black, for example, tell us that the biggest part of retail shrinkage does not result from shoplifters, but rather from employee theft.[4] Of course, reliable estimates of such losses are not available, but more importantly for our purposes here, seldom do such losses ever show up on the police statistics.

Second, even of the thefts that are recognized, not all are reported to the authorities. The National Opinion Research Center victim survey of 1967, for example, reveals that only about 32 percent of burglaries and 44 percent of larcenies are reported to the police. Cobb attempts to deal with this problem by doubling the loss figures reported by the Norfolk police, a procedure suggested by the President's Commission. Whether this adjustment allows for an adequate assessment of total dollar loss is not clear. The nonreporting of theft, it should be noted, is not a random matter. Quite probably, the greater the value of stolen goods, the more likely the theft will be reported. Whether the adjustment procedure suggested by the President's Commission adequately compensates for this fact is not clear. Further, it is not clear if this estimate procedure allows for the tendency of victims to overestimate the value of their stolen goods when reporting to the authorities.

Third, there would appear to be some disagreement over the value of fenced goods. Cobb puts the value at 20 percent for most items, but some suggest a figure of one third and still

others a value as high as 40 percent. Unfortunately, there is no "hard" evidence that allows us to answer this question. Certainly though, some types of stolen items have a higher fenced value than others. As a professional fence recently pointed out to me in an interview, a "hot" pistol (say, worth $100 retail) is worth quite a bit more to him than a $100 vacuum cleaner, "which you can't give away." The same could apply to the value of jewelry compared to other "hard to move" items. In short, the fenced value of 20 percent that Cobb uses for jewelry, furs and miscellaneous items (which is the largest single category of theft) would seem somewhat suspect.

The question of fences brings up another issue that must be examined. In Cobb's analysis, benefits to thieves are assessed as if all stolen goods are fenced at the going rate. This would appear to be a highly questionable assumption. Again we are faced with a lack of evidence, but I would submit that probably proportionately few stolen goods are fenced by thieves. Further, I would argue that proportionately few thieves steal with the intention of fencing the loot. Many probably steal with the intention of keeping the goods for themselves, and of course, much stolen property is discarded, particularly by young thieves. All of these factors make it extremely difficult to assess the cash value of stolen goods to thieves.

There is one additional aspect of "fencing" goods that Cobb glosses over without due consideration. In his analysis he implies that fences are readily available to retrieve stolen goods, and that thieves know of their whereabouts. I put these questions to an introductory sociology class very recently with these results. First, only approximately two-thirds of the class knew what a fence was. Second, only a few out of a class of over 100 thought that they knew where they could sell stolen goods (to a fence, that is). And third, even though each of these students had been personally involved in some theft, and some in major thefts, none had ever tried to fence stolen goods.

[4]Norman Jaspan and Hillel Black, *The Thief in the White Collar* (Philadelphia: J.B. Lippincott Co., 1960).

In sum, Cobb's attempt to construct an index of the economic benefits of theft is highly commendable, but it would appear to suffer from some major shortcomings that must be recognized.

The Costs of Theft

As Cobb points out, the costs to thieves are extremely difficult to evaluate. He recognizes a number of areas of consideration: the physical costs of the actual work involved in committing thefts; the disposable income lost while incarcerated if apprehended and convicted; fines levied in addition to, or in place of, incarceration; and the psychic costs of the loss of freedom and the negative stigma of a "bad reputation." To these I might add the costs of nuisance arrests (he and Becker cite this as a factor earlier in the selection), the cost of lawyer's fees, the cost of bail, the psychic costs of guilt and shame, and the costs of physical injury that might result from unwilling victims and the police.

Mr. Cobb chooses only to examine two cost factors in his analysis: the loss of disposable income as a result of incarceration, and fines levied on convicted thieves. Using these two factors he constructs his overall index of costs to thieves by combining the figures for fines for convicted thieves with the figures for the total lost disposable income of incarcerated offenders calculated according to the work histories of the convicted thieves.

SOME CONCLUSIONS

Having constructed indices of total income benefits and total income losses for two years, Cobb compares these estimates to see if theft "pays" in Norfolk, Virginia. For both years combined, total losses are put at $281,885, while benefits equal $750,460, a net difference of $468,575. From these figures, he argues that for those who served prison sentences, the average yearly costs would have to exceed $3,225 per year before one could say that theft is not profitable. Clearly, he concludes, thieves are making a wise economic choice.

But what of psychic costs? Cobb sees the loss of freedom as a major road block in his analysis, but he dismisses "bad reputation" as a possible cost. Why? Because in many cases, he says, and especially in the ghetto, "ex-cons" are held in esteem.

I must take strong issue with Cobb for summarily dismissing legal stigma as a cost. On the contrary, I see it as an important cost consideration. First, while probably some persons with a police record are viewed with esteem in the ghetto, probably many others are seen as losers. Second, theft is definitely not solely confined to ghetto residents. Investigations of confessed thieves reveal that no socioeconomic class in this society has a corner on this market.[5] Hence, the costs of legal stigma cannot be so easily disregarded. Nor does Gunning's 1970 research on the costs of the loss of freedom seem of much importance, as Cobb recognizes. Clearly additional research is required in this important area. Ignoring psychic costs, though, Cobb concludes that thieves in Norfolk are making a wise economic choice. I must conclude that because of some major problems in Cobb's benefit index of theft, I am unconvinced of this conclusion.

Charles H. Logan

I never have understood why some economists, like Cobb, insist on transforming ordinary prose into symbolic formulas, which are harder to type, take longer to read, and often, as in the

---

[5] See James S. Wallerstein and Clement Wyle, "Our Law-Abiding Law-Breakers," *Probation*, vol. 25 (April 1947), pp. 107–12; Ivan F. Nye, *Family Relations and Delinquent Behavior* (New York: John Wiley, 1958); Robert A. Dentler and Lawrence Monroe, "The Family and Early Adolescent Conformity and Deviance," *Marriage and Family Living*, vol. 23 (August 1961), pp. 241–47; Harwin L. Voss, "Ethnic Differentials in Delinquency in Honolulu," *Journal of Criminal Law, Criminology, and Police Science*, vol. 65 (September 1963), pp. 322–327; and Albert J. Reiss and Albert L. Rhodes. "The Distribution of Juvenile Delinquency in the Social Structure," *American Sociological Review*, vol. 36 (October 1961), pp. 720–32.

present instance, add nothing in the way of precision. Gary Becker's statement that the number of offenses is a function of probability of conviction, punishment if convicted, and "other variables" is still just a vague generalization whether he states it that way or as:

$$O_j = O_j (P_j, f_j, u_j).$$

A more serious consequence of reducing our thinking to manipulation of the terms of economic equations is that it produces dangerous simplifications. In Cobb's decision model, for example, he is forced to consider the prices of apprehension, punishment, and rehabilitation purely in terms of one common dimension: expenditures. But when nonmonetary costs are also considered, it is clear that the financially cheapest arrangement may entail the greatest overall human cost. Unfortunately, such multidimensional cost accounting does not fit into neat economic models.

The most fascinating part of Cobb's selection—the determination of whether or not theft does, in fact, "pay"—is an illustration of this, perhaps inherent, problem of simplification. Cobb's ingenious calculations and adjustments produce what can be accepted as perhaps the best available estimate of the net monetary benefits of theft to thieves in the aggregate (though I'm surprised that he did not include tax "exemption" in his calculations). But, as Cobb realizes, this does not really tell us—or potential thieves—whether or not theft "pays" in the largest sense of the term.

It is necessary to ask about the usefulness of attempting to calculate the net economic costs and benefits of theft. Suppose we could say for sure that theft is twice as profitable in Baltimore as it is in Cumberland. This might tell us something about the effectiveness of law enforcement in these two cities, but not necessarily, since the profitability of theft is determined by other factors as well. Likewise, the information might be of some interest to thieves who take a scientific approach to their work, but if they are intelligent they will realize that the figures are not relevant to individual thieves, only to thieves as a group. If criminologists are equally intelligent, they too will refrain from drawing inferences about the rationality of the average theft from figures that prove the overall profitability of stealing. Such an inference (that stealing is an individually profitable, hence rational, act) might be correct; but it is also at least equally possible that a small number of individuals gain the bulk of the profits while the majority of thieves are losers, who, therefore, are behaving "irrationally" in the economic sense. At any rate, it is evident that Cobb's selection has little to do with individual thieves, and nothing directly to do with motivation.

*

51. Economic Crises and Crime

M. HARVEY BRENNER

URBANIZATION AND ECONOMIC GROWTH

The area of urbanization and economic development has probably been the largest single source of theoretical development in the social sciences. From the works of Toennies, Durkheim, Weber, Simmel, Worth and others, there has developed a long-held assumption that the urbanization processes inherently contain elements of social disintegration and pathology. The basic notion appears to be that the bonds which traditionally united elements of the society, namely those relating to family, kin, and ethnic group, gradually lose their importance as society becomes industrialized and the power base shifts from kinship sources to those connected with the national political economy. In the course of this political transformation, the fundamental indicators of social position change from those ascribed, on the basis of kin relations to the social structure, to those based on economic achievement in the industrial sector. Thus, increasingly, economic achievement alone comes to represent the definition of social value in the society. An additional result is that those sources of community integration, which were based on kinship and ethnic ties, come to be

▶SOURCE: *"Part One: Time-Series Analysis (1900–1970). Effects of the Economy on Criminal Behavior and the Administration of Criminal Justice in the United States, Canada, England and Wales and Scotland," in United Nations Social Defence Research Institute, Economic Crises and Crime. Publication No. 15. (May 1976). Rome: U.N.S.D.R.I., pp. 30–59.* (Editorial adaptations.)

replaced by those based on economic interrelationships. Therefore, with the long-term development of economic growth, there is a gradual increase in the degree to which social integration is dependent on the economic function of society.

The obvious implication of this conception is that with continued economic growth the entire fabric of social integration becomes more vulnerable to even minor disturbances in the national economy. Thus, social pathology in general and criminal behaviour in particular would increasingly come to be explained by instrumentalities of the polictical economy.

Another important component of urbanization and economic development, which is also instrumental in diminishing the influence of ethnic ties, is that of population heterogeneity. Under conditions of urban economic development, the industrial locations draw ethnically mixed populations from many areas into categories of employment defined only by industry and occupation. Thus, in the same economic region, there will be found groups of very different backgrounds engaged in similar occupations and utilizing the same goods and services made available through the urban network. With this heterogeneity of populations, there occurs subcultural pluralism with a multitude of often conflicting value and normative systems. The subcultural pluralism logically leads to moral relativism on the part of increasingly large proportions of the urban population. The resulting vagueness in moral values concerning appropriate conduct and goals, theoretically would, in turn, lead to increasing acceptance and practice of behaviour previously considered unequivocally immoral.

Issue of "rational" versus "irrational" models of criminal behaviour as related to economic changes.

The principal sources of hypotheses on which the present work is based derived from the medical and psychological disciplines (psycho-biological) on the one hand, and the economic, sociological and political (socio-cultural) on the other. The psycho-biological formulations centre around the impact of psychological stress on aggression, especially violence. In this mechanism, stresses which overwhelm the individual tend to bring about behaviour which is eruptive and irrational in the sense that it is not under the control of the individual.

The socio-cultural view, by contrast, is that economic and political conditions change in such a way as to make it more probable that the individual will resort to illegal methods in order to gain income or social position. These processes are at least assume to be "rational," or under individual control. The conception of illegal injury, whether it involves violence or deprivation of property, is that it represents a form of aggression. The mode of aggression used may itself be comparatively "irrational" or "rational" but it is rarely either purely one or the other. Probably both psycho-physiological and instrumental gain is influencing the criminal behavioural process. Moreover, it is not easy (nor perhaps even correct) to discriminate between psycho-physiological and material gain.

The position taken in this research is that the criminal behaviour attributable to economic change contains elements of both psychological stress and the means of coping with it through either violence or comparatively utilitarian crime. In this sense, both the psycho-physiological and socio-cultural models are operative. In this conception a property crime

could well be considered an act of violence, or injury against another person, though not involving immediate physical harm. The loss in property, however, could ultimately result in substantial psychological harm.

Nevertheless, different forms of criminal response to economic stress could be categorized by the degree to which conscious or unconscious factors dominate the response pattern. In this case, the degree of "rationality" does not logically depend on the extent of violence in the criminal act. By this we do not intend to argue that such stress-responses represent forms of mental illness, but rather that they are coping mechanisms to overwhelming stress situations of which the criminal subject may be more or less aware. Yet it is probable that a "solely" violent act without additional criminal implications, such as assault, can be construed largely within the "more nearly irrational category." Also, it is probable that a solely utilitarian act of larceny may be largely "rational" under this definition.

OPERATIONAL MEASURES OF THEORETICAL CONSTRUCTS

In translating the theoretical views into operational measures which reflect on the state of the economy, we are considering six types of measurement. These are:

1.   General cycles of economic upswing and recession.

2.   Economic instability, or departures from smooth economic growth in general.

3.   Change in the structure of economic inequality.

4.   The extent to which specific (socio-economic or demographic, population subgroups tend to gain or lose employment and income during economic upturns and recessions, again as compared with the general population.

5. Secular changes in income distribution among population subgroups.

6. Secular changes in income levels according to population subgroups.

The basic mechanisms alluded to by these sets of measures concern:

(a) Changes in the level of economic well-being.

(b) Changes in comparative socio-economic position (or status) on the part of any specific subpopulation to the population as a whole (overall median) or to any other specific subpopulation (reference group, as in Merton).

(c) The general extent of economic inequality in a population, where the measure would approximate the standard deviation (among subgroups) of overall population income.

(d) The exact profile (pyramidal structure) of income distribution. This issue concerns the relative proportions of income distributed among the various subpopulations which may be inherently pathological or salutary.

(e) Economic instability, or the degree to which levels of income and employment, in the general population or in any subpopulation, is subject to fluctuation. From a psychological standpoint, this is a problem of coping with, or adjusting to, situations of change per se. These economic instabilities are measured by the absolute difference between smooth economic trends and the raw economic data that they are taken to represent.

(f) Urbanization, as measured by population size, density and heterogeneity.

(g) Increasing dominance of the economy as a mode of societal integration, as measured by the extent to which national or international economic phenomena are causes of the socio-economic situation of subpopulations.

MEASUREMENT OF THE EFFECTS OF ECONOMIC CHANGE ON CRIME AND CRIMINAL JUSTICE SYSTEM (CJS) ACTIVITY

1. Measurement of adverse effects of economic change:

(a) Fluctuations in the rate of employment and unemployment (in combination with measures related to personal income, we can estimate the impact of "underemployment" or "misemployment").

(b) Effects of inflation: annual percentage changes in the Consumer Price Index.

(c) Intermediate range (1–5 years to long-term) patterns of national economic growth. This measure may be inversely related to the crime rate where:

  (i) Income distribution is not widened among specific subpopulations.

  (ii) There are no substantial concomitant economic instabilities.

(d) Differential trends in income and employment among the various subgroups.

(e) Differences between income and employment levels of selected minority groups, on the one hand, and the median of per capita income unemployment for the population aggregate on the other.

(f) Combinations of several of the above stated measures in order to derive a comprehensive econometric model of adverse effects of economic change.

2. Measures of the incidence of criminal behaviour and effects on the CJS:

(a) The problem: that at any single point in time criminal justice statistics do not accurately reflect the incidence or prevalence of crime in society, and that there is a substantial "dark figure" of unmeasured crime; and furthermore that the size of this "dark figure" varies greatly depending on which criminal justice indicator is used. In sum, the CJS statistics represent the "tip of the iceberg" of existing criminal activity, even if we consider crimes known to the police. This problem has traditionally been so overwhelmingly difficult that in comparing nations, provinces, cities, or even sub-units of citiee, the issues of comparable reporting have prevented accurate assessment of relative crime rates.

(b) In the present study, this problem of statistical validity and reliability is handled in several different ways:

(1) While it is true that cross-population comparisons, at a single point in time, are extremely treacherous, there is considerably less danger in assessing trends over time for a specific locality since the same reporting system (with the same biases of reporting) can usually be assumed to prevail during the period of the trend analysis under consideration. Thus, various nations or other regional units may be compared with respect to variations in their trend levels if one does not assume the accuracy of the absolute levels (or rates) represented in the trends, but rather focusses simply on proportionate increases and decreases over time. In addition, multivariate time-series analytic methods have been established to separate the effects of different influences on the criminal statistical trends, and even the problem of trend changes in reporting can to some degree be estimated or at least statistically controlled.

(2) A major safeguard in the assurance of both the validity and reliability of time trends in criminal statistics as they reflect *fluctuations* in criminal behaviour, is the use of multiple statistical indicators of crime drawn from CJS sources. These sources include police, criminal court, and prison. Thus, the range of data include the following indicators: crimes known to the police, arrests, crimes brought to trial, conviction and other dispositions, and imprisonment. All of these data are cross-classified by major crime. A major effort, then, is to observe the degree to which there is correspondence among the various administrative categories of criminal justice statisitcs in their specific relationships to economic indicators. To the extent that there is good correspondence, we can be relatively certain that the relationships are not based on any one type of measure, but rather that all available sources of criminal justice data point to the same conclusions. This enhances the likelihood that specific problems in the validity or reliability of any single category of criminal justice data will be compensated for by the use of other indicators which do not present the identical problems.

For example, one of the most crucial issues in the validity of criminal justice statistics trends in representing trends in crime is that they may be influenced by long-term changes in the propensity of the general public to report crime. In particular, it has been suggested that over time the public might have shown a lowered tolerance of (what had earlier been thought of as) comparatively minor crimes, and thus might be more willing to report such crimes to the police. While such a suggestion, if factually accurate, would influence the rate of incidence of certain (comparatively minor) crimes known to the police, it would probably not influence the rate of imprisonment which we would assume to deal almost entirely with relatively serious crimes.

In any case, we would at least assume that as one moved from crimes known to the police to arrest, to prosecution, to conviction, and finally to imprisonment, if the relationships to economic indicators became *successively* weaker, then the reporting issue may well be the source of the problem. If, on the other hand, there were little differences among these criminal statistical indicators in their relation to the economy, then we would assume comparatively minor impact due to reporting. Finally, if we found that the criminal statistical indicators occurring later in time—the very latest representing imprisonment—showed the strongest relations to the economy, then we would assume that the reporting factor probably does not influence the later indicators (especially imprisonment), yet they may influence the earlier indicators (especially crimes known to the police) to some extent.

(3) A third safeguard in assuring the validity and reliability of the estimated relationships between criminal statistical *trends* and economic indicators is that they will pertain to a great variety of different crimes—a number referring to violent behaviour and another group dealing with property crimes. To the extent that we observe consistency in the relationships across each of the group of violent crimes, and the group of property crimes, we can infer generalizability of the relationships. We therefore counteract the possibility that the relationships are a result of any one type of crime or, as is often the case in this type of research, that a gross figure for crime is used which may indicate the predominant influence of one offence or category of offences.

(4)   A fourth method of assuring validity and reliability in the relationships found is that they will be matched for consistency across four major geographical and political units, namely the United States, Canada, England and Wales, and Scotland. This comparison is particularly pertinent because the Anglo-American legal tradition is common to all, yet the definitions of crime, public tolerance of crime, reporting systems, and criminal justice administrative procedures may vary considerably. We thus control, in part, for the effects of these differences through a determination of the consistency of the results (while exposing the most important differences in these systems).

(5)   One of the most important sources of obtaining validity and reliability of research results using criminal statistical data is to offer comparisons which are derived from outside of the CJS, and are otherwise not subject to the types of criticism that have been directed toward CJS statistics. The data we use in this respect derive from vital statistics of each of our four areas and pertain to homicide. Homicide is a diagnosis, within the specifications of the ICDA (WHO), by which the attending physician or officially designated coroner ascertains that mortality has occurred as a result of violence done to the deceased by another person. These data have been subject to the least amount of negative scholarly critique and, at worst, proba-

bly under-represent the true incidence of homicide by a small fraction.

In addition, as in the case of the other CJS-derived statistics, the four major political regions are compared. Also, additional multiple checks on consistency of results for homicide are obtained since the data are examined for each of several (i.e., ten) different age-groups, cross-classified by sex and, for the United States, further cross-classified by race.

Finally, the homicide data offer a comparison (for consistency in terms of validity and reliability) with CJS statisitics on murder in the sense that the homicide data pertain to victims who died, while the CJS data pertain largely to alleged criminals (apart from crimes known to police).

(6)   Another means of checking the reliability and validity of findings is to make comparisons among techniques used to establish the findings in the first place. There are four sources of comparison among techniques: differential trend examination, bivariate versus multivariate analyses, varying methods of establishing significant associations, and observations of the relationships over different spans of time. Altogether, to the extent that consistent findings are obtained among the different procedures, we increase confidence in the findings obtained.

The issue of differential trend analysis involves, first, the difference between removing, versus not removing, secular trends (since there are important schools of thought which suggest one or the other procedure). Also, there is the question of examining different levels (or intervals) of temporal change (1–11 or more year changes) in order to observe at which trend and interval levels the relationships can be found. Can we predict even on an annual basis, and can we predict for very large proportionate changes as well as medium-size changes? Also, can we predict to moderate-size changes rather than only to dramatic changes?

The second question concerns the distinction between observing the impact of different economic (and other social) indicators on crime versus observing their combined multivariate effect, where internal statistical controls have been employed. Does the explanation of the interactive multivariate model show consistency with the relationships indicated by simple correlation techniques?

Thirdly, do the two major techniques of over-time analysis, namely regression and spectral, lead to similar conclusions?

Fourthly, do analyses performed over different spans of time, namely 1920–1940 versus post World War II, lead to similar conclusions?

(7)   The next source of ascertaining validity and reliability of the findings pertains to explanation and interpretation of the findings themselves. Ideally, it is hoped that the findings are consistent with other established research findings in the area, and with theoretical positions that are most sophisticated given the state of the discipline at that time. In line with these considerations, in following standard scientific procedure one constructs hypotheses derived from previously constructed empirical generalizations and theory and either supports or falsifies them as a result of the research effort.

(8)   Again, some of the answers to questions about the reliability and validity of the trend data in CJS statistics are ascertained in connection with the findings of consistency of relationships vis-à-vis measures that are derived independently from the CJS statistics (the exogenous economic and social indicators). Given consistency of findings among all of the many types of cross-classifications of the CJS data *in relation to the economic and other indicators,* we can assume in large measure, general reliability at least of the trend components of the CJS data.

(9)   Finally, the existence of the consistent relationships themselves, despite the significant reporting problems inherent in the CJS data, would argue that the relationships found are *underestimates* of the true relationships, and thus the findings could be assumed to be stronger were the data to have carried greater validity and reliability. Yet the findings

themselves are very strong in terms of statistical significance and variance explained. It is therefore not difficult to accept the conclusion that these are underestimates, and are thus the most conservative estimates, of the true relationships.

RESEARCH METHODS

1.   Data

The data gathered range over the twentieth century and as far into the present as feasible. They generally begin with the year 1900. These data include mortality, crimes known to the police, arrests, trials, and imprisonments for all major crimes including: *(a)* murder, *(b)* manslaughter, *(c)* wounding, *(d)* assault, *(e)* rape and other sexual offences, *(f)* offences related to possession and abuse of dangerous drugs, *(g)* robbery, *(h)* embezzlement, *(i)* forgery, *(j)* fraud, *(k)* burglary (housebreaking, shopbreaking and entering), and *(l)* larceny and other theft. Where possible, the data are cross-classified by age, sex, and race. In addition, data on prison release by crime are obtained in order to analyse the impact of economic change on the discharge and parole processes.

The national-level economic indicators include employment, unemployment, and per capita personal income and inflation. These data have proven most representative of fluctuations in national economic-industrial indicators, and on the individual level bear a close relationship to per capita economic loss and gain.

2.   Analysis

(a)   *Data transformations*

Three forms of the economic and criminal justice data are used in these analyses. We generally begin with the data transformed so as to eliminate the long-term trends. This process is accomplished after the data have been converted to rates, having first been divided by the appropriate population denominator. The long-term trends are estimated by fitting the best of five models of long-term changes (one linear type, two logarithmic types, a positive and negative reciprocal model, and a logistic type). The most appropriately fitting model is determined by the magnitude of the simple correlation coefficient representing the relationship between each hypothetical trend and the raw economic and criminal justice data. Once the proper trends have been fitted, they are algebrically subtracted from the respective economic and criminal justice series and the cyclic fluctuations remain. This data transformation is used only to investigate the cyclic effect of fluctuations in employment, income and inflation.

The second mode of "transformation" involves no alteration at all in the raw economic and criminal statistics. The use of the criminal statistics in their raw form enables determination of the total amount of variation in the criminal statistical trends that are due to trends in the economic indicators.

Finally, the third type of data transformation involves conversion of the economic and criminal statistics, arrayed over time, into percentage changes. Typically, four levels of percentage change were utilized: annual, 3-year, 5-year, and 10-year changes. These data conversions allow us to examine the question of which levels of trends give evidence for the relationship between the economic and criminal statistics. It is theoretically possible that the relationships exist only at the level of 3–5 year changes, since these are the levels which are closest to cyclic fluctuations in national economic indicators. It is also possible that the relationships exist only at a relatively broad level of change, such as 10-year fluctuations, since the relationships may be mostly confined to comparatively large structural changes in the national economy. It is also possible that the relationships are so potent that they are predictable on a year to year basis, in which case they would be measurable at the level of annual percentage changes. The last possibility is that the relationships between economic and criminal statistics are so potent as to be measurable at all four of these levels of national economic change.

(b) *Measure of association*

Standard methods of time-series are used, including:

(1) Simple correlation (controlling for autocorrelated residuals).

(2) Distributed lag analysis, through multiple regression, in order to determine the proportion of variance in the criminal justice indicators which are related to economic changes at lags of specific years (behind economic changes, from one to three years).

(3) Fourier analysis, to determine whether the relationships are active over short (1–3 years), middle-range (3–5 years), and long periods (7–11 years) of recession on economic decline.

These relationships are being separately examined for the following groupings of years in order to determine whether the correlations obtained will show equal strength and predictability over time.

(a) 1900–1910

(b) 1900–1920

(c) 1922–1941

(d) 1936–1970

(e) 1941–1970

(f) 1948–1970

Graphic analysis of the relationships will also be an important component of the final presentation of data. Such analyses enable the viewer to observe the magnitude of change in the economic and criminal justice indicators in relation to each other. They have traditionally had greater face validity among persons not fully acquainted with the more complicated mathematical aspects of time-series analysis.

SUMMARY OF FINDINGS

1. Relationships between cyclic fluctuations in employment (and personal income) and criminal statistics.

(a) *Distinction between pre- and post-World War II relationships*

In the four major political units (United States, Canada, England and Wales, and Scotland), the overall relationships between instabilities in the economy and the major sources of criminal statistics show remarkable correspondence. In general, the rate of unemployment (or declines in employment and in personal income) show significant and strong relationships to increases in trends of criminal statistical data, for all major categories of crime and sources of criminal statistics.

In each country, however, it is also observed that the apparent significance of these adverss short-term economic fluctuations show a substantially heightened influence on the criminal statistics after the Second World War or, more generally, with the passage of time. This is indicated especially by the simple (or zero-order) inverse relationships between these economic fluctuations and the criminal statistics within one year of a decline in employment and income. In other words, without considering lags of criminal statistical data to economic fluctuations, the later decades of the twentieth century show substantially higher inverse correlation coefficients. The difference, in fact, between the strength of these correlations since World War II, as compared with the previous period, might lead one at first blush to imagine that the significant relations exist only since approximately 1946.

Since a conclusion would be extremely misleading, however, a more sophisticated analysis, which takes into consideration the dispersion of the lagged effects of economic stress over a period which includes 0–3 years (distributed-lag analysis), shows that the *overall* impact of the effects of these sources of economic stress on criminal statistics has probably not changed significantly from the pre- to post-World War periods. Rather, what appears to have happened is that particularly for Canada, England and Wales, and Scotland, the lagged effects are quite pronounced during the pre-war period while minimal since then. There has been, then, a speeding up of the reaction time to short-term economic adversity coincident with accelerated rates of inflation and economic growth during the last thirty years.

(b) *Distinction between violent crimes against property and property crimes without violence*

The difference in reaction time (or distributed-lag effects) between the pre- and post-war eras is most pronounced when one considers the extent of physical violence involved in the criminal behaviour. Since the Second World War the relationships appear to be quite similar regardless of the extent of violence associated with crime. Perhaps the only remaining point of discriminaiton is that with increasing violence associated with crime there is somewhat more of a tendency toward a distributed-lag relationship with a lower inverse correlation for any single year.

Prior to the Second World War, however, there tends to be a substantially weaker simple correlation relationship for crimes of violence only, as compared with those involving violence with economic gain, or property crime alone. It therefore appears that the single most important source of the acceleration of reaction time to economic adversity has occurred with crimes of violence, even those involving violence with property crime.

(c) *Distinction in these relationships among the four national regions*

There is a difference between the change in the relationship between adverse economic fluctuations and criminal statistics over time when one compares the United States particularly with England and Wales, and Scotland. It is especially for England and Wales, and for Scotland that the acceleration of the inverse relationship with economic fluctuations is observed. By contrast, the United States, while indeed showing some heightened sensitivity during the later years, also showed very substantial and rapid reactions of criminal statistics particularly during the period 1921–1940, which included the Great Depression. In the United States incarceration in state and federal institutions, for example, for all major crimes show relationships so strong that virtually no other factors other than adverse national economic changes explain the trends. Canada appears to lie somewhere between the extraordinary sensitivity of pre-World War II United States and the more delayed and dispersed reactions of the English and Scottish criminal statistics. In the Canadian case, it is found that the majority of separate crime categories do show increased statistical sensitivity since the Second World War, yet there is a large minority of important categories of crime that do not show such an increased sensitivity.

2. The relationship between economic growth, as measured by changes in Gross National Product, and criminal statistics.

The long-term effects of economic growth during the twentieth century on criminal statistics generally show strongly postive relationships. This finding appears to coincide with the general effects of urbanization, but, perhaps more importantly, with the effects of structural (or technological) unemployment, underemployment (or misemployment) and *comparative* decline in socio-economic status is more generally referred to as the problem of inequality in income distribution and job allocation. It appears to be engendered by two types of economic trends. The first of these pertains to economic swings of comparatively lengthy and deep variation, in which a substantial aggregate of the population is experiencing change in employment and income. Under these conditions of intermediate-range economic changes

(a standard component of the economic growth process), that element of the population which ordinarily shows the highest rates of unemployment and the lowest income experiences only a minor decline in absolute income and employment levels. That lowest socio-economic group, however, simultaneously experiences a *comparative substantial increase* in socio-economic status in relation to the considerably larger declines in employment and income levels experienced by other population groups, (a situation which pushes the other groups into an economic situation which is similar to that of the more chronically unemployed and impoverished).

By contrast, in the case of intermediate-range economic upswings or long-term economic growth, while these lowest socio-economic groups do show increases in employment and income levels, those increases do not begin to compare with those for the general population. In other words, there is substantial *comparative* decline in socio-economic status among the lowest income and occupational skill groups during these periods of substantial economic acceleration or long-term economic growth.

In industrial societies, especially since the Second World War, the premium qualifications for middle to high income employment have been based on education and technologically sophisticated skills. The lack of acquisition of such skills by the lowest socio-economic groups, frequently in conjunction with the movement of such groups from rural to urban areas, has helped to create great disparities in income and subcultural living styles.

In all political regions examined, therefore, the secular effects of economic growth have served to increase the trends in criminal statisitics. These pathological effects of rapid economic development have been far more pronounced since the Second World War, but were in evidence to some degree even prior to 1941. These trends, prior to 1941, were probably most important for Canada, less important for England and Wales, and Scotland, and least in evidence for the United States.

The pathological effects of economic growth are most apparent for crimes of violence unrelated to economic gain, moderately related to violent property crimes and least strongly related to crimes related to property alone. In many instances, in the four major political regions, certain exclusively property crimes do not show trend increases related to economic growth (e.g. occasionally burglary and grand larceny).

(a) *Economic growth, trends in income inequality, and crime rates*

A number of different explanations can be proposed as to the causal factors behind the positive correlation between long-term trends in economic growth and crime rates, especially since the Second World War. The issue of changes in income inequality (or relative income change) are among the more prominently cited sources of feelings of deprivation. The finding that relative income deprivation explains the positive relationship between crime and long-term economic growth, due to increasing economic inequality among specific population subgroups would be in line with the general thesis that it is the *sense* of economic deprivation which leads to crime. This finding would be coincident with those of this study which indicate that with *downturns* in the economic cycle, and with inflation, there are substantial increases in rates of criminal behaviour. Furthermore, it is illogical to make the direct interpretation that it is precisely the increase in income which is the antecedent of crime rate increases for the long-term trend, since exactly the opposite is indicated for small-to-moderate economic fluctuations of the "cyclical" variety.

In this study we have experimented with one major variable by which we hoped to operationalize an important component of the potential impact of changes in income inequality. This variable is the degree of income change of the population at different age-groups in relation to the general growth of population income over time since 1948. The reason that age

was specified relates specifically to the variable it was intended to explain, namely homicide. It had been found previously in this study that the size of the population under age 30 was an important factor in the homicide rate since World War II. The further question was raised as to whether the youthful population was put at risk for homicide especially under conditions where their relative income had decreased in relation to that of a population as a whole.

The experiment indicated that since World War II there has indeed developed a very substantial relationship between the income gap of persons between ages 14 and 25 who are not living in families and the rate of homicide. This relationship appears to be so significant that it diminished the statistical importance of unemployment changes as well as the long-term trend in economic growth. Most important, however, is that focussing on age provides only a single indication of the possible impact of changes in income inequality over time on criminal behaviour. A similar type of quantitative operationalization of income inequality through time should be performed at least for specific income groupings (e.g., the lowest tenth of the population of income distribution), occupational, industrial and ethnic groups. Such operationalizations of multiple indicators of income inequality should extend greatly the potential for explaining the effects of long-term economic growth on the sense of deprivation felt by specific subpopulations.

(b) *General explanation of positive relationship between economic growth and crime rates*

Long-term economic growth appears to reduce pathological effects which may involve (a) increased social inequality, or *relative* inequality, (b) urbanization, with its problems of decreased significant interpersonal relationships as related to population size, crowding, and reduced family structure. There may be a minor positive impact of general economic growth, in terms of urbanization, on pathology due to the "civilizing" effects of urban life, and a probable decrease in tolerance for personal violence. The following is an outline of some of the more important factors which may impinge on the crime rate:

- Changes in relative income distribution: or the issue of inequality or relative inequality.

- True differentials in *relative income* change coincident with economic growth (the problem of relative social mobility), according to income or unemployment level by:

  - Occupation, industry

  - Income group

  - Age

  - Educational level (i.e., differentials in social mobility as measured by education level alone)

- Increased perception of relative deprivation by comparatively low-income groups due to the (apparent) increasing dependence of economic growth on heightened consumer demand. This heightened consumer demand is, in turn, brought about by the communications industry in general, and advertising in particular. The following variables may be used to measure the growth and potency of these industries:

  - Expenditures, or extent, of GNP related to communications in general

  - Expenditures for advertising (also manpower involved in advertising)

  - Expenditures and manpower in television

  - Growth of market research and related industries

- Increasing minority status of lowest income groups, according to:

  - Income rank

  - Occupation

  - Ethnicity

- Greater *sensitivity* to loss due to the national median level of greatly increased economic affluence:

  - The higher the income level over time, the greater is the absolute income loss due to unemployment (or underemployment).

  - The higher the national median level of income, the greater the relative personal loss due to unemployment, underemployment, or inflation. The isolating effects of economic loss during periods of economic affluence, probably imply, in addition, that short-term and sharper economic downturns have a harsher proportional effect than larger sources of economic downturn in which a greater proportion of the population is involved.

- The problem of urbanization

- Physical dimensions of urbanization

- Size and heterogeneity

  - Comparative insignificance of the individual in terms of personal status.

  - A larger number, but less individually significant and close, personal relationships—leading to a decrease in the social control exerted by individuals upon one another;

  - Decreased community integration leading to decreased effectiveness of police and decreased community relations engendering lowered inhibition to injure one's neighbours (1) Less accurate perception of who actually "belongs" or resides in the community; (2) The issue is raised as to who will become involved in helping others; (3) Decreased relationships with local police; (4) Lowered inhibition to harm others due to lessened protection normally afforded by close interpersonal relations.

- Population density: the issue of crowding and stress levels.

  - The issue of privacy

  - The relative importance of the individual person and his influence on his life situation

  - Competition for resources, or pressure on the distribution of resources.

- Environment

  - Noise levels

  - Pollution and odour intensity.

- Decline in family structure (and structure of other primary groups)

  - Indicators of family structure (1) Family size; (2) Divorce rate; (3) Separation rate; (4) Illegitimate birth rate; (5) Number of persons residing together; (6) Marital status including singles and widowed, by age; (7) Growth of school education

  - Causal indicators (1) Growth of the female labour force; (2) Migration patterns, international, rural-urban, and inter-city; (3) Social mobility.

3. The relationship between inflation, as measured by annual percentage changes in the Consumer Price Index (CPI), and criminal statistics.

There is little statistical doubt that the annual rate of inflation bears a significant positive relationship to the criminal justice statistical indicators. These relationships appear to behave very much like those observed for economic growth as measured by the Gross National Product (which has been deflated). Ordinarily, in fact, the rate of inflation, measured by CPI, and the GNP would be very highly correlated (at a level of correlation greater than 95). Since we wished to sharply distinguish the effects of general economic growth from those relating to

inflation per se, annual percentage changes in the CPI were used to represent inflation, while the GNP (deflated) did not undergo transformation. Nevertheless, the greatly attenuated measure of inflation which (according to correlation coefficient measures) bears little relationship to GNP, does show relations to the criminal statisitics which are similar to those found for GNP.

In general, for all four major political regions there is a positive relationship of inflation to the criminal statistics during the full period covered by the twentieth century data. These relationships do not become very important, however, until after the Second World War for most of these regions and for the majority of crimes. As in the case of economic growth, they are most important for the violent crimes without reference to economic gain, least important for the purely property-labelled crimes, and moderately important for those crimes in which violence is associated with economic gain. For the United States, and England and Wales, the relationships between inflation and the criminal statistics are not important until the late 1940's and for the United States, in particular, they seem to be absent until that time.

4. Interaction among the three major national economic indicators (unemployment, GNP, and CPI) and criminal statistics.

Summarizing the combined effects of the three national economic indicators on the criminal statistics, it is found that when used together in the same predictive equation, they explain considerably more variation in the criminal statistics than any one does alone. The three economic indicators seem to have both independent effects and interactive effects. Each one of the three by itself exerts a measurable and statistically significant impact on the criminal data. The combined effect of these three indicators is such that for a great many categories of crime more than 90 per cent of the variation in trends in criminal statistics can be accounted for. This is often true for the entire period from the early 1900's through the late 1960's, but is especially noteworthy since the Second World War.

For the most part, cyclic fluctuations in employment and income appear to be the dominant factors affecting the crime rates prior to the Second World War; but even where they are dominant they may not explain more than 40–60 percent of the variance in the majority of crime categories. Since the Second World War, however, the effects of economic growth and inflation have been especially pronounced so that in combination with the cyclic economic instabilities, the complete set of three economic indicators frequently accounts for over 90 per cent of the variances in the criminal statistics.

The cyclic economic fluctuations, particularly relating to employment patterns, have been traditionally the most important sources of influence on the crime rate. They continue to retain their significance during the last three decades but become equal in importance to the economic disequilibria and inequalities subsumed in the economic growth indicator and including the features of long-term structural unemployment, underemployment, and chronically low and unstable income. Of the three economic indicators, inflation has exerted the least important influence, although that influence has been statistically significant. It has been especially significant in combination with declining, or comparatively low levels of employment and income, since it further acts to reduce real income levels. Inflation is also a variable which during the last few years, has shown very great potential for economic disruption at a level at least potentially equal to that of unemployment or economic inequality.

5. Combined effects of economic and non-economic factors on estimates of crime.

Apart from those factors which are inherently related to absolute or relative change in socio-economic position, it is also necessary to consider factors which influence the crime rate in conjunction with national economic changes. These additional factors could influence the crime rate either by directly interacting with the economic change factors or having an additional independent effect which either moderates or exacerbates the effects of economic change. Two factors which interact directly with the effects of economic change refer to the demography and community structure of a nation. Two major examples of such factors are 1) the expansion and contraction of the size of the comparatively youthful population involved in serious criminal behaviour, and especially violent behaviour, and 2) the extent of urbanization. The size of the youthful population at risk for crime, i.e., 20–30, depends on fluctuations in the birth rate—which are in turn generally positively related to long-term economic changes. Similarly, the extent of urbanization, as measured by the number of persons living in cities greater than village size (i.e., more than 10,000 persons), is a function of long-term economic development, which has been especially pronouced since the second World War even in industrialized countries.

A set of factors which would theoretically have an effect either moderating or making more acute the effects of economic change would be the efficiency and effectiveness of the CJS. While the operations the CJS are not necessarily dependent on the economy, outlays of national revenue for CJS expenditures, in the area of manpower and facilities for example, certainly are.

The impact of changes in the size of the population under age 30, the extent of urbanization, and the ratio of arrests, prosecutions, and convictions to crimes known by the police were investigated in terms of their independent and combined effects of the crime estimates. In addition, these effects were measured in combination with those due strictly to economic changes.

We have been able to experiment with these three groups of variables on the United States data on homicide and England and Wales data on major crimes in each segment of the CJS process (from crimes known to the police through imprisonment). It is quite clear that the size of the youthful population is a significant predictive factor in our measures of the crime rate. This is particularly true for homicide but somewhat less important for our measures of crime funds derived from CJS data.

The extent of urbanization also turns out to be a potent variable in the statistical explanation of crime indicators. It appears to have a positive relationship to property crime in general, at least as indicated by the British data, since 1948 pertaining to robbery, burglary, and larceny. In the case of homicide, on the other hand, it appears to have a comparatively mild effect and even an inverse relationship at times. It is possible, then, that urbanization has the effect of diminishing the extent of violence over the long-term trend while increasing the rate of property crime somewhat. It should be kept in mind that these relationships for urbanization pertain to the period following World War II. Prior to the war, there seem to be few significant observable relationships for urbanization during the twentieth century.

The impact of measures of effectiveness of the CJS does appear to be significant and consistent among the crime indicators with which experimentation has taken place (i.e., the data for England and Wales). While the results are significant, the measures do not explain a substantial proportion of the variation in crime rates as compared with the major economic indicators; the proportion of variance explained by the CJS measures range from approximately 3–12 per cent. Nevertheless, these results are theoretically and practically significant, particularly considering that the relationship is always in the hypothesized direction—namely that the higher the ratio of arrests, prosecutions and convictions is to crimes known to the police, the lower is the crime incidence. This apparent effect on crime incidence of the CJS measures would lead to a deterrence explanation, and the greatest effect is observed on crimes known to the police. There is little or no negative effect, however, of the CJS measures on crimes which result in imprisonment—that is, the more serious offences. Indeed for crimes resulting in imprisonment, there is a significant positive correlation with the CJS measures, probably indicating the importance of police and prosecution functions in obtaining conviction even for major crimes.

In general, the demographic, urbanization and CJS data, while showing statistically significant results, do not appear to alter substantially the observed impact of national economic indicators on the measures of crime incidence. These additional factors do, however, serve to round out the explanatory model by which the trends in crime statistics can be understood.

6.   The relationship between homicide mortality and national economic indicators.

There are two outstanding distinctions between the homicide data and the data representing changes in crime incidence derived from CJS sources. In cases of both types of data, the attempt is to ascertain relationships between national economic changes and criminal behaviour. In the case of the homicide data, however, the primary source derives from vital statistics reports of actual deaths. In addition, the homicide data are perhaps closest to representing "irrational" aggression, in the sense that most homicide occurs among individuals who are closely acquainted and especially among family members. Therefore, the homicide data are possibly the "purest" representatives of criminal activity without obvious utilitarian motive.

For each of the four major areas under investigation, the homicide findings are somewhat different from those pertaining to other crimes (as derived from CJS data sources). The primary difference relates to the period between the first and second World Wars, whereas after the second World War the findings for homicide and the CJS-based data are virtually identical. For the period 1920–1940, data on homicide for the four major areas are consistent in showing the following relationships to national economic indicators: (1) a positive correlation with the inverted unemployment index, and (2) an inverse relationship to changes in the Gross National Product (GNP). By contrast, for the CJS-derived data (i.e., robbery, larceny) these criminal indicators are inversely related to both the inverted unemployment index and GNP. It therefore appears that while criminal activity was in general strongly inversely related to all the major economic indicators during 1920–1940, homicide is inversely related to the major national economic indicator (GNP) but is positively related to changes in the employment rate (as measured by 100 minus the proportion of persons unemployed per civilian population).

Before attempting to interpret this apparent contradiction in findings, it is important to make reference to the only other study in recent times which dealt with the effects of national economic changes on homicide rates, namely that of A. F. Henry and J. F. Short, *Suicide and Homicide.* Using an index of industrial production for the United States, Henry and Short found a positive correlation with the homicide rate during the twentieth century through 1950. The explanation given by these authors focussed on the issue of relative, as distinguished from absolute, deprivation. They argued that since persons committing homicide are typically of considerably low socio-economic status, and during economic downturns such individuals lose less proportionately than the majority of the population, it is important to focus on the possible adverse effects of economic upturns for these individuals. Thus, while during economic downturns a sizable proportion of the population is actually reduced to a very low level of socio-economic status, during economic upturns the relative gaps between the lowest and higher income groups increases, and even in the best of times the lowest group shows high rates of unemployment.

The difficulty with Henry and Short's explanation is that they generalized to all economic downturns regardless of magnitude. However, while their interpretation might well be correct for an extraordinarily deep and lengthy economic depression, it probably would not hold for the more usual short-term economic recession which involves a minority of the population. It is only in the case of a long and deep economic depression that economic change is so intense as to propel a significant number of the population to a status nearly equivalent to that of the lowest socio-economic stratum—in such a way, furthermore, that it is plainly visible to individuals for the lowest socio-economic positions. In the ordinary economic recession, however, probably the typical individual who experiences major income or employment loss is largely unaware of the effects on others, and in fact is likely to blame himself for the loss rather than attribute it to a national phenomenon.

The finding in this study of a positive relationship to homicide rates for the inverted unemployment index during 1920–1940 is coincident with this thesis. Observation of the unemployment rate during this period shows extremely dramatic changes during the period 1929–1936, essentially covering the Great Depression, but minor fluctuations during the other years of 1920–1940. Therefore, the entire relationship between homicide and the inverted unemployment index is dominated by the deep and lengthy economic adversity of 1929–1936. By contrast, the relationship between GNP and the homicide rate is in the proper direction for the hypothesis that absolute economic deprivation produces an increase in the homicide rate; i.e., the correlation is inverse. The validity of the absolute income loss hypothesis is supported by observation that while GNP fell substantially during the Great Depression, other fluctuations in GNP during 1920–1940 were far more important than were those in unemployment (comparing 1929–1936 with the remainder of the period 1920–1940).

It is therefore reasonable to conclude that during the period 1920–1940 the economic stress which precipitated very large increases in the homicide rate in all four major regions was due to both (1) absolute adverse changes in socio-economic status for substantial proportions of the general population, and (2) relative adverse changes in socio-economic status for the very lowest socio-economic groups normally having very high unemployment rates. In addition to the typically adverse effects of economic loss during periods of economic downturn (represented by changes in GNP during 1920–1940), we must also consider the positive effects of major increases in unemployment, during an extraordinarily deep economic depression, on those who were already in an unstable economic situation (as represented by changes in the employment rate, especially during 1929–1936). In the case of the latter group of individuals of very low socio-economic status, their homicide rate apparently diminished during the early part of the depression (1929–1932), only to increase greatly during the second period (1932–1936) which was an upturn (after the low point of 1932) for most of the population.

There is, then, a real difference between the effects of the economy on homicide as distinguished from other crimes during the 1920–1940 period dominated by the Great Depression. The homicide rates apparently responded to both absolute and relative economic deprivation, while other major crimes (all involving property) responded to absolute deprivation alone. The distinction between homicide and property crime in their relation to national economic indicators during the period of the international depression may lie in significant differences between the populations who committed these crimes. It appears in general to be the case that more of the population who committed property crimes during this period were affected by absolute income loss than is true of the population committing homicide. While both populations did respond in the *same* way to absolute income loss, there was appa-

rently an *additional* population of persons who committed homicide who were responding to the relative economic loss of other persons, and who were probably themselves of very low socio-economic status.

It is important to keep in mind, however, that while relative economic loss did have a significant effect on the homicide rate during the Great Depression, the *overwhelming* effect on the homicide rate resulted from absolute economic loss as it did in the case of major property crimes. In both instances, the international depression is associated with extremely large increases in the rate of criminal behaviour. Indeed, even for homicide in particular, the rates during the Great Depression were the highest recorded during the twentieth century. During the period since the second World War, however, the patterns for both the homicidal and property crimes are identical; they increase sharply during periods of short-term reductions in employment and income. In summary, then, recession and depression both overwhelmingly have the effect of increasing crimes against property and persons.

7.   Effects of economic indicators on components of the criminal justice system.

Perhaps the single most consistent set of findings in this multinational study is that the relations between economic indicators and criminal statistics are very similar for data derived from each component of the criminal justice system. The CJS-component data include: crimes known to the police, crimes cleared, pre-trial police and judicial activity, trial proceedings, sentencing, and incarceration. All of these show the similar and substantial effects of adverse economic conditions.

In addition, individuals acquitted, both prior to trial and as a result of trial, also reflect adverse national economic conditions. These acquittals may be a result of overload on the CJS which may produce less effective police and prosecution functioning, or possibly a greater rate of arrest of innocent citizens in response to public demand for resolution of a considerably higher rate of crime victimization.

Finally, we observe that the rate of discharge from prison is also considerably greater during periods of economic adversity. This is no doubt partly a result of new waves of inmates "pushing out" an older population of inmates under the management aegis of the prison administration. It is entirely probable that this released population, newly vulnerable to the same types of situations which brought them to the CJS in the first place, will return to prison under similar conditions within a short period.

8. Interpretation of the general relationship.

Interpretation of the relationships between measures of national economic changes and criminal statistics is based on the link between those empirical relationships and theories as to crime causation. The two outstanding findings of the present study are that both absolute economic loss and comparative decline in socio-economic status (as a result of greater gain in such status by the majority of the population) are the pre-eminent causes of variations in criminal statistical trends.

Absolute economic loss is indicated by real "cyclic" declines in employment and income, as measured chiefly by fluctuations in the unemployment rate. Economic loss is additionally measured by annual percentage changes in the rate of inflation.

Comparative decline in socio-economic status of the lowest socio-economic groups is indicated by accelerated levels of economic growth involving high rates of structural (or technical) unemployment and low (and unstable) income levels. This situation of accelerated economic growth levels, in which significant minorities participate minimally, is also heightened during periods of intermediate-range economic upswings.

Overall, then, to use traditional economic phraseology, the major causes of variation in criminal statistics lie in economic instability and economic inequality. In both of these cases, however, the common basis of causation lies in comparatively low socio-economic status, whether that situation has occurred unexpectedly or represents a chronic pattern. It is clearly no accident, therefore, that the principal theories of crime causation relate to the same condition of comparatively low socio-economic status.

Frustration-aggression theory, which relates most closely to violent crime but is easily applicable to "expressive" forms of property crime which have instrumental overtones, is basically linked to conditions of thwarted socio-economic aspirations. Similarly, the development of subcultural deviance as a "reaction-formation" to socio-economic integration would stem from comparatively low socio-economic status. Differential-association theory would be especially relevant to the formation of subcultures of potential delinquents based on enlargement of the poor socio-economically malintegrated individuals, principally brought about by cyclic or structural unemployment patterns.

The issue of urbanization as a factor linked to economic growth, and potentially to criminal behaviour, bears additional discussion. From a general theoretical standpoint, it can be argued that long-term urban development is instrumental in replacing ethnic and socio-cultural modes of societal integration with those based on economic integration alone. Thus, with long-term economic growth the society's means of integration depends increasingly heavily on the stability of the economy and the "justice" or equity of its distributive mechanism.

From a purely empirical standpoint, in addition, the typical pattern of urbanization involves a population dynamic in which the occupational structure and industrial development are the bases for urban residential patterns. In the industrialized societies investigated in the present study, a typical pattern is for lower socio-economic groups, as defined by occupation and industry, to congregate in discrete residential areas. These residential areas of lower socio-economic status then expand or contract according to regional patterns of economic growth and stability.

During the last two to three decades, it has been frequently observed that urban rates of criminal activity have increased to extraordinarily high levels. In line with the previous discussion of the frequent pathological effect of economic growth on subpopulations of comparatively low socio-economic status, it appears likely that the growth in urban crime since the Second World War is related to (1) the migration of population of low socio-economic status and low technological skill and education into urban industrial and service occupations, and (2) the simultaneous out-migration of higher socio-economic groups somewhat beyond the political boundaries of these cities.

Professional and Organized Crime

WHILE MANY RECENT VENTURES INTO THEORY AND CRIMINAL TYPOLOGIES HAVE proven to be unproductive, much valuable theory and research have developed regarding two, rather special forms of criminal behavior: the competent, experienced criminal, sometimes referred to as the "professional criminal;" and criminals who band together within a formal organizational framework in order to maximize collective efficiency, safety, and profits, the so-called "organized criminal."

Attacking both elements of the concept "professional thief," Klein persuades the reader that "thief" as this has been defined and used by Edwin Sutherland is both ambiguous and vague; "professional" as that term is commonly defined by social scientists is said not to be easily applicable to the thief. Finally, the term "professional" was found to lack both specificity and uniformity in usage.

One of the most persuasive statement on work capabilities, talents, and skills found with career criminals is that of Letkemann in his description of offenders who engage in crimes involving face-to-face confrontation with their victims. In this selection, he deals with the experienced bank robber. The importance of preevent planning and the subtle, psychological alternatives in victim-management strategies during the robbery are very clearly and dramatically described.

The major sources of illegal income of persons in organized crime are by common attribution, lending money at usurious rates (loansharking), and illicit gambling. Seidl's dissertation is the most detailed and least stereotyped investigation yet made of loansharking. Viewing the activity from an economic perspective, the author portrays the borrower-lender agreement, the collection process, and two types of borrowers: the "rationed" and the "unrationed."

In the area of illegal gambling, the Fund for the City of New York's investigation of the "numbers game" offers information on the manner in which odds are calculated, winners are determined, as well as the social structure of this enterprise. Horse betting is examined in several selections from a recent investigation by the Select Committee of the U.S. House of Representatives. The first of these reveals how horse races have often been "fixed" by the use of electrical devices, illegal drugs, "ringer" horses, and the deliberate "pulling" of horses. The same committee, with considerable attendant publicity, pursued the role of two superstar entertainers, Sammy Davis, Jr. and Frank Sinatra in organized criminal activities in horseracing. Sinatra was accused of somehow being linked with putative criminal leaders and having invested money in a race track operated in a suspicious manner.

Ianni portrays a black criminal group that undertook operations in an enterprise known as "gypsy" or non-legally sanctioned cabs. For a number of years it has been said that one continuing threat posed by organized crime is that it tends to infiltrate legitimate businesses for various economic, legal, social, and subtle psychological purposes. One example of this pattern is revealed in MacMichael's selection, describing the manner in which very notorious and widely feared members of organized crime, such as Johnny Dio and Thomas Eboli, have infiltrated the kosher meat and bagel industries in New York City.

Laswell's study of organized crime in the Bedford-Stuyvesant area of Brooklyn is quite distinctive from any other investigation. He analyzes crime in terms of skill, affection, respect, and rectitude. His startling finding is that the gross income of organized crime in the neighborhood almost equals total welfare payments or total Social Security and unemployment payments for the area. Organized crime was found to be a major employer in Bedford-Stuyvesant, second only to governmental employment.

By an anthropological study of the Lupollo family, Ianni describes the rules of appropriate conduct in organized crime, which center primarily around the concepts of family loyalty, "acting like a man," and secrecy. Raising the issue of whether an organization known as the "Mafia" or "Cosa Nostra" truly exists or is largely the creation of the mass media, Congressional committees, or some law-enforcement officials, Dwight Smith compares the myth with the reality. Finally, Ianni, in "The New Mafia" treats black, Latin, and Italian-American groups as they view for their share of the power and profits of organized crime. He portrays entry into the system, criminal linkages, the operating codes of behavior, and future hierarchies among these ethnic groups.

52. The Professional Thief

JOHN F. KLEIN

INTRODUCTION

MOST CRIMINOLOGY TEXTBOOKS WHICH DISCUSS criminal behaviour patterns make reference to the professional thief.[1] A review of such texts indicates that, for most, Sutherland's *The Professional Thief* is the keystone of analyses of professional criminal behaviour patterns.[2] Unfortunately, Sutherland's definition of the professional thief does not possess the rigour and clarity which we might expect from a well-formulated concept. While definitions of what constitutes a professional thief may be gleaned from his analysis at several points, a clear, concise, and unitary definition is not offered. The professional thief is defined at the outset of his analysis as [Sutherland, 1956: 3-4].

"... one who steals professionally. This means, first, that he makes a regular business of stealing. He devotes his entire working time and energy to larceny and may steal three hundred and sixty-five days a year. Second, every act is carefully planned. ..."

▶ SOURCE: *"Professional Theft: The Utility of a Concept,"* Canadian Journal of Criminology and Corrections (April 1974), 16:133–143. Reprinted by permission.

[1] For example, see Bloch and Geis 1962: 191–215; Clinard and Quinney 1967: 428–437; Gibbons 1968: 245–257; Haskel and Yablonski 1970: 83–86; Reckless 1967: 287–298; Quinney 1970: 270–273; and Sutherland and Cressey 1970: 281–186.

[2] Einstadter 1969: 65 states that "A body of literature on professional crime has centered largely on an extension or modification of Sutherland's conceptions of the essential social characteristics of professional theft and his unifying theoretical statement of differential association."

Third, the professional thief has technical skills and methods which are different from those of other professional criminals. ... Fourth, the professional thief is generally migratory. ... In addition to these four characteristics, professional thieves have many things in common. They have acquaintances, congeniality, sympathy, understandings, agreements, rules, codes of behavior, and language in common."

Later, Sutherland [1956: 14] seems willing to accept two criteria as the basis for being a professional thief:

"The distinctions most sought after among thieves are money and proficiency in their chosen lines."

Shover [1972:541] maintains that

The professional thief then is the thief who, on the basis of these criteria, enjoys high status both among thieves and those legitimate people who are knowledgeable about thieves.

Lemert [1958], in his analysis of the systematic cheque forger, employs the four criteria previously mentioned as well as a fifth criterion, that of differential association with other criminals. Similarly, Clinard and Quinney [1967: 428–437] draw heavily on Sutherland's formulation in developing their typological definition of the professional criminal behaviour pattern.

A basis issue which is implicit in the above is that of the extent to which we are justified in using the term "professional" and the meaning of the term "thief."

Another issue is that of the utility of the concept: A concept represents a selection of certain phenomena that are grouped or classified together.

> Concepts are not statements; they are names or labels [Brodbeck, 1968: 7].

As such, then,

> A concept is neither true nor false, only propositions are. A concept is neither valid nor invalid, only arguments are. Yet there is a distinction of "good" and "bad" among defined descriptive terms [Bergmann, 1957:50].

Phillips [1971: 47–50] mentions several criteria which are employed in evaluating the utility of a concept in terms of the advancement of scientific knowledge: determinancy, uniformity of usage, charity, scope, and systematic import. Determinancy refers to a concept's degree of freedom from vagueness and ambiguity—that is, how precisely it specifies or connotes a particular set of phenomena [Phillips, 1971: 47]. The degree to which the usage of the concept is the same for all users of the language will affect the concept's value for the communicative process. The latter three criteria are, however, more fundamental in evaluating the utility of a concept. Phillips [1971: 48] states that:

> Scope refers to the inclusiveness of the class of situations to which the concept applies [i.e., its boundaries] . . .; clarity, to the concept's potential for moving down the ladder of abstraction to an objective determination or measurement; and systematic import, to the degree to which the concept is incorporated in propositions and theories. Both the scope of the propositions and their degree of clarity affect systematic import.

Systematic import is synonymous with Bergmann's [1957: 50] criterion of significance.

Employing the above mentioned criteria, it is our aim to evaluate the utility of the concept of the professional thief as it is used in contemporary criminology. Our contention is that the concept is inadequate and misleading, that it tends to obfuscate more than it clarifies in furthering our understanding of criminal behaviour patterns.

I. PROFESSIONAL?

Pavalko [1971: 16–17] in his review of the literature on professionalism, identifies three basic uses of the term professional:

1.   The term is frequently used to convey an evaluation of the work referred to; in this sense it is honorific.

2.   Sometimes the term is simply used to denote the full-time performance of a particular kind of work for pay in contrast to engaging in the activity as a part-time basis or without pay.

3.   It is used to convey the idea of great skill or proficiency at some task. However, none of these usages reflects the rigour with which the term is generally used within the sociology of occupations.

Pavalko prefers to view the concept of profession as one extremity of an occupation—profession continuum. He (Palvalko) [1971: 16] claims that

> ". . . substantial consensus has emerged on these dimensions and it is possible to identify key features of work groups that appear to occur in combinations and clusters that function to differentiate occupations from professions."

Moore [1970: 5–6] presents the following ideal-typical description of a professional:

> "The professional practices a full-time *occupation* which comprises the principal source of his earned income. . . . A more distinctively professional qualification is that of a commitment to a *calling,* that is, the treatment of the occupation and all of its requirements as an enduring set of normative and behavioral expectations. Those who pursue occupations of relatively high rank in terms of criteria of professionalism are likely to be set apart from the laity by various signs and symbols, but by the same token are identified with their peers—often in formalized *organization.* An important next step in professionalism

is the possession of esoteric but useful knowledge and skills, based on specialized training or *education* of exceptional duration and perhaps of exceptional difficulty. The qualification of useful knowledge implies that next higher scale position of professionalism: in the practice of his occupation, the professional is expected to exhibit a *service orientation*, to perceive the needs of individual or collective clients that are relevant to his competence and to those needs by competent performance. Finally, in the use of his exceptional knowledge, the professional proceeds by his own judgment and authority; he thus enjoys *autonomy* restrained by responsibility."

Carr-Saunders and Wilson [1933: 491] state that

"We have found that the application of an intellectual technique to the ordinary business of life acquired as a result of prolonged and specialized training, is the chief distinguishing characteristic of the profession."

Given the above criteria for professional status, it is a moot point that the characteristics attributed by Sutherland and others to professional thieves do not meet these criteria of professionalism. Sutherland himself hedges somewhat on this issue. While he attempts to demonstrate that some thieves should be classified as professionals, he appears willing to concede that their professionalism is more on the level of professional athletics [Sutherland, 1956: 215–217]. However, using Sutherland's line of reasoning, we would have to classify almost anyone who has a full-time occupation which requires some degree of skill as a professional thus robbing the concept of much of its utility.[3] It might be more accurate to categorize the type of thief described by Sutherland as a craftsman rather than a professional. In any case, the term as used by Sutherland and others is essentially honorific in respect to the individual's proficiency at theft.

[3]In fact, The President's Commission on Law Enforcement and Administration of Justice [1967: 96] did precisely this in defining professional crime as "Crime committed for personal economic gain by individuals whose major source of income is from criminal pursuits and who spend the majority of their working time in illegal enterprises."

II. THIEF?

Almost as unfortunate as Sutherland's choice of the term "professional" was his choice of the term "thief." A more precise term would have been that of "grift" which, in criminal argot, denotes a certain class of theft. A contemporary *Dictionary of Criminal Language* [California, 1962: 11] defines a grifter as a "small time gambler or con man: one who lives without working but does not commit crimes which usually result in arrest." It is noteworthy that this same dictionary does not define "thief," presumably because the criminal usage of the term conforms sufficiently to common usage. *The Random House Dictionary of the English Language, Unabridged Edition* defines a thief as a "person who steals, esp. secretly or without open force. . . . A THIEF takes the goods or property of another by stealth without the latter's knowledge. . . ." As we shall see, this definition expresses a degree of generality which Sutherland clearly never intended in his use of the term "thief."

While it is our view that a distinction should be made between engaging in grift and engaging in the more general act of theft, Sutherland appears to be somewhat uncertain on this point. In the glossary of *The Professional Thief* [Sutherland, 1956: 238] he gives the following definition: "GRIFT, v.—To steal; n.: theft." Apparently, on this basis he uses the terms theft and grift and thief and grifter interchangeably throughout the work. However, elsewhere he qualifies the term grift [Sutherland, 1956: 43].

"The principal rackets of professional thieves are the cannon (picking pockets), the heel (sneak-thieving from stores, banks, and offices), the boost (shoplifting), pennyweighting (stealing from jewelry stores by substitution), hotel prowling (stealing from hotel rooms), the con (confidence game), some miscellaneous rackets related in certain respects to the confidence games, laying paper (passing illegal checks, money orders, and other papers), and the shake (the shakedown of, or extortion from, persons engaged in or about to engage in illegal acts)."

It is probably not too crucial in evaluating the utility of a concept that the criterion of uniformity of usage be too rigourously invoked when looking at *all* users of the language; however, it does not seem too unreasonable that, at the very least, one individual using a concept should be bound by that criterion.

Conversations which we have had with some 125 criminals, many of whom call themselves thieves, revealed that the term, which is invariably used honorifically, connotes much more than does the previously given dictionary definition of "thief."[4] There are several factors involved in labelling oneself a thief and being so labelled and accepted by others in the "life":

1. The person's criminal acts are against property and these acts do not involve the immediate knowledge on the part of the victim that his property is being stolen. This criterion excludes the act of robbery (an exception to this appears to be the case of the skilled armed robber who, with a mob, engages in a few well-planned robberies per year) but permits the inclusion of such acts as the conversion of fraudulent or fictitious negotiable instruments.

2. Being a thief involves a primary commitment to the act of theft. If the individual's commitment stems from some other form of deviation (e.g., the person's commitment to theft is a function of his alcoholism or drug addiction), then he would not be called a thief.

3. The thief possesses a rather distinctive world view. This world view is perhaps best summarized by a statement made by thieves on several occasions: "ten per cent of the people are honest; five per cent are honest thieves; and the rest are simply thieves." One informant who has had a long-term commitment to theft told of a time when he decided to give up the life of a thief by taking a job as a used car salesman.

"He reported quitting the job after a week to return to stealing: 'It seemed so dishonest—I just couldn't live with myself' was the rationale given."

What is important in the above is not only a commitment to the act of theft *per se* but, in addition, the thief's possession and support of a rather distinctive set of values. This does much to explain the assertion of some informants that a true thief never *retires*, he simply *tires*—tires of the tension associated with the act of theft and the prospect of incarceration. Thus, a person may no longer steal yet he may be regarded as a thief by other thieves and retain a similar self-concept. To be a thief, then, involves a complex interaction between attitudes and behaviour: one must be (or have been) committed to the act of theft *and* must espouse those values which thieves claim to have in common.

The ambiguity in Sutherland's conceptualization of the term "thief" has been noted by others. For example, Irwin [1970: 8–12] makes a distinction between the thief and the grifter who is involved in "indirect" theft. This distinction corresponds to Gibbons [1968: 246–257] distinction between the professional thief and the professional "heavy."

Such vagueness and ambiguity as is found in the conceptualization of the professional thief may lead to the unfortunate consequence of myth making. An ancillary consequence of this may be an unrealistic, ineffectual, and overly punitive approach in dealing with certain offenders [Klein, 1973]. This being the case, we shall examine some evidence relating to the existence and characteristics of what some have termed "the professional thief."

III. EVIDENCE

Turk [1969: 15] states that:

"... the code-conscious 'professional' who is strictly limited to a field of illegal activity in which he exercises his skills with great discrimination appear to be more the creation of journalism, romanticism, and commercialism than an empirically demonstrable social type."

[4]In the course of his teaching and research the author has been able to establish contacts with criminals both in and out of prison.

There exists some evidence bearing upon this assertion. The President's Commission on Law Enforcement and Administration of Justice [1967: 98] did a survey of "professional" criminals in the mid-1960's. It was found that such individuals, individuals who were relatively skilled and committed to a life of crime, were often quite versatile. Most did not demonstrate the degree of specialization and commitment to a single type of crime that Sutherland hypothesized.

Strictly speaking, the evaluation of any evidence pertaining to the existence and structure of professional theft (in Sutherland's terms) should be restricted to descriptions of the types of grift analyzed in *The Professional Thief*. Research on the above has been quite limited. Maurer's studies of the confidence game [1940] and of pickpockets [1964] support Sutherland's descriptions of these grifts. However, Maurel [1940: 47] notes a demise in the practice of the confidence game as legal conditions changed prior to World War II. Similarly, Maurel [1964: 132–134] alludes to a demise of the type of professional pickpocket described by Sutherland and himself. While Cameron [1964] refers to the existence of the professional booster, her analysis of department store shoplifting is, for the most part, restricted to that of the amateur or "snitch." As well, the boosters who she actually describes would seldom be classified as professionals. For example, Cameron [1964: 49] states that "In part, this category [boosters] is composed of alcoholics and narcotics addicts. . . ."

The reports of Rhodes [1934], Dilnot [1929 and 1930], and Byrnes [1886, reprinted 1969: 285–308] are very much in accord with Sutherland's descriptions of professional cheque forgers (a type of grift which received short shrift in *The Professional Thief*). Lemert [1958] is unable to find much support for Sutherland's description in his study of cheque forgers in the 1950s.

However, Lemert's findings may not weaken Sutherland's description as much as some might maintain. Sutherland [1956: 75–78] notes that there was some debate among grifters themselves as to the accuracy of his (that is, Cromwell's) description of professional cheque forgers' behaviour patterns. As well, Sutherland [1956: v] warns that "the conditions described in this manuscript are essentially those of the period 1905–25"—a period which was prior to the time of the widespread use of personal and payroll cheques. Finally, if as Sutherland [1956: 217] maintains, the professional grifter is relatively immune to severe penalties, then one should not do as Lemert did and draw a sample from a prison population in order to determine the characteristics of a particular type of grifter. It *may* be that Lemert's conclusions are primarily an artifact of his research design.

In any case, we suggest that the controversy regarding the nature of "professional" forgery operations has yet to be resolved. For example, the investigation into organized criminal operations in Quebec [see *Edmonton Journal*, April 17, 1973, p. 23] has heard evidence on a 1.5 million dollar fraud using forged cheques to purchase securities. This incident bears a striking resemblance to some of the operations recounted by Sutherland [1956] and Maurel [1940].

The concept of professional theft has been applied to forms of theft outside of the boundaries of grift. While such research is not truly appropriate given our concerns, it does shed some further light on the utility of the concept in terms of its degree of generality (that is, its scope).

In applying the concept of professional theft to armed robbery, Einstadter [1969] found that robbery gangs have little in common with the professional thieves (read grifters) investigated by Sutherland [1956].

Conklin [1972] maintains that professional armed robbers do exist. However, in making this claim he exercises considerable license in defining a professional. Conklin [1972: 64] defines professionals as

". . . *those who manifest a long-term commitment to crime as a source of livelihood, who plan and organize their crimes prior to committing them, and who seek money to support a particular life style that may be termed hedonistic* [italics his]."

We hold this definition to be inadequate in that it excludes any mention of the person's actual level of skill and his degree of success in committing such crimes. [For a similar view as to some of the problems with this type of definition see Stebbins [1971] and Jackson [1969: 15–65].

Shover [1972], however, finds that Sutherland's model is not inapplicable to the career of the burglar. He [Shover, 1972: 540] states that

". . . the anatomy of, and careers in, systematic burglary conform more closely to this [Sutherland's] model than, apparently, do armed robbery and systematic check forgery."

He refers to the professional burglar as a "good" burglar [Shover, 1972:541]:

"Good burglars are those who (1) are technically competent, (2) have a reputation for personal integrity, (3) tend to specialize in burglary, and (4) have been at least relatively successful at crime. And success in turn is determined by (a) how much money one has made stealing, and (b) how much time, if any, he has done."

If nothing else, such a definition removes some of the aura associated with the use of the term professional.

IV. CONCLUSIONS

A basic difficulty with the concept of professional theft is that it lacks both determinacy and uniformity of usage. As we have seen, there appears to be little consensus among criminologists as to the meaning of professional theft—not only in terms of what constitutes professional status but also in terms of the boundaries of the term theft.

While law enforcement officials use the terms professional thief and professional criminal, discussions with such officials have yet to reveal an explicit definition of the same which is characterized by determinacy and uniformity of usage. The police have seldom been known to underestimate or under-rate the degree of a person's criminal involvement; when they apply the adjective "professional" to a criminal they

may be saying more about the extent to which the criminal threatens their own self-concept than they are about the objective characteristics of the criminal. If a person is sophisticated enough or *lucky* enough to avoid arrest and conviction for a relatively long period of time even though the frequency of his depredations are well known, he presents a real challenge, if not an outright threat, to the police's self-concept of professionalism and the police's status in the community. If nothing else, however, this enhanced status which is ascribed to some criminals by the police does provide grist for the mills of sensational journalism. This, of course, helps to further reify the concept in the mind of the public.

If the label of professional involves status enhancement, then it is not surprising that some criminals are willing to call themselves professionals or, at least, apparently aspire to this status when writing their autobiographies [see, for example, Benton [1936]; Martin [1970]; and Rudensky [1970]. However, to read some of these autobiographies might make one more inclined to apply the honorific adjective to the noun "convict" than to "thief."

Unfortunately, some criminologists apparently are not immune from the tendency to reify the concept of professional theft and, in doing so, rely upon biographical and autobiographical data which may give only questionable support to their generalizations about professional theft.[5]

Sutherland's [1956] original formulation of professional theft leaves much to be desired in terms of its *clarity*. Subsequent modifications of the concept in which some researchers choose to use those aspects of Sutherland's formulation which permit them to discover certain types of

---

[5]For a recent example of this problem see Chambliss' *Box Man: A Professional Thief's Journey* 1972. The thief's account of his life in crime (primarily safe-cracking) raises questions as to whether the term "professional" is all that appropriately applied and Chambliss' 1972: 167–179 does not always receive what most social scientists would consider to be adequate support from one's data.

professional thieves in their midst do nothing to improve the concept's clarity. This leads to a further difficulty with the concept—that of *scope*. Most modifications of the concept have made it much more difficult to determine its actual scope. Given the implied scope of Sutherland's original formulation (that is, the grifter), it appears likely that the grand age of the grift as described by Sutherland came to an end prior to World War II. The various applications of contemporary conceptual modifications tend to give us, collectively, a residual category describing theft by individuals who are relatively persistent, skilled, and successful in carrying out certain types of theft. The collective evolution of the concept of professional theft as a residual category lessens whatever *systematic import* it might have originally possessed. If the concept is unable to help us empirically identify a clear behaviour pattern or "career line" among certain types of offenders involved in crimes against property, then we should not expect it to be of any great significance in the development of a theory of criminal behaviour. What is required, then, is a concept (or set of concepts) which is more closely allied to theoretical considerations.

VI. SUGGESTIONS FOR FURTHER RESEARCH

Two recent approaches which seem promising in terms of avoiding some of the problems which have been associated with the use of the concept of professional theft are those of Stebbins [1969 and 1971] and Mack [1972]. Stebbins [1969: 47–48] calls for an integration of the traditional objective approach to the study of careers (career patterns and individual-objective careers) with a subjective approach in which the

"... career is composed of both the more private meanings of such phenomena as stages, time and direction of movement, alternative career lines, recruitment, contingencies and so forth, and of meanings not represented in the objective stances."

Stebbins [1969] argues that the concept of career is useful in areas other than just the study of occupations if we wish to understand changes which take place in an individual's identity and socialization over time. Such an approach appears to hold promise in terms of gaining an understanding of the process of becoming committed to a certain type of deviant career [see Stebbins, 1971].

Mack [1972] has examined official and unofficial police records and discerned what he terms "the able criminal." Unlike most research which has attempted to identify and describe specific types of able criminals [for example, Shover's [1972] "good" burglar; Conklin's [1972] professional armed robber; and Lemert's [1958] systematic cheque forger], Mack treats ability as though it is relatively independent of any given legal offence category. There appear to be sound empirical reasons for doing so insomuch as there is some evidence which suggests that relatively successful property offenders do not specialize in terms of a single legal offence category to the extent that some would like to believe [President's Commission on Law Enforcement and Administration of Justice, 1967: 96–101].

It is our view that research aimed at understanding the *process* by which an individual becomes committed to a deviant career [cf. Stebbins, 1969 and 1970] along with the simultaneous exploration of the *structure* of the deviant career [cf. Mack, 1972] holds more promise for the theoretical development of criminology than approaches which restrict themselves to specific legal categories of offenders. Such an approach should permit us to delimit concepts which relate to specific facets of the constellation of variables that comprise a criminal behaviour pattern. In turn, this should bring us closer to the development of a more theoretically useful and sophisticated typology of criminal behaviour patterns—one which is relatively independent of crude legal offence categories.

REFERENCES

Benton, Roger. *Where Do I Go From Here?* New York: L. Furman, 1936.

Bergmann, Gustav. *Philosophy of Science*. Madison, Wisc.: University of Wisconsin Press, 1957.

Bloch, Herbert A. and Gilbert Geis. *Man, Crime, and Society: The Forms of Criminal Behavior*. New York: Random House, 1962.

Brodbeck, May, ed. *Readings in the Philosophy of the Social Sciences*. New York: The Macmillan Company, 1968.

Byrnes, Thomas. *1886 Professional Criminals of America* (New York: Chelsea House), 1969.

California, Board of Corrections. *A Dictionary of Criminal Language*. Sacramento, Calif., 1962.

Cameron, Mary Owen. *The Booster and the Snitch*. New York: Free Press, 1964.

Carr-Saunders, A. M. and P. A. Wilson. *The Professions*. Oxford: The Clarendon Press, 1933.

Chambliss, Bill. *Box Man: A Professional Thief's Journey*. New York: Harper Torchbooks, 1972.

Clinard, Marshall B. and Richard Quinney. *Criminal Behavior Systems: A Typology*. New York: Holt, Rinehart, and Winston, 1967.

Conklin, John E. *Robbery and the Criminal Justice System*. Toronto: Lippincott, 1972.

Dilnot, George. *The Bank of England Forgery*. New York: Scribner's, 1920. *The Trial of Jim the Penman*. London: Geoffrey Bles, 1930.

Einstadter, Werner J. "The Social Organization of Armed Robbery", *Social Problems*, 17:1, 64–83, 1969.

Gibbons, Don D. *Society, Crime, and Criminal Careers*. Englewood Cliffs, N.J.: Prentice-Hall, 1968.

Haskell, Martin R. and Lewis Yablonsky. *Crime and Delinquency*. Chicago: Rand McNally, 1970.

Irwin, John. *The Felon*. Englewood Cliffs, N.J.: Prentice-Hall, 1970.

Jackson, Bruce. *A Thief's Primer*. Toronto: Collier-Macmillan, 1969.

Klein, John F. "Habitual Offender Legislation and the Bargaining Process", *Criminal Law Quarterly*. August 1973.

Lemert, Edwin. "The Behavior of the Systematic Check Forger", *Social Problems*, 6:2 (Fall), 141–148, 1958.

Mack, J. A. "The Able Criminal", *British Journal of Criminology*, 12:1, 44–54, 1972.

Martin, John Bartlow. *My Life in Crime*. Westport, Conn.: Greenwood Press, 1970.

Maurer, David. *The Big Con*. Indianapolis: Bobbs-Merrill, 1940. *Whiz Mob*. New Haven, Conn.: College & University Press, 1964.

Moore, Wilbert E. with Gerald W. Rosenblum. *The Professions: Roles and Rules*. New York: Russell Sage Foundation, 1970.

Pavalko, Ronald M. *Sociology of Occupations and Professions*. Itasca, Ill.: F. B. Peacock, 1971.

Phillips, Bernard S. *Social Research: Strategy and Tactics*. Toronto: Collier-Macmillan, 1971.

President's Commission on Law Enforcement and Administration of Justice. *Task Force Report: Crime and Its Impact—An Assessment*. Washington, D.C.: U.S. Government Printing Office, 1967.

Reckless, Walter, C. *The Crime Problem, 4th ed.* New York: Appleton-Century-Crofts, 1967.

Rhodes, Henry T. F. *The Craft of Forgery*. London: John Murray, 1934.

Rudensky, Morris (Rod). *The Gonif*. Blue Earth, Minn.: The Piper Co., 1970.

Shover, Neal. "Structures and Careers inBurglary", *Journal of Criminal Law, Criminology & Police Science*, 63:4 540–549, 1972.

Sutherland, Edwun H. *The Professional Thief*. Chicago: Phoenix, 1956.

——— and Donald R. Cressey. *Criminology, 8th ed.* (Toronto: Lippincott), 1970.

Turk, Austin T. *Criminality and the Legal Order*. Chicago: Rand McNally, 1969.

53. The Skilled Bank Robber

PETER LETKEMANN

INTRODUCTION

THE INFORMATION RECEIVED FROM THE FORTY-five subjects interviewed for this study includes comments on a wide variety of criminal behavior. Without wishing to provide yet another detailed typology of crimes, I believe it is useful to differentiate between those crimes committed surrepititously and those involving direct confrontation with the victim. The one involves the taking of property without the owner's consent or knowledge, the other involves the demand for property and its being "given" to the thief by the victim. Roughly speaking, this follows the legal distinction between burglary and robbery. The primary difference sociologically is that robbery involves direct interaction between thief and victim, whereas burglary does not. It follows, therefore, that the skills associated with robbery must include those necessary for the management and manipulation of people. This is not to minimize the importance of mechanical and technical skills, but to indicate that victim confrontation adds an additional dimension to the skills necessary for success in nonsurreptitious crime. Sutherland points out that, in terms of status, professional thieves distinguish between those criminals whose work depends primarily on manual dexterity as opposed to those whose work depends on "wit, 'front' and talking ability":

▶SOURCE: *Crime as Work. Spectrum Book. Englewood Cliffs, N.J.: Prentice-Hall, Inc., 1973, pp. 90–116. Reprinted by permission of Prentice-Hall, Inc., Englewood Cliffs, N.J.*

". . . burglars, robbers, kidnappers, and others who engage in the 'heavy rackets' are generally not regarded as professional thieves, for they depend primarily on manual dexterity, or force. A few criminals in the 'heavy rackets' use their wits, 'front' and talking ability, and these are regarded by the professional thieves as belonging to the profession."[1]

The inference, as I see it, is that violent crimes, for example those involving the threat or use of violence by way of weapons are thought to require little or no ability to manipulate people. Since the mechanical skills, besides the ability to use a gun, also appear to be minimal, the robber appears to share neither the social skills of the con artist, nor the technical skills of the burglar.

My subjects recognized that some lines demand greater ability in conning the public (obviously, for example, con artists) and that some lines involve no contact with the public at all. Among the latter, however, are some lines, such as burglar-alarm experts who, although not in face-to-face contact with the public, speak of their work in terms of their ability to outsmart the public. The same is true of safecrackers, who violate the ultimate symbols of financial security. Therefore, although the manual aspect of the above lines varies (the safecracker doing much more purely physical labor), each is perceived as an intellectual rather than a physical conquest.[2]

[1]Sutherland, *The Professional Thief,* p. 198.

[2]There are exceptions to this, and examples of snobbishness can be documented. For example, no. 35, who was a burglar, recalled his difficulty in opening his first safe. I

It is my purpose to analyze the accounts given by armed robbers, with a view to discovering the assumptions on which the robber proceeds and the skills used in the action.

Just as safecracking was used to illustrate various dimensions of burglary, so group bank robbery will be used here to illustrate facets of robbery. This choice is partly arbitrary, for similar basic patterns can be seen in general armed robbery as well. To focus on bank robbery, however, provides a useful contrast with our previous discussion of safecracking, which is also used to extract money from banks. My subjects frequently suggested that the increasing difficulty of burglarizing a bank is the cause for the rise in bank robberies.

In terms of organization, robbery may involve a highly organized group of persons working as a team; on the other hand, it may be a loose, temporary liaison between several persons, or it may take the form of a lone gunman doing a stick-up. The victims may also vary, from banking institutions to the corner grocer or a lone pedestrian. As indicated later in this chapter under "Procedural Variations," bank robbery may take various forms.

My choice of group bank robbery enables us to look both at the interaction between the group and the bank employees, and at the sociological processes within the group itself. The group formation, the testing of loyalties, and the allocation of responsibilities will be dealt with later under the more general topic of teaching and learning criminal skills. In this chapter, we will look at the act of group robbery itself, so that the technical, organizational, and social skills involved may be documented and described before we ask how they are learned and transmitted.

A. PRE-EVENT PLANNING

If the group is a loose, temporary liaison initiated by a transient robber, the choice of partners will be made at least partly on the basis of the skills required for a particular job. If the group is a coalition of some duration, various responsibilities will be understood and fulfilled by members prior to the event itself. Legal, medical, and financial arrangements may or may not form a part of an individual's prerobbery preparation, depending on his experience and ability to pay.

"THE ONLY TOOLS YOU BASICALLY NEED THEN ARE MASKS AND GUNS? Oh no. Definitely, you need more than that. Now this is where organization is the big thing. You see, well—first of all you've got—well, I was shot. Well, I'm shot, see? Now just supposing I'd have got away, where am I going to go? St. Paul's Hospital? Am I gonna go to St. Mary's Hospital? General Hospital? Oh no—I've gotta have a doctor. You've gotta, so therefore you've gotta have a doctor. You've gotta take care of all these things. You just don't—you've gotta have, in case you go to jail, you've gotta have a lawyer. You've gotta have all these things taken care of long before you go into planning a bank job. Well, where would I have gone if I'd have got shot? Well, I couldn't have stayed in a hotel room, bleeding like a sieve. Right away, if I'd have got out, I'd have just phoned my doctor so and so, and said, "I'm here, get up here right away!" You see, you've gotta pay them off, you see. There's lots of them in Western City. Same also if I'd have got caught, I would have needed a lawyer right away, quick. Things like that. You've got to take care of all these things.

"WHAT ABOUT BAIL MONEY? Oh, I had that all taken care of. Bail money was taken care of." (no. 7)

It may be for reasons such as these that organized criminals tend to operate within specific areas, despite the fact that such operation draws "heat" on them. The transient criminals enjoy anonymity, but must choose partners from among relative strangers, and sacrifice the insurance provided by arrangements with doctors, lawyers, and bondsmen.

The bank will have been cased beforehand by the one who initiated the robbery. He may or may not have consulted with a partner (before the casing) as to the feasibility of the job. In cases of transient, two-, or three-man groups, casing

---

asked why he had not sought advice from an experienced safecracker. "I wasn't that much interested in it," he said. "Actually, I just rate a safecracker, even the best, only as a laborer." (no. 35)

may be done by all members of the group as they drive leisurely down the streets. In all cases of bank robbery related to me, no member of the group was entirely "cold" (for example, had not as much as seen the bank to be done). The general procedure is for the one who initiated the job to case the place, decide on a suitable time, and then take his partners with him on a dry run the day before the hold-up.

"OKAY. LET'S SAY IT'S THE DAY BEFORE—THE DAY BEFORE YOU WANT TO DO THIS. WHAT DO YOU HAVE TO DO THE DAY BEFORE? Well, we usually get our car the night before, and we—well, we naturally check over our weapons. We go through the dry run so to speak, you know. The best exit out. DO YOU DO THAT WITH YOUR OWN CAR? Oh yes. DO YOU MAKE ANY DRAWING AT THAT STAGE? No. BUT YOU'RE ALL TOGETHER AT THIS TIME, RIGHT? Right.

"DO YOU SPEND THE NIGHT TOGETHER? We have at times, yeh. But not all the time, not all the time. We—usually, if we're gonna meet in the morning we just sort of casually saunter into a coffee shop, just like the working stiff, you know. Saunter in and have a cup of coffee. And before you know it there's three of us there and we have our coffee and then we saunter out.

"AND YOUR CAR IS READY TO GO? Yeh, that's right—it's all been taken care of. WHEN DID YOU GET THIS CAR? The night before. AND IT'S A STOLEN CAR?[3] That's right. SUPPOSE THE COPS ARE LOOKING FOR THAT CAR BY THAT TIME? That's very unlikely, because we have the plates and that all doctored up.

"AT WHAT POINT DO YOU DECIDE WHO DOES WHAT? Well, it's pretty well understood; like you always have one who makes the suggestion, "Let's rob a bank." So, naturally, if you're going to rob a bank, you make the suggestion, you're the one who's going to lay the groundwork for it. So they—well, they just more or less accept you as the leader." (no. 7)

---

[3]Later no. 7 stated:

You never steal your own car—you have somebody do it for you, and pay them off. There's no use incriminating yourself in a car theft, when you're gonna pull a bank job. Therefore, it's worth to you to give some fellow a hundred dollars to get you a car. What's a hundred dollars of the bank's money? Nothing! (no. 7)

Bank robbers rely heavily on the architectural uniformity of banks. Banks are frequently located on street corners, and this is convenient for getaways. Glass doors permit the robber-doorman to see who is coming in, whereas, as a robber noted, the persons coming in have more difficulty seeing through the glass because of light reflection. The present trend toward low counters, possibly motivated by the bank officials' desire for a more personal and less prisonlike atmosphere, is looked upon favorably by bank robbers:

"WHAT ABOUT THE HEIGHT OF THE COUNTER? IS THIS A FACTOR? Well, sometimes you see, you might have to jump the counter. Well, if you get some of these real high counters, well—they're tough to get over. Well, you lose a few seconds by getting over the counters, and some of these banks, like, they have these gates like, with—well, you can't reach over and open them because the catch is too far down, so therefore you've got to jump over this counter, you see. The lower the counter, the better I like it. You just hop over the—and hop back, and also you can see just exactly what the man is doing with his hands at all times." (no. 7)

Just as architectural uniformity is assumed, so the presence of mechanical alarm systems is assumed. The use of hidden TV cameras and other devices (the presence of which are advertised with warning stickers) are not a deterrent to the experienced bank robber because he will be "covered" (wearing a mask) anyway, and so he cares little whether he is seen only by bank personnel on the scene or by others via TV. Since the presence of alarm systems is taken for granted, they are neither "cased" nor the object of special attention. The robber assumes they are in working order and that they have gone off the moment he enters the bank.

Although these purely mechanical factors are assumed constant, other factors vary and may affect the difficulty of doing a bank. Some of these may be assessed beforehand. The disposition of the manager is inferred by his apparent age. Those robbers who prefer to deal with as few employees as possible may make daily observations as to the most opportune time. No attention is paid to the number of customers in a bank, except insofar as this indicates the probable number who may wish to enter the bank during the robbery. Persons wishing to enter at this time are much more of a risk to the robber than those already inside. The danger lies in the customer noting that something is wrong before he, or she has entirely entered. Such a customer cannot be prevented from leaving at that point, and becomes the first "alarm." When this happens, the doorman will call his men out immediately.

The safecracker who wants to do a bankjob assumes the presence of money at all times. Primarily, he must consider the *technical* availability, which involves the architecture of a building permitting an "in," the make of the safe, and so forth. The bank robber, on the other hand, must consider the *immediate* availability of money. Unless he is planning a rural robbery, during which he will have time to rob the vault as well as the teller's tills, the bank robber expects to take only what is in the tills.[4] He assumes that the amount carried in tills varies according to day of the week, time of day, and paydays.

The following outline was presented by no. 41:

"The time—on a Monday, if possible. On a Friday, people withdraw for the weekend: Only got two thousand six hundred dollars on a Friday from three cashiers. Business deposits on Monday—each cashier will have no more than five thousand dollars—some under the box, some above. Businesses need change for the weekend, they don't want to deposit till Monday. On Saturday banks are closed. Businesses may make a night deposit—if so, that deposit will also be counted on Monday morning" (no. 41).

The bank robber may plan his robbery on the basis of inferences made from the location of the bank:

"If a bank is near factories, you can be sure it will carry a lot of cash on paydays, which as a rule are on Friday." (no. 39)

---

[4]Larger banks, with more tills, are preferred because of their greater cash potential.

Given a suitable commercial context, the thief may wish to assess more specifically the economic potential, particularly with reference to its temporal fluctuations:

"So you see, there's quite a few mills around here, so I sat down and bought some beers for a couple of guys who work in mills, and just in conversation, you know, kind of—the conversation got around to working in these mills and that, and I mentioned that I knew a guy who worked at the mill and who could—and the guy owed me some money and I asked them when—when does this group get paid. I'd like to collect. I'd like to catch him on a day he gets paid. So they told me. So I figured, well, a lot of these guys cash their cheques here and more do on Thursdays than on Fridays, so sure enough I went down the next—the following week on Thursday, and sure enough, and they came around like a couple of trained rats. So I said, the money's there all right—I'll get it here." (no. 2)

While interviewing an urban bank robber I had little success in having him respond to the question, "What time of day is the best time to hit a bank?" He finally responded by saying, "Well, you can't tell, you see—you may not be able to find a parking spot." He noted that sometimes robbers are obliged to cruise around the block repeatedly before a suitable parking spot materializes. The urban bank robber can neither double-park nor park some distance from the bank. The problem of parking, which may be only an annoyance to the shopper, is a vital consideration to the bank robbers. Furthermore, banks, in order to draw customers by providing parking space, also draw unwanted "customers."

The urban parking consideration makes further planning difficult. Knowledge of police patrol must be synchronized with uncertain parking opportunities, which vary within the urban setting. One robber pointed out that parking is seldom a problem in the suburbs. In those instances where parking violations are anticipated, the robber follows what he considers to be "normal" parking violations, that is, violations that will not attract attention. Just as persons in law enforcement offices construct concepts of the "normal" or "typical" crime, so it is assumed by the robber that the layman distinguishes between routine parking violations and atypical ones:

"SUPPOSE YOU CAN'T FIND A PARKING SPOT? Oh, we double-park. You see, in these small towns, especially country towns, you see, we're driving a pickup truck; if people see a truck double-parked, motor running, they think it's a farmer who's gone into the bank for a minute—so it takes away all suspicion. We make sure it's an old truck, but with a fairly good motor in it." (no. 8)

B. PROCEDURAL VARIATIONS

Although the detailed differences that make every robbery unique cannot be dealt with here, I will indicate how some situational contingencies and individual preferences shape the procedures employed. The emphasis, however, will be upon those variations necessitated by social, geographical, and other structural factors.

Our procedure here will be to present a first-hand account, recorded verbatim, of a small-town bank robbery, its most distinctive feature being that it is rural. Its ruralism distinguishes it from an urban robbery in terms of speed required, parking opportunities available, and risk of police intervention.

Example

"The way we do in the provincial field when I hit that town, we usually hit them that have somewhere in the neighborhood of five thousand population. They have generally one police that police the whole town, you know. So we're not afraid of this guy—he's nothing. We drive the car, and two of us would be behind the seat and with the door open, the hoods on, the guns ready. The driver would start to slow down when he comes to the bank and call 'three, two, one.' And then we open the door and we run as fast as we can. Into that bank. Because whoever comes in first, he's got ten dollars more than the rest of us got, you know. It's just to—yeh, just to give us an urge, you know. IS THAT RIGHT? Yeh. And the first guy that enters the bank goes over the counter. The second guy which follows him, which is very fast, goes for the

manager's office. The third guy stays by the door.[5] And the driver comes in last.[6] NOW, WHAT DOES HE DO WITH THE CAR? The car—the doors are open, and it stays like that. Now, I look at the people in the street—I watch them so that nobody will come near the car.

"IS IT PARKED WHERE ALL THE OTHER CARS ARE? No, no. Parking— we don't care about parking, whether or not. We drive right in front of the bank where the door is the closest to it, even if it's on the sidewalk, and there's a thing that goes on the sidewalk. And if there's one there we go right on the sidewalk. Period! Because we figure that as soon as we open the door of the car, we assume that the alarm is going off right there.

"And we act accordingly. So we are tense right there, you know. We are full of tension. And once the action starts, you got no tension any more.[7] You know, you're so busy watching; looking there, watching there—'On the floor there!' Watching that car pass by, you know. 'Get the fuck out of there!' And things like that, you know. You're not afraid anymore. But I'm afraid before I go into the bank though. The moment I sit on that back seat or I'm driving that car

---

[5] The work positions are determined by the central concern of the operation, namely speed. All persons must be capable of performing equally well in different positions; however, the door-man has the most dangerous position, requiring the greatest degree and variety of skills. The fact that, in this group, the door-man would be the first to enter and temporarily take up a different position is unusual. It may be accounted for by the fact that all members of this group are highly experienced. The more common pattern, I was told, is better expressed by no. 7:

I usually go in last. If I'm the leader I go in last. Now this is my own—some guys do it differently. But I go in last and I come out last. (no. 7)

[6] The role of the driver varies with the rural-urban factor. In an urban bank robbery, the driver would likely remain in the car and have the car already moving as the partners return and jump inside. He will try to look inconspicuous, perhaps with a newspaper in his hand. He is responsible for watching for opposition, either civilian or police. Besides having driving ability, he must be absolutely reliable. He is expected to remain on the scene should the police arrive.

[7] The lack of tension while on the job is in contrast to the anxiety of the employees—an anxiety induced and deliberately aggravated by the robbers. It must also be viewed as a necessary skill—the situation, in which mistakes may mean death, demands quick, rational decisions.

coming to the bank, I'm looking all over the place and I'm full of tension. I'm ready to bunch up. If somebody would say, 'boo!' behind me, you know, I'd go right through that roof!

"WHAT ABOUT THE DRIVER—IS HE WEARING A HOOD? Everything.

"WELL, AREN'T YOU BEING NOTICED THEN, BY PEOPLE ON THE STREET? It's funny. It's funny how people— I've noticed that. It's been noted too—that most of— I'll tell you more than that—on three banks we walked into the bank, we got out, and the people were walking by, and they thought it was Halloween or something phony.[8] They didn't know it was something real

reverse the tank and we set fire to it or sometimes we don't even bother with that.

"WELL, LET'S SEE NOW. YOU'RE TWO MEN TO THE CAR WHEN YOU DRIVE INTO THE TOWN HERE. And you know—suppose the bank is here and the street is here, and there's a connecting street here. Now, we stop the first car here. We got hoods on. But as you stop here the two guys goes out and I'm right in front. They just jump in and we keep going. And then we come back and if everything goes good, everything goes good here we don't worry about that car—we leave it there. We just keep going. Because this car is completely useless to us anymore. This car is just put there in case of emergency. I SEE.

Diagram,

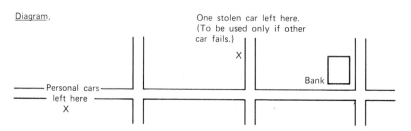

One stolen car left here.
(To be used only if other car fails.)

——— Personal cars ———
——— left here ———
         X

happening. You know, they realize when people start to scream, 'Holdup, bandit!' and things like that. Then they say, 'Oh, my god—how close I was to that guy!' You know.

"SO, YOU'RE NOT GOING TO BE BOTHERED ABOUT A PARK SPOT? Oh no, not in a provincial. In the city you would have to. You know, because then the police are patrolling the street all the time, yeh. You got to park at the proper place or otherwise you are going to have opposition right there and then. WELL, WELL.

"NOW, LET'S STAY WITH THE SEQUENCE HERE, YOU GENERALLY TRAVEL IN TWO CARS? Two cars, yes. Two stolen cars. Like, my car and my partner's car. Two guys per car, you see, and the stolen car; we drive them two days before. They're parked there and they're there, and we drive back with our own car. Because these are the cars that we're going to go through the roadblock with, and the two stolen cars, they are going to be dumped out or sometimes we

[8]This illustrates how the public is accustomed to some deviation from the normal in society, and how the robber can take advantage of this.

"AND YOU SAY THAT THERE'S NO SET ORDER AS TO WHO GETS IN THE BANK FIRST? No. The one who runs fastest is the one who goes in. I stay at the door, but suppose now I run faster than my partner—I go in. The first thing I do—I'll jump over the counter,[9] you know. I give the order 'On the floor!' and then everybody goes on the floor, and I'll smash somebody—the one who is closest to me. I'm going to have to smash him in the face. 'On the floor, in the corner!'[10] Now, by that time, by the time I say that, my three other partners are in. The one is already going into the office and I backstep right to the door, and then I take my position. And now I watch the car outside. I watch the employees. If someone gets up, or something like that. And I watch the people which are on this side of the counter also.[11]

[9]Even the most important position is temporarily left vacant in the interest of speed. It is most important that the tellers are moved away from their counters and alarm buttons as quickly as possible.

[10]When recalling another robbery, no. 28 elaborated further on the psychology of this initial violence. See discussion p. 109.

[11]The robber is continuously assessing the probable meaning of his victims' movements.

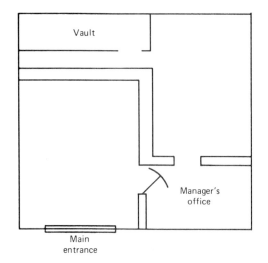

Vault

Manager's office

Main entrance

WHAT DOES HE DO DOWN THERE? Well, he gathers all the people—there may be—he bursts—sometimes he got guys with their pants halfway down—grabs the guy, 'Up you go!' Yeh, no choice. You can't say, 'Well, have your crap and please come up,' you know.

"WHY DON'T YOU JUST HAVE HIM STAY THERE AND JUST BE SURE NONE OF THEM LEAVE? Oh, well, we can't because you see, this guy here, by the time he stays down there all the time, suppose actions start here at the door—somebody starts popping shot in through that window—I want to—I want this guy to be up there pretty fast, you know. And he leaves that guy down there, you know—how do I know that he hasn't got a gun concealed in there somewhere down there? He'll bring them up and push them all up in one corner. Now we know that all the people are in one corner—they cannot be of any harm to us. If there happened to be a police officer in the bunch, I'm watching that guy there all the time. If a guy goes and makes a move there, he got his hands on his head you know. And if he makes a move I got time to react to him, and I say, 'What are you doing there?' And if I got a suspicion it may be a police officer I may just knock him off, you know—give him a good blow in the head and knock him cold, or things like that. But you cannot have dispersion in the bank. If the guy is down near here, and suddenly action occur, and this guy wants to know what's going on, and so you have to leave this guy here and run upstairs.

"NOW, BANKS ARE MOSTLY BUILT THE SAME WAY, I GUESS. BUT SOMETIMES THEY ARE A LITTLE DIFFERENT. DO YOU, BEFORE YOU COME THERE THAT DAY, GO THROUGH THAT BANK AND SEE WHERE THE WASHROOM IS, AND WHERE THIS IS AND WHERE THAT IS? No. Sometime we do that but very often not, because I don't want to be identified after. OH, I SEE. But sometime we know—you see, the provincial banks in ———, for example. They build in a certain manner. A National Bank maybe in a slightly different manner, but it's so close that after you have done maybe two or three banks it comes automatic. Just two or three. It's reflex action. You get in and you see that the manager's office—you don't have to worry, is the—is this the assistant? Yes it is—it's the manager's office. You **burst the door open** and see what's there and push them out. Period! And you see a door connecting downstairs; well, right away you say—this is a bank that I'm sure, that must be the toilet in there, you know. And away out one goes, you know.

"NOW, IF YOUR BANK IS BUILT LIKE THIS,[12] LIKE MANY OF THEM ARE, WITH THE DOOR HERE, AND THE BANKING COUNTER, AND THIS IS THE MANAGER'S OFFICE—YOU'VE GOT TO JUMP OVER THAT COUNTER. THERE'S A DOOR HERE AND A DOOR THERE. IF YOU MUST JUMP OVER THIS WAY, HOW DO YOU MANAGE THIS FELLOW IN THE FRONT? I don't worry about him. If I'm the one that comes in the bank first, I don't worry about him. I just jump in the corner here, on top here, and the door will likely be closed anyway, eh? And there will probably be someone having an interview with this manager. I don't bother with him. Because the manager, also—they know about that. They still freeze in their office, just thinking, 'Is that a joke, or something?' you know. And the—by the time he starts to react, like it takes only maybe three seconds, the whole sequence there. I give a yell, 'All on the floor!' and then by the time I give my yell people look at me—they are kind of undecided and I'll smash the first guy and back I go, because my partner is on the side of the counter and one is busting the door open and 'Out you go!' and there you are, you know. And I'm back at the door here—I take my position.

"OKAY, YOU'RE BACK HERE. NOW, TWO FELLOWS, NO, THREE . . . ? Three. We usually work four. Now, one guy goes in here—he gets everything in there. One will go to the toilet, or wherever, the washroom or the employees washroom—sometimes they are downstairs, you know. He goes down there and he cleans everything out there, and the third one . . .

"OKAY NOW, ONE GUY IS CLEANING OUT THE BATHROOMS, ONE GUY IS IN THE MANAGER'S OFFICE, ONE—YOU'RE AT THE DOOR, AND ONE FELLOW IS SCOOPING UP THE MONEY. Scooping—well, first you make sure that all the people are in the corner. Take a fast look into the vault, and then he scoops the cash. Then, by that time the two other guys will enter the vault with the manager, and we have—we try to have the first safe opened.

"There's always a big safe—there's four tellers in that bank. The association—insurance association, will not cover more than five thousand dollars, for example, in teller's, [till] where they call 'risky area,' right? So now they have the first door in the safe and there's four small other safes. You know, a case like that. Now, you call, 'first teller.' First teller comes in and opens her safe. Now, anything in excess of her money she puts in that safe until four o'clock and then she counts it. Now, you scoop that money in, and you open them four safes.[13] We never have time to go for the treasury,[14] which is another safe—that sits way at the—most of the time at the end of the vault.[15] And this big safe is what they call the 'treasury.' All the money, rolling money, you know, of the bank is there. So we get them four as fast as we can.

"NOW, THOSE FOUR HAVE TO BE OPENED BY THE TELLERS? Yeh—we call them 'first teller, second teller, third, and fourth.' SO, THEY'VE GOT TO COME AND OPEN THESE? Yes. Well, we get the manager to call them. You know, we grab the manager by the head, and you know, 'Come on, move!' 'Call the first teller, you cocksucker!' And he calls them in, Mrs. so-and-so, and we're ready to go. And they are all pretty excited and they don't like the pressure of sharp commands like that, and dirty language—we use very often too,

you know. To upset them as much as possible we can. Don't let them think—we don't want them to think, you know. Get them as nervous as possible—in a hysteria situation, where they are just ready to collapse, you know.[16]

"DOESN'T THAT PRODUCE THE DANGER OF SOMEONE IN FACT GETTING HYSTERICAL? Yeh, it did on me once. A woman—she was maybe forty-five or fifty or so—an eldery woman. She had a satchel—is that a satchel—how do you call a women's . . . ? PURSE? Purse. And when she got—when she went into the corner first and then she backtracked and she said, 'I want to get out of here, I want to get out of here!' And now, I saw her right away—she's hysterical. I got a machine gun[17] and the first thing that I always do on a job like this, never let the person be able to touch my weapon, because that's where accidents mostly occur. If I got a gun I'm pointing at you, you grab my gun and the trigger blows and I kill you and I have no intention. I keep the damn thing away from me, you know. And I put myself in a position, if the guy comes—I could still cover myself, or blast him if he's dangerous. This lady—she went for the door there; I just back away and I held my machine gun like this [at his side, as far back as possible], and I said, 'Go!' you know. And she—that's what she wanted—I knew that—she wanted to get out of there, you know. And when she went by me I was just—one of my hands—flap! Right on the side of her—she fell right on the floor and she cooled down. She started to cry, and she said, 'Don't shoot, mister!' I said, 'Sure, I won't shoot you—just go back into the corner.' And she went on the floor, you know—going back into the corner. Well, I didn't have no other opposition from that. But that's where they say it is dangerous sometime with a person like that. If I had had no experience, for example—if I would have been in a position of my first bank robbery, I would have probably shot her right there and then, because I would have been in a state of shock myself. You see, I would have said, 'Well, she cannot go out, I cannot permit her to go out!' You know, and I'm afraid she comes close to me, and I would shoot her. But today I wouldn't do that.

---

[13]Note the robber's above-average knowledge of banking procedures.

[14]Although the rural bank robber has not the time to get all the money kept in the bank, he does attempt access to considerably more than his urban counterpart. Urban robbers, who spend less than two minutes in a bank, will not ask for any of the money in the vault, but must be content with till money. (That is, unless they have planned for special monies, such as safety deposit monies—to be discussed later.)

[15]Uniform architecture, undoubtedly an economic consideration for banks, is of advantage to the bank robber as well.

[16]Some robbers attempt to dispel fear, others induce it.

[17]Again, there is a lack of consensus as to which weapons are best. One was firm in his belief that a shotgun is best "because you can cover everyone in a bank with a shotgun." (no. 41)

"I SEE. WOULD YOU SAY THAT THE MORE EXPERIENCED BANK ROBBERS ARE LESS DANGEROUS? They're less dangerous—the less dangerous they become. IS THAT RIGHT? I mean—providing that it's not a police opposition. You know, I mean—to a civilian in a bank they're not harmful—there is no danger in that—there's no danger attached to that providing that there's no weapon being shown. But as soon as somebody should pull a weapon somewhere, and when that is—you know, a bullet may go astray and kill somebody. But normally speaking, it's less dangerous having to do with professional criminals in banks like that than having to do with what we call the amateur.

"OKAY. HOW LONG DOES THE WHOLE OPERATION TAKE? HOW LONG ARE YOU IN THE BANK? It would never exceed more than four to seven minutes, at the most. I don't know—depending on the—on how we, how much time is devoted into having the safe opened inside the vault, you know.[18]

"AND ALL THAT TIME YOUR CAR IS SITTING OUT HERE. Oh yes. AND YOU ARE STANDING HERE, WATCHING IT. Yeh. IS THE MOTOR RUNNING? Oh, yeh. Everything is

[18] Regarding time duration and factors that determine time, four to seven minutes are usual in rural robbery. This is based on the length of time it would take for the local policeman to augment his force. Also, only in places where customer traffic is light could all incoming customers be accommodated in this length of time.

   "NOW THIS ALWAYS AMAZES ME. HOW DO YOU KEEP THESE GIRLS AT THE COUNTER FROM PRESSING THESE ALARM BUTTONS? Well, sometimes you can't tell, sometimes it's very difficult. This is why you can spend only such a short time in the bank. 'Cause in these cages, if there's a high counter you cannot see their hands when you first walk in. If they happen to spot you first, they've only got to move their hand a matter of inches and they can press a silent alarm, or somebody could be standing at the counter and he just needs to move his foot a few inches and he could press a silent alarm. This is why you're in the bank only maybe at the most thirty to forty seconds, 'cause you've got to be out of there—you can't stand no three or four minutes in the bank. By that time the police are there and the whole place is surrounded. So you can't count on them not pressing the silent alarm—you've got to go fast and take no chances." (no. 7: urban bank robber)
The technology demands speed: "HOW DOES THE GUY WHO'S COLLECTING THE MONEY KNOW WHEN THE TIME IS UP?" "I usually holler. I tell him, 'thirty seconds, let's go!' You can count off thirty or forty seconds pretty accurately." (no. 7).

running—the car door open. SUPPOSING SOMEBODY WANTS TO GET IN THERE? I shoot. YOU SHOOT AT THEM? Oh yeh. I would just open the door and say, 'Out, or I shoot!' I would say—if a guy comes into my car and sees the door is open and I assume right away that this guy—he's a police officer or something—he has no business there. And I would shoot, probably very close to him, in order for him to duck, and that would be the first thing I'd do. Then I would bust the door open and go after this guy. You see, so he won't have time to react there. In case he's armed. You see, if he's a police officer, for example, that's the best way to catch them. You shoot first, close to them, and duck down. Now he is in a state of shock for maybe two or three seconds. By the time he got his gun, and he doesn't know now—he's ducked down—he doesn't know where you are. I'm out of that door—I'm running. And I got into that—behind the car, you know. One way I shoot him and then the other way I get him cold turkey by the way back. And if he's got a gun, I'll probably shoot, because I don't want to take a chance for him to turn around, you know, and shoot at me.

"SUPPOSING A CUSTOMER WANTS TO COME INTO THE BANK WHILE YOU ARE IN THERE? Oh yeh—he comes in. He goes with the rest. SO YOU LET THEM ALL IN? Oh yes. He goes with the rest.[19]

"SUPPOSE THE MANAGER DOESN'T COOPERATE? Ah, he will cooperate, because there's two ways of having a

[19] It is important to bank robbers that customers come all the way into the bank:

   "WHAT DO YOU DO WITH CUSTOMERS WHO COME IN WHILE YOU'RE IN THERE? Oh, I make them lie right down, lie right down. Actually, not too many come in. You see, you're in there only about thirty seconds. So if somebody does come, why you let them in and you're there and you say, 'Down.' and they just—usually just get right down—they just drop right down—the don't even look.

   "SUPPOSE I'M COMING IN AND I HAVE THE DOOR HALF-WAY OPEN AND SEE WHAT'S GOING ON, AND THEN I DECIDE NOT TO ENTER—WHAT WOULD YOU DO WITH A GUY LIKE THAT? Nothing. YOU MEAN YOU'D LET HIM GO? Well, the minute I start chasing him I'm taking my eyes off the people and I'm leaving my partner unguarded. So usually when something like that happens, whether we're finished or not there's other banks, we come right out. You know, usually—actually, they never actually see you in there. I'm usually behind a partition or something like that." (no. 7)

manager very easily to cooperate. First of all this guy's in a state of shock. You have hoods on your head, you have a heavy weapon in your hand and you see two or three guys there, swearing language—he knows we're vulgar—he knows—we made him know that we are brutal, subhuman bastards, you know. We project that image to him, you know. And usually they are in a state of shock, but if it's a very cold customer we would say, 'Well, listen, you open the door or we shoot the first one!' And one of my partners would grab the—a woman by her hair, you know, and she would scream every time, 'cause it's sorrowful, you know, and then the man he would say, 'Well, these damn fucking subhuman bastards, he's going to kill her,' you know, and this, you talk two or three times like that and usually he'll go all the way.

"OKAY, YOUR SEVEN MINUTES ARE UP. NOW YOU'RE GOING TO LEAVE THIS PLACE, RIGHT? Right. WHO GETS OUT FIRST? I do. YOU GO OUT FIRST? That's the bloody part of it. I got to go first. I run. You see, I open the door—the door is usually kept open at all times anyway, because in them banks you open the door like this, and you put the thing like this [the gun at his side and as far back as possible], and I would take a run—I run—the car is never farther away than, for example, twice the width of that room here, and not even that; to get into the car I'd jump in, you see, in the back seat. And the driver comes second,[20] and the third and fourth. And we go.

"WHY DO YOU SAY THAT YOU DON'T LIKE TO LEAVE FIRST? Because I'm afraid all the time that one of the Second-World-War heroes, or one of them square johns, maybe, have a rifle at the other side of that house, there in the street, or something, and he's waiting for the first bastard to get out, and give him a potshot, you know. So that's why I'm always leary—lorry, how do you say that? LEARY? Leary—I took to them window and I haven't too much time to devote there myself—I go to get out fast, you know, and it's very hard to look inside a window—you just have to take a chance. So that's why I tried to make it as fast as I can. (LAUGHTER)

"HAVE YOU EVER BEEN SHOT AT WHILE YOU WERE GOING OUT? No, but my partner has—he lost his

---

[20]As indicated earlier, some urban bank robbers prefer that the driver remain in the car and act as a look-out man. He will also have the car already moving as the robbers catch it "on the fly."

thumb like that, and he told me the story the same night, you know—he scared the shit out of me.

"SO YOU SAY WHILE YOU'RE DOING THAT YOU'RE NOT SCARED? No—before and after. DO YOU NEED A BIT OF STRONG WHISKEY BEFORE? No—the guy who would—no. I drink a glass of porter with two eggs at six o'clock in the morning. And I don't drink anything else till the job is over. . . . But none of us would be tolerated if he had alcohol into him, or goofball or—the police they are quite fast to say that the guys were goofed up, you know. Goofballs and things like that—some of them are, but not any of the gang that I was working with. Because it's very dangerous. Because a guy now is overly too much—overly confident—he's overly confident to the point that he is a danger to myself more than he is a danger to society." (no. 28)

Number 28 continues with the details of the group's return to their own car. The money and equipment is buried, the stolen car taken some distance down the road and abandoned, and the robbers are left with their own car that contains everything associated with an innocent fishing trip—beer, fishing rods, and some fish bought earlier at the market.

"NOW, THAT FISHING THING YOU TALKED ABOUT—THE LAKE WOULD BE SOMEWHERE IN HERE, I SUPPOSE. Yeh, suppose there's no lake there—we'll look for a creek, or a—any God-damn thing—a small thing, just to say that we have an excuse for a law, you know, for a point of law. You know, if we—if our lawyer says, 'What were you doing in that region?' 'Well, we were fishing in that region. You know, we felt like going for an outdoor—going, you know—going in a field for a—having a—enjoy ourself!' We had a case of beer in the car—we had fishing rods and things like that, nature—a compass, you know—a compass and things like that, to go into the bush. So they—we got something to justify our being in that region, for the lawyer. In case it goes to court. That's the main thing. And then we go through the road block.

"NOW, I WOULD IMAGINE THESE FELLOWS AT THE ROAD BLOCK WOULD FAIRLY SOON KNOW WHOM TO LOOK FOR. Yes, they do, but then, what can they do? What can they do? The police officers, you know him, let's say you recognize me—well, I say, 'How are you doing?' 'Well! How are you doing! You bastard! You just been there, eh?' 'Well, gee, I don't know anything—I just come from the creek there.' 'Is that a fact? Let's search the fuckin' car first, right?' 'Okay, I'll help you—I'll help you search my car—you want me to strip right here—I'll strip with pleasure. You know, the more they search me the better you give me a beef in case I go to court. Because my lawyer will question you, and as soon as you say that you've searched this person so thoroughly that you couldn't barely pass a dollar bill there, then home-free I am.

"AND HE CAN'T ARREST YOU, IF HE HASN'T ANYTHING ON YOU? Well, he could possibly say, 'Well, okay, I'll bring you in for, say what—24 hours.' Well, I don't care about that. I'll go twenty-four hours anytime for five thousand dollars—you know that part.

"WHAT WOULD YOUR NORMAL TAKE BE IN A BANK LIKE THAT—A SMALL PLACE? Yeh—they never have reached more than twenty or twenty-five thousand at the most. That's the very most. SO THAT GIVES YOU FOR FOUR PEOPLE . . .? That's about five thousand each. Well, usually we average about three thousand each. THREE THOUSAND EACH.

"OKAY. NOW, HOW SOON DO YOU COME BACK FOR THE MONEY IN THE BUSH? We usually come back somewhere between four and seven days. So, because they're smart, them guys too—they know we plant the money. I mean, they watch us." (no. 28)

C. DIMENSIONS OF VICTIM MANAGEMENT

The skills required for crimes involving the avoidance of the victim are significantly different from the skills required for crimes involving victim confrontation. Surreptitious crimes tend to revolve around mechanical competences, whereas crimes involving victim confrontation revolve around victim management. The term "management" is chosen to differentiate this process from what might be termed "victim manipulation," as in confidence games.[21]

My focus on victim management is not in-

[21]Under some conditions victim manipulation develops into a situation of victim management. Erving Goffman, "On Cooling the Mark Out," *Psychiatry* 15, no. 4 (November 1952).

tended to obscure other differences, nor to suggest that criminals develop mechanical or social skills to the exclusion of the other; I have earlier pointed out that thieves may engage in both types of crimes. The focus arises, instead, from the distinctions made by the criminals themselves, and from inherent differences in mechanical versus social skills.

1. Surprise and Vulnerability
The bank robber relies on surprise to bring about momentary mental and physical paralysis of bank employees:

"The door would fly right open and the people inside, they freeze!" (no. 28)

Such paralysis is crucially important to the bank robber: it allows him quickly to take up his position in the building; further, he hopes to be able to back all cashiers away from their counter before they have had a chance to regain enough composure to push an alarm button.

Criminals believe that bank employees' susceptibility to surprise and their consequent vulnerability varies with the time of day and the day of week. A bank robber insisted mornings are the best time:

"OKAY. NOW WHAT TIME OF DAY? Always in the morning. Catch them by surprise. They've still got sleep in their eyes and sort of hung over if they drink. Catch them by surprise. About ten o'clock." (no. 7)

A bank robber who preferred Monday mornings, said:

"On Monday, everybody's asleep; not asleep, but not going anywhere. People are dull. On Monday, people are not on the street in the morning—people are either asleep or at work." (no. 41)

The criminal is also aware that his surprised victim is not in a position to react efficiently, even if he should try to. A burglar involved in the "live prowl" stated:

"WERE YOU PREPARED IN ANY SENSE IN THE EVENT OF BEING CAUGHT? Well, you don think of that. 'Course I always made sure, like you say, that there were ways out. 'Cause I never thought of being cornered by anyone there, because most people when they wake up, they're stunned, you know, anyhow; they're not that wide awake, so you're wide awake, you know. You're going to get out of the place." (no. 21)

This resembles the bank robber's inducement of near hysteria in order to create an imbalance in the degree of rationality the robber and the victims are respectively capable of.

In addition, the victim is not equipped with the skills required to reverse his position of weakness, even if he should recover from his surprise:

"But in the long run, your chances of ever using a gun on a professional thief are very small—you're better off without a gun—you'll probably get your head shot off because he's doing something he does every day and you're doing something you've never done before."[22]

2. Establishing Authority and Managing Tension

The initial moment of surprise and shock is the first step in establishing a robber-victim relationship. During this time, the entire group may be herded into one corner of the bank, or ordered to lie prostrate on the floor. In either case, the posture and physical location of the victims are such as to enhance the robber's control over them.

Once having established control, some robbers encourage the return of rational thought to the victim, while others prefer to extend the state of shock until the robbery is completed. In either case, the particular style adopted seems to be a matter of personal preference rather than a choice based on features of the specific robbery itself. Through experience, robbers adopt a style they find effective in managing the victim. The robber quoted next seeks to maintain victim management by continuing the state of shock in his victims.

". . . the door would fly right open and the people inside, they freeze. You know, when there's a big

[22]Martin, *My Life in Crime,* p. 69.

smash around everyone they freeze on the spot and look around, whether it's a joke or not. And you see them guys, you know; and they have hoods on their heads, and the gun, you know. And then there's one command—'Hit the ground!' you know—'Hit the dirt!'—I don't know how to say that—'Hit the floor—bunch of dogs!,' you know. That's the way we say that: 'Fuckin' dog, hit the floor, or we kill each and everyone of you!,' you know. So they are froze there—their reaction is one of very extreme fear and they drop on the floor and sometime we select the strongest person—the manager especially or another teller which is very big—a six footer, or something like that, you know. And we won't say a word, we just walk up to him and smash him right across the face, you know, and we get him down. And once he's down the people, the girls especially, they look at him and they say, 'My God—big Mike, he's been smashed like that—I'd better lay down too, and stay quiet. You know—it's sort of like psychology, to obey us immediately, everybody will follow the leader. The manager is the leader, and I see you go down—Jesus Christ, I'm going to follow you—I'm going down too, you know!" (no. 28)

Another bank robber, in contrast, is anxious to avoid hysteria:

"That's how I used to operate. I'd stand right there and the manager and the whole works at bay. I might have them lay down on the floor, 'cause you couldn't just have them standing there with their hands up, because it's too noticeable. You just walk in, and anyone you think is going to panic, well you just talk real quiet to them and you say, 'Don't panic and everything will be all right; just take it easy and there'll be no trouble, see?'

"DID YOU USE TO FIRE ANY SHOTS INTO THE CEILING OR ANYTHING LIKE THAT? No—I used to talk very softly—I'd talk very softly, very quietly, and I'd never raise my voice. I always figure that if you holler and show panic, it would make the people panicky. If you just walk in quietly, just like you're transacting ordinary business, it kinda reassures the people that you know exactly what you're doing, and that you mean them no harm. But if you go in there hustling and bustling and firing and shooting, you're going to have people start to scream, and everything else. And it's pretty hard to hold back people screaming no matter what pressure they're under.

"BUT ISN'T THERE THE PROBLEM THAT IF YOU SPEAK SOFTLY THERE MAY BE SOMEONE AT THE BACK AT AN ADDING MACHINE . . .? Oh well, they automatically know. You don't speak that softly. You know, when we walk in we say, 'This is a holdup!' and they automatically hear you. But then after that you just sort of—no worry, no rush. It's just a matter of routine—load up the money, and your shopping bags and go out. Oh, we make sure that everybody hears you, that's for sure. We don't just walk in there and say, 'Well, this is a holdup, hand over the money.' We give a good bellow when we walk in."[23] (no. 7)

Bank robbers emphasize self-confidence as the key to successful bank robbery. They directly relate self-confidence to the ability to control people who are under stress. The manner in which this confidence is communicated is secondary, but it is essential that it be communicated.

Number 45 stressed the importance of making it clear to those in the bank that his group "meant business":[24]

"They can tell by the sound of your voice, by what you say and how you go about things, whether or not you mean business. If you're shaky, they'll know."[25] (no. 45)

The role of "voice" in establishing authority and in managing tension is considered critical to bank robbery, and to armed robbery in general. The methods used are visual (masks, hoods), auditory (vocal commands), and physical.

[23]This is similar to the approach used by the robber described in "The Heist . . ." by DeBaum. On page 74, he states:

"So far as may be, the mob are calm and polite on the job. 'Cowboying' or the wild brandishing of pistols and shouting of orders in all directions is frowned upon; fear has made more heroes than courage ever has."

DeBaum pays detailed attention to some aspects of victim management in armed bank robbery. [Everett DeBaum, "The Heist: The Theory and Practice of Armed Robbery," *Harpers* 200 (February 1950): 69–77.]

[24]This raises the question of why bank personnel find it difficult to accept the reality of a robbery.

[25]Number 45 was described to me by other criminals as "very good in banks," and as having a "very good voice for banks."

"SO WHAT WOULD YOU SAY ARE THE DANGERS IN THIS KIND OF AN OPERATION? Uh—well, panic on the part of the store owner. WHAT FORMS CAN THAT TAKE? Uh—I've experienced a man literally freezing—couldn't speak. He just pointed to show where the money was. SO THAT DIDN'T CAUSE YOU MUCH TROUBLE? No, no. But on occasion I've had women scream. WHAT DO YOU DO IN THAT CASE? Well, on a couple of occasions I've just belted them on the side of the head with the pistol. KNOCK THEM OUT OR WHAT? No. SO THAT'S ONE WAY OF DEALING WITH WOMEN WHO SCREAM? Or slap them in the face with the fist. The man I worked with was well over six feet and a very powerful built man with a deep resonant voice, and I saw him just with a loud voice, and with the tone of his voice, he would bring people out of a shock state.

"IS THE MANNER IN WHICH YOU SPEAK VERY IMPORTANT? Very much so—yeh—you have to be positive at all times. DID YOU EVER HAVE ANY TROUBLE, LET'S SAY, WITH A WOMAN WHO WOULDN'T COOPERATE? I didn't, no." (no. 27)

Another example regarding the use of language:

"Now, her mother and brother they were at the back of the bank, you know, of the house, and they heard that, because, you know, my talking during a bank holdup is very different from the talking we have now—it's full of tension and very commanding, you know. In order to impress the people as much as we possibly can." (no. 28)

What bank robbers seem to be describing has certain similarities with what Max Weber has defined as "charisma." Robbers refer to these qualities, such as voice and physical build, as inherent, rather than as techniques that might be learned. It is more difficult, however, to delineate the various dimensions of what robbers refer to as "confidence." Some clues have been provided; in crime, as elsewhere, success breeds success:

"AND YOU WERE PRETTY SURE THAT YOU COULD KEEP THIS UP WITHOUT TROUBLE? Oh yes, definitely—most of the guys that I've met, and I've met a tremendous amount of criminals, you know, that were involved in a bank robbery, and we feel very confident; as a matter of fact, anyone who does two banks and he succeeds going all through and he has no police suspicion on him, he becomes over confident, you know. You say, 'Well, now I'm a master criminal and I know how to do it. They didn't catch me, they're not aware that I'm working on it, and everything goes smoothly—it will work forever like that.' You know, you get conident like that." (no. 28)

Number 28 points out that confidence can be dangerous, encouraging false notions of immunity from danger. Yet it appears to be precisely this confidence that facilitates successful robbery. In a sense, the robber cannot afford to consider possible or even probable consequences of his action, lest such considerations deprive him of the confidence needed to complete the task successfully.

Number 40 noted that, objectively and rationally, the probability of a prison sentence ought to deter the criminal. He added, however, that the criminal cannot afford to consider these matters, particularly just before a holdup, because he will lose his confidence. At that stage, it is rational *not* to consider failure, since by so doing you will bring it upon yourself all the more surely.

Although the degree of tension felt by a robber appears to vary from person to person, it is clear that he must manage his own tension besides his victims'. Number 28 said he is very tense before a holdup, whereas to no. 7 it was just "like getting up and having a shave and having coffee and going to work."

The ability to manage one's own tension affects work roles. It is generally agreed that it is essential for the door-man to be armed but that the other accomplices can do without weapons. Only those who have demonstrated their ability to control themselves will be given guns:

"The man with experience carries the gun; the reason he carries the gun is that he won't pull the trigger right away. Everybody is nervous; if a guy is too nervous you don't give him a gun—it's too dangerous." (no. 39)

Another stated:

"Getting the money is the easiest job for the least experienced or nervous person." (no. 41)

Experienced criminals may demand that less experienced partners be unarmed, or armed with less effective weapons. An experienced burglar who worked with two less experienced partners insisted they carry knives rather than guns:

"You think twice with a knife. A person going with a gun, if he has to use it, he'll use it right away, whereas a person with a knife, if he can dodge it, he will. Say, for instance, if you saw a guy in the place, instead of panicking and blowing the guy's head right off, with a knife you can move back into the shadow, and you don't panic, you just relax. With a gun you're likely to shoot the guy, with a knife you gotta stab him which means you come in close contact with him to stab him." (no. 10)

Ability to manage their own fears is also requisite for the driver of the holdup car, particularly when it is necessary for the driver to remain in the car during the holdup. His opportunity to leave the scene in relative safety is in stark contrast to the situation of his partners. Whether or not the driver remains in the car appears to be related both to the reliability of the driver and the degree of pressure he is exposed to:

"In the old days, they used to leave the driver of a bank car outside, and most times they'd come out and the car would ge gone! Now, you take the driver with you and he's the first one out. DO YOU THINK THAT IS WHY THEY TAKE THE DRIVER WITH THEM? Definitely, no other reason." (no. 15)

Another respondent:

"YOU LEAVE THE MOTOR RUNNING? Yes. WITH NO ONE IN THE CAR? That's the way I would do it. Sure, because if something happens and this guy panics and takes off with the car—which has happened, but not to me." (no. 36)

Experienced bank robbers feel their work is made more difficult, and the victim's situation more dangerous, by the tendency of the mass media to depict bank robberies as phony, "toy gun stuff." Robbers feel they are now constrained first of all to convince their victims the event is "not a joke." This may require more brutal action on their part than they would otherwise need to use. They need to convince any potential "heroes" among their victims that they cannot be subdued, TV dramas to the contrary.

The establishment of authority is no doubt enhanced by the display and use of weapons. The discussion above is intended to indicate, however, that the gun is only one of various persuasive devices used by robbers. This is not to deny that the successful use of other resources such as loud commands and physical violence is possible only because he has a gun. Nevertheless, much of the robber's activity during a robbery is necessitated only because he does not want to use his gun. He is, therefore, rightly dismayed at the condescension of those who fail to appreciate that his techniques revolve around the nonuse, rather than the use, of guns.

Such condescension is obvious in the statement of a con man serving a sentence for armed robbery:

"He had great pride in his previous achievements as a con man but said that anyone could stick a gun in a sucker's belly and get some money and that anyone who did this and landed in prison for it should feel ashamed."[26]

If guns are carried for purposes of intimidation only, then why not use toy guns? The answers were unanimous: "It's too dangerous—you've got nothing to protect yourself with." (no. 39) Such protection may be needed because of police or potential heroes among robbery victims. Robbers have only contempt for the hero type, whose action is considered irrational and extremely dangerous. Whenever the robber meets resistance from his victims and is forced to shoot, he is almost certainly going to "win," given his experience and advantageous position. Such "winning," however, has serious legal implications. Also, the scuffle will likely disrupt the orderly retrieval of money, forcing him to leave empty-handed. The bank robber does not want trouble—he wants money:

"Well, this is where the public makes an awfully tragic mistake. It's a tragic mistake and I think maybe there would be a lot less people getting shot in hold-ups if people were just told that the money is there—give it to the man and leave it to the police. And you've seen in the paper time and time again where people have been shot chasing them down the street. Mind you, they may catch the odd one, but they've only got to shoot one man and it's tragic, you know what I mean. And actually I don't want to shoot anybody, but if it's me or you, you're going first, I'll tell you that right now." (no. 7)

Although the robber will hesitate to use his gun on a civilian, confrontation by police is seen as resulting inevitably in a "shootout." "Why not put your hands and surrender when cornered?" I asked. That seemed incomprehensible: "They'd mow you down. They can just say we resisted arrest." (no. 39)

Bank robbers do not anticipate resistance from a single patrolman but are prepared for it should it occur. Such resistance would be interpreted as a stupid "hero act," similar to a civilian's:

"Have you ever heard of a smart detective getting shot? No, the only ones you ever hear of getting shot are some dumb patrolmen. What do you think so-and-so [a detective] would do if he pulled up alongside a car and a guy raised a chopper? [Submachine gun] You think he'd be a hero? No—he's got brains. He'd get away from there as fast as he could. But he'd eventually find out who that was. Where a dumb patrolman hasn't got enough sense to do that."[27]

Police are expected to arrive in a group, or more likely, to be waiting in the bank. The experienced robber, however, does not expect to be apprehended while at work. If he is to have "trouble," he expects it upon arrival at the bank, or after he has left. To meet it upon arrival indicates an information leak, considered by robbers as their most serious uncontrollable contingency.

The successful management of victims during a robbery demands the continuous and correct

---

[26]Sutherland, *Professional Thief*, p. 42.

[27]Martin, *My Life in Crime*, p. 100.

interpretation of the victim's behavior. As such, it is important the robber understands correctly the non-verbal communication that is going on—a particularly difficult task, since the degree of tension encourages abnormal behavior. Robbers pointed out numerous examples of bizarre behavior on the part of the victims. The most common observed in banks took the form of bank customers offering their own valuables to the robbers, presumably to enhance their own chances of survival. On the other hand, some customers will go to great lengths to hide their own wallets, rings, and jewelry. Such actions must be interpreted as a threatening move. When this occurs, the robber may issue a warning, or shoot. One respondent, an experienced robber, said he was in prison now because of an error he had made in this regard:

"The guy wouldn't stop moving—I didn't know what he was doing, so I let him have it. Later, I found out he was just trying to hide something under a rug."

The data and analysis . . . enable us to compare and contrast the work of the safecracker with that of the armed robber. They share those concerns generated by the illegality of their work. Both must avoid apprehension and con-viction, and reduce the risk of such by way of insurances such as arrangements with friends, bondsmen, and lawyers. Both share certain skills needed for casing, though the specific nature and application of these skills differ. Despite the above similarities, the contrasts in specific work patterns are striking. The behavior of an armed robber at work is very different from that of a safecracker. Since an armed robber manages people in crisis, and the safecracker uses mechanical skills, an analogy between a psychiatrist and a mechanic may be appropriate. The mere fact that both of the latter work roles are legal, does not blind us to their important differences. In the study of crime, however, we have permitted the fact of its illegality to obscure significant behavioral differences.

Having delineated the various skills and procedures appropriate to both surreptitious and overt crimes, we now turn to the question of how these skills are learned and transmitted. Although learning normally precedes behavior, the reverse chapter sequence used here is necessitated by the fact that it is difficult to appreciate the complexities of the learning process unless the substance of that learning is first understood.

54. Running a Fencing Business: The Front

CARL KLOCKARS

THE FRONT

VINCENT IS A BUSINESSMAN; HE BUYS AND SELLS merchandise in order to make a profit. Some of his merchandise is stolen; some of it is not. There is only one advantage to trading in stolen goods: one can buy them cheaper than legitimate goods and thus make a greater profit.[1]

At any given moment, roughly eighty percent of the retail stock on Vincent's shelves is legitimate. This does not mean that the merchandise costs the same as it would in a department store. Rather, Vincent prides himself in buying dead stock, damaged merchandise, factory close-outs, overruns, and the like at especially low prices. Having traded legally and illegally for more than twenty years, Vincent enjoys a large number of contacts in the business world whom he solicits for such buys. For example, Vincent

▶SOURCE: *The Professional Fence*. New York: The Free Press, 1974, pp. 77–93. (Editorial adaptations.) Reprinted by permission.

[1]The fence's profit margin may or may not be greater than that of the legitimate businessman; it all depends upon what kind of fence one is. If one is a "secret" dealer selling goods to customers who do not know those goods are stolen, the mark-up is usually higher than in the legitimate market, because the dealer bought the goods below wholesale price and sells them as if they were legitimate. If one is a "public" fence like Vincent, one's profit margin is generally similar to that in the legitimate market. Although goods are purchased at lower than wholesale prices, they are also sold at lower than regular retail prices. Thus the "public" fence's profits tend to come from the volume of his trade and the rapidity with which he can sell merchandise on account of its being offered at lower prices than in the legitimate market.

recently bought three cases of name-brand wigs from a friend in a drug distribution center. In drugstores the wigs normally sold for $7.99, but the drugstores that bought them found them difficult to sell even when they were marked down to $5.99. Thus the supply house found itself stuck with cases of wigs no one would buy. Vincent bought three cases for $125. At 120 wigs per case, that represents a wholesale cost to Vincent of 35¢ per wig. Although the price tag on them in his store reads $6.00, Vincent is selling them quickly at $4.00.

Vincent has a number of explanations for why he is able to sell legitimate merchandise that a neighborhood drug, clothing, variety, or general merchandise store cannot sell.

"First, I buy right. I'm a cash buyer and I know where to buy. That means I got better prices. Nobody can stay with me when it comes to buyin'. And I don't mean hot stuff either. I mean legitimate. When it comes right down to it, some stuff I can buy legitimate cheaper than I can buy it hot.

"I told that to a judge once, you know, Judge Mac-Fee. He says to me, 'Mr. Swaggi, how many years have you been buying merchandise?' I tell him, 'All my life, Your Honor.' So he says, 'And didn't you suspect something when that man offered to sell you this merchandise for that price?' 'No sir, Your Honor,' I said, 'I can buy merchandise so cheap you wouldn't believe it, Your Honor.' Then my lawyer asked me, 'Mr. Swaggi, would you tell the court what the big sign which hangs over the door of your store says?' 'Sure,' I says, 'it says, "Everything less than Wholesale," and that's true, Your Honor.' 'Well,' the judge says, 'I'm going to have to go down to your store one of these days and see some of those bargains.'

"Take perfume, for instance. When a line don't move for six months, the dealers 'll give it away. Ten cents on the dollar for what was goin' retail for six ninety-five. You gotta know what you're doin' and I been at this business for a lotta years, buddy.

"Next, I sell my merchandise. You go to a store today, what happens? You see something you want and you bring it to the cash register yourself. That ain't sellin', that's buyin'. With me, I ask the customer what he wants, show him what I got, have 'em try something on, tell 'em how good it looks on him or how much his wife would like it. That's sellin'. What the hell are you in the store for if it ain't to sell? Hell, if you didn't have to sell, all you'd need is some girl at a cash register to take the money."

Vincent's aggressive but pleasant salesmanship and his lower prices on legitimate merchandise are important factors in keeping his customers coming back. The fact that his customers know he has stolen merchandise to sell at prices lower than at any legitimate outlet also figures importantly in his trade in legitimate goods.

"See, most people figure all of the stuff in my store is hot, which you know it ain't. But if they figure it's hot you can't keep 'em away from it. It's just like the old hustler bullshit all over again. People figurin' they're gonna get something for nothing. You think I'm gonna tell 'em it ain't hot? Not on your life. In fact I tell 'em it is hot. I got this guy who comes to my store, you know who he is, only we can't put his name in the book on account of he's so well known. Anyway, he's got a loudspeaker in his car. Sometimes when he drives by he'll say, 'Ladies and Gentlemen, I want to call your attention to Mr. Vincent Swaggi's store on the corner of the street. All stolen merchandise, Ladies and Gentlemen, all stolen merchandise.' See, that's the kinda bullshit I gotta put up with the clowns I know. But when you come right down to it, he's helpin' my business by sayin' that.

"There was a store in this city some years ago. The guy who owned it took an arrest for being a fence. After that he never bought nothin' hot. But he'd pass the word around to his customers in the neighborhood that on such and such a night he was gettin' a

truckload of hot suits. Well, he'd have the truck pull up to the back of his place and unload the suits, maybe ten, eleven o'clock at night. By midnight they'd all be sold, twenty-five bucks apiece and every one legit. So he makes only eight or nine bucks a suit. Five, six hundred suits in an hour ain't bad. Plus his customers would help him unload the truck!"

Far more important to Vincent's business than the psychological edge his trade in legitimate goods gives him in dealing with retail customers are the multiple advantages that such a legitimate business identity gives to his trade in stolen merchandise. Collectively, these advantages are commonly referred to as a "front." To explain the interplay between illegal and legal trade which constitutes the front, it is necessary to explicate the legal elements of the offense of receiving stolen goods.[2]

[2]Federal law prohibits receipt of stolen goods in ten sections of title 18 of the United States Code: 18 U.S.C., sec. 641 (receipt of property stolen from the United States); 18 U.S.C., sec. 659 (receipt of property stolen from an interstate or foreign carrier or depot); 18 U.S.C., sec. 662 (receipt of stolen property within the special maritime or territorial jurisdiction of the United States); 18 U.S.C., sec. 842 (h) (receipt of stolen explosives); 18 U.S.C., sec. 1660 (receipt of property taken by an act of piracy or robbery); 18 U.S.C., sec 1708 (receipt of property stolen from the U.S. mails); 18 U.S.C., sec 2113 (c) (receipt of property stolen from a federally insured bank); 18 U.S.C., sec. 2312 (receipt of a stolen vehicle moving in interstate or foreign commerce); U.S.C., sec. 1315 (receipt of stolen goods, securities, moneys or fraudulent State tax stamps which are part of interstate or foreign commerce). Sec. 341 of title 18 prohibits conspiracy to commit any of these offenses and therefore is also a receiver statute. In addition every state has a statute prohibiting the receipt of stolen property: Ala. Code tit. 14 sec. 338; Alaska Stat. sec. 11.20.350; Ariz. Stat. Ann. sec. 13-621; Ark. Stat. Ann. secs. 41-3934, 41-3938; Cal. Pen. Code. sec. 496; Colo. Rev. Stat. sec. 40-5-2; Conn. Sess. Laws, Pub. Act. no. 828 sec. 128 (1969); Del. Code Ann. tit. 11 secs. 791, 792; Fla. Stat. Ann. sec. 811.16; Ga. Code. Ann. sec. 26-1806; Hawaii Rev. Stat. sec. 761-1 to 761-10; Idaho Code sec. 18-1307; Ill. Ann. Stat. ch. 38 sec. 16-1; Ind. Ann. Stat. sec. 10-3030; Iowa Code Ann. sec. 712.1; Ky. Rev. Stat. Ann. sec. 433.290; Kan. Stat. Ann. sec. 21-3701; La. Rev. Stat. sec. 14:69; Me. Rev. Stat. Ann. tit. 17 sec. 3551; Md. Ann. Code art. 27 sec. 466; Mass. Sess. Laws ch. 681 (1971); Mich. Comp. Laws Ann. sec. 750.535; Minn. Stat. Ann. sec. 609-53; Miss. Code Ann. sec. 2249; Mo. Stat. Ann. sec. 560.270; Mont. Rev. Codes Ann. sec. 94-2721; Neb. Rev.

Receiving stolen goods can be legally adjudged a crime if and only if it is proven that (1) the goods in question are in fact stolen goods; (2) the accused did in fact have them in his possession; and (3) he had reasonable cause to know they were stolen. In running his fencing business Vincent constantly employs procedures that render the discovery or proof of one or more of these elements difficult or impossible.

The Goods Are Stolen

In order to establish that particular goods are, in fact, stolen it is necessary that the owner be able to identify them.[3] The extent of Vincent's legitimate trade assures that an especially precise identification of stolen property will be necessary.

"Look, you got a store, I got a store. Some shine [thief] takes a load of merchandise from you and sells it to me. Even if detectives find out it's me that's got it, how you gonna know it's yours? Say it's suits, Botany suits. How are you gonna know they're yours? I got Botanys, you got Botanys, every store in town's got Botanys. On stuff like that you don't even have to cut

Stat. sec. 28-507 to 28-510; Nev. Rev. Stat. sec. 205.275; N.H. Rev. Stat. Ann. sec. 582-10; N.J. Stat. Ann. secs. 2A: 139-1 to 2A: 139-4; N.M. Stat. Ann. sec. 40A-16-11; N.Y. Pen. Law secs. 165.40 to 165.65; N.C. Gen. Stat. secs. 14-71, 14-72; N.D. Cent. Code sec. 12-40-19; Ohio Rev. Code Ann. sec. 2907-30; Okla. Stat. Ann. tit. 21 sec. 1713; Ore. Rev. Stat. sec. 165-045; Pa. Stat. Ann. tit. 18 sec. 4817; R.I. Gen. Laws sec. 11-41-2; S.C. Code of Laws sec. 16-362; S.D. Comp. Laws sec. 22-37-18; Tenn. Code Ann. secs. 39-4217, 39-4218; Tex. Pen. Code art. 1430; Utah Code Ann. sec. 76-38-12; Vt. Stat. Ann. tit. 13:2561 (cf. Vt. Proposed Crim. Code sec. 1957); Va. Code Ann. sec. 18.1-107; Wash. Rev. Code Ann. sec. 9.54.010; W. Va. Code sec. 61-3-18; Wis. Stat. Ann. sec. 943.34; Wyo. Stat. sec. 6-135.

[3]This is a practical, common-language statement, not a precise or comprehensive summary of the law on the matter. On some occasions circumstantial evidence of the theft has been held as sufficient proof. See *James v. State*, 8 Ala. App. 255, 62 So. 897 (1913); *Bell v. State*, 220 Md. 75, 150 A 2d 908 (1959). Generally, the identity of the goods as stolen must be clearly established. Some statutes that contain statements such as "intent to deprive the rightful owner" require that that owner be "strictly" established. See *State v. Bean*, 49 Del. 247, 113 A. 2d 875 (1950); contra, *Williams v. State*, 216 Tenn. 89, 390 S. W. 2d 234 (1965); *State v. McGraw*, 140 W. Va. 547, 85 S. E. 2d 849 (1955).

the labels out. Somebody brings me suits like that, name brand, I don't even have to touch 'em. Just put 'em right up on the rack.

"Now, of course, if you got suits nobody else is supposed to have, say Sears or Macy's, then you just cut the labels off and you own 'em. And there ain't a thing nobody can do once you got those labels off.

"Now most of your small stuff, shirts, sweaters, children's toys, women's blouses, all you gotta do is take 'em outta the cartons. The carton's got numbers on it. Get rid of the carton and you're set. Leave the labels in and put 'em on the shelves.

"[I ask about items with serial numbers.] Well, take typewriters. If it's from a house burglary, that's no problem. It's almost certain the guy don't know his serial number. Do you know the serial number on your TV set and camera and typewriter? [I answered, 'Yes.'] Well, you know what you're doin' so you don't count. Anyway, most people don't. Now if it's from a factory or an office and they come in on you, then they're gonna know it's what they're lookin' for so you gotta scheme somethin' else. But I got this guy who I can send typewriters to who owns a typewriter store. All he's gotta do is change a few numbers and put it in the window. When you buy from him, he gives you a two-year service contract so he don't have no back-ups.[4]

"See, with me I got bills, too. Suppose some detectives come in and say somethin' I got ain't legit. Well, first they gotta have a warrant. It's not like the old days, anymore, when they could just walk in and grab what they wanted. Now they gotta have a warrant and it's gotta say exactly what they're lookin' for. Say they find what they want. Chances are I got a bill for it. [I ask how he just happens to have a proper bill.] Look, how many things you think I buy legitimate, with bills, each year? Hundreds! I gotta keep all those bills you know, for Uncle Sam. So two months ago I bought

[4]By "back-ups" Vincent means interference by the police or others that could stop the orderly flow of illegitimate merchandise and possibly result in the arrest of the dealer. In the particular instance referred to above, the service contract ensures that for two years following the sale of the typewriter with altered serial numbers only the illegitimate dealer will be called to repair it. The procedure prevents any serious "back-ups" because in the state in which Vincent does business the time assigned by the statute of limitations for the crime of receiving is eighteen months.

seventy-five suits at auction. You know what that bill says, 'One Lot of Suits Sold to Vincent Swaggi, Paid in Full.' It don't matter what those detectives have on that warrant then. Those are my suits.

"I do that with bills a lot. Like a while ago I had a guy bringin' me electric razors and hot combs. Every day or so he'd bring me a dozen of each. So what did I do? I bought two dozen legitimate from the supplier he was workin' for. Now, if there's a back-up, I'm covered."

It would be laborious to explain in detail all of the ways in which Vincent manages to alter and conceal the identity of stolen merchandise. When necessary, gems can be taken from their settings, minks refashioned, serial numbers changed, labels removed. Suffice it to say that most goods can be sufficiently altered or merged with legitimate stock to avoid identification. There are limits, however, imposed by time and skill, and certain merchandise may be sold only to customers who are willing to assume the risk of possessing identifiable stolen property. Such sales are made without bills or receipts, and as of their conclusion possession of the property is no longer a matter of concern for Vincent. Nevertheless, during the time Vincent possesses such identifiable items he sacrifices the cover that his legitimate business front gives him for this aspect of the offense of receiving.[5]

[5]It may be helpful to mentally keep separate those advantages (for Vincent's trade in stolen merchandise) accruing simply from his owning a business, from those which he creates by his own acts in order to give the appearance of legitimacy. Simply because he owns a store, (1) Vincent has the right to hold various quantities of diverse merchandise; (2) he has the right to hold bills of purchase; (3) he has the right not to be disturbed in the holding of merchandise unless there is precise knowledge (probable cause to suspect) that some part of it may well be stolen merchandise; and (4) since his particular trade is often with distressed merchandise, his possession of goods that are altered to avoid identification is not especially suspect. By his own acts, Vincent creates the appearance of legitimacy or obliterates the appearance of illegitimacy by (1) changing or destroying identification numbers, (2) removing identifiable characteristics, (3) falsely claiming that particular receipts cover stolen property, (4) forging those receipts, (5) maintaining receipts with vague descriptions of merchandise, and (6) intentionally mixing stolen stock with legitimate stock.

He Had Possession of the Goods

The law requires, as we have said, that for a criminal prosecution one must also prove *possession* of stolen goods. In order to do so, the police must first find the stolen property and then establish the fence's possession or control of it.[6] To the end of thwarting the discovery of stolen property in his possession, Vincent employs certain devices and requires certain procedures on the part of those who would sell to him. Principal among the devices employed is the drop.

The Drop. There are two common senses in which "drop" is used in the vocabulary of fences and thieves. In the first, it refers to a place other than the fence's place of business in which the fence stores stolen goods, usually for a short time, in order to keep their location secret from the police, from thieves, or from both.[7] It is this sense of "drop" that is meant when a fence says, "I kept the merchandise in a drop." When the word is used in this way, it is normally preceded, in a prepositional phrase, by "in." Another sense of "drop" is meant when a thief says, "The fence told me to leave my swag at a drop." Here the thief means a location other than the fence's place of business at which the fence instructed the thief to leave the merchandise or transfer possession of it to the fence or his agent. In this case the fence might then put the merchandise

[6]Statutes on receiving stolen property are not limited to physical possession. Many include provisions for "effective control," "concealment," "buying," etc. (e.g., Alaska Stat., sec. 11.20.350; Fla. Stat. Ann., sec. 811.16). Vincent does a substantial part of his business with samples of merchandise. In such situations he may not only not physically possess the merchandise he has bought and sold; he may not even see it. Vincent claims that "there is an old saying in the fencing business: "If you didn't see it, you didn't buy it.' " I am not sure about the antiquity of the saying, but there is no doubt that it accurately reflects the difficulty of proving possession.

[7]The definitions given in the two major collections of criminal cant and argot are a rough approximation of this first meaning. See Eric Partridge, *A Dictionary of the Underworld* (New York: Bonanza Books, 1961), pp. 207–08; and Hyman E. Goldin, Frank O'Leary, and Morris Lispus, eds., *Dictionary of American Underworld Lingo* (New York: Twayne Publishers, 1950), p. 62. Neither mentions the technical distinction elaborated on in this section.

in a drop of the first sort, or might take it directly to a buyer. When "drop" is used in this sense, it is normally preceded, in a prepositional phrase, by "at."

The two meanings of "drop" correspond to different institutional arrangements. A drop of the first kind is a relatively permanent location, which the fence may own or control. It may be a house, garage, parked trailer, warehouse, or any other location which is stable and secure for storage. The drop of the second definition may be only an impromptu, agreed-upon location at which goods will be taken from the thief by an agent of the fence. It may be an empty warehouse, a street corner, a loading platform, or a rented truck with the engine running. The usage of different prepositions with the two meanings of the word reflects these different arrangements. In the first sense, "in" suggests the control which the fence exercises over his "drop." In the second sense, "at" suggests but a temporary meeting place selected for the purpose of transaction.

Vincent's explanation for the use of hiding-place drops is brief and direct: "You put it in a drop so nobody knows where it is. They can't stick you with it if they can't find it." Drops for the purpose of transaction are a much more complicated matter.

"The whole idea of havin' a guy leave his stuff at a drop is so he don't know where you got it. Maybe he's tryin' to set you up or maybe he's got a tail on him. You never want to let him know where you got the swag. So you set up a drop.

"There's lots a ways to do it but if I think there's trouble I'll just have 'em leave it on the pavement. Say it's a driver and I think he might have a tail on him. I'll tell him I'll meet him at such and such a corner in my truck. When he gets there I'll tell him to just keep drivin' until I blow my horn. When I do, he stops and puts the cartons on the pavement right there and takes off. Then I park my truck and watch the load for ten minutes. Maybe I'll go in and have coffee somewhere, I dunno what I'll do. So after ten minutes if nobody stops and I see he ain't bein' tailed, out I go and pick up the stuff.

"Most of the time you don't have to worry about that stuff, but, you know, sometimes you gotta take precautions.

"Like one time—oh, this is goin' back maybe ten, twelve years—I had this guy bringin' me small appliances. Waffle irons, toasters, fry pans, you name it. I had him puttin' it in a garage I had somebody rent for me. He'd put the stuff in and I'd take it out the next day. Now this guy was a rubbish truck driver. He was workin' with a guy on the inside. Anyway, in with the rubbish every day were a few appliances. I told him any time you think you're bein' followed go straight to the dump. Don't worry about the stuff, just dump it. One night, sure enough, the company put a tail on him. He spotted them and went right by my garage to the dump. Those security guys arrested him but they couldn't make nothin' stick. On top of that, they sat all night at the dump waitin' for somebody to come pick up the stuff.

"Also, you gotta remember that when you're talkin' drops you're talkin' bulk merchandise, loads of stuff. It don't make no sense to talk about drops for jewelry. You just put it in your pocket or in a drawer somewhere.

"You wanna know where your fences get their drops, just look in the newspaper some night. Find how many garages are for rent. You send somebody there to give a phony name and for twenty bucks a month you got a drop. Hell, I musta had a hundred different drops in my life. Use one for six months, then get another one."

Although drops are a part of the mechanics of Vincent's illegitimate business, he uses them infrequently. In recent years Vincent claims that he has "quieted down." He therefore prefers to avoid deals in which the possibility of difficulty is substantial. Instead, Vincent protects himself in other ways against possible proof that he possessed particular stolen goods, most importantly by the speed with which he can sell the merchandise he receives.

"I'll tell you something. The most important thing in this business is moving the merchandise, how fast you can get rid of what you got. Look at it this way. Take your average detective. He's workin' on a case that happened two months ago. He ain't gonna get to your case for weeks. Well, maybe if he's workin' on one particular guy he's gonna be on his tail. But mostly they are so overworked they ain't gonna get to what you're doin' for weeks.

"I would say that most of my stuff is in and out inside of three hours. I get somethin' in the morning and by noon it's all gone. When it comes right down to it chances are I got it sold before the guy who owns it knows it's stolen. See, with speed like that there's no way nobody's gonna nail you.."

Another protection in the matter of possession of stolen property is the number of outlets he has for various merchandise.

"A good fence is somebody who can get rid of anything. It don't matter what it is, I can handle it. Now, me, I'm known for furs and jewelry and general merchandise mostly, but in my life I would say I've handled just about any item you could name.

"If you got the contacts that means you ain't gonna be sittin' on your merchandise no three or four days."

Finally, Vincent demands from the people who sell him stolen merchandise certain behavior patterns in the transfer of goods to him.

Store Demeanor

"You see, I school my thieves and drivers. Watch sometime when one of my boosters comes in the store. First thing he does, he puts his bag down by the front door. Then he just looks around at the shelves like he's lookin' for something to buy. When I'm ready I'll give him the OK to come over and tell me what he's got. Remember I still ain't looked at his merchandise. Maybe I'll give him a little bullshit about how I ain't interested in what he's got, but then I'll have him bring it over. See, all that time if somebody's followin' him they're gonna come in. So if I didn't buy nothin' there's nothin' nobody can do."

Use of Samples

"Now that's for a booster. With somebody who got some cartons you do it a little different. First he's gonna only show you some samples if he's got a whole load. He ain't gonna carry all the cartons in the store if he don't know you're gonna buy 'em. If the samples are what you're interested in you ask him where he's got the rest of his load. Say he got it in a truck. Well,

then you can have 'em leave it at a drop or whatever. Maybe you'll have 'em around to your loading platform. Say you do, and it's somethin' I ain't gonna sell in my store. Well, most of the time I make a call and I can have a buyer by the time he gets his truck around to the loading platform. I'll tell 'em to leave his truck there. Then, say, I make a price with him. I'll tell him tto go around the corner and get me some cigars or a cup of coffee. If the guy who I'm sellin' it to is close by, I'll have him have his truck there when the thief gets back. We load it in the other truck and the deal's over, just like that. Twenty minutes everything's finished, an' nothin' hot ever came in my store."

Marks Identifying Goods as Stolen Not Permitted in Store

"I had this guy a couple of years ago who was murder on post office trucks. He'd follow a guy 'till he went in a big office building for a delivery, then, Zap, he'd hit the truck. Now ya see with post office trucks all the packages is wrapped, so you don't know what you're gettin'. So I had to school him: you forget the big boxes right off. They ain't worth shit. What you're lookin' for is the small ones with jewelry. See, you gotta check the wrappings. The heavier the wrapping the more it's worth.

"I made him take all the wrappings off before he brought it in my store. And I made him throw 'em away, too. You don't want all those post office numbers around. After he does that he's clear. He can walk in and sell it to you with the FBI standin' right there. There ain't no problem at all."

Store Name on Carton

"Your drivers, of course, are a whole different thing entirely. First of all, I wanna make it clear and you can put this in the book like I told you: most of your drivers are honest, hard-working men with families to support. They'd never steal a thing. I have lots of drivers who bring me stuff like that. They wouldn't take nothin' but if they get an overload it comes right to me. I had that deal with some drivers goin' on fifteen years. Now they know what to do. They take off the label on the carton and just write the name of my store on it. Then they just drop it off. If they're in a rush they just come back later and I'll pay 'em then. You got a bunch of drivers like I do and they're your bread and butter. Never no trouble, no bullshit.

"[I ask if it wouldn't be better if they didn't write the store name on the carton.] What am I? What am I? A businessman, right? You know any businessmen who get cartons with no labels on 'em? No, right? He puts my name on it and it's just another delivery. No name and it's swag. Suppose I go out on the sidewalk to get it and some security's been tailin' him. What am I doin'? I'm outside my store, pickin' up a package with my name on it. If it ain't mine, it ain't mine, but I gotta open it up to find out, don't I?"

The Use of Other Fences

"I'll tell you somethin' I do which you never seen me do that's right what you're talkin' about. Say I got a guy who I ain't too sure about, but I want his merchandise. All I do is send him down to another fence and tell him to buy it for me. Like the other day I had this guy who said he knew Leggins [one of Vincent's more dependable thieves]. Now I told Leggins always, never to send anybody to me unless he checks it out with me first. So I get suspicious. Well, the guy's got three cartons of panty hose in his car and I can use it, so instead of me buyin' it direct, I tell him I can't use it but I'll make a call and see if I know somebody who can take it off his hands. So I call Red (a fence in another area of the city) and tell him to buy it from him at a certain price, and I send him down there. Then I send Tony down to pick it up. Red made twenty bucks on the deal and there wasn't no trouble. Sometimes you just get a funny feelin' about a deal so you do somethin' like that.

"[I ask why Red was willing to do that for only twenty dollars.] Well, for one thing he don't know what he's doin'. He thinks the reason I'm sendin' him down there is because we can't come to a price. See, I told him to buy it for eighty and Tony will be there with a hundred. So the thief walks in and I told him to try to get ninety offa Red. Red's only gonna give eighty and he might try to Jew him down to sixty. If he does, so what? I'm gonna give a hundred either way. So he's got a sure twenty, maybe more, for three minutes work. For a little guy like Red that adds up."

The strategies Vincent uses to avoid proof of possession of stolen property depend in large part on his legitimate business identity. That identity covers the comings and goings of vendors of stolen merchandise, who are otherwise not distinguishable from customers and legiti-mate deliverymen. It renders the moving of merchandise, the discussions of price, the examination of cargoes, and the dealings with samples all entirely normal. It makes the deposit of unattended cartons at the front or back of Vincent's store an everyday practice for Vincent in common with his wholesaler neighbors. Hence it is not only by designing elaborate pro-cedures that Vincent succeeds in frustrating at-tempts to prove his conduct illegitimate, but also by making his illegitimate conduct indistin-guishable from the normal activities of the legitimate business world. Nowhere is this more in evidence than with respect to the require-ments of the law in establishing the third ele-ment of the offense of receiving stolen property.

He Had Reason To Believe the Goods Were Stolen

Even if one can prove that a fence possesses or has possessed certain property and that that property was indeed stolen, it is still necessary to prove that at the time of purchase the fence had reasonable cause to believe the property was sto-len. This is normally determined in court by demonstrating that the price the fence paid was substantially below market levels.[8] The fence's

[8] Again I must add that my statements here are rather crude condensations of collections of statutes and rulings that are almost as diverse as the occasions of purchase they are designed to cover. The problem the law has tried to tackle is the "state of mind" implication in this element of receiving. To that end, some states have introduced statutes which imply a rebuttable presumption of guilt when the character of the buyer, seller, or goods seems suspect.

Goods: E.g. Mont. Rev. Codes Ann., sec. 94-2721; N.J. Stat. Ann. sec. 2A:139-1; N.Y. Pen. Law., sec. 165.55.

Buyer: Cal. Pen. Code, sec. 496; Idaho Code, sec. 18-1307; Mich. Comp. Laws Ann., sec. 750.535; N.Y. Pen. Law, sec. 165.55.

Seller: Mont. Rev. Codes Ann., sec. 94-2721; N.J. Stat. Ann., sec. 2A:139.1.

These attempts, however, appear to raise some serious constitutional questions about the shift such statutes effect regarding the presumption of innocence (Christie and Pye, "Presumptions and Assumptions in Criminal Law: Another View," *Duke Law Journal*, 1970, p. 919, quoted in U.S., Con-gress, Senate, Select Committee on Small Business, *An*

protection against possible proof of this element of receiving rests, therefore, on devices establishing a record of reasonable price and intending to cast doubt on the question of whether a reasonable businessman would have suspected that the goods he purchased were stolen.

"[Question to Vincent: 'Let's say you got caught red-handed. They caught the thief an hour after he sold you some stuff, they come in, it's half in the cartons, half on your shelf, the numbers match up and everything. What would you do?'

"What you need is a bill and a check. You don't even need a real billhead, any piece of paper is OK. You got that and you're home free.

Analysis of Criminal Redistribution Systems and Their Impact on Small Business, 92d Cong., 2d sess., pp. 16–17):

One of the few almost universally recognized presumptions in the State courts is the jury instruction that, in a prosecution for the knowing possession of stolen goods, knowledge that the goods are stolen may be inferred from the unexplained possession of recently stolen goods. Typically, this so-called presumption is not the result of any legislative action but merely the result of a State supreme court's approval of a jury instruction of this effect or affirmance of a conviction in which the only evidence of knowledge was the unexplained possession of recently stolen goods. The only important issue involved here is whether a sufficient rational connection exists between the unexplained possession of such stolen goods. For, whether or not the jury is instructed on the point, it is very likely to make this inference even if no specific reference is made to a presumption. Accordingly, even if all "presumptions" were struck down—[a] position that Justice Black advocated in *Turner*—because they place the burden of coming forward on the defendant and because they deny the defendant the right to have the evidence on which he may be convicted presented to the jury, the defendant is still confronted with the same dilemma. If the jury is likely to convict him on the basis of the evidence of recent possession that has been presented by the prosecution, he will have to come forward with evidence, regardless of his constitutional right to remain silent. The situation is not like that in a narcotics prosecution, where the jury is told, from unexplained possession it may infer that the narcotics were distributed in a package not bearing tax stamps or were illegally imported—something that would not ordinarily occur to the jury.

"[I ask how he gets the thief to write him a bill.] He don't write the bill, I do. I take a piece of paper and—say I buy three cartons of MacGregor sweaters, #2605—I write that on the paper. I put down the numbers and all. Then I write 'Sold to Vincent Swaggi' for say, $200, Paid in Full, check number so and so. Then I make up some phony name and tell Tony to sign it.

"[Here I ask in disbelief how the thief they just caught ends up with check number so and so?] He don't. Just listen to me for a minute, will you Carl? Then I take the check outta my book and write it up for two hundred to the phony name and Tony signs it again on the back. Then I take it down to my bank and deposit it with the rest of my stuff for that day.

"[Still lost, I ask, 'So what does that do?'] It gives me a legitimate deal, that's what it does. See, so when you get in court now you got proof you paid the right price. [Vincent looked at me and explained what he thought I should have seen instantly.] Look, I say this man came in and said his brother-in-law is going out of business and he wants to get rid of these few cases of sweaters. He knows I'm in general merchandise so he comes in to ask if I want to buy. I say yes and I make up a bill 'cause he don't have any and he signs it. Then I give him a check. He takes the check and then asks me if I'll cash it for him. I say OK and that's it. See now? I got a bill and a check which just goes in and out of my bank and I get a cancelled check, date and everything, for my receipt."

This anecdote describes a procedure which in its general form (phony bill, check to fictitious name, deposit as record of transaction, and appropriate description of the transaction in court) is a very strong defense against conviction for receiving stolen goods. Since it occupies a central place in the operations of Vincent's illegitimate dealings it is important to analyze both its limitations and its implications.

The false bill—cancelled check procedure is not applicable to all varieties and quantities of goods. For example, one would not be able to claim that a relative going out of business was interested in selling a truckload of general merchandise represented to be the remainder of his store's inventory, if the merchandise still bore price tags of a known department store. Nor could one construct an adequate explanation of this kind for possession of a truckload of liquor or other commodity that requires a special license for one to trade in it. Further, cashing a check at Vincent's store of an amount adequate to establish a reasonable purchase price on a very large quantity of merchandise would appear to be exceedingly suspect. Nevertheless, for the vast majority of general-merchandise goods in the medium quantities in which a store like Vincent's would normally trade, the false bill—cancelled check procedure creates a believable image of normal business practice.

The scheme does have a technical fault. It is the matter of two fictitious signatures, one appearing on the check, the other on the bill. There is little likelihood that they would match the handwriting of the thief. This does not seem to trouble Vincent, who claims that with just two signatures to work with, "Handwriting analysis is a bunch of baloney." Actually Vincent has produced this evidence only at preliminary hearings and at the police station, where such analysis, reliable or not, did not occur.

The fence must also have the capacity to "stand-up" under police interrogation and in court in order to carry off his story and, eventually, convince a jury that he is telling the truth.

"A fence has to be tough, somebody who can take it without falling apart, if you know what I mean. Let's face it, the cops know you bought hot stuff and they think they got a good case. So you pull some bullshit which they know is gonna get you off, they're gonna get pissed off.

Then if it goes that far and you gotta go to court, the D.A. is gonna be after you. You just gotta stick by your story, that's all, and not let it bother you."

Vincent considers his courtroom abilities one of his strongest assets and so is not troubled by the necessity for this additional skill required to work the scheme described in his anecdote.

The availability of the phony bill–cancelled check procedure may explain the rather casual way in which Vincent regards the various artifices and manipulations by which he protects his trade in stolen goods. On more than one occasion thieves have entered the store with stolen merchandise without following the procedures for store demeanor that Vincent requires. When that happens Vincent seems neither upset nor worried and more often than not he will assume the thief is in a hurry and not mention it to him. On one occasion Tony, whose job it usually is to remove stolen merchandise from cartons and then dispose of them, insisted it was one-thirty, his lunch time, and the cartons would have to wait until after he had eaten. Vincent was not pleased by this behavior on Tony's part, and although he complained about how stupid his brother was, he did not remove the cartons himself. It may credit the phony bill-cancelled check scheme with too much effect to say that it is responsible for the casual way in which Vincent occasionally takes his serious business; he also knows that less than one purchase of stolen goods in a hundred will involve any police investigation that reaches him.

But infrequent police investigation does not adequately explain Vincent's infrequent use of storage-type drops for stolen merchandise. Secret locations under fictitious names are simply not normal business procedures; if trouble developed, explaining a hidden storage area might prove to pose more problems than the advantages such an area offered. Vincent has often described to me how he sees his dealings in stolen property as having developed a certain sophistication and elegance during the years he has been working at it.

"Carl, the way I look at it, when I started out I was a ward leader; then after a while I was a politician; now I'm like a statesman. I don't have to worry about that little stuff anymore. I'm past that already." . . .

55. Loan-Sharking

JOHN M. SEIDL

DEFINING CRIMINAL LOAN-SHARKING AND ITS ILLEGAL ASPECTS

CRIMINAL LOAN-SHARKING COMPRISES THREE major elements. the first is the lending of cash at very high interest rates by individuals reputed to be connected with underworld operations. With few exceptions, interest rates are much higher than those available at legitimate lending institutions. The second element is a borrower-lender agreement which rests on the borrower's willingness to pledge his and his family's physical well-being as collateral against a loan. The corollary of the borrower's willingness is the lender's willingness to accept such collateral with its obvious collection implications. The third element is a belief by the borrower that the lender has connections with ruthless criminal organizations. The borrower is induced to repay his loans based on this reputation and his expected needs for future loans. If loan-shark reputations and future loan needs are inadequate repayment incentives, however, the lender is willing to resort to criminal means to secure repayment.

*

Interest charges which borrowers pay for loan-shark funds are not a function of supply and demand or marginal cost and marginal revenue relationships. Rather they are traditional prices which have been established over time. There is a small-loan rate which is charged by loan-sharks who work industrial plants, docks, construction sites, and neighborhoods catering to blue collar and lower middle class borrowers. Individual loans ranging from $50.00 to $1000.00 are common for these small (in capital assets) loan-sharks; an average loan is probably somewhere between $150.00 and $400.00

The street corner loan-shark racket of the 1920's and 1930's was known as the "6 for 5" racket.[1] Twenty percent continues to be an important element in the small-loan charge today. The rate in some urban areas for small-loans is 20 percent per week—"6 for 5." The interest charges—called "vig," "vigorish," or "juice" by borrowers and lenders alike—is due each week as long as the principal is outstanding. The principal can be reduced only in lump-sum or, in some cases, half-lump-sum payments.[2]

---

[1] "6 for 5" means that the interest on a five dollar loan for one week is one dollar. Thus if a borrower repays the principal and interest in one week on a five dollar loan, he repays six dollars. If he does not desire to repay the principal, he pays weekly interest which is one dollar or 20 percent per week. Turkus and Feder, 1951, pp. 120-125; Boehm, *New York Journal American*, February 19, 1940, p. 7; Stanton, *New York American*, November 7-9, 1935; "Loan-Shark Victim Driven Insane: Four More Shylocks Go to Prison," *Bronx Home News*, December 3, 1935, p. 1; People v. Faden, 271 N.Y. 435; 3 N.E. (2nd) 584 (1935); aff'd. 247 App. Div. 777; N.Y. Sup. 405 (1936).

[2] Twenty percent per week is the most common charge in some urban areas. It is not the only charge. In some cases

▶SOURCE: *Upon the Hip: A Study of the Criminal Loan Shark Industry. Ph.D. Dissertation, Harvard University, 1968, pp. 20-31, 39-40, 45-59, 88-94. (Editorial adaptations.) Also published by U.S. Department of Justice, Law Enforcement Assistance Administration, December 1969, reprinted by permission.*

[One] major element of criminal loan-sharking is the borrower-lender agreement. It is not easy to borrow money from a loan-shark. A potential borrower must first find an illegal lender. For someone acquainted with the underworld this is not a difficult task; he already knows a loan-shark or at least someone who can "steer" him to one. For an individual not acquainted with the underworld, finding a loan-shark is more difficult. He must look for a "steerer" or "shill"[3] who can introduce him to a loan-shark. "Steerers" normally work in service jobs requiring the continuous meeting of people: For example, bartenders, taxi drivers, hat check girls, elevator operators, barbers, and doormen.[4]

One can also try to find a loan-shark by first looking for a bookmaker. Normally wherever there is a "bookie," there is a loan-shark nearby to whom the "bookie" can direct a potential borrower. The advantage of beginning the search with a "bookie" is that "bookies" are more plentiful and people are more familiar with bookmaking organizations than with loan-shark organizations.[5]

Generally loan-sharks do not solicit business. Borrowers seek loan-sharks. There are exceptions to this general rule. Loan-sharks normally attend large dice and card games run by the underworld to provide losers with an on-the-spot lending service.[6] Some loan-sharks also solicit business in banks approaching potential borrowers whose loan requests have been turned down.[7]

Once a potential borrower makes the acquaintance of a loan-shark, it is still not easy to obtain a loan. For the first loan, the new borrower must have a "voucher" or guarantor. The guarantor must be known and trusted by the loan-shark. The guarantor normally guarantees only the principal in a transaction, although in some cases he may have to guarantee both interest and principal.[8] Once a loan has been suc-

borrowers can negotiate small-loans for five or ten percent per week, but this is normally on a second or succeeding loan. The important understanding is that a borrower does not shop for low lending rates. Loan-sharks do not compete for each other's customers. A variation in lending charges is a matter between borrower and lender and depends upon their personal relationship.

[3]"Steerers" or "shills" direct potential borrowers to loan-sharks. Depending upon their relationship with the loan-shark and the borrower-lender transaction that follows the introduction, "steerers" may or may not receive a "finders fee." New York State Commission of Investigation, 1965, pp. 27-28. Interviews, New York: Disbarred Attorney; Dominic; Salerno; Philadelphia: Mark; Members of the Intelligence Section; Boston: Doyle; Members of the Intelligence Section; Members of the Special Service Unit; Chicago: O'Donnell, Siragusa.

[4]Same as above.

[5]New York State Commission of Investigation, 1965, p. 35; *Burroughs Clearing House*, April 1965, p. 41. In many cases there is a business relationship between "bookies" and loan-sharks. "Bookies" have been known to sell selected customer debts to loan-sharks. They sometimes require a heavy bettor, who has "a lot on the cuff" (substantial credit bet-

ting), to borrow from a loan-shark to pay off his gambling debt. Interviews, New York: Salerno; Dominic; Jimmy; Disbarred Attorney; Cronin and Procino; Detroit: Piersante, Swartzendruber; Boston: Detective Edward Twohig, District No. 4, Boston Police Department; Members of the Special Service Unit; Members of the Intelligence Section; Chicago: Duffy, Peterson; Philadelphia: Members of the Intelligence Unit.

[6]The loan-shark at a gaming session is often referred to as "the man with the box" or "the man with the bank." Interviews, New York: Salerno; Kelly; Disbarred Attorney; Boston: Howland; Members of the Intelligence Section; Detroit: Paul Komives, attorney in a private law firm, formerly Assistant U.S. Attorney and Counsel for a One Man Grand Jury of Wayne County that investigated criminal organizations; Piersante; Chicago: O'Donnell.

[7]This is a prevalent practice in the New York garment district owing to the seasonal nature of garment manufacturing, the small capital stock of most firms, and the need for cash to meet payrolls, suppliers, etc. One loan-shark would get "a nod of the head or a wave of the hand" from a bank official to indicate a potential borrower in immediate need of cash who had been refused credit by the bank. New York State Commission of Investigation, 1965, pp. 68-70. Interviews, New York: Tyler; Disbarred Attorney.

[8]Infrequently the guarantor is required to pay off a loan when the actual borrower leaves the area or makes himself unavailable in some other manner. Interviews, New York: Disbarred Attorney; Jimmy; Dominic; Philadelphia: Mark; Kevin; Thomas; Ted. All law enforcement officials interviewed pointed out the need for a guarantor on the initial loan from a loan-shark.

cessfully negotiated and all or a part of it repaid, the borrower has established his credit with the loan-shark; a guarantor is no longer needed for second and successive loans.[9]

The amount of money a loan-shark desires to or is able to lend a borrower varies. It can be a function of the loan-shark's personality, his evaluation of the borrower's repayment capabilities, or the organizational constraints imposed upon him. Some loan-sharks arbitrarily decide, without reliance upon meaningful economic facts, what amount they will lend a customer.[10] Some loan-shark organizations run credit and asset checks on potential borrowers. They can accomplish this, with connections, through legitimate credit channels; or the organization can attempt to make the check with its own resources. Credit checks are run most often in large-loan transactions when portions of a business are offered as collateral.[11]

Many loan-sharks will lend only that amount which they believe a borrower can afford to repay. They determine repayment capabilities based upon the borrower's income or his expected profits as a result of the loan.[12] Some loan-sharks attempt to lend the borrower a little more than he can afford to repay so that he becomes "hooked." The "hooked" borrower is continually in debt to the loan-shark. Oftentimes the size of a customer's weekly payment to the loan-shark requires that he borrow new money on payday to supplement his already depleted earnings. Some borrowers are never able to repay the principal, because weekly interest payments make saving for the principal payment impossible.[13]

[9]Same as above.

[10]Interviews, New York: Disbarred Attorney.

[11]New York State Commission of Investigation, 1965, p. 29. Interviews, New York: Dominic; Detroit: Olzlewski and DePugh; Cleveland: Successful Defense Attorney; Boston: Members of the Intelligence Section; Members of the Special Service Unit.

[12]Interviews, New York: Dominic; Jimmy; Philadelphia: Mark; Ted; Thomas; Kevin; Cleveland: Successful Defense Attorney.

[13]Interviews, New York: Salerno; Kelly; Cronin and Procino; Winthers; Chicago: Duffy; O'Donnell; Siragusa.

There is never any misunderstanding between the loan-shark and the borrower about their relationship or the collateral for the loan. Seldom does any paper pass between borrower and lender;[14] a handshake usually confirms the bargain. The borrower realizes that he is offering his body and his family's well-being as collateral. He must understand, if he seeks the loan-shark and then secures the proper guarantor. Loan-sharks usually make the relationship clear in their first meeting with a potential borrower. In some cases the underlying threat is communicated subtly; in other cases it is made explicitly clear.[15]

[Another] major element of criminal loan-sharking is the collection process. Two important generalizations must be discussed before turning to the more detailed aspects of collection procedures. A loan-shark organization's reputation for violence and ruthlessness is the most important factor inducing borrowers to repay their loans.[16] An organization's reputation may stem from a number of things; but

[14]Paper does pass between the borrower and lender on rare occasions. A loan-shark in Philadelphia always required new borrowers to give him a check made out to cash for the total principal on the first loan; this was in addition to the okay of a guarantor. The checks were seldom cashed. They served as a continual inducement to borrowers to make their payments. Interviews, Philadelphia: Davis; Mark; Ted; Kevin; Thomas.

[15]The Disbarred Attorney (Interviews, New York) told the author that his partner left no misunderstanding about the collateral that the borrower was putting up. He explained the possibility of beatings should there be collection problems. The borrowers in Philadelphia (Interviews, Philadelphia) all said that their loan-shark matter-of-factly warned them when he handed them money, "If you can't make the payments, don't take the money." Everyone the author interviewed regarding loan-sharking agreed that there is never any misunderstanding in the borrower-lender agreement about collateral.

[16]This point was emphasized by all the individuals interviewed by the author. The borrowers stressed that repayment was a function of a loan-shark's reputation and their anticipated needs for future loans. Interviews, New York: Jimmy; Philadelphia: Mark; Kevin; Thomas; Ted. Dominic and the Disbarred Attorney (Interviews, New York) stressed this point emphasizing that the loan-shark works hard to establish and maintain his reputation which is his key collection tool. All the law enforcement officials interviewed also

from the borrower's viewpoint reputation is a function of two perceptions—of the loan-shark from whom he borrows and of the organizational structure and operational methods of the loan-shark industry.[17]

There are a number of important factors which affect a borrower's perceptions of his loan-shark. The physique, appearance, and demonstrated or rumored physical prowess of the loan-shark and his associates are important factors.[18] Arms carried by the loan-shark and his associates as well as their demonstrated or rumored willingness to use them are important factors.[19] Foreboding qualities about the loan-shark's temperament, character, or attitudes that are made known directly or indirectly to the borrower affect his perception of the loan-shark from whom he borrows.[20] Finally, the loan-shark's connections with criminal organizations, whether they be real or imagined, are an important ingredient in the borrower's perception of his loan-shark.[21]

A borrower's perception of the loan-shark industry is the second important factor in the establishment of a reputation. This perception hinges on the borrower's previous contacts with the underworld and his exposure to criminal organizations and their enforcement methods through communications media.[22] If the reputation is formidable, it makes the loan-shark's job easy by removing many of his potential collection problems.[23]

A second important generalization about the collection process is that the use of actual violence is minimized. Potential violence causing fear and anxiety is utilized whenever necessary to motivate delinquent borrowers. Actual violence can become counter-productive from an organizational standpoint, however, for it may bring increased scrutiny of loan-shark activities by public, law enforcement, or underworld elements. It also hampers lending profitability. It makes repayment more difficult for the individual who is victimized and discourages new or continued borrowing from customers who now view the risks of borrowing differently.[24]

---

agreed that reputation was a loan-shark organization's greatest asset in the collection process.

[17]Interviews, New York: Dominic; Jimmy; Disbarred Attorney; Philadelphia: Ted; Kevin; Thomas; Mark.

[18]Law enforcement officials and other people acquainted with the underworld interviewed by the author maintained that loan-shark associates who act as enforcers reveal their trade merely by presenting themselves. It is probable that if violence is required in the collection process enforcers not known to the borrowers will be used. Associates of loan-sharks, nevertheless, are chosen for their appearance as well as their skill to insure that implicit and explicit threats are as effective as possible. Interviews, New York: Salerno; Disbarred Attorney; Kelly; Chicago: Siragusa; Duffy; O'Donnell; Boston: Doyle; McClain; Members of the Intelligence Section; Detroit: Piersante; Olzlewski and DePugh.

[19]A loan-shark organization was lending money in a large book binding factory in New York. The plant had two shifts and a different loan-shark worked each shift. The loan-shark who worked days was about six foot four inches tall and weighed 260 pounds. He utilized his physical appearance and rumored toughness to establish his reputation. The loan-shark who worked nights was a slightly built individual who carried a Beretta; this was the subject of many rumors within the plant and was instrumental in establishing his reputation. In addition, it was rumored that the loan-sharks were connected with a large-scale criminal organization headquartered in Greenwich Village. Interviews, New York: Members of the C.I.B.

[20]Interviews, New York: Disbarred Attorney; Salerno; Kelly; Cronin and Procino; Detroit: Olzlewski and DePugh; Boston: Howland; Doyle; Chicago: Siragusa; O'Donnell.

[21]See n. 3, p. 51. The Philadelphia borrowers (Interviews, Philadelphia) all pointed out that they personally liked the brothers who who loaned them money; however, a third brother, rumored to an be important member of the large-scale criminal organization in South Philadelphia, was supposedly backing the other two brothers. This rumor helped to establish a fearsome reputation for the loan-shark brothers. The importance of underworld connections in the establishment of a reputation was pointed out by most of the law enforcement officials interviewed by the author.

[22]The borrowers interviewed by the author all referred to the ruthless violent enforcement methods of loan-sharks as an accepted fact. When questioned about their own knowledge of these enforcement methods, they all cited newspapers, magazines, rumors, etc., to support their beliefs. Typical of their answers was, "Everybody knows about loan-sharks and the way they operate." Interviews, New York: Jimmy; Philadelphia: Mark; Thomas; Kevin; Ted.

One borrower was aware of these methods from firsthand experience as a result of repayment troubles. Interviews, New York: Jimmy.

[23]Same as n. 2, p. 50.

[24]Interviews, New York: Salerno; Kelly; Disbarred Attor-

The detailed aspects of the collection process can be described in terms of six steps.[25] The first step is the weekly payment meeting between the borrower and the lender. These meetings are on the same day every week, sometimes at a specific time. The meetings not only provide for the collection of payments, but they also establish borrower-lender rapport.[26] Some loan-sharks are not interested in establishing a special relationship with their borrowers. In these cases, payments may be made at a drop with no meeting between borrower and lender.[27]

---

ney; Dominic; Detroit: Olzlewski and DePugh; Piersante; Boston: Howland; Doyle; McClain; Members of the Intelligence Section; Members of the Special Service Unit; Philadelphia: Rizzo; Members of the Intelligence Section; Cleveland: Elden Meyers, Chief, Intelligence Division, Cleveland District Office, Internal Revenue Service; Providence: Stone.

Chicago is an exception to the rule of minimum violence. Chicago loan-sharks are more violent than the loan-sharks in any of the other cities visited by the author. They are much quicker to explicitly threaten delinquent borrowers and to resort to physical beating in the collection process. Peterson, *A Report on Chicago Crime for 1965*, 1966, p. 99; "River" and "Stone" Cases, Files of the Intelligence Division, Chicago Police Department; Statement of loan-shark victim to a State's Attorney, October 18, 1963, Files of the Intelligence Division, Chicago Police Department. Sandy Smith, *Chicago Sun Times*, November 18, 1965, pp. 3-4; "Loan-Shark Gang Bared in Chicago," *New York Times*, January 16, 1966; Illinois Crime Investigating Commission, *Report of the Proceedings Held and Evidence Taken at a Hearing Before the above Entitled Commission*, January 1966, three volumes. Interviews, Chicago: Duffy; Siragusa; O'Donnell.

[25] The six steps are a general characterization of the collection process in as a comprehensive a manner as possible. They are analogous to the steps on an escalation ladder in any type of dispute. Every collection dispute need not include all six steps nor does each step have to take place as described. There are a number of factors which shape the specifics of a collection situation. Especially important factors include: The borrower, the lender, the loan-shark organization, the underworld, and the sum of money involved.

[26] New York Commission of Investigation, *Testimony of Public Hearing Loan Shark Investigation*, December 1964; Illinois Crime Investigating Commission, January 1966. Interviews, New York: Disbarred Attorney; Dominic; Jimmy; Salerno; Detroit: Piersante; Olzlewski and DePugh.

[27] Statement of loan-shark victim to a State's Attorney, October 18, 1963, Files of the Intelligence Division, Chicago Police Department. Interviews, Philadelphia: Ted; Thomas.

The first step in the collection process is the only step that many borrowers are personally acquainted with. Should they miss a weekly payment, however, they will become aware of the second step. A loan-shark moves quickly to establish contact with a delinquent borrower reminding him of his obligation. The type of reminder is not standard and depends upon the size of the loan outstanding, the borrower's previous record, and the loan-shark's psyche. Reminders at this stage are usually pleasant, but the loan-shark does penalize the borrower for his tardiness. Normally the penalty is a fine which is added to the already late payment. In some cases, a loan-shark will fine a borrower by increasing the principal.[28]

Harassment is the third step and likely the first aggressive action the loan-shark takes to induce repayment from delinquent borrowers. This can take the form of a continuously ringing telephone at the borrower's home in the early morning hours or constant telephone interruptions at work. It can include circumstances contrived by the loan-shark to embarrass the borrower in public.[29]

Implicit threats are used next to induce re-

[28] New York State Commission of Investigation, December 1964, pp. 38-43, 124-135, 136-162, 164-192, 378-416; Illinois Crime Investigating Commission, January 1966; "Stone," "Farm," and "River" Cases, Files of the Intelligence Division, Chicago Police Department. Interviews, New York: Disbarred Attorney; Dominic; Jimmy; Members of the C.I.B.; Salerno; Detroit: Piersante; Olzlewski and DePugh; Boston: Doyle; McClain; Members of the Intelligence Section; Members of the Special Service Unit; Providence: Stone.

[29] A large-loan loan-shark in New York would harass his delinquent customers unmercifully after they had missed one or, at the most, two payments. He would do anything to infuriate the borrower, so he would pay just to get the loan-shark off his back. The loan-shark would spit in a delinquent borrower's face in public, call him vile names in front of his wife, or ring his doorbell or phone in the early hours of the morning. Interviews, New York: Disbarred Attorney. Also New York State Commission of Investigation, December 1964; Illinois Crime Investigating Commission, January 1966. Interviews, New York: Salerno; Kelly; Dominic; Jimmy; Philadelphia: Kevin; Thomas; Boston: Members of the Special Service Unit; McClain.

payment. The loan-shark accompanied by enforcers, whose appearances easily reveal their occupations, may visit a delinquent borrower's home or place of employment. Phone calls are made to members of the borrower's family. Callers simply state their name and ask that the borrower be reminded of a specific appointment which is important if business troubles are to be averted. General demonstrations of violence are also used by loan-sharks. The demonstration is not directed specifically at a borrower, but rumors circulate which indicate that the violence was the work of a loan-shark or his associate.[30]

Explicit threats directed at various aspects of the borrower's psyche are the fifth step in an escalating collection process. Usually the borrower is threatened with violence against his own person or against his family, relatives, or property. The language is raw and vulgar frequently communicated to a wife who is unaware of her husband's borrowing. The threats portend property destruction, physical beatings, accidents, torture, or death.[31]

Sometimes loan-shark organizations use demonstrations of violence to explicitly threaten a delinquent borrower. A bombing or a fire preceded by a warning and followed by threatening pressure is an effective method.[32] Oftentimes loan-shark organizations will claim responsibility for underworld violence which is none of their doing; they adopt it and utilize it skillfully

as a demonstration of their willingness to act violently when sufficiently provoked.[33]

Some loan-shark organizations use a class "B" movie technique to threaten victims. They pick up a delinquent borrower and take him "for a ride" in a big black cadillac or its equivalent. Usually the destination is the waterfront. Here the borrower is verbally threatened as well.[34] When violence is required, loan-sharks often use it to explicitly threaten other customers. If a delinquent borrower is beaten, other borrowers may be required to observe the result of the enforcer's treatment.[35]

Actual violence, the sixth step, is used when loan-shark organizations feel that a borrower is *not trying* to meet his obligations. A key consideration is the size of the outstanding loan; for at some point, especially in the large-loan business, the loan-shark must consider the credibility of his own reputation and that of his organization.[36]

Violence related to delinquent borrowers' repayment problems can be very harsh and painful. The weapons most often used are enforcers' fists and feet. Other weapons used are iron pipes, brass knuckles, baseball bats, bicycle chains, sledge hammers, and razor blades.[37] Most loan-shark violence involves physical beating which may or may not be severe enough to include broken limbs. The intentional murder

---

[30]New York State Commission of Investigation, December 1964; Illinois Crime Investigating Commission, January 1966. Interviews, New York: Dominic; Jimmy; Salerno; Disbarred Attorney; Detroit: Olzlewski and DePugh; Boston: McClain; Doyle; Chicago: Siragusa; O'Donnell; Providence: Stone.

[31]Same as n. 1, p. 55. Also *Burrough's Clearing House*, April 1965, p. 41. Typical threats include showing the borrower two sticks of dynamite and telling him his house will be blown up without regard to his wife and children; or warning the victim that his daughter may have an accident on her way home from school. "Two Plead Not Guilty to Loan-Shark Charges," *Boston Herald*, October 28, 1966, p. 12.

[32]New York State Commission of Investigation, December 1964, pp. 494-504; Interviews, New York: Salerno; Detroit: Piersante; Boston: Doyle; Providence: Stone.

[33]Interviews, Detroit: Olzlewski and DePugh; Boston: Howland; Doyle; Members of the Intelligence Section.

[34]Interviews, Detroit: Olzlewski and DePugh.

[35]Statement of loan-shark victim to a State's Attorney, October 18, 1963, Files of the Intelligence Division, Chicago Police Department. Interviews, Chicago: O'Donnell; Boston: Doyle.

[36]Interviews, New York: Jimmy; Dominic; Salerno; Disbarred Attorney; Detroit: Piersante; Olzlewski and DePugh; Boston: Doyle; Members of the Special Service Unit; Members of the Intelligence Section; Philadelphia: Mark; Thomas; Kevin.

[37]Sandy Smith, *Chicago Sun Times*, November 18, 1965, p. 3; *Burrough's Clearing House*, April 1965, p. 41; "Enforcers Back Up Loan Sharks," *Boston Globe*, March 17, 1963, p. 1; Illinois Crime Investigating Commission, January 1966. Interviews, Chicago: Siragusa; Duffy; O'Donnell.

of delinquent borrowers, however, is extremely rare.[38]

Throughout any period of payment delinquency, a loan-shark continues to increase the repayment burdens of an already overburdened borrower with the assessment of fines. There are provisions within most large-scale criminal organizations for adjudication in cases where the borrower *strongly* feels that the loan-shark's claims are completely out of proportion to what is owed. These disputes normally arise after interest payments have been made for a long time and total much more than the original principal. A "sit-down" or meeting is held presided over by an underworld figure of greater recognized importance than any of the participants to the dispute. He arbitrates the dispute normally prescribing a lump sum settlement to be paid by the borrower within a given time period.[39]

*

Rationed borrowers desire more credit in the upperworld than legitimate lending institutions are willing to supply or than they think legitimate lending institutions are willing to supply. In either case, they turn to loan-sharks to supplement their credit needs. Some rationed borrowers are unaware of the legitimate lending alternatives available to them. Thus they do not fully exploit upperworld lending possibilities.[40]

Other rationed borrowers are aware of legitimate alternatives but fail to contact lending agencies. They believe their requests will not receive favorable consideration.[41] Most rationed borrowers, however, do not possess the required creditworthiness, based upon present lending laws and practices, to secure the loan they desire.[42] Unrationed borrowers, on the other hand, can secure needed credit in either the upperworld or the underworld. They borrow from loan-sharks because of the peculiar lending service offered.[43]

The peculiar lending service offered by loan-sharks is an important factor which stimulates loan demand among rationed and unrationed borrowers. It s importance is easier to isolate in unrationed borrower demand, because it is obvious that these individuals borrow from a loan-shark due to the lending service he offers.[44] The service also entices rationed borrowers who not only appreciate the availability of funds but the convenient lending methods of loan-shark organizations. Many rationed bor-

[38]Interviews, New York: Disbarred Attorney; Salerno; Kelly; Detroit: Olzlewski and DePugh; Piersante, Boston: Doyle; Members of the Special Service Unit; Members of the Intelligence Section; Chicago: O'Donnell; Duffy.

[39]Testimony of Assistant District Attorney Frank Rogers, New York State Commission of Investigation, December 1964, pp. 46-47. Interviews, New York: Disbarred Attorney; Salerno; Kelly; Detroit: Piersante.

[40]Some borrowers do not know the lending alternatives available to them; some do not visit every legitimate lending institution that is available. If a borrower is turned down once or twice, he probably assumes that he will be turned down by all lending institutions. Yet there is a percentage of rationed borrowers who could have secured needed credit in the upperworld if they had explored completely all possible upperworld alternatives. Large-loan borrowers are less likely to be unaware of lending alternatives than small-loan borrowers because of their different educational and occupational backgrounds. Interviews, New York: Disbarred Attorney.

[41]This seems reasonable especially if in the past borrowers have had questionable credit ratings or unpleasant experiences with lending institutions. One large-loan and one small-sloan borrower interviewed by the author borrowed from loan-sharks because each believed his request for money from legitimate lending institutions would not receive favorable consideration. It also should be noted that they preferred the loan-shark lending service to upperworld lending techniques. Interviews, Philadelphia: Mark; Thomas.

[42]Most law enforcement officials interviewed believed that loan-shark borrowers were predominantly poor credit risks who borrowed in the underworld because they could not secure credit elsewhere. Of the three small-loan borrowers interviewed by the author, only one admitted that he had initially borrowed from loan-sharks because he believed he could not secure credit at legitimate lending institutions owing to his creditworthiness. Interviews, Philadelphia: Thomas.

Large-loan borrowers, on the other hand, are predominantly rationed borrowers who are unable to secure loans because of upperworld lending institutions' creditworthiness criteria. Interviews, New York: Jimmy; Dominic; Disbarred Attorney.

[43]Interviews, New York: Jimmy; Dominic, Philadelphia: Mark, Thomas; Ted; Kevin.

[44]Interviews, Philadelphia: Ted; Kevin; Mark; Thomas.

rowers would not pay the loan-shark charges for an unduly formal and complex lending service.[45]

Four important characteristics comprise the loan-shark lending service. The importance of each characteristic varies with individual borrowers. The first characteristic is (a) secrecy. No one needs to know about the loan including the borrower's family, his neighbors, his employers, or his creditors.[46]

(b) Second, the loan is made on an informal basis.[47] the borrower is not kept waiting[48] or interviewed by "stuffy" or "pompous" loan officials. He is not required to fill out long complicated forms which is particularly embarrassing for individuals without language facility. Secret screening of a borrower's credit history or personal background is unusual in a small-loan transaction and not too common in large-loan transactions. The borrower is seldom subjected to an overt credit investigation among his friends, neighbors, fellow employees, or employers. The loan-shark borrower does not require a formal co-signer, nor does the borrower need to offer material collateral usually required by institutional lenders.[49]

Third, the loan is made quickly and conveniently.[50] The speed with which one is able to secure a loan depends upon one's previous dealings with a loan-shark. Customers who have successfully borrowed from a loan-shark can secure successive loans quickly. Those who have underworld connections will not find it too difficult to negotiate an initial loan. Customers without underworld connections will find securing an initial loan more troublesome. The convenience factors are almost always present in a loan-shark transaction. Proceeds of the loan are cash and usually made available to the borrower immediately. Oftentimes the loan-shark comes to the borrower, visiting his place of business or neighborhood.[51] Seldom does a borrower have to travel far to meet his loan-shark. Hours of operation are not a problem; loan-sharks lend money every day and night of the week.[52] Many

---

[45]Interviews, New York: Jimmy; Philadelphia: Thomas.

[46]The importance of secrecy was stressed by all loan-shark borrowers interviewed. Interviews, New York: Jimmy; Philadelphia: Ted; Kevin; Thomas. In some cases, there was a desire to hide spending habits; in other cases, there was a desire to hide a thin week in sales and commissions. One small businessman desired to hide the regular purchase of new inventory from his wife. Interviews, Philadelphia: Mark.

[47]The informal aspects of the loan-shark service were emphasized as an important positive feature by all borrowers interviewed. One unrationed borrower, who claimed he could have negotiated a loan with either a bank or a finance company, just did not like to go through the red tape involved in borrowing in the upperworld. Interviews, Philadelphia: Kevin; Thomas; Mark; Ted; New York: Jimmy.

[48]Allen Jung concluded in a study of personal finance company attitudes toward borrowers that there ". . .was [a] desire of loan representatives to keep prospective borrowers waiting in a private office." The reasons for using this tactic against borrowers was not clear. Jung concluded that loan officials probably believed that waiting had a psychological effect upon the borrower which increased the chances of negotiating a profitable loan. Jung also pointed out that attitudes among loan officials in banks were "completely different." Jung, *Public Opinion Quarterly*, Fall 1961, pp. 414-416.

[49]The informal aspects were of special interest to the author, for it appears that borrowers preferred to honor an informal commitment rather than a formal one. All the borrowers interviewed believed they had incurred an obligation to pay their loan-shark, because the loan-shark had provided them with an important service. The loan-shark had taken a definite risk lending money on a handshake while minimizing red tape. This obligation to pay was in addition to repayment motivations induced by loan-shark reputations and borrowers' anticipated needs for future loans. Small-loan borrowers believed it would be easier to discuss repayment troubles; as a result of sickness, family problems, or loss of work; with their loan-shark than with an impersonal credit department or lending agency. Large-loan borrowers believed their obligation stemmed from the risk taken by a loan-shark when he lends large sums so informally. They held factors in special contempt because of their reputedly high interest charges yet their unwillingness to accept risk by completely tying up a debtors' assets. Interviews, New York: Jimmy; Dominic; Philadelphia: Mark; Thomas; Kevin; Ted.

[50]The loan-shark borrowers interviewed by the author stressed speed and convenience as important components of the loan-shark lending service. All the borrowers were regular customers, so they could obtain their loans quickly and easily. Interviews, New York: Jimmy; Philadelphia: Mark; Kevin; Ted; Thomas.

[51]Interviews, Philadelphia: Mark; Ted; Thomas; Kevin.

[52]One borrower told a story of being in a night club in

loan-sharks even simplify repayment proce-dures for borrowers by personally collecting from them on payday.

Mark, an antique dealer and loan-shark bor-rower, illlustrated the convenient nature of loan-shark borrowing. When he read or heard about a sale that he wanted to attend, he would call his loan-shark and ask to meet him at the corner of 15th and Chestnut Streets in downtown Philadelphia. Mark could request that the meeting take place within an hour or within a week depending upon the cir-cumstances. The loan-shark would arrive as re-quested, hand Mark an envelope with the needed cash, and Mark would go on to the sale.

It is interesting that Mark seldom checked the contents of the envelope. He was certain he could trust his loan-shark.[53]

The fourth important characteristic of the loan-shark lending service is the regular availa-bility of funds. Loan-sharks provide a continu-ous source of available cash for borrowers who meet their repayment schedules. The borrower does not need to worry about the effect of tight money on his borrowing potential, nor need he worry over the frequency of his borrowing. As long as he meets his payments, the loan-shark is willing to keep him supplied with loans.[54]

North Philadelphia; he was somewhat drunk. It was 11:30 p.m. a few days before Christmas. Outside it had been snow-ing since late afternoon. He had run out of money and cal-led his loan-shark. The loan-shark came out in the snow from South Philadelphia to lend the borrower $200 on the spot. The borrower told the author, "I would gladly pay $40 interest over 10 weeks for a service like that. Where else could I borrow $200 at that time of night under those condi-tions?" Interviews, Philadelphia: Thomas.

[53]Interviews, Philadelphia: Mark.

[54]Availability was emphasized by all borrowers inter-viewed. Two borrowers admitted that easy avail-ability meant they borrowed more money than they needed or would have borrowed if it had been harder to negotiate a loan. One stated that he stayed in debt to the loan-shark when he knew he was the only one in the au-tomobile agency borrowing. He believed that if he stopped borrowing the loan-shark would stop visiting the agency and he would "lose his angel." Interviews, Philadelphia: Kevin; Thomas; Ted; Mark; New York: Jimmy.

56. The Numbers Game

FUND FOR THE CITY OF NEW YORK

IN THE NUMBERS GAME'S MOST POPULAR FORM, A player chooses any three-digit number from 000 through 999. The player thus has one chance in 1,000 of winning. In New York City, a winner is paid off at advertised odds of 500 to one in some games, 600 to one in others. *Betting on numbers is not an offense under the penal law, but the operation of a numbers game is.*

The winning number is determined by betting totals or payoff odds on selected races at horse racing tracks. Belmont or Aqueduct results are used during their season. At other times of the year, those of Florida's Hialeah or Maryland's Pimlico and Bowie are used. Since the tracks are closed on Sunday, numbers are played six days a week.

Two systems are used to determine the winner. The "Brooklyn" number is simply the last three digits of the track's total parimutuel handle for the day.

The more widely-used "New York" number is more complicated and combines the payoff odds for win, place and show horses in the first seven races. The first digit is calculated after the third race, the second after the fifth race and the last after the seventh. For this reason, betting the New York number is sometimes called playing "3-5-7".

The New York number was introduced because bettors feared that operators might be able to fix the simpler Brooklyn number. But the New York number also makes possible two variations of the standard bet:

Bolida, a wager on the first two or the last two digits of the final winning number.

Single Action, a separate bet on each digit as it is calculated.

These side bets give players a chance to make several wagers each day, and bets on one or two-digit numbers vastly improve a player's chances of winning—although at a lower payout.

Table A. Odds of Winning and Payout Odds

	Three Number Bet	Bolida	Single Action
Odds of winning	1 in 1,000	1 in 100	1 in 10
Payout	600 500 } to 1	60 to 1	7 to 1

Players can further increase their winning opportunities by betting a "combination" (i.e., betting on any of their three-digits' possible combinations). A bettor who "combinates" or "boxes" a number has six chances to win. The payout is reduced correspondingly: a six-way combination payout is 100 to one. If a player

▶SOURCE: *Legal Gambling in New York. New York: The Fund for the City of New York, 1972, pp. 20–34. (Editorial adaptations.) Reprinted by permission.*

boxes a number in which two of the digits are the same (such as 484), there are only three chances to win and the payout odds should be 200 to one. Banks, however, are often able to pay out at the six-way odds of 100 to one.

While banks advertise that they pay $500 or $600 on a winning $1 bet, winners actually receive less. Players traditionally tip their runner ten percent of any prize. In some areas, runners deduct this tip automatically. More often, tipping is voluntary, but goodwill between player and runner is important so tips are usually paid. Tipping alone cuts net winnings to $450 or $540 on a $1 numbers wager.

Prizes are reduced even further by the practice of "cutting" popular numbers. In this case, the advertised payout is usually 400 to one. Many numbers can be included. Round hundreds are generally cut, along with triple digits (000, 111, 222, etc.). So are traditionally lucky numbers such as 711 and numbers that could be played as a hunch by many bettors (e.g., the batting average of a baseball hero or the number 317 on St. Patrick's Day, March 17). Some banks issue printed cards listing cut numbers for the week, but most players learn of them by word of mouth.

Number cutting is a protective device. The operator of a conventional lottery makes sure of a random distribution of numbers by selling serially-numbered tickets, so that he can predict with perfect accuracy how many players will win. A race track's parimutuel odds are established by the amount of money wagered on each horse, so that the track makes money no matter how many bettors pick the winning horse. Numbers operators, on the other hand, pay off at fixed odds and cannot control the number of winners. On any given day, therefore, they can lose heavily. For this reason, they cut heavily played numbers so that they will have to pay less if these numbers win. Number cutting, however, can be used by the operator to boost his profits as well as to protect himself against losses. . . .

To learn the winning number, it is a simple matter for bettors on the Brooklyn number to look up the last three digits of the parimutuel handle in any newspaper. While the process is more complicated, players can also calculate the New York number as race results come in over the radio or later from newspaper charts. This is seldom necessary, however. In areas where numbers are played regularly, word of the winning number circulates quickly. People can be seen holding up fingers as they pass one another in the street, and some stores post the winning number in their windows.

Winners are sometimes paid off the same evening, but usually they collect the following day. Runners may station themselves in a prominent place to make payoffs. Winning customers are good publicity for a runner. And the presence of a runner disbursing prize money is good for business in a bar or restaurant.

If disputes arise between runners and their customers, neither party has recourse to the courts and there is no formal system for settlement. Ultimately the bank must decide whether it will pay, but there is no evidence that many players are dissatisfied enough to abandon the game. When a player claims that his runner has failed to record a winning bet, the bank may consult its records for the previous week. If the winning number is one that the bettor has customarily played in the past, the bank may agree that the runner has erred. But it will usually settle for half the amount claimed.

The most distinctive characteristic of the numbers game is the player's freedom to pick the number on which he bets. While all numbers have an equal chance to win, most players bet on numbers that have some personal significance. A variety of publications touting lucky numbers are available, and some newspapers carry cartoon tips.

Many bettors select their numbers on the basis of dreams. This does not mean that a number is involved in the dream. But for a dollar or two, a player can buy a book that assigns a number to almost any dream character or situation.

One publication, *Rajah's Lucky Number-Dream Book*, includes these suggestions:

Sniffing	584
Doctor	734
Doctoress	896
News—bad	453
News—good	112
Money	402

Once they have picked a lucky number, players often continue to bet it for weeks or months. Control over selection of a number is essential to most players, a fact that must be kept in mind in any attempt to design a competitive legal game, whatever complications it may entail.

Numbers are played in offices, factories and residential areas. Two-thirds of all players bet in their home neighborhoods, although law enforcement officials believe that more money may be wagered in factories and offices. Since three fourths of all players are employed, most of the action in neighborhood games takes place early in the day as bettors leave for work.

Players place their bets with a runner or collector, who may operate on the street or in a neighborhood bar, store or other business place. Many runners are stationary. Some are operators of legitimate retail businesses who accept bets as a sideline, either as a service to customers or a source of added income.

In office games, numbers bets are frequently collected by service employees such as messengers, elevator operators, sandwich delivery men and newsstand dealers. In factories, union shop stewards often take numbers bets. Not only do they enjoy freedom of movement in the plant, but they are in a position to interfere with other workers who try to act as collectors.

The numbers organization is a three-tiered pyramid. There are many runners and collectors at the bottom. They report to a much smaller number of controllers on the next level. Controllers are the agents or associates of a relative handful of bankers at the top. The functions of runner, controller and banker are roughly analogous to those of salesman, district manager and president of a legitimate business. While there are variations among individual numbers organizations, depending on size, area and the style of the operators, the following descriptions are typical:

RUNNERS, the most exposed agents of the game, deal directly with bettors and take the greatest risks with the law. For this reason, they are paid a commission of 25 percent of their receipts. They may also receive, as a fringe benefit, bail and legal counsel in case of arrest. Runners can make a great deal of money, but they are low-level employees.

A runner may operate from a stationary place of business or, if he is a mobile salesman, have a "turf" in which he enjoys exclusive rights. His turf may be a geographic area or a particular group of customers. The desirability of a geographic turf depends on the density of players. Hence offices and factories are highly prized.

In a neighborhood game, a runner may spend his early morning hours accepting bets from players on their way to work. If he works full time as a runner, he may then go from shop to shop taking wagers directly or collecting from sub-agents. In apartment buildings, a tenant may collect bets for him. If a mobile runner is worried about the police, he may operate in hallways where he is less conspicuous.

The perfect runner, as Malcolm X described him in his autobiography, retains all bets in his head. In fact, runners usually keep a coded record. Before the day's first winning number is selected, the runner must turn in this record and the money received to his controller, either directly or by means of a prearranged drop. If a runner turns in his work late, the bank may refuse to pay off his winners, since conceivably they could have learned the first digit of the winning number before betting—significantly improving their chances.

A runner may bank some of his own bets. Single action, for example, is seldom financed by a bank. A runner who risks keeping some of his regular bets, however, can find himself in serious trouble if he is hit heavily.

The traditional belief is that runners furnish three important extra services to their customers: traveling to players to collect their bets; allowing players to bet on credit; and making loans for purposes other than betting on numbers. The Quayle survey found that these services are offered and used far less frequently than they are popularly assumed to be. Only one-third of all players enjoy personal collection service. Fewer than one in five ever bets on credit. And a mere nine percent borrow from runners. Almost all of those who receive such services, moreover, are larger bettors.

CONTROLLERS are of two types. A few "spot" controllers deal directly with bettors, acting as both runner and controller and collecting both commissions. The controller's share is five percent of total receipts. These controllers usually employ, for a flat wage, lookouts, "streeters" (local people who steer recognized residents to the spot controller's frequently-changing location) and "writers" who record bets.

The more typical controller collects bets and money from his runners and turns them over to his bank before the start of the third race. This intricate operation, designed to protect the game's security, must be carried out swiftly. As the runner insulates the controller from the police, the controller acts as a buffer shielding the banker.

Security measures are an essential element in the controller's operation. Betting slips are placed in sealed envelopes marked with his code identification. If his organization is paying protection money to the police, that fact may also be indicated by code. When such envelopes are seized in a raid, they are to be returned to the controller. The transfer of slips and cash to the bank may be hedged with elaborate precautions. The bank's pickup man, often with a car or taxi waiting, makes a quick stop to collect from the controller or a prearranged drop. Timing is important, especially when an unprotected drop is involved. Because pickup men can provide the police department with a good lead to the banker, decoys or relay teams are frequently used to foil pursuers.

Betting slips must be transferred daily, but controllers may retain some or all of the money collected. Some is used to pay off winners and only the profits are transferred, as infrequently as once a week.

BANKERS, acting either as affiliated entrepreneurs or as member-agents of larger criminal organizations, are the managers of individual numbers games. They accept the financial risks, covering short term losses and keeping the profits. Their identity is rarely known except to their own controllers. Individual bankers, in fact, seldom have direct knowledge of other operations. In an illegal activity, it is to everyone's advantage that few participants know anything about the others.

Each bank keeps a running audit of its game. To do this, it is staffed by a few full-time salaried "adders," equipped with adding machines. It may also subscribe to a racing wire service for prompt receipt of the race payoffs. As controllers' envelopes arrive, bets are transferred to adding machine tape, along with the controllers' codes. Lists of played numbers may also be made for quick reference.

If a banker notices a particularly heavy play on a given number, threatening a loss for the day if the number wins, he may choose to cut his risk by turning over some or all of these wagers to a layoff bank—a bank with sufficient capital to cover large hits. If the heavily-played number wins, the layoff bank provides funds to pay the winners. If the number does not win, the layoff bank keeps the money wagered.

As winners are determined, the bank either arranges for controllers to pay off hits through their runners or waits for money requests to come up through the communications chain. The only records kept are the controllers' envelopes containing runners betting slips and day's adding machine tapes. These are usually held for a week, and are used to settle any disputes that arise.

Security is vital to banks, which are usually located in apartments, stores or hotel rooms far from either the area of collection or the banker's own home or legitimate business. Wherever they are located, banks do not usually remain for long. In a time of intense police activity, a bank may move more than once a week.

This tedious but essential preoccupation with security is one of the economic wastes in the illegal numbers game. Not only must outright bribes be paid, but operating efficiencies are more difficult to achieve in an organization constantly on the move. The commissions paid to runners, moreover, are disproportionate to the effort they would need to make if their activities were not against the law. A substantial portion of their commission must be regarded as compensation for risks.

Estimates of the numbers game's annual handle in New York City range from $240 million to $1.5 billion. The findings of the Quayle poll, supported by the informed opinion of police officials, suggests that the game attracts between $500 million and $600 million a year.

The Quayle group based its estimate on the responses to survey questions about the frequency and size of players' bets. Almost 40 percent of betters played numbers daily, and another 30 percent two or three times a week. On a day when they play, only 18 percent of numbers players usually bet less than $1. Using a detailed breakdown, Quayle projects the game's annual volume as $580 million.

The game's profitability is more difficult to assess than its size. But some reasonable calculations can be made from estimates of the probable costs of operating a numbers bank.

Most of the handle goes for two major items: sales commissions to runners and controllers and prize payouts to winners. The runner's commission is 25 percent; controllers receive another five percent. Total sales costs, therefore, are 30 percent.

Payout levels are 500 to one in some areas of the city, 600 to one in others. The use of cut numbers reduces the actual payout, however.

Most banks are believed to cut between 25 and 100 numbers. The effect is to reduce the net payout to winners by about 1.5 percent for banks paying 500 to one and about 2.5 percent for banks paying 600 to one.

In the present, illegal game, protection from the law is another unavoidable element of cost. Available data on this item are not entirely satisfactory. Testimony in one trial showed that a Bronx banker paid about five percent of his handle to the police.[1] But he was the operator of a small bank, whose relative protection costs are higher than those of a large bank. Five percent is probably an upper limit for protection costs.

A banker also has office costs. He must pay a pickup man, whose salary in one documented case was $75 a week.[2] The banker must also pay adders, at a reasonable estimate of $150 a week, and office rent. There are economies of scale in office costs as there are in protection costs. Two percent for office costs is probably a reasonable upper limit for a typical bank.

As tabulated in the table below, operating costs and prize payouts total 85.5 percent for a bank that pays advertised odds of 500 to one and 94.5 percent for a bank that pays 600 to one. If half of the banks in New York City pay 600 to one (with a 5.5 percent profit on sales) and that the other half pay 500 to one (14.5 percent profit on sales), annual profits from the illegal game are $58 million.

The current numbers game, as an illegal enterprise, is a protected market for criminal operators, since legitimate business by definition cannot compete. Individual numbers operators, moreover, require a number of illicit services whose most efficient suppliers are large-scale, diversified criminal organizations.

Illegal numbers operators need, most of all, access to large amounts of money in case they

[1]"People of the State of New York vs. Robert Stanard," Bronx County Supreme Court, part 20, June 1970. p. 533.

[2]"People of the United States vs. Raymond Marquez," Federal District Court, Southern District of New York, December 1970. p. 450.

Table B. Estimated Operating Costs and Profit (as a percentage of sales)

Bank Which Pays Winners 500 to One

Sales costs, runners	25.0%
Sales costs, controllers	5.0
Payback to winners, net	48.5
Protection	5.0
Office costs	2.0
Total costs	85.5
Profit	14.5

Bank Which Pays Winners 600 to One

Sales costs, runners	25.0%
Sales costs, controllers	5.0
Payback to winners, net	57.5
Protection	5.0
Office costs	2.0
Total costs	94.5
Profit	5.5

are hit heavily. A banker's credibility depends on his ability to pay winners within a day. Over the long haul, his receipts are sure to exceed his payout. But on a given day—or even over a short period—he may have to pay out in prizes more money than he takes in.

A banker can turn to a layoff bank. If he does not, and cannot pay his winners out of his own cash reserves, he must borrow. Since he obviously cannot call on legitimate commercial lenders, he must rely on loan sharks. Both layoff banking and illicit lending in New York City are controlled by organized crime.

Illegal numbers operators also need protection from the law. Organized crime, by means of its capital and the contacts made through its wide range of activities, is in a position to provide protection. A large, diversified criminal organization can influence the attitude of public officials, the posture of the media and the practices of law enforcement personnel. A numbers banker can buy some protection on his own. But low-level bribes are not likely to be as effective as the multi-faceted connections of a more powerful criminal group.

An individual numbers banker may also need other forms of protection. If he wishes to earn a steady living from the game, he wants to avoid the disruption of wars over territory. It is also in his interest to maintain a low payout and to avoid having it forced up by price competition. Organized crime is in a position to determine and enforce divisions of territory and payout levels.

Diversified criminal organizations also benefit significantly from their close association with numbers bankers. The yield from numbers is substantial, involves relatively low risks, and flows steadily. Such activities as importing drugs or selling stolen property may produce more income, but it is intermittent. Organized crime does not receive all of the $58 million annual profit that we estimated the numbers game brings in every year, but through direct participation, tribute and fees from layoff banking and loans it captures the substantial majority.

The game also supplies steady jobs for members of large criminal organizations. These members are employed more or less full time in numbers, but are still available when needed for assignments in other sporadic criminal enterprises such as hijacking or transporting shipments of narcotics.

As the most highly visible of all criminal activities, the numbers game is peculiarly susceptible to police interference and requires an extensive network of contacts with public officials at several levels. Thus it provides a convenient entry point to the law enforcement structure. Many agencies and individual public officials wield decision-making power over the numbers game: to arrest, to order a crackdown, to investigate, to prosecute, to sentence. As a consequence, corruption related to the game is pervasive.

The pattern of corruption varies among overlapping levels of the numbers organization and the law enforcement system. A runner faces the constant danger of arrest because of his exposed position. A uniformed precinct patrolman may "score" with a runner by threatening an arrest unless he is bought off. An individual incident like this may turn into a formal system of periodic payments.

A controller, who is responsible for the work of his runners, may be involved in a package deal with many precinct patrolmen. He may also have to protect himself from plainclothesmen who have the authority to follow collectors and pickup men across precinct boundaries. A controller, therefore, may have to establish a "pad"—a system of fixed, regular tribute—for the plainclothes force.

Bankers require more sophisticated protection (e.g., advance information on police activities or placement of sympathetic officers in sensitive positions). At the top, large criminal organizations may use direct bribery less than contributions to political parties or the influence gained through control of legitimate business enterprises to buy protection.

One of the worst effects of corruption is that officials involved have a stake in preserving the illegal activity. Corrupt police perform several services for numbers operators. They accept stand-in arrests (booking a substitute with little or no criminal record for the real offender); settle disputes between controllers over the services of a particular runner; and act as enforcers for protected operators by harassing their competitors. Some police have been known to help secure financing for a numbers operation that had gone bankrupt.

57. Fixing Horse Races

SELECT COMMITTEE ON CRIME, U. S. HOUSE OF REPRESENTATIVES

RACE FIXING

BECAUSE HORSERACING AND OTHER FORMS OF legalized gambling can affect the integrity of State government, they should be the best policed of activities. We have determined that inadequate security at many thoroughbred tracks and harness raceways has led to race fixing which threatens not only the integrity of the industry in which the sport is sanctioned but that of the State itself.

This committee has heard of schemes as simple in design as that of a dishonest jockey hoping an electrical charge applied to his mount will put him into the winner's circle.[1] We have also heard of elaborate conspiracies in which an entire race was effectively tied up by knocking out half the field of horses with drugs.[2]

Fixed races have been discovered at both thoroughbred, or flat tracks, and harness raceways. What has come to public attention, we fear, are only the most flagrant examples of a significant problem which the industry chooses not to face due to its misguided desire to protect the image of the sport.

*

▶SOURCE: *"Organized Criminal Influence in Horseracing,"* *Report by the Select Committee on Crime, 93rd Congress, 1st Session, House of Representatives. Report No. 93–326 (June 25, 1973), pp. 1–10,14 (Editorial adaptations.)*

[1]Hearings before the Select Committee on Crime entitled "Organized Crime in Sports (Racing)" (hereinafter referred to as "Hearings"), testimony of Alexander MacArthur, pt. 2, pp. 527–528.

[2]Crime Committee Hearings, testimony of Bobby Byrne, pt. 3, pp. 1103–1139.

An attempt to prod a horse through the jolt of an electric whip at an Illinois track focused attention on the need to inspect equipment as well as horses at the track. The jockey involved was not a newcomer to the sport but Lane Suire, the country's fourth ranked rider. MacArthur said:

There was a collision coming into the homestretch on the third race . . . . One jockey [Suire] was injured . . . one horse had to be destroyed for a broken leg. It was a pretty good collision out there.

*

It was directed to our attention by one of the ground personages, that he picked up a whip out there. Upon examination he saw that this whip had what appeared to be a battery device in it. I might add the men told me a very sophisticated one. * * * Because of the suggestion of an irregularity, I immediately asked the steward, the chief State steward, Ted Atkinson, to go in and indulge in some important curiosity and then check the jockeys' quarters in other racetracks. And I am advised and regret to inform you that in Fairmont, Ill., that night, we entered the jockey quarters and conducted a search and found another one of these devices in the footlocker of another jockey.[3]

*

Mr. PHILLIPS. Essentially a device to speed a horse up and help fix the race; is that correct?

[3]Hearings, testimony of Alexander MacArthur, pt. 2, pp. 527–528.

Mr. MACARTHUR. It is a device very definitely engineered to increase the speed of the horse. Besides the moral aspect of it, which is plenty in my book, because I won't even allow a cattle prod to be used on my cattle because it stresses them. I think it is a terrible way to treat an animal that is supposed to be your friend.[4]

*

Mr. FITZGERALD. . . . I have studied the betting pattern of the race. The horse's name was "Little Solaris." It was appropriately priced at where it belonged, and it is our belief that he [Suire] inadvertently touched this device to the horse. He certainly would not have deliberately done so at the turn. He was in a crowded condition at a turn and he wouldn't normally do this, but we suspect he brought the whip down along the side of the horse and the prongs touched the horse and the horse veered, as the pictures illustrate, into other horses, tripped, went down, broke his leg; had to be destroyed there. . . .[5]

*

In another incident, a nine-State, 12-track fraud in which superior or "ringer" horses were substituted under the names of slower thoroughbreds was described by witness Paul Berube, an investigator for the Thoroughbred Racing Protective Bureau. The scheme was such a substantial financial undertaking that "it would be my opinion that organized crime is definitely involved in perhaps the financing of this whole operation," Berube told the committee.[6]

Berube's testimony underscored the need for Federal statutes to make such schemes, which can be interstate in character, subject to heavy fines.

Six horses running under 12 different identities had one thing in common—the fraudulent foal certificates under which they ran were of slower thoroughbreds. (Foal certificates contain information about the animals and are comparable to birth certificates for humans). The "ringer" or substitute horses ran in at least 41 races at the 12 different tracks. Some ringers finished as much as seven lengths in front of the field. Berube named nine States in which he detected the use of forged foal certificates and substitute horses: Michigan, New Hampshire, Massachusetts, Rhode Island, New Jersey, Pennsylvania, Maryland, Delaware, and Florida. He also named a total of 12 tracks at which the practices were detected: Hazel Park, Rockingham Park, Suffolk Downs, Narragansett Park, Atlantic City, Garden State Park, Liberty Bell, Bowie, Laurel, Pimlico, Delaware Park, and Florida Downs.[7]

Berube testified that the 18-month period in which the scheme was in operation covered the period from November 1970 to March of 1972. "Of the races in which ringers were run, there were at least 14 winners."

*

The committee also heard about an incident which occurred on June 6, 1971, in which many of the 17,900 patrons on a "hot June Monday night" rioted at Yonkers Raceway in New York. The Yonkers race became the target of a Federal investigation by the New York Strike Force on Organized Crime whose chief, Daniel P. Hollman, had no authority to act unless there was evidence of some interstate violation involved. The possibility that the race had been fixed was so apparent, however, that Hollman decided to look into the case to determine whether there was any interstate activity on which to charge a violation when it became apparent State officials were not going to act.

[The fans] rioted after a particular fifth race, and they had good reason to riot. They had been "had" by inside information, as far as they were concerned. They didn't know where it was, what had happened, but they

---

[4]Id., p. 528.

[5]Hearings, testimony of Gerald F. Fitzgerald, pt. 4, p. 1838.

[6]Hearings, testimony of Paul Berube, pt. 2, p. 780.

[7]Id., p. 780.

knew they had been had and a good many of the fans rioted.

*

What sparked the rioting was this: The fifth race went off. I think it was a pace of 1 mile. There were eight horses in the race.

They came around the second time, and the No. 6 horse, "Moonstone Bay" won, and No. 7 "Mr. Ace," finished second. The exacta paid a very low amount, $42.60, which was about a hundred dollars less than what it should have paid. And this is what triggered that riot.[8]

This meant that a higher percentage of bettors were holding exacta tickets than the odds would dictate. As it turned out, a number of the ticket holders turned out to be drivers, trainers and others with access to the paddock area. Several holders of large blocks of winning tickets never cashed them in, presumably when it was discovered that an investigation was underway. One unknown purchaser of a block of twenty-two $20 tickets to this day hasn't claimed them. "Those tickets are worth $10,000," Hollman said. "In all the history of Yonkers, they know of no other situation where that has occurred.[9]

*

. . . Syndicate enforcer Joe Barboza gave the committee a chilling rundown of the muscle tactics he employed on jockeys in New England on behalf of mobster Henry Tamello to fix races. Barboza testified that New England crime boss Raymond Patriarca had once boasted of owning "half of the horses in New England" through third party fronts—an obvious accounting error.
Barboza testified:

Tamello, Patriarca's right-hand man, had five jockeys under his control.

Mr. BRASCO. Do you know whether or not Mr. Tamello ever asked these jockeys to do anything in terms of any race they were riding in?

Mr. BARBOZA. All I know is that after he would talk to them, he would say that he got them to pull the races for him.

Barboza related an example of the tactics he said Tamello used to intimidate jockeys to the point where they would pull horses for him. This particular incident took place in the Ebb Tide bar located near Suffolk Downs. Barboza said Tamello told him to corner a jockey who owed a $1,500 bar tab to Castucci—

and start to pressure him and I will come in there and I will stop you. Don't hurt him, but just really come on strong.

So I went in there and said, "You owe $1,500, you know . . . to the Ebb Tide. Richard Castucci. How come you haven't paid him? You may be a good strong guy, you know, you have all kinds of publicity, you think you are a bad man as far as riding horses," and so forth. "Everybody caters to you but I am not catering to you. * * * I pulled out a knife and put it at his throat and said I was going to slice it. And Henry came in and said, "What's this? What's going on?" Henry says, "Get away from him. He's a good kid. Are you crazy?" I said, "He owes Richard Castucci $1,500 and he hasn't paid."

Henry Tamello says, "I want to pay for him. I am telling you, don't bother this kid any more. He can do anything he wants in here. I want to cover his tab, pay his tab," and so forth.

I walked out of the cloakroom. Henry Tamello stayed there with the jockey maybe 15–20 minutes, and he came out, and he had a jockey that was going to pull horses for him.[10]

*

Mr. BYRNE. At one particular meet alone we would have access to like a dozen jockeys. But we used two key ones. Two key jockeys, three key jockeys, and they would be buddy-buddy.

[8]Hearings, testimony of Daniel P. Hollman, pt. 2, p. 646.
[9]Id., p. 657.

[10]Hearings, testimony of Joseph Barboza, pt. 2, p. 737.

Remember, them kids, some of them are making good money. But the average jockey, he doesn't make any money.[11]

So a guy, like the same guys again—he has got a weakness for money. He wants to make money. He says, "Gee, look, these guys ride around in big cars, good clothes, living in the best. Here I am out among the horses all day long for a 10-percent piece of the purse, and probably a little workout in the morning. I have to get up early in the morning." You know, they say, "I have got to get with this, I want to go where the money is."[12]

*

Mr. PHILLIPS. In relation to some of this money, was some of it paid to jockeys to hold horses?[13]

Mr. BYRNE. Right. Some jockeys you can buy cheap and others, one guy in particular, he is expensive. Other jockeys will do it. Like one jockey we had, he had no qualms, he knew we would take care of him. And if we made a score, and we were using the jockeys and trainers, we made a score, we would take care of him. He never had to worry about money. We didn't give him too much because the more you give them, the more they want. If you give them a couple hundred now, they want $400 next time. So if he asked for $200, you give him $150.[14]

*

Byrne explained that he and his cohorts obtained the drug from a cooperative veterinarian—that veterinarian had been previously barred from Rhode Island racetracks.

Mr. PHILLIPS. In all of these situations where you actually hit [drugged] the horse, the horse ran out of the money?

[11]Id., p. 1106.
[12]Id., p. 1106.
[13]Hearings, question by Chief Counsel Joseph A. Phillips, pt. 3, p. 1101.
[14]Hearings, testimony of Bobby Byrne, pt. 3, p. 1102.

Mr. BYRNE. Definitely, out of the money.

Mr. PHILLIPS. In every case?

Mr. BYRNE. It was working so good that we have, like our four live ones, and we would stand on the backstretch at different tracks, or at the top of the stretch, and we used to bet among ourselves who was going to buy the beer and lunch and how the four live ones were going to finish, and we have the winning tickets in our pocket.

*

Mr. PHILLIPS. In a 10-horse race you leave four, and an eight-horse race you leave four or three?

Mr. BYRNE. We leave three. Our practice is to leave three in an eight-horse field.[15]

*

Mr. PHILLIPS. How did you actually hit him, with a hypodermic needle?

Mr. BYRNE. Right. In the neck. You could hit him in three places. You could hit him in the neck, or breast, or rump. But the most effective place to hit him is right in the neck, because it travels, it travels faster. This particular drug we use, it travels, it hits them faster. For the first half-hour it is noticeable that the drug is in there because the horse is standing there like he is drunk. After that it wears off and he is kind of dopey.

But it hits his brain and his heart. It flows through the blood stream fast; whereas the other places it takes a little bit longer. It is effective, but not as good as in the neck. The neck is the best place to hit him with it.

Depending on the circumstances at the time, you might—like depending on the race and the time you get to this horse, how many cc.'s of this drug you would use. Like, say, the best time to hit, say it is like a race is going to come off after 4:30 or 5 o'clock. The ideal time to hit a horse with 5 cc.'s of this drug is between

[15]Id., pp. 1092–1093.

8 and 10 o'clock. And by the time he goes to race, he can go to his post position and no one notice nothing. You couldn't detect it without a test on him. You could surmise.

They run out a few trainers that are pretty sharp, but they would have a hard time. There are certain things they look for, but if you hit it right and enough dosage, they will never detect it. And they don't check the losers. That is why people think we were hitting favorites, I mean hitting the horse to win. But what we were doing was hitting them to stop them.

We didn't want them to win and they never check the ones who lose the race. They only check the winners.[16]

*

[16]Id., p. 1091.

58. Celebrities As "Fronts" for Organized Crime

SELECT COMMITTEE ON CRIME U. S. HOUSE OF REPRESENTATIVES

CELEBRITIES AS FRONTS

BECAUSE NEITHER COULD SAY "NO" TO A GOOD business deal, entertainers Sammy Davis, Jr., and Frank Sinatra each found himself the unwitting front in corrupt racing schemes orchestrated by middle men with close ties to major racketeers.

Each was invited to describe to the Select Committee on Crime how his character and reputation was misused in order to deceive racing officials in three different States.

Mr. Davis came willingly to relate how his "investment" in a horse farm returned nothing but bad checks in Kentucky and a police investigation in New Jersey; Mr. Sinatra appeared under threat of subpoena to plead ignorance of events which parlayed a 5-percent investment to a seat on the board of directors and the title of vice president of a Massachusetts racetrack in which New England crime boss Raymond Patriarca bragged of having a heavy interest.

In 1968, while playing the Copa-Cabana in New York City, Sammy Davis, Jr., first met a customer who appeared to be a fan.

I noticed that several nights he would come back with various parties and they always sent over a bottle of champagne, or came by the dressing room and that is how we came to know each other,"

▶SOURCE: *"Organized Criminal Influence in Horseracing,"* Report by the Select Committee on Crime, 93rd Congress, 1st Session, House of Representatives, Report No. 93–326. (June 25, 1973), pp 71–78. (Editorial adaptations.)

Davis said of "Corky" Vastola. He was introduced to me, Davis said, as "Tommy Vastola, and I called him Tommy, or TV."[1]

Mr. PHILLIPS. Did you understand at the time when you did meet him what his occupation was?

Mr. DAVIS. No; I did not. I did not ask, either.[2]

One man who did know filled in the answer for the committee—Capt. William Baum of the Intelligence Division of the New Jersey State Police. Had Davis sought Vastola's character references, instead of the other way around, it is doubtful they would ever have done business together.

" 'Corky' or 'Sonny' Vastola's correct name is Gaetano Vastola," Baum told the committee.

Our best intelligence—that is a group intelligence of State Police, Federal, and local authorities—indicates that Mr. Vastola is a principal organized crime figure in the central shore area of New Jersey today. That would include Monmouth and Ocean Counties.

He is closely aligned with the principal organized crime figures in this State, including Sam DeCavalcante and Anthony Russo. In fact, his uncle is Dominic Ciaffone, also known as "Swats" Mulligan out of Brooklyn,

[1]Hearings, testimony of Sammy Davis, Jr., pt. 2, p. 552.
[2]Id., p. 562.

N.Y., who was listed as a soldier in the Genovese family. He also, has an extensive criminal record.

Mr. Vastola has a number of business interests in the New York area, including an interest in the Queens Booking Agency, 1650 Broadway, which has booked many principal entertainment figures throughout the country.[3]

The booking agent Vastola had in mind for Davis was a middle man named Steward Siegel. Davis further related:

. . . I got a call from Tommy and he mentioned there was a man that had a legitimate deal and he felt it might be good for me, and that the man would call.

The man did call. I set up an appointment with him and we met. The deal sounded good to me. I then told my legal people, who are at my office in Philadelphia, to please check it out. It sounded good. It sounded like a marvelous, good, legitimate deal.

*

It was a deal for a farm to be used to breed horses. They were going to buy horses, sell horses in Europe, bring them back to the farm, which would be called Sammy Davis, Jr., Farms.

For the use of my name and my association, I was to get so much preferred stocks for a small amount of dollars, and so forth. That was my participation.

In other words, he wanted to use my name. He thought it would be good and I was terribly aware of the fact it might open up some jobs for people. That is all I know. I said, "Hey, I don't know anything about it, but I will try it."[4]

The particular track, according to Captain Baum, was Riverdale Horse Farm in Dover Township, Ocean County, N.J.

A check revealed that the farm is 12½ acres and the purchase price originally was for $30,000. The present value is between $150,000 and $200,000 according to people in the local area. The farm is deeded in the name of Joseph and Angelina Annunziata from Brooklyn. The farm was purchased from a Nathan and Ada Boyer.

Mr. PHILLIPS. Is Joseph Annunziata the father-in-law of Corky Vastola?

Mr. BAUM. That is correct.

Anticipating the future promotional aspects of advertising a trotting horse stable that bore his name, Davis said he "naturally jumped the gun a little bit, as I am prone to do occasionally, and I took some pictures in (jockey) silks and all that."

Naturally, Davis presumed the photographs would be held until his attorneys finished drawing up all the papers promoting his new investment. Davis presumed wrong.

Mr. DAVIS. It was announced prematurely. "I didn't announce it. I cannot even remember where it was at this point, Counsel. But I do remember that I was working and I read about it. Somebody from the press called and said, "Hey, I hear you got a farm of horses.""

I said, "I know there was a deal going on but I don't know whether it has been solidified or not."

And the next call I got was I owed somebody a lot of money because I bought one of their horses. It was in that kind of quick succession.[5]

The horses Davis bought, or more accurately, the horses bought by Siegel in Davis' name, were

[3]Hearings, testimony of William Baum, pt. 2, pp. 570–571.
[4]Hearings, testimony of Sammy Davis, Jr., pt. 2, p. 553.

[5]Id., pp. 553–554.

four yearlings purchased October 2, 1971: Jet Wave, $4,700; Petite Time, $2,300; Sweet Trick, $1,100, and Prince Singer, $700.

Mr. PHILLIPS. All of this was done by Mr. Siegel without any knowledge or authority from you; is that correct?

Mr. DAVIS. Absolutely.[6]

Meanwhile, Siegel resold Jet Wave for the purchase price—$4,700—to Dr. Alvan Field of Beachwood, N.J. After returning the other three animals to the nationally known auction firm of Tattersalls in Lexington, Ky., Siegel disappeared. Reports are that he is operating a gambling casino in Yugoslavia.

Davis was left with a lot of collection notes to answer.

This will serve to advise you that litigation will be filed by Tattersalls against Sammy Davis, Jr. Farms, Inc., and Steward Siegel for the recovery of $8,800. We intend to notify, as is customary in such cases, all members of the news media. . . .

*

Davis told the committee that, since he had no interest in the horse farm, he refused to pay all the bills Siegel ran up before vanishing.

"I didn't lose any money, except legal fees," he said. "Sometimes," Davis said, reflecting on his testimony and his ill-fated racing venture, "I'm afraid we are guilty of leaving the door open a little too wide."[7]

Before Joe "the Baron" Barboza, syndicate enforcer, linked the name of Frank Sinatra with that of New England organized crime boss Raymond Patriarca, the Select Committee on Crime had decided to call Mr. Sinatra as a witness.

Of concern to the committee was an 11-month period in late 1962 and early 1963, in which Sinatra ascended to the board of directors

and was elected vice president of Berkshire Downs Race Track in Hancock, Mass. The now defunct flat track was at the same time a principal target for organized crime investment. Patriarca, himself, was later heard to claim that he and his associates had sunk up to a quarter-of-a-million dollars in the track through middle men who wouldn't so easily raise the eyebrows of police and racing officials. But Berkshire Downs Race Track was not uppermost in Frank Sinatra's mind when he strode into the hearing room accompanied by business manager and attorney Mickey Rudin.

Sinatra was more concerned, he said, in clearing his name which he said was impugned when Congressman Sam Steiger asked witness Barboza—

a simple question and this bum went running off at the mouth. I resent it. I won't have it. I am not a second-class citizen. Let's get that straightened out,

a scorned Sinatra advised the Committee.[8]

The committee's counsel advised Mr. Sinatra that—

Berkshire Downs, as you know, is a race track in Massachusetts. The evidence we uncovered in relation to Berkshire Downs reflected a man by the name of Raymond Patriarca and a man by the name of Tommy Lucchese were principals and had interests in that particular track. Those particular individuals are members of organized crime. They are racketeers.

We also found, prior to Mr. Barboza testifying, that you were vice president of record of that particular track. So, long before Mr. Barboza testified, this committee had scheduled you as a witness in this particular proceeding and had taken actions to contact you to invite you to appear and testify in relation to Berkshire Downs.

[6]Id., p. 562.
[7]Id., p. 565.

[8]Hearings, testimony of Frank Sinatra, pt. 4, p. 1412.

I think that you should recognize that you are not here in relation to Mr. Barboza's testimony. That was not the intent of the committee in calling you. It was in relation to Berkshire Downs.[9]

Mr. SINATRA. I understand that clearly, but I wanted to make a point.

When he came to discuss his investment in Berkshire Downs Race Track, Sinatra and his attorney pictured it as little more than a petty cash speculative venture. Also invited to share in the deal was Sinatra's old sidekick, singer Dean Martin, who was offered a similar 5 percent investment in the track for $55,000, ultimately turned it down, as he later told an FBI agent.[10]

Mr. RUDIN. While I don't want to demean a $55,000 investment to people who do not have the ability to earn the type of income Mr. Sinatra has the ability to earn, and Mr. Martin has the ability to earn, but it was the kind of a thing a couple of fellows sitting around a club might say "I am taking a piece of that. Do you want a piece of it for the fun of it. Maybe we will hit it lucky." Extent of the conversation.

The catalyst for Sinatra's involvement with the horses was a Miami home builder, Salvatore A. Rizzo. FBI tapes indicate that Rizzo was also the conduit for organized crime's investment in Berkshire Downs.

Rizzo, according to Sinatra, approached him after a performance at the 500 Club in Atlantic City, N.J., in 1962. Lots of customers did this, the singer added. Some, like Rizzo, succeeded.

Mr. PHILLIPS. Well, could you tell us, to the best of your recollection, how Mr. Rizzo met you?

Mr. SINATRA. I was working in a club in Atlantic City and I met him there, which is common.

Mr. PHILLIPS. Would you tell us more about it?

Mr. SINATRA. That's all I can tell you about it.

Mr. PHILLIPS. Did he introduce you to himself and say, "I am interested in the racetrack?"

Mr. SINATRA. Apparently somebody might have introduced me to him, but I don't remember who it was.

Mr. PHILLIPS. Was it anybody you had any reliance on?

Mr. SINATRA. I can't remember that.

Mr. PHILLIPS. Well, I am trying to learn, Mr. Sinatra, how it is that Mr. Rizzo could make such a favorable impression on you in such a short period of time.

Mr. SINATRA. Many people have come to me in my lifetime and made impression on me with business deals. Some I accepted and some I didn't accept. Lots of people get to me.[11]

This fact is the probable reason that Rizzo unexpectedly decided to invoke the fifth amendment privilege to all questions concerning the Berkshire Downs affair and his association with Sinatra when he was subpoenaed as a witness before this committee. Yet, in his appearance before the Florida State Beverage Commission, Rizzo answered, under oath, that he had known Sinatra for 15 to 20 years. The questions and the answers that Rizzo made before the Florida commission in an effort to obtain a liquor license included:

Q. Did Frank Sinatra invest money in your track up there? [Referring to Berkshire Downs.]

A. Yes.

Q. Do you know how much, just in round figures?

A. I think he invested $70,000 for five points of 100.

---

[9]Hearings, statement of Chief Counsel Joseph A. Phillips, pt. 4, p. 1413.

[10]Hearings, testimony of Milton A. Rudin, pt. 4., p. 1417.

[11]Hearings, testimony of Frank Sinatra, pt. 4, p. 1414.

Q. Does that equal 20 shares?

A. No, just 5 percent.

Q. How long have you known Mr. Sinatra?

A. Fifteen or 20 years.

Another committee witness, former Berkshire Downs Race Track Comptroller Charles Carson, also testified that Rizzo had bragged of knowing Sinatra for years.

It was in fact Rizzo's assemblage of secret coinvestors with Sinatra which brought Berkshire Downs to this committee's attention. Committee member Sam Steiger informed Sinatra:

> The basis of the concern of this committee is the fact that Mr. Patriarca, who has been identified as a Mafia figure in New England, was indeed a heavy investor. Now, the basis of this assumption is a series of "phone taps and bugged conversations which the Justice Department had in Mr. Patriarca's office over a long period of time. And for your information, on the 24th of August 1962, Mr. Patriarca was informed that the track was going to put Frank Sinatra on the board of directors of Hancock Raceway to add a little class to the track. And I will tell you, Mr. Sinatra, in my opinion, it was desperately in need of a little class at that point.

But we had a similar experience, the committee had, in which another entertainer, Mr. Davis, was apparently used in a similar fashion.

Addressing Sinatra's attorney, Rudin, Chairman Pepper asked:

Chairman PEPPER. Did Mr. Rizzo tell you Mr. Patriarca had any ownership in that track?

Mr. RUDIN. Mr. Rizzo did not tell me about anybody else having an ownership, but indicated that he was going to seek other investors. Had

he mentioned the name Patriarca, it would have meant nothing to me.

A more familiar name would have been Tommy "Three Fingers Brown" Lucchese, notorious New York City racketeer, now deceased, who was a secret angel in the financing of Berkshire Downs Race Track.

Mr. PHILLIPS. Mr. Rudin, did you know Tommy Lucchese?

Mr. RUDIN. I had met Mr. Lucchese.

Mr. PHILLIPS. On how many occasions?

Mr. RUDIN. Maybe once or twice.

Mr. PHILLIPS. Where?

Mr. RUDIN. I met him, I believe, once in Atlantic City. He came in to see Mr. Sinatra and Mr. Martin perform, and I believe I was introduced to him in a restaurant in New York once.

Mr. PHILLIPS. Do you know whether he had any business dealing with Mr. Sinatra and Mr. Martin?

Mr. RUDIN. I know of no business dealings with Mr. Sinatra.

Mr. SINATRA. I can answer that question. I never had any business dealings in any sense or form with Mr. Lucchese. He was a man I met two or three times at the most, shook hands, and that was the end of it. . . .

Mr. PHILLIPS. Mr. Sinatra, Mr. Lucchese had a substantial interest in Berkshire Downs.

Mr. SINATRA. That's his problem, not mine. I wasn't aware of it.[12]

Berkshire Downs became very much Sinatra's problem with his election as vice president and member of the board of directors.

[12]Id., pp. 1420–1421.

"We became aware of it when we read about it in the sports page," Sinatra said.

Chairman PEPPER. Mr. Rizzo did not tell you about it?

Mr. SINATRA. No, sir.

Chairman PEPPER. And you did not know about your election as an officer and director of the track?

Mr. SINATRA. No, sir. That is essentially one of the two reasons why we got out of the business deal.[13]

The second reason was an investment Sinatra had made in the Sands Hotel and gambling casino in Las Vegas, Nev. Under Nevada gaming laws, no person who has a gambling interest in any other State may invest in a Nevada gaming operation. A visible, managerial position at Berkshire Downs Race Track would seriously jeopardize Sinatra's far greater investment in Las Vegas.

Sinatra's attorney, Rudin, began taking steps to withdraw both his client's association with the track and Dean Martin's as well.

Rudin said:

And in the correspondence, when questioned about the fact they named Mr. Martin as an officer and director, Mr. Rizzo said he thought that Mr. Sinatra wanted Dean to have an interest in the track and therefore he named Dean as an officer and director.[14]

I would also like to point out, on March 4, 1963, I wrote to the counsel for the Hancock Raceway Association, in which I pointed out to them I had previously written. I had learned in the press that Mr. Sinatra was being listed as an officer and director. And in this letter, I identified the fact I had a full power of attorney and, therefore, this letter was written not

only as an attorney at law, but as an attorney in fact, in which I said to the extent that Mr. Sinatra may be or may be deemed to be a director or officer of Hancock Raceway, Inc., would you please regard this letter as a request that the record of the corporation duly note that he is not an officer or director.

In any event, he hereby resigns from such position in the event he has been so elected, regardless of whether or not he has accepted.

Because under the laws of the State of Massachusetts, if they elect him as an officer, he might have been an officer. I just wanted to go firmly on record that he was not an officer. But if by their law he was an officer, he was resigning, which he had to the right to do as well.[15]

Sinatra was luckier than other investors in Berkshire Downs Race Track. On July 10, 1963, a check covering his original $55,000 investment was supposedly sent to and allegedly received by Rudin a few days later.

Rudin testified:

Mr. Rizzo was just a small episode in our [Sinatra and attorney] very complicated business life over the past 17 years. It was particularly a small episode because that was the year we were beginning to work on a merger of a record company and establishing a foreign distribution for a record company, and that absorbed my time and thinking.[16]

Summarizing what was the reaction of most committee members to the explanation of Sinatra's involvement with Berkshire Downs Race Track, Congressman William Keating said:

I recognize your statement and accepted it earlier that a $55,000 investment to some is large and you don't demean that. In some areas,

---

[13]Id., pp. 1419–1420.
[14]Hearings, testimony of Milton A. Rudin, pt. 4, p. 1419.

[15]Id., p. 1423.
[16]Id., p. 1416.

$55,000 is not a large investment. I understand that and I think you were very careful the way you said it, but the point I was trying to make, there is more than just the amount of the investment involved.

There is Mr. Sinatra's reputation that has to be considered and I think you indicated that in all of these types of investments, that really would require some further investigation.

*

59. Gypsy Cabs and Organized Crime

FRANCIS A. J. IANNI

DURING THE COURSE OF FIELD WORK IN BROOKLYN, we learned from Tomas Correa that he had sold a stolen car to Frank White, an owner/driver in the Superfast Cab Company in Manhattan. Through this initial contact, one of our field assistants traced out and observed a complex web of relationships in a burgeoning new venture into minority entrepreneurship that has been developing in a number of American cities over the past decade. Usually called "gypsy cabs," it involves the use of automobiles for hire as taxis despite the fact that they do not meet the legal standards and conditions for taxicabs. Through the use of a variety of semi- and openly illegal practices, the "gypsies" operate in ghetto areas where legally licensed taxis seldom venture. Despite the patent illegality of the gypsy system, many cities have now tacitly accepted the practice while admitting to its illegality and publicly calling for regulation of the new industry. The history of how gypsy cabs came into existence, how and why they continue to operate, their role in ghetto life and their relationship to organized crime activities illustrate the mixture of legal, semi-legal and illegal activities that make up that segment of the American economy we call organized crime. The story of gypsy cabs is also an object lesson in the social chaos and conflict that can result when the legitimate aspirations of

▶SOURCE: *Black Mafia. New York: Simon and Shuster, 1974, pp. 246–251; 258–264. (Editorial adaptations.) Reprinted by permission.*

minority groups are blocked and they resort to illicit and illegal means to escape poverty.

Since 1937, there have been a set, limited number of taxicabs legally eligible to cruise the streets of New York City looking for passengers. In that year the Haas Act was passed, limiting the number of outstanding taxicab licenses or "medallions" to 13,566, which were then purchasable for $100 apiece. Since then a number of medallions have been retired, leaving the actual total at large in 1973 as about 11,700.

The rationale for limiting the number of cruising taxis was presumably (1) to ensure a healthy, stable, prosperous cab industry, unthreatened by a glut of cabs surviving marginally as business enterprises and by the cutthroat competition that would probably result; and (2) to ensure that although the public might never be the beneficiaries of too many cabs vying for their business, they might at least not be the victims of drastic shortages.

Over the years this system made rich men out of many medallion holders: the value of a single medallion went from $100 in 1937 to highs ranging between $25,000 and $30,000 in recent years and some fleet owners dominated the industry, holding hundreds of medallions. For twenty years or so the system seemed to work reasonably well to keep cabs on New York City's streets, or at least on those streets of highest public visibility, in the midtown, downtown, and white residential sections of Manhattan.

However, New York is a big city. It encompasses far more than East Side, West Side, Broadway and Wall Street. And as the years passed, into the late 1950s and early 1960s, the failures of the medallioned taxi industry—which has come to be known as the "yellow" cab industry, after the color that all its cabs are now required to be painted—became more pronounced. As crime, and more importantly the fear of crime, increased, more and more taxi drivers steered clear of New York's black and Puerto Rican areas. It was a plain fact that during these years attacks on cab drivers began to increase markedly, especially in black and Puerto Rican areas and especially after dark, and so finding a yellow cab in Harlem at night became increasingly difficult. But at the same time the same fear of crime, along with other factors such as marginal increases in employment and prosperity, served to enlarge the demand for taxi service in black and Puerto Rican areas. As the early 1960s became the late 1960s, that demand, along with so many other long-stifled aspirations, began emerging out of the ghettos with fresh articulation, and with a persistence backed by emerging political power.

Medallioned taxis have never been the only way one could get a car legally to take you someplace in New York City. Rather, they have been the only cars legally entitled to pick you up off the street when you flag them down and to measure the amount you will be charged on a meter. It has, however, always been possible to look in the classified pages of the phone book, find a "car service," a "public livery" service or a "radio car" service, call them, and arrange for one of their cars to pick you up. Charges for the service are computed at either a flat rate or at a rate determined by some kind of "zone" system (for example, if you go from 23rd Street to 28th Street, that's one zone, but if you go from 23rd Street to 146th Street then that is about five zones and will cost you five times as much). It has also always been possible for an entrepreneur to go into this kind of "public livery" business easily. He has not had to purchase an expensive medallion; rather, all he has had to do

is (1) obtain an "O" (taxi) or a "Z" (special omnibus) registration and license plates from the State Department of Motor Vehicles, which will issue them automatically on proper proofs of ownership and insurance; and (2) purchase the appropriate equipment such as a two-way radio for his business. From the late 1950s onward "car services" based on two-way radios and telephone orders began to proliferate, not only in ghetto areas but also in quiet white residential neighborhoods of the outlying boroughs, where yellow cabs seldom cruised and where old people especially were in need of door-to-door transportation. These car services were perfectly legal operations so long as they did not pick up passengers off the street or carry taxi meters, practices limited to bona fide medallioned cabs, and many services abided by these rules and continue to abide by them today.

However, it is easy to see how such car services might not fully satisfy the needs of many citizens for quick, convenient, personalized transportation, especially in ghetto areas. For they require both a phone call and a wait, and for a man on a Harlem street late at night or for an old woman trying to get home from a clinic or from shopping, neither of these are very satisfactory preconditions. Moreover, zone systems are more cumbersome and more difficult to understand than simple meters. While it's true that in some cities all taxis operate on zone systems and that in many other cities cabs are available only on a telephone basis, nevertheless, it's easy to understand how in a city where metered cabs cruise in profusion "downtown," ghetto residents would demand similar service for their own heavily populated, intensely urban areas.

It is equally easy to understand how it might have come about that "car services," unmedallioned public livery vehicles, began picking up fares off the ghetto streets. It is so easy to do. There's the man or woman out there on the street corner, flagging you down. You look in your rearview mirror and there are no cops anywhere in sight, or if they are, they're not paying attention. Moreover, there certainly aren't any yellow cabs around to complain. It only takes a few seconds for you to stop, for the guy to jump in, and then you're off. You've done the passenger a favor, and since for the moment you've had no radio business you're also improving your income a touch. Undoubtedly this is how the gypsy cab was born. And, considering the demand, it's easy to see how such street pickups could have become standard practice for many "car service" drivers, or even how many men could have taken to driving or buying public livery cars on the assumption that a good portion of their income would derive from hails off the street.

What might be somewhat more difficult to explain, and where current gypsy operations are most obviously in open violation of the law, is how taxi meters finally found their way onto the dashboards of so many "car service" vehicles and how these same cars can blatantly post their meter rates on their doors, just as yellow cabs do. To really understand this requires considering the social climate of the 1960s and the relationship between political power and law enforcement. For an unmedallioned vehicle to have a meter and to post its rates on the door were and continue to be illegal acts. Neither is it the type of marginal or covert illegality that is difficult to uncover and even more difficult to prove. The meters and posted rates are there for anyone to see. But it was and continues to be true that black and Puerto Rican neighborhoods needed the gypsies, because yellow cabs were also violating the law by *not* picking up passengers in ghetto areas. In fact, it was, and is, commonly charged by blacks that they even had trouble being picked up *downtown* by yellow cab drivers fearful of being asked to drive to Harlem. The police were not pressured by City Hall to make arrests of gypsies since the political consequences of pressing the issue were not acceptable to politicians. Remember also that this was the period of widespread unrest and even rioting in the ghettos and neither the politicians nor the police were anxious to provoke confrontations with ghetto dwellers. And so, once again, the

characteristically American accommodation with crime in the ghetto—which holds that so long as ghetto residents keep it among themselves and it doesn't spill outside, it is not a major problem—prevailed. The two voices that most men will heed are the voice of their own conscience and that of police, and in the 1960s neither of these was telling "car service" drivers in the ghetto that they mustn't pick up their brothers and sisters.

And so out of "public livery" status, out of radio-dispatched, unmetered "car services" grew the gypsy cab industry. Today it is flourishing, one of the few minority-group enterprises that emerged out of the 1960s "push" to do so—and, needless to say, without any poverty program help at all. Go to any of the black or Puerto Rican parts of Manhattan, to Harlem or El Barrio or Broadway on the Upper West Side, or up into the South Bronx or the Grand Concourse, or over to Brooklyn, in Bedford-Stuyvesant, or even in downtown Brooklyn, and you will see them. Indeed, in these neighborhoods they will seem to be everywhere. No uniform shiny yellow on the cabs here. Rather, every other color that to an owner's eye looks handsome—fire engine red or metallic blue, a fair number of purples, and lots of two-tone jobs: They are big old cars, with their rear ends hanging down, or their front ends, always bad suspension somewhere, and dents—and always with the rates posted on the side, just like the yellows except slightly cheaper: 45¢ the first fifth-mile, 10¢ for every fifth thereafter, and decals all over saying "car service," and even a couple of little lights on the roof, "proof" that this is a real live taxicab. And inside you will see, attached to the dash where it is supposed to be, the meter, and behind the wheel a black or Puerto Rican face.

*

THE SUPERFAST CAB COMPANY

In the spring of 1970, James Taylor, Frank White and Edward Wilson, all black males residing on the Upper West Side of Manhattan, in the neighborhood of 103rd–106th Streets between Broadway and Amsterdam Avenue, came together to form what they called the Superfast Cab Company. They did not incorporate or take any other action that required a lawyer, but they did agree that each of them would obtain an appropriate car, a taxi meter, and Superfast Cab Company insignia and would begin to cruise the streets of the West Side looking for fares. They further agreed that they would try to expand their business as quickly as possible so as to be able to afford two-way radios and a dispatching system, and for that purpose each contributed a portion of his initial weekly earnings to a kitty. James Taylor already owned a '66 Chevy, which he turned into a Superfast cab by having Superfast decals made up and purchasing certain other decals and two small yellow lights for his hood from a store specializing in such accessories and a taxi meter from Roberto Quevedo, further uptown, whose large garage was then—and is now—supplied with large amounts of stolen automotive merchandise by Rafael Pagan and other junkie/thieves. The meter purchased by Taylor, along with the meters similarly purchased by Edward Wilson and Frank White, were stolen by Pagan from other New York City cabs—two from yellows, one from a gypsy (to Pagan it has never mattered which).

Neither Edward Wilson nor Frank White owned cars at the time the partnership was formed, and so for them buying a car was the first big step. Wilson, who had previously driven a yellow cab in Manhattan and was looking for a way to set out on his own, to "have something" for himself and his large family, was in the strongest cash position of the three initial partners, and he purchased a '68 Ford from a legitimate used-car dealer. White, who was rather strapped for funds, bought a stolen car from Tomas Correa in Brooklyn, a '67 Ford at a fraction of the price that Wilson paid for his '68. This is how the purchase worked: Frank first went to Correa, to whom he had been introduced by a mutual friend, and then to an automotive junkyard, where for very little money

he purchased a wrecked '67 Ford four-door sedan. He took the registration papers and right on the premises removed from the car its door-tag and other official identifications. Then he went back to Correa, whose thieves in three days' time stole an all-but-matching '67 four-door sedan. He took the car to a legitimate auto painter where, for $39.95, he had it painted maroon and then switched the door tags. Thus Frank White, for all appearances and at a total investment of about $400, came to own a "properly" registered full-sized late model car, completely appropriate for use as a taxicab.

One thing that should be noted about this initial partnership, and that puts the Superfast company in a slightly different category than many other nascent gypsy operations, is that all three of its personnel had prison records. Indeed, although they came eventually to live in the same neighborhood, all three served time together when they were quite a lot younger, and prison undoubtedly did much to cement their friendship. Prison, it should also be noted, provided them with the range of acquaintances that led them to the stolen parts supplier Roberto Quevedo and through him to the stolen car supplier Tomas Correa—although even without ex-con friends they probably would have been able to find similar suppliers eventually.

The three friends worked hard, cruising chiefly in their own immediate neighborhood, and within a year they had prospered sufficiently so that White shed his stolen car and bought a legitimate one, which was cause for a great celebration at a local club one night. The truth is that White had been rather embarrassed by his stolen car from the first; he was not admired at all for his "shrewdness" in paying much less for a car than Wilson, but rather had been looked slightly down upon for the lack of substance that his illegitimate vehicle suggested. Prosperity also brought into the Superfast company two new owner/drivers: William Prentice, an old prison buddy who lived in Central Harlem, and Ramon Suarez, an ex-yellow driver who lived in the 103rd–106th neighborhood. Shortly thereafter the five men further expanded their venture by working a deal with one Leroy Atkins, whose affiliation with a now-defunct gypsy outfit had left him with some two-way radio equipment. The five drivers purchased three radios from Leroy (and two from Roberto Quevedo) and in addition each agreed to pay him $25 per week, in exchange for which he and his wife, Marion, would operate a radio-dispatch business for them fifty-five hours per week. Superfast began advertising, posting its new number by the phone in local groceries and bars, sending circulars around; and of course the owners told all their relatives and friends. Their prosperity increased, but Leroy and Marion grew dissatisfied with their end of the bargain, whereupon Superfast took on two more new drivers, Jose Rodrigues and Kenny Rivers, each of whom enlarged Atkins' income by $25 weekly. In exchange for the additional money, Leroy and Marion agreed to operate the dispatcher's office several more hours per week. Superfast's drivers had already discovered the importance of being available whenever their clients called.

The business continues to do well. The seven owners keep their cars almost constantly on the streets by renting them out for twelve- or twenty-four-hour shifts whenever they themselves choose not to drive. Each owner has three or four drivers who rent from him, usually on established schedules and at set rates of $15 for twelve hours and $20 for twenty-four. This is known in the cab business as the "horse-hire" method of rental. The driver pays his flat fee and is then permitted to keep all the money he takes in during the twelve- or twenty-four-hour period, exclusive of his gas and incidental expenses. James Taylor, who drives perhaps sixty hours a week himself and rents his cab out for another forty-eight, can clear $225 in a good week. Superfast has, however, been plagued by some problems. For one, there has been the problem of keeping the radio manned. Gradually, the number of hours worked by the Atkins family has grown, and they now have a ten-hour-per-week employee; but whenever a customer calls Superfast and no one answers the phone, there is still created a dissatisfied customer. Superfast is still not really big enough to maintain a credible, wholly reliable radio business, although the radios do bring in substantial income and do provide a cover for the drivers' gypsy cruising. Another problem has been the police. The drivers have long since discovered the patrolmen they must make monthly small "contributions" to, but the patrolmen still come around with their periodic summonses, claiming that "the sergeant's putting the heat on," or whatever. Nobody at Superfast has yet made contact with a sergeant. And then there are the supraprecinct police, the Tactical Patrol Force and the Highway Patrol and so forth, who, whenever they're in the neighborhood and in the mood, cause the gypsies trouble. There's no way for a small outfit like Superfast to bribe these roving cops. Insurance has been another problem because of the large cash outlays that many insurers require and because of difficulties in getting certain ones to pay off. But Superfast been fortunate recently in latching on to an agent who obtains low rates for their cars by having them registered in Mount Vernon and who nevertheless has found insurance companies that seem to pay off regularly and promptly. Last but not least is the problem of crime—that is to say, of crimes committed against the drivers themselves. Cab drivers have long been choice targets for muggers in New York, and gypsies, who work the black and Puerto Rican neighborhoods where many of the muggings take place, have not been exempted simply by the fact that they share skin color or ethnicity with the attackers. Five of the seven Superfast owners have been mugged at one time or another while driving, and at least four of their "horse-hire" drivers have too. But Superfast is now fighting back. All the owner/drivers now carry guns while they drive, concealed against the possibility of police inspection but nevertheless readily at hand, under the seat or dash somewhere. Most of the guns are .25 caliber. And, more importantly, they have worked out systems for helping one another out. A buddy system that is perhaps in many ways a vestige of prison life ensures that other cabs will be quick to help in case of emergency. In this regard, the two-way radios are obviously a deterrent to crime. Many muggers know that it's easy for a driver to phone in his location and situation if it appears at all threatening or after the fact of an attack. Superfast drivers have a code: if a guy gets in who appears a likely mugger, the driver will call in, "Cab 6, calling a signal 1 from Broadway and 88th, heading north on Broadway, to 104th and Manhattan Avenue." Or if the guy becomes more threatening, pulls something from his pocket or seems about to, "Cab 6, calling a signal 3 from Broadway and 101st." Or in case ultimately of attack, "Cab 6, calling a signal 5 from Manhattan Avenue and 102d." Leroy or Marion Atkins will always quickly relay this information on to the other cabs, and in the relatively small neighborhood where Superfast ordinarily operates, help is seldom far off.

It is worth noting the various criminal activities that Superfast and its drivers get involved in, ancillary to the fundamental illegality of gypsy cruising. Herminia Rivers, a prostitute, often uses Superfast cabs to get from one assignation to another, because she lives in the Superfast neighborhood and because she considers the Superfast people, in contradistinction to yellow cab drivers, "one of us." More seriously, Robert Murphy is a heroin addict and small-time pusher who occasionally horse-hires the cab of Frank White in order to peddle drugs out of it. White is aware that Murphy pushes but does not know the use to which he puts the cab. On the other hand, he should be able to guess. Heroin addicts will pay a premium to be able to purchase their drugs in the safety of a cab parked in a quiet parking lot or simply driving around somewhere, as opposed to having to purchase on the street.

Another criminal activity is the bribing of police officers, already mentioned. Still another is the evasion of income taxes. During the first year none of the drivers paid any taxes at all. Then they heard about two or three gypsy firms whose drivers had all been stuck with big bills for back taxes, and on the advice of a Broadway accountant, all except William Prentice have, during the past two years, been reporting at least a portion of their earnings to the IRS. Of the total tax due from seven owners, the various income tax bureaus now receive perhaps 35 percent. All the other drivers tell Prentice that he should report at least *something,* for their sake and the sake of the company if not for his, but they have thus far not insisted on it. The last major criminal area in which Superfast is still involved is thievery, or at least the receipt of stolen goods. Jose Rodrigues and Kenny Rivers are still driving stolen cars, obtained through Tomas Correa. In fact, Kenny has two of them: he drives one for three months, then garages it for three months, shifting his meter and radio back and forth between them, to save wear and tear on both. And all the drivers still purchase the largest portion of their automotive accessories—tires, batteries, radios especially—at vastly discounted prices from Roberto Quevedo. It happened once recently that a spare tire purchased by William Prentice turned out to have been stolen by one of Quevedo's boys from James Taylor's cab. Taylor made a positive identification of it, then all of Superfast confronted Quevedo with the evidence. He gave them a free tire, pleaded for their continued business and promised to inform Rafael Pagan and the others to steer clear of Superfast transportation. It was a rare coincidence, of course, in a city or even a neighborhood full of automobiles, and so Superfast will continue dealing with Quevedo; but it's doubtful that Quevedo could actually prevent his junkies from doing the same thing again, since there is small chance that they would even listen, and if they listened, how would they ever remember the name, and if they remembered the name, still, would they forbear if they needed the money and had the chance?

But despite the various criminal activities in

which Superfast and its drivers have become at least tangentially involved and despite the illegal nature of their business itself, it is important to see that these men—all of them, to a man—are simply using the opportunities presented to them by illicit business to gain for themselves and their families the security and prestige of respectable middle-class society. They are striving for legitimacy, and it's tough to be "legitimate" in America if you're poor. The gypsy cab business, with or without its ancillary criminal activity, is the best if not the only way open to these men for "making it." They are mature individuals. James Taylor is forty-eight and all except Kenny Rivers are over thirty. Every one of them is married with children, ranging up to five children in the case of Edward Wilson. And they are running their business along lines that can only be called a model of middle-class commercial acuity: they are building up a clientele, trying to be friendly, trying to provide good service, gaining a good reputation. And, in the best tradition of American business, they are, with reference to the law, getting away with whatever they can get away with, cutting whatever corners they can.

60. The Infiltration of Organized Crime into the Kosher Meat and Bagel Businesses

DAVID C. MACMICHAEL

NEW YORK

THE RECENT NEW YORK STATE HEARINGS INTO THE legitimate business activities of organized crime and the continuing Waterfront Commission investigations provide a large amount of material on the subject.

The New York State Investigative Commission report, "An Investigation of Racketeer Infiltration into Legitimate Business," purports to show that through the use of personal and economic threats organized criminals are coming to infiltrate and control a wide variety of businesses in New York in a way that "endangers the economy and welfare of the people of this city and state." Unfortunately, the Chairman of the Commission pointed out, not only is fear preventing victimized businessmen from seeking the aid of law enforcement, but some businessmen shameful to say, are actually inviting criminal participation in their businesses.

[Several] cases were presented during the hearings:

*

[One] case examined in some depth by the Commission was that of the kosher meat industry. In the last ten years or so innovations in

meat packaging have resulted in rabbinical authorization for kosher meats properly wrapped in plastic to be handled and displayed without previously required ritual precautions. The result has allowed the sale of kosher meat products in all groceries, meat markets, delicatessens and so forth and produced a minor boom in the kosher meat business. While the long established firms occupying "high or moderate competitive positions in the industry," to quote the New York State Commission report, enjoyed the benefits of the boom without any special effort, a number of new firms attempting to secure positions in the cheap and lower quality end of the market were not above employing as salesmen people with organized crime backgrounds in order to place their products in markets which are not infrequently owned or controlled by identified members of Mafia (or Cosa Nostra) families.[1]

One such firm was the American Kosher Provisions Industry (AKPI) owned by a Hyman Kleinberg. In 1959 he saw himself losing busi-

▶SOURCE: *The Behavior of Organized Crime Figures in Legitimate Business. Stanford, California: Stanford Research Institute (December 31, 1970), pp. 30–31; 34–40. (Editorial adaptations.) Reprinted courtesy of SRI International.*

[1]Testimony at the hearings brought out clearly the fact that stores of this sort serve as important outlets for highjacked meat. More than a quarter of a million tons of meat are highjacked in the New York area annually and the ability of men like Gambino to sell stolen meat at below market prices gives them, naturally, a great competitive edge. As one witness who had had to close a store in close competition with one of Gambino's candidly testified this situation was very good for the consumer but tough on the meat packers.

ness to his chief competitor, Consumer Kosher Provisions, Inc. and guessed that the latter's employment of Max Block,[2] former President of the Amalgamated Meatcutters Union who had recently been ousted after exposure by the McClellan Committee as a labor racketeer, might have something to do with the situation. Nothing simpler than to hire Block away at a higher salary ($50,000 a year) and also one Lorenzo Brescio, a member of the Vito Genovese Mafia family and a former bodyguard for Lucky Luciano. With the assistance of these two, AKPI soon outstripped Consumer and the latter firm was in desperate straits by 1963.

In that year the notorious John Dioguardi (John Dio) was released from the Federal Penitentiary at Atlanta where he had been serving a term for extortion. Dio, a member of the Lucchese family, wielded enormous power in the Teamsters Union,[3] and Herman Rose, the owner of Consumer, hired him as a salesman because, as Rose stated to investigators, people like Dio had the entree to the big food chains.

With Dio's help Rose first tried to negotiate a merger with AKPI. When this attempt failed in 1964, Rose decided that the best tactic for Consumer was to go into bankruptcy, which occurred in January 1965, and that another previously dormant corporation of his First National Kosher Provisions, should take up the struggle with AKPI. Dio later was convicted of bankruptcy fraud in connection with the demise of Consumer, but for the next several years he led First National in a conquest of the low-priced kosher meat business in New York. Eventually, his own salary reached $250,000 a year, and by January 1966 he succeeded in driving AKPI into bankruptcy.

According to the investigations of the Nassau County District Attorney, William Cahn, Dio's success as a salesman was based almost totally on his ability to guarantee labor peace to those supermarket chains which took his product and dropped AKPI's. This conclusion is supported by the statements of supermarket executives who testified, usually anonymously and on the Commission's promise that the names of their firms would not be revealed.

For purposes of this study there are several interesting aspects to the kosher meat case. First, the legitimate owners of the companies vied for the services of organized crime figures who, they believed, could give them a competitive advantage. Second, a fierce competition developed between two firms, each with a leading organized crime racketeer in an important position. With the exception of the abortive attempt at merger of AKPI and Consumer in 1964 there was no appearance of conspiracy by organized crime *as such* to control the market. Third, the competition was only rarely based on considerations of price, quality, or service but almost entirely on which competitor was better able to prevent supermarket labor disputes from arising. Fourth, one of the firms did engage in a fraudulent bankruptcy as a competitive tactic. (And, incidentally, that fraud was rapidly detected and resulted in a return to prison for Dio.) Finally, there was no indication that the consumer suffered through increases in cost or reduction in quality except at the time Consumer was going into bankruptcy and deliberately reduced quality and service in order to hasten the loss of accounts.

Interestingly enough, although the struggle involved two different Mafia families no violence was reported throughout. Also it has to be inferred that markets owned or controlled by other organized crime were involved as purchasers. Unfortunately, the testimony at the hearings did not reveal what tactics were used to persuade them to take one brand or another.

The case of the bagel shops again involved organized crime figures (including the ubiquitous John Dio) in the expanding market for tra-

---

[2]Block is, or was, also the owner of the Black Angus restaurant in Manhattan, an eatery famous for its food and infamous as the preferred gathering place for the organized criminals of New York.

[3]Dio had been important in James Hoffa's successful effort to topple David Beck and gain the presidency of the International Brotherhood of Teamsters.

ditional Jewish food specialties. Most of the testimony introduced at the New York hearings established clearly that such racketeers as the late Thomas Eboli (Tommy Ryan) and Gerardo Catena established a number of bagel shops and, further, that they employed the services of John Dio in getting their products introduced into leading supermarkets.

Once again, however, the careful reader of the testimony is struck by the absence of evidence regarding price gouging, violence, or fraud in the conduct of these businesses. Of particular interest is the testimony of Harold Fleishmann, representing Local 338 of the Bagel Bakers Union, regarding his successful efforts to unionize the Mafia-owned shops.

Fleishmann's first experience with this new type of owner occurred in 1964 when he got word that a new shop, the Bagel Boys, was opening in Brooklyn. The owners, later identified as members of the Genovese Mafia family, at first expressed no interest in the union. Told by Fleishmann they would be picketed they offered him a bribe which he refused. Then they offered to sign a contract with the understanding that they need not abide by it. This offer, too, was refused. That night one of the union officers received a telephoned threat against his family. This was ignored (and no attempt was ever made to carry out the threat) and the next day union pickets were on the scene.

The picket line was successful, the picketers even distributing free bagels to dissuade prospective customers from entering the shop. After a few days of this the Bagel Boys owners' announced that they had signed with another union. This turned out to be a phony under a notorious hoodlum named Benny Ross. The union continued picketing, informing the public of Ross' background, and the Bagel Boys made another try, announcing a contract with a racketeer-controlled jewelry workers union. This, too, was exposed, and eventually the shop signed with Local 338.

Fleishmann testified that the experience was repeated several times during ensuing months.

In every case the shop either signed or gave up the fight and went out of business. There was only minor violence at any time—a fistfight on one occasion; someone threw hot water on a picket on another—and after the incident mentioned above, no additional threats.[4]

Other testimony on the bagel business dealt with the activities of the ubiquitous John Dio in getting his friends in the supermarkets to buy the products of his friends in the bagel business. However, there was no evidence to show price gouging or delivery of poor quality goods. On the contrary, Dio assisted one Ben Willner of W&S Bagels to introduce his machine-made product with the result that retail bagel prices in the metropolitan area dropped more than 15 percent.

There is reason to suspect, although no testimony was introduced alleging this, that Willner's eventual bankruptcy and the consequent sale of his plant to Thomas Eboli at a time when Eboli and his associates were organizing an interstate bagel operation (Bagel U.S.A.) represented a classic takeover. However, the evidence presented to the Commission might as well have supported an opposite contention. Dio several times introduced Willner to his highly placed friends in the big market chains in order that the bagel maker could solicit them, unsuccessfully, for loans to stay in business.

In bagels, as in kosher meats, there was competition between firms with organized crime connections. In Teaneck, New Jersey, in 1965 a Bagel Boys shop planned to open at a location coveted by an established bagel bakery. When representatives of the rivals met it developed that the Eboli-backed Bagel Boys were not the

---

[4]Testimony during the hearings revealed that at the time of the events described here bagel bakers were the highest paid bakery workers in the United States. The standard union contract provided a wage of $210.00 a week plus generous pension benefits. It was not unusual for bagel bakers to make $15,000 to $17,000 annually. One of the owners described by the Commission as a racketeer, complained bitterly about high labor costs and makework practices imposed by the union.

only ones with Mafia support. The New Jersey family boss Gerardo Catena was a silent partner in the established firm. Eventually the two agreed to allow Bagel Boys to open a retail shop in Teaneck but to refrain from engaging in wholesale operations in the area. It was also revealed that not only did Bagel Boys try to violate this agreement by seeking wholesale outlets but that both parties were paying John Dio to use his influence in gaining them access to the major supermarkets. However, in no case was violence threatened or employed.[5]

The Commission hearings show Mafia bagel bakeries as rather ordinary small businesses, plagued by labor problems, haggling and competing over business sites, and paying off to the man with connections in order to distribute their products. One even sees Thomas Eboli's son, Xavier, taking such a personal interest in Bagel Boys that he waits on customers and works parttime as a baker in various shops until his annoyed father makes him quit to pay more attention to his insurance brokerage business.

The amounts of money involved in bagel baking are apparently small. Investments of $500, $1,000, and $1,500 dollars are the rule. Dio reportedly got $10,000 to introduce Bagel Boys to the larger supermarkets in New Jersey. When Bagels U.S.A. went public in late 1968 the business was capitalized at $300,000. With regard to the incorporation of Bagels U.S.A. it should be noted that in early 1970 the bad public character of the people involved in the corporation caused the Securities and Exchange Commission to prohibit the circulation of the firm's prospectus.

*

---

[5]The deCarlo and de Cavalcante transcripts reveal the wide extent of competition between Mafia families in the greater New York area. One conversation has deCarlo envying Chicago, Detroit, and Cleveland which each have only one family so that the members are able to make a decent living.

61. Organized Crime And an Inner City Community

HAROLD D. LASSWELL
JEREMIAH B. McKENNA

RESEARCH METHODS

Introduction

THE MASTER PLAN FOR NEW YORK CITY, PUB-
lished by New York City Planning Commission in 1969, describes Bedford-Stuyvesant as
the heart of he largest ghetto in the nation.[1]
"Poverty is woven into the fabric of life and is
inseparable from it," the Planning Commission
Report goes on to say. Yet the community is also
described as relatively well organized and politically sophisticated.

Before 1936, Bedford-Stuyvesant was a fashionable, upper middle income section of Brooklyn. The development of residential homes occurred between 1870 and 1930, but the depression caught the area with an oversupply of
homes for sale. In 1936, the city extended a new
subway line to Bedford-Stuyvesant which provided a rapid transit link with Harlem. There
followed a migration of the more prosperous
blacks from overcrowded Harlem to Bedford-
Stuyvesant taking advantage of the easy availability of residential homes for sale.

By 1940, Bedford-Stuyvesant was 60% white
and 38% black. The crossover came in 1947
when the black population surpassed the white,

▶SOURCE: *The Impact or Organized Crime on an Inner City
Community. Report by Policy Sciences Center, New York (September, 1972), pp. 38–41; 163–171. (Editorial adaptations.)*

[1]New York City Planning Commission, *Plan for New York
City 1969*, Section 3, Brooklyn, p. 40.

drawn during the early forties by the job opportunities provided to black semi-skilled laborers
by the near-by, bustling Brooklyn Navy Yard.
By 1950, the community was 56% black and
44% white with the rate of increase in the black
population averaging 18% per year. At the time
of the 1960 census, Bedford-Stuyvesant had become 74% black and in the last year of the project survey, 1970, the figure reached 94%. It is
estimated that the unemployment rate is double the city-wide average and if you add those
who are employed at less than a living wage, the
figure jumps to 42% of the labor force out of
work or only marginally employed.

The Bedford-Stuyvesant community presented major obstacles to the researcher. Factual
data pertaining to conditions in the community
are fragmentary and scattered throughout a
myriad of official and non-official agencies. The
major share of the project staff's time and effort
was consumed in the collection effort.

Another problem encountered was in the
disparate boundaries set by the various agencies
for their version of Bedford-Stuyvesant. Practically every official agency had a different geographic definition of the Bedford-Stuyvesant
community. This situation required the careful
analysis of all data collected from official sources
to insure that the extracted material referred
only to the project definition of Bedford-
Stuyvesant. Because the central focus of the project was organized crime, the project definition
of Bedford-Stuyvesant included the geographic

boundaries of the 77th and 79th Police Precincts, which are the prime data collection points for the facts pertaining to local crime. The area defined by the precinct boundaries is the core of Bedford-Stuyvesant but somewhat smaller than the area denominated Bedford-Stuyvesant by most other official agencies.

Control was imposed on the data collection process by organizing it around the eight value categories of the social process used by the policy sciences for the construction of social process models or contextual analysis of problems confronting decision makers. There is no special illumination contained in the eight categories, but they do provide a comprehensive checklist. . . . At this point, it is sufficient if a value is defined as a desired goal pursued in the course of the social process. The eight value categories provide the means of slicing into the "big, blooming ongoing confusion" which constitutes the realities of life or what is denominated the social process. The categories are power, enlightenment, wealth, well-being, skill, affection, respect and rectitude. . . .

The working definition of organized crime originally posed . . . was *non-ideological, concerted criminality of sufficient weight and scope of power to inhibit public control.* Weight of power was defined as the degree of participation in the making of decisions and scope of power referred to the number of values controlled in the exercise of such power. The near total inhibition of the community power process demonstrates the *weight* of organized crime's power. . . . The scope of the power involved, i.e., the other values implicated in the inhibition of the community power process, consist of the obvious one of wealth (at least $250,000 per year) but also enlightenment (the counterintelligence of police operations obtained through these bribes), skill (the indictments described a well-organized and carefully managed arrangement between the gamblers and the corrupt police) and rectitude (a reverse form of morality where the police involved identified with an internal code that legitimatized the bribery).

It is, therefore, not community apathy that permits organized crime to operate but rather the ability of organized crime to inhibit the power process directed against it. . . .

Enlightenment

What is the flow of information between the community and organized crime? The newspapers serving the community are almost totally silent on organized crime. Because of the corruption of the law enforcement effort, successful prosecutions do not come to the focus of attention of the community. The significant number of corrupt police officers have interrupted the flow of intelligence concerning organized crime which would normally pass through the police department to the other law enforcement agencies, such as prosecutors. The latter agencies, denied such intelligence, are unable to alert the community in their usual way to the magnitude of the operations of organized crime.

On the other side of the enlightenment process, organized crime appears to have a steady flow of information coming to it of the community's plans and operations directed against it. The revelations concerning police corruption in the policy and narcotics operations are an indirect source of enlightenment to the community of the weight and scope of organized crime's power. The cumulative impact of these various investigations reinforces the expectations of community residents as to their powerlessness.

The effect of this interaction under the value of enlightenment has been that there are almost no demands directed at law enforcement agencies from community groups to control organized crime. There are certainly demands made to rid the community of the addicts and addict-pushers, but the demand is directed at the visible, street-level addicts and pushers (the unorganized segment of organized crime) and not at the higher and well-organized levels of the narcotics operation. As a result, public pressure has not been focussed upon organized crime in Bedford-Stuyvesant.

Organized crime has available to it at least 1,666 community residents as its eyes and ears to monitor the operations of law enforcement that are directed against it. When these numbers are considered together with the demonstrably successful penetration of the law enforcement process, one is forced to conclude that organized crime's enlightenment processes are far superior to the community's and interact in a way what negates the community enlightenment process directed against it.

An indirect interaction of organized crime and the community enlightenment process can be seen in the impact of the narcotics traffic on the area's schools. The project's estimates of numbers of addicts in the period 1963-1970 are not broken down according to age because many of the sources studied in reaching the estimates did not break down their figures by age groups. However, the Narcotics Register did catalogue new drug abusers according to age groups and the figures show an increasingly large number of school age persons coming onto the Register. An extrapolation from the Register figures for the under-nineteen age group being newly reported from the project area shows the following:

Prior to 1964	1964	1965	1966	1967	1968	1969	1970
96	50	86	204	322	501	766	1133

Another indicator of organized crime's interaction with the community enlightenment process is the number of school staff personnel arrested for the possession or sale of narcotics. The only figures available are for the entire city, but the Board of Education concedes that at least 41 teachers and 106 non-pedagogical employees had been arrested for drug crimes in recent years.

Organized crime has employed addicted school age children to sell drugs in the schools. Again the only available figures are citywide, but they nevertheless indicate a very serious problem. In 1968, 765 school age children were ar-

rested in the city for the felonious possession or sale of drugs. In 1969, the figure rose to 1,150 and moved to 1,449 in 1970. Total narcotic arrests, felonies and misdemeanors, in the 16 to 20 age group in 1968 were 7,701; in 1969 were 12,733 and in 1970 zoomed to 17,705.

The estimated gross take of $69.5 million to organized crime from Bedford-Stuyvesant almost equalled total welfare payments into the area of $76 million and total social security and unemployment insurance payments of $71.9 million. The 1970 payroll for the policy operation of $12.9 million makes organized crime the major employer in the area, second only to the government. Police sources tell us that many of the small stores in the project area take policy bets and use the cash profit to extend credit to the large welfare population in the area. It is the only way the small stores can compete with the large chains. The policy controllers and runners are also known to lend funds to their better customers who are temporarily short (the custom is that the loan is interest free). This indicates that the tremendous cash flows generated by the policy operation are crucial to whatever credit economy there is in the project area.

The tremendous amounts of wealth extracted from the already depressed community economy provide the means by which organized crime corrupts and inhibits the power processes of the community. The 1970 gross of $88 million to organized crime is larger than the total federal income tax collection of $57 million from the project area and the federal government puts back into the area far more than organized crime does.

Well-Being

This area of the social process includes comfort, health and safety. . . . In 1970 the reported narcotics crime rate in the project area reached

Wealth

A simple chart of the interaction of organized crime with the community wealth process would read:

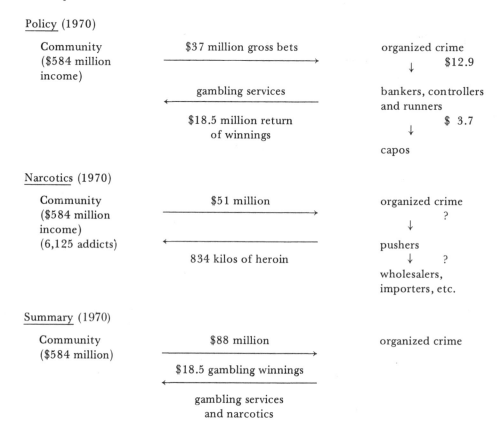

Policy (1970)

Community ($584 million income)	$37 million gross bets →	organized crime ↓ $12.9
	← gambling services	bankers, controllers and runners
	$18.5 million return of winnings	↓ $ 3.7
		capos

Narcotics (1970)

| Community ($584 million income) (6,125 addicts) | $51 million → | organized crime ↓ ? |
| | ← 834 kilos of heroin | pushers ↓ ? wholesalers, importers, etc. |

Summary (1970)

Community ($584 million)	$88 million →	organized crime
	$18.5 gambling winnings ←	
	gambling services and narcotics	

52.47 per thousand of population. It can be predicted that each new addict above the figure of 6,125 will increase that rate by a factor of .006 to .007 per thousand of population. Narcotics is also responsible for an increase in the homicide rate as the police estimate that almost 40% of the killings in the city are related to drugs. Homicides in the project area increased from 48 in 1963 to 89 in 1969.

There are many indirect effects on community well-being caused by narcotics-related crime. Interviews with physicians in the project area disclosed that almost no new medical practices were being established in the area. It had become very dangerous for doctors to function in the area since they are a prime target for robbery committed by desperate addicts. As the result, the physicians serving the area are rapidly aging out and their median age went past 60 during the year 1970. The net result of this is to place greater strains on the public health facilities in the area which are concededly already overtaxed.

Another interaction occurs with respect to the housing base of the community. Interviews of community leaders and community residents indicated that the high narcotics-related crime rate in the community impacted upon the housing turnover rate. Buyers are unwilling to purchase a home in the Bedford-Stuyvesant area and the property owner, seeing no incentive to improve his property in anticipation of a profitable turnover at a future date, allows the housing to deteriorate. Mortgages are not sought, although other indications were that they were a little easier to obtain. Maintenance of housing stock is neglected. The community expectation is that Bedford-Stuyvesant is not the most desirable place to live and, therefore, not the place to put down roots.

It has become trite to observe that narcotics is the largest single killer of persons between the ages of 15 and 44 in New York City. The statement holds true for Bedford-Stuyvesant. However, an equally important indicator of the impact of narcotics on community well-being is the rate of serum non-transfusion hepatitis cases in an area. Serum non-transfusion hepatitis is usually caused by an addict's self-administered injection with a contaminated needle. The trend for the project area is as follows:

1963	1964	1965	1966	1967	1968	1969
9	10	24	27	41	77	87

The figures for central Harlem, with supposedly a larger addict population, provide an interesting comparison.

1963	1964	1965	1966	1967	1968	1969
12	15	14	35	51	88	192

In 1970, the city-wide rate per 100,000 broken down by age group was as follows:

Age Group	Rate Per 100,000
10-14	2.9
15-19	93.0
20-24	70.8
25-34	18.7
35-44	3.5
45-65	0

Each such hepatitis case presumably required extensive hospitalization in a facility servicing the project area. There are no figures available as to the number of hospital beds in the area occupied by a person under treatment for a narcotics-related illness. But every secondary indicator suggests the figure is large. The rate of reimbursement to a hospital from public funds for the care extended to those unable to pay is $110 per day per person.

The project staff also attempted to determine how many of the reported robberies involved an injury to the victim. Unfortunately, the records of cases where the police reported medical assistance was rendered to a victim of a crime were only available for a three year period in just one of the precincts, the 77th, which was the smaller of the two. In 1967, 60 persons were injured as victims of a violent crime within the 77th precinct; in 1968, the figure dropped to 30; but in 1969, it rose to 184.

In conclusion, the impact of organized crime on community well-being in the project area is significant and perhaps the most significant single factor in the deterioration of the project area's health, safety and comfort.

Skill

The skill process in the community is the provision of the opportunity to receive instruction and to exercise an acquired proficiency. It is a vital component of the social process of any community because the improvement of the skill level of a community results in improvements in the enlightenment, wealth, well-being and respect levels as well. The narcotics traffic has impacted on the skill processes of Bedford-Stuyvesant by removing almost 6,125 persons from the skill sharing process. The narcotics addict does not identify with the community's skill process, makes no demands upon it for the improvement of a skill, and expects little advantage from the skill process. The narcotics-related crime rate has drained off significant portions of the community's wealth that would otherwise have been available to spend on the improvement of skills.

The community member who does acquire a

significant degree of skill in whatever form does not identify with the community in the process of acquiring that skill. The disruption of the community processes as a result of the narcotics-related crime rate destroys the identification with the community formerly possessed by those who take the leadership in the shaping and sharing of the skilll process. The natural inclination is to emigrate from the community in order to better pursue the improvement of skill in a condition of greater safety, health, and comfort.

Affection

The primary institution of a community specialized to affection is the family. The family promotes feelings of love, friendship, and loyalty. The policy operation impacts on the family in Bedford-Stuyvesant by reducing the wealth assets of the family that would be ordinarily devoted to the acquisition of other values for the family. The impact of the narcotics traffic upon the Bedford-Stuyvesant family is far more disruptive. The 6,000 plus addict population are an enormous financial drain on their families. The addict is frequently arrested, requiring legal services, bail and the like, all of which are a financial drain on the family.

The narcotics-related crime rate directly affects the variety of civic, religious and fraternal organizations functioning in the area. People are afraid to leave their homes after dark so that community civic life dries up. Fear of crime becomes fear of the stranger to the damage of the whole dimension of friendship in community. Interviews with civic leaders in the community confirmed that their organizations recruited only a fraction of their potential membership due to the fear of crime. The diminution of community civic life keeps the area disorganized and unable to develop an effective response to the deteriorating situation.

Interviews of panel members indicated that a new dynamic had to be considered in the interaction process. The expectations of the community (their perspectives) had been conditioned to anticipate increased growth in the addict population and the narcotics distribution network. It was, therefore, increasingly risky to organize a counter-force to the narcotics traffic. Organizational efforts were limited to economic improvement and the like. The community therefore looked to outside sources for an attack on the problem.

Respect

Respect is coextensive with recognition. Organized crime has interacted with the respect perspectives of the community in several ways. The area residents uniformly deplore the conditions of safety prevailing in their community and realize that Bedford-Stuyvesant is not regarded as a desirable place to live. However, in the course of interviews with the leadership of the Bedford-Stuyvesant community, it was interesting to note that they ranked their community as superior to other adjacent communities such as Ocean Hill-Brownsville and Crown Heights because of the more serious narcotics problem in other areas.

In a central-city, deprived community, probably the most important value to the residents of the community is wealth. Respect will be accorded to the members of the community possessing or displaying the greatest wealth. In Bedford-Stuyvesant one of the most respected figures is the policy collector. He is usually a person of obvious affluence who is visible in the community throughout the day. To the community residents he is a symbol of "upward mobility," although it has been attained through his employment in illegal policy operations.

The loss of respect for one's community has significant effects. It undermines the motivation of area residents to mobilize a counter-attack on the conditions of deterioration. The attitude of "why bother" or "what's the point of it" works against the community organizing itself. It leaves organized crime the largest organized group in the community, and it is axiomatic that power flows to the best organized groups. The interaction of organized crime with the community process of respect is critical to the continuing success of organized crime, since no meaningful counter-criminal program can take hold in the community until the interaction process is reversed in favor of the community.

Rectitude

The process of interaction around this value is difficult to measure but is nevertheless observable. The acceleration of the crime rate dramatically evidences the demoralization of the project area. Increasing numbers of the area's youth are dropping out of the dominant culture and joining the narcotics sub-culture, which is really a counter-culture. As noted previously, the addict population is doubling every two years.

Even the non-addict population gets sucked into the counter-culture. A huge black market has taken hold in the community as the addict population disposes of the fruits of its crimes. Those who have been victimized in the process are increasingly tempted to trade in the black market to recoup their own losses as cheaply as possible. The black market for stolen property then develops its own dynamic and in the process undermines the conventional ethics of hard work and honesty.

One indicator of the standards of rectitude in a community is its illegitimate birth rate. The figures for Bedford-Stuyvesant parallel the other depressing statistics in this report.

Year	Number of Live Illegitimate Births	Rate per Total Live Births
1963	1,917	23.9%
1964	2,053	26.9%
1965	2,095	28.9%
1966	2,239	32.4%
1967	2,400	36.7%
1968	2,556	40.2%
1969	2,789	41.4%
1970	3,246	43.5%

The project staff counted 96 churches within the project area. A survey of the churches in the 77th precinct showed that every church in that area had been established before 1963. Ordinarily, churches are not the locale of a crime, and an increase in crimes committed upon "sacred" ground provides an indicator of the breakdown in rectitude in a community. The trend of crimes committed on church premises in the area is as follows:

1962	1963	1964	1965	1966	1967	1968	1969
11	27	31	45	—	64	68	90

By 1970, it was approaching the point where there was one reported crime per church in the project area.

There were no available records of church membership or attendance so that no indicators could be drawn of the number of community residents identified with the rectitude institutions of the project area. The clergymen interviewed in the course of the research noted a decline in church membership which they attributed in part to the crime rate and in part to the in-migration of new residents who lack any church affiliation. All were agreed there had been a serious decline in community standards of morality.

The impact of organized crime on the process of demoralization of the community could not be segregated in measurable terms but there is secondary evidence in the form of narcotics-related crime rates, etc., which indicated there was an interaction process. . . .

62. Rules of Appropriate Conduct in Organized Crime

FRANCIS A. J. IANNI

WE BEGAN OUR STUDY OF THE LUPOLLO FAMILY with two basic questions in mind: How is the family organized to achieve shared goals? What are the techniques of social control used to motivate members in that pursuit? In the last two chapters, we have described the family's organization as we saw it. Now we turn to the code of rules which not only shapes the behavior of family members but also distinguishes the "good" or successful member from the less-successful one. In the sense we use it here, control within social systems begins with values which establish preferential guides to action. Ultimately, it comes to take the form of specific rules which attempt to apply those values to everyday situations. Thus, while values direct behavior, it is the rule which states which actions will be approved and which forbidden. Rules also carry with them sets of sanctions to be applied when they are broken.

Before we describe the Lupollo family's code of conduct, . . . it may be worthwhile to look at the code of rules which other investigators have found applicable to Italian-American criminal syndicates. Like the popularly known pattern of organization and roles we discussed earlier, these rules of conduct have usually been derived by analogy. That is, rather than looking directly at the behavior of criminal-syndicate members and extrapolating a code from their words and actions, investigators have tried to apply to syndicates codes drawn from observations of other groups.

CODES OF RULES DERIVED BY ANALOGY

"The Mafia Code"

One favorite analogy for the code of conduct in Italian-American criminal syndicates is the "code of the Mafia." The report of the Task Force on organized crime, for example, reasons that since "there is great similarity between the structure of the Italian-Sicilian *Mafia* and the structure of the American confederation of criminals it should not be surprising to find great similarity in the values, norms, and other behavior patterns of the two organizations."[1] Continuing with this reasoning, the report then goes on to present two summaries of "the *Mafia* code"; one statement was made in 1892, the other in 1900.

1. Reciprocal aid in case of any need whatever. 2. Absolute obedience to the chief. 3. An offense received by one of the members to be considered an offense against all and avenged at any cost. 4. No appeal to the state's authorities for justice. 5. No reve-

▶SOURCE: *A Family Business: Kinship and Social Control in Organized Crime* by Francis A.J. Ianni, with Elizabeth Reuss Ianni © 1972 Russell Sage Foundation, New York, pp. 135–139. (Editorial adaptations.)

[1]The President's Commission on Law Enforcement and Administration of Justice, *Task Force Report-Organized Crime: Annotations and Consultant's Papers,* Washington, D.C.: Government Printing Office, 1967, p. 47.

lation of the names of members or any secrets of the association.

1. To help one another and avenge every injury of a fellow member. 2. To work with all means for the defense and freeing of any fellow member who has fallen into the hands of the judiciary. 3. To divide the proceeds of thievery, robbery and extortion with certain consideration for the needy as determined by the *capo.* 4. To keep the oath and maintain secrecy on pain of death within twenty-four hours.[2]

The report notes that "the *Mafia* code" is quite similar to the tenets of American organized criminals—loyalty, honor, secrecy, honesty, and consent to be governed, which may mean "consent to be executed." As the report freely admits, "the *Mafia* code" is similar to the code of any secret organization, from Mau Mau to the Irish Republican Army, and even to public organizations opposed to existing authority and seeking to overthrow it.

Unless the premise of direct descent of Italian-American criminal syndicates from the *Mafia* is accepted, there seems to be no more reason for attributing these reported similarities in behavioral code to *Mafia* origins than to the general behavioral needs of all secret organizations opposed to existing power. The antiquity of the reports used to reconstruct the *Mafia* code also reduces the utility of the analogy. Again, unless it is assumed that the early immigrants to the United States brought the code from Sicily and that it remains largely unaffected by American culture, then it would seem more sensible to compare the current codes of behavior in Sicilian *Mafia* and Italian-American crime syndicates.[3]

The Code of American Prisoners

The Task Force Report and more recently both Donald Cressy and Ralph Salerno also find striking similarities between the behavioral code of organized-crime syndicates and the code of prisoners in American penal institutions.[4] Both Salerno and Cressey recognize the similarity of the prisoners' code to that of underground organizations in general, and see the similarity as growing out of similar needs to control behavior.

The Code of Organized-Crime Families

While each of the major sources admits the absence of any codified set of rules in organized-crime families, all present descriptive lists drawn either from analogies with the codes we have just described or from the experience of the writers in observing organized criminals. Cressey holds that the "thieves' code" is essentially the conduct code for organized-crime families:

1. Be loyal to members of the organization. Do not interfere with each other's interest. Do not be an informer. . . .

2. Be rational. Be a member of the team. Don't engage in battle if you can't win. . . . The directive extends to personal life.

3. Be a man of honor. Respect womanhood and your elders. Don't rock the boat. . . .

4. Be a stand-up guy. Keep your eyes and ears open and your mouth shut. Don't sell out. . . . The "stand-up guy" shows courage and "heart." He does not whine or complain in the face of adversity, including punishment, because "If you can't pay, don't play."

5. Have class. Be independent. Know your way around the world. . . .

Ralph Salerno derives his list from study of organized crime during a career with the New York City Police Department:

1. Secrecy. Most members reveal as little as possible to the police, but the silence of the "Cosa Nostra" segment of organized crime has been so complete that

---

[2]*Ibid.,* p. 47; The first summary was taken from Ed Reid, *Mafia,* New York: New American Library, 1964, p. 31, and the second from A. Cutrera, *La Mafia ed i Mafiosi,* Palermo, 1900.

[3]Cf. Francis A. J. Ianni, "Time and Place as Variables in Acculturation Research," *American Anthropologist,* Vol. 60, No. 1, February 1958, pp. 39–45.

[4]Donald Cressey, *Theft of the Nation,* New York: Harper and Row, 1969; Ralph Salerno and J. S. Tomkins, *The Crime Confederation,* New York: Doubleday and Co., 1969.

until the famous Apalachin meeting in November 1965, many law-enforcement officials doubted its very existence.

2. The organization before the individual. As in the case of secrecy, this rule is one that many in the outside world subscribe to. In military service the individual is expected to put the good of the organization ahead of his own, even if his life depends on it. Our gallery of national heroes is made up of people who made such a choice; the heroes of organized crime are those who went to the death house with their mouths shut.

3. Other members' families are sacred. In most social groups it would be considered unnecessary to specifically prohibit members from making seductive approaches to their associates' wives and daughters. But "Cosa Nostra" is an organization of Italian-Americans and as Luigi Barzini has observed, all Italian males, married and unmarried, are in a constant state of courtship. The rule helps protect the organization from vendettas over such "matters of honor." It makes it possible for a member to be inattentive to the female relatives of another member without this lack of interest being considered unmanly. This sense of chivalry does not, of course, extend to the families of strangers. They can, and often are, taken advantage of.

4. Reveal nothing to your wife. There are three reasons for this rule. In the first place, a member might become estranged from his wife and since "Hell hath no fury . . ."—it is important that she not know anything that she could use to hurt him. Keeping wives in the dark about illegal activities diverts law enforcement attention from them and the rest of one's family. The overall policy that business is not discussed with one's wife is part of a general desire to dissociate the home and family from criminal activities.

5. No kidnapping. The rule against kidnapping [of other members] for ransom is probably a holdover from Sicily where this form of coercion and extortion was widespread.

6. You don't strike another member. This is another rule designed to avoid internal vendettas that could easily arise if an argument were allowed to turn physical. The restraint of often fiery temperaments that it demands is a graphic demonstration of the authority that the code carries.

7. Orders cannot be disobeyed. While self-explanatory, this rule is much broader than similar injunctions found in military or religious organizations. Orders must not only be obeyed, they must be properly carried out. Going through the motions, or hewing to the letter of one's instructions is not enough. This is true even though orders are not detailed or explicit.

8. Promotions and Demotions. Members are promoted in rank—soldier to *capo* to underboss etc.—to fill vacancies created by death, illness, and retirement. The rank of a member who is in prison, however, is kept by him, though his job may be performed by a substitute until he is paroled. At the same time, all members of the same rank are not necessarily equal. A highly successful soldier, for example, may operate a number of different businesses or rackets and have many people working for him. His economic power and influence will tend to make him more important than his technical rank would indicate.

9. Transfers. The majority of members spend their lives within the same family or group. The rules and traditions encourage this loyalty. Under special circumstances, though, there can be a transfer to a family in another jurisdiction.

10. All arguments to higher authority. Most of the disputes that are important enough to go to higher authority involve business practices, sales territories, new operations and the like.

11. Always be a stand-up guy. A "stand-up guy" is by definition, a man who lives by the rules and, if necessary, will die for them. He keeps his mouth shut to the police, he puts the organization ahead of himself, he respects the families of others. He is a man of honor who can be relied on. In the parlance of those in the Confederation he "has character," he is true to the code. In other words, the injunction, be a stand-up guy epitomizes what the code says a real man should be.

12. Justice. The law is the basis for the administration of justice, which is handled within each family. The authority for judgments comes down from the boss in the same way that it might from the village chief of a primitive tribe. The boss, however, does not personally preside except in very serious cases.[5]

[5]Salerno and Tompkins, 1969, pp. 111–128.

All these attempts to define the "code of the *Mafia*" are based on a fundamental, unproven assumption—for there to be a single "code" which covers *all* Italian-American criminal syndicates, there must be a single national organization. Any code of rules must be derived from some shared set of values; the only way *the* "code of the *Mafia*" could exist would be in the context of a unified organization. Cressey, Salerno, and the others assume that such an organization exists. We found no evidence for it in our study of the Lupollo family and our data are limited to what we were able to see and hear. Thus we have investigated the code of the Lupollos, *not* the code of the *Mafia*. Our method was to observe and record behavior and then to seek regularities that had enough frequency to suggest that the behavior resulted from the pressures of the shared social system rather than from idiosyncratic behavior. We also questioned family members and others about rules, usually by asking why some member of the family behaved in a particular way. Thus, our reconstruction of rules of conduct comes both from our own observations and from the explanations of observed behavior given by the people living under those rules.

In the Lupollo family as in the card game of bridge, there are two levels of the rules. There are game or ground rules, which structure the game, and then there are informal rules for playing the game intelligently. Similarly, in the Lupollo family there are those basic rules which structure the framework of acceptable conduct, and those supplementary rules which define who plays the game well and who plays it poorly. We found three basic ground rules for behavior in the Lupollo family: (1) primary loyalty is vested in "family" rather than in individual lineages or nuclear families, (2) each member of the family must "act like a man" and do nothing which brings disgrace on the family, and (3) family business is privileged matter and must not be reported or discussed outside the group. These three rules are basic for maintaining membership within the group, but each subsumes a number of informal rules which explain why some members are more successful at the game than others.

THE LUPOLLO CODE OF CONDUCT

Rule 1. Loyalty to the Family

Several studies of family structure among Italians both in the United States and overseas have reported that what seems at first an *extended family*—a unit which extends horizontally and vertically to include all kin in a socially and economically self-sufficient unit—is actually an *expanded family*, nuclear families in separate households who maintain close social relationships but do not function as an integrated economic unit.[6] Among the impoverished peasants in the south of Italy, this has always been a matter of necessity rather than choice. Poverty and the scarcity of land precluded any holdings large enough to sustain extended families except among the nobility or land-owning classes. When the peasant migrated, the new conditions of his life also precluded common residence or joint economic enterprise for the vast majority. The Lupollo family, however, while they live as separate households, are an integrated extended family in every sense. They are economically and socially self-sufficient and do not venture far outside the family group. Friends of individual members either become part of the family circle or are seen only occasionally.

It is to the extended Lupollo family (which includes the Alcamo, Salemi, and Tucci lineages) that primary loyalty is given. On the surface, at least, this loyalty supercedes loyalty to lineage and even to individual nuclear families, and is expressed in a number of ways. Members

---

[6]Cf. Donald Pitkin, "Land Tenure and Farm Organization in an Italian Village," Unpublished Ph.D. Dissertation, Harvard University, 1954, p. 114; Herbert Gans, *The Urban Villagers*, Glencoe: The Free Press, 1962, pp. 45–46; and Philip Garigue and Raymond Firth, "Kinship Organization of Italianates in London," in Raymond Firth (ed.), *Two Studies in Kinship in London*, London: Athlone Press, 1956, p. 74.

speak of the family as a unit; they are almost completely dependent on friendship, business, and social relations within the family circle; they tend to settle in physical proximity to other family members. Most fundamentally, however, this loyalty finds expression in the closeness that members feel for the family and for one another.

Once Bobby Lupollo and I talked about how close members of the family were with one another. Bobby had remarked that he thought running was better exercise than basketball, that he was going to mention this to his cousin Freddy, and that perhaps Freddy and Bobby could then get Tommy and Paulie to start jogging in a "running club." I asked Bobby why it was that he usually thought of his relatives whenever he mentioned starting some new social or business venture:

"Our family is very close like all Italian families, but ours is even closer than most. Ever since I could remember everything we did was done together. If I decided that I wanted to to to the circus, my father [Joey Lupollo] would get Tommy or Freddy to go with us, too. Even when we were dating we used to go to the same places together. I was Tommy's best man when he was married and he was mine. When I was in college I was a pledge in a fraternity—no, two different fraternities—but never became a brother because I didn't have anything in common with the other fellows. Even now that we are married we go out together, not because our wives get along together so well—they don't and Linda [Bobby's wife] is always after me to make new friends. It's because we were raised more like brothers than like cousins. Look, I can stand naked in front of you [we were in the dressing room at an athletic club] and I can stand naked in front of my wife but I can't stand naked in front of the two of you, not without all of us feeling ashamed or my wife saying that I'm some kind of a crude guinea bastard. It's something like that with my cousins. I can say and do things in front of them that I wouldn't say or do even in front of my wife, because we're close. If I find a good business deal or see a movie that I like I always think about how they would like it too. We're a family that believes in sticking together. All Italians are that way but when it comes to business we're more like Jews than like Italians. I

know that if I tell Tommy about a good deal he'll remember me when he finds a good one. Even my father is that way with Pete Tucci and he doesn't like him too much."

As Bobby's remarks indicate, the bonds which we normally associate with the nuclear family are, among the Lupollos, generalized beyond, into the extended family relationship which has been produced by the merger of personal and social interests with economic interests. This conforting sense of family is accepted by all of the fifteen members of the central family. Basil Alcamo—with Paulie, the most alienated from the family—often explains business or social arrangements which run counter to his own idea of good practice by the phrase "it's in the family." He resents Joe's old-fashioned business ideas, but he never expresses any thought of striking out on his own, nor does he refuse to go along with what he considers bad deals arranged by Joe. He protests, but only toward his "brothers" in his same age-grade rather than to Joe and his peers or to the younger family members, and he eventually accepts the decision like any dutiful "son." How much he complains to his father, Phil, and whether Phil is responsive to his complaints has not been determined; but publicly he submits to the family authority structure just as other members do. Paulie, on the other hand, never protests openly. In private conversation, however, he complained to me of the favoritism shown the Lupollo and Alcamo lineages at the expense of the Salemis.

One revealing deviation from the injunction to maintain family loyalty occurred when Freddy married Monica, a woman of Irish descent, against his parents' wishes. Soon after their marriage in 1967, they began socializing with her friends and their husbands. By 1968, the "defection" had become a problem in the family. The family's reaction included harsh and biting comments about Monica, her ancestry, and Freddy's lack of masculinity in letting her "lead him around by the balls." Their extra-familial friendships were frowned upon. Phil Alcamo commented that whenever the women of the family gathered they talked of Monica and her airs. According to Phil, who got the information secondhand from his wife (who is also non-Italian), the women's comments ranged from "she thinks we're not good enough for her" to speculation that Monica was not interested in her friends, but in their husbands. Freddy's mother bore the brunt of the collective displeasure. Finally, in exasperation and embarrassment, she would join in the chorus of disapproval and her most caustic comment was always ". . . she says she wants to give me respect, I don't need respect from her, I'm not her mother." This pressure had its effect. Freddy and Monica began turning more toward the family and gradually dropped their outside associations. After that, Phil thought Monica was not so bad "for an Irish."

The rule of loyalty to the family includes a number of subsidiaries. The most important among these is "no outside business interests which might conflict with the family." Here are two situations exemplifying this rule and its application.

In early 1968, Tony Lupollo bought a tract of land on the Toms River in New Jersey, and planned to build a motel-marina. Although the land had been purchased through Brooklyn Eagle Realty, Tony's business venture was a private one. By early 1969, ground had been broken for the motel and some of the marina piers had already been built. Then, in the summer of 1969, trouble developed over the township's zoning ordinances. News of the difficulty reached Joe Lupollo. Joe was furious at Tony both because his own interests in New Jersey would be jeopardized by any dispute involving a member of the family, and because, according to Phil, "Tony never had the balls or the head to tell his father he was doing it." Later in 1969, Phil said that Tony had sold the land at a loss and that a good way "to get his ass up" would be to ask him when the motel would be finished.

The second incident took place in early 1970, and involved Joe's son Marky, who is considered to be a poor judge of business. Marky decided

that since New York was without an Italian discotheque, whoever started one would make a killing. For weeks he talked of nothing but how he would set it up, with Italian singing stars and rock groups coming over to play, and how people of all ages would flock to it. One night at dinner, Marky commented on the possibility of getting a well-known Italian singer to come over for the opening of the club, which he had already named "The Villa." Joe turned to him and said (in Italian), "I don't want to hear anymore about the club, now or ever again." Later, Phil Alcamo explained that "anyone with any sense should realize that a nightclub is the one sure way of getting into trouble, since all kinds of bums go to nightclubs and just like Joe Namath you can find yourself associated with people you don't know and who don't owe you anything." His mother (Phil said) had always told him that "if you go around with a cripple you learn to limp." Marky never mentioned "The Villa" again.

A second subsidiary to the rule of family loyalty calls for mutual aid to other family members. There are no status differences in who can call upon whom for aid. In the two years of this study, there were situations in which a member with high prestige called upon a lower-prestige member for help, as well as those in which a high-prestige member helped a person with lower prestige. The explanation is always given in terms of family. For example, Phil gave several thousand dollars to Tony after the motel-marina fiasco. When his son Basil took him to task, pointing out that Tony could have gotten it from his father and that gratitude was not one of Tony's outstanding virtues, Phil answered simply, "he's family, Basil, how can I say no?"

A third subsidiary rule says, "Don't interfere in the business of another family member." It is an expression of the security which comes with family membership. In its most basic form, it is the insurance which goes with knowing that others will not interfere in one's best interest so long as you do not give them cause to distrust you. The rule is expressed in many ways. Pete

Tucci is the best example within the family of the importance of "playing the game" properly in this area. He has no base of power other than his relationship with his father-in-law, Joe Lupollo. Since none of his children have gone into the family business, he has no paternal relationship which would allow him to call on others for support, and yet the vulnerability of his position obviously does not worry him. His role in managing the food-processing sector of the family business is an important and lucrative one, which would be profitable to any other member—better connected—who craved it. Yet, so long as Pete does not try to move into someone else's area, he is secure. No one really thinks very highly of him—he is considered little more than "Joe's boy" in the business—but he does not have the role of isolate. He is *a member of the family,* and as long as he gives it his first loyalty he enjoys its collective security.

The basic rule of loyalty to the family over all else and the subsidiary rules which define the way to use the rule to one's best advantage give the family a group solidarity against anyone or anything outside the family. While the younger members of the family do not seem to show it as belligerently as their parents and grandparents, it is still an important behavior guide for them. They are known in the Italian-American community as members of the family, and without exception they see the future of that organization as their own.

The rule of loyalty does not ensure smooth social relationships within the family. There are squabbles, and rivalries, and cliques, and the various lineages do stick together; but the family as a unit absorbs these differences and continues to function. When there are attacks from outside the group, the force of family cohesion comes into play and the divisions disappear.

Not all members of the family use the rules equally well. Those with high respect or prestige show more awareness of and conformity to the subsidiary rules than those with low respect or prestige. Only when someone seems to be ignoring the rule of loyalty itself, as when Freddy

began finding new friends and when Tony got involved in the potentially troublesome motel-marina, is the question of loyalty raised. Marky's desire to start the Italian nightclub was simply considered foolish and everyone could laugh at it; Freddy and Tony actually lost some respect as a result of their actions, and group pressure was exerted to bring them back into line.

Rule 2. "Act Like a Man."

The concept of "being a man" goes by many names in the Lupollo family. At various times it is expressed as "being a stand-up guy," or "having balls." At the same time, however, the notion of being a man carries with it a distinct sense of humility and willingness to accept decisions, even when they are troublesome to ego, without resort to complaints, whines, or other unmanly actions. In fact, the rule of being a man seems so close to the concept of *omertà* found in the south of Italy that it is tempting to assume that *omertà* is its origin. To one who has watched both systems in operation, however, it is logical to conclude that both *omertà* and the injunction to be a man are part of the social contract created when a group of men bond themselves together in a secret society. In such bonding, the alliance demands that each man depend on the others in the group to protect their common interest, and to act like a man in the company of other men.

The importance of being a man within the Lupollo family is part of the code for each generation, and no one escapes its demands. But the demands differ according to one's status in the family. Generally, the higher the status the more important it is to present a public image of self-control, willingness to accept decisions, and interpersonal power which demands respect from others. Being a man is also mediated in non-"business" relationships. Joe Lupollo, for example, is stern and authoritarian even with his grandchildren in all matters related to the family business, but he is permitted to show grandfatherly concern for them in social and personal relationships even in public. The younger members of the family have learned to read the particular role he is playing and to react accordingly. Freddy, for example, will actually tease his grandfather about his old-fashioned suits and shoes in front of other members of the Lupollo lineage, but whenever members of other lineages or persons outside the family are present he is respectful and correct in relations with Joe. This same pattern of situational determination of the content of the requirement to be a man is true throughout the family between father and son, godfather and godson, and brothers.

In many ways, the behavior involved is similar to the Chinese or Oriental concept of "face." That is, just as "losing face" is a much more obvious and observable social and behavioral feature than gaining it, so those behaviors and group reactions which appear when someone is *not* being a man are more obvious in the Lupollo family than the behaviors and reactions appearing when someone *is*. In this negative aspect, it appears that being a man has two different dimensions, one primarily social and one primarily personal. The social aspect of being a man is part of the awarding of respect within the family and, while it does characterize family members to outsiders, it is much more obvious and important within the group itself. It is the *groups'* valuation of the individual member in terms of how they define him as a man worthy of trust and so respect. Since group functioning depends on mutual trust and confidence that other family members will perform in ways appropriate to being a man, behaviors which are not so defined can cause serious problems for the individual and the group. During this study, only one incident occurred which approached a loss of respect and consequent loss of status for a family member. Early in 1969, Joe's son Marky evidently entered into a business arrangement with Albert Cuccio, who is a cousin of Domnick Maisano of the East Harlem De Maio family. Marky kept it from his father and other members of the family. In the spring of that year Marky left for Florida and did not return until late June. One of the younger members of the

family told me that Marky had gone away for a while because his father was so furious with him that it was best to "keep out of the old man's sight" for a while. Joe was particularly upset because Cuccio was reputedly involved in the drug trade, and thus Marky had possibly compromised the family by being seen with Cuccio. What made matters worse for Marky was that he had behaved badly when confronted by his father and his Uncle Charley. Marky apparently tried to implicate his brother Joey and refused to take responsibility for his own actions. Evidently just being seen with Cuccio was sufficiently dangerous that his subsequent refusal to admit his error was viewed as cowardly and disruptive of family discipline. Marky's son Tommy was particularly upset, because some of the criticism spilled over to him.

While we have little information on even this case of loss of status within the group as a result of behavior contrary to the requirement to be a man, we venture to suggest these rules: (1) loss of respect within the group can come from behavior defined as contrary to the requirement to "be a man" and (2) such loss reaches beyond the individual to affect his closest relatives and associates. Being a man in this collective sense means earning and keeping the respect and trust of one's associates. In the case just described, Marky violated the first rule of family loyalty by endangering the group through association with a reputed drug baron and then, having been discovered, did not accept the responsibility for his actions and lost the respect of his fellows for not acting like a man.

There is a second dimension to being a man which is personal in that it is part of an individual's "reputation." While the social aspect of being a man is essentially internal to the group and suggests that the individual can be depended upon to behave in a fashion which will not bring danger or disgrace to the group, the reputational aspect of being a man is much more a matter of his image outside the family. In earlier chapters some of these external "reputations" were described—Freddy's being a "ladies' man" and Phil Alcamo's being an "astute political animal." Such reputational aspects of "being a man" can change without any great effect on the person's role within the family, for they are part of the individual's role in the *external* environment. They can be enhanced or diminished, changed by personal effort or clever maneuvering, and even borrowed through association with the right people. The social aspect of being a man, however, is not only defined within the group, it is maintained or lost as a whole. After Marky returned from Florida, his position within the group seemed to have diminished to the point that it created serious personal and social difficulties for him.

The reputational aspect of the injunction to be a man is supported in family legendry by numerous oft-told tales of family members or their associates who have shown that peculiar combination of personal courage mixed with humility which is defined as being a man. In one such story, the protagonist, a relative of the Salemi lineage who was known as *"Don Cece,"* was picked up by the police in front of one of the storefront social clubs in Greenwich Village for questioning. One of the police officers, a detective inspector, knew enough about the importance of respect in the world of the families that he decided to shame *Don Cece* (who was then in his early sixties) by having two patrolmen beat him to the ground and handcuff his hands behind his back. When they lifted him to his feet, his face was bloody and his glasses had been knocked off onto the sidewalk. One of the patrolmen, somewhat abashed by what he had done, picked up the glasses and started to put them back on *Don Cece*'s nose, but *Don Cece* turned his head aside and said (in Italian for the benefit of his audience), "I have seen and remembered all I need to this morning." The Lupollos always tell the story in the same manner that second- and third-generation Italian-Americans tell tales of their immigrant forebears' courage, endurance, and simplicity in face of the adversity of the ghetto. Here, however, the moral is very obviously not the stoic

perseverance of the peasant immigrant but the refusal of someone in a family to allow himself and so his family to be publicly shamed.

Rule 3. The Rule of Secrecy

The third set of conduct rules fit under the basic rule that family business matters are privileged and are not to be reported or discussed outside the group. An obvious reason for secrecy in the Lupollo family is their involvement in illegal activities. But even in the legitimate business enterprises the degree of secrecy goes beyond that found in other business organizations. This could be explained by the linkages between the illegal and legal activities, except that secrecy extends even beyond legitimate business activities, to include the social and personal behavior of individual members of the family. This extension of secrecy is manifest in a number of characteristic behaviors among family members. The most obvious is that family members use a jargon made up of words and phrases which have meaning only to family members. Some of the "code" refers to business activities. The family-controlled Absford Linen Service, for example, is always called "the Long Island place" or "Vince's place" (Vincent Corallo is the owner of record) in conversation. The same approach is used with personnel: Vincent Corallo is referred to as "the fellow in Long Island" or "Patsy's brother-in-law." But the jargon carries over into all conversation, and even when social or kinship relations are being discussed the same descriptive terms are used. In addition, in the second and third generations (but less so in the fourth generation), Italian and Sicilian words and phrases are used in their original meanings as part of a conversation in English. Marky, for example, might say to Patsy, "I know that guy from meeting him a couple of years ago and he is a real *cafone* (idiot)." The use of Italian and Sicilian terms in English sentences is not an uncommon practice among other Italian-Americans of the same generations, but here it combines with the use of jargon to provide a shared language which serves to protect the conversation from those not part of the group.

There is another function of secrecy in the Lupollo family beyond concealing or obscuring information. In Sicilian *Mafie,* the differentiation of individuals as members or outsiders is one of the purposes of secrecy. Those individuals who share the secrets are fellow members; those who do not are outsiders. Secrecy in this sense serves as a bonding mechanism among the members of the group. Not only does it assign individuals to a membership or outsider status, it establishes a comaraderie among group members. In the Lupollo family, this shared sense of membership excludes those members of the various lineages who are not part of the family business and all female members of the lineages as well. Rosa Parone, who is Phil Alcamo's sister and operates the family-related Melrose Cigarette Company, is the only woman who has any contact with any of the family businesses, and most of the actual business operation is actually handled by her son James. Even the brothers and sisters of members are excluded. Usually, where one part of a group joins together and agrees to hold certain secrets in common, the action invites hostility from those who are not members. In the Lupollo family, however, this does not seem to be so.

Finally, secrecy serves as a means of establishing and maintaining dominance and social distance not only between family members and nonmembers but within the family as well. Some secrets are more secret than others, and are shared by only some members of the group. In part this circumstance relates to the structure of authority in the family. Joe Lupollo and his brother Charley have access to all family information; some they share with other members, but some they do not. In part the differentiation is an outgrowth of the relationship between the respect-rating structure of the group and secrecy. There are some members of the family who enjoy low respect and do not have access to as many secrets. But in part it is also the natural result of the various power networks, which make for greater confidentiality among some

members than others. In the Lupollo family, despite the cardinal importance of the basic rule that loyalty to the family comes before loyalty to lineage, there seems little question that, for example, Phil Alcamo and his son Basil share a father–son confidentiality, as do Joe Lupollo and his favorite son Joey.

Every business organization has secrets of some kind. Business practices, tactics, and strategy to some degree are always private and privileged information. A difference in the Lupollo family business, however, is that the rule of secrecy is more inclusive than in most business operations, and violations are considered independent acts against the collective welfare of the group. The injunction against disclosure of information is not specific to the illegal sectors of the business operations, but cover virtually all areas of the family operations. The preferred behavior is not just reluctance to disclose business secrets which might aid competitors, but complete silence in the face of any inquiries, formal or informal, official or private, about business affairs. In a sense, then, this rule reflects not only the businessman's reluctance to make business matters public, but also the strength of the bond among family members which defines all others as "outsiders." Here again it is the kinship bond, both real and fictive, which effectively serves as the basis of enforcement; to violate the injunctions against disclosure of information is not a bad business practice, it is an act of disloyalty to the family. And family in this context excludes wives, those members of the various lineages who are not directly involved in the family business, and all others.

ENFORCING RULES OF CONDUCT

Rules of conduct are meant to be enforced, and a system of sanctions always has to be established. Previous studies of organized crime have stressed the coercive sanctions or the allocation of punishments, including death, as the principal means of control in Italian-American criminal syndicates. It would be naïve to suggest that such sanctions do not exist in the Lupollo family, but this study did not produce any evidence of them. Within the family, the canon of reciprocity forms the motive force behind rules of conduct. Individuals within the group have obligations toward others and, in turn, have expectations concerning how others will relate to them. Because the group is small and close primary relationships exist within the group, violations of the rules of conduct are not frequent. Where they do occur, they tend to be idiosyncratic behaviors rather than outright disobedience. This shared understanding of what is right and what is wrong in terms of behavior keeps conflict over rules at a minimum. And, since in groups of this type rules tend to be enforced only when something provokes enforcement, it is usually sufficient for the offending behavior to become public within the group for behavior to become appropriate once again. Thus in the examples of rule violation we described earlier—Freddy's turning outside the family for friendship and the actions of Patsy and Marky that jeopardized the welfare of the group—it was sufficient for group attention to be focused on the violations. There are, however, some members of the family who blow the whistle on infractions of rules with some consistency. Joe Lupollo, as head of the family, seldom intervenes except when his anger is aroused—as when he felt Marky was behaving foolishly in attempting to open a nightclub—or where an infraction is of such magnitude that his authority is questioned. Generally, Charley Lupollo questions the behavior of other family members.

Usually this is done publicly without much rancor, as any uncle or father might do in a traditional Italian-American family. What is different is that Charley takes the initiative for citing rule infractions in every area of behavior, from business practices to social protocol, and he acts in the name of his brother Joe. This surrogate position is obvious both in his approach to the erring family member and in the reaction of the miscreant. Charley will, for example, chide Patsy for being late to some gathering and suggest that Joe expected everyone to be there on time. Patsy's response will differ depending on whether Joe is scheduled to be there or not; in neither case, however, will Charley pursue the point. He lets his suggestion that Joe will be offended serve as warning enough.

In addition to Charley, Phil Alcamo and Joey Lupollo are also frequent critics of rule violators. Phil usually cites rule violations on the part of members of the next lower generation in the family—Patsy, Marky, Basil and so on—while Joey reserves his criticism for the younger members of the group, who are also his next-generation relatives. Our limited experience with rule violation and consequent enforcement makes it difficult to differentiate rule enforcers in the family with any certainty, but it seems that Charley's role as Joe's surrogate is a fairly formal one, while Phil is acting as an informal rule enforcer as a result of his age and respect ranking in the group. Joey, on the other hand, acts both in his role as heir-apparent and as the role model for his younger relatives within the family.

63. The Myth of the Mafia

DWIGHT SMITH

OUR PRIMARY SOURCES FOR PRESENT-DAY IMAGES of organized crime are three threads in the broader conceptual fabric of "crime." One thread is the official and reportorial approach to real persons identified with organized crime. The second thread is the novelist's approach to the fictional criminal who used to be called a "gangster" or "racketeer" but, since 1969, has been known as a "Mafioso." The third and ordinarily least visible thread is the scholarly approach to a sociological concept, organized crime. These were essentially independent views at the outset, but after 1950 they became increasingly intertwined as public attention was drawn to a particular law-enforcement view of organized, conspiratorial crime. More recently, since the President's Crime Commission report was issued in 1967 and *The Godfather* was published in 1969, the three threads have continued unbroken, but with a difference: they have each become infected with the "Mafia" label.

The sustained use of a single label results from a series of entrepreneurial efforts. It began in the fifties with the moral entrepreneurship of the Federal Bureau of Narcotics, which was intent upon portraying a supercriminal opponent as a partial excuse for its inability to halt heroin smuggling. By the sixties, other law-enforcement officials appropriated use of that supercriminal "Mafia" label as a justification for tipping the legal balance away from indi-

vidual privacy and toward internal security. As that objective was being met, with enactment of the 1968 and 1970 omnibus crime control acts, literary entrepreneurs intent upon a post-Puzo gravy train reappropriated the label as their rallying point for (as Puzo has since described it for *New York Magazine*) "the Godfather business."

These separate uses of a single name entailed projection of images that were not wholly consistent. But consistency and precision have seldom concerned those who have applied the "Mafia" label, and under the circumstances in which it has been used, its bearers have had little reason to issue clarifications or to demand corrections.

The consequent diffusion of popular meaning for "Mafia" is important if one wishes to understand the problems associated with "educating the public" about organized crime. In January 1970, for example, at the height of popularity for the "Mafia" label and as the federal government was in hot pursuit of various New Jersey luminaries identified through the so-called "DeCavalcante Tapes," references frequently were made to "Mafia" connections. In a typical column, Charles Grutzner, then the *New York Times* expert-in-residence, identified eight men variously as "a major New Jersey mafioso," "the last Mafia 'boss of all bosses,'" "reputed captains in the Genovese Mafia family," "then Mafia boss in Chicago," "boss of a New York-based Mafia family with some rackets in New Jersey," "then under-boss to the late Mafia 'boss of bosses,'" and "a soldier in [a] Mafia family." These references implied a rather extensive shared view of an organization and the way it

▶SOURCE: *The Mafia Mystique.* New York: Basic Books, 1975, pp. 289–298, 223, 224, 230. (Editorial adaptations.) Reprinted by permission.

was understood to work. Grutzner went beyond this, however; after identifying his Mafiosi cast, he wrote of "organized crime groups" and "members of organized crime." Within the context of the article the two forms of address became almost interchangeable. But only almost; had Grutzner referred only to "organized crime groups" and "members of organized crime," his readers generally would have had a much less distinct image of his subjects than was conveyed by identifying them with "Mafia."

The question posed by the labeling process is not simply whether the subjects of the column were properly identified with "Mafia." Rather, the question is twofold: Is it proper at all to transfer the imagery of "Mafia" to organized crime? And if one does, what risks are undertaken because "Mafia" is subject to multiple interpretations? Leaving aside for the moment the first question, it appears that Grutzner probably had keyed in his mind a particular set of images, drawn at that time from the Crime Commission report. The chances are that participants in the federal strike force in New Jersey were keyed to the same set of images. But what of the "average" *Times* reader? The idea of "a major New Jersey mafioso" may have triggered some strong images, but were they sufficiently similar to the images intended by the writer? Did the reader visualize the Crime Commission's Mafia, or was his imagery fashioned more directly by Mario Puzo? And if the latter, did he "see" the gangster-outlaw, the gangster-businessman, or the gangster-servant?

The principal excuse for the lack of clarity has been secrecy: *omertá*. The excuse itself has added an extra pejorative kick to the basic rhetoric which, from 1950 to 1969, was largely exposé-oriented and based on information obtained from a law-enforcement point of view. The few attempts at portraying organized crime from a different perspective—examples being Daniel Bell's "Crime as an American Way of Life" in 1953 and articles for *The Annals* of the American Academy of Political and Social Science by Robert Woetzel and Thorsten Sellin in 1963, and Gilbert Geis in 1966—gave little comfort to believers in a Mafia conspiracy and were generally ignored. The state of knowledge is illustrated by the selections in Guy Tyler's 1962 book of readings, *Organized Crime in America* (which Geis described in 1966 as "the best single source of information on organized crime"). Three-quarters of them were written originally either as anecdotal accounts of crime or as exhortations to the faithful. Writings about Mafia and organized crime have been noted for emotional content, not "disciplined objectivity." They were judged for their ability to arouse strong negative sentiments among the public at large, not for their appeal to the intellect.

The principal effort to add intellectual substance to prevailing sentiment was Donald Cressey's work for the President's Crime Commission, "The Functions and Structure of Criminal Syndicates." He intended to encourage other social scientists to enter the search for new questions and new evidence concerning organized crime. As it turned out, he was the first to answer his own call, but in so doing he retreated to old questions for which new evidence simply recapitulated old answers and reinforced old stereotypes. The search for reality was thus dominated by established conventions. When a wider audience responded with new questions that led to new answers that did not reinforce the old stereotypes, Mafia watchers found it easy to reject or ignore what they had to say.

But the questions remain, annoying though they may be. Cressey's invitation was successful, even if it led in directions his supporters had not expected. As we search for reality among the images of novelists and newsmen, an alternative approach to the meaning of "Mafia," and an alternative way of interpreting the phenomenon we call organized crime, are waiting for us.

*

LAW ENFORCEMENT GIVES UP ITS GHOST

The problem of analyzing the reportorial use of "Mafia" can be illustrated dramatically if we consider the number of articles under the entry

"Mafia" in the *New York Times Index* for each year since 1950, when the Kefauver hearings began. Consider:

Year	Number of References	Year	Number of References
1950	5	1962	2
1951	11	1963	67
1952	1	1964	57
1953	2	1965	81
1954	3	1966	98
1955	3	1967	148
1956	0	1968	182
1957	4	1969	359
1958	11	1970	319
1959	10	1971	246
1960	4	1972	268
1961	1	1973	160

. . . earlier focal points—the 1950–51 Kefauver hearings and the 1957 Apalachin incident with its repercussions until 1960 in Congress and the courts—are modestly evident. They pale in significance, however, in comparison with the quantum jumps in "Mafia" notoriety after Valachi in 1963*, the Crime Commission in 1967, and Puzo in 1969. A new level of interest was established that shows only partial signs of abating. Such a change can hardly be explained as random choice, and it cannot be expected to have occurred without some effect on the name itself. Under what circumstances, then, did "Mafia" popularity change? And what happened to "Mafia" imagery as a result?

There were, of course, a series of events with news value and some justification (though sometimes strained) for assemblage under a common label. December 1968 was the turning point, as William J. Brennan 3d, an assistant state attorney for New Jersey, spoke at a dinner meeting of Sigma Delta Chi (the professional journalists' society) in Kenilworth, New Jersey, and told his

¹See Editors' Note at the end of this selection.

audience that organized crime had infiltrated nearly every facet of life in New Jersey, including politics. It was hardly a surprising message for that group, especially since Brennan was known to be directing a special state investigation of organized crime—until he added that there were "three legislators [in New Jersey] who are entirely too comfortable with members of organized crime."

If we bear in mind the circumstances in which he spoke—most particularly that he represented a Democratic administration and referred to a Republican-controlled legislature—it is clear that the speech generated more news than his limited comment justified. It was the catalyst for a political issue that was as valuable for William Cahill's subsequent and successful New Jersey gubernatorial challenge as the Apalachin incident had been for Nelson Rockefeller's 1958 campaign. Politics aside, however, Brennan provided an inadvertent platform for the journalists whom he addressed. Though his references were limited to "organized crime," he precipitated an argument apart from the gubernatorial campaign (but including legislative hearings) that lasted more than a year and became immediately identified in the press as a "Mafia probe."

Other events followed. In 1969, Sidney Franzblau, defense lawyer for Simone DeCavalcante in a conspiracy-extortion case, demanded disclosure from the Justice Department of any wiretapping or eavesdropping in his case and was rewarded with two thousand pages of FBI reports on conversations held in his client's office from 1964 to 1965. "Sam the Plumber," as DeCavalcante had come to be known, was alleged (and the media were quick to pick it up) to be the head of the sixth-largest Mafia family in the New York metropolitan area. Later that fall, Peter Maas's *Valachi Papers* was published, and it gained substantial ex post facto legitimation from popular interpretations of DeCavalcante's conversations. Meanwhile, in January 1969 the House ethics Committee had begun debating a probe of *Life* magazine's 1967 report that New Jersey Congressman Cornelius Gallagher had too cozy a relationship with the reputed Mafia leader Joseph Zicarelli, and in September San Francisco's Mayor Joseph Alioto had been accused by *Look* magazine of a similar arrangement with West Coast Mafiosi. Vito Genovese had died in a federal prison in Missouri in February, thereby inviting speculation as to his probable successor as "boss of all bosses." And in March, *The Godfather* had been published. All things considered, it was a banner year for "Mafia" hunters.

The year 1970 promised to be equally productive, thanks partly to a carryover of interest in the previous year's events; but the climate changed dramatically in July, when Attorney General John Mitchell placed an embargo on official use of "Mafia" or "Cosa Nostra" by Justice Department officials. "It has become increasingly clear," he wrote in a well-publicized confidential memorandum to his division heads, "that a good many Americans of Italian descent are offended. They feel that the use of these Italian terms reflects adversely on Italian-Americans generally, and there is no doubt that their concern is genuine and sincere." When Governor Rockefeller issued a similar directive in August, the moratorium was virtually complete. (Connecticut Governor Thomas Meskill's ban for his state the following March was belated, but consistent.) Cynics were quick to point out that it was an election year, that there were quite a few Italian votes in New York, and that Joseph Colombo's picketing of the New York City office of the FBI—alleging harassment of Italian-Americans—had received surprising support that climaxed in the Italian-American Unity Day rally at Columbus Circle on June 28. Organized crime did not cease with the banning of two ethnic names, and there was no suggestion that the press was covered by national or state edicts, but the fact remains that of the 359 *New York Times* references to "Mafia" in 1970, only one-sixth of them came in the five months after Mitchell's order became public. The ban was not rescinded, but the media became independently bold by mid-1971, as another Unity

Day rally was scheduled. When it became the scene of an attempted assassination of its organizer, Joseph Colombo, and when one of his rivals, Joseph Gallo, was gunned down the following April—just weeks after the successful premiere of *The Godfather* in New York City—the "Mafia" label was able to claim an identity independent of government control. Its value as the media's rallying point for public opinion, and its ability thereby to compete for news space, could only have been exceeded (as it later was) by an event like the Watergate scandal.

The news that accompanied "Mafia" was not invented: it happened. That it appeared under the umbrella of that one label is a circumstance that was facilitated by two independent conditions. First, a revised federal policy emerged that encouraged public talk about the Mafia. Second, the media revised its assessment of the risk of libel that might stem from the use of "Mafia."

Sidney Franzblau had demanded disclosures in June of that year because he fully expected the government to refuse and, as a result, to have his client's case dismissed. Though the FBI's file on DeCavalcante was inadmissable as evidence, and thus incapable of generating indictments, its contents suited an extensive publicity program the Justice Department had been working on, with Attorney General Mitchell's encouragement, for more than a year. The department's aim, said the *Times* in discussing release of the tapes, was "to expose the profound depths to which the Mafia had penetrated into basic American institutions, not excluding the Congress of the United States," and to generate a public reaction sufficient "so that we can get in there and clean the situation up."

Mitchell's predecessors had held that if information did not meet standards of admissibility, as a prelude to rigorous testing and cross-examination under the eyes of a court, then it did not qualify for public release. One might expect that as clandestinely installed FBI bugs began producing "good" stories[2] to which a public would "obviously" respond, the internal pressure for a revised disclosure policy gained strength. When it came to a question of privacy versus crime control after January 1969, opinion had shifted from the old Kennedy-Katzenbach-Clark philosophy to the newer Mitchell policy. Franzblau's "demand" then descended on the department almost as an answer to prayer.

The press appears at first to have responded closely to ghe government's disclosure policy, emphasizing "Mafia" when government officials did and deemphasizing it when they did not. The pattern would confirm the media message at Oyster Bay in 1966 that law-enforcement desires for the "right" publicity would pass unfulfilled if the risk of libel were too strong. As their defense the news media needed either truth or a public proceeding that could be fairly and accurately reported. The elusiveness of truth and the ordinary limits on pretrial publicity had already been demonstrated. The difference in 1969 came from the combination of a series of intercepted conversations from De-Cavalcante's office and a theoretical formulation of "Cosa Nostra" that the President's Crime Commission had produced two years earlier. They gave substance to "Mafia" that had been missing in earlier circumstances, and the media seemed to respond.

But how reliable was the evidence? Under close examination it offers little more than earlier probes. The Kefauver Committee suffered in retrospect by a habit of taking whatever its witnesses said as proof of a Mafia: assertions were self-evident, and denials were obvious subterfuges. Aside from feeding official suspicion and encouraging a visceral desire to believe in a particular hypothesis concerning conspiracy, the Apalachin incident had proved little more than the observation that racketeers were like policemen, lawyers, dentists, doctors, and people in other trades and professions who like to congregate and who are reticent about their private dealings. Valachi seemed more credible because he was an insider, but after defining a set of organizing principles—built around the

sharing of illicit gain, mutual help, and the allocation of illicit territories—he recalled a series of events in his own life that appeared at nearly every point to contradict what he had said Cosa Nostra was all about.

The new evidence of the late sixties was primarily the result of eavesdropping and wiretapping. When examined critically, however, their revelations were often ambiguous. As Gordon Hawkins has observed, the DeCavalcante file was prefaced with a qualification from the FBI:

"Some conversations were merely summarized. These pages of conversations and parts of conversations were frequently summarized in subsequent memos. Then these subsequent memos were occasionally summarized, incorporating selected material apparently obtained from other investigative sources." ["A Nationwide Crime Syndicate: Assessing the Evidence," p. 20]

If some conversations were summarized, others were obviously verbatim; but that hardly solved the basic problem of context. Was there any reason to assume that in any given conversation all its participarticipants knew, or told, the truth? One of Simone DeCavalcante's conversations suggested that Joseph Magliocco had been poisoned on orders of Joseph Bonanno in 1963 and had not died of a heart attack as his death certificate indicated; but an autopsy prompted by that conversation failed to reveal any trace of poison. Anthony DeCarlo (in a separate series of conversations) thought he had been told the truth by Anthony Boiardo about the murder of "the little Jew," but three days later Anthony Russo told him a considerably different story of the same event. As Charles Grutzner observed in the *Times*, this contradiction was one that gave "substance to the F.B.I.'s note of caution, inserted among the transcripts, that members of organized crime sometimes boast falsely to their associates to make themselves appear more powerful and influential than they really are."

They did more than innocently repeat misinformation and boast. Instead of a monolithic superorganization emphasizing loyalty, honor, respect, and absolute obedience—characteristics of Cosa Nostra cited by the President's Crime Commission in 1967—the tapes described a number of warring factions whose members could be characterized in terms of treachery, disrespect, and disobedience.

. . . A parallel problem of interpretation lay behind [Joseph] Valachi's confessions. But though he and agent Flynn may well have talked past each other rather than participating in a mutually shared conversation, at least they were in the same room and could engage in a certain amount of cross-testing. That possibility was completely lacking in the DeCavalcante eavesdropping and wiretapping material. Misunderstandings, misstatements, boasting, lies, and manipulative statements for effect all started from the same cold, impersonal base as did statements of fact and truth. Any interpretation of them—and summaries, or summaries of summaries, obviously depended on third-party interpretation—had to be based on what the primary listener expected to hear. The results were thin ice indeed for the news organization that needed to be protected from libel.

A longer look at the media and the Mafia suggests that fear of libel was not the real issue. Government agencies stopped talking publicly about "Mafia" and "Cosa Nostra" in 1970 after Attorney General Mitchell's order to do so, and that silence was reflected in the press. But through the label ban continued, "Mafia" returned once again as the prime descriptor of organized crime, libel or no libel. The second wave points to the second condition governing application of the label: the news media recognized the commercial value of linking certain events to the Puzo-generated public interest in "Mafia." After *The Godfather*, "Mafia" sold newspapers. For example, consider the columns of newsprint commanded by Joseph Gallo's release from prison, his well-publicized marriage, his violent death, and the search for (and prosecution of) his assassins. The news was well in excess of what the events in his life deserved. He was more important to the business manager's balance sheet than he was to the custodians of obituary files. As we note that his death and the official acts following it generated twice as many news stories as the combined responses to the Giuseppe Masseria and Salvatore Maranzano murders forty years earlier, questions of balance and perspective in the news become obvious.

*

EDITORS' NOTE

Joseph Valachi had been talking to government agents for nearly a year when news of his apparent defection was first made public. His information was said to provide a "breakthrough" in the fight against organized rackets. The level of detail to which he was willing to testify stood in sharp contrast to the silence of his Apalachin predecessors. A cloud of mystery had grown around organized crime since 1957, and when it unexpectedly lifted, as both the *Washington Star* and the *Saturday Evening Post* broke the government's security shield in early August 1963, the press had a field day. In the two weeks following the original reports, for example, the *New York Times* carried the Valachi story in its headlines almost every day, even though it had no direct link to what he was saying.

Once the fact of Valachi's confessions was known publicly, Justice Department sources were happy to cooperate with the media. Private but highly publicized meetings were scheduled with the police department and the district attorneys of New York City to discuss ways in which dormant murder cases could be revived and other crimes reconsidered with the additional evidence that Valachi supplied. Nuggets of testimony were leaked to appreciative newsmen. By the time Valachi appeared in public, there was little he could add (other than his physical presence) to what was already known.

He began testifying on September 27, 1963. His immediate audience was the Permanent Subcommittee on Investigations of the Senate Government Operations Committee. It was the same group that had investigated organized crime and gambling two years earlier; before it now was a Senate request, approved in May, to study organized crime and narcotics. The original agenda included two topics: narcotics trafficking and the treatment of addicts. The record does not specify when Senator McClellan learned of Valachi's revelations, but we might guess that it was early in the development of the subcommittee's schedule when he and Attorney General Robert Kennedy agree that the forthcoming hearings would be a good stage for Valachi's national debut.

Valachi testified publicly for five days between September 27 and October 9. He was followed by law-enforcement personnel from New York City, Chicago, Detroit, Buffalo, Florida, and New England who testified as to their belief in what he had said about a Cosa Nostra and added what they knew of its personnel, organizational structure, and operations in their own jurisdictions. As new witnesses were ready to turn to the subcommittee's original agenda, the Treasury Department asked for a postponement, in order to avoid jeopardizing a large narcotics conspiracy trial that was about to begin in New York. When the hearings resumed the following summer, Valachi was not in evidence, and questions concerning narcotics, as distinct from "Cosa Nostra," were aired with considerably less publicity. As a result, the record really contains two different hearings under a common name.

The gambling hearings of 1961 had been successful. Congress subsequently passed six bills proposed by the Justice Department concerning gambling in interstate commerce, and their influence on national betting services and mechanical gambling devices was beginning to be seen. A companion legislative opportunity was now pending, as the Justice Department focused on a conspiracy strategy against the narcotics trade. In pursuit of that strategy, it was hoped that Valachi's testimony would add force to the department's request for authority to wiretap and an expanded framework for granting immunity to informers.

The tactic failed, both for Valachi as a star attraction and for the legislative program of the Justice Department—at least for that session of Congress. "Valachi's televised appearances before the subcommittee were a disaster," wrote Peter Maas five years later, as he placed the blame on Valachi's inability, after years of avoiding publicity, to cope with the circuslike atmosphere of the hearing room and on the subcommittee's essentially undisciplined—and thus disordered—approach to his appearance. The silent print of hearings documents reveals little of Valachi's mood, though one can sympathize with the possible traumatic effects of television cameras and a deluge of interrogators. The record gives ample evidence, however, of a generally unprepared group of senators who seemed more concerned with their own media coverage than with the systematic development of Valachi's story. But one must look beyond the hearing transcripts for the structure and continuity that give perspective to his confessions.

*

Valachi had called it "Cosa Nostra" ("our thing"); the subcommittee occasionally used that name, but it was obviously more comfortable with "Mafia.'" This distinction in nomenclature, and the subcommittee's preference for "Mafia," is particularly interesting in light of subsequent scholarly arguments that the significance of Valachi's testimony rested on the name change to "Cosa Nostra" and its reflection of the Americanization—and bureaucratization—of the kinship structure of an older social phenomenon.

The subcommittee also concluded that Valachi lacked any redeeming social value other than his testimonial accuracy, and that he was motivated solely by desires for revenge and self-preservation. "His role as an informer," read the final report, "was not dictated by conscience, nor was it a result of remorse for his crimes." Though the absence of remorse thus precluded forgiveness, it did not stand in the way of accepting his testimony. The subcommittee announced that his disclosures where of vital importance "because, for the first time, an underworld insider has broken the code of silence to give reliable indications of the tremendous size of the criminal combine, and to give details of activities and relationships of its leaders and members. His information about the genesis of the present Mafia organization has been of great value to federal and local law-enforcement agencies."

Valachi's reliability was, then, the key to his testimony. The subcommittee felt that it had been assured by other witnesses, who fell into two categories: those who could supply independent corroboration of what Valachi had said specifically about New York City, and those who could demonstrate that what Valachi had described as the criminal structure in New York City could be replicated in the crime files of other cities.

*

64. The New Mafia

FRANCIS A.J. IANNI

ORGANIZED CRIME IS MORE THAN JUST A CRIMINAL way of life; it is an American way of life. It is a viable and persistent institution within American society with its own symbols, its own beliefs, its own logic and its own means of transmitting these systematically from one generation to the next. As an integral part of economic life in the United States it can be viewed as falling on a continuum which has the legitimate business world at one end and what we have come to call organized crime at the other. Viewed in this way, organized crime is a functional part of the American social system and, while successive waves of immigrants and migrants have found it an available means of economic and social mobility, it persists and transcends the involvement of any particular group and even changing definitions of legality and illegality in social behavior.

At present organized crime is in a period of transition. Italian domination has begun to give way to that of a new group: the blacks and Hispanics. During the next decade we will see the presently scattered and loosely organized pattern of their emerging control develop into a new Mafia. This black and Hispanic involvement can be examined as part of the process of ethnic succession. They, like other minorities before them, are inheriting a major instrument to social and economic mobility.

▶SOURCE: *"New Mafia: Black, Hispanic and Italian Styles,"* *Society (March/April 1974), 11 (3): 26–39. Published by permission of Transaction, Inc., from Society, Vol. 11, #3. Copyright © 1974 by Transaction, Inc.*

How does this new group differ from its predecessors? What is common and what is different in these groups in comparison to the Italians who preceded them? To answer these questions it is necessary to examine the networks of criminal operation in order to determine the types of relationships which bring people together, foster some kind of criminal partnership, then lead to the formation of organized criminal networks.

To research the nature of crime in America a major study using anthropological field work techniques was undertaken. All of the classifications, descriptions and anecdotes which follow are drawn from field work. Information was received either from members of networks or from those familiar with criminal networks. Although we focused on the patterns of blacks and Hispanic crime activists, previous research on Italian-American patterns was utilized for comparison.

ORGANIZATION OF CRIME NETWORKS

The first step in determining the pattern or patterns of organization in the networks we observed was to ask the questions: What brings and holds people together in these networks? How are relationships of mutual dependence and responsibility established among people who will engage in organized crime? From our analyses of the networks we found two distinct types of linkages: *causal relationships*, which serve to introduce individuals to each other and into joint criminal ventures; and *criminal relationships*, which are based on a common core of activity in crime. We identified six sets of causal relationships in our networks. All are marked by a sense of mutual trust in the personal characters of those within the relationship.

Childhood

While childhood gangs are an obvious place to look for such friendships, the childhood friendship does not require a gang to establish a potentially criminal relationship. Reggie Martin and Jimmie Brown were childhood friends on 143rd Street, and later, when both were grown and successful in their individual criminal ventures, they joined together to "launder" some of their illicit profits through a joint enterprise in boutiques. The long-term relationship which grows out of childhood friendships is not, of course, restricted to crime circles and is also found in legitimate social relationships. It seems particularly potent in organized crime networks, however. In every case of childhood friendship which grew into an adult criminal partnership, the individuals involved were of the same ethnic or racial grouping and usually of approximately the same age. Obviously, this is not the result of any innate criminality in any of the ethnic groups but rather results from the fact that street society, where kids meet, is based on residential patterns which tend to follow racial and ethnic lines as well as socioeconomic ones. Reggie Martin and Jimmie Brown could just as easily have been meeting in the Grill Room of the Yale Club and discussing the formation of a joint stock venture if their childhood circumstances had been different. But youngsters growing up in the ghetto have a different set of experiences, a different set of role models and so a different pattern of life chances. One of our interviewees in Central Harlem makes just this point:

"Again I stress the point of making the right kind of friends, from the time you're a little kid, then building up the right kind of respect among your associates, and carrying yourself so that those people who have always known you can continue to depend on you, to think that you are okay. For every friend you have, you have that much more chance to get in on deals, to make it in crime. You are able to be in touch; people will give you their address, their telephone number. Otherwise you are outside looking in—you are nobody. It's a thing in New York that people just don't take you in unless you know somebody. It's a city thing, a poverty thing."

The Recruits

A second type of linkage develops when an experienced criminal in the neighborhood sees a young boy or gang of young boys with talent and recruits them into organized criminal ventures. This is the most common mode of entry into organized crime and represents the first step in criminal apprenticeship. The War Dragons, a young gang, were recruited in this way following a successful whiskey theft. Recruitment was also the means by which Rolando Solis was brought into the lower echelons of the Cuban Connection (a drug ring) as the first step up the ladder of criminal success. Thus recruitment may involve either individuals, as in the case of Rolando, or groups, as with the War Dragons. Like all social relationships, however, this causal link between younger and older crime activists is two-sided; not only does the older criminal seek out the younger, the youngsters also seek to be recruited and to emulate their elders in crime. It is this role-modeling which gives generational continuity to organized crime and accounts, in part, for its persistence in society.

There were numerous examples throughout the obsevations and interviews of both blacks and Puerto Ricans which document this apprenticeship system. The process is described by a black from Paterson, New Jersey:

"You can know who is connected and who is involved but you can't go to them and say, 'Hey, man, I want to be one of you!' You can know for certain that Joe Blow is the biggest man in Paterson. He knows me and I know him but I can't approach that man about it. If I ask him something about that directly he might cuss me out. This is the way it happens. If he has been watching me and he likes what he sees and he wants to give me a little play, he might tell me one day to go see Joe. He won't ever turn around and commit himself to me the first time. You just take this for granted that you don't approach these guys at that level . . . ."

Finally, there is the simple, but telling observation by one of our field assistants about the lack of positive influences and legitimate role models for ghetto youngsters:

"The ones you see are the ones that interest you. If it had been doctors and lawyers who drove up and parked in front of the bars in their catylacks, I'd be a doctor today. But it wasn't, it was the men who were into things, the pimps, the hustlers and the numbers guys."

Prison Acquaintanceship

Incarceration can provide very strong and durable links among men who have already been involved in crime and who in the prison atmosphere come to feel themselves segregated from society and find natural linkages among themselves. The chances of these prison links leading to later joint criminal activity and forming the basis for organized crime networks seem to be quite high. Moreover, a multiplier effect is at work here since sometimes being a friend of a friend is enough to establish a link among ex-convicts. The role of prison experience bringing blacks and Puerto Ricans together in crime networks is also an important difference between these groups and the Italians who preceded them. Prison experience, often beginning early in the crime activist's experience, is found very commonly among the blacks and Puerto Ricans in the networks which we have described but seems to have been absent to any sizable degree among Italian-Americans. The strength of kinship and family which binds Italian syndicates together is not found among blacks and is less pronounced among Puerto Ricans than it is among Italians. Thus, the linkages among Italian-Americans are formed early enough so that apprehension and consequent incarceration seem to be less common among Italians than among blacks and Puerto Ricans.

Throughout the networks we found numerous examples of the importance of prison experience in bringing crime activists into contact with each other.

"When if I do need him outside [prison], I go to his neighborhood. Everybody is leery of telling me where I can find him or even telling me they know him. But the minute I mention that I did time with him and where, then immediately they come around. They get less scared I may be a cop. When I get to my friend he can take me around so all the people know I'm OK because we did time together."

Prison experience also fosters the strong relationship between a man and "the man who watches my back." The mutual loyalty has been forged during periods of trouble in prison. One inmate protects another. This is one of the strongest links found in black and Puerto Rican crime networks and rivals childhood friendship as a bond.

"It sounds strange, but you make your best friends in prison. I could remember a time when something would go down like a strike or something like that. It is like going to a shooting gallery. Someone's waiting to put a shiv in your ribs. But you got friends. The guy in front of me, I'd watch his back; the guy in the back of me watches mine and down the line."

Wives and Lovers

A fourth type of linkage is the infrequent but potent causal type of relationship which seems to exist between individuals in black and, to a lesser extent, Puerto Rican organized crime networks and their wives or lovers. Black and Puerto Rican members of organized crime networks involve women, particularly their lovers, in their criminal activity. Women may be involved in theft rings or in numbers operations. Sometimes they attain fairly high positions within an organization. Here there is a distinctive difference between the emerging black and Puerto Rican organized crime networks and those found traditionally among Italian-Americans. Once again it may represent the strength of family and kinship among Italian-Americans but it may also be a result of the less highly organized and consequently less professionalized relationships among blacks and Puerto Ricans. It is interesting to note that in our field experience we have found that Cubans who are much more highly organized than either Puerto Ricans or blacks, do not use women in their crime groups. The usual reason given for this by the informants was that the Cubans are "more like the Italians."

"Among the blacks there have always been women involved in numbers and dope. You find the same thing in the Puerto Rican race sometimes where they are runners in the numbers; they don't actually 'run' numbers from place to place but they do have people come to their house and you leave your number and your money there. Where you don't find any women is with the Cubans. If a Cuban woman gets into drugs or into hustling her ass, she is dead in the Cuban sections, and she better get out as fast as she can."

Kin
Although family is less important than among the Italian-Americans, kinship ties will sometimes foster a criminal linkage among blacks and Puerto Ricans. Our experience indicates that there is some greater reliance upon kinship among Puerto Ricans than among blacks and that once again, the Cubans seem more like the Italians in that among them, kinship is an important element. One interesting point is that all the kinship ties in our study were between brothers; none were between a father and a son. This could be a function of the limited size of our sample but it could also be a function of the relatively short period of time in which organized crime networks such as those we have described have been in existence in black and Puerto Rican societies. However, the the importance of kinship ties, even among blacks, was commented on by a number of informants:

"There is a great deal to the observation that trust is given more easily to a boy if he has a relative—a father, uncle, brother, an aunt—involved in crime. Many times, people want to know who a guy is, that is they want to know his pedigree. A guy is accepted more easily if he has a 'crime-heritage.' "

Partners
The sixth and most common causal type of linkage is the meeting of two men, either through intermediaries or casually, who happen to be in complementary business positions, and consequently form a linkage for common profit. A feeling of mutual trust is established. These kinds of relationships, premised on business can lead to a great deal of criminal activity. Characteristically, some of the activities are legitimate and some are illegal, but the activity tends to move from one form of organized crime operation to another. Some partnerships are episodic as when a particularly good opportunity arises and two or more individuals along with their associates will join together briefly for a common venture. In other cases the relationship grows over a period of time as expertise and special skills are required for the continuation of certain types of activities. In either case, the rules of good business practice are as true here as in the world of legitimate business:

"I find that in order for people to put the right kind of opportunities in your path on the streets there must be respect given to the people in positions in crime. They, in turn, must respect your ability as a person or a hustler, or whatever. In this way—through a system of mutual respect—there is the chance that you will be given the opportunity for profit-making in crime. Drug addicts, for instance, are never really successful because they are not respected—they are hooked on dope and cannot be trusted."

CRIMINAL LINKS IN CRIME NETWORKS

In addition to these causal types of linkages in the networks, there are also a number of substantive "criminal relationships," links which develop out of joint criminal operations within a network. Here it is the activity rather than the people which fosters the relationship.

Employer-Employee Relationship
This is the most common by far, just as it is in the legitimate business world. The employer

hires the employee for a salary to do certain things that the employer requires of him. In nearly every one of the networks we find many such relationships. Our study revealed men such as Thomas Irwin who employed a group of theives, and George the Fence and his employees in the whorehouse, Roberto Mateo and the neighborhood women who worked for him, and Jimmie Mitchell who employed a group of pushers.

Joint Venture

A second type of substantive criminal relationship is provided in the partnership and joint-venture type of linkage in criminal networks. The partners or associates share equally in the risks, responsibilities and profits. This relationship differs from the employer-employee relationship in that the two individuals involved are in association without a dominant-submissive relationship; there are no fixed leaders or followers. In some cases, however, one partner does seem to have greater authority and perhaps more influence than the others. The childhood gang often operates in this fashion and it appears that older groups do also.

Buyers and Sellers

A third type of relationship is that which occurs between the buyer and seller of goods. This type of relationship is, of course, very important in the narcotics, boosting and stolen car trades. However, we have found in most of our networks that this type of relationship exists in a number of the activities of networks. In some cases, it is a well established pattern such as those where illegally acquired goods such as guns or cars are sold either through a middle-man or directly as part of the network. In others it tends to be episodic, as when an individual or group learns that someone has some "hot" goods to sell.

Related to the buyer and seller of goods relationship is the buyer and seller of services relationship. In all networks this involves chiefly a specialized criminal skill, such as locksmithing.

Other skills such as prostitution or numbers running are less specialized but still important in the networks which include these activities. In the buyer and seller of services relationship, there is usually an established pattern so that the same locksmith, for example, is used repeatedly.

Leaders and Followers

There is also a complex linkage that exists between a leader of an informal gang and his followers. The most significant examples of this appear in prison life, although it does appear in other networks in some form. This relationship seems to be too informal to maintain a stable operation except in prisons where incarceration keeps inmates in close, continuous association. Here our data are too thin on heirarchical placement, dominance, submission and other organizational features to allow us to do more than speculate that these informal relationships represent first stages in the formalization of leadership in organized crime networks.

Esprit de Corps

Another type of linkage is that which exists among and between fellow employees, or among and between followers in a gang. Although this type of relationship seldom brings a criminal venture into existence, it is often on this type of relationship that the success of a venture rests. Poor coordination of effort and a lack of cohesion in the group seem to have doomed some of the criminal efforts described in our networks. For example, Luis Santos was a leader of a gang whose downfall was caused by this lack of cohesion. In a traditional legitimate business relationship this would be described as morale, or esprit de corps, within the company.

There are also a few relationships which are somewhat less common than the foregoing but they do emerge with some frequency and seem important to a number of criminal operations. The first of these is that which obtains *between a granter and a grantee of a privilege*, as when, in the Paterson network, Bro Squires inherited his brother's business and his connections and followers as well. In effect this relationship defined property and territorial rights in much the same way as in Italian-American organized crime circles. Another type of relationship which seems to be present in our networks is that which is engendered by bribes and favors; that between *the giver and the recipient of the bribe or favor*. Here the basis of the relationship is the exchange of goods and services based upon mutual needs and the assumption that the exchange is in some fashion mutually beneficial. This is not an uncommon activity even outside of organized crime, but the relationship is an important one for keeping the networks in operation and protected:

"Even to survive with the law you have to be connected. The cops will not take money from just anyone. They are in the business of being a cop for money and they are interested in pulling in bribes, but they want it in a safe way. The safety comes in knowing the guy from whom they take money. The cop takes the money from a successful man and grants him his protection so that the man can carry out his numbers or dope thing which allows the money to keep flowing to the cop."

Finally, there is a substantive relationship which is not as frequent but should be noted. This is *the relationship engendered by a simple, direct assault*. For example, one of our informants described a policeman in Central Harlem who shakes down addicts to obtain narcotics for resale on the street. We do not have a great deal of data on the use of violence and assault as techniques for compelling behavior in organized crime. Our informants reported repeatedly that violence does occur but is not an important factor since it is the certainty of relationships and the mutual profit among members of the network which keeps it in operation. It is important, however, to remember that criminal business is not always tidy, and consequently violence certainly does occur.

Identification of the causal links which lead to the formation of networks and the criminal links which sustain them helps to clarify the nature of criminal networks and the functional bases on which they are organized. There seem to be two forms of behavioral organization into which all networks can be divided. One type is characterized by the term *associational networks*.. These are networks held together by close personal relationships where strong emphasis is placed on mutual trust, and causal links are the usual agents of their formation. We found two forms of associational networks in our field experience.

The first of these is the childhood gang as a beginning criminal partnership. In these associational networks, black or Puerto Rican youngsters growing up in the same neighborhood were involved in criminal activities and then through the process of recruitment became involved in organized crime as a group. The friendships and ties among these youngsters were such that they continued into adulthood. It is important to point out, however, that youthful gangs as such should not be included under organized crime networks because although they might occasionally participate in organized criminal activities, they are not organized entirely for participation in such activities. Rather their importance is as a beginning step and as a source of recruitment into organized crime.

It is this partnership of old neighborhood friends which is most characterized by the sharing of risks and profits, by unclear lines of authority, by expressed concern over many aspects of the personalities of the members, and by the youthfulness of the partnership's members. This type of network seldom lasts beyond early adulthood, but individual relationships may be maintained long after.

The importance of these childhood relationships in building a "rep" and in forming crime networks is obvious in this excerpt from an interview:

"You've got to be forceful and be willing to do things like putting your life out on the line because somebody just took $10,000 from you. You also have to always be thinking about your business and what you're going to do with it. What happens to it depends on who comes along. Everything works on the basis that you are liked, either because you have qualities that are likeable or because you have qualities that are recognized, such as being a nice guy but still being a regular guy, somebody that is good to be with or a bright kid. These things lead to your being discovered. These are the things that oldtimers look for. It is a tradition."

The second major type of associational network which we found was the prison court, where individuals within prison band together along very strict racial lines and form strong bonds with each other. In addition to racial segregation these prison courts are characterized by strong leadership and a sensitivity to being together under a coercive and authoritarian system. As is true of childhood associations the relationships which are formed tend to be highly personalized and consequently tend to be very lasting. They have the character of partnerships since they do depend on mutual trust and responsibility as well as compatibility of the individuals.

While the chief purposes of the prison court do not include the commission of crime, there is impressive evidence in our data that prison activities are linked to external criminal activities and that base recruitment and basic relationships which serve to structure organized crime networks in the post-release period are often first formed in prison courts. These prison courts are characterized by (1) a single strong leader and his followers, (2) by strict racial segregation, and (3) by extreme sensitivity to the closed environment of prison life. It is within these courts that the exchange of favors—the concept of mutual rights and obligations— seems to become well established. The possession or lack of material advantages is an important factor in the adjustment of relations within the prison court. Thus, the individual who is able to provide goods or services is able to achieve a leadership position with the group. The relationships thus established become binding in the sense tht there are expectations built up on both sides of each interpersonal relationship.

The second type of behavioral organization is the *entrepreneurial network*. This seems to be a more advanced form among blacks and Puerto Ricans than the associational types. It is the model of the small businessman, the individual entrepreneur, whose illegal activities are carried out through a network of individuals related to him in that activity. In many respects, these crime networks are similar or identical to the kind of network that would coalesce around an individual who establishes his own small legitimate business. The pattern of this type of structure is quite familiar throughout our research and is found in networks ranging from Thomas Irwin's gang of thieves to the gypsy cab industry. Its characteristics seem always the same. One man is basically in charge of the activity by virtue of the fact that he pays the salaries or commissions of the other men. There is not a great deal of hierarchical arrangement among the employees. Most employees seem to have some direct contact with the boss and they identify with him more than they do with other members of the network except in those specific cases where we have seen direct partnerships or long standing relationships among the employee-members. The boss or center of the network is in most cases the only one in the net who has accumulated any risk capital. In fact, if an employee does accumulate risk capital he is likely to try to go off and set up some enterprise of his own. Again it seems that the salaried or commissioned employees, even when they are out on the street, are likely to view their activities as little different from "a job." Similarly, the boss, if the business of the network is successful, is likely to have many of the traits of any good small businessman—economy, prudence, firmness, a sensitivity to when he is being cheated or lied to, and status as a businessman in his neighborhood. It is this relationship between the illegal business set and the community which is most significant as we review the data in the various networks. There are probably no more secrets or confidences within the group of employees in these networks than there would be within any comparable group of employees in legitimate small business. What is different is that despite the illegal nature of the activities, many co-ethnics and neighborhood associates of these networks view them as legitimate.

THE CODE

Like any legitimate organization, criminal networks require a code of rules which regulates relationships between the network and the outside world. It is the code which keeps the network functioning, defines relationships within it, and establishes who is inside and who is outside the net. Control systems of this sort begin with values which define what is "good" and what is "bad." Ultimately, however, human behavior, whether in organized crime or in legitimate enterprises, is guided by specific rules which attempt to operationalize these values and apply them to everyday situations. Thus, while values give us some general sense of what is expected, it is the rule which states what actions will be approved and which forbidden. Rules do not stand alone but are usually grouped into codes or sets of rules which cover specified classes of behavior and the sanctions to be applied when the rule is broken. The rules which govern behavior in organized criminal networks follow just as surely all of these characteristics and direct behavior just as forcefully as do more legitimate codes.

Like so much in the study of organized crime, descriptions of codes for organized criminals have usually been derived by analogy—that is, rather than looking directly at the behavior of criminal syndicate members and extrapolating a code from their words and actions, investigators have tried to apply codes drawn from observations of other groups. One favorite source of analogies for rules of conduct in American criminal syndicates is the "Code of the Mafia," which originated in Sicily. The Task Force on Organized Crime set up in the Johnson Administration, for example, points out that since "there is great similarity between the structure of the Italian-Sicilian Mafia and the structure of the American confederation of criminals, it should not be surprising to find great similarity in the values, norms, and other behavior patterns of the two organizations."

The reason, suggests the report, is that organized crime in America is an off-shoot of the Mafia. As the report freely admits, however, the Mafia code itself is also quite similar to those which govern any secret societies such as Mau Mau, or even to those of secret organizations who, like the Irish Republican Army, seek to overthrow the authority in power.

Both Ralph Salerno and Donald Cressey, two leading experts on organized crime in America, further compare these rules of behavior to the Prisoners' Code, an unwritten but widely accepted set of rules which operates among inmates in American prisons. This similarity may be credited to the need of any underground organization for secrecy and control.

Deriving rules of behavior by analogy, however, can only be a valid technique if the values of the organization or group being studied are similar to those of the organization or group from which the analogy is borrowed. There is no certainty that present-day organized crime groups share the values of the Mafia in Sicily in 1900 or, for that matter, of prisoners and theives. In my recent study of the Lupollo "family," rules were derived from observed behavior rather than by analogy. Our method was to observe and record social action within the Lupollo family and then to seek regularities in behavior which have enough frequency to suggest that the behavior results from the pressures of the shared social system rather than from idiosyncratic behavior. We also asked family members and others about rules, usually by asking why some member of the family behaved in a particular way. Thus, reconstruction of rules of conduct came both from our own observations and from the explanations of observed behavior by the people living under those rules.

In analyzing the data we found three basic rules which organize behavior in the Lupollo family: (1) primary loyalty is vested in the family rather than in the individual lineages or families which make up the overall organization; (2) each member of the family must act like a man and do nothing which brings disgrace on the family; (3) family business is privileged matter and must not be reported or discussed outside the group. These three rules were the basics for maintaining membership within the group but there were a number of informal rules under each which explain why some members are more successful at playing the game than others.

In studying black and Hispanic organized crime networks, we again tried to extract rules from observed behavior rather than by analogy. A similar but functionally different code of rules exists for each of the two forms of organization we found in our networks.

In associational network—prison and youthful partnerships—rules seem more likely to speak to intimate personal characteristics:

1. *Don't be a coward.* This rule, which is found in both the prison court and in the youthful networks, enjoins the individual to be a man but has a more physical connotation than we found to be true among the Italian-Americans. Essentially, it indicates that the individual is always willing to fight for his own rights and safety and to a lesser extent for those of his colleagues in the network.

2. *Don't be disloyal.* Here again, the injunction is less positive in terms of its relationship to the group than we found among the Lupollos. What is called for here is a feeling of membership in a group and a basic loyalty rather than the intensely socialized family membership code among the Italian-Americans. Loyalty in this context means acceptance of membership in a group with the consequent requirements that outsiders be rejected.

3. *Don't be a creep.* Here, the rule calls for a normalizing of behavioral relationships among members in the network. What this rule does is to exclude from membership aberrant individuals—those who are somewhat deficient or who cannot for some reason enjoy full membership—and consequently establishes rules of behavior.

These rules are of course not written and they are usually expressed in terms of punitive or critical actions toward any behavior which violates them. No one says "Be loyal," but when an act by a member of the network is perceived as disloyal by his fellows, he will be subject to verbal and sometimes physical abuse as well. Neither are these rules normally taught in any formal manner; they are learned by experience and taught by example. In effect, these are expected norms of behavior which are socialized into individual network members as a result of their membership in the network in day-to-day experiences.

In prison perhaps more than in the youthful partnerships (and for obvious reasons) shrewdness and the capacity to keep calm seem to be required. Thus, in the prison network we found greater emphasis upon a fourth rule: "Be smart," which enjoins the individual to learn to acquiesce to some regulations which cannot be ignored but at the same time to determine ways to beat the system. This rule, which we found only in the prison networks, is also a rule in what we have earlier called the code of American prisoners. Prisoner-to-prisoner injunctions such as "don't whine . . . don't cop out . . . be tough . . . play it cool and do your own time . . ." are responses to the imposed authoritarian environment which is found in prisons but not in the youthful gangs.

In the entrepreneurial networks, rules speak much more to the impersonal requirements of the activities of the network than to the personal qualities we have described in the prison and youthful gang networks. In these business-related networks we found three major rules:

1. *Don't tell the police.* This rule also includes the caution against telling anyone who is likely to tell the police either through malice or weakness. While the rule is strongest within the networks themselves we found that it reaches beyond the networks into the community and that (just as we found among the Italian-Americans) there is a great reluctance on the part of the community to inform on organized crime activities. To some extent this is the result of fear but it also results from an antagonism toward the criminal justice system and a stronger identification on the part of the community members with their co-ethnics in the networks than with the criminal justice system.

2. *Don't cheat your partner or other people in the network.* This rule places a highly "moral" standard on interpersonal behavior within the network but does not carry outside that group. Thus an individual is expected not to cheat with money inside the network but is not enjoined against doing it externally.

3. *Don't be incompetent in your job.* This rule sets standards of excellence within the network and again it establishes confidence among its members. What this rule suggests is that an individual—thief, numbers runner, prostitute, pimp, locksmith, dealer of stolen goods, narcotics pusher, or hijacker—should do his job well.

These rules seem far less related to personal characteristics than they are to business relationships, because the relationships are more situational or episodic than is true in the prison court or in the youthful gangs. Individuals come together in these entrepreneurial models largely for mutual profit and their dependence upon each other is related entirely to advancing that profit. In the prison court or youthful gang model, however, personal relationships develop out of long-term, intense interaction and are designed to build trust.

While the rules which govern associational networks emphasize personal characteristics and those of entrepreneurial networks emphasize conduct, there is an important relationship between them. The more highly personalized rules take place within networks which

might be considered training and testing grounds for the more profitable but also more demanding entrepreneurial networks. Thus recruitment of blacks and Puerto Ricans into sophisticated organized crime networks usually seems to come as a result of prior experience either in a youthful gang or in prison where they are identified as promising individuals. Unfortunately, our data about youth gangs and prison experience among Cubans is quite sparse and we cannot support similar observations there. We do know from our informants that Cubans must go through a preliminary street experience before they are accepted into more important positions. Among blacks and Puerto Ricans, however, enough information is available to codify this process by adding a fifth rule, to be used as a general guide for the entrepreneur type of network which we described earlier: In order to join the "organization" one must have passed through some kind of accredited criminal training course in which it can be assumed that the personal qualities valued in organized crime were duly tested.

Among youthful criminal partnerships, lines of authority seem in general to be poorly drawn—there is little sense of who is obliged to follow whose orders except in particular circumstances. On the other hand, in prison and in the small criminal businesses, certain lines of authority seem to be clearly drawn. In prison, one man in each court is the leader, based on personal qualities and criminal expertise, and all of the others are his followers. In the entrepreneurial network the authority pattern is simple: whoever pays the salaries gives the orders.

Comparing the code of rules for the black and Hispanic network structures with the code of the Lupollo family, there are some obvious similarities and some important differences as well. Both the Italian and the black and Hispanic codes establish who is inside the net and who is an outsider. Those rules demanding loyalty and secrecy serve to establish the boundaries of the network or family and set up behavioral standards as well. It is, of course, not surprising that an organization or network which is engaged in illegal activity should require of its members that they show their loyalty to the group by respecting its confidences and maintaining secrecy. Secret societies of any sort, whether criminal, fraternal, or revolutionary could not long survive without requiring both loyalty to the organization and some degree of secrecy. Thus the similarity in the two codes results from the generic nature of organized crime as joint clandestine activity. The other similarity between the two codes also derives from the nature of organized criminal activity. These injunctions, which are described in terms such as "be a stand-up guy," "be competent in what you do" or "don't be a coward" are rules which reinforce the feeling of trust among the members of the network or family.

There are also some important differences between the sets of codes. While each of the major rules found among the Lupollos is also found in black and Hispanic networks, these rules do not seem to operate with the same degree of force within the black and Puerto Rican organized crime networks. While the Italian code subordinates the individual and stresses protection of the family—usually a larger organization than a typical black or Puerto Rican network, the latter codes tend to emphasize the individual and secondarily stress loyalty to the network. This may be because of the relatively recent development of networks in comparison to the long history of the Italian crime family.

FUTURE HIERARCHIES

A description of the future of organized crime must be speculative. It is instructive, however, to look at the present pattern of organization, which we found in our study, and the degree of control or power now possessed by the blacks and Hispanics. At present, their networks could not be characterized as big operations, like Italian-American crime families with many layers of authority and countless functionaries and associates, many of whom are not aware of the roles of the others. Black and Hispanic organized crime networks have not yet reached that level of development. We do, however, have enough data on hierarchical arrangements and placement within some of the networks to conclude that while they are growing in complexity, they are still dependent on external sources for supplies and protection. In the Paterson network (the most highly developed of the black networks we examined), the two lowest levels, the street operators who sell drugs, numbers or their bodies as well as their immediate supervisors, the numbers controllers, pimps and small-scale drug suppliers, are all black. It is the next highest, "boss" level which now seems in ethnic transition as Bro Squires, a black, struggles to replace Joe Hajar, a white, as the big man on the hill. Both Squires and Hajar, however, are still dependent on the Italians for police and political protection as well as for drug supplies.

In Harlem and in Bedford-Stuyvesant, black networks seem to be free of such dependence on the Italians for protection, but not as yet for drugs except in those cases where they are switching to the Cuban Connection. Internally, these networks do not seem to have developed any new forms of hierarchical arrangement as yet. In the numbers games, the traditional pattern of the carefully articulated runner-controller-banker hierarchy which is still in use by the Italians is also used by both blacks and Puerto Ricans. As we followed the networks upward through the layers of individual black and Puerto Rican entrepreneurs, each with his own little entourage of employees and followers, however, it became obvious that while only in Paterson did we find a direct connection with an Italian syndicate, most of these individual entrepreneurs must relate to Italian families or alternately to the Cuban Connection for drug supplies and for other high-level services such as lay-off banking. Nowhere in our networks did we find blacks or Puerto Ricans who have risen to the point where they are providing major services to other criminals. Neither did we find any systematic pattern of exchange of such services among the various networks. Where we did find any contact among the networks, the individual entrepreneurs seem to be connected to one another either through occasional joint ventures or through straight, one shot deals for sales or services.

This lack of organizational development in black and Puerto Rican criminal structures coincides with both the newness of blacks and Puerto Ricans in control positions and with the nature of the types of criminal activities which we discovered in these networks. Just as the lack of a sufficient period of time in control positions has hindered any large-scale organizational development, it has also tended to keep the networks in specific types of criminal activities rather than allowing them to achieve hegemony in any one territory. Once again the only exception was in Paterson, where the Italians are still in control. Throughout the networks, however, there is evidence of some embryonic diversification of criminal activity involved in the networks as black control is consolidated. The combinations seem to be fairly stylized: prostitution and drugs, theft and petty gambling, numbers and narcotics are typical patterns. We also found evidence that black crime activists are starting to acquire some legitimate fronts: a boutique, for example, serves to shade some illegal activities, while a gypsy cab is sometimes used for drug transactions and prostitution.

Within this emergent system, mobility is based upon both efficiency needs and power through the accumulation of wealth and territorial control. There is a set of fairly strict rules and norms governing such movement. So it was among the Italians and the evidence suggests that it is becoming so among blacks and Hispanics in organized crime. Successful operations are gaining power increments over time through the scope, extent and intensity of their dealings. In crime organizations as in more legitimate business enterprises, small operations grow into larger ones and then join with others to maintain territorial control over rich market areas. The market for illegal goods and services is not restricted to the ghetto but at present, with the exception of prostitution, the black or Puerto Rican organized crime networks are excluded from the larger markets which are still dominated by Italians. This same condition prevailed among the Italians in the earlier part of the century until prohibition provided a source for extra-ghetto profit and power and allowed the Italian mobs to grow into control. But since the present networks among blacks and Hispanics are still relatively small operations, they continue to specialize and have yet to develop into large empires or even interconnected baronies. There are of course a number of indications of connections among networks in the same line of business and some of the activities we observed were on their way to becoming large, but the evidence from our study seems to indicate that the present pattern of loosely structured, largely unrelated networks has now reached its highest stage of development and that what seems to be necessary for these networks to become elaborated into larger combines, like those now present among Italians are: (1) greater control over sectors of organized crime outside as well as inside the ghetto; (2) some organizing principle which will serve as kinship did among the Italians to bring the disparate networks together into larger criminally monopolistic organizations; and (3) better access to political power and the ability to corrupt it.

The first of these conditions, monopolistic control over some sector or sectors of organized crime, can only come about by wresting or inheriting such control from the Italians or, alternately, by developing new forms of illicit goods and services for sale to the public. The current sectors of organized crime—drugs, stolen goods, gambling, prostitution and loan sharking are presently in a state of transition and their availablity to blacks and Hispanics as a source of illicit profit differs. At present, the numbers game is the major organized crime sector coming into obvious and immediate control of blacks and, to a lesser extent, Puerto Ricans. But the short period of control by blacks in this area seems certain to come to an early end. The reasons for its demise are precisely the same as was true in an earlier period when the game's popularity attracted the interest and attention of Jewish and Italian crime syndicates. Now it is the government which seems to be attracted to the immense profits which accrue in this form of gambling. Over the last decade a number of forms of gambling have been legalized, largely as a means of gaining additional revenue for near-brankrupt cities and for state governments as well. In New York, for example, the first step was the establishment of a lottery, ostensibly to defray the cost of education. The success of the lottery, and the lack of a public outcry against it, led to the legalizing of gambling on horse races through the establishment of the Off-Track Betting system. The latter was proposed simply as a means of diverting profits from gambling away from organized crime and directly into the public coffers.

There are now proposals in a number of cities to legalize the numbers as well. Here, however, the conflict between community sentiments and a revenue-hungry government is already beginning to emerge. When Off-Track Betting was established in New York, a number of spokesmen for the black community indicated that now the white middle class had managed to legalize its own preferred form of gambling and even added the convenience of placing the betting parlors throughout the city, doing away with the need to even go to the track. The numbers, however, was a black thing and it remained illegal. Thus, they said it was illegal for blacks to gamble but not for whites. The ghetto dweller's sense of white establishment hypocrisy in legalizing most other forms of gambling while continuing to condemn the numbers is not difficult to understand. On March 6, 1973, the New Jersey edition of the *New York Times* ran a full-column story reporting a police raid on a Puerto Rican numbers operation in East Harlem. The article described the raid by over 40 policemen and detectives, the arrest of 13 people and the confiscation of thousands of dollars worth of equipment. At the bottom of the column, there appeared the black-bordered box which is now present in every issue of the paper:

The winning New Jersey
daily lottery number yesterday was:
25113

The movement to legalize the numbers seems assured of success within the next few years. The proposals being advanced by a number of blacks is for a system of community control through licensing or franchising arrangements and even the granting of amnesty to present black numbers operators who can run the legal numbers games. The chances for such community control are minimal and even in the unlikely event that it does occur, the important point here is that the numbers, at present the most lucrative form of black organized crime, will certainly disappear through legalization in the near future.

Prostitution, while predominantly organized by black pimps and already operating outside the ghetto, does not actually offer a large enough financial base for further expansion so that among the present forms of organized crime, loan sharking, the theft and sale of goods, and drugs remain as possibilities. Loan sharking and the sale of stolen goods do not seem possible as means of expansion outside the ghetto for black crime activists. It is difficult to imagine that most white Americans would deal with a black salesman pushing stolen goods and even more difficult to envision whites borrowing money from black loan sharks. Thus, while these forms of illicit enterprise may well expand in the ghetto, it is not very probable that blacks can use them as a basis for extending their control over organized crime outside it.

The one sector of organized crime which does seem to present some possiblity for black and Hispanic monopolization as a basis for expansion both within and outside the ghetto is drug traffic. First, narcotics and the drug traffic have the same pattern of relationships which surrounded alcohol and bootlegging during the prohibition era. Although there is not as wide a public acceptance of drugs and social opprobrium of hard drug use remains strong, all of the other conditions previal. Drugs are illegal but in demand. In order for drugs to be produced and wholesaled, some safe haven is necessary for the crime operatives, a place in which they can be assured of at least tacit protection from police by their neighbors. The present movement toward tougher drug laws and stiffer penalties will reduce competition in the drug traffic so that blacks can begin to supply drugs outside the ghetto. Here, as in prostitution, the willingness of disenfranchised blacks to take risks that other groups need not take to escape poverty will combine with the color blindness of the needs of drug users to break down the racial barriers which impede loan sharking and the sale of stolen goods.

Finally, there is the possibility of corrupting police and other governmental officials without whose protection no form of organized crime could long endure. When the numbers are legalized, the major source of police graft will disappear leaving drugs one of the few remaining sources for the payment of substantial sums to police. All of the conditions for control of distribution within the ghetto are now operative and all that seems necessary is for the blacks and Hispanics to take over the sources of supply and then move into extra-ghetto distribution. In the East Harlem-Brooklyn Hispanic network, the Cuban Connection is already developing these sources. The importance of cocaine as a street drug has grown tremendously in the last two years and the Cuban Connection has grown apace. Both the police and the underworld, until recently preoccupied with the heroin trade, are now realizing the enormous profits which can be made in cocaine. Its growing popularity among the affluent drug public in penthouses and luxury apartments as well as on the street is equally obvious today. If blacks, either in concert or in competition with Hispanic groups, can take over control of this area then they can develop a national and even in-

ternational base for operations. Then, as happened among the Italians, they can take their profits and reinvest them in other illicit enterprises. Whether they can also follow the pattern of Italians and use these same monies as a basis for movement into legitimate areas is, however, another question.

The second condition for the elaboration of black organized crime networks into larger combines is the development of some organizing principle which will serve to coalesce black and Hispanic organized crime networks as kinship did for the Italians. Hispanics in organized crime—particularly the Cubans—may well adopt and adapt the existing family model of organization used by the Italians. As we have noted, the bonds of kinship seem stronger in the Hispanic networks we observed than they did among blacks. In fact, there is growing evidence that Hispanics are working in concert with Italian families to a much greater extent than is true of blacks. In September of 1972, for example, Cubans operated the gambling concessions at the San Gennaro festival, New York's annual Italian street fair. Until 1972, of course, the gambling tables and wheels were always operated by Italians. Obviously some arrangement must have been made for the Italians to allow the Cubans to operate, even under franchise, in the heart of Little Italy. While there is a cultural base for a family-type organization among Hispanics, this is not true among blacks.

Instead of family or kinship, however, the blacks may be able to use black militancy as their organizing principle. Previous ethnic groups involved with organized crime—the Irish, the Jews and the Italians—were desperately trying to become white Americans. Now, however, the blacks are beginning to become important in organized crime at a time when being black, being a brother or a sister, serves to create a family-type structure based upon militancy. Even the terminology—brother, sister, mother—expresses a sense of rights and responsibilities to the "family of blacks." More importants, blacks and Puerto Ricans involved in organized crime may rightfully feel themselves bound together by the oppressiveness of a system which rejects their attempts at social and political mobility and that during this period when much of black power is negative power—that is demanded and given out of fear—banding together to beat the system by any means may serve as a powerful incentive and organizer.

Patronage, acceptance and admiration define the attitudes of many of the blacks and Puerto Ricans we spoke with toward blacks and Puerto Ricans in organized crime. The reasons are not difficult to find; the crime activist is making it and he is making it in spite of and in conflict with an oppressive white establishment. Also, the activities he engages in—gambling, boosting and fencing, prostitution and loan sharking—are not considered socially harmful by many ghetto dwellers or indeed by many non-ghetto dwellers. Community attitudes toward crime activists change sharply when the drug problem is discussed, but solidarity is even apparent here. The narcotics trafficker is universally detested in the ghetto. Yet the local pusher, even though he is black or Puerto Rican (perhaps because he is black or Puerto Rican) is often not held responsible for the problem of drug addiction. The community's attitude toward the drug pusher is ambiguous. On the one hand, he is a visible symbol of the narcotics traffic and as such becomes an easy target for verbal, sometimes physical abuse. People living in the community, overwhelmed by the magnitude of the drug problem and not knowing how to deal iwth it, identify the problem with the pusher. The pusher comes to represent the narcotics problem and the shame and fear comjunity residents feel about drugs. At the same time, community residents assign the responsibility for widespread drug addiction to forces operating on the community from the outside. A conspiracy theory of drugs is widely held in the black and Puerto Rican communities. According to community residents, the widespread use of drugs in the ghetto is the result of a white establishment plot to kill off black and Puerto Rican

youths by allowing or even encouraging drugs in these areas. The role of Italian-American criminal syndicates in narcotics importing and sale is also widely accepted in the ghetto. Community people believe it is Italian-Americans, not blacks and Puerto Ricans, who profit most from the drug trade. Again, this belief mitigates the community's attitude toward the local pusher.

Like most Americans living in our consumer society, ghetto dwellers are hungry for money and for the goods and services it can procure. Ghetto dwellers are cut off from many legitimate ways of obtaining financial security. At the same time they have fewer opportunities than middle-class Americans to achieve the psychological security that can reduce the incidence of crime. When a man is financially secure, happy in his work, has a stable family life and lives in a stable community, he has little reason to consider criminal activity as a vocational possibility. But blacks and Puerto Ricans, like other ethnics before them, see organized crime as one of the few available routes to success, to financial and thus psychological security. In every society, criminals tend to develop under those social conditions which seem to offer no other way of escaping bondage. Poverty and powerlessness are at the root of both community acceptance of organized crime and recruitment into its networks. Conditions of poverty also nurture community desires for the services organized criminal operations provide. Escapism accounts in part for both widespread drug use and numbers gambling; the resentment that poverty and powerlessness arouse in the subordinated population makes drugs and gambling attractive as mechanisms of rebellion. Organized crime is esteemed for the very reason that society outlaws it.

It is important to note in this context of ethnic succession that none of these characteristics of or attitudes toward organized crime are culture bound: the structures of poverty and powerlessness, rather than the structures of the black and Puerto Rican cultures, seem most responsible. It is of course probable that certain subcultures are more prone to certain kinds of specific behavior as a result of the normative structure of those cultures. As we observed among the Italian-Americans, for example, the cultural model provided by Mafia and other secret criminal organizations in the south of Italy led to a high degree of organizational development in the criminal syndicates operating in the United States. Certainly, if there is a movement toward higher organization within black and Puerto Rican networks, this movement will respond to the culture imperatives of those groups. This, however, is very different from a cultural propensity toward organized crime. Organized crime involves a calculated pattern of offense to one or more of a culture's norms. Its presence is perhaps predictable whenever one culture in a dominating way holds such norms over the head of a lively and energetic dominated subculture. In such a situation, organized crime will probably persist until an adequate degree of assimilation and accommodation takes place. In effect, it can be hypothesized that organized crime results from a conflict of cultures and, further, that organized crime as we know it in the United States requires an underclass of minority-status ethnics in order to be operative.

There seems to be little question that assimilation and accommodation with the larger American society are the chief aims of black and Puerto Rican organized crime activists. This is not to suggest that they are not criminals and that they are not involved in illegal activities but rather that as was true of the Italians, the Jews and the Irish before them, the greater motivation is to achieve social, occupational and residential mobility. Even while they themselves might never articulate such aims, even when their goals are limited by the scope of their own neighborhood, nevertheless they still exhibit single-minded striving for the material wealth and social security which motivates others in society as well. If some of our informants cannot themselves quite imagine movement toward respectability and security then certainly they want

this this for their children and their children's children.

Eventually all of these factors could serve to bring together the presently scattered organized crime networks into a classical Mafia. Mafias are first and foremost a form of social protest which can, like the classical Mafia in Sicily and its counterpart among the earlier Italian immigrants to the United States, use crime as a weapon of protest. This protest is expressed in a general attitude toward the law which tends to develop where that law is considered unresponsive or hostile and alien to the culture of the rebellious group. This condition exists in black and Hispanic ghettos today and the coalescence into a new Mafia could prove to be a more effective organizational principle than kinship was among the Italians in organized crime, because its social base is more resistant to social change than kinship bonds are.

The third condition for the elaboration of black and Hispanic crime networks is better access to political power and the ability to corrupt it. The evidence here is more difficult to deal with because it is to some extent contradictory. On the one hand, it is well established in the social history of the city that ethnic groups succeed to power in politics as they do in crime and that the two forms of mobility are often connected. There is evidence that blacks are moving ahead in politics in the large urban areas just as they are in organized crime. What is less evident is that the necessary connections between politics and its corruptability and black movement in organized crime will coincide. While it is a maxim in the underworld that graft and corruption are color-blind and that police and politicians will take graft regardless of the color of the hand that delivers it, it is difficult to imagine that blacks will be able to insinuate themselves into the kinds of social relationships with white politicians within which deals are made, bribes are offered or sought and protection developed. Again, the black movement in both politics and crime like so many other processes of social advance among them, comes at a time when much of the power and profit has already been milked from the system by the groups which preceded them. The rampant corruption of our political system reaching up to and now obviously including the White House, could put the costs of corruption to a point where it is prohibitive. This already seems to be the case in New York City where the revelations of the Knapp Commission on bribe taking by the police seems to have doubled the costs of bribery in just one year's time.

While the growth of a new Mafia is fairly well known or at least perceived in black and Puerto Rican neighborhoods, it would not be unfair to say that, aside from the occasional newspaper headlines, there is little public knowledge that it is going on. To judge from its actions, the greater society seems to consider black and Puerto Rican organized crime as one of the small prices it must pay for the continuance of the many psychological and economic comforts that accrue from the existence of an ethnic underclass. Indeed, when measured against the cost of eliminating such crime, the costs are small. The most visible cost—of the thefts and muggings by narcotic addicts—touch only a few people in the large urban areas. In many respects there is also a continuation of that traditional attitude of the criminal justice system: so long as ghetto dwellers keep their crimes within the ghetto and do not spill outside, leave them to themselves. It is when the muggings and the robberies have reached the non-ghetto areas that there is a strong outcry. This attitude, which has traditionally been part of our law enforcement value system, allows organized crime to thrive within the ghetto. Once the organized crime networks find profitable sources of revenue outside the ghetto then the growing economic, political and social impact of organized crime becomes a matter of public interest and social policy. In the meantime, blacks and Hispanics must continue to face the same basic dilemma which confounded earlier generations of Irish, Jews and Italians: How do you escape poverty through socially approved routes when such routes are closed off from the ghetto? Organized crime resolves the dilemma because it provides a quick if perilous route out.

Drug-Related Crimes

IN THIS SECTION WE CONSIDER DRUGS AND THEIR RELATIONSHIP TO CRIME, A TOPIC that has caused great public concern since the late 1960s. The level of drug use, despite massive governmental efforts, has not noticeably diminished. The initial selection is taken from a draft report of the National Institute of Drug Abuse. It presents a comprehensive statement on the putative and still arguable association between heavy drug use and subsequent criminality.

The universal loathing, not so much of drug addicts but of drug merchants ("pushers" or dealers) all but precludes any objective analysis of the several economic strategies available to the heroin supplier as a rational businessmen, in order to avoid the omnipresent risk of arrest. Moore's selection, is then unusual in that it objectively describes these reasonable alternatives precisely and fully. He indicates what "tradeoffs" are necessitated by each choice; one cannot maximize both profit and safety therefore compromises are required for any dealer response.

The final selection by Wilson explicates the punitive versus the medical approaches to the problem of heroin abuse and also describes the values and limits of the peer group and the contagion models of explanation of drug misuse.

65. Drug Use and Crime

THE NATIONAL INSTITUTE ON DRUG ABUSE

THE ASSOCIATION BETWEEN DRUG USE AND CRIMINAL BEHAVIOR

IT IS GENERALLY RECOGNIZED THAT THERE IS AN association between drug use and criminal behavior, but there is considerable disagreement concerning the nature of the relationship. The assumption that underlies many national drug and crime policies is that drug use is a principal cause of criminal behavior. Others doubt that reduction in drug use will have the expected impact on crime. In this selection, attention is focused on what is known about this relationship.

Utilizing samples of arrestees, prisoners, individuals in treatment, and, to a lesser extent, persons in the general population, investigators have conducted many relevant studies. Surveys of arrestees and prisoners indicate that large proportions of apprehended offenders are either current or past users of drugs (5, 6, 10, 12, 24, 27).[1] Studies of persons in treatment yield high proportions of clients with criminal histories (4, 8, 16, 25, 28, 40). Similarly, general population surveys indicate that the proportions of respondents who admit to criminal acts are higher among those who report illicit drug use than among those who do not admit use.

▶SOURCE: *Drug Use and Crime. Draft Report of the Panel on Drug Use and Criminal Behavior. Sponsored by the National Institute on Drug Abuse. (August 1976), pp. 3:1–30; 5:1–18. (Editorial adaptations.)*

[1]The numbers in parentheses refer to the references found at the end of the selection.

Clearly, there is a strong *statistical* association between drug use and crime.

An association by itself, however, is not sufficient evidence of a causal relationship. While scholars have adopted a variety of philosophical positions on the concept of cause, there is general agreement among social scientists that the evidence of causal relationships in complex human behavior will be less than perfect. Rather than abandoning the concept of cause entirely, many social scientists conceive of causality in probabilistic terms. In this sense, there are three kinds of information that would indicate the probability of a causal relationship. First, one must demonstrate that there is a statistical association between an independent (causal) variable and a dependent variable (effect). In addition, it is necessary to show that the presumed cause is linked to its effect in a logical sequence and that other variables cannot explain the effect equally well (20).

Unfortunately, in much of the available research, effort has been directed almost exclusively at the establishment of a statistical association between drug use and criminality. Because of the limited information on the causal relationship between drug use and crime, the researchers claim that the association is a spurious one that cannot be refuted.

Therefore, the question of whether or not there is a causal relationship between drug use and criminality requires more systematic investigation. There are now three conflicting hypotheses, and some support for each of them, in the drug literature: (1) drug use leads to crime; (2) involvement in crime leads to drug use; and (3) both crime and drug use are the results of some other factor(s). While a convincing answer to the question of whether drug use and criminality are causally related may not be possible on the basis of the available data, there are a number of sub-questions which are highly relevant for public policy and which may be addressed on the basis of existing information. *What proportion of the criminal activity of drug users is attributable to the financial requirements of drug use? To what extent are changes in the level of criminal activity associated with changes in the schedule or level of drug use?* At the aggregate level we need to know the degree to which drug use affects the crime rate and the extent to which the crime rate can be affected by reducing drug supply and demand.

There are two alternative strategies—the explanatory and the descriptive. The descriptive approach assumes the need for more complete information on why crimes occur or the motivation for criminal behavior. An explanatory approach involves developing models, testing hypotheses generated from the models, and rejecting, accepting, expanding, or revising the models on the basis of sound empirical data. This approach has two principal advantages. First, empirical data can be organized into a meaningful framework. Second, the actions of individuals can be explained in terms of the general behavioral model. There is, though, the disadvantage that data that do not fit the model may be overlooked or discarded.

The descriptive approach is preferred by those who feel that information on the criminal behavior of drug users and the drug use of criminals is too incomplete for the development of adequate explanatory models. The descriptive approach involves an attempt to gather as much data as possible prior to the construction of models. A vast amount of data has been and can be collected. A disadvantage of this approach is that the amount and variety of available data can make the task of building models extremely

difficult, but without a model researchers have little guidance regarding the data needed.

The descriptive approach was selected for several reasons. Though a variety of explanatory models are available—some pertaining only to drug use, others exclusively to criminality—there is little consensus on the most appropriate model. Too, different kinds of models would be required for analyses at the individual level than at the aggregate level. It was recognized that fundamental problems of definition and measurement had to be faced prior to the selection or development of explanatory models. It was decided, therefore, to pose three sets of related questions. The answer to each question would, in turn, allow more precise determination of the nature and extent of the association between drug use and criminality.

The first question is: *What proportion of criminals have ever used drugs and what proportion of drug users have ever committed crimes?* With such knowledge, we can estimate the maximum possible effectiveness of drug policies in reducing crime, assuming all crimes committed by drug users are caused solely by drug use. It should be noted, though, that the fact that criminals have at one time used drugs and that drug users have at one time committed crimes does not mean that drug use causes crime.

The second set of questions concerns the patterns of criminal behavior and drug use. Because of our interest in the antecedents of criminal behavior, we need to ascertain the temporal order of criminal behavior and drug use. *Does involvement in criminal behavior precede drug use or does drug use precede criminal behavior? Do both criminal behavior and drug use initially occur within a restricted time span?*

Knowing the temporal order still leaves a number of questions unanswered. *Do criminals intensify their involvement in income-generating criminal behavior after onset of regular use of addictive or expensive drugs? Do changes in income-generating criminal behavior accompany changes in the cost of drug habits?*

A statistical association or simultaneous increase in drug use and crime does not, in itself, prove that drug use is a cause of crime. It is reasonable to assume that other factors such as employment and law enforcement can have substantial impacts on both criminal behavior and drug use. The question would then be: *Are any other factors associated with criminal behavior and drug use? What is the relative impact of particular patterns of drug use on patterns of criminal behavior in comparison with the impact of other variables?* Answers to this series of questions will allow us to gain a better understanding of the causal relationship between drug use and crime and to construct more complete and accurate explanatory models. The end result should be a basis for more informed and more effective drug-crime policy.

A. NATURE AND EXTENT OF CRIMINALITY ASSOCIATED WITH DRUG USE

Our initial question is: *What is the nature and extent of criminality among different types of drug users, and what is the nature and extent of drug use among criminals?* To answer this question, we are limited to studies of identified drug users or detected criminals and to general population surveys.

In surveys of the general population, we can ask both questions, but these samples would include few of the most serious types of offenders or addicts. Among persons who admit to committing or are charged with particular types of crime, we can ask: *What are the probabilities that these persons use drugs?* In studies with samples of treatment clients or addicts, we can ask: *Among persons who are known to have had particular drug use patterns, what are the probabilities that these persons commit crimes?*

One way to obtain answers to these questions is to examine both an individual's drug use and criminal histories. That individual could then be classified as a particular type of user or criminal on the basis of one or more instances of drug use or crime at any time in the individual's life.

A more restrictive approach would be to look at crime and drug use within a particular time frame. This is the preferable alternative. Both approaches are described in more detail in the following discussion.

1. Crimes Committed by Drug Users

The basic question regarding the crimes committed by drug users is: *Among different types of drug users, what is the probability that these persons commit crimes?*

In order to answer this question we have chosen to focus on three mutually exclusive types of drug users, excluding those who have been only experimental users. The first type consists of users who have used only marihuana. A second type includes those who use other drugs in addition to or instead of marihuana but do not use addictive narcotics. The final category of users is composed of those who have used illicit addictive narcotics or opiates. Obviously, drug use is a vastly more complex phenomenon than these levels suggest. Clarity and the need for comparability suggested this method of categorization for this discussion.

(a) Marihuana Users   There is a widespread acceptance of the belief that use of marihuana leads to crime. Though that idea is rejected here, it was considered appropriate to include marihuana use in this discussion of crime.

At one time a single "toke" from a marihuana "weed" was purported to lead to "reefer madness," an irreversible deterioration in morals, and an increase in criminality (2). Despite the results of volumes of careful, well-designed research over the past 80 years, the belief that marihuana use as a cause of crime has persisted. In 1967, the President's Commission on Law Enforcement and the Administration of Justice remarked on the opposing views on the question of the association between crime and marihuana use:

"Here differences of opinion are absolute and the claims are beyond reconciliation. One view is that marihuana is a major cause of crime and violence. Another is that marihuana has no association with crime and only a marginal relation to violence. Proponents of the first view rely in part on reports connecting marihuana users with crime. . . . Those who hold the opposite view cannot prove their case, either. They can only point to the prevailing lack of evidence" (38: p. 13).

In a 1972 survey by the National Commission on Marihuana and Drug Abuse, a majority (58%) of the adults aged 18 and over believed that marihuana users often commit crimes they would not have otherwise committed; and many (52%) believed the crimes were committed to obtain money to buy marihuana. These beliefs were even more prevalent among youth aged 12–17. Two-thirds of these young respondents expressed agreement with both statements (1).

More recent and definitive reports have strongly asserted that marihuana is not a direct cause of crime. The 1973 National Commission on Marihuana and Drug Use concluded that marihuana use neither instigates crime nor increases existing levels of crime.

"In essence, neither informed current professional opinion nor empirical research, ranging from the 1930's to the present, has produced systematic evidence to support the thesis that marihuana use, by itself, either invariably or generally leads to or causes crime, including acts of violence, juvenile delinquency or aggressive behavior. Instead the evidence suggests that sociological and cultural variables account for the apparent statistical correlation between marihuana use and crime or delinquency" (30: p. 76).

Reviews of recent studies and analyses of secondary data during the preparation of this summary have supported the Commission's conclusion. From 1973–76, four major studies based on large probability samples of general youth populations have provided data on the relationship between marihuana and delinquency (14, 17, 22, 23, 24). Review of these studies established two points: (1) including delinquency, marihuana use is a part of a general pattern of deviance or criminal behavior and (2) any causal linkage that exists between marihuana use and deliquency is complex and indirect (14).

(b) "Other" Drug Users—Excluding Addictive Narcotics or Opiates Evidence of a relationship between crime and the use of "other" drugs is sparse and conflicting. The President's Commission indicated that an association between the use of drugs such as amphetamines and barbiturates and crime may exist. In one study of an arrestee population, an examination of arrest charges indicated that a higher proportion of the few current users of amphetamine and barbiturates identified through urinalysis were charged with crimes against the person than were users of other drugs or nonusers (12). Though based on a relatively few cases, this result may warrant further followup. The pharmacological properties of cocaine, solvents, and some nonbarbiturate sedatives suggest that use of these drugs can lead to violent actions; however, few examples could be directly linked to use. A review of the literature provides little support for a conclusion that use of amphetamines is related to crime. Amphetamine use is not necessarily conducive to crime, nor is it particularly prevalent among criminal groups. Criminal amphetamine users have substantial criminal histories prior to their first use of such drugs. It has been suggested that the pharmacological effects of amphetamines in interaction with situational factors can induce behavior resulting in crime (18).

Drugs which have not been studied extensively in the past may become important problems in the future. For example, cocaine is an extremely expensive stimulant. Its use is now, apparently, largely limited to those who can afford the luxury without resorting to crime. There is evidence, though, that cocaine use has increased several fold in recent years. The spread of use to larger populations may lead to its eventual association with crime.

(c) Narcotics and Opiate Addicts Users of addictive narcotics and opiates are the most likely population subgroup to be involved in criminal behavior. The President's Commission on Law Enforcement and Administration of Justice recommended that research focus

primarily on users of these drugs and that non-drug and drug-defined offenses be distinguished.

"Drug addicts are crime-prone persons. This fact is not open to serious dispute, but to determine its meaning is another matter. Analysis is best restricted to heroin because of the applicable laws, because of the information available, and because drugs with addiction liability present the clearest issues" (37: p. 221).

The National Commission on Marihuana and Drug Abuse reached similar conclusions about the types of crimes generally committed by opiate users:

"Use of opiates, especially heroin, is associated with acquisitive crimes such as burglary and shoplifting, ordinarily committed for the purposes of securing money to support dependence, assaultive offenses are significantly less likely to be committed by these opiate users, especially in comparison with users of alcohol, amphetamines and barbiturates" (30: p. 165).

This conclusion was supported in a recent review of literature on crime and addiction.

"Contrary to early studies, the most recent evidence suggests that addicts commit primarily those crimes that yield a financial return regardless of whether they are violent or not" (19: p. 261).

Thus, the consensus appeared to be that income-generating crime is more common among opiate addicts. To check this assumption, the Panel examined types of crimes that heroin users commit both throughout their lives and within a particular time span.

1. *History of criminal behavior*—Three samples of heroin users were examined. These included those in treatment, those arrested, and those in a general population survey. Foi each group, those ever arrested for or admitting to ever committing each of several types of crimes are shown in Tables I, II, and III. The arrest histories of treatment clients in 12 programs are shown in Table I. The percentages of program clients found to have an arrest history range

from 55 to 100 percent. Table I illustrates the very important point that few researchers have differentiated between drug offenses and other types of crime, and that most depend on arrest charges rather than self-admissions. In the studies in which types of crime were differentiated, it was found that between 66 and 80 percent of the addicts had committed at least one income-generating crime. In a sample of Baltimore addicts, 46 percent of the police contacts were for property offenses or robbery (32). In a sample of persons arrested in six cities in 1971, those ever charged with at least one robbery or property offenses were much higher for heroin users (45% and 91%) than for other types of drug users (Table II). Similar criminal histories from the general survey of males aged 20 to 30 are shown in Table III. Substantially higher proportions of the self-admitted heroin users admitted a robbery, breaking and entering, and shoplifting than other types of users (44). These data from treatment, arrest, and general population sources all support the conclusion that heroin users are much more likely than the other types of users to admit to or be charged with a robbery or property offense at some time in their lives. However, little or no information is available regarding the frequence with which these users committed these offenses.

A logical next question is: *Do drug use and crime occur concurrently?* To answer this question, the Panel examined criminal behavior and drug use within specified time periods.

2. *Concurrent criminal behavior and drug use*—The proportions of heroin users who committed particular types of offenses may be inferred from looking at recent drug use and criminality. For treatment populations, the DARP data showed that about one-third of the clients reported illegal income as a major source of support in the 2 months prior to enrollment in treatment (8). Among arrestee populations (Table IV), regardless of the city or year, a large number of heroin users had a current charge for a property crime or robbery (6, 10,12, 24,

Table I. Arrest Histories of Treatment Clients

Treatment Program	Number in Sample	Percentage of Arrest Types			
		Robbery	Income-Generating Crime	Nondrug Defined Crime	Any Crime
DARP	42,293	NA	NA	NA	82%[a]
New Jersey					
Methadone maintenance	249	NA	NA	NA	83%[a]
Drug free	198	NA	NA	NA	57%[a]
Heroin addicts	476	32%	87%	NA	100%[b]
Lexington Hospital					
Kentucky addicts	266	5%	22%	47%	60%[b]
NARA sample	1,096	2%	13%	NA	90%[b]
Pennsylvania					
Methadone maintenance	224	NA	NA	56%	84%
New York City					
Beth Israel meth. maintc.	912	NA	NA	NA	91%[a]
ASA drug free	958	NA	NA	NA	55%[a]
Phoenix House	1,148	NA	68%	NA	80%[b]

Sources: DARP (40), New Jersey (28), Lexington-Kentucky addicts (33), Lexington-NARA (45), Pennsylvania (3), NYC-Beth Israel (9), NYC-ASA (42), NYC-Phoenix House (29).

[a]Arrests (records or self-reported arrests).
[b]Self-reported crime.

Table II. Arrest Histories of Drug Users in Arrestee Samples in Six Cities, 1971

Type of Offense[a]	Percentage for Four Levels of Drug Use			
	Heroin Use	Other Drug Use	Marihuana Use	Non-drug Use
Robbery	45	32	31	23
Property	91	78	73	69

Source: (13).
[a]Ever charged with robbery or property offenses.

27). The proportion of heroin users who were arrested and charged with robbery varied from 56 percent in Chicago to 11 percent in Los Angeles and San Antonio. General population surveys yield small numbers of respondents who admit to current drug use and criminality, but a similar pattern is indicated. A high proportion of current users of heroin admit engaging in income-generating predatory crimes.

Data from these studies consistently confirm that identified heroin users commit primarily property crimes.

Their most serious offense is commonly robbery. Without data on undetected or untreated drug users, it is questionable whether we can generalize to all drug users on the basis of these data.

A substantial number of criminals in TASC programs, jails, or prisons had never been in treatment and consequently would have been less likely identified as users (5, 43).

Another study found that drug users who are identified by means of urinalysis but who deny current drug use in interviews are more likely to have been charged with a serious crime against the person (12). These findings suggest that un-

Table III. Criminal Histories of Drug Users in a National Sample
of Males Age 20-30

Type of Offense[a]	Percentage for Five Levels of Drug Use				
	Heroin Use	Other Opiate Use	Other Drug Use	Marihuana Use	Non-drug Use
Armed robbery	11	2	1	1	1
Breaking & entering	39	26	17	9	5
Shoplifting	72	66	53	47	28
No crime	18	28	44	47	68

Source: (44).

[a]Admitting ever committing armed robbery, breaking and entering, or shoplifting.

Table IV. Arrest Charges for Identified Current Heroin Users in
Arrestee Samples in Nine Cities, 1969-74

Year and Location of Arrest	Percentage of Most Serious Charges			
	Property	Robbery	Serious Person	Total
1969 Washington, DC	44	15	9	68
1971 Washington, DC[a]	64	24	19	107
New York, NY	55	24	7	86
Chicago, IL[b]	34	56	4	94
St. Louis, MO	64	14	14	92
New Orleans, LA	73	27	0	100
San Antonio, TX	75	11	6	92
Los Angeles, CA	68	11	11	90
1973 Washington, DC[a]	42	42	6	90
Philadelphia, PA	66	19	9	94
1974 Miami, FL[c]	39	12	7	58

Sources: Washington (6, 24), Philadelphia (10), Miami (27), other cities (12).

[a]Included multiple arrest charges; therefore, totals exceed 100%

[b]Chicago had two jail intakes. The one used in this study received the more serious
types of offenders.

[c]Minor offenders included in the calculation of percentages.

detected drug users may be involved in different kinds of crime than those who are readily identified as users.

2. Drugs Used by Criminals

From the preceding discussion, it is clear that known heroin users commit or have committed a large number of crimes, particularly income-generating ones. *What proportion of all crime they commit is open to conjecture.*

Answers have been suggested by public officials. For example, police administrators have estimated that 30 to 70 percent of all crime is committed by heroin users (36).

For the Panel's purposes, this question may be phrased as follows: *Among different types of crimi-*

nals, what is the probability that the offenders are particular types of drug users? Stated in this manner, we can examine the nature and extent of drug use in known criminal populations to find at least a partial answer. One source of information, of course, is the tallies of heroin users or addicts on arrest dockets or in jails. Table V shows that a high proportion of the persons arrested for income-generating offenses are current users of heroin.

In a study in Washington, D.C., 27 percent of the persons arrested in 1969 for nondrug offenses were heroin users; comparable figures for 1971 and 1973 were 31 and 16 percent, respectively (6, 24). These figures may not be typical of other cities. Wide variation was found in a central jail intake study in six cities in 1971 (12). In New York, 60 percent of all those arrested for property crimes were current heroin users; in St. Louis, New Orleans, Chicago, San Antonio, and Los Angeles, the figures ranged from 20 to 25 percent. The percent from a Dade County (Miami) study was 19 percent (27). The

differences were even more dramatic for robbery. The proportions of identified heroin users among those arrested for robbery varied from 80 percent in New York to 17 percent in St. Louis. An LEAA survey of 10,000 inmates in state correctional facilities found 13 percent were using heroin at the time of the arrest that led to their current incarceration (5).

The counts of heroin users in jails and prisons give us roughly the same range (13 to 60 percent) as that of police administrators (30 to 70 percent). Neither is particularly helpful in deriving a precise estimate. The figures indicate that a disproportionate share of arrestees charged with robbery and property crimes is current heroin users.

Whether heroin users, in turn, actually commit a disproportionate amount of all reported and unreported crime remains an open question. The discovery of high percentages of addicts at various points in the criminal justice system may simply mean that heroin addiction is dangerous to one's freedom or that addicts are

Table V. Identified Current Heroin Use Among Samples of Arrestees Charged in Nine Cities, 1969-74

Year or Location of Arrest	Percentages of Users Charged			Percentage of Users Identified
	Property	Robbery	Serious Person	
1969 Washington, DC	49	42	31	27
1971 Washington, DC[a]	68	52	40	31
New York, NY	60	80	23	53
Chicago, IL[b]	21	22	3	15
St. Louis, MO	22	17	13	16
New Orleans, LA	24	35	0	14
San Antonio, TX	22	33	6	14
Los Angeles, CA	21	19	14	19
1973 Philadelphia, PA	22	24	7	11
Washington, DC[a]	43	40	25	16
1974 Miami, FL[c]	19	27	10	16

Sources: Washington (6, 24), Philadelphia (10), Miami (27), other cities (12).
[a]Included multiple arrest charges.
[b]Chicago had two jail intakes. The one used in this study received the more serious types of offenders.
[c]Minor offenders included in the calculation of percentages.

visible to authorities and easily caught. Robbery is a high risk offense and heroin use is a high risk behavior. Since the criminal "skill level" of heroin addicts has not been the topic of extensive research, the validity of any generalizations from an arrestee sample to the general criminal population is in doubt.

Less than 20 percent of all property crimes known to the police result in arrest (15). It is not known whether the remaining 80 percent of all property crimes that are not cleared by arrest involve the same proportions of drug users and nonusers as appear on the arrest dockets. Those who are arrested or jailed may not be a random sample representative of the persons who commit income-generating property crimes or robberies. It is for these reasons that we conclude that estimates based on arrest or prisoner data regarding the amount of crime committed by addicts must remain suspect.

B.   PATTERNS OF DRUG USE AND CRIMINALITY

One way to obtain a better understanding of the association between drug use and crime is to observe how criminal behavior changes when patterns of drug use change. The major focus of past research was on the sequence of initial drug use, initial criminal behavior, and increments in criminal behavior after the onset of addiction. It was assumed that drug use or addiction could only become more serious. Any increase in criminality after the onset of addiction was, therefore, attributed to the addiction. There is now evidence that drug use and, perhaps, addiction patterns are reversible and variable. The more appropriate general question now is: *What variations in criminal behavior are associated with variations in drug use?*

There is considerable evidence to show that drug-using criminals are involved in crime before drug use and that their criminal involvement increases after the onset of addiction (19). It has been suggested since 1950 that those who used heroin regularly had already committed income-generating crimes and were apprehended by law-enforcement agents before they started to use heroin. Further, once they were addicted, their involvement in crime intensified. However, other researchers doubt that the crime-drug use sequence is that simple:

"Among addicts that are criminals prior to addiction, there is no reason to believe that addiction is the causal factor in increasing criminality. While crime may increase, it may have increased anyway, given the fact that most contemporary addicts are at an age which is also a high risk age for crime. There is such a substantial lack of control of important variables in most studies that it is impossible to evaluate the effect of addiction on criminal behavior" (19: p. 260).

Another investigator also suggests that the causal relationship is quite complex:

At the present time most known opiate addicts have been delinquent prior to their being identified as users and most continue to be arrested after release from hospitals and prisons. Changes in the association between delinquency and opiate use occur over time and differ among cultural subgroups. At present there is a tendency for individuals after release to experience an increase in arrests over preaddiction experience, these arrests primarily being for narcotics offenses and secondarily in connection with crimes against property . . . (7: p. 57).

Comparison of the nature and extent of criminal activity before the onset of drug use with that after initial drug use is useful, but may be misleading. Similarly, examination of the rates at which addicts commit crimes before and after becoming addicted would provide only a partial answer. We need to determine if either the onset of drug use or addiction is a critical point in a criminal career. *Do criminals intensify their involvement in criminal behavior after the onset of regular daily use of addictive or expensive drugs?* To answer this question we must assess what individual criminality would have been without drug use or addiction on the basis of their background characteristics and prior criminality. Predicted rates of crime could then be compared with actual postdrug-use or postaddiction rates of criminality.

Based on the evidence that drug use may be episodic, we can ask questions about the variability in criminality between and during episodes of drug use. *Do changes in income-generating criminal behavior accompany changes in the cost of drug habits, or variation in use patterns?* Data regarding changes in patterns of criminality within and after periods of nonmedical use of illicit opiates (particularly heroin) are needed to answer this question. It could then be determined how criminality changes after regular drug use or addiction is interrupted or terminated.

Episodic drug use could be studied by using an individual as his or her own control. Criminal behavior during periods of regular drug use could then be compared with criminal activity during periods of infrequent use or abstention. A study which used episodes found that arrests during periods of opiate use were five times greater than the number during periods of nonuse (3). In another survey of young males a higher proportion of the few identified heroin users admitted committing various crimes during periods in which heroin was used than in other periods (44).

In a study of Baltimore narcotic addicts, data were collected by episodes of use. Consequently, criminal behavior before, during, between, and after episodes of regular use could be compared (31). It was found that arrests, especially for property crimes, were more common during episodes of regular use than in periods of nonuse. Periods of nonuse, however, were often initiated by incarceration. It is apparent these respondents were in correctional facilities during part or during all of their periods of nonuse. It would be misleading to compare crime during episodes of regular use with periods of nonuse when an episode of nonuse included substantial time spent in custody. Preliminary analyses showed that the marked difference between criminality during periods of regular use and nonuse virtually disappeared when a crude control was made for time spent in correctional facilities.

C. THIRD FACTORS ASSOCIATED WITH DRUG USE AND CRIMINAL BEHAVIOR

Many social, psychological, and economic factors have been found to be associated with both drug use and criminal behavior. It is reasonable to assume that some of these variables are causally related to criminality. This has led some writers to conclude that, compared to other factors, drug use itself has less impact on criminality than generally believed. The National Commission on Marihuana and Drug Use outlined the argument:

"Most of the researchers who have found that the majority of their sample populations were arrested before the onset of dependence agree that criminal behavior is not a by-product of dependence but results, as does the drug dependence itself, from psychological and social deviance which predates dependence and is ordinarily apparent by adolescence. This conclusion challenges the theory that drugs cause crime and stresses that drug dependence and criminality are two forms of social deviance, neither producing the other. . . . It is generally agreed that drugs have the ability to exacerbate existing psychopathology, delinquency and criminality. However, such ability is conditional upon the preexistence of psychological and social maladjustment prior to the onset of drug use or dependence" (30: p. 172).

Such arguments are in conflict with the assumptions underlying many of the current drug abuse policies. The primary assumption among these is that drug use is a major cause of crime.

To accurately assess the impact of drug use on crime, we need to ask: *What is the relative impact of particular patterns of drug use on patterns of criminal behavior in comparison with the impact of other variables?*

Researchers must include variables other than drug use and crime in their analyses. The outcome of these analyses will help to answer a fundamental question facing policymakers: *What proportion of crime, particularly income-generating property crime, can be attributed to the financial requirements of drug habits?*

Other factors can be taken into account in two ways. First, the researcher can examine the relationship between drug use and criminal behavior within selected population subgroups. The variables which are used to define the subgroup are thereby controlled. The second approach is to statistically control for the effect of other variables. Multivariate analytical techniques can be used to determine the marginal impact of drug use on crime compared to the effects of other variables.

The few investigators that have taken other variables into account have looked primarily at the crime-drug relationship within particular cultural, sex, ethnic groups, or birth cohorts. In the studies conducted prior to 1950, it was generally found that addicts did not have criminal records prior to addiction. In the past 25 years, the pattern seems to have changed; that is, an increasing proportion of addicts have fairly extensive contact with the criminal justice system prior to addiction (19). The crime-drug use pattern has changed, and clear evidence of this fact was reported in a description of the addict populations in the Lexington hospital in 1936 and in 1965 (35, 41):

"Thus, Smith et al. characterized a typical addict in Pescor's sample as white, from the South, and in his middle twenties at addiction. Generally, he became medically addicted to morphine and had a noncriminal history. In contrast, the typical addict in the mid-sixties was black, urban, young, nonmedically addicted to heroin, and had a long history of delinquency and crime prior to drugs. This contrast between early and recent samples of officially recorded opiate addicts can be observed in several studies" (19: p. 235).

This suggests that a fundamental shift in the composition of the addict population has occurred in recent decades.

The few investigations of female drug-using offenders (4, 16, 21, 39, 46) indicate that female users depend on different sources of illicit support more than their male counterparts. A comparison of the criminal behavior and narcotic use patterns of black and white Baltimore addicts revealed substantial differences in the nature and extent of criminal behavior for the two groups (31, 32).

From these analyses, it may be concluded that not one but many associations exist between drug use and criminal behavior.

If the link between drug use and criminal behavior is to be fully understood, then many patterns need to be examined by sex, ethnic group, and other characteristics.

Population subgroup differences also should be taken into consideration when developing a national policy. A single strategy may well have differential impacts on various segments of the population. That is, a policy may be effective for some segments, but could exacerbate problems in other parts of the population.

In multivariate analytical techniques, the relative association of a number of explanatory variables with the dependent variable can be examined. The need for such an approach is illustrated by two examples. Results of two studies showed that increases in treatment enrollment were accompanied by decreases in communitywide crime rates (11, 26). However, there was also a concurrent increase in the size of the police force. Although treatment enrollment may have been the major cause of the reduction in crime, failure to systematically consider other possible explanatory variables leaves the results of such studies open to debate.

In a second example, the supply reduction strategy was ostensibly at work during the 1972 heroin panic. At that time, the Turkey-Barcelona-Marseille connection was broken. A dock workers' strike may have augmented the effect. Presumably if heroin users abandoned the market at this time, their need to commit crimes to support their habits should have dropped precipitously, and new recruits to heroin use would have been effectively discouraged. The shortages would most affect those geographic areas served by the affected distribution network. An examination of aggregated data of serum hepatitis shows that the volume of novice users and property crime rates calculated for three U.S.regions declined during this period. As shown in Figure 1 and Figure 2, the two indicators for the Mid-Atlantic region move together in the expected direction.

It is difficult to rule out the possibility that the relationship is a spurious one. It is important to note that in 1972 the FBI changed the manner in which it reported property crimes. There was also a tremendous increase in treatment slots for drug users during this time.

Consideration of salient situational variables and personal characteristics is mandatory in any analysis of the relationship between drug use and crime. We know that many of the same variables associated with individual drug use—such as sex, age ethnicity, employment, and education—are also associated with criminal behavior. Law enforcement policies, criminal justice practices, treatment availability, and unemployment rates are some of the factors that would likely affect crime rates in a community. What we need to know is, after taking such factors into account, *how much more of an individual's criminality or a community's crime rate can we explain by looking at an individual's drug use patterns or the prevalence of drug use in a community?*

D. CAUSAL MODELS OF DRUG USE AND CRIMINAL BEHAVIOR

Although sophisticated analytical techniques will provide a more complete and detailed description of the association between drug use and criminality, a description alone is not enough. The Panel's adoption of a descriptive rather than explanatory approach is not an endorsement of atheoretical research efforts.

The questions of why crime is committed and why drugs are used are, of course, the paramount issues. The nature and extent of a complex causal relationship between drug use and criminal behavior can be more fully understood only when we learn more about how and why individuals become involved in various forms of criminal behavior and in the use of different drugs, and how and why these behaviors change over time.

The development and testing of explanatory models of drug use and criminal behavior are essential. Initial models based on our current

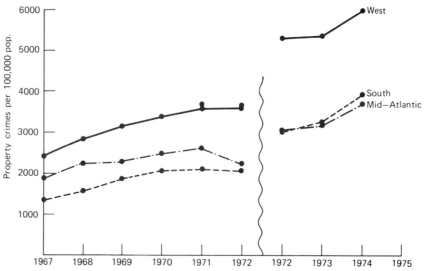

Figure 1.   Regional property crime trends, 1967-74. (Source: NIDA Division of Research.)

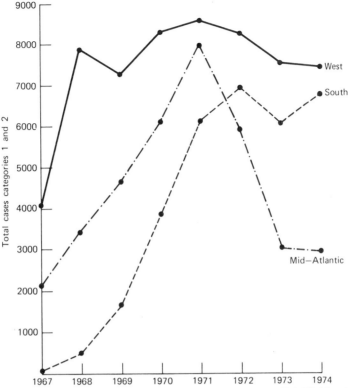

Figure 2. Regional hepatitis trends, 1967-74. (Source: NIDA Division of Research.)

knowledge would necessarily be crude. Longitudinal data must be collected and analyzed to provide an overview of the criminal and drug use careers of individuals and histories of the trends in drug use prevalence and crime rates in communities. Well-designed prospective and retrospective longitudinal studies must be encouraged.

From such studies, we can obtain the kind of empirical data necessary to test and refine models of behavior.

Attention must be devoted to the identification of important intervening variables such as education, peer group membership, and employment on the individual level as well as law enforcement practices and social program impacts on the community level. We need to know not only how much criminal behavior is a direct result of the financial requirements of addicts but also how much is due to more indirect effects. For example, *does drug use lower motivation to seek work, affect the physical and mental capacities needed to perform on the job, and increase the chances of being excluded from legitimate employment opportunities?* If it does, these effects may lead an individual into a career of crime.

Research using sophisticated models of human behavior, data collected in well-designed longitudinal studies, and appropriate multivariate techniques hold the promise of providing answers to these key questions of causality. The questions are not academic. Knowledge of the processes underlying drug use and criminal behavior will enable us to identify the strategic points for intervention in social programs designed to comprehensively attack the problem of crime.

*

THE DRUG USER AND MARKET BEHAVIOR

The manipulation of drug prices is commonly thought to be within the realm of government policy. Further, the increase of drug prices is thought to be an efficient policy instrument for reducing drug use. In the long run, it is also judged to be efficient for reducing criminal activities associated with drug use. The 1975 *White Paper on Drug Abuse*, for instance, advocated "supply reduction efforts to make drugs difficult to obtain, expensive, and risky to possess, sell or consume."An increase in price via successful supply reduction, according to the paper, can: "(1) minimize the number of new users, (2) increase the number of old users who abandon use, and (3) decrease the consumption of current users." The paper warns that one adverse effect of supply reduction is that "crime rates increase, as users attempt to meet the rising cost of scarce, illegal drugs." Further, supply reduction must be coupled with demand reduction since "reduced drug availability increases pressure on drug users to seek treatment" (50: pp. 2–4).

*

. . . The consumer in . . . is the drug user— the ultimate target of both drug suppliers and those who would either prevent the consumer from entering the drug market or attempt to reduce the consumer's level of use.

The drug consumer may or may not have committed nondrug crimes. As shown in the previous sections of this report, significant associations exist between illicit opiate use and involvement in various forms of criminality, especially between narcotic use and income-generating criminal acts. Few past or current researchers deny these associations. What has been debated at length but not resolved conclusively is whether or not there is a systematic relationship that links the consumption of heroin and other narcotic or expensive drugs with income-generating criminal activity. While the behavior of the drug user can be partially explained at the theoretical level by sociological, psychological or physiological forces, the argument for relating criminality to drug use is perhaps strongest from an economic perspective.

The usual mechanism for relating heroin and other narcotic use to income-generating criminal activity is based directly on the economics of the habit. Few addicts, the argument goes, have the legal incomes to support habits costing $30-$70 a day. The addict either resorts to income-generating criminal activity to provide the necessary funds or reduces drug consumption. A profound physiological craving, the sheer pleasure of the drug, or fear of withdrawal are often cited as reasons why reduced consumption is an unlikely choice. Thus, it is generally believed that consumption continues at the same or increased quantity level and requires the commission of crimes.

A number of explicit or implied assumptions in the above paragraph should be questioned. We thought it necessary to examine central issues regarding the drug use-criminal behavior relationship in an economic framework. For the current purpose which is consistent with the objective of developing policy relevant information, two issues were delineated: (a) the drug user's response to changes in drug prices and (b) methods of supporting a drug habit. The two issues are further developed by the following questions:

How does drug consumption behavior and associated criminality to support drug use change as a function of changes in price due to changed availability, law enforcement or other reasons? At the aggregate level, what is the effect on criminality of price changes and the relative importance of other factors including availability of treatment, unemployment rates, and urbanization?

What proportions of drug user's income-generating activity are licit and illicit? Or what proportion of income supporting a drug habit is from illicit sources, in particular income-generating crimes? What proportion of drug user income is committed to supporting drug use?

Aspects of these issues and questions are discussed in the following section which is based primarily on a paper prepared for this report (53). We attempt in this section to summarize briefly the current knowledge about each of the two central issues. It becomes apparent from the following paragraphs that few aspects of the issues have been convincingly resolved.

A. DRUG USER REACTIONS TO DRUG PRICE CHANGES

The direction and extent of variation in drug expenditures due to changes in drug prices depend on the quantity of drugs that would be consumed at alternative prices. This relationship is stated in economic terms as "price elasticity of demand"—the percentage change in the quantity of the purchased good (narcotic drugs) divided by the percentage change in its price.

1. Demand Considerations

It is often assumed that heroin users are reluctant to reduce their consumption when price rises. This implies that the price elasticity of demand for heroin is extremely low; that is, in terms of quantity consumed, it is not very responsive to changes to the price of heroin. Thus, although an increase in price of heroin may decrease the quantity consumed, the total expenditures will increase. In the extreme, if there is no decrease in consumption when price rises (a price elasticity of zero), the percentage increase in expenditures will equal the percentage increase in the price. This assumption of an inelastic demand for heroin is an integral part of the usual mechanism which tells us that heroin consumption leads to income-generating crime: with increased prices come increased expenditures which require increased income. If the heroin user's income-generating opportunities are limited to criminal activities, the need will be to commit either more crimes or more lucrative crimes.

The above comments on the consumption of heroin have been made without consideration of alternative drugs. Other drugs, particularly those which can substitute for heroin, may affect the demand for heroin, whatever the extent of its elasticity. If the consumer of heroin has excellent low-cost (or lower cost) narcotic substitutes such as inexpensive, illegal ("street") methadone or access to legal methadone maintenance, then the quantity of heroin consumed may be "sensitive" to increases in the price of heroin. Thus, with substitutes available, increased heroin prices may not lead to increased need for income, legal or illegal.

There is considerable evidence of methadone diversion and the proliferation of illegal markets for methadone. Methadone does serve as a substitute and is even referred to as the "preferred drug" by some researchers (47). Others have described it as "a supplemental substance . . . a convenient means of avoiding some of the more typical vicissitudes of street life encountered by most 'street addicts' " (64, p. 264). In at least one previous high-heroin-use locality, ethnographic reports describe methadone as the main drug for 85 percent of the drug users. The methadone is mixed with and consumed in patterns which include "wine, pills, and coke." The other 15 percent of the drug users consume only heroin (61). The main point is that the consumption of methadone as at least a partial substitute for heroin "softens" the elasticity of demand for heroin, is far less expensive than heroin, and requires less income for regular consumption.

It is known that consumption patterns differ among users, and it is expected that these patterns have an impact on the demand for heroin. As summarized in a paper prepared for this report, "all addicts are users but not all users are addicts" (53). Four categories of drug users adopted by the National Commission on Marihuana and Drug Abuse are (1) infrequent recreational users, (2) frequent recreational and circumstantial users, (3) intensive users, and (4) compulsive users (58). Each succeeding category is meant to describe greater use frequency and quantity per unit of time. For each category, different behaviors are assumed. Lesser sensitivity to changes in the price of narcotics is assumed for each category. Although there are no reliable figures on how consumers are spread across user categories, the National Institute on Drug Abuse estimates that only 1 in 10 heroin users is addicted. Recent research contradicts the belief that heroin use leads inevitably to destructive compulsive use for all users. Case studies indicate that some users can occasionally use heroin or "chip" without becoming addicted (65). This finding is consistent with other earlier findings (60).

Occasional users and multidrug users make up substantial proportions of the heroin-consuming population. Thus, the direction and extent of the net total effect of a heroin price change on income-generating crime depends on the mix of users and the availability of substitutes in the affected market. At the individual level, data have not been available to estimate consumer reactions to price. *How many users are in the various categories? How and why do users move across the categories? Does the use of substitutes by heroin users vary across categories of users?* These questions have not been satisfactorily answered. It is known from ethnographic observations of small numbers of users that relatively less expensive substitutes are used during periods of heroin shortage or the inability to finance purchases. Use of these substitutes may be short-term (47, 61).

To specify the type of reaction each type of user has to price increases, it would be necessary to obtain consumption and price data (among other things) both cross sectionally and over periods of time at the individual level. Considerable effort would be required to overcome problems of measuring consumption and prices; however, methodologies exist which can be adapted to this purpose. Somewhat more work has been done on user reactions to price changes at the aggregate level.

2.   Evidence of Reactions to Price Changes

Evidence of the impact of drug treatment on criminal behavior has been considered from the individual, the clinical, and the aggregate levels where communitywide or neighborhoodwide reported offenses were related to treatment enrollment. In the first part of this section, we briefly consider the treatment-crime relationship from the perspective of drug price changes and treatment enrollment. In the second part, we consider the relationship between heroin prices and criminal activity.

(a) Supply Reduction, Treatment, and Crime   Treatment is the main federal policy strategy for reducing the total demand by eliminating the individual need for expensive narcotics. Eliminating the need to consume illicit narcotics concurrently eliminates expenditures for those narcotics. To the extent that narcotic drugs lead to income-generating crime, enrollment in treatment and the subsequent reduction in demand for narcotics should decrease crime. Thus, there should be an inverse relationship between treatment slots filled (enrollment in treatment) and measures of crime, particularly income-generating crime.

The findings of several studies of the impact of aggregate enrollment in treatment on crime are consistent with this hypothesis. In summary, these studies contend that simultaneous demand reduction via the increased availability of treatment and supply reduction via increased law enforcement have been accompanied by *increased numbers enrolled in treatment* and *decreased numbers of reported criminal offenses*. These studies are discussed in a paper prepared for this report (53, pp. 1–17). The investigators of these studies do not interpret their findings as causally linked, although such an interpretation would be tempting and plausible. The studies were conducted in Washington, D.C., and San Antonio, Texas, during or immediately following increased law enforcement efforts of 1969–74 which were at least partially directed to reducing heroin supplies. It should be noted that a supply reduction strategy does not have to physically remove the heroin or the heroin dealers from the market (although this would reduce supply); it simply has to raise the cost to the suppliers of doing "business" so that they sell smaller quantities at prevailing prices. This amounts to the same thing as charging higher prices for a given quantity. The purpose of supply reduction, then, is to increase the price of heroin. Ultimately, the objective of supply reduction is to decrease the consumption of heroin, the number of users, and to keep new users out of the market. Success of the strategy depends to a large part on the impact of price changes on demand.

Thus in these communities for this period of time, the positive aspects of the policy model advocated by the *White Paper* appeared to be effective. Supply reduction efforts appeared to increase the cost of heroin; treatment was made available and enrollment increased following an apparent heroin supply reduction and concurrent price increase; and a reduction in reported crime was also recorded. Furthermore, the results of these studies are also consistent with the relationship among at least some broader, more aggregate indexes of heroin availability, heroin use and income-generating criminal activity. . . .

We should, however, interpret the results of these studies with caution because of significant criticisms of methodology or measurements and plausible alternative explanations for the results. Criminality measurements were *reported* offenses for specified crimes in the communities. One criticism is that some crimes go unreported and that this underreporting may vary over time and by the mix of crimes committed by addict and nonaddict criminals. The major criticism is that the reported crimes are in no way *necessarily* related to the addict population since the increased law enforcement efforts

were not restricted to the heroin-using population. In other words, the criminal activities of the heroin users and persons in treatment could have remained unchanged or could have increased, and the criminal activities of the nonusing criminal population could have decreased and accounted for the net reduction in reported offenses. Another criticism is that there are no measurements of the "seriousness" or "social cost" of the crimes reduced. Thus, the increased law enforcement may have had an impact directly on the relatively low-cost, low-yield crimes committed in large numbers by relatively inefficient criminals. Simply put, it is not possible to distinguish from these studies the different impacts of law enforcement on the heroin- and nonheroin-consuming criminal populations and the crimes they commit.

(b) Prices and Criminal Activity   A study of the relationship between heroin prices and the level of criminal activity was based on monthly price data for July 1970 through June 1972 (49). The major hypothesis was that if addicts must consume a fixed quantity of heroin during a specified period and support their habit through criminal activity, a rise in the price may be expected to lead to an increase in activity. Alternatively, criminal activities may go on independently of fluctuations in the price of heroin. This would be the case if the heroin user is flexible enough to (1) substitute other drugs for heroin, (2) decrease heroin consumption, or (3) abstain from heroin use altogether when the price of heroin rises. While the more immediate effect of a price rise may be an increase in criminal activity, the long-run effect may discourage regular use, encourage abstinence, and thereby decrease criminal activity among addicts.

Possibilities other than the two in this study do exist. For example, the addict-criminal may choose to participate in legal activities to increase earnings. Or the addict-criminal may change a pattern of criminal activity and opt for crimes with greater risk but greater rewards; such a change may not increase the numbers of reported offenses (the measure used in the study) since they may be committed at the same rate or less frequently.

The study used data on prices of purchases, amount of purchase in grams, and purity of purchases to construct a standardized heroin price series separately for nine cities. These series were used to test the relationship between the price of heroin and criminal activity in each city. Reported criminal offenses by category by month were the dependent variable. The price series by month, average temperature by month, and month of observation were the explanatory variables.

The results are presented only for New York City; results for the other eight cities are reported as "mixed and, in many ways, ambiguous." For New York City, the results show a positive and generally significant relationship between the price of heroin and criminal activities associated with income generation; those not associated with income generation are generally not significant.

This study recasts the question from *Do drug users commit crimes?* to *How much crime is attributable to drug use, and how does this vary across the categories of crime?* It asks whether the variation in the retail price of heroin was systematically related to variation in reported criminal offenses and, if so, to what extent. The findings for New York City indicate a positive relationship between the heroin price index and reported criminal activity.

In summary, the findings for New York City are consistent with the hypothesis that there is a systematic, positive relationship between the consumption of heroin and criminal activities—that is, an increase in the price of heroin *leads to* an increase in criminal activities. These findings are also consistent with several alternative hypotheses. For instance, higher prices may result from increased demand brought about by increased income, and addict-criminals may commit more crimes to increase earnings to purchase more heroin. Thus, instead of a rise in price leading to a rise in crime, a rise in crime would lead to a rise in price. Both are examples

of a *positive* crime-heroin price relationship. Another possibility is that drug markets (particularly heroin prices) are *unrelated* to criminal activities but that both are systematically related to one or more variables that were excluded from the study.

A similar methodology was extended and applied to time-series data for the city of Detroit (63). As in the previous study, variation in reported criminal offenses was related to variation in explanatory variables, including the constructed heroin price series. Significant changes from the previous study were that the analyses were conducted for neighborhoods rather than cities and that an indication of police activity (proportions of crimes cleared by arrest) was incorporated. The investigators reported results consistent with the earlier study. That is, changes in the heroin price series have both a positive and generally significant impact on reported crimes. The impact varies by type of neighborhood.

In summary, these studies provide measures of the net effects of changes in heroin prices on *total* crime; however, little is contributed to our understanding of crime attributable to drug use. Aggregate crime includes crimes committed by the addict and nonaddict, the user, and the nonuser. In the studies, these are associated with changes in a heroin price series. Several alternative explanations for the associations that were found are possible, and each calls for different policy prescriptions.

The basic link between drug use and crime is reliance on criminal activity to support a habit. The following presents some current knowledge about drug abuser income.

B.   SOURCES OF INCOME OF DRUG USERS

It is clear from the section of this report dealing with the association between criminal behavior and drug use that a great deal of income-generating crime is committed by drug users. What is unclear is the proportion of the total number of income-generating crimes committed by drug users, as opposed to others. Also unclear is the extent to which the need to support a habit enters into the drug use-crime relationship for individual users. This section describes the sources of support of drug use, employment among addicts, and expenditures for drugs.

1. Sources of Support

We stated earlier that income generated from illegal sources may to some extent and for some users influence the demand for narcotics. In that framework, successful criminals spend earnings from criminal activities on a consumption good—heroin. Regardless of the direction of causality—crimes to drugs or drugs to crime—the sources of support for a drug habit are important determinants of the social costs of drug use. Drug use is supported through a variety of legal and illegal sources and activities other than property crime. These include drug distribution system activities such as selling; legal activities such as employment and public assistance; and revenues from victimless crimes such as gambling and prostitution.

A 1971 study of the major occupations of 125 addicts in a Chicago "heroin copping community" indicated that 38 percent described themselves as "hustlers" and cited thievery and other forms of criminality as sources of support; 34 percent were primarily engaged in drug distribution; and 28 percent had legitimate jobs. The 28 percent generally had habits which involved less frequent and less expensive use (55).

In another study, 259 users entering a medical clinic for heroin addiction treatment offered another view of means of support (59). While Table VI shows that thievery et al. were by far the most important primary source, it also indicates that less than 50 percent of the support is from activities which might be property-type crimes.

Another study estimated that addicts derive 45 percent of their funds for the purchase of heroin from the heroin distribution system. Of

Table VI. Means of Support among Drug Patients[a] at the Haight-Ashbury Medical Center

Means of Support	Primary Support	Secondary Support
Job	15%	3%
Spouse	4	1
Welfare	4	1
Other legal	13	18
Thievery, burglary, or "hustling" stolen goods	39	10
Dealing	21	7
Pimping or prostituting	5	2
Total	100%	

Source: (12).
[a] Among the 259 patients were 44 nonrespondents.

the remaining 55 percent, more than a third was obtained from legal sources and victimless crimes such as prostitution and gambling (57, pp. 69–71).

A recent study of 254 females in Seattle, Washington, provides some insight into the female addict support systems (56). In this study prostitutes were defined as those with an arrest charge or self-report for prostitution or loitering for purposes of prostitution. Addicts were defined as those who had used addictive narcotic drugs for at least 6 months and who experienced withdrawal symptoms in treatment or jail. The 254 women included 64 addicts, 60 addict-prostitutes, 66 prostitutes, and 64 other offenders.

All of the women, addicted and nonaddicted, were asked to describe their illegal support systems. Prostitutes and addict-prostitutes, predictably, depended primarily on prostitution for their support and secondarily on drug sales and larceny, in that order. Nonprostitute addicts and female offenders relied primarily on drug sales. Secondary support for the nonprostitute addict was shoplifting, followed by larceny and prostitution; for the female offender it was shoplifting, forgery, and prostitution (56, pp. 10–11).

When asked to approximate the *percentages* of monthly and yearly incomes from each illegal activity, nonprostitute addicts reported relying on drug sales for about 68 percent of their total income. Female offenders derive about 26 percent of their income from this source, about 25 percent from forgery, and about 19 percent from shoplifting. Addict-prostitutes earned about 73 percent of their income from prostitution, with the remainder earned by a variety of activities.

From the studies cited above and from other reports, drug selling accounts for 30–50 percent of the means of support for drug habits. The important point is that drug selling for support probably removes the financial onus from the heavy users. Other users are less desperate in terms of habit-need and, thus, less compelled to commit crimes for support.

2. Addicts as Workers

Conventional behavior by the narcotics-using population has tended to be overlooked because research has centered on the relationship of drug addictions and social pathologies. Employment status has been important in much of the research centered on treatment evaluation; however, little has been devoted to the effect of employment status on drug addiction and criminal activity prior to treatment.

A 1964–68 study of the 1,230 persons in New York City admitted to methadone maintenance treatment shows 33 percent was employed immediately prior to admission—the period which the literature suggests is one of "social dysfunction" (52). This is particularly significant in light of the admissions criteria requiring at least 5 years of addiction to heroin and a record of arrests and incarceration; neither criterion is conducive to maintaining employment.

The National Commission on Marihuana and Drug Abuse, after an extensive review of literature on drug addiction and criminal behavior, reported that 41–66 percent of the various study populations were employed immediately prior to arrest, incarceration, or treatment (58, p. 169). The New York State Narcotic Addiction Control Commission estimates that 53 percent

of the regular users of heroin are employed, 34 percent are still in school, and 13 percent are unemployed (48). It is not known how many of the unemployed were actively seeking employment.

In an analysis of a subsample restricted to outpatients reported to a drug treatment information system as having been in treatment for at least a year, 47–50 percent had worked during the 60 days prior to entering treatment, 26–20 percent had worked at least 31 days, and the mean was 40 days (62, p. 267).

While the rates of employment in legitimate activities may seem low, they must be viewed within the context of legal market opportunities. There is little information for local market areas. We gain some insight by referring to and subjectively revising national statistics for the labor market conditions likely to prevail for "typical" persons in areas of greatest drug use. The Bureau of Labor Statistics reports in 1974 for blacks who were 16–24 years of age and not enrolled in school that the unemployment rate was 18 percent if a high school graduate and 32 percent if not. By 1975 these rates were 24 percent if a high school graduate; 35 percent if not (51, Table 2, p. 3). Those graduating from high school in 1975 faced an unemployment rate of 17 percent if white and 43 percent if black; for 1974–75 high school dropouts, it was 28 percent if white and 61 percent if black (51, Table 2, p. 3).

Two points should be stressed about these employment and unemployment data. First, a significant number and percentage of addicts, it appears, are employed and earning legitimate incomes. Their employment patterns do not differ greatly from those of a comparable socio-demographic population. If one includes, in addition to earned income, the revenues received by addicts through local, state, or federal transfer programs and the support received from the drug distribution system, then a substantial part of the expenditures for support of a drug habit may be legitimately obtained. If so, computations based on the assumption that drug habits are supported entirely through criminal activities would be overstatements. Second, it may be the need for income rather than the need for drugs that is the driving force behind much of the presumed drug-related criminal activity. In this case, drug use in general is simply one component which may accompany the criminal life-style. For the marginally employed or those unemployed either periodically or for long periods, income-generating criminal activities may be a rational form of "employment"—that is, the best opportunity available.

REFERENCES

1. Abelson, H. I., Cohen, R., Schrayer, D., & Rappaport, M. Drug experience, attitudes and related behavior among adolescents. In the National Commission on Marihuana and Drug Abuse, *Drug use in America: problem in perspective,* Appendix, Vol. I. Washington, D.C.: U.S. Government Printing Office, 1973, 488–810.

2. Anslinger, H. J., & Cooper, C. R. Marihuana: assassin of youth. *American Magazine,* 1973, *124* (19).

3. Ball, J. C. A selective review of the crime-drug literature with reference to future research implications. National Institute on Drug Abuse, *Drug use and crime* (final report), 1976, pp. 215–229.

4. Ball, J. C., Levine, B. K., Demaree, R. G., & Newman, J. F. Pretreatment criminality of male and female drug abuse patients in the United States. *Addictive Diseases: An International Journal,* 1975, *1* (4), 481–489.

5. Barton, W. I. *Drug histories of prisoners.* Survey of inmates of state correctional facilities. Paper presented at the National Drug Abuse Conference, New York, March 25–29, 1976.

6. Bass, U. F., Brock, V. C., & DuPont, R. L. Narcotics involvement in an offender population at three points in time. *American Journal of Drug and Alcohol Abuse,* 1976, *3* (3).

7. Blum, R. H. Mind-altering drugs and dangerous behavior: narcotics. The President's Commission on Law Enforcement and Administration of Justice, Task Force Report: *Narcotics and drug abuse.* Washington, D.C.: U.S.Government Printing Office, 1976.

8. Demaree, R. G., & Neman, J. F. Criminality indicators before, during, and after treatment for drug abuse: DARP research findings, National Institute on Drug Abuse, *Drug use and crime* (final report), 1976, pp. 457–487.

9. Dole, V. P., Nyswander, M. E., & Warner, A. Successful treatment of 750 criminal addicts. *Journal of the American Medical Association,* 1968, *206*,2708–2711.

10. *Drug use and drug users in an arrestee population.* Final Report of the Philadelphia TASC's Mass Urine Screening Program, 1974.

11. DuPont, R. L., & Greene, M. H. The dynamics of a heroin addiction epidemic. *Science,* 1973, *181*, 716–722.

12. Eckerman, W. C., Bates, J. D., Rachal, J. V., & Poole, W. K. *Drug usage and arrest charges.* Washington, D.C.: Drug Enforcement Administration, 1971.

13. Eckerman, W. C., Poole, W. K., Rachal, J. V., & Hubbard, R. L. Insights into the relationship between drug usage and crime derived from a study of arrestees, National Institute on Drug Abuse, *Drug use and crime* (final report), 1976, pp. 387–407.

14. Elliott, D. S. & Ageton, A. R. The relationship between drug use and crime among adolescents, National Institute on Drug Abuse, *Drug use and crime* (final report), 1976, pp. 297–321.

15. Federal Bureau of Investigation. *Crime in the United States—1973.* Washington, D.C.: U.S. Government Printing Office, 1974.

16. File, K. N., McCahill, T. W., & Savitz, L. D. Narcotics involvement and female criminality. *Addictive Diseases,* 1974, *1* (2), 177–188.

17. Gold, M., & Reimer, D. *Changing patterns of delinquent behavior among Americans 13 to 16 years old, 1957–1972.* Report #1 of the National Survey of Youth, 1972. Ann Arbor, Michigan: University of Michigan, Institute for Social Research, 1974.

18. Greenberg, S. W. An empirical review of the literature on the relationship between crime and amphetamine abuse. *Contemporary Drug Problems,* 1976 (in press).

19. Greenberg, S. W., & Adler, F. Crime and addiction: an empirical analysis of the literature, 1920–1973. *Contemporary Drug Problems,* 1974, *3*(2), 221–270.

20. Hirschi, T., & Selvin, H. *Principles of Survey Analysis.* New York:The Free Press, 1973.

21. James, J., Gosho, C. T., & Watson, R. The relationship between female criminality and drug use, National Institute on Drug Abuse, *Drug use and crime* (final report), 1976, pp. 441–455.

22. Jessor, R., Jessor, S. L., & Finney, J. A social psychology of marihuana use: longitudinal studies of high school and college youth. *Journal of Personality and Social Psychology,* 1973, *26* (1), 1–15.

23. Johnston, L. D., *Drugs and American Youth.* Ann Arbor: University of Michigan Institute for Social Research, 1973.

24. Kozel, N. J., DuPont, R. L., & Brown, B. S. Narcotics and crime: a study of narcotic involvement in an offender population. *International Journal of the Addictions,* 1972, 7 (3), 443–450.

25. Long, G. L., & Demaree, R. G. Indicators of criminality during treatment for drug abuse. *American Journal of Drug and Alcohol Abuse,* 1975, *2* (1), 123–136.

26. Maddux, J. F., & Desmond, D. P. *Association of crime with treatment of heroin users in San Antonio.* Paper presented at the National Drug Abuse Conference, New York, 1976.

27. McBridge, Duane C. Drug use patterns and arrest charges in Dade County, National Institute on Drug Abuse, *Drug use and crime* (final report), 1976, pp. 409–418.

28. Nash, G. *The Impact of Drug Abuse Treatment upon Criminality: A Look at 19 programs.* Upper Montclair, New Jersey; Montclair State College, 1973.

29. Nash, G., Waldorf, D., Foster, K., & Kyllingstad, A. The Phoenix House program:the results of a two year follow-up. In G. DeLeon (Ed.), *Phoenix House: Studies in a Therapeutic Community (1968–1973).* New York: MSS Information Corp., 1974.

30. National Commission on Marihuana and Drug Abuse. *Drug use in America: problem in perspective.* Washington, D.C.: U.S. Government Printing Office, 1973.

31. Nurco, D. N. Crime and addiction: methodological approaches taken to correct for opportunity to commit crimes. National Institute on Drug Abuse, *Drug use and crime* (final report), 1976, pp. 489–508.

32. Nurco, D. N., & DuPont, R. L. *A preliminary report on crime and addiction within a community-wide population of narcotic addicts.* In Proceedings: The Thirty-eighth Annual Scientific Meeting of the Committee on Problems of Drug Dependence, Assembly of Life Sciences, National Research Council, Richmond, Virginia, 1976.

33. O'Donnell, J. A. Narcotics Addicts in Kentucky (PHS Pub. No. 1881). Washington, D.C.: U.S. Government Printing Office, 1969.

34. O'Donnell, J. A., Voss, H. L., Clayton, R. R., Slatin, G. T., & Room, R. G. W. *Young men and drugs—a nationwide survey,* NIDA Research Monograph 5. Washington, D.C.: U.S. Government Printing Office, 1976.

35. Pescor, M. J. A statistical analysis of the clinical records of hospitalized drug addicts. *Public Health Reports* (Supplement No. 143), 1938, 1–23.

36. Pomeroy, W. A. *Police Chiefs Discuss Drug Abuse.* Washington, D.C.:The Drug Abuse Council, 1974.

37. President's Commission on Law Enforcement and Administration of Justice. *The challenge of crime in a free society.* Washington, D.C.:U.S. Government Printing Office, 1967.

38. President's Commission on Law Enforcement and Administration of Justice. Task Force Report. *Narcotics and drug abuse.* Washington, D.C.:U.S. Government Printing Office, 1967.

39. Raynes, A. E., Climent, C., Patch, V. D., & Ervin, F. Factors related to imprisonment in female heroin addicts. *The International Journal of the Addictions,* 1974, *9* (1), 145–150.

40. Sells, S. B. (Ed.). *Effectiveness of Drug Abuse Treatment* (2 vols.). Cambridge, Massachusetts: Ballinger, 1974.

41. Smith, W. G., Ellinwood, W. H., & Vaillant, G. E. Narcotics addicts in the mid 1960's. *Public Health Reports,* 1966, *81* (5), 403–412.

42. System Sciences, Inc. *A comparative analysis of 24 therapeutic communities in New York City funded by the Addiction Services Agency of the City of New York.* Bethesda, Maryland: System Sciences, 1973. (Mimeographed)

43. Toborg, M. A., Levin, D. R., Milkman, R. H., & Center, L. J. *Treatment alternatives to street crime (TASC) projects.* National Evaluation Program Phase I. Summary Report Series A Number 3. U.S. Department of Justice, Law Enforcement Assistance Administration, February 1976.

44. Voss, H. L. Young men, drugs and crime, National Institute on Drug Abuse, *Drug use and crime* (final report), 1976, pp. 351–385.

45. Voss, H. L., & Stephens, R. C. Criminal history of narcotic addicts. *Drug Forum,* 1973, *2,* 191–201.

46. Zahn, M. A., & Ball, J. C. Patterns and causes of drug addiction among puerto Rican females. *Addictive Diseases,* 1974, *1* (2), 203–213.

47. Agar, M. H., & Stephens, R. C. The methadone street scene: the addict's view. *Psychiatry,* 1975, *38,* 383.

48. *An Assessment of Drug Use in the General Population.* New York State Narcotic Addiction Control Commission, 1971.

49. Brown, G., & Silverman, L. The retail price of heroin: estimation and applications. *Journal of the American Statistical Association,* 1974, *69* (347), 603.

50. Domestic Council Drug Abuse Task Force. *White paper on drug abuse, a report to the President.* Washington, D.C.: U.S. Government Printing Office, 1975.

51. *Employment of school age youth, October 1975* (Special Labor Force Report). Washington, D.C.: Department of Labor, 1976.

52. Gearing, F. R. Methadone maintenance treatment five years later—where are they now? *American Journal of Public Health,* 1974, *64* (Part II, Supplement).

53. Goldman, F. Drug markets and addict consumption behavior, 1976.

54. Goldman, F. *The relationship between drug addiction and crime* (Draft Report), January 1976.

55. Hughes, P., Crawford, G., Barker, N., Schumann, S., & Jaffe, J. The social structure of heroin copping community. *American Journal of Psychiatry,* 1971, *123* (5), 554.

56. James, J., Gosho, C., & Watson, R. The relationship between female criminality and drug use, National Institute on Drug Abuse, *Drug use and crime* (final report), 1976.

57. Moore, M. *The Economics of Heroin Distribution, Policy Concerning Drug Abuse in New York* (Vol. 3). New York: Hudson Institute, 1970.

58. National Commission on Marihuana and Drug Abuse. *Drug use in America: problem in perspective* (Second Report). Washington, D.C.: U.S. Government Printing Office, 1973.

59. Newmeyer, J. The Junkie Thief. Mimeographed. San Francisco: Haight-Ashbury Free Medical Clinic (1972). Reproduced in L. Gould, Crime and the addict, *Drug and the Criminal Justice System* (J. Inciardi and C. Chambers, Eds.), 1974.

60. Powell, D. H. A pilot study of occasional heroin users. *Archives of General Psychiatry,* 1973, *28.*

61. Preble, E., & Miller, T. *Methadone, wine and welfare.* Presented at the Workshop on the Ethnography of Drugs and Crime, conducted by Research Triangle Institute and the University of Miami, 1976.

62. Sells, S. B. *The Effectiveness of Treatment for Drug Abuse: The Evaluation of Treatment* (Vol. 1). New York: Ballinger, 1974.

63. Silverman, L. P., & Spruill, N. L. Urban crime and the price of heroin (mimeographed). Revised July 1975, forthcoming in the *Journal of Urban Economics.*

64. Smith, R. B., & Watkins, T. D. A study of addicts' career experiences with methadone. *American Journal of Drug and Alcohol Abuse,* 1976, *3,* 264.

65. Zinberg, N. E., & Jacobson, R. C. The natural history of "chipping." *American Journal of Psychiatry,* 1976, *133* (1), 40.

66. The Pusher as a Rational Business Man

MARK MOORE

DEALERS' RESPONSES TO THE THREAT OF ARREST AND IMPRISONMENT

THE MOST IMMEDIATE AND IMPORTANT CONSEQU-ence of legislating against the manufacture, distribution, and possession of heroin is that every heroin supplier is faced with some possibility of being arrested, convicted, and imprisoned. Lost income, restricted opportunities upon release, the loss of freedom, and isolation from normal society all represent losses associated with imprisonment. To a greater or lesser degree, depending on their activity and the activity of the police, heroin suppliers must expect to absorb these losses.

A useful technique for analyzing the effects of threatening heroin dealers with arrest and imprisonment is to assume that the expected losses represent costs to individual heroin suppliers. In this view, the threat of arrest resembles a tax imposed on dealers. The higher the probability of arrest and imprisonment, and the greater the penalties, the greater is the tax imposed on heroin dealers.

If this view is accepted, then economic theory allows two general predictions about the response of heroin suppliers to increased risks. First, they will attempt to pass the increased costs of supplying heroin onto the consumer through higher prices. Second, they will seek to reduce these risks by engaging a variety of strategies to reduce the chance that they will be arrested, convicted, and imprisoned.

Price Increases as a Response to Enforcement Pressure

The conventional analysis of the impact of enforcement efforts concentrates on the price response of heroin dealers. The reasoning is usually the following:

1. An expanded enforcement effort increases the risk of arrest and imprisonment to dealers.

2. To compensate themselves for the increased risk (and to cover increased operating costs) dealers raise their prices.

3. Since the demand for heroin is perfectly inelastic, the increased price results in no reduction in the amount of heroin that is consumed.

4. Since consumption is not reduced and since the price has increased, gross revenues and profits increase.

5. The increased profits mobilize old dealers to be more aggressive and attract new dealers into the business.

The conclusion of this analysis, then, is that increased enforcement pressure results in higher prices for heroin, no less heroin consumption,

▶SOURCE: *By and Bust. Lexington Mass, Lexington Book, 1977, pp. 5–47. Reprinted with permission.*

and richer heroin dealers. In addition, many analysts conclude that the higher profits will motivate old dealers to seek new customers and new dealers to enter the market.[1]

This analysis is misleading. The major problems are (1) the restrictive (and probably incorrect) assumption about the elasticity of demand; and (2) logical errors in reasoning about the relationship between gross revenues, profits, and the attractiveness of the business. In addition, the conventional analysis fails to present explicit assumptions or hypotheses about the structure of the distribution system. Since industry structure will decisively influence the price response to increased threats of arrest, it is difficult to evaluate the conventional argument.

A more careful analysis of the response of the distribution system to increased enforcement pressure is presented below. However, before advancing to the more careful analysis, it is important to confront directly the misleading parts of the conventional analysis. Consequently, we explore the assumption of a perfectly inelastic demand for heroin, and the implications of relaxing this assumption. In addition, we consider the issues of whether heroin distribution is more attractive or less attractive following a general increase in the risk of arrest and imprisonment.

The conventional assumption that the demand for heroin is *perfectly* inelastic is based on beliefs about the overwhelming addictiveness of heroin. In this view, the mechanisms of tolerance and withdrawal lock heroin users onto narrow, steadily rising paths of heroin consumption. If the user falls off this path, either deliberately or by accident, he faces agonizing withdrawal symptoms. The pain of withdrawal is sufficiently agonizing (and the pleasure of relieving the pain sufficiently euphoric) to insure very strong resistance to reductions in heroin

consumption—even if maintaining a given level of use requires extraordinary effort and imposes extraordinary risks on the user.[2]

Although this view is colorful and widely believed, there are two major problems with relying on it as a justification for the assumption of a perfectly inelastic demand for heroin. First, the aggregate demand for heroin is composed of the demand from many different kinds of users—addicts, casual users, neophyte users. The addiction model applies to only a fraction of the total users. Second, the addiction model turns out to be a poor description of the consumption of even hard-core users.

Consider, first, the demand by hard-core addicts. Within this group, one might expect the assumption of a perfectly inelastic demand to be most accurate. However, even for this group, consumption is likely to decrease at least a little and perhaps substantially as the price of heroin increases. The reasons to expect decreased consumption are the following.

First, the demand for heroin from this group will certainly be affected by the enforced periods of abstinence that result from arrests. Since the probability of arrest is likely to increase with the level of addict crime, and since the level of addict crime will increase as addicts seek to maintain their level of real income in the face of increased heroin prices, these users will take increased periods of enforced abstinence. Although we may not place any great social value on such enforced periods of abstinence,

[1]For expositions of this conventional analysis, see Donald Phares, "The Simple Economics of Heroin and Organizing Policy," *Journal of Drug Issues,* Spring 1973, pp. 186–200; or Harold L. Votey and Llad Phillips, "Minimizing the Social Cost of Drug Abuse: An Economic Analysis of Alternatives for Policy," *Policy Sciences* 7:3(September 1976).

[2]For scientific descriptions of tolerance and withdrawal, see Hannah Steinberg, *Scientific Basis of Drug Dependence* (New York: Grune and Stratton, 1969). For more popularized accounts of the phenomena, see Edward H. Brecher, *Licit and Illicit Drugs* (Boston: Little, Brown and Co., 1972), pp. 64–90; or James Delong, "Drugs and their Effects," in Drug Abuse Survey Project, *Dealing with Drug Abuse* (New York: Praeger Publishers, 1972). For anecdotal accounts of the subjective reactions of users to these effects, see William Burroughs, *Junkie* (New York: Ace Books, 1953); Seymour Fiddle, *Portraits from a Shooting Gallery* (New York: Harper and Row, 1967); or Jeremy Larner and Ralph Tefferteller, *The Addict in the Street* (New York: Grove Press, 1964).

they will affect the total consumption of heroin and absolute levels of revenue to the industry.

Second, under the pressure created by high prices for heroin, and in the presence of adequate treatment capacity, many users will seek treatment rather than remain on the street hustling for heroin.[3] In New York City, users may choose from methadone programs, therapeutic communities, and detoxification programs for help in reducing heroin consumption. Although it is clear that heroin consumption does not fall to zero in these institutions, it is likely that it declines significantly,[4] and these de-

clines will affect the total consumption of heroin.

Third, even without the institutional "help" offered by jails or treatment programs, heroin users can reduce their heroin consumption. There is evidence that heroin users can consume heroin at levels far below their "habit size" without experiencing withdrawal symptoms,[5] that addicts detoxify themselves frequently,[6] that addicts voluntarily abstain from drug use for relatively long periods,[7] and that addicts

[3]The extent to which high prices will motivate current users to seek treatment is controversial. However, interviews with addicts who enter treatment programs consistently show that a large fraction of these users attribute their decision to enter treatment to increased pressures of maintaining an expensive habit. In Patrick Hughes et al., "The Impact of Medical Intervention in Three Heroin Copping Areas," paper presented at the Fourth National Methadone Conference, (San Francisco: January 1972) the following results from interviews with users who were being recruited for treatment were reported: "[T]hey [the users] were not particularly interested in treatment while they had a successful hustle and access to quality heroin. Interest increased only when they came on hard times, i.e., they were arrested, lost their drug dealership role or their drug connection." (p. 5) Similarly, in Gila J. Hayim, "Changes in the Criminal Behavior of Heroin Addicts: A One Year Follow-Up of Methadone Treatment" (The Center for Criminal Justice, Harvard Law School, 1972), p. 9, it is reported that "over 2/3 of the patients listed such factors as 'being tired of hustling,' 'the habit is getting too expensive,' or 'would like to find an honest job,' as important reasons for joining the program."

In summarizing a review of many studies of reasons for seeking treatment, McGlothlin reported that "about 25–50% of current methadone admissions appear to be largely motivated by the push of legal and other pressures. They come into treatment under legal pressure, the demands of relatives, the panic of withdrawal, the need for habit reduction, etc." (See William H. McGlothin et al., "Alternative Approaches to Opiate Addiction Control: Costs, Benefits, and Potential," Bureau of Narcotics and Dangerous Drugs, 1972, p. 20).

Finally, at an aggregate level, a strong relationship between increased prices of heroin and increased treatment enrollment is demonstrated in Robert L. DuPont and Mark H. Greene, "The Dynamics of a Heroin Addiction Epidemic," *Science* 181 (1973): 716–722.

[4]Methadone programs using urinalysis to discover heroin use routinely find "dirty urines." For example, Gearing re-

ports: "Although many of the patients test the methadone 'blockade' of heroin one or more times in the first few months, less than 1% have returned to regular heroin usage while under methadone maintenance treatment." Similarly, Richman reports that 28 percent of a group of 587 patients treated in methadone-maintenance programs had at least once reported "dirty urine." See Frances R. Gearing, "Successes and Failures in Methadone Maintenance Treatment of Heroin Addiction in New York City," and Alex Richman, "Utilization and Review of Methadone Maintenance Patient Data," in Proceedings of the Third National Conference on Methadone Maintenance, National Institute for Mental Health (1970), pp. 8, 26.

[5]Heather Ruth, "The Street Level of Economics of Heroin Addiction in New York City:Life-styles of Active Heroin Users and Implications for Public Policy," Unpublished manuscript (New York: 1972).

In interviews with 42 street addicts, Ruth found that although the average habit size was estimated at 20.5 $2 bags of heroin per day, the estimate of the average amount of heroin necessary to avoid withdrawal was 5.4 $2 bags per day. As she states, "The most important finding is that there is room for much economic flexibility in the range between 'minimum' heroin to avoid withdrawal and 'habit.'" (p. 31).

[6]Richard Brotman and Alfred M. Freedman, *Continuities and Discontinuities in the Process of Patient Care for Narcotic Addicts* (New York: New York Medical College, 1965), p. 73.In a sample of 200 hard-core users in treatment, the median number of previous detoxication was 5. Moreover, 60 percent of those reporting detoxication reported they were undertaken voluntarily at home.

[7]Mark H. Moore, "Policy Towards Heroin Use in New York City" (Ph.D. diss., Harvard University, 1973), Appendix 1, pp. 677–701, contains descriptions and an analysis of the evidence on voluntary abstinence. The basic sources on the phenomenon are the following:John C. Ball, and Richard Snarr, "A Test of the Maturation Hypothesis," *Committee on Problems of Drug Dependence,* National Academy of Science (Washington, D.C.: National Research Council, 1969); Henrietta Duvall, Ben Locke, and Leon Brill, "Follow-up Study of Narcotic Drug Addicts Five Years After Hospitalization," *Public Health Reports*78:3 (March 1963);

substitute other drugs for heroin. Again, although we have much different attitudes about the social value of these different responses, the fact that hard-core users have this much flexibility about their heroin consumption suggests that they can respond to price increases by reducing their consumption.

Consider, next, the demand of users of heroin who are not addicted. It used to be widely believed that nonaddicted users constituted only a small minority of all heroin users. The physiological mechanisms of tolerance and withdrawal were sufficiently powerful to insure that nearly all experimenters would become addicts. However, more recent evidence indicates that hard-core users constitute a minority of all users. There are many users who use heroin sporadically over a long period and never become deeply involved. Since the physiological mechanisms that could justify the assumption of a perfectly inelastic demand have not begun to operate in this group, their demand for heroin must be considered to be relatively elastic. The inclusion of this group in the aggregate demand for heroin has the effect of making the aggregate demand much more elastic.

In sum, the aggregate demand for heroin is not likely to be perfectly inelastic. It includes the demand of consumers who are not addicted. Even those who are addicted can reduce their consumption in the face of price increases. Thus, it is not surprising that current estimates of the price elasticity of heroin resemble the price elasticities of such ordinary goods as

John O'Donnell, "The Relapse Rate in Narcotics Addiction: ACritique of Follow-up Studies" (Albany: Narcotic Addiction Control Commission, 1968); John O'Donnell, "A Follow-up of Narcotic Addicts: Mortality Relapse and Abstinence," *American Journal Orthopsychology* 34 (1964); Lee Robins and George Murphy, "Drug Use in a Normal Population of Young Negro Men," *American Journal of Public Health* 57:9 (September 1967); George Vaillant, "A Twelve Year Follow-up of New York Narcotic Addicts:The Relation of Treatment to Outcome," *American Journal of Psychiatry* 122 (1966); "The Natural History of a Chronic Disease," *New England Journal of Medicine,* December 8,1966; and Charles Winick, "Maturing Out of Narcotic Addiction," *United Nations Bulletin on Narcotics* 14:1 (January-March 1962).

physician services, oil and gasoline, and auto repair: when prices for these goods increase, consumption declines. Specifically, in the case of heroin, it is estimated that a 10 percent increase in price results in a 2 percent decrease in consumption. Some new users are discouraged from experiments; and some chronic users seek treatment, voluntarily abstain, or wind up in jail.

Note that this estimate of elasticity indicates that the demand for heroin is "inelastic" (i.e., the percent decrease in consumption is less than the percent increase in price); but the demand is not "*perfectly* inelastic" (i.e., there is some reduction in consumption). This is an important distinction. If the elasticity lies between zero and one, we know that price increases will *reduce* heroin consumption, and *increase* gross revenues to the heroin industry. We *like* the effect of reducing consumption. We do *not* like the effect of increasing gross revenues since we are concerned that increased gross revenues may imply more stealing by addicts and greater profits for heroin dealers. We leave the issue of whether price increases result in increased stealing for another section. The issue of whether increased gross revenues necessarily imply greater profits and a more attractive business are discussed directly below. At this stage, the important point to understand is that the demand for heroin is *not* perfectly inelastic, consumption will *decrease* as price increases—although not by an equal amount.[8]

[8]There is a legitimate issue of whether a 2 percent decrease in the consumption of heroin for a 10 percent increase in price is a "significant" reduction. The answer to this question depends partly on which populations of users decrease their consumption, and partly on how hard it is to increase the price by 10 percent. If all of the decrease in consumption comes from current users marginally adjusting their consumption, then little of significance is achieved. If the decreased consumption results primarily from driving experimenting users out of the market before they advance to chronic, intensive levels of use, then a very valuable social effect is achieved. This would imply a significant decline in the growth of the heroin-using population. In addition, the fact that the price of heroin has doubled nationwide (and tripled on the East Coast) in the period from 1970 to 1974 suggests that it may not be hard to raise the price of heroin by much more than 10 percent. Thus, although the sig-

The fact that price increases caused by increased threats of arrest and imprisonment result in increased gross revenues leads many to assume that profits to dealers have increased and that the business has become more attractive as a result of enforcement pressure. This seems like a paradoxical result. It seems incredible that increased enforcement pressure would make the heroin business more attractive. In fact, the conclusion that the business becomes more attractive *is* incorrect. However, the problem in the reasoning that leads to the incorrect conclusion is somewhat subtle.

The basic problem comes from failing to distinguish between money profits and "utility" and failing to remember which concept is being employed at different stages of the analysis.[9] In most commercial enterprises, this distinction between money profits and utility disappears. We can assume that all the things that could potentially influence a person's view of the attractiveness of a business are small compared to the impact that money has on his total satisfaction. Consequently, in gauging the attractiveness of the business, we look only at the difference between costs and revenues defined strictly in terms of money.

In the heroin business, the assumption that money profits are all that matter is not so readily defensible. It is likely that the threat of arrest and imprisonment also looms large in a dealer's calculation of the attractiveness of the business. Indeed, it is reasonable to expect that the anxiety of living with the threat is unpleasant even if the dealer is never actually arrested. Thus, in describing the calculations of heroin dealers, it is important to talk in terms of *utility* rather than simply money profits and to remember that utility will be affected not only by changes in money profits, but also by changes in levels of risk to the dealer.

The conventional analysis relies on the idea of utility in the early stages of the analysis. The threat of arrest and imprisonment enters the analysis as a cost to dealers with cost being defined in utility terms. In response to this reduced utility, dealers make two adjustments: they invest time and money in strategies to reduce the risk, and they demand more money to compensate themselves for the increased risk of staying in the business. Notice that the dealers demand more money not to *increase* their utility, but rather to *maintain* their utility at levels that existed prior to the increased threat of arrest and conviction. It is only the *reduction* in utility occasioned by the increased threat that forces the price adjustment. Presumably, if it had been possible to increase utility through price increases before the increased threat of arrest and imprisonment occurred, dealers would have done so. Whether dealers can succeed in offsetting reduced levels of utility by price increased depends on both the precise elasticity of demand and the market structure. This analysis is presented in detail below. However, it is worth noting here that there is no way that the industry as a whole can become more attractive with an increased threat of arrest and imprisonment. At best, dealers can exactly offset the reduction in utility that occurs with the increased threat. And this result occurs only with very restrictive assumptions (e.g., a competitive market operating in an inelastic portion of the demand curve). In the more likely cases, dealers' efforts to increase prices will be restrained either by consumer resistance or by competition, and the business will be *less* attractive than the situation prior to an increased threat of arrest and imprisonment.

---

nificance of this effect is uncertain, one can make an argument that says the effect is very important: one can easily increase the price of heroin by 50 percent, and thereby both prevent new use among many experimenters and drive current users into treatment.

[9] The concept of "utility" is introduced here to capture two somewhat different ideas. One idea is simply to remind us that variables other than money are included in the objective functions of heroin dealers. A second idea is to remind us that people have different attitudes toward uncertain results—some are risk favoring and some are risk avoiding. For a complete and precise description of this second idea of utility, see Howard Raiffa, *Decision Analysis* (Reading, Mass.: Addison-Wesley, 1968).

The conventional analysis reaches a different conclusion about changes in the attractiveness of the heroin business because it suddenly changes from a calculation in terms of utility to a calculation in terms of money. In the very last step of the analysis, money suddenly becomes the terms one uses to gauge the attractiveness of the business. Gross money revenues have increased, money costs have probably not changed all that much, therefore money profits must have gone up. If money profits have increased, the business must have become more attractive. What this reasoning ignores is the fact that the analysis *began* with a significant *reduction* in utility that resulted from an increased threat of arrest and imprisonment. Thus, the conventional analysis forgets that the dealers were made worse off before prices and revenues increased, and that these increases are motivated by an effort to offset the losses.

Probably the easiest way to see the failure of the conventional analysis is to draw a strict analogy between an increase in the threat of arrest and imprisonment and a tax on the operation of the dealers. A tax is applied. Prices, amount consumed, and gross revenues change in response. But in calculating the impact of the tax on profits, the cost of paying the tax is suddenly ignored. In effect, the conventional view of high prices and high profits overstate the attractiveness of the heroin business just as looking at the pretax profits of a highly taxed industry would grossly overstate the profitability of the industry. Because there is no neat way of calculating the costs associated with the prospect of arrest and indicating this cost on a financial statement, we grossly overestimate the attractiveness of the heroin business. When we include these costs, the industry does not look so attractive in spite of the large money profits.

Thus, two major conclusions of the conventional analysis about price responses by heroin dealers are incorrect. It is likely that heroin use *decreases* rather than remains constant. It is also likely that the attractiveness of the business *decreases* rather than increases.

Given the weakness of the popular analysis of pricing responses by the heroin distribution systems, it is important to develop an alternative analysis. We are interested in predicting the impact of an increased threat of arrest and prosecution on:

1. The quantity of heroin demanded.

2. The price of heroin.

3. The total revenues earned by heroin distributors.

4. The attractiveness of the business.

Economic theory indicates that these effects will depend on:

1. The degree of competition in the distribution system.

2. The price elasticity of demand in the relevant range of demand.

3. Whether the threat of arrest is perceived as a lump-sum tax or as a variable-cost tax.

It is not obvious what we should assume about these factors. It is not clear whether the distribution system is competitive, monopolistic, or hybrid. It is not clear whether existing supplies of heroin are in the elastic or inelastic portions of the demand curve for heroin. Finally, it is not clear whether the threat of arrest should be treated as a lump-sum tax or a variable-cost tax. Consider this last problem.

Treating the threat as a lump-sum tax implies that the heroin dealer cannot affect the magnitude of the tax by adjusting the scale of his operation. The threat of arrest could have this aspect if a dealer was known to be involved in heroin dealing and avoided arrest only by paying large bribes on a regular basis and by successfully disciplining his employees and customers. For such dealers, an increased threat of arrest adds only to fixed costs (e.g., bribes and administrative overhead to monitor and discipline employees). Moreover, such dealers must consider themselves vulnerable to informants and illegal arrests by the police in spite of their fixed cost strategies to avoid arrest. Both the heavy reliance on fixed-cost strategies and the residual risks give the threat of arrest the appearance of a lump-sum tax.

Treating the threat of arrest as a variable-cost tax implies that the dealer can adjust the magnitude of the tax he pays by adjusting the scale of his activity. The threat of arrest may have this aspect for retail dealers who are not well-known by the police. For such dealers, reducing the number of transactions or reducing the quantity they sell could significantly reduce both the probability of arrest and the magnitude of the sanctions. Thus, it is not clear what we should assume about dealers' perceptions of the threat of arrest and imprisonment.

Because of the uncertainty about these different factors, we have made predictions for each possible case. Table I defines eight different sets of assumptions about conditions prevailing in the heroin industry, and deduces the effects of increasing the threat of arrest for each set of assumptions about the industry.[10] Although Table I yields no powerful general conclusions, one can make several significant observations.

First, in every case, the supply of the product is unchanged or reduced, and the price is unaffected or increased. In *no* case does the supply increase and the price decrease. This is an important regulatory effect to achieve.

Second, a price increase is not always associated with an increase in total revenues. The only case in which a price increase occurs and yields greater total revenues is the case of competitive suppliers producing in an inelastic range of the demand curve. In all other cases, price increases yield less total revenues simply because dealers were operating in an elastic range of the demand curve prior to the increased risk. In effect, they had made everything that could be made out of the users' desires for heroin before the threat increased.

Third, even in those circumstances in which a price increase yields increased total revenues, it is not clear what happens to the utility and money profits of the industry. It is possible that the costs (i.e., the threat of arrest) have increased by a larger amount than total revenues have increased. In this case, utility will also certainly fall. It is also possible that the costs will have increased by less than the total revenues increase. In this case, money profits would obviously increase, but utility will not necessarily increase. In general, the more inelastic the demand and the smaller the costs, the more likely it is that utility will rise. This suggests that if we are working on an already restricted supply (i.e., one that is close to an *elastic* range of the demand curve), and if we impose a substantial cost, utility is unlikely to increase.

In sum, in many cases, the heroin industry does not respond at all in terms of price to an increased threat of arrest: the dealers simply have to accept the reduction in utility associated with the increased anxiety. In other cases, although the dealers respond by reducing supply and increasing prices, these actions do not necessarily yield increased total revenues. In the cases where dealers can increase total revenues, their utility need not increase. Thus, dealers cannot always respond successfully to an increased threat of arrest simply by restricting supply and raising prices. Unless they are competitive dealers operating in an inelastic portion of the demand curve facing a variable-cost tax that is small relative to the gain in revenue associated with a reduction in supply, they will be worse off than they were before the threat of arrest increased.

Investment in Strategies to Reduce a Threat of Arrest

A second response to the threat of arrest and imprisonment is for heroin dealers to spend time and money to decrease the probability of arrest and imprisonment. Since the sanctions are applied by social agencies that are suscepti-

[10]I am indebted to Francis M. Bator, professor of political economy, Kennedy School of Government, Harvard University, for assistance with this table.

Table I. Predicted Impact of an Increased Threat of Arrest on Gross Revenues and the Attractiveness of the Heroin Business for Alternative Assumptions about Industry and "Tax" Structure

Assumptions about Industry Structure, Tax Characteristics, and Elasticity of Demand	Predicted Effects On:			
	Quantity Consumed	Price	Gross Revenues	Attractiveness of Business
1.0 Monopolistic structure:				
1.1 Lump-sum tax	No change	No change	No change	Decrease
1.2 Variable-cost tax[a]	Decrease	Increase	Decrease	Decrease
2.0 Competitive structure:				
2.1 Elasticity >0; and <1				
2.1.1 Lump-sum tax	No change; or decrease[b]	No change; or increase[b]	No change; or increase[b]	Decrease; or uncertain[c]
2.1.2 Variable-cost tax	Decrease	Increase	Increase	Uncertain
2.2 Elasticity >1				
2.2.1 Lump-sum tax	No change; or decrease[b]	No change; or increase[b]	No change; or decrease[b]	Decrease
2.2.2 Variable-sum tax	Decrease	Increase	Decrease	Decrease
3.0 Monopolistic competition:				
3.1 Lump-sum tax	No change; or decrease[b]	No change; or increase[b]	No change; or decrease[d]	Decrease or uncertain[c]
3.2 Variable-cost tax	Decrease	Increase	Increase	Uncertain

Note: This table is produced from simple manipulations of microeconomic theory.

[a] The reason that supply, gross revenues, and attractiveness decline is that monopolists will choose to restrict supply until they are operating in a region of the demand curve where the price elasticity is greater than 1. Consequently, when the tax hits, it forces them into an even more elastic portion of the demand curve.

[b] A decrease in supply, increase in price, and increase in gross revenues will occur if the tax is large enough to drive some marginal dealers out of business. Note that the number of marginal dealers forced out of business depends on the "opportunity costs" of dealers as well as the size of the tax.

[c] The attractiveness of the business *to dealers who remain in business* is uncertain. It depends on the size of the tax, the number of marginal dealers who leave the business, and the precise elasticity of demand. If many go out of business and the demand is very inelastic, the business may become more attractive for those dealers who stay in business. If only a few go out of business, the demand is not very inelastic, and the tax is large, then the business may become less attractive.

[d] This assumes that the dealers have already restricted supply and priced at a level that is close to the elastic portion of the demand curve.

ble to deception, corruption, and incompetence, broad opportunities exist for heroin dealers to manipulate the situation strategically to their own ends. The strategies available to dealers can be grouped as different lines of defenses against the enforcement agencies; as one line of defense is penetrated, the next line may still provide sufficient protection.

The first line of defense is to conceal all connections with the heroin industry. The objective is to avoid becoming known as a dealer. The second line of defense is to avoid creating evidence that could be used to convict a dealer for criminal offenses. The third line of defense is to corrupt or manipulate the agencies that apply sanctions to heroin dealers.

Concealing All Connections with the Heroin Industry   To conceal one's relation with the heroin industry, one must avoid (or reduce the frequency of) activities and associations that threaten to expose one. More specifically, one must

1. Avoid activity that is visible and uniquely connected with the production, distribution, or consumption of heroin.

2. Avoid associations with people known to be active in the heroin industry.

3. Prevent people who know one is involved in the heroin industry from telling others that one is involved.

It is not easy or inexpensive for dealers to follow these guidelines. Indeed, there are some activities and associations that must be continued in spite of the fact that they create substantial risks for those involved in the trade. Moreover, the more religiously one adheres to these guidelines, the less successful one will be in producing, selling, and using heroin.

Consider, first, the problem of avoiding activity known to be associated with the production, distribution, and consumption of heroin. If one is a producer of heroin, one must purchase anhydrous acetic acid to continue production. If one is a distributor of heroin, one must purchase adultrants (mannite, quinine) and containers (medicine capsules, glassine envelopes) to continue successful distribution. If one is a consumer, one must inject heroin into one's veins. Each of these activities leaves traces: records of transactions in the case of purchase of supplies, scars in the case of injection. These traces are both durable and visible. Moreover, to some extent, they are probative of connections with a heroin industry. Thus, the activities make association with the heroin industry quite visible. Although one can substitute other activities that produce less durable and visible signs, or are less probative of connections with the heroin industry, all substitutes are more costly to producers, dealers, and consumers. Thus, in seeking to avoid tell-tale activities, heroin dealers and consumers will find it either impossible or costly.

Consider, next, the problem of avoiding identification with people known to be involved in the heroin industry. This problem is at least as expensive to resolve as the problem of avoiding tell-tale activities. The basic problem is that suppliers and dealers must communicate among themselves to make the market work smoothly. Addicts need to talk to other addicts to find their way to heroin markets in which "good bags" are being sold. If they shun the company of known addicts to avoid identification, they cut themselves off from valuable information. Similarly, dealers need to be able to communicate with consumers. If they fail to advertise to known users to avoid identification, they cut themselves off from valuable markets in which to sell. Thus, avoiding identification with known users and dealers often results in giving up significant advantages that come from being able to communicate freely.

The third problem—keeping those who know of one's involvement in the heroin industry from telling others that one is involved—is by far the most difficult. The major problem is that the police can suddenly change the contingencies facing one's associates. Although prior to an arrest it is generally in the interests of an associate to be discreet and tight-lipped, following an arrest it may be strongly in his interests to trade information for money or reduced penalties. Unless a dealer can wield incentives contingent on an associate's silence that are at least as powerful as the incentives wielded by the police, the dealer will be betrayed.

Notice that the dealer has two strategies in guarding against betrayal. One strategy is to confront all his associates continuously with sanctions sufficient to guarantee their silence under all possible threats by the police. This strategy yields a generalized immunity from the police. A second strategy is to adjust the sanctions that confront his associates according to changes in their situations; that is, he can confront his associates with sanctions sufficient to guarantee their silence against modest pressure or inducements of police most of the time, and then change the sanctions when an associate comes under stronger police pressure or is weakened for some other reason. This strategy yields a selective immunity.

Both strategies have serious problems. The

problem with the generalized immunity is that it is very expensive. It is difficult to distribute continuously a set of rewards and penalties that are sufficiently large to guard against all threats by the police. The problem with selective immunity is that it does not always work. It is difficult for a dealer to discover when an associate's incentives have changed, difficult for him to wield incentives that are as large as those wielded by the police, and difficult for him to communicate to the potential informant that the informant is now facing a different set of contingencies from the dealer as well as a new set of contingencies from the police. Thus, the dealer can neither respond electively to a sudden need to control a potential informant, nor guarantee that there are no potential informants among his associates.

These examples indicate that there are serious problems in maintaining the first line of defense. Strategies to avoid activities and association with the industry are expensive and only partly successful. In spite of this general observation, there are several strategies that have offered some protection. Although the price of the strategies is high, many dealers have found them worth the investment.

One strategy is to limit the number of people with whom heroin is exchanged. This strategy has at least five advantages in concealing one's relation to the heroin distribution system.

First, a small number of customers and associates implies that few people have direct, first-hand knowledge of a dealer's connections with the heroin industry. This reduces the chance of a casual information leak, and reduces a dealer's vulnerability to sustained efforts from enforcement agencies to gain information.

Second, a small market allows the supplier to monitor his customers and associates closely for signs of defection. Close monitoring allows the dealer to respond more reliably and more quickly when an associate becomes likely to betray him.

Third, if customers are restricted to a single, small market, they will come to identify their interests with keeping the dealer in operation.

He becomes their vital "connection." To the extent that customers do come to identify their interests with keeping the dealer in business, it will be easier for the dealer to insure against casual information leaks.

Fourth, the small market will establish face-to-face relations between customers and suppliers. Because face-to-face relations bolster norms against leaking information, these relations will facilitate the dealer's problem in disciplining his customers and associates.

Fifth, the small market allows inexpensive, simple communication between the dealer and his customers. This allows the dealer to adjust his pattern of dealing (e.g., hours of operation, place of operation, techniques for concealing the exchange of money for heroin, etc.) without having to increase significantly the time he spends with his customers. In effect, a small market is quieter and more agile in responding to new threats than a large market.

Thus, operating with 5 to 15 customers and associates has significant advantages in maintaining the first line of defense compared with operating with 30 to 50 customers and associates.

The strategy of operating in small markets is not without liabilities. One very important disadvantage is that a dealer must abandon opportunities for aggressive market expansion. Note that market expansion is dangerous for dealers at two different stages—the period in which the dealer operates and maintains a large market, and the period in which the dealer is recruiting new customers to enlarge his market. Of these stages, the second is by far the most dangerous.

The period of operating and maintaining a large market is dangerous for all the opposite reasons that operating a small market is safe. A large market implies both that there are more people who can betray the dealer, and that the dealer's ability to control and discipline his customers is less. Consequently, the dealer must consider himself more than proportionately vulnerable.

The period of recruiting new customers is dangerous simply because the dealer has the least information and control over new customers at the moment of recruitment. Moreover, the dealer must consider all potential recruits particularly suspect. Dealers must assume that other dealers avoid or exclude customers whom they judge to be risky and retain customers known to be trustworthy. Consequently, an eager, unattached customer is more than proportionately likely to be a marginal, high-risk customer. In effect, because all dealers are interested in screening out undercover agents and informants, the pool of unattached customers must be more than proportionately stocked with informants and undercover police. Thus, both because a dealer has little control over new customers, and because he must assume he is picking customers from a high-risk pool, the moment of recruiting a new customer is particularly risky.

There are several important implications of this analysis of the unusual risks associated with expanding a market. The first implication is that contrary to common beliefs, heroin dealers are not likely to be aggressive marketers of heroin. Although the industry as a whole would be better off if dealers engaged in aggressive market expansion, it is not in the interest of any individual dealer to do so. Indeed, stepping out of a protected market into an unknown market is the most dangerous move a dealer makes. Whatever incentives there are for market expansion leads dealers to try to steal their competitors' best customers rather than venture into unknown markets. Thus, the "pushing" phenomenon is probably a myth.[11]

[11]Patrick Hughes et al., "The Social Structure of a Heroin Copping Community," *American Journal of Psychiatry* 128:5 (November 1971): p. 48. There is strong empirical evidence supporting this conclusion. In a detailed examination of activity in a heroin copping community, Hughes et al. made the following observation: "Dealers in this neighborhood were not 'pushing' heroin. The addicts, in fact, were in a seller's market—they had to seek out the dealers." Also consistent with this deduction are the findings that users only rarely report that they received their first shot of heroin from a pusher.

The second implication is that dealers will rely on a variety of screening mechanisms to help them distinguish reliable customers from unreliable customers. They will look for track marks, insist on references or introductions from people they know, listen for false notes in the customers' use of street jargon, and look for tell-tale physical characteristics such as clean fingernails or inappropriate clothes and haircuts. These screening devices will result in discrimination against some classes of potential customers.[12]

The third implication is that dealers will choose to operate and expand in areas where there are pervasive norms against cooperating with the police. In such areas, the risks associated with recruiting additional customers and operating with a large number of customers will be less. This observation may account for the fast spread of heroin in the ghetto, and, since youth in the suburbs may now be internalizing strong norms against cooperating with the police, may not bode well for the future of drug use in suburbs.

Thus, it is difficult for dealers to expand and operate large markets without exposing themselves to significant risks. Although abandoning opportunities for expansion is a great price to pay for the protection provided by small markets, many dealers find the sacrifice worth making. Others who have become greedy have regretted the consequences.[13]

[12]It is argued that a fundamental objective of the enforcement strategy is to create discrimination against new users of heroin. This effect can be achieved precisely because dealers will react to the threat of arrest by setting up screening procedures. All the police must do is disguise themselves as the customers they would like to protect. In effect, the police contaminate a pool of potential customers by counterfeiting the customers.

[13]There is a general tendency for the police to arrest the least cautious heroin dealers. Many people take this as a sign of the inevitable failure of enforcement efforts. However, in many cases, it is precisely the least cautious dealers who are the most important dealers to arrest. The reason is that their aggressiveness could result in the recruitment of large numbers of new users or a dramatic increase in the aggregate

A second disadvantage of selling only in small markets is that since the supplier continues to distribute heroin, he continues to expose himself to people who cannot be completely trusted. Although the bonds between customer and supplier are greater in small markets than in large markets, they are a long way from foolproof. The fragility of these bonds implies that there is still a substantial risk in distributing heroin.

A more robust strategy is not only to restrict the size of the market, but also to invest heavily in procedures for screening and disciplining customers. This strategy differs from the first only in the relative emphasis it places on screening and discipline.

The dealer could tighten screening procedures by applying a more conservative rule in selling to new customers, or by gathering additional information about new customers. For example, the dealer could insist on three references from people known to him before deciding to sell. Or, the dealer could attempt to find out more about his customers by investigating their arrest record, asking other dealers about them, or by covertly observing their activities and encounters for a given time. The combination of more evidence and a more conservative standard could effectively reduce the risk of betrayal.[14]

The dealer could strengthen discipline by increasing the rewards and penalties he controls, and by increasing the reliability of his monitoring system. For example, the dealer can beat or kill those who betray him or share his market with those who remain silent. However, to make such rewards reliably contingent on the customer's silence, the dealer must be able to discern which of his customers is likely to have betrayed him. This requires the dealer to monitor his customers' activity and status. He can discover which have come under police pressure by monitoring arrests through newspaper accounts, court appearances, or police records.[15] He can occasionally covertly trail his customers to observe their activities and encounters. If the dealer succeeds in monitoring his customers' behavior, and can credibly threaten them with significant rewards and punishment, the dealer can, again, significantly reduce the risk of betrayal.

---

supply of heroin. The caution of other dealers makes them inefficient suppliers and marketers of heroin and therefore less important targets of police action.

[14]The process of screening is important throughout this analysis. Consequently, it is valuable to establish a fairly precise analytic conception of the process. Basically, dealers try to distinguish trustworthy customers from traitorous customers. They cannot directly observe the degree of trustworthiness. They can only observe characteristics they believe are correlated with this characteristic ("signals"). Because the correlation between the signals and the actual characteristics is uncertain, dealers will make errors in deciding to sell. The errors will be of two different types: they will sometimes decide to sell to traitorous customers and will sometimes refuse to sell to trustworthy clients. The frequency with which they make both types of errors will depend on the strength of the correlation between the signal and the actual characteristic: the stronger the correlation, the fewer the errors. However, dealers can adjust the proportion of errors of each type they make by adjusting their criteria for deciding to sell to a user. If they decide that a weak signal of trustworthiness is sufficient for them to sell, the dealers will reduce the frequency with which they refuse to sell to a trustworthy client, but only at the price of increasing the frequency with which they agree to sell to a traitorous customer. In effect, in setting up a screening procedure, a dealer can adjust two different components: he can change the "signals" he examines (absorbing some costs to observe signals more highly correlated with the desired characteristics than the signals that are inexpensively available); or he can alter his criterion for deciding whether to sell or not on the basis of the observed signals. Presumably increased enforcement pressure pushes dealers towards increased expenditures to observe higher quality signals and more conservative criteria in evaluating the signals. From the point of view of policy objectives, forcing dealers to invest in elaborate screening and rely on conservative standards are very valuable effects: many new users will be discouraged by the process and denied access to markets. For a brilliant analysis of the role of signals in the labor markets, see Michael Spence, *Market Signalling, Discussion Paper No. 4,* Public Policy Program, Harvard University, 1972.

[15]An analysis of a fencing operation showed that fences were heavily dependent on newspapers for information. See Carl B. Klockars, *The Professional Fence* (New York: The Free Press, 1974), pp. 74–75, footnote 1.

Note that to some extent screening and discipline are redundant. If one screens *in* customers who are naturally inclined to be discreet even when confronted with police pressure, one reduces one's need for effective discipline. Similarly, if a dealer can discipline his customers successfully, he reduces his need for effective discipline. Effective discipline implies that a customer will be strongly motivated to be discreet and silent regardless of his initial characteristics. Note, also, that effective discipline functions as a screening device. Those customers who are anxious about their ability to avoid or withstand police pressure may prefer not to participate in a market where there is effective discipline. In effect, the threat of effective discipline deters many marginal customers.

Given this redundancy, it is generally unwise for dealers to invest in both screening procedures and discipline procedures. The only case in which it would make sense to invest in both procedures is when the dealer is willing to spend large amounts of time and effort to guarantee a very high level of security. In cases where a dealer is not inclined to absorb the great expense and inconveniences of being very cautious, it is worthwhile to invest in only one procedure. Generally, it seems that effective discipline is less expensive and more valuable in providing security than effective screening. Consequently, one would expect marginal dealers to use a few rudimentary screening devices and to invest heavily in procedures to discipline their customers. As dealers become more risk averse or wealthier, they will continue to purchase improved discipline rather than improved screening. At some high level of risk averseness or wealth, dealers will begin to invest in more expensive screening devices.

The advantages of small markets combined with tight screening and effective discipline are obvious. All the natural advantages of small markets accrue. In addition, one sells only to customers who are unusually trustworthy and maintain a high degree of effective control over their behavior.

The major disadvantage of this strategy is that it is extraordinarily expensive. It is time consuming to gather evidence on the trustworthiness of customers. Monitoring the behavior of customers and rewarding or punishing them at every turn requires a great deal of time and the assumption of significant additional risks of being linked to the heroin industry.

Similarly, controlling large incentives such as a capacity to kill or injure or a willingness to share profits in the market require the assumption of additional risks or large monetary expenditures. The costs of tight screening and effective discipline make this strategy much more expensive than simply reducing the size of one's market.

This strategy also has the same disadvantages with respect to lost opportunities for market expansion as the first strategy. Indeed, problems with market expansion are exacerbated with this second strategy. Tight screening will exclude many possible customers. The effective discipline may frighten additional customers. These effects will slow, and ultimately constrain, market expansion in a way that the first strategy does not.

A third strategy is for suppliers never to engage personally in any illegal activity, and to keep their identity known only to one or two agents who do the work for them.[16] In effect, this strategy simply adds a level to the distribution system. The advantage of adding this level is that the supplier divides by a factor of 5 to 10 the number of people with whom he must deal. All the advantages of dealing with an extremely small group follow. The supplier may more effectively screen his own activity and connections without losing control over the consumers. Indeed, he may be able to increase dramatically the number of consumers he can control.

The major disadvantage of the strategy is that

---

[16]For evidence that dealers employ this tactic see Staff and Editors of *Newsday, The Heroin Trail* (New York: Signet, 1973), p. 205. For the costs of using agents, see Richard Woodley, *Dealer* (New York: Holt, Rinehart and Winston, 1971), p. 68.

a supplier often finds himself in a very precarious position via-à-vis his agents. The agents are both an extremely valuable resource to the supplier (since they screen him from many risks) and a dangerous liability (since they are in a position to expose his apparently secure position). Because the agents have a strategic position, they may exploit their position for sizeable rewards. The supplier is faced with the difficult problem of controlling these agents without giving up all the profits that accrue to his particular heroin market.

Frequently, a critical resource that makes the supplier valuable to the agents is the supplier's relation with the supplier above him. If the agents can be made to believe that the supplier's relation to a higher level supplier is the critical factor guaranteeing the supply of heroin that keeps them all rich, then the supplier becomes the goose that lays the golden egg. Such a position allows him to maintain a hold on a share of the profits. The importance of this position to the supplier implies that the supplier will do everything in his power to keep his agents from establishing a reliable relation with the higher level supplier.

Note that the supplier's interest in limiting access to his supplier often coincides with the higher level supplier's interest. The higher level supplier prefers that he be shielded from the agents by the lower level supplier since he would like to minimize the number of people who know of his activities. It is this interest that makes the supplier's efforts to keep the agents away from his supplier likely to be successful. This probability of success, in turn, provides some stability in the strategic maneuvering between the agents and supplier.[17]

[17]These observations have important implications for the potential value of enforcement strategies that rely on "buying up the ladder." A common enforcement tactic is to make an escalating series of undercover buys from the same dealer. The objective is to motivate the dealer to pass the undercover agent on to the higher level dealer. In fact, both the current dealer and his supplier will resist this tendency. The current dealer will have strong incentives to retain such

In sum, the strategies to conceal one's relation with the heroin industry are:

1. Restricting markets to a small number of users.

2. Screening customers very carefully.

3. Monitoring and disciplining customers.

4. Using agents to shield the dealer from the customers.

It is no accident that these strategies are organizational strategies. The problems to be solved in maintaining the first line of defense are to screen the inevitable transactions of the business from casual observation. The brunt of the screening efforts must lie with establishing a sharp boundary beyond which evidence of the transactions cannot be seen, and reducing the amount of activity and negotiation necessary to complete the transactions. The discipline and the number of individuals are critical variables in establishing the boundaries and determining the amount of explicit negotiation and uncoordinated activity that are necessary. Consequently, these are the variables that must be manipulated to limit the probability that a heroin supplier will be identified with the heroin industry.

Avoid Creating or Being Caught with Evidence The second line of defense is to avoid creating evidence that provides probable cause for a search, justifies an arrest, or supports a conviction. In the course of their activities, dealers may create evidence that will support convictions on a variety of charges. However, the most persistent and pervasive threat is that they will be discovered while possessing or exchanging heroin. Consequently, the central problems in maintaining this line of defense are

a good customer for himself. The higher level dealer will want to avoid being exposed to the strange customer. Thus, the incentives operating in the distribution system reduce the chance of success for this strategy. This issue is discussed more extensively below.

to hide or dispossess heroin while continuing to exchange and control inventories of heroin.

Maintaining this line of defense is inconvenient for dealers. Both concealing and dispossessing heroin impede the exchanges that are vital to the dealer's business. If heroin is well hidden, then it ceases to be readily accessible—either because the heroin is so well hidden that it takes a long time to disassemble and reassemble the hiding place, or because frequent access to the heroin gives away the location to any observer. As a result, to maintain the security of their heroin, dealers are restricted to a small number of transactions per day.

Dispossession of one's heroin also tends to make heroin inaccessible. In addition, dispossession carries the risk that the dealer will lose control of his inventories. Distant, unwatched caches of heroin are tempting marks for thieves. Similarly, if a dealer does not personally participate in transactions involving his heroin, he risks being defrauded. His customer can claim that the heroin he paid for was not where it was supposed to be, or can take more heroin than he paid for. Thus, in order to minimize the chance that a dealer is caught with evidence, he must sacrifice convenience and security in possessing and exchanging heroin.

Several features of the world generally facilitate the dealers' effort to avoid being caught with heroin. First, since heroin is light, small in volume, and requires no special packaging to be preserved, it can be hidden securely in many different places and dispossessed quickly if the need ever arises. It can be stored in compartments small enough to be unnoticeable, and exchanged in handshakes or kisses. It can be swallowed or flushed down toilets when the police arrive at the doorstep. If heroin was larger or heavier, it would be easier to notice and harder to dispossess.

Second, the police are restricted to looking for heroin in only a small number of places. One reason for this restriction is limited resources. There are only a small number of eyes employed to look for heroin. Equally significant are constitutional limitations on search and seizure. The police are prohibited from looking for heroin except in situations where they can establish probable cause for a search. The implication of the limited capacity of the police to look for evidence of heroin is that dealers can afford to be somewhat incautious about concealing and dispossessing heroin. Even if dealers are occasionally careless, there is a good chance that the police will not notice.

Although these factors reduce the pressure on dealers to conceal and dispossess their heroin, they do not totally negate the police threat. Indeed, there are three strategies the police can use to make legitimate arrests in spite of these difficulties. First, they observe people known to be active in the heroin industry and stop them at points where they are likely to have stored or exchanged heroin. Second, they obtain information about the location of drugs from informants. Third, they penetrate the organizations that store and exchange drugs and directly observe the location of the heroin. In order to reduce their risk to very low levels, dealers must devise and employ strategies that frustrate the strategies of the police.

One effective way for dealers to frustrate police efforts to secure evidence is simply to maintain the first line of defense (i.e., avoid being identified as a dealer). If one can avoid being "known" as a dealer, one can avoid being closely observed. If one can screen out undesirable customers (e.g., informants and undercover police), one can prevent the police from learning about the location of one's heroin. Thus, the strategies that are effective in maintaining the first line of defense are also important and effective in maintaining the second line of defense. But there are additional strategies that will frustrate police efforts to secure evidence even after the first line of defense has been penetrated.

Perhaps the most important strategy is for dealers to blend their illegal activities of possessing and exchanging heroin into the normal, legitimate activities of their daily lives.[18] Heroin can be stored in the apartment of a mother or girl friend and tapped or replenished during the course of casual, routine visits. Heroin can be exchanged while shaking hands, having a beer, or buying a newspaper. Complicated arrangements to exchange heroin covertly can be negotiated during casual encounters on the street or telephone calls. In a society where citizens cannot be stopped and searched without probable cause to believe that a crime is being committed, a great deal of behavior that can be used to cover heroin transactions is constitutionally protected. As a result, heroin dealers can enjoy significant latitude in operating if they are careful to blend illegal activities into constitutionally protected activities.

Notice that for this blending strategy to be successful, the same activity used to cover exchanges of heroin must occur frequently and *not* involve a heroin transaction. In effect, a dealer is trying to hide a "signal" (his illegal activities) in general background "noise" (outwardly similar activities that do not involve exchanges of heroin). Consequently, for the signal to be taken merely as noise, the dealer must increase the amount of noise.

To some extent, a dealer can accomplish this himself. If a dealer wants to use his mother's apartment as a safe place to store heroin and he wants to be able to have ready access to it, he must become an extremely dutiful son. He must visit his mother on many occasions when he does not bring or take away heroin. Similarly, if a dealer wants to pass heroin on the street through casual encounters, handshakes, and embraces, he must spend a lot of time encountering, handshaking, and embracing when he is not exchanging heroin. In effect, the constant motion, interaction, and hustle that is typical of heroin dealers serves the same function as the incessant wiping, scratching, and arm crossing of major league baseball coaches: an observer attempting to figure out the sign is uncertain about which activity is the real sign. Thus, dealers can create a great deal of noise by themselves.

However, to a greater extent, dealers rely on others around them to create the background noise that conceals them. Since many others in the cultural milieu of heroin dealers behave as heroin dealers do in all respects but possessing and exchanging heroin, it is difficult to distinguish the dealers from the nondealers. Both adolescents and ghetto residents spend time "hanging out" in public areas. In addition, there is a great deal of movement and interaction. The sheer volume of activity, all of which *could* involve exchanges of heroin, makes it difficult to identify the small number of encounters that actually *do* involve exchanges of heroin. Since ordinary behavior is precisely the behavior required to continue dealing in heroin, the general background noise totally obscures the actual exchanges of heroin.[19]

One observes the same phenomenon in analyzing the behavior of heroin smugglers. Every day tons of cargo are unloaded in New York City ports and airports. Only pounds of heroin must be concealed in this huge volume to maintain the local heroin market. Sailors getting off ships, diplomats being checked through cus-

---

[18]For the role of blending strategies in protecting heroin laboratories, see Staff and Editors of *Newsday, The Heroin Trail*, p. 76. For the importance of blending strategies in the fencing business, see Klockars, *The Professional Fence*, pp. 77–82.

[19]Some personal experience convinced me of the difficulty of distinguishing the "signal" from the "noise." While riding in an unmarked car with New York City narcotics detectives, I asked them to point out any heroin transactions they observed. They would often point to encounters and groups of people on the street whom they believed to be involved in heroin deals. I was unable to distinguish the groups they identified from the hundreds of other encounters and groups we passed. I suspect that the differences the detective noticed were not particularly significant in identifying the transactions—particularly so because they were unable to say what distinguished the events described as heroin transactions from other events that appeared similar to me.

toms, bottles of wine being loaded on trucks, cars being picked up by private purchasers may all conceal heroin. But they conceal heroin in such a small proportion of total cases, that it is not worth investigating all possible cases closely.[20] In effect, the problem that the customs official faces in attempting to single out the few bottles of wine that contain plastic bags of heroin from a large shipment of wine in a busy port is analogous to the problem that patrolmen and narcotics agents face in trying to decide which of the 40 groups standing on street corners are currently engaged in exchanging heroin.

Thus, both retail dealers and smugglers can effectively blend illegal activity into their own legal activity and the legal activity of others who look and behave much like they do. Blending protects dealers because it capitalizes on the small size of heroin and the budgetary and constitutional restrictions on the police to keep the dealers from being investigated too closely and too frequently.

A third strategy to avoid creating evidence is simply to hide the heroin well enough to frustrate a close investigation. A variety of mechanical devices are used. Heroin has been hidden in secret compartments of suitcases, cupboards,

and chests; in automobile gas tanks; in specially constructed bottles that have wine only in the top third of the bottle; and in padded wire frames made to simulate a pregnant woman's stomach. These devices often have the advantage of being fairly inexpensive. They have the disadvantage of being easily penetrated by a thorough police search.

Generally, this strategy of hiding heroin with mechanical devices is used merely to complement a blending strategy. The dealer relies primarily on blending to ward off a thorough search, and employs clever hiding places only to reduce the probability of a chance discovery. The devices are not designed to frustrate a very thorough search.

However, some devices are successful in frustrating very serious searches. Some hiding places can be both very carefully concealed, and very difficult to gain access to. Internal components of a car, human beings, or other large mechanisms afford both a high degree of concealment and impose a heavy burden on anyone who wants to look hard enough to find the heroin.[21] Consequently, these devices afford much greater protection to dealers.

Very intricate and complicated hiding places have several disadvantages. First, they reduce the dealers access to heroin as much as they reduce the access of the police. As previously noted, this cramps the style of a dealer who needs to make transactions. Second, they tend to require the work of specialists who are knowledgeable about the mechanisms in which the heroin is concealed.[22] Unless a dealer has the

---

[20]The problem Customs faces is illustrated dramatically by the following example: "An appreciation of this 'needle in a haystack' situation can be obtained from the following theoretical, but typical, example. One cargo invoice covers a shipment of 10 containers, each container holds 100 cartons, each carton contains 24 teapots in individual boxes, and one teapot contains heroin.

"Actual detection of the heroin in that teapot would be a formidable task even if it were known that the heroin was secreted somewhere within this shipment. If, however, this were not known or suspected, the task of detection becomes staggering, if not impossible, particularly when one considers the situation in its entire context—one teapot, one of 24 boxes, in one of 100 cartons, in one of 10 containers, in one of many shipments covered by one of 1.4 million invoices. This, in brief, gives an idea of the problem faced by Customs in its efforts to impede the flow of heroin into the country." See Comptroller General of the United States, "Heroin Being Smuggled Into New York City Successfully" (Washington, D.C.: General Accounting Office, 1972), p. 16.

[21]For a good example of very difficult hiding places, recall the "French Connection" case. A search of several hours failed to locate the heroin and the police were nearly discouraged from continuing the search. It is also worth noting that restrictions on "strip searches" of people entering the country make internal parts of human beings effective hiding places for small, but not insignificant amounts of heroin. In reading through a sample of cases on the Southwest Border, I was surprised of how frequently heroin was concealed in body cavities.

[22]The existence of specialists in building "traps" is reported in the anecdotal literature. See Vincent Teresa with

necessary, specialized skills himself, he must expose his activity to an additional person. Such exposure is always a risk. Third, the hiding places tend to be expensive.

A fourth problem with intricate hiding places is of a slightly different order. Because the intricate hiding places are expensive and require the work of a specialist, a dealer may decide to use the same hiding place on several different occasions. This may lower average costs and bind the specialist closer to his organization. Moreover, because the hiding place is intricate, the dealer may feel very confident in its effectiveness. All of these factors lead the dealer to use the same device frequently. Frequent use of the same device ultimately makes the dealer vulnerable. Once discovered, the dealer's modus operandi becomes a powerful piece of evidence the police can use to discover, arrest, and convict the dealer. There is a nice paradox here: it is partly because the devices are so effective that they become the dealers' Archilles' heel. He is lulled into a false sense of confidence and comes to rely too heavily on something that becomes increasingly vulnerable as he increasingly relies on it.[23]

Thus, both simple and intricate hiding places contribute to the security of the dealers. But both have important disadvantages as well.

A fourth major strategy to prevent the police from obtaining persuasive evidence is simply to dispossess the heroin. Because the police must establish possession to secure a conviction, and because the police design tactics on the assumption that dealers have heroin in their immediate possession, an effective strategy for dealers is to keep heroin far away from themselves. They can do so at several different stages: while storing heroin in inventories, while exchanging heroin, or when confronted by the police.

Inventories of heroin can be dispossessed by creating caches for heroin that are remote from a dealer's daily activity.[24] The advantage of these caches is that the dealer can go about most of his daily life without fearing a police search. Then, when he needs to gain access to his heroin, he can take special measures to avoid being followed. He can lose himself in crowds or streets, outrun potential pursuers, or refuse to go when he suspects he is being successfully followed. In effect, a cache allows a dealer to economize on his efforts to avoid being followed.

A cache has several disadvantages. First, like intricate hiding places, it reduces the number of transactions a dealer may make. Second, caches are vulnerable to rip-offs. Although one can hire guards, one must worry about their trustworthiness. Third, a cache can often be linked to a particular individual. Because of the threat of rip-offs, dealers often establish their caches in property they or their friends or relatives control and own.[25] Although this device reduces the threat of a rip-off, it facilitates police efforts to prove that the dealers possessed heroin. Names on leases or titles of property where heroin is stored become powerful pieces of evidence in conspiracy or possession cases. Thus, in establishing a cache a dealer must either leave his heroin exposed hoping that it will go unremarked and confident that it will be difficult to trace the heroin to him; or he must make provisions to guard his heroin knowing that when he does so, he may not have adequately protected his heroin and has certainly made it easier for the police to connect him to the cache.

Dispossessing heroin in exchanges is slightly more complicated. But it is also very important

---

Thomas C. Renner, *Vinnie Teresa's Mafia* (Garden City: Doubleday and Co., 1975), pp. 123–128. See also, *Newsday, The Heroin Trail*, p. 71.

[23]This is an application of a general point developed in Erving Goffman, *Strategic Interaction* (Philadelphia; University of Pennsylvania, 1969). See particularly, p. 62.

[24]For the role of "caches" see Woodley, *Dealer*, pp. 31–32, *Newsday, The Heroin Trail*, p. 256. For similar operations in the fencing business, see Klockars, *The Professional Fence*, pp. 83–86.

[25]In the distribution system described in *Newsday, The Heroin Trail*, p. 256, all the caches were controlled by relatives.

since the police are particularly alert to and interested in any encounter of a "known dealer" with a "known junkie" that could cover a heroin transaction. The strategies that are effective in dispossessing heroin during exchanges are complicated "drop" systems. Drugs are left in locations at times when the dealer is not observed to be picked up at times when the purchaser is not observed. Such strategies have the advantage of allowing legitimate or constitutionally protected activity (e.g., meeting on the street, talking on the phone, "lending" money, etc.) to substitute partly for the illegal activity of buying and selling heroin, since the heroin part of the transaction occurs at another time in a more discreet way than would otherwise be possible. An additional advantage is that it is hard to prove that drugs in one location were in fact controlled by a man who is not there in person. Consequently, even if discovered, the behavior and purposes of the drop system are hard to prove in court.[26]

The strategy has the disadvantage of making the dealer vulnerable to unobserved thefts (since his drugs are exposed for at least part of the time), and sometimes to absconding by the purchaser. The consumer is also vulnerable to double crosses by the dealer. The uncertainties that mark these transactions and the complex behavior that must be coordinated to make the transaction successful imply that the negotiations among consumers and suppliers consume large amounts of time. This is particularly true when communication between the supplier and the consumer is not facilitated by past experience with one another. The large amount of time required is a disadvantage of the strategy. Finally, the strategy is often vulnerable to informers since the strategies cannot change quickly without dramatically increasing the time

a dealer must spend on negotiating new arrangements with his customers.

Dispossessing heroin when confronted by the police is a surprisingly effective tactic for dealers. Dealers can drop the heroin to the street, flush heroin down toilets, or swallow it when arrest and search seem imminent. This tactic is effective in subverting police efforts for three reasons.

First, because there is a demanding legal test for possession, the dealer has many ways of legally dispossessing the heroin. Heroin must be found in the immediate possession of a person, or in a place that is owned and used primarily by the person, for possession to be demonstrated. Since the streets are not owned by anyone, all the dealer must do is drop heroin to the street unobserved to avoid a conviction.

Second, the procedures required in conducting a legal search often provide dealers with sufficient time to dispossess their heroin. If the police must knock or otherwise announce themselves and wait a reasonable period between entering or taking custody of someone by force, the dealer may be able to throw the heroin away, swallow it, or otherwise dispossess it.

Third, since the police have often *not* followed these procedures and have given perjured testimony in narcotics cases, virtually all police testimony about the circumstances surrounding the discovery of heroin is suspect. As a result, it is now possible for dealers to dispossess the heroin in a standard way, to have the police observe the dispossession and testify accurately that the dispossession occurred, and to have the court disbelieve and heavily discount the policeman's testimony. In effect, the police have given dealers additional latitude in dispossessing heroin by attempting to restrict their latitude through improper procedures and perjured testimony. Not only can dealers take advantage of the wide latitude given them if the police adhere strictly to legal procedures, but, in addition, they can often escape when their dispossession efforts have been clumsy and easily ob-

---

[26]For elements of proof necessary to establish possession, see Charles H. Whitebread and Ronald Stevens, "Constructive Possession in Narcotics Cases: To Have and Have Not," *Virginia Law Review* 58 (1972): 751.

served by the police. The courts simply do not believe the police cries of wolf, and the wolf goes undetected. Thus, dispossessing heroin when confronted by the police affords an effective strategy to avoid creating persuasive evidence of wrong doing.[27]

One thing to notice before leaving the strategy of dispossession is that using agents in transactions can serve the function of dispossessing heroin. However, it serves this function only if the agent cannot be traced to the dealer. Consequently, to dispossess heroin through the use of agents, the dealer must be able both to guarantee the silence of the agents and to instruct and direct the agent without leaving durable signs of one's communication with the agent. Using agents to dispossess heroin has the additional problem of making the dealer vulnerable to frauds and take-offs.

A fifth and final strategy to frustrate police efforts to secure evidence is to move the drugs constantly from hiding place to hiding place. This strategy has a serious liability in that the police generally watch the activity of individuals in limiting the number of places the drugs could be and this strategy dramatically increases the activity associated with storing drugs. Another disadvantage is that such a strategy often involves many people and much negotiation to keep the drugs in motion. Both requirements are liabilities. Still, the strategy has the advantage of quickly making obsolete any detailed information the police might have about the location of drugs. Consequently, it may be worth its disadvantages when there is reason to believe that the police are receiving good information about the location of heroin. This strategy works simply because there is a lag between obtiing reliable information about the location of drugs,

and police action to discover the drugs in the possession of the dealer.

Thus, in addition to the strategies that maintain the first line of defense, the following strategies are effective in frustrating police efforts to secure evidence:

1.   Blending illegal activities into one's own legitimate activities and the activities of others.

2.   Constructing simple or elaborate hiding places for heroin.

3.   Dispossessing heroin by:
    (a)   Storing it in caches.
    (b)   Using drop systems to exchange heroin.
    (c)   Getting rid of the heroin when confronted by police.

4.   Moving heroin from place to place to make any information about the location of the heroin quickly obsolete.

Judicious use of these strategies allows dealers to frustrate police efforts to secure evidence even when dealers are known to the police.

Corruption of Enforcement Agencies   The third line of defense is to corrupt, manipulate, or demoralize enforcement agencies so they are unwilling to apply the authorized sanctions against heroin dealers. The major tactic for demoralizing enforcement agencies is bribery. The purpose of bribing law-enforcement officials is to purchase indulgence for acts that would otherwise be prosecuted. In effect, dealers purchase a "license" to continue their illicit activities.[28] There are two interesting questions about the dealers' use of bribery. First, who will the deal-

---

[27]Jerome M. Skolnick makes an important distinction between police "knowledge" of guilt and "evidence" necessary to show guilt, and suggests that this has a major impact on the way police use their discretion. See *Justice Without Trial* (New York:Wiley and Sons, 1966), pp. 150–151.

[28]See Simon Rottenberg, "The Clandestine Distribution of Heroin: Its Discovery and Suppression," *Journal of Political Economy* 76 (1968): 83–86. A "franchise" system for pickpockets in subways is reported in Leonard Shecter with William Phillips, *On the Pad* (New York: Berkley, 1973), p. 166.

ers bribe? Second, what kinds of "licenses" will they be able to purchase?

The problem of whom to bribe requires a nice calculation. A bribe offered to the wrong official results in a bribery conviction. Less extreme, but .still significant, is the chance that a dealer will pay an expensive bribe to one official only to be arrested shortly thereafter by another official.[29] On the other hand, a bribe offered to the right official can prevent an imminent arrest, or relieve the dealer of having to behave cautiously. In general, dealers will decide whom to bribe by reckoning the dollar cost of the bribe (and the risk of offering it) against the protection a successful bribe can offer.[30] A variety of factors will influence the dealers' calculations.

In gauging the *risk* of offering a bribe, the dealer will consider such factors as:

1. The number of officials involved in the bribe.

2. The extent to which the actions of the officials are carefully scrutinized by others.

3. The amount that an official has to lose if he is discovered taking a bribe.

4. The morale and integrity of officials in specific positions.

The more people who are involved, the more closely scrutinized, the more they have to lose, and the higher the morale of the organization, the more risky and expensive the bribe.

In gauging the potential *benefits* of a bribe, the dealer will consider such factors as:

1. The magnitude and immediacy of the threat posed by a specific official.

2. The extent to which the official monopolizes threats against the dealer or can protect the dealer from threats posed by other officials.[31]

3. The scope of the license conferred (i.e., the variety of criminal acts that are tolerated and the period over which the license is effective).

The more substantial and immediate the threat, the more effectively an official monopolizes threats, and the broader the license conferred, the more valuable is the bribe.

Note that the potential benefits of bribing any particular official depend a great deal on the position of the dealer. Unless they happen to be neighbors, it does a street dealer operating in Bedford-Stuyvesant little good to bribe a patrolman in Richmond. Similarly, unless a large-scale importer engages in casual retail sales, it may do him little good to bribe a local narcotic detective. Because the police are geographically and functionally specialized, a dealer is threatened only by certain kinds of police. It follows, then, that only a few officials are valuable for any particular dealer to bribe. It also follows that there are few *general* propositions about the value of bribes offered to different officials. It all depends on the position of the dealer. However, to illustrate the dealer's calculations and to probe for significant weaknesses in the enforcement apparatus, it is useful to consider the problem from the point of view of an experienced street dealer. Since this group of dealers is large, any conclusions about the vulnerability of different officials are likely to identify a major portion of the existing corruption problem.

Consider, first, the choice between bribing police officials and court officials. In general, the police are the more attractive targets. Since much police work occurs without written records or close supervision, a policeman can take

---

[29]For a description of a criminal's reaction to being arrested by different police than he was paying, see Shecter with Phillips, *On the Pad*, p. 116.

[30]To make these calculations successfully, some kind of "brokers" would have to develop who helped criminals locate the people who were vulnerable and valuable to bribe. Such people seem to exist. William Phillips appears to have played this role. See Shecter with Phillips, *On the Pad*, p. 29.

[31]For an explicit calculation of the adequacy of the protection provided related to the cost of the bribe, see Shecter with Phillips, *On the Pad*, p. 30.

a bribe with little risk of exposure.[32] Moreover, since the police initiate cases against dealers, their indulgence can totally eliminate the threat of prosecution. Court officials, on the other hand, operate with many written records and fairly close public scrutiny. Consequently, the risks of exposure are significant. Moreover, since they are restrained by written records, they can only marginally affect the outcome of a case. Thus, a heroin dealer should try to bribe police rather than court officials. The costs to them are lower, and the protection more effective.

Among kinds of police officials, the choice is less obvious. Consider three types of officials—a uniformed patrolman, a narcotic detective, and a superior officer. From the point of view of the dealer, the patrolman has the advantages of operating with significant discretion, of facing low opportunity costs if he is exposed, and often, of being judged to have relatively low morale. He has the twin disadvantages of neither posing a significant threat nor being able to protect dealers against threats posed by others. Thus, although his price is low, his protection is often not very significant.

The narcotics detective typically operates with even greater discretion than the patrolman. However, both his morale and opportunity costs if exposed may be much higher. Consequently, he may be more expensive than the patrolman. He is often worth the additional price because he poses a substantial threat to a dealer and can often offer broad, effective protection. He is certainly worth the price if his morale is judged to be low.

The superior officer is probably the least likely target. He personally rarely poses a significant threat and he cannot reliably control his subordinates without dramatically increasing

his own risk of exposure. The risk of exposure is an important deterrent because he has a relatively long way to fall if discovered. Thus, a superior officer is likely to be too expensive and his protection too unreliable to be an attractive target for bribes.

Among police officers, then, a narcotics detective is the most attractive target as long as one can count on them having low morale. A uniformed patrol officer is the next most attractive target, and a superior officer the least attractive target.

Among court officials, the choice is more obvious. Consider three kinds of officials—judges, district attorneys, and court clerks. Judges and district attorneys are much alike. Since their decisions and actions are recorded and noted by others such as arresting officers, corroborating witnesses, and assorted court officials, and since there are fairly well-known standards that prescribe the appropriate conduct of a case, both D.A.'s and judges face substantial risks of exposure. Moreover, they both stand to lose significantly if they are exposed. Finally, the greatest benefit they can offer is often merely a reduction in penalties. Consequently, these officials are likely to be expensive and relatively ineffective.

Court clerks are more vulnerable and potentially more valuable because they operate without close scrutiny, and can exercise significant influence. They can lose papers, affect the pace of cases by scheduling hearings, or give cases to one judge or another. Any of these decisions could have an important effect on the outcome of a case. Because their actions are rarely noted, and because clerks face low opportunity costs if exposed, they might be easily tempted. Thus, among court officials, court clerks represent a very attractive target for bribes.

The second question about bribing officials concerns the kinds of licenses that dealers can buy. Logically, many different licenses are possible. The bribe can include only heroin dealing or can extend to a wide variety of criminal acts. It can stipulate the scale and location of the

[32]For general description of the environments within which police work and the significant discretion they enjoy, see Jonathan Rubinstein, *City Police* (New York: Farrar, Straus and Giroux, 1973); Skolnick, *Justice Without Trial*; or James Q. Wilson, *Varieties of Police Behavior* (Cambridge, Mass.: Harvard University Press, 1968).

permitted activity. It can nullify a recent arrest or guarantee against a future arrest. It can require repetitive payments or include only a one-shot encounter. In spite of the variety of logically possible bribes, it seems likely that only a small number of licenses will actually be available. Moreover, the available licenses will tend to be at the extremes—broad and repetitive (the "pad"), or narrow and one-shot (the "score"). Finally, the bribes will tend to be retrospective rather than prospective.

Two arguments support the view that there will be a small number of bribes. First, in arranging a bribe, there is not likely to be much explicit communication.[33] To avoid creating damaging evidence, both parties will prefer to rely on tacit understandings of what is expected of each. In order for these tacit understandings to work well enough to support the market, they must be fairly simple and well-known. Complicated or detailed descriptions of mutual obligations will simply not survive. Since the contracts must be defined crudely and used tacitly, only a small number will be available.

Second, it is difficult for both parties to observe whether the other party stays within the bounds of the contract. A heroin dealer can hide a burglary ring behind his heroin dealing without being discovered by the bribed official. As a result, the official is cheated out of the larger payment he would deserve for allowing both heroin dealing and burglary to continue unmolested. A bribed policeman can "finger" the heroin dealer who is bribing him to another policeman. Consequently, the dealer is cheated out of the protection he thought he had purchased. Given that such *gross* transgressions of the terms of the contract are possible, all *detailed* stipulations about specific responsibilities are meaningless. Again, one can conclude that only crude categories of licenses will be available.

The argument supporting the view that only extreme types of licenses will be available (i.e.,

narrow, one-shot licenses or broad, repetitive licenses) is based on an analysis of the strategic relationship between dealers and police once the initial bribe is offered and accepted. Once the first bribe is arranged, a complicated relationship begins. Each party can continue to extort the other. The dealer can threaten to expose the official's corruption. The official can threaten a new arrest on old evidence. As in most strategic situations, the outcome of these mutual threats is uncertain. An experienced, tough, greedy cop might be able to bully an inexperienced dealer. However, in general, as the relationship continues through additional encounters, the dealer's bargaining position strengthens relative to the official.

The reason for this shift is that the dealer's threat to expose an official's corruption gradually becomes more credible than the official's threat to arrest the dealer. Immediately after the first arrest, the dealer will typically not have powerful evidence documenting the official's corruption. As a result, the official need not take the threat of exposure too seriously. As additional encounters occur, the dealer can accumulate increasingly powerful evidence of the official's corruption. The dealer can arrange to have witnesses, take photographs, or record the dealings on tape. Moreover, it becomes increasingly difficult for the official to arrange alibis or explanations for each of the dealer's specific allegations. Meanwhile, the official does not necessarily accumulate more evidence against the dealer. At best, the official will be able to charge the dealer with bribery or additional counts of narcotics offenses—charges that will be relatively unimportant in court. The effect of this asymmetric accumulation of evidence is that the official's threat of a new arrest gradually becomes less credible than the dealer's counterthreat to expose the official's corruption if he is ever arrested.[34] The official must take the dealer's threat seriously not only because he

---

[33]For dialogues involved in transacting a bribe, see generally Shecter with Phillips, *On the Pad*.

[34]For situations involving asymmetric accumulation of evidence, see Shecter with Phillips, *On the Pad*, pp. 30, 254.

knows the dealer can make a strong case, but also because he knows it will cost the dealer very little to implicate the official if the dealer is arrested. Indeed, the dealer may have a positive incentive to "give up" the corrupt official if he thinks the betrayal will ingratiate him with the D.A. and the judge.[35] Thus, the dealer's counterthreat often controls the strategic situation between dealers and corrupt officials.

If the official is aware of this dynamic, one of two actions is available to him in his initial encounter with the dealer. He can sell a very narrow license by agreeing to let the dealer go for that one offense and warn him that the next offense will certainly be prosecuted. Alternatively, he can sell a very broad license at a price that will compensate him for the risk he runs in granting a broad license and for the pains he must take to prevent the dealer from accumulating evidence of his corruption. If the official tries to sell a medium-broad license at a lower price, chances are that he will eventually be forced to provide the protection of a broader license without getting paid for it. Thus, due to an asymmetry in the rates at which dealers and officials accumulate threats as they continue in their relationship, a wise official will exploit the advantage he has in their initial encounter to sell either a very narrow license (minimizing the chance that he will be extorted in the future) or a very broad license (guaranteeing that he will be paid well for something he might eventually be forced to provide in any case).

The proposition that retrospective bribes (which indulge past offenses) are more common than prospective bribes (which guarantee against future arrests) is based on two different arguments. First, a prospective bribe is inherently more uncertain than a retrospective bribe. As previously noted, it is difficult to negotiate explicitly on the terms of a bribe. It is also difficult to enforce the implicit terms of the bribe. Because a prospective bribe specifies future and therefore inherently uncertain obligations, these problems of communication and enforcement will be exacerbated. On the other hand, since a retrospective bribe concerns events that have already occurred, the bargaining over the license will be facilitated. Both dealers and officials will have a relatively clear idea of what is being bought and sold. Thus, retrospective bribes will be much easier to arrange than prospective bribes.[36]

Second, a prospective bribe has an additional disadvantage in that it requires a dealer to expose his position before he is certain that the police know who he is and have accumulated evidence against them. In soliciting an "insurance bribe," the dealer must abandon his first two lines of defense. For this reason, new dealers will often *not* solicit prospective bribes.

These arguments do not imply that there are *no* prospective bribes. In spite of the problems, it is not hard to see how prospective bribes could occur. As we have seen, a retrospective bribe can easily become a prospective bribe if the official's resistance crumbles before the dealer's threat of exposure and the lure of additional money.[37] It is also possible that the police have organized their corruption by establishing "franchises" for dealers. We know that such arrangements exist.[38] Thus, the arguments merely indicate that prospective bribes will be a little more

---

[35]A situation in which the police are afraid of exposure by the people who bribe them appears in Shecter with Phillips, *On the Pad*, p. 202.

[36]An important piece of indirect evidence indicating that retrospective bribes are important is the fact that dealers carry "wads" to pay off the police when they are arrested. See Shecter with Phillips, *On the Pad*, p. 111; and Woodley, *Dealer*, pp. 97–98.

[37]For a description of the development of prospective bribes ("pads") in narcotics, see Shecter with Phillips, *On the Pad*, p. 202.

[38]There are several basic sources on corruption that report these arrangements. See generally, "Commission to Investigate Allegations of Police Corruption and the City's Anti-Corruption Procedures," *Commission Report* (New York: Fund for the City of New York, 1972); New York State Permanent Commission of Investigations, *Narcotics Law Enforcement in New York City* (New York: New York State Commission of Investigation, 1972) and Shecter with Phillips, *On the Pad*.

difficult to arrange and a little less common than retrospective bribes.

This conclusion has important policy implications. If a dealer can arrange a prospective bribe, he reduces his incentives to behave cautiously to avoid arrest. He can be aggressive in seeking customers, and careless with inventories of heroin. As such, he is a particularly efficient and dangerous dealer. On the other hand, if a dealer can arrange only retrospective bribes, he continues to have strong incentives to behave cautiously. What he fears as a consequence of arrest is not jail, but extortion from the officials. As long as the officials charge a high enough price for their indulgence, the incentives for dealers to behave cautiously will remain strong, and they will continue to behave inefficiently.[39] For this reason, we prefer that police and dealers arrange retrospective bribes rather than prospective bribes. Consequently, it is reassuring to discover that prospective bribes will be relatively easy to discourage: even if we cannot eliminate all bribery, we may be able to eliminate the most dangerous kind.

In summary, then, we can offer the following observations about bribes. First, who one should bribe depends on one's position in the distribution system. Second, for street level dealers, the police are much more attractive targets than court officials, and lower level police are more attractive targets than higher level police. Third, dealers will be restricted to a small number of kinds of licenses—very narrow, one-shot licenses, or very broad, repetitive licenses. Fourth, retrospective bribes will be more common than prospective bribes. Thus, the most attractive bribe from the point of view of a street level dealer is a narrow, ad hoc, retrospective bribe offered to the arresting police officer.

One should keep in mind that tactics other than bribery can demoralize enforcement agencies. Narcotics dealers can become so dangerous

that the police become reluctant to go after them. They can invest in so many defensive tactics that it becomes unprofitable for the police to investigate them rather than other criminals who are easier to catch. They can become so skillful and aggressive in exploiting their legal rights that enormous resources must be spent prosecuting them and few are convicted—even when there are strong cases against them. All of these tactics would have the effect of deflecting police attention from narcotic dealers to other criminals.

An apparent disadvantage of these tactics is that they depend on *collective* action by the heroin dealers. Police administrators are influenced to shift their priorities only if *many* dealers become very dangerous, very hard to catch, or very hard to convict. If only a few dealers make the investments and take the risks to become dangerous, hard to catch, and so on, the general reputation of all heroin cases will not be significantly changed. The police will continue to investigate and arrest heroin dealers.

This is only an *apparent* disadvantage because it happens that dealers face individual incentives motivating them to behave in a way that produces the collective benefit for all other dealers. The least careful dealer supplies an important externality to all other more careful dealers: he becomes the most likely target of police efforts and absorbs some portion of the police resources. As a result, the police have fewer resources to attack the next most careful dealer, and they run out of resources long before they reach the most careful dealer. Any individual dealer, then has a strong incentive to be a little more cautious than the last dealer arrested by the police. Since all dealers face these incentives, there is a general tendency to strive to be more cautious than other dealers. This leads to a high level of investment in defensive tactics for the industry as a whole and results in heroin dealers enjoying a general reputation as being very difficult to catch.

There are undoubtedly very complex dynamics in this situation. In a period when

---

[39]For an example of a gambler who behaves cautiously not to avoid imprisonment but rather to avoid payoffs, see Shecter with Phillips, *On the Pad* p. 238.

police pressure is very great, the individual incentives will cause dealers to strain to be the dealer who is slightly more careful than the last dealer caught. As a result, it will become generally more difficult for the police to make arrests in the area, and they may be dissuaded from continuing to apply the pressure. Once the police reduce the pressure, there will be some incentive for individual dealers to exploit the situation by becoming less careful. The dealers who become less cautious and do not get caught because of reduced police pressure benefit from the collective good previously provided by the strong desire of everyone not to get caught. These dynamics could easily produce the oscillation in narcotic arrests and narcotics distribution that we observe.

In summary, the main tactics for demoralizing enforcement agencies are bribery and being harder to arrest and convict than other criminals. The individual incentives of dealers cause both tactics to be employed. We observe the effect of these tactics in the low morale of agencies charged with enforcing narcotics laws, and in increasing public skepticism about the value of enforcing these laws.

Different Tactics for Different Types and Levels of Dealers   Virtually none of these tactics for avoiding arrest and successful prosecution are mutually exclusive. Consequently, dealers are likely to employ combinations of the tactics. In effect, dealers choose portfolios of tactics that are designed to maximize the objectives of profits and security at a low cost to themselves.

The portfolio chosen by any particular dealer depends partly on his position in the distribution system, and partly on his own individual attitudes toward risk, profit, and violence. For example, a dealer who imports heroin must be particularly concerned about the various tactics for hiding heroin since he knows there will be at least a cursory examination at the border. A dealer selling at the retail level must be interested in all the various devices for screening out informants and undercover police. A newcomer in the heroin business has the advantage

of being able to rely on anonymity to protect him. But to preserve that protection, he must develop discrete procedures for advertising his product, and strong procedures for screening his customers. An old timer cannot rely on anonymity and makes larger investments in tactics to avoid producing or being caught with evidence. A dealer who is very interested in profits and less interested in security may charge high prices and aggressively market his product. A more cautious, less acquisitive dealer will charge low prices and keep his clientele small, loyal and tight-lipped. Thus, portfolios chosen by different types of dealers will vary considerably.

Table II analytically defines several different types of dealers. Table III offers hypotheses about the portfolio of tactics they will use. To some extent, these tables are drawn from specific descriptions of dealers in the literature.[40] However, to a greater extent, the types of users are created simply by imagining the logical possibilities. The hypotheses about portfolios of tactics are based in logical inferences from assumed rational maximizing behavior. Thus, the reader should not take these tables too seriously.

What is important to understand is the general idea that types of dealers differ. The differences are important for two reasons. First, we care differently about different types of dealers—partly because some types appear more evil and criminal than the others, and partly because some types have a larger impact on the drug-abuse problem than others. Second, the different types of dealers are differentially vulnerable to different enforcement tactics. "Bad Actors" may run organizations that are

[40]The major sources describing dealers are the following: Richard H. Blum et al., *The Dream Sellers: Perspectives on Drug Dealers* (San Francisco: Jossey-Bass, 1972); Burroughs, *Junkie*; Fiddle, *Portraits from a Shooting Gallery*; Evert Clark and Nicholas Horrack, *Contrabandista!* (New York: Praeger, 1973); Larner and Tefferteller, *The Addict in the Street*; Robin Moore, *The French Connection* (New York: Bantam, 1971); *Newsday, The Heroin Trail*; Preble and Casey, "Taking Care of Business"; Woodley, *Dealer*.

Table II. Types of Dealers Defined in Terms of Positions and Attitudes towards Profits, Risk, and Violence

Position and Type of Dealer	Length of Time in Business	Strength and Direction of Daeler's Attitudes towards:		
		Profits	Risk	Violence
I. Retail dealers				
A. "Accommodating dealers"				
1. Cautious	Recent	Moderate; positive	Strong; negative	Strong; negative
2. Reckless	Recent	Moderate; positive	Indifferent	Strong; negative
B. "Old Standby"				
1. Not ambitious	Old	Moderate; positive	Moderate; negative	Moderate; negative
2. Ambitious	Old	Strong; positive	Indifferent	Moderate; negative
C. Entrepreneur	Old	Strong; positive	Strong; negative	Moderate; negative
D. "Bad Actor"				
1. Not ambitious	New or old	Moderate; positive	Moderate; positive	Indifferent
2. Ambitious	New or old	Strong; positive	Indifferent	Indifferent
II. Wholesale dealers				
A. Free lance				
1. Cautious	New	Strong; positive	Moderate; negative	Moderate; negative
2. Reckless	New	Strong; positive	Indifferent	Moderate; negative
B. Independent seller	Old	Strong; positive	Strong; negative	Indifferent
C. Franchised firm	Old	Strong; positive	Strong; negative	Indifferent

difficult to penetrate by recruiting informants, but relatively easy to penetrate with "cold," undercover purchases. "Accommodating Dealers" may be extremely vulnerable to general surveillance. The implication of these observations is that we may be able to tailor the overall enforcement strategy by selectively investing in enforcement tactics that attack the types of dealers who cause the greatest problems or appear to be the most evil and criminal. For now, it is sufficient merely to suggest the possibility. Thus, although one cannot be certain about the distribution of types of dealers, the potential importance of this judgment to the design of an enforcement policy encourages one to speculate and to keep the issue in mind when looking at any evidence about the heroin-distribution system.[41]

THREATS FROM OTHER CRIMINALS

The threat of arrest and imprisonment is probably the most significant problem created by illicitness. However, illicitness has an additional effect: not only are the dealers threatened by the police—they are also effectively denied police protection. No police and courts will respond to a heroin dealer's complaints that his property has been stolen, implied contracts broken, or his business embezzled by employees. No social conventions will establish strong commitments between employers and employees. The dealer can rely on nothing other than his own ability to protect, retaliate, or inspire respect among his criminal associates. In the face of enormous opportunities for gain and fragile social institutions, "honor among thieves" can disintegrate rapidly.[42] Thus, the isolation that

results from illicitness exposes heroin dealers to threats from other criminals.

These threats from other criminals create two particular problems for dealers. One problem is how to protect property and enforce contracts when the police and courts will not do so. The second is how to attract and manage reliable employees.

The Problem of Enforcing Contracts and Protecting Property

For most businesses, the costs of enforcing contracts and protecting property are largely external. The society provides police services and courts to protect property and insure that business is carried on in an orderly fashion. Moreover, the existence of well-known laws and specialized institutions for enforcing the laws establishes norms and expectations that insure a great deal of voluntary compliance as well as enforced compliance. Although it is true that legitimate businesses pay taxes to support the legal system and must pay lawyers to take advantage of the existing legal system, it is also true that the costs of supporting the system are widely shared, and the costs of using the system are small compared to the enormous benefits.

For illegal businesses, the situation is quite different. Protection and contract enforcement are *not* provided or supported by the public at large. The full costs of the service fall directly on the illegal businesses. Moreover, these costs are likely to be very significant for two reasons.

First, the heroin business is extremely vulnerable to thefts. It is very easy to steal drugs from "drops" and strong incentives exist for addicts to do so. It is riskier, but still very profitable, for people to rob distributors for "rip-off" drugs they were supposed to sell as intermediaries or the supplier. Furthermore, because they operate in areas where there are many other criminals, distributors are often known and picked as

[41]See Richard Blum et al., *The Dream Sellers*, for statistical information on types of dealers.

[42]For evidence on the importance of threats from other criminals for heroin dealers, see Woodley, *Dealer*, pp. 5–7; Teresa with Renner, *Vinnie Teresa's Mafia*, p. 178. Klockars reports similar problems for fences. See the *Professional Fence*, pp. 113–129. For violence and rip-offs among users,

see Larner and Tefferteller, *The Addict in the Street*, pp. 78–99, 206; or Fiddle, *Portraits from a Shooting Gallery*, pp. 124, 128.

Table III. Portfolios of Defensive Strategies for Different Types of Dealers

| | Level of Investment in Tactics to Avoid Arrest | | | |
| | Conceal All Connections with Heroin Industry | | | |
Position and Type of Dealer	Keep Markets Small	Screen Customers	Discipline Customers	Employ Agents
I. Retail dealers				
A. "Accommodating dealers"				
1. Cautious	Heavy	Heavy	—	—
2. Reckless	Modest	Modest	—	—
B. "Old standby"				
1. Not ambitious	Heavy	Heavy	—	—
2. Ambitious	Modest	Modest	—	Modest
C. "Entrepreneur"	Heavy	Heavy	Small	Heavy
D. "Bad actor"				
1. Not ambitious	Modest	Modest	Heavy	—
2. Ambitious	Small	Small	Heavy	Small
II. Wholesale dealers				
A. Free lance				
1. Cautious	Heavy	Heavy	Modest	—
2. Reckless	Small	Small	Modest	—
B. Independent seller	Heavy	Heavy	Heavy	Modest
C. Franchised firm	Modest	Modest	Heavy	Heavy

targets by criminals. This vulnerability means that dealers must be able to provide relatively extensive protection or face significant losses.

Second, for many parts of the market there is no existing, specialized organization that performs the function cheaply and effectively. The result is that efforts at protection and contract enforcement are often undertaken by small, inefficient ad hoc organizations. The benefits that might be obtained through the economies of scale and increased efficiency of a large, specialized agency are not always available to reduce the burden of contract enforcement and protection. Thus, dealers must provide extensive services in this area, and may not be able to buy efficient forms of the service.

There are three strategies that suppliers may use in solving the problem of contract enforcement and protection. One strategy is to purchase these services from organizations that are willing and able to supply them for heroin dealers. A second is to wield rewards and penalties that make voluntary compliance with contracts desirable from the point of view of their consumers and others. A third is for the supplier to make his own activity a necessary condition for consumers or agents to enjoy any benefits from stealing or breaking contracts with him.

In the underworld, "muscle" (i.e., a capacity for violence) is a generally valuable resource. It can be used for protection, enforcing contracts, or simply for extortion.[43] Consequently, there are many groups operating in the underworld who are in the business of "contingent violence."[44] Included among these groups are the

[43]See generally, Thomas C. Schelling, "What is the Business of Organized Crime," *Journal of Public Law* 20:1 (1971), for a provocative analysis that suggests that "muscle" is the major business of organized crime.

[44]"Contingent violence" implies that violence is

Table III. *(cont.)*

Position and Types of Dealer	Level of Investment in Tactics to Avoid Arrest			
	Avoid Creating or Being Caught with Evidence			
	Blend Illegal Activity into Legal Activity	*Conceal Heroin*	*Employ "Drops" and "Caches"*	*Move "Drops" and "Caches"*
I. Retail dealers				
A. "Accommodating dealers"				
1. Cautious	Heavy	Modest	Modest	—
2. Reckless	—	—	—	—
B. "Old standby"				
1. Not ambitious	Heavy	Heavy	Heavy	Modest
2. Ambitious	Heavy	Heavy	Heavy	Modest
C. "Entrepreneur"	Heavy	Heavy	Heavy	Heavy
D. "Bad actor"				
1. Not ambitious	Modest	Modest	Modest	—
2. Ambitious	Modest	Modest	Modest	—
II. Wholesale dealers				
A. Free lance				
1. Cautious	Heavy	Heavy	—	Heavy
2. Reckless	Modest	Heavy	—	—
B. Independent seller	Modest	Heavy	Heavy	Heavy
C. Franchised firm	Heavy	Heavy	Heavy	Heavy

police, local gangs, local vigilante groups, or the "syndicate." Often the heroin dealer is a *victim* of these organizations. However, heroin dealers may also be able to use these groups to protect their property, enforce contracts, or eliminate competition. There is some evidence that heroin suppliers have used gangs they were paying off to drive competitors out of business or catch and murder consumers who absconded with goods. Other evidence indicates that police have been used selectively to arrest and jail addicts, agents, or thugs who were causing problems for the major heroin suppliers.[45] The problem, of

course, is finding muscle strong enough to stand up to other predatory muscle groups in the area, and then paying them enough to keep them loyal. To the extent that the supplier can find cheap, effective, and loyal muscle for sale, purchasing these services from others is a desirable strategy.

Note that the heroin dealer's relations with muscle groups is *very* uncertain. They can suddenly escalate their demands and seek very large shares of the dealer's profits. The dealer may have little bargaining power to fend off such moves. It is also never clear in what coin the muscle groups will demand payment. They can always ask for money, but they can also gain policy control over the dealer's organization. They can insist on more aggressive marketing or profit-maximizing strategies, and can restrict a dealer's operation to particular geographic areas. At an extreme, they can demand that a

threatened as a consequence of specific actions. It is designed as an incentive—not as an expressive act.

[45]The possibility that the police might be manipulated for these purposes is a major problem in managing informants. See Malachi L. Harvey and John C. Cross, *The Informer in Law Enforcement* (Springfield, Mass.: Charles C. Thomas, 1960), pp. 33–39.

Table III. (cont.)

| Position and Type of Dealer | Level of Investment in Tactics to Avoid Arrest | | |
| | Corrupt Enforcement Officials | | |
	Offer Ad Hoc; Prospective Bribes	Offer Ad Hoc; Retrospective Bribes	Purchase Licenses
I. Retail dealers			
A. "Accommodating dealers"			
1. Cautious	—	—	—
2. Reckless	—	—	—
B. "Old standby"			
1. Not ambitious	—	Modest	—
2. Ambitious	—	Modest	Small
C. "Entrepreneur"	—	Heavy	Modest
D. "Bad actor"			
1. Not ambitious	—	—	—
2. Ambitious	—	Modest	—
II. Wholesale dealers			
A. Free lance			
1. Cautious	Modest	Heavy	—
2. Reckless	—	Small	—
B. Independent seller	—	Heavy	Modest
C. Franchised firm	—	Heavy	Heavy

dealer occasionally "take a fall."[46] The high cost and uncertainty of relying on outside muscle groups is a major disadvantage of this strategy.

The second alternative is for the supplier to discipline his agents and consumers with his own stock of rewards and penalties without hiring an outside enforcer and guardian. The problems in this effort are the same as those involved in trying to discipline the small market organization—a strategy considered above. The dealer must be willing to kill or give up some large share of his profits to provide sufficiently large rewards and penalties to protect himself from thefts. Note that if discipline is effective with respect to the goal of reducing the proba-

bility of arrest and conviction, it will also be effective with respect to the problem of contract enforcement. Note also that if a dealer develops his own capacity for violence, this can be used for some bargaining advantage vis-à-vis other muscle groups. It is this triple advantage of violence that justifies its enormous costs to dealers.[47]

The third alternative is to structure the situation so that even if agents, consumers, or outsiders are successful in stealing from a supplier, they will fail to convert the fruit of their theft into a benefit without the active compliance of

---

[46]At some stage, such "muscle" groups may come to resemble what is commonly called "organized crime," but which may only be a very impressive group of extortionists. See Schelling, "What is the Business of Organized Crime."

[47]These observations suggest the importance of cultivating a reputation as a violent man. For the difficulty of hiring "muscle" and the importance of establishing a reputation for violence, see Woodley, *Dealer*, pp. 84–87. For the importance of a violent temperament in most underworld business, see Teresa with Renner, *Vinnie Teresa's Mafia*, pp. 118–121,154–155.

their victim. In most cases, this is, of course, impossible. Money stolen from a supplier is very liquid and easily convertible to benefits for the thief. Heroin stolen by an addict is also easily convertible to desired benefits. However, for one important case, there may be a serious problem.

Consider the case of a man who has just stolen a large quantity of heroin from a dealer and would like to turn it into cash. For several reasons, he has a difficult time selling the stolen heroin. Some people who might buy in quantity from him are afraid to do so since they risk their relation with the victimized supplier if they do. Since many close friends of the thief in the heroin industry may be afraid to buy from him, he may be forced to sell in strange markets. Selling in strange markets is both extremely difficult and extremely dangerous. It is difficult because he cannot "advertise"that he has some heroin to sell. It is dangerous because those consumers who do find him are likely to be people who do not have regular markets. These will be undesirable consumers and will, by definition, include an extraordinarily large percentage of informers or undercover police. Finally, the victimized supplier can always "tip" the police about the location and activity of the thief. In such a situation, it should be clear that it is not particularly desirable to steal from a supplier even when he does not have any muscle that can be immediately applied.[48]

In sum, contract enforcement and protection may be secured by

1. Purchasing the services from organizations that are in a position to sell muscle.

2. Relying on one's own capacity for violence to discipline his own organization effectively.

3. Making one's own compliance necessary for a thief or absconder to convert the stolen

commodity into benefits the thief may internalize.

The Problem of Reliable Employees

It is clear from previous discussions that heroin dealers are exceedingly vulnerable to activities by their employees. It is also clear that strategies to insure effective discipline (e.g., small numbers of employees, contingent violence, reasonable shares of large profits, etc.) are effective in controlling employees. Consequently, some of the problems of reliable employees have already been analyzed.

However, there is an additional aspect of this problem that deserves explicit attention. It is clear that there are some people who are "stand-up guys" (i.e., people who will neither expose nor steal from their associates). By definition, such people have internalized a set of norms that make them particularly valuable employees. To the extent that stand-up guys are plentiful and easy to identify, dealers will be able to reduce investments in strategies to insure effective discipline. In effect, they can substitute careful recruitment, selection, and training for later investments in control systems. Consequently, strategies to increase the supply of stand-up guys or improve dealers' ability to distinguish stand-up guys from others will be important in determining the level of security that dealers are able to achieve.

Note that the *rate* at which dealers can recruit reliable employees will have a decisive influence on the potential impact of enforcement efforts. If the police can arrest dealers and their employees faster than they can be replaced, the direct effects of enforcement action will accumulate steadily and the size of the illicit market will be steadily reduced. If employees can be replaced more quickly than they can be arrested, the direct effects of enforcement efforts will be transient. Consequently, the factors influencing the supply of reliable employees and the screening devices employed by dealers will have an important effect on the potential impact of enforcement efforts.

---

[48]The difficulty of people in this situation is vividly (if somewhat surrealistically) described in Robert Stone, *Dog Soldiers* (New York: Ballentine, 1974).

To a large extent, factors influencing the aggregate supply of stand-up guys are beyond the control of individual heroin dealers. Stand-up guys are the products of subcultures that distrust existing social institutions and view arrest and imprisonment as routine events. The conditions that produce such subcultures are probably deeply rooted in the structure of our society, and are not likely to be influenced by individual heroin dealers.

However, on a local and temporary basis it is entirely possible that *collectively* heroin dealers can affect the supply of stand-up guys. In areas that are badly disorganized, heroin dealers can contribute to the isolation of the community and provide examples that will influence the supply of stand-up guys. The supply of heroin will insure a high prevalence of heroin use in the community. Within the heroin using community, heroin dealers will be powerful figures. Their values and preferences are likely to be dominant. Thus, it is no accident that heroin is difficult to displace from areas where it is already endemic. Within such areas, it is likely that heroin dealers have succeeded in insuring a large supply of reliable employees.

Even if dealers are not operating in areas where there are subcultures producing stand-up guys, there are options for them to increase the supply of reliable employees. They can exploit personal relations by recruiting employees from the ranks of relatives, lovers, or friends.[49] They can provide general services to large numbers of people to create obligations that increase the employees' reliability. Or, they can secure incriminating evidence against individuals and insure reliability through blackmail. These strategies are particularly valuable to dealers simply because they build up loyalty to a *particular* dealer. As a result, this dealer need not compete for these reliable employees with other heroin dealers. They are reliable only to the dealer who has the personal relation, owns the obligation, or controls the incriminating evidence. Thus, individual dealers can extract monopsonistic advantages from this group of employees; they will pay less for their services than for employees who are equally reliable, but whose reliability is more general across dealers.

Regardless of the actual supply of reliable employees to a given dealer, the dealer will face the problem of screening stand-up guys from others who are less reliable. There are many inexpensive screening procedures. Dealers can screen on the basis of race, addiction status, criminal record, or the testimony of others who he trusts. However, these inexpensive screens have the disadvantage of being imprecise—they screen *out* many people who would turn out to be reliable employees, and they screen *in* many unreliable types.[50]

More expensive screening procedures are those that involve long periods of probation during which potential employees are closely observed, tested, and kept ignorant about much of the operation. Probation is expensive because one must pay for close supervision and delay the benefits of using the new employee. However, it has some enormous advantages. A common test during probation periods is the requirement that the employee commit some crime. Such tests provide an opportunity not only to gauge an employee's reliability, but also to gather incriminating evidence that can be used to blackmail the employee. In effect, these tests not only gauge reliability, but increase it. In addition, such tests will certainly screen out all police. The possibility of such elaborate tests, and the safety that comes from not exposing one's operation to untested employees are the benefits that justify the substantial costs of probationary periods.

[49]Relatives are generally among the safest people to recruit. It is interesting that relatives were recruited to protect the security of the "Ultra Secret" in World War II. See F. W. Winterbotham, *The Ultra Secret* (New York; Harper and Row, 1974), p. 76.

[50]The problem is strictly analogous to the problem of screening customers.

67. A Day in The Life of a Street Addict

MICHAEL AGAR

PROBLEMS IN LEXICAL VARIATION

THE TERMINOLOGY OF HEROIN ADDICTS IS DIF-
ficult to analyze systematically. The addicts are
regionally and racially heterogeneous. There
are, of course, other dimensions of heterogeneity, although these two alone are sufficient to make the point. Although urban heroin
addicts share many of the same situations and
problems, their speech can vary. Whereas some
terms are specific to the addict culture nationwide, others are used in nonaddict cultures, and
still others may be specific to a regional, racial, or
other subgroup. To give a quick example, *junkie*
is a well-established term. *Jones,* on the other
hand, is not. In Boston, *jones* is a "heroin habit";
in Detroit, it refers to "heroin" itself.

*

HUSTLING

To *cop*, the *junkie* needs *bread*, but *hustling* is certainly not the only way to get it. Like the *square*,
the *junkie* could hold a legitimate job, using his
wages to purchase heroin. Alternatively, he
could sell his car, his furnishings, or even his
home to raise cash to support a habit. In fact, a
progression from legitimate support to support

▶SOURCE: *Ripping and Running; A Formal Ethnography of
Urban Heroin Addicts. New York: Seminar Press, 1973, pp.
43–56. (Editorial adaptations.) Reprinted by permission.*

through illegal activities (*hustling*) fits one popular stereotype of the addict.

In many cases this is a false picture. First of
all, an addict who does not *hustle* is not a *street
junkie* or *stone dope fiend*. By definition this type
usually obtains his *bread* from *hustling* activity.
Second, almost all the *junkies* who assisted in this
study were competent *hustlers* before they became *street junkies*. Rather than being driven into
hustling activity due to increasing costs, they
applied previous skills while developing more as
well. . . . In fact, several *street junkies* claimed that
the newer *junkies* are more likely to enter *the life*
without prior *hustling* experience. Such incompetence makes them more dangerous and unpredictable.

As already implied, *hustling* skills are not restricted to *street junkie* culture. *Hustles* provide
an alternative source of financial support and
are used by numerous different groups for this
purpose. . . .

Due to time limitations on this study, *hustles*
were not given the detailed analysis that is
applied to *copping* and *getting-off*. Two specific
hustles, the *burn* and the *rip-off*, are treated in
detail because of their relevance to *junkies* engaged in the *cop* or *get-off* events. On the whole,
though, the domain of *hustles* is neglected here.
Since *hustling* is the activity least specific to *street
junkie* culture, and since other sources are available, that area was sacrificed to the pressures of
time.

Although no extensive analysis was done,
some preliminary interviewing did touch on the

domain of *hustles*. A tentative discussion might be appropriate to familiarize the reader with some of the alternatives available and some of the considerations important in selecting among them.

A *hustle* can be operationally defined as the set of responses to any of the following queries in a context where the respondent knows that the questioner knows that he is a *street junkie:*

1. What's your game?

2. What's your thing?

3. What do you do?

There are undoubtedly other forms taken by the query; these three are examples.

Although most *junkies* will give only one response to the queries, this does not imply that they actively practice only one *hustle*. Most have a primary *hustle*, but will draw on a wider *hustling* repertoire as the opportunity arises. An earlier analysis of folkloristic material suggests that diverse *hustling* ability is an attribute of high status. . . .

Numerous different *hustles* are used by *street junkies*. Perhaps the most common are *stealing, dealing, pimping,* and *confidence games*. Prostitution is often used by females, but it is not discussed here. Again, high status accrues to the individual who can draw from all categories of *hustling*. In conversations with *junkies*, frequent mention of a "click-click" mind occurred. The metaphor emphasized that the good *junkie's* mind never stops working. Any situation in which he finds himself can be exploited by the clever *junkie* toward the attainment of money or *dope*.

The categories listed above include several more specific categories of *hustles*. . . .Confidence *games*, as their name suggests, are routines where the *junkie* obtains the confidence of the target of the *game*, or the *mark*. Basically, the *game* convinces the *mark* that he will receive something for his money or services, when in fact the *junkie* has no intention of delivering. *Confidence men*, whether *junkies* or not, must be good intuitive psychologists with poise and a sense of authority. They must correctly "read" the *mark* and immediately formulate a strategy to encourage his trust.

Confidence games vary. Some, for example, are *played* for what the *mark* has in his pocket (*short con*), whereas others entice the *mark* to obtain money for a large investment (*long con*). Some are used by a *con man* operating alone, whereas others rely on teams. Perhaps the most frequent kind of *con game* used by the *street junkie* is the *burn*. This term has been used to label events where an insufficient amount of heroin is given for the money. Actually, this is only one kind of *burn*, but the one most frequent in *junkie–junkie* interaction.

When the domain is enlarged to include *burns* usually directed toward *squares,* several other types appear. One is the *Murphy,* where a *mark* is sold the services of a prostitute who never shows up. Another is the *hot TV game*. In this form of the *burn*, the *junkie* enters a bar or other neighborhood setting and talks about the availability of an inexpensive color TV. Eventually some potential *mark* approaches him, and the *junkie* tells him that the set is *hot* ('stolen'). Usually, the *mark* remains interested because of the inexpensive price tag.

At this point, the *junkie* instructs the *mark* to follow him. They drive to a large appliance warehouse where several trucks are loading shipments in plain sight of the *mark*.The *junkie* tells the *mark* to wait and enters the warehouse. He approaches a driver who is loading his truck and asks him for a match, converses about the weather, etc. This occurs in sight of the *mark*, sitting in his car across the street. The *junkie* returns to the *mark's* car and tells him that the deal is arranged.

The *mark* is to give the *junkie* the money for the TV. The *junkie* will give it to the driver. When the driver leaves, the *mark* should follow him until in a quiet neighborhood. The driver will stop and give the *mark* his new color TV set, reporting it stolen from his truck when he returns to the warehouse. The *mark* will have his TV, and the *junkie* and the driver will share the money.

Of course, no such thing will occur. The *junkie* does not know the driver, but he must get the *mark's* confidence to get his money. This is the crucial moment of the *game*, since the *mark* must be absolutely convinced to release his money. A person who is *hip* would suggest that he hold the money and give it to the driver when they stop in the quiet neighborhood, but if the person was *hip* he probably would not have been chosen by the *junkie* as a *mark*.

The *junkie* must now demonstrate his psychological proficiency. He must decide what sort of tactic to follow with the *mark* to reassure him—kindness, anger, disgust, disinterest—all are possible tactics. Assuming the *mark* gives him the money, the *junkie* reenters the warehouse, again converses innocuously with the driver, smiles and waves to the *mark*, and leaves the scene. Eventually, the truck will leave with the *mark* following, and sooner or later the *mark* will realize that he has been *burned*.

This example of a *burn* is included to illustrate the general mechanisms of the *confidence games*. A second category of *hustles* is labeled *dealing*. As noted by Preble and Casey . . . there are many different kinds of *dealers*. At the higher levels are importers of nearly pure heroin, men who are never *junkies* and whose life centers on luxury. At the lowest level is the *junkie* who sells a few *bags* to support his own habit. Numerous levels exist between these two. For the *street junkie*, an involvement with *dealing* extends only to an occasional purchase of some heroin for quick resale. If a *street junkie* moves up a level or two in the dealing hierarchy, he is no longer a *street junkie*. The two categories are contrasted in conversations, as in "I'm no big time *dealer*; I'm just a *junkie* like you." A *dealer's dope* is purer and less expensive. His life is easier in that his *hustle*

comes to him; he occupies a seller's market. On the other hand, he runs a higher risk of arrest, incarceration, and robbery from *street junkies*. For the *street junkie*, then, *dealing* is only an occasional, low-level affair.

The *junkie's* involvement in *pimping* is similar to *dealing*. As with *dealers*, there are different kinds of *pimps* who operate on different levels. At the highest level are those with a number of attractive, high-priced girls who serve elite clientele. At the lowest level is a *pimp* with one girl who is physically unattractive and available at low cost. Again, *street junkies* tend toward the lower end of the scale. The most frequent form of *pimping* is to have one *old lady* who works the *streets* and turns her *bread* over to the *junkie*. Often, the *old lady* is a *junkie*, too.

Finally, there is the category of *stealing*. The kind of *stealing* practiced by *street junkies* varies. Some methods are very simple and straightforward. For example, there are different forms of *boosting* ('stealing property') such as *till-tapping* ('stealing from cash register') or *tail-gating* ('stealing from a parked delivery truck'). Other kinds of *stealing* are more complicated, as in the form of breaking and entering called *crib-cracking* ('entering homes'). This form of stealing often involves skills related to lock picking, signals that the residents are absent, and so on.

There are also forms of *stealing* which involve the presence of a victim, such as *dipping* ('pickpocketing'). Another example of this type of *stealing* is the *rip-off*. The *rip-off* involves direct physical confrontation where goods or money are stolen by threatening the victim. Different forms of the *rip-off* include simply grabbing the valuable object, such as a purse, and running, or using a weapon like a knife or pistol to force the victim to surrender. As with the *burn*, the kind of *rip-off* that will concern us here is the type related to *junkie–junkie* interaction, where one may *rip-off* another for his *bread* or *stuff*.

In picking a particular *hustle*, a *junkie* will consider several aspects. First, certain *hustles* require certain kinds of personal skills that not all-junkies have. *Confidence men,* as mentioned earlier, must be poised, authoritative, and quick-witted. *Pimps*, it is said, must be *cold*, capable of concealing and controlling emotion in the face of their *prostitutes'* demands or pleas. *Dealers* must also be *cold*, to resist the pleas of sick *junkies* who do not have enough to *cop*. *Junkies* who want to steal from others in a face-to-face situation must display some bravado to cower their victims. If a *junkie* is not prepared or not able to display these attributes, he is less likely to choose the *hustle*.

Of course, other attributes of the *hustle* are also important. Some, like the *confidence game,* pay off in cash, which can then immediately be used to *cop*. Others, like *boosting*, result in property, which must then be exchanged for cash (*fenced*) before *copping*. Another factor involves risk, both in the possibility of arrest and in the chance of being attacked by other *junkies*. *Dealing*, for example, is high in risk on both counts. *Dealers* must constantly guard against arrest, and they are frequent targets of a *rip-off* by junkies. As we have seen though, *dealing* pays off in providing the most reliable, highest quality source of *stuff*.

Two final factors that might be mentioned include length of penal sentence and payoff. Again, *dealing* and *boosting* provide good contrasts. *Dealing* pays well, but the *dealer* risks a sentence of several years if apprehended. *Boosting*, on the other hand, pays much less, but carries only a misdemeanor charge in most cases. In short, there are several attributes of *hustles* that are considered by a *junkie* when he selects a particular one. To repeat, this discussion is only to familiarize the reader with the broad outlines rather than providing a systematic analysis.

Hopefully, this section gives the *square* some feeling for the variety of *hustles* and process of selecting among them. Since this book is an analysis of events among *street junkies*, the only *hustles* that receive extensive treatment are the *burn* and the *rip-off*. These two are the most likely ones that one *junkie* would use against another while *copping* or *getting-off*; hence, they appear as topics in conversations. . . .

COPPING

Copping ('scoring, making a connection'), in the context here, refers to a category of events where the desired outcome is the exchange of money or goods for heroin. In its broader sense to *cop* can be glossed as 'to get', as in to *cop* some food. Furthermore, one could exchange money/goods for other drugs and correctly label the event *copping*. For the *street junkie*, though, *copping*, as contrasted with *hustling* and *getting-off*, usually refers to *copping* heroin.

The individual from whom one *cops* is called a *dealer (the man, connection).* Although *dealers* may operate in numerous settings, such as bars or pizza parlors, most either deal on the streets (*street dealer*) or in an apartment or house (*house connection*). Since this is not an analysis of *dealers*, reasons for selecting the streets or a house as a setting by *dealers* will not be examined. The *street dealer* and *house connection* are not the only kinds of heroin *dealers* . . . although they are the usual kind dealt with by the *street junkie*. Whichever *dealer* is contacted, the units of exchange must be known. *Junkies* almost always use cash for their purchase; *dealers* will seldom accept goods as payment, since the trouble in *fencing* ('illegally selling') the material is not worth the effort.

The *junkie* finds his heroin, or *stuff (smack, skag, shit, jones, boy)*, packed differently from region to region (see Table I). The largest amount he usually purchases is a *bundle* or a *spoon*, costing around $30.00. Larger units, such as the

Table I. Sample of Heroin Packaging from Three Cities

Type of Packaging	New York	Los Angeles	Detroit
Bag	$2, $3, $5	$10, $20	—
Cap	—	—	$1
Spoon[a]	$25	$35	$5
Half-load	$30	—	—
Half-quarter	—	—	$30

[a]Obviously the New York *spoon* is a larger measure than the Detroit *spoon*.

piece ('ounce'), are usually purchased only by *dealers*.

Unfortunately, it is difficult to describe the packaging system precisely. Quality, quantity, and price can vary, sometimes across a wide range. Lingemann, for example, estimates that *bags* of heroin can vary from 1% to 80% heroin. The rest of the mix usually contains milk sugar or other easily soluble powders resembling heroin and quinine, which tastes and gives a *rush* (glossed later) like heroin. A *dealer* will *cut* ('adulterate') the heroin as much as he can without losing customers. Since this amount varies from *dealer* to *dealer* and from day to day, quality concommitantly varies.

Quantity also varies. *Dealers* sometimes give a *short count* by removing a small amount from each unit. Furthermore, *dealers* are often not overly precise when they divide the heroin for packaging. Similarly, price can vary. For example, in 1969 a *bag* that cost $5.00 in New York cost $10.00 in Boston. Generally, the more distant an area is from the point of entry, the more middlemen are involved in the transaction. Thus, either the price will increase, or the quality will decrease through additional *cuts*.

Within an area, prices can rise in the event of a shortage of heroin, or *panic*. Prices can also vary in different neighborhoods. For example, one New York informant reports that a *trey* ($3.00 *bag*) can vary in price $1.00 either way. A Caucasian who is afraid to *cop* in Harlem can purchase the *bag* for $4.00 in a "safe" area, whereas the *junkie* who is known in Harlem can purchase it for $2.00.

For these and other reasons, the packaging system is a loose system at best. The *street junkie* must learn through experience if a quantity is acceptable as a member of the category. Furthermore, although visual inspection offers some clues to quality, he must learn to *taste* ('take a small fix') a small amount and judge the quality from physical sensations. Table I gives the units usually found in New York, Los Angeles, and Detroit. The *bag* and the ½ teaspoon *spoon* are classified by price; there is the *deuce* ($2.00),

the *trey* ($3.00), the *nickel* ($5.00), and the *dime* ($10.00). In Los Angeles, heroin is sometimes packaged in folded *papers* or *balloons*. The *cap* is a small gelatin capsule. Larger units in Table I include the *half-load* ('15 trey-bags') or the *half-quarter* ('⅛ ounce').

The next level, not shown in the table, is represented by the *bundle* ('25 nickel bags') or the *quarter-piece* ('¼ ounce'), each selling for about $70.00 to $80.00. Although it would be advantageous to buy at this level, since the more you buy, the lower the price, most *junkies* cannot do so. Since the abstinence syndrome begins 4 to 6 hours after the last injection, time pressure impedes the accumulation of large sums of money.

GETTING-OFF

The final event category considered here is labeled *getting-off (taking-off, shooting up, fixing)*. The desired outcome in all of these events is the injection of the dissolved heroin into a vein. To *get-off*, the *junkie* must have the necessary paraphernalia. Among these are the set of *works (outfit)*. There is some disagreement as to just what is included in the *works*. All agree that it must include a hypodermic needle or *spike (pin)* and either a *gun* ('hypodermic syringe') or a *dropper* and *bulb*.

The *spike* size is usually 26 gauge. The *dropper* may be an ordinary glass eyedropper or a dropper from Murine, a commercially available eye relaxant. The Murine *dropper* may be preferred because the 26 *spike* fits snugly over the end. Because of its relatively small size, though, many will not use it. Since most *junkies* have some trouble getting a *hit* ('needle into the vein') they want to use all the heroin they intend to in one *fix*. This often requires more volume than the Murine dropper can provide. Thus, many will prefer the larger *dropper*.

If the ordinary *dropper* is used, some thread is wrapped around the tip to ensure a snug fit with the *spike*. Another type of *collar* is the *Gee*, a strip of paper torn from a $1.00 bill and similarly wrapped. Rather than using the standard rubber *bulb*, the *bulb* from a baby pacifier is removed and fastened to the top of the *dropper*. The larger *bulb* is preferred, since it increases both the pressure that can be used to *draw up* the heroin and the total volume of the *works*.

Although some *junkies* use a *gun*, most will not for two reasons: First, the injection must usually be administered with one hand, since the other usually holds the *tie*. The *dropper* is much easier to handle with one hand than is the *gun*, especially if one wants to *boot*. Second, most addicts must probe to get a *hit*. With the *dropper*, a *hit* is indicated when the pressure in the vein forces some blood into the *works*. This is called a *flag* (*register*). With a *gun*, the *junkie* must pull back on the plunger to test for a hit. This often jerks the *spike* out of the vein. Thus, unless a *junkie* has good *ropes* ('veins') that are easy to *hit*, he will prefer the *dropper*.

Three other items are included in the *outfit* by some informants. A small piece of wire is useful to clean the *spike* if it becomes clogged. A razor blade may be included to open heroin packaged in *balloons* (as in Los Angeles), or to divide a quantity into equal piles. *Cotton* may be carried and used to filter the dissolved heroin into the *works*. The *cotton* catches the undissolved material and minimizes the possibility of clogging the *spike*. Others may use part of a cigarette filter or a piece of Kleenex for this filtering process. In addition, the *junkie* will need a *cooker*. This can be any small, nonflammable receptacle in which the heroin can be dissolved. Two frequently used *cookers* are a spoon with the handle bent to prevent spillage or a bottle cap with a hairpin handle attached.

Finally, the addict needs a *tie*, unless he has exceptionally good *ropes*. A *tie* is any flexible material that can be applied like a tourniquet to force the veins to stand out. This facilitates getting a *hit*. Some examples of *ties* are a belt, a nylon stocking, or a thin piece of cord. If a belt is used for an injection into the arm, for example, the belt is wrapped around the mid-upper arm and cinched tightly. The *junkie*, who is sitting, then leans forward on the elbow of the belted

arm with the belt running under the elbow to the left hand. Held tightly, the veins bulge and the right arm is free to use the *works*. By releasing his grip, the tension on the belt is relaxed.

This is only one example. There are different ways of using different *ties*. Furthermore, the arm is not the only area for injection. Any vein can be used, for example, in the hands, legs, or feet. Some *hit* in the neck, and there are rarer cases who use a vein in the tongue. Other veins are usually used sooner or later, since constant use of one vein usually results in venal collapse. Furthermore, unsterile needles or accidental subcutaneous injection may cause abscesses, also necessitating a move to another spot.

Given the necessary equipment, the addict must know how to use it. First he must *crack the bags* and place the heroin in the *cooker*. The *works* are filled with water, and the water is squirted into the *cooker*. He then heats the mixture over a burning match or candle to dissolve the heroin. The *cooker* is set on some surface and the cotton (or other filter) is dropped into the mixture. The tip of the needle is placed in the cotton and the mixture is drawn into the *works*. The *tie* is applied, and the addict probes for a vein until the *flag* comes up. Usually, he then loosens the *tie* to ensure that the needle does not slip out. He can then *shoot-up* the entire *fix*, or he can *boot* (*jack, milk*).

If he *boots*, he shoots in a fraction of the fix, then releases the *bulb*, thus drawing in blood. He then reapplies pressure to the *bulb*, *shooting* the blood–heroin mixture (*gravy*). He can continue to *boot* until the *works* are empty of heroin. He may do this for one of two reasons. First, he may want to test the quality by fixing a bit at a time. Second, he may want the multiple *rush* (glossed later) that comes with *booting*. The disadvantages of *booting* include the possibility of clogging the needle as the mixture cools. Finally, one can *boot*, obviously, only when one has adequate time to do so.

As the drug first enters the body, the *junkie* experiences the *rush* (*flash*, 'initial physiological effects'). The *rush*, as well as the other physical effects discussed later, are usually said to be impossible to describe to a *square*. The *rush* is sometimes compared to a "driving force" or to an orgasm. Two important implications of the *rush* should be noted. First, popular knowledge has it that heroin use has no effect on a *junkie* after his tolerance builds up. While this is true for some effects (to be discussed), it is not for the *rush*. Unless he has purchased a *blank* ('bag of fake heroin'), the *junkie* experiences the *rush* no matter how addicted he is. A second implication is that intravenous injection is preferred because it is a means to a quicker, better *rush*. *Snorting* ('sniffing heroin like snuff') and *skin-popping* ('subcutaneous injection') are possible techniques of administration, as is simple ingestion. But none of these produce a *rush* as rapid or powerful as intravenous injection.

A second kind of effect is the *high*, described as a feeling of general well-being. This effect (and the *nod*, discussed later) decreases with increased tolerance. That is, as the *junkie* becomes more addicted and acquires a higher tolerance to heroin, it takes increasing amounts to make him *high*. The *high* is longer lasting than the *rush*, though the length of time varies with the tolerance of the *junkie* and the dosage.

A third effect is the *nod*, usually described as a state of unawareness, a kind of chemical limbo. *Nods* can vary from *light* to *heavy*. A *light nod* produces such effects as slightly dropping eyelids and jaw, whereas a *heavy nod* is a state of complete unconsciousness. The *nod* is less frequent than the *high*, since a higher dose of heroin relative to the *junkie's* tolerance is necessary to bring it about.

A fourth effect, . . . is the feeling of being *straight*. A *junkie* is *straight* when he is not sick. If the *fix* removes whatever withdrawal symptoms the *junkie* is experiencing, then it gets him *straight*. Four to six hours after the injection, symptoms of withdrawal begin to appear (runny nose, watery eyes, chills, among others) and continually worsen until another shot is administered.

Unless he has purchased a *blank* the *junkie* will get a *rush* and get *straight*. Depending on the amount in his *fix* and the quality [i.e. *garbage* ('poor quality'), *decent* ('normal'), or *dynamite* ('high quality')], he may get *high* and possibly *nod*. If the dose is too high or the quality too good, he may *O.D.* ('overdose') and die.

*

68. The Problem of Heroin

JAMES Q. WILSON
MARK H. MOORE
I. DAVID WHEAT, JR.

IT IS NOW WIDELY BELIEVED THAT MUCH OF THE recent increase in predatory crime is the result of heroin addicts supporting their habits; that heroin use has become a middle-class white as well as lower-class black phenomenon of alarming proportions; and that conventional law-enforcement efforts to reduce heroin use have not only failed but may in fact be contributing to the problem by increasing the cost of the drug for the user, leading thereby to the commission of even more crimes and the corruption of even more police officers. These generally held opinions have led to an intense debate over new policy initiatives to deal with heroin, an argument usually described as one between the advocates of a *"law-enforcement"* policy (which includes shutting off opium supplies in Turkey and heroin-manufacturing laboratories in France, arresting more heroin dealers in the United States, and the use of civil commitment procedures, detoxification centers, and methadone maintenance programs) and the partisans of a *"decriminalization"* policy (which includes legalization of the use or possession of heroin, at least for adults, and the distribution of heroin to addicts at low cost, or zero cost, through government-controlled clinics).

The intensity of the debate tends to obscure the fact that most of the widely accepted opinions on heroin use are not supported by much evidence; that the very concept of "addict" is ambiguous and somewhat misleading; and that many of the apparently reasonable assumptions about heroin use and crime—such as the assumption that the legalization of heroin would dramatically reduce the rate of predatory crime, or that intensified law enforcement drives the price of heroin up, or that oral methadone is a universal substitute for heroin, or that heroin use spreads because of the activities of "pushers"who can be identified as such—turn out on closer inspection to be unreasonable, unwarranted, or at least open to more than one interpretation.

"PUNITIVE" VS. "MEDICAL" APPROACHES

Most important, the current debate has failed to make explicit, or at least to clarify, the philosophical principles underlying the competing positions. Those positions are sometimes described as the *"punitive"* versus the *"medical"* approach, but these labels are of little help. For one thing, they are far from precise: Putting an addict in jail is certainly "punitive," but putting him in a treatment program, however benevolent its intentions, may be seen by him as no less "punitive."Shifting an addict from heroin to methadone may be "medical" if he makes the choice voluntarily—but is it so if the alternative

▶SOURCE: *"The Problem of Heroin," The Public Interest (Fall 1972)* 29:3–14. *(Editorial adaptations.) Reprinted by permission.*

to methadone maintenance is a criminal conviction for heroin possession? And while maintaining an addict on heroin (as is done in Great Britain and as has been proposed for the United States) is not "punitive"in any legal sense, neither is it therapeutic in any medical sense. Indeed, there seem to be no forms of therapy that will "cure" addicts in any large numbers of their dependence on heroin. Various forms of intensive psychotherapy and group-based "personality restructuring" may be of great value to certain drug users, but by definition they can reach only very small numbers of persons and perhaps only for limited periods of time.

But the fundamental problem with these and other labels is that they avoid the central question: Does society have only the right to protect itself (or its members) from the harmful acts of heroin users, or does it have in addition the responsibility (and thus the right) to improve the well-being (somehow defined) of heroin users themselves? In one view, the purpose of the law is to insure the maximum amount of liberty for everyone, and an action of one person is properly constrained by society if—and only if—it has harmful consequences for another person. This is the utilitarian conception of the public interest and, when applied to heroin use, it leads such otherwise unlike men as Milton Friedman, Herbert Packer, and Thomas Szasz to oppose the use of criminal sanctions for heroin users. Professor Packer, for example, recently wrote that a desirable aspect of liberalism is that it allows people "to choose their own roads to hell if that is where they want to go."

In another view, however, society has an obligation to enhance the "well-being"of each of its citizens even with respect to those aspects of their lives that do not directly impinge on other people's lives. In this conception of the public good, all citizens of a society are bound to be affected—indirectly but perhaps profoundly and permanently—if a significant number are permitted to go to hell in their own way. A society is therefore unworthy if it permits, or is indifferent to, any activity that renders its members inhuman or deprives them of their essential (or "natural") capacities to judge, choose, and act. If heroin use is such an activity, then its use should be proscribed. Whether that proscription is enforced by mere punishment or by obligatory therapy is a separate question.

The alternative philsophical principles do not necessarily lead to diametrically opposed policies. A utilitarian might conclude, for example, that heroin use is so destructive of family life that society has an interest in proscribing it (though he is more likely, if experience is any guide, to allow the use of heroin and then deal with its effect on family life by advocating social services to "help problem families"). And a moralist might decide that though heroin should be illegal, any serious effort to enforce that law against users would be so costly in terms of other social values (privacy, freedom, the integrity of officialdom) as not to be worth it, and he thus might allow the level of enforcement to fall to a point just short of that at which the tutelary power of the law would be jeopardized. Still, even if principles do not uniquely determine policies, thinking clearly about the former is essential to making good judgments about the latter. And to think clearly about the former, it is as important to ascertain the effects of heroin on the user as it is to discover the behavior of a user toward society.

THE USER

There is no single kind of heroin user. Some persons may try it once, find it unpleasant, and never use it again; others may "dabble" with it on occasion but, though they find it pleasurable, will have no trouble stopping; still others may use it on a regular basis but in a way that does not interfere with their work. But some persons, who comprise a large (if unknown) percentage of all those who experiment with heroin, develop a relentless and unmanageable craving for the drug such that their life becomes organized around it: searching for it, using it, enjoying it, and searching for more. Authorities differ on whether all such persons—whom we shall call "addicts,"though the term is not well-defined and its scientific status is questionable—are invariably physiologically dependent on the drug, as evidenced by painful "withdrawal"symptoms that ocur whenever they cease using it. Some persons may crave the drug without being dependent, others may be dependent without craving it. We need not resolve these definitional and medical issues, however, to recognize that many (but not all) heroin users are addicts in the popular sense of the term.

No one knows how many users of various kinds there are, at what rate they have been increasing in number, or what happens to them at the end of their "run." That they *have* increased in number is revealed, not only by the testimony of police and narcotics officers, but by figures on deaths attributed to heroin. Between 1967 and 1971, the number of deaths in Los Angeles County attributed to heroin use more than tripled, and although improved diagnostic skills in the coroner's office may account for some of this increase, it does not (in the opinion of the University of Southern California student task force report) account for it all. A Harvard student task force has used several techniques to estimate the size of the heroin-user population in Boston, and concludes that there was a tenfold increase in the decade of the 1960's. Why that increase occurred, and whether it will continue, are matters about which one can only speculate. The USC group estimated that there are at least fifty thousand addicts in Los Angeles; the Harvard group estimated that there are six thousand in Boston; various sources conventionally refer (with what accuracy we do not know) to the "hundred thousand" addicts in New York.

No one has proposed a fully satisfactory theory to explain the apparent increase in addiction. There are at least four speculative possibilities, some or all of which may be correct. The rise in real incomes during the prosperity of the 1960's may simply have made possible the purchase of more heroin as it made possible the purchase of more automobiles or color television sets. The cult of personal liberation among the young may have led to greater experimentation with heroin as it led to greater freedom in dress and manners and the development of a rock music culture. The war in Vietnam may have both loosened social constraints and given large numbers of young soldiers easy access to heroin supplies and ample incentive (the boredom, fears, and demoralization caused by the war) to dabble in the drug. Finally, the continued disintegration of the lower-income, especially black, family living in the central city may have heightened the importance of street peer groups to the individual and thus (in ways to be discussed later in this essay) placed him in a social environment highly conducive to heroin experimentation. There are, in short, ample reasons to suppose (though few facts to show) that important changes in both the supply of and demand for heroin occurred during the last decade.

Heavy users of heroin, according to their own testimony, tend to be utterly preoccupied with finding and consuming the drug. Given an unlimited supply (that is, given heroin at zero cost), an addict will "shoot up" three to five times a day. Given the price of heroin on the black market—currently, about $10 a bag, with varying numbers of bags used in each fix—some addicts may be able to shoot up only once or twice a day. The sensations associated with heroin use by most novice addicts are generally the same: keen anticipation of the fix, the "rush"when the heroin begins to work in the bloodstream, the euphoric "high," the drowsy or "nodding" stage as the "high" wears off, and then the beginnings of the discomfort caused by the absence of heroin. For the veteran addict, the "high"may no longer be attainable, except perhaps at the risk of a lethal overdose. For him, the sensations induced by heroin have mainly to do with anesthetizing himself against withdrawal pain—and perhaps against most other feelings as well—together with a ritualistic preoccupation with the needle and the act of injection.

The addict is intensely present-oriented. Though "dabblers" or other episodic users may save heroin for a weekend fix, the addict can rarely save any at all. Some, for example, report that they would like to arise in the morning with enough heroin for a "wake-up" fix, but almost none have the self-control to go to sleep at night leaving unused heroin behind. Others report getting enough heroin to last them for a week, only to shoot it all the first day. How many addicts living this way can manage a reasonably normal family and work life is not known, but clearly many cannot. Some become heroin dealers in order to earn money, but a regular heavy user seldom has the self-control to be successful at this enterprise for long. Addicts-turned-dealers frequently report a sharp increase in their heroin use as they consume much of their sales inventory.

It is this craving for the drug, and the psychological states induced by its use, that are the chief consequences of addiction; they are also the most important consequences about which, ultimately, one must have a moral or political view, whatever the secondary effects of addiction that are produced by current public policy. At the same time, one should not suppose that all of these secondary effects can be eliminated by changes in policy. For example, while there are apparently no specific pathologies—serious illnesses or physiological deterioration—that are known to result from heroin use *per se*, the addict does run the risk of infections caused by the use of unsterile needles, of poisoning as a result of shooting an overdose (or a manageable dose that has been cut with harmful products), and of thrombosed veins as a result of repeated injections. Some of these risks could be reduced if heroin were legally available in clinics operated by physicians, but they could not be eliminated unless literally everyone wishing heroin were given it in whatever dosage, short of a lethal one, he wished. In Great Britain, where pure heroin is legally available at low prices, addicts still have medical problems arising out of their use of the drug—principally,

unsterile self-injections, involuntary overdoses, and voluntary overdoses (that is, willingly injecting more than they should in hopes of obtaining a new "high"). If, as will be discussed below, heroin were injected under a doctor's supervision (as it is not in England), the risk of sepsis and of overdoses would be sharply reduced—but at the cost of making the public heroin clinic less attractive to addicts who wish to consume not merely a maintenance dose but a euphoria-producing (and therefore risky) one.

WHY HEROIN?

No generally accepted theory supported by well-established facts exists to explain why some persons but not others become addicts. It is easy to make a list of factors that increase (statistically, at least) the risk of addiction: Black males living in low-income neighborhoods, coming from broken or rejecting families, and involved in "street life" have much higher chances of addiction than upper-middle-class whites in stable families and "normal" occupations. But some members of the latter category *do* become addicted and many members of the former category do not; why this should be the case, no one is sure. It is easy to argue that heroin use occurs only among people who have serious problems (and thus to argue that the way to end addiction is to solve the underlying problems), but in fact many heavy users seem to have no major problems at all. Isidor Chein and his co-workers in their leading study of addiction in New York (*The Road to H*) found that between a quarter and a third of addicts seemed to have no problems for which heroin use was a compensation.

Though we cannot predict with much confidence who will and who will not become an addict, we can explain why heroin is used and how its use spreads. The simple fact is that heroin use is intensely pleasurable, for many people more pleasurable than anything else they might do. Heroin users will have experimented with many drugs, and when heroin is hard to find they may return to alcohol or other drugs, but for the vast majority of users heroin remains the drug of choice. The nature of the pleasure will vary from person to person—or, perhaps, the interpretive description of that pleasure will vary—but the desire for it remains the governing passion of the addicts' lives. All of us enjoy pleasure; an addict is a person who has found the supreme pleasure and the means to make that pleasure recur.

This fact helps explain why "curing" addiction is so difficult (for many addicts, virtually impossible) and how new addicts are recruited. Addicts sent to state or federal hospitals to be detoxified—i.e., to be withdrawn from heroin use—almost invariably return to such use after their release, simply because using it is so much more pleasurable than not using it, regardless of cost. Many addicts, probably a majority, resist and resent oral methadone maintenance because methadone, though it can prevent withdrawal pains, does not, when taken orally, supply them with the euphoric "high" they associate with heroin. (The intravenous use of methadone will produce a "high" comparable to that of heroin. The oral use of methadone is seen by addicts as a way to avoid the pain of heroin withdrawal but not as an alternative source of a "high.") Persons willingly on methadone tend to be older addicts who are "burned out," i.e., physically and mentally run down by the burdens of maintaining a heroin habit. A younger addict still enjoying his "run" (which may last five or 10 years) will be less inclined to shift to methadone.

THE "CONTAGION" MODEL

When asked how they got started on heroin, addicts almost universally give the same answer: They were offered some by a friend. They tried it, often in a group setting, and found they liked it. Though not every person who tries it will like it, and not every person who likes it will become addicted to it, a substantial fraction (perhaps a quarter) of first users become regular and heavy users. Heroin use spreads through peer-group contacts, and those peer groups most vulnerable to experimenting with it are those that include a person who himself has recently tried it and whose enthusiasm for it is contagious. In fact, so common is this process that many observers use the word "contagious" or "contagion" deliberately—the spread of heroin use is in the nature of an epidemic in which a "carrier" (a recent and enthusiastic convert to heroin) "infects" a population with whom he is in close contact.

A recent study in Chicago has revealed in some detail how this process of infection occurs. Patrick H. Hughes and Gail A. Crawford found that a major heroin "epidemic" occurred in Chicago after World War II, reaching a peak in 1949, followed by a decline in the number of new cases of addiction during the 1950's, with signs of a new epidemic appearing in the early 1960's. They studied closely 11 neighborhood-sized epidemics that they were able to identify in the late 1960's, each producing 50 or more new addicts. In the great majority of cases, not only was the new user turned on by a friend, but the friend was himself a novice user still exhilarated by the thrill of a "high." Both recruit and initiator tended to be members of a small group that had already experimented heavily with many drugs and with alcohol. These original friendship groups broke up as the heavy users formed new associations in order to maintain their habits. Strikingly, the new user usually does not seek out heroin the first time he uses it, but rather begins to use it almost fortuitously, by the accident of personal contact in a polydrug subculture. In these groups, a *majority* of the members usually try heroin after it is introduced by one of them, though not all of these become addicted.

Such a theory explains the very rapid rates of increase that have occurred in a city such as Boston. The number of new users will be some exponential function of the number of initial users. Obviously, this geometric growth rate would soon, if not checked by other factors, make addicts of us all. Since we are not all going to become addicts, other factors must be at work, though their nature is not well understood. They may include "natural immunity" (some of us may find heroin unpleasant), breaks in the chain of contagion (caused by the absence of any personal linkages between peer groups that are using heroin and peer groups that are not), and the greater difficulty of finding a supply of heroin in some communities than others. *Perhaps most important, the analogy between heroin use and disease is imperfect: We do not choose to contract smallpox from a friend, but we do choose to use heroin offered by a friend.*

THE MYTH OF THE "PUSHER"

If heroin use is something we choose, then the moral and empirical judgments one makes about heroin become important. If a person thinks heroin use wrong, or if he believes that heroin use can cause a serious pathology, then, other things being equal, he will be less likely to use it than if he made the opposite judgments. Chein found that the belief that heroin use was wrong was a major reason given by heroin "dabblers" for not continuing in its use. The extent to which the belief in the wrongness of heroin use depends on its being illegal is unknown—but it is interesting to note that many addicts tend to be strongly opposed to legalizing heroin.

The peer-group/contagion model also helps explain why the fastest increase in heroin use has been among young people, with the result that the average age of known addicts has fallen sharply in the last few years. In Boston, the Harvard student group found that one quarter of heroin users seeking help from a public agency were under the age of 18, and 80 per cent were under the age of 25. A study done at American University found that the average age at which identifiable addicts in Washington, D.C., began using heroin was under 19. Though stories of youngsters under 15 becoming addicts are commonplace, most studies place the beginning of heavy use between the ages of 17 and 19.

It is persons in this age group, of course, who are most exposed to the contagion: They are intensely involved in peer groups; many have begun to become part of "street society," because they had either dropped out of or graduated from schools; and they are most likely to suffer from boredom and a desire "to prove themselves." It is claimed that many of those who become serious addicts "mature out" of their heroin use sometime in their thirties, in much the same way that many juvenile delinquents spontaneously cease committing criminal acts when they get older. Unfortunately, not much is known about "maturing out," and it is even possible that it is a less common cause of ending heroin use than death or imprisonment.

If this view of the spread of addiction is correct, then it is pointless to explain heroin use as something that "pushers" inflict on unsuspecting youth. The popular conception of a stranger in a dirty trench coat hanging around schoolyards and corrupting innocent children is largely myth—indeed, given what we know about addiction, it would almost have to be myth. No dealer in drugs is likely to risk doing business with strangers. The chances of apprehension are too great and the profits from dealing with friends too substantial to make missionary work among unknown "straights" worthwhile. And the novice user is far more likely to take the advice of a friend, or to respond to the blandishments of a peer group, than to take an unfamiliar product from an anonymous pusher.

An important implication of the peer-group/contagion model is that programs designed to treat or control established addicts may have little effect on the mechanism whereby heroin use spreads. Users tend to be "infectious" only early in their heroin careers (later, all their friends are addicts and the life style seems less glamorous), and at this stage they are not likely to volunteer for treatment or to come to the attention of police authorities. In the Chicago study, for example, Hughes and Crawford found that police efforts directed at addiction were intensified only after the peak of the epidemic had passed, and though arrests increased sharply, they were principally of heavily addicted regular users, not of the infectious users. *No matter whether one favors a medical or a law-enforcement approach to heroin, the optimum strategy depends crucially on whether one's objective is to "treat" existing addicts or to prevent the recruitment of new ones.*

CRIME AND HEROIN

The amount of crime committed by addicts is no doubt large, but exactly how large is a matter of conjecture. And most important, the amount of addict crime undertaken solely to support the habit, *and thus the amount by which crime would decrease if the price of heroin fell to zero, is unknown.* Estimates of the proportion of all property crime committed by addicts range from 25 to 67 per cent. Whatever the true fraction, there is no reason to assume that property crimes would decline by that fraction if heroin became free. Some addicts are criminals before they are addicts and would remain criminals if their addiction, like their air and water, cost them virtually nothing. Furthermore, some addicts who steal to support their habit come to regard crime as more profitable than normal employment. They would probably continue to steal to provide themselves with an income even after they no longer needed to use part of that income to buy heroin.

Just as it is wrong to suppose that an unwitting youth has heroin "pushed" on him, so also it is wrong to suppose that these youth only then turn to crime to support their habit. Various studies of known addicts have shown that between half and three quarters were known to be delinquent *before* turning to drugs. In a random sample of adult Negro males studied in St. Louis (14 per cent of whom turned out to have records for using or selling narcotics), 60 per cent of those who tried heroin and 73 per cent of those who became addicted to it had previously acquired a police record. Put another way, one quarter of the delinquents, but only four per cent of the nondelinquents, became heroin addicts.

That addicts are recruited disproportionately from the ranks of those who already have a criminal history may be a relatively recent phenomenon. The history of heroin use in New York City compiled by Edward Preble and John J. Casey, Jr. suggests that in the period before 1951 heroin use grew slowly and often occurred through "snorting" (inhaling the powder) rather than "mainlining" (injecting liquefied heroin into a vein). The heroin used was of high quality and low cost, and its consumption took place in social settings in which many users were not criminals but rather entertainers, musicians, and the like. The heroin epidemic that began around 1951 was caused by the new popularity of the drug among younger people on the streets, especially street gang members looking for a new "high." (Indeed, one theory of the break-up of those gangs romanticized in *West Side Story* is that heroin use became a status symbol, such that the young man "nodding" on the corner or hustling and dealing in dope became the figure to be emulated, rather than the fighter and the leader of gang wars. A group of heavy addicts, each of whom is preoccupied with his own "high," will soon find collective action—and thus gang life—all but impossible.) Mainlining became commonplace, the increased demand led to a rise in price and a decline in quality of the available heroin, and the level of heroin-connected crime increased.

Some supportive evidence for the increase in the recruitment of addicts from among the ranks of the criminal is found in a study of white male Kentucky addicts carried out by John A. O'Donnell. He traced the careers of 266 such persons who had been admitted to the U.S. Public Health Service Hospital in Lexington from its opening in 1935. The earlier the year in which the person first became addicted, the less the likelihood of his having a prior criminal record. Only five per cent of those addicted before 1920, but 47 per cent of those addicted between 1950 and 1959, had a criminal record before they became addicted. Furthermore, the younger the age of a man when he first became addicted, the more likely he was to have committed criminal acts *before* addiction. The proportion of addicts with criminal records, and perhaps the rate of increase of those with such records, would probably be greater among a more typical population of addicts—for example, among urban blacks.

Once addicted, however, persons are likely to commit more crimes than they would have had they not become addicted. The common and tragic testimony of street addicts dwells upon their need to find the money with which to support the habit, and this means for many of them "hustling," stealing heroin from other users,- dealing in heroin themselves, or simply begging. The O'Donnell study in Kentucky provides statistical support for this view, though no estimate of the amount by which crime increases as a result of addiction.

The kinds of crimes committed by addicts are fairly well known. Selling heroin is perhaps the most important of these—the Hudson Institute estimated that almost half of the annual heroin consumption in New York is financed by selling heroin and related services (for example, selling or renting the equipment needed for injecting heroin). Of the non-drug crimes, shoplifting, burglary, and prostitution account for the largest proportion of addict income used for drug purchases—perhaps 40 to 50 per cent. Though the addict wants money, he will not confine himself only to those crimes where property is taken with no threat to personal safety. Muggings and armed robberies will be committed regularly by some addicts and occasionally by many; even in a burglary, violence may result if the addict is surprised by the victim while ransacking the latter's home or store.

The amount of property taken by addicts is large, but probably not as large as some of the more popular estimates would have us believe. Max Singer (in *The Public Interest,* No. 23, Spring 1971) has shown that those who make these estimates—usually running into the billions of dollars per year in New York City alone—fail to reconcile their figures with the total amount of property known or suspected to be stolen. He estimated that no more than $500 million a year is lost to both addicted and non-addicted burglars, shoplifters, pickpockets, robbers, and assorted thieves in New York each year. If *all* of that were taken by addicts (which of course it isn't) and if there were 100,000 addicts in the city, then the average addict would be stealing about $5,000 worth of goods a year—not a vast sum. Even the more conservative figure of 60,000 addicts would raise the maximum average theft loss per addict to only $8,000.

Despite the fact that many addicts were criminals before addiction and would remain criminals even if they ended their addiction, and despite the fact that the theft losses to addicts are considerably exaggerated, there is little doubt that addiction produces a significant increase in criminality of two kinds—stealing from innocent victims and selling heroin illegally to willing consumers. More accurately, the heroin black market provides incentives for at least two kinds of anti-social acts—theft (with its attendant fear) and further spreading the use of heroin.

Sex Offenses

THIS SECTION ON SEX CRIMES FOCUSES ON FORMS OF OFFENSES THAT HAVE newly arisen or have come to prominence through social movements such as the women's rights movement in its concern over the crime of rape. Rape is, of course, an ancient offense, but recent concern has largely centered on the victim and the manner in which she is handled within the criminal justice system. A large number of polemic articles and books have appeared but, incredibly, very few careful studies have been produced that seriously examine the rapist himself. The Queen's Bench Foundation pilot study of 164 rapists is a limited but admirable examination of the general demographic characteristics of the rapists, plus some fascinating, if tragic, data on the elements of the sexual assault itself, particularly factors that go into the selection of the rape victim by the assailant.

Teenage prostitution appears to be on the increase. Gray examines the early sexual experiences, "turning out" (becoming a prostitute), occupational problems, and associated hazards with pimps and customers. Another urban development involves the rapid proliferation of so-called "massage parlors" that are frequently a front for a new form of the older houses of prostitution. The massage parlor setting, the masseuse role, the meaning of sexual professionalism, problems of rate busting and arrest are all detailed by Rasmussen. Finally, a seldom-described comparatively specialized form of illegal sexual activity, homosexual prostitution, is considered by Gagnon and Simon. They trace the "gay" as a client, characteristics of the sexual interaction, and elements of risk and types of prostitutes.

69. The Rapist and His Crime

QUEEN'S BENCH FOUNDATION

RESEARCH METHOD

THIS RESEARCH WAS INITIATED AS A PILOT STUDY to explore the dynamics of sexual assault from the perspective of the sexual offender. To date prevention information has evolved exclusively from victim accounts and analysis of crime reports; studies of rapists have focused on psychodynamics of offenders and treatment. Our research is directed towards understanding what precipitates a man to rape a particular woman, and what stops him.

As with the victim study, this research analyzed incidents of completed and deterred sexual assault, and in particular it focused on (1) factors contributing to commission of the crime, (2) characteristics of the crime scenes, and offender and victim behaviors before, during, and after the assault, (3) methods of resistance used by rape and attempted rape victims, (4) differences between completed and deterred sexual assaults, and (5) the relationship between resistance and injury.

Inquiry was guided by a series of specific questions:

1. What is a man seeking when he rapes or attempts to rape?

2. Does a rapist plan his attack?

3. Is a victim selected beforehand? If so, why is a particular woman selected?

4. Does an assailant perceive the woman he attacks as having influenced[1] his commission of the crime?

5. To what extent does his decision to rape include violence?

6. In the assailant's perception, is the amount of violence influenced by the victim? If so, to what extent?

7. What factors cause intensification of the degree and type of violence inflicted upon the victim?

8. What factors are associated with deterrence of rape?

9. How does an assailant respond to victim resistance?

10. How does an assailant account for his rape or other sexual assault?

11. Finally, what ideas do rapists have for ways in which a victim can deter a rape attack; and what can women do to avoid being raped?

Because injury and possibility of death are major issues in considering resistance to rape, this study concentrated on offenders who used "excessive violence" in commission of the as-

▶SOURCE: *Rape: Prevention and Resistance. San Francisco: Queen's Bench Foundation, 1976, pp. 59–76, 79–87, 92–94. (Editorial adaptations.) Reprinted by permission.*

---

[1]"Influence" is used here in a neutral sense, not to impute blame on the victim. It reflects the *assailant's perception* of the chain of events and factors which affected his commission of the crime.

sault, (i.e., force or threat of force exceeding the violence of rape itself). Special attention was addressed to factors pertinent to exacerbation of aggression and violence: what triggered the violence, was the injury intentional, what types and degrees of injury were inflicted, and what might victims have done to prevent infliction of injury?

The selection of excessively violent rapists for the study provided important insights regarding victim injury, however, it must be remembered that the research findings reflect the choice of this sample population: if the research had included non-excessively violent rapists, the correlations of violence with other elements of the attacks would have been significantly reduced. What was important in this study was the exploration of the factors which influenced violence *in those cases where it occurred.*

The lack of prior research on rapists determined the exploratory nature of this study. This report is therefore a compilation of the data received in response to a series of more detailed questions encompassing the issues outlined above, a discussion of the significant relationships between certain variables in the study identified through data analysis, the identification of those variables that seemed to impinge most significantly upon violence and deterrence, and finally, a few suggested hypotheses and tentative explanations for key trends observed in the data.

Definitions

For the purpose of this study, specific meanings were assigned to the following terms:

1. "Rape" was defined as forced vaginal or anal penetration of a woman, or forced oral copulation (fellatio and cunnilingus).

2. "Attempted rape" was an assault which stopped short of vaginal or anal penetration or oral copulation, but in which the assailant's intent (through verbal or physical indications) to commit such an act was clear.

3. "Excessive violence" meant force or the

threat of force excessive of that necessary to accomplish a rape and exceeding the violence of rape itself, e.g., serious bodily harm to the victim, use of a lethal weapon, strangulation or other forms of force which might result in serious bodily harm or death but which do not necessarily leave noticeable injuries, prolonged beating of the victim; severe restriction of the victim's physical movements by binding or physical force, etc.

4. "Deterrence" signified the interruption of a specific attack (i.e., rape was not accomplished).

5. "Prevention" was used in a larger sense, to mean the curbing of rape attacks in general, before the inception of particular incidents.

6. Mentally Disordered Sex Offenders (MDSO) is defined by Section 6300 of the Welfare and Institution Code of California, as "any person who by reason of mental defect, disease, or disorder is predisposed to the commission of sexual offenses to such a degree that he is dangerous to the health and safety of others."

Data Collection

The interview method was the primary data collection technique, supplemented by a review of participant's medical records which contained information on the offense described during the interview. Unlike a self-administered questionnaire (which is often met with a low response rate among research participants), the interview approach seemed to hold greater potential for a high response rate and for comprehensiveness and clarity in responses. Since the research was exploratory in nature, the interview format allowed an opportunity for the interviewer to probe and to raise other questions in order to assist the participant in recollecting details of the assault and to clarify obscure or inconsistent responses. The review of participants' medical charts was useful for the verification of background data on the offender and the offense.

Development. Two types of research instruments were used: an interview schedule and data sheets for the background information from the offender's records. Preparation of the interview protocol was preceded by a detailed examination of Queen's Bench Foundation's 1975 interviews with rape victims and a review of the available literature on rapists. The draft interview schedules were submitted to the Research Committee at Atascadero State Hospital. (This committee includes hospital staff who have conducted research on sex offenders and who have supervised therapy programs for rapists; their comments aided the refinement of the interview schedules.) The final format was approved by the Research Committee prior to implementation of the research.

The interview schedule was partially structured, with the majority of the questions open-ended. The schedule included 49 questions arranged in three broad categories:

1. A series of background questions covering demographic variables, age, ethnicity, education, etc., and prior criminal record (both sexual and non-sexual offenses).

2. The participant's account of the rape incident, followed by specific questions regarding the assault, arranged sequentially: what was happening in the participant's life *immediately prior to the rape*; what factors led to the attack itself; why was a particular woman selected; what signalled the beginning of the rape; how did the victim respond; what violence was used; and what injuries were inflicted.

3. Questions regarding victims' resistance and rape deterrence in the specific case under investigation, and prevention of rape in general.

Administration. Research staff met with the sex offenders selected as eligible for the study (see "Subject Population" below) to explain the purpose, nature, and procedures for the research, and to answer questions regarding the study. The voluntary nature of the research was stressed, and participants were offered $2.50 to participate. Offenders who chose to participate in the research signed consent forms and were scheduled for interviews.

The research was conducted over a period of four days at Atascadero State Hospital. Interviews, each lasting between one and two hours, were conducted by six women staff members of Queen's Bench Foundation; 3 interviews were conducted in Spanish. For security purposes, all but three interviews were conducted in a large multi-purpose room, however, the individual interview tables were several yards apart to insure full privacy during the interviews. The remaining three interviews were conducted in private rooms connected to the wards; one interview was conducted under maximum security. With the permission of the participants the majority of interviews were audio-taped.

Confidentiality. Stringent precautions were taken to preserve confidentiality, both to protect the offender from misuse of information and to reduce bias in the data collection. The questions were limited to only those offenses for which the participant had been *charged*, and all names mentioned during the interviews were erased from the audio-tapes. All interview schedules and data sheets are identified by numbers, and no list exists to match participants names to those numbers. Access to research materials is limited to Queen's Bench Foundation staff, Atascadero State Hospital, and those deemed to have legitimate research interests.

Subject Population

Contacts with the California Department of Corrections and Department of Health resulted in the selection of Atascadero State Hospital as the most feasible site for research with a rapist population.

Atascadero State Hospital has a current population of approximately 1,000 men, including approximately 18% of all convicted rapists in California. It is a maximum security institution specializing in particular in the treatment of mentally disordered sex offenders (MDSO's). The offender/patients are returned to the courts when the hospital recommends their release from the hospital, either because they have improved and are not a danger to others or because they are *not* improved and are still a danger but would not benefit from further treatment.

Of the hospital's total population, 16.4% (164 patients) are rapists. A brief demographic summary follows:

1. MDSO's comprise 42% (420) of the total population. Of these, 55% are pedophiles (child molesters); 40% are rapists; and 5% are other sexual offenders, e.g., exhibitionists, voyeurs, etc.

2. The remaining 58% (580) are categorized as not competent to stand trial. This group included those men whom the courts have declared not guilty by reason of insanity or not able to stand trial, transfers from the Department of Corrections for purposes of accomodation, and conservatees, i.e., men who are unable to provide themselves with clothing and shelter.

Because the researchers anticipated severe psychiatric disorders among the offenders, this possible sample bias was closely investigated. Hospital authorities assured us that despite the MDSO (Mentally Disordered Sexual Offender) classification of the offender/patients, the men at Atascadero were (with few exceptions) not seriously mentally disordered and that they were fully capable and suitable for participation in the study.

The research sample was necessarily clustered in type, i.e., it included all the men at the hospital who fell within the excessively violent rapist category. Because of the particular sentencing system for commitment to the hospital, representativeness in the sample cannot be assumed, and the hospital population differs from other convicted rapist populations (e.g., at prisons) on characteristics such as racial composition, socio-economic status, etc.

The Atascadero population did provide several advantages. Some of the men had been exposed to research at the hospital before, and they seemed eager to contribute to what they saw as an academic and potentially therapeutic project. Because of participation in therapy groups at the hospital, they were open about their rape experiences, although their therapy exposure may have introduced a degree of treatment bias into their responses (e.g., in the usage of psychiatric and psychological terms and explanations for past behavior). Hospital records were made available for verification of interview information, as well as for the collection of additional data. Finally, the population's accessibility and the interest and support of the hospital staff were valuable to the entire data collection process.

The seven program directors who had rapists under their supervision assisted with selection of the subjects. The project goals and the need for a specific type of participant (i.e., excessively violent rapists) as well as the criteria for identifying this particular type of rapist were explained to the program directors. Then rape and attempted rape offenses committed by prospective participants were discussed with ward staff, and Queen's Bench Foundation staff reviewed the hospital medical charts of the rapists to determine eligibility for the study.

The initial sample pool included 83 excessively violent rapists. The research was discussed with all the men in this pool, and 82 signed up for interviews.

Seven (7) of the original 82 offenders did not show up for the interview, in most cases because of medical or disciplinary restriction or because they were no longer interested in participating. A total of 75 interviews were conducted, however two homosexual rape cases were excluded from data analysis because of unique features of their crimes.

Overall, the participants were overwhelmingly young, white, high school graduates, primarily skilled or service workers, with varied criminal backgrounds.

76.8% were 29 years old or under.

75.3% were white.

68.5% were single.

50.7% were high school graduates.

68.5% had previously held skilled jobs (furniture maker, construction, automechanic, welder, truck driver, etc.) or service jobs (cook, maintenance worker, gardener, laborer, etc.); 24.7% (18) had held semi-professional jobs (optical technician, psychiatric technician, police cadet, etc.).

78.1% had incurred previous charges for non-sexual offenses (burglary, attempted murder, assault with a deadly weapon, larceny, drunk driving, etc.).

57.5% had been charged previously with attempted rape, 76.2% (32) were charged with one previous offense, and 23.8% (10) with two such offenses.

69.9% had at least one prior rape charge.

45.2% had prior charges for sexual assault other than rape or attempted rape (oral copulation, kidnapping, sodomy, child molesting, etc.).

Data Analysis

The small sample size exerted considerable constraint on the data, limiting the type and number of statistical tests that could be used for analysis. Testing[2] and analyses were limited to 73

---

[2] Very briefly, the frequency distribution stage of data analysis provides the basic *distributional characteristics*, degree of variability, etc. of each of the variables to be used in subsequent statistical analysis. Pearson's correlation measures the *strength of relationship* between two variables. Factor analysis enables *data reduction* by providing new factors/variables for subsequent statistical analysis. One function of multiple regression is to allow an analysis of the relationship between a criterion (dependent) variable and a set of predictor variables. Among other uses it indicates the extent to which certain variables predict another. (For a full descrip-

interviews, and proceeded in the following sequence:

1. Frequency distribution for a descriptive summary of all the responses.

2. Pearson's correlational analysis for the identification of relationships between parts of variables in the study.

3. Two sets of factor analysis to allow consolidation of the numerous items measuring victim resistance and offender violence, and an additional correlational analysis using the new variables generated by the factor analysis.

4. A multiple regression analysis using rape deterrence and completion of rape as dependent variables. This was based on several relationships established by Pearson's correlation.

RESEARCH FINDINGS

Demographic Characteristics

The frequency of various characteristics of victims and offenders in this research shows striking similarity to characteristics derived from other studies discussed in the literature on rape; in addition, demographic characteristics which emerged from this research were consistent with demographic characteristics found in the Queen's Bench Foundation victim research.

Age. Offenders and their victims were between 16 and 35 years at the time of the sexual assault. Most were 23 years and under. The offender study found the following age groupings:

69.9% (51) of the offenders compared to 63% (49) of the victims were 25 and under *at the time of the offense.* Within this group, 13% (10) of the victims were between 10 and 15 years old at the time of the offense.

---

tion, see: Hubert Blalock, *Social Statistics*, New York: McGraw-Hill Book Company, 1960.)

20.5% (15) offenders compared to 9.3% (5) victims were between 26 and 30 years in age.

4.1% (3) offenders compared to 2.7% (2) victims were between 31 and 35 years old at the time of the offense.

5.3% (4) offenders compared to 13.3% (10) victims were 36 years and above.

These figures are not large enough to draw strong conclusions, but they indicate that rape is not entirely a peer phenomenon. There were several instances where offenders attacked women several years older or younger than themselves:there were 10 victims under 15 years in age, and 3 who were 50 and over.

Ethnicity.   Typically offenders were of the same race and ethnic group as their victims.

75.3% (55) of the offenders compared to 74% (54) of the victims were white.

Marital Status

93.2% (67) of the offenders were single (includes divorced or separated) compared to 60.3% (44) victims who were single.

6.8% (5) of the offenders and 12.3% (9) of the victims were married.

Number of Assailants.   The vast majority of instances (94.5%) involved a solitary assailant and a solitary victim. Three cases involved two assailants, and one involved four. There were four cases with two victims.

Victim/Offender Relationship.   The majority of rape attacks (78%) in this study involved strangers.

78% (57) of the offenders were strangers to the victims; although 20.5%(15) of these men had seen their victims before, acquaintance was extremely superficial.

21.9% of the cases involved victims and offenders who were friends of some sort.

In two instances, victim and offender were related.

Times and Dates of Offense

62.9% (46) of the offenses were committed between Thursday and Sunday with frequencies peaking on Friday (20.5%) and Sunday (17.8%).

50.7% (37) occurred at night; 34.2% (25) were committed during the afternoon, and 15.1% (11) during the morning.

Characteristics of Sexual Assault
The Setting of the Attack.   Almost as many offenders first encountered their victims at home as outside.

39.7% (29) of the offenders first encountered the victim in her home or nearby, e.g., getting into her car.

27.4% (20) encountered the victim on the street.

27.4% (20) encountered the victim at some other public place, e.g., bar, restaurant, grocery store, parking lot, bowling alley, school campus, etc.

5.5% (4) met the victim at the assailant's or a mutual friend's home.

Assailant activity at the time of the first encounter with victims shows an important trend with respect to the assailant's motivations that day.[3]

52.1% (38) stated that they were out looking for a victim to rape.[4]

23.3% (17) said they were either just "hanging

---

[3]Due to multiple responses to interview questions, percentages throughout this text will not necessarily add to 100%.

[4]Most of these men explicitly said "rape." Others said "sex" but when probed further, indicated they knew it had to be forcible sex. A small number said they were hoping to seduce their victims but anticipated opposition from the women and expected they would have to force compliance.

out," standing around looking for something to do, or sitting around drinking and talking at a public place, such as a bar, restaurant, or school campus.

21.9% (16) were driving their cars (10) or riding or walking casually on the street (6).

2.7% (2) said they were burglarizing the victim.

Rapist's Activity Prior to the Sexual Assault. The offenders generally mentioned a recent disappointment which caused a high degree of frustration, depression, or anger just prior to their rape attacks. Several acknowledged planning the rape, and many described the disappointing or depressing experiences as *causal* to the rape. A considerable number recalled consuming alcohol after their disappointments but before their rapes. The following summarizes the events preceding the rapes.

76.7% (56) of the offenders said they were feeling frustrated, depressed, angry, or rejected before they planned and/or committed their attacks.

57.5% (42) felt very strongly so, and 19.2% (14) felt somewhat so.

There was some variation in the source of the disappointment, but typically, it resulted from an argument or fight with a wife or girlfriend.

47.9% (35) attributed their disappointments to an argument or fight with wives or girlfriends.

20.5% (15) said that it was not necessarily a recent experience but rather a welling up of previous disappointments that were intensified by a recent incident.

13.7% (10) experienced a disappointment over work or money, with parents or siblings, or with other friends.

The extent of alcohol and drug use among the offenders immediately before their rape attacks was high. However, it should be noted that a correlational analysis of the data (discussed later) did not show any significant relationship between alcohol or drug use and intent to rape or actual rape.

61.6% (45) had been drinking before their assaults; 41.1% (30) drank liquor such as rum, whiskey, or wine, while the remainder drank beer.

35.6% (26) said they had been drinking heavily, 15.1% (11) moderately, and the rest only had a little to drink that day.

38.4% (28) had used drugs of some sort, mostly marijuana (32.6%); 61.6%(45) reported no drug use.

Planning of the Rape. The assailant's activity during his assessment and planning of the rape suggests some important trends. For example, 79.5% (58) said *that they were watching their victims before they approached them*. Significantly too, 20.5% (15) reported they had seen their victims twice on the day of the rape incident; they committed their attacks the second time. Although this number is relatively small, its implications should be considered: in *certain instances* the rapist may assess and plan a rape attack after locating a potential victim, returning later to execute the rape. *A considerable amount of forethought about rape* was indicated by the offenders' responses to a question about what they were thinking of when they approached their victims that day.

68.5% (50)—over two-thirds—of the men said they were thinking of rape.[5]

26% (19) stated they were thinking of something casual, such as ordinary conversation,

---

[5]Here again, many of these men explicitly said "rape." The others said "sex" but with further questioning, indicated they knew the sex had to be forcible as they did not expect the victims to comply.

companionship, helping the victim by giving her a ride someplace, etc., or of nothing in particular.

4.1% (3) were thinking of robbing the victim.

One offender claimed that it was the victim who approached him.

The offenders were next asked what they were hoping would happen when they approached their victims.

71.2% (52) said they were hoping the victim would comply with their expectations.

21.9% (16) said they were not hoping for anything in particular.

2.7% (2) stated they were hoping to acquire money.

The next series of questions probed deeper into the nature of the offender's planning of the assault. The men were asked, for example, about intent to have sexual contact that day, intent to use violence, possession of weapon, type of weapon, regularity of possession of weapon, and familiarity of victim.

67.1% (49) said they intended to have sexual contact that day.

67.1% (49) said they had not intended to use violence that day, *but 32.9% said that they anticipated having to use violence that day.*

69.9% (51), however, *in spite of the sizable proportion who reported no intent to use violence, had a weapon that day in their possession.* About half of the armed attackers, 35.6% (26) stated that they usually carried a weapon.

47.9% (35) were armed with knives including butcher knives, paring knives, or switchblades; 15.1% (15) were carrying guns; and 6.8% (5) had other kinds of weapons—often meat forks. One offender had a club which he had made

himself; another had a screwdriver; another had handcuffs; and one had a rock. Some of the rapists used rope and clothing found at the victims' house to tie or gag the women.

78% (57) of the offenders defined their victims as strangers, but *38.4%(28) indicated they had a particular woman in mind before the rape, and 34.2% (25) identified that woman as the eventual victim.*

The response patterns in this set of items suggests a clear trend in the phenomenon of rape in this study: it is quite evident from the distributions noted above, that in the planning stages of the attack, the majority of the offenders were thinking of *forcible* sex.

Victim Selection.   The participants' were asked what factors influenced their selection of a particular victim. Close to two-thirds (61.7%) of the offenders stated they chose a particular victim because she was available ("she was there") and/or defenseless. Selection factors were further delineated as follows (see Figure 1):

82.2% (60) of the offenders said they chose a particular victim because she was available.

71.2% (52) said because she was defenseless.

46.6% (34) said because they saw her as sexy (for example, she may have been dressed in clothes they found sexually arousing; several commented that they felt other men might not perceive her to be "sexy").

42.5% (33) said because they found her physical appearance attractive. (There was little consistency in their criteria for attractiveness.)

39.7% (29) stated they chose their victims because they were the "right age" (which ranged from young girls 15 and under to women their own age, to 50 and over).

24.7% (18) claimed they selected their victims because they saw them as "loose"women (waitresses, hitchhikers who looked like hippies, and

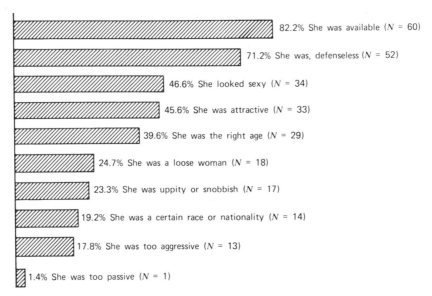

Figure 1. Factors in selection of rape victim.

women who were said to have had sexual relationships with more than one man, for example, were described as "loose women.")

For other offenders, the selection of the victim was based on entirely different grounds: 23.3% (17) cited victim aggressiveness, and 17.8% (13) cited victim snobbishness as well as aggressiveness.

Initiation of the Sexual Assault. The research explored in detail the sequence of the events constituting the sexual assault, beginning with the assailant's first interaction with the victim, victim behavior and rapists' perceptions of her during the interim period before onset of the attack, the initiation of the attack, victim response at this point, and finally, assailant reaction to the victim's response.

When asked about their first interaction with their victims,

39.7% (29) of the offenders stated that they had spoken *casually* to their victims on the street or in another public place, such as a bar, re-staurant, bowling alley, grocery store, or parking lot.

35.6% (26) accomplished their first interaction by *immediately grabbing* the victim and attacking her.

13.7% (10) awakened their victims from sleep.

12.3% (9) said they had knocked on the victim's door to gain entry.

Of particular importance are the cases in which the offender's first interaction occurred after *breaking into* the victim's house: 20.5% (15) of the offenders checked around the victim's house and entered through an unlocked door or window, cut holes through window screens, or knocked on the victim's door and forcibly pushed their way into her house when she opened the door. Two offenders said they were in the process of burglarizing the victim's house when they first interacted with their victims. Two other men were managers of apartment buildings where their victims lived and had easy access to the victims. One had given up his managing job when he committed the rape, but he knew the building very well and came by to visit other people quite often. When he came back to rape, he effortlessly entered the victim's apartment by climbing through a friend's bathroom into an airshaft and down some pipes to the victim's bathroom window. The other offender simply took his keys and entered his victim's apartment.

Of particular importance also are the cases in which the attack was preceded by an interim period of casual conversation: 50.7% (37) offenders indicated that they spoke to the victim casually before becoming openly aggressive in the attack. Duration of this interim period varied but was usually less than an hour.

20.5% (15) of the offenders spent 15 minutes or less in conversation.

21.9% (16) spent between 16 minutes and an hour.

The rest (6) spent two hours or more in conversation.

Usually, offender-victim activity during this interim period included walking, "sitting around" outdoors, or travelling (for example, to the victim's destination or a secluded area). The responses for these two items grouped as follows:

17.8% (13) were walking or "sitting around" outdoors with the victim.

12.3% (9) of the offenders were driving.

9.6% (7) of the offenders were talking with the victims while they (the victim) were at home relaxing (lying on bed, watching television, reading, etc.) or doing household chores.

24.7% (18) said they took their victims some place during this time: 13.7% (10) took her to some private place (victim's bedroom, other part of victim's house, a secluded area off a main street, etc.); 6.8% (5) took her to their house or car; 4.1% (3) took her to the victim's destination.

The offenders' description of their victims' behavior during this interim period showed some similarity. About two-thirds of the men who reported casual conversation described their victims' behavior as friendly.[6]

32.9% (24) of the offenders in the study felt that the victim was friendly.

15.1% (11) described her as scared.

9.6% (7) thought she was calm.

8.2% (6) found her sympathetic.

8.2% (6) described her as snobbish.

In four cases, a period of conversation occurred after the offender had executed an immediate attack on the victim. These four men said they had grabbed their victims, and after successfully intimidating them, tried to calm them through "casual" talk.

It was usually the offender who signalled the beginning of the attack, most often through physical force, the use of a weapon, or physical restraint of the victim: (See Figure 2.)

61.6% (45) of the men used physical force.

57.5% (42) used a weapon and a verbal threat.

43.8% (32) physically restrained the victim; e.g., choking.

Only 13.7% (10) said that they used an oral threat only; oral threats were otherwise accompanied by another signal.

A few of the offenders, 15.1% (11), cited the

---

[6]There is an overlap in these percentages because the victims were placed in more than one category quite often; e.g., a victim was sometimes described as friendly and scared, or friendly and calm, etc.

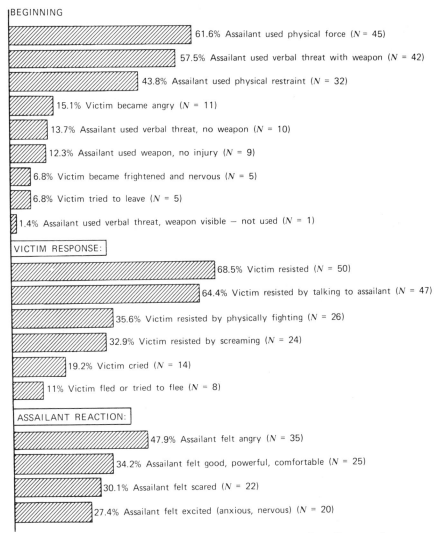

Figure 2.   Signals at beginning of attack, victim response, and assailant reaction.

expression of anger on the part of the victim as signalling the beginning of the attack, and a smaller percentage cited victim nervousness, 6.8% (5), or the victim's attempt to leave, 6.8% (5).

Despite the initiating role offenders played in signalling the beginning of their rape attacks, *45.2% (33) of the offenders claimed that their victims had "provoked" the attack.* A slightly larger percentage, 52.1% (38), stated that their victims did not

influence the attack. Of the 33 men who felt that their victims had contributed to the rape,

24.7% (18) explained that provocation was in the form of victim resistance (physical, oral, or verbal, including insulting the assailant).

17.8% (13) claimed that the victim's attractiveness or friendliness and cooperativeness provoked the attack.

One of the remaining two offenders said he was angered by his victim's passiveness, while the other claimed that he became angry and raped the woman because she confused his attempt to rob her with an attempt to rape.[7]

Victim Resistance and Assailant Reaction. The offender frequently reported that their victims were taken by complete surprise when they were attacked. Yet despite this fact and the frequency with which the offenders used weapons (usually to intimidate victims at the beginning of the attack), *a sizable proportion, 68.5% (50) of the women resisted in some way.* (See Figure 2.)

64.4% (47) questioned their attackers asking, for example, "What are you doing?""Why are you doing this?" "Leave me alone!" "Don't hurt me." "Stop" or "Get out of here!"

35.6% (26) physically fought with their assailants.

32.9% (24) screamed.

19.2% (14) started crying.

11% (8) fled or attempted to flee

The offenders, on the other hand, reported a variety of emotional reactions to the victim's behavior at this point.

47.9% (35) said they felt very angry.

34.2% (25) said they felt powerful, good, dominant, or comfortable.

27.4% (20) said they felt excited (i.e., nervous or anxious).

30.1% (22) said that they felt scared.

It was at this stage, when victims resisted, that many of the men intensified their violence.

54.8% (40) offenders became *angrier* during the attack, and 32 of these attributed this change to victim resistance at the beginning of the attack.

Injury was caused in 61.6% (45) of the rape attacks, 46.5% of which ranged from moderate to extensive injury (such as cuts, severe choking which caused the victim a great deal of discomfort, and injuries from being repeatedly kicked, dragged, beaten, bruised). Very severy injury occurred in 22.7% (17) incidents, and included stabs, bruises, lacerations, etc., which produced a great deal of bleeding or swelling, or which resulted in unconsciousness.

75.3% (55) of the men had a weapon with them during the assault,[8] although only a relatively small proportion, 16% (12), actually used their weapons to inflict injury. *Physical strength* caused most of the injury, 45.2% (33), usually in the form of bruises, cuts, lacerations, and scratches.

54.8% (40) of the men said that the injuries were intentional, not necessarily because they wanted to hurt, but because their expectations were not being met.

Despite the extent and degree of assailant violence, in 32.9% (24) of the attacks, the woman successfully resisted the sexual assault. The men committed the following acts:

65.8% (48) of the men successfully consummated their rapes through coitus.

38.4% (28) had fellatio performed on them.

20.5% (15) performed cunnilingus on their victims.

8.2% (6) sodomized their victims.

Violence in Offenders. Since the role of vio-

---

[7]This offender stated that he saw the woman's confusion, and although he never robs and rapes during the same attack, he raped this victim after robbing her because "she offered it."

[8]This percentage is greater than that for possession of weapons prior to the attack because some offenders went into the victim's kitchen and got knives when she began to resist.

lence was a focus in this study, several questions addressed the events which intensified the violence. *A large majority, 89% (65), said there was a particular point at which they decided to "scare"(i.e., intimidate) or hurt their victims.*

53.4% (39) explained that they had decided to *scare* their victims at the beginning of the attack to force submission; 30.1% (22) decided to scare the victim when she resisted; and four offenders said they decided to scare their victims when they felt that the victim might "blow it" and they would get caught.

24.7% (18) of the men stated that they decided to *hurt* the victim when she started to resist either at the beginning of the attack or during the attack; 8.2%(6) decided to hurt the victim initially to intimidate her into submission; and three said they decided to hurt the victim either when they could not achieve an erection to consummate the rape, or after completing the rape when they thought about the possibility of getting caught. Some men who injured victims stated they did not intentionally hurt them.

Assailant's Expectations.   To further explore what women could have done to mitigate chances of injury, the offenders were asked if there was anything the victim did to cause his intensified violence and how he would have preferred her to respond. They were also asked what she could have done to *stop* him from escalating the violence.

24% (18) stated they were satisfied with the way their rape attacks had progressed.

45.2% (33) said they would have liked their victims to have complied with them, fulfilling their expectations (usually surrender).

12.3% (9) said their expectations would have been met by victim support, sympathy, or "concern (for them) as a person."

11% (8) wanted their victims to struggle more

vigorously, or to act scared so that their feelings of power could have been enhanced.

Over half, 56.2% (41), of the men stated that the victim could have inhibited them from further intimidating or harming her.

27.4% (20) explained that victims could have accomplished this by struggling more vigorously, screaming, or being more assertive (verbally and through body movement); 20% (15) claimed that victims could have accomplished this by simply complying and "enjoying" the experience; and *only 8.2% (6) felt that the expression of "concern as a person" for them by the victim would have been effective.*

Deterrence of Sexual Assault.   Half the offenders, *50.7% (37), believed they could have been deterred.* Quite a few said that if their victims had put up a big struggle they would have "freaked" and run away.

37.1% (27) explained that their victims should have resisted more vigorously orally, physically, and verbally.

6 said that the victim's "concern for the offender as a person" would have deterred them.

5 stated that they would not have proceeded to have intercourse if their victims had complied outright.

Causes of Rape.   When questioned about what they felt influenced them to commit rape, the offenders mentioned a number of factors: poor social relations with women, general inability to develop interpersonal relations, lack of self-confidence, negative self-concept, etc. (See Figure 3.) Developmental psycho-social dynamics of rapists were not a focus of the study and was not explored further.

*

Correlated Data and Regression Analysis
As noted previously, data analysis after the fre-

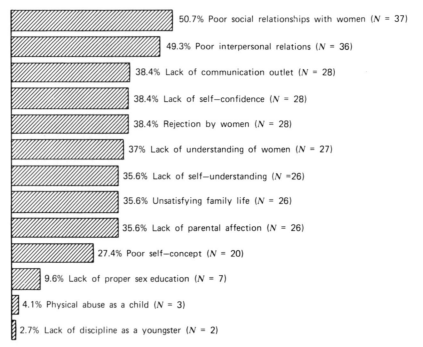

Figure 3.   Causes of rape or attempted rape: offenders' opinions.

quency distribution included the following methods:

1.   Pearson's correlation between the items where relationships were anticipated.

2.   Scale construction of the variables resistance and violence preceded by a factor analysis of the respective item sets, and followed by Pearson's correlation between the new scaled variables resistance and violence, and deterrence.

3.   A multiple regression analysis to determine the extent of predictability of each of six independent variables with respect to deterrence.

Significant findings revealed by these procedures are presented in the format of the questions stated in the research purposes.

1.   What is a man looking for when he rapes?

According to most of the respondents in this study, 50.7% (37), *power* or *dominance* over their victims was their primary goal: "to overpower and control" them. This theme was expressed in a variety of forms:

A 24 year old who had raped a 28 year old woman recounted a story characteristic of others related in the course of the study:

"I walked off from a County farm; I had rape on my mind. I intended to rape off this chick I know . . . but some people came . . I went over to this lady's house . . . I was talking to her, stalling time, really planning how to rip her off . . . By 'rape', I don't just mean intercourse. I mean to go through all the changes—me getting what I wanted. If she had agreed to give me a head job, I would have said, 'No' and not raped her. If she had said, 'yeah, let's go to bed', *I would have said, 'No', as she would have been in control.*"

A 34 year old offender defined rape as *misdirected violence* aimed at the achievement of dominance and power, which he believed most people achieve through communication and love. A 33 year old man who raped a 19 year old hitchhiker explained his rape as a means of expressing a *power-fantasy*:

'My fantasy was—before I stopped—that she was teasing me. So I had an attitude of 'I'll show you' . . . *I wanted power over her* . . . power to overcome my fear of women."

Another 20 year old who raped a 40 year old woman explained:

"She was cooperating. It was fulfilling my fantasy (from before I woke her up). She was doing it just like it was nothing. My fantasy was she would give me what I wanted because I had the knife and she was scared. *I wanted her to be scared to keep me in control.*"

For many of the offenders, exertion of dominance and power included elements of revenge and humiliation. Often it was not sufficient to control the victim, but the offender wished to "put her down" as well. For example, a 21 year old who raped a 42 year old woman said that initially he was seeking sex, but his account suggests more:

"I asked her to go out; she said 'another time' . . . I was interested in sex . . . I continued to tell her I wanted to take her out. She got even more upset . . . She slapped me and called me a punk . . . I got upset, so I knocked the shit out of her. 'I'll show you; you just don't do that to me.' I degraded the shit out of her. I was just getting even dealing with myself . . ."

When the offenders were questioned specifically regarding their intentions as they approached their victim, the vast majority—91.8% (67)—spontaneously identified "rape" as their aim; few came close to implying "innocent" intentions though many said sex was on their mind—65.8% (48). Probing of their expectations regarding this intended sex revealed that they anticipated it would be forcible sex, and often their fantasies included strong elements of dominance and violence.

8.2% (6) said their initial aim was merely a casual visit.

8.2% (6) said their initial aim was to rob the victim.

Offender's Aims of Dominance, Humiliation and Revenge significantly correlated with Casual Conversation Prior to the Rape.

Several of the men explained that they usually spoke to their victims for a short while (52.4% between 2 to 30 minutes) before executing the assault. Apparently this period was used to elicit certain kinds of behavior in their victims (e.g., sometimes resistance, sometimes fright, etc.) and to set the process of dominance in motion.

2.   Does the rapist plan the attack?

According to the majority of the participants in this study, the answer is "Yes." The majority (65.8%) indicated they had planned to have sex that day, while 91.8% described rape as their intention. Of the latter, 9.3% specified that they were considering rape if the victim did not cooperate. None of the offenders anticipated compliance initially although they contemplated and desired it. In this context data, analysis revealed that:

1.   Intent to Have Sex correlated significantly with:
Aim to Rape
Having a Particular Woman in Mind
Knowing the Victim

2.   Assailant's thoughts as he approached the woman correlated very highly with what he was hoping would happen when he encountered her

3.   Assailant's Tendency to Watch and closely observe the victim (79.5%) correlated significantly with Victim being a Stranger (78%)

4.   Assailant's Possession of a Weapon (69.9%) correlated highly with his use of Weapon to intimidate the victim (though most had stated they had no previous intentions to use the weapon)

In addition, it was clear in at least seven cases (Peeping Toms) that some rapists make a comprehensive assessment of a prospective victim and her environment, returning later to execute the rape.

"One 24 year old related that he had been out walking one night, after leaving a party because he didn't know many of the people. He saw a woman get out of a Volkswagen van and go to her apartment. He saw the light go on in her house, knocked on her door, and asked if she knew where _____ lived. When she said she didn't, he asked her if her husband was home. She said, 'I'm not married.' He went home for a knife and returned to the apartment to rape her."

Another 24 year old described one of his many rape attacks as follows: One evening he drove around for about an hour checking apartments for a victim, because single women often live in complexes. He found a woman's name on a mailbox and rang her bell, but no one answered. He entered the house through an open back window, unlocked the back door and left. After watching for about 15 minutes, the victim returned and he watched through the window 2–3 minutes. She puttered about the kitchen, then went to the bedroom and took off some clothes. 'I was outside, building up my nerve. Then I went into the house, looked at her a few seconds, went to the bedroom door and showed her my gun . . .'"

3. Is a victim selected beforehand, and why is a particular woman selected?

Although victims were predominantly strangers (78%), assailants did engage in a selection process, often eliminating certain women until they found a suitable victim.[9] For example, 38.4% reported having a particular woman in mind; 34.2% said that this woman did become the victim. Often, they were looking for a *particular kind of victim* rather than a certain preselected woman. Further probing revealed that in addition to availability and defenselessness, perceived promiscuity or "looseness"[10] of wo-

men, apparent naivete, and ambivalent behavior were cited as decisive influences in the selection of victims. However, race, physical appearance (e.g., heavily built women), or assertive body language were factors which led to elimination of prospective victims. Several men said that the presence of males (i.e., if a man was in the victim's house or if the victim was married) would have made them change their minds immediately.

4. Does the assailant perceive the woman he attacks as having influenced his commission of the crime?

The participants were almost equally divided in their responses to this question: 52.1% said that they had already decided to rape when they selected the victim, but another 45.2% felt that their victims had preceipitated the assault. When those who responded that the victim had "precipitated" the offense (33) were asked about the manner in which the victim incited the attack, 18 cited victim resistance and 13 cited victim attractiveness. However, both of these explanations are disputable.

In the instances involving victim resistance, the victim was resisting an attack already in progress. Victim attractiveness might contribute to rape in a passive sense, as the victim is not necessarily consciously participating in the fantasy which spurs the rapist to attack. Moreover, the criteria for attractiveness among these men varied considerably: some preferred older women, finding them more attractive and "sexy", others preferred females much younger than themselves. Others were attracted to women clothed a particular way; for example, one man considered tight pants an "invitation" while another was "turned on" by bare feet.

5. To what extent does the decision to rape include violence?

No clear answer to this question emerges from the data. Despite the extensive use of vio-

---

[9] . . . 82.2% chose a victim who was "available" and 71.2% chose a woman they perceived as defenseless and vulnerable.

[10] A perception of the rapist; often these men had never seen the woman before.

lence in the sample (see "Victim Resistance and Assailant Reaction"), the frequency of weapon possession (69.9%) and the degree of victim injury, the participants generally claimed that they had not intended to use violence (67.1%). Although only 32.9% acknowledged their intent to use violence, 91.8% stated they had the intention to rape (i.e., intended to use force to win compliance), and 50.7% claimed they sought dominance, humiliation and/or revenge and 61.6% actually caused injury to their victims. On the basis of these data, it appears that *the decision to rape did include violence.* However, it is not possible to ascertain the exact extent to which violence was anticipated during the decision-making stage.

6. In the assailant's perception, is the amount of violence used influenced by the victim? If so, to what extent? What are the contributing factors?

The answer to the first part of the question is "Yes, sometimes," but a range of elements contributed. The assailants frequently became frightened during their rape attacks: *30.1% acknowledged getting scared after they had initiated the assault,* particularly when victims attempted to resist and especially when the victims screamed. Typically, they were afraid of getting caught.

Sometimes assailants instigated passive victims to resist by threatening to kill the victim even though she was complying. When the victim began to cry or plead for her life, the assailant then reacted violently. Often these men indicated their sense of accomplishment during the attack depended on their dominance of the victim, so they needed some form of resistance. Others saw ready compliance on the part of their victims as usurpation of the rapists' control of the situation—a control they needed before they could consummate the act of rape. For example, 27.4% reported becoming excited when the victim resisted their attacks. One participant stated:

"I hit her because I wanted to hit her—to let her know I was in command . . . Her responses weren't making me feel as good as I wanted to, so I decided to scare her to create this."

The data produced several correlations of varying degrees of significance among the items comprising victim response and the amount of violence used by the assailant.

Assailant Anger correlated with:
Victim influence of the offense (i.e., the assailant's perception that she had "provoked" him).
The victims' subsequent resistance.

Assailant's Use of Physical Force correlated with Victim Resistance.

Intensification of Assailant Anger correlated with:
Victim Resistance during coitus or attempted coitus.
Victim Anger.
Injury to the Victim.

Extreme Violence significantly correlated with Victim Uncooperativeness[11] (low or passive resistance) as interpreted by the assailant during the assault.

The most extreme violence was apparently elicited by resistance during coitus: 40% of the victims resisted during coitus and suffered increased violence as the assailant forced compliance.

7. What factors cause intensification of the degree and type of violence inflicted upon the victim?

This study indicates a great deal of violence, however, the sample bias must be noted: The subject population included only excessively violent rapists, approximately one-half the Atas-

[11]Extreme Violence and Uncooperativeness (low resistance) were both new variables generated by factor analysis.

cadero MDSO population. If the excluded population of rapists who were not excessively violent were included, the incidence and degree of violence would have been significantly reduced.

Correlations in the previous sections show that victim resistance (especially screaming, but also physical resistance), feelings of fright on the part of some assailants after they had initiated their assaults, fears of being caught if their victims "blew it" either during the assault or afterwards, victim anger, victim calmness or appearance of control during the attack instead of fright, and sometimes victim passiveness tended to precede an increase and/or an intensification of assailants' violence, ranging from wielding a weapon to actual infliction of injury. In approximately 7% of the cases studied, offenders recalled becoming extremely angry and sometimes more violent when they could not get an erection to consummate the rape.

The study also indicated that the rapes which were motivated by the *desire for revenge* upon certain individual women were often more violent than the others. In what was clearly the most excessively violent of all the sexual assaults described in the study, a 24 year old participant recalled the following experience:

"I asked her to go to the party . . . she started calling me a son-of-a bitch, etc., and accused me of robbing her house . . . This was five days after I had gotten out of the County Jail . . . I was getting really paranoid as she said she was going to call the police . . . (Later that night around 11:30 p.m.) I saw her standing there in a negligee drinking a beer . . . Then I thought, 'This nasty bitch is no good for anything but to be used. I'm going to fix her now so she doesn't screw anybody else.'"

Armed with a butcher knife, this offender entered this woman's house, and beat her continuously until daylight, dragging her all over the house, kicking her repeatedly, cutting her (she sustained several lacerations in her vagina), and eventually stabbing her through one hand to the floor. He left her thinking he had killed her.

Typically, participants said they increased their violence when their expectations for the rape were not being met by the victim; 68.5% wanted their victims to comply with their expectations.

8. How does the assailant respond to victim resistance?

The responses of assailants to victim resistance in this study showed some variation (see Figure 2). A large percentage (54.8%) reported getting more violent, sometimes losing control. Often the response was anger (47.9%). On the other hand, 34.2% felt powerful, dominant or good; 30.1% felt scared; and 27.4% felt excited.[12]

The data analysis with respect to the variables constituting this question were:

Victim Resistance during coitus or attempted coitus correlated with Assailant Getting Scared.

Victim Screaming correlated with Assailant Getting Scared;

Victim's Physical Resistance (Fought) correlated with Assailant Getting Angry;

Victim Anger correlated with Assailant Getting Angry;

Victim's Resistance correlated with Assailant getting *Angrier*.

The data analysis at this stage also revealed a very important correlation: *Extreme Violence correlated significantly with Deterrence*. Victim resistance was also related to intensification of violence. What the correlation suggests is that despite the precipitation of anger and increased violence manifested by some rapists during an assault, rape can still be deterred in some instances.

In three particular rape incidents where the men were armed (two with guns, one with a

---

[12]Percentages overlap because of multiple answers—many offenders had mixed reactions.

knife), the victims succeeded in deterring the rape without incurring any injury. In each case they remained quite calm, persistently resisting the attack by verbal objection and simultaneously attempting to persuade the assailant to put the weapon away. The offenders reported that they became extremely scared when they realized that they had not succeeded in intimidating their victims. In one of the incidents, the woman over-powered the rapist and grabbed the gun, then made him leave her house. In the second, the woman struggled physically while verbally questioning her attacker about what he was trying to do, until she eventually wrested the knife from him. In the third case, the woman complied with her assailant's demands while she persuaded him to put his shotgun away. When the gun was safely out of sight, she grabbed her clothing and fled. It is important to note, however, that two of these attacks involved people who knew each other before the incident although there had been no sexual relationship between them.

9. How does the assailant account for his rape and other sexual assaults?

The respondents provided a wide variety of answers to this question, many of which sounded rather "cliche", probably due to the offenders' exposure to psychiatric and psychological theories about sexual assault. One offender who wanted his victim to "enjoy the sexual intercourse more" complained about the "John Waynism" in men in this society and the over-emphasis upon competition that characterized the male role in American society. He added that he turned to sexual crimes after his return from Vietnam: his experience in Vietnam left him with an emptiness which he felt motivated his commission of rape.

A number of other respondents attributed their crimes to their lack of trust and social relationships which, they claimed, would have provided them with a "sounding board" for articulation of fantasies and social and psychological

problems. A few mentioned their emotional make-up and personal needs (e.g., the need to feel powerful) as contributing influence to their commission of rape.

Overall, however, the offenders profiled themselves as losers. Underlying almost all the factors they cited as motivating their crimes was a general feeling of inadequacy which they attributed to a number of sources: rejection by women, lack of self-confidence, poor self-concept, lack of affection from anyone, lack of control over their lives, etc. *Not one participant in the study referred to the lack of a sexual outlet as a reason for the crime.* This supports the hypothesis that sexual intercourse is only a secondary concern of the rapists.

*

Peeping Tom Rapists

Peeping Toms are generally considered harmless men who achieve sexual gratification by surreptitiously watching women (frequently scantily dressed or undressing) in their homes. In short, Peeping is seen as an end in itself. Our data, although very limited with respect to peeping Tom cases, suggested otherwise. Seven rapists in the research sample reported "doing some Peeping Tom stuff" prior to their rapes. In the particular incidents discussed in the interviews, peeping preceeded the sexual assault, and in all cases the rape was completed.

Five of the seven Peeping Toms were single, one was married, and one was separated. They ranged in age from 19 to 30 years. Six were 24 years old or under. Some of the more outstanding characteristics of their assaults are as follows:

6 had rape as their aim; 1 said he had sex in mind, later stating he knew it had to be forcible.

6 were armed with weapons (one had a gun; the others had knives, meat forks, etc.) The 7th—a 20 year old—raped an 86 year old woman using considerable physical force as she put up a vigorous struggle.

5 of the 6 who were armed said they did not usually carry weapons. Only 1 said he usually carried a weapon.

6 said they did not have a particular victim in mind that day, but that they selected their victims after watching them through their windows and assessing the victim's vulnerability as well as the "safety" of the attack (i.e., from discovery). The 7th offender said he had raped his victim before and was passing her house on this particular day watching. He saw the woman naked through her window, and soon after, he entered her house by cutting a hole through a bathroom window screen.

All 7 claimed they did not intend to use violence that day, but 6 of them were armed, and the weapons were used in every case to intimidate the victims. The victims in three of the incidents received serious injury as a result of physical force on the part of the assailant: two were choked with considerable force, one was choked and knocked unconscious, and another was gagged with a towel.

6 broke into the victim's house by climbing through unlocked windows or entering through unlocked doors. Only one offender said that he entered the victim's house by first knocking and speaking to his victim. He pushed his way through the partially opened door after he discovered that the woman was unmarried and alone.

3 of these offenders said that they returned to their victim's house after their rapes to rape her again, but only one was successful. One changed his mind after he heard "shuffling" when he partially opened an unlocked window; he thought there was a man this time in the victim's apartment. The other did not get an answer when he knocked on the victim's door and her lights were off, so he thought she was not at home.

While the offenders in these rape incidents were watching their victims prior to the attack, the victims seemed to have been totally unaware of the potential attacker until the first interaction. And according to the offenders, the women were terrified when they were attacked. Faced with weapons at their throats or backs, none of them resisted physically. Four attempted to resist verbally, e.g., shouting, "Get out! Who are you?," "What are you doing here?," etc. Two victims screamed loudly. In one of these cases the assailant stuffed a towel into the victim's mouth gagging her, then knocked her unconscious—"because she was taking away my control of the situation." In the other case—that with the 86 year old woman—the offender stated that the victim hollered throughout the attack. This did not deter him (he completed the rape in about five minutes), but when he was leaving he saw several neighbors arriving at the house, responding to the victim's cries.

Unlike the majority of the other rape attacks, the Peeping Tom rapes were completed in 30 minutes or less, frequently in less than 15 minutes. All the victims were strangers to these offenders. It is important to note too that these rape attacks were extremely violent. For example, despite victim's entreaties and lack of vigorous physical resistance, the offenders showed no pity or consideration. One offender bluntly stated: "The first 30 seconds was the payoff. *I had the power to make her do anything.*" Another stated that although his victim was crying, "I didn't have any feelings at the time. We were just two pieces of meat." He knocked her unconscious before he left her apartment.

Significant in the Peeping Tom rapes is the *planning of the attack*, which in turn, seems to increase the probability that the rape attack will be completed. Typically, the Peeping Tom rapists watched their victims for a while (between 5 to 30 minutes). One of the men said that he was feeling very destructive that night, so he took a butcher knife and proceeded to slash cars. After this, he thought "about doing some Peeping Tom stuff," went to a nearby apartment building "to look for women", and caught sight of a woman through an open window. He observed her for a while, decided to rape her, and entered her house through an unlocked front door. The woman yelled when she saw him, but he showed her his knife and ordered her to follow him as he held the knife at her back. He added

"She was scared and quiet. She walked ahead, and I got sexually excited watching her. I felt her bottom. She gave me a scathing look and said, 'Is that all you want?' That made me feel small and angry with her. I cowered at first, but then put on my tough act. Suddenly, a car came by. I ran to hide, leaving her behind. I yelled for her to follow me, and she did. From then on, things changed. I felt she liked me . . . I also had the power back. She obeyed me."

This offender raped the woman soon after, and returned the next day to take her out. He also said that he planned another rape after this one. He was surprised to learn from the police that the victim in the previous rape incident had reported him.

In many ways, these seven offenders did not differ greatly from the other offenders. Nonetheless, there was a certain consistency in their mode of attack which usually began with peeping. These characteristics suggest that we should begin to re-examine the Peeping Tom phenomenon more critically. It might be, as was clearly the case in our sample, that sexual offenders who "peep" might not be as harmless and humorous as is often assumed. Rather, peeping might be the initial stage in a chain of events that lead to a rape attack. Their possession of weapons coupled with their expressed desire to dominate and control their victims (although not necessarily to inflict injury) was indicative of more than simple visual enjoyment.

A similar connection between exhibitionism and rape has been observed by the research staff at the Rape Crisis Center in Pueblo, Colorado. They are finding, at least tentatively, that a few of the rapists in their sample exposed themselves (exhibitionism), then proceeded to make contact with women immediately, or hid and attacked them shortly thereafter. We must note that these possibilities are being suggested only as tentative relationships. Further investigation is necessary.

70. Teenage Prostitution

DIANA GRAY

THE PROBLEM

PROSTITUTION HAS LONG BEEN A SUBJECT OF FASCI-
nation, curiosity, and—occasionally—empirical research (see, for example, Benjamin,
1964, 1960; Bryan, 1966, 1965; Davis, 1937;
Gagnon, 1968; Glover, 1945; Greenwald, 1970,
1969, 1958; Henriques, 1962–1963; Hirschi,
1962; Hollender, 1964; Jackman et al., 1967;
Maurer, 1939; Murtagh, 1957; Reckless, 1933;
Reitman, 1936; Schreiber, 1967; Winick, 1962;
Winick and Kinsie, 1971). When researched,
there are two questions to which studies of prostitution have typically addressed themselves.
They attempt either to account for the existence
of prostitution as a phenomenon in a society or
to explain why particular women enter prostitution. This study is concerned with the latter
question.

Unfortunately, most studies investigating entrance into prostitution rely on interviews with
older prostitutes of call-girl status who are experienced in the profession (Bryan, 1966, 1965;
Greenwald, 1970, 1969, 1958). Information on
the early lives of prostitutes and relevant factors
which brought them into the life are primarily
retrospective and may be subject to recall error
or rationalization on the part of the subjects
(Winick and Kinsie, 1971: 38). And in spite of
the long-standing interest in prostitution generally, teenage prostitution has been a rare focus

▶SOURCE: *"Turning Out: A Study of Teenage Prostitution,"*
Urban Life and Culture (January 1973), 1:401–425. Reprinted by
permission of the publisher, Sage Publications, Inc.

of investigation in the sociology of deviant behavior. Frequently it is thought to be so low in
incidence as to not be a fruitful area of inquiry.
Winick and Kinsie (1971: 31), using the FBI
Uniform Crime Reports, note that only 16% of the
women arrested for prostitution were under age
21 and conclude that very few girls in their early
teens work as prostitutes (Winick and Kinsie,
1971: 52).

Yet even casual observation while I was a
juvenile parole counselor in Seattle revealed
that streetwalking was not an uncommon enterprise among adolescent girls.[1] *Newsweek* (1971)
reported that in New York the arrests for prostitution of girls under 25 has increased from
24% to 74% in the past 10 years. In other major
cities, official records show a decline in the average age of prostitutes.

There are several aspects of deviant behavior
which can be brought into sharper focus by a
study of young girls entering prostitution.
Among these are: socialization into a deviant
role; supportive cultural conditions (Hirschi,
1969); legitimate and illegitimate opportunities
(Cloward and Ohlin, 1960; Sutherland, 1955);
and social variables in the acquisition and the
maintenance of deviant behavior (Burgess and
Akers, 1969: 554).

The opportunity to learn prostitution needs

[1] Approximately one-third of my caseload of thirty girls
became involved in streetwalking activities. During this same
period, other juvenile parole counselors also reported having teenage prostitutes in their caseloads.

to be a preexisting condition in the environment before a girl can become a prostitute, according to differential-association theory (Reckless, 1950: 230). But, given that girls are exposed to the opportunity to learn prostitution, the existing literature is not clear as to what factors make a girl "vulnerable to enter prostitution."In his study of twenty call girls, Greenwald (1969) found that the majority came from broken homes, and all reported marital discord between their parents. He also found that many of these girls had an early pleasurable sexual experience with an adult male for which they were rewarded. Greenwald (1969: 195) hypothesized that lack of close parental ties coupled with early, rewarded sexual experience made these girls vulnerable to prostitution.

Two theoretical approaches, social control theory (Hirschi, 1969) and social reinforcement theory (Burgess and Akers, 1969), which have been used to describe the etiology of delinquent behavior in general, provide a fruitful perspective for viewing the natural history of the teenage prostitute. Social control theory asserts that deviant behavior occurs when one's bond with society is weak or broken (Hirschi, 1969: 16). This bond is composed of a sensitivity to the opinion of others, fear of consequences for breaking the rules, involvement in conventional activities, and a belief in the rules of society (Hirschi, 1969:16–23). Social reinforcement theory applies the principles of differential reinforcement to an understanding of the process whereby these bonds are strengthened or weakened and the process whereby deviant activities are sustained. Inadequate social reinforcement for conventional behaviors provide the vehicle which moves the individual toward eventual commitment to unconventional activities (Burgess and Akers, 1969:554–555).

Entry into prostitution appears to be entry into a relatively closed system which would provide for little occupational mobility. It is not clear from existing studies what occupational and life-style alternatives are available to, or are perceived by, the young girls who enter prostitution.

Beyond some of these relatively obvious points, the literature on prostitution does not yet have much in the way of empirical or theoretical insights into the conditions and the consequences of entering prostitution at an early age. Indeed, information on becoming a prostitute by those still at an early point in the process, rather than recollections well after the fact, is sorely inadequate. It is clear, then, that even an exploratory study among a limited number of teenage prostitutes would serve to fill some lacunae in sociological knowledge.

THE STUDY

In this investigation, no specific hypotheses were laid out in advance; rather, many areas, as indicated by the literature on prostitution and theories of deviant behavior, were explored in order to give rise to possible explanations of adolescent prostitution (of the streetwalking variety) and, in general, to construct a natural history of early entry and progression into prostitution from the perspective of the teenage prostitute herself.

The study was conducted in Seattle, Washington, between August 1970 and June 1971. A relatively open-ended, unstructured interview schedule designed to elicit conversation about various areas of the young prostitute's experience was administered to seventeen teenage prostitutes. These interviews were tape-recorded and later transcribed for analysis. Participation by the girls was completely voluntary, and the girls received $5.00 for the interview. In addition to the seventeen prostitutes, four girls were included in the study who had not prostituted but who had been exposed to the opportunity to do so. Though this number is small, analysis of these cases provided some insights into the etiology of adolescent prostitution.

The majority of the girls interviewed (15) were incarcerated at the time of the interview, either in a juvenile institution or in the city jail. They ranged in age from 13 to 21 with the mean age of 16.9. The sample was composed of 11 black girls and 10 white girls. The majority of the girls were born and raised in the Seattle area.

THE FINDINGS

Social Background of Teenage Prostitutes

Other studies of prostitutes have emphasized inadequate family relationships as a causal factor leading to prostitution. All the girls in this study came from the lower or lower-middle socioeconomic level as measured by family income, occupation of parent, and education of parents. They tended to come from homes broken by separation or divorce and with many siblings. Home relationships in general were poor. Typical feelings are reflected by this statement: "To be honest with you, there wasn't anything good about it because I had so many problems with my father. What he said went, and what I had to say wasn't important. What he said goes."

By the time these girls reach adolescence, parental ties and attachments to their family have become weak. Relationships with both mother and father are poor due to inadequate supervision, lack of intimacy in communication patterns, and consistent failure of the parents to provide positive social reinforcement in the form of attention, affection, or effective communication. One girl placed in a foster home at her mother's request explains:

"I tried to communicate with my mother.... I wrote down exactly how I felt and I mailed them but she wouldn't write down her feelings in letters. Even when we talked, she didn't have any interest in what I wanted to talk about . . . what I suppose about her now is that she really—that at the time—she didn't really want me and my sister."

According to social control theory, lack of intimate ties with the conventional order will free a person to commit delinquent acts since he has nothing to lose through a negative evaluation by parents or conventional others. The girls who become prostitutes at a young age come to think little of their parents' reactions to their behavior at a time when their contact with their peers is providing them with many opportunities to participate in unconventional behavior. However, this was true of all the girls in this study, even those who had not prostituted. (All had been adjudicated delinquent.) Lack of intimate attachments to parental figures does not necessarily lead to prostitution, but it does contribute to the social conditions which make the girl vulnerable to enter the life.

A similar conclusion can be reached about the impact of school and legitimate work experiences. The teenage prostitute is likely to have quit school voluntarily due to experiences of repeated failure to adjust to the academic setting. As a result of such experience, she does not see education as relevant to her future or as a source of reinforcement for her now or later in her life. Ties to educational values, then, are broken before entry into prostitution and, as does the breaking of home ties, set the stage for the girl's future role as a streetwalker.

Eleven of the adolescent prostitutes had held prior legitimate jobs which were usually short-term, part-time, and part of special OEO programs such as the Neighborhood Youth Corps. These jobs (clerical, nurses aides, day care aides, day work) were neither highly glamorous nor financially remunerative, but they were indicative of the legitimate employment opportunities available to most of the women in the work force who were known to the girls. Thus, although they were exposed to the legitimate models and paths to the conventional goals of society, the rewards were insufficient to hold them.

In addition, none of the teenage prostitutes expressed as a future goal the role of wife and mother, a conventional aspiration for most adolescent females in this society, nor did they report a steady attachment with a boyfriend which might eventually lead to marriage and motherhood. Most saw the possibility of achieving a happy marriage for themselves as slim, probably due to experiences in their family of orientation.

All these findings are explicable in terms of a social control theory: there is a breaking (or lack) of ties with the conventional social order as a result of social and emotional deprivation in their family life, of academic failure and frustration at school, and of boredom and dissatisfaction with the world of legitimate work. None of these experiences leads directly to prostitution, but all can be seen as facilitating a girl's vulnerability to be influenced to try out unconventional behavior.

Early Sexual Experiences

The majority of the girls reported knowing fairly accurately, prior to age twelve, what behavior was entailed in the act of sexual intercourse. One states:

"I learned it [sexual intercourse] living in the ghettos. I heard about it when I was really small. No person ever told me anything. You just find out. You learn things together and you experience things together. I guess I learned it ever since I was seven or eight or maybe younger. . . . I kept it between me and my friends because my mother never talked."

Knowledge about sexual intercourse was most frequently acquired from peers. Menstrual periods began with a minimum of information, usually gleaned from peers or from inadequate preparation by some adult such as:

"She had said, 'Well, you're going to have a menstrual period, what's called a menstrual period, and you're going to be bleeding in your underpants. When you do, come and tell me.' And then it was about two months later I came running home screaming."

The mean age for first coital experience was 12.9; the black girls experienced it about two years earlier than the white girls. Just how the timing and nature of the first coital experience of the girls in this study compare to those of other adolescent girls in the same social setting who are not prostitutes is very difficult to surmise. Good research on normal adolescent sexual behavior is scanty and outdated (Reevy, 1960: 53) but what there is suggests that although these girls experience coitus at a relatively early age, their sexual behavior is not especially unusual when compared to that generally found among females of their social background and educational level.[2]

Further evidence for this is suggested by the reports the girls give about their first sexual partners. The first coital experience generally occurred for the black girls with a boyfriend within about five years of her own age. The behavior was fairly spontaneous but never, according to her reports, initiated by the girl:

"I was scared. He kind of pushed himself on me, you know. Pushed me. I didn't really like it. And then he made me mad. He was telling some of his friends, you know. I broke up with him. He was the first person I ever did that with, and I broke up with him because I didn't care for him any more."

White girls were more likely than black girls to have their first coital experience with a stranger or casual acquaintance. Participation was voluntary, due partly to the girls' curiosity and partly to their hopes that it would be the experience as physically and psychologically enjoyable as their peers had described. One girl explains: "The first time I was kind of curious because I had heard so much about it. I just wanted to know what it was all about because I'm a very curious person. I like to know and experience things."

Regardless of race, the girls reported finding the initial coital experience somewhat disappointing, and often unpleasant. The reaction

---

[2]Only 3% of the females in Kinsey's (et al., 1953: 288) sample, irrespective of the age at which they had married, experienced coitus by fifteen years of age. There tended to be a span of one or two years between first coital experience and marriage, so that those females who married at a younger age tended to have their first coital experience at a younger age (Kinsey et al., 1953: 286–287). Kinsey, using years of schooling completed as an indicator of social class, found that those with grade school educations have a higher incidence (11%) of coital experience by age fifteen than did those women with higher educational attainment (Kinsey et al., 1953:338). Likewise, Burgess and Wallin (1953: 340) found a higher rate of premarital coitus during engagement for lower-educated females. Gebhard et al. (1958: 31) also found that females of lower socioeconomic levels have a greater incidence of premarital intercourse and at an earlier age than other levels of social class.

reported by this young woman was not uncommon:

"I cried a long time. I don't know. I had a funny feeling. I didn't want to do it and then I did, so then it was funny. But I had to cry about it. We had been going together for a month but I hadn't let him touch me. I was kind of the shy type. And then when I did, it was intercourse."

After this first experience she might not participate in intercourse for a time and feel somewhat betrayed by the experience: "My girl friend and I had been talking about it. Then, afterwards, I went and told her that I didn't see what the big deal was—going to bed with a guy. I didn't see nothing neat about it."

Incidents of forced or unpleasant sexual experiences were reported by some of the girls, but for the most part these did not constitute the first sexual experience. Unpleasant experiences may not have even resulted in coitus but were usually defined as offensive due to the particular male involved or to his manner of sexual approach. In all such cases except one, the male involved was more than five years the senior of the girl and was either a stranger, a casual acquaintance, or a relative rather than a boyfriend. The girls were most likely to report responding to the experience with fear.

Incestual relationships were not reported by the girls in the study, although one described sex-play with her brother when they were children. Most of the girls reported that, although the initial experience of sexual intercourse was not one to rave about, they did learn later to find coitus pleasant and enjoyable. It does not appear that the girls were traumatized by these initial experiences.

A tendency toward promiscuity or early, rewarded sexual experience with an adult male do not appear for this group. For the majority, promiscuity began at the time of, not before, becoming a prostitute. Therefore, their initial sexual experiences do not seem to set them apart from other adolescent females of their social class and educational background who do not prostitute.

Turning Out

The data up to this point have clarified some of the conditions which seem to be necessary for the making of the adolescent prostitute. The girls in the study show similarity with respect to their social class, their lack of conventional ties, and their initial sexual experiences. All these similarities are present prior to the girls' entry into prostitution, according to their reports. Yet these factors alone are not sufficient to explain that entry. Many girls who share these same features do not become teenage prostitutes. Therefore it is important to examine those elements which introduce the girl to prostitution and lead up to her decision to enter this occupation.

Prostitution existed as a concept in the minds of most of the girls by the time they were eleven years old, before they had any sexual experiences of their own. Information was picked up through conversation with family members or peers. One reports:

"The only thing that I got out of it was that they'd call them 'ho's'and they talk about how they dress sharp, and how they'll all be riding around in their car with their man, and the big nice cars and all this stuff. The guys and the girls would talk about it. I always said, 'Look, I wouldn't ever do that.' But at the same time there was a kind of a rising feeling. It sounded exciting."

As they did with initial responses to first hearing about sexual intercourse, many of the respondents reported that they felt intrigued by the description of prostitution which appeared exciting and glamorous in common conversation.

All the girls in the study report having known someone on a fairly intimate basis who was involved in the occupation of prostitution before they themselves turned out. For seven of the girls, it was a relative; for the remaining ten, a friend. Even though the parent or other relative might be engaging in unconventional behavior of which they knew the young girl was aware, they made attempts to pass on conventional values, warning her against the pitfalls of their way of life. One girl reports her sister-in-law's admonitions:

"I thought she was nice. She always dressed up all the time. She looked real nice. I didn't see anything wrong with it [prostitution];. Well, my brother, he was a pimp and my sister-in-law and I got to be real close. She used to tell me all the time she'd better not ever catch me doing it. She'd always talk to me against it. She just said she didn't think it would be right for me."

However, since these girls were not closely tied to their families—whether conventional or unconventional—anticipated family disapproval would seem to have been minimally consequential to them as they weighed the pros and cons of prostituting.

Most reported that they deliberately sought out persons who "were in the life"before making any firm decision to enter it themselves. They flirted with the idea and were curious to learn more about prostitution by acquainting themselves with some of the more prominent players.

"I went with my girl friend to this after-hours place. They [the pimps] would call us 'bitch this and bitch that.' They would talk about money. This was the first time I snorted coke . . . and I felt funny. I didn't go home. I was too loaded. We were all sitting around and I had the cocaine tray and he pulled up a chair and started talking to me. He asked me my age and I said I was nineteen. I had on a wig and everything [She was actually fourteen]. . . . He asked me why I'd been coming down here all the time 'cause he'd been admiring me but we hadn't been seeing each other. So I explained to him. I told him I always wanted to see how the 'fast life' was. I had to find who I really wanted to be with, see how the life was. Then the next day I left and went to San Fran with him."

It was the attractiveness of certain things about prostitution that led the young girl into exploring possible entry into the life. The material rewards have long been recognized and re-ported as primary causal factors in leading women into prostitution. But the initial attraction for the girls in this study was social as well as material. Reasons such as being drawn to "the fast life," liking her pimp, seeing a "way to be somebody important," or becoming someone "to be admired," were as likely to be mentioned as the money or clothes. This suggests that the young prostitute seeks, through unconventional behavior, the social reinforcement which she does not obtain in other realms of her life. Social rewards are recognized as readily as material rewards by the girls even prior to their entry into prostitution.

They are also aware at the outset that pros-titution has its negative side. Girls report per-ceiving both physical and social-psychological unpleasantries as part of prostitution. The most frequently mentioned response about the nega-tive aspects of prostitution was the necessity of having sexual intercourse with the customer.[3] The next most frequently perceived negatives were the dangers of arrest and venereal disease, and the day-to-day hazards of hustling on the streets.

When considering the precipitating factors surrounding the final decision to prostitute, the girl's immediate living situation and financial circumstances prove to be important. Most of the girls reported that, at the time, they were runaways from home or from a juvenile correc-tional institution. Other girls were under parole supervision or living in a foster home. For the most part, then, they had unstable living condi-tions at the time they turned-out. However, only half the girls felt that they turned-out due to financial or social pressures. Nine reported that it arose from their own curiosity, boredom, or desire to rebel. Eight girls claimed that they "turned themselves out." Nine felt that they began due to the persuasion or influence of another person, although this persuasion was generally minimal, as in the following account:

"I had stayed gone all night from my foster home, and I had spent the night at my cousin's house. He told me to go home. I was walking up the street, and a couple of guys that had seen me before at the store came up and started talking to me. So I decided I

---

[3]That is, they viewed the behavior required of them in the "work" of prostitution as possibly contrary to their own val-ues of sexual permissiveness and to their own preferences for sexual relations. Thus, intercourse *with the customer,* al-though not intercourse per se, tended to be regarded as distasteful by the girls prior to their attempting to prostitute.

wasn't going home. They asked me to stay with them. About two weeks later I started prostituting. One of the guys, I know he brought it up. I said okay."

The mean age for the first act of prostitution for this group is 14.7 or approximately 2 years more than the mean age for first coital experience. The youngest age reported was 12 and the oldest age of entry was age 18.

The girls reported little or no training period prior to their first act of prostitution. However, some received minimal supervision during their first few weeks on the streets. These juveniles required very little skill and training to carry out an act of prostitution. Generally they were able to engage in their first act without any job-related briefing. They operated on the basis of the informal information acquired up to this point in their life through association with others in, or on the periphery of, prostitution. One girl describes her first attempt:

"We got the idea in our heads that we were going to try it. We went down on Pike, downtown, and we were walking down there. I didn't say anything. I didn't know how the girls called out to ask for a date. We both went down there and we didn't say anything . . . then another girl explained that I would have to call out to them and speak to them. I did like she told me and caught my first trick. I took him to a trick house and he spent $25."

Although nearly all began without any training, approximately two-thirds of the girls reported that later they were explicitly briefed by the pimp or another prostitute in how to wash the customer, check him for venereal disease, and get him to wear a condom. But even then, only about one-third reported ever being instructed in other specific techniques, such as watching for cops, guarding against pregnancy, picking up customers, or locating trick houses. They learned these things by trial and error on the job. Nor were they schooled in specific sexual techniques: usually they were taught by customers who made the specific requests. Many of the girls reported never having encountered fellatio or other sexual variations before they worked the stroll. The typical briefing a novice might

receive from the pimp emphasized the proper attitude toward work and outlined the employer-employee relationship:

"Well, he explained some to me and I already knew some about it. . . . He told me it was going to be rough and the police was heavy. And he told me that when the cops come up and park, there's always a cafe there and you go in a cafe until they leave. But don't get caught in there. Like if you're just standing around jiving and there ain't no police and no vice out there, he's going to know you ain't out to make no money; you're just out to play. You can go in there and have a cup of coffee, smoke a cigarette and relax, but don't go in there to be jiving around and talking to those other 'ho's' and mess[ing] around, 'cause he know then that you ain't out to get the money."

Dealing with the finances was one of the first key learning areas for the young novice. The price per trick ranged from $15 to $50 with many of the younger girls reporting an average of $25 per trick, with four to eight tricks a night. Price arrangements were made through bargaining procedures:

"When you meet a customer, you generally ask him if he wants a date. He would say yes. Then he would ask you how much. You try not to state a definite price. 'Well, how much can you spend, honey?' or something like this. It would usually be around $20 or $25."

Only three of the girls reported retaining all of their earnings. Three others reported splitting the money 50–50, and the remaining eleven turned over all or the bulk of their earnings to their pimps. One informant explains:

"One-hundred percent went to him. He'd go out and buy me clothes and stuff like that. And we'd save maybe $10 or $20. The thing we worked out was this: this girl I was with—we could go out every other night. Both of us could go out every other night and we'd get money to go out to nightclubs. We'd spend money on clothes and stuff, and go out and have a good time. They make sure you don't get out of line."

On the other hand, the majority of the girls reported being satisfied with how the money was handled. Learning to be willing to turn over their earnings to the pimp was a major area of socialization, and many report they had difficulty accepting this rule:

"There was a dress I really wanted and he wouldn't get it for me. I got real mad. He would take me down to work and I started running off every night. You know, I would make some money down there but I would run off and keep it for myself. He found out where I was hiding. He came over there looking for me. He caught me so I gave him the money 'cause I didn't know what to do. He slapped me in my face. He said as much as I had been working I had better come up with more than $20. He told me I was 'with him' and I had better go down there and work. . . . I didn't say nothing because I was mad. He started yelling at me about running off and not giving him the money. He said, like this was the right thing, to give him the money. But I don't know. I didn't think it was the right thing—for him to use somebody like that."

However, the pressure to play by the rules of the game are great, and the girls learn that they will receive a great deal of social reinforcement from their "man" when they are able to provide him with large sums of money. One of the youngest informants reports:

"He told me this wasn't for the money; he really liked me. He told me he couldn't really hurt me unless I did something he already told me about and I go out and disrespect him. He said we were meant to be together. That made me feel pretty good; so it was love too. He said, 'You not only make the money for me, you're making it for the two of us.' And that really made me feel good. I had what I wanted then. I had him. And really, that's all I wanted but at first I couldn't understand the game because I figured like this: Why did I have to give him all the money? And he had all his main ladies over my head. I couldn't stand this. I wanted to be number one. But I was with him with love all the time, but I didn't know that he was too. So then, after that, I started going out steady."

This social reinforcement serves to offset the unpleasantness of having to surrender the money to the pimp.

Rip-Offs
Along with learning to receive payment for sexual intercourse, many girls were encouraged to rob their customers when possible. This technique of "creeping" or "ripping-off" was far more lucrative than regular trade, as one girl explains:

"I did a lot of those [rip-offs] when I was in Seattle last time because I found that a flat-back ain't never going to get you nothing. It's too low down for me. Sometimes I had, not what you call a stable-sister, but a partner. When they [the customer and the partner] go to the bathroom to wash up, I rip the money off and go back downstairs. I catch a taxi cab and leave her half there. Either she'll get it when she comes downstairs or whatever. I've made $600 to $700. One time in San Francisco, just at the beginning, we ripped-off $900. One of my stable-sisters ripped-off $1,500 from a merchant marine."

The girls considered themselves especially clever when they were able to take money from a "date" and escape without the necessity of having sexual relations with him. Only four girls reported never having robbed a trick. Twelve reported that they did it sometimes or often.

The Pimp
Pimp-prostitute relationships ranged from impersonally business-like to shockingly brutal. Stories such as this were not uncommon:

"He had a six-foot bullwhip and he hit me in the head with it. He told me he was going to take me home and kick my ass. . . . It scared me so bad that I said to myself, 'Slick, you're in for it now.' We got home and he beat me with that bullwhip and told me to go to sleep."

One problem in interpreting their reports of the relationship lies in the context in which the girls viewed their pimps' behavior. They tended to feel that verbal chastisements or physical abuses of themselves were justified. One girl described how, after a night's work, her pimp repeatedly threw cold water in her face. She did not express anger at this behavior but interpreted it as a training procedure. She explained:

"If the tricks would say or do something that upset us very much and we smart off, there could be big trouble. They wouldn't come back or it could bring in the vice. So what we were supposed to do was call

Tommy or tell the guy to get his clothes on and get out. We could have Tommy or someone else take care of him. Sometimes it was hard not to lose your temper, so he was teaching us."

For the most part, then, the relationship is seen as satisfactory: "We had fights, like we were married—married people have fights. He beat me up a couple of times, but not very bad. . . . But after our fights he'd just be so lovey-dovey. He'd give me anything I wanted."

The pimp does not necessarily physically force the adolescent girl to prostitute against her will. Rather, girls seek out their male partners and consider them an essential part of the life.

"It was important to me that I was with him because when you get with those little nobodies, they go to jail and don't know what to do. They might get fifteen to twenty years. But you know, one that's been off in the game who knows exactly what he's doing, hey, you got a good chance. And if you want to make something of yourself out there in the fast life, you got to get a for-real man. You got to get somebody who knows about the game so you can really be off in it."

They believe they need a man to "take care of business" and to give them social status on the stroll. They accept the idea that they are not a "qualified ho" until they are so-and-so's lady. One subject explains this view of pimps:

"I always managed to get with a different guy, another guy who was more important, who had more strength than the other guys did. They have to have respect for another man's women at all times, except for the real young fools that are running around on the street. And then when I got with James, that was the top. Nobody messed with me at all."

The pimp is not essential to the girl's turning-out or to her apprenticeship, but he is essential if the novice is to remain in the life with any degree of status or respect from the other players.

But even here, the juvenile prostitute fails to gain any permanent social-emotional attachment. The relationship with the pimp is fraught with conflict and instability. Frequent switching from pimp to pimp is not uncommon. The be-

ginning of the relationship may be marked by a mutual attraction, characteristic of the adolescent crushes her age-mates might be having, but this early affection is often later replaced by fear and hostility. The pimp-prostitute relationship, although it reverses the "financial provider" role of conventional marriage, does show similarities to some kinds of conventional marital behavior. The pimp serves as the major decision maker, authority, and controller of the funds. The couple may argue, frequently over money, but as long as the pimp does not administer too severe or brutal a beating the prostitute will accept the occasional use of physical force in their relationship as part of the life.

Sisters of the Night

The girls report that contact with other prostitutes is likely to be intimate only among those working for the same man. Even then, relationships are not necessarily friendly: "He had other girls for awhile. But I was jealous, so I ran them all off. I'd treat them real mean and they didn't like it so they would leave."

Although not especially close to one another, girls sometimes display esprit de corps while on the stroll. They may go to the aid of a girl being hassled by the police or a trick and may occasionally give aid in turning a trick:

"We all helped each other because we were all out there for the same thing. So whenever we could help each other, we did. It was no hassle. Like if one of the tricks had a whole lot of money and they wanted somebody to go along for a rip-off, it was okay. Sometimes you'd double-date. It was all cool, because we were all out there for the same thing."

Other Relationships

Once the young prostitute moves into the regular routine of street life, her social contacts are centered around those people in prostitution. This process has been noted by others (Gagnon, 1968: 594; Hirschi, 1962) and seems to be related to the length of time the girl spends in the life. Family relationships are to some degree still maintained with varying degrees of success.

Once she has left home, the girl may feel that her relationship with her parents improves, though it is still characterized by indifference. The black girl is more likely to maintain at least an average relationship with her family, while the white girl is more likely to experience complete parental rejection. This may be a result of the fact that the lower-class black family, despite its disapproval of the profession, has long been aware of prostitution as a possible alternative for its daughters. It seems more willing than does the white family to allow its prostitute daughters to remain community members and occasional visitors at home. In commenting on her family's reaction, one black girl reports:

"My family knows about it, but since I left home and have been supporting myself, I gets along better with them than when I lived there. My dad, he don't say nothin' about it. My mother says that she wished I wasn't out there, but she will still accept me back and I am still her daughter no matter what I did."

White girls report that their parents tend to reject them, and they interpret this as resulting more from concern over how the behavior reflects on the family socially, than from real grief over their actions.

"Yeah, she read about it in the papers when I got arrested for prostitution. So I explained it to her and it just hurt her so bad, *she said.* But she didn't really care 'cause she was trying to find some way of getting rid of having to support me, so it didn't bother her all that much. She said it did, and carried on a scene, but it didn't bother her at all."

As these quotes illustrate, once in the life, the earlier tenuousness of parental ties undergoes no change. In fact, at this point, the indifference seems to become reciprocal; at this juncture in her life experiences, parental reaction to her prostitution appears to have no bearing at all on the girl's behavior.

Place of Business

Virtually all the teenage prostitutes report at least some experience as a streetwalker. The majority had spent most of their time on Seattle streets, and all preferred working the streets to working in houses of prostitution: "I liked working the streets best. It's just—sitting in a house—you get all bored and everything . . . just sitting in a house waiting for customers. Out on the stroll; that's where it's happening."

However, increasingly stringent law enforcement practices in Seattle in 1970–1971 were being felt by the girls and were influencing their choice of where to work:

"It's tight. They are really trying to shut this off. Yeah, lots of people are going into houses now. They do get tired. It's monotonous going back and forth to jail. They crack down a heck of a lot more than they used to. I know there was a time when we used to walk on each other's heels down on Jackson. It was so crowded with forty to fifty girls a night. You don't see that anymore."

The Tricks

None of the girls volunteered descriptions of customers; such information had to be elicited by the interviewer. One received the impression that the customer was merely incidental, or, at best, a "necessary evil" in the game and that there were other subjects of greater interest to discuss. The majority said their customers were "mostly old men," but when pressed, described the typical trick as white, in his middle thirties or forties, a working or businessman. A few claimed doctors, lawyers, ministers, and even a juvenile court judge as customers as well. One girl reported dating mostly servicemen and all occasionally did so, as servicemen were felt to be lucrative tricks, especially after payday. The merchant seaman was another favorite. The girls were under the impression that the majority of their customers were married.

The encounter with the trick is relatively brief, usually taking less than thirty minutes for the entire transaction. The girl contacts the trick, for example, in downtown Seattle and they agree to a "date." After reaching an understanding on price and service, they catch a cab to a trick house in the Central District. The girl then spends approximately ten to fifteen minutes with the trick, washing him, checking him for venereal disease, and having sexual intercourse. More than likely, unless the customer pays extra, neither party completely disrobes. They then return downtown, perhaps in the same cab, but disembark at different locations.

A girl who has been on the street for awhile generally develops a trade with a few "steadies": usually the big spenders or men who have been "business-like" in their past dealings. Eleven of the seventeen girls reported having at least one steady. Contact was usually made by her being in a certain place at a certain time each week so that he could find her; she did not contact him. Often she did not know his full name or telephone number.

Services requested of the girls were not confined to regular sexual intercourse. Twelve of the girls reported requests for such variants as fellatio, cunnilingus, anal sex, intercourse with multiple partners, homosexual contact, sado-masochistic activities, urination or defecation, or use of obscenity.

The chances of being assaulted by a customer is as likely for the young prostitute as being assaulted by her pimp. Few girls who have spent any time on the stroll have been able completely to avoid an undesirable, often frightening experience with a client:

"All he wanted was sex. He wanted to have intercourse but he didn't know how to approach me about it. Like I ask him, 'What do you want done? What do you want done?' He keeps telling me he didn't know. So I say, 'Hey, I am going to take the money and go if you don't tell me what you want.' And he grabbed me and choked me so bad that I was unconscious."

Most of the girls learn to take precautions to avoid assault, such as not dating alone, not going in the trick's car, and not going to the trick's residence. They prefer to use public transportation and local trick houses to transact their business. But even experienced girls at times may misjudge a trick or take chances, especially if there appears to be a considerable sum of money involved. These are the times that the girls are most vulnerable and may find themselves in dangerous situations.

Incarceration

Incarceration and the correctional institution experiences may be perceived positively or negatively by the girls. From their remarks, it appears that little of their experience in correctional institutions is addressed to the problems of street life or to their lack of conventional attachments in the community. Rather, the primary focus is on conformity to the norms of the particular institution, as evidenced by their behavior in school and living areas. If the girls are able to develop important ties with conventional adults in the institution, they are likely to have a satisfactory institutional experience. Since these relationships are seldom continued when the girls leave the institution, however, they have little or no effect on their subsequent unconventional behavior.

An examination of the role of the police and the incarceration experiences in the life of the juvenile prostitute complete the ring of vulnerability by which the girl comes to be surrounded. She is the target of attack from all sides: from the pimp, the trick, the other "ho's" and the cops. Indeed, due to this social milieu in which the young prostitute must operate, she is not now likely ever to develop any long-term affectionate attachments with anyone, be they conventional of unconventional. She stands isolated and alone.

SUMMARY

Employing materials from intensive interviews with a number of teenage prostitutes and utilizing the social control and social reinforcement perspectives, I have tried to develop a model of the process by which an adolescent girl becomes a prostitute. Her childhood is marked by early emotional and social deprivation in family relationships, which leads her to break emotional ties with parents and evince lack of concern over their reactions to her behavior. In addition, she experiences failure and lack of reinforcement in school and work settings. Thus, she is left with few, if any, ties to the conventional order. This leaves her free, then, to behave in unconventional ways. It is neither unlikely nor illogical that if she confronts failure in conventional paths, she will seek out other avenues that do bring reinforcement. Of course, her unconventional behavior need not be delinquent.For this group of girls, however, the opportunity to learn prostitution was easily accessible in their social milieu of unconventional relatives and peers and relatively early sexual experience. Given the absence of conventional ties in a setting where the opportunities to prostitute exist, her involvement in the life should be predictable. Prostitution provides both social and material reinforcement on a schedule such that reward is immediate, intermittently large, and requires little effort to obtain. Punishment is, initially, usually mild and infrequently administered and thus ineffective as a deterrent. And once the adolescent girl begins to prostitute, she finds herself entangled in a system which provides strong incentive to continue but limited outside contact. It seems likely, therefore, that she will make prostitution a lifetime career. Two elements might break the cycle: (1) the formation of a close, intimate attachment to a conventional person who strongly disapproves of her involvement; or (2) the removal of the opportunity for her to engage in prostitution. Given the nature of the life style of the prostitute, the chance of developing an enduring relationship with someone outside the life is negligible. In addition, in the atmosphere of the prevailing sexual standards and attitudes in our society, the demand for prostitution as a market commodity is not likely to diminish rapidly. Prostitution will then continue to be an avenue of employment for some women in society despite its illegality.

REFERENCES

Bell, R. R. (1966) Premarital Sex in a Changing Society. Englewood Cliffs, N.J.:Prentice-Hall.

Benjamin, H. (1964) Prostitution and Morality. New York: Julian.

——— (1960) "Prostitution," in A. Ellis and A. Abarbanel (eds.) Encyclopedia of Sexual Behavior. New York: Hawthorne.

Bryan, J. H. (1966) "Occupational ideologies and individual attitudes of call girls." Social Problems 13 (Spring): 441–450.

——— (1965) "Apprenticeships in prostitution." Social Problems 12:287–296.

Burgess, E. and P. Wallin (1953) Engagement and Marriage. Philadelphia: J. B.Lippincott.

Burgess, R. L. and R. L. Akers (1969) "A differential association-reinforcement theory of criminal behavior," in D. Cressey and D. A. Ward (eds.) Delinquency, Crime, and Social Process. New York: Harper & Row.

Cloward, R. A. and L. E. Ohlin (1960) Delinquency and Opportunity. New York:Free Press.

Davis, K. (1937) "The sociology of prostitution." Amer. Soc. Rev. 2(October): 744–755.

Ellis, H. (1911) The Psychology of Sex. Philadelphia: F. A. Davis.

Gagnon, J. H. (1968) "Prostitution," pp. 592–598 in Volume 12 of D. Sills (ed.) International Encyclopedia of Social Sciences, Volume 12. New York: Macmillan and Free Press.

Gebhard, P. H., W. B. Pomeroy, C. E. Martin, and C. V. Christenson (1958) Pregnancy, Birth and Abortion. New York: Harper.

Glover, E. G. (1945) The Psychopathology of Prostitution. London: Institute for Scientific Treatment of Delinquency.

Greenwald, H. (1970) The Elegant Prostitute: A Social and Psychoanalytic Study.New York: Walker.

——— (1969) "The call girl," pp. 194–199 in W. A. Rushing (ed.) Deviant Behavior and Social Process. Chicago: Rand McNally.

——— (1958) The Call Girl: A Social and Psychoanalytic Study. New York: Ballantine.

Henriques, F. (1962–1963) Prostitution and Society. London: MacGibbon & Kee.

Hirschi, T. (1969) Causes of Delinquency. Berkeley: Univ. of California Press.

——— (1962) "The professional prostitute." Berkeley J. of Sociology 7:37–41, 47–48.

Hollender, M. H. (1964) "Prostitution, the body and human relatedness." International J. of Psychoanalysis 42: 404–413.

Jackman, N. R., R. O'Toole, and G. Geis (1967) "The self-image of the prostitute,"in J. H. Gagnon and W. Simon (eds.) Sexual Deviance. New York: Harper & Row.

Kinsey, A. C., W. B. Pomeroy, C. E. Martin, and P. H. Gebhard (1953) Sexual Behavior in the Human Female. New York: Pocket Books.

Maurer, D. W. (1939) "Prostitutes and criminal argots." Amer. J. of Sociology 44: 546–550.

Murtagh, J. M. and S. Harris (1957) Cast the First Stone. New York: McGraw-Hill.

Newsweek (1971) "Prostitutes: the new breed." (July 12): 78.

Reckless, W. C. (1950) The Crime Problem. New York: Appleton-Century-Crofts.

——— (1933) Vice in Chicago. Chicago: Univ. of Chicago Press.

Reevy, W. R. (1960) "Adolescent sexuality," in A. Ellis and A. Abarbanel (eds.) Encyclopedia of Sexual Behavior. New York: Hawthorne.

Reitman, R. L. (1936) The Second Oldest Profession. New York: Vanguard Press.

Schreiber, H. (1967) The Oldest Profession: A History of Prostitution. New York: Stein & Day.

Sutherland, E. H. (1955) Principles of Criminology. Philadelphia: J. B. Lippincott.

Winick, C. (1962) "Prostitutes' clients' perceptions of the prostitutes and of themselves." International J. of Social Psychiatry 8: 289–297.

——— and P. M. Kinsie (1971) The Lively Commerce: Prostitution in the United States. Chicago: Quadrangle.

71. The New Masseuse

PAUL K. RASMUSSEN
LAUREN L. KUHN

MASSAGE PARLORS HAVE BECOME A COMMON SIGHT throughout America in the last several years. They began in the great metropolitan areas, especially in San Francisco, Los Angeles, and New York, and it is in these areas that they have come to full bloom. But they are also springing up in out-of-the-way cities throughout the country. During a recent visit with his in-laws in a midwest city, one of our research colleagues was slightly shocked to see a little red building nestled among all the government buildings downtown—with a big sign proclaiming "Joyous Massage." But the full shock came only when his in-laws showed him another little building, with a small sign proclaiming "Bon Vivante Massage" announcing complete services, including overnight lodging, all just blocks from his in-laws' home—and also showed him the circular the parlor had delivered to all nearby residents.

Western City, with a metropolitan population of one million and a core city population of half a million, has not been in the forefront of the massage parlor explosion. But it has kept pace with most of the nation and is far more representative of the nation than those cities in the vanguard. In the past four years the number of massage parlors has jumped from 3 to 150. Business is booming, with an ever-wider segment of the population discovering the pleasures of the "fine art of the massage." Doctors, lawyers, and dentists enjoy this new-found pastime as much as salesmen, clerks, and laborers. And the controversy over the parlors rages in the city and county meetings, in courtrooms, and in the mass media.

The controversy over massage parlors centers on the question of sex. Are the parlors health spas, as their owners and supporters claim in public pronouncements, or are they centers of prostitution, as the police and their political attackers proclaim? Each side has extensive arguments and facts to support their claims. The opponents point to the sometimes sexy ads— "Nights of Paris Massage—A Girl for Every Taste." They also point to the "sexual format" of the massage itself.

The basic pattern of the massage puts a male customer in a room alone with a female masseuse, both in some state of undress. This sets the stage for such attacks as: "I'll bet I know which stiff muscle gets the most attention"—a comment which stems from the belief that a man and a woman alone in a room, both semi-nude and both touching each other, "have gotta be sexually involved." On the other hand, the supporters point to the healthful aspects of massage. Moreover, there are a lot of men in Western City who, from their own experience, claim the parlors are "straight." This was the experience of a friend, who claimed: "I don't know what you've found out, but I went to the Devil's Den, hoping to get laid, and all I got was a straight massage—sex never came up, dammit."

▶SOURCE: *"The New Masseuse: Play for Pay," Urban Life (October 1976), 5(3): 271–292. Reprinted by permission of the publisher, Sage Publications, Inc.*

Media coverage and court cases further add to the controversy and public confusion. Most people in Western City really do not know whether sexual services are offered or not, and many figure it is an even chance. The police contend that the "obvious is true." As one very experienced vice-squad officer told us: "We've been able to find only five straight parlors in Western City and even those we're not sure about—the rest are all houses of prostitution."

Our initial approach to the parlors, which involved classic "negotiations of entree" as social researchers, turned up some beautiful and sometimes outraged denials. One male researcher spent two months at a parlor becoming good friends with all the women, but especially one masseuse named Launa. Their friendship grew very intimate and our researcher had every reason to believe he had established the trust and confidence necessary for an honest exchange of information. Since Launa was candid about other things in the parlor, it made sense to also accept her claim that the parlor, for the most part, was straight and they were playing off other parlors' reputations to get customers while staying out of trouble with the police. But there was also evidence to the contrary. Our researcher witnessed, on several occasions, a fifty-dollar bill finding its way into the woman's purse and another friend claimed he had been to the parlor and received sexual services.

We decided to adopt an insider, in-depth approach. Fortunately, the female researchers on our team were able to get to know some masseuses quite well informally. They told us how it was done and once we knew, we were able to use that information to obtain other facts. Subjects were less inhibited, and we discovered there are indeed basic and extensive changes taking place on the American sex scene.

THE SETTING

Generally, massage parlors reflect the area they are in and the clientele they serve. In downtown business districts, they are converted store fronts and cater mostly to the tastes of the nearby military personnel. In residential areas, they are remodeled homes with the gruff atmosphere of their working-class customers. In the suburbs, they are housed in the local shopping centers complete with the decor of the suburbanite bar. They generally are dimly lit inside with drapes drawn, but all have the bright neon light proclaiming "massage." Most have waiting rooms furnished with a couch, several chairs, and a desk. The rest of the parlor is subdivided into private rooms for massage and facilities for bathing. The private rooms have a massage table covered with sheets or towels, a chair to hang clothes, and a shelf stocked with oils, powders, and lotions. The bathing facilities include things such as a shower, bath tub, and sauna.

Layla's Massage is typical of most parlors. It is located in a small shopping center along with several other businesses and looks strangely out of place with its drapes drawn. It is certainly not the typical store front. In fact, you might assume that the place is closed, but upon closer inspection you see the "open" sign. As a masseuse, you might feel rather self-conscious as you approach the parlor. The man from the barber shop next door is peering at you with curiosity and the secretary in the real estate office is also checking you out. After all, they think they know what you do.

The bells on the door jangle loudly as you enter. The change in atmosphere is a little overwhelming. You have stepped from the bright sunlight and hustle bustle of the outside world to the quiet, dimly lit surroundings of the massage parlor. It takes a moment to adjust your eyes to the relative darkness. Before you see the couch, table, and the reception desk up front, you hear the stereo playing softly. The soft blue lighting, the current issues of *Playboy* and *Penthouse* on the table, the picture of a provocative woman on the wall, all blend to create a seductive, sensuous atmosphere. It takes awhile, but slowly the atmosphere begins to affect how you feel. You begin to think sexy and act sexy.

Now you are ready for the day's work so you take your place behind the desk and wait for your first customer.

THE MASSEUSE'S ENTRY TO THE SCENE

Masseuses come from all walks of life. Their family backgrounds can range from the upper classes of society to the very lowest. Their ages range from eighteen to thirty. Their physical appearances vary also, from the very attractive to the average, but all the women are at least pleasant in appearance. Generally, the women have a liberal view of sex and have had an early exposure to sexual relations. Most have an ambiguous view of their personal social worth, and all need money. Like most members of Western City, they have a vague understanding about the sexual nature of the massage parlors and are willing, within limits, to perform certain sexual acts.

There are severe social constraints against becoming a masseuse. Unlike the customer, it is not possible for the masseuse to claim a "temporary loss of sanity" due to drinking too much or being pressured by "the boys." She is out there day after day, repeatedly exchanging sex for money. As a result, her choice of occupation says something about her "substantial self." As one masseuse put it:"At first, I couldn't look at myself as a prostitute, everyone knows that a prostitute is the lowest form of human existence. But then I just couldn't deny the facts, it was me out there, the real me out there, taking money for sex. I guess that's prostitution."This self-image as a prostitute must also be shared in many cases by close friends and intimates. This raises the obvious question, why would anyone choose such a profession?

Motives

It has always been a very common belief that women who choose to become prostitutes do so only as a last resort. This assumption was made in the early studies of prostitution (Parent-Duchatelet, 1837), by the different commission reports of the 1900s (Chicago Vice Commission, 1911; Kneeland, 1913), and by the more recent studies (Greenwald, 1958; Barlay, 1968). The prostitutes either lack the skills necessary to get other jobs, are so unattractive that no one would marry them, come from so low a social background that no one would want them, or they have been seduced into the profession not knowing what they were getting in to. In short, they have rather limited chances for success in life. Even those who seem to be "on the side of" the prostitute call for the banding together of the prostitutes to fight jointly their economically exploited circumstance (Verlade and Warlick, 1973). Our investigation of massage parlors strongly contradicts these views. In fact, quite the opposite is true.

The pay and the working conditions are very favorable. There are basically two common payment schedules for the masseuse. The first and most common is commission. The masseuse receives from 40% to 50% of the massage fee. The second is an hourly wage and ranges from $2-$3 an hour. In either case, she keeps all the money for sexual services. The cost of a straight half-hour massage ranges from $5-$15 and entails simply the masseuse massaging the customer. Variations on the basic massage include the topless or bottomless massage, the switch, where the customer massages the masseuse for part of the time, and the double massage where two women massage the customer. Each of these variations costs more, adding around $5 to the basic massage price.

The sexual services are called "extras" and are paid for in addition to the basic massage fee. Sexual services fall most commonly into three categories:(1) manual stimulation (locals, hand jobs) costing around $10, (2) oral sex (french, blow jobs) averaging $15, and (3) intercourse (lays, balling) ranging around $30. Variations of these types are sometimes offered and as with the massage increase the price. For example, manual or oral sex can be done bottomless or topless. On rare occasions customers desire and receive unusual sex such as anal intercourse

(Greek), being urinated on (golden showers), or being tied (bondage).

In the course of one eight-hour shift, a masseuse will have anywhere between two and six customers, each earning her an average of $25. This breaks down to anywhere from $50 to $150 per day, or $12,000 to $36,000 per year. A good income is definitely an important motive for becoming a masseuse. As one university graduate masseuse put it:

"If I could find a straight job that paid as well, I'd take it in a minute. But where can anyone just out of college find a job that pays twenty-four thousand dollars a year? Where could anyone find a job like that? It's good money and I enjoy it."

Even though some masseuses work only part-time they easily earn enough to live a good life.

Another important motive for becoming a masseuse is the "fast life"that is part of the business. By the fast life we mean the excitment and fun one experiences as part of the everyday existence on the job. The fast life cannot be any better explained than by a happily married masseuse:

"I quit the parlor for six months or so. The police were really hassling the parlors then. But I couldn't stand the boredom—not having a purpose in life. Now I'm back, living in two worlds. At home, I sit and read with my husband. That's the routine part. I feel comfortable there, I've got my man and nobody is going to hassle me. I can go out to a bar and the men won't try to pick up on me. Other women don't see me as a threat. I've known him for a long time and we've been through a lot together. He puts up with the worst side of me—when I'm on the rag and a real bitch—when I'm super depressed and down on life. Times that I wouldn't want to lay on anyone else. But this life is so predictable, so stable, that it's taken all the fun out of sex. I mean, for me to really enjoy sex, there's got to be some mystery to it. I really get off making it with someone new. Learning what's in his head, overcoming all the new problems of getting it on in bed. It's really exciting doing something that just bout everyone else thinks is wrong. What I really dig is looking across the room catching someone's eye—instant turn on. It's like this guy who came into the parlor. He had a good body and his eyes, you could really tell that in his eyes he really wanted me. I climbed right up on the table and got it on—good straight fucking. And that's how it is. I live in my stable world, doing what's necessary to get by. And then I live the fast life for all the fun and excitement."

Not only do the masseuses make good money, but they also enjoy the life style that is associated with it. They have not been forced into the profession because they lacked the skills, appearance, or opportunity for another profession. They clearly have not been seduced into the business out of ignorance. This is not to say that there are no problems associated with the job.

Limits

Most women starting out in the business set limits on what sex they are willing to perform. Some women will just do hand jobs, others will do just hand jobs and blow jobs and still others will perform anything including lays. While there are exceptions, the general path progresses from hand jobs, to blow jobs, to lays. This progression is further reflected in the price structure. Lays are universally more expensive than the other types of sex. The limits imposed by the women also go further than just the type of sex. Some women will perform lays only with regular customers that they find particularly nice or attractive.

The purpose of setting limits is similar to that in our general society. It helps maintain a positive self-image as well as a positive evaluation of one's self by others.This point was made clear by the statement of one novice masseuse when she said: "I've just done hand jobs since the first day on the job. After all, I go to church and believe in God. There's really nothing wrong with locals, the penis is just another part of the male body and needs to be massaged too." Boyfriends or close intimates also find limits important, as the boyfriend of one masseuse put it: "I'm really glad Mary decided to stick to just BJ's. That doesn't bother me so much.We still have something that is just between us. I really don't think I could handle it if I knew that anyone with the right amount of money could have her."

Meanings of Sex. Although limits set in the parlors function in much the same way as in our general society, they take a different path. rom our numerous discussions with customers and wit members of society in general, the progression in our society develops first with hand jobs, then to lays, and finally blow jobs. Further, customers in parlors overwhelmingly prefer oral sex. Using an economic model of supply and demand, one would expect BJs to be the most expensive. The general society sees oral sex as the extreme and even has laws against it. But BJs cost less than lays. So it appears that masseuses and customers disclosed several practical reasons for this. Customers claimed they liked BJs because they did not get them at home, and could lay back and enjoy the sensual variations possible with the human mouth; some mistakenly believed they could not contract venereal disease. Masseuses, on the other hand, pointed out the advantages of not having to undress, the economy of labor, and the increased ability to accommodate numerous men. Other possible explanations include the symbolic meanings attached to various body parts. The hand is the least intimate part of the body, often extended to strangers during the custom of "handshaking." The mouth is next, such as kissing a friend. And the most intimate part of the body is the genital region, commonly contacted by only the most intimate of lovers. This reasoning concurs with our findings of guilt neutralization: as long as one leaves the most intimate form of body contact to one's mate, one is not being unfaithful. All of these reasons come into play, so that oral sex is the most popular form of sex for masseuses and customers.

Breaking Limits

Whatever the reasons, limits are set by the women and as in our general society, men are always trying to seduce the women into breaking them. We found three ways this was commonly done. First, customers may ask for another masseuse who will do as he likes, or he may simply not return to the parlor. This prevents the woman from building up her clientele, a major source of her earnings and the major protection against police detection. One masseuse explained why she started doing BJs: "I'd been working here for about two weeks, and I just wasn't getting the money. The other girls were giving head and it didn't take the customers long to figure it out. I just sat there and watched all this money walk right out the door. So I figured if I was going to make it in this business I'd have to start giving BJ's." The second approach is more subtle. Customers would come in and become friends of the women. Another masseuse who started out with just hand jobs and later started giving BJs and lays explained how this happened:

"My boyfriend and I decided that I'd just do hand jobs, there was plenty of money with just that. But then I got to know a few of the guys really well. They'd take me out to lunch or just sit around the parlor and talk. After a while, I figured I'd ball these guys if they weren't in the parlor, so why not? But I really had to hide it from my boyfriend, he'd just shit if he knew."

The third way is open hostility from the customer. One masseuse who had maintained her limits described one time when it happened to her:

"The first thing I noticed when I walked in the room was his hat, he'd hung it over the light and the room was really dark. He'd signed up for a switch and wanted to massage me first. Right away he started getting really kissy. Then he said, 'I bet you make love real good.' When he found out he wasn't going to get laid, he got really pissed. He started swearing at me, put his clothes on, and left after he put his cigarette out in my coffee."

The pressures to conform to customer desires are especially strong and masseuses who stay in the business generally conform. While they may not break all limits, they generally must offer some form of sexual service. One veteran to the scene said:

"When I first started working here I decided: absolutely no sex. I could give a good massage and that should be enough. Then came along my first customer. He had been in the hospital for two months without any sex and just wanted to get off. He had the scars and all, so I felt really sorry for him. I decided that I'd make an exception, just this once. Since then, I make a lot of exceptions—to the point that the exceptions have become the rule."

PROFESSIONALISM

It is common for a masseuse to assert that she is a professional. One reason for this is that she considers herself an expert in her field. Not in the art of massage, ironically, but in her ability to deal openly with sex and to cater to the specific sexual needs of her customers. As one masseuse put it: "I am definitely a professional here. I have a skill and the skill is sex. It's not like everyone else.I do sex in the parlor as a job, and I'm good at it. I know a lot of techniques and I practice them all the time. Most men tell me that I'm better than their wives or lovers."

Disinterest

An important aspect of professionalism is disinterest. By disinterest we mean that a masseuse is able to look at her job objectively and not become emotionally involved. Disinterest allows the masseuse to justify the fact that she is getting paid for sex. If she were really involved in sex with customers, it would be difficult to rationalize getting paid for it, and customers would no doubt wonder if they should be getting paid to satisfy her. However, there is a conflict of interest here because in many cases a man expects the masseuse to get involved to a certain degree and to enjoy him personally or to get turned on by him. His ego is at stake and he wants to feel that he is capable of sexually arousing a woman. And so at the risk of losing clientele because of her lack of emotion and interest, a masseuse is compelled to "get into it" to a certain extent; in other words, to fake it. In this case a masseuse might breathe harder, or moan a little, but not to the point of having an orgasm. Of course, she is probably often sincerely interested in a customer but there are always times when she must appear happier or friendlier or

more interested than she feels, and also times when she is compelled to feign sexual excitation that she does not feel.

Occasionally, quite the opposite is true. Girls feign disinterest even though they are sexually aroused. As one masseuse said:

"I had this nice old guy come in and he paid me $20.00 to perform oral sex on me. He said all he wanted was to make me feel good. He started off really slow which made me feel really at ease . . . he knew what he was doing . . . and then all of a sudden I got sexually aroused. I laid there on my back trying to control my breathing and stomach muscles, so he wouldn't know. After it was all over he asked me if I had gotten off. I told him no, but I did enjoy it."

What is important is that the involvement remains a pseudo-involvement; objectivity is essential. The problems that arise as a result of becoming involved are best illustrated in the case of Carla. Because she enjoyed sex, being a masseuse gave her an opportunity to do what she liked and to get paid well to do it. But liking one's work too much can present problems:

"It just seems unfair to accept money for something that you enjoy. So when I do get off on a customer I really feel guilty about charging him. When I first started out, I didn't charge guys that I got off with. But it turned out that I wasn't making any money. I also got really emotionally involved with the customers. I just couldn't handle it. So I changed parlors and tried to remain aloof from the situation. When I do get off, I really try to hide it. I just don't think that's professional."

Play Acting

If a masseuse is professionally oriented and fairly perceptive, she will try to psych-out a customer's "type" as soon as he walks in the parlor. Masseuses become very adept at picking up clues about what kind of woman a customer will best respond to, i.e., does he try to develop a rapport with the masseuse, does he come on very sexually, does he like to be told what to do. Within a few minutes a masseuse can usually determine what "his type of woman" is and then cater to his particular needs by putting on her own performance. It is part of her professionalism. As one masseuse said: "When I walk out of that room, with my money in hand, you can't believe the feeling of success I have. Like, you know, a job well done. I know that I really made the guy happy and I was paid well to do it."

It might be added that this "act" aspect of the work is rarely discussed. It is extremely important for the man to feel that the situation is real. He wants to believe that the girl is not putting him on, even though, deep down inside, he might know that this is true. For the moment, he suspends the obvious and enjoys the pleasure of the performance.

INTERNAL DYNAMICS OF MASSAGE PARLORS

One nearly universal concern of people is the maintenance of a respectable concept of self. Most people want others to see them in a positive light and everyone wants to see themselves in a positive light. People develop a wide range of tests to evaluate their social worth. For example, success in sports demonstrates skills of the body, educational levels attained are taken as proof of intelligence, and leadership ability is evidence of personal charisma. These tests rank people, so that one either wins or loses in sports, has a degree or does not, is the leader or the one being led. There are certain restrictions placed on too much success. For example, if a person's chances are too slim to pass the test, he may simply withdraw from the test, try to change the ground rules of the particular test, or, in the extreme, resort to open violence. Further, people often band together and become part of a team, so that one's individual value is tied to that of the team. But regardless of whether it is a group or individual effort and regardless of the kinds of restrictions placed on the testing, the essence of the relationship is competition. You gain or lose a positive image of self at the profit or loss of others.

Competition is also an important aspect of the masseuse's job. They cannot rely on their occupational category for a respectable image. In fact, quite the opposite is true; the stigma of a masseuse is something to be overcome. The test for the masseuse revolves around the relative number of customers who choose her and the amount of money she can exact for her extras. By having more customers than other girls, she is able to claim a higher self-image. By receiving money for sex, she not only can compare her income with others, but also she can claim superiority to the customer.

Marketing Self

There are several techniques which the girls use to improve their chances of success. Perhaps the most difficult thing to manipulate is physical appearance. The *Playboy* centerfold has become the sexual ideal, and it is for this type of image that masseuses strive. Few women, if any, are born this way, and so they attempt to compensate for their deficiencies by wearing flattering clothes, choosing a becoming hairstyle, buying the appropriate make-up, and so on. Certainly the braless look can be very sexy, and the least amount of clothing a woman wears generally points in her favor when it is time for the customer to make a decision.

Body Language. The use of body language and seduction rhetoric is more easily manipulated than physical appearance, and does not require anything in terms of a money investment. Only time and a willingness to learn from others are needed. People are very conscious of body language, and masseuses use this knowledge to their advantage in their initial encounters with customers. If a masseuse is anxious to give a man a massage, she can easily communicate this through eye contact, body touching and body posture, relative body position, and body movement. In the case where one masseuse is more attractive than another, the latter may compensate by coming on strong with her body language, and this type of presentation of self makes her more desirable to the potential customer than even a more attractive woman.

Seduction Rhetoric. Seduction rhetoric is also used by masseuses. For example, a masseuse might be sitting in a chair with a pose that appears to be very casual but is actually well planned, give a customer "the look," and say, "You know, I could give you a r-e-a-l-l-y good massage." The implication is clear here; the customer is being assured that he will get sex once he signs up for a massage.

Both body language and seduction rhetoric are marketing techniques that are used primarily in the reception room before the massage has begun. It can really be to a woman's advantage to get a new customer first, as many men will return to the same masseuse provided they like her. Once the massage has begun, however, there are other marketing techniques that may be used to make one masseuse more desirable than another. As indicated, some women specialize in lays and locals and no frenches, or just locals and frenches, or just locals. One masseuse who decided to do only locals was competing with other women who offered a broader range of sexual services. Consequently, in order to build up a clientele, she had to market herself and her hand jobs very well. She accomplished this in two ways. Rather than standing next to the customer and masturbating him, which is the more common position, she completely undressed and sat on the man's stomach, facing his penis. Then she came up with the idea of a "Hopi Indian ball massage." She would lightly massage the balls of her customer with oil before giving him the local. In other words, she spent a lot of time and imagination in dealing with her customers. She also described the procedure to the customer ahead of time, which titillated his sense of the exotic or bizarre, and in addition it allowed the masseuse to charge more than the regular $5-$10 for a hand job.

However, a customer usually comes to a parlor with a particular sex act in mind, and a masseuse who is willing to accommodate his desires will generally have more customers than the girl who specializes. It is no less true in parlors than in general business that it is a good policy to please your customers. This takes on greater significance when the parlors are located in areas which are dependent upon return clientele.

All of these marketing techniques are employed by the general public to some extent. Although people might not be selling themselves directly, in a subtle way they are marketing themselves continually in various social situations. The major difference is that while in general society marketing takes place over a prolonged period of social interaction, in parlors it is generally a "one-shot deal." Because marketing in parlors occurs over a briefer period of time, it is necessarily more overt and less subtle than marketing that takes place in social situations. How a woman markets herself, in a massage parlor or the society at large, is largely dependent upon her own individual taste; and this is a product of social and class origin. You can find a masseuse who is reminiscent of the hardcore hooker stereotype just as easily as you can find a woman who presents herself in a tasteful, sophisticated manner.

Rate Busting

As in general society, there are problems in marketing oneself too well. In massage parlors, this problem presents itself in the form of the "rate-buster." As stated earlier, to a large extent masseuses establish their personal worth by their relative success. This structures their relationships to each other as a competitive one. For one masseuse to be successful, it is necessary that another masseuse be less successful. This necessity is generated by the fact that women are competing for the same rewards. Rate-busters are women who manage marketing too well and they end up getting more than their share of customers. Understandably, other masseuses resent rate-busters and consequently they must find some way in which to deal with them. In our research, we found several common ways of doing this.

Rumors.   In the event the woman is new, and has not secured her position in the parlor, unfavorable rumors can be circulated that threaten her job standing. The kinds of rumors range from stealing money, breaking house rules of behavior, using drugs, getting arrested, and spreading disease. Linda, an extremely attractive and a rather well-educated woman, had just been hired and was assigned to work several shifts with Lee, a reasonably attractive woman who had been doing well in the business. However, many of Lee's customers became interested in Linda and started seeing her. At this time, Lee went to the boss and complained that Linda was not "checking customers out" sufficiently and her actions were setting the parlor up for an eventual "bust." In addition, Lee claimed that Linda was cold and unfriendly toward customers, and therefore discouraged business. Because Lee had been working at the parlor much longer than Linda had, the boss tended to take her word over Linda's. It was necessary for Linda to gain support from girls of other shifts to deal with Lee's harassment.

Beating Them at Their Own Game.

A second way in which rate-busters are dealt with is to beat them at their own game. If women are finding it difficult to compete, they might react by attempting to redo their image, i.e., wear sexier clothes, try a new hairdo, have better come-ons, or whatever.

Price Cutting.

However, the most common way to deal with rate-busters is to undercut them in price. For example, if a rate-buster charges $30 for a lay, another woman might start charging $15 or $20, and as a result, she would get more business. An illustration of this is the case of Sandy, a masseuse who was rather overweight and generally not very attractive, but was rather well endowed. It was probably on this basis that she was able to get customers at all. She began doing lays for $10 or $15, which was considerably under the going rate of $30. All of a sudden, Sandy began getting a lot of business. Customers would start coming in and requesting Sandy all of the time while the other, better-looking girls sat around and wondered what was happening. In time, customers began complaining to the other masseuses that they were charging too much: "Why should I pay you thirty dollars when Sandy will do a lay for ten?" What happened was that now Sandy herself had in fact become the rate-buster, and now it was up to the other masseuses to deal with the problem of her

getting more business. In this case, they did this by complaining to the boss, who consequently put pressure on Sandy to charge the going rate unless she wanted to lose her job. When Sandy complied, she was still in the same predicament of not being able to compete.Eventually she quit the job.

Ostracism.

Obviously, there are some problems in trying to beat the competition. There is definitely a strain between competition and cooperation. Prices are not only determined by what people will pay, but also by what people will ask. In the massage parlor situation it is in the interest of all the girls involved to cooperate and to organize the prices set for extras. While everyone as a general rule will act in her own interest, in this case it benefits individual interest to act in the group's interest. If rate-busting were to go unchecked, the end result would be chaos. Masseuses would not end up making any money, and a great deal of hostility and resentment would be generated in the group.

The last way to deal with rate-busters is socially to ostracize them. This is done, not only in terms of the work setting in the parlor, but also outside in social settings. Social pressure is a common technique found in regular society; it is not unique to the parlor. For example, by refusing to talk or interact with another person, or by acting very critical and sarcastic, one can make another individual feel extremely frustrated and uncomfortable. Sherry was a girl who received this treatment as a result of the tremendous business she did. This might not have been so bad in itself, but she had a tendency to flaunt it, i.e., telling everyone how many "requests" she had had that evening, bragging about the amount of money she had made, and so on. Her coworkers reacted negatively to this, and before long she was either given the "silent treatment," criticized openly, or talked about behind her back.

The Threat of Arrest

One of the greatest occupational hazards that a masseuse must deal with is getting arrested. There are several ways in which a girl is likely to be busted. By far the most common way is for a vice-squad officer to pose as an undercover agent and handle the arrest himself. The law governing prostitution is California State Penal Code 647(a) and (b), which covers solicitation and the commission of a lewd act. There are several lines of defense that a masseuse may adopt to protect herself from being arrested on either or these charges. One is to be able to detect that a customer is a vice-squad officer by means of a "checking-out procedure."

Checking Out.   Some of the techniques for detection are very intangible. A woman must rely heavily on her sense of perception and intuition in checking out customers. From the moment that a customer walks in the door, the masseuse picks up clues that allow her to determine whether or not the guy might be a cop. First of all, she will probably categorize the customer according to a certain type; she will pick up on whether he is obviously in the military, a businessman, a salesman, a young surfer type, or whatever. Within each of these categories is the possibility that the man is a vice-squad officer in disguise. More specifically, a masseuse will check out a guy's haircut (is the guy's hair short, but not short enough to be in the military, is he a long-hair?); clothing (is he wearing a work uniform or a suit or faded jeans and T-shirt?); mannerisms (how he carries himself—is he confident or rather shy?); language (does he use jargon that is unique to his apparent occupation, how articulate is the customer given the vernacular he should know?).

In addition to his general appearance, there are other characteristics that a masseuse looks for in checking out her customers. Some customers come in and appear to be quite nervous. This may be indicative of a man's genuine uneasiness because this is his first visit to a parlor, or it may be the kind of nervousness that a person displays when he is trying to cover up something; or it may be the kind of nervousness that is brought on by being sexually aroused. Masseuses must also be wary of customers who attempt to develop rapport with them right away.

They learn to distinguish between the guy who is just being friendly or the guy who is just an obnoxious nuisance, or the guy who is really trying to glean some inside information about the masseuse or the parlor. Again, exactly how the women do this is largely dependent upon their intelligence and perception. A masseuse who is alert and aware will do a much better job of screening a potential customer than the girl who is disinterested or spaced out.

Another clue that arouses a masseuse's suspicion is if the customer inquires if extras are available and he does so right out at the front desk. This can mean one of two things: the guy is not familiar with the massage parlor scene and so he does not "know" that extras are to be discussed with the individual masseuse in the massage room; or, the guy is a vice-squad officer or an informer who is trying to set up the parlor. Most massage parlor owners insist that masseuses always claim that the place is straight when asked over the phone or at the desk. However, for the guys who are genuine customers this is a bad deal. They will probably leave and never come back unless they learn the inside line from a friend. For this reason, a masseuse may insinuate that extras are available or she may come right out and say it. As a general rule, however, masseuses are concerned enough about their own welfare that they will not do this, even though it means losing a few customers now and then.

Masseuses are also suspicious of men who come in the parlor in twos. Vice-squad officers have a habit of doing this, and it is the ideal situation for them. This way there are two people to testify against the masseuse in court. It is generally a good idea not to do extras with men that come in the parlor in twos, especially if there are only two masseuses working. Once the massage is paid for, a man may ask for a receipt. If he does, this also arouses suspicion. Most men are not interested in carrying a massage receipt in their pockets as evidence of their visit, and as massages are not tax deductible, there is no logical reason to keep it—unless, of course, you are an undercover agent, and in that case you might choose to keep it. From the moment that the man walks in the door until he has paid for his massage, the perceptive masseuse will pick up all of the clues we have mentioned and then she will form an overall impression.This checking-out procedure continues as the masseuse leads her customer down the hall to his room. During this time she may inquire, "Have you been here before?" and if the answer is yes, she may press him later for information regarding which masseuse he had, and so on. In order not to arouse suspicion by asking this question, a masseuse may comment in response to the man's answer, "Oh, then you know where the bathroom and shower are?" At this point the masseuse shows the customer to his room, instructs him to undress and lie on the table, and says that she will be back shortly. She gives him enough time to undress and then returns to the room.

Upon entering the room, the masseuse continues with her checking-out procedure. The first thing she notices is the man's body position: is he lying face down or face up; is he completely naked or partially clothed; is he using a towel to cover his genitalia; is he lying on the table in a relaxed position, seemingly ready for the massage or is he sitting on the table looking like he is ready to talk. The masseuse takes all of these things into account in the first couple of seconds that she enters the room.

If the man appears to be relatively passive, the masseuse will initiate the conversation. This is to her advantage: she can control everything that is said and done during the course of the massage. She may begin by greeting him, asking him if he prefers lotion, powder, oil, or alcohol. As she begins to massage, she will ask him a series of questions that, on the surface, appear to be nothing more than friendly interest. These questions are all calculated to give the masseuse a clearer picture of the customer's background and interests. She will inquire about the man's job, his family, where he lives, and what he does in his spare time. She will ask if he gets massages often, or how he found out about this particular

parlor, or what other parlors he has frequented. She will always be looking for consistencies and inconsistencies in his "story"; i.e., if the man claims that he is a local construction worker, are his hands rough and calloused? If he is a salesman, can he discuss marketability of his product with specific knowledge of other competitive products? By this time, the masseuse has a very definite feeling about the customer; whether he is "cool" (not an undercover agent), or whether many of the things he has said do not check out and he is "weird." It is this positive or negative evaluation which determines the willingness of the masseuse to engage in sex. If he is weird he will receive a straight massage and nothing more. If he is cool and knows how to play the game, he will have his sexual desires fulfilled.

The Word Game

Another important technique used to protect the masseuse from legal constraint is the word game. The effectiveness of the word game is derived from the nature of the laws against prostitution and, ironically, also from the moral attitudes of our society. A prostitute is guilty of breaking the law if she either (1) solicits her customer, i.e., asks him if he would like to pay for her services or, (2) commits a lewd act, i.e., takes part in a sex act. The purpose of the word game is for the masseuse to get the customer to solicit her for the sex act, thus freeing her from prosecution under solicitation. In order for one to be guilty of committing a lewd act, an actual sex act must occur and since it takes "two to tango" this means the vice officer would have to take part also in the sex act. While this is within the limits of the law, as a "feigning accomplice," it is generally not within the moral limits of our society. Hence, the moral codes of our society themselves prevent enforcement.

There are several methods a masseuse can use to get the customer to solicit her. The massage itself is sometimes enough, with the erotic finger tip massage coming close and sometimes touching erogenous zones of the body. Other techniques include "Take my hands and place them where you want me to massage" or "Our time is almost up, is there anyplace *else* you would like massaged?" Other innovative techniques are sometimes added, such as asking if he is in any way connected with the law enforcement agency, what identification he can produce to prove who he really is, the actual signing of a statement to the effect that he solicited her, and the taping of the whole conversation to be used in court if necessary. But, generally, the masseuse has little trouble getting the customer to solicit her, the slightest sign of sexual interest is usually enough. A typical solicitation would be:

L: Do you give extras?

M: What do you mean by extras?

L: Like give head or things like that?

M: Are you soliciting me?

L: Well, yes.

M: Ya, I do, but it's really expensive now.

L: How about $20.00

M: Yes.

Law Enforcement

Arrests that have been made regardless of the word game and checking-out procedures are generally the result of a girl too new to the scene or a vice officer who is not aware of the legal restrictions placed on his behavior. One such case, involving Cheri, resulted from a little of each circumstance. Cheri was arrested the first day on the job for soliciting a hand job. Since it was her first day she lacked the skills to sense the presence of a vice-squad officer. On the other hand, the vice-squad officer, not understanding the nature of the law, played the word game and made the solicitation, not only once, but many times. The case went to trial by judge and was dismissed immediately on the sole testimony of the arresting officer. The grounds for the dis-

missal were: (1) no act of solicitation was made by the masseuse, hence no infraction of 647(b) and, (2) no lewd act had occurred—647(a). While the case was dismissed, it was not without great personal loss to Cheri. She still had to pay $1,000 to a lawyer, to spend many hours in court, and to live with a certain amount of emotional strain.

The conviction rate for arrests involving prostitution is extremely low. Cases are either plea bargained to the lessor offense of disturbing the peace or thrown out of court altogether. So, except for some harassment by police, massage parlor sex-for-money becomes quasi-legal.

CONCLUSION

Traditional theories of prostitution have taken the functional view (Merton, 1938) that prostitutes have internalized the values (ends) of society but lack the legitimate means to achieve them. For example, the prostitute values the financial rewards of our society but lacks the education or job skills necessary to achieve them. She turns to prostitution as the last resort. The women become exploited by the pimps, owners, and customers (Verlarde and Warlick, 1973) which leads to deep emotional problems such as low self-esteem (Greenwald, 1958).

Many findings in this article conflict with these traditional theories. Part of these differences can be attributed to basic attitudinal changes in our society. The liberation movements of both women and homosexuals, the acceptance of public nudity, and sexual freedom, all carry the same message: "The body is a source of pleasure and should be used for pleasure." While all members of society have not endorsed this new attitude, its impact is evident in the increased sexual nature of entertainment and the explosion of public nudity on the stages, the beaches, and in many other places. Clearly, this new attitude is very different from that of the past: "save yourself until you're married." The effect on prostitution is obvious. Now a girl can say: "I'm only doing what I like, and if someone wants to pay me for it, that's great. I can use the money."

The massage parlor front is equally important. By playing the word game and checking out each customer, prostitutes have a quasi-legal status. The masseuses are simply giving a massage, and if one should ask for sexual pleasure, he not she, is breaking the law. Furthermore, the massage parlor front gives the masseuses freedom of choice. If a customer comes in whom the women do not like, for whatever reason, they can give him nothing more than a straight massage. This allows the masseuse to maintain her self-respect. As one masseuse put it: "I'm not a common prostitute, I only do those customers that I especially like." This also fits with new American sex values: "If it feels good, do it; at least if you really like the other person."

The changes in society's attitudes and the existence of the massage parlor front have interested a new type of employee in prostitution. While other forms of prostitution have been dominated by girls from lower-class origins, the new masseuse is typically a middle-class girl with some college education. To some degree, then, the differences in our findings can be explained by the fact that massage parlor sex is really different than traditional forms of prostitution. The existence of this new middle-class masseuse seriously questions the assumed causal relationship between prostitution and social pathological behavior (Greenwald, 1958). The "sick" behavior which has been reported seems to be a product of a lower-class background and the life styles common to this class.

We feel the major source of this traditional bias is the methods which have been used to study prostitution. Most of the studies which have been done on prostitution focus on the lower-class prostitute who is in jail. Similarly, the subject matter of sexual behavior creates intense emotional conflict in all those associated with it. Since there is conflict, it is difficult not to take sides. If you are a male, you become either a customer or a boyfriend; and if you are a female, you become either straight or "in the business." Each of these roles limits the type of information you receive. Hence, it is important to have researchers playing each role to get all sides. As mentioned at the beginning of this paper, it took a female "insider-informant" to break through the straight front presented to our male researcher. There were many other incidences where the method of team field research allowed us to go beyond our sole reliance on the member's accounts. In many cases, we were able to match our own individual experiences and feelings against those given by members. In other cases, we spent the time necessary to break through the member's deceptions. Without exception, we have all felt it impossible to gain an in-depth understanding without the benefit of the diverse characteristics and information of a team.

Finally, returning to the question which concerned us in the beginning, we have found that there is indeed a basic change taking place within American society over the social forms of sex-for-money. There are at least a few other studies of massage parlors that are reliable in some degree, although in all cases we have found that they were "fronted-out" in some important ways by failing to use women who could deal with the inside informants as friends. These have revealed the same basic pattern as our findings. Obviously, there may be some important differences in what goes on behind the parlor fronts from one part of the country to another, but the burden of proof now rests with those who contend that these are not fronts for sex-for-money acts. We expect that, as the evidence accumulates around the country, it will be clear that America now has complex forms of quasi-legalized forms of sex-for-money and they are on a large and growing scale. We suspect this quasi-legal form is a half-way form, something less than legal because of continuing opposition to sex-for-money, but something more legal than prostitution has been in our society. This ambivalent situation is made possible by changing social feelings and values about sex. While past experience shows the hazards of predicting social events, we would predict these new forms of sex-for-money, carried out discreetly and perhaps with controlled hygienic conditions will become fully decriminalized in the years ahead.

REFERENCES

Barlay, S. (1968) Sex Slavery. London: Heinemann.

Chicago Vice Commission (1911) The Social Evil in Chicago. Chicago: Gunthorp-Warren.

Davis, K. (1955) "Prostitution," in R. Merton and R. Nisbet (eds.) Social Problems. New York: Harcourt Brace & World.

Greenwald, H. (1958) The Call Girl. New York: Ballantine Books.

Kneeland, G. (1913) Commercialized Prostitution in New York City. Montclair, N.J.: Patterson Smith.

Merton, R. (1938) "Social structure and anomie." Amer. Soc. Rev. (October).

Parent-Duchatelet, A. J. B. (1837) Prostitution Dans la Ville de Paris. 2 vols. Paris: J. B. Bailiere.

Verlarde, A. and M. Warlick (1973) "Massage parlors: the sensualist business." Society (December).

72. Homosexual Prostitution

JOHN H. GAGNON
WILLIAM SIMON

LIKE ALL FORMS OF COLLECTIVE SEXUAL DEVIANCE, male homosexuality tends to create at its periphery a substantial number of persons who are involved in the staging or performance of various parts of the homosexual life. The owner of the homosexual meeting place, the bartenders, the owners and clerks in boutiques for men, the models, the makers and purveyors of erotic photographs and films of males are all service personnel generated by the existence of a homosexual subculture. The majority of personnel in these service occupations are themselves homosexual, and are more likely to be publicly homosexual than homosexuals in other, more conventional occupations. These are occupations which can tolerate and even promote the exaggerated feminine or camp elements of the homosexual life style. In a very important sense, these occupations are the ones that promote a great deal of continuity in the homosexual subculture and, by virtue of their visible nature, produce a public image of homosexuality that is at variance with the behavior of the largest number of the subculture's members. Even though these occupational locations are the most deviant from the point of view of the larger culture, as a result of their public nature they do not require so much concealment of homosexual interests. Therefore, they may not be so psychologically costly in terms of keeping major components of the self secret from the larger society.

In addition to these roles which promote homosexual presentations that are public in nature, there is one other central figure in the homosexual world who often depends in large measure for his success on being, or at least presenting himself as, exclusively heterosexual. This is the male prostitute.[1] The male prostitute plays for the male homosexual many of the same roles that the female prostitute does for heterosexual men, but the role takes on additional complexity since the male prostitute faces a client population that has a subcultural aspect quite unlike that of the female prostitute's heterosexual client. Furthermore, there are certain aspects of male prostitution that arise specifically from the way in which male homosexual preferences are organized in this culture.

One of these central differences is that the female prostitute is paid so that her client can have an orgasm, while in nearly all of the cases the male prostitute is paid for his orgasm. Therefore, unlike the female prostitute, the male prostitute must have sufficient sexual arousal from the contact to become erect and have orgasm. Thus, unlike the female prostitute, the male prostitute is limited in the number of contacts he may have over a short period of time by the refractory period to sexual stimulation that

▶SOURCE: *Sexual Conduct: The Social Sources of Human Sexuality. Chicago: Aldine, 1973, pp. 165–175. Reprinted by permission.*

[1]Estimates of the frequency of contact with prostitutes by homosexuals are presently unknown.

follows orgasm in the male. While there are males who can have more than one orgasm over a single twenty-four hour period (and there is evidence from non-Western cultures that this is a more common physical capacity than Western men exhibit), the capacity for two or three orgasms per day is usually limited to the young and the healthy. The requirement of arousal to the point of orgasm in these sexual encounters on the part of men who are either predominently interested in females or make such a presentation has consequences for both patterns of recruitment to the occupation and to levels of economic reward. Since the female prostitute needs to have neither arousal nor sexual pleasure, she may engage in prostitution without sexual interest in her partner and have contact with substantial numbers of males over relatively short periods of time.

THE HOMOSEXUAL AS CLIENT

Much of the content and character of contacts with homosexual prostitutes arises from the character of the homosexual lifestyle itself. Even though a substantial number of homosexuals do go to prostitutes, paying for sex is evidence that one is unable to compete for it on the free market—that is, that one is unattractive or inept at making a sexual approach. It is clear from our discussion of female prostitution that a certain proportion of a prostitute's clients are those physically unable (the ugly, the handicapped) or socially unable to operate in normal sociosexual encounters. While these persons represent some of the customers of prostitutes—those who find the usual channels of sexual access too difficult to manage—they are clearly not the majority.

Once again, like prostitution in the heterosexual world, there are elements of erotic degradation in paying for a sexual encounter. However, unlike the heterosexual world where the paying of money degrades the woman—making her into a more erotic object, an object to which anything can be done without consequence—in the homosexual world the payment of money often has the effect of degrading the customer.[2] In the heterosexual world, power in some limited sense in the interaction falls to the customer following the exchange of money; in most acts of homosexual prostitution the customer remains the supplicant of the prostitute. The range of sexual techniques permitted will be highly stereotyped and limited, especially when the partners are playing out a situation in which the heterosexuality of the prostitute is what is being paid for.

This commitment to the heterosexual character of the male prostitute is often central to the relationship. Much of the sexual content of some homosexuals' lives is stereotyped around the heterosexual pattern. The contact between heterosexuals is well differentiated in terms of sets of defined modes of approach and withdrawal, linked to the playing out of nonsexual gender roles. Such self-other differentiation is often sought by homosexuals in seeking persons with whom to have sexual contact. Commonly, this search for differentiation occurs along some symbolic axis that relates to masculine or feminine role presentations that the homosexual (as much as the heterosexual) mistakes as a commitment to heterosexuality or homosexuality. It is this drive for differentiation from the self that often leads homosexuals to contacts with men in uniform, truck drivers, stevedores, or men in other masculine-typed occupations, to men of other races, and to prostitutes who are commonly referred to as "rough trade." Two motives may be untangled in these kinds of contacts. The first is one of self-degradation. Contact with men who are symbolically more powerful gives the sexual act a greater sense of tension through increased risk. At the same time, a desire for power over the heterosexual is also evoked. By the act of arousing the prostitute and "making" him ejaculate, the homosexual male acts out a drama in which

[2]Thomas Painter, "Male Homosexuals and their Prostitutes in Contemporary America," 2 vols. (unpublished, 1941).

he is in power over the heterosexual male. He also reduces his own deviance by confirming his belief that there is an element of homosexuality in all men.

A less complex set of motivations exists among those male homosexuals who, like heterosexuals, are in positions where their sexual needs must remain anonymous and protected.[3] The homosexual businessman or executive is even more vulnerable than the heterosexual who engages in deviant sexual activity. Contact with prostitutes provides an outlet that does not have the risks that creating a series of close sexual friendships might, nor does it necessarily contain the risk comparable to that of going to locales where known homosexuals congregate. (Not untypically, such homosexuals fear disclosure to other homosexuals almost as much as they fear disclosure to nonhomosexuals.) This is especially true when contact with prostitutes occurs outside of the city or neighborhood where the individual lives or works. There are risks in contacts with prostitutes, as we shall see, but often these risks are run by men who find that conventional access to homosexual contacts is denied them. Another group of men in this class, who go to prostitutes out of convenience or because of restrictions of sexual opportunity, are those males who are themselves homosexual but have heterosexual families. These men, often bisexual, go to prostitutes because they are unable to create other liaisons due to the great social risks involved.

A final major component in going to male prostitutes is a desire among many homosexuals for young men. Here, many of the components of heterosexual contacts are to be found in homosexual relationships. The society of the United States is youth-oriented in both its heterosexual and homosexual worlds. The physical attractiveness of the young is a major element in sexual desirability. To gain access to the young and the attractive, it is often necessary to pay some kind of price whether one is heterosexual or homosexual—in today's world the young desire the young. In order for an older male to enter this world, he must pay either in money or in allowing access to rewards that would not normally be available to the young. While real affection can and does exist in both worlds between people of disparate ages, this is not a common phenomenon, and such encounters are often contaminated by other considerations.

THE TRANSIENT MAJORITY

Unlike the female prostitute, whose first paid encounter often comes after a fairly substantial career of unpaid heterosexual contact, for many men (perhaps the majority) payment for a homosexual experience is either part of a single homosexual experience or one of just a few experiences.

A substantial number of young men in relatively isolated social situations (out of money, without friends, traveling, and the like) are approached by homosexuals who offer them money for a simple act of fellatio. The encounter goes no further in terms of physical intimacy. It begins and it is over within a few moments. Sometimes the encounter will involve returning to the homosexual's quarters and staying the night, but more commonly the encounter will have little social dimension. Such an experience may occur while young men are hitchhiking, living transiently in a youth hostel or hotel, or wandering in a marginal bright lights section of a community.[4] For the heterosexual young man this social isolation, the fleeting nature of the contact and the money serve to reduce any sense of personal homosexuality. He must, however, have the minimal capacity to symbolically transform the homosexual act by neutralizing it into a merely

[3]For the distinction between overt and covert homosexuals see Maurice Leznoff and William A. Westley, "The Homosexual Community," *Social Problems* 3 (April 1956):257–67.

[4]Reiss, "The Social Integration of Queers and Peers."

physical response or to imagine a heterosexual stimulus. Without these circumstances of isolation and the minimum ability to transform the situation, he will be unable to sustain his sexual response. Outside of this circumstance, it is unlikely that he will pursue homosexual relationships.

Another relatively common situation for transient homosexual prostitution occurs when a collection of young men, often in the military service in a strange community, are seeking heterosexual adventure. Often their search is in vain. In a state of mild sexual excitement and commonly somewhat intoxicated, they may be approached either singly or as a group by a male homosexual. If the young man is approached singly, his reaction will be similar to the young man who is approached in social isolation. If the group is approached, what occurs is dependent on the prior experience of the members and the power structure of the peer group itself. If the consensus is for cooperating, the group values themselves serve to neutralize the homosexual character of the event in addition to the mechanisms cited above.

Another common collective situation that can lead to paid homosexual encounters comes out of the street group culture of many U.S. cities. Many lower-class young men spend a great deal of time in gang behavior engaging in delinquent and quasi-delinquent activities.[5] Depending on many characteristics of the local community and the gang, some or many members of the gang will engage in transitory contacts with homosexuals for pay. The act is perceived by the heterosexual participants as ways to make money when they are out of funds. Depending on the local gang culture, such encounters may be relatively aggressively pursued, or they will be waited for almost passively. Gangs can develop a fairly long-term contact with a series of males who buy liquor for underage members, supply them with money, drive them around in

their cars, and do over favors. The contacts are viewed in much the same light as contact with female prostitutes or contacts with promiscuous girls in the neighborhood.

All of these relationships with males who are predominantly heterosexual have serious elements of risk. The etiquette of the contact requires that the client very carefully refrain from raising the homosexual nature of the contact, that the physical contact be only with the genitals, and that there is no expectation of reciprocity.[6] The image of the self as heterosexual on the part of the prostitute is very delicately balanced, and if there is an imputation that the prostitute is enjoying the act out of homosexual motivations serious violence can result. Some of these reactions may well be what has been clinically described as homosexual panic. The prostitute, formerly secure in his heterosexual self-image, suddenly suspects that he is being aroused by the homosexual content of the transaction. The reaction is often a retreat to physical violence, since assaulting the homosexual now reasserts his dominance and his masculinity. This potential is especially true in group encounters with young men where, after the sexual contact occurs, the group of men assault the homosexual in order to continue to see themselves and each other as heterosexual. This same process also occurs in delinquent gangs where the homosexual contact is followed by assault and robbery of the homosexual. Among some delinquent gangs, members deliberately play the role of prostitute in order to rob the customer. Since the homosexual was engaged in what is illegal behavior, he has no recourse to the police. As we will see, the robbery and blackmail of the homosexual occurs among more professional prostitutes as well.

These transients make up the majority of men who in their lives have had a homosexual contact for pay. The vast majority remain heterosexual and continue to see their

---

[5]Ibid., p. 199.

[6]Ibid., p. 214–26.

homosexual contacts as merely "playing the queers."

APPRENTICES, HUSTLERS, AND CALL BOYS

The apprentices in the life of homosexual prostitution are drawn from the subgroup of originally heterosexual males and some homosexual males. For many young men living at the edge of conventional social life, living lives of bare economic subsistence and lacking skills or training, the first accidental homosexual encounter may lead to still others. The relatively easy money, the personal attention, the comparatively exciting life can be attractive to the young, unattached male. If he is physically attractive he will find that by going to certain street locations in large cities or to specifically homosexual gathering places he will be approached by a substantial number of men who will pay him for sexual contact.[7] He may be advised to these locations by his first customer. If he wishes to continue in the trade, he will learn that there are modes of receiving money and maintaining the normative character of the relationship. The life on the street leads to further detachment from conventional life. He will come into contact with other prostitutes and they will describe and discuss customers, homosexual techniques, and the ways of the life. His newness on the street will at first assure him of customers simply because he is new. Like any prostitute his physical attributes, including penis size, will be talked about in the client world, creating his market price and desirability. To the degree that he maintains a physical attitude of nonreciprocity in homosexual acts, he will retain a certain set of customers; but he will find that the longer he is around the life the greater the suspicion is that he is, in fact, homosexual himself. As a protection against homosexual ideation and reaction, many of

these young men have extensive contacts with the pre-prostitute females who are to be found in the same half-world of the street.

In some cases, young men who are themselves homosexual also go through this process as their way into a homosexual lifestyle. An earlier homosexual commitment takes on its beginning form through prostitution, just as if the individual were totally heterosexual. This role-playing is often a transitory phenomenon, and a young male with strong prior homosexual proclivities begins to reciprocate in the paid encounters. If such young men are attractive, they will continue to be paid for sexual relationships that either do or do not involve reciprocity, but their own homosexuality will drive away those customers who are paying for the illusion or the reality of heterosexual conquest or degradation.

Time and self-conception combine to move the young man from apprenticeship to hustler status. When the young man moves from sporadic, unsought encounters to spending time on the street or other locations where he is available to clients on a full-time or weekend basis, his status changes both for himself and for others. Once a young man has appeared on the street often enough and has had sex with enough men, he may maintain his self-image as heterosexual but becomes identified as a hustler. This status, however, is not nearly as irreversible a situation as the movement into female prostitution.

The bulk of even these young men will, as apprentices or hustlers, drift out of the world of prostitution if they remain heterosexual, since the search for newness and variety is endemic in this sector of the homosexual comminity. New faces and new bodies will replace these young men in the street and bar culture, and they will disappear back into the mainstream of the society or take up other delinquent occupations. Some of these originally heterosexual males will drift into a homosexual self-image and fall into conventional roles in the homosexual world. Those who were previously disposed to

[7]H. Lawrence Ross, "The 'Hustler' in Chicago," *The Journal of Student Research* 50 (September 1959): 15.

homosexuality will do much the same. It is this small proportion, of all those who came in as transient members of the world of homosexual prostitution, who verify the homosexual folklore that "this year's trade is next year's competition," meaning that this year's prostitutes will be paying prostitutes next year. This occurs often enough to keep the folklore going, but it is an insignificant source in terms of recruitment to adult homosexuality. From this street population a few will go on to other roles as courtesans and call boys.

For those young men marked by substantial physical attractiveness and quick wits, it is possible to move into more specialized prostitute roles. The street or bar hustler can, if he has good manners and social graces, move upward socially through his physical attributes. He may attach himself to an older male who is affluent and become his lover, attendant, or servant; or he can become a relatively highly paid call boy. This later occupation can be performed singly or through a male madame. Like the call girl, this is the pinnacle of the profession, and it is organized in much the same manner as the highest echelon of female prostitution. The profession at this level is marked by discretion, since the clients are men of considerable substance and reputation. The prostitute must by this time be prepared to participate in nearly any kind of sexual activity, either actively or passively, either heterosexually or homosexually. The most complex and extended group of this sort known to the authors includes both males and females who can be supplied in almost any numbers or combinations.

Movement into this world is much the same as movement into the world of female prostitution. Individuals become almost totally detached from conventional lifestyles, and customers are regulars who return relatively frequently. Unlike the erratic and disordered street world, this can be a world of considerable stability and continuity. The homosexual call boy's goal is very similar to that of the call girl—to move into a permanent relationship with someone who is extremely affluent. The job, however, has the same disadvantages as well. It is dependent, for most of its members, on continuing good looks and amenability. At the same time, detachment from conventional lifestyles and work habits encourages (except for the best organized call boys) general dissipation and laziness that decreases attractiveness. The male prostitute begins to live in a world dominated by other prostitutes and by the accoutrements of prostitution, its attitudes, and exploitative lifestyles. One real advantage, however, is that this world seems more protected from the police and less vulnerable to arrest than is the world of the female prostitute.

CONCLUSION

Like all worlds of secondary deviance organized to facilitate the lives of other deviants, the world of homosexual prostitution is a shifting and diffuse community.[8] Its values and norms overlap and differ from the values and the norms of the world of female prostitution, but at the center of each is the confluence of sex and money. In the one, the money serves to create the image of eroticism on the part of the client; in the other, the money serves to protect the self-image of the prostitute. For the males, the taking of money is often the first step toward the world of prostitution; for the female, the taking of money is the last step in the process. Both prostitute types are continuous with the character and values of the world that they serve, the female with the world of the heterosexual as a deviant alternative, the homosexual prostitute as a form of deviance for the deviant.

[8]The cost of sexual encounters with male prostitutes, unlike contacts with females, has not increased with general affluence. This may be a function of the large number of transients and apprentices who drive down the price. See T. C. Esselstyn, "Prostitution in the United States," *The Annals of the American Academy of Political and Social Science* 375 (March 1968): 133.

White Collar and Corporate Crime

PUBLIC ATTENTION HAS BEEN DIRECTED TO CRIMES OF POLITICIANS, ILLEGAL political contributions by major corporations, and other kinds of offenses committed by upper-class and powerful segments of American society, particularly in the wake of Watergate.

One of the most heavily publicized events of our time is the scandal arising from the blatant political corruption of Spiro Agnew while governor of Maryland and as Vice-President. The criminal information instigated by U.S. Attorney George Beall in federal court in Baltimore reveals a picture of bribes and other corrupt practices, which revealed the crassest kind of dishonesty at the very highest levels of government.

Many large corporate businesses in America have become subjected to very serious criticism, in part, at least, for illegal political contributions. The Gulf Oil Corporation, in its own publication, mercilessly reveals the flow of corporate funds "laundered" through the Bahama Exploration Co., Ltd., involving, in 12 years, about five million dollars distributed among various state, federal, and local government personnel. In another influential industry, the automotive business, Farberman argues that a criminogenic market structure exists that exerts economic control and pressures some new car dealers to enter into fraud, kickbacks, "shortsales," and other illegal or unethical practices against customers.

A classic example of white-collar crime at the highest corporate level, similar in some ways to the electrical industry's conspiracies in the 1950s, encompassed 15 manufacturers of plumbing supplies who agreed to fix prices illegally on their bathroom fixtures. The selection, by Demaree, reveals how their complicated plans were formulated and ultimately uncovered. The final item is a rather informal but fascinating statement on the illegal and exploitive behavior by some members of the medical profession, the occupational elite in America. We are told that some doctors have manipulated insurance companies, overcharged, engaged in pseudosurgery, received fees for services never rendered, and have cheated at taxes.

73. The United States vs. Spiro Agnew, Vice-President

GEORGE BEALL
BARNET D. SKOLNIK
RUSSELL T. BAKER, JR.
RONALD S. LIEBMAN

TEXTS OF CHARGE AGAINST VICE PRESIDENT AND OF GRAND JURY CRIMINAL INFORMATION

THE UNITED STATES ATTORNEY FOR THE DISTRICT of Maryland charges that:

On or about the 23rd day of April, 1968, in the District of Maryland, Spiro T. Agnew, a resident of Annapolis, Maryland, who during the calendar year 1967 was married, did wilfully and knowingly attempt to evade and defeat a large part of the income tax due and owing by him and his wife to the United States of America for the calendar year 1967, by filing and causing to be filed with the District Director of Internal Revenue for the Internal Revenue District of Maryland, at Baltimore, Maryland, a false and fraudulent joint income tax return on behalf of himself and his said wife, wherein it was stated that their taxable income for said calendar year was the sum of $26,099 and that the amount of tax due and owing thereon was the sum of $6,416, whereas, as he then and there well knew, their joint taxable income for the said calendar year was the sum of $55,599, upon

▶SOURCE: *Documents filed in the case of the United States vs. Spiro T. Agnew, U.S. District Court for the District of Maryland. Exposition of the Evidence Against Spiro T. Agnew Accumulated by the Investigation in the Office of the U.S. Attorney for the District of Maryland, October 10, 1973.*

which said taxable income there was owing to the United States of America an income tax of $19,967.47.

GEORGE BEALL
United States Attorney

THE UNITED STATES ATTORNEY FOR THE DISTRICT OF MARYLAND AS OF OCT. 10, 1973

Introduction

The following statement is respectfully submitted to the court by the Government at the arraignment of Spiro T. Agnew. It constitutes a detailed recitation of the facts and evidence developed by the investigation to date, which establish in part the source of the unreported funds which constitute the basis of the charge filed today. The presentation of this statement in court today was a material condition, requested by the Department of Justice, to the agreement reached between the Government and Mr. Agnew.

SUMMARY

I. The relationship of Mr. Agnew, I. H. Hammerman 2d and Jerome B. Wolff.

In the spring of 1967, shortly after Mr. Agnew had taken office as Governor of Maryland, he

823

advised Hammerman that it was customary for engineers to make substantial cash payments in return for engineering contracts with the State of Maryland. Mr. Agnew instructed Hammerman to contact Wolff, then the new chairman-director of the Maryland State Roads Commission, to arrange for the establishment of an understanding pursuant to which Wolff would notify Hammerman as to which engineering firms were in line for state contracts so that Hammerman could solicit and obtain from those engineering firms cash payments in consideration therefore.

Hammerman, as instructed, discussed the matter with Wolff, who was receptive but who requested that the cash payments to be elicited from the engineers be split in three equal shares among Agnew, Hammerman and Wolff. Hammerman informed Mr. Agnew of Wolff's attitude; Mr. Agnew informed Hammerman that the split of the cash monies would be 50 per cent for Mr. Agnew; 25 per cent for Hammerman and 25 per cent for Wolff. Hammerman carried that message to Wolff, who agreed to that split.

The scheme outlined above was then put into operation. Over the course of the approximately 18 months of Mr. Agnew's remaining tenure as Governor of Maryland, Hammerman made contact with approximately eight engineering firms. Informed periodically by Wolff as to which engineering firms were in line to receive state contracts, Hammerman successfully elicited from seven engineering firms substantial cash payments pursuant to understandings between Hammerman and the various engineers to whom he was talking that the substantial cash payments were in return for the state work being awarded to those engineering firms. The monies collected in that manner by Hammerman were split in accordance with the understanding earlier reached: 50 per cent to Mr. Agnew, 25 per cent to Hammerman and 25 per cent to Wolff. An eighth engineer contacted by Hammerman flatly refused to make payments and, instead, complained—first to his attorney and later to Governor Agnew himself—about Hammerman's solicitation. Wolff, informed of

the complaint, reduced the share of work being awarded to the complaining engineer, but decided not to cut that engineering firm off completely from state work for fear of further exacerbating the situation.

Wolff, as chairman-director of the Maryland State Roads Commission, made initial tentative decisions with regard to which engineering firms should be awarded which state contracts. These tentative decisions would then be discussed by Wolff with Governor Agnew. Although Governor Agnew accorded Wolff's tentative decisions great weight, the Governor always exercised the final decision-making authority. Often Wolff would present the Governor with a list of engineering firms competent in Wolff's judgment for a state job, and the Governor would make the final selection of which particular firm would be awarded that job.

Hammerman also successful solicited, at Governor Agnew's instruction, a substantial cash payment from a financial institution in return for that in-situation's being awarded a major role in the financing of a large issue of state bonds.

II. The relationship between Mr. Agnew and Allen Green.

Shortly after Mr. Agnew's election in November, 1966, as Governor of Maryland, he complained to Allen Green, principal of a large engineering firm, about the financial burdens to be imposed upon Mr. Agnew by his role as Governor. Green responded by saying that his company had benefited from state work and had been able to generate some cash funds from which he would be willing to provide Mr. Agnew with some financial assistance. Mr. Agnew indicated that he would be grateful for such assistance.

Beginning shortly thereafter, Green delivered to Mr. Agnew six to nine times a year an envelope containing between $2,000 and $3,000 in cash. Green's purpose was to elicit from the Agnew administration as much state work for his engineering firm as possible. That purpose was clearly understood by Governor Agnew both because Green occasionally expressed his appreciation to the Governor for state work being received by his company and because Green frequently asked for and often received from the Governor assurances that his company would get further state work, including specific jobs.

Between Mr. Agnew's election and inauguration as Vice President, Wolff contacted Green, at Mr. Agnew's instruction, for the purpose of preparing for Mr. Agnew a detailed written computation of the work and fees which had been awarded to Green's company by Governor Agnew's administration. After assisting Wolff in the preparation of such a compilation, Green subsequently met with Mr. Agnew, who noted that Green's company had received a lot of work from Governor Agnew's administration and stated that he was glad that things had worked out that way. Mr. Agnew then went on to complain about the continuing financial burden which would be imposed upon him by his position as Vice President and to express the hope that Green would not stop his financial assistance to Mr. Agnew. To Green's surprise, Mr. Agnew went on to state expressly that he hoped to be able to be helpful to Green with respect to the awarding of Federal engineering contracts to Green's company.

As a result of that conversation, Green continued to make cash payments to Vice President Agnew three or four times a year up to and including December, 1972. These payments were usually about $2,000 each. The payments were made both in Mr. Agnew's Vice Presidential office and at his residence in the Sheraton-Park Hotel, Washington, D.C. The payments were not discontinued until after the initiation of the Baltimore County investigation by the United States Attorney for the District of Maryland in January, 1973.

III. The relationship between Mr. Agnew and Lester Matz.

Lester Matz, a principal in another large engineering firm, began making corrupt payments while Mr. Agnew was County Executive of Bal-timore County in the early nineteen-sixties. In those days, Matz paid 5 per cent of his fees from Baltimore County contracts in cash to Mr. Agnew through one of Mr. Agnew's close associates.

After Mr. Agnew became Governor of Maryland, Matz decided to make his payments directly to Governor Agnew. He made no payments until that summer of 1968 when he and his partner calculated that they owed Mr. Agnew approximately $20,000 in consideration for the work which their firm had already received from the Governor's administration. The $20,000 in cash was generated in an illegal manner and was given by Matz to Governor Agnew in a manila envelope in Governor Agnew's office on or about July 16, 1968. In handing the envelope to Governor Agnew, Matz expressed his appreciation for the substantial amounts of state work his company had been receiving and told the Governor that the envelope contained the money that Matz owed to the Governor in connection with that work.

Matz made no further corrupt payments to Mr. Agnew until shortly after Mr. Agnew became Vice President, at which time Matz calculated that he owed Mr. Agnew approximately $10,000 more from jobs and fees which the Matz firm had received from Governor Agnew's administration since July, 1968. After generating $10,000 in cash in an illegal manner, Matz met with Mr. Agnew in the Vice President's office and gave him approximately $10,000 in cash in an envelope. Matz informed the Vice President at that meeting that the envelope contained money still owed to Mr. Agnew in connection with work awarded to Matz's firm by Governor Agnew's administration and that more such monies would be owed and paid in the future. Matz did make several subsequent payments to the Vice President; he believes that he paid an additional $5,000 to Mr. Agnew in cash.

In or around April, 1971, Matz made a cash payment to Vice President Agnew of $2,500 in return for the awarding by the General Services Administration of a contract to a small engineering firm in which Matz had a financial ownership interest. An intermediary was instrumental in the arrangement for that particular corrupt payment.

FULL EXPOSITION

I.   The relationship of Mr. Agnew, I. H. Hammerman 2d and Jerome B. Wolff.

I. H. Hammerman 2d is a highly successful real estate developer and mortgage banker. He has entered into a formal written agreement with the Government, pursuant to which he has tendered his complete cooperation to the Government with respect to the present investigation. Under the terms of this agreement, Hammerman will plead guilty to a charge of violating a felony provision of the Internal Revenue Code. As a result of that plea, Mr. Hammerman will be exposed to a maximum sentence of three years in prison. In return, the Government has agreed not to charge Mr. Hammerman with any other crime relating to the subject matter of this investigation and to bring his cooperation to the attention of the court at the time of his sentencing. The Government has not agreed to make any specific recommendation with respect to the period of incarceration, if any, to which the Government believes it would be appropriate for Mr. Hammerman to be sentenced, and, in particular, the Government has made no representation to Mr. Hammerman that it will recommend to the court that he be placed on probation.

Jerome B. Wolff is an engineer and also an attorney. He is the president of Greiner Environmental Systems, Inc. Wolff has tendered his complete cooperation to the Government in the present investigation. The Government has not entered into any agreement with Wolff as to what consideration, if any, he may expect in return for his cooperation, other than the assurance that his own truthful disclosures to the Government will not be used against him in any criminal prosecution.

At the Government's request, both Hammerman and Wolff have executed sworn written statements that recount their relationships with Mr. Agnew. Their testimony, the corroborative testimony of other witnesses, and various corroborative documents, would prove the following:

Hammerman has known Spiro T. Agnew for many years. When Mr. Agnew ran for Baltimore County Executive in 1962, however, Hammerman actively supported his opponent. The day after the election, Hammerman called to congratulate Mr. Agnew and asked to see him. They met in Hammerman's office and again Hammerman congratulated Mr. Agnew on his victory. Hammerman told Mr. Agnew that he knew all campaigns had deficits, and he offered Mr. Agnew a post-election contribution of $10,000. Mr. Agnew refused, but he told Hammerman that he would expect a contribution three times as large when he ran for office again.

Friendship Develops   Between 1963 and 1966, while Mr. Agnew was the Baltimore County Executive, he and Hammerman developed a close, personal friendship. During the period and continuing up until early 1973, they often discussed Mr. Agnew's personal financial situation. Mr. Agnew complained about it, and told Hammerman that he had not accumulated any wealth before he assumed public office, had no inheritance, and as a public official received what he considered a small salary. Mr. Agnew believed, moreover, that his public position required him to adopt a standard of living beyond his means and that his political ambitions required him to build a financially strong political organization. During the period when he was County Executive, Hammerman entertained him introduced him to substantial political contributors, and gave him substantial gifts.

At the outset of the 1966 Maryland gubernatorial campaign, Hammerman found himself in a difficult situation. Some of his closest business associates were involved in the Democratic candidates' campaign, but Mr. Agnew insisted that Hammerman choose between them and him. Hammerman decided actively to support Mr. Agnew, contributed $25,000 and raised an even larger amount in campaign funds for Mr. Agnew. Hammerman was one of Mr. Agnew's financial chairmen and devoted considerable time, energy and money to his campaign. After he became Governor and later Vice President, Hammerman continued to entertain him, travel with him and provide him with other financial benefits. These benefits were not related to the monies discussed below.

In the late nineteen-fifties, while Wolff was Deputy Chief Engineer and later Assistant Director of Public Works for Baltimore County, Mr. Agnew became a member of the Baltimore County Board of Zoning Appeals. Mr. Agnew and Wolff became acquainted as a result of Wolff's appearances as a witness before the Board.

Wolff left employment with the County approximately six months after Mr. Agnew took office as County Executive. Mr. Agnew and he became good friends between 1963 and 1967 while Wolff was in business as a consulting engineer, and Wolff became an unofficial adviser to him. Mr. Agnew arranged for him to receive contracts from the County. Wolff greatly admired Mr. Agnew and believed that Mr. Agnew was sincerely attempting, with considerable success, to do a good job as County Executive.

Questions From Friends   Friends in the consulting business asked Wolff, while Mr. Agnew was County Executive, how much Wolff was paying for the engineering work that he was receiving from Baltimore County. They seemed to assume that he was paying, as it was well known in the business community that engineers generally, and the smaller engineering firms in particular, had to pay in order to obtain contracts from the County in those days. Only a few of the larger and well established firms were generally considered to be immune from this requirement.

It is Wolff's belief, based upon his experience and his understanding of the experience of others, that engineering firms generally have to struggle for 10 to 15 years in order to become established. During this period, and for some time thereafter, they generally make payments—sometimes through middlemen—to public officials at various levels of government throughout Maryland in order to receive public work. Sometimes they reach a point where they are sufficiently established as qualified engineers that they do not generally have to make illegal payments in order to obtain a fair share of the public work.

It was Wolff's belief that a certain close associate of Mr. Agnew's (referred to hereafter as "the close associate" or "the middleman") was his principal middleman in Baltimore County. The close associate courted engineers, developers and others and bragged a great deal about his relationship with Mr. Agnew. Although Wolff was in a favored position with Mr. Agnew, on two or more occasions while Mr. Agnew was County Executive, the close associate requested money from Wolff in return for contracts Wolff wanted or had obtained from the county. Wolff paid him $1,250 in cash in April, 1966, and in addition made a payment to another associate of Mr. Agnew's, ostensibly as legal fees. Wolff's present recollection is that he also made one or two other payments to the close associate.

Another Middleman Seen   It was Wolff's belief that another individual also acted as a middleman for Mr. Agnew. Wolff learned from others that a certain Baltimore engineer was paying for work through that other individual. It is Wolff's recollection that in his office, Mr. Agnew once remarked to Wolff that the engineer in question was paying 10 per cent for the work that he received from the county. Wolff inferred from Mr. Agnew's comment that Mr. Agnew was surprised that that engineer was paying as much as 10 per cent, in view of the fact that the going rate was generally 3 per cent. Through conversations with still another engineer, Wolff learned that he also was making payments for county work.

During Mr. Agnew's 1966 campaign for Governor, Wolff gave him $1,000 in cash as a campaign contribution. Wolff also worked in Mr. Agnew's campaign. Wolff knew that he had a potential personal stake in Mr. Agnew's candidacy, as Mr. Agnew had sometime earlier indicated to him the possibility that he might appoint Wolff as chairman-director of the State Roads Commission if Mr. Agnew were elected Governor.

Wolff had first become acquainted with Hammerman during the period when Wolff had been an assistant engineer employed by the Baltimore County Public Works Department. Hammerman considered Wolff to be a brilliant engineer, and Wolff had handled in an efficient manner various problems that Hammerman had had with county agencies in connection with Hammerman's building ventures. A close personal friendship had developed between them. Hammerman had been so impressed with Wolff that he had advised him that if he ever decided to leave county government, Hammerman would retain him as the engineer for his building projects. After Wolff had left county government in 1963 and established his own engineering business, he had done virtually all of Hammerman's engineering work.

After his election as Governor, Mr. Agnew told Hammerman that he intended to appoint Wolff chairman-director of the Maryland State Roads Commission. Hammerman objected strenuously because he wanted to retain Wolff's engineering services. Mr. Agnew responded, however, that Hammerman should not be too upset about Wolff's appointment because, Mr. Agnew told Hammerman, "You won't lose by it."

On or about March 1, 1967, Wolff took office as Governor Agnew's appointee as the chairman-director of the state roads commission. Governor Agnew had Wolff monitor every consulting engineering and construction contract that came through the state. It became obvious to Wolff that, in view of the provisions of the states road commission legislation, he would in effect control the selection of engineers and architects for contracts to be awarded by the state roads commission, subject only to the ultimate decision-making authority of Governor Agnew.

Shortly after Wolff took office, Governor Agnew asked Hammerman to come to his office in Annapolis, Md. At this meeting, Governor Agnew advised Hammerman that there was in Maryland a long-standing "system," as he called it, under which engineers made substantial "cash contributions" in return for state contracts awarded through the state roads commission. Governor Agnew referred to the substantial political financial demands that would be made on both himself and Hammerman, and said, in effect, that those who would be benefitting (the engineers) should do their share. Governor Agnew said that Hammerman could help him by collecting cash payments from the engineers, and told him to meet with Wolff to set things up.

Hammerman subsequently met with Wolff and told him of the discussion he had had with Governor Agnew. Wolff readily agreed to participate and suggested that the payments be equally divided among the Governor, Hammerman and Wolff. Hammerman then met again with the Governor and told him of the suggested division of the payments. Governor Agnew at first replied that he did not see why Wolff should receive any share of the money, but he agreed to the division as long as he received 50 per cent of the total payment. He told Hammerman that he didn't care what Hammerman did with his share.

Hammerman went back to Wolff and told him that Mr. Agnew insisted on 50 per cent of the money, and that Hammerman and Wolff should equally divide the rest between themselves. Wolff agreed.

Implementation Described   Over the course of the subsequent 18 or 20 months that Mr. Agnew served as Governor of Maryland, the scheme agreed to by Mr. Agnew, Hammerman, and Wolff was fully implemented. Wolff kept Hammerman informed as to which engineers were to receive state contracts and Hammerman kept Wolff informed as to which engineers were making cash payments. It was soon generally understood among engineers that Hammerman was the person to see in connection with state roads engineering contracts. As a result Hammerman soon found himself meeting with individual representatives of certain engineering firms. They would inform Hammerman of their interest in obtaining state work, and Hammerman would reply he would see what he could do. In some cases an engineer would specify the particular work in which he was interested; in most cases, the engineers would not specify any particular job.

There was no need for Hammerman to make coarse demands or to issue threats because the engineers clearly indicated that they knew what was expected of them. The discussions were generally about "political contributions," but the conversations left no doubt that the engineers understood exactly how the system worked—that is, that cash payments to the Governor through Hammerman were necessary in order for their companies to receive substantial state contracts. The "contributions" were almost always in cash, and many of them were made when there was no campaign in progress.

No Specification on Amount   Although Wolff had told Hammerman that "contributions" should average between 3 per cent and 5 per cent of the contract amount, Hammerman did not specify any exact amount to be paid, and accepted any reasonable sum. Sometimes the "contribution" was made in one payment, sometimes in several. When a contract was about to be awarded to one of the engineers who was known to be willing to make payments, Wolff would advise Hammerman that the engineer had been selected for a certain job. Hammerman would then contact the engineer and congratulate him. His congratulations were intended as signals that a cash "contribution" was due, and the engineer would then meet Hammerman and bring him the money.

Pursuant to his understanding with Mr. Agnew and Wolff, Hammerman retained 25 per cent of the payment and delivered to Wolff his 25 per cent share. Hammerman generally held Mr. Agnew's 50 per cent share in a safe-deposit box until Mr. Agnew called for it. From time to time Mr. Agnew would call Hammerman and ask how many "papers" Hammerman had for him. It was understood between Mr. Agnew and Hammerman that the term "paper" referred to $1,000 in cash. Hammerman would tell Mr. Agnew how many "papers" he had and Mr. Agnew would ask Hammerman to bring the "papers" to him. Hammerman would then collect the cash from the safe-deposit box and personally deliver it to Mr. Agnew to his office in Annapolis or in Baltimore or wherever else Mr. Agnew would designate.

Cash Was Transferred   The cash which Wolff received from Hammerman was initially kept in Wolff's home. It was then transferred to two, and later, three safe-deposit boxes, two in Baltimore and one in Washington. Most of the money was spent on ordinary personal expenses over a period of more than four years. A small portion of it was used by Wolff to make payments to other public officials in order to obtain work for the two consulting firms which he had sold before he had become chairman of the state roads commission, but in which he still had a financial interest. Wolff kept detailed contemporaneous documents on which he recorded the dates, amounts, engineering firm, sources of the monies that he received from Hammerman as his share of the proceeds of the scheme. These records are among a large volume of corroborative documents that Wolff has turned over to the United States Attorney's office.

The selection process for the state roads contracts generally worked in the following manner: Usually, based upon previous discussions with Governor Agnew, Wolff would make preliminary decisions with regard to the consulting engineering and architectural firms to be awarded contracts. He would then obtain the approval of the State Roads Commission. Governor Agnew would then make the final decision.

During Mr. Agnew's tenure as Governor of Maryland, Wolff met with him from time to time to discuss the status of various projects and the decisions which had to be made with respect to engineering, management and sometimes architectural contracts. Wolff generally prepared agendas for these meetings in advance. Governor Agnew appeared to have confidence in Wolff's technical ability and generally accorded substantial weight to Wolff's preliminary decisions as to which consulting firms should be awarded contracts, generally concurring with Wolff's selection. Where important or unique projects were involved, Wolff would present Governor Agnew with a list of several possible firms from which Governor Agnew would select the firm to be awarded the contract.

Governor Agnew always had and from time to time exercised the power to make all final decisions.

Factors Influencing Wolff   Several factors influenced Wolff in his own decision-making in the selection process outlined above:

1. It was the basic premise of Wolff's selection process that an engineering firm had to be competent to do the work before it could even be considered for a contract. Any engineering firm which, in Wolff's judgment, was competent to perform a certain assignment which might be given consideration.

2. Both Governor Agnew and Hammerman would from time to time ask Wolff to give special consideration to a particular engineering firm, which might or not be making cash payments, and he would then try to do so. He remembers, for example, that the Governor on one or more occasions asked him to give work to two specific engineering firms. Hammerman also recommended to Wolff, presumably because of Hammerman's friendship with one or more particular engineers, that work be given to at least one company that, according to Wolff's understanding, had not made any cash payments.

3. Wolff's decision-making (and he recalls that this was a matter that he discussed with Hammerman in particular) was intended to avoid substantial and noticeable deviations from general fairness—that is, he tried to avoid a situation in which any firm reserved more or less work than could be justified on a purely legitimate basis. Wolff always viewed the process as one of accomplishing competent public work for the state of Maryland, very similar to that which would have been accomplished if all the selections had been made strictly on their merits, while at the same time serving the mutual ends of Mr. Agnew, Hammerman, and himself.

Appearance of Fairness   Wolff believed it was important not to deviate too obviously from the appearance of fairness and even-handedness in the selection of engineers. For example, he became aware—he believes initially as a result of a conversation he had with Governor Agnew—that Hammerman had apparently approached a certain engineer to solicit cash payments in connection with potential state work, and that the engineer had complained to Governor Agnew that state contracts should not be awarded on this basis.

The Governor was very upset, as Wolff understood it, because Hammerman had apparently been especially heavy-handed with the engineer, and apparently because the Governor felt that the engineer might make his complaint public. For these reasons, Wolff continued thereafter to give the engineer's firm some work.

The investigation also established that the same engineer also complained to his attorney, a close personal friend of Mr. Agnew's, about Hammerman's solicitation. Shortly after the engineer had complained to his attorney, and several months before the engineer complained directly to Mr. Agnew, the attorney met with Mr. Agnew and gave him a detailed account of Hammerman's solicitation and of his client's outrage. He warned Mr. Agnew that Hammerman's activities could undermine all the attorney believe Governor Agnew was attempting to accomplish.

Although he indicated that he would look

into the matter, Mr. Agnew never reported back to the attorney. He did several months later meet personally with the engineer, at the attorney's insistence, but the investigation has established Mr. Agnew did nothing whatever to stop Mr. Hammerman's continuing solicitations of cash payments from engineers in return for state work and that he (Mr. Agnew) continued for several years thereafter to accept his 50 per cent share of these cash payments.

4. The fact that a certain firm was making cash payments was a definite factor in the firm's favor. It was, therefore, accorded special consideration in the decision-making process. Holt believes that a comparison of the amount of work given to certain firms before, during and after Governor Agnew's administration would confirm this.

Selection of Firms   On the other hand, there were times when a firm was selected for a specific job without regard to whether or not the firm was making cash payments. Some local Maryland firms had outstanding expertise in certain fields of engineering. This made them obvious choices for certain jobs, whether or not they were making cash payments. Even such firms, however, can never be completely sure that such considerations would be decisive in the decision-making process, so that even some of those companies were vulnerable to solicitations for cash payments.

5. Various other factors worked for or against particular firms or individuals in the selection process. For example, Wolff definitely favored Lester Matz and Allen Green, and their companies, not only because he understood they were making cash payments directly to the Governor, but also because Wolff was receiving money from certain illegal dealings that he had with Matz and Green that did not involve Governor Agnew. Conversely, one engineering firm was disfavored by Wolff because in his view that firm had taken positions contrary to the best interests of the Commission.

The evidence accumulated to date, both testimonial and documentary, establishes that Hammerman obtained, and split with Mr. Agnew and Wolff, cash payments from seven different engineering firms in return for State engineering contracts, and from one financial institution in return for a lucrative arrangement with the State involving the financing of certain State bonds. Those seven engineering firms and the one financial institution will not be named in this statement in order to avoid possible prejudice to several presently anticipated prosecutions.

It is worth noting, however, that Hammerman specifically recalls discussing with Mr. Agnew whether or nor the particular financial institution would be awarded the lucrative State bond business, and that during that discussion Mr. Agnew commented that the principals at the particular financial institution in question were "a cheap bunch" who "don't give you any money." Mr. Agnew informed Hammerman that he did not intend to award that institution the bond business in question unless a substantial "contribution" were made. Hammerman carried that message to the appropriate person; a substantial cash "contribution" was made; the institution got the bond business.

Green and Matz 'Contributions'   Hammerman also remembers that, while Mr. Agnew was Governor, Hammerman observed that Allen Green and Lester Matz, two engineers whom he had known for some time, were receiving very substantial amounts of State Bonds work. Hammerman mentioned that fact to Wolff and, since he had not received any money from Green and Matz, asked Wolff if he should approach them. Both Green and Matz had indicated to Wolff that they were approach them. Both Green and Matz had indicated to Wolff that they were making their payments directly to the Governor. Wolff therefore told Hammerman that both Green and Matz were making "contributions" and that Hammerman should "stay away." Hammerman did so.

It is Wolff's understanding and belief that both Green and Matz continued to make cash payments directly to Mr. Agnew after he had become Vice President. Wolff bases this conclusion on conversations that he has had with both Green and Matz since January, 1969, in which each of them has indicated to Wolff that he had made payments directly to the Vice President.

At a certain point, which Wolff believes was after Mr. Agnew's election as Vice President in November, 1968, but prior to his inauguration as Vice President on January 20, 1969, Mr. Agnew asked Wolff to determine the details of payments that had been made by the State Roads Commission under his administration to the engineering company owned and operated by Allen Green. Wolff then discussed this request with Green, who subsequently prepared a list that he submitted to Wolff. Wolff then prepared a final list, a copy or duplicate of which he gave to Mr. Agnew. When Wolff handed Mr. Agnew the list, they did not discuss it to any extent, according to Wolff's present recollection. Mr. Agnew just put it away.

Wolff would testify that much of his understanding concerning Mr. Agnew's actions and reactions to specific situations was inferential, since he and Mr. Agnew did not discuss Wolff's relationship with Hammerman or others or the fact that he and Mr. Agnew were acting, either jointly or individually, in a corrupt manner. Wolff believes his relationship with Mr. Agnew flourished because of their mutual sensitivity to their own positions and their mutual respect for one another. He does recall, however, an occasion on which he was in the Governor's office in the State House. Governor Agnew and he were standing in front of the fireplace after a meeting, and the Governor said to Wolff in substance: "Look after yourself but be careful."

II.   The relationship between Mr. Agnew and Allen Green.

Allen Green is the president and one of the principal owners of Green Associates, Inc., a Maryland engineering company which has, over the years, performed various types of engineering work.

Green has signed a formal written agreement with the Government under which he has agreed to plead guilty to a criminal felony violation of the Internal Revenue Code that will expose him to a maximum sentence of three years in prison. He has given the Government his complete cooperation in this investigation. In return, the Government has promised him that he will not be prosecuted for any offense related to this investigation other than the one to which he will plead guilty, and that at his sentencing the Government will bring his cooperation to the attention of the Court. The Government has expressly refused to promise Green that it will recommend to the Court at his sentencing that he be placed on probation.

At the Government's request, Green has executed a sworn written statement detailing his relationship with Mr. Agnew. Green's testimony, the corroborative testimony of other witnesses, and various corroborative documents would prove the following:

Green has been an engineer in Maryland for 21 years. During this period, he has often made cash payments on behalf of his company in return for various State and local consulting contracts and in order to remain eligible for further contracts. He used cash for the simple reason that checks could have been traced and might have led to the discovery of these illegal payments. These payments formed a pattern over the years and reflected his understanding, based upon experience, of the system in which a firm such as his had to participate in order to insure its survival and growth in the State of Maryland. This system had developed long ago in Maryland and in other States as well.

Engineering contracts have not been awarded on the basis of public bids in Maryland. Instead, the selection of engineers for State roads contracts has rested exclusively in the discretion of public officials—in Maryland, the Governor and the members of the State Roads Commission. They have had virtually absolute control. There are many engineering companies which seek contracts, but price competition was not allowed under the ethical standards of this profession until October of 1971. Therefore, engineers are very vulnerable to pressure from public officials for both legal and illegal payments. An engineer who refuses to pay can be deprived of substantial public work without effective recourse, and one who pays can safely expect that he will be rewarded.

A few companies developed in time a size, expertize, and stature that insulated them to some extent from this system. One or two developed and expertise, for example, in large bridge design, that other local companies could not match. One or two grew so large and had been awarded so many substantial contracts that the State could not do without their services unless out-of-state consultants were employed. In these ways, a few companies in effect "graduated" in time from the system to a position of lesser vulnerability, and they could afford to resist and perhaps in some instances, refuse to participate. In fact, Green believed that his own company was in recent years in the process of moving into this class.

It was seldom necessary, in Green's experience, for there to be any express prior agreement between an engineer and a public official in Maryland. Under this system, which each State administration perpetuated, the connection between payments and contracts rested on a largely tacit understanding under which engineers knew that if they did not pay, they would not receive very many contracts and that if they did pay, they would receive favored treatment. Therefore, when a politician requested a payment or when an engineer offered one, it was not necessary for anyone expressly to refer to the connection between payments and contracts because everyone understood the system, and could rely upon it without actually talking about it.

Green came to know Spiro T. Agnew in mid-1963, when Mr. Agnew was the County Executive for Baltimore County, Maryland. Although his company received some engineering contracts from the county, Green does not recall making any cash payments to Mr. Agnew or to anyone in his administration during these years. Green cultivated his relationship with Mr. Agnew and occasionally had lunch with him. By 1966, they had developed a close relationship.

$8,000 in Campaign Contributions   In connection with Mr. Agnew's successful 1966 campaign for Governor, Green gave him approximately $8,000 to $10,000 in campaign contributions. He did so in part because he genuinely admired Mr. Agnew and believed that he would make an excellent Governor. He also knew, however, that Mr. Agnew would be grateful for his support, and he anticipated that Mr. Agnew would express his gratitude by giving the Green company state work if he were elected.

After the inauguration, Green met with Governor Agnew on several occasions in his new offices, usually in Baltimore, but sometimes in Annapolis. At one of these meetings Governor Agnew expressed his concern about the substantial financial obligations and requirements imposed upon him by virtue of his new position. He told Green that, as the titular leader of the Republican party in Maryland, he would need substantial funds in order to support his own political organization. In addition, he believed that he would be called upon to provide financial assistance to other Republican candidates around the state.

Furthermore, he complained that it was extremely difficult for a person in his limited financial situation to bear the personal expenses of high public office, in the sense that his new position would require him, he believed, to adopt and maintain a life style that was beyond his means. He said that he had served as County Executive at substantial financial sacrifice because of the small salary and that, although the Governor's salary represented an increase in income, it would still be insufficient to meet the additional demands that he believed his new position would impose upon him.

Complaints by Agnew   This was neither the first nor the last occasion upon which Mr. Agnew mentioned to Green his concern about his personal financial difficulties. He had voiced similar complaints while County Executive, and he continued from time to time to mention his personal financial difficulties thereafter.

Green inferred from what Mr. Agnew said, the manner in which he said it, and their respective positions that he was being invited in a subtle but clear way to make payments. He, therefore, replied that he recognized Mr. Agnew's financial problems and realized he was not a wealthy man. Green told him that his company had experienced successful growth and would probably continue to benefit from public work under the Agnew administration. He, therefore, offered to make periodic cash payments to Governor Agnew, who replied that he would appreciate such assistance very much.

On the basis of Green's experience, he had developed a policy that, where required, he would make payments in amounts that did not exceed an average of 1 per cent of the fees that his company received on public engineering contracts. This informal calculation included legitimate political contributions as well as cash payments. He knew that many politicians believed that engineers were wealthy and often demanded payments in much greater amounts, frequently 5 per cent and sometimes higher. Although he believed that some engineers made payments in these amounts he knew that such percentages were unrealistic, given the economics of the engineering industry. An engineering firm could not, in his judgment, make a profit on public work if payments in these excessive percentages were made. He had come to the conclusion that his company could not afford to pay more than 1 per cent and, in areas where more was demanded, he had simply refused to pay and had sought work elsewhere.

Therefore, Green calculated, largely in his head, that it would be appropriate for him to make approximately six payments a year to Mr. Agnew in amounts of $2,000, $2,500 or $3,000 each.

Payment Appointments   The exact amount to Green for such purposes at the time of the payment. After the meeting at which this subject had first been discussed, Green scheduled appointments with Governor Agnew approximately six times a year. At the first such meeting, he handed an envelope to Governor Agnew that contained between $2,000 and $3,000 in cash. Green told the Governor that he was aware of his financial problems and wished to be of assistance to him. Governor Agnew accepted the envelope, placed it in either his desk drawer or his coat pocket, and expressed his gratitude. Over the next two years, they gradually said less and less to each other about each payment; Green would merely hand him an envelope and Governor Agnew would place it in either his desk drawer or his coat pocket with little or no discussion about it.

During these meetings, Green and Governor Agnew would discuss a number of matters, but Green almost always made it a point to discuss state roads contracts with him. Indeed, Green's principal purpose in meeting with him was always to increase the amount of work that his company received from the state. They would discuss state contracts in general, and frequently, specific upcoming road and bridge contracts in particular. Green would express his desire that his company receive consideration for proposed work and would occasionally ask for specific contracts that he knew were scheduled to be awarded by the State Roads Commission. Green knew from experience and from what he learned from Wolff that Governor Agnew played a substantial role in the selection of engineers for State Roads Commission work. Governor Agnew would often tell him in these meetings that his company could expect to receive substantial work generally, and on occasion, he promised Green specific contracts. On other occasions, however, Governor Agnew would tell Green that a contract had already been or was to be committed to another company.

Green admits that his principal purpose in making payments to Governor Agnew was to influence him to select the Green company for as many state roads contracts as possible. Based upon his many years of experience, it was his belief that such payments would probably be necessary and certainly helpful in obtaining substantial amounts of State Roads Commission work.

A Tacit Understanding   With one exception (to be related later in this statement), Mr. Agnew never expressly stated to Green that there was any connection between the payments and the selection of the Green company for State contracts. According to Green, the understanding was a tacit one, based upon their respective positions and their mutual recognition of the realities of the system; their relationship was such that it was unnecessary for them to discuss openly the understanding under which these payments were given and received. The circumstances were that Green gave Governor Agnew cash payments in substantial amounts and asked for contracts, and from time to time, Governor Agnew told him that contracts would be awarded to the Green company.

Green paid Governor Agnew approximately $11,000 in each of the years he served as Governor of Maryland (1967 and 1968). Green generated the necessary cash to make these payments through his company by various means that violated the Internal Revenue Code and that were designed to obscure the purpose for which the cash was used.

Green also recalls that during the early part of the Agnew administration, the Governor occasionally asked him to evaluate the competency of certain engineering companies which he was considering for State Roads Commission work. On at least one occasion, the Governor also asked him if certain companies could be counted upon to provide financial assistance if State work were received.

Under the Agnew administration, the Green company received substantial work from the Maryland State Roads Commission. It was awarded approximately 10 contracts, with fees approximating $3,000,000 to $4,000,000.

On a few occasions during these years Green was asked by Jerome B. Wolff if he was taking care of his "obligations" with respect to the sub-stantial State work that the Green company was receiving and Green replied that he was.

Green saw little or nothing of Governor Agnew between his nomination as the Republican candidate for Vice President in the summer of 1968 and the election in November. He made some campaign contributions by check to the Nixon-Agnew ticket in the 1968 election.

List of Contracts Prepared   In November or December, 1968, after Mr. Agnew was elected Vice President but before his inauguration, Wolff came to Green with a list that he had prepared of the contracts that the Green company had received from the State Roads Commission under the Agnew administration. Wolff told Green that Governor Agnew had asked him to prepare the list, and Green concluded that the list had been requested and could possibly be used as a means of assessing what he owed to Governor Agnew in return for those contracts.

Wolff and Green discussed the contracts and fees and, in effect, bargained about the matter. Green argued that some of the contracts that appeared on the list had in fact been awarded to his company under the Tawes administration and that the Agnew administration was simply implementing a contract for which the selection had been made previously. Wolff, however, reminded him that the Agnew administration could have canceled at least some of the contracts, or could have awarded portions of the contracts to other firms. Subsequently, Green prepared a revised list of his own and submitted it to Wolff.

Some time thereafter, but still before the inauguration, Green met with the Vice President-elect in his Baltimore Governor's office. He gave Mr. Agnew a payment during the meeting. Mr. Agnew began the conversation by making some reference to the list and indicated that the Green company had received a lot of work from the State Roads Commission. Mr. Agnew said that he was glad that things had worked out that way.

He then reiterated that he had been unable to improve his financial situation during his two years as Governor and that, although his salary as Vice President would be higher than his salary as Governor, he expected that the social and other demands of the office would substantially increase his personal expenses. For these reasons, he said he hoped that Green would be able to continue the financial assistance that he had been providing to him over the preceding two years, and, Mr. Agnew continued, he hoped he could be helpful to Green with respect to Federal work.

A Tacit Understanding   This was the only occasion upon which Green can now recall that Mr. Agnew made any such express statement to him about the connection between payments and favors. Green did not believe that it was necessary expressly to refer to specific favors in return for payments. Indeed, throughout Mr. Agnew's gubernatorial tenure, it had never been necessary to state expressly that Green would receive anything in return for the payments that he had made, because a tacit understanding on this matter was more than sufficient to satisfy Green and to accomplish his purposes.

Green replied by telling Mr. Agnew that he would be willing to continue to be of financial assistance, but that he was not certain that he could continue to make payments in amounts as great as those he had made during the previous two years. Green knew that contracts awarded by the Agnew administration would generate income to his company over the next several years, and that therefore he could continue to make payments for several years. Green also hoped that his company's Federal work might increase in amount as a result of Vice President Agnew's efforts on his behalf.

He did tell Mr. Agnew of one important concern: that the new administration in Annapolis might take credit for, and possibly demand payments in connection with, projects that had actually been awarded to the Green company by the Agnew administration. Mr. Agnew, however, confidently indicated that he did not believe that would happen.

Green continued to make cash payments to Mr. Agnew after he became Vice President. Payments were made three or four times a year and were personally delivered to Mr. Agnew by Green either in the Vice President's office in the Executive Office Building in Washington or at his apartment in the Sheraton Park Hotel in Washington. Green made his last payment during the Christmas season in December of 1972. As Green recalls it, these payments invariably amounted to $2,000 each. As before, the money was always in a plain envelope, and the two men were always alone when the payment was made.

Fearful on Tapes   Green particularly recalls the first occasion upon which he paid money to Mr. Agnew in his offices in the Executive Office Building. Green was quite impressed with Mr. Agnew's office and position and felt very uncomfortable about the transaction that was about to occur. In addition, Green had some concern that the conversation between him and Vice President Agnew might be overheard or even taped. For all of these reasons, Green did not believe that it was appropriate or wise to continue to speak of personal financial assistance. Therefore, he stated to the Vice President that this money was part of his continuing and unfulfilled commitment to Mr. Agnew with respect to "political contributions." Thereafter, Green usually made a similar statement when he delivered money to Mr. Agnew in his Executive Office Building offices. Green recalls that on the first occasion he made such a statement to Mr. Agnew. Green raised his eyes to the ceiling in order silently to suggest to Mr. Agnew the reason for the unusual and inaccurate statement.

In 1969 and 1970, Green paid Mr. Agnew $8,000 a year, four payments of $2,000 each in both years. In 1971 and 1972, he paid Mr. Agnew $6,000 a year, three payments of $2,000 each in both years.

In Green's meetings with Vice President Agnew, he frequently asked about Federal engineering contracts for his company, and Mr. Agnew generally indicated to him that he was attempting to be as helpful as he could. Green soon realized, however, that the Vice President did not exercise any substantial control over Federal work, and, in fact, the Green company received only one Federal job during this period.

The payments were discontinued after December 1972, because of the investigation conducted by the United States Attorney's office into corruption in Baltimore County, Maryland.

Over the six year period between 1966 and 1972, Green's cash payments to Mr. Agnew totalled approximately $50,000.

III.   The relationship between Mr. Agnew and Lester Matz.

Lester Matz has been an engineer in Maryland for approximately 24 years. He is the president of Matz, Childs and Associates, Inc., and Matz, Childs and Associates of Rockville, Inc., two Maryland engineering companies. John C. Childs is his principal business associate in these two companies. Matz has tendered his complete cooperation to the Government in this investigation. The Government has not entered into any agreement with him as to what consideration, if any, he may expect in return for his cooperation, other than the assurance that his own truthful disclosures to the Government will not be used against him in any criminal prosecution. At the Government's request Matz has executed a sworn written statement that recounts his relationship with Mr. Agnew. His testimony, the corroborative testimony of Childs and other winesses, and various corroborative documents, would prove the following:

Between 1956 and 1963, Matz and Childs supplied various engineering services to private developers, principally in the metropolitan Baltimore area. Although they wanted to do as much public work as possible for the Baltimore County Government, they found it extremely difficult to receive any substantial amount of county work. They observed that a relatively small number of engineering companies received most of the substantial county engineering work during these years, and that most, if

not all, of these companies were closely associated with County Administration or public officials. They simply could not break into this group, despite their repeated efforts to do so.

They, therefore, welcomed Mr. Agnew's candidacy for Baltimore County Executive in 1962 because they believed that his election would present their company with an opportunity to be one of the few engineering companies that, they believed, would inevitably form around his administration and receive most of the substantial county engineering work. Matz had known Mr. Agnew casually for possibly two years, and during the 1962 campaign, he and Childs made a $500 cash contribution directly to Mr. Agnew. *Close Personal Friendship*   Prior to the 1962 election, Matz had also worked professionally with one of Mr. Agnew's close associates. Indeed, by this time the three of them (Mr. Agnew, Matz and the close associate) had already begun to develop what would in the next four years become a close personal friendship. Very shortly after Mr. Agnew assumed office as County Executive for Baltimore County. Matz was contacted by the close associate. During this conversation the close associate told Matz that the two of them were going to make a lot of money under the Agnew administration. Although he did not elaborate on this comment, Matz inferred from what he said during this conversation that under the Agnew administration, the two of them could expect substantial favors from the Baltimore County government.

Shortly thereafter, Matz was invited by the close associate to meet with Mr. Agnew. At this meeting there was no specific discussion about payments for county work, but Mr. Agnew told Matz that he had a lot of "confidence" in his close associate. Matz inferred from what Mr. Agnew said during this meeting that he should work through the close associate and make any payments through him.

After Mr. Agnew became County Executive, the close associate contacted Matz and asked him to prepare a chart which would set forth the amounts of money that could reasonably be expected from engineers on the various kinds and sizes of consulting contracts that the county generally awarded. Matz calculated the profits that could generally be anticipated under the various types of contracts, and he determined that, on the average, 5 per cent of the fee was not unreasonable, although the percentage varied depending on the size and nature of the contract. He gave a copy of the chart to the close associate.

The chart showed the expected profit on each type of contract and the percentage that engineers could reasonably afford to pay on it. Matz later showed his retained copy of this schedule to Mr. Agnew in his office and told him that he had given a copy to the close associate. Mr. Agnew looked at the chart and thanked Matz for his effort on the matter. Matz cannot recall today whether Mr. Agnew returned the copy to him.

Not 'Political Contributions'   When Matz gave a copy of this schedule to the close associate, he was told that he would be expected to make payments to the close associate for county contracts. The close associate said that as Matz's company received fees from the county, payments were to be made to him in the appropriate percentages, 5 per cent on engineering contracts and 2½ per cent on surveying contracts. He led Matz to believe that this money would be given to Mr. Agnew. These payments were not described by the close associate as "political contributions;" they were payments made in return for contracts.

Thereafter, Matz discussed this proposition with Childs. They were not surprised that payments would be necessary because it was generally understood that engineers had been making such payments for consulting work in a number of Maryland jurisdictions. They agreed that this would be a satisfactory arrangement. In fact, they were delighted that they would be among the small group of engineers who would be close to the Agnew administration and that they would, therefore, receive their share of the substantial county engineering consulting work. Al-

though the 5 per cent payments were not insubstantial, the company could afford to make them, and Matz and Childs both believed that the payments would make a substantial difference in the amount of work that their company would receive from the county.

During the balance of Mr. Agnew's tenure as County Executive, Matz and Childs would find out what contracts were coming up in the county, and Matz would then contact the close associate to ask him for as many of these contracts as possible. The close associate always seemed well aware of the work to be let, and, from time to time, he would advise Matz that his company had been awarded a particular contract. Matz then knew that, under their arrangement, the necessary payments were due, and he would therefore deliver the required cash payments personally to the close associate in the latter's office.

On most occasions, Matz placed the necessary cash in plain white envelopes. Usually he paid in installments rather than in one total payment in advance. Matz and Childs believed that even if they had refused to make these payments, their company would have received some county contracts, but that, as before, the company would not have received any substantial amount of work. In short, they believed that the payments made a great difference in the amount of work they received.

Methods of Raising Cash   At first Matz and Childs personally generated the necessary cash to make these payments. As the size of the various cash payments they were making increased, however, they found it necessary to employ other methods by which to generate these cash funds in their company. These methods violated the Internal Revenue Code and were designed to secure the purpose for which the cash was used.

During the first year or two of the Agnew administration in Baltimore County, the company's county work increased. Matz, however, was not satisfied because he believed that his company was entitled to an even larger share of the county's work, due to his reliability in making payments. He told the close associate that he was dissatisfied, and the close associate arranged a meeting with Mr. Agnew.

The three men met at Mr. Agnew's house. At this meeting, Matz complained, that his company had not received enough county work. Both Mr. Agnew and the close associate promised that they would help the company to receive more county work, and, in particular, Mr. Agnew told him that he would speak on Matz's behalf to the appointed county officials who were nominally responsible for the selection of engineers for county consulting contracts.

In the 1966 gubernatorial campaign, Matz and Childs made campaign contributions to Mr. Agnew, in part because they believed that Mr. Agnew would make an excellent Governor. They also, however, had another substantial reason for supporting Mr. Agnew. Under Governor Tawes's administration, their company had not received any substantial amount of work from the Maryland State Roads Commission. They realized that their inability to secure any substantial amount of state work was the result of the fact that they were not among the small group of engineering firms that were closely associated with the Tawes administration and that had received most of the state work awarded by that administration. Both men were therefore excited about Mr. Agnew's candidacy because they believed that if he were to be elected Governor, their company could begin to receive substantial amounts of work from the State Roads Commission by continuing to make payments to Mr. Agnew through his agents.

New Projects and Contracts   Several months after the Agnew administration took office, the State Roads Commission began to generate new projects and to award new contracts, and Matz's company began to receive substantial amounts of State work. On several occasions during the spring and summer of 1967, the close associate called Matz and attempted to perpetuate the arrangement under which payments had been made for contracts in the past. Matz was reluc-

tant, however, to continue this arrangement, for several reasons.

First, he knew that if he paid Governor Agnew through any middleman, the credit to which he was entitled by virtue of these payments would be somewhat diluted because the middleman himself would receive a substantial portion of the credit. Second, he suspected that the close associate had, without Mr. Agnew's knowledge, retained for himself some of the money that had been paid to him by Matz between 1963 and 1966. Third, he knew that Mr. Agnew believed that the close associate had given him poor advice on certain matters that had resulted in bad publicity and embarrassment to Mr. Agnew.

Sometime early in Governor Agnew's administration, Matz met with Governor Agnew alone in his offices. During this conversation Matz told Mr. Agnew that he believed that the close associate lacked the discretion necessary safely to represent Mr. Agnew's interests and that sooner or later he would lead the two of them into trouble. Therefore, rather than continuing to pay through the close associate, Matz suggested that his company establish a savings account into which he would deposit the money that he owed on State contracts. After Mr. Agnew left office, Matz could pay him the money accumulated in this account, perhaps under the guise of legal fees. Governor Agnew liked the idea, and at a later meeting he referred to the idea again with approval.

These factors and, in particular, these conversations with Mr. Agnew, led Matz to conclude that he could dispense with the close associate and pay Mr. Agnew directly. He therefore told the close associate that he would take care of his obligations directly. Subsequently, however, he abandoned the savings account idea because he feared that it would involve too many records of payments and thereby lead to the disclosures of the scheme. Instead, he decided to make his cash payments to Mr. Agnew directly.

Taking Care of 'Obligations'   The amount of

work that Matz's company received from the State Bonds Commission continued to increase substantially, and, on at least one occasion. Matz was asked by Wolff if he was taking care of his "obligations" with respect to his contracts. Matz told Wolff that he was taking care of his obligations "directly."

Although Matz's company received several substantial State contracts in 1967, he made no payments that year. On the basis of his experience, he assumed that he would have to pay 5 per cent of the fees that his company received from the State on these contracts. The contracts and fees that their company was receiving from the State roads Commission were much more substantial than those it had ever received before, and Matz and Childs therefore decided that they would defer payments until after they had received fees from the State.

No payment was made until the summer of 1968, by which time Matz knew that he was behind in his obligations. He was anxious to fulfill them because he wanted to maintain his reputation as a man who could be trusted to fulfill his obligations, in order to insure that he would continue to receive substantial amounts of work from the State Roads Commission. Although his company was in a financial position to make the large payment that was due, he knew that it would be extremely difficult to generate safely the substantial amount of necessary cash, particularly if he continued to rely exclusively upon his usual methods for generating the money with which to make cash payments.

Outside the Company   Sometime in late June or early July, 1968, Matz calculated that he owed Governor Agnew approximately $20,000 on the basis of 5 per cent of the fees that his company had already received from the state. He reviewed this calculation with Childs, who agreed with it. They did not believe that they could safely generate this amount of cash from within the company and, therefore, decided to go outside the company.

Matz approached an old client and friend of his who was in a business in which he customarily dealt in large sums of cash. Since Matz knew that he would be receiving substantial fees from the state within the next several months, on which he would owe Governor Agnew approximately an additional $10,000, he told his friend that he needed $30,000 in cash in the very near future. He did not disclose to his friend why he needed this money.

They agreed upon the following scheme: Matz's company would by corporate check "lend" his friend $30,000; his friend would then generate $30,000 in cash through his own company which he would return to Matz. The "loan" would be repaid to Matz's company by $1,700 quarterly checks for principal and interest; and Matz would return these "loan repayments" to his friend in cash. This scheme was satisfactory to Matz because his regular procedures were adequate to generate $1,700 in cash on a quarterly basis.

The friend reluctantly agreed to assist Matz in this manner. He immediately generated $20,000 in cash, which he delivered to Matz. Matz showed this $20,000 in cash to Childs before he delivered it to Governor Agnew. The friend promised that he would supply Matz with the additional $10,000 in cash as soon as he could generate it, and he did so within the following several months. Thereafter, the "loan" repayment scheme was implemented.

Matz then called Governor Agnew's office and set up an appointment with the Governor. The meeting occurred in mid-July, 1968. Matz met with the Governor alone in his office and handed him a manila envelope that contained $20,000 in cash. Matz expressed his appreciation for the substantial state contracts that his company had received and told the Governor that the envelope contained the money that his company "owed" in connection with these contracts. The meeting was a very short one and very little else was said.

To the best of Matz's present recollection, he made no further payments for state work to Mr. Agnew while he was Governor of Maryland. During the 1968 national campaign, however,

Matz's firm contributed to Mr. Agnew's campaign. He also acted as a fund raiser for Mr. Agnew in 1968. Matz also recalls that at some point in 1967, Governor Agnew called him and asked him to contribute $5,000 to Nelson Rockefeller's campaign for the Republican Presidential nomination, a campaign which Mr. Agnew was then publicly supporting Matz asked if he wanted cash or a check, and Mr. Agnew asked for a check which Matz subsequently sent to him. When Rockefeller later withdrew, Mr. Agnew returned the money to Matz with a letter.

A couple of months after Mr. Agnew had assumed the office of Vice President, Matz decided that it was time for his company to make another payment in connection with contracts that had been awarded by the State of Maryland under the Agnew administration. He was willing to make this payment, even though Mr. Agnew no longer controlled the contracts awarded by the Maryland State Roads Commission, because he wanted to maintain his reputation as a man who would meet his obligations in order to influence Vice President Agnew to assist him in securing Federal engineering contracts for his company.

Matz called the Vice President's office in Washington and set up an appointment to meet with Mr. Agnew. On a piece of yellow legal-size paper, Matz calculated the sum then owed to Mr. Agnew for work received by Matz's company from the State of Maryland. He took this piece of paper with him when he went to the Vice President's office. He met with Mr. Agnew, showed him the calculations, and briefly reviewed them for him. He then handed him an envelope, containing approximately $10,000 in cash. Matz told him that the envelope contained the money that his company "owed" in connection with the State Roads Commission contracts that he had been awarded under Mr. Agnew's administration in Annapolis. Mr. Agnew placed this envelope in his desk drawer.

Matz also told the Vice President that the company might "owe" him more money in the future as these contracts continued to generate fees, and that he would fulfill these obligations. They agreed that Matz was to call Mr. Agnew's secretary when he was ready to make the next payment and to tell her that he had more "Information" for Mr. Agnew. This was to be a signal to Mr. Agnew that Matz had more money for him. After this meeting, Matz returned to Baltimore and told Childs of the payment. He also told Childs that he was shaken by his own actions because he had just made a pay-off to the Vice President of the United States Matz also told Wolff, who was then working or about to begin working on the Vice President's staff, that he had made a direct payment to the Vice President.

Agreement on $2,500   Although Matz believes that he made several additional cash payments totalling approximately $5,000 to the Vice President, he never completely fulfilled his obligations to Mr. Agnew with respect to the State Roads Commission contracts, in part because Mr. Agnew had very little, if any, influence with respect to Federal engineering contracts.

Sometime in late 1970 or early 1971, Matz received a telephone call from the close associate who told him that there was an upcoming Federal project and that some or all of the engineering contracts could be controlled by the Vice President. He told Matz that, as usual, he would be expected to make a payment in order to receive a contract. At first, Matz resisted on the ground that he was entitled to this job without a payment by virtue of his prior payments, but the close associate insisted, and Matz agreed to a payment of $2,500. Matz asked that the contract be awarded to a certain small company in which Matz, Childs and Associates had an interest, and that small company was later awarded the contract. Thereafter, Matz received another telephone call from the close associate, during which they agreed that the payment would be made in the Vice President's office.

Matz contacted the president of the small company and explained that a payment was necessary in connection with the contract. The man at first balked and refused to make any such payment, but he subsequently agreed to participate. An appointment was then made for Matz to meet with Vice President Agnew in the latter's office in Washington. This meeting occurred in the spring of 1971. The evidence is somewhat contradictory as to whether or not the close associate was present at the meeting. Matz placed an envelope containing the $2,500 cash on the Vice President's desk and stated that the envelope contained the money required for the contract. When he left the meeting, the envelope had not been removed from the desk, but moments later Matz re-entered the office and noticed that the envelope was gone. Matz received $1,000 from the president of the small company as his contribution to this payment.

In the spring of 1972, the close associate called Matz and asked him for $10,000 for the 1972 Nixon-Agnew campaign. Matz declined. When the close associate continued to press him, Matz complained about these solicitations to Mr. Agnew, who told Matz to say that he gave at the office.

Respectfully submitted,
George Beall
United States Attorney
BARNET D. SKOLNIK
Assistant United States Attorney
RUSSELL T. BAKER, JR.
Assistant United States Attorney
RONALD S. LIEBMAN
Assistant United States Attorney

October 10, 1973

74. Illegal Political Contributions by Gulf Oil Officials

JOHN J. MCCLOY
NATHAN W. PEARSON
BEVERLEY MATTHEWS

IN THE UNITED STATES, A DIRECT OR INDIRECT contribution by a corporation in a campaign for a federal office, such as President, Senator or Representative, is and has been an illegal act under the so-called Corrupt Practices Act since the original legislation was passed in the early part of this century (18 U.S.C. § 610). A number of the states have passed similar statutes which were in effect during the period here involved. It is not too difficult to interpret or apply these statutes. No corporation or responsible corporate official, certainly none with legal counsel worthy of the name, can successfully plead ignorance of these laws. It is, therefore, not surprising that for an extended period of time payments out of corporate funds for domestic political campaigns and purposes were made by Gulf under circumstances which clearly indicate that those who authorized, dealt with and made use of the funds went to considerable pains to suppress knowledge of them and their use.

It is common knowledge that enforcement over the years since the passage of the Corrupt Practices Act has been marked by great slackness on the part of federal authorities. Indeed, enforcement by both federal and state authorities until the Watergate prosecutions has been practically non-existent. Nor is there much

doubt that political contributions and payments have been induced in large part by strong importunities on the part of expectant recipients and their representatives as much as by a calculated effort on the part of contributors to induce governmental favors from elected officials. Nonetheless, the fact remains that well-known laws were honored in the breach rather than the observance by both donors and donees. It is hard to escape the conclusion that a sort of "shut-eye sentry" attitude prevailed upon the part of both the responsible corporate officials and the recipients as well as on the part of those charged with enforcement responsibilities.

*

GULF'S DOMESTIC POLITICAL CONTRIBUTIONS

It is not too much to say that the activity of those Gulf officials involved in making domestic political contributions with corporate funds during the period of approximately fourteen years under review was shot through with illegality. The activity was generally clandestine and in disregard of federal, as well as a number of state, statutes. That the practice was engaged in during a period of pre-Watergate corporate and political morality when there was widely prevalent only a lip-service attitude toward such laws on the part of many contributors, contributees and, apparently, enforcement officers as well, cannot constitute justification.

▶SOURCE: *Report of the Special Review Committee of the Board of Directors of Gulf Oil Corporation, 1975, pp. 2–4, 31–37, 51–52, 62–76. (Editorial adaptations.)*

843

The results of the Committee's domestic investigation follow.

Generation of Cash through Bahamas Ex.: The "Usual Procedure"

The Committee's domestic investigation has focused generally on two broad areas: the origins and operation of the Bahamas Exploration Company, Limited (Bahamas Ex.) arrangement for the generation of cash, including the surreptitious delivery of cash to Gulf officers and others in the United States, and the distribution of cash to federal, state and local political figures. This section describes the Bahamas Ex. arrangement, its termination and, in 1973, its reactivation through two other Gulf Bahamian subsidiaries, Midcaribbean Investments Limited, and Gulf Marine & Services Company, Ltd. The succeeding section summarizes the Committee's efforts to reconstruct the political activities of Wild and his colleagues in disbursing funds to domestic politicians.

Origins of the Arrangement.   Gulf's main off-the-books political fund was developed more than 15 years ago and only a few individuals with knowledge of the original concept are alive today. Moreover, in most cases, the scope of knowledge of those who still are available was intentionally limited by the deceased chief executive officer who appears to have conceived the project and set procedures in motion to carry it out. Nonetheless, the Committee believes it has learned the basic facts surrounding the opening phase of the arrangement, principally as a result of its interviews with Bounds, who at the time (1959–1960) was an Administrative Vice President of Gulf and is now 70 years old and retired. At the time of the interviews, Bounds was in poor health and apparently under constant medication. In addition to his general affliction, he was recovering from a rattlesnake bite, the results of which were painfully evident. The interviews were an obvious ordeal for him. Despite these obstacles, his ability to recollect events occurring 15 years ago generally somewhat impressed the Committee

and his recollection was buttressed to some degree by notes Bounds had made contemporaneously with the early phases of the Bahamas Ex. arrangement.

Bounds told the Committee that the original idea of an off-the-books political fund was developed in 1959 by William K. Whiteford, the dynamic and colorful Chairman of the Board and Chief Executive Officer of Gulf at the time, who felt that Gulf would get no effective support from the Department of State in connection with its overseas expansion program.[1] According to Bounds, Whiteford decided to create a fund out of which political contributions or payments could be made, presumably to help Gulf maintain a political atmosphere conducive to its foreign expansion plans. At the same time, Whiteford sought a source of funds from which Gulf would make contributions in domestic elections.[2]

A series of meetings was attended by Whiteford, Archie Gray, Esq. (then Gulf's General Counsel), Bounds and possibly David Searls, Esq., who followed Gray as General Counsel (both Gray and Searls, as well as Whiteford, are deceased). According to Bounds, it was determined at these meetings that if funds were generated outside the United States and were handled by a foreign corporation with no

---

[1] Some documentary confirmation of Whiteford's knowledge, as well as some insight into his personality, is provided by the following jocular statement made by Whiteford, an outside director of The Bank of Nova Scotia, in a letter to Mr. W. C. Harris upon his appointment as Vice President of the Bank (a position largely honorary in nature):

"This is good news, especially to me, as the next time I have to make a confidential arrangement to secure political funds I can put the blame on the Bank should this great institution and W. C. Harris, Vice President, fail to protect my anonymity."

Harris, who was questioned by counsel, stated that he had no recollection of the letter and no knowledge of any political activities of Whiteford. Because of Whiteford's personality, he said, he would not have attached much importance to a facetious comment such as that quoted above.

[2] According to Bounds, the method previously used to generate funds for this purpose—pressuring company executives to contribute—had proved unsatisfactory.

deductions on Gulf's United States tax returns, there would be nothing illegal about the arrangement. Bounds believed this conclusion may have been based upon an opinion from outside counsel, but the Committee has been informed that no written opinion has been located in Gulf's files, despite a thorough search. Nor, according to the Committee's information, is there a record of any written opinion in the files of the law firm thought to have rendered the opinion.

Bounds recalled that Whiteford was emphatic that knowledge of the existence of this arrangement should be kept from "the Mellons"[3] and the "Boy Scouts." The "Boy Scouts" were, according to Bounds, Brockett and Dorsey, each of whom later became Board Chairman, as well as, Bounds said, Davis (presumably Mr. I. G. Davis), subsequently an Executive Vice President.

Under the original arrangement, the money transferred from Pittsburgh to Bahamas Ex. was to be returned in cash to the United States by courier to Claude Wild in Washington, D.C. However, Bounds said that before the Bahamas Ex. arrangement went into effect, Whiteford decided that Wild was not competent to handle the foreign payments, which were, according to Bounds, initially considered much more important than the domestic aspect of the operation. As a result, when the Bahamas Ex. arrangement began to operate, cash was delivered to Wild and others in various places in the United States for the purpose of making domestic payments, and to Bounds and Grummer in Pittsburgh for foreign use.

Bounds stated that Whiteford initially anticipated utilizing Sir Stafford Sands, a well-known attorney in The Bahamas who had represented Gulf on various occasions, as the individual who would control the proposed off-shore fund. Sands agreed to handle the account, but wanted a courier who could carry funds between The Bahamas and the United States and some one who could keep track of the accounts. Bounds believed that it was after Whiteford's first discussion with Sands in regard to the fund that Viglia of the Comptroller's office in Tulsa was sent to Nassau to serve as the bookkeeper and courier.[4]

Bounds' recollection and records of events taking place during this period indicate that Whiteford decided to handle the foreign payments personally.[5] However, Whiteford told Bounds to be the contact with Viglia in order to keep the operation secret. To facilitate deliveries, Whiteford told Bounds to get a safe and install it in Bounds' office in the Gulf Building in Pittsburgh. Whiteford then had the combination changed so that he alone had it. At the same time, Whiteford obtained a key to Bounds' office. A code was established by which Viglia could be notified when deliveries to the United States were to be made, and to whom.

Prior to the first delivery from Nassau in 1960, Whiteford apparently met with Bounds and Gray (described by Bounds in his notes as Whiteford's "watch dog" of the operation). Whiteford told them that he had talked to top management of some other major oil companies and learned that all of them had set up arrangements similar to that which Whiteford planned.[6] Whiteford pointed out that at least some of these other corporations did not main-

---

[3]At about this time the Mellon family and related interests together held the single largest block of Gulf stock.

[4]According to Bounds, Sands subsequently asked for a commission on all funds handled in the account. Whiteford refused the demand and decided to set up the fund without Sands' participation.

[5]Bounds believes that Whiteford planned to handle his foreign distributions through some one located in New York and perhaps another individual in London. Bounds never learned who these people were. However, he was quite convinced that whenever deliveries of cash were made to him in Pittsburgh, Whiteford removed the funds from the safe and sent them overseas via his contacts in New York or London. The Committee has not been able to identify the other individuals, if any, who might have been involved, or to verify that Whiteford obtained or made use of the funds.

[6]The Committee has made no attempt to investigate the activities of other companies or to confirm Whiteford's understanding in regard to them.

tain any records of these arrangements and reaffirmed that he wanted no records to be kept of Gulf's political fund. This was the sum of Bounds' recollection.[7]

Mr. William Grummer, Gulf's Comptroller from 1958 to 1964, told the Committee that in early 1960 he was informed by Bounds that he had had a conversation with Whiteford regarding the need to have cash funds available for making certain unspecified payments. Bounds commissioned Grummer to set up such an arrangement from an accounting point of view, and Grummer did so. First, however, Grummer inquired of Gray (then General Counsel) as to the propriety of Bounds' request and Grummer's compliance with it. Bounds had not told Grummer either the purposes or order of magnitude of the funds. (Grummer told the Committee that he could not recall the amount of the initial transfer to the Bahamas but it probably was $100,000 or $200,000.) Gray told Grummer that he was aware of Bounds' request, and that it was approved by Whiteford and all right for Grummer to proceed as requested. According to Grummer, neither Bounds nor Gray indicated who else might be involved in the arrangements.

Grummer then set up the arrangement for purposes of corporate accounting. Bounds had indicated that the funds would not be tax-deductible and, therefore, that the bookkeeping for the arrangement should be outside of IRS scrutiny. Grummer suggested using Bahamas Ex. since it was an off-shore company with no U.S. tax implications. In addition, although that company was a license holder, it had no active

[7]Due to the length of time which has passed since Bounds' retirement from Gulf and the passage of his former Gulf colleagues from the scene, it has not been possible to obtain satisfactory confirmation of many details of Bounds' recollection. There are a number of aspects of his account which stretch credulity, such as how the very sizeable amounts of cash came and went from his Pittsburgh safe, with his alleged complete lack of knowledge as to how it was to be, or was, used. Nevertheless, the Committee is inclined to accept the basic truth of Bounds' account of how the "arrangement" came about.

operations. Bounds advised Grummer that Mr. H. R. Moorhead in the Treasurer's Department would be in charge of setting up the arrangement for the actual funding.

Moorhead (Gulf's Treasurer from 1949 to 1972) told the Committee that in about 1960 Bounds said to him in a telephone conversation that "we have a very sensitive account, put it somewhere and deposit X amount of money." Moorhead told him, "then send me a memorandum in writing and sign on the matter and I will take care of it." According to Moorhead, Bounds resisted the request for written authorization but, after some dispute on the point, Moorhead finally did get the signed, written request from Bounds and acted upon it.

Moorhead also recalled another discussion with Bounds relating to the opening of and access to a safe deposit box in Nassau, The Bahamas. Bounds told Moorhead that from time to time certain individuals might want to withdraw cash from the Bahamas bank account he had set up and, since it was a sensitive matter, they wanted to be able to hold the cash in a separate safe deposit box with another bank.

*

Summary of the Arrangement. Between January 1960 and July 1972, a total of $5,186,000 of Gulf funds was transferred to the Bahamas Ex. account with The Bank of Nova Scotia. Of this amount, at least $4,530,000 was returned to the United States, principally by Viglia, and some $108,000 was used to purchase a helicopter for a Bolivian general. The Committee has been unable to learn how much more was returned to the United States by Grummer, the only other known carrier.

The principal steps in supplying cash from Bahamas Ex. to Wild, as the system operated from 1966 to 1972, are outlined in the following diagram.

*

Disbursement of Cash for Political Purposes

The Committee has made no effort to investigate the nature of Gulf's domestic political con-

MOVEMENT OF FUNDS UNDER THE
BAHAMAS EX. ARRANGEMENT—1966–1972

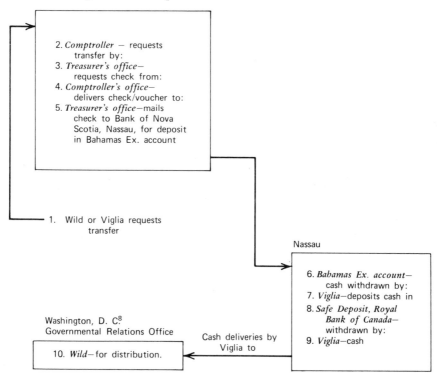

PITTSBURGH
Gulf Corporate Headquarters

2. *Comptroller* — requests transfer by:
3. *Treasurer's office*— requests check from:
4. *Comptroller's office*— delivers check/voucher to:
5. *Treasurer's office*—mails check to Bank of Nova Scotia, Nassau, for deposit in Bahamas Ex. account

1. Wild or Viglia requests transfer

Nassau

6. *Bahamas Ex. account*— cash withdrawn by:
7. *Viglia*—deposits cash in
8. *Safe Deposit, Royal Bank of Canada*— withdrawn by:
9. *Viglia*—cash

Washington, D. C[8]
Governmental Relations Office

10. *Wild*—for distribution.

Cash deliveries by Viglia to

tributions, if any, before the period covered by the Undertaking. It does appear, however, that the Bahamas Ex. arrangement and related political payments may well have stemmed from Gulf's announcement in September 1958 that "in the future the Corporation will take an increasingly active interest in practical politics." In succeeding months, that aim was developed into "A Political Program for Gulf Oil Corporation," a pamphlet which was disseminated to employees and shareholders in June 1959 over the signature of Mr. Archie D. Gray, a Senior Vice President, now deceased. In summarizing the Program, Gray noted the "creeping en-

croachment" by government toward industry generally and toward the oil industry in particular. He decried arbitrary import quotas for oil, attacks on the depletion allowance, conflicting regulatory schemes and the lack of consideration afforded Gulf's efforts to present facts to governmental investigating committees. Gray observed:

"In short, we have seen the development of a situation in which Gulf—and the industry—had been subjected to increasing attack while in the political climate of our times, it increasingly has been denied a fair hearing."

To combat this situation, Gulf's Political Program encouraged its employees to become involved personally in politics on the local level

[8]Actual deliveries of cash by Viglia to Wild were made in various cities in the United States, not always in Washington.

and set up an employee network of regional political supervisors. The Program also envisioned a Washington office to be staffed by a top-notch legislative analyst, also to be a registered lobbyist, and a political writer who was to serve in a public relations capacity as well. This conscious effort to participate in politics to a greater degree was noted both by Bounds who referred to the same pamphlet in his interviews, and by Wild, who regarded the Political Program as a significant change in Gulf's political outlook.

The Contributors: Wild and His Emissaries. When Wild finally agreed to testify before the Committee in December 1975, he stated that his first connection with Gulf took place when David Searls, Gulf's General Counsel, now deceased, approached him in 1959 for the purpose of interviewing him for a position with Gulf. Later, Searls, Gray and Bounds interviewed him and he was employed as a legislative analyst in Washington in accordance with the Program. Wild, a lawyer, was at the time employed by Mid-Continent Oil & Gas Association. Wild stated to the Committee that those in charge of Gulf—and notably Whiteford—felt that Gulf had been "kicked around, knocked around by government" for a long time and that the time had come to do something about it. Gulf had decided to have its voice heard in government circles.

One of the things that Searls and Gray wanted Wild to do was to build an organization around the country that would give Gulf some "muscle" in politics. For this purpose, they said they would provide Wild with about $200,000 a year. According to Wild, Gray and Searls realized that to be effective on the political scene contributions were "a part of life" and this was the purpose of the $200,000 yearly amount they mentioned. Wild took the job, which paid $25,000 annually, in late 1959.

Wild became the head of Gulf's Government Relations Department in Washington in 1963 and was made Gulf's Vice President for Government Relations in 1968. He held that title until March 1974 when, following the disclosure described earlier in this report, he retired. Wild was later retained by Gulf on an emergency basis as a consultant in legislative matters from August 1974 to April 1975.

In the early years of his employment, Wild reported, as a formal matter, to the head of the Washington office[9], although in practice he considered himself more responsible to Gray, Searls and Whiteford. In 1963 he began to report to Savage, the General Counsel. Following Savage's retirement in 1969, Wild reported to Brockett until 1972, and then to Dorsey.

As had been anticipated when he was hired, beginning shortly thereafter Searls and Gray did make money available to Wild for political purposes. As his first assignment, to meet a commitment Searls had made earlier to Senator Lyndon B. Johnson, Wild delivered over a period of months $50,000 in cash to Mr. Walter Jenkins, an aide of Mr. Johnson.

Wild received a total of between $200 and $300 thousand, in cash, from Searls and Gray between late 1959 and late 1961,[10] all of which was distributed by Wild or at his direction. On some occasions, Searls and Gray specified who the recipients were to be but otherwise Wild was to use his own judgment. Wild recalls discussing with Whiteford the fact that he was making contributions and on at least one occasion. Whiteford directed him to make a specific contribution. However, Wild told the Committee that, at least until late 1961, he "had no reason to assume" that the funds with which he was supplied came from "anything but a legitimate fund of contributions or gifts made by various people in the company."

In the summer of 1961, just before Bounds was "exiled" to California, he told Wild that

---

[9]From 1958 to 1964 the Gulf Washington office was directed by Kermit Roosevelt, who was interviewed by Committee counsel. The Committee has concluded, and Wild, among others, agrees, that Roosevelt had no knowledge of Wild's activities.

[10]Apparently these sums were obtained by Searls and Gray through the Bahamas Ex. arrangement.

some dissatisfaction had developed with the method of transferring funds to Wild and that the arrangement was to change. Bounds then for the first time mentioned Viglia and told Wild that when he needed funds he should call Viglia. But Bounds cautioned that Viglia was never to come to Wild's office, that no records were to be maintained and that Viglia was not to be told what Wild was doing with the funds. Bounds also instructed Wild that he was not to talk to any one except Viglia about the deliveries and that Bounds would handle the rest.

Beginning in the fall of 1961, when Wild needed funds he telephoned Viglia and Viglia delivered the cash requested by Wild. Wild stored the cash in a safe deposit box. Wild and Viglia met at various points throughout the United States but never in a Gulf office. Viglia told Wild when more money was needed in the Bahamas and, until Bounds retired in 1964, Wild called Bounds and Bounds arranged for the transfer; thereafter, Wild made the requests for transfers to two of the three Comptrollers who held that office—first Anderson and then Deering. Wild said he could not recall making any requests from 1964, when Bounds retired, to 1966, when Anderson became Comptroller. Henry was Comptroller during 1964–1966.

Wild stated that he had no knowledge of the mechanics involved in transferring the funds to the Bahamas and it was his understanding that he could call for as much money as he needed.

In late December 1965, Viglia gave Wild a list showing the dates on which he had made his cash deliveries, the amounts and the Gulf official or other person to whom the delivery was made. In addition to Wild, Viglia's list showed that Bounds, Henry and one G. C. Parker (a former officer of Parker Drilling Company, now deceased) had received cash. Viglia later supplemented this list to document further deliveries; Wild never showed the original or supplemental list to any one else. However, when he learned that Viglia had made deliveries to others, Wild became concerned that these deliveries might be attributed to him. Therefore,

he put Viglia's list in a sealed envelope and gave it to Savage, telling Savage that if there were any legal inquiries or problems, the envelope should be opened. Wild did not tell Savage what the envelope contained. Apparently, they never discussed the envelope, or its contents, again. Sometime later, after Savage retired, his secretary found the envelope in a desk drawer and destroyed it, without examining its contents.

Wild was responsible for disbursing the cash he received from Viglia, personally took charge of national political figures and was to some extent involved in making political payments in Texas. However, from time to time, Wild needed the assistance of others in making payments to political figures because, as he put it, it was "physically impossible for one man to handle that kind of money." In his Washington office, Wild used Messrs. Frederick A. Myers, Thomas P. Kerester and Norval Carey to make deliveries. In other parts of the country, Wild was assisted by his regional vice presidents— Messrs. Harris Winfree, James Winfree, Arthur V. Harris, James LeSage, Kenneth R. Murphy, J. Neil Miller and Bernard Markwell—and by others who were associated with Gulf or with Wild in various capacities, including Messrs. W. B. Edwards, Herbert C. Manning, Ralph Lewis, Ira Butler, Larry Temple, William Abington and Pat O'Connor.

Some of those assisting Wild apparently were authorized to use their discretion in making payments to politicians while others were directed to make particular contributions. According to Wild, the only criterion which was ever used was that the money be spent in the general interest of Gulf and the oil industry. He told the Committee that payments were initiated mostly by requests from the recipients, but on occasion he perhaps did volunteer. Although the payments were pointed towards campaigns, that distinction was not a realistic one because, in Wild's view, people in or wanting to enter political life campaigned constantly and were not bashful about seeking assistance at any time.

Wild informed the Committee that he could

not recall telling any of those who disbursed funds for him of the fact that corporate funds were being used; nor could he recall any of these emissaries asking about the source of the funds.

As mentioned, Wild reported to Savage from 1963 until 1969. Wild told the Committee that Savage was "uncomfortable" about the arrangements for political payments and the situation was discussed between them over a two- or three-year period. In 1966 and 1968, Wild said, he gave Savage, at the latter's request, a general accounting, jotted down on a sheet of legal foolscap, of the amounts he had received and spent. According to Wild, Savage said he did not like the arrangement but that they were on a merry-go-round and the question was how to get off. Wild further stated that Savage "wanted to move away from what we were involved in and I did, too, frankly, but obviously we didn't move away fast enough."

The alternate arrangement which Savage eventually developed was the employee fund that came to be known as the Gulf Good Government Fund.[11] This employee political fund (a vehicle for making legal political contributions) had its formal genesis in a memorandum from Savage to Dorsey dated January 15, 1970. By January 21, 1970, Dorsey had approved the arrangement suggested by Savage.[12] For the

years 1970 through 1972, the Fund collected $77,008.91, $71,177.34 and $74,718.33, respectively. The money was collected by Minks, Savage's successor as General Counsel, who made several disbursements at Wild's request and forwarded the balance to Wild. Wild was responsible for making other disbursements from the Fund.

Beginning in 1970, the first Good Government Fund checks[13] were transmitted to politicians and political campaign committees. However, it is clear that the Bahamas Ex. arrangement, Viglia's deliveries of cash to Wild, and Wild's distribution of substantial amounts of cash to political figures continued unabated for more than two years after the Good Government Fund was established.

On advice of counsel, Wild declined to identify for the Committee the recipients of political payments from Gulf corporate funds because of discussions then going on with the Watergate Prosecution. But Wild did state that he had nothing at all to do with political payments made outside the United States, except he confirmed that he had arranged for a payment to the Bolivian ambassador to build certain field hospitals and that he had made a payment on April 5, 1972, earmarked for the campaign committee of a certain senator (identified from sources other than Wild as Senator Mark Hatfield) at the request of the Kuwait Ambassador.[14]

The Committee was interested to learn from Wild which of Gulf's officers and employees had knowledge of his political contributions. Because of the importance of the officers to whom Wild reported—principally the three Board

---

[11]Apparently the Good Government Fund was in some respects not unlike "BIPAC"—the Business and Industry Political Action Committee—which was established to serve as the political action arm of business and industry, as a counterpart to COPE (a labor political action organization). BIPAC distributed literature to its members and made contributions to political campaigns. Requests for contributions ranging from $25 to $99 ($100 being the minimum contribution required by law at that time to be reported), were regularly made within the Gulf organization. The Committee found no evidence that undue pressure was used in such requests or that corporate funds were contributed to BIPAC, except in connection with certain educational programs and the like which were thought to constitute legitimate charitable contributions.

[12]Good Government Fund contributions were voluntary and were made in amounts of one-half of one per cent of the base salary of employees at a designated salary class and

above. With one or two exceptions, all contributions from the Good Government Fund were made by check, payable to the recipients.

[13]The fund was not named until sometime in 1972, but in the meantime checks were drawn against funds collected from Gulf employees and deposited in a segregated checking account.

[14]Wild stated that one-third of the contribution came from the Good Government Fund and that the balance came from the other funds Wild had available.

Chairmen, Whiteford, Brockett and Dorsey—Wild's relationship with them was of particular interest. . . . True to the original admonition of Bounds in 1961, Wild took care to keep the details of the operation largely to himself. Nevertheless, it seems significant that when certain Gulf officers had need of funds for political contributions, or had received solicitations for such contributions, even before formation of the Good Government Fund, they sought out the assistance of Wild.

The Recipients: Federal, State and Local. Although Wild declined on counsel's advice to identify for the Committee those candidates and politicians who he knew received Gulf corporate funds,[15] the Committee, its counsel and accountants obtained at second-hand from members of the Eckert firm who met with Wild the names of a number of recipients he had identified to them in the early stages of their investigation.[16] The Committee also has reviewed Wild's testimony before the Senate Watergate Committee and has obtained some first-hand information from others who were connected with Wild's activities. This information is somewhat fragmentary and therefore not entirely satisfactory. Yet in some cases it is quite clear as to payments to federal, state and local political figures.

While the Committee recognizes that second-hand information is inferior to direct testimony of Wild, much of the material it initially developed in its own investigation has since been repeated under oath in depositions in the SEC action against Wild and it has received considerable publicity. Hopefully, when the Watergate Prosecution and the SEC have concluded their investigations into the manner in which Gulf corporate funds were distributed, a more complete account can be presented. In the meantime, to fulfill its obligations under the

Undertaking, the Committee has no alternative but to summarize, as objectively as possible, such information as the Committee has been able to obtain of the use of Gulf funds by Wild and his colleagues for domestic political contributions.

Funds Dispensed Directly by Wild. Over a 14 year period, it seems that Wild received something over $4 million from the funds generated in the Bahamas.

The only direct testimony of Wild specifying those to whom he made payments is found in his public testimony before the Senate Watergate Committee on November 14, 1973. Wild, accompanied by Leo T. Kissam, Jr., Esq., was questioned on that occasion about his contributions to the 1972 Presidential election campaign.

Wild testified that in early January or February 1971, Mr. Lee Nunn, who formerly had been with the Republican Senatorial Campaign Committee, came to Wild's office and told him that the Committee to Re-Elect the President would handle the 1972 Nixon campaign outside the normal Republican channels. Nunn was hopeful that Wild could arrange for a $100,000 contribution and suggested that if Wild wanted verification of Nunn's role in the effort he should get in touch with Attorney General John Mitchell. Wild met with Mitchell in his office at the Department of Justice, and Mitchell indicated that the Committee to Re-Elect the President was a legitimate operation and that Mitchell had full confidence in Nunn. Wild testified that Mitchell made no mention of any campaign contributions or expressions of any special considerations to be given to Gulf. Wild decided, without consultation with any other Gulf officer or employee, to make a contribution of $50,000. To obtain the funds, Wild testified, he called Viglia, who brought him the $50,000 in cash from the Bahamas Ex. account in April or May of 1971. Wild gave the cash to Nunn.

Calling on Wild again in January 1972, Nunn told Wild that it would be a very expensive campaign and he would like another $50,000. Nunn implied to Wild that this was "kind of a quota that they were expecting from large corpora-

---

[15]Wild told the Committee that he could not recall ever telling any recipient that corporate funds were involved.

[16]Substantially the same information was later made public through the SEC deposition of Wright, the Eckert firm partner with the most detailed interview notes.

tions." Nunn suggested that Wild might like to meet with Mr. Maurice Stans and Nunn set up an appointment. Wild met with Stans on February 4, 1972, while Stans was still Secretary of Commerce but after he had announced his intention to resign that office. Stans, who knew of the previous $50,000, indicated that he was hopeful of obtaining $100,000 from the large American corporations. Wild told Stans that he would have to think about it. Wild then called Viglia, obtained the additional $50,000 and delivered it personally and in cash to Stans, who by then had moved his office to the Committee to Re-Elect the President.

In early 1972, Mr. William Brawley of Senator Henry Jackson's staff called Wild for an appointment, and Wild agreed to meet with Senator Jackson and his assistant, Mr. Sterling Monroe. The Senator indicated that he was having a difficult time raising money and was hopeful that Wild would be helpful; Wild said he would see what he could do. Wild then arranged through Viglia to obtain $10,000 and delivered it to Monroe. Also in early 1972, at the request of Carl Arnold, a very close friend, Wild arranged to give him $15,000; Wild presumed that Arnold passed the money on to a committee handling Congressman Wilbur Mills' campaign. Again, the source of the money was Viglia and Bahamas Ex.

In the course of questioning by members of the Senate Watergate Committee, these interchanges between Wild and Senator Ervin took place:

"Senator Ervin. . . .

"How did you figure that the best interests of Gulf would be promoted by making a contribution [to CREEP]?

"Mr. Wild. Well, Senator, you have to make decisions in the context of the situation that exists at the time, and I arrived at the decision that if we wanted to be, were going to be treated, in an equal way I knew other corporations were going to be treated, in an equal way I knew other corporations were going to on [sic] other individuals, a big effort was going to be made and if there was not some participation on my part or our part, we may be, you know, on what, whether you call it a black list or bottom of the totem pole, I would just like [them] to answer my telephone calls once in a while and that may not happen sometimes."

*

"Senator Ervin. Mr. Wild, don't you think it is very unfortunate that we have so much regulation of business in America that business necessarily is susceptible of being coerced by people in authority to make a campaign contribution which, if left to themselves, they certainly would not make?

"Mr. Wild. I could not have said it better."

Shortly after being retained by Gulf in July 1973, members of the Eckert firm, together with Minks, met with Wild to question him about the matters Wild had disclosed to Dorsey. There were more than six such meetings held in July, August, September and October of 1973. In addition to these meetings, members of the Eckert firm accompanied Wild when he was interrogated by lawyers for the Watergate Prosecution on October 4, 1973, and by the staff of the Senate Watergate Committee on October 23 and November 13, 1973. Thomas D. Wright, Esq., of the Eckert firm, took notes of some of the meetings with Wild and prepared memoranda of the October 4 meeting with the Watergate Prosecution and the October 23 meeting with the staff of the Senate Watergate Committee.

In May 1975 Committee counsel reviewed Wright's notes with him.[17] On September 22 and 23, 1975, Wright's sworn deposition was taken by the SEC staff in the action against Wild. That testimony was made public in late November 1975.

In his meetings with the Eckert firm lawyers, as those meetings were recounted by Wright to the SEC, Wild identified a number of national political figures to whom he had given money. Wild revealed that in prior years Senator Hugh Scott or his law firm was on an annual retainer

---

[17]Counsel also reviewed the notes of Mellott with him but, generally speaking, they were not as detailed as Wright's and thus were not as useful for refreshing Mellott's recollection of what Wild had said in his presence.

of some $20,000 a year from Gulf. Wild reported that Savage did not like this arrangement, that it was changed, and that for many years thereafter Wild had given Senator Scott $5,000 in the spring and $5,000 in the fall of each year in cash. According to Wright, the funds were made available to the Senator after he described to Wild his need for money for personal matters or for some office matter— never as a political contribution. Wild said that he gave these funds "as a gift for unrestricted use without regard to political campaigns."[18]

According to Wright, Wild told him in one of their interviews that even after the initial Watergate publicity erupted in 1973 the Senator again requested funds from Wild. Wild apparently told the Senator that he could not provide money any longer, but the Senator seemed unable to understand why. The matter was left that they would talk again around Christmas of that year. The Senator renewed his request at that time, and Wild repeated that there were no longer any funds and that his pipeline had been cut off.

Wright's notes included the comment, "all senators on Watergate except Ervin." Wright testified, however, that he did not recall any reference by Wild to the amount of any contribution or whether any contributions were from corporate funds or Good Government Funds or as to exactly what was meant, except "there was some reference in some way Mr. Wild had as-

sisted all of the senators in Watergate, except Senator Ervin."[19]

Mention was also made of Senators Russell Long and Daniel K. Inouye but Wright did not testify that Wild had in fact said that contributions had been made to either of them.

Wright testified that Wild said that he gave $25,000 to Pat O'Connor, "a personal confidant" of Senator Hubert Humphrey, during the Senator's 1968 campaign, and in March or April 1968 he gave $25,000 in cash to Maurice Stans in connection with Mr. Nixon's nomination effort. Some time during the summer of 1970 Wild had lunch at the White House with Harry Dent, Danny Hofgren and Herbert Kalmbach, who requested $50,000 from Wild to assist in electing a Republican Senate. Wild subsequently agreed to give $25,000 and the delivery was made to a Mr. Gleason. Another cash contribution of $25,000 was given to Mitchell for the Nixon campaign on October 4 of that year.[20] After the 1970 election Colson asked Wild for $5,000 to satisfy a debt which had been incurred by Senator J. Glenn Beall, Jr. in connection with his Maryland senatorial race, and the contribution was made to a Sandy Lankler in 1971.

[18]In accordance with the Committee's practice of seeking to verify the information which it had received concerning recipients of contributions. the Chairman wrote to Senator Scott on October 23, 1975, advising that the Committee had received "information indicating that in the spring and fall of each year [back to 1960] you or your representative had received the sum of $5,000 from a representative of Gulf" and requested the Senator "to confirm or deny the foregoing information, adding such additional comments as you may care to make." By letter dated November 28, 1975, the Senator neither confirmed nor denied the receipt of $5,000 twice during each year but acknowledged the receipt of political contributions and stated, among other things, that "as a political figure I have never knowingly received corporate contributions from Gulf Oil Company through any of its representatives."

[19]The Committee has been able to determine that only two Senators on the Senate Watergate Committee—Senators Baker and Weicker—received checks from Gulf's lawful Good Government Fund. Any cash given members of the Watergate Committee by Wild must be presumed to have been corporate funds from Bahamas Ex. and an unlawful contribution. For example, while Senator Baker has furnished the Committee with a copy of a letter from Wild dated March 14, 1974, assuring the Senator that the contribution Wild made to his campaign "came from a Company employee fund and had no relationship to the other contributions which received such notoriety," only $2,500 of the $5,000 given Baker in March 1972 was paid by check from the Good Government Fund. There is no indication that the remaining $2,500, which was paid in cash, came from the employee fund.

[20]The Eckert firm lawyers asked Wild whether Mitchell was "in any way doing any favors for Gulf" and were told that nothing in the way of a *quid pro quo* was expected. Wild volunteered that there had been a visit to Mitchell's office in 1969 or 1970 in which the Attorney General was advised of Gulf's acquisition of the Sequoia Refinery.

Wright also testified that, between 1969 and 1972, Wild made several donations to both Democratic and Republican Committee dinners. He contributed $5,000 for each dinner to the Democrats, and $10,000 for each dinner to the Republicans.

During Wright's testimony, various schedules of receipts and disbursements, previously produced to the Watergate Prosecution and the SEC, were described and marked as exhibits. Wright explained that the schedules showed receipts and disbursements by Wild of both Good Government Fund money and Bahamas Ex. money for the years 1968 through 1972 in connection with federal elections. Interviews of Eckert partners indicated that since the schedules were intended to reveal information only in connection with federal elections, they omitted any expenditures in connection with state and local politics and payments not made as campaign contributions. For example, the schedules did not include the regular semiannual payments which Wild said he made to Senator Scott. Similarly, the total receipts listed on the schedules for each year were intended to reflect only those funds ultimately used in connection with federal elections. This explains why the receipts listed on the schedules ranged from only $20,000 to $25,000 for 1969 to a maximum of something less than $200,000 for 1972, during a

period when Wild was receiving regular deliveries totaling nearly $400,000 a year from the Bahamas Ex. account.

According to Wright, Wild mentioned other requests from political figures but the Committee is not able to conclude, without more evidence than is available to it, that a political payment was involved. For example, Wright told the SEC staff of Wild's statement that highly placed aides of President Nixon sought to have Gulf sponsor a re-telecast of the wedding of Tricia Nixon Cox and to engage a Washington public relations firm. The television program was re-run and achieved high ratings. Apparently, the public relations firm was not hired.

Wright told the SEC lawyers that Wild had estimated the amounts from Bahamas Ex. that had been directed annually to state and local political activities as follows: Pennsylvania—$75,000; Texas—$50,000 to $60,000; California—$15,000; Louisiana—$50,000 to $60,000; Virginia—$10,000; Atlanta—$10,000 to $15,000; Mississippi—sporadic; Arkansas—sporadic; New Mexico—$10,000. However, Wright's testimony was not specific as to the state and local recipients earlier identified by Wild. This void was filled in part by information developed by the Committee from others who were associated with Wild's political efforts, some of whom later testified before the SEC.

75. Crime and the Auto Industry

HARVEY A. FARBERMAN

SOCIOLOGISTS HAVE COME UNDER ATTACK FOR IG-
noring the role powerful elites play in controlling society's central master institutions by establishing political and economic policies which set
the structural conditions that cause other (lower
level) people to commit crimes[1] (Gouldner,
1968, 1970; Quinney, 1970; Liazos, 1972;
Taylor et al., 1974). My aim here is to suggest
how one elite, namely, automobile manufacturers, creates a "criminogenic market structure"[2]

▶SOURCE: *"A Criminogenic Market Structure: the Automobile Industry,"* The Sociological Quarterly (Autumn 1975), 16:438–457. Midwest Sociological Society. Reprinted by permission.

[1]Typical explanations for this neglect include the observation that sociologists of deviance often work out of a symbolic interactionist perspective, and that this perspective has
an ideological-theoretical bias which offers tacit support to
power elites (Thio, 1973); that it has a philosophical-
methodological bias which focuses attention on the passive,
powerless individual and thus cannot conceptualize trans-
cendent, unobservable, active groups (Schervish, 1973); and,
finally, that it tends toward a grounded-emergent rather
than a logico-theroretic style of theory construction and thus
is vulnerable to the unequal power distribution embodied in
everyday life and, consequently, has a conservative bias
(Huber, 1973). For a reply to some of these points, see Stone
et al. (1974).

[2]I borrow the term "criminogenic market" from Leonard
and Weber (1970), who contend that the most useful conceptual approach to occupational crime is to see it as a *direct
consequence of legally established market structure.* In ths present
study, by "criminogenic market structure" I mean the deliberate and lawful enactment of policies by those who manage
economically concentrated and vertically integrated corporations and/or industries which coerce lower level (dependent) participants into unlawful acts. Those who set the conditions which cause others to commit unlawful acts remain

by imposing upon their new car dealers a pricing policy which requires high volume and low
per unit profit. While this strategy gives the
manufacturer increased total net aggregate profit
(by achieving economies of scale and by
minimizing direct competition among

non-culpable, while those who perform under these conditions remain eminently culpable. A micro illustration
suggestive of this approach was played out in the heavy electric industry where the U.S. government was able to show
that a cartel existed among corporations which resulted in a
price-fixing conspiracy. Nevertheless, the actual corporate
officials who were indicted and convicted came from the
second and third echelon of the corporate hierarchy and,
upon exposure, were legally and morally disavowed by the
first level echelon. Division heads and vice presidents were
censured and repudiated by presidents and directors for
contravening corporate policy. Those indicted and convicted, however, never for a moment thought of themselves
as contravening corporate policy, nor of having done anything but what was expected of them—their jobs (Smith,
1961). Although this case describes activity *within* a corporation, I wish to extrapolate it to an entire industry. Thus, at
the pinnacle of the economically concentrated auto industry
sit four groups of manufacturers who control 92 percent of
the new car market and who, on the distribution side of the
industry alone, set economic conditions which control approximately 31,000 franchised new car dealers, approximately 4,000 used car wholesalers, and approximately
65,000 "independent" used car retailers. Despite the fact
that those on the top cause the conditions which compel
others into untoward patterns of action, they do not reap the
public's wrath. At the same time that new car and used car
dealers consistently trail far behind every other occupational
grouping in terms of public esteem, there never has been a
presidential administration—beginning with Franklin
Roosevelt—without an automobile *manufacturing executive* in
a cabinet or sub-cabinet position!

oligopolist "rivals"), it places the new car dealer in a financial squeeze by forcing him to constantly free-up and continuously re-cycle capital into fixed margin new car inventory. This squeeze sets in motion a downward spiral of illegal activities which (1) inclines the new car dealer to engage in compensatory profit taking through fraudulent service operations, (2) under certain conditions, generates a "kickback" system which enables used car managers of new car dealerships to exact graft from independent used car wholesalers, and (3) forces the independent used car wholesaler into illegal "short-sales" in order to generate unrecorded cash for kickback payments. I shall present the evidence which provides the grounding for this model as I came upon it in the research process. What follows, then, is a natural history which reconstructs the stages of my investigation.[3]

THE BASE SITE

My principal research site was a medium-sized used car wholesale operation located in an eastern metropolitan area.[4] There are approximately forty other wholesale operations in this area,[5] the top three of which sell between 6,000 and 8,000 cars per year.[6] My base operation, which sold 1,501 cars in 1971 and 2,124 in 1972,[7] carried a 125-car wholesale inventory and a repair shop at one location and a 25-car retail inventory at another location. There were 16 employees altogether, including three partners (an older one who runs the office and two younger ones who function as buyers), three additional buyers (who also sell wholesale when not on the road), a retail manager, a retail salesman, two shop workers, a bookkeeper, and two-to-five drivers. The firm also retains the services of a lawyer and an accountant.[8]

Entry into my principal research site and later into other operations was relatively easy, for during my high school and college days I had made pin money selling used cars on a lot owned by the older partner. Later I came across two old acquaintances from high school days who hustled cars when I did; one is now a new car agency general sales manager, and the other a partner in a "family-owned" new car dealership.

Although I was always more an observer than a participant, I increasingly was expected to answer phone calls, take messages, move cars

---

[3] For a discussion of this presentation format see H. Becker (1970:37).

[4] For a breezy, journalistic description of the used car wholesaling scene see Levine (1968:26–29). For sociological insight into various levels of the auto industry see: Brown (1973) for independent used car retailing; Vanderwicken (1972) for franchised new car dealing; and Robbins (1971) for manufacturing.

[5] This figure derives from enumeration by wholesalers themselves. I was forced to rely on this source for three reasons. First, the appropriate State Departments of Motor Vehicles informed me that their statistical information does not distinguish between new and used and wholesale and retail dealers. Nevertheless, they intend to introduce such breakdowns within the next few years. Second, the *U.S. Bureau of the Census, County Business Patterns, 1970* places fundamentally different *kinds* of wholesale automobile establishments into the same reporting category. Thus, wholesale body and fender shops, junk yards, auction sales, freelance wholesalers, and regular wholesalers appear in the same category. Moreover, the census also includes businesses that

are legally chartered in a state but not actually doing business there. Consequently, for my purposes the census was not helpful. Third, the various county *Yellow Pages* phone books in which used car wholesalers advertise did not allow me to distinguish "cut-book" wholesalers, who free lance and work out of their home addresses, from regular wholesalers, who have substantial business premises, a staff of employees, and sizeable inventories.

[6] This figure also comes from wholesalers themselves.

[7] I compiled these figures from the dealers' "Police Book." For each car in stock, dealers must enter 23 items of descriptive information. Detectives from the Motor Vehicle squad routinely inspect this book.

[8] Subsequent to the completion of my study, three more operations were opened: a retail lot with a thirty-car capacity, a wholesale lot with a forty-car capacity, and a twelve-stall body and fender shop. Each of these operations was situated on land or in buildings purchased by the corporation. The staff also increased with the addition of three more buyers, two retail salesmen, seven body and fender men, one mechanic, and a pool of part-time drivers which fluctuates from three to ten on any given day.

around the wholesale lot, and deliver cars as part of a "caravan" with the regular drivers. Eventually, I gained access to all files. At about the same time the firm offered me a gasoline credit card, reimbursement for my private telephone bill, maintenance work on my own car, and drivers to pick me up at the airport when I returned from out-of-town trips. I did not decline the maintenance work or the airport service[9]; however, I did break off field appearances—but maintained social contact—when the firm adopted one of my opinions as the basis for its expansion policy, and it became clear that my role as an investigator had somehow given way to that of an advisor or consultant.

From December 1971 to August 1973, I spent an average of one day a week including evenings and weekends at my principal site, on the road, and at the homes of or out socializing with various members of my base organization and their families. Sometimes, though, I would hang around the lot for two or three consecutive days in order to get some sense of th continuity and rhythm of the operation. I always carried a notebook and, when necessary, made entries in full view of all present. I also tape-recorded extensive in-depth interviews with the consent of participants, but only when I knew more or less what I wanted information about, thus not abusing the privilege. These "formal" interviews al-

lowed me to nail down—for the record—what I had observed, participated in, or been told during the course of everyday activity or conversation over the course of nearly two years. The insight and information gleaned from these informal conversations were the basis for the "formal" interviews, the first of which I held during the sixth month of my field appearances.

SERENDIPITY

I should note here that I did not start out to study a criminogenic market structure. Rather, I wanted to follow up on a speculative hypothesis which grew out of some previous research on low income consumers (Farberman, 1968; Farberman and Weinstein, 1970). As a result of the latter study in particular, I had hypothesized that low income consumers strengthened their bargaining position vis-á-vis high status or expert sales or service people by changing the normative ground of the transaction from universalism to particularism, and thereby were able to coerce the expert other to respond as a concerned friend rather than as a mercenary stranger. Consequently, I began the present investigation to see if I could discover if people who bought used cars employed (wittingly or unwittingly) a set of bargaining tactics. I therefore observed over 50 transactions between retail customers and used car salesmen and, indeed, have been able to identify several bargaining tactics, associate them with distinct types of customers, and provide a theoretical interpretation.

My interest in the systemic nature of occupational crime developed without my realizing it for sometimes, while I wrote up notes in the office after watching a sales transaction, I would vaguely overhear or observe the sales manager and customer "write-up" the deal. I began to notice that occasionally the customer would make out a check *as well as* hand over some cash. This was accompanied by the customer's saying how "taxes were killing the little man" and "if you didn't watch out, the Governor would bleed

---

[9]During one of these trips, I parked my car—a small 1965 Buick Special—on the wholesale lot. As a gag, and in addition to whatever prudential motives may have been involved, the firm sold my car and with the proceeds put me into a large 1970 Oldsmobile. The firm, at considerable expense to itself, and, in the words of one of the partners, "felt that a Professor, who you also call Doctor, should drive around in a better car." At one and the same time the "gag" shows deference to my status, takes liberty with my property (albeit improves it) and coerces me into a more conventional status appearance. This gambit smacks of something approaching a hazing ritual. It is fun, yet it prepares the initiate for further entree into the club by manipulating him into club conventions. I imagine field workers often run this sort of gamut before they gain entrance into the secret place. Unhappily, these experiences usually remain unrecorded.

you to death." Out of simple curiosity I began *deliberately to observe* the "write-ups"—something I had originally paid no attention to since I thought the transaction was actually over after the bargain had been made and the salesman had "closed" the deal. It was at the "write-up," however, that a new research problem emerged, because what I had witnessed—and what, in fact, led me off in a new direction—was an instance of "selling short," or "a short-sale," an illegal act which constitutes the first link in a chain of activity that goes back to Detroit.[10] In the section which follows, I will describe (a) what a "short-sale" is; (b) how it benefits and costs both the retail customer and the dealer; and (c) why the dealer feels compelled to engage in it.

THE SHORT-SALE

A "short-sale" begins to develop when a retail customer observes the sales manager compute and add on to the selling price of the car the state sales tax—a hefty eight percent. Often, the customer expresses some resentment at the tax bite and asks if there is any way to eliminate or reduce it. The sales manager responds in a sympathetic fashion and allies himself with the customer in a scheme to "cut down on the Governor's share of the deal" by suggesting that the customer might make out a check for less than the actual selling price of the car. In turn, the manager will make out a bill of sale for the lesser amount. The customer then will pay the difference between the *recorded* selling price and the *actual* selling price in cash. A car which normally costs $2,000 would carry an additional 8 percent (or $160) state sales tax, thus actually costing the customer $2,160. If a bill of sale which records the selling price as $1,500 is made out, however,

[10]Although my initial research problem situated me so that I luckily tripped over and recognized a new problem, the new problem actually links to the old problem so that my understanding of the dynamics of customer/salesman interaction is enlarged by my understanding of the systemic dynamics of "short sales." In fact, deliberate—as opposed to accidental—problem transformation may be integral to the methodologic of contextual, vertical analysis.

then at 8 percent the taxes would be $120, for an apparent total of $1,620. Although the customer still pays $2,000 for the car ($1,500 by check and $500 in cash), he "saves" $40 in taxes.

Almost as important as saving the $40 is the obvious delight the customer typically takes at finally discovering himself in a situation where he can "even the odds," "give the big guys what for," and "make sure the little guy gets his two cents too." The attitude and mood which washes through the short-sale suggests a welcome, if minor, triumph in the back-stepping of everyday life. As an observer witnessing this "petty" collusion between little Davids against remote Goliath, I had a rather difficult time identifying it pursuant to the criminal code—as a conspiracy to defraud the government through tax evasion. Obviously, the meaning, value, and sentiment attached to the act by at least one of the participants (the customer) is totally incongruous with the meaning, value, and sentiment attached to it by the criminal code. Thus does a minor victory in everyday life co-exist in the same act with a punishable transgression of law. The victory is often more symbolic than material, however, since, if the customer at any future time has an accident or theft, his insurance company, in part, will initiate compensation calculations based on the selling price recorded in the bill of sale—a sum which understates the actual price paid.

But, if the customer derives both a small material savings and a large measure of delight, what does the dealer derive? For one thing, a lot of money; more precisely, a lot of *unrecorded* cash. At the moment the customer "saves" $40 in taxes the dealer gains $500 in cash. The "short sale" to the customer allows the dealer to "steal-from-the-top." In any given year an accumulation of these short sales can total to tens of thousands of dollars. In an effort to determine if "stealing from the top" was anything other than rank venality, I questioned one of the partners in my principal site.

Q: You've just said that it's [stealing-from-the-top] O.K. for the customer but bad for you. I don't understand that. Jeez, look at the money!

A: Yeah, sure, but who the hell wants to live with any of the retail customers. You see what goes on. They don't know shit about a car. They look at the interior, turn on the radio, check the odometer, kick the tire, push the windshield wiper button, turn on the air conditioner, open up the trunk, look at the paint. What the fuck has any of that got to do with the *condition* of the car? I mean, the way the fucker runs. If I put money into all this crap, I can't put it into improving the mechanical condition. Three weeks later the fucking car falls apart and they're on my ass to fix it. Then I got to live with them. They drive me off the wall. Then that broad down the consumer affairs office wants to know why I don't give the customer a fair shake. Shit, why the hell don't she educate the customers? It would make things a lot easier.

Q: Listen, if they're such a pain, why do you put up with them?

A: What do you mean?

Q: I don't know what I mean, but there is usually a bottom line and it's usually money!

A: Well, if you mean that they bail me out every now and then, sure.

Q: What do you mean?

A: Well, you know those creeps [buyers] I got on the road buying for me, you know what their philosophy is? "If you don't buy, you don't earn." They pay big numbers; what do they care; it's my money. If they get in too high on a package [group of cars] or a piece [one car], and I can't blow [wholesale] it out, then I look for a retail shot [sale]. But that means I can't turn over my money quickly, I got to lay with it out on the lot and hope some yo-yo [retail customer] comes along. Believe me, it's a pain in the ass. This whole business is in and out, in and out. Anything that slows the turnover costs money.

Q: O.K., so retail customers generally are a pain, but you put up with them because they bail you out on bad buys, but that still doesn't get to it. What about those retail sales that are "short" sales, that's where the bread is. That's what I'm trying to get at.

A: All right, listen: A wholesaler runs a big grocery store; if it's not on the shelves, you can't buy it. Without cars to sell, I can't sell cars. Look, we make enough legit, but you can't pay graft by check. Those bums get you coming and going.

Q: What bums?

A: You ever wanta meet a crook, go see a used car manager [of a new car dealership]. They clip a quarter [$25], a half [$50], a yard [$100], maybe more [on each car]. Put a package together and take it out [buy it from them] and they'll zing you for a week's pay. They steal their bosses blind.

Q: So, you have to pay them to get cars. You mean something under the table?

A: Yeah, the "vig."

Q: The what?

A: The grease, the commission, the kickback. How I'm gonna stay in business with no cars? You tell me.

Q: Incidentally, how many of your retail sales do you figure are "short"?

A: Maybe 70–75 per cent. I can't be sure.[11]

---

[11]Since the operation in question is primarily a *wholesale* not a retail house, the proportion of retail sales typically do not exceed 25 percent of total sales. Of these, however, about 75 percent are "short" sales. Thus, of 2,124 total sales, 398 are short. At a minimum of $100 stolen from the top per short sale, approximately $39,000 is generated in unrecorded cash. Used car *wholesalers* may well engage in retail selling for cash and, therefore, are clearly different from used and new car *retailers* who *avoid* cash sales in favor of "credit" or "installment" sales. This latter point was vividly disclosed at a hearing before California's Corporations Commissioner when Sears, Roebuck and Company requested a license to make low cost automobile loans *directly* to

Q: Tell me, do you ever wind up with more than you need for the kickbacks?

A: Sure, am I gonna lie to you? So I put a little away [in safety deposit boxes]. You think I'm the only one? But if it's buried, you can't use it. Better it should be in the business; I could use it—besides, who needs the aggravation?

Q: Are you ever able to get it [buried money] back into the business?

A: Yeah.

Q: How?

A: Aw, you know.

Apparently, the dealer's reasons for engaging in "short-sales" include, but are not confined to, rank venality. After all, most, but not all, of the unrecorded money is passed along in the form of "kickbacks"; only the residual excess actually finds its way directly into his own hands, and even this excess must be buried or occasionally laundered.[12] The principal reason the dealer

engages in short sales is to come up with kickback cash in order to keep his sources of supply open, and this imperative is more than enough to keep him involved with "short-sales," even though it means he has to deal with retail customers—the very bane of his existence.

The antagonism the dealer holds toward the retail customer is incredibly intense and appears to have two sources. First, it stems from the dealer's apparent inability to sell the customer what the dealer considers to be the *essential* element of a car—namely, its *mechanical condition*. Instead, he is compelled to sell what to him is non-essential—*physical appearance*. If he is to improve the car's physical appearance, then he must skimp on improving its mechanical condition. This, in the long run, works to his own disadvantage since he must "live with the customer" and, in some measure, make good on repairs affecting mechanical condition. Put another way, the wholesaler's *conceptualization* of the car and the retail customer's *conceptualization* of the car do not overlap. Where the wholesaler wishes to sell such *unobservables* as a good transmission, a tight front end, a solid chassis, and an engine without knocks in it, the typical retail customer wishes to buy such *observables* as a nice paint job, a clean interior, etc. The wholesaler and the retail customer basically have a hard time "coming-to-terms," that is, abstracting out of the vehicle the same set of concrete elements

---

customers, thus by-passing dealers. Direct loans, in effect, would turn consumers into cash customers. This the dealers emphatically did not want as the following testimony reveals:

> Q: . . . Do you want to sell cars for cash?
> A: I do not want to sell them for cash if I can avoid it.
> Q: You would not want to sell the cars you do for a cash price, then?
> A: No, sir.
> Q: Does this mean that you are not really in the business of selling automobiles?
> A: It does not mean that at all.
> Q: But you don't want to sell automobiles for cash?
> A: It means that I want to sell cars for the most profit that I can per car. Finance reserve (dealer's share of the carrying charges) and insurance commissions are part of the profit derived from selling a car on time.

Moreover, these dealers have no qualms about extending credit to poor risk customers; the car always can be repossessed and resold (Quoted in Macaulay, 1966:186).

[12]*"Burying money"* means putting it in a safety deposit box. Ironically, this money becomes a source of long-term anxiety instead of long term security. First, it remains a concrete symbol of criminality and is at odds with the dealer's self-image. Second, it also always is the target of potential investigatory disclosure although known instances of such activity

are virtually unheard of. Third, the dealer resents the accumulation of "idle" cash and is frustrated by his inability to "turn it over" easily and make it productive. *Laundering* occurs in tight money situations when capital *must* be made available. It invokes a symbiotic relationship between the dealer and a "bookie." The bookie is hired on as a "commissioned agent" of the dealership. The dealer "pays" him a weekly salary using a legitimate business check; in return, the bookie gives the dealer an equal amount in cash. The dealer provides the bookie with a W2 form and the bookie declares and pays taxes on this "income." The dealer then "declares" the income brought in by the bookie. Since this income derives from nonexistent buying or selling it is subtly apportioned and spread over actual transactions. The dealer also periodically writes a letter to the bookie's probation officer testifying to the bookie's reliable and gainful contribution to the business.

to invest with meaning and value. The vehicle literally *means* different things to each of them and the establishment of a shared meaning which is *mutually* valued is extremely problematic.

The second source of the dealer's antagonism stems from his overwhelming dependence on these ignorant customers. This dependence heightens dramatically when the dealer's own professional "house" buyers make bad buys; that is, pay too high a "number," or price for the car, which makes it impossible for the car to be quickly re-wholesaled. If the car is in basically sound mechanical condition, it will be "shaped" out in hopes of "bailing out" through a "retail shot." Though a bad buy can be redeemed through a retail sale, this route of redemption bodes ill for the house buyer since it reflects on his competence. It bodes ill for the dealer as well since he must tie up money, men, and space waiting for a fickle retail customer to get everyone off the hook. Thus, the dealer's antagonism toward the retail customer stems from his own dependence, for short-sales and bail-outs, on ignorant yo-yo's who don't know anything about cars. The dealer's redemption, then, lies in the hands of "idiot saviors," an unhappy situation at best.

KICKBACKS AND SUPPLY

In any event, based on what I had seen, heard, and been told, I concluded that the wholesale used car dealer engaged in "short-sales" principally to insure his supply of used cars. Since this conclusion was derived exclusively from observation and interview, I wanted to check it out against the dealer's inventory files. In the following section, I seek evidence of two things: (a) that the predominant source of the wholesaler's inventory, in fact, is the used car department of new car agencies; and (b) that used car managers in new car agencies universally receive kickbacks.

Accordingly, I classified all vehicles in my base site for the years 1971 and 1972 by their source of origin. Table I indicates that, of the 1,501 vehicles bought in 1971, 1,134 or 75.5 percent came from used car departments of new car dealers; of the 2,124 bought in 1972, 1,472 or 69.3 percent came from the same source. These figures corroborate the used car wholesaler's overwhelming dependence on the used car department of the new car agency for supply. They also suggest that there may well be a decreasing supply in the number of used cars available on the market altogether. From 1971

Table I. Units[a] within, and Vehicles Generated by, Various Sources of Supply

Source of Supply	1971		1972	
	Units	Vehicles	Units	Vehicles
1. Used car depts. of new car agencies	72	1134	94	1472
2. Rental, lease or fleet companies	9	145	18	104
3. Off-the-street customers	116	116	172	172
4. Dealers auctions	2	38	1	38
5. Body and fender shops	6	35	6	105
6. Retail used car dealers	11	27	17	193
7. Wholesale used car dealers	3	6	4	40
	219	1501	312	2124

[a]The generic term "units" encompasses "establishments" as in categories 1-2 and 4-7, and customers as in category 3.

Source: Dealer's Police Books

to 1972 there was a 6.2 percent decrease (75.5 to 69.3) in the proportion of cars from used car departments of new car dealers even though the number of new car agencies dealt with increased from 72 to 94.[13]

Given an overall paucity of used cars on the market, it would seem that used car managers of new car agencies are in a perfect position to exact tribute from the independent used car wholesaler whose major source of supply is in their hand. I thus proceeded to check out the universality of kickbacks. I classified all inven-

[13]These figures are consistent with national trend figures provided to me by Thomas C. Webb, research assistant, National Automobile Dealers Association (personal communication, March 11, 1974). Estimations of the number of used cars sold "on" and "off" the market in 1960 and 1973 indicate that, of the 20.7 million used cars sold in 1960, 14.9 million or 71.6 percent were sold "on" the market, whereas of the 31.4 million used cars sold in 1973, 18.7 million or 59.6 percent were sold "on" the market. Thus, there was a net decrease of 12.0 percent. A possible explanation for the decreasing supply of used cars on the market may be the consequence of an already established social-economic trend toward the multiple car family. Whereas a decade ago only 15 percent of the total population owned more than one car, today 30 percent do. Indeed, one out of every three families whose head of household is between the ages of 35–44 owns two cars and one out of ten whose head of household is between 45–54 owns three cars (MVMA, 1974:38–39). What this probably means is that cars are *handed down* from husband to wife to children and literally "run-into-the-ground." In other words, we may well be seeing the reemergence of "second-hand" cars. Cars change hands but outside the commercial nexus i.e., "off-the-market." An additional factor which may be contributing to this trend is declining public confidence in auto dealers. Not too long ago a poster showed a picture of former President Nixon with a caption which asked, "Would you buy a used car from this man?" The credibility of the new and used car dealer apparently has never been lower. Confirmation of this comes from several different polls which seek to determine the public image of new and used car dealers compared to other occupational groups. Auto dealers uniformly trail way behind others in terms of the trust they inspire in the buying public (Leonard and Weber, 1970). Still another compatible and contemporary factor is the deteriorating condition of our national economy where the combination of rising prices and decreasing purchasing power inhibit overall consumer demand and thus retard new car sales and accompanying trade-ins.

tory by the *specific* new car agency it came from, and then asked the older partner of my base operation to indicate at which agencies kickbacks were paid. As shown in column 4 of Table II, kickbacks were paid on 304 (out of 1,134) vehicles in 1971 and on 614 (out of 1,472) vehicles in 1972. Moreover, column 3—much to my surprise—shows that *all* of these cars come from only *seven* (7) agencies in both 1971 and 1972 and each of these agencies carried a Giant Motors franchise. Note, however, that these seven constitute only a small proportion of the total number of G.M. agencies dealt with, which is 35 in 1971 and 51 in 1972. Moreover, only 10 percent of *all* agencies in 1971 and less than 7 percent in 1972 required kickbacks. Nevertheless, in 1971 these agencies did, in fact, provide nearly 27 percent of all supply coming from used car departments of new car agencies and 20 percent of total supply. Similarly, in 1972 they provided 56 percent of supply from used car departments and 31 percent of all supply.

A closer examination of these seven G.M. agencies, however, discloses some common characteristics. First, an inspection of their zip codes and street addresses reveal that all seven are located in the same high density, urban area. Second, a rank ordering of all new car agencies by the number of cars they supply, as shown in Table III, reveals that these seven are the top supply sources and, by agreement among house buyers, are large agencies. Third, the remaining eight agencies among the top 15 supply sources all are located in suburban areas and are described by house buyers as medium sized.

With this information in hand, I again questioned the older partner of my base operation.

Q: Listen, didn't you know that you only paid kickbacks at large, urban, G.M. agencies? Why did you guys give me the impression that you paid kickbacks to *all* used car managers?

A: Really?

Q: Really, what!?

Table II. Kickbacks by Vehicle, Agency, and Franchise

Franchise	No. of Agencies 1971	No. of Agencies 1972	No. of Vehicles 1971	No. of Vehicles 1972	Kickback Agencies 1971	Kickback Agencies 1972	No. of Kickback Vehicles 1971	No. of Kickback Vehicles 1972
Giant Motors	35	51	571	976	7	7	304	614
Fore	10	16	159	209	—	—	—	—
Crisis	15	16	256	191	—	—	—	—
U.S.	1	2	1	5	—	—	—	—
Foreign	8	6	143	62	—	—	—	—
Unknown	3	3	4	29	—	—	—	—
	72	94	1,134	1,472	7	7	304	614

Table III. Number of Dealerships by Number of Vehicles Supplied: 1972

Number of Dealerships	Number of Vehicles Supplied
2	100+
1	75+
4	50+
8	25+
79	1+

A: Really, you thought we paid off all the managers? Well, I guess these are the big houses for us—it seems like a lot. I'll tell ya, the hicks are O.K. They don't know from conniving. The city is full of crooks.

Q: Really? Don't you think it has anything to do with these particular agencies, maybe the way they're set up or maybe with G.M.? After all, the other manufacturers have agencies there too.

A: No, it's a freak thing! It just means that seven crooks work at these places.

Q: Aw, come on. I don't believe that.

A: Listen, your barking up the wrong tree if you think it has anything to do with G.M.

Q: But why only at G.M.? and why only at G.M. agencies in the city?

A: Look, there's more G.M. agencies than [Fore] and [Crisis]. G.M. sells more cars, they get more trade-ins, they have solid used cars operations. These crooks go where the action is. They're good used car men, they get the best jobs. But they're crooks. I'm telling you, believe me!

Q: But if they're crooks, and you know it, why don't their bosses know it?

A: Look, the bosses aren't stupid. They know what's going on. If the used car man pushes the cars out, and turns over capital, and doesn't beat the boss too bad—they're happy.

Q: I guess I must be thick, I'm still not convinced.

A: All right. The boss is busy running the new car operation. He brings in a sharp used car man and bank rolls him. The used car man pays rent to the boss for the premises and splits profits with him depending on the deal they work out. O.K.? The used car man takes the trade-ins, he keeps the good stuff and wholesales the bad. He wholesales me an off-model, say, for two grand. He tells his boss, the car brought $1,875.00. I send a check for $1,875.00, and grease him a buck and a quarter. At $1,875.00, he still made a legitimate fifty or a hundred on the car—the boss gets half of that. As long as the used car man doesn't get too greedy, there's no problem. The boss takes a short profit but frees up his capital. Believe me, that's crucial, especially if he's paying one percent a month interest on his bank roll to begin with.

Q: So, what you're saying, is that the best agencies are in the city, that they're G.M., that G.M. dealers know their used car men are beating them, but that they don't get uptight as long as they make something and can free-up their capital.

A: Yeah.

Q: Listen, you've got a point, but isn't there another way to look at this? Isn't it possible that the boss does more than just tolerate being ripped off a little by his used car man? Isn't it possible that he's working with the used car man and beating his own business. In other words, he's splitting the kickbacks or something like that?

A: Look, anything's possible, but all I know is that the used car managers are a bunch of crooks. The bosses, I can't say; as for [Giant Motors], forget it, they're a legit concern.

Q: Maybe you're right but it sure would make sense if the bosses [G.M. dealers] did both— you know, turn over money and beat their own business. Hell, you do it and you're the boss, why shouldn't they?

A: Well, I have to. I don't know about them. Just don't go off half-cocked. Be careful before you lean on anybody.

This interview material has two intriguing aspects. Despite the dealer's strenuous insistence that kickbacks are the artifact of corrupt and venal individual used car managers, there is also the suggestion that such venality can take place precisely because large, urban G.M. agencies sell a lot of cars and therefore have an abundance of trade-ins, the best of which are recycled back into the agencies' used car retail line while the surplus is wholesaled out. The power to determine how this surplus is dispersed into the wholesale market places the used car managers

of the involved agencies in the position to demand and receive "kickbacks." Moreover, the new car dealer himself, who is under pressure to free up capital in order to avoid paying excess interest on money borrowed to purchase new car inventory, may have an incentive to "look-the-other-way," and perhaps even split "kickbacks" as long as his used car manager keeps moving cars and freeing capital.

THE FINANCIAL SQUEEZE

In the section which follows, I seek to check out (a) the existence of a financial squeeze on dealers, and (b) whether this squeeze inclines dealers to tolerate or even participate in kickbacks. By way of checking these points, I contemplated interviewing some people in the "kickback" agencies. The more I thought about how to guide myself in such interviews, the more I realized I was facing an interesting dilemma. I wanted to do the interviews precisely because I had discovered that the agencies were paid kickbacks by the wholesalers. Yet, in each case the kickback was being paid specifically to the manager of the used car department of the agency and I was not sure if the manager was acting on his own or was acting with the knowledge of his principal. If he was acting on his own, and I disclosed this, I might then put him in jeopardy. If he was acting with the knowledge of his principal, it was certain I would have an unreliable interview since in these cases I did not have personal bonds strong enough to insure truthful responses. Since I did not wish to deceive or jeopardize any of the respondents, and since I did not feel I could be truthful—as no doubt I would have had to disclose just how I had discovered the "kickback" arrangement, and thus transgress the trust that I had established with the wholesalers and run the risk of jeopardizing their ongoing business relationships with the new car dealers—I developed another approach. I decided to interview G.M. dealers in "non-kickback" agencies and try to elicit information which would allow me to pinpoint the key differences between kickback and non-kickback agencies, thereby nailing down an interpretation of the "kickback" phenomenon.

I managed to arrange interviews with three different dealers. The following quoted interview lasted five hours, was granted on the basis of a personal tie, and therefore is most reliable and valid. In addition, the elicited material is highly representative of the other interviews. The general thrust of my questioning was first to ask the dealer to talk about issues which are problematic in the running of his own business, and then to comment on the "kickback" phenomenon at the urban agencies. I was interested mainly in knowing if the pressure to turn over capital and avoid interest payments would encourage a dealer to "look-the-other-way" on "kickbacks" or even split them.

Q: How long have you been a dealer?

A: A dealer? About 20 years. About five or six years after [I finished] college, my dad and I went in as partners. It's mine now.

Q: Have you enjoyed it?

A: Well, it's been good to me for a goodly number of years, but frankly, during these past three to four years the business has changed markedly. It's a tougher, tighter business. I'm more tied down to it now than ever before. I can't be as active in the community as I would like. You know, that's important to me.

Q: Why is that the case? Is the business expanding?

A: Not really, well it depends on how you measure it. I work harder, have a larger sales and service staff than ever, I've expanded the facilities twice and refurbished the fixtures and touched up several times, and yes, I'm selling more new cars than before, but is the business expanding? Well, I suppose, yes, but not the way I'd like it to.

Q: Could you elaborate on that?

A: Well, the point is—and I know this will sound anomalous, well, maybe not to you—but I wish I could ease off on the number of new cars and pick up somewhere else, maybe on used cars.

Q: Why is that?

A: It boils down to investment—return ratios. The factory [manufacturer] has us on a very narrow per unit profit margin [on new car sales]. But if I had the money and the cars, I could use my capital more effectively in used cars.[14]

Q: In other words, G.M. establishes how much profit you can make on each new car you sell?

A: Just about. And more than that, they more or less determine how much [new car] inventory I have to carry, and the composition of that inventory.

Q: So, you have to take what they give you—even if you don't want or need it. How do you pay for the inventory?

A: I borrow money at prevailing interest rates to finance the inventory. And, sometimes it gets tight. Believe me, if I am unable to sell off that inventory relatively quickly, I'm pressed. I have got to keep that money turning or that interest begins to pinch.

Q: Is it fair to say that you compensate for narrow margins on new cars by making wider margins on used cars?

A: Not really, not in practice, at least not out here [in the suburbs]. Used cars, good used cars, are hard to come by. I imagine the city dealers have an easier time getting trade-ins. We get a lot of repeat customers, but I don't believe they trade up. They just buy new cars. Actually, we tend to pick up additional re-

[14]Leonard and Weber (1970:4) estimate that a dealer can make a gross profit margin of $400 on a $2,000 used car but only $150-200 on a $3,200 new car. Indeed the new car dealers I interviewed all indicated a desire to be able to sell more used cars.

venue from our service repair operation. I'm not particularly proud about it, but there is a lot of skimping going on. It's quite complicated. The factory has a terrible attitude toward service repair generally, and the [mechanics] union is overly demanding and inflexible. It's rather demoralizing and, frankly, I'm looking out for myself, too.

Q: Could you expand on that?

A: I prefer you not press me on that.

Q: If you had a choice, how would you prefer to set up your operation?

A: Well, if I had a choice—which I don't—I would rather have a low volume, high margin operation. I could get by with smaller facilities, a smaller staff, put less time into the business, and not constantly face the money squeeze.

Q: Do you think the really large city dealers would prefer the same kind of alternative?

A: I guess so, but it's hard to say. Their situation is somewhat different from mine.

Q: In what way?

A: Well, first of all, some of them, especially if they're located in [megalopolis] have even less control over their operation than I do. Some of them really run factory stores. That is, G.M. directly owns or controls the agency. Those outfits are really high-volume houses. I don't see how they can make a go of it. The factory really absorbs the costs.[15]

[15]According to White (1971), Detroit manufacturers generally avoid owning their own retail outlets or "factory" stores since a network of financially independent but exclusively franchised dealers helps to spread the risk of doing business, defrays cost, and provides local management with entrepreneurial incentive. Edwards (1965) also suggests that a franchise dealer system establishes local identity for products as well as provides facilities which handle trade-ins and repairs. Nevertheless, as a matter of prestige and because no individual dealer can afford the extremely high cost of land in this particular megalopolis, manufacturers usually own retail outlets directly.

Q: You did say that they probably had strong used car operations or, at least, had a lot of trade-ins. Do you think that helps?

A: Possibly.

Q: Do you think a really sharp used car man could do well in that kind of operation?

A: Well, he would do well in any operation in which he had used cars to work with.

Q: He could both retail and wholesale?

A: Oh, yes, if he had the cars to work with.

Q: Is it likely, in the wholesale end, he could demand and receive "kickbacks" from wholesalers?

A: Well, it's been known to happen. You know, those wholesalers, they're always willing to accommodate a friend. But it would only pay them to do that in relatively large operations where they could anticipate a fairly steady flow of cars.

Q: So, it would certainly make sense for them to accommodate friends in large, high volume, urban G.M. agencies?

A: Sure.

Q: Do you suppose the used car managers split kickbacks with their bosses?

A: Well, it's possible, but more than likely, the boss is more interested in moving those cars out quickly any way he can, so he can turn over that money and place it back into new car inventory.

Although this material does not permit any educated guess as to whether the dealers might split kickbacks with their used car managers, it does provide some assurance that new car dealers are under pressure to sell off cars relatively quickly in order to turn over capital and thus reduce interest payments. This pressure may be enough of a stimulus to, at least, incline the dealer to "look-the-other-way" if and when his used car man partakes in graft. As long as the used car man doesn't become too greedy and cut into the boss's pocket, his activity will be tolerated. Of course, we may still speculate, but not conclude, that if a "boss" is merely managing or only controlling a minimal share in a new car agency which is principally owned directly by G.M., he may be inclined to collude with his used car manager against "his own" agency. In any event, it is safe to presume that dealers feel under constant pressure to continuously recycle capital back into new car inventory and to get out from under interest payments. Corroboration of this comes from Vanderwicken (1972:128) who did a financial analysis of a medium-sized Fore agency located in a suburb of Cleveland, Ohio, and reported that:

"The average car is in inventory thirty days before it is sold. Quick turnover is important to a dealer, the instant a car leaves the factory, he is billed for it and must begin paying interest on it. This interest is one of [the dealer's] biggest single expenses."

Additional support also comes from Fendell (1975:11) who asked a New Jersey [Fore] dealer how he was coping with decreasing consumer demand and received the following response:

"I'm making deals I lose money on just to get the interest costs off my back. Those cars sit out there, costing me money every second. [Fore] has been paid in full for them a long time ago."

The dealer went on to say that his interest rates run between 10.25 percent to 11 percent per year.

MANUFACTURERS' PRICING POLICY

The constant and unremitting emphasis on new car inventory and the capital squeeze it places dealers in apparently is no accident. To the contrary, it is the calculated outcome of the manufacturers' pricing policy. According to Stewart Macaulay (1966:8), manufacturers and dealers enter into relationships for the mutual goal of making profit; however, their strategies for making that profit may differ.

"For example, a . . . dealer might be able to make a hundred dollars profit on the sale of one car or a ten dollar profit on each sale of ten cars . . . [it makes a great deal of difference to the manufacturer] because in one case it sells only one car while in the other it sells ten . . . It must sell many units of all the various models it makes. . . ."

This imperative to sell *many* cars stems from the manufacturers effort to achieve economies of scale, that is, savings in production and other costs as a result of massive, integrated, and coordinated plant organization. George Romney, when President of American Motors, testified before a Senate Judiciary Subcommittee on Antitrust and Monopoly and reported that:

"A company that can build between 180,000 and 220,000 cars a year on a one-shift basis can make a very good profit and not take a back seat to anyone in the industry in production efficiency. On a two-shift basis, annual production of 360,000 to 440,000 cars will achieve additional small economies . . ." (quoted in Lanzillotti, 1968:266.)

An economist, Joe S. Bain (quoted in Edwards, 1966:162) estimates that an even higher minimal production volume is needed for savings.

In general, 300,000 units per annum is a low estimate of what is needed for productive efficiency in any one line.

Thus, in order to cut costs to a minimum, the manufacturers—as in days gone by—must continue to engage in mass production,[16] which leads to mass distribution and the need for a dealer network into which the manufacturer can pump massive doses of new cars in a *controlled* fashion. According to economist Lawrence J. White (1971:139), this translates into a "forcing model," which may be defined as "the require-

---

[16] In principle, much the same strategy was used in the early 1900s when Henry Ford introduced mass production techniques and reduced the price of the Model "T" from $950.00 in 1909 to under $300.00 in the early 1920s and, as a result, boosted sales from 12,000 to two million and captured 50 percent of the market (Lanzillotti, 1968). Rothchild (1973) undoubtedly is correct when she observes that the auto industry continues to rely on ancient and probably obsolete formulas.

ment that the retailer sell a specified number of units as a condition of holding his franchise."[17] In effect, this allows the manufacturer to manipulate dealer inventories in a way that serves the oligopolist interests of an economically concentrated industry. Oligopolist "rivals" recognize their interdependence and avoid direct competition. Placing new dealerships in each others' territory would only call forth counter placements which, rather than expanding total auto sales, would perhaps cut into one's own already established dealerships. Thus,

"it would be better to concentrate on lowering the [profit] margins of existing dealers, which could only be met by equal actions . . . by one's rivals and which . . . has the effect of expanding the overall demand for the product" (White, 1971:142.)

All the manufacturer need do then to reduce per unit margins, which increases total net aggregate profit for the manufacturer, is to increase dealer inventory volume. This puts pressure on the dealer to free up capital from alternative investment possibilities such as used cars or to borrow capital at prevailing interest rates. Either way the dealer faces a financial squeeze and has a powerful incentive to sell off his inventory as quickly as possible, which industry trend statistics bear out. Despite the fact that new car dealers can achieve more efficient investment-return ratios from used car inventory—that is, if it is available—the ratio of new to used car sales from 1958 to 1972 per franchised new car dealer reflects an increasing preoccupation with new car sales. Examination of Table IV, column 3, indicates that over the last decade and a half new car dealers have been forced away from used cars and into new cars. In 1958, the ratio of used to new car sales was 1.77, but steadily declined until it reached 1.00 in 1970. And after 1970 it actually reversed itself so that in 1972 it was .81.[18]

[17]For a further mathematical articulation of this model, see Pashigan (1961:33–34; 52–56) and White (1971:137–145).

[18]Interestingly enough, the decreasing ratio of used to

This pressure to slant one's operation overwhelmingly in the direction of new car sales

Table IV. Cars Sold per Franchised New Car Dealer: 1958-1972

Year	New	Used	Ratio Used to New
1958	125	221	1.77
1959	168	272	1.62
1960	191	285	1.49
1961	175	271	1.55
1962	208	302	1.45
1963	225	317	1.41
1964	239	311	1.30
1965	283	354	1.25
1966	285	336	1.18
1967	269	328	1.22
1968	302	326	1.08
1969	309	389	1.26
1970	281	292	1.00
1971	331	—	—
1972	354	275	.81

Sources: Compiled from *The Franchised New Car and Truck Dealer Story*, Washington, D.C., National Automobile Dealers Association, 1973, p. 32, and *Automobile Facts and Figures*, Detroit: Automobile Manufacturers Association, 1971, p. 33.

new car sales more or less parallels the increasing market penetration of foreign auto makers. In 1963 foreign auto makers held 6.0 percent of the American market; that percentage increased to 14.6 percent by 1972. And the very year the ratio of used to new car sales declined to 1:00 or parity in 1970, G.M. lost nearly 7.1 percent of its previous market share (NADA, 1973:5). Put another way, increasing market penetration by foreign firms may have placed greater pressure on American auto makers to push harder on new car sales. One plausible way to accomplish this would be to require the dealer distribution network to put still more capital into new car inventory thus enabling the manufacturer to increase the volume of sales and thereby hold its market share. There is another compatible interpretation for the dramatic and unprecedented 7.1 percent market loss sustained by G.M. in a one year period. This interpretation is held widely by dealers themselves, namely, that G.M. was attempting to prevent rumored anti-trust action by the justice department and was inclined to show itself under competitive siege. In the following year, 1971, G.M. recouped all but 1.6 percent of its previous loss and has held subsequently at about 45.4 percent of the total market.

places the dealer in a tight margin operation. Vanderwicken (1972:121) observes that ". . . most people have a vastly exaggerated notion of a car dealer's profits . . . the average car dealer earns less than 1 percent on his volume, a miniscule margin far below that of most other retailers." He also provides a breakdown for the Ford agency he studied. Thus, on a car that the customer paid the dealer $3,337.00, the dealer paid the manufacturer $3,025.00. The dealer's gross margin was therefore $312.00 or 9 percent. (Average gross margin for retailers in other industries runs between 20–25 percent). Nevertheless, of this $312.00 the dealer paid $90.00 in salesman's commission, $43.00 in wages and salaries, $30.00 in advertising, $28.00 in interest, $27.00 miscellaneous, $24.00 in taxes, $22.00 in rent and maintenance, $16.00 in preparation and pre-delivery work, $9.00 in free customer service, and $7.00 in employee benefits—giving him a net profit of $16.00 per unit. As the boss of the Ford agency remarked, "Our low margins reflect the manufacturer's constant clamor for volume . . . the manufacturer sure as hell gets his . . ." (Vanderwicken, 1972:124).[19]

Should the dealer seek to protest this situation because it locks his time, effort, and money exclusively into fixed margin new car sales, he finds himself under subtle coercion. Quick delivery from the factory becomes problematic and so does a substantial supply of "hot" models (Macauley, 1966:173). Moreover, unfavorable sales comparison with "factory" stores, which sell cars below average retail price, raises questions of effective management (Leonard and Weber, 1970:416). And should such subtle coercion fail to reach home, there is always the threat of franchise termination—a threat which cannot be dismissed as idle given the elimination of over 3,300 dealerships between 1961 when

there were 33,500 and 1970 when there were 30,200[20] (NADA, 1973:30). If a franchise is cancelled, it is unlikely that another manufacturer will step in and offer a new franchise or that a new dealer will offer to buy one's premises, equipment, stock, and reputation. Consequently, new car dealers apparently accommodate to this "forcing" procedure and avoid direct reaction. Nevertheless, it appears that they do undertake a form of indirect reaction.

DEALER REACTION

An expert witness who testified before the Senate Judiciary Subcommittee on Antitrust and Monopoly in December 1968 reported on a series of "rackets" which dealers perpetrate on the public in order to supplement their short new car profits. These "rackets" include charging for labor time not actually expended, billing for repairs not actually done, replacing parts unnecessarily, and using rebuilt parts but charging for new parts (Leonard and Weber, 1970). In addition to fleecing customers, they also attempt to retaliate against manufacturers whom they accuse of having a hypocritical attitude on service work. Virginia Knauer (Sheppard, 1972:14), special assistant to the President for consumer affairs, reports that complaints about auto service repair lead the list of all complaints. According to Knauer, local car dealers themselves complain that the manufacturers simply do not care about service repairs because if they did, they would adequately compensate dealers for pre-delivery inspection and for warranty work and they certainly would not set up—as one of the Big Three did—a regional competition in which prizes were awarded to regions that *underspent* their warranty budgets (Leonard

---

[19]The per unit net of $16.00 does not reflect per unit revenue from financing or insurance which can boost that figure by 200 percent. Little wonder retail dealers want to avoid cash customers.

[20]It is difficult to know what percentage of these 3,300 was the result of attrition, voluntary termination, bankruptcy, or direct and indirect franchise cancellation. It is probably safe to assume, however, that the existing network of franchises reflect manufacturers' perferences relative to location and pricing strategy.

and Weber, 1970). Indeed, the resentment held by the dealers toward the factory on the issue of service work, as well as the manner and magnitude of retribution engaged in by the dealers against the factory, has been of such proportion that one manufacturer, General Motors, recently fired its entire Chevrolet Eastern Zone office, which has jurisdiction over no less than 60 Chevrolet dealers, for colluding with those dealers against the factory, in the cause of more just compensation for dealer's service work for dealer's service work (Farber, 1975).

It would seem, then, that the forcing of fixed margin new car inventory works to the manufacturers' advantage by increasing total net aggregate profit without risking direct competition. This high volume low per unit profit strategy, however, precipitates a criminogenic market structure. It forces new car dealers to free up money by minimizing their investment in more profitable used car inventory as well as by borrowing capital at prevailing interest rates. The pressure of interest payments provides a powerful incentive for the dealer to move his inventory quickly. The need to turn money over and the comparatively narrow margins available to the dealer on new car sales alone precipitate several lines of illegal activity: First, it forces dealers to compensate for short new car profit margins by submitting fraudulent warrantee statements to the manufacturers, often with the collusion of the manufacturers' own representatives. Second, it forces dealers to engage in service repair rackets which milk the public of untold sums of money. Third, it permits the development of a kickback system, especially in large volume dealerships, whereby independent used car wholesalers are constrained to pay graft for supply. Fourth, the wholesalers, in turn, in order to generate unrecorded cash, collude with retail customers in "short-sales." Fifth, to the extent that short-sales spawn excess cash, the wholesaler is drawn into burying and laundering money. In sum, a limited number of oligopolist manufacturers who sit at the pinnacle of an economically concentrated industry

can establish economic policy which creates a market structure that causes lower level dependent industry participants to engage in patterns of illegal activity. Thus, criminal activity, in this instance, is a direct consequence of legally established market structure.

REFERENCES

Becker, Howard S.
1970   Sociological Work: Method and Substance. Chicago: Aldine Publishing Company.

Brown, Joy
1973   The Used Car Game: A Sociology of the Bargain. Lexington, Mass., Lexington Books.

Edwards, Charles E.
1965   Dynamics of the United States Automobile Industry. Columbia: University of Southern Carolina Press.

Farber, M. A.
1975   "Chevrolet, citing 'policy violations,' ousts most zone aids here." The New York Times, Sunday, January 12, Section L.

Farberman, Harvey A.
1968   A Study of Personalization in Low Income Consumer Interactions and Its Relationship to Identification With Residential Community, unpublished Ph.D. thesis Department of Sociology, University of Minnesota.

Farberman, H. A., and E. A. Weinstein
1970   "Personalization in lower class consumer interaction." Social Problems 17 (Spring): 449–457.

Fendell, B.
1975   "Dealers struggle for survival." The New York Times, Sunday, February 2, Section A.

Gouldner, Alvin
1970   The Coming Crisis of Western Sociology. New York: Basic Books.
1968   "The sociologist as partisan: sociology and the welfare state." American Sociologist 3 (May):103–116.

Huber, Joan
1973   "Symbolic interaction as a pragmatic

perspective: the bias of emergent theory."
American Sociological Review 38 (April):
274–284.

Lanzillotti, Robert F.
1971   "The automobile industry." Pp. 256–301 in
W. Adams (ed.), The Structure of American Industry, 4th edition. New York: The
MacMillan Company.

Leonard, W. N. and N. G. Weber
1970   "Automakers and dealers: a study of
criminogenic market forces." Law and Society 4 (February):407–424.

Levine, L.
1968   "Jerome Avenue." Motor Trend 20
(December):26–29.

Liazos, A.
1972   "The poverty of the sociology of deviance:
nuts, sluts, and perverts." Social Problems
20 (Summer):103–120.

Macaulay, Stewart
1966   Law and the Balance of Power: The Automobile Manufacturers and Their Dealers.
New York: Russell Sage Foundation.

Motor Vehicle Manufacturing Association
1972   Automobile Facts and Figures. Detroit:
MVMA.

National Automobile Dealers Association
1973   The Franchised New Car and Truck Dealer
Story. Washington, D.C.: NADA, Table 6,
p. 30.

Pashigan, Bedros P.
1961   The Distribution of Automobiles, An
Economic Analysis of the Franchise System. Englewood Cliffs, N.J.: Prentice Hall.

Quinney, Richard
1970   The Social Reality of Crime. Boston: Little,
Brown and Company.

Robbins, Harold
1971   The Betsy. New York: Trident Press.

Rothchild, Emma
1973   Paradise Lost: The Decline of the Auto-Industrial Age. New York: Random House.

Schervish, P. G.
1973   "The labeling perspective: its bias and potential in the study of political deviance."
The American Sociologist 8 (May):47–57.

Sheppard, Jeffrey M.
1972   The New York Times, Sunday, November
5. Section A.

Smith, R. A.
1961   "The incredible electrical conspiracy." Parts
I and II, Fortune (April-May).

Stone, G. P., D. Maines, H. A. Farberman, G. I. Stone,
and N. K. Denzin
1974   "On methodology and craftsmanship in the
criticism of sociological perspectives."
American Sociological Review 39
(June):456–463.

Taylor, I., P. Walton, and J. Young
1974   "Advances towards a critical criminology."
Theory and Society 1 (Winter):441–476.

Thio, A.
1973   "Class bias in the sociology of deviance."
The American Sociologist 8 (February):1–12.

Vanderwicken, Peter
1972   "How Sam Marshall makes out with his
'deal.'" Fortune 86 (December):121–130.

White, Lawrence J.
1971   The Automobile Industry Since 1945.
Cambridge: Harvard University Press.

76. Price Fixing in the Plumbing Fixture Industry

ALLAN T. DEMAREE

NEARLY A DECADE HAS PASSED SINCE DISCLOSURE of the multibillion-dollar price-fixing conspiracies in the electrical industry shook the conscience of the business world and sent seven men to jail. Now, in one of the biggest criminal price-fixing cases since the electrical affair, a federal judge has again sentenced respected executives to prison for violating the antitrust laws. A little-publicized and often bizarre case, it resulted in convictions for fifteen manufacturers of plumbing fixtures, companies ranging in size from tiny Georgia Sanitary Pottery, with all of seventy-six employees in an antiquated plant in Atlanta, to American-Standard, a diversified, multinational corporation with more than $1 billion in sales a year, the acknowledged leader of the industry.

The first price-fixing meeting in this case was held, astonishingly enough, just six months after the electrical-industry executives had been sentenced to jail, an event that was widely reported in the press. Although the volume of sales affected by the price fixing was considerably smaller than in the electrical conspiracies, several of the eight executives convicted were of higher rank, the fines imposed on them were heavier, and the jail sentences longer. Three companies and three executives, who stood trial in Pittsburgh for sixteen arduous weeks, are now appealing their convictions. The others pleaded

no contest, have served their jail terms and paid their fines.

The case holds valuable lessons about the nature of price-fixing conspiracies. The executives involved were hardly robber barons of nineteenth-century lore, building great trusts and amassing outrageous fortunes. They were harried, uneasy men. Their industry had grown highly competitive, and price cutting had become fierce. Other industries sheltered themselves from savage price competition by following a pattern of price leadership, by creating brand preferences, or by investing in the high technology that yields patent monopolies. The plumbing industry was not able to escape price competition with such strategies, and as profits slid, responsible executives drifted into price fixing. Many of them could rationalize their plight: they weren't really breaking the law, or if they were, they weren't "gouging" the public, just seeking an "adequate" profit. But in fact, of course, they *were* breaking the law, and in doing so they fell victim to all the misfortunes visited upon the ordinary criminal—treachery, threats of blackmail, deceit, distrust of one another, and, not least, their own stupidity.

The importance of the case lies not only in the tangled web these executives spun for themselves or in the harsh penalties ultimately inflicted upon them. Even more significantly, it stands as an insistent reminder of the continuing need for vigorous and rationally conceived antitrust enforcement, a task that must begin inside the corporation itself. While much in cur-

►SOURCE: *"How Judgements Came for the Plumbing Conspirators,"* Fortune *(December 1969), pp. 96–99, 170, 175–176, 178, 180, 182. Reprinted by special permission: 1969 Time, Inc.*

rent antitrust policy is speculative and controversial, no one can doubt that flagrant price-fixing violations of the sort encountered here do great damage to the fabric of free enterprise.

ACRES OF UNWANTED TUBS

The defendants are men who feel buffeted by fate. Their industry is inextricably linked to the fortunes of another—construction, which itself is notorious for ups and downs. The end of World War II brought the greatest home-building boom in American history and, as a result, manufacturers of plumbing fixtures fared fabulously. Demand far exceeded supply, sales expanded rapidly, and profits soared. Then, almost simultaneously, several events occurred to throw the market into turmoil.

Most important, the building boom faltered, first in 1956 and then again, after a brief recovery, in the early Sixties. Suddenly the industry found itself saddled with overcapacity. Acres of unwanted tubs and toilets stood, row upon row, mutely commenting on the fickleness of the marketplace. To make matters worse for the old-line producers of cast-iron and vitreous-china fixtures, "outsiders" charged in with new, cheaper products stamped of steel and molded of plastic-coated fiber glass.[1] Distribution patterns changed radically, too, as mass merchandisers like Sears, Roebuck and Montgomery Ward, and other direct-to-user outlets, began siphoning business away from the industry's old standbys, the independent wholesale distributors. New managements at the manufacturing level, particularly Thomas Mellon Evans who took over Crane Co. (third largest in the industry) in 1959, further jostled competitors by introducing new marketing techniques. As manufacturers vied for shares in a contracting market, prices fell and profits plummeted.

[1]Most bathtubs and some lavatories, the industry term for bathroom sinks, are cast of iron and coated with porcelain enamel. Most lavatories, urinals, and water closets (again the industry term) are made of vitreous china fired in kilns.

BIG BOY AND THE LITTLE POTTERS

Traditionally, the industry's manufacturers have been grouped into two levels—the full-line companies like Standard, Kohler, Crane, and Eljer (now a division of Wallace-Murray Corp.), which produce both enameled cast-iron and vitreous-china fixtures, and the short-line companies, mostly small potters that produce only china. The small potters have always sold their wares for less than the major companies, whose products enjoyed greater market acceptance. During the industry's plush years the price differential was narrow. But as soon as the market turned down, the small potters were forced to drop their prices, the differential increased, and this in turn aggravated price pressures already being felt by the majors.

In the spring of 1960 the small potters who had begun shaving prices were taught an acute lesson about the power of their bigger competitors, particularly American Standard. That corporation reacted to the competition with what came to be called the White Sale, a drastic drop in prices that lasted six weeks. The move was initiated by Daniel J. Quinn, now sixty-eight, an affable and shrewd Irishman who had risen from a salesman peddling plumbing ware on the streets of New York to vice president for plumbing sales. Quinn was known throughout the industry as the Big Boy, not only because he carried 245 pounds on a six-foot frame, but also because he symbolized Standard's dominant position.

It was with one eye cocked toward the Big Boy that representatives of most of the small potters gathered at the O'Hare Inn in Chicago on August 8, 1961. The room was reserved by Oscar Gerber, the president and a principal owner of Gerber Plumbing Fixtures Corp. in Chicago; he habitually wore a silver tie clasp in the shape of a commode. The meeting was called under the auspices of the Plumbing Fixture Manufacturers Association, the industry's trade association, as many more such gatherings would be in the years to come. Formal P.F.M.A. sessions, which discussed legitimate association business, were attended by William E. Kramer, the Washington-based executive secretary, and by his friend, James C. McKay, a partner in the Washington law firm of Covington & Burling, who acted as legal counsel. Kramer arranged the meetings, planned the agenda, and kept minutes. McKay, as one potter remembers, "always called our hand if we got into prices—he was very saintly about it all." So the prices were fixed in rump sessions after Kramer and McKay had withdrawn.

At that first meeting, the potters reached what Gerber later termed, somewhat euphemistically, "a general oral understanding as to price sheets," or more specifically, an agreement to raise prices 5 percent on the four highest-volume china fixtures. Thus began what might be called the "little conspiracy." With two important exceptions, the ten companies involved were all small potters, like Gerber, with from $1 million to $6 million in sales. The exceptions were Crane and Universal-Rundle Corp., the latter controlled by Sears, Roebuck. Both manufactured cast-iron tubs as well as chinaware. They gained entrée to the little conspiracy by virtue of the fact that in addition to their higher-priced chinaware, they also produced a secondary line that sold for the same prices the little potters charged.

A BREAKDOWN OF TRUST

It was easier for the potters to agree on prices in a hotel room than to hold them in a declining market. Unlike the electrical conspirators, they were dealing in shelf items sold to hundreds of independent wholesalers who whipsawed one producer against another. Although they tried, they found no effective way to police prices; rumors of "chiseling" swirled through the industry. "The trouble was," recalls Raymond F. Gammons Jr. of little Georgia Sanitary, "we wouldn't trust each other outside the damn room." Prices deteriorated so badly in the fall of 1961 that Raymond Pape, Crane's thin, frenetic marketing manager, drew the conclusion that

his was the only company abiding by the agreement. He did the "honorable" thing, called his competitors, and said he was pulling out.

Early the next year, however, the potters again met under the guise of the P.F.M.A., first in January at Chicago's Morrison Hotel and then the following month in suite 600 of the Knickerbocker in the same city. On each occasion, they waited until Kramer had left the room, and then turned the talk to prices. They discussed reports that Standard was down to four days' production a week at some plants, and Stanley S. Backner, Universal-Rundle's marketing vice president, predicted that if the small potters didn't raise prices, Standard would get "disgusted" and lower the boom.

At the January session they agreed on prices, then polled the members to be sure there were no misunderstandings. In February they renewed the agreement and also set new prices for B-grade china, fixtures marred by imperfections. The conspirators were like members of Alcoholics Anonymous, Pape remarked. They had to meet repeatedly to "reassure" themselves. As the meeting broke up, Oscar Gerber warned the others not to allow incriminating memoranda to creep into their files, and Stan Backner cautioned a colleague not to throw notes in the wastebasket. They departed in a jovial mood.

THERE'S A BUG IN SUITE 600

The industry thought the world of Bill Kramer. Then thirty-six and P.F.M.A.'s executive secretary for six years, Kramer was a man of glib tongue and impressive stature, standing a strapping six-foot-three. Friends in the industry described him as "brilliant," "the all-American boy," and "a supersalesman who could talk the buffalo off a nickel."

But there was a lot about Bill Kramer they didn't know. For one thing, they didn't know he had brought a companion along to the February meeting, a young private investigator who was built like a running guard and was named

Anton (Tony) Fanflik. The two men took considerable care not to disclose their relationship. They flew from Washington in the same plane, but Kramer flew first class and Fanflik went coach. They rode to the Knickerbocker in the same taxicab, but neither spoke a word to the other. Fanflik registered as "Frank Edwards" and took a room adjacent to suite 600.

A man who takes pride in his craft, Tony Fanflik spent seven hours painstakingly bugging suite 600. He especially wanted this job to be successful, for Kramer was a good client, who had previously paid Fanflik's firm, Van Will Associates, Ltd., to install a recorder on his telephone, shadow a government official, and secretly record the meeting at the Morrison a month earlier. To Fanflik's chagrin, the Morrison bugging had picked up nothing and he agreed to make up for it by bugging the Knickerbocker free of charge.

When he moved a piece of furniture, Fanflik meticulously marked its location on the carpet with straight pins so he could replace it exactly. He disassembled the television and planted a miniature transmitter inside. He lodged other bugs under a couch, behind the drapes at the windows, under a serving bar in the bedroom, and in the bathroom. The next day, as the potters sipped drinks and fixed prices, Fanflik tended four recording machines quietly turning in his own room next door. Minutes after the meeting broke up, Fanflik walked down the hall to Kramer's room and handed him a stack of tapes as he stood shaving in the bathroom. "I was happy as a pig in slop," Fanflik recalls. "I got my client what he wanted."

A SUDDEN COLLAPSE IN MAY

Just three months after the Knickerbocker meeting, the little conspiracy was broken by precisely what the potters had feared—a sudden 20 percent price cut by American-Standard in May, 1962. The cut was recommended by Dan Quinn and concurred in by his boss, Joseph J. Decker, president of the plumbing and heating division,

a lean, tough-looking man with heavy black brows and a deep raspy voice. Quinn's market intelligence had indicated that if there really was a conspiracy among the small potters, "it wasn't doing any good."

The big May drop that ended one conspiracy ultimately led to a second, far more important one involving American-Standard and all the other majors—seven companies that produced 98 percent of the enameled cast-iron bathtubs sold in the U.S. It began on a cool September evening, the night before a P.F.M.A. meeting, at the Sheraton-Chicago Hotel where Dan Quinn had a hospitality suite. At first things hardly seemed hospitable. The top marketing men from most of the big companies were there: Standard, Kohler, Crane, Eljer, Universal-Rundle, Rheem, and Borg-Warner. Several told Quinn bluntly that his price cut, which had plunged bathtubs down as low as $40, was "unprecedented" and "ruinous."

Feelings of desperation weren't confined to Quinn's competitors. Standard's own profit picture was so bleak that Joseph Grazier, then president, feared the company would fail to earn its dividend. Grazier was livid when he first learned of the cuts while touring plants in Europe; he had previously recommended against price cuts and was not used to having his advice cavalierly ignored. From the time he returned in June, Grazier pressed his subordinates for price increases, but they didn't think the market was ready.

All the "crying" in Quinn's suite indicated that the market was ready, however, and before the evening was over an understanding had been reached. Memories vary as to just how explicit this agreement was. Discussions lasted over drinks anywhere from three to five hours; some men left early, others drifted out to dinner and returned. Charles J. Callanan, who had worked under Quinn at Standard for ten years before becoming Rheem's national product manager, remembered explicitly which prices would be raised and by how much, perhaps because Rheem's plumbing-ware division had consistently lost money even at higher prices and he was particularly concerned that an increase go through. On the other hand, Norman Held, a square-built, square-faced Kohler vice president and director, was the last to arrive in Quinn's room and the first to leave, and he claims not to recall any specific prices being mentioned. By merely dropping in, however, Norm Held violated Kohler's own Spartan "anti-fraternization" rule, a strict standard fashioned by a tough and puritanically independent management, which barred even a casual drink with competitors.

ORDERS FROM THE OLD MAN

On October 12, Standard led off with the agreed increase, lifting prices on enameled cast-iron bathtubs 6 percent, and the others followed. But the problem remained what to do about china prices, which the major companies had not felt they could raise in October because the small potters' prices were then so low. The next month, the P.F.M.A. members gathered again, this time at Washington's rambling Shoreham Hotel, where after a breakfast meeting several men lingered to discuss the market. Robert Casner, Crane's feisty, impatient, vice president, told his competitors that "the old man"—Crane's Chairman Tom Evans—had ordered him to raise prices on china, and he would do so regardless of what the rest of the industry did. By the time the meeting broke up, one participant recalls, it looked as if the industry would follow Crane's lead "in some form or another."

When Crane's move came in January, it was a whopper. Crane increased prices on widely selling china fixtures by as much as 40 percent. Other manufacturers, immediately interviewed by reporters, joined in the delicate minuet that so frequently is choreographed in the press as an industry tiptoes toward a price rise. "Based on the needs of the industry," said Standard's Joe Grazier, "higher prices should prevail." John B. Balmer, Murray Corp. president, chimed in: "Chinaware needs adjustment at least equally as much as the iron adjustment we

made last fall." But privately many producers figured a 40 percent increase was simply too much to stick.

As the days passed, Crane felt uncomfortably like the general who looked back to find his troops weren't following. Ray Pape, the nervous fellow who had figured prominently in the short-line conspiracy, began telephoning competitors. Either Pape or his boss, Bob Casner, talked with their counterparts at Briggs, Universal-Rundle, Rheem, Eljer, and possibly Standard, complaining that these companies were slow to follow and urging them to come at least part way along. After a week of anxiety, Standard increased its prices 7 percent, Crane gladly dropped back, and the rest of the industry followed suit.

"THEY KNOW THIS IS AGAINST THE LAW, DON'T THEY?"

At about this time Kramer called his lawyer friend, McKay, and spun out a tale calculated to turn an antitrust lawyer's hair gray. He told how the prices were rigged on china and went on to describe what he considered the final link in the industry's chain of conspiracy. This was a plan to quit producing bathtubs coated with regular enamel, even though these tubs accounted for a big share of the market, and to supply only more expensive acid-resistant enamel instead. Eliminating regular enamel, which could be stained by detergents and household acids, would markedly improve the quality of the cast-iron tubs on the market and strengthen the manufacturers in competition with plastic-coated fiber glass, which was acid resistant. The companies planned to request that the Department of Commerce revise its commercial standard for bathtubs so as to specify the use of acid-resistant enamel only. That was all perfectly legal. The illegality crept in when the manufacturers met and agreed on new prices, higher ones on the average, to be announced simultaneously with the switch to all acid-resistant enamel.

"They know this is against the law, what they're doing, I suppose, don't they?" asked McKay.

"Well," said Kramer, "I don't know whether they know consciously that it is. I don't think they think about it consciously."

Both men laughed. Then McKay said he thought the industry's action would arouse suspicion on the part of the antitrust authorities, and Kramer asked why the government had never done anything before.

"Because," said McKay, "I think actually they've never successfully agreed on prices before."

"Oh, you really think that?"

"Well, I think they have for a very short time, and I think they've thought they had an agreement and then they, uh, it pootered out and—"

"Well, how long does it have to go on?"

"Doesn't have to—well, I mean for the customer to get sore about it, you know, it has to go on for a little time. Of course, they violated the antitrust laws before; but they just—it hasn't been a successful violation. But this sounds like the bathtub increase is successful and it sounds like if this pottery increase is successful and also if they are successful in eliminating non-acid-resisting tubs . . . well, I think there's a fair chance that someone's going to squawk, that's all, and then you might have a grand jury and then you have subpoenas, and then you're in trouble, especially if those ass-holes are writing memoranda about this."

Kramer doubted that anyone would be that stupid.

"It's not affirmative stupidity," McKay said, "it's just thoughtlessness, despite the fact that over the years I've tried to tell them not to write any memoranda. But I can't tell them how to violate the law and get away with it." McKay was so angry at the industry now that he sputtered. "I think they're stupid to, uh—I think the industry is stupid anyway. I think they ought to, if they only had price leadership you know, which they don't have—that would be the thing—that is, you know, that isn't violative of anything . . .

"But to get together and hold these meetings—and you know perfectly well with ten or twelve people at these meetings, someone is making memoranda, writing up what goes on, and they're using the words, 'Well, today we agreed that we will eliminate non-acid-resisting enamel on bathtubs and . . . if we hold to this agreement as everyone said they would, this means that we should get an extra two or three dollars per bathtub . . .' You know perfectly well that there is a memorandum like that that's around or will be around."

"Well," Kramer replied, "it must have been around for a long time because we've been having these meetings for a long time."

"I know, but nobody has . . ."

"Squawked."

". . . Nobody has served a subpoena on them, and subpoenaed that stuff which is sitting in the files."

WON'T YOU COME HOME, BILL KRAMER?

The Department of Commerce, following the industry's request, revised its commercial standard in July 1963. American-Standard led off with the agreed price changes and the industry followed suit. Later that month, Dan Quinn, then president of P.F.M.A., called McKay to say he was disturbed because the association's Plastics Research Fund containing more than $130,000 had never been audited. When McKay talked to Kramer about this, Kramer said he had delayed the audit because Kohler had not yet decided whether to contribute to the fund. The amount each company paid was based on its sales, and if the fund were audited now, then again after Kohler paid, everyone in the industry would know Kohler's market share—a statistic each company jealously guarded. Because of Quinn's concern, however, Kramer assured McKay that he would order the fund audited as soon as he returned from a vacation he was about to take.

That was a promise Kramer never kept. For, as it turned out, he had been secretly embezzling from the Plastics Research Fund and other accounts for more than a year. He had invested part of the proceeds in a sixty-two-foot Chris-Craft luxury yacht on which he, his wife, and four children now took off for a vacation cruise in the Bahamas. By the time they embarked, there wasn't enough money left in the till to cover the P.F.M.A. payroll.

When McKay finally reached him at the Harbour Club in Nassau, Kramer admitted taking some $170,000, most of it from the unaudited Plastics Research Fund. An Ernst & Ernst special audit later put the missing funds at $214,000, including unauthorized payments to Van Will Associates, investigator, which Kramer had charged on P.F.M.A.'s books as "audio-visual expenses." He had spent $52,000 for the yacht and thousands more for repairs. Kramer spurned McKay's plea that he return, and added ominously that if the P.F.M.A. harassed him he would report the members' price fixing to the government and back the charges up with tape recordings, which until then no one in the industry knew existed.

Two days later, P.F.M.A.'s executive committee met in emergency session at Washington's Mayflower Hotel to hear McKay report on the embezzlement and threat. Some of the men present must have felt a keen sense of danger, among them Oscar Gerber, who had reserved the meeting rooms at the O'Hare Inn, warned of memoranda at the Knickerbocker, and later admitted to an "understanding as to price sheets." Dan Quinn, however, had entered into agreements more subtly and to this day steadfastly maintains his innocence. In any case, nobody knew how much evidence Kramer had and no one let on to McKay that he was the least bit worried.

A place at the head of the oblong table was saved for Daniel J. Cronin, a representative of Aetna Casualty & Surety, who, less than a year earlier, had talked Kramer into doubling his bond to $100,000. The tone of the meeting was conciliatory, despite obvious signs of embezzlement and threats of blackmail. "We had mercy

in our hearts," says Dan Quinn. Cronin marveled at their understanding nature and left with the opinion that all would be forgiven if Kramer would only return.

PANDORA'S DESK DRAWER

But Kramer would not come back. The executive committee dispatched McKay and Ray Pape to Nassau over the Labor Day weekend, but by then Kramer had sailed for other islands. Later, when he returned to Nassau, Kramer telephoned McKay in Washington, charging the $80 call on his P.F.M.A. credit card, but again he refused to return. Shortly thereafter, P.F.M.A. attached the proceeds from the sale of Kramer's home and backyard pool. The Internal Revenue Service launched an investigation of his tax liability, and the Federal Bureau of Investigation began searching for him on suspicion of transporting stolen funds across state lines. An inexorable chain of events had begun that would soon overwhelm both Kramer and members of the plumbing-fixtures industry, great and small.

In November, the full association met in Washington and elected to replace Kramer with Stan Backner, a stalwart of both the little and big conspiracies who at sixty-two was heading toward retirement as vice president of Universal-Rundle. The very next day, as Backner was beginning to redecorate P.F.M.A.'s dowdy offices, two I.R.S. agents arrived to pick up Kramer's canceled salary checks, needed in the tax investigation. The agents were about to leave when Backner, friendly and cooperative, stopped them at the door. "By the way," he said, "I'm throwing out a bunch of Kramer's stuff. Want to take a look at it?" He led the agents to Kramer's old desk where, in one of the drawers, they came upon three boxes of magnetic tape. Remembering Kramer's threat, Backner must have blanched at the sight, but he remained calm and allowed the agents to take the tapes with them. I.R.S. later turned the tapes over to the Justice Department along with three others

Kramer had left in the trunk of his Thunderbird.

Kramer was arrested in Fort Lauderdale, Florida, in February, 1964, and for the next year the plumbing-fixture industry quietly squirmed. What was in those tapes? How much did Kramer know? What could he prove if he decided to cooperate with the government?

Once Kramer had been indicted and released on bond, he began bargaining with the government. He had many more telltale tapes, he said, which were far better than the ones that had already fallen into the government's hands (they included the recording of the Knickerbocker meeting and scores of telephone conversations). He would happily trade them for the Justice Department's promise to drop all charges against him. The best deal he could get, however, was an agreement that the government would not object if he entered a plea of no contest and took his chances on the sentence. Dissatisfied, Kramer kept the tapes and chose to stand trial in Baltimore.

As his defense, Kramer contended that the plumbing-fixture executives had promised him a reward for assisting in the price fixing, organizing meetings, acting as a clearinghouse for price information, and running the P.F.M.A. as a front. "There came a time," his lawyer said later, "when Mr. Kramer became convinced that those rewards were not going to be forthcoming . . . he felt he was entitled to take self-help." To assist Kramer in proving his charges, a federal judge subpoenaed reams of documents from eleven manufacturers, including price sheets, catalogues, and notices to wholesalers.

JUSTICE BUILDS A CASE

On the day set for the trial, dozens of prospective jurors gathered in the richly paneled courtroom while Kramer's lawyers paced nervously in the hallway, prosecuting attorneys and court attachés milled around the bench, and observers from both the companies and the government waited to see what Kramer would prove. Their expectations were disappointed. Flying in from Maryland's Eastern Shore in a private plane, Kramer was suddenly overcome by the inadequacy of the defense he had been able to prepare. He directed the pilot to land at another airport and jumped bond.

While the F.B.I. was combing the countryside for Kramer, the Department of Justice was wasting little time. John C. Fricano, a quick and aggressive antitrust attorney who had been assigned to head the investigation, moved to empanel a federal grand jury in Pittsburgh—a jury that was ultimately to consider evidence for sixteen months, hear thirty-five witnesses, and subpoena more than 50,000 documents from company files. In the beginning, Fricano had nothing much in the way of evidence except the six tapes that I.R.S. had uncovered, which were of poor recording quality and dubious evidential worth, plus a threatening five-page letter that Kramer had written to McKay from Nassau, and which McKay turned over to the F.B.I.

Then, in the summer of 1965, things began breaking the government's way. Kramer tired of running and hiding. He was nearly penniless, his family was on welfare, and his yacht had been sold. He sent sixteen reels of tape to his wife, told her to turn them over to the Department of Justice, and then surrendered. A year later the grand jury returned two indictments, one naming ten companies in the little conspiracy, the second naming the eight major bathtub manufacturers. All the companies except Standard, Kohler, and Borg-Warner pleaded no contest, as did the executives, except for Dan Quinn, his boss, Joe Decker, and Kohler's Norman Held.

From the masses of documents subpoenaed by the grand jury, Fricano culled out four that proved especially telling when the big conspiracy case finally came to trial this year. Three were internal memoranda from the files of American-Standard, Crane, and Wallace-Murray's Eljer division. The fourth comprised six pages of notes scrawled in Ray Pape's hand on a Hotel Corp. of America memo pad. Each document dealt with new prices to be announced when the industry switched to all acid-resistant enamel.

At first glance, Standard's memorandum looked innocuous enough, nothing more than a typewritten worksheet listing proposed prices for various sizes and shapes of bathtubs. It was dated March 1, 1963, four months before the prices were to be announced, and on the bottom some notes were penned in Dan Quinn's precise block letters. What was interesting about the worksheet was its striking similarity to the internal memoranda that came from the files of Crane and Eljer, both of which were written after the date of the Standard worksheet but more than a month before the new prices were announced. All three documents—Standard's, Crane's, and Eljer's—proposed new tub prices that were the same down to the last penny. Moreover, they all proposed identical prices for acid-resistant lavatories and other "smallware," and a 25 percent spread between white and colored products. These similarities would have been an incredible coincidence, to say the least, had the prices been arrived at independently.

"IMAGINE IF YOU WILL, A HOTEL ROOM"

How had these companies found out about each other's prices? To answer this question, Fricano dwelled long on the fourth piece of circumstantial evidence, Ray Pape's notes on the Hotel Corp. of America pad. The Palm Beach Biltmore, an H.C. of A. hotel, was the scene of a P.F.M.A. meeting that Quinn and Pape both attended in March. Under the circumstances, it was remarkable that Pape's notes not only contained the same prices as were on Quinn's worksheet, but also referred directly to it, even to the point of using Standard's own brand names. Standard's list, for example, showed a $2 markup for its "Restal" tub; then this was crossed out and a $2.50 markup written in by hand. Pape's notes said: "Restal raise 2.50 noted."

Fricano's summation to the Pittsburgh jury

was dramatic. First he reviewed testimony on the Palm Beach meeting. Then, waving Quinn's worksheet high in one hand and the Pape notes in the other, he concluded:

"If there should be a shred of doubt, one small shred, is it not disspelled, is it not dissipated, is it not taken away by the documents, the originals of which I hold in my hand, and the copies which you had in yours? . . . You saw the consistency and the changes that appeared in these two documents, the changes which could only have been found out and determined in that hotel room at Palm Beach, no other place . . .

"Ladies and gentlemen, imagine if you will, a hotel room, a group of men sitting in this hotel room talking between themselves, sitting there. Quinn is sitting there with his worksheet discussing each price, taking up each price with these men. Consider, if you will also, a man sitting there, Ray Pape, next to his boss Casner, the vice president of Crane, and taking down the things that are being said. Because that is what happened, ladies and gentlemen. There they are." Fricano waved the notes. "Right there."

THE HIGH COST OF CRIME

The jury returned a verdict of guilty on the three corporations and three individuals who had chosen to stand trial. Last August, Judge Louis Rosenberg pronounced sentences: For Daniel J. Quinn, Standard's $53,000-a-year vice president for plumbing sales, the Big Boy whose service to the industry began nearly a half a century ago: $30,000 and a year in jail, to be suspended after he serves one day. For his boss, Joseph J. Decker, fifty-four, the $64,000-a-year president of the plumbing and heating division, and a Standard employee for thirty-five years: $40,000 and a year in jail, suspended after he serves sixty days. For Norman Held, fifty-seven, the son of a Kohler foreman, a man who began at Kohler forty years ago on graduation from Kohler High School, worked his way up to a directorship and $50,000 a year, and broke the "anti-fraternization" rule along the way: $30,000 and a year in jail, suspended after he serves fifty days.

Their appeal, now pending, challenges the evidentiary rulings of Judge Rosenberg, a former Pittsburgh city official whose nomination to the bench by John F. Kennedy was strongly opposed by the organized bar. They also claim that Fricano's extensive cross-examination of Held, which highlighted Kohler's acrimonious, eight-and-a-half-year labor dispute, prejudiced the largely blue-collar jury whose foreman was a Teamster official.

Five other executives who pleaded no contest have already served jail sentences up to thirty days and paid fines totaling $110,000. Highest ranking among them was John B. Balmor, sixty-three, white-haired, erect, and expensively tailored, the former $150,000-a-year president and chief executive of Wallace-Murray Corp. and now chairman of the executive committee. Also included were Crane's $63,000-a-year vice president, Bob Casner, who told competitors that "the old man" wanted prices up, and Stan Backner of Universal-Rundle, who had invited the I.R.S. to browse in Kramer's office.

Judge Rosenberg levied fines totaling $752,500 against the companies. Crane and Universal-Rundle pleaded no contest in both conspiracies and received the statutory maximum fine, $50,000, in each case. Standard, Kohler, and Borg-Warner, the three that stood trial on the big conspiracy, were each fined $50,000 and are appealing.

For companies earning many millions a year, a $50,000 fine is picayune. (Richard McLaren, the Assistant Attorney General in charge of antitrust, has urged Congress to increase such penalties tenfold.) But far more disturbing than fines these days are the damage suits filed by consumers, large customers, wholesale distributors, and retailers—all those in fact who can make a reasonable case that they were damaged by price fixing. Under the antitrust laws they may sue for three times the amount of actual damages. The number of these suits has increased by leaps and bounds since the electrical cases, which General Electric and Westinghouse settled for more than $350 million. Hundreds of plaintiffs, including thirty-two state governments, have now filed suit against the plumbing-fixture manufacturers. This stern lesson should persuade corporate managements that they have the best of selfish reasons to undertake their own vigorous antitrust enforcement.

WHEN BILL KRAMER CAME HOME

Bill Kramer didn't get off easily either, although the judge who eventually sentenced him in Baltimore took into consideration his cooperation with the Department of Justice. He was sentenced to eighteen months in jail and was paroled after serving four months. A free man now, he is living in a suburb of Washington, where he taught scuba diving in local swimming pools last summer and is currently at work on two books, one on the plumbing industry and the other on the inevitability of nuclear war. A gentle person with animals, he took in a wild baby rabbit, which he bottle-fed and later released, and a motherless woodchuck, which he walks on a leash and has trained to use Kitty Litter placed in the bottom of an acid-resistant bathtub.

77. Medical Swindlers

HOWARD LEWIS
MARTHA LEWIS

TO THE PATIENT IT'S A PIECE OF PAPER THAT THE doctor fills out so he will be paid by health insurance. To the insurance carrier it's a means of learning what services the doctor has performed. To some doctors it's temptation.

A physician's conscience is his chief restraint as he completes a health insurance form. Within limits, almost any carrier will pay the doctor for the services he sets down. To this extent, insurance carriers are open to exploitation, and a small minority of doctors treat an insurance form like a blank check. The amount they swindle and the costs of policing them lead to higher premiums for policyholders. Among insurance swindlers turned up recently are:

• A doctor who billed Blue Shield for removing his daughter's appendix—twice.

• A physician who used an ordinary styptic pencil to stop minor bleeding—but charged an insurance company for cauterizing a major wound.

• An M.D. who billed an insurance plan for doing a certain procedure 29 times at $400 apiece—whereas all the other physicians in the program performed a total of one.

All of which explains why personnel who review health insurance claims may cast a cold eye

not only at the fee the doctor charges but also at the services he lists. Overtreating is a favorite way for insurance swindlers to milk a program.

One doctor billed the Veterans Administration for weekly injections he was giving a former serviceman who suffered from flat feet. When the V.A. questioned the validity of such treatments, the doctor said that the shots contained "vitamins to tone up the muscles of his feet."

"Poppycock!" replied the V.A.'s chief medical officer. "There is no justification in all of medicine for such 'therapy.'"

"Look here," responded the doctor. "You bureaucrats don't treat patients. So don't tell *me* how to treat them!"

Another doctor snowballed the costs of treating an insured case after a policyholder wanted a small wart removed from the back of his hand. The doctor arranged to have the procedure done in a hospital, thereby raising the insurance payment to him from $15 to $37.50.

This simple operation required only Novocain, which the doctor himself administered by injection. But the hospital's anesthetist billed the insurance company for $25, and the hospital charged for a day's room and board even though the patient was never in a hospital bed. The bills for removal of a wart measuring less than a quarter of an inch totaled about $200, all so the doctor could collect the higher insurance payment.

Some doctors bilk insurance plans by giving unnecessary diagnostic tests. One doctor was

▶SOURCE: *The Medical Offenders. New York: Simon and Schuster, 1970. Pp. 127–135. Reprinted by permission.*

doubling his income from the routine office visits of Blue Shield subscribers by performing extra "diagnostic" procedures—an examination of the rectum and bowel, for example, even if the patient had a sore throat.

IN NEVER-NEVER LAND

While those tests were unnecessary, they were at least performed as reported. Some insurance cheats, however, perform merely token services, then report major procedures for payment. In this medical never-never land, sprains become fractures, bumps emerge as concussions, scratches deepen into cuts.

One New York dermatologist put in a claim for removing a breast tumor. When Blue Shield investigated, it found that he had actually treated a benign skin condition. In another pseudosurgery, a G.P. submitted 157 claims for the incision and draining of carbuncles (severe infections that burrow beneath connective tissue). On investigation, Blue Shield found he had treated not a single carbuncle. Rather, he had cared for skin pustules of the minor sort common in acne.

Insurance carriers have special problems with physicians who own their own hospitals, reports A. B. Halverson of the Occidental Life Insurance Company of California. Proprietors of these institutions stand to benefit if procedures are blown up to require lengthy hospital stays. It is a rare appendectomy that requires even ten days' hospitalization. But at one Southern California hospital, Occidental found that the physician-owner took out a normal appendix and kept the insured patient hospitalized for twenty-four days.

At the same hospital, investigators found, a supposed "seven-inch wound requiring hospitalization" was really a minor cut less than an inch long. As a result of Occidental's detective work, this hospital withdrew claims totaling more than $3,000.

More obvious to claims reviewers is the physician who reports performing complicated surgery in his office. To get the substantial insurance payment for surgery, exploitative doctors have claimed they surgically removed internal hemorrhoids, excised pilonidal cysts, even took out organs. If true, the lack of hospital facilities and staff would have constituted a grave threat to the patient's life. In most cases, Dr. Arthur A. Fischl of Group Health Insurance has found, the office "surgery" is a minor procedure inflated in the insurance report by a physician who lacks hospital privileges.

In a six-month period, one general practitioner submitted eight claims for repairing dislocations of major joints. Blue Shield became suspicious when it learned the doctor had accomplished the treatments in his office, without the aid of x-rays. In each claim, the "dislocation" proved to be a strained ligament.

As a matter of routine, many insurance plans inform the patient of the payment that has been made to the doctor. Sometimes the patient recognizes that the doctor has exaggerated his service. In Arkansas, a policy-holder learned that his doctor had been paid $150 "for performing an appendectomy." The patient replied:

"I'm glad you paid my doctor $150 but he didn't take out my appendix. He removed a wart from my neck."

In policing claims, insurance carriers rely on such reactions from patients. Laymen, who generally expect high standards of behavior from doctors, are often quick to blow the whistle on a suspected swindler. One otolaryngologist billed an insurance plan for extensive nasal surgery and bone removal. He got the usual fee of $350. Routinely the insurance carrier sent the patient notification of the payment. Almost at once, the patient wrote to complain.

"How come so much money?" he protested. "The doctor did nothing but pack my nostrils."

INFLATED FEES

After Dr. Morton E. Berk, of Honolulu, finished three years of service on his medical society's health insurance committee, he was asked the His reply:

"Abusers of health plans. Until . . . they are castigated by their colleagues and treated like the thieves they really are . . . abuse will undoubtedly continue."

Insurance carriers estimate that between 1 and 5 percent of all claims submitted suggest abuse. A principal type of tampering entails charging a higher fee than normal because an insurance plan and not the patient will pay. An Occidental Life Insurance study of 6,000 claims has shown that, comparing patients with equal incomes, physicians charge an average of as much as 20 percent more when the coverage permits them to set their own fee for a service. This is in contrast with what they would charge if the coverage incorporated a fee schedule, generally based on prevailing rates.

As a result of such findings, the Health Insurance Council, an industry group, has made this observation:

"Some physicians apparently feel that a patient with insurance protection . . . has moved beyond the financial bracket which normally would be determined by his annual income. On that basis and following the pattern of charging according to the ability to pay, the fees charged sometimes appear to be higher than might be expected in the absence of insurance."

An example of such fee raising in action has been reported by Joseph M. Adelizzi, managing director of the Empire State Highway Transportation Association, whose members provide health insurance coverage for employees. Originally a surgeon set $75 as his fee for a service for a patient connected with the association.

"Good," the patient said. "I have health insurance that will pay up to $75."

"In that case," the surgeon told him, "my fee is $125 and you'll have to pay only $50."

The Santa Monica, California, local of the International Association of Machinists provides a health insurance plan for members. A physician treated one machinist with 28 days of house calls. The bill he submitted was for $1,625, or

some $60 per visit. The union refused to pay, so the doctor reduced his bill by $1,000, to $625. This netted him over $20 per house call—and other local physicians declared that he was still getting away with robbery.

In another California case, a surgeon operated on an eleven-year-old boy for a hernia and undescended testicle. Believing the family carried insurance, he submitted a bill for $3,500. Although the policy had not yet gone into effect, the insurance company protested in behalf of the boy's parents. Ultimately they got a revised billing of $500.

According to insurance company evidence presented in court, fee disputes surrounded a New Orleans surgeon who submitted a bill for an elbow operation on a patient insured by the Hartford Accident and Indemnity Company. The company protested that the $4,550 fee was excessive. The surgeon agreed to reduce it to $3,000, and the company sent him a check for that amount.

But, in a bookkeeping error, the company failed to record that the sum had been paid. Thus the company later sent the doctor another check for the same amount.

Meanwhile, the same patient required another operation. Instead of submitting a bill for the additional surgery, the surgeon credited the mis-sent check toward his fee. The insurance company now went to court to get back the duplicated payment.

"Not only should I not give the $3,000 back," the doctor said. "I demand an additional $900 because the second operation was worth $3,900."

The court, however, disagreed. It instructed the doctor to return $1,500, leaving him $1,500 for the second operation. Even that, said the Court of Appeal, "is more than ample for the services rendered."

Five months later, the doctor was back in the Court of Appeal. This time he was suing the Travelers Insurance Company for $4,325 for operating on the arm of a man injured in a motorboat accident. The fee was "unreasonable and excessive," said the company. During the trial of the case, two surgeons took the witness stand.

"What would be a reasonable charge for the services this surgeon rendered?" each was asked.

"A thousand dollars," answered one.

"Six hundred dollars," said the other.

Striking its own, more liberal compromise, the court ruled that the fair fee would be $1,275, less than a third of what he had asked.

SOMETHING FOR NOTHING

Claims reviewers occasionally spot insurance frauds who perform no service at all for the fees they seek to collect.

In Louisiana, a physician treated many patients who were employees of the same company and thus were covered by the same insurance carrier. The doctor became suspect after he filed so many false claims in their names that the carrier had to raise the premium it was charging the employer. The evidence gathered against the doctor was transmitted to federal authorities, who successfully prosecuted him for mail fraud.

Similarly, a New York ophthalmologist submitted 170 claims in a single year for removal of foreign bodies from the cornea, the transparent coating of the eyeball. Blue Shield investigators found that in none of the claims were foreign bodies removed or even present.

Nor is the presumed patient necessarily present. Federal officials charged that a private practitioner in Dallas got $6,654 from the Veterans Administration for allegedly treating patients. At least $258 had been claimed for treatment while the veterans were actually being cared for in government hospitals. One of the supposed patients had died before the dates on which the doctor reported seeing him.

In exchange for the privilege of using a hospital's facilities, attending physicians customarily perform chores for the institution. Some of these duties can be onerous, such as serving in clinics or on burdensome committees. By contrast, one of the most nominal of assignments is general stand-by service. In effect this merely requires the doctor to be reachable by phone in case the regular staff needs help.

Although the stand-by physician's connection with the hospital is generally just that uninvolving, some doctors use stand-by as an unauthorized excuse to bill for services performed during the period by the hospital staff. Two Baltimore doctors thus collected $480 from Blue Shield for presiding at deliveries—though the doctors on stand-by were no closer to the hospital than their home phones. They were found out after a Blue Shield subscriber complained that $80 for delivering his child had been paid to a physician who had never even seen his wife.

Claims reviewers also watch for physicians who are obligated by their hospitals not to charge for their services yet do so anyway. A Newark, New Jersey doctor was found guilty of defrauding a medical-surgical plan of over $5,500. The state successfully contended that he had collected insurance fees for surgery performed at a hospital that was supported by the county to provide exclusively free medical care.

The return from defrauding a health-care program can be greater than from robbing a bank. One Long Island doctor was indicted on 373 felony and misdemeanor counts, including 122 counts of grand larceny, for filing false claims for the treatment of Welfare Department beneficiaries.

The doctor ultimately admitted cheating the program in almost every way possible: He filed claims for patients he had not seen. He billed the county for treating whole families when he had actually seen only one member. He charged for tests he never performed and for injections he never gave. He exaggerated services beyond resemblance to what was really done. He even entered into collusion with two druggists to submit to the county fraudulent prescriptions.

In all, the doctor confessed to offenses totaling over $100,000.

THE TAX CHEATS

The health insurance form is not the only document that some dishonest physicians abuse before signing. Form 1040, the federal income tax return, also comes in for occasional swindling.

The medical profession produces a disproportionately high number of tax evaders, about four times the rate for the public at large. In a typical year, between 20 and 25 of some 1,400 persons convicted of tax violations are M.D.s. While only 1 out of every 240 taxpayers is a physician, doctors account for about 1 out of 60 taxpayers convicted of tax evasion. Almost always the doctor is a respected citizen. Charles K. Rice of the Justice Department's Tax Division has reported that tax fraud is a white-collar crime. Most convicted defendants are business and professional people who have never had previous trouble with the law.

"It may seem strange, but as a group the percentage of fraud cases arising among doctors of medicine is far out of line with other professions," commented Judge Ernest H. Van Fossan after retiring from the U.S. Tax Court. Judge Van Fossan went on to speculate: "Why this is so would be an interesting study, but possibly the table drawer into which [a physician] tosses fees which he receives in cash or the deep pocket in which he places them may be the answer."

Every year a half dozen or so physicians go to prison as a result of criminal violations of income tax laws. Deliberate concealment of income is the principal offense. After practicing abroad for a number of years, one G.P. settled in a New England city. Feeling that cash payments would be too hard for tax agents to trace, he recorded only a fraction of his cash receipts. The rest went for living expenses and acquiring new possessions.

During a routine audit, a tax agent noted that the doctor owned a large house, a flashy car, and other trappings of high living. The doctor's reported income would not allow him to consume quite so conspicuously, so the I.R.S. man inves-

tigated further. As new facts were uncovered, the doctor attempted to misdirect the investigation by continuously changing his explanation of where he got his funds.

Finally the agent reconstructed the doctor's income for the previous eight years, showing that he had failed to report an average of $13,000 a year. The doctor pleaded guilty and paid $15,000 in fines and back taxes. He also served 90 days in jail.

A tax-evading physician with other sources of income sometimes reports only his earnings from his practice and conceals the rest. A California practitioner provided special services for an insurance company and a county old-age program. He reported his income from his private patients. But—according to charges to which he pleaded nolo contendere—he converted his monthly checks from the insurance company and the county into cashier's checks. These were as good as cash (and safer), and he turned them into currency whenever he needed money.

This method enabled him to hide about two thirds of his income one year and over half his income the next. With his unreported earnings he bought jewelry, household furniture, a trip to Hawaii. Ultimately his spending called attention to him. He was required to pay back taxes and fines totaling $34,000. Moreover, his state board of medical examiners ruled that he had committed a felony involving moral turpitude, put him on probation, and suspended his license to practice for 180 days.

Anyone in business needs a bookkeeping system to keep track of who has paid how much and what is owed by whom. Tax evaders, to disguise their true income, often keep secret records. In a southern community, an internist resigned from the staff of a local hospital. Word got around that he had refused to keep medical records the way the hospital required. The story reached the ears of a Treasury agent. Suspicious, he followed up the case for two years.

The doctor had been concealing income by recording small fees for minor services while actually receiving large fees for major services. Thus a $350 hysterectomy would go down as a $75 dilation and curettage, and the $275 difference would be stashed away. This concealment was the reason the doctor could not submit to the cross-checks that the hospital demanded on its records.

A jury convicted the doctor of willfully failing to report total income of some $23,000. His penalty: payment of back taxes and fines of $17,000 and a prison sentence of five years.

Another physician who tampered with his books was a West Coast surgeon. His financial records seemed meticulous, but an I.R.S. agent was puzzled by strange symbols that kept recurring. Treasury experts deciphered the hieroglyphics as an elaborate code that denoted payments not included in the surgeon's tax reports.

The doctor also misrepresented his deductible business expenses. "What about this gift you deducted?" the agent asked.

"It was a promotional expense, for practice building," replied the doctor.

"Really?" said the agent. "Then why did you have the gift shop enclose a card saying 'Happy Mother's Day'?"

To the charges, the doctor pleaded nolo contendere. He was sentenced to pay $20,000 in fines and back taxes and received a six-month prison term.

To lift the curtain on a tax evasion, the I.R.S. may need outside help. In one case, the intervening force was death. A New York City gynecologist lived modestly with his wife in a three-room apartment on the lower East Side. He spent little of his earnings from his thriving practice. Instead, he put most of his income into thirty-seven trust accounts that he secretly maintained in as many savings banks. On his income tax returns he mentioned none of the amounts he deposited.

The accounts came to light after the doctor died. Tax agents discovered that he had been accumulating the extra money by falsifying his records. One year he listed only 200 patients on his books. Actually he had treated 600.

The Tax Court ruled that the beneficiaries of the trust accounts would need to satisfy back taxes and penalties totaling over $150,000. The office nurse, who had inherited 11 of the accounts, thus had to surrender some $50,000.

Often tax evaders are revealed by informers. Over many years of practice one doctor regularly concealed cash and juggled his books. With each $1,000 of unreported income, he bought investment bonds under fictitious names. He placed these bonds in safe-deposit boxes that he rented under assumed identities.

Meanwhile, someone who knew the doctor became more and more interested in his financial affairs. The Treasury Department will not reveal the precise identities of tax informers. It will say, however, that informers are often bookkeepers, accountants, and employees of banks and brokerage houses—persons in a position to sense that income is not being properly reported. With physicians, informers are also frequently disgruntled patients, colleagues, even wives and children.

Whoever it was in this case developed a comprehensive file on the doctor's dealings, including many of the fictitious names the doctor used and the location and amounts of many of the concealed bonds. He (or she) informed the I.R.S. The agents found the report was true and pressed charges against the doctor.

For his efforts the informer received a near-record $41,000. The doctor's back taxes, interest and penalties totaled no less than $2,400,000.

Contemporary Crimes

IN THIS FINAL SECTION. WE DEAL WITH VARIOUS FORMS OF CRIMINAL BEHAVIORS that largely reflect our times. These are primarily offenses that have newly sprung into existence or that have recently proliferated enormously.

The first selection depicts the manipulation and abusing of one of the minor deities of our time, the computer. Parker reveals how the computer has been used in bank embezzlements and other criminal acts involving government, consumers, and various business operations. The selection produces instances of physical attacks on computers, software and data, along with the theft of computer hardware, software, and computer services. An unusual area of criminal endeavor is considered in the article by McCaghy and Denisoff. They describe the unauthorized duplication of musical records to sell to such customers as collectors, entrepreneurs, and counterculture pirates.

The crime of shoplifting is the subject of Cobb's dissertation. This offense seems to offer almost insuperable methodological problems for research including differentiating employee theft from shoplifting. The actions of a talented shoplifter are detailed: concealment, identification of the store security staff, and the range of techniques engaged in.

A federal advisory committee was commissioned to examine false identification documents and the manner in which they are used to fraudulently secure welfare payments, aid to families with dependent children, Medicare, and food stamps.

Certainly one of the strongest and most pervasive fears in modern urban communities relates to being victimized while trapped underground in a subway system. The Transportation Research Institute report reveals the extent and method of armed and strong-arm robbery and assaults against the public and members of the transport system.

The final selection by Willrich and Taylor deals with a crime that apparently has never occurred but that is of increasing concern to governments throughout the world and to members of the scientific community. Nuclear theft, we learn, could be carried out by a single individual, a criminal group, a terrorist group, a member of the nuclear enterprise, or a political faction within a country. The stolen material could be used for ransom, extortion, or black-market sale. Though the event has apparently never taken place, its consequences would be almost unimaginable.

78. Computer Abuse

DONN B. PARKER
SUSAN NYCUM
S. STEPHEN OURA

FOUR STUDIES OF COMPUTER ABUSE

FOUR STUDIES HAVE BEEN MADE AT STANFORD RE-
search Institute of specific types of computer
abuse. The study on bank embezzlement[1] was
done for the American Bankers Association,
Operations and Automation Division; this study
was particularly valuable because it was possible
to statistically compare the computer-related
cases with general bank embezzlement cases,
whereas a direct comparison of all recorded
cases to general white-collar crime is not possible
because of the lack of data on the latter.
Another study was done for the Lawrence
Livermore Laboratory on reported cases involving multi-access or time-sharing computer systems[2]. The third study was on computer abuse
in civil government; its results were presented[3]
to the California State Assembly Committee on
Efficiency and Cost Control, which was investigating the security problems that might be encountered in centralizing the State's computing
facilities. The fourth study on consumer and
business computer abuse covers primarily retail
sales and services and is drawn from several
sources.

All four studies are briefly summarized below.

▶SOURCE: *Computer Abuse: Final Report Prepared for the National Science Foundation (November 1973). Menlo Park,
California: Stanford Research Institute. Pp. 35–46, 55–61, 91–
101, 104–108, 110–111. (Editorial adaptations.)*

Bank Embezzlement

Out of 140 recorded cases of all types of computer misuse in the SRI data bank when this study
was carried out, 18 involved banking, and 12 of
these—most of which occurred since 1970—
constituted embezzlement. These recorded
cases appear to represent only a small fraction
of the actual incidents of unauthorized acts in
banking. In comparison, the Comptroller of the
Currency reported 272 defalcations of all types
of $10,000 or more in 1971.

The study of computer-related case histories
supports the past findings of embezzlement research by criminologists. The definition of embezzlement varies among legal jurisdictions but
is best defined here as criminal violation of trust.
Donald Cressey, one of the foremost
criminologists on white-collar crime, states his
well-tested hypothesis as follows:

"Trusted persons become trust violators when they
conceive of themselves as having a financial problem
which is non-shareable, are aware that this problem
can be secretly resolved by violation of the position of
financial trust, and are able to apply to their own conduct in that situation verbalizations which enable
them to adjust their conceptions of themselves as
trusted persons with their conceptions of themselves
as users of the entrusted funds or property."[4]

Computer technology has introduced new factors concerning the types of perpetrators, the
forms of assets threatened, and embezzlement
methods.

Programmers, system analysts, and computer

and keypunch operators, either alone or in collusion with bank employees traditionally associated with embezzlement, represent new occupations in positions of trust and temptation. Asset data electronically and magnetically stored within computer systems are becoming popular targets, along with the negotiable instrument forms of assets.

Computer-related embezzlement methods include old elements of kiting, lapping, creating fictitious float, and manipulating checks, cash, and inactive accounts; but they now are perpetrated in EDP environments requiring modification or at least detailed knowledge of the computer programs and data file structures. Computer programs represent more exact and predetermined processes compared with the work procedures assigned to people in the previous manual systems, presenting a different environment for the embezzler.

The characteristics of the average bank embezzler have not changed much in the past 35 years. According to the FBI he is about 32 to 36 years old, he is married, and he has two children. However, one significant embezzlement feature has changed: the average bank embezzlement now continues for more than three years before discovery, a year longer than the period shown in 1935 statistics. According to the FBI, most embezzlers are not motivated by living beyond their means.

Of the cases examined in one study, 41 percent involved the unauthorized extension of credit to a customer and resulted in no personal benefit to the embezzler. In 22 percent of the cases, the perpetrator used stolen funds to engage in other business. Only 19 percent of the perpetrators were living beyond their means or were gambling.

Two kinds of simple embezzlement (without collusion) are associated with computer systems. External embezzlement is performed outside the computer system but requires the manipulation of input and output based on a knowledge of the computer application. Internal embezzlement originates from within the computer system staff. It requires the following:

1. Access to a computer.

2. Access to data files.

3. Access to computer programs.

4. System knowledge.

5. Means of converting fraudulent activity to personal gain.

Embezzlement can consist of both internal and external fraud when perpetrated by several people in collusion.

* * *

As indicated in Table I, one-third of the cases involved collusion—which was apparently needed to acquire all the necessary skills and access not possessed by any single party to the collusion. In 111 cases of general embezzlement involving losses over $10,000 reported in 1971, the position of the embezzler was known; only 13 of the 111 cases involved collusion. Table I compares the positions of embezzlers in computer-related and general cases.

Methods used by the computer-related bank embezzlers included four instances of unauthorized program changes to delete items in exception reports, one of changing credit limits, and one of accumulating into a favored account the round-down remainders from arithmetic calculations (this case is not verified). One theft of a computer program is recorded. The rest of the methods required input/output data manipulation using detailed knowledge of the computer programs. Two of these cases involved inactive account manipulations; one involved control total balancing; another took advantage of falsely created float by inputting checks as cash deposits; another involved check processing and Magnetic Ink Character Recognition (MICR) code defacing; and one took advantage of parallel operation of manual and computerized systems during the transition to a computer. Only one case of inactive account manipulation and the false float case were external embezzlements. All the others involved only EDP personnel or were cases of collusion involving both internal and external employees.

Table I. Positions Held by Bank Embezzlers

Position	Number of Embezzlers
Computer-related cases (11 total)[a]	
Vice president, EDP	4
EDP clerk	3
Programmer	3
Computer operator	2
Chief teller	1
Systems analyst	1
Vice president	1
General cases (111 total)[b]	
Operations vice president, manager, clerk	32
Loan officer, manager	29
Teller	22
President	14
Cashier	8
Director, stockholder, officer	5
Bookkeeper	3
Trust officer	3
Auditor	1
Computer operator	1
Proof department supervisor	1
Systems analyst	1

Source: Stanford Research Institute and Treasury Department.
[a]Collusion in four cases; the perpetrators in one case were not identified.
[b]Collusion in 13 cases.

It is possible that embezzlement, fraud, forgery, and business-related thefts will decrease as the prevention and detection potential of computers is developed. The potential for cost-effective protection of business, financial, and informational activity and data is far greater in EDP environments than in the manual environments they replace. The computer is an ideal tool to detect embezzlement activity, but how to use it effectively requires further development. The growing speciality of EDP audit in banks offers hope that audit control techniques will catch up with the advancing state of the art of computer usage.

The separation of responsibility in the new types of staff now in positions of trust appears to be the single most effective deterrent to internal embezzlement, from an operations point of view. External embezzlement control is a matter of building appropriate detection methods into the production application programs to alert EDP audit personnel about anomalous activity.

Multi-access Computer Abuse

Of a total of 129 cases on file at the time this study was done, 19 involved multi-access computer systems. Two of the cases were thefts of entire operating systems and occurred in 1971. The remaining 17, all occurring since 1969, were limited to input/output manipulation of applications. Seven cases involved penetration of the operating systems. Four of the seven were unauthorized use of services; one was industrial espionage; another was vandalism; and the purpose of the last is undetermined. Five of the 19 cases occurred in university environments, the rest in businesses.

These 19 cases represent only 15 percent of the total recorded cases, probably because of the small number of multi-access systems, compared with on-site batch systems, that were in operation in the 1969–72 period. The small proportion may also be explained by the known time lag in discovering incidents, and it is suspected that more multi-access system penetrations are not detected compared with the more obvious physical access usually associated with other types of systems.

The total number of cases and the number of multi-access cases would almost certainly be far higher if a methodical search were conducted among academic institutions. Although more unique and sophisticated methods would probably be discovered, there is usually less serious damage, loss, or injuries in the university facilities than in business and government environments. However, there is a sinister potential for proliferation of acts in an academic environment. Students rationalizing these acts as games and legitimate challenges with relatively benign results could become a generation of computer users in business and government with different, ethical standards and great expertise in subverting computer systems. A study of cases in academic environments and a study of the attitudes and social values of students gaining such expertise would be valuable in predicting the trends and nature of computer-related crime.

A significant increase in multi-access cases can be predicted on the basis of the proliferation of such systems that contain, control, and process valuable assets. The historic laissez-faire philosophy of computer users toward proprietariness of data, programs, and computer services—and sometimes the user's image of the computer as an attractive subject of attack but not possessing personal attributes—are factors that support this expected increase.

Discussions with managers and systems programmers from computer time-sharing service companies, including four perpetrators of unauthorized acts, indicate that it is common practice to gain legitimate or unauthorized access to competitors' systems. Once access is gained, the perpetrators test the system's performance and features, take copies of programs and data files, test the security access control, and—on penetration into a privileged mode—take private information and subvert the operating system to make subsequent attacks simple. As a final act, they usually "crash" the system. In one example, the perpetrator was discovered by the victimized company and hired by the company to plug the hole he had found in the system. This young, skilled systems programmer performed the penetration by adapting his knowledge of his own company's system to the subject system. He later rationalized that this type of activity is not unethical or illegal, and challenged anybody to prove that it is in the absence of legal precedence, contractual agreements limiting activity, or visible protective signs or warnings.

A trend of increasing incidence of multi-access systems abuse could be reversed by (1) increasing the security of the systems to a point where only the most knowledgeable systems programmers associated with a system could penetrate it, (2) establishing norms of professional conduct inhibiting such activities, and (3) providing detection and warning features to confront an individual with the nature of his act and as a basis for legal action.

Government Computer Abuse

A total of 24 cases of computer abuse are recorded as having occurred since 1967 in local, state, and federal government facilities[3]. Most of the cases occurred at the city and county levels. Table II indicates the breakdown of the cases by type, position of the main perpetrators or suspects, and number of perpetrators in collusion.

Table II. Government Computer Abuse Cases

	Number
Case type	
Theft of address lists	5
Vandalism	4
Manipulation of checks	4
Confidentiality violation	4
Manipulation of payroll files and checks	3
Unauthorized sale of EDP services	2
Vote-counting fraud	2
Position of main perpetrator or suspect	
EDP employee	16
Elected official	2
Citizen	2
Private businessman	1
Manager of claims	1
Welfare employee	1
Policeman	1
People in collusion (10 cases)	
6834	30
7034	11
7226	5
6741	5
7245	5
7241	5
7121	2
7044	2
7322	2
7227	?

Source: Stanford Research Institute.

None of these cases involved manipulation of computer programs, in contrast to other, non-government environments. This fact might be coincidence, or it might possibly be because a lack of controls in programs in government installations made unauthorized acts easy simply by manipulating input and output data. Another possibility is that unauthorized acts perpetrated within computers are so difficult to discover that no cases are known even though they may be numerous. Collusion has a high frequency of occurrence, and the number of perpetrators is surprisingly large per case. The reason may be the need for different skills, knowledge, and access to carry out an act within the compartmentalized and highly technical computer environment of government.

Consumer and Business Computer Abuse

It might be assumed that if retail and other businesses were abusing people before computers were in use, they are still doing it in the same ways and to the same degree today with computers. Westin and Baker indicate that this might be true in their study of privacy and data banks[5]. Some factors may alter this position and are presented below in a conjectural fashion for the purpose of choosing the more fruitful areas for further investigation.

The Association for Computing Machinery, one of the major professional societies in the computer field (27,000 members), has 46 members serving as volunteer ombudsmen throughout the United States to aid people having difficulties in transactions involving the use of computers. A letter sent to these ombudsmen requested that they report on consumer problems they have encountered. Eight ombudsmen replied, but in only two incidents was ombudsman activity reported: one involved investigation of vote counting system failures in Detroit, the other involved assisting the State of Illinois Attorney General in prosecuting a fraudulent computer dating service that was not, in fact, using a computer.

Annual reports for 1970, 1971 and 1972 of the State of New York Attorney General's Bureau of Consumer Fraud and Detection[6] indicated 20,400 to 22,700 investigations of consumer fraud per year completed. Five examples connected with computer use were cited, but there were no records indicating the total number of such cases. The examples given included computer dating bureaus that bilked customers, a computer programming school that failed to refund tuitions when it terminated classes, and public utility companies' failure to provide sufficient help to consumers in handling billing errors. Barnett Levy, Assistant Attorney General in Charge, stated that most consumer frauds involve computers in some form simply because of the pervasive use throughout retail business.

Levy is looking for opportunities to attack excesses in personalized computer letter advertising. He claims that making letters look as though they are individually typed, with personal information about each addressee imbedded in the text and signed by a fictitious person, is a fraudulant practice.

The New York State Attorney General has been successful in preparing legislation to control excesses in computer dating services, trade schools and billing practices. However, little of this legislation directly relates to the roles played by computers.

The SRI case history file includes 13 cases, all perpetrated since 1970, of alleged abusive acts by businesses against consumers that resulted in law enforcement actions or litigation. (Many abuses identified only in newspaper accounts do not reach the formal complaint stage and are not included in the SRI file.) The 13 cases include computer processing of insurance policies, fraudulent use of mailing lists, unfair and fraudulent billing practices, incomplete criminal records retention, and dating services and trade schools engaging in false advertising.

Business fraud against consumers is normally one-to-many, one perpetrator with many victims. Computer abuse acts by consumers against retail businesses or government agencies may be just as frequent as abuses against consumers, but on a one-for-one, victim-perpetrator basis. The SRI case file contains 20 such cases against businesses. These cases include consumer vandalism against computers, computer input manipulation, counterfeiting to perpetrate fraud and unauthorized use of computer time-sharing services.

The American Federation of Information Processing Societies and Time magazine conducted 1,001 telephone interviews with a statistically drawn probability sample of the population of the United States in July and August, 1971[7]. The pertinent results are summarized below:

- Computer Problems—34 percent of those surveyed reported that they have had a problem "because of a computer." Billing problems were most frequent, accounting for almost half of the difficulties reported. Others included problems with banks, paychecks, schools, computers at work, credit cards (only 2 percent) and, to a minor extent, with magazine subscriptions purchase orders, credit, and taxes (1 percent each). About 75 percent of those surveyed reported they received an incorrect computerized bill. Of the 24 percent who reported difficulties, 71 percent placed the blame on the personnel of the billing company while 12 percent felt the computer itself was at fault.

- Computers and the Consumer—the public view of the use of computers in providing consumer benefits is generally positive. Approximately 89 percent felt computers will provide many kinds of information and services to us in our homes; 65 percent felt computers are helping to raise the standard of living; and 68 percent believe computers have helped increase the quality of products and services. However, on some topics, attitudes were less positive: 48 percent felt computers make it easier to get credit versus 31 percent who disagreed. Again, 48 percent felt the use of computers in teaching children in school should be increased, versus 25 percent who felt such use should be decreased.

Stories about the perverse nature of computer abuse, such as the well-circulated ones of persistant computer-produced dunning of consumers to pay $0.00 for a service or product is a popular topic in newspapers. It is easy to see how these incidents can occur and just as easy to see how they will disappear with improved design of computer applications, growing business experience in using computers, and public tolerance of these types of problems. However, intentional, premeditated abuse by both sides—business and consumers—must be documented and investigated if it is to be finally controlled. The excesses of credit reporting services have already attracted controls in the form of the federal Fair Credit Reporting Act.

The following scenario depicts circumstances often leading to consumer problems. A business will go about automating a customer billing function by assigning a team of systems analysts and programmers, and may even include an accountant from the accounts receivable department familiar with the function but unfamiliar with computers. A budget and schedule are established. The specifications for the computer system are written according to what is thought the manual procedures accomplish. These, in turn, are interpreted by the EDP staff who write the computer programs. In the end, the specifications are not complete or not correct, the programmers do not interpret them correctly, the programs are not complete and do not work correctly, and the budget and schedule have run out.

At this point anguish sets in. All of the niceties, controls, and features to handle extraordinary and infrequent billing situations are dropped, and the programs are forced into production before the business is prepared to cope with a new and radical way of functioning. Most of the people who handled the unusual cases and complaints are given other assignments because it was assumed they would not be needed—that was one of the purposes of automating. The new billing system starts operation in a highly limited and rigid state. Customers are bombarded with wildly incorrect billings. Since the correction facilities of the programs were never fully completed, attempts at correction produce even more seriously incorrect results.

By this time, the viability of the business is affected and management becomes seriously concerned for the first time. The EDP staff is put on probation, consultants are called in, more money is now being spent than ever before on billing, but gradually the system is corrected and enhanced to full operational capability. Not as much money is being saved as hoped, but some is. Billing becomes more efficient, and customers grudgingly admit they now have few problems and are getting better service than before. The people previously responsible for handling errors and complaints have been retrained in the new system and fulfill this function. New and improved features are added to the system to handle unusual cases, to control fraud, and to produce improved performance reports. When everything is finally running smoothly, volume increases, and then, for several reasons, the system becomes overloaded and obsolete and a new, different computer is needed. This causes the whole conversion process to start all over again.

This sad story is common throughout business and is often the cause of consumer problems. Fortunately the art of putting applications on computers is improving; it is leaving the "cottage craft" stage and becoming an engineering-type discipline. Thus problems in automation are gradually being overcome. A similar history can be related in other applications such as vote counting by computer.

A technical problem in the automation process can often force rethinking of acceptable ethical business practices. This is best illustrated by an example that occurred in Washington D.C. A bank there normally posted deposits and withdrawals in demand deposit accounts manually and in the order in which transactions occurred. A customer could make a deposit, then a withdrawal, and be assured they were posted in

that order, thus avoiding overdraft situations. The process was then placed in the computer in a batch mode of operation. Each night all withdrawals were batched and posted to all accounts and when overdraft conditions were found, penalties were automatically debited. Then deposits were batched and posted to all accounts. One of the bank's customers, a computer expert by chance, deposited a sum of money and then wrote a check the same day on part of the deposited sum. He was charged with an overdraft and complained to a bank officer who explained the way the computer system worked—the deposits and withdrawals are handled separately and not time-stamped, and there was nothing that could be done. Obviously unsatisfied with that, the customer finally found the manager of the computer operation and was shown exactly what the program directed the computer to do. The customer suggested this be changed and was told that it could be changed but it was standard banking procedure. He finally was able to convince the bank to send a notice to all customers explaining how the system functions and advising customers how to avoid overdrafts. Does this solve the problem?

*

LEGAL ASPECTS OF COMPUTER RELATED CRIME

For the purposes of this discussion, the incidents in the SRI data base have been classified into two categories. In the first, the question is what crimes, if any, have been committed. The second category contains those incidents in which the crimes are easily identifiable but in which the computer has had a direct impact in terms of mode of perpetration and form of detection. There is some overlap, of course.

In the first category are attacks on and theft, misappropriation, or misuse of hardware, software, and services. The second category of cases is analyzed in terms of the computer operation, i.e., input, processing, output, and control. Implicit in both types of incident are acts of conspiracy and obstruction of justice on the part of offenders, and procedural and constitutional considerations regarding their rights and the rights of others.

Attacks, Thefts, Misappropriation, and Misuse

Physical Attack on Computers.   Physical attack on computer components was particularly prevalent during the recent period of campus unrest. Students and others, seeing the computer as a tool of warmongers or the establishment, sought to destroy it or capture it and hold it for ransom until various demands had been met by college administrations. In some cases the computer was attacked after the building or room which it occupied was broken into. Then it was bludgeoned, set on fire or flooded, or its cables severed. Fire bombing took place, and in the case of the University of Wisconsin (7012), the explosion took the life of a researcher.

Though dramatic, these acts for the most part constitute traditional elements of crimes to the person and property—malicious mischief, arson, burglary, bombing, murder, riot. Where the computer facility was occupied and shut down but not otherwise damaged, we may find extortion and criminal trespass. When perpetrators took away tapes or other materials in the course of their activities, we can find larceny and in some instances robbery.

Attack on Software and Data.   Another type of vandalism occurred which left the hardware unharmed but attacked the software and data in the machine. Perpetrators in these instances did not necessarily enter the machine room physically but "broke into" the computer via card reader or on-line terminals, which were hardwired or connected to the system via phone lines. The legal questions here include: do these acts constitute malicious mischief, can we find a burglary, and what violation has occurred through such misuse of telephone services?

Perkins defines malicious mischief as the malicious destruction of or damage to the property of another[8]. Immediately we have a definitional problem—are software and data inside the machine property? The Model Penal Code

220.3 includes as criminal mischief "purposely or recklessly causing another to suffer pecuniary loss by deception or threat," thus broadening the base of liability. Nevertheless, the question of software as property has not been before many courts, and where it has, the issue has been treated in matters of theft of software, discussed later.

Should the act of damage to software or data constitute a felony, is a breaking and entering of an appropriate subject area burglary? In a jurisdiction which recognizes the breaking into a vending machine as burglary[9], could we find the nonphysical entrance to a computational machine a breaking? Further, not every initial penetration is unauthorized. A valid user may utilize what can be equated to his "key" to gain access to one part of the computer system and then, once inside, penetrate further into privileged areas in order to effect the damage.

At present, the use of the phone services to assist in perpetration of this type of activity falls only within the legal sanctions against obscene or harassing telephone calls[10]. It may be appropriate to consider legislation more specific to the particular issue.

Theft of Hardware.   The unlawful taking of hardware is another set of incidents. Inasmuch as this hardware is tangible personal property, the issues are traditional and the crimes include larceny, embezzlement, obtaining money under false pretenses, and associated offenses.

Theft of Computer Services.   Theft of computer services presents some interesting questions. These incidents occur in one form when the perpetrator gains unauthorized access to all or a privileged part of a system, e.g., via telephone connection or onsite card reader. The name, account number, and passwords of others may be entered via terminal, punched card, or credit card. Thereafter, the perpetrator uses computer resources without paying. Can services such as computer time legally be the subject of a theft? The Model Penal Code 223.7 is helpful.

"A person is guilty of theft if he obtains services which he knows are available only for compensation, by deception or threat or by false token or other means to avoid payment for the service. "Services" includes labor, professional service, telephone or other public service, accommodation in hotels, restaurants, or elsewhere, admission to exhibitions, use of vehicles or other moveable property . . ."

One of the recorded incidents (7042) involved a terminal in one state (Ohio) accessing the computer in another state (Kentucky). Here the court found a violation of 18 USC 1343 ". . . devise or intending to devise any scheme or artifice to defraud or obtain money or property by means of false or fraudulent pretenses, transmits or causes to transmit by wire . . . . in interstate commerce any . . . signals to execute such scheme." Then the court went on to say that if the law of Kentucky considered what was taken (computer services) as property, a theft of property could also be found.

Where the specific identification of another person, organization, or account is utilized in perpetration, the elements of forgery may also be present. Perkins enumerates the requirements of the offense as (1) a writing of such nature that it is a possible subject of forgery (has some value or purpose other than its own existence), (2) which writing is false, and (3) was made false with intent to defraud. The modern trend toward credit card-like access to the machinery may bring this mode of entry within the meaning of the credit card fraud sanctions.

The other prevalent form of theft of computer services is the misappropriation of services by employees authorized to use the computer services who convert them to their own use, e.g., set up a private service bureau or do work for outsiders on an overhead account. Here, an additional question may merit consideration—is it relevant that the machine was "idle" at the time of the misuse, in which case there would technically be no pecuniary loss?

Theft of Software. In at least one jurisdiction, software has been considered property ithin the meaning of the criminal code. Hancock v. State, Court of Criminal Appeals of Texas, 1966 402 S.W. 2d 906 (6421), held that computer programs were property within the meaning of the state statutes defining offenses of theft. Sub-

sequently, the perpetrator appealed from a denial of a writ for habeas corpus in which he contended he was unlawfully convicted of a felony theft (Hancock v. Decher, U.S. Court of Appeals, 5th Circuit 1967, 379 F 2d 552). The U.S. Court of Appeals affirmed the denial of habeas corpus, saying that the Court of Criminal Appeals construction of state theft law to include computer programs within the definition of property for theft purposes—which definition in turn included "all writings of every description, provided such property possesses any ascertainable value"—was not so unreasonable nor arbitrary as to be violative of due process. Further, the court found that the evidence amply supported the finding that the defendant committed the offense of stealing property worth more than $50, and that the trial court properly did not accept defendant's argument that the programs had ascertainable value only as paper, but considered them as writings under the property definition of the applicable provisions of the theft sections of the penal code.

The theft of software or data from within a computer raises the thorny problem of finding a taking, since the program is not removed from its owner's possession but at most copied. It is suggested that the focus be not on the property aspect of the act but on the dilution of value and loss of control. Similarly, where the elements of embezzlement are otherwise present, the focus should be on the breach of duty to the employer[12].

Should the software qualify as a trade secret—and here it must be assumed that state trade secret protection is viable[13]—there are a number of statutes available. In the Ward case (7121), the Superior Court of California[14], affirmed by the Court of Appeals, found probable cause that the defendant had stolen, taken, or carried away an article representing a trade secret, which trade secret consisted of a computer program, the article being a copy of the program Ward caused to have printed out by his employer's computer, which he thereafter carried to his office in violation of California Penal Code 499c(b)(1). Further, the court found probable cause that having unlawfully obtained access to the program, without authority the defendant made a copy consisting of two printouts of an article representing that trade secret, and was thus in violation of 499c(b)(3).

The court, however, clearly pointed out that "article," as defined in 499c(a), must be tangible, although the trade secret it represents need not. Therefore, the mere transmission of electronic impulses over telephone lines from the trade secret owner's computer to the computer of the defendant's employer would not constitute an article. Thus, the question remains unresolved as to the liability of one who transmits impulses from one computer to another and simply uses the program in some way without causing a printout or other tangible article to be made.

Unauthorized Alteration of Software or Data.   Where data are not copied but altered within the host machine, the existing statutes prohibiting altering of records[15] appear applicable—assuming there is found no difficulty in identifying a computer record as a record within the meaning of the section.

Unauthorized Surveillance.   Unauthorized surveillance poses questions of invasion of privacy, whether accomplished by access from a terminal to the files or by interception of impulses from the computer by electronic or mechanical devices. The latter may come within the perview of federal or state wiretapping statutes, e.g., California Penal Code Section 634.

Word has come, as yet unconfirmed, of a recent Texas decision which held that installations monitoring transactions for internal security purposes must utilize the equivalent of a "beeper" on a phone line to let the user know his activity has been monitored.

Crimes Involving Computer Operation

The second category of computer abuse incidents may be addressed from an operational viewpoint. The speed of the computer, its capability to manipulate large amounts of data, and the differences between the man-machine interface and the man-paper interface in manual systems have tended to alter both the mode of perpetration of certain business crimes and the method of their detection. Operationally, these matters can be classified as input, processing, output, and control.

Input.   Incidents concerning input—data capture and entry into the system—include the instance of the keypunch operator who in the course of her duties as an employee of city government created the master file of parking meter offenses (7226); as a kindness to fellow employees, she ignored the manual record of their violations when punching the master list. This classification also includes the creation of entirely false records and the altering of amounts, names, etc., on otherwise authentic documents. A Canadian incident, for example, concerned the employee who altered the account number of deceased pensioers to his own and thereby collected their pension payments (71312).

Processing.   Processing refers to the manipulation of information within the machine. Included here are transfers between accounts and masking of information. For example, one of the earliest reported cases involved a programmer who put in a patch to the system to cause it to ignore overdrafts on his account (6631). He was convicted of, and given a suspended sentence for, alteration of bank records.

Output.   Output incidents include the case of the employee who hit the repeat button on the printer and caused multiple copies of his legitimately prepared paycheck to be made (71314). A French incident involved an employee who was authorized to round salary figures to two decimal places instead of three (7133); he apparently added the remaining money to his own check.

Control.   Control is defined here as the ability to affect the total computer system. Many perpetrators have had to have that capability to carry off their schemes. Included here are the Union Dime Savings embezzlement of $1.5 million (7331) and the Equity Funding incident (7332). Where an individual has been able to accomplish his goal unaided by others, it is frequently due to his higher level of supervisory responsibility. One perpetrator became a vice president of his organization before he was caught. Other opportunities for unassisted activity come from lack of separation of functions or lack of controls over access to separated functions. Certain perpetrators have conspired with other insiders or with an outsider to carry off their plans. In New Jersey, bank employees and outsiders worked in concert (7033). The outsiders opened accounts. The insiders transferred funds from little used accounts to the accomplices' accounts. The insiders intended to alter the bank records (an additional crime) so as to conceal the transfer, but a fortuitous computer conversion by the bank occurred before this could be accomplished and the transfers were uncovered.

Large scale activity can indicate great agility and technical expertise on the part of a single perpetrator, conspiracy among several, or reliance on a high degree of credulity and lack of imagination on the part of keypunchers, operators, and programmers who do not see or question the implications of what they are directed to do.

Control can also be defined as an affirmative activity by management, auditors and, where applicable, government officials. The computer has made the audit and reporting function both easier and more difficult. One could argue that a different standard of performance in terms of procedures employed to carry out one's responsibility has been thrust upon these groups by virtue of the computer. A computer-prepared report may be the best source of information to raise suspicions of untoward acts, yet at least in one case that record was not scrutinized by management until after the perpetrator had been exposed for other reasons (6631).

At the same time, undue reliance on a computer report and failure to look behind it to the truth or existence of the data it purports to reflect may subject the overly credulous to liabilities under federal and state securities, banking, insurance, and corporation acts. Yet, on the other hand, too close monitoring may raise privacy issues.

Possible New Legal Approaches

In summary, a host of legal issues has evolved in the recorded case histories. Many of these present unique questions of interpretation if addressed under existing law. It has been suggested by Professor Kaplan, consultant to this study, that a reasonable means of avoiding dissimilarity in approach to these issues is to draft a uniform computer abuse act that would identify in particular these special activities.

On the other hand, the current low level of agreement among computer specialists as to what constitutes ethical or legal activities in their field is a counter-indication that a modification is appropriate at this time.

It may be prudent to concentrate current efforts on extending the research which this initial study has begun into more detailed identification of problem elements, thus helping to ensure that future legislative recommendations will be relevant and practicable.

SUMMARIES OF SELECTED CASES

Hancock vs Texas, Texas—Program Theft

A programmer stole $5 million worth of programs he was maintaining for his employer and attempted to sell them to a customer of his employer. He was convicted of grand theft and lost two appeals based on programs not being property as defined by theft laws. He served five years in prison.

*

MICR Deposit Slips Fraud, New York City—Fraud

A depositor put a large sum of money in his account and asked for 1000 MICR-coded deposit slips. He placed them on counters in the bank and accumulated money in his account from other depositors.

*

Washington MICR Deposit Slips Fraud, Washington D.C.—Fraud

A depositor exchanged blank deposit slips on the counter in the bank with his own MICR-coded slips. He accumulated $250,000 in four days from other people's deposits. He then withdrew $100,000, disappeared and has never been caught.

*

Bennett vs U.S.A., Minneapolis—Altering Bank Records

A programmer altered his demand-deposit accounting program to ignore overdrafts in his checking account for about six months. He accumulated overdrafts of $1357 before he was caught by manual accounting when the computer failed. He made restitution and received a suspended sentence.

*

Youth Corps Payroll Fraud, New York—Embezzlement

A data center employee printed Youth Corps payroll checks for nine months at 100 checks per month for a total loss of $2,750,000.

*

Programmed Bigotry, New York

A programmer was accused of bigotry because he programmed a computer to eliminate black people in screening and selecting new employees.

*

New York University Vandalism, New York

Students held the Atomic Energy Commission computer for $100,000 ransom. Incendiary devices were defused before damage was caused. Two people were indicted on bomb conspiracy charges.

*

Pharmaceutical Company Vandalism, New Jersey

An employee destroyed on-line data files after being given notice of termination.

*

Publishers Mailing List Theft, Chicago

Three million customer addresses were stolen by three night shift computer operators.

*

New Jersey Bank Embezzlement, New Jersey

The computer systems vice president, senior computer operator, and three nonemployees of a bank were charged with transferring money from infrequently used savings accounts to newly opened accounts. They were detected when converson to a new computer disrupted work.

*

Los Angeles Welfare Embezzlement Theft, Los Angeles

Eleven County Department of Social Service employees used terminated state welfare numbers, changing names and addresses, to issue checks to themselves.

*

New York Two-Bank Float Embezzlement, New York-Jamaica, Queens

A bank vice president and four others deposited checks designated as cash deposits, which are recorded for immediate credit. Checks drawn on the account were good until the deposit checks were found not to be covered by another bank. The act was discovered when a bank messenger failed to deliver $440,000 worth of checks to the clearing house. The scheme worked for four years, with a total theft of $900,000.

*

IRS Tax Credit Embezzlement, Washington, D.C.

An IRS adjustment clerk transferred unclaimed tax credits from one account through a chain of other accounts and finally to a relative's account. The act was discovered when auditors traced a complaint of no refund of a $1,500 tax credit.

*

Minnesota Dating Bureau Fraud, Minneapolis

A dating bureau was accused by the State Attorney General of falsely advertising that clients would be matched with compatible dates by computer.

*

Computer Service Theft, Detroit

Two engineers accidentally used a password one digit different than theirs. It belonged to the president of the time-sharing firm and allowed access to privileged customer and accounting data. Thus it allowed the engineers to use unlimited amounts of computer time and obtain customer information and proprietary program listing. Discovery was made by computer operators who noticed use of the password at unusual times. The engineers were fired, no other action was taken.

*

Life Insurance Company, Paper Tape Failure Vandalism, New York

Three on-strike computer maintenance technicians activated a field office data collection system by prerecorded computer messages via telephone. The instructions were not to rewind paper tape, causing the next read command to read blank tape endlessly. Perpetrators were discharged and indicted under an obscene telephone call law.

*

Railroad Theft, New York

A suspected organized crime attempt to manipulate input to a computerized inventory system to steal rolling stock.

*

Program Extortion, Theft, Los Angeles

A programmer is alleged to have taken all his employer's programs to hold for extortion. The case was dropped for lack of evidence.

*

Registered Voters List Civil Suit, Los Angeles

A computer service used a registered voters address list for commercial purposes. A suit was filed by the state. It was settled out of court when the defendant paid $22,000.

*

NCIC Information Theft, Chicago

A policeman is alleged to have obtained from the FBI National Crime Information Center (NCIC) the dossier of a man involved in a transaction with the policeman's brother-in-law.

*

Doctor's Claim, Fraud, Canada

A manager of claims of a government medical aid service introduced false doctor's claims into a computer system and directed payments to a fictitious doctor's office.

*

Collection Agency Fraud, Texas

A computerized collection agency sent new bills to people who had paid the bills the previous year. They relied on the discouragement of people fighting computerized systems.

*

Tapes and Disks, California—Vandalism

Employee of a Berkeley or San Francisco messenger service carrying tapes and disks between computer sites claims he used a magnet to destroy information. Presumed to be a case of malicious mischief.

*

Insurance Company—Vandalism

A tape librarian, disgruntled because she was fired, replaced all of the magnetic tapes in the vault with new, blank tapes during her 30-day notice period. The loss was estimated at $10 million.

*

Telephone Company Order Systems, Los Angeles—Theft

The president of a telephone equipment distributor used a phone to enter orders for equipment, then picked the equipment up in a truck disguised as a telephone company truck. His company sold the equipment for several years before he was caught and convicted. He served two months in jail and now operates a computer security consulting firm.

*

Data Preparation Fraud, Lansing, Michigan—Unauthorized Act

According to Computerworld, five keypunch operators were discarding traffic tickets issued to their own and fellow workers' cars. A metermaid became suspicious after ticketing one car several days in a row. A three-part ticket with one copy to the supervisor as a control has been instituted.

*

MICR, Reno—Counterfeiting Fraud

Phony airline payroll checks with counterfeited MICR codes passed successfully through a check reader, but were noticed in manual handling. No suspects have been identified.

*

Computer Service, Texas—Theft
A high school student found a privileged password of the services analyst on a listing in a waste basket. He also obtained detailed specifications of the system. He used large amounts of computer time, played computer games, and obtained other customers' data. He was discovered when a computer operator noticed scratch tapes being read before being written. Restitution was made.

*

State of Illinois—Theft
A computer operator was bribed for $10,000 to steal a tape reel of river registration addresses normally sold by the Driver Registration for $70,000.

*

Homes in Chicago—Burglary
$1 million in negotiable securities was stolen from burglarized homes. A raid on the suspects' residence produced a computer output listing of affluent supermarket owners.

*

Equity Funding Life Insurance, Los Angeles—Alleged Fraud
Equity created 56,000 fake insurance policies and sold them to re-insurers. Insurance Commissioners in at least three states are investigating. The estimated loss is $2,000 million.

*

Dividend Payments—Embezzlement
A clerk caused the computer to issue dividend checks to former shareholders, but addressed to an accomplice, and then to erase records of the checks. The clerk was convicted for embezzling $33,000.

*

BIBLIOGRAPHY

1. D. B. Parker. Embezzlement by Computer, Proc. American Bankers Association, Operations and Automation Division. 1973.

2. D. B. Parker. Threats to Computer Systems, Final Report for U.S. Atomic Energy Commission, University of California, Lawrence Livermore Laboratory, California. March 14, 1973.

3. D. B. Parker. Testimony Before the State of California Assembly Committee on Efficiency and Cost Control. June 14, 1973.

4. D. Cressey. Other People's Money (Wadsworth, Belmont, California) 1971.

5. A. Westin, M. Baker. Databanks in a Free Society (Quadrangle Books, New York) 1972.

6. Louis J. Lefkowitz. Annual Reports, State of New York Attorney General's Bureau of Consumer Fraud and Detection, 1970, 71, 72.

7. AFIPS, Time Magazine National Survey of Public Attitudes Toward Computers. Time, Inc. 1971.

8. R. Perkins. The Criminal Law at 337 (2nd ed.). 1969.

9. See e.g., Chapter 38 Ill. Rev. Stats. Sec. 16–5.

10. See e.g., California Penal Code Section 653m (West 1969).

11. See e.g., California Penal Code Section 484d-i (West 1969), Perkins supra note 1 at 374.

12. Note Theft of Trade Secrets: The Need for a Statutory Solution 120 Columbia Law Review 378. 1971.

13. J. Gambrell. Problems of Software Protection, Preceedings of the AFIPS, Stanford Law School, Joint Conference on Law, Computers, Society. June, 1973 (in press).

14. Ward. V. Superior Courts of the State of California, County of Alameda, Superior Court of the State of California. March 22, 1972. 3CLSR206. (Robert Bigelow. Computer Law Service (Chicago: Calahan Cc.) 1972.)

15. See e.g., California Penal Code Section 471.1.

79. Record Piracy

CHARLES H. MCCAGHY
R. SERGE DENISOFF

WRITERS IN THE AREAS OF SOCIAL PROBLEMS, DEviant and criminal behavior have had to deal with the issue of how *private problems* are translated into or recognized as *public issues* (Ross and Staines 1972). The difference between the two was described by C. Wright Mills (1959, p. 8) when he suggested that "personal troubles"

"... occur within the character of the individual and within the range of his immediate relations with others; they have to do with his self and with those limited areas of social life of which he is directly and personally aware."

"Public issues" extend beyond the individual and involve threats to values cherished by "publics" and may concern a "crisis in institutional arrangements" (Mills 1959, p. 9).

Among supporters of the conflict paradigm it is axiomatic that legislation and its enforcement reflect the differential political power of interest groups. They presume that the formulation and application of law is based less upon a consensus concerning the need for remedy or control than upon the ability of the influential to translate their private problems into public issues. Criminalization is one process used by the powerful to solve their problems and protect their interests.

▶SOURCE: *"The record Industry as powerless giant." "An example of differential interest group influence on the criminalization process." Unpublished paper. Pp. 41. Reprinted by permission.*

"Law is a form of public policy that regulates the behavior and activities of all members of a society. It is *formulated* and *administered* by those segments of society which are able to incorporate their interests into the creation and interpretation of public policy. Rather than representing the institutional concerns of all segments of society, law secures the interests of particular segments supporting one point of view at the expense of others" (Quinney 1970, p. 40).

For the adherents of the conflict approach criminalization begins with interest group activity in the legislative arena (Turk 1966, pp. 347–351; Quinney 1970, pp. 16–20). These groups attempt to gain advantage over others by seeking laws consistent with their own needs. Even after the legislation has been enacted special interests are seen as operating through all levels of the enforcement process.

It is assumed that the size of such interest groups and the number of people they represent are usually extremely small in relationship to the power they wield. Thus, *power* is the crux of legislation. As Chambliss and Seidman (1972, p. 70) claim:

"Most laws, then, emerge as a consequence of the activities of the relatively small minority of the population who hold positions of political and economic power. The remaining small proportion of the legislation can be accounted for by more amorphous interest groups. On occasion, a particular social class can effectively influence legislation through the expression of "public" sentiment. ..."

The implication of this position is that once

the powerful find their interests threatened, protective legislation or enforcement will be forthcoming. This appears especially true in cases where the "power differential" (Turk 1966, p. 349; Quinney 1970, pp. 39–40) is great and where concerted legislative efforts are brought to bear by the oligarchical units (Denisoff and McCaghy, 1973, *passim*).

This argument is qualified by the political climate of a particular period. As Schur (1971, p. 105) indicated, the proper *zeitgeist* is important if three significant aspects of rule-making are to be operative:

". . . social forces that permit (or 'create') categorization of a particular kind of behavior as 'deviant,' the sequence of events culminating in specific efforts at rule-making and rule-enforcement, and the rule-making processes themselves, for example, legislative debates, hearings, and commission reports."

The writings of Sutherland (1950), Gusfield (1963), Becker (1963, pp. 147–163), and Odegard (1928) are but a few of the case studies of interest group influence on legislation. Nearly all such studies have recorded outcomes favorable to the powerful. Therefore, it is generally assumed that those with access to the polity will obtain legal policies consistent with their interests provided, of course, such policies do not conflict with other powerful interests.

The legislative career of the American phonograph record industry raises some doubts, however, about the broad interpretation concerning the oligarchical role in the criminalization process. This industry's experience clearly indicates that rule-making even by a "powerful" group is a problematic undertaking. For decades the recording industry attempted to obtain special legal protection from the unauthorized use of its products. The targets of the legislative efforts evidently possessed the requisites to be legally sanctioned: (1) Their actions were "deviant" according to all influential parties concerned and it was agreed that their actions should be curtailed; (2) They were virtually powerless in the political realm; and (3) They had acquired an appropriate set of labels

attesting to their deviance: "pirates," "bootleggers," and in some cases "radicals." Yet despite the apparent great power differential and a series of legislative initiatives, the criminalization process was stalled for nearly 70 years due to a lack of laws, and then by lack of enforcement.

This paper examines the factors which confronted this particular interest group in its attempt to eliminate a threat to itself by legislation. It is concluded that the possession of an economic power advantage, even in the absence of contest by other power groups, is not a sufficient condition for obtaining an advantage through the criminalization procedure.

PERIOD OF INTEREST GROUP CONFLICT

Thomas A. Edison invented the phonograph in 1877 when he reproduced sound using tin foil cylinders. Just ten years later with the formation of the American Graphophone Company an industry began whose product was sound reproduction: aggregates of sound affixed to material objects (cylinders, discs, tapes, wires, etc.) and representing the creative efforts of composers, performers, and engineers. By the turn of the century this product, as well as piano rolls, were being duplicated by others for sale without the authorization of the original manufacturers. Manufacturers attempted to register their products under the existing copyright law which made unauthorized *writings* subject to civil remedies and criminal penalties. Only piano rolls and some perforated disks were permitted to be registered, apparently because they exhibited a discernible pattern constituting an "arrangement," while similar patterns on phonograph records were not intelligible to the eye hence not amenable to copyright.[1]

The first attempt to make sound reproductions copyrightable was in 1906 during hearings on revision of the copyright law. A bill was in-

[1] A detailed discussion of manufacturers' attempts to acquire legislation during the period up to 1955 will be found in a study by Ringer (1961).

troduced to the Committee on Patents specifying that copyrights could be obtained for "devices, applicances and contrivances for reproducing to the ear, speech or music." Due to a recent Supreme Court decision, the constitutionality of copyrighting products which were not intelligible writings became uncertain.[2] Rather than confront the constitutional issue Congress enacted the 1909 copyright law (Title 17, United States Code) containing no provision concerning sound reproductions. Thereafter the Copyright Office consistently refused to register them.[3]

During these same hearings, the legislators expressed a fear of a monopoly within the sound reproduction industry. To forestall this possibility, Congress included in the 1909 act a provision known as the "compulsory license."[4] Under this provision once a copyright owner of a musical work, usually the publisher, permits it to be recorded it is no longer exclusive. Anyone may record it providing they give notice to the copyright owner of their intention to do so, and they pay a royalty of two cents for each record manufactured. It was this issue rather than unauthorized reproduction (or "dubbing" as it was then called) which occupied the manufacturers' attention for the following decades. Between 1912 and 1932 a series of bills were introduced into Congress which included provisions for copyrighting records. But "dubbing" was practically ignored in the battles among the author-publisher groups, performers, and manufacturers concerning whether the compulsory license was discriminatory against authors and composers.

By 1921 the recording industry was well established with sales of over $100 million annu-

[2]*White-Smith Music Publishing Co.* vs. *Apollo Co.*, 209 U.S. 1 (1908).

[3]Much later, in 1955, a Federal Court decision did indicate that sound reproductions were potentially copyrightable under the Constitution: *Capitol Records, Inc.* vs. *Mercury Records Corporation*, 221 F.2d 657 (2d Circ. 1955). But this did not alter the fact that the present law excluded them.

[4]17 U.S.C. Sec. 1(e) and 101(e). See Henn (1960, pp. 1–11) for a history of the provision.

ally. But starting in 1922 these sales were seriously undercut by the growth of radio broadcasting. In 1932 during hearings over copyright law revision record manufacturers for the first time since 1906 strongly urged copyright for records. Their suggestions, however, were directed not only at dubbers but broadcasters as well. Strong opposition was forthcoming from broadcasters and publishers alike. The tenor and results of these hearings were indicative of subsequent attempts to gain legislation up until 1950: copyright privileges for manufacturers met with increasing opposition from performers, publishers, broadcasters, jukebox concessionaires, and film producers (Ringer 1961, pp. 21–37). These opponents contended that common law concerning unfair competition was sufficient to combat piracy and that the extension of copyright privileges to manufacturers would jeopardize their own interests.

Ringer (1961, p. 37) sums up the situation between 1925 and 1955:

"As the importance of radio in the music publishing and recording industries grew, there was a proportionate increase in the pressure to secure copyright in sound records, and in the concerted opposition to such proposals on the part of author and user groups. The performers and manufacturers each sought protection for themselves and opposed it for others. . . .

"Throughout the hearings there was a great deal of confusion between protection against the actual reproduction of a particular recording and protection against imitation or mimicry of a general style or manner of performance. These and other technical deficiencies of the bills were widely criticized. Virtually all of the opponents of the measure (sic) attacked their constitutionality on the ground that performances and recordings are not creative, and are labor rights or mechanical objects rather than 'writings.' Essentially, however, the arguments, pro and contra, were dictated by economic self-interest, and revolved around the problem of radio broadcasting. There was practically no direct opposition to the principle of protection of sound recordings against unauthorized dubbing."

Up through 1950, record piracy was comparatively limited in both sales volume and scope.[5] The immediate post-war pirates appealed almost exclusively to collectors interested in jazz, blues, and swing; their products were essentially obscure and otherwise unavailable pre-war recordings. Hundreds of such items were available on various "pirate" labels (e.g., Wax, Jazz-Time, Jolly Roger, the Hot Jazz Club of America). But they seldom sold more than 1,000 copies of any one item (*Variety* July 5, 1950, p. 35). Given the restricted market, these "collectors' pirates" did not particularly concern the record companies:

"Doubtless there would never have been such a prolific mushrooming of 'contraband' labels if the big companies who control rights to these masters had followed through with reissues sufficient to keep the jazz wing happy. Most majors, when queried as to why they let the reissue business go to the pirates, reply: 'Why—ah, it's wasn't worth the trouble to put out that moldy stuff. It never sold anyway' " (Ramsey 1950).

Twenty years later John Hammond of Columbia Records expressed the reaction of his company to the jazz pirating: "The bootlegging isn't much of a concern to Columbia, because in the case of old jazz records it serves a few collectors not numerous enough to support a general release" (*Downbeat* March 4, 1971, p. 14).

Without protection from the Federal copyright statute record manufacturers were not completely lacking means of legal recourse

concerning rights to their products. Protection could be sought under common law. The common law recognizes a property right in assets which have been gained through the expenditure or investment of money, skill, time, and effort.[6] An injunction against a counterfeiter under this theory of unfair competition occurred as early as 1904;[7] a 1950 case set a precedent in interpreting the theory which is used by record manufacturers for combatting pirates in recent times.[8]

This protection, however, was restricted by numerous drawbacks such as limited jurisdiction, lack of uniformity, and uncertainty of case outcome (Ringer 1961, p. 47; Recent Cases 1970, p. 846n). Some of these disadvantages were discussed in a *Billboard* article entitled: "Diskeries Impotent as Bold Pirates Muscle In" (May 19, 1951, pp. 1+). The paper reported industry complaints that since no criminal violation was involved, pirates must be tracked down to face civil actions by the companies themselves. This was both a fruitless and expensive operation. In other cases, after difficult detective work locates a pirate, he simply "flies the coop" leaving the manufacturer little to show for his effort.

Twenty years later a spokesman of the record industry testified before Congress on the ineffectualness of common law protection:

". . . Even if a record company were successful in enjoining a pirate in one state, the pirate could merely move to another state and begin his operations all over again. The record industry has spent hundreds of thousands of dollars chasing after pirates by bringing lawsuits in state courts throughout the United States. Finally, the state remedy is also inadequate because only the record company bringing the action

---

[5]"Piracy," when more precisely used in the music industry, refers to the unauthorized use of sound reproductions from one or more legitimate records when producing a record to be passed off as an original. "Counterfeiting" involves the unauthorized production of a record in which the genuine article is copied in all respects including label, jacket, etc. "Bootlegging" refers to the unauthorized manufacture and distribution of what is otherwise a legitimate record; the usual case is when a record pressing plant deliberately overruns an order to a consumer and disposes of the excess copies without permission (*Billboard* November 4, 1967, p. 3; Diamond 1968, p. 856n). The most recent practice of marketing unauthorized reproductions of live performances is also referred to as "bootlegging" in the industry. The term "piracy" will be used in this article as a general term to cover these and all forms of unauthorized duplication of sound reproductions. Entertainment industry publications frequently use the term "disklegging" in this sense.

[6]For discussions of common law theories as they apply to piracy, see: Ownbey (1960) and Protection (1967, pp. 749–753).

[7]*Victor Talking Machine Co.* vs. *Armstrong*, 132 Fed. 711 (S.D.N.Y. 1904).

[8]*Metropolitan Opera Association, Inc.* vs. *Wagner-Nichols Recorder Corp.*, 199 Misc. 786, 101 N.Y.S. 2d 483 (Sup. Ct. 1950).

can benefit from it. A pirate enjoined by one company simply could begin pirating records manufactured by another" (U.S. Congress, House 1971, p. 29).

Although common law protection against piracy was a poor substitute for that possible under Federal statutory law, the record industry obviously lacked the political strength to overcome the array of interest groups opposed to manufacturer control over sound recordings. Of the 31 bills introduced in Congress between 1906 and 1951 which offered statutory protection at the Federal level, none passed. Nor was any state to give such protection until the mid-1960's, although several bills were introduced, especially in New York during the 1950's. Only one municipality, Los Angeles, the home of the record industry, had a law prohibiting the production and sale of records without authorization of the "owner of reproduction rights."

Prior to the 1950's it is evident that the record industry failed in its legislative attempts due to a relative lack of power. Its opponents in the publishing and broadcasting industries outweighed it in political influence. But after 1950 the publishers, broadcasters, and recording people began to reach a shakey *modus vivendi* consistent with Durkheim's (1964, pp. 200–232) notion of "complimentary differences." Publishers and recording companies made money from airplay, and radio stations found in records a cheap way of filling broadcast time. While each had their own interests, they were intertwined with the other.

PERIOD OF CRISIS AND COALESCENCE

In 1951, the record industry took note of a new phenomenon in piracy: current hits were being issued under counterfeit labels with one pirate pressing 50,000 records per week in four plants (*Billboard* September 1, 1951, pp. 1+). But the initial targets of the first major post-war assault of pirates involved "collectors' pirates." The first case concerned recordings of Metropolitan Opera Saturday matinee broadcasts and the second, in 1951, concerned Dante Bollentino,

who marketed pirate jazz records under the "Jolly Roger" label.[9]

Bollentino made the mistake of issuing Louis Armstrong recordings made from 1925 to 1932, subsequent to Columbia's releasing the same material. The company and the artist filed a complaint with the New York Supreme Court against Bollentino and Paradox Industries Inc. for re-recording under misleading brand labels records made from Columbia. Bollentino pleaded he had not violated any law; instead, he was serving the public by keeping old jazz records available to the people (*Newsweek* February 11, 1952, p. 71). Columbia argued that they constantly reissued jazz classics, thus there was no justification for Jolly Roger to do so (*Billboard* February 9, 1952, pp. 21+). Shortly after Columbia obtained an injunction against further pirating of these records, publishers holding copyrights sued Bollentino for damages stemming from infringement since he had neither secured licenses to use the music nor paid royalties. The publishers were awarded $5,002.50 for damages and legal fees. *Billboard* (June 14, 1952, pp. 44+) heralded the results as being the most important case in years against record pirates. In view of the trivial award, however, an attorney for Bollentino was more accurate when he described the judgment as "pyrrhic" (U.S. Congress, House 1962, p. 27).

Nevertheless, the Bollentino case did mark a new phase in the piracy battle: another group besides the record manufacturers was beginning to show concern over lost revenues. But unlike manufacturers, the publishers did have some recourse through the copyright law. But it was becoming questionable whether this was enough to deter pirates.

In May of 1955, the music publishers launched a second attack by causing the arrest of Joseph Krug, who was accused of copyright infringement in pirating radio broadcasts of the Glenn Miller orchestra made during the Second

---

[9]See Livingston (1970, pp. 61–62) and Piracy on Records (1953, pp. 436–441) for discussions of these cases.

World War. More important than Krug's arrest was the declared intention of the publishers to sue dealers, distributors, or whoever had any part in the handling or manufacture of the records. In October, 1957, the U.S. Court of Appeals, 2nd Circuit, ruled in favor of the publishers: distributors and dealers were liable for payment of the statutory royalty of two cents for each unlicensed record sold by them plus court costs and attorneys' fees; however, unlike the Bollentino case, no damages were awarded.

The initial reaction to the decision among record dealers was apprehension over the requirement to police their merchandise. Publishers were jubilant. *Billboard* headlined: "Court Decision Sunday Punch to Disk Piracy" (October 7, 1957, p. 27). Time was to temper such enthusiasm. By May, 1962, Julian T. Abeles, Counsel for Music Publishers' Protection Association, Inc., testified that because the liability was "trifling" the decision was simply another "pyrrhic victory," and of no deterrence to major retail record outlets (U.S. Congress, House 1962, p. 30). The publishers were beginning to move into the manufacturers' camp in recognizing the inadequacies of existing legal weapons.

The further frustrations of the record industry in the late fifties is exemplified by the case of George Hilger. Hilger was arrested in Chicago in February, 1958, in connection with organized crime's involvement in pirated records containing counterfeit labels. Hilger had in his possession 12,500 such disks, which appeared to represent only the tip of an enormous iceberg. For infringing on the trademarks, a misdemeanor in Illinois, Hilger was fined $50.

In commenting on the Hilger case, an unnamed "legal source" criticized the record industry for being negligent with its own products:

"The record industry is at fault . . . because it has never effectively lobbied for laws to forbid the making of bogus disks. Furthermore, all the offended companies threatened to bring civil suits against Hilger, but so far not a single suit has been filed. The industry . . . doesn't seem to care about legally de-

fending itself against pirates. It's a hit-and-run industry . . . preoccupied with today's hit and running furiously after another" (*Billboard* March 2, 1959, p. 1).

There is no arguing the ineffectiveness of lobbying efforts to that date, and there was indication that the giants of the industry were less active for legislation than smaller firms. In a survey by *Advertising Age*, spokesmen from RCA, Columbia, Capitol, and MGM expressed indifference over the piracy situation: "This sort of thing happens to the small companies which can't defend themselves" (*Advertising Age* March 9, 1959, p. 12). The indifference of giants was rapidly truncated by the appearance of the "entrepreneurial pirate."

"Collectors' pirates" operate in what Livingston (1970) calls a "shade of grey" area: they provide a small public with a product otherwise unavailable, their profits are generally marginal, and their economic impact on legitimate record companies is negligible. The opposite of these characteristics describe the "entrepreneurial pirates." Like buccaneers of the 17th century, the success of these pirates depends on the success of others. A flourishing market must be already established for a product before they will enter into the competition. They have no intention of establishing a monopoly, for to drive record companies out of business would only defeat their own sources of income.

The record industry deals in a high risk product. To understand the nature of this risk it is necessary to briefly examine the process by which a recording achieves marketability. A company issuing an original record absorbs copyright costs of two cents per pressing, musicians' fees, advertising and promotional costs, federal excise taxes, and other production expenses incurred between the record's conception and its release on the market. Before the company sells a single record it has already absorbed substantial costs:

"To create almost any album, a record company will expend no less than $55,000 in prerelease costs, and that is before the first record or tape is actually manufactured. . . .

"Then, when the record company feels moderate confidence in its product and undertakes its manufacturing, distribution, and promotion, it will have spent and risked between $180,000 and $200,000" (U.S. Congress, House 1971, p. 39).

Once the record is released, the company has essentially lost control over the record's fate. Success is dependent on the whims of the public and its cultural gatekeepers: radio station managers, disk jockeys, and to a lesser extent record critics (Denisoff in press; Hirsch 1972). Only one of ten albums in 1971 was successful enough to break even (U.S. Congress, House 1971, p. 29). But if one should become a hit, time becomes critical. The originating company must quickly produce enough records to supply a demand which is likely to peak and decline in a short period: usually three months.

Once a record is a hit the "entrepreneurial pirate," although occasionally paying copyright royalties, has only to pay for the duplication of the sound reproduction on a material of inconsequential cost: less than 30 cents per single record, $1.50 for L.P.'s, and 95 cents per tape (Piracy on Records 1953, p. 434; *Wall Street Journal* November 30, 1970, p. 1). He operates without the element of chance since he deals only in recordings or performers with demonstrated saleability. Entering the market with a competitively priced product already in demand, he is assured of profit. All risk and expense involved in producing a hit have been absorbed by the legitimate company; the only risk facing the pirate up to 1972 was dependent upon the company's efforts in initiating legal action.

By 1960 the "entrepreneurial pirates" had established themselves as part of the record scene in America. Evidence of how well they succeeded can be judged from the developments during that year. Whereas piracy had previously been primarily restricted to singles, unauthorized albums now began to appear. This meant that pirates had reached a new stage of organization: they were not only pressing records but manufacturing their own album covers as well (*Billboard* May 16, 1960, pp. 2+). While pirates once concentrated on hit records they were now pirating a performer's follow-up to a hit in anticipation of its own hit status (*Billboard* May 23, 1960, pp. 1+). Pirates became quite blatant—in Cleveland, for example, a large truck was making rounds carrying hit master disks and advertising "press your favorite records from your favorite labels" on the spot (*Billboard* May 16, 1960, p. 9). Also, it was increasingly evident that organized crime was implicated in counterfeiting operations, an indication of the profits involved (*Billboard* December 12, 1960, pp. 3+).

It is impossible to accurately assess the magnitude of the economic impact of entrepreneurial piracy on the record industry. All estimates by industry spokesmen must be considered in the context that they are given, namely, in attempt to justify legislative action. By 1959, industry spokesmen were estimating that 20 percent of his records (*Billboard* December 14, 1959, pp. 3+) and one-third of all records sold (*Billboard* June 15, 1953, pp. 3+) were pirated. The following year, industry spokesmen claimed that five percent of the record industry's annual gross of $20 million per year was being siphoned off by pirates (*Billboard* October 10, 1960, pp. 2+). This figure of $20 million was to be cited frequently in the next few years, especially during congressional hearings in 1962 (U.S. Congress, House 1962, *passim*). At these same hearings, a representative of publishers estimated that "at least 40 percent of the current record sales represent 'pirate' booty" (U.S. Congress, House 1962, p. 36). Retrospectively, most estimations of that period appear to be exaggerations (*Wall Street Journal* November 30, 1970, p. 1). Nonetheless, a growing threat to the interests of the recording industry was becoming increasingly evident. Industry trade associations heightened their lobbying in Congress.

The Record Industry Association of America, Inc. (RIAA), comprised of the largest and many medium-sized record manufacturers, had been seeking state legislation against piracy as early as 1952 (*Billboard* March 1, 1952, pp. 1+).[10] The more recently founded (1959) American Record Manufacturers and Distributors Association (ARMADA), comprised of smaller and medium-sized manufacturers and large distributors from major cities, considered the combatting of piracy a principal goal (*Billboard* June 27, 1960, p. 2; and June 26, 1961, pp. 6+). Both organizations actively initiated several civil suits and supplied evidence in actions in piracy cases. But their principal goal was expressed by ARMADA president, Art Talmadge, when he claimed that stiff federal legislation was the "ultimate remedy": "Possibly an amendment to the Copyright Act, which would put the fear of the Lord and the F.B.I. into the hearts of the bootleggers" (*Billboard* October 10, 1960, pp. 2+).

In the meantime, the Copyright Office from 1955 to 1961 had prepared a series of studies as part of a copyright revision program. In 1961 it published its recommendations which included: "Sound recordings should be protected against unauthorized duplication under copyright principles, but detailed recommendations are being deferred pending further study" (U.S. Congress, House 1961, p. 18). While this gladdened the manufacturers, one other recommendation did not: the elimination of the compulsory license (U.S. Congress, House 1961, pp. 32–36).

By all indications it seemed the time was ripe for the record industry to obtain legislation protecting their products: the interest group conflict of the pre-1955 period had disappeared, diverse interests had coalesced into lobbying groups favoring the legislation, and the industry's sales in 1962 were $687 million. Clearly a "power group" by political and economic standards, the industry also possessed a great "power differential" over the targets of such legislation since they had virtually no power at all.

[10]The largest firms accounted for 85 percent of dollar volume of business in 1954: RCA Victor, Columbia, Capitol, Decca, MGM, Mercury, and London (Henn 1960, p. 45).

PERIOD OF LEGISLATIVE POWERLESSNESS

In mid-1962, hearings began on a bill (H.R. 6354) to provide up to $10,000 fine or up to ten years imprisonment for interstate transport of recordings with forged or counterfeited labels, and for interstate transport of recordings "reproduced without the permission or authorization of the owner of the master recording." The bill would also amend the copyright law to provide damages on counterfeited records. Unlike previous hearings on the copyrighting of records, manufacturers, publishers, and composers were in accord favoring the bill's passage. Testifying in favor of the bill were representatives from ARMADA, RIAA, Music Publishers' Protective Association, Inc., some record manufacturers, and the American Guild of Authors and Composers.

Opposition to the bill was expressed by the National Association of Broadcasters, the Register of Copyrights, and the Librarian of Congress. While favoring the intent and various aspects of the bill, these opponents argued that a number of complicated copyright issues concerning sound recordings were unresolved. In particular, they were referring to the compulsory license provision. Consequently, they felt that since a general revision of the copyright law was in progress, the bill was the kind of piecemeal legislation which should be avoided at that juncture. The main argument of the opponents appears to be summed up in the following quotes: the first by the General Counsel of the National Association of Broadcasters, the second by the Register of Copyrights:

"Because of the complexity and the technical nature of copyright matters in general, it is our opinion that piecemeal changes in the overall law are not advisable (U.S. Congress, House 1962, p. 76). Piecemeal legislation on a matter of such importance in advance of general revision is, of course, to be avoided unless absolutely necessary" (U.S. Congress, House 1962, p. 79).

Evidently the $20 million annual losses to piracy claimed by representatives of the industry did not qualify as calling for "absolutely necessary" changes in the copyright law. The resulting law (Public Law 87–773) left the copyright law untouched and represented an otherwise emasculated version of the original bill: penalties were provided solely for interstate commerce in recordings with forged or counterfeited labels and the requested harsh penalties were diluted to a maximum fine of $1,000 and/or no more than one year imprisonment. Such were scarcely likely to "put the fear of the Lord and the F.B.I. into the hearts of bootleggers." In practice, the law was seldom used up through 1971, if only because most of the unauthorized duplication did not involve counterfeiting (U.S. Congress, House 1971, p. 16).

Thus the record industry was again rebuffed by Congress and apparently only as a matter of legislative convenience. The question is: Why did a "power group" remain impotent in its efforts to initiate the criminalization process against generally recognized "deviants?" A major part of the answer we believe lies in the image of the music industry in Congress at that time. The entire entertainment industry had just emerged from the television quiz show scandals of the late 1950's. These were shortly followed by the payola scandals within the record industry itself. During congressional hearings on the payola issue recriminations were not only exchanged between competitors within the industry but also were heard from Congressmen as well. Members of the Harris Committee took the opportunity to lament both the quality of popular music and the ethics of the industry. During testimony by Dick Clark, Representative Steven Derounian charged that popular music was selling sex in disguise (U.S. Congress, House 1960, p. 1342). The chairman of the subcommittee, Representative Oren Harris, typified the tendency of the hearings when he told Clark:

"I do not think you are the inventor of the system;

"I do not think you are even the architect of it . . .

"I think you are the product that has taken advantage of a unique opportunity . . ." (U.S. Congress, House 1960, p. 1351).

The "system" referred to was the industry itself and Congress appeared more interested in applying controls upon industry practices than in protecting it. Payola strained the manufacturers' image of integrity. Congress was not persuaded that the interests of an industry, itself being considered for sanctioning, needed special protection on their own merits. Neither was it persuaded that other important interests, the public's for example, were significantly endangered by piracy of recordings.

In the latter half of the 1960's, the recording industry enjoyed a spurt in profits generated by the growing popularity in albums. The apparent power of the recording industry concommitantly rose as many large conglomerates purchased record companies. Columbia Broadcasting System, Radio Corporation of America, Trans-America, Gulf-Western, and EMI now had a strong interest in protecting their investments. *Forbes*, the financial magazine, ran a feature story on the industry, "$2 Billion Worth of Noise" (July 15, 1968) praising it as an excellent "growth" industry.

In 1967, the same year the record industry first surpassed $1 billion in sales, a copyright revision bill (H.R. 2512, 90th Congress, 1st Session) containing protections for sound recordings passed the House but not the Senate.[11] In the meantime, several states, including New York and California—home bases for the recording industry—enacted statutes intended to suppress piracy. Two Supreme Court decisions cast doubts on the constitutionality of these laws, however, as well as suits under the common law of unfair competition.[12] The laws were challenged on the theory that states were attempting

---

[11]The Senate's rejection had nothing to do with sound recordings but with the CATV issue.

[12]*Sears, Roebuck & Co.* vs. *Stiffel Co.*, 376 U.S. 225 (1964), and *Compco Corporation* vs. *Day-Brite Lighting, Inc.* 376 U.S. 234 (1964).

to exert jurisdiction in an area preempted by the Constitution.[13]

As Congress and the courts deliberated, sound piracy continued to rise. The most serious inroad of piracy into the record business came with the development of tapes and cartridges for which the industry had great sales hopes. Again, there was a flurry of estimates of the damage. By 1969 it was claimed that one-third of the retail sales in prerecorded tapes represented pirated goods (*Billboard* May 10, 1969, pp. 45+; and *Wall Street Journal* December 3, 1969, pp. 1+). The reputed "king" of the 4-track tapes, Earl Muntz of Stereo-Pak, claimed 80 percent of the prerecorded 4-tracks and 30–35 percent of the recently developed 8-tracks were pirated (*Billboard* November 8, 1969, pp. 1+). A month later, Muntz abandoned his prerecorded tape business because he was unable to compete with the pirates (*Billboard* December 6, 1969, p. 13). The prerecorded 4-track market belonged to the pirates and it was predicted that the 8-track would soon go the same path (*Billboard* January 24, 1970, p. 20).[14] Industry executives as late as 1972 were blaming the failure of tape sales to reach their potential due to pirates.[15]

---

[13]See U.S. Congress, House (1971, pp. 31 and 65). For comments opposing this interpretation see Diamond (1968, pp. 857–858); Recent Cases (1970); and Comments (1971).

[14]Duplication of tapes is obviously a simpler, far less expensive process than involved for records. This fact was not lost on one tape equipment manufacturer who, in 1969, advertised: "You may never buy a record again" and "You never need buy a record or tape again." This type of promotion drew criticisms of varying degrees from the music industry. See Anderson (1969) and *Billboard* (August 16, 1969, pp. 1+).

[15]During the Spring of 1972, the second author conducted a series of interviews with executives and attorneys at the following record companies: Columbia, Capitol, Warner/Reprise, United Artists, Elektra, and A&M. These interviews were designed in part to verify statements found in trade journals concerning pirating and to obtain other information on the companies' reactions toward pirating.

PERIOD OF THE POLITICALIZATION OF PIRACY

In the summer of 1969, a new type of pirate emerged to plague the industry. The pirates' first product was a set of two unmarked records packaged in a white double sleeve with the words *Great White Wonder* rubber-stamped in a corner. The records contained private performances by Bob Dylan and were released without his or his company's permission.

Although the new pirates were providing the public with unreleased material, they were unlike the "collectors' pirates" in two important respects. In the first place, the demand for their product was much greater hence potentially more profitable. Secondly, the rationales associated with the products were to go beyond the simple service theme of the "collectors' pirates." The early statements of these new pirates were certainly reminiscent of those of the collectors'. A producer of one Dylan pirate album said:

"Well, sir, some of these are better than the shit that Columbia has released. They just keep on sitting on them so you might say, in a sense, we're liberating the records and bringing them to all the people, not just the chosen few" (*Los Angeles Free Press* December 19, 1969, p. 52).

Symbolically, however, the products of these "counterculture pirates" represented the ideological *Zeitgeist* of the period: the New Left, campus demonstrations, and acts of political extremist that were unpopular with Congress and the public. Rock music of the 1960's was bestowed with an elaborate ideology by the politically radical counterculture.[16] This ideology

---

[16]The term "counterculture" is synonymous with "contraculture" as defined by Yinger (1960, p. 629): "... The normative system of a group contains, as a primary element, a theme of conflict with the values of the total society, where personality variables are directly involved in the development and maintenance of the group's values, and wherever its norms can be understood only by reference to the rela-

possessed two major tenets. The first posited rock music as a revolutionary force to destroy the dominant social structure of *Amerika* or the "death culture." The most elaborate explication of this proposition has been articulated by John Sinclair, founder of the White Panther Party, who portrayed rock as the core of the new culture providing "inspiration and the breath to go on." "Everything was built upon the music, and it was going to be the force that would carry us through to the glorious world of the future" (Sinclair 1971, p. 19). Rock music was to reveal the manifest interests of young people and contribute unity and purpose to them.

The second tenet of the rock ideology has already been implied by Sinclair. Sinclair (1972) joined by Abbie Hoffman (1969), Craig Pyes (1970), and others viewed the music as the basis of a new people's culture. Much of the rhetoric of this posture was derived from the utopian socialists (Green 1971) and encompassed the notions of "parallel-structures" and "counter communities" popular with segments of the New Left in the mid-1960's. The fundamental thrust of this position was the creation of a new world within the "decaying" structure of the old. However, as Sinclair (1971, p. 20) argued, the people's culture was being "ripped off" or exploited by the creators and manufacturers of the music:

"We started out making a new life-form in which all of us could participate equally, and now we have the same thing we were trying to get away from, only it's worse because our original creative impetus has been blunted and perverted and channeled into the same old dead-end Hollywood shuck which insists that the only relationship we can have to our vital art-expression is as consumers, as buyers and consumers who just keep paying more and more for less and less of what we need. . . ."

tionships of the group to be surrounding dominant culture." Cf. Parsons' (1951, p. 355) "counter-ideology" and Roszak's (1969, pp. 48–49) "counter-culture."

Sinclair and some rock journalists (Karpel 1971; Lydon 1971; Lippincott 1970) charged the music industry with over-pricing records, concerts, and festivals and of "selling out" the people. Indicative of the feelings of many radicals are those of A. J. Weberman, the founder of the Dylan Liberation Front, when he shouted at the singer: ". . . you *used* the struggle of the black people to get yourself ahead . . . you ripped-off their music. *You owe them quite a bit*" (*Rolling Stone* March 4, 1971, p. 44).

The sales success of *Great White Wonder* prompted the release of two additional pirate records by Dylan: *Stealin'* and *John Birch Society Blues* in December, 1969. Shortly thereafter the "live" or concert facsimile became a standard pirate product. The first rock concert album was *LIVEr Than You'll Ever Be*, performances of the Rolling Stones, nearly a year prior to the London Records' release of many of the same performances on *Get Yer Ya Ya's Out*. *LIVEr* is as significant as *Great White Wonder* in that it was the prototype of a major aspect of countercultural pirating. It established that "any kid can take his tape recorder to a Rolling Stones' performance and become a millionaire" (*Time* June 28, 1971, p. 72).

The rock and underground press argued that record conglomerates were unsympathetic to the needs of the "new community." Greil Marcus (1970) of *Rolling Stone* reviewed a number of unauthorized recordings and noted:

"In a way, the bootleg phenomena may well force artists to respond to what the public wants—or lose a lot of bread. One obvious way to squelch the *Great White Wonder* album, without arousing any bad feelings, would have been to issue the basement tape; the way to kill the new live Stones' album would be to release a similar LP that was even better."

In a similar vein, the pirates presented themselves as serving the public:

"I explain it mainly through the failure of the establishment record companies to provide the listener with anything stimulating, innovative, and worthwhile. After all, the summer of 1969, when the underground record industry began, was an incredible period of record industry hype and shuck. Such utterly atrocious jive as "Grand Funk," "Ten Wheel Drive," "Blind Faith," "Santana," and "Chicago" were served up to the listening public. Amidst all of this came underground records which were exciting and stimulating in an artificial and illusory way. People bought them because there was nothing else to buy and they wanted to have something that their friends didn't have" (*Los Angeles Free Press* April 10, 1970, p. 10).

"Bob Dylan is a heavy talent and he's got all those songs nobody's ever heard. We thought we'd take it upon ourselves to make this music available" (*Rolling Stone* September 20, 1969, p. 6).

But the political implications of the pirating operations were inescapable. *Kaleidoscope* (March 18, 1970), a Madison, Wisconsin underground paper, condemned the "gigantic profits" of the recording companies and went on to say:

"Now . . . some of us who feel that freak-rock belongs to the people from where it came have liberated Dylan and Beatles tapes and returned the music to the people."

The report then described how "community" members had taped parts of the Beatles' *Get Back* and Dylan's Isle of Wight appearance, and had pressed 1,000 records with a picture of John Sinclair on the cover which would be sold for three dollars. The earnings would be "returned to the community" as contributions to a bail fund. The article ended proclaiming: "This album is a step toward reclaiming the people's music from filthy-capitalist record companies."

The "counterculture pirate" was thus an artifact of an alternative lifestyle; his product had political significance. Of course, the economic significance was there as well. Record companies were at first hesitant to respond to this new threat because they underestimated its long-term consequences. According to an attorney then with Columbia Records, the company philosophy concerning the trend begun by *Great White Wonder* was, ". . . if we ignore it perhaps it

will just go away."[17] But the pirate albums became increasingly more successful evoking a sense of corporate "indignation":

"Nothing fostered moral indignation as much as having it hit you in the money belt. . . . As albums followed upon albums, and as the volume started to increase, they [the company] became increasingly aware of the total impact of them, and it became a major problem to them. Then they decided that perhaps there was moral indignation on top of economic indignation."

In 1971, the record industry once more presented its case to Congress.

THE GIANT FINDS ITS MUSCLE

By 1971 the record industry surpassed $1¼ billion in sales. Meanwhile it was claiming to be sorely beset by pirating: the generally accepted estimates were one of every four prerecorded tapes, representing $100 million in sales, and one of every twenty records, $60 million in sales (U.S. Congress, House 1971, pp. 5, 25, and 38; *Wall Street Journal* November 30, 1970, p. 1). The promised copyright revision was still not in sight. In June House hearings convened on a bill, already passed in the Senate without hearings, to amend the copyright law as it applied to sound recordings.

The proponents for the bill were again a formidable array of trade associations: American Federation of Musicians, RIAA, National Association of Record Merchandisers, Inc. (into which ARMADA had merged in 1965), and National Music Publishers Association, Inc. The only dissent was from "legitimate pirates" who had paid "all statutory royalties" under the compulsory license provision, plus the juke box industry which had some reservations (U.S. Congress, House 1971, pp. 67–119). The Deputy Attorney General's Office and two previous dissenters, the Librarian of Congress and the Copyright Office, all claimed the piracy mat-

[17]Interview with second author.

ter was now too "urgent" to await copyright revision.

In addition, support for the bill came from two new parties. The Department of State was in the process of negotiating an international treaty on record piracy and felt that passage of the bill would enhance the United States' bargaining position (U.S. Congress, House 1971, pp. 6–10, 18, and 32). Since the treaty negotiations had implications for international trade relations, the Department of Commerce also urged the bill's passage (U.S. Congress, House 1971, p. 123). In October of 1971 Congress passed Public Law 92–140, an amendment to the copyright law, to permit the copyrighting of sound reproductions.

The law effected only recordings made between February 15, 1972 and January 1, 1975. The latter date was set on the assumption a general copsright revision would be passed by that time. The former date posed a problem for the industry since it meant that prior recordings would not be subject to Federal protection.

The industry thus faced two tasks: first, to ensure the copyright law was enforced and second, to seek ways by which pre-1972 recordings could be protected. To these ends the industry put on a great show of strength in November, 1971 when it announced the formation of an "industry council" to combat piracy (*Billboard* November 6, 1971, p. 3). This consisted of: RIAA, NARM, the Harry Fox Agency, International Tape Association, American Federation of Television and Radio Announcers, American Federation of Musicians, and American Guild of Authors and Composers. In practice, however, the primary burden was carried by RIAA and NARM.

Unquestionably, the industry was particularly successful in encouraging states to enact legislation. By mid-1973, 17 states had passed laws prohibiting unauthorized reproduction of records and tapes. The majority of these laws were enacted within the previous three years, and similar statutes were pending in at least three other states. The most severe penalties were in-

corporated in the Minnesota law, passed in June, 1973: possible fine of not more than $100,000 and/or imprisonment up to 10 years.

The constitutional status of thee laws remained in question however, until June, 1973 when the Supreme Court ruled in a five to four decision (Goldstein vs. California 93 S.Ct.2303 (1973)) that the California anti-piracy law did not conflict with the jurisdiction of the Congress in legislating copyright law. Thus the way was clear for state protection of pre-1972 recordings. A factor in the majority decision was an economic one. In the words of Chief Justice Burger:

"The California statutory scheme evidences a legislative policy to prohibit 'tape' and 'record piracy,' conduct that may adversely affect the continued production of new recordings, a large industry in California."

But while the industry was being successful in the legislative and judicial areas, the enforcement of legislation evidently remained a weak point. The first arrest under the copyright amendment did not occur until November, 1972 and the first indictments not until May, 1973 (*Billboard* May 5, 1973, pp. 1+). RIAA officials claimed in June of 1973 that piracy was now costing the industry $200 million a year (*Billboard* June 30, 1973, p. 3). In a legal memorandum distributed to its members by NARM it was frankly admitted:

"In many cases, it is difficult to persuade law enforcement officers to apply their limited resources to prosecution of recording piracy cases" (Arent *et al.* 1973, p. 2).

Thus, according to industry sources, piracy continued to expand despite legislative victories.

However, the legislative prospects continued to look bright. Additional states were expected to pass anti-piracy laws since the Goldstein decision had apparently cleared up constitutional questions. More importantly, a copyright revision bill (S. 1361) was again introduced in Congress by Senator John L. McClellan in April, 1973. The revision bill contained provisions similar to the amendment protecting sound reproductions, but the industry was encouraged by the possibility that the panalty of one year maximum could be expanded to as many as three years (*Billboard* June 2, 1973, pp. 3+). Suddenly things became cloudy: history seemed about to repeat itself.

In May payola scandals again struck the industry. The president of CBS Records was dismissed and various allegations were made in the news media concerning the industry's involvement in drug trafficking (drugola) plus organized crime's connection with rock groups. Senator John L. McClellan was uncertain as to the impact of these charges on the copyright bill's progress, although he had no intention of delaying action on revision (*Billboard* July 7, 1973, p. 13). Meanwhile, congressional probes were called for and a phrase, "need for a change in corporate moral climate" (*Billboard* July 7, 1973, p. 13), was often heard—but for the music industry the tune was scarcely a new one.

ANALYSIS AND DISCUSSION

Despite the apparent economic power of the recording industry, historically its ability to influence legislation has been highly problematic. Until recent years the "personal troubles" of the industry remained so regardless of the plethora of attempts to place pirating into the realm of "public issues" and thus translating its interests into public policy.

The reason for the industry's impotence prior to 1950 is not inconsistent with the conflict-power conception of the legislative process (Quinney 1970, pp. 37–40). The industry was unable to overcome the opposition of other powerful interest groups, namely the music publishers and broadcasters. The manufacturers' search for copyright protection initially appeared to legislators and opposing interest groups as a matter of self-enrichment rather than of defense against pirates. Pirates were regarded as corporate gadflies instead of real economic threats.

Following 1950 this situation changed. Publishers, manufacturers, and broadcasters began to recognize an interdependence among themselves. While each was aware of their own interests, these could be reconciled with the concerns of the manufacturers: publishers were also losing royalty monies because of the pirates. Radio stations, while not directly affected by the pirates, needed the cooperation of the record industry to service their music libraries. As long as radio stations could continue to operate as usual they presented only nominal opposition to the proposed legislation. This *modus vivendi* plus the formation of trade associations allowed the industry to mount several lobbying campaigns against what was rapidly being perceived as a considerable economic threat. Yet, despite the cessation of interest group conflict, the power differential, and access to the decision-making process legislative remedy was not forthcoming at the Federal level.

Even in a capitalistic society in which economic power is considered synonomous with access to decision-making processes and where protection of private, especially corporate, property is of high priority, the possession of such power is not a sufficient condition to create public policy. The record industry's experience is not consistent with Quinney's (1973, p. 88) claim that "government and business are inseparable." The industry, despite its economic resources, for years was scarcely part of the "ruling class" in its influence:

"The ruling class . . . in capitalist society is 'that class which owns and controls the means of production and which is able, by virtue of the economic power thus conferred upon it, to use the state as its instrument for the domination of society' (Miliband 1969, p. 23). The existence of this class in America, rooted mainly in the corporations and financial institutions of monopoly capitalism, is well-documented. This is the class that makes the decisions that affect the lives of those who are subordinate to this class" (Quinney 1973, p. 89).

In the instance of the record industry, its strongest support at the Federal level has come from the judicial branch when it allowed the states to act where the legislature chose to ignore. Meanwhile, the legislative branch has consistently acted independently as another interest group.[18] This supports the arguments of the "pluralist" students of power such as Dahl and Riesman when they argue that diverse interests exist within all levels and that power alone does not determine legislative outcome (see Domhoff and Ballard 1968, and Parry 1970).

The question, then, is why the industry heretofore has been unsuccessful in the legislative arena. It appears that it is due in large part to the industry's own deviant image in comparison with that of the pirates. Despite its "respectable" corporate ties, the industry has been involved in a number of public scandals, each coming with uncanny timing in relationship to proposed legislation. The exposure of payola, drug use by musicians, and the beliefs by segments of society that popular music is mindless noise, or worse, has labeled the industry as less than an upstanding corporate citizen. Furthermore, until 1973 the industry rarely showed any contriteness over charges of wrongdoing and avoided even "cosmetic" self-regulatory bodies as adopted in baseball, film, and broadcasting. The president of MGM Records, Mike Curb, recently acknowledged this problem when he told *Billboard* (August 11, 1973, p. 4):

"In my opinion, the general feeling in Washington is that we look worse than the bootleggers because of the [drug and payola] allegations."

A related image problem stems from what record pirating means to the public: the "collec-

tors'" and "contraculture" pirates provide otherwise unavailable material while the "entrepreneurial pirate" offers a lower price. Insofar as the public is concerned, the pirate is simply a form of competition to the companies. Those who benefit are not only "hippies" but supporters of "law and order" who purchase $2.00 records of Loretta Lynn and Merle Haggard at weekend "swap meets."

The record industry experiences other problems which insulate it from Congress. The industry has traditionally been headquartered in New York and Los Angeles. Only in recent years has it developed any stature in Nashville (Hemphill 1971). As one Capitol executive indicated, "That gives you 4 senators" leaving 96 with little if any political benefit in aiding a "suspect" industry. The industry's ability to lobby in Congress was further frustrated by the very nature of the record business. It is highly competitive with 90 companies attempting to produce hits. Only 50 belong to RIAA and mutual cooperation is, except in trade associations, rare. Several record companies with tape operations have even supplied pirates with equipment to manufacture their products. Other companies have benefited from loosely interpreted copyright laws. Consequently legislators can and do pose the question, "Who's in charge?" Frequently, an answer is not immediately forthcoming. Without the subsequent aid of NARM, which has members in nearly all 50 states, the industry could have missed influencing an indifferent Congress even in 1971.

Even at this late date, the relationship of the legislative branch to the recording industry is a generally sour one. Senator James Buckley has on numerous occasions criticized it for not correcting some industry practices and more significantly objected to its lack of cooperation (Ferretti 1973a and 1973b).

In the area of Federal legislation the recording industry has been a powerless giant. While it does have a number of unique features which have been a hinderance its experience raises a question about the role of economic power in

---

[18]It is important to differentiate between the legislative and executive processes (see Walton 1966, and Bachrach 1967). The legislative branch is more open to conflicting interest groups, hence it is susceptible to exchange and bargaining. On the other hand, in the executive branch it is possible for private problems to be translated into public issues by fiat, the problems of Penn Central Railroad, Lockheed, and ITT being cases in point. In Congress, given its many constituencies and members, similar decisions would have to be reached by a majority of its members (Dexter 1969, and Matthews 1960).

the criminalization process. The Supreme Court by a five to four decision validated the industry's quest for legal protection, but this is a far cry from a neat theorem linking power differentiation to the creation of public policy.

One can argue, as does Jackson Toby (1955) in his famous "Aunt Bertha" illustration, that a single case does not negate a sociological generalization. This is quite true. However, further investigations of this kind seem warranted to learn the mechanics and key variables in the criminalization process. Most studies of passages of legislation have taken place after the fact. We especially lack studies of *unsuccessful* cases. While the conflict theorists may be correct in identifying interest groups as prime players in the criminalization process, the outcome of any legislative game must be recognized as an uncertainty.

REFERENCES

Anderson, William, 1969. "Editorially Speaking: A License to Steal." *Stero Review* 22 (March): 4.

Arent, Fox, Kintner, Plotkin, and Kahn. 1973. *Unfair Competition Suits by Recording Distributors and Retailers Against Sellers of Pirated Tapes and Records.* Memorandum Prepared for National Association of Recording Merchandisers, Inc.

Bachrach, Peter. 1967. *The Theory of Democratic Elitism: A Critique.* Boston: Little, Brown & Co.

Becker, Howard S. 1963. *Outsiders: Studies in the Sociology of Deviance.* New York: Free Press.

Chambliss, William J. and Robert B. Seidman. 1971. *Law, Order, and Power.* Reading, Mass.: Addison-Wesley.

Comments. 1971. "Comments . . . Copyright Law—Federal Preemption—State Statute Forbidding Tape Piracy Held Not to be in Conflict With the Copyright Act—*Tape Industries Association* vs. *Younger.*" *New York University Law Review* 46 (March): 164–176.

Denisoff, R. Serge and Charles H. McCaghy. 1973. *Deviance, Conflict, and Criminality.* Chicago: Rand McNally.

Denisoff, R. Serge. In Press. *Solid Gold: The Popular Record Industry.* New Brunswick, N.J.: Trans-action Books.

Dexter, Lewis A. 1969. *The Sociology and Politics of Congress.* Chicago: Rand McNally.

Diamond, Sidney A. 1968. "Sound Recordings and Copyright Revision." *Iowa Law Review* 53 (February): 839–869.

Domhoff, G. William and Hoyt B. Ballard. Editors. 1968. *C. Wright Mills and the Power Elite.* Boston: Beacon Press.

Durkheim, Emile. 1964. *The Division of Labor in Society.* (Translated by George Simpson). New York: The Free Press. 200–232.

Ferretti, Fred. 1973a. "Buckley Wants Record Industry Investigated By 4 U.S. Agencies." *New York Times* (June 26): 47.

——— 1973b. "Record Industry 'Will Cooperate' in Payola Study." *New York Times* (July 2): 19.

Green, Gil. 1971. *The New Radicalism: Anarchist or Marxist.* New York: International Publishers.

Gusfield, Joseph R. 1963. *Symbolic Crusade: Status, Politics, and the American Temperance Movement.* Urbana, Ill.: University of Illinois Press.

Hemphill, Paul. 1970. *The Nashville Sound: Bright Lights and Country Music.* New York: Simon and Schuster.

Henn, Harry G. 1960. *The Compulsory License Provisions of the U.S. Copyright Law.* Study No. 5, July, 1956. In the Senate Committee Print, *Copyright Law Revision*, Studies Prepared for the Subcommittee on Patents, Trademarks, and Copyrights of the Committee on the Judiciary. Washington: Government Printing Office.

Hirsch, Paul. 1972. "Processing Fads and Fashions: An Organization-Set Analysis of Cultural Industry Systems." *American Journal of Sociology* 77 (January): 639–659.

Hoffman, Abbie. 1969. *Woodstock Nation.* New York: Random House.

Karpel, Craig. 1971. "Das Hip Kapital." *Creem* 3 (March): 25–33.

Lippincott, T. Proctor. 1970. "The Cultural Vultures." In *Age of Rock.* Edited by J. Eisen. New York: Vintage Books.

Livingston, William. 1970. "Piracy in the Record Industry." *Stereo Review* 24 (February): 60–69.

Lydon, Michael. 1971. "Rock For Sale." In *Conversations With the New Reality: Readings in the Cultural Revolution*. Edited by Editors of *Ramparts*. San Francisco: Canfield Press.

Marcus, Griel. 1970. "The Bootleg LP's." *Rolling Stone* 51 (February 7): 36.

Matthews, Donald R. 1960. *U.S. Senators and Their World*. New York: Random House.

Miliband, Ralph. 1969. *The State of Capitalist Society*. New York: Basic Books.

Mills, C. Wright. 1959. *The Sociological Imagination*. New York: Oxford University Press.

Odegard, Peter. 1928. *Pressure Politics*. New York: Columbia University Press.

Ownbey, Lloyd C., Jr. 1960. "Comment: The Civil Remedies for Disklegging." *Southern California Law Review* 33 (Winter): 190–207.

Parry, Geraint. 1970. *Political Elites*. New York: Praeger Publishers.

Parsons, Talcott. 1951. *The Social System*. Glencoe, Ill.: Free Press.

Piracy on Records. 1953. "Piracy on Records." *Stanford Law Review* 5 (April): 433–458.

Protection. 1967. "Protection of Sound Recordings Under the Proposed Copyright Revision Bill." *Minnesota Law Review* 51 (March): 746–774.

Pyes, Craig. 1970. "Rolling Stone Gathers No Politix." *Sundance* (October): 34–35.

Quinney, Richard. 1970. *The Social Reality of Crime*. Boston: Little, Brown.

———. 1973. "Crime Control in Capitalist Society: A Critical Philosophy of Legal Order." *Issues in Criminology* 8 (Spring): 75–99.

Ramsey, Frederic Jr. 1950. "Contraband Jelly Roll." *The Saturday Review* 33 (September 30): 64.

Recent Cases. 1970. "Recent Cases . . . Copyright—Unfair Competition—Unauthorized Reproduction of Another's Recording for Resale Violates State Unfair Competition Doctrine." *Vanderbilt Law Review* 23 (May): 840–847.

Ringer, Barbara A. 1961. *The Unauthorized Duplication of Sound Recordings*. Study No. 26, February, 1957. In Senate Committee Print, *Copyright Law Revision*, Studies Prepared for the Subcommittee on Patents, Trademarks, and Copyrights of the Committee on the Judiciary. Washington: Government Printing Office.

Ross, Robert and Graham L. Staines. 1972. "The Politics of Analyzing Social Problems." *Social Problems* 20 (Summer): 18–40.

Roszak, Theodore. 1969. *The Making of a Counter Culture*. Garden City. New York: Doubleday.

Schur, Edwin M. 1971. *Labeling Deviant Behavior*. New York: Harper and Row.

Sinclair, John. 1971. "Liberation Music." *Creem* 2 (No. 17 n.d.): 18–22.

———. 1972. *Guitar Army: Street Writings/Prison Writings*. New York: Douglas Book Corp.

Sutherland, Edwin H. 1950. "The Diffusion of Sexual Psychopath Laws." *American Journal of Sociology* 56 (September): 142–148.

Toby, Jackson. 1955. "Undermining the Student's Faith in the Validity of Personal Experience." *American Sociological Review* 20 (December): 717–718.

Turk, Austin T. 1966. "Conflict and Criminality." *American Sociological Review* 31 (June): 338–352.

U.S. Congress, House. 1960. *Responsibilities of Broadcasting Licenses and Station Personnel*. Hearings Before a Subcommittee of the Committee on Interstate and Foreign Commerce on Payola and Other Deceptive Practices in the Broadcasting Field, Part II. Washington: Government Printing Office.

———. 1961. *Copyright Law Revision*. Report of the Registrar of Copyrights on the General Revision of the U.S. Copyright Law. House Committee Print. Washington: Government Printing Office (July).

———. 1962. *Counterfeit Phonograph Records*. Hearing Before Subcommittee No. 3 of the Committee on the Judiciary on H.R. 6354, May 10, Washington: Government Printing Office.

———. 1971. *Prohibiting Piracy of Sound Recordings*. Hearings Before Subcommittee No. 3 of the Committee on the Judiciary on S. 646 and H.R. 6927, June 9 and 10, Washington: Government Printing Office.

Walton, John. 1966. "Substance and Artifact—The Current Status of Research on Community Power

Structure." *American Journal of Sociology* 71 (January): 430–442.

Yinger, J. Milton. 1960. "Contraculture and Subcul-

ture." *American Sociological Review* 25 (October): 625–635.

80. Shoplifting

WILLIAM E. COBB

SHOPLIFTING, ALONG WITH EMPLOYEE THEFT, IS unique among those crimes of theft which were investigated in that there is little consensus about the magnitude of the problem. The literature on these two crimes contains radically different estimates of their frequency of occurrence. The source of this estimation problem is the inability of retailers to accurately measure flows of inventory and, hence, inventory shortages.

Shortages (shrinkage in inventory not accounted for by sales records) can be segregated into two primary types. There are *apparent shortages* which are the direct result of errors (especially errors of omission) which appear on the accountant's ledger. There is no actual physical shrinkage but, on a dollar basis, the inventory will appear to have been reduced by more than total sales. The second type of shrinkage can be labeled *real shortage*. This real shortage of inventory stock is the result of losses to shoplifters and employee thieves.

APPARENT SHORTAGES: BOOKKEEPING ERROR

There are two basic methods of retail inventory measurement: cost accounting and retail accounting. Under the *cost method*, the book inventory control is used to accumulate cost figures, adding such information as purchases and transportation costs to the initial inventory amounts. At each physical inventory date, each inventory item is referenced to vendor's invoices in order to obtain cost information. Since this is both expensive and time consuming, the cost method is used infrequently. Most stores have adopted the *retail inventory method*. Physical inventory values are compiled at marked retail prices. That is, inventory stock is recorded according to selling price, not cost.[1]

The major source of bookkeeping error in both methods of inventory accounting would seem to be the up and down gyration of prices in a store. If the price of an item is raised (marked up) and the accountant fails to record the increase, an apparent surplus will exist at the time that the physical inventory is taken. Conversely, if the price of an item is lowered (marked down), failure to record the mark-down will result in an apparent shortage.

The general trend in retail stores is to "overprice" a product when it is initially placed in stock. The price is then reduced and the retailer advertises a "sale" in honor of some birthday, holiday, anniversary, or other "special" occasion. Since price changes of this nature far outnumber price increases, the random occurrence of a failure to record will probably be a failure to record a price reduction. Hence, normal store

▶SOURCE: *The Economics of Shoplifting. Ph.D. Dissertation, Virginia Polytechnic Institute and State University, 1973. Pp. 2–6, 36–51. (Editorial adaptations.) Reprinted by permission of William E. Cobb, West Virginia College of Graduate Studies.*

[1]For a good description of the retail method, see *Retail Inventory Made Practical* (New York: National Retail Merchants Association, 1971).

policy accompanied by less than perfect bookkeeping should lead to apparent shortages.

In addition to the pseudo-sales which merchants often advertise, there are often legitimate temporary reduction in the prices of certain items in order to attract customers. If the number of items purchased at the "sale" price is not accurately kept, apparent shortages will once again appear on the accountant's ledger. According to one retailer, Walter E. Reitz of the Hecht Company in Washington, D.C., "In these domestic departments where they mark the whole stock down for a sale, purchase at the new price, and mark so much of it back after the sale, we have found some departments making gross errors—$15,000 or $18,000, in some cases."[2]

Apparent shortages, in and of themselves, are of little concern to the retailer. His major interest is minimizing real shrinkage (theft). It is difficult to separate the shortage, which his books reveal, into apparent and real shortages. As Reitz has said:

"The whole shortage situation resolves itself around the fact that there is a difference between a physical and a book inventory. Part of these errors are, of course, in the control division, in the accounting. Some of them are made by the people that initiate paper, in the receiving and marking and so forth. The difficulty is, we have never been able, I guess—any of us—to know to what degree we have errors.

"The most important thing you can do is try to keep the errors at a minimum. We make a lot of errors because [sic] although the percentage is small, the numbers are so high.[3]"

A great number of security experts argue that bookkeeping error accounts for only 5 percent of the total reported shrinkage. On the other hand, the following passage points up the difference of opinion which exists on this subject.

"Some of the panel members agreed, however, that in general at least half and probably a much greater proportion, of all shortages can be rightfully attributed to errors in record-keeping and to system breakdowns, aside from any question of theft, either internal or external. Those who would attribute as much as 75% of total shortages to record keeping, etc., pointed out the tremendous number of instances occurring daily where opportunities exist for errors and omissions which contribute to the shortage picture. They felt that the cumulative total of such daily incidents greatly outweighed occasions of theft by either employees or the general public and that this fact must be taken into consideration in any attempt to allocate responsibility.[4]"

REAL SHORTAGES: SHOPLIFTING AND EMPLOYEE THEFT

If, in fact, bookkeeping error accounts for over 50 percent of reported shortages, quite obviously shoplifting and employee theft account for less than 50 percent. Many security experts vehemently disagree with this. They argue that 25 to 40 percent of shrinkage is the result of shoplifting, 60 to 75 percent is the result of employee theft, and the residual is relegated to bookkeeping error.[5]

One author, Joseph G. Metz, a former member of the National Commission on the Causes and Prevention of Violence, argues that, ". . . all businesses lose five times as much money to their own employees as they do to the outside shoplifter."[6] On the other hand, a study reported by the Virginia Retail Merchants Association indicated that, of the amount lost through theft, both shoplifting and internal pilferage, 78 percent was stolen by shoplifters and 22 percent by pilfering employees.[7] One of the problems to

[2]This statement was made at a panel discussion of retailers and then published as, Stock Shortages: Their Causes and Prevention (New York: National Retail Merchants Association, 1959), p. 37.

[3]Ibid., p. 34.

[4]Ibid., p. 62.

[5]C. H. Almer, The Fight Against Shoplifting in Sweden and West Germany: A Comparative Study (Boras, Sweden: AB Boras Tryckservice, 1971).

[6]Joseph G. Metz, The Economics of Crime, Economic Topic Series (New York: Joint Council on Economic Education, 1971), p. 4.

[7]Virginia Retail Merchants Association, The Retail Review, September, 1970.

be dealt with in the text is the estimation of the relative weights of shortages as between shoplifting and employee theft.

*

APPREHENSION OF SHOPLIFTERS: TECHNOLOGICAL CONSTRAINTS

To summarize, merchandise in retail stores is positioned so that customers—and thieves—can handle it. Merchants wish neither to offend shoppers with store policy nor to arrest them falsely. In this section, the effect of these two factors on shoplifting techniques is discussed. Emphasis is placed on the physical impossibility of apprehending most shoplifters.

As with the previous two costs, both the cost (loss) of stolen merchandise and the cost of detecting shoplifters are related to apprehension effort. The four costs are summed to provide a relationship between apprehension effort and the total loss of dollars which results from shoplifting.

*

Successful Shoplifting: An Overview

Successful shoplifting requires only that the thief be briefly shielded from the view of the clerk or store detectives; this can be accomplished by the use of display racks or counters, the position of the body or clothing of the thief, or the position of the body of a confederate or innocent shopper. No action will be taken against the thief unless store personnel *observe the concealment* or theft and *observe all activity of the thief from that moment until apprehension.* Exceptions to this rule occur only when electronic detection apparatus is in use.[8]

A theft is either successful or unsuccessful in the split second required to conceal the merchandise. *The place and method of concealment are important only because of the time constraint involved.* Since the crucial factor is insurance that no one witnesses the theft, concealment must be a quick maneuver.

Once certain of freedom from electronic surveillance, the thief must also insure that no clerk or detective witnesses the theft. The method used is a function of the ingenuity of the shoplifter. Any action which distracts from the movement of the hands contributes to the success of the theft. It is difficult to steal any item without the use of the hands. Since both clerks and detectives are aware of this fact, they watch the hands of shoppers relatively carefully.

Clerks are generally unconcerned about theft and seldom watch shoppers at all. It is easy to neutralize clerks either by sending them away for some type of merchandise or by spending enough time in their area so that they lose interest in making a sale. Disposing of the store detective is only slightly more difficult.

Identifying the Store Detective

If the thief is able to identify the store detective, shoplifting is made more simple.[9] In order to show that such identification requires only a minimum of effort, it is necessary to examine the magnitude of the job facing the store detective. Because of the proof-positive doctrine, the store detective must observe any theft for which he makes an arrest. Clearly the large number of shoppers which enter a store precludes observation of each one of them. The detective must make some conscious selection of whom he ought to keep under surveillance.

How can the detective choose when to follow whom? General consensus among security experts is that there is little, if any, correlation between an individual's physical characteristics (sex, age, race, or general appearance) and his proclivity to shoplift. These same experts give

[8]The professional thief who suspects possible television surveillance will conceal an item in an obvious manner, discreetly replace it on the counter or rack, then move to a quiet corner of the floor to observe any on-rushing detectives. If there is a closed circuit television hook-up in use, detectives will come running to the "scene of the crime." Since customers seldom run through a store, the thief can presume that the area is being scanned by cameras. This is a proven method for discovering "dummy" television cameras.

[9]Store detectives are normally incognito so that the potential shoplifter must consider all shoppers as potential detectives.

only general impressions about the hours, days, and months in which shoplifting is greatest.

The small amount of data which is available can be misleading. For instance, it is generally true that more females than males are arrested for shoplifting. A report published by Management Safeguards, Inc., of New York revealed that from a random sample of 1,647 shoppers followed in four general merchandise stores, 80 females shoplifted while only 29 males stole.[10] These two facts seem to indicate that females are more likely than males to shoplift. Security personnel, confronted with these statistics are quick to argue that more shoplifters are female simply because more shoppers are female. When the Management Safeguard statistics were adjusted to account for the fact that only 34.7 percent of their sample was male, the resultant data still showed that 5 percent of male shoppers stole while 7.4 percent of female shoppers were shoplifters (see Table I). The test for the significance of the difference between two proportions reveals that this difference is significant—once more indicating that women, in fact, are more likely than men to shoplift.

Security experts counter this statistic with the argument that women steal "more" because women spend more time in the store per shopping trip than do men. A study which will be detailed in Chapter VI indicated that males do spend less time than females per shopping trip to a store—16 percent less on the average. Using this figure, the Management Safeguard results can be adjusted, showing that the number of female shoplifters per female customer-minute spent in the store is 1.23 times the number of male shoplifters per male customer-minute. Once more the difference is significant.

The data do seem to indicate that the detective should spend relatively more time watching females.[11] However, I have found no security expert who agrees with this policy. Detectives are explicitly trained to make no selection on the basis of physical characteristics.

The detective is not left without a method of selecting suspects, however. The detective realizes that the thief will wish to be aware of any potential witnesses to the crime. He knows that the thief will be watching clerks and customers, alertly awaiting the opportunity to steal. Experience proves that the honest customer seldom takes his eyes off the merchandise. In fact, it is the objective of the store manager to set up his displays to encourage this behavior. He wants the customer to look at his merchandise, to handle it, and to buy it.

Thus, while the honest customer looks at *merchandise,* the shoplifter looks at *people* around him. The detective is aware of this difference and watches the eyes of shoppers for a clue as to their intentions. Quick eye movements reveal many, if not most, potential shoplifters.

The detective, then, *is* able to narrow the number of suspects. But the system he uses can also be used by the potential shoplifter to identify the detective. Just as the eye movements of the thief reveal him to the detective, the eye movements of the detective reveal him to the thief. The detective who pretends to be a shopper spends more time watching people around him—in order to watch eye movements and catch thieves—than he spends looking at merchandise. To a third party, the detective and the shoplifter behave in an almost identical manner.[12]

Common Techniques of Shoplifting (Without Booster Devices)

The *large shopping bag* is a most effective tool of the shoplifter. It is not uncommon for a legitimate shopper to place a shopping bag at his feet while he examines merchandise on a display

---

[10]Saul D. Astor, "Shoplifting Survey," *Security World,* VIII (March, 1971), pp. 34–5. As will be discussed in Chapter VI, there are some apparent weaknesses in Astor's study.

[11]It is worth noting that every male arrested while I was doing "field work" for this study wore a hat of some kind. This should pose an interesting research project for

psychologists which could aid the store detective in creation of a "profile" for the average shoplifter.

[12]I personally tested this method of pinpointing undercover store detectives. Unannounced, I visited a large department store and, within ten minutes, had identified all security personnel with 100 percent accuracy.

Table I. Male/Female Shoplifting Frequency Comparison

City	Males Followed	Male Shoplifters	%	Females Followed	Female Shoplifters	%
New York store #1	156	10	6.5	344	32	9.2
New York store #2	135	7	5.7	226	12	5.3
Boston	149	4	2.6	255	14	5.4
Philadelphia	132	8	6.0	250	22	8.8
Totals	572	29	5.0	1,075	80	7.4

Source: Saul D. Astor, "Shoplifting Survey," *Security World,* VIII (March, 1971), 34.

counter or rack. These shopping bags normally gape open at the top unless secured in some manner. The careful shopper, fearful of the pickpocket and sneak thief, will often place the bag on the floor between his legs in order to protect merchandise already purchased. This habit is a boon to the shoplifter who mimics this behavior. The shoplifter will stand very close to the display containing the desired merchandise, placing a large shopping bag on the floor between his legs. He will "handle" the merchandise until certain that he is unobserved and, at that moment, quickly drop the object into the open bag. Unless store personnel are alert during the split second the merchandise is dropped, the theft has been successfully accomplished as soon as the thief picks up the bag. No one can demand to look into the bag unless the customer-thief is first arrested; and, because of the danger of a false arrest suit, arrest is unlikely unless the thief carelessly lets someone see him drop the item into his bag.

Large purses are also effective places of concealment for stolen items. Once restricted to use by women, the introduction of male purses has generalized the technique somewhat. There is a myriad of legitimate reasons for a purse to be opened in a retail establishment so that an open purse attracts no undue attention. The thief simply waits until he is free from observation and quickly inserts the merchandise into the purse.

All manner of clothing can be used for *concealment* or *pseudo-concealment* of stolen merchandise. A sweater or coat carried over the arm provides adequate concealment for items hastily placed under it. Loose or bulky clothing, especially an overcoat, conceals merchandise worn or quickly inserted under it.

"Pseudo-concealment" is a rather audacious and clever method of shoplifting. The price tags are removed from clothing, jewelry, gloves, scarves, billfolds, pocketbooks, or other items which are normally worn or carried by shoppers. The thief then wears or carries the merchandise as if it were his own. Under many shoplifting laws, even if the thief is seen removing the tags, he breaks no law until he attempts to leave the store with the unpurchased items. If the thief suspects that he was seen removing tags, he simply walks around the store, determining if he is being followed. If not followed, the thief quickly exits with the merchandise. If he is being followed, he returns the items and can move on to a new department or store.

In one retail establishment a young lady was seen entering a fitting room with four pairs of stockings. An alert employee saw her exit the fitting room carrying no stockings. The store manager detained the female and called the police. Upon their arrival, officers observed that the suspect was wearing *all four* pairs of the stockings—one over the other. The suspect, however, had violated no law. She had not left the store with unpurchased items. Neither had she concealed any items—the stocking were clearly visible even though she was wearing them. The suspect returned the merchandise and was allowed to leave the store.

Ticket and cap switching is another relatively

safe method of shoplifting. Cap switching is made feasible because of the desire of manufacturers to make one size cap or lid for varying sizes of a product. Alert sales clerks may sometimes notice that an item has the wrong price on it. Incorrect prices on merchandise are often the fault of stock personnel. For this reason, if a clerk does notice a mistake, he normally apologizes to the customer and reveals the true price. The shoplifter can pretend to be irritated and return the item to its shelf or rack. Ticket and cap switching is most effective in a discount or grocery store where all items are purchased at the exits. Cashiers in these stores seldom pay attention to the prices of most items.

Two methods of shoplifting involve *the use of sales receipts*. In one instance, the thief either saves a receipt from a previous purchase at the store, or picks up a loose one from the floor or a trash bin of the store. This procedure allows the thief to steal an item priced the same as that on the receipt. However, most receipts are numbered so that an alert employee or detective can determine on which day the receipt was issued.

The experienced thief can avoid the embarrassment of this discovery, if he uses a confederate. The confederate buys an item, gets a legitimate receipt, leaves the store, and gives the receipt to the actual shoplifter. The shoplifter will then enter the store to steal an item identical to the one purchased. Even if apprehended, he will possess a correct receipt. Store personnel might suspect something "shady," but they will be forced to apologize for the inconvenience of detaining the thief. Not only has a successful theft been carried out, but also a false-arrest suit may be possible.[13]

[13]When an arrest is made, detectives immediately go to the department from which the stolen merchandise was taken and note the number on the store receipt register. (These number, ordered consecutively, coincide with the customers' receipt numbers.) If the detective did not follow this procedure, it would be possible for the arrested thief, out on bond, to purchase an item identical to the one which he was arrested for stealing. When he comes to trial, he could present a legitimate sales receipt as proof that he purchased the item.

Team stealing of any type is, by far, the most difficult to detect. Some members of the team can draw attention to themselves while others rob the store. Phony arguments, fights, or fainting spells are a few methods of distraction. With a large team, no distraction is necessary. Since only a few seconds are required for successful concealment, store personnel cannot adequately observe several potential thieves at once. During research which was undertaken for this dissertation, a team theft was observed. Nine male juveniles entered the clothing department of a store. Several were identified by store personnel as previous shoplifters. Additional detectives were called and eventually seven members of the security force were watching the youths. Even with an almost one-to-one ratio of detectives to the potential thieves, the boys were able to cluster around a display counter in such a way as to make accurate observation impossible. The detectives could only make their presence known in the hope of scaring off the boys. This failed and the detectives became suspicious, and rightly so. On another floor another group of youths were apparently helping themselves to merchandise secure in their belief that their nine confederates were keeping the store detectives busy. Not one of the fifteen youths involved was apprehended.

One unsophisticated, but effective, method of shoplifting is *to grab merchandise and run* from the store with it. If no store detective is nearby, this is a safe technique. Few sales personnel are willing or able to give chase. Most detectives are willing, but few are able to catch a fast running shoplifter. If the sneak thief is pursued, he need only "ditch" the merchandise in some obscure place. No crime can be proven if the merchandise is not recovered.

A risky, but oft used, technique is the *hiding of an item* or items inside large merchandise to be purchased. This is an unsafe method since, if the clerk decides to inspect the larger item, it is difficult for the thief to deny intent to steal.

There is one situation in which this procedure is relatively safe. In most grocery stores the customer is provided with large brown bags which may be used in the produce department. It is easy to place expensive steaks in the bottom of these bags and cover them with potatoes. Few grocery store cashiers are going to inspect a bag of potatoes. The thief gets steak for about 30 per pound.

A most amazing technique of shoplifting is commonly referred to as *"crotch-walking."* An item is placed between the legs of the thief and gripped with the upper thighs. A long dress or coat conceals the merchandise. With a little practice, the shoplifter is able to appear to be walking normally while moving only the legs from the knee down. Large females have been known to walk out of a store carrying large watermelons or portable television sets in this manner. There is one report of a "female professional who escaped with a fifteen pound ham between her thighs by climbing an eight foot fence and outrunning two male detectives, all without dropping the booty."[14]

The final category of shoplifting techniques to be discussed in this section is perhaps the most widespread of the methods employed. A general name for this classification is *"the fitting room theft."* For many years customers were permitted to carry bundles of clothing into fitting rooms with no questions asked. If a large number of items were taken into the fitting room, even an alert clerk found it difficult to ascertain that all were returned to the display racks. Store personnel are more careful today. They do not allow many items to be taken into a fitting room at one time. This is not an effective measure, though, since it is difficult for a clerk to keep track of even a few items, especially when his department is busy.

One unique fitting room theft involves men's pants or jeans. The thief examines several pairs of pants. After examining one pair, he folds it into a very small bundle and lays this bundle on the display counter beside other pants which he is "looking over." When he feels that no one is alert, he slides the folded pair of pants into the waistband of another pair. He then carefully

picks up several pairs of pants—including the pair which now conceals the folded pants—and requests a fitting room. Even if the clerk keeps track of the number of pairs of pants carried into the fitting room, he will not be aware of the hidden pair. Once in the fitting room, the thief can loosen his belt and place the folded pants in the back of his own pants. An overcoat completely conceals the stolen item.

If the shoplifter wishes to get a sports coat to go with the pants, he may wear a topcoat with a zip-out lining. He will unzip the lining and remove his topcoat, leaving the lining on as a vest-sweater. He then will "try on" the sports coat which he desires. If unobserved, he will quickly put on his topcoat over the sports coat, which now is worn *between* the lining and his overcoat. Once he zips up the lining, the sports coat is concealed even if he opens the overcoat.

Another fitting room theft is called the "packaging technique." An item is carried into a fitting room. Hidden wrapping paper and ribbons are then used to gift wrap the merchandise. Nothing is less suspicious to store personnel than a wrapped package.

Common Techniques of Shoplifting (With Booster Devices)

Some shoplifters plan the crime far enough in advance so that they are able to prepare special clothing and containers to be used in commission of the theft. Such devices are called "boosters." Although the theft may prove to be easier with such paraphernalia, the shoplifter must balance this benefit against the stiffer penalty that can be expected if he is apprehended while using these aids. Judges tend to be less lenient when there is evidence of premeditation. For this reason, the use of boosters appears to be the exception rather than the rule.[15]

One aid in shoplifting is known as a *"booster box."* A large box is wrapped and actually tied with string. This usually puts the sales clerk at

---

[14]McCabe, "Shoplifting in Iowa," p. 12.

[15]To some extent, this fact seems to offer credence to the view that severity of punishment *is* taken into account by shoplifters.

ease since a thief cannot discreetly untie a box and place merchandise inside. However, the string is a ruse. One end of the box is constructed so that merchandise can be inserted. This is normally accomplished with a hinged end which flips open inwardly.

A purse can be an effective booster box. A false bottom will allow merchandise to be placed in the purse without the obvious action of opening it.

Another common device is *the "drop bag."* Cloth bags—pillow cases, or their equivalent—are pinned or sewn into coat linings. Merchandise can easily be slipped inside the coat and into the bag.

For the shoplifter who does not like the drop bag, a variety of hooks and fasteners can be designed which may be placed inside a garment or on a belt. Heavy items are more cumbersome with these aids than with the drop bag.

Coats with "slashed pockets" are appropriate with drop bags or hooks and fasteners. The pockets of the coat are removed so that the hands are loose under the coat, while appearing to be resting in the pockets. The sales clerk can be distracted by one hand while the "pocketed" hand reaches out of the coat, seizes the desired merchandise, and inserts it into the drop bag or places it on the fasteners.

Double elastic waist bands which form hidden pockets inside skirts and trousers can be substituted for the drop bag or the hooks and fasteners. All of these boosters require that some type of coat be worn to conceal the merchandise. They are appropriate only in cool or damp weather.

The simple *umbrella* is a very effective booster device, although, again, the thief must be certain that the weather is appropriate for carrying one. Fasteners are placed inside the umbrella to hold the ribs open. The umbrella is then carried over the arm so that it hangs below the counter level. It is then an easy task to discreetly remove an object from the counter and drop it into the umbrella.

Before leaving the discussion of who shoplifts and how they do it, one interesting point comes to mind. Two categories of shoppers are provided unlimited license to steal—using whatever techniques they choose. Security personnel have an unwritten policy of releasing all elderly or pregnant persons who are caught shoplifting. (At least one large chain department store has put this policy in writing. "It is the general policy of ____ to prosecute shoplifters and pilferers, except when obvious (a) mental cases, (b) seniles, or (c) pregnant women are involved.") It has been learned through bitter experience that courts seldom convict these persons. The courts sympathize with the condition, age or pregnancy, of the accused. If one considers the "five-finger discount" awarded to the elderly—all ethical considerations set aside—their potential level of income rises dramatically. The policy of releasing these individuals is a type of income redistribution to them.

The methods which were described above are not the only ones used by shoplifters, but do represent a large percentage of thefts which occur.

81. The Criminal Use of False Identification

FEDERAL ADVISORY COMMITTEE ON FALSE IDENTIFICATION, U.S. DEPARTMENT OF JUSTICE

INTRODUCTION

THE MISSION OF THE TASK FORCE IS TO INVESTI-gate the national impact of false identification fraud on programs that involve payments by local, state, and federal governments to individuals.

Four areas, each of which involves programs of national scope, were investigated by the Task Force. These areas included the Aid to Families of Dependent Children (AFDC) and Medicaid programs administered by the Assistance Payments Administration, Department of HEW; the Food Stamp Program of the Department of Agriculture; and four programs administered by the Social Security Administration: Supplemental Security Income (SSI), Health Insurance (HI), Disability Insurance (DI), and Retirement and Survivors Insurance (RSI).

Programs administered by the Veterans Administration and the Department of Housing and Urban Development that involve government payments were not investigated.

Questionnaires were prepared for each of the four areas investigated. Eighty-six sets of questionnaires covering AFDC, Medicaid and Food Stamps were sent to Directors of Welfare in each state as well as Guam, Puerto Rico and the Virgin Islands; Welfare Quality Control Directors in several states; state and county auditors in several states; and the Inspectors General of New York and Michigan. Twenty sets of questionnaires covering the four Social Security Administration programs were sent to Social Security Headquarters and Regional Offices throughout the country.

Approximately 40% of the questionnaires have been returned. Evident thus far is the apparent lack of information relative to the frequency of false ID fraud and its fiscal implications. This lack of information should not be taken to mean that a problem does not exist. Results of several investigations carried out independently by individual states and localities will be cited that show significant impact from false ID fraud in government payments programs. Several of the returned questionnaires have contained expressions of deep concern about the use of false identification and the hope that something can be done to alleviate the problem. The Office of the Commissioner of Welfare, Department of HEW, has recommended on several occasions to the National Welfare Fraud Association that information on frequency and impact of false ID fraud should be collected by the states and reported to the HEW National Center of Social Statistics in Washington, D.C.

THE FALSE ID PROBLEM

False ID fraud in government-assisted w and social insurance programs has sig

▶SOURCE: *The Criminal Use of False Identification.* *Washington, D.C.: U.S. Department of Justice, 1976, pp. A-7–A-25.*

national problem potential because of the ubiquitous nature and staggering dollar volume of such programs. For example, in January 1975, a nationwide average of 11.1 million AFDC recipients were receiving benefits at the rate of $730 million each month; this represents an annual cost to taxpayers of $8.8 billion. The federal government issued over 100 million benefit checks in fiscal 1975 under SSI, DI, and RSI programs; these checks represented a total dollar value of over $13.7 billion. Benefits under the HI program (which includes Medicare) amounted to an additional $9.2 billion in fiscal 1975.

Government payments programs have generally displayed a steady growth in beneficiaries over recent years; the growth of some programs, such as Food Stamps, has been spectacular. In 1965, recipients of Food Stamp benefits numbered 400,000 and total benefits were $36 million. As of January 1975, the program had expanded over a hundredfold to encompass 19.1 million recipients and a payment level of $5.2 billion per year. Programs of this scale present many opportunities for abuse by fraud, whether by false ID or not. Even if only a small percentage of the transactions between government and the beneficiaries of these programs are fraudulent, the total dollar loss to taxpayers in direct payments and costs of fraud detection and prosecution can be very high. Thus, although our surveys have indicated that false ID fraud is generally viewed as only a small part of total program abuse, the Government Payments Task Force has concluded that such fraud constitutes a significant national problem that is deserving of further study.

Government payment programs are sub-
'ed to false ID fraud in both "application"
'se" phases of the programs and these are
' below.

rograms studied by the Task Force
ort of application for future be-
is "application phase," applic-
entify themselves and any
behalf program benefits

are sought. The types of identification documents currently required by state agencies were found to vary widely, ranging from none at all to a self-consistent set of official documents. The most commonly used documents in false ID fraud in this phase appear to be birth and baptismal certificates, state-issued driver's licenses, and Social Security cards.

Fraudulent documents are obtained in a number of ways. Birth certificates are usually genuine documents that have been altered and then photocopied. Baptismal and some birth certificates, on the other hand, can be easily generated by forging data on official appearing blanks bought at stationery stores or through mail order companies. Fraudulently used driver's licenses are obtained through theft and counterfeiting; they can also be obtained by application, using a false birth certificate as a "breeder" document. Although the Social Security card was never intended to be used as an identity document, it is used extensively as such in both legitimate and fraudulent transactions. Until recently, little identification was required to establish a new Social Security account. Thus, it was possible for an individual to establish accounts under several aliases. This has led to the collection of multiple benefits not only from Social Security programs but also from other government payments programs in which the multiple Social Security cards served as "identity documents" at application. Social Security cards have also been obtained by theft or counterfeiting. Unofficial "permanent" Social Security cards made of metal can also be obtained by supplying mail-order firms with an account number that is assumed or fictitious; these unofficial cards are sometimes used successfully for identification.

The period between application for government benefits and the receipt of benefits varies from a few days (or weeks) in the case of emergency relief payments to several months (or years) in the case of certain Social Security programs.

False ID has been employed in the "use"

phase when persons fraudulently assume the identity of others to collect their benefits. This use of false ID occurs most commonly in the cashing of stolen government checks or Food Stamps. Apparently, many banks and businesses are willing to cash these instruments without adequate identification of the endorser.

The following sections present analyses by the Task Force of surveys of AFDC, Medicaid, and Food Stamp programs. The analyses describe the range of requirements for recipient identification in application and use phases of the programs, and give available data on the scope of the false identification problem.

Aid to Families with Dependent Children

Twenty-eight responses to the questionnaires on the use of false identification to obtain Aid to Families with Dependent Children (AFDC) have been received. Respondents represent twenty-five states, one county (Los Angeles), one territory (Guam), and the Commonwealth of Puerto Rico.

The AFDC process begins when an applicant (generally one adult and one or more children) indicates verbally or in writing that they are in need of public assistance. Initial application may be made by phone, in writing or by personal appearance at a local political subdivision. Eligibility for public assistance under the AFDC program is limited to U.S. citizens and legal aliens permanently residing in the U.S. eligibility criteria include resource and income limitations, financial need and deprivation. When application is made and the welfare organization is satisfied that the applicant is indeed eligible, instructions are generally forwarded to an office of the state welfare organization from which grants are issued. In some states, grants are prepared centrally within counties, in others by the state welfare office and still others by the state controller or treasurer.

Once AFDC eligibility is established, states are not required to issue an AFDC identification document to recipients. Of the twenty-eight respondents to the questionnaire, 5 issue a photo ID, 2 issue an ID with no photo and 21 issue no ID at all.

The financial assistance provided to AFDC recipients is usually in the form of a semi-monthly check or warrant. Nationwide, as of January 1975, there were an average of 11.1 million AFDC recipients receiving benefits each month.

It is evident that a wide variety of documents are acceptable for the initial identification of AFDC applicants. The types of documents accepted and the number of respondents accepting them follow:

1. Birth Certificate 22
2. Social Security Card 16
3. Drivers License 14
4. Welfare ID (if former recipient) 7
5. Credit Cards 6
6. Employer Identification Card 10
7. Selective Service Card 10
8. Military Identification Card 10
9. Military Discharge Papers 13
10. Food Stamp ID 8
11. Union ID Card 8
12. Immigration and Naturalization Documents 17
13. Baptismal Records 5
14. Marriage Certificates 4

Of interest is the fact that five states returning questionnaires make no attempt to verify an applicant's identity. Some states only require identification to verify the birth of the children for whom assistance is sought, but none for the adult applicant who will also receive assistance. Most jurisdictions rarely, if ever, check the authenticity of "breeder" identification documents.

The importance of an effective identification program is illustrated by a report[1] of the Office of the New York State Comptroller.

The New York Legislature, according to this report, mandated that the New York City Human Resources Administration issue photo identification cards to all recipients of public assistance in the AFDC program. "The primary purpose of the Photo ID was to (reduce or) prevent the cashing of lost and stolen checks."

This report found that "as of May, 1973, *about 3,000 cases were closed as a result of the Photo ID program. This represented a savings of about $7.2 million a year in payments to ineligible recipients.*"[2] This reduction in caseload apparently came about either as the result of fictitious cases being closed or an "unwillingness" to be photographed on the part of some recipients.

The types of documents accepted as a means of identifying recipients when benefits are obtained (e.g., when AFDC checks are cashed), depends on the criteria established by the banks and merchants who cash the checks. Unfortunately, a significant number of banks and merchants require little if any identification when cashing government checks.[3] Checks are cashed under the false assumption that government issued checks are automatically "good." Evidence of this can be seen in Figure 1, a chart prepared by the Department of the Treasury, Fiscal Service, Operations Planning and Research Staff in a study entitled "Report on Forged Treasury Checks."

The basis of the Treasury report was a review of all forged checks for which a formal affidavit of forgery was filed with the Treasurer of the United States during the month of August, 1972. A total of 3,978 forged instruments were reviewed. The chart, comparing the types of identification used with the establishments accepting them, reveals that 81.3% or 3,236 forged checks did not contain written evidence on the check that an ID was used at the time of cashing. The study found that "the rate of acceptance of drivers' licenses and Social Security cards as a means of identification is particularly high in department stores and other establishments whereas these identification forms (except for one instance) are unacceptable to check-cashing firms. Also, use of the Regiscope[4] as a means of identification is relatively low in commercial banks (4.6%) and department stores (4.1%), relatively high in grocery (24.4%) and liquor (25%) stores, and extremely high in check-cashing firms (66.6%)."

The survey requested specific information on the extent and impact of AFDC identification-related fraud. Data requested included the number of fraud cases investigated in which false ID was used, the fiscal impact of the fraud, estimates of the percentage of total AFDC frauds that involve false ID, administrative costs of prosecuting false ID, and types and use of false ID encountered.

Twenty-three of twenty-eight responses to all these queries left the questions blank or stated that the information was either not available or unknown. The states supplying some of the requested information estimated that less than 2% of AFDC fraud cases involved the use of false identification. However, one state readily admitted that because fraud reports do not generally specify the nature of the fraud, true percentages are likely to be much higher. As a result, the Task Force has concluded that the frequency of the use of false identification remains undetermined because of the lack of adequate information at all levels of government and the private sector.

Because of the dearth of information, it is necessary to turn to specific welfare fraud reports in order to demonstrate the seriousness of the false identification problem. It should be

---

[1] *Audit Report on Photo ID Program, New York City Human Resources Administration,* Report No. NYC-22-74, Feb. 15, 1974.

[2] Emphasis added.

[3] See Appendix A, Part 2, Report of the Task Force on Commercial Transactions.

[4] A device that photographs both the check and the individual cashing the check.

Figure 1. Establishment Where Checks Cashed Relative to Identification Shown

Financial/Commercial Establishment Where Cashed	Endorser's Identification																			
	Driver's License		Social Security		Regiscope Picture		Employment I.D.		Check Cashing Card		All Other Forms[a]		Total I.D. Forms[b]		Items Showing I.D.		Items Not Showing I.D.		Total Items	
	No.	% of Col. 7	No.	% of Col. 7	No.	% of Col. 7	No.	% of Col. 7	No.	% of Col. 7	No.	% of Col. 7	No.	% of Total in this Col.	No.	% of Col. 10	No.	% of Col. 10	No.	% of Total
	(1)		(2)		(3)		(4)		(5)		(6)		(7)		(8)		(9)		(10)	
Commercial bank	49	18.6	31	11.7	12	4.6	22	8.3	24	9.1	126	47.7	264	30.8	231	19.1	979	80.9	1210	30.4
Grocery store	17	14.3	17	14.3	29	24.4	3	2.5	10	8.4	43	36.1	119	13.9	99	15.9	522	84.1	621	15.6
Liquor store	5	20.8	3	12.5	6	25.0	1	4.2	—	—	9	37.5	24	2.8	22	13.5	141	86.5	163	4.1
Check-cashing firm	1	5.6	—	—	12	66.6	—	—	1	5.6	4	22.2	18	2.1	18	16.5	91	83.5	109	2.8
Department store	14	28.6	8	16.3	2	4.1	6	12.2	2	4.1	17	34.7	49	5.7	38	32.8	78	67.2	116	2.9
Other Estbmt.[c]	6	33.3	4	22.2	2	11.1	—	—	—	—	6	33.3	18	2.1	18	8.6	192	91.4	210	5.3
All others	17	16.3	14	13.5	14	13.5	8	7.7	2	1.9	49	47.1	104	12.2	92	13.6	585	86.4	677	17.0
Total legible items	109	18.2	77	12.9	77	12.9	40	6.7	39	6.6	254	42.6	596	69.6	518	16.7	2588	83.3	3106	78.1
Items not legible	44	16.9	20	7.7	10	3.8	13	5.0	1	.4	172	66.2	260	30.4	224	25.7	648	74.3	872	21.9
Total items	153	17.9	97	11.4	87	10.2	53	6.2	40	4.7	426	49.8	856	100.0	742	18.7	3236	81.3	3978	100.0

[a] Covers all other forms of I.D. presented, including principally military I.D. (32), Credit Cards (17), fingerprints (7), voter card I.D. (7).

[b] The total number of I.D. forms presented is greater than the number of items bearing I.D. information because in 114 cases two forms of I.D. were shown on one item.

[c] Covers six other types of establishments, each cashing more than ten checks, as follows: gasoline station (55), drug stores (54), bar (44), savings & loan associations (36), realty firm/housing authority (11), and nursing home (10).

pointed out that the available reports are not limited to obvious problems of false identification, but include numerous other fraudulent practices such as forgery, which is a false ID crime, the check itself being the false ID. It is abundantly clear that if proper identification is required at the time a public assistance check is cashed, millions of dollars can be saved annually.

One of the most serious problems encountered by jurisdictions that mail checks to welfare recipients is mail theft. A Pennsylvania study[5] has found that "Pennsylvania welfare checks are stolen with much greater frequency" than any other checks sent by mail. A prime reason for this is due to the length of time it takes Pennsylvania to complete an investigation on reports of lost or stolen checks. In September and October, 1974, it was found that investigations of non-receipt complaints currently in progress in the Philadelphia area were for "checks issued in July of 1971." It should be noted that similar delays are common in many of the larger metropolitan areas throughout the country.

Most states, including Pennsylvania, upon receiving a report of a lost or stolen check, have the recipient complete an affidavit and issue a replacement check within twenty-four or forty-eight hours. These affidavits are used as the basis for collecting information to be used in any subsequent investigation. The Pennsylvania Grand Jury found that the majority of non-receipt claims *cannot* be resolved after a search of the files of the State Treasury Department. Statistics indicate that "approximately 41% of the cases are determined to involve checks that have been stolen or forged." Another 20% of the cases are determined to constitute fraud, that is, a check was received and cashed by the welfare recipient but subsequently reported as lost or stolen, in order to obtain a double payment. A study by the New York State Comptroller[6] found that over *thirty percent* of the checks for which replacements have been issued are subsequently determined to have been fraudulently cashed.

These percentages are shocking when one considers the number of replacement checks issued. The Pennsylvania Federal Grand Jury found the following:

"For the month of January, 1971, the incredible total of over twenty-six thousand replacement checks was issued in Philadelphia alone. Since the average welfare check amounts to approximately one hundred and eight dollars, the value of these replacement checks was more than two million six hundred thousand dollars. In 1972 and early 1973, ten thousand replacement checks, totalling over one million dollars, were being issued each month in Philadelphia alone. That figure is currently reduced to four or five thousand replacement checks per month, with an approximate value of one-half million dollars. This reduction, however, should not lull us into believing that there has been a proportionately great reduction in the *rate* of theft of welfare checks. The continued and diversified enforcement efforts of the Postal Inspectors and some improvements in the processing of these checks have reduced the theft rate. However, most of the reduction of monthly replacement checks from twenty-six thousand to five thousand is the result of a substantial reduction in the number of checks being delivered by the mails."

The Fraudulent Deplicate Check Claims audit in New York City revealed that in fiscal year 1974, the City's public assistance payments were approximately $1.2 billion. The audit found that "during the year ended October, 1973, HRA (Human Resources Administration of New York City) replaced 310,000 checks worth $28 million which had been reported lost or stolen." They also found that "as of November, 1973, there was a backlog of 110,000 fraudulently cashed checks worth $9.7 million on which no recoupment action had been taken."

These figures are substantiated by the *Report*

---

[5]*Report of the Federal Grand Jury for the Eastern District of Pennsylvania on Welfare Check Theft and Fraud in Pennsylvania and the Administrative Processing of Pennsylvania Welfare Recipient Complaints on Non-Receipt.*

[6]*Audit Report on Fraudulent Duplicate Check Claims, New York City Human Resources Administration, NYC-50-74.*

on Investigation of Welfare Fraud by Office of the Queens District Attorney for the Year 1974. This report states that "the most serious problem faced in the administration of Public Assistance and one for which there are no adequate present safeguards is the multiple collection of welfare payments by people using several aliases." The report further states that "it appears that the only way to eliminate this type of welfare cheating is to require a form of identification which is absolutely unique to each individual and which is not capable of fraudulent duplication."

A recent article in the Washington Post on check thieves and their victims, with emphasis on federally issued checks, indicates that upwards of $15,000,000 are lost due to forgery. The article stated:

"The check thieves steal about $50,000 a day by forging government checks. Most of those direct losses are carried by the banks and businesses that cash the forged checks. The indirect costs borne by various government departments that investigate and replace the stolen checks runs into the millions each year."

A recent review conducted by the New York State Office of Audit and Quality Control showed that welfare checks issued by the State of New York alone account for $12,000,000 in fraudulently cashed checks each year. It is likely that if similar studies were made of fraudulently cashed government checks issued in other major metropolitan areas across the county, these figures would double or triple. It is unlikely that the New York and Philadelphia metropolitan areas are the only ones experiencing these problems.

The most common characteristics of individuals who have come under investigation for using fraudulent identification in order to obtain AFDC benefits are as follows:

1. 20–30 years of age.

2. Female.

3. Unemployed.

4. Has completed 12 years of education.

5. Resides in a metropolitan area.

6. The fraud occurred in a metropolitan area.

7. Had no prior criminal record.

8. Has resided in present residence six months.

Apparent thus far is the fact that the amount of detectable fraud is commensurate with the effort made to detect it. As an example, of 343 cases sent to the prosecutor by the Special Investigative Section of the Department of Social and Health Services in the State of Washington, 338 or 98.5% resulted in guilty verdicts. This occurred in the first year of their operation beginning August, 1973. The annual report of the Special Investigation Unit for Suffolk County, New York, stated that "as a result of activities by the Special Investigation Unit in the year 1974, over one million dollars in fraud was uncovered, and resulted in an additional savings to the County of $900,000 in Public Assistance cases being closed."

The Treasury Department[7] expresses the frustration of those in government concerned with the fraudulent cashing of checks and the question of proper identification. They state:

"It is apparent that check-cashing establishments, and particularly banks, do not take proper precautions. They are accepting checks (in some cases for large dollar amounts) with questionable endorsements and forms of identification which are not, obviously, reliable. It is entirely conceivable that strict observance of the simple maxim 'Know your endorser—require identification' would reduce substantially the incidence of encashment of stolen and forged Treasury checks."

Medicaid

Twenty-six responses to the questionnaires on the use of false identification to obtain Medicaid

---

[7]"Report on Forged Treasury Checks," Department of the Treasury, Fiscal Service Operations Planning and Research Staff.

benefits have been received by respondents representing twenty-four states, one county (Los Angeles) and one territory (Guam).

While all states issue some form of Medicaid identification card and/or Medicaid labels, the conclusion that must be drawn from the responses received is that states have little, if any, knowledge concerning the use of false identification in the Medicaid program. A common response is that states are "not required" to keep Medicaid fraud statistics and, therefore, do not.

The states that did provide some information indicate that the problem appears to be more in the nature of provider fraud rather than recipient fraud. One state that found some recipients using Medicaid cards belonging to other persons discovered that in most instances the imposters were themselves eligible for Medicaid or other medical assistance but had lost or mislaid their own Medicaid ID.

The Task Force is, therefore, unable to provide any meaningful data relative to the use of false identification in obtaining Medicaid benefits.

The Task Force believes that states should be required to maintain uniform and detailed statistics on Medicaid fraud. In addition to providing meaningful national data, such statistics would serve as administrative tools for corrective action at all government levels.

Food Stamps

The Food Stamp questionnaire was mailed to Welfare Departments of all U.S. states and territories. Twenty-four responses have been received; respondents represent twenty-two states, one county (Los Angeles), and one territory (Guam). Maryland's response consisted of twelve separate questionnaires filled out by officials of as many counties.

The Food Stamp application process begins when an individual or family applies for benefits at a local or state welfare office (in many urban areas, community service organizations serve under contract to the state as registration offices). Eligibility for Food Stamp benefits is li-

mited to U.S. citizens and legal aliens in permanent residence and is based on income level, number of dependents, and certain other eligibility requirements. Recipients of federally-supported state assistance programs such as Aid to Families with Dependent Children (AFDC) are automatically eligible for Food Stamp benefits. If the local registration office is satisfied that the applicant meets eligibility criteria, the application is forwarded to an office of the state welfare department for a final determination. Upon a favorable determination, the applicant is provided with a Food Stamp ID card and (in most states) his first Authorization to Purchase (ATP) card. The Food Stamp ID is usually not a photo ID card; in Massachusetts, for example, it is a machine-readable card containing the applicant's name, Social Security Number, and signature. The name and signature of an authorized proxy may also appear on the card. The ATP document is also a machine-readable card containing the authorized face value of food coupons to be purchased and the purchase price. The purchase price is determined by the need of the applicant and ranges from zero to slightly less than the face value of the coupons. Food Stamps may be purchased at state-authorized outlets, which are usually banks but may be retail stores or community service agencies. The "stamps" (more properly coupons) are issued by the federal government. ATP are presently issued monthly; revalidation, which entails redetermination of eligibility and issuance of a new Food Stamp ID, is required every three months.

It is apparent that there is no nationally-accepted standard for identification of Food Stamp applicants upon registration. Eight states require no identity documents at this point. Fourteen of the twenty-six respondents accept a Social Security card as identification at registration; nine accept a driver's license, and eleven accept immigration and naturalization documents. Several respondents noted "if applicable" on immigration documents, implying that selection was exercised in demanding proof of citizenship. One respondent (a Southwestern state) indicated that ID was required "only if citizenship is questioned." All the documents suggested as choices[8] are accepted by at least three of the respondents. Other documents not listed but accepted by one or more respondents include library cards, income documents, bills, and "personal papers." Some of the respondents indicated that the responsibility of the state agencies is to determine the eligibility and need level of the applicant, not his true identity.

The standards for identification of recipients picking up Food Stamps in person are apparently tighter and more uniform than those applying at registration. Twenty-three of the twenty-six respondents accept a current Food Stamp ID at this point; several respondents accept *only* this document for Food Stamp pickup. Ten respondents would accept the Food Stamp ID of a former recipient, six a driver's license, and five a current welfare ID. Only one respondent indicated that most of the documents listed as choices[9] are accepted; none indicated that no ID is required for Food Stamp pickup.

The Food Stamp ID was also most frequently mentioned (nineteen responses) as the usual document required when Food Stamps are used to purchase food. Nine respondents indicated that an old Food Stamp ID would be accepted. Four respondents stated that the required ID would depend on the "sales outlet" at which the stamps were used, while two believed that no ID is usually required by food stores.

Specific information was requested to the extent and impact of Food Stamp Fraud. The number of fraud cases investigated in which false ID was used, the fiscal impact of the fraud, estimates of the fraction of total Food Stamp frauds that involve false ID, administrative costs of prosecuting false ID, and types and use of false ID encountered. Unfortunately, the most

common response (ten of twenty-six) to all these queries was "Information Not Available." One respondent's comment summarized the apparent attitude of many state welfare departments: "No record kept (of this type of information) since there is no requirement to do so." Almost as common (nine responses) was the comment that false ID fraud is nonexistent in the respondent's jurisdiction.[10] This was not only the response of such sparsely populated rural states as Oklahoma, North Dakota, and Montana, but also of urban states such as Connecticut and Delaware.

Completely in contrast to these responses was the report submitted by the State of Arkansas. This report covered only Non-Public Assistance Food Stamp recipients in North Pulaski County, which includes only 2.5% of statewide Food Stamp recipients. Nevertheless, in FY 73–74, this county (which includes part of Little Rock, Ark.) recorded 57 cases of false ID fraud carrying a loss to the Federal government of $18,740. All cited cases involved false ID at the time of application; seven cases also included the use of false ID at the time of food purchase. In 31 cases, imposter identification was used; counterfeit identification was used in 24 cases; and altered identification in 2 cases. The state estimated its administrative cost in prosecuting these cases to be $3500.

The Arkansas data are extremely significant, considering the relatively small sample of Food Stamp recipients that yielded all these cases. Two possible explanations of the data are suggested: either Little Rock, Ark. is a hotbed of false ID fraud, or the problem is being overlooked (and therefore declared nonexistent) in most of the nation. Some additional information, quoted from the Arkansas response, suggests that the latter explanation is more nearly correct:

"Since April 1974, the prosecuting attorney in Pulaski County has been extremely concerned with all

---

[8]The list of suggested documents appears in the description of AFDC programs in this report; current and expired Food Stamp ID's were added to this list.

[9]Same as suggested for Food Stamp application.

[10]If no records are maintained, it is questionable as to whether such a statement can be given much credence.

aspects of recipient abuse of the Food Stamp Program and has been very active in the prosecution of food stamp fraud cases. To date, three hundred and ten (310) felony charges of false pretense have been filed against one hundred and twenty-seven (127) persons in Pulaski County. Thus far eleven (11) persons have been found guilty with sentencing ranging from five (5) years in the State Penitentiary to one (1) year suspended."

Substantive data on false ID fraud was also received from Los Angeles County, California. However, no special breakout for Food Stamp fraud could be provided: the figures given refer to welfare fraud of all types. False ID fraud cases investigated increased from 24 in FY 70–71 to 103 in FY 73–74. Estimated welfare and Food Stamps payments to recipients as a result of this fraud totalled $24,170 in FY 70–71 and $85,148 in FY 73–74.

The documents most frequently used in false ID fraud in Arkansas are Social Security Cards and Food Stamp ID documents. Social Security Cards are obtained by application under one or more false names; unofficial "permanent" Social Security cards made of aluminum are obtained by mail order and sometimes used as ID documents. The most frequent abuse of the nonphotographic Food Stamp ID is the "loan" of it to unauthorized parties who then use it in purchasing Food Stamps. Apparently, the intermediate ATP document is not used in Arkansas.

California listed baptismal and birth certificates and driver's licenses as the most frequently abused ID documents. Birth certificates are commonly used to support the existence and ages of claimed dependent children; blank baptismal certificates are available in stationery stores, while birth certificates are most frequently genuine documents that are altered and then photocopied. Most of the driver's licenses used in false ID fraud in California were counterfeit documents.

Arkansas and California showed good agreement in their profile of the typical suspect in false ID investigation; both identified a young (18–30) unemployed woman resident in a metropolitan area. California described the typical suspect as not having a prior criminal record, while Arkansas could not supply data on prior criminal records. Both states cited metropolitan areas as the most common locales for ID fraud.

None of the twenty-six respondents to the Food Stamp survey indicated a belief that false ID fraud represents a majority of total Food Stamp fraud cases. However, the Arkansas response, which contained the most detailed data on false ID fraud, estimated the proportion of false ID cases as 10% of the total fraud cases. Much more common methods of fraud include falsification of income, medical expenses, or number of dependents. In Los Angeles County, the percentage of welfare fraud cases investigated that involved false ID was less than 1% for all years reported (FY 70–74 inclusive). Estimates of false ID fraud as percentages of total Food Stamp fraud supplied by other respondents ranged from below 1% to 5%; no basis for these estimates was given.

Analysis of ID Fraud Data.   These estimates establish clearly that the use of false ID is perceived as a minor problem with respect to overall abuse of the Food Stamp program. Three comments, however, appear to be in order. They are: (1) Based on the wide variance of the Arkansas response from the national sample, *false ID fraud is probably much more widespread and considerably more frequent than most state welfare departments realize;* (2) *All of the methods of false ID use that were detected are very primitive.* This includes the unauthorized use of Food Stamp ID, phony or duplicate Social Security Cards, and counterfeit driver's licenses; and (3) More sophisticated methods of false ID (such as Infant Death Identity) could be in widespread use but not currently detected.

Disposition of Cases.   Cases of Food Stamp fraud, when discovered, are referred to the local prosecutor's office (usually county-level) for disposition. The cost-sharing provisions of the Food Stamp program do not provide a strong incentive for state and local prosecution of Food Stamp fraud; in fact, they provide the states with a strong disincentive. The states pay a portion of the administrative costs of the program, including costs for the apprehension and prosecution of offenders. The entire cost of the coupons fraudulently obtained, on the other hand, is borne by the Federal government. Therefore, added emphasis on fraud results in *added costs to the state, yet all funds recovered must be returned to the Federal government.* Stolen or forged Food Stamp ID and ATP cards can be used at banks and retail stores to obtain and "spend" coupons where no effort is made to confirm the identity of the bearer. The Food Stamp ID used in most states is not a photo ID and can, in certain cases, be used by a proxy to purchase coupons for a designated recipient. These characteristics make it relatively easy to counterfeit or to use if stolen. Federal guidelines for state action (FNS [FS] Instruction 736–1) make it extremely unlikely that states will elect to prosecute any but the most flagrant abusers of the Food Stamp program. Finally, several respondents to the Food Stamp survey indicated that communication is poor between state and local welfare officials regarding abuses of the Food Stamp program.

82. Subway Crime

TRANSPORTATION RESEARCH INSTITUTE

WHERE DOES THE ISSUE OF TRANSIT SECURITY FIT
into our thinking about public transit systems?
To begin with, the question of security is often
seen from two somewhat related economic viewpoints. Both proceed from a concern over the
financial solvency of the system. One places emphasis on the direct cash drain crime imposes on
mass transit; the other on indirect losses due to a
decline in passenger revenues.

From the first point of view, crime on a transit
system is seen as a pernicious theft of proceeds.
Such costs include damage to the property and
equipment itself by means of vandalism, cash
losses in station booth robberies, and unrealized
revenue whenever someone rides without paying. The system is seen as victim; its capital assets and cash stores directly assaulted. The loss
of $10,000 at station booths through robbery or
the replacement cost of $10,000 for vandalized
seats or windows are regarded as equally corro-
sive to the precarious financial balance sheet of a
transit system.

From the second point of view, a deteriorating image of a transit system also costs money.
But here the costs are in terms of lost patronage.
That is, patrons use mass transit less as they lose
confidence in its ability to provide a secure ride.
Hence the very same $10,000, lost through
booth robberies or vandalism, could be alternatively lost if 200 occasional riders (say, those rid-

ing one time per week) refrain from using the
system at all. In one year this small group would
account for about 10,000 roundtrip rides.

From either viewpoint, crime on mass transit
is a costly affair. But the matter doesn't stop
there. A third point of view must be considered,
and that is the degree to which transit crime
contributes to the urban dweller's sense of in-
security. Just how all this detracts from the
overall quality of life in our cities is not easily
measured by the cost accountant's yardstick.

Its sporadic visibility to the general public
notwithstanding, crime on our public transit systems is and, as we have seen in the section on
history, has been an ever-present problem.
Characteristically, scant attention is paid to
transit crime save for the periodic alarm generated by a single dramatic instance or the occasional rash of crime catastrophies. Thus, on
March 12, 1965, a seventeen–year old was murdered on the "A" train of the New York City
Subway System during the night. Mayor
Wagner called for an increase in the transit
police from 1200 to 3100 men at an annual cost
of over $13,000,000. On May 9, 1968, a
Washington, D.C. bus driver was shot during
the course of a robbery and on May 17 of that
year another driver was murdered during a
robbery attempt. Mobile police units of the Metropolitan Police Department were assigned to
escort busses to dangerous areas and were
positioned at terminals where busses awaited
passengers. An exact fare procedure was instituted as an anti-bus robbery measure, a remedy
soon adopted by most major cities in the United

▶SOURCE: *Security of Patrons on Urban Transportation Systems. Pittsburgh: Transportation Research Institute, Carnegie-Mellon University, 1975, pp. 5, 9–11, 33–38, 43. (Editorial adaptations.) Reprinted by permission.*

States. On July 5, 1971, a prominent and popular physician was murdered during a robbery attempt in a Chicago Subway station. Shortly thereafter, the Mass Transit Unit of the Chicago Police Department instituted a "decoy" strategy to apprehend would-be robbers. These are but a few of the measures taken in response to publicized crime occurring on public transit in the United States. Significantly, serious attention to crime as a problem indigenous to mass transit had to await evidence that a crisis existed. Then, characteristically, response followed a reactive pattern. Once the public was believed to be reassured, especially if crime temporarily receded, little further systematic attention was given to the issue.

*

MEASURING RISK

On the one hand, transit crime shares with all other crime certain methodological problems of measurement. On the other hand, it has some unique features of its own. The common problems shared with all crime types are (a) discretion of the police in reporting crimes, both with regard to whether they are recorded at all and also with regard to the classification of those that are recorded; (b) the failure of some crimes to come to the attention of the police; and (c) the lack of any uniformly applied scale of seriousness for crimes or format for reporting such details as would be needed to rate the seriousness of the crime.

As a consequence, it is possible, for example, for police statistics to show a decrease in the reported number of robberies on some transit system, and yet it would require considerable effort to determine whether the problem of robbery has in fact lessened or whether the actual explanation is one or more of the following:

• A smaller fraction of robberies on the transit system are being recorded.

• Some types of crimes previously recorded as robberies are now being recorded as purse snatches or something other than robbery.

• There is a smaller number of robberies, but they are now more serious or involve more victims than previously.

Certain types of crimes, such as possession of drugs, loitering for purposes of prostitution, vandalism, and others that the FBI classify as "Part II," are so unlikely to be reported by members of the public that the number of them that are recorded is a direct function of the extent of police effort. For this reason, the FBI does not even compile statistics on the numbers of Part II crimes, but only on the number of arrests for such crimes. However, in the context of transit systems, these "less serious" crimes may nonetheless have an important impact on the public's perception of safety on the system. So the absence of reliable methods for gauging the frequency of these activities, while not a problem peculiar to transit systems, is not to be overlooked as a serious methodological difficulty.

In general, research into mass transit crime is going to require more complete and different information than is currently available. Special household surveys have already been conducted to determine victimization rates in some cities, but these are too expensive to be carried out routinely. Unfortunately, the National Crime Survey, which is being conducted by the Census Bureau for the Law Enforcement Assistance Administration, categorizes the locations of crimes in such a way that transit crimes cannot be distinguished from crimes in stores, restaurants, or other commercial establishments. Thus this instrument, which was designed to permit distinguishing "reported" crime rates from "true" crime rates, will not be of use for analysis of transit crime.

Computerized systems can furnish valuable information from police reports, but only if the information appears on the reports in the first place. A very helpful and probably necessary innovation is the development of a standardized police crime report form which would be used to report transit crime across the country. The New York transit police are currently using a form which contains more information as to location of crimes than most standard forms and might profitably be used as a starting point for developing a new standard form.

There is also a problem of determining the extent to which crime rates are affected by anti-crime measures. Even such general phenomena as changes in people's values, attitudes, lifestyles and income levels are all relevant to transit crime. If transit crime rates decreased in a city where unemployment levels dropped and per-capita income rose significantly, transit operators would probably be mistaken to believe that some particular change in security had caused the change.

Turning now to those problems of crime measurement that are unique to transit systems, we encounter the following particular difficulties.

1. An unambiguous determination of whether a crime is or is not related to the transit system is not always possible. Part of the problem here is related to the operation of the crime reporting system. Especially in cities where a special police force protects the transit system, a simple separation may be made between crimes reported to the transit police and crimes reported to the city police. If a person reports a crime that occurred on the transit system to the city police, it may not be entered into statistics for transit crime. Indeed, it is a common experience for researchers to inquire of city police as to whether they may obtain tabulations of bus robberies and find that no such statistics are kept.

Should the researcher desire to produce a special tabulation, it may be necessary to inspect the text of numerous crime reports if there is no special place on the form for the police officer to indicate that the crime occurred on a bus.

Aside from these problems related to the crime reporting system, there is also an ambiguity as to whether or not some types of crime should appropriately be considered transit crimes. Included in this category are robberies and assaults of persons who are either waiting for buses or walking to or from transit systems. For practical reasons the latter are usually excluded from transit crime, since at present most crime reports do not note where a person was going when he was the victim of a crime on the street. However, the fact that a patron of a transit system must pass through areas he knows to be of higher risk than the places he normally frequents is not an unimportant characteristic of these systems. The adoption of a uniform crime reporting format and system in all major cities would be a considerable aid to research.

2. The next methodological problem peculiar to transit crime is that some classes of crimes do not have patrons as victims in any meaningful sense. Instead, the system itself is the "victim." Included in this group are robberies of fare collectors, vandalism of transit system property, and theft of service (getting a free ride). Other crimes, such as robberies of concessionaires, are neither directed against the system nor against the riding public. Such differing sorts of crimes may have very different effects on transit ridership. Vandalism, for example, may discourage ridership by the sort of continuous, if subdued and latent threat it suggests, while robberies of fare collectors may pass almost unnoticed by the vast majority of customers in the actual vicinity of the robberies.

In attempting to calculate a victimization rate for patrons of the system, it seems appropriate to exclude all crimes of the types just mentioned, and yet it seems likely that the public's perception of the extent of transit crime is influenced by events such as these. Even if a transit system could assure that there would be no crimes against the public, daily reports of robberies and shootings of transit system employees would be adequate to convince the public that the system is unsafe.

Finally, there are classes of crimes for which the public in some generalized sense is the victim, and yet no particular patron is the victim.

These include public drunkenness, sales of drugs inside the transit system, littering, and the like. In attempting to measure the amount of transit crime and compare it with crime elsewhere, is it appropriate to include or exclude such incidents? Do these incidents, some of which are anti-social but not criminal, have an impact on ridership?

3. Next, we come to the thorny problem of developing appropriate normalized measures of crime *rates* that will permit comparing the extent of crime among transit systems, among different parts of the same transit system, or among different times of day in one part of a system. Measures traditionally used for comparing municipal crime rates, such as robberies per 100,000 population, are clearly inadequate in the context of transit crime. Primarily this is because the size of the system is ignored in a per-population measure. A city that chose to have no public transit could achieve a rate of zero transit robberies per 100,000 population.

Other measures that have been used or proposed include crimes per revenue passenger, crimes per vehicle-hour, and crimes per vehicle-mile. The American Transit Association compared several systems according to these measures and showed that relative rankings depend on which one is used. In addition, the study criticized all the measures for failing to distinguish between revenue passengers and "users." "A person riding twice a day 300 days a year counts as 600 revenue passengers, but he is only one user." The ATA proposed an *exposure index* for measuring crime rates. A modified version of this index appears suitable for comparing on-system with off-system crime rates, but further research is needed on this issue.

4. The next problem is that of availability and reliability of the information needed to calculate appropriate transit crime indices. Presumably, transit systems do not usually collect the data required to calculate the exposure to risk. Indeed, the exposure index in the ATA

study is calculated on the assumption that the average time spent in the system is 15 minutes. This appears extremely questionable, especially for fixed-rail systems, suggesting that no reliable statistics were located. (Average time spent in the system ought to mean the amount of time elapsed from the moment the patron enters the system until the moment he leaves, and therefore it would include various waiting times as well as travel times.)[1] Origin-destination studies will be required to establish more accurate estimates of "average time." Since some new systems have ticket-in ticket-out procedures for collecting fares, it may be possible in the future to study the times spent on the system in considerable detail.

A comparison of crime inside and outside the system is valid only if what is compared are "true" crime rates. Using *reported* crime rates may distort the comparison if reporting practices differ between on-system and off-system crimes.[2] But as was mentioned above, we are far from having any reliable victimization data to compare with reported transit crime figures.

5. Even if suitable on-system and off-system crime rates can be calculated, there remains the methodological difficulty that the potential transit system patron is not logically faced with a choice between using the transit system or staying at home or in his neighborhood. Instead, he is faced with a choice between using the transit system and using some other means of reaching his desired destination. Since the probability of being robbed while riding in one's personal automobile must be extraordinarily low, it may

---

[1]It is noteworthy that other definitions of "average time" are possible. Some researchers believe that the problem of security begins when a patron decides to go somewhere.

[2]The hazards for researchers who use police crime reports are highlighted by the recent resignation of Robert Rapp, longtime chief of the New York Transit Police, under circumstances where he admitted to "encouraging the making of false entries concerning the times of commission of crimes in official departmental reports." The Rand study (3) was partially based on assembling information from transit police reports whose accuracy is now placed in doubt.

well be that no reasonably achievable crime rates on transit systems will ever compare favorably with such alternatives in regard to safety from crime.

6. In order to more fully understand what choices are available to the transit patron and to better understand who the patron is, patron stratification studies as to sex, race, age and income need to be done.

7. In using transit crime rate data to evaluate various intervention and prevention activities, the possibility that crime is being displaced to other times or targets should be explored fully. However, the number of transit crimes is ordinarily small in comparison with the number of crimes committed against reasonable substitute targets, so determination of the extent of displacement effects may be extremely difficult.

*

What We Presently Know about Transit Crime
For the purposes of this report, personal security is seen relative to three classes of crime; 1) Robbery, 2) Assault and/or Battery, and 3) Crimes against People (rape, murder, indecent exposure, etc.).[3] It is clear from many current critiques that crime statistics are among the most difficult to collect and compare meaningfully. In large part this is a result of the changing definition of crime, procedural changes in administration of criminal justice, and changes in methods of recording and reporting crime. (7)

What is more important is that crime itself may not be as relevant to a personal perception of safety as publicity about crime. The President's Commission on Law Enforcement and the Administration of Justice reported:

[3]*Robbery* is the taking of property from a person by force or the threat of force. *Assault* is the conduct of an individual when he unlawfully places another person in apprehension of receiving a battery. *Battery* is intentionally and knowingly and unlawfully causing bodily harm to another or making physical contact of an insulting or provoking nature.

"The first (conclusion) is that the public fears most the crimes that occur least often, crimes of violence.

"Second, the fear of crimes of violence is not a simple fear of injury or death or even of all crimes of violence, but, at bottom, a fear of strangers.

"Third, this fear of strangers has greatly impoverished the lives of many Americans, especially those who live in high-crime neighborhoods in large cities. People stay behind the locked doors of their homes rather than risk walking in the streets at night. Poor people spend money on taxis because they are afraid to walk or use public transportation. Sociable people are afraid to talk to those they do not know.

"Fourth, the fear of crime may not be strongly influenced by the actual incidence of crime as by other experiences with the crime problem generally. For example, the mass media and overly zealous or opportunistic crime fighters may play a role in raising fears of crime by associating the idea of "crime" with a few sensational and terrifying criminal acts." (12)

Keeping those views in mind let us examine what is known about patron crime that originates in the mass transit environment.

Review of Selected Studies on Rapid Transit Security
Significantly, of the very few reported studies of personal security in transit systems (1, 2, 3, 5, 6, 8) only four have dealt with fixed guideway systems (2, 3, 5, 8) and none have dealt with automated vehicles. For this reason it is well to caution that any conclusions or recommendations for automated fixed guideway systems are bound to be opinions based on extrapolation.

Profiles of Transit Crime
Whatever its relative importance to crime in other urban systems, it is instructive to examine the how, when, where and what of transit crime. In this regard the Chicago study does provide us with a set of rapid transit crime profiles:
Rapid Transit Robbery. Rapid transit robbery was about evenly divided between armed and strong-armed offenses. Very few attempts were reported; most reported robberies were carried through to completion.

The majority of these crimes occurred in the evening between 6 p.m. to midnight. In contrast, few robberies occurred in the morning or early afternoon. The heaviest robbery periods occurred on Friday and Saturday nights.

Victims were almost always lone individuals. Over 50% were male and Caucasian and most were under 50 years of age. C.T.A. employees (mostly station agents), students, and service workers were prevalent among the victims.

A substantial number of these robberies were perpetrated by groups of two or three offenders. Offenders as a whole were overwhelmingly male and Black; most were under 30 years of age.

Most robberies occurred on station platforms where most of the victims were waiting for their trains. Those which occurred within the station lobby almost always involved station agents. Virtually none occurred in station restrooms. Where the robbery took place on a rapid transit vehicle, it usually occurred while the train was in motion between stations. Few witnesses, if present, reported crimes.

Weapons (most commonly revolvers and knives) were used in a majority of cases, though a significant number of offenders used no weapons at all except their hands or feet. When used, weapons were almost always displayed. Few victims were struck, stabbed, or shot by weapons, but many were punched or kicked. Though a majority were not injured, those who were, often required hospitalization. Proportionately more Caucasian than Black victims received injuries.

Money alone, or money and credit cards, jewelry, wallets, or purses were taken in most cases. Losses were generally under $20, though many multi-victim and station agent robberies netted the robber in excess of $100.

Offenders attempted to exit the rapid transit system as quickly as possible following their crimes. Where the robbery occurred on a platform, the offender usually fled onto the street via stairs or ramps, avoiding the station lobby wherever possible. Few offenders boarded trains. Where the robbery occurred on a rapid transit vehicle, virtually all the offenders exited the train at the first regular stop. Very few either moved to another car or pulled the emergency stop.

Most robberies were self-reported by the victim. Police responded quickly, arriving on the scene within five minutes of the report of the crime in a substantial number of cases. Where officers did arrive while the crime was still in progress (or had been completed only a short time before) the apprehension rate was substantially higher than where a delay occurred between the commission of the crime and the arrival of the police.

Relatively little of the stolen property was recovered.

Battery (and Assault).   Most batteries involved either the infliction of minor injury without the use of a weapon, or physical contact of an insulting or provoking nature.

Batteries were about evenly distributed across the week with slightly more occurring on Wedneday and Thursday. They tended to be committed earlier in the day than robberies (almost half occurred between 4 and 10 p.m.). The evening rush-hour was the peak battery period. As with robbery, few batteries occurred during the morning or early afternoon hours.

Rapid transit batteries were distributed geographically across the system in about the same proportions as robberies, occurring as they did in those portions of the system located in high crime neighborhoods.

Almost all battery victims were lone individuals. Most were male and Caucasian. C.T.A. employees (very few station agents, however) students, and service workers were the most prevalent groups of battery victims.

Slightly more batteries than robberies occurred on trains, though the majority were still carried out on station platforms. Most victims were waiting for their trains while on their way home from the loop.

Just over 50% of the batteries were perpetrated by lone offenders—although a substantial number were carried out by gangs of four or more. Most offenders were male, Black, and under 30 years of age.

Most rapid transit batteries involved no weapon other than the threatened or actual use of hands or feet. Victims were generally kicked or punched or were struck by a weapon; very few were stabbed or shot. However, most victims who were injured required hospital attention.

Like their robbery counterparts, battery offenders attempted to escape the system completely following their crimes.

Most victims reported the crime themselves. As with robbery, police responded quickly, generally arriving on the scene of the crime within five minutes of receiving the report. Apprehensions were made in almost 33% of the cases.

Crime Against Persons.   Most crimes against persons were minor in nature, generally involving indecency in public. A few, however, were serious: murder, justifiable homicide, or rape. Most occurred during the morning rush-hour or early evening from 5 to 10 p.m.

Most victims were again lone individuals. Unlike the other crimes however, the majority were perpetrated against women, mostly C.T.A. personnel (generally station agents), students, or clerical workers.

Almost all crimes against persons were committed by lone individuals, though several offenders were involved in some of the more serious crimes. Significantly fewer of these offenders (though still a majority) were Black than was true for either robbery or battery offenders.

Few weapons were used in these crimes, though the victim was seriously injured in a large percentage of the cases in which a knife or firearm was involved.

Almost 50% of these crimes were committed on a rapid transit vehicle—generally while the train was between stations. In these on-train crimes, the offender usually left the train at the first possible stop. Most in-station crimes against persons were committed on platforms, though a significant number did occur within station lobbies. Almost 50% of these in-station offenders escaped by boarding trains.

As with the other rapid transit crimes, most victims reported the incident themselves. Police generally responded quickly once the crime was reported.

Crime on the New York Subway

The Chicago findings are reinforced and extended somewhat by similar conclusions from the Rand Study of the New York subway system. In the Rand Study they concluded:

1.   Except for changes clearly attributable to anticrime activities of the Transit Police or the Transit Authority, the rate of serious crime in the subway system has tended to increase steadily from year to year.

2.   When a particular type of crime proves to be lucrative and relatively safe, additional offenders will be attracted to it, possibly in lieu of other criminal opportunities. This apparently happened in 1969 with bus robberies, for which the data suggest that some individuals who otherwise would have been committing subway robberies were robbing bus drivers instead.

3.   The geographical locations of subway crimes are not evenly spread throughout the system but are focused on a small number of stations and the portions of train routes that run between those stations. The high-crime locations can be easily identified from historical data and tend to be where surface crime rates are also high. A finding congruent with the Chicago Study.

4.   Subway robbers are predominantly young and Black, but there are substantial differences between those who rob passengers and those who rob token booths. Many passenger robbers are school-age children, and the bulk of their crimes are committed in the afternoon just after school hours. Few passenger robberies involve the use of guns, but many are violent crimes. By contrast, token booth robbers are somewhat older and frequently used guns, but do not often use violence.

5.   In 1970 about half of all robberies took

place in the station while in 1971 more than 70 percent of the robberies took place in the station and the remaining 30 percent aboard the train. Again, confirming the findings of the Chicago Study.

Summary: What We Know About Rapid Transit Crime

In Table I we have taken the conclusions from the previous transit studies cited and stated them as facts in Column 1. In Column 2 we

Table I.

Conclusion	Confidence	Probable Relevance
1. Majority of crimes occur in the evening	H	H
2. Heaviest robbery period is Friday and Saturday night	H	M
3. Robbery victims are lone individuals	H	H
4. Transit employees were most frequent robbery victim group	M	M
5. Robberies frequently are perpetrated by groups of two or three	H	M
6. Offenders were most often young male blacks	M-L	M-L
7. Most victims are robbed on the station platform while they await the train	H	H
8. When robbery occurs in the train it usually occurs while train is in motion between stations	H	H
9. Very few witnesses report transit robberies	H	H
10. Weapons (revolvers or knives) were used in a majority of cases	M	L
11. Majority of robbery victims are not injured	H	M
12. Money jewelry, credit cards were most often stolen	H	M
13. Robbers tried to escape as quickly as possible	H	H
14. When robbery occurred in station, robber fled to the street	H	H
15. When robbery occurs in train robber flees at next stop	H	H
16. Robbers rarely pull emergency stop	H	H
17. Most robberies were self reported by the victims	H	H
18. The shorter the delay between crime and arrival of police, the greater the apprehension rate	H	H

Table I. (continued)

Conclusion	Confidence	Probable Relevance
19. Those stations where robbery is highest have high surface crime	H	H
20. Most batteries occur during the evening rush hour	M	H
21. Geographic distribution of battery is similar to robbery	L	H
22. Most battery victims are lone individuals	M	M
23. Most batteries occur on station platforms	L	M
24. About half of the batteries are carried out by lone individuals	M	L
25. Half the batteries are carried out by gangs of four or more	M	L
26. Those who commit battery are young, male and black	M	M-L
27. Most batteries involve no weapon	H	L
28. Most victims who were injured required hospital attention	L	M
29. Those commiting battery attempted to exit the system as fast as possible	M	H
30. Most victims of battery reported the crime themselves	H	H
31. Most crimes against persons (CAP) occurred during morning rush hour	L	M
32. Most CAP's were minor, involving indecency	H	M
33. Most victims were lone individuals	L	M
34. 50% of CAP's are committed on trains in motion between stations	M	H
35. When the CAP occurred in the station the offender escaped by getting on the train	L	H
36. Most patrons would feel more secure if they knew emergency assistance could be readily obtained	H	H
37. Perception of crime on a system has a definite effect on ridership patterns	M	H

Table II. Scenario for Rapid Transit System User

Action	Security Rank Perceived	Actual	Hazard Area/ Factor
1. Arrival at station		6	Parking lot
2. Enter station	1 (most dangerous)	4	Stairways, Escalators, Elevators, etc.
3. Fare collection	—	3	Handling currency
4. Waiting for vehicle	3	1	Isolation
5. Entering vehicle	—	5	Crowding
6. Riding	3	2	Isolation, unknown arrival environment
7. Exiting vehicle	—	7	Unfamiliarity
8. Exiting station	1	8	Stairs, escalators, ramps, etc.

express our opinion as to the reliability of these conclusions. Our reliability rating is given in three qualitative terms; high-medium-low and indicates the extent to which we feel that the fact stated would be true in most transit system. In Column 3 is our opinion as to the relevance of the fact to the design of any proposed rapid transit system. Again we have used high-medium-low ratings. When the relevance is rated as high, it is our opinion that there are definite pesonal security implications in the choice of system designs relating to the fact stated.

Implications for Small Vehicle Systems
Crime Exposure Scenario for Typical Transit User. The typical user of a rapid transit system will go through a fairly stereotyped sequence of events in riding from origin to destination. We can describe that sequence with the scenario shown in Table II. Also shown are the areas or factors that pose potential personal security risks. The rankings are based on findings in the

Chicago study, the actual risk from crime data analysis, perceived risk from the attitude survey.

The initial hazard listed in Table II is arrival at the station. In some areas there will be parking lots provided for a "park and ride" type of service. This service encourages commuters to leave their autos at central suburban locations and to proceed to the central business district on the rapid transit system. In our survey of existing systems we have not found reports of crimes (other than auto theft) with any frequency. Auto theft or thefts of articles from autos is on the increase in the park and ride facilities of the Bay Area Rapid Transit System (BART).[4] While this is not a problem that would cause fear of bodily harm, it could reach a point where ridership decreases because of the unwillingness of commuters to leave their cars unattended at the transit facility lots.

Entry into the station usually will involve stairways, walkways, ramps, elevators or es-

[4]Personal Communication from Ralph Lindsay, Director, Security Services BART.

calators. Very few existing systems have elevators, although they are specified in most proposed systems to transport the aged and handicapped. While the elevator will undoubtedly provide a potential hazard, we have not been able to gather data on its magnitude.

Walkways, stairways, escalators etc. provide a hazard in so far as they contain areas which are not under direct observation by the user.

Fare collection is a problem area in systems such as Chicago and New York where token booth employees make up a substantial proportion of the robbery victims. Automated fare collection systems will not pose this hazard, but will nevertheless provide the only place in the transit scenario when a potential victim will usually be handling his currency. Automated fare collection systems have significantly reduced the number of robberies where they have been used and will undoubtedly reduce the number of transit robberies in a proposed system.

The most dangerous segment of the transit scenario is in waiting for a vehicle. Waiting is most dangerous at night in a large station with many areas which cannot be observed by the patron. There are two separate but related aspects to this portion of the scenario, the length of the waiting time and number of people waiting per unit area. It appears from studies cited that if people can wait in groups they are safer. Thus, when there are but a few people waiting, they should have a small waiting area. Typically, as waiting time increases the number of people waiting in queue will also increase and the area in which to wait must be increased. With scheduled service this implies variable sized waiting areas. Current systems in New York and Chicago attempt to some extent to solve this problem by closing exits and limiting ready access to platform areas at off-peak periods. One of the recommendations from the Chicago study was for movable barriers which could be used to reduce platform size and thereby increase the number of people waiting per unit area thus making their wait safer.

Entering the vehicle is an act which places people in close proximity to one another and is the site of most assault and battery crimes. It is reasonable to believe that many factors are at work here, most of which can be classed as frustrations. Again, station size is an important variable. When the patron density is high and crowding takes place, these "expressive" crimes are more likely.

Riding on the vehicle is the second most likely time for a crime to occur of the eight activities in the scenario. Approximately one-third of all robberies, one-third of all assault/battery crimes and one-half of all crimes against persons are committed on the trains.

Exiting the vehicle presents special characteristics during rush hours where high density traffic may again be the focus of assault and battery. This condition is actually much safer however than entering, probably as a result of the greater patron density in entering vehicles at the end of the work day when frustration tolerance is likely to be lower. In other words, in the morning on the way to work there are large numbers of patrons exiting the trains in the central business district (CBD) stations. These patrons have not yet faced the day's frustrations. In the evening when there are a great number of patrons entering at the CBD stations the frustration tolerance is lower and the assault rate is higher.

Exiting the station is the safest portion of the scenario even though it takes place over the stairs, walkways, etc. which are perceived to be the most dangerous portions of the system. Perhaps it is the rapid purposeful movement of most patrons at the exit points which is responsible for this safety factor. When patrons arrive at their destination they move quickly out of the system thus reducing the chance of crime in the system.

REFERENCES

1. Gray, P., Robbery and Assault of Bus Drivers. *Operations Research,* March-April, 1971, p. 257–269 based on *Reduction of Robberies and Assaults of Bus Drivers* (Final Report), Stanford Research Institute and

the University of California, Palo Alto, California, December, 1970.

2.   Shellow, R., Bartel, E. W., Cooley, W. L., Roszner, E. S. and Pazour, J., Improvement of Mass Transit Security in Chicago: *A Report to the City of Chicago Department of Public Works Recommending Specific Security Measures for Demonstration on Chicago Transit Authority Facilities.* Carnegie-Mellon University, June 30, 1973.

3.   Chaiken, J. M., Lawless, M. W., and Stevenson, K. A., *The Impact of Police Activity on Crime: Robberies on the New York City Subway System.* The New York City Rand Institute, publication R-1424-NYC, January, 1974.

4.   Shellow, R., Romualdi, J. P. and Bartel, E. W., Crime in Rapid Transit Systems: An Analysis and a Recomended Security and Surveillance System. *Highway Research Records* (in Press).

5.   Thrasher, E. J., Schnell, J. B., Smith, A. J. and Dimsdale, K. R., *Vandalism and Passenger Security. A Study of Crime and Vandalism on Urban Mass Transit Systems in the United States and Canada.* An American Transit Association Study, National Technical Information Service, PB-226-854145, September, 1973.

6.   Sinha, K. C. and Roemer, F. P., *Problem of Personal Security in Buses Along a Transit Route in Milwaukee and its Effects on Ridership.* Presented at the 53rd Annual Meeting of The Highway Research Board, Washington, D.C., January 21–25, 1974.

7.   *Crime in the Nation's Five Largest Cities,* U.S. Department of Justice, National Criminal Justice Information and Statistics Service, Washington, D.C., April, 1974.

8.   *Broad and Columbia Subway Development Study: Final Report.* Broad and Columbia Subway Group. Prepared for U.S. Department of Transportation, Assistant Secretary for Environment and Urban Systems, August, 1971.

83. Nuclear Theft

MASON WILLRICH
THEODORE B. TAYLOR

INTRODUCTION

IT IS ALL TOO EASY TO IMAGINE INNUMERABLE possibilities for nuclear theft—a parade of horrors. It is extremely difficult, however, to determine where the line should be drawn between credible and incredible risks, between risks that should be safeguarded against and those that can be safely ignored. An assessment of the risks of nuclear theft is even more speculative than an analysis of the risks of major accidents in the operation of nuclear power reactors. With respect to reactor operation, risks to public safety arise primarily from the possibilities of malfunctioning machines. In regard to nuclear theft, however, the risks to national and individual security arise primarily from malfunctioning people.

Nevertheless, the safety risk analysis applicable to reactor accidents and the analysis of security risks applicable to nuclear theft have two difficulties in common. In the first place, both types of analysis deal with very low probability risks of very great damage. It is noteworthy, however, that the damage which might result from a nuclear theft is potentially much greater than the damage that could result from the maximum credible accident in the operation of a nuclear power reactor. Second, as to both

areas of risk, there is, and hopefully will continue to be, a lack of actual experience involving substantial damage to the public on which to base predictions.

As fuel for power reactors, nuclear weapon material[1] will range in commercial value from $3,000 to $15,000 per kilogram—roughly comparable to the value of black market heroin. The same material might be hundreds of times more valuable to some group wanting a powerful means of destruction. Furthermore, the costs to society per kilogram of nuclear material used for destructive purposes would be immense. The dispersal of very small amounts of finely divided plutonium could necessitate evacuation and decontamination operations covering several square kilometers for long periods of time and costing tens or hundreds of millions of dollars. The damage could run to many millions of dollars per gram of plutonium used. A nuclear explosion with a yield of one kiloton could destroy a major industrial installation or several large office buildings costing hundreds of millions to billions of dollars. The hundreds or thousands of people whose health might be severely damaged by dispersal of plutonium, or the tens of thousands of thousands of people

▶SOURCE: *Nuclear Theft: Risks and Safeguards. Cambridge, Mass.: Ballinger Publishing Co., 1974, pp. 107–120. (Editorial adaptations.) Reprinted with permission from Nuclear Theft: Risks and Safeguards. Copyright 1973, Ballinger Publishing Co.*

[1]Throughout we use "nuclear weapon material" to mean material that can be used in fission explosives or, in the case of plutonium, in dispersal devices either directly or with chemical conversions that are much simpler processes than those involved in reprocessing irradiated nuclear fuels or in isotope enrichment.

who might be killed by a low-yield nuclear explosion in a densely populated area represent incalculable but immense costs to society. These intrinsic values and potential costs should be borne in mind throughout our analysis of the risks of theft of nuclear weapon material from the nuclear power industry.

The analysis which follows focuses exclusively on the potential security risks involved in the development and use of nuclear power. We have avoided analogies to a multitude of other security risks, some of which appear equally deserving of study and concern. For example, biological or chemical agents might be diverted from their intended medical or industrial uses for use in very powerful weapons, or they might be produced in clandestine laboratories operated by criminal groups. Chemical high explosives have been frequently used for criminal and terrorist purposes, often with devastating effects. Thus, it is important to view the security risks implicit in nuclear power as a cost to be weighed against the benefits of nuclear energy as a source of electric power, and also as an integral part of the general problem of violence that afflicts society.

With these cautionary thoughts in mind, we may explore the possibilities for and consequences of diversion of nuclear material from the nuclear power industry to illicit use. Our analysis is mainly intended to provide readers with a more informed basis for making their own judgments concerning the credibility of the risks involved—judgments which can be expected to differ widely since they will be necessarily based on individual views of human nature.

We consider the risks of nuclear theft by different types of potential thieves: one unstable or criminal person acting alone; a profit-oriented criminal group; a terrorist group; a nuclear enterprise; and a political faction within a nation. For each type of potential risk, we outline the reasons for theft, the scope of the risk, and various methods of thievery. Finally, we examine the main problems associated with nuclear black

market operations. The nature and extent of such a market, if any, generally affects the specific risks of theft previously considered.

Although our study concerns primarily the theft of nuclear material from the U.S. nuclear power industry, the risk analysis is also applicable to possibilities in other countries with nuclear power industries. Indeed, some of the risks would seem to be greater in other countries than in the U.S., while others may be greater in the U.S. than elsewhere. Moreover, material stolen from the U.S. nuclear power industry might be used to threaten the security of people in foreign countries and their governments. Similarly, material diverted from the nuclear industry in a foreign country might form the basis for a nuclear threat within the U.S.

THEFT BY ONE PERSON ACTING ALONE

Reasons

The possible reasons for one person to attempt to steal nuclear weapon material from the nuclear power industry cover a broad spectrum. On one end of the motivation spectrum is financial gain, and on the other is a sick expression of extreme alienation from society as a whole. In between lie such motives as settling a grudge against the management of a nuclear plant, or a strong conviction that nuclear weapon proliferation is a good thing. Money would seem to be the most likely general motive for an individual to steal nuclear material, assuming a buyer were available. (The terrorist would normally be operating as part of a group rather than alone.)

More specifically, the lone person who contemplates theft of nuclear weapon material may do so with any of a large number of particular uses for the material in mind. Possible uses include the following:

Black Market Sale. The entire amount of stolen material might be sold in one transaction, if a large quantity of nuclear material would bring a premium price. Alternatively, small amounts might be sold over long periods of time in separate transactions, if the thief viewed his ill-gotten gains as something like a very precious metal to be liquidated in installments as income is needed.

Ransom of Stolen Material.   If carefully worked out, the thief might be able to obtain at least as high a ransom for the stolen material as he would be able to get by sale in a black market. The nuclear enterprise stolen from would be one possible target of such a blackmail scheme; another might be the U.S. government. The nuclear enterprise, the government, and—depending on his tactics—the thief himself, might have a strong interest in keeping from the public any information about a nuclear theft. This possibility raises two questions: In what circumstances do the American people have a right or a need to know about a theft of material from the U.S. nuclear power industry? And, furthermore, do other governments have a right or a need to be informed about such a theft, if circumstances indicate that the stolen material has likely been taken out of the country?

Fabrication of a Weapon and Actual Nuclear Threat.   The manufacture of a fission explosive or plutonium dispersal device may be within the capabilities of one person working alone, assuming he possesses the requisite technical competence. But what would the individual do with his nuclear weapon? As with stolen material, he might sell the device in the black market or ransom it. Any level of government—municipal, state, or federal—might be a target for blackmail of this type, and a governmental authority might be prepared to pay a very high price to gain possession of the device. The blackmailer would, of course, have to establish the credibility of the nuclear threat, but this would not seem difficult. One easy way to do so would be to send the authorities a design drawing of the device, perhaps together with a sample of the nuclear material used and photographs of the actual device.

As with the ransom of stolen nuclear material, the blackmailer could make his demands and conduct the entire transaction in secret, or he might from the outset or at some stage in the negotiations make his demands known to the public. The governmental authorities would probably wish to keep the matter secret, at least until an emergency evacuation became necessary. If the nuclear threat were disclosed to the public, serious panic could result. The threatener would have to be sure that, whatever his demands, they were satisfied prior to or simultaneously with the government's gaining possession of the device. This might be very difficult to arrange, especially for a lone individual.

Nuclear Hoax.   If a design description plus a sample of nuclear material would establish the credibility of a nuclear threat, why would the threatener have to actually fabricate and emplace a fission explosive or plutonium dispersal device in order to obtain satisfaction for his demands? If government authorities were willing to pay off a nuclear bluff or hoax, the potential profit or political utility of a small amount of nuclear weapon material would be increased substantially. One or a series of such hoaxes would greatly complicate the problem facing a government. Even the appearance of succumbing to a nuclear threat, whether genuine or not, might be an added incentive to potential thieves.

If a person perpetrates a nuclear hoax on a government that has previously experienced one or more bomb threats, made payoffs, and recovered the devices, the hoax will probably be successful. If, however, a government has made payoffs as a result of credible hoaxes, but not recovered any devices, it may establish a policy of no more payoffs. This could create a situation of extreme danger. The next credible bomb threat might be the real thing, and a nuclear catastrophe would be the probable result.

On the one hand, a government policy of paying off all credible nuclear bomb threats would probably increase the frequency of such threats to intolerable levels. The results could be a large drain on financial resources, great anxiety in people living in urban areas, and widespread loss of confidence in the ability of governmental institutions to cope with the security problem. On the other hand, if a policy of not paying off on any nuclear bomb threat were adopted, it might have to be accompanied by strict and enforceable urban evacuation plans which could be carried out immediately upon receipt of a credible threat. If credible nuclear threats occurred often, an urban community would be paralyzed at enormous costs to society as a whole. The alternative would be to assume the risk and ignore any nuclear bomb threat.

If the government adopted a policy of trying as best it could to distinguish between the actual nuclear threat and the hoax, the consequences of a wrong choice would again be nuclear catastrophe. Therefore, the acceptability of such a policy would depend on a foolproof method of discriminating between the real threat and the hoax. It is difficult to imagine such a method.

Scope of the Risk

Fortunately, not everyone is a potential thief of nuclear material. The greatest risk of nuclear theft by one individual acting alone is posed by persons authorized access to nuclear material at facilities (mainly nuclear industry employees), and to persons authorized control over nuclear material during shipment between facilities in the various fuel cycles. This considerably narrows the scope of the risk of individual theft. But it also means that someone who is in a position to steal nuclear material by himself may well possess the technical knowledge required to handle it safely and use it destructively.

However, anyone can make a nuclear threat simply by lifting a telephone. A very large number of people could make a nuclear threat that is credible—at least up to a point—but still be a hoax. At least one such threat has already occurred. . . .

Options

The lone thief who is an employee in a nuclear facility or somewhere in the transportation system for nuclear material has two basic options for acquiring material for fission explosives or radiological weapons: (1) he can attempt to steal a large amount of material at one time; or (2) he can take a small amount each time in a series of thefts. One possible scenario for a large theft by an individual from a nuclear facility would be to fake an accident involving the risk of employees being exposed to high radiation levels, or some other emergency condition which requires the immediate evacuation of all persons from the facility. The thief might then be able to make off with a significant quantity of material through the emergency safety exits. Individual acts of theft of nuclear material in transit or in storage during transit could also result, if successful, in the loss of large amounts of material.

The possibility and significance of a series of thefts of small amounts of nuclear material would depend on the detection threshold and the elapsed time between the events and discovery of their occurrence. It seems that materials accountancy alone would provide insufficient protection against small thefts by a plant employee given the limit of error of material unaccounted for (LEMUF) in any such system, and the knowledge the employee would normally have of what the LEMUF was.

THEFT BY A CRIMINAL GROUP

Reasons

There are two reasons why a criminal group might want nuclear weapon materials. One is obvious: money, which might be obtained through black market or ransom dealings in the materials themselves, in fabricated fission explosive devices, or in fabricated plutonium dispersal devices. The corollary reason is that the possession of a few fission explosives or radiological weapons might place a criminal group rather effectively beyond the reach of law enforcement authorities. A criminal organization might use the threat of nuclear violence against an urban population to deter police action directed against its nuclear theft operations. The organization might also use nuclear threats to extort from the government a tacit or explicit relaxation of law enforcement activities directed against a broad range of other lucrative criminal operations.

Scope of the Risk

To what extent would criminal groups become interested in the potential for financial gains in illicit trade in nuclear material? It may be argued that the potential gains are so large that a wide variety of criminal organizations would attempt to exploit the possibilities of nuclear theft. To the contrary, however, it may be argued that criminal groups primarily interested in money are likely to be politically conservative, and that they would not develop a black market in a commodity such as nuclear material which could have revolutionary political implications. Moreover, a large nuclear theft might prompt a massive governmental crackdown and lead to a widespread public outcry, whereas the continued existence of organized crime on a large scale might depend on the susceptibility of some government officials to corruption and on a degree of public indifference.

The possession of a few nuclear weapons as a deterrent against law enforcement may be viewed by a criminal group as more of a risk than a benefit. In order to obtain the advantage of a deterrent effect, the criminal group possessing such weapons would have to be willing to inflict large scale, indiscriminate harm on society. Moreover, like nuclear war between nations, if the deterrent failed and a criminal group either used nuclear weapons or failed to use them, the group itself would probably not survive the crisis as an organization.

Options

It seems very likely that a criminal group would be able to develop a capability to apply sophisticated means, including substantial force if necessary, in order to carry out a nuclear theft. Therefore, the analysis which follows focuses on the technical capabilities a group might have for dealing with nuclear material, not its capabilities to use force or stealth to obtain it.

Minimal Nuclear Capability.   At a minimum, a group contemplating nuclear theft would have to be able to recognize precisely the material it wanted and to understand the procedures required for its safe handling. Regarding the tactics of nuclear theft, a criminal group with such a minimal nuclear capability would have two basic options. In the first place, it could attempt to infiltrate nuclear industry or transportation facilities through which nuclear material passes, and then attempt to steal very small quantities of material without being detected. Secondly, it could attempt to burglarize a nuclear facility or hijack a vehicle carrying a nuclear shipment and take a large amount at one time.

If successful with either a series of small nuclear thefts or a single large one, a criminal group with minimal technical competence would posses material that it could sell to others or use to blackmail the enterprise stolen from. These are basically the same options available to one person acting alone. However, an organized group would have much greater capabilities than one person to make arrangements for either the black market sale or the ransom of stolen material to a nucleur enterprise or a governmental authority.

Capability to Manufacture Nuclear Weapons.   A criminal group could acquire the technical competence to fabricate nuclear weapons in a number of ways. A group member with a well-developed scientific and mathematical talent could develop the required competence on his own without formal training; or a group member with some aptitude and a college education might be sent to a year or two of graduate school; or the group might recruit, or kidnap and coerce someone already possessing the requisite technical skills. Alternatively, someone with the requisite skill might decide to pursue a career in crime rather than lawful industry and take the initiative to form his own criminal group in order to profit from nuclear theft.

A favorable location could be selected for the weapon manufacturing facilities. This might be in the midst of an intensively industrialized area or it might be in a remote and inaccessible region. Some foreign government might be willing to host a clandestine manufacturing operation outside the U.S. Any government opposed to nuclear weapon proliferation might find it extremely difficult to deal with a criminal group which had the capability to manufacture nuclear weapon devices if the group's manufacturing facilities were located on territory under the jurisdiction of a government that was amenable or indifferent to such proliferation.

The capabilities and preferences of potential buyers—terrorist groups, national governments, or political factions within national governments—could well be the decisive factor determining whether a profit-oriented criminal group would develop its own capability to manufacture nuclear weapons. For example, national governments interested in the clandestine acquisition of nuclear weapons might prefer to purchase the requisite material in order to manufacture weapons tailored to their particular requirements. However, terrorist groups might provide a ready market for fabricated nuclear explosive devices.

Capability to Manufacture Nuclear Weapon Material. It seems very unlikely that a criminal group could develop its own capability to produce significant amounts of plutonium or uranium–233. The operations required are numerous and complicated, and on too large a scale. There are a number of reasons why it is also unlikely that a criminal group would be capable of enriching uranium, at least in the near future. The technology to separate uranium isotopes by means of centrifugation, one alternative method to diffusion (which requires huge facilities), is being developed in various countries under conditions of governmental or commercial secrecy. The operation of centrifuges would be a demanding task technically. The criminal group would have to steal a number of centrifuges in order to acquire a capability to produce significant quantities of high-enriched uranium from stolen low-enriched or natural uranium. Given the cost of one centrifuge, inventory controls capable of detecting the theft of one or more centrifuges would seem justified. If a theft were promptly detected, it would seem that the government would have a relatively long time to recover the stolen centrifuges. However, the successful development and widespread application of laser techniques for isotope separation would seem to have substantial implications for the spread of uranium enrichment capabilities, possibly to criminal groups as well as to many commercial enterprises.

THEFT BY A TERRORIST GROUP

Reasons

Although financial gain should not be excluded as a possibility, the dominant motive of a terrorist group attempting to obtain nuclear material would probably be to enhance its capabilities to use or threaten violence. An important, though secondary purpose might well be to provide itself with an effective deterrent against police action. In these respects, a terrorist group possessing a few nuclear weapons would be in a qualitatively different position offensively and defensively from such a group possessing only conventional arms. Hence, theft of fuel from the nuclear power industry might place nuclear weapons in the hands of groups that were quite willing to resort to unlimited violence.

Scope of the Risk

The scope of the risk of theft by terrorist groups would seem to depend largely on how widespread terrorist behavior becomes in the future. Although any assessment in this regard is highly speculative, present trends appear discouraging. The incidence of violence initiated by various terrorist groups seems to be increasing in many parts of the world. Terrorist organizations are increasing their technical sophistication, as evidenced by the armaments and tactics they use. Such groups are also rapidly developing transnational links with each other in order to facilitate the flow among countries of arms and ammunition and even of terrorist personnel. Whatever works as a terrorist tactic in one part of the world appears likely to be picked up and possibly emulated elsewhere. One wonders how in the long run nuclear power industries can develop and prosper in a world where terrorist activities are widespread and persistent. For if present trends continue, it seems only a question of time before some terrorist organization exploits the possibilities for coercion which are latent in nuclear fuel.

Options

Terrorist groups might become a large source of black market demand for nuclear weapons. However, such a group may prefer, for various reasons, to develop its own capabilities of stealing and using nuclear materials. A terrorist group may wish to be independent of any ordinary criminal enterprise; the group may believe that a spectacular nuclear theft would serve its purposes; or the group may be able to obtain the material it wants more cheaply by stealing it than by buying it on the black market. It is difficult to imagine that a determined terrorist group could not acquire a nuclear weapon manufacturing capability once it had the required nuclear weapon materials. In this regard, a terrorist's willingness to take chances with his own health or safety, and to use coercion to obtain information or services from others, should be contrasted with the probably more conservative approach of persons engaged in crime for money.

The theft options of a terrorist group would not differ substantially from those available to a profit-oriented criminal group. But whereas there may be incentives working on all sides to keep the fact of theft by a profit-oriented criminal group secret from the public, there may be reasons why a terrorist group would want a successful nuclear theft to be well publicized. Theft of a large amount of nuclear material would not only acquire for the terrorist group a significant capacity for violence or the threat of violence, but also the process of executing a successful theft could itself generate widespread anxiety. People would become concerned, not only in the country where the theft occurred, but also in a country or countries against which the group's activities might be ultimately aimed. However, one important reason why a terrorist group may prefer to keep its nuclear theft operations a secret, if possible, would be its own vulnerability to swift and forceful government action during the period between nuclear theft and completion of the fabrication of fission explosive devices or radiological weapons.

The ability of a government, whether U.S. or foreign, to deal with an emergent terrorist nuclear threat would depend on the location of the group's base of operations, particularly the location of its weapon manufacturing facilities. This may be unknown and hard to determine, or it may be located on territory subject to the jurisdiction of a government that is for some reason not prepared to take decisive action against the group involved.

Once a terrorist group possesses fission explosives or radiological weapons, the group's options for their coercive use, both aggressively and to deter enforcement action against it, cover the complete range of options discussed previously for an individual acting alone and for profit-oriented criminal groups. However, if a terrorist group were involved, doubts concerning the credibility of many options previously considered would be substantially removed, and the inner logic of the possibilities for nuclear coercion would control. These possibilities would be exploited by a group of people who might be quite free of the practical, intellectual, or emotional restraints that tend to inhibit the use of violence by other groups.

DIVERSION BY A NUCLEAR ENTERPRISE

Options

We consider here only the risk that the managers of a nuclear enterprise might divert to an illicit use some of the material flowing through facilities under their operational control. The most likely diversion option would be for the managers of processing facilities to manipulate material balances within the margins of uncertainty in the accountancy system. The nuclear material input of a fuel reprocessing or fabrication plant is not known to anyone exactly. Therefore, the input could be stated to be at the lower limit of the range of uncertainty, or in other words at the lower limit of the limit of error of material unaccounted for (LEMUF). The output could then be stated to be either at the lower or at the upper limit of the LEMUF. If the material output were stated to be at the lower limit, the excess material, if any, could be diverted and secretly kept or disposed of. If, however, the output were stated at the upper limit, the plant management might be able to charge its customers for more material than was actually present.

Reasons

The managers of a nuclear enterprise may want to divert material in order to cover up previous material losses known to the management but not yet discovered by the AEC authorities. The managers may want to have some clandestine material on hand simply as a convenient way to remove material accountancy anomalies as they arise—an easy way to balance the books. Furthermore, the managers of a nuclear facility may view manipulation of material balances as a way to increase slightly the profitability of the enterprise. . . .

Scope of the Risk

The risk that nuclear enterprise managers might manipulate material balances to their own advantage seems to be inherent in the nuclear power industry because of the high intrinsic value of the materials involved and the fact that no one will know exactly how much is actually flowing through a major facility. In addition to the presumed honesty of nuclear plant managers, however, there are limitations on the scope of this particular diversion risk. If an "arms

length" commercial relationship exists between the operators of distinct steps in the fuel cycle, the possibilities for diversion by materials balance manipulations would be lessened. In addition, since one person could probably not get very far in a complicated manipulation process, a conspiracy within the plant would be necessary. This would substantially increase both the difficulty of diversion and the risk of detection.

Government materials accountancy requirements could arguably have the effect of either increasing or reducing incentives within industry to manipulate nuclear materials balances. Vigorous government enforcement of stringent materials accountancy requirements might increase the incentives for plant managers to cheat the system in order to be sure they could balance the books and keep their facilities operating efficiently. However, a lax governmental attitude towards materials accountancy might reduce incentives for discipline within industrial operations, open up opportunities for much larger manipulations of materials balances, and perhaps create conditions in which large scale diversions by criminal or terrorist groups could occur without timely detection.

DIVERSION BY A POLITICAL FACTION WITHIN A NATION

Scope of the Risk

The government of a nation is normally not of one mind. The possession by a faction or interest group within the government of enough nuclear material in a suitable form to make a few weapons might significantly affect the internal balance of political forces within a nation. This particular risk of nuclear diversion would seem negligible in the U.S. However, it could be substantial in a nation where force was commonly used as a means of transferring governmental power and authority. It should be noted that in countries where force is frequently used as an instrument for political change, the line between political faction and criminal group would sometimes be difficult to draw. This diversion risk is considered briefly here because of its potential bearing on U.S. foreign relations and its relevance to the possible development of a nuclear black market.

Reasons For Diversion

The overriding reason why a political faction within a government might want to divert nuclear weapon material would be to enhance its power to achieve its own immediate or future political objectives. The specific objectives might be either domestic or international.

In terms of domestic politics, preemptive diversion by a political faction in order to shore up its power base is one possibility. Protective diversion by a faction fearing it was about to be suppressed or outlawed is another. In either of these circumstances, the reason for nuclear diversion would be to assure stability or to deter the use of violence against themselves. The credibility of the threat or use of nuclear force in a *coup d'etat* would seem difficult to establish, however.

In terms of international policy, whether or not to acquire nuclear weapons is an issue that is likely to be on the governmental agenda of many non-nuclear-weapons nations from time to time in the future. Adherence to the nuclear non-proliferation treaty and acceptance of International Atomic Energy Agency safeguards cannot be expected to settle the issue permanently, although such governmental action should substantially strengthen the position of those within a government who are opposed to the acquisition of nuclear weapons. Those who favor the development of such weapons may view diversion of material from nuclear industry as a convenient and effective way to confront the government with a *fait accompli*, and to reverse in fact the non-nuclear-weapon decision.

Options

A political faction planning a nuclear diversion might have two ways to accomplish the result that would not be available to criminal or terrorist groups. First, the owners or managers of an industrial facility with an inventory of nuclear weapon materials might actively support one faction against another in an internal power struggle. Therefore, they might be quite willing to transfer some of the material under their control to the faction they were supporting, and perhaps to provide assistance in weapons manufacture. Second, the armed forces, or particular units of the armed forces, might be persuaded to participate in the plot and to seize the nuclear material that the governmental faction wanted.

Finally, it may be noted that in a country where violence is considered to be a necessary catalyst for political change, a political faction may decide to drop out of the government, take to the hills, and begin a civil war. A group which carried with it a significant quantity of nuclear weapon material would be in a far different political position than one which took along only conventional arms and chemical explosives.

NUCLEAR BLACK MARKET

The existence or lack of a market for stolen nuclear material, and the characteristics of such a market, would substantially affect the diversion risks previously considered. In general, the profit incentives for nuclear diversion would be increased greatly if stolen nuclear material were easy to dispose of in transactions on a black market. Although the obstacles in the way of black market development appear quite large, the potential for profits by the middlemen in the market could also be very great.

Sellers in a nuclear black market might be any of the potential thieves previously discussed. A ready market could increase not only the incentives for thefts, but also the probability that stolen material could be successfully ransomed as an alternative to marketing it. The existence of a well-developed black market would perhaps be especially pernicious, because it would ease the problems an individual acting alone would otherwise face in disposing of any nuclear material he might steal.

Terrorist groups and national governments

are the more likely customers in a black market. There would also seem to be possibilities for the operators of a nuclear black market to stimulate demand. Terrorist groups often appear to emulate each other's tactics. Moreover, an initial sale or two of nuclear weapons to petty dictators with dreams of glory might thereafter enable the operators in a nuclear black market to play on the fears of more responsible leaders, who would then have no way of knowing which nations had secret nuclear weapon stockpiles. A nuclear black market could offer the governments of nations without *any* previous civilian or military nuclear capabilities opportunities for acquiring nuclear weapons. Such a development could, therefore, greatly increase the dangers of nuclear weapon proliferation throughout the world.

A black market in nuclear material would seem to require a subtle and complex structure, possibly composed of several loosely affiliated groups. The market would probably become transnational in scope since demands for stolen nuclear material or fabricated weapons would not necessarily come from a country that has the sources of supply. Weapon fabrication or material processing services may or may not be part of the market operations. If they were, these activities might take place in remote areas or where a government was willing to look the other way.

A criminal or terrorist group might thus target its efforts on especially vulnerable nuclear fuel or facilities anywhere in the world. The stolen material might then be passed through various middlemen and processing steps and sold ultimately to purchasers in other countries far away from the scene of original theft.

The evolution of a nuclear black market would be a hazardous and uncertain affair. It may be doubted whether such a market could ever achieve the institutional stability or long term viability that would pose a major threat. If one or more major nuclear thefts occur, governments everywhere may be prompted to act swiftly and decisively to foreclose any possibilities for disposition of stolen material. From the preceding analysis it would seem, however, that a few successful thefts could increase incentives for black market formation, and that an incipient nuclear black market would increase the likelihood of nuclear theft or other types of diversion attempts. It should be noted that no national government acting unilaterally could prevent a nuclear black market from developing if the conditions were ripe. Like the risks of nuclear theft, the dimensions of a nuclear black market are potentially global.